PLANT ASSETS (Chapter 10)

Presentation

Tangible Assets	Intangible Assets
Property, plant, and equipment	Intangible assets (Patents, copyrights, trademarks, franchises, goodwill)
Natural resources	

Computation of Annual Depreciation Expense

Straight-line	$\dfrac{\text{Cost} - \text{Salvage value}}{\text{Useful life (in years)}}$
Units-of-activity	$\dfrac{\text{Depreciable cost}}{\text{Useful life (in units)}} \times \text{Units of activity during year}$
Declining-balance	Book value at beginning of year $\times$ Declining balance rate* *Declining-balance rate = 1 $\div$ Useful life (in years)

Note: If depreciation is calculated for partial periods, the straight-line and declining-balance methods must be adjusted for the relevant proportion of the year. Multiply the annual depreciation expense by the number of months expired in the year divided by 12 months.

CONCEPTUAL FRAMEWORK OF ACCOUNTING (Chapter 12)

Characteristics	Assumptions	Principles	Constraints
Relevance	Monetary unit	Revenue recognition	Materiality
Comparability	Economic entity	Matching	Conservatism
Reliability	Time period	Full disclosure	
Consistency	Going concern	Cost	

SHAREHOLDERS' EQUITY (Chapter 14)

Comparison of Equity Accounts

Proprietorship	Partnership	Corporation
Owner's equity	Partner's equity	Shareholder's equity
Name, Capital	Name, Capital	Capital stock
	Name, Capital	Retained earnings

No-Par Value vs. Par Value Stock Journal Entries

No-Par Value	Par Value
Cash	Cash
Common Stock	Common Stock (par value)
	Paid-in Capital in Excess of Par Value

DIVIDENDS (Chapter 15)

Comparison of Dividend Effects

	Cash	Common Stock	Retained Earnings
Cash dividend	↓	No effect	↓
Stock dividend	No effect	↑	↓
Stock split	No effect	No effect	No effect

BONDS (Chapter 16)

Premium	Market interest rate < Contractual interest rate
Face Value	Market interest rate = Contractual interest rate
Discount	Market interest rate > Contractual interest rate

INVESTMENTS (Chapter 17)

Comparison of Long-Term Bond Investment and Liability Journal Entries

Event	Investor	Investee

Purchase / issue of bonds	Debt Investments
	     Cash
		Cash
		     Bonds Payable

Interest receipt / payment	Cash
	     Interest Revenue
		Interest Expense
		     Cash

Comparison of Cost and Equity Methods of Accounting for Long-Term Stock Investments

Event	Cost	Equity

Acquisition	Stock Investments
	     Cash
		Stock Investments
		     Cash

Investee reports earnings	No entry	Stock Investments Investment Revenue

Investee pays dividends	Cash
	     Dividend Revenue
		Cash
		     Stock Investments

STATEMENT OF CASH FLOWS (Chapter 18)

Cash flows from operating activities (**indirect method**)
Net income

Add:	Losses on disposals of assets	$ X
	Amortization and depreciation	X
	Decreases in current assets	X
	Increases in current liabilities	X
Deduct:	Gains on disposals of assets	(X)
	Increases in current assets	(X)
	Decreases in current liabilities	(X)
Cash provided (used) by operating activities		$ X

Cash flows from operating activities (**direct method**)
Cash receipts
  (Examples: from sales of goods and services to customers, from receipts
  of interest and dividends on loans and investments) $ X
Cash payments
  (Examples: to suppliers, for operating expenses, for interest, for taxes)   (X)
Cash provided (used) by operating activities $ X

RAPID REVIEW

Weygandt, Kieso, Kimmel
Accounting Principles, Seventh Edition

PRESENTATION OF NON-TYPICAL ITEMS (Chapter 19)

Prior period adjustments (Chapter 15)	Statement of retained earnings (adjustment of beginning retained earnings)
Discontinued operations	Income statement (presented separately after "Income from continuing operations")
Extraordinary items	Income statement (presented separately after "Income before extraordinary items")
Changes in accounting principle	Income statement (cumulative effect adjustment presented just above "Net income")

MANAGERIAL ACCOUNTING (Chapter 20)

Characteristics of Managerial Accounting

Primary Users	Internal users
Reports	Internal reports issued as needed
Purpose	Special purpose for a particular user
Content	Pertains to subunits, may be detailed, use of relevant data
Verification	No independent audits

Types of Manufacturing Costs

Direct materials	Raw materials directly associated with finished product
Direct labor	Work of employees directly associated with turning raw materials into finished product
Manufacturing overhead	Costs indirectly associated with manufacture of finished product

JOB ORDER AND PROCESS COSTING (Chapters 21 and 22)

Types of Accounting Systems

Job order	Costs are assigned to each unit or each batch of goods
Process cost	Costs are applied to similar products that are mass-produced in a continuous fashion

Job Order and Process Cost Flow

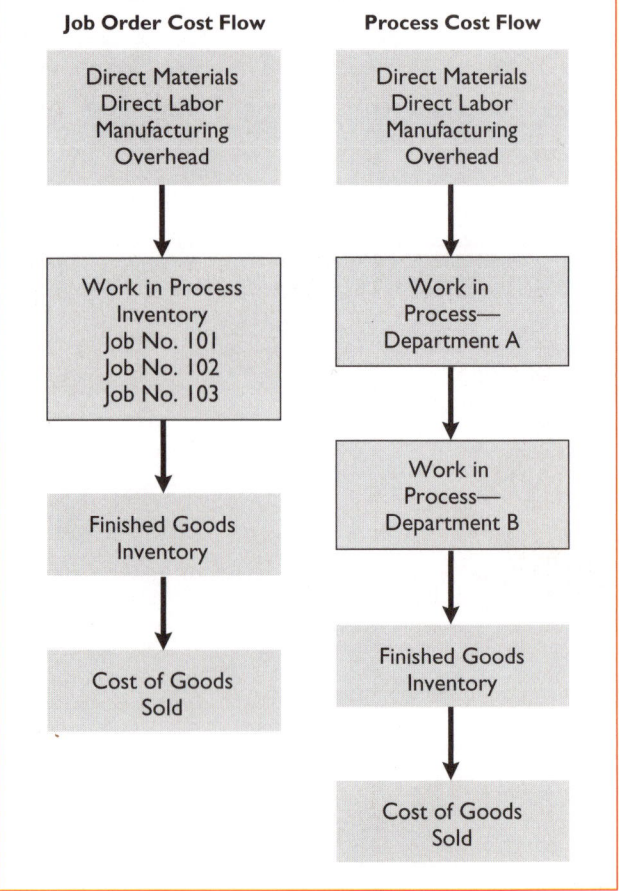

eGrade Plus

with EduGen

www.wiley.com/college/weygandt

Based on the Activities You Do Every Day

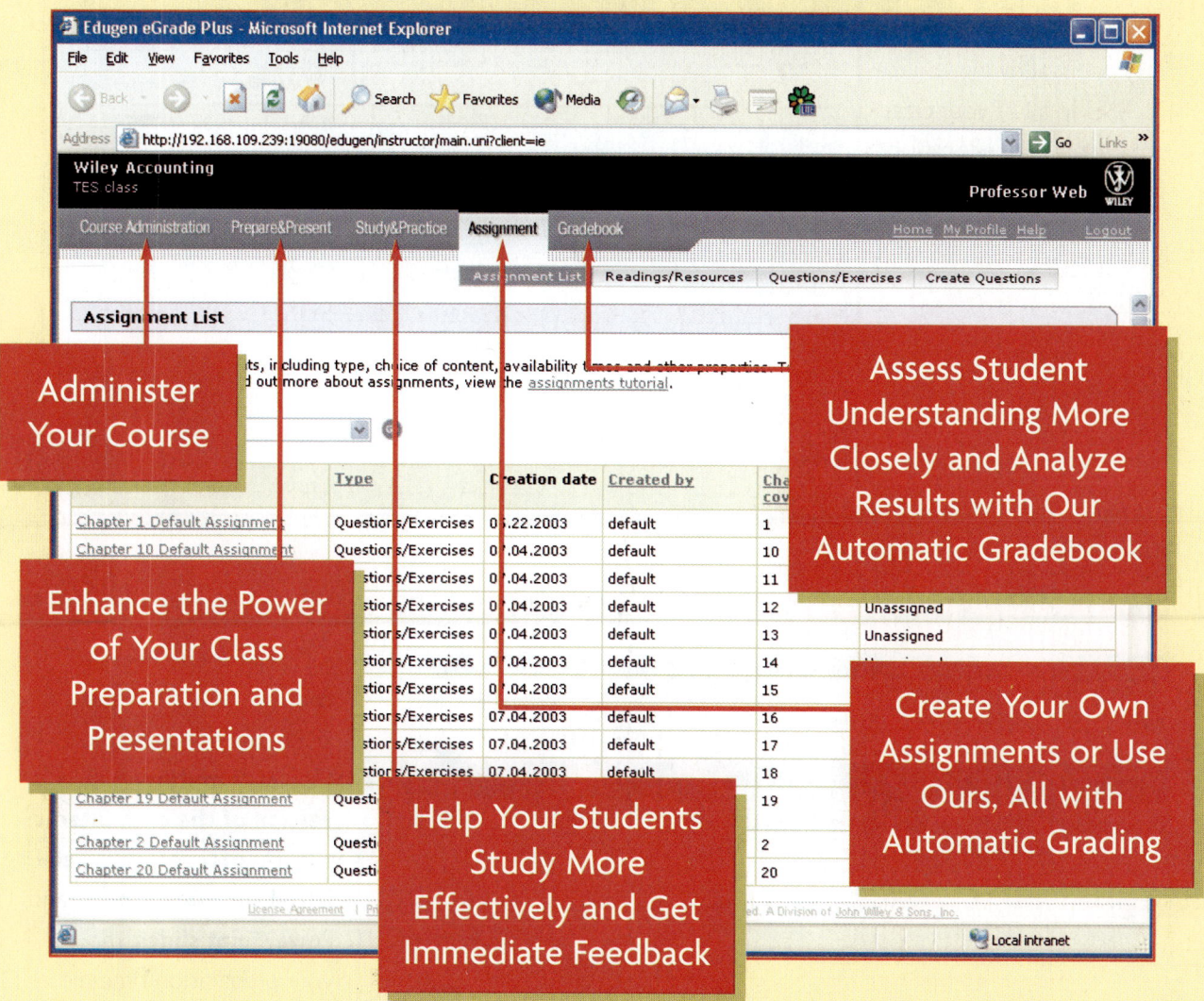

Administer Your Course

Enhance the Power of Your Class Preparation and Presentations

Help Your Students Study More Effectively and Get Immediate Feedback

Assess Student Understanding More Closely and Analyze Results with Our Automatic Gradebook

Create Your Own Assignments or Use Ours, All with Automatic Grading

All the content and tools you need, all in one location, in an easy-to-use browser format. Choose the resources you need, or rely on the arrangement supplied by us.

Now, many of Wiley's Book Companion Sites are available with EduGen, allowing you to create your own teaching and learning environment. Upon adoption of EduGen, you can begin to customize your course with the resources shown here. eGrade Plus with EduGen integrates text and media and keeps all of a book's online resources in one easily accessible location. eGrade Plus integrates two resources: homework problems for students and a multimedia version of this Wiley text. With eGrade Plus, each problem is linked to the relevant section of the multimedia book.

Administer Your Course

Course Administration tools allow you to manage your class and integrate your Wiley website resources with most Course Management Systems, allowing you to keep all of your class materials in one location.

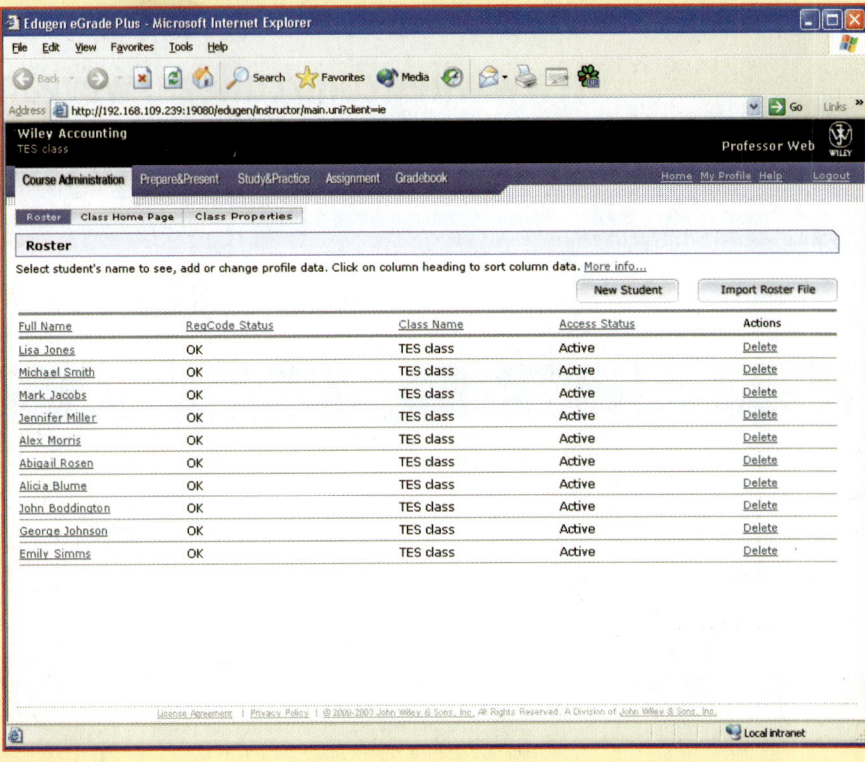

Enhance the Power of Your Class Preparation and Presentations

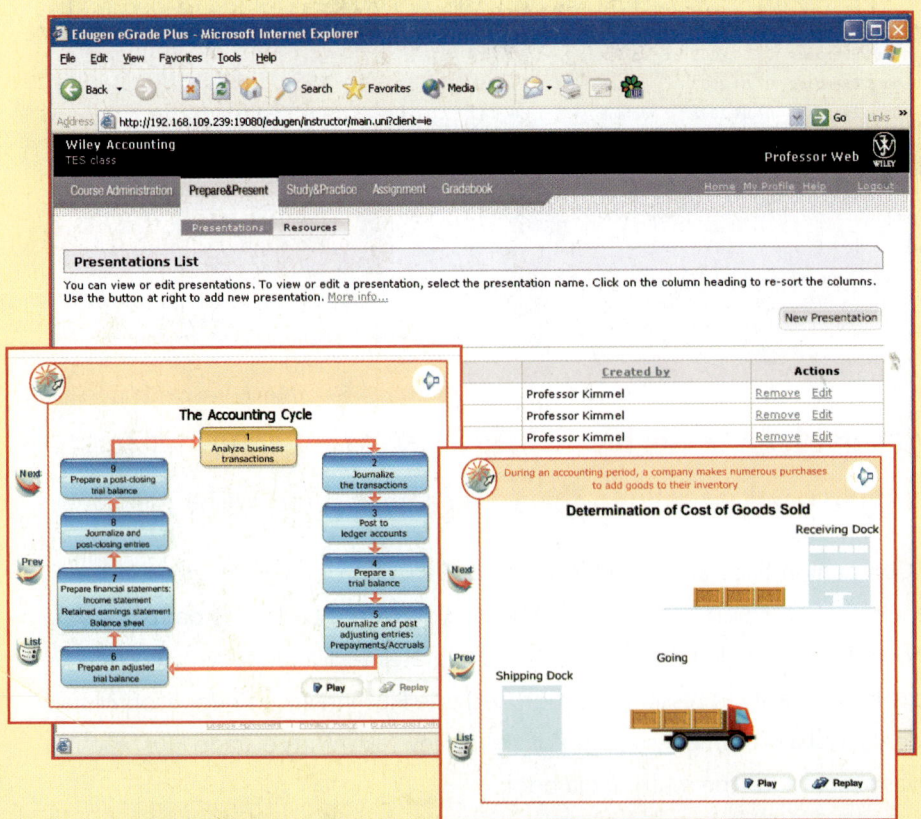

A **"Prepare and Present" tool** contains all of the Wiley-provided resources, such as **a multimedia version of the text, interactive chapter reviews, web-based tutorials, videos,** and **PowerPoint slides,** making your preparation time more efficient. You may easily adapt, customize, and add to Wiley content to meet the needs of your course.

Create Your Own Assignments or Use Ours, All with Automatic Grading

An **"Assignment"** area allows you to create **student homework** and **quizzes** that utilize **Wiley-provided question banks,** and an **electronic version of the text.** One of the most powerful features of Wiley's premium websites is that student assignments will be automatically graded and recorded in your gradebook. This will not only save you time but will provide your students with immediate feedback on their work.

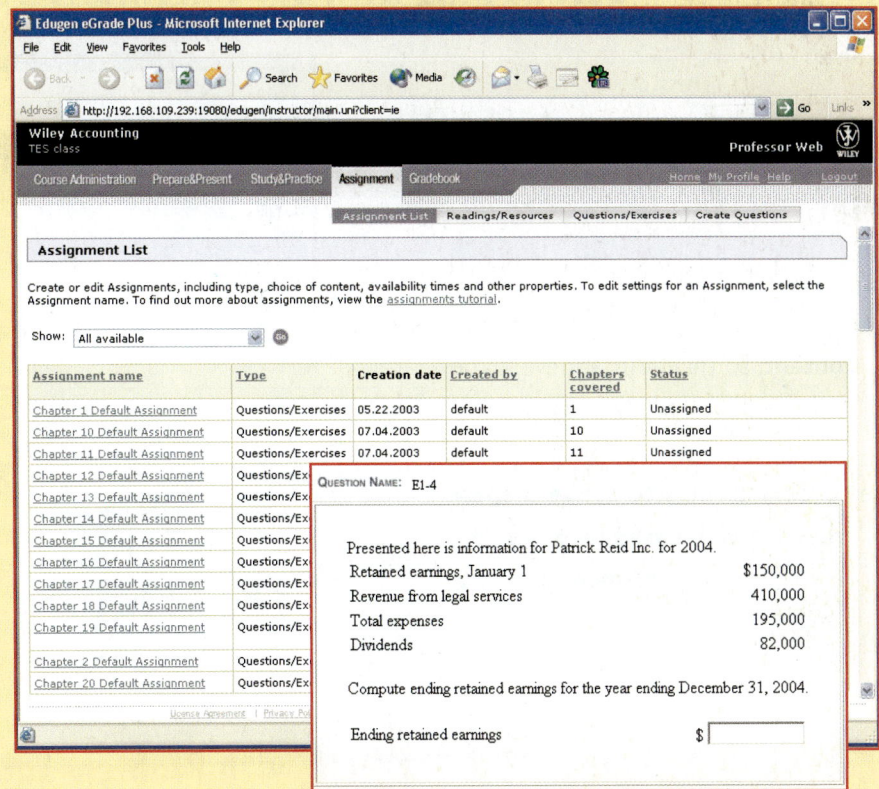

Assess Student Understanding More Closely

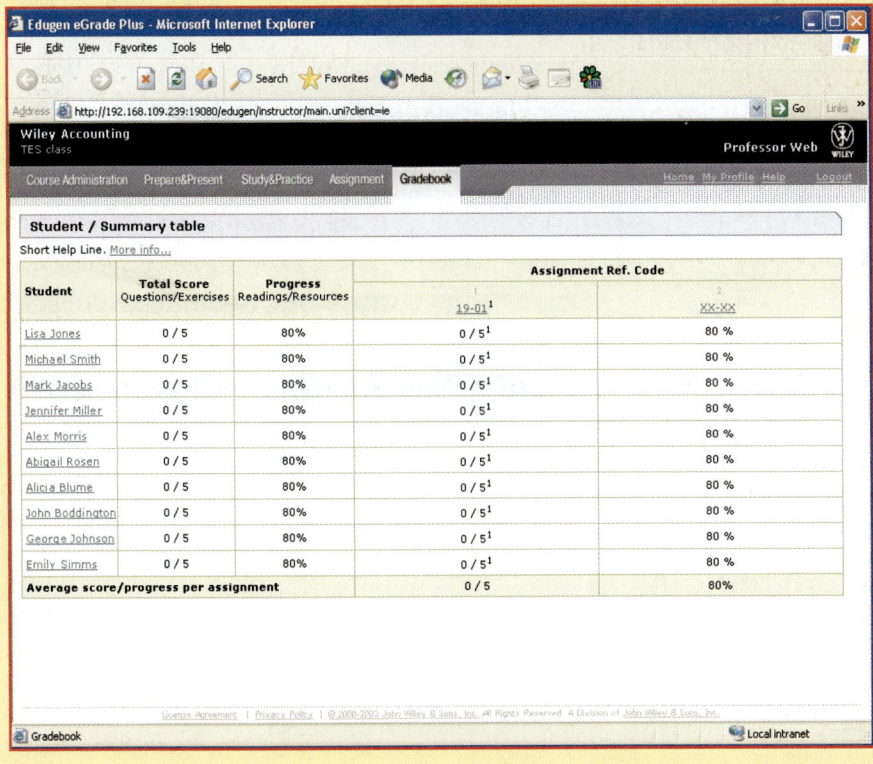

An **Instructor's Gradebook** will keep track of your students' progress and allow you to analyze individual and overall class results to determine their progress and level of understanding.

Students,
eGrade Plus with EduGen Allows You to:

Study More Effectively

Get Immediate Feedback When You Practice on Your Own

Our website links directly to **electronic book content,** so that you can review the text while you study and complete homework online. Additional resources include **interactive chapter reviews, web-based tutorials,** and **self-assessment quizzing.**

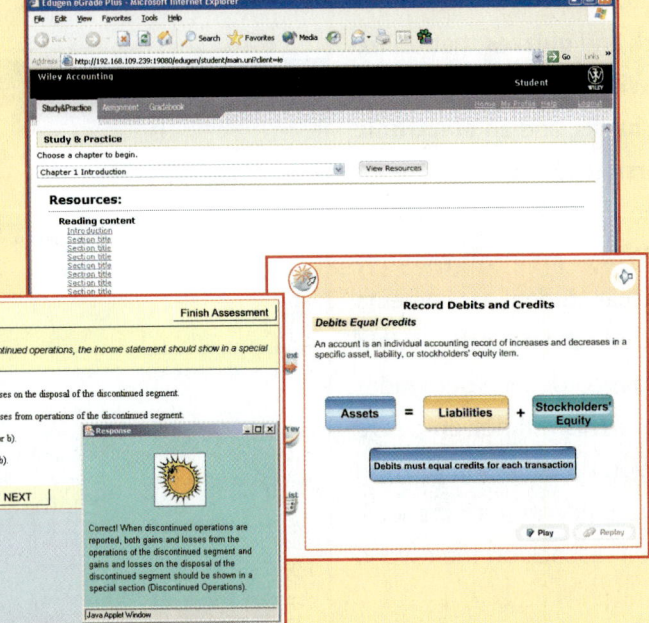

Complete Assignments / Get Help with Problem Solving

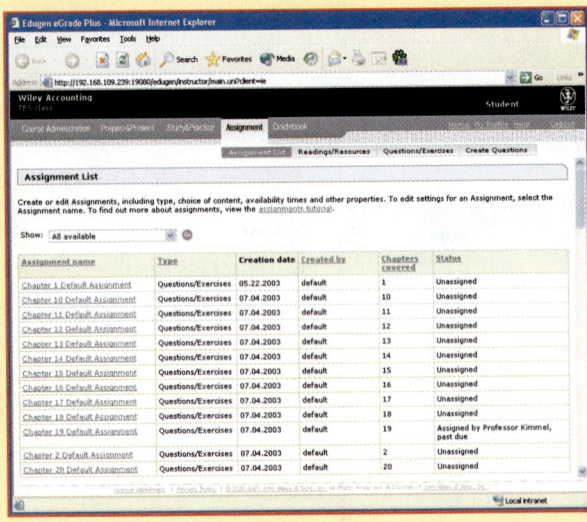

An **"Assignment"** area keeps all your assigned work in one location, making it easy for you to stay on task. In addition, many homework problems contain a **link** to the relevant section of the **electronic book,** providing you with a text explanation to help you conquer problem-solving obstacles as they arise.

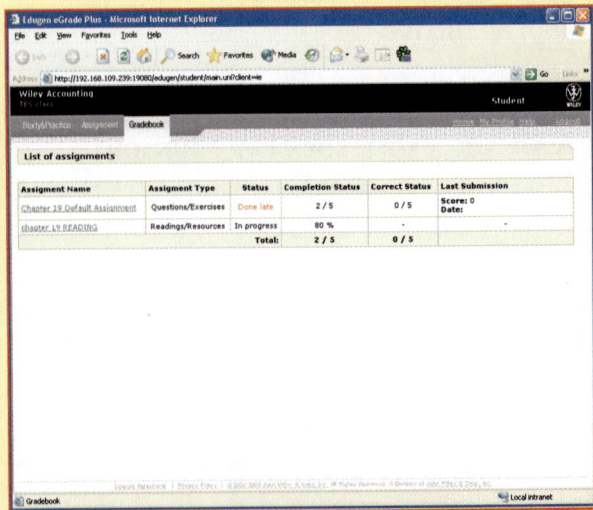

Keep Track of How You're Doing

A **Personal Gradebook** allows you to view your results from past assignments at any time.

7TH EDITION

Accounting Principles

Jerry J. Weygandt *PhD, CPA*

ARTHUR ANDERSEN ALUMNI PROFESSOR OF ACCOUNTING
University of Wisconsin
Madison, Wisconsin

Donald E. Kieso *PhD, CPA*

KPMG EMERITUS PROFESSOR OF ACCOUNTANCY
Northern Illinois University
DeKalb, Illinois

Paul D. Kimmel *PhD, CPA*

ASSOCIATE PROFESSOR OF ACCOUNTING
University of Wisconsin—Milwaukee
Milwaukee, Wisconsin

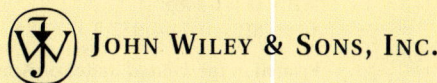
JOHN WILEY & SONS, INC.

Dedicated to
Amaya Mari, Christina Mari, and Max Joseph, and their grandmother, Enid
Morgan Marie, Cole William, and Erin Danielle, and their grandmother, Donna
Croix David, Marais Kachina, and Kale David, and their mother, Merlynn

PUBLISHER   *Susan Elbe*
ASSOCIATE PUBLISHER   *Jay O'Callaghan*
SENIOR MARKETING MANAGER   *Steve Herdegen*
PRODUCTION SERVICES MANAGER   *Jeanine Furino*
MEDIA EDITOR   *Allie Keim*
DEVELOPMENT EDITOR   *Ann Torbert*
PRODUCTION MANAGEMENT   *Ingrao Associates*
SR. DESIGNER   *Dawn L. Stanley*
ASSOCIATE EDITOR   *Ed Brislin*
TEXT AND COVER DESIGNER   *Jerry Wilke*
PHOTO EDITOR   *Sara Wight*
ILLUSTRATION EDITOR   *Sandra Rigby*
ART STUDIO   *Precision Graphics*
COVER PHOTO   © *Peter Turner/The Image Bank/Getty Images*

This book was set in Times Ten by GTS/Techbooks and printed and bound by Von Hoffmann Press. The cover was printed by Von Hoffmann Press.

To order books or for customer service please, call 1(800)-CALL-WILEY (225-5945).

We are grateful for permission to use the following material: The PepsiCo logo throughout the text and the PepsiCo 2002 Annual Report in Appendix A. Pepsi is a registered trademark of PepsiCo, Inc. Used with permission. The Coca-Cola 2002 Annual Report in Appendix B: Printed with permission of The Coca-Cola Company.

Copyright © 2005, by John Wiley & Sons, Inc.

Library of Congress Cataloging-in-Publication Data

Weygandt, Jerry J.
  Principles of financial accounting/Jerry J. Weygandt, Donald E. Kieso, Paul D. Kimmel.—7th ed.
    p. cm.
  Includes indexes.
  ISBN 0-471-44884-2 (pbk.: alk. paper) ISBN 0-471-44857-5 (cloth: alk. paper)
   1. Accounting. I. Kieso, Donald E. II. Kimmel, Paul D. III. Title.
  HF5635.W5244 2005
  657—dc22

                                                                              2003065000

ISBN: 0-471-44857-5
WIE ISBN: 0471-47952-7

Printed in the United States of America

10 9 8 7 6 5 4 3

Student Owner's Manual: How to Use the Study Aids in This Book

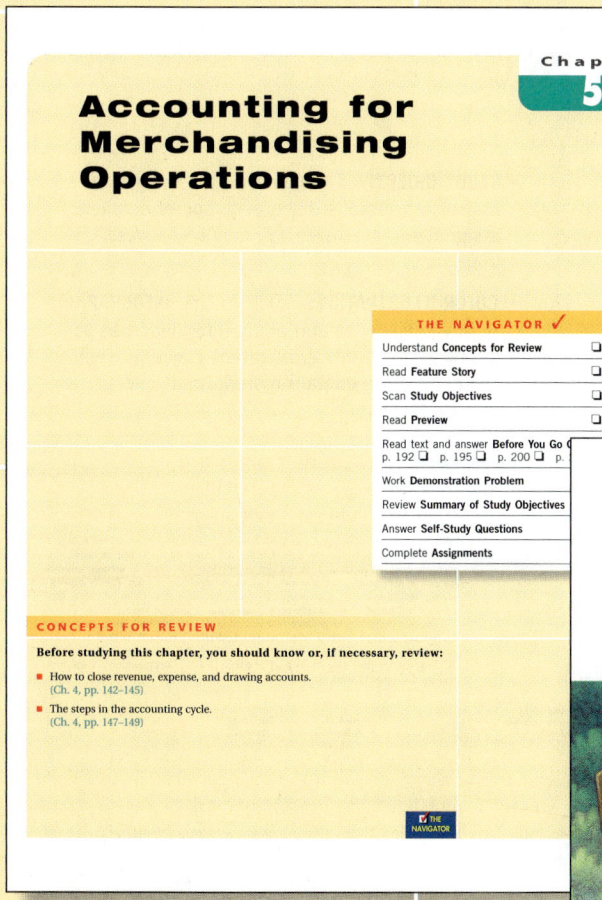

THE NAVIGATOR is a learning system designed to guide you through each chapter and help you succeed in learning the material. It consists of (1) a checklist at the beginning of the chapter, which outlines text features and study aids you will need, and (2) a series of check boxes that prompt you to use the learning aids in the chapter and set priorities as you study.

▼ The **FEATURE STORY** helps you picture how the chapter topic relates to the real world of accounting and business. References to the Feature Story throughout the chapter, will help you put new ideas in context, organize them, and remember them. Many Feature Stories end with the Internet addresses of the companies cited in the story.

▲ **CONCEPTS FOR REVIEW,** listed at the beginning of the chapter, are the accounting concepts learned in previous chapters that you will need to know in order to understand the topics you are about to learn. Page references point you to the earlier material, if you need to review before reading the chapter.

▶ **STUDY OBJECTIVES** at the beginning of each chapter give you a framework for learning the specific concepts covered in the chapter. Each study objective reappears in the margin where the concept is discussed. Finally, you can review the study objectives in the **SUMMARY** at the end of the chapter text.

PREVIEW OF CHAPTER 2

In Chapter 1, we analyzed business transactions in terms of the accounting equation. The cumulative effects of these transactions were presented in tabular form. Imagine a restaurant and gift shop such as The Mug and Musket using the same tabular format as Softbyte to keep track of every one of its transactions. In a single day, this restaurant and gift shop engages in hundreds of business transactions. To record each transaction this way would be impractical, expensive, and unnecessary. Instead, a set of procedures and records are used to keep track of transaction data more easily.

This chapter introduces and illustrates these basic procedures and records. The content and organization of Chapter 2 are as follows.

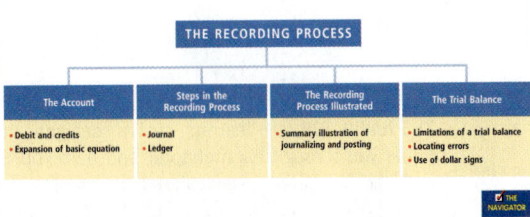

THE RECORDING PROCESS

The Account	Steps in the Recording Process	The Recording Process Illustrated	The Trial Balance
• Debit and credits • Expansion of basic equation	• Journal • Ledger	• Summary illustration of journalizing and posting	• Limitations of a trial balance • Locating errors • Use of dollar signs

THE NAVIGATOR

The Account

An account is an individual accounting record of increases and decreases in a specific asset, liability, or owner's equity item. For example, Softbyte (the company discussed in Chapter 1) would have separate accounts for Cash, Accounts Receivable, Accounts Payable, Service Revenue, Salaries Expense, and so on. In its simplest form, an account consists of three parts: (1) the title of the account, (2) a left or debit side, and (3) a right or credit side. Because the alignment of these parts of an account resembles the letter T, it is referred to as a T account. The basic form of an account is shown in Illustration 2-1.

STUDY OBJECTIVE 1
Explain what an account is and how it helps in the recording process.

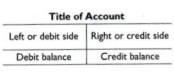

Illustration 2-1
Basic form of account

Title of Account

Left or debit side	Right or credit side
Debit balance	Credit balance

► The **PREVIEW** links the Feature Story with the major topics of the chapter and describes the purpose of the chapter. It then outlines the topics that are discussed. This narrative and visual preview helps you organize the information you are learning.

► **STUDY OBJECTIVES** reappear in the margins where the related topic is discussed. End-of-chapter assignments are keyed to study objectives.

► **COLOR ILLUSTRATIONS,** such as this **INFOGRAPHIC,** help you visualize and apply information as you study. They reinforce important concepts and therefore often contain material that may appear on exams.

► **KEY TERMS** and concepts are printed in blue where they are first explained in the text. They are listed and defined again in the end-of-chapter **GLOSSARY.**

► **KEY FORMULAS** that you will need to know and use are boxed off.

► **HELPFUL HINTS** in the margins are like having an instructor with you as you read. They further clarify concepts being discussed.

Book value at the beginning of the first year is the cost of the asset. This is so because the balance in accumulated depreciation at the beginning of the asset's useful life is zero. In subsequent years, book value is the difference between cost and accumulated depreciation to date. Unlike the other depreciation methods, the declining-balance method does not use depreciable cost. That is, **salvage value is ignored in determining the amount to which the declining-balance rate is applied.** Salvage value, however, does limit the total depreciation that can be taken. Depreciation stops when the asset's book value equals expected salvage value.

A common declining-balance rate is double the straight-line rate. As a result, the method is often referred to as the **double-declining-balance method.** If Barb's Florists uses the double-declining-balance method, the depreciation rate is 40% (2 × the straight-line rate of 20%). The computation of depreciation for the first year on the delivery truck is:

Illustration 10-13
Formula for declining-balance method

Book Value at Beginning of Year	×	Declining-Balance Rate	=	Annual Depreciation Expense
$13,000	×	40%	=	$5,200

The depreciation schedule under this method is as follows.

Illustration 10-14
Double-declining-balance depreciation schedule

BARB'S FLORISTS

	Computation			Annual	End of Year	
Year	Book Value Beginning of Year	× Depreciation Rate	=	Depreciation Expense	Accumulated Depreciation	Book Value
2005	$13,000	40%		$5,200	$ 5,200	$7,800
2006	7,800	40		3,120	8,320	4,680
2007	4,680	40		1,872	10,192	2,808
2008	2,808	40		1,123	11,315	1,685
2009	1,685	40		685*	12,000	1,000

*Computation of $674 ($1,685 × 40%) is adjusted to $685 in order for book value to equal salvage value.

HELPFUL HINT
The method recommended for an asset that is expected to be more productive in the first half of its useful life is the declining-balance method.

You can see that the delivery equipment is 69% depreciated ($8,320 ÷ $12,000) at the end of the second year. Under the straight-line method it would be depreciated 40% ($4,800 ÷ $12,000) at that time. Because the declining-balance method produces higher depreciation expense in the early years than in the later years, it is considered an accelerated-depreciation method. The declining-balance method is compatible with the matching principle. The higher depreciation expense in early years is matched with the higher benefits received in these years. On the other hand, lower depreciation expense is recognized in later years when the asset's contribution to revenue is less. Also, some assets lose usefulness rapidly because of obsolescence. In these cases, the declining-balance method provides a more appropriate depreciation amount.

When an asset is purchased during the year, the first year's declining-balance depreciation must be prorated on a time basis. For example, if Barb's Florists had purchased the truck on April 1, 2005, depreciation for 2005 would become $3,900 ($13,000 × 40% × 9/12). The book value at the beginning of 2006 is then $9,100 ($13,000 − $3,900), and the 2006 depreciation is $3,640 ($9,100 × 40%). Subsequent computations would follow from those amounts.

▶ **BEFORE YOU GO ON** sections follow each key topic. **REVIEW IT** questions prompt you to stop and review the key points you have just studied. If you cannot answer these questions, you should go back and read the section again.

REVIEW IT questions marked with the PepsiCo icon direct you to find information in PepsiCo, Inc.'s 2002 Annual Report, packaged with new copies of the book and printed in Appendix A. Answers appear at the end of the chapter.

Brief **DO IT** exercises ask you to put to work your newly acquired knowledge. They outline an **ACTION PLAN** necessary to complete the exercise, and they show a **SOLUTION.**

---

50   CHAPTER 2   The Recording Process

BEFORE YOU GO ON...

Review It

1. What do the terms debit and credit mean?
2. What are the debit and credit effects on assets, liabilities, and owner's capital?
3. What are the debit and credit effects on revenues, expenses, and owner's drawing?
4. What are the normal balances for PepsiCo's Cash, Accounts Payable, and Interest Expense accounts? The answers to this question are provided on page 85.

Do It

Kate Browne has just rented space in a shopping mall in which she will open a beauty salon, to be called "Hair It Is." Long before opening day and before purchasing equipment, hiring employees, and remodeling the space, Kate has been advised to set up a double-entry set of accounting records in which to record all of her business transactions.

Identify the balance sheet accounts that Kate will likely need to record the transactions needed to open her business. Indicate whether the normal balance of each account is a debit or a credit.

ACTION PLAN

■ Determine the types of accounts needed: Kate will need asset accounts for each different type of asset she invests in the business, and liability accounts for any debts she incurs.
■ Understand the types of owner's equity accounts: Only Owner's Capital will be needed when Kate begins the business. Other owner's equity accounts will be needed later.

SOLUTION   Kate would likely need the following accounts in which to record the transactions necessary to ready her beauty salon for opening day: Cash (debit balance); Equipment (debit balance); Supplies (debit balance); Accounts Payable (credit balance); if she borrows money, Notes payable (credit balance); K. Browne, Capital (credit balance).

Related exercise material: BE2-1, BE2-2, E2-1, E2-3, and E2-10.

THE NAVIGATOR

Classified Balance Sheet   155

DECKERS OUTDOOR CORPORATION	
Balance Sheet (partial)	
(in thousands)	
Current liabilities	
Notes payable	$ 3,951,000
Accounts payable	12,916,000
Allowance for returns	1,255,000
Salaries and commissions payable	2,342,000
Taxes payable	732,000
Other current liabilities	912,000
Total current liabilities	$22,108,000

Illustration 4-22
Current liabilities section

Liquidity

Illiquidity

Users of financial statements look closely at the relationship between current assets and current liabilities. This relationship is important in evaluating a company's liquidity—its ability to pay obligations that are expected to become due within the next year or operating cycle. When current assets exceed current liabilities at the balance sheet date, the likelihood for paying the liabilities is favorable. When the reverse is true, short-term creditors may not be paid, and the company may ultimately be forced into bankruptcy.

Long-Term Liabilities

Obligations expected to be paid after one year or an operating cycle, whichever is longer, are classified as long-term liabilities. Liabilities in this category include bonds payable, mortgages payable, long-term notes payable, lease liabilities, and obligations under employee pension plans. Many companies report long-term debt maturing after one year as a single amount in the balance sheet. They then show the details of the debt in the notes that accompany the financial statements. Others list the various sources of long-term liabilities. In its balance sheet, Brunswick Corporation reported the following.

ALTERNATIVE TERMINOLOGY

Long-term liabilities are also called *long-term debt* or *noncurrent liabilities.*

BRUNSWICK CORPORATION	
Balance Sheet (partial)	
(in thousands)	
Long-term liabilities	
Notes payable	$437.2
Bonds payable	124.4
Guaranteed debt	15.5
Other long-term debt	12.4
Total long-term liabilities	$589.5

Illustration 4-23
Long-term liabilities section

◀ **FINANCIAL STATEMENTS** appear regularly throughout the book. Those from actual companies are identified by a logo or photo. Often, numbers or categories are highlighted in red to draw your attention to key information.

◀ **ALTERNATIVE TERMINOLOGY** notes present synonymous terms that you may come across in practice.

◀ Note that the names of **REAL COMPANIES** are highlighted in red type.

Limitations of a Trial Balance

A trial balance does not guarantee freedom from recording errors, however. **It does not prove that all transactions have been recorded or that the ledger is correct.** Numerous errors may exist even though the trial balance columns agree. For example, the trial balance may balance even when (1) a transaction is not journalized, (2) a correct journal entry is not posted, (3) a journal entry is posted twice, (4) incorrect accounts are used in journalizing or posting, or (5) offsetting errors are made in recording the amount of a transaction. In other words, as long as equal debits and credits are posted, even to the wrong account or in the wrong amount, the total debits will equal the total credits.

ETHICS NOTE

Auditors are required to differentiate *errors* from *irregularities.* An *error* is the result of an unintentional mistake; it is neither ethical nor unethical. An *irregularity* is an intentional misstatement, which is viewed as unethical.

Locating Errors

The procedure for preparing a trial balance is relatively simple. However, if the trial balance does not balance, locating an error in a manual system can be timeconsuming, tedious, and frustrating. Errors generally result from mathematical mistakes, incorrect postings, or simply transcribing data incorrectly.

What do you do if you are faced with a trial balance that does not balance? First determine the amount of the difference between the two columns of the trial balance. After this amount is known, the following steps are often helpful:

▶ **ETHICS NOTES** point out ethical issues related to the nearby text discussion.

▶ **ACCOUNTING EQUATION ANALYSES** appear in the margin next to key journal entries. They will help you understand the impact of an accounting transaction on the financial statements, on the owners' equity accounts, and on the company's cash flows.

▶ **ACCOUNTING IN ACTION** examples give you more glimpses into how actual companies make decisions using accounting information. These high-interest boxes are classified by four types of issues—business, ethics, international, and e-business. The **E-BUSINESS INSIGHTS** report on how technology is affecting business transactions.

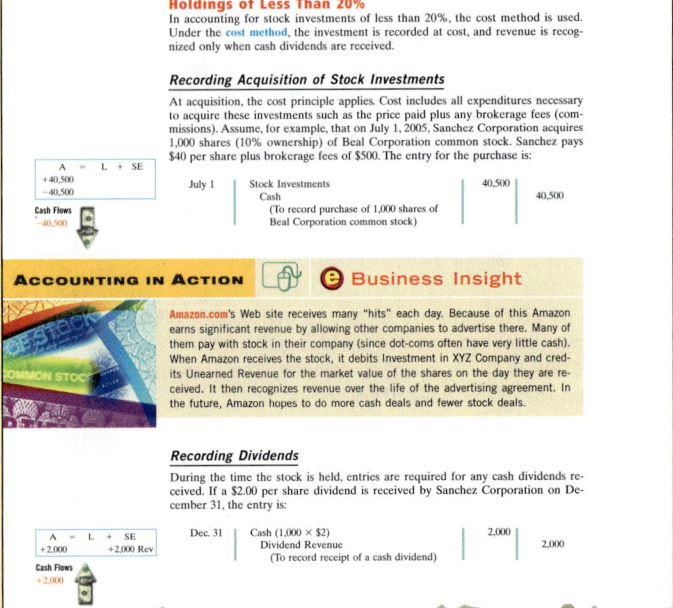

Holdings of Less Than 20%

In accounting for stock investments of less than 20%, the cost method is used. Under the **cost method**, the investment is recorded at cost, and revenue is recognized only when cash dividends are received.

Recording Acquisition of Stock Investments

At acquisition, the cost principle applies. Cost includes all expenditures necessary to acquire these investments such as the price paid plus any brokerage fees (commissions). Assume, for example, that on July 1, 2005, Sanchez Corporation acquires 1,000 shares (10% ownership) of Beal Corporation common stock. Sanchez pays $40 per share plus brokerage fees of $500. The entry for the purchase is:

A = L + SE			
+40,500			
−40,500			
Cash Flows			
−40,500			

July 1	Stock Investments	40,500	
	Cash		40,500
	(To record purchase of 1,000 shares of Beal Corporation common stock)		

ACCOUNTING IN ACTION | **e Business Insight**

Amazon.com's Web site receives many "hits" each day. Because of this Amazon earns significant revenue by allowing other companies to advertise there. Many of them pay with stock in their company (since dot-coms often have very little cash). When Amazon receives the stock, it debits Investment in XYZ Company and credits Unearned Revenue for the market value of the shares on the day they are received. It then recognizes revenue over the life of the advertising agreement. In the future, Amazon hopes to do more cash deals and fewer stock deals.

Recording Dividends

During the time the stock is held, entries are required for any cash dividends received. If a $2.00 per share dividend is received by Sanchez Corporation on December 31, the entry is:

A = L + SE			
+2,000	+2,000 Rev		
Cash Flows			
+2,000			

Dec. 31	Cash (1,000 × $2)	2,000	
	Dividend Revenue		2,000
	(To record receipt of a cash dividend)		

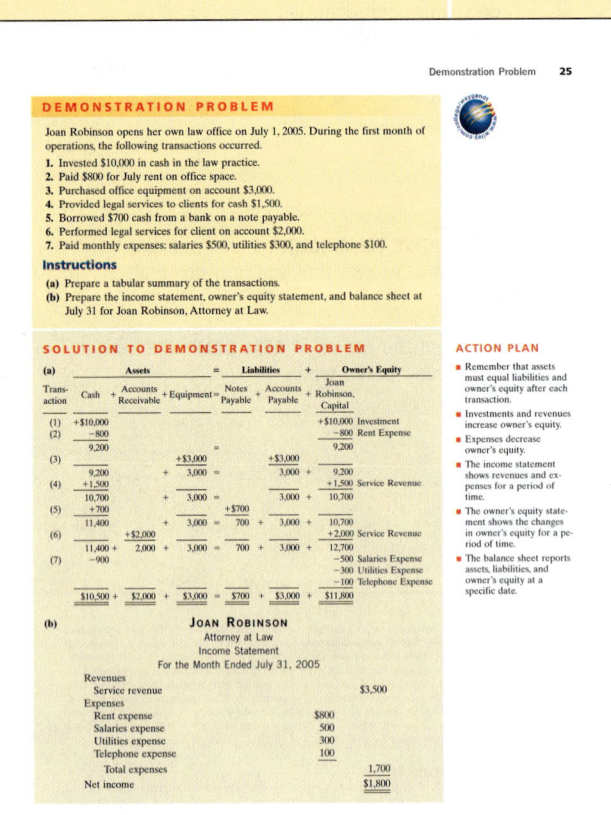

Demonstration Problem **25**

DEMONSTRATION PROBLEM

Joan Robinson opens her own law office on July 1, 2005. During the first month of operations, the following transactions occurred.

1. Invested $10,000 in cash in the law practice.
2. Paid $800 for July rent on office space.
3. Purchased office equipment on account $3,000.
4. Provided legal services to clients for cash $1,500.
5. Borrowed $700 cash from a bank on a note payable.
6. Performed legal services for client on account $2,000.
7. Paid monthly expenses: salaries $500, utilities $300, and telephone $100.

Instructions

(a) Prepare a tabular summary of the transactions.
(b) Prepare the income statement, owner's equity statement, and balance sheet at July 31 for Joan Robinson, Attorney at Law.

◀ A **DEMONSTRATION PROBLEM** is the final step before you begin homework. These sample problems provide you with an **ACTION PLAN** in the margin that lists the strategies needed to approach and solve the problem. The **SOLUTION** demonstrates both the form and content of complete answers.

Where indicated, an interactive version of the Demonstration Problem is available with eGrade Plus.

▶ The **SUMMARY OF STUDY OBJECTIVES** reviews the main points related to the Study Objectives. It provides you with another opportunity to review what you have learned as well as to see how the key topics within the chapter fit together.

▶ The **GLOSSARY** defines all the **KEY TERMS** and **CONCEPTS** introduced in the chapter. Page references help you find any terms you need to study further. The **WEB ICON** tells you that you can review these terms interactively on the Website.

◀ In some chapters, **APPENDIXES** that follow the summary of the main part of the chapter offer expanded coverage of accounting procedures or further discussion of certain topics.

▶ **SELF-STUDY QUESTIONS** provide a practice test, keyed to Study Objectives, that gives you an opportunity to check your knowledge of important topics. Answers appear at the end of the chapter. The **WEB ICON** tells you that you can answer these **SELF-STUDY QUESTIONS** interactively on the book's Website. There is an additional **SELF-TEST** at the Website that can further help you master the material.

◀ **QUESTIONS** allow you to explain your understanding of concepts and relationships from the chapter. Use them to help prepare for class discussion and tests.

Inset: Glossary page 425

Glossary   **425**

SUMMARY OF STUDY OBJECTIVES

1. **Describe how the cost principle applies to plant assets.** The cost of plant assets includes all expenditures necessary to acquire the asset and make it ready for its intended use. Cost is measured by the cash or cash equivalent price paid.

2. **Explain the concept of depreciation.** Depreciation is the allocation of the cost of a plant asset to expense over its useful (service) life in a rational and systematic manner. Depreciation is not a process of valuation, nor is it a process that results in an accumulation of cash.

3. **Compute periodic depreciation using different methods.** There are three depreciation methods:

Method	Effect on Annual Depreciation	Formula
Straight-line	Constant amount	Depreciable cost ÷ Useful life (in years)
Units-of-activity	Varying amount	Depreciation cost per unit × Units of activity during the year
Declining-balance	Decreasing amount	Book value at beginning of year × Declining-balance rate

expenditures are generally debited to the plant asset affected.

6. **Explain how to account for the disposal of a plant asset.** The accounting for disposal of a plant asset through retirement or sale is as follows:
   (a) Eliminate the book value of the plant asset at the date of disposal.
   (b) Record cash proceeds, if any.
   (c) Account for the difference between the book value and the cash proceeds as a gain or loss on disposal.

7. **Compute periodic depletion of natural resources.** Compute depletion cost per unit by dividing the total cost of the natural resource minus salvage value by the number of units estimated to be in the resource. Then multiply the depletion cost per unit by the number of units extracted and sold.

8. **Explain the basic issues related to accounting for intangible assets.** The accounting for intangible assets and plant assets is much the same. One difference is that the term used to describe the write-off of an intangible asset is amortization, rather than depreciation. The straight-line method is normally used for amortizing intangible assets.

GLOSSARY

Accelerated-depreciation method Depreciation method that produces higher depreciation expense in the early years than in the later years. (p. 410).

Additions and improvements Costs incurred to increase the operating efficiency, productive capacity, or useful life of a plant asset. (p. 413).

Amortization The allocation of the cost of an intangible asset to expense over its useful life in a systematic and rational manner. (p. 418).

Asset turnover ratio A measure of how efficiently a company uses its assets to generate sales; calculated as net sales divided by average total assets. (p. 422).

Capital expenditures Expenditures that increase the company's investment in productive facilities. (p. 413).

Copyright Exclusive grant from the federal government that allows the owner to reproduce and sell an artistic or published work. (p. 419).

Declining-balance method Depreciation method that applies a constant rate to the declining book value of the asset and produces a decreasing annual depreciation expense over the useful life of the asset. (p. 409).

Depletion The allocation of the cost of a natural resource to expense in a rational and systematic manner over the resource's useful life. (p. 417).

Inset: Chapter 1 Appendix page 28

28   CHAPTER 1   Accounting in Action

APPENDIX   THE ACCOUNTING PROFESSION

The Accounting Profession

What would you do if you join the accounting profession? You probably would work in one of three major fields—public accounting, private accounting, or not-for-profit accounting.

Public Accounting

STUDY OBJECTIVE 9
Identify the three major fields of the accounting profession and potential accounting careers.

In *public accounting*, you would offer expert service to the general public in much the same way that a doctor serves patients and a lawyer serves clients. A major portion of public accounting involves *auditing*. In this area, a certified public accountant (CPA) examines the financial statements of companies and expresses an opinion as to the fairness of presentation. When the presentation is fair, users consider the statements to be **reliable**. For example, **PepsiCo** investors would demand audited financial statements before extending it financing.

Taxation is another major area of public accounting. The work performed by tax specialists includes tax advice and planning, preparing tax returns, and representing clients before governmental agencies such as the Internal Revenue Service.

A third area in public accounting is *management consulting*. It ranges from the installing of basic accounting systems to helping companies determine whether they should use the space shuttle for high-tech research and development projects.

Inset: Self-Study Questions page 695

Questions   **695**

SELF-STUDY QUESTIONS
Self-Study/Self-Test

Answers are at the end of the chapter.

(SO 2) **1.** Debt investments are initially recorded at:
   a. cost.
   b. cost plus accrued interest.
   c. fair value.
   d. None of the above.

(SO 2) **2.** Hanes Company sells debt investments costing $26,000 for $28,000, plus accrued interest that has been recorded. In journalizing the sale, credits are to:
   a. Debt Investments and Loss on Sale of Debt Investments.
   b. Debt Investments, Gain on Sale of Debt Investments, and Bond Interest Receivable.
   c. Stock Investments and Bond Interest Receivable.
   d. No correct answer given.

(SO 3) **3.** Pryor Company receives net proceeds of $42,000 on the sale of stock investments that cost $39,500. This transaction will result in reporting in the income statement a:
   a. loss of $2,500 under "Other expenses and losses."
   b. loss of $2,500 under "Operating expenses."
   c. gain of $2,500 under "Other revenues and gains."
   d. gain of $2,500 under "Operating revenues."

(SO 3) **4.** The equity method of accounting for long-term investments in stock should be used when the investor has significant influence over an investee and owns:
   a. between 20% and 50% of the investee's common stock.
   b. 20% or more of the investee's common stock.
   c. more than 50% of the investee's common stock.
   d. less than 20% of the investee's common stock.

(SO 4) **5.** Which of the following statements is *not true?* Consolidated financial statements are useful to:
   a. determine the profitability of specific subsidiaries.

   b. determine the total profitability of enterprises under common control.
   c. determine the breadth of a parent company's operations.
   d. determine the full extent of total obligations of enterprises under common control.

(SO 5) **6.** At the end of the first year of operations, the total cost of the trading securities portfolio is $120,000. Total fair value is $115,000. The financial statements should show:
   a. a reduction of an asset of $5,000 and a realized loss of $5,000.
   b. a reduction of an asset of $5,000 and an unrealized loss of $5,000 in the stockholders' equity section.
   c. a reduction of an asset of $5,000 in the current assets section and an unrealized loss of $5,000 in "Other expenses and losses."
   d. a reduction of an asset of $5,000 in the current assets section and a realized loss of $5,000 in "Other expenses and losses."

(SO 5) **7.** In the balance sheet, a debit balance in Unrealized Gain or Loss—Equity is reported as a:
   a. contra asset account.
   b. contra stockholders' equity account.
   c. loss in the income statement.
   d. loss in the retained earnings statement.

(SO 6) **8.** Short-term debt investments must be readily marketable and be expected to be sold within:
   a. 3 months from the date of purchase.
   b. the next year or operating cycle, whichever is shorter.
   c. the next year or operating cycle, whichever is longer.
   d. the operating cycle.

THE NAVIGATOR

Inset: Questions

QUESTIONS

1. What are the reasons that corporations invest in securities?

2. (a) What is the cost of an investment in bonds? (b) When is interest on bonds recorded?

3. Jose Gonzalez is confused about losses and gains on the sale of debt investments. Explain to Jose (a) how the gain or loss is computed, and (b) the statement presentation of the gains and losses.

4. Sablow Company sells Gish's bonds costing $40,000 for $45,000, including $1,000 of accrued interest. In recording the sale, Sablow books a $5,000 gain. Is this correct? Explain.

5. What is the cost of an investment in stock?

6. To acquire Jackson Corporation stock, R. Toni pays $62,000 in cash, plus $1,500 broker's fees. What entry

should be made for this investment, assuming the stock is readily marketable?

7. (a) When should a long-term investment in common stock be accounted for by the equity method? (b) When is revenue recognized under this method?

8. Diaz Corporation uses the equity method to account for its ownership of 25% of the common stock of Victor Packing. During 2005 Victor reported a net income of $80,000 and declares and pays cash dividends of $10,000. What recognition should Diaz Corporation give to these events?

9. What constitutes "significant influence" when an investor's financial interest is below the 50% level?

10. Distinguish between the cost and equity methods of accounting for investments in stocks.

BRIEF EXERCISES

Journalize entries for debt investments.

(SO 2)

BE17-1 Buslik Corporation purchased debt investments for $46,800 on January 1, 2005. On July 1, 2005, Buslik received cash interest of $2,340. Journalize the purchase and the receipt of interest. Assume that no interest has been accrued.

Journalize entries for stock investments.

(SO 3)

BE17-2 On August 1, Hyun Company buys 1,000 shares of Morgan common stock for $35,000 cash, plus brokerage fees of $600. On December 1, Hyun sells the stock investments for $40,000 in cash. Journalize the purchase and sale of the common stock.

Record transactions under the equity method of accounting.

(SO 3)

BE17-3 Iguana Company owns 30% of Hyde Company. For the current year Hyde reports net income of $180,000 and declares and pays a $50,000 cash dividend. Record Iguana's equity in Hyde's net income and the receipt of dividends from Hyde.

Prepare adjusting entry using fair value.

(SO 5)

BE17-4 The cost of the trading securities of Homura Company at December 31, 2005, is $64,000. At December 31, 2005, the fair value of the securities is $59,000. Prepare the adjusting entry to record the securities at fair value.

Indicate statement presentation using fair value.

(SO 5, 6)

BE17-5 For the data presented in BE17-4, show the financial statement presentation of the trading securities and related accounts.

Prepare adjusting entry using fair value.

(SO 5)

BE17-6 Karpman Corporation holds as a long-term investment available-for-sale stock securities costing $72,000. At December 31, 2005, the fair value of the securities is $68,000. Prepare the adjusting entry to record the securities at fair value.

Indicate statements presentation using fair value.

(SO 5, 6)

BE17-7 For the data presented in BE17-6, show the financial statement presentation of the available-for-sale securities and related accounts. Assume the available-for-sale securities are noncurrent.

Prepare investments section of balance sheet.

(SO 5, 6)

BE17-8 Dobbs Corporation has the following long-term investments: (1) Common stock of Kubek Co. (10% ownership) held as available-for-sale securities, cost $108,000, fair value $115,000. (2) Common stock of Ely Inc. (30% ownership), cost $210,000, equity $250,000. Prepare the investments section of the balance sheet.

◀ **BRIEF EXERCISES** help you focus on one Study Objective at a time and thus help you build confidence in your basic skills and knowledge.

EXERCISES

Journalize issuance of common stock.

(SO 3)

E14-1 During its first year of operations, Klumpe Corporation had the following transactions pertaining to its common stock.

Jan. 10   Issued 70,000 shares for cash at $5 per share.
July 1   Issued 40,000 shares for cash at $8 per share.

Instructions
(a) Journalize the transactions, assuming that the common stock has a par value of $5 per share.
(b) Journalize the transactions, assuming that the common stock is no-par with a stated value of $1 per share.

Journalize issuance of common and preferred stock and purchase of treasury stock.

(SO 3, 4, 5)

E14-2 Garza Co. had the following transactions during the current period.

Mar. 2   Issued 5,000 shares of $1 par value common stock to attorneys in payment of a bill for $30,000 for services provided in helping the company to incorporate.
June 12   Issued 60,000 shares of $1 par value common stock for cash of $375,000.
July 11   Issued 1,000 shares of $100 par value preferred stock for cash at $110 per share.
Nov. 28   Purchased 2,000 shares of treasury stock for $80,000.

Instructions
Journalize the transactions.

▶ **EXERCISES,** which are more difficult than Brief Exercises, help you continue to build confidence in your ability to use the material learned in the chapter.

PROBLEMS: SET A

P4-1A The trial balance columns of the work sheet for Undercover Roofing at March 31, 2005, are as follows.

Prepare a work sheet, financial statements, and adjusting and closing entries.

(SO 1, 2, 3, 6)

UNDERCOVER ROOFING
Work Sheet
For the Month Ended March 31, 2005

Account Titles	Trial Balance Dr.	Trial Balance Cr.
Cash	2,500	
Accounts Receivable	1,800	
Roofing Supplies	1,100	
Equipment	6,000	
Accumulated Depreciation—Equipment		1,200
Accounts Payable		1,400
Unearned Revenue		300
I. Spy, Capital		7,000
I. Spy, Drawing	600	
Service Revenue		3,000
Salaries Expense	700	
Miscellaneous Expense	200	
	12,900	12,900

Other data:
1. A physical count reveals only $140 of roofing supplies on hand.
2. Depreciation for March is $200.
3. Unearned revenue amounted to $130 after adjustment on March 31.
4. Accrued salaries are $350.

Instructions
(a) Enter the trial balance on a work sheet and complete the work sheet.
(b) Prepare an income statement and owner's equity statement for the month of March and a classified balance sheet at March 31. I. Spy did not make any additional investments in the business in March.
(c) Journalize the adjusting entries from the adjustments columns of the work sheet.
(d) Journalize the closing entries from the financial statement columns of the work sheet.

(a) Adjusted trial balance
$13,450
(b) Net income $ 760
Total assets $9,040

◀ **SPREADSHEET EXERCISES** and **PROBLEMS,** identified by an icon, are selected problems that can be solved using the spreadsheet software *Solving Principles of Accounting Problems Using Excel.*

◀ **CHECK FIGURES** in the margin provide key numbers to let you know you're on the right track.

PROBLEMS: SET B

P4-1B Sherlock Holmes began operations as a private investigator on January 1, 2005. The trial balance columns of the work sheet for Sherlock Holmes P.I. at March 31 are as follows.

Prepare work sheet, financial statements, and adjusting and closing entries.

(SO 1, 2, 3, 6)

SHERLOCK HOLMES P.I.
Work Sheet
For the Quarter Ended March 31, 2005

Account Titles	Trial Balance Dr.	Trial Balance Cr.
Cash	11,400	
Accounts Receivable	5,620	
Supplies	1,050	
Prepaid Insurance	2,400	
Equipment	30,000	
Notes Payable		10,000
Accounts Payable		12,350
S. Holmes, Capital		20,000
S. Holmes, Drawing	600	
Service Revenue		13,620
Salaries Expense	2,200	
Travel Expense	1,300	
Rent Expense	1,200	
Miscellaneous Expense	200	
	55,970	55,970

Other data:
1. Supplies on hand total $680.
2. Depreciation is $1,000 per quarter.
3. Interest accrued on 6-month note payable, issued January 1, $300.
4. Insurance expires at the rate of $200 per month.
5. Services provided but unbilled at March 31 total $830.

Instructions
(a) Enter the trial balance on a work sheet and complete the work sheet.
(b) Prepare an income statement and owner's equity statement for the quarter and a classified balance sheet at March 31. S. Holmes did not make any additional investments in the business during the quarter ended March 31, 2005.
(c) Journalize the adjusting entries from the adjustments columns of the work sheet.
(d) Journalize the closing entries from the financial statement columns of the work sheet.

(a) Adjusted trial balance
$58,100
(b) Net income $ 7,280
Total assets $49,330

▶ Each **PROBLEM** helps you pull together and apply several concepts from the chapter. Two sets of **PROBLEMS—A** and **B**—are keyed to the same Study Objectives and provide additional opportunities for practice.

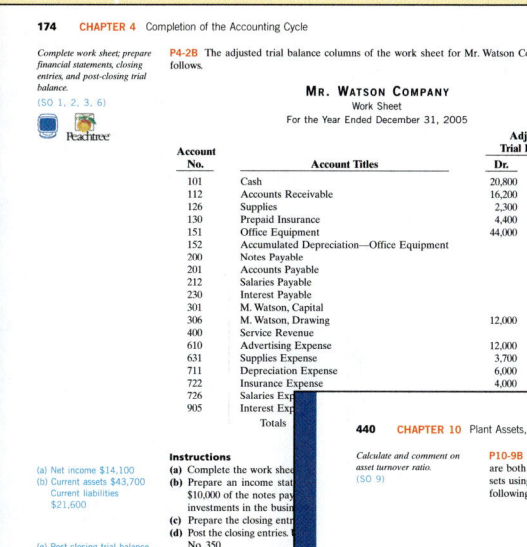

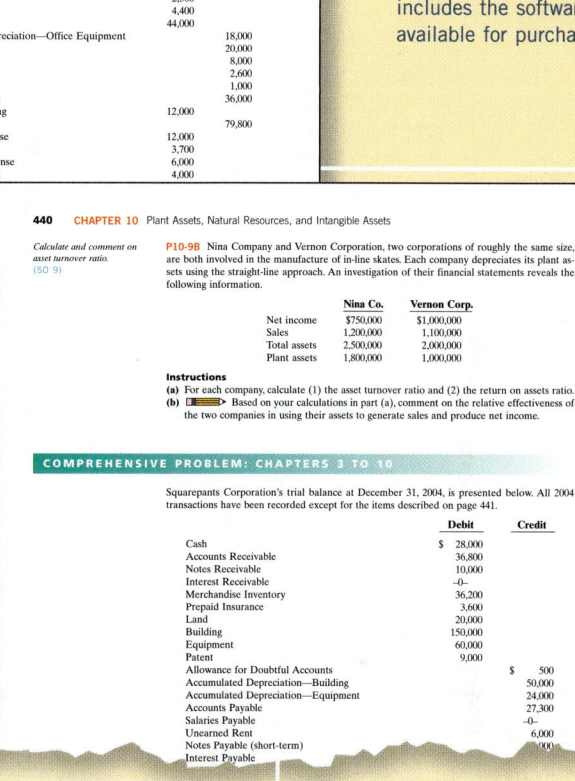

▶ **GENERAL LEDGER PROBLEMS,** identified by an icon, are selected problems that can be solved using the *General Ledger Software* package.

◀ Problems marked with the **PEACHTREE** icon can be worked using *Peachtree Complete Accounting® to Accompany Principles of Accounting*. A separate student workbook that includes the software is available for purchase.

▶ Certain Exercises and Problems, marked with a pencil icon help you practice **BUSINESS WRITING SKILLS,** which are much in demand among employers.

▶ **COMPREHENSIVE PROBLEMS** in seven chapters give you the opportunity to put to use concepts covered across multiple chapters.

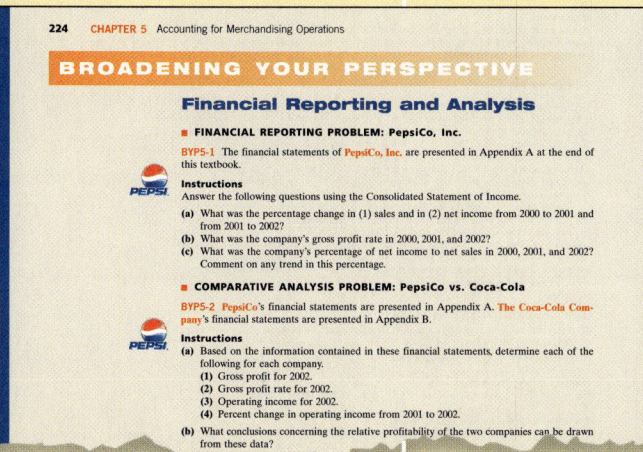

◀ The **BROADENING YOUR PERSPECTIVE** section helps you pull together various concepts from the chapter and apply them to real-world business situations.

◀ In the **FINANCIAL REPORTING PROBLEM** you study various aspects of the financial statements of PepsiCo, Inc., which are printed in Appendix A.

◀ A **COMPARATIVE ANALYSIS PROBLEM** offers the opportunity to compare and contrast the financial reporting of PepsiCo with a competitor, The Coca-Cola Company.

■ **INTERPRETING FINANCIAL STATEMENTS: A Global Focus**

BYP5-3 Recently it was announced that two giant French retailers, **Carrefour SA** and **Promodes SA**, would merge. A headline in the *Wall Street Journal* blared, "French Retailers Create New Wal-Mart Rival." While **Wal-Mart**'s total sales would still exceed those of the combined company, Wal-Mart's international sales are far less than those of the combined company. This is a serious concern for Wal-Mart, since its primary opportunity for future growth lies outside of the United States.

Below are basic financial data for the combined corporation (in French francs) and Wal-Mart (in U.S. dollars). Even though their results are presented in different currencies, by employing ratios we can make some basic comparisons.

	Carrefour/ Promodes (in billions)	Wal-Mart (in billions)
Sales	Fr 298.0	$137.6
Cost of goods sold	274.0	108.7
Operating expenses	9.6	22.4
Net income	5.5	4.4
Total assets	155.0	50.0
Average total assets	140.4	47.7
Current assets	63.5	21.1
Current liabilities	85.8	16.8
Total liabilities	114.2	28.9

Instructions

Compare the two companies by answering the following.

(a) Calculate the gross profit rate for each of the companies, and discuss their relative ability to control cost of goods sold.

◄ **INTERPRETING FINANCIAL STATEMENTS: A GLOBAL FOCUS** ask you to read parts of financial statements of actual international companies, interpret this information, and apply concepts from the chapter to specific situations faced by these companies.

■ **EXPLORING THE WEB**

BYP12-2 The **Financial Accounting Standards Board (FASB)** is a private organization established to improve accounting standards and financial reporting. The FASB conducts extensive research before issuing a "Statement of Financial Accounting Standards," which represents an authoritative expression of generally accepted accounting principles.

Address: www.rutgers.edu/accounting/raw, or go to www.wiley.com/college/weygandt

Steps

1. Choose FASB.
2. Choose **FASB Facts**.

Instructions

Answer the following questions.

(a) What is the mission of the FASB?
(b) How are topics added to the FASB technical agenda?
(c) What characteristics make the FASB's procedures an "open" decision-making process?

► **EXPLORING THE WEB** exercises guide you to Web sites where you can find and analyze information related to the chapter topic.

Critical Thinking

■ **GROUP DECISION CASE**

BYP3-5 The Happy Travel Court was organized on April 1, 2004, by Alice Henry. Alice is a good manager but a poor accountant. From the trial balance prepared by a part-time bookkeeper, Alice prepared the following income statement for the quarter that ended March 31, 2005.

HAPPY TRAVEL COURT
Income Statement
For the Quarter Ended March 31, 2005

Revenues		
Travel court rental revenue		$90,000
Operating expenses		
Advertising	$ 5,200	
Wages	29,800	
Utilities	900	
Depreciation	800	
Repairs	4,000	
Total operating expenses		40,700
Net income		$49,300

Alice knew that something was wrong with the statement because net income had never exceeded $20,000 in any one quarter. Knowing that you are an experienced accountant, she asks you to review the income statement and other data.

You first look at the trial balance. In addition to the account balances reported above in the income statement, the ledger contains the following additional selected balances at March 31, 2005.

Supplies	$ 6,200
Prepaid Insurance	7,200
Notes Payable	12,000

You then make inquiries and discover the following.

1. Travel court rental fees include advanced rentals for summer month occupancy $20,000.
2. There were $1,300 of supplies on hand at Mar[ch]
3. [P]repaid in[surance...]

◄ The **GROUP DECISION CASE** helps you build decision-making skills by analyzing accounting information in a less structured situation. These cases require teams of students to evaluate a manager's decision, or they lead to a decision among alternative courses of action. They also give practice in building business communication skills.

■ **COMMUNICATION ACTIVITY**

BYP3-6 In reviewing the accounts of Karibeth Co. at the end of the year, you discover that adjusting entries have not been made.

Instructions

Write a memo to Kari Beth Renfro, the owner of Karibeth Co., that explains the following: the nature and purpose of adjusting entries, why adjusting entries are needed, and the types of adjusting entries that may be made.

■ **ETHICS CASE**

BYP3-7 Santa Fe Company is a pesticide manufacturer. Its sales declined greatly this year due to the passage of legislation outlawing the sale of several of Santa Fe's chemical pesticides. In the coming year, Santa Fe will have environmentally safe and competitive chemicals to replace these discontinued products. Sales in the next year are expected to greatly exceed any prior year's. The decline in sales and profits appears to be a one-year aberration. But even so, the company president fears a large dip in the current year's profits. He believes that such a dip could cause a significant drop in the market price of Santa Fe's stock and make the company a takeover target.

To avoid this possibility, the company president calls in Diane Leno, controller, to discuss this period's year-end adjusting entries. He urges her to accrue every possible revenue and to defer as many expenses as possible. He says to Diane, "We need the revenues this year, and next year can easily absorb expenses deferred from this year. We can't let our stock price be hammered down!" Diane didn't get around to recording the adjusting entries until January 17, but she dated the entries December 31 as if they were recorded then. Diane also made every effort to comply with the president's request.

Instructions

(a) Who are the stakeholders in this situation?
(b) What are the ethical considerations of (1) the president's request and (2) Diane's dating the adjusting entries December 31?
(c) Can Diane accrue revenues and defer expenses and still be ethical?

Answers to Self-Study Questions
1. c **2.** a **3.** d **4.** d **5.** d **6.** c **7.** a **8.** b **9.** b **10.** c ***11.** a

Answer to PepsiCo Review It Question 4, p. 99
Per Note 4, **PepsiCo**'s 2002 depreciation expense is $929 million; 2001 depreciation expense is $843 million.

► **COMMUNICATION ACTIVITIES** help you build business communication skills by asking you to engage in real-world business situations using writing, speaking, or presentation skills.

► In the **ETHICS CASES,** you will reflect on typical ethical dilemmas, analyze the stakeholders and the issues involved, and decide on an appropriate course of action.

► **ANSWERS TO SELF-STUDY QUESTIONS** provide feedback on your understanding of concepts.

► **ANSWERS TO** *REVIEW IT* **QUESTIONS** based on the PepsiCo financial statements appear here.

► After you complete your homework assignments, it's a good idea to go back to **THE NAVIGATOR** checklist at the start of the chapter to see if you have used all the chapter's study aids.

 REMEMBER to go back to the Navigator box on the chapter-opening page and check off your completed work.

Special Student Supplements That Help You Get the Best Grade You Can

The Accounting Principles Website

The book's Website at *www.wiley.com/college/weygandt* provides a wealth of materials that will help you develop conceptual understanding and increase your ability to solve problems. For example, you will find PowerPoint presentations and Web quizzing. Be sure to check the site often.

Take Action! CD-ROM

This dynamic accompaniment to the main text contains interactive study reviews for every chapter. The CD is an excellent resource for both class preparation and review.

Working Papers

Working Papers are partially completed accounting forms for all end-of-chapter exercises, problems, and cases. They are a convenient resource for organizing and completing homework assignments, and they demonstrate how to correctly set up solution formats. The Working Papers are available in various groupings, so take care to order the set that matches the book you are using (check the number of chapters in your book). Also available on CD-ROM are *Excel Working Papers,* which are Excel-formatted, partially completed accounting forms.

Study Guide

The Study Guide is a comprehensive review of accounting. It guides you through chapter content, tied to study objectives. It provides resources for use during lectures and also is **an excellent tool when preparing for exams.** Each chapter of the Study Guide includes a chapter review (20 to 30 key points); a demonstration problem; and for extra practice, true/false, multiple-choice, and matching questions, and additional exercises, with solutions. The Study Guide is available in two volumes, Volume I for Chapters 1–13 and Volume II for Chapters 14–27.

Problem-Solving Survival Guide

This tutorial is designed to improve your success rates in solving homework assignments and exam questions. Each chapter includes an overview of key topics and a review of study objectives; a purpose statement and link to study objectives for each homework assignment; tips to alert you to common pitfalls and misconceptions; and reminders to concepts and principles. Multiple-choice exercises and cases similar to common homework assignments or exam questions enhance your problem-solving proficiency. The Problem-Solving Survival Guide comes in two volumes, Volume I (Chapters 1–13) and Volume II (Chapters 14–27).

General Ledger Software for Windows

 The General Ledger Software program allows you to use a computerized accounting system to solve the end-of-chapter text problems that are identified by the icon shown here.

Peachtree Complete® Accounting

 A workbook and accompanying CD teach you how to use Peachtree Complete® Accounting Software. Selected problems in the book, denoted by the Peachtree icon, can be solved using this software package.

Solving Accounting Principles Problems Using Excel

 A manual guides you step-by-step from an introduction to computers and Excel, to completion of pre-programmed spreadsheets, to design of your own spreadsheets. Accompanying spreadsheet templates allow you to complete selected end-of-chapter exercises and problems, identified by the icon shown here.

Practice Sets

Practice sets expose you to real-world simulations of maintaining a complete set of accounting records for a business. They integrate the business events, accounting concepts, procedures, and records covered within the textbook, and they reinforce the concepts and procedures learned. Four different practice sets are available: Campus Cycle Shop; Heritage Home Furniture; University Bookstore; and Custom Party Associates.

Financial Accounting Tutor (FacT) CD

This self-paced CD-ROM is designed to review financial accounting concepts. It uses simple examples that introduce concepts gradually and reveal the logic underlying the accounting process. Discussions and examples are followed by brief, interactive problems that provide immediate feedback.

For more information on any of these student supplements, check with your professor or bookstore, or go to the Wiley Website at *www.wiley.com/college/weygandt.*

How Do I Learn Best?

This questionnaire aims to find out something about your preferences for the way you work with information. You will have a preferred learning style, and one part of that learning style is your preference for the intake and the output of ideas and information.

Circle the letter of the answer that best explains your preference. Circle more than one if a single answer does not match your perception. Leave blank any question that does not apply.

1. You are about to give directions to a person who is standing with you. She is staying in a hotel in town and wants to visit your house later. She has a rental car. Would you
   a. draw a map on paper?
   b. tell her the directions?
   c. write down the directions (without a map)?
   d. pick her up at the hotel in your car?

2. You are not sure whether a word should be spelled "dependent" or "dependant." Do you
   c. look it up in the dictionary?
   a. see the word in your mind and choose by the way it looks?
   b. sound it out in your mind?
   d. write both versions down on paper and choose one?

3. You have just received a copy of your itinerary for a world trip. This is of interest to a friend. Would you
   b. call her immediately and tell her about it?
   c. send her a copy of the printed itinerary?
   a. show her on a map of the world?
   d. share what you plan to do at each place you visit?

4. You are going to cook something as a special treat for your family. Do you
   d. cook something familiar without the need for instructions?
   a. thumb through the cookbook looking for ideas from the pictures?
   c. refer to a specific cookbook where there is a good recipe?

5. A group of tourists has been assigned to you to find out about wildlife reserves or parks. Would you
   d. drive them to a wildlife reserve or park?
   a. show them slides and photographs?
   c. give them pamphlets or a book on wildlife reserves or parks?
   b. give them a talk on wildlife reserves or parks?

6. You are about to purchase a new CD player. Other than price, what would most influence your decision?
   b. The salesperson telling you what you want to know.
   c. Reading the details about it.
   d. Playing with the controls and listening to it.
   a. Its fashionable and upscale appearance.

7. Recall a time in your life when you learned how to do something like playing a new board game. Try to avoid choosing a very physical skill, e.g., riding a bike. How did you learn best? By
   a. visual clues—pictures, diagrams, charts?
   c. written instructions?
   b. listening to somebody explaining it?
   d. doing it or trying it?

8. You have an eye problem. Would you prefer that the doctor
   b. tell you what is wrong?
   a. show you a diagram of what is wrong?
   d. use a model to show what is wrong?

9. You are about to learn to use a new program on a computer. Would you
   d. sit down at the keyboard and begin to experiment with the program's features?
   c. read the manual that comes with the program?
   b. call a friend and ask questions about it?

10. You are staying in a hotel and have a rental car. You would like to visit friends whose address/location you do not know. Would you like them to
    a. draw you a map on paper?
    b. tell you the directions?
    c. write down the directions (without a map)?
    d. pick you up at the hotel in their car?

11. Apart from price, what would most influence your decision to buy a particular book?
    d. You have used a copy before.
    b. A friend talking about it.
    c. Quickly reading parts of it.
    a. The appealing way it looks.

12. A new movie has arrived in town. What would most influence your decision to go (or not go)?
    b. You heard a radio review about it.
    c. You read a review about it.
    a. You saw a preview of it.

13. Do you prefer a lecturer or teacher who likes to use
    c. a textbook, handouts, readings?
    a. flow diagrams, charts, graphs?
    d. field trips, labs, practical sessions?
    b. discussion, guest speakers?

Count your choices:

a.	b.	c.	d.
V	A	R	K

Now match the letter or letters you have recorded most to the same letter or letters in the Learning Styles Chart. You may have more than one learning style preference—many people do. Next to each letter in the chart are suggestions that will refer you to different learning aids throughout this text.

Learning Styles Chart

 **V** *Visual*

INTAKE: TO TAKE IN THE INFORMATION	TO MAKE A STUDY PACKAGE	TEXT FEATURES THAT MAY HELP YOU THE MOST	OUTPUT: TO DO WELL ON EXAMS
• Pay close attention to charts, drawings, and handouts your instructor uses. • Underline. • Use different colors. • Use symbols, flow charts, graphs, different arrangements on the page, white space.	Convert your lecture notes into "page pictures." To do this: • Use the "Intake" strategies. • Reconstruct images in different ways. • Redraw pages from memory. • Replace words with symbols and initials. • Look at your pages.	**The Navigator** **Feature Story** **Preview** **Infographics/Illustrations** **Photos** **Accounting in Action** **Accounting Equation Analyses** **Key Terms in blue** **Words in bold** **Demonstration Problem/Action Plan** **Questions/Exercises/Problems** **Financial Reporting Problem** **Comparative Analysis Problem** **Interpreting Financial Statements** **Exploring the Web**	• Recall your "page pictures." • Draw diagrams where appropriate. • Practice turning your visuals back into words.

A *Aural*

INTAKE: TO TAKE IN THE INFORMATION	TO MAKE A STUDY PACKAGE	TEXT FEATURES THAT MAY HELP YOU THE MOST	OUTPUT: TO DO WELL ON EXAMS
• Attend lectures and tutorials. • Discuss topics with students and instructors. • Explain new ideas to other people. • Use a tape recorder. • Leave spaces in your lecture notes for later recall. • Describe overheads, pictures, and visuals to somebody who was not in class.	You may take poor notes because you prefer to listen. Therefore: • Expand your notes by talking with others and with information from your textbook. • Tape record summarized notes and listen. • Read summarized notes out loud. • Explain your notes to another "aural" person.	**Preview** **Infographics/Illustrations** **Accounting in Action** **Review It/Do It/Action Plan** **Summary of Study Objectives** **Glossary** **Demonstration Problem/Action Plan** **Self-Study Questions** **Questions/Exercises/Problems** **Financial Reporting Problem** **Comparative Analysis Problem** **Exploring the Web** **Group Decision Case** **Communication Activity** **Ethics Case**	• Talk with the instructor. • Spend time in quiet places recalling the ideas. • Practice writing answers to old exam questions. • Say your answers out loud.

 ## Reading/Writing

INTAKE: TO TAKE IN THE INFORMATION	TO MAKE A STUDY PACKAGE	TEXT FEATURES THAT MAY HELP YOU THE MOST	OUTPUT: TO DO WELL ON EXAMS
• Use lists and headings. • Use dictionaries, glossaries, and definitions. • Read handouts, textbooks, and supplementary library readings. • Use lecture notes.	• Write out words again and again. • Reread notes silently. • Rewrite ideas and principles into other words. • Turn charts, diagrams, and other illustrations into statements.	**The Navigator** **Feature Story** **Study Objectives** **Preview** **Review It/Do It/Action Plan** **Summary of Study Objectives** **Glossary** **Self-Study Questions** **Questions/Exercises/Problems** **Writing Problems** **Financial Reporting Problem** **Comparative Analysis Problem** **Interpreting Financial Statements: Global Focus** **Exploring the Web** **Group Decision Case** **Communication Activity**	• Write exam answers. • Practice with multiple-choice questions. • Write paragraphs, beginnings and endings. • Write your lists in outline form. • Arrange your words into hierarchies and points.

 ## Kinesthetic

INTAKE: TO TAKE IN THE INFORMATION	TO MAKE A STUDY PACKAGE	TEXT FEATURES THAT MAY HELP YOU THE MOST	OUTPUT: TO DO WELL ON EXAMS
• Use all your senses. • Go to labs, take field trips. • Listen to real-life examples. • Pay attention to applications. • Use hands-on approaches. • Use trial-and-error methods.	You may take poor notes because topics do not seem concrete or relevant. Therefore: • Put examples in your summaries. • Use case studies and applications to help with principles and abstract concepts. • Talk about your notes with another "kinesthetic" person. • Use pictures and photographs that illustrate an idea.	**The Navigator** **Feature Story** **Preview** **Infographics/Illustrations** **Review It/Do It/Action Plan** **Summary of Study Objectives** **Demonstration Problem/ Action Plan** **Self-Study Questions** **Questions/Exercises/Problems** **Financial Reporting Problem** **Comparative Analysis Problem** **Interpreting Financial Statements: Global Focus** **Exploring the Web** **Group Decision Case** **Communication Activity**	• Write practice answers. • Role-play the exam situation.

For all learning styles: Be sure to use the book's website to enhance your understanding of the concepts and procedures of the text.

Acknowledgments

From the first edition of this textbook and through the years since, we have benefitted greatly from feedback provided by numerous instructors and students of accounting principles courses throughout the country. We offer our thanks to those many people for their criticism, constructive suggestions, and innovative ideas. We are indebted to the following people for their contributions to the most recent editions of the book.

Reviewers and Focus Group Participants for the Sixth Edition

Victoria Beard, *University of North Dakota*
Ken Couvillion, *San Joaquin Delta College*
Linda Dening, *Jefferson Community College*
Albert Fisher, *Community College of Southern Nevada*
George Gardner, *Bemidji State University*
Marc Guillian, *University of Louisiana—Lafayette*
Kathy Horton, *College of DuPage*
Margaret Hoskins, *Henderson State University*
Inam Hussain, *Purdue University*
Sharon Johnson, *Kansas City Community College*
J. Suzanne King, *University of Charleston*
Terry Kubichan, *Old Dominion University*
Melanie Mackey, *Ocean County College*
Jamie O'Brien, *South Dakota State University*
Shelly Ota, *Leeward Community College*
Peter J. Poznanski, *Cleveland State University*
David Ravetch, *University of California—Los Angeles*
Paul J. Shinal, *Cayuga Community College*
Beverly Terry, *Central Piedmont Community College*

In addition, special thanks to Kathy Horton and the students of the *College of DuPage* and to Alphonse J. Ruggiero and the students of *Suffolk Community College* for their reviews that contributed to the development of the Sixth Edition.

Reviewers and Focus Group Participants for the Seventh Edition

Matt Anderson, *Michigan State University*
Yvonne Baker, *Cincinnati State Tech Community College*
Peter Battelle, *University of Vermont*
Michael Blackett, *National American University*
David Boyd, *Arkansas State University*
Leon Button, *Scottsdale Community College*
Trudy Chiaravelli, *Lansing Community College*
Kenneth Couvillion, *San Joaquin Delta College*
Thomas Davies, *University of South Dakota*
Peggy DeJong, *Kirkwood Community College*
Kevin Dooley, *Kapi'olani Community College*
Edmond Douville, *Indiana University Northwest*
Pamela Druger, *Augustana College*
John Eagan, *Erie Community College*
Richard Ellison, *Middlesex Community College*
Richard Ghio, *San Joaquin Delta College*
Jeannie Harrington, *Middle Tennessee State University*
William Harvey, *Henry Ford Community College*
Zach Holmes, *Oakland Community College*
Paul Holt, *Texas A&M—Kingsville*
Verne Ingram, *Red Rocks Community College*
Mark Johnston, *Washtenaw Community College*
Shirly Kleiner, *Johnson County Community College*
Jo Koehn, *Central Missouri State University*
Robert Laycock, *Montgomery College*
Maureen McBeth, *College of DuPage*
Jerry Martens, *Community College of Aurora*
Shea Mears, *Des Moines Area Community College*
Pam Meyer, *University of Louisiana—Lafayette*
Robin Nelson, *Community College of Southern Nevada*
George Palz, *Erie Community College*
Bill Rencher, *Seminole Community College*
Renee Rigoni, *Monroe Community College*
Jill Russell, *Camden County College*

Alice Sineath, *Forsyth Tech Community College*
Jeff Slater, *North Shore Community College*
Ken Sinclair, *Lehigh University*
James Smith, *Ivy Tech State College*
Carol Springer, *Georgia State University*
Lynda Thompson, *Massasoit Community College*
Sue Van Boven, *Paradise Valley Community College*
Christian Widmer, *Tidewater Community College*

Marianne M. Rexer, *Wilkes University*—eLearning Courseware
Paul Jep Robertson, *New Mexico State University*—eLearning Courseware
Diane Tanner, *University of North Florida*—Test Bank II
Dick Wasson, *Southwestern College*—Excel Working Papers, Working Papers
Mike Watters, *Henderson State University*—eLearning Courseware

Special Thanks

We sincerely appreciate the competent support and devotion to our projects by associate editor Ed Brislin. Our thanks also go to the authors of the Seventh Edition supplements:

Mel Coe, *DeVry Institute of Technology, Atlanta*—Peachtree Workbook
Joan Cook, *Milwaukee Area Technical College*—Campus Cycle Practice Set, Heritage Home Furniture Practice Set
Denise M. English, *Boise State University*—Solving Problems Using Excel Workbook
Larry Falcetto, *Emporia State University*—Test Bank, Instructor's Manual II
Patricia Fedje, *Minot State University*—Custom Party Associates Practice Set
Sarah L. Frank, *University of West Florida*—Web CT, Blackboard
Jessica Frazier, *Eastern Kentucky University*—Instructor's Manual I
Candice Humphrey, *Northeast Iowa Community College*—University Bookstore Practice Set
Marilyn Hunt, *University of Central Florida*—Problem-Solving Survival Guide
Naomi Karolinski, *Monroe Community College*—PowerPoint Presentation Slides
David R. Keoppen, *Boise State University*—Solving Problems Using Excel Workbook
Douglas W. Kieso, *University of California, Irvine*—Study Guide
Steve Lustgarten, *Baruch College*—eGrade Plus
Laura McNally—eGrade Plus
Gary Lubin, *Merck*—General Ledger Software
Sally Nelson, *Northeast Iowa Community College*—University Bookstore Practice Set, General Ledger Software manual
Rex A. Schildhouse, *University of Phoenix, San Diego Campus*—Peachtree Workbook
Margaret O'Reilly-Allen, *Rider University*—eLearning Courseware

We also thank those who have ensured the accuracy of our supplements:

Jack Borke, *University of Wisconsin—Platteville*
Larry Falcetto, *Emporia State University*
Clyde Galbraith, *West Chester University*
Jennifer Laudermilch, *PricewaterhouseCoopers*
Barbara Muller, *Arizona State University*
Laura Ruff, *Milwaukee Area Technical College—West*
Teresa Speck, *St. Mary's University*
Chris Tomas, *Northeast Iowa Community College*
Dick Wasson, *Southwestern College*

In addition, special recognition goes to Karen Huffman of Palomar College for her assessment of the text's pedagogy and her suggestions on how to increase its helpfulness to students; to Gary R., Morrison of Wayne State University for his review of the instructional design; and to Nancy Galli of Palomar College for her work on learning styles. Thanks also to "perpetual reviewers" Robert Benjamin of Taylor University, Charles Malone of Columbia Basin College, and William Gregg of Montgomery College for their continuing interest in the book and their regular contributions of ideas to improve it. Finally, special thanks to Wayne Higley of Buena Vista University for his technical proofing.

Our thanks also to Ann Torbert for her special talents and outstanding editorial and development work that maintains and raises the quality of this book; her contributions merit coauthorship.

We appreciate the exemplary support and professional commitment given us by publisher and vice president Susan Elbe, executive editor Jay O'Callaghan, marketing manager Steve Herdegen, associate editor Ed Brislin, program assistant Brian Kamins, program assistant Kristin Babroski, media editor Allie Keim, vice president of higher education production and manufacturing Ann Berlin, production manager Jeanine Furino, designer Dawn Stanley, illustration editor Sandra Rigby, photo editor Sara Wight, project manager Suzanne Ingrao of Ingrao Associates, permissions assistant Yolanda Pagano, product manager Carole Kuhn at TechBooks, and project manager Karin Vonesh at Elm Street Publishing Services. They provided innumerable services that helped this project take shape. Finally, our thanks for the support provided by Will Pesce, President and Chief Executive Officer, and Bonnie Lieberman, Senior Vice President of the College Division.

We thank PepsiCo, Inc. and The Coca-Cola Company for permitting us the use of their 2002 Annual Reports for our specimen financial statements. Suggestions and comments from users—instructors and students alike—will be appreciated.

Jerry J. Weygandt
Donald E. Kieso
Paul D. Kimmel

Brief Contents

Detailed Contents

CHAPTER 7

Accounting Information Systems
275

CHAPTER 8

Internal Control and Cash
317

CHAPTER 9

Accounting for Receivables
361

CHAPTER 10

Plant Assets, Natural Resources, and Intangible Assets
399

CHAPTER 20

Managerial Accounting   815

CHAPTER 21

Job Order Cost Accounting   851

CHAPTER 22

Process Cost Accounting   889

CHAPTER 27

Incremental Analysis and Capital Budgeting

About the Authors

Jerry J. Weygandt, PhD, CPA, is Arthur Andersen Alumni Professor of Accounting at the University of Wisconsin—Madison. He holds a Ph.D. in accounting from the University of Illinois. Articles by Professor Weygandt have appeared in the *Accounting Review, Journal of Accounting Research, Accounting Horizons, Journal of Accountancy,* and other academic and professional journals. These articles have examined such financial reporting issues as accounting for price-level adjustments, pensions, convertible securities, stock option contracts, and interim reports. Professor Weygandt is author of other accounting and financial reporting books and is a member of the American Accounting Association, the American Institute of Certified Public Accountants, and the Wisconsin Society of Certified Public Accountants. He has served on numerous committees of the American Accounting Association and as a member of the editorial board of the *Accounting Review;* he also has served as President and Secretary-Treasurer of the American Accounting Association. In addition, he has been actively involved with the American Institute of Certified Public Accountants and has been a member of the Accounting Standards Executive Committee (AcSEC) of that organization. He has served on the FASB task force that examined the reporting issues related to accounting for income taxes and is presently a trustee of the Financial Accounting Foundation. Professor Weygandt has received the Chancellor's Award for Excellence in Teaching and the Beta Gamma Sigma Dean's Teaching Award. He is on the board of directors of M & I Bank of Southern Wisconsin and the Dean Foundation. He is the recipient of the Wisconsin Institute of CPA's Outstanding Educator's Award and the Lifetime Achievement Award. In 2001 he received the American Accounting Association's Outstanding Accounting Educator Award.

Donald E. Kieso, PhD, CPA, received his bachelor's degree from Aurora University and his doctorate in accounting from the University of Illinois. He has served as chairman of the Department of Accountancy and is currently the KPMG Peat Marwick Emeritus Professor of Accountancy at Northern Illinois University. He has public accounting experience with Price Waterhouse & Co. (San Francisco and Chicago) and Arthur Andersen & Co. (Chicago) and research experience with the Research Division of the American Institute of Certified Public Accountants (New York). He has done postdoctorate work as a Visiting Scholar at the University of California at Berkeley and is a recipient of NIU's Teaching Excellence Award and four Golden Apple Teaching Awards. Professor Kieso is the author of other accounting and business books and is a member of the American Accounting Association, the American Institute of Certified Public Accountants, and the Illinois CPA Society. He has served as a member of the Board of Directors of the Illinois CPA Society, the AACSB's Accounting Accreditation Committees, the State of Illinois Comptroller's Commission, as Secretary-Treasurer of the Federation of Schools of Accountancy, and as Secretary-Treasurer of the American Accounting Association. Professor Kieso is currently serving on the Board of Trustees and Executive Committee of Aurora University, as a member of the Board of Directors of Kishwaukee Community Hospital, and as Treasurer and Director of Valley West Community Hospital. From 1989 to 1993 he served as a charter member of the national Accounting Education Change Commission. He is the recipient of the Outstanding Accounting Educator Award from the Illinois CPA Society, the FSA's Joseph A. Silvoso Award of Merit, the NIU Foundation's Humanitarian Award for Service to Higher Education, a Distinguished Service Award from the Illinois CPA Society, and in 2003 an honorary doctorate from Aurora University.

Paul D. Kimmel, PhD, CPA, received his bachelor's degree from the University of Minnesota and his doctorate in accounting from the University of Wisconsin. He is an Associate Professor at the University of Wisconsin—Milwaukee, and has public accounting experience with Deloitte & Touche (Minneapolis). He was the recipient of the UWM School of Business Advisory Council Teaching Award, the Reggie Taite Excellence in Teaching Award, and a three-time winner of the Outstanding Teaching Assistant Award at the University of Wisconsin. He is also a recipient of the Elijah Watts Sells Award for Honorary Distinction for his results on the CPA exam. He is a member of the American Accounting Association and has published articles in *Accounting Review, Accounting Horizons, Issues in Accounting Education, Journal of Accounting Education,* as well as other journals. His research interests include accounting for financial instruments and innovation in accounting education. He has published papers and given numerous talks on incorporating critical thinking into accounting education, and helped prepare a catalog of critical thinking resources for the Federated Schools of Accountancy.

Accounting in Action

The Navigator is a learning system designed to prompt you to use the learning aids in the chapter and set priorities as you study.

THE NAVIGATOR ✓

Understand **Concepts for Review**	❏
Read **Feature Story**	❏
Scan **Study Objectives**	❏
Read **Preview**	❏
Read text and answer **Before You Go On** p. 8 ❏ p. 14 ❏ p. 20 ❏ p. 24 ❏	
Work **Demonstration Problem**	❏
Review **Summary of Study Objectives**	❏
Answer **Self-Study Questions**	❏
Complete **Assignments**	❏

CONCEPTS FOR REVIEW

Before studying this chapter, you should know or, if necessary, review:

- How to use the study aids in this book.
  (Student Owner's Manual, pages vii–xiv)
- How you learn best.
  (Student Owner's Manual, pages xvi–xviii)
- The nature of the special student supplements that accompany this textbook.
  (Student Owner's Manual, page xv)

Concepts for Review highlight concepts from your earlier reading that you need to understand before starting the new chapter.

THE NAVIGATOR

FEATURE STORY

Financial Reporting: A Matter of Trust

In 2002 the financial press was full of articles about financial scandals and accounting misdeeds. It started with Enron, but then spread to Xerox, Qwest, Global Crossing, and WorldCom, among others. Many of the articles expressed concern that as an increasing number of misdeeds came to public attention, a mistrust of financial reporting in general was developing. These articles made clear just how important accounting and financial reporting are to the U.S. and world financial markets and to society as a whole. Without financial reports, managers would not be able to evaluate how well their company is doing or to make decisions about the best way to make their company grow in the future. Without financial reports, investors and lenders could not make informed decisions about how to allocate their funds. There is no doubt that a sound, well-functioning economy depends on accurate and dependable financial reporting.

In order to make financial decisions as either an investor or a manager, you need to know how to read financial reports. In this book you will learn about financial reporting and some basic tools used to evaluate financial reports. In the first chapter we introduce you to the real financial statements of a company whose products most of you probably are familiar with— PepsiCo, Inc. We have chosen the financial statements of PepsiCo because they are a good example from the real world. An appendix to this textbook contains the statements in their entirety, and a copy of the PepsiCo, Inc. 2002 Annual Report accompanies this text.

PepsiCo manufactures Pepsi-Cola, the number two soft drink beverage in the world. PepsiCo also manufactures the number one bottled water (Aquafina), the number one sports drink (Gatorade), the number one ready-to-drink tea (Lipton), and the number one ready-to-drink coffee (Frappuccino). In addition, PepsiCo is the largest manufacturer of snack foods in the world. Its Frito-Lay chips dominate the U.S. market, with 59% of all snack chip sales and the world market with over 32%. In all, PepsiCo ranks among the world's largest packaged good and beverage companies, with over $25 billion in sales, $23 billion in assets, and 140,000 employees. PepsiCo is not only large; it is also quite profitable, ranking twenty-eighth among all U.S. companies, with $3.3 billion in net income.

www.pepsico.com

✓ THE NAVIGATOR

STUDY OBJECTIVES

After studying this chapter, you should be able to:

1. Explain what accounting is.
2. Identify the users and uses of accounting.
3. Understand why ethics is a fundamental business concept.
4. Explain the meaning of generally accepted accounting principles and the cost principle.
5. Explain the meaning of the monetary unit assumption and the economic entity assumption.
6. State the basic accounting equation, and explain the meaning of assets, liabilities, and owner's equity.
7. Analyze the effects of business transactions on the basic accounting equation.
8. Understand what the four financial statements are and how they are prepared.

✓ THE NAVIGATOR

The opening story about PepsiCo, Inc. highlights the importance of having good financial information to make effective business decisions. Whatever one's pursuits or occupation, the need for financial information is inescapable. You cannot earn a living, spend money, buy on credit, make an investment, or pay taxes without receiving, using, or dispensing financial information. Good decision making depends on good information.

The purpose of this chapter is to show you that accounting is the system used to provide useful financial information. The content and organization of Chapter 1 are as follows.

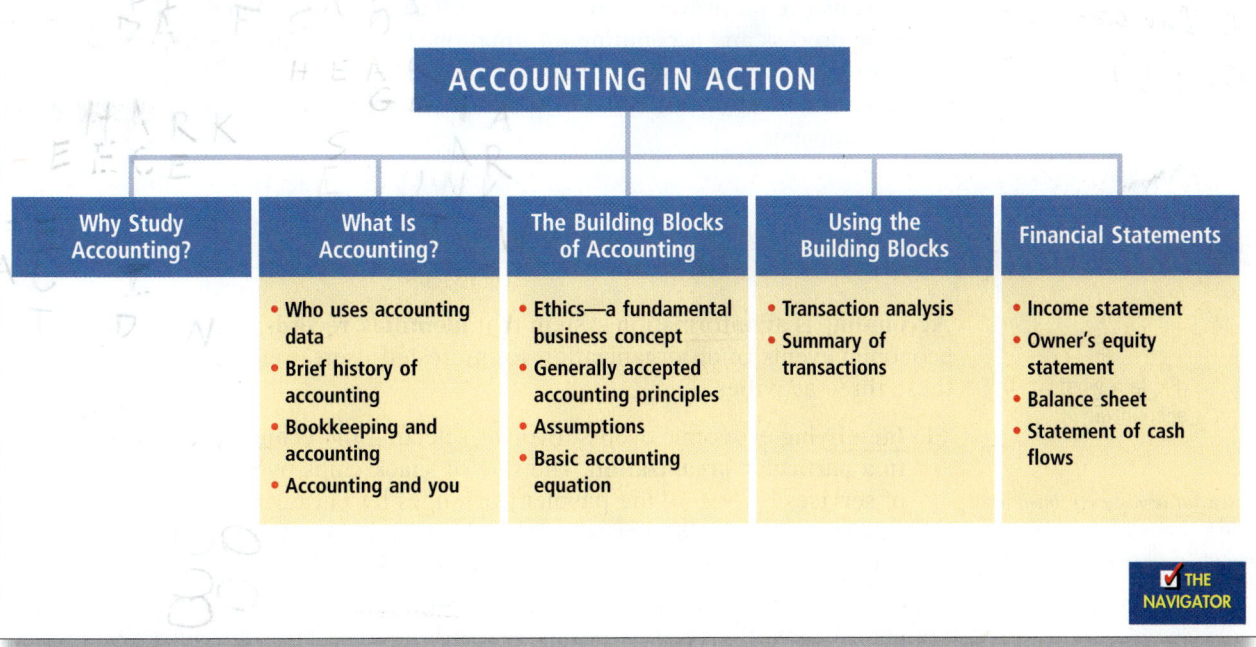

The **Preview** describes and outlines the major topics and subtopics you will see in the chapter.

Why Study Accounting?

As indicated in the Feature Story, accounting scandals and corporate misdeeds made headlines on a weekly basis for over two years. **WorldCom**'s $3.8 billion restatement of inflated earnings contributed to losses to shareholders of $179.3 billion and to job losses of 17,000. **Enron**'s variety of schemes that inflated income by $586 million, leading to financial restatements and bankruptcy, caused investor losses of $66.4 billion and job losses of 6,100. **Xerox Corp.**, using "accounting tricks" to fool investors, restated five years of earnings to reclassify more than $6 billion in revenue.

Numerous proposals to improve business practices and accounting oversights have come from federal agencies and regulators, the investment community, and the accounting profession. As a consequence, new laws have been passed to legislate business behavior as well as accounting and auditing practices. The Sarbanes-Oxley Act, signed into law in July of 2002, increases the resources for the government to combat fraud and to curb poor reporting practices, and it introduces sweeping changes to the structure of the accounting and auditing professions.

One thing is very evident from these recent embarrassing, illegal, or unethical business events: **Accounting is important**. **Good accounting is essential** to sound business and investing decisions. **Bad accounting cannot be tolerated**. At the slightest hint of a company's accounting improprieties, investors sell their stock and batter its stock price.

Recent events prove the worth of studying, understanding, and using the accounting process and accounting information. This textbook is your introduction to accounting as a valuable tool of business record keeping, communication, and analysis. Make the most of this course—it will serve you for a lifetime in ways you cannot now imagine.

What Is Accounting?

STUDY OBJECTIVE 1

Explain what accounting is.

Essential terms are printed in blue when they first appear, and are defined in the end-of-chapter glossary.

References throughout the chapter tie the accounting concepts you are learning to the story that opened the chapter.

Accounting is an information system that **identifies**, **records**, and **communicates** the economic events of an organization to interested users. Let's take a closer look at these three activities.

1. **Identifying** economic events involves selecting the **economic activities relevant to a particular organization**. The sale of snack chips by **PepsiCo**, the providing of services by **Sprint**, the payment of wages by **Ford Motor Company**, and the collection of ticket and broadcast money and the payment of expenses by major league sports teams are examples of economic events.

2. Once identified, economic events are **recorded** to provide a history of the organization's financial activities. Recording consists of keeping a **systematic**, **chronological diary of events**, measured in dollars and cents. In recording, economic events are also classified and summarized.

3. The identifying and recording activities are of little use unless the information is **communicated** to interested users. Financial information is communicated through **accounting reports**, the most common of which are called **financial statements**. To make the reported financial information meaningful, accountants report the recorded data in a standardized way. Information resulting from similar transactions is accumulated and totaled. For example, all sales transactions of **PepsiCo** are accumulated over a certain period of time and reported as one amount in the company's financial statements. Such data are said to be reported **in the aggregate**. By presenting the recorded data in the aggregate, the accounting process simplifies a multitude of transactions and makes a series of activities understandable and meaningful.

A vital element in communicating economic events is the accountant's ability to **analyze** and **interpret** the reported information. Analysis involves the use of ratios, percentages, graphs, and charts to highlight significant financial trends and relationships. Interpretation involves **explaining the uses**, **meaning**, **and limitations of reported data**. Appendix A of this textbook illustrates the financial statements and accompanying notes and graphs from **PepsiCo, Inc.**; Appendix B illustrates the financial statements of **The Coca-Cola Company**. We refer to these statements at various places throughout the text. At this point, they probably strike you as complex and confusing. By the end of this course, you'll be surprised at your ability to understand and interpret them.

The accounting process may be summarized as shown in Illustration 1-1.

Illustration 1-1
Accounting process

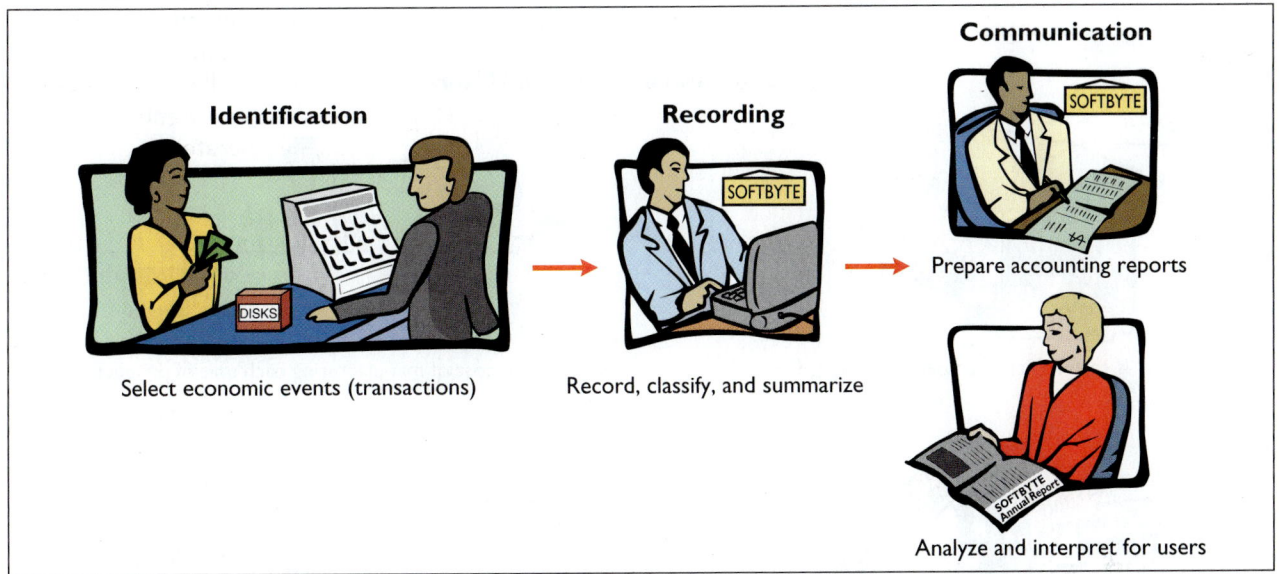

Communication

Identification   **Recording**

Select economic events (transactions)   Record, classify, and summarize

Prepare accounting reports

Analyze and interpret for users

Accounting should consider the needs of the users of financial information. Therefore, you should know who these users are and something about their needs for information.

Who Uses Accounting Data

Because it communicates financial information, accounting is often called "the language of business." The information that a user of financial information needs depends upon the kinds of decisions the user makes. The differences in the decisions divide the users of financial information into two broad groups: internal users and external users.

Internal Users

Internal users of accounting information are managers who plan, organize, and run a business. These include **marketing managers**, **production supervisors**, **finance directors**, **and company officers**. In running a business, managers must answer many important questions, as shown in Illustration 1-2 (page 6).

To answer these and other questions, users need detailed information on a timely basis. For internal users, accounting provides **internal reports**. Examples are financial comparisons of operating alternatives, projections of income from new sales campaigns, and forecasts of cash needs for the next year. In addition, summarized financial information is presented in the form of financial statements.

External Users

There are several types of **external users** of accounting information. **Investors** (owners) use accounting information to make decisions to buy, hold, or sell stock. **Creditors** such as suppliers and bankers use accounting information to evaluate the risks of granting credit or lending money. Some questions that may be asked by investors and creditors about a company are shown in Illustration 1-3 (page 6).

The information needs and questions of other external users vary considerably. **Taxing authorities**, such as the Internal Revenue Service, want to know whether the

STUDY OBJECTIVE 2

Identify the users and uses of accounting.

Helpful Hints help clarify concepts or items being discussed.

HELPFUL HINT

The IRS requires businesses to retain records that can be audited. Also, the Foreign Corrupt Practices Act requires public companies to keep records.

Illustration 1-2
Questions asked by
internal users

Questions Asked by Internal Users

Is cash sufficient to pay bills?

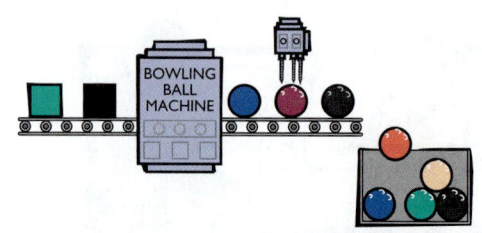

What is the cost of manufacturing each unit of product?

Can we afford to give employee pay raises this year?

Which product line is the most profitable?

Illustration 1-3
Questions asked by
external users

Questions Asked by External Users

Is the company earning satisfactory income?

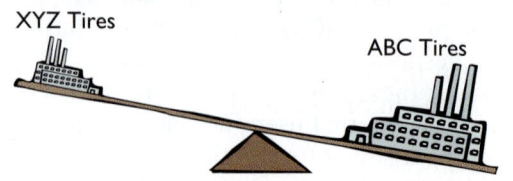

How does the company compare in size
and profitability with competitors?

Will the company be able to pay its debts as they come due?

company complies with the tax laws. **Regulatory agencies**, such as the Securities and Exchange Commission and the Federal Trade Commission, want to know whether the company is operating within prescribed rules. **Customers** are interested in whether a company will continue to honor product warranties and support its product lines. **Labor unions** want to know whether the owners can pay increased wages and benefits. **Economic planners** use accounting information to forecast economic activity.

Accounting in Action examples illustrate important and interesting accounting situations in business.

ACCOUNTING IN ACTION

International Insight

Concern over the quality and integrity of financial reporting is not limited to the United States. Recently the Chinese Ministry of Finance reprimanded a large accounting firm for preparing fraudulent financial reports for a number of its publicly traded companies. Afterward, the state-run news agency noted that investors and analysts actually felt that the punishment of the firm was not adequate. In fact, a 2001 survey of investors in China found that less than 10% had full confidence in companies' annual reports. As a result of these concerns the Chinese Institute of Certified Public Accountants vowed to strengthen its policing of its members.

Brief History of Accounting

The **origins of accounting** are generally attributed to the work of Luca Pacioli, an Italian Renaissance mathematician. Pacioli was a close friend and tutor to Leonardo da Vinci and a contemporary of Christopher Columbus. In his 1494 text *Summa de Arithmetica, Geometria, Proportione et Proportionalite,* Pacioli described a system to ensure that financial information was recorded efficiently and accurately.

With the advent of the **industrial age** in the nineteenth century and, later, the emergence of large corporations, a separation of the owners from the managers of businesses took place. As a result, the need to report the financial status of the enterprise became more important, to ensure that managers acted in accord with owners' wishes. Also, transactions between businesses became more complex, making necessary improved approaches for reporting financial information.

Our economy has now evolved into a post-industrial age—**the information age**—in which many "products" are information services. The computer has been the driver of the information age.

Distinguishing Between Bookkeeping and Accounting

Many individuals mistakenly consider bookkeeping and accounting to be the same. This confusion is understandable because the accounting process **includes the bookkeeping function**. However, accounting also includes much more. **Bookkeeping usually involves only the recording of economic events**. It is therefore just one part of the accounting process. In total, **accounting involves the entire process of identifying**, **recording**, **and communicating economic events**.

Accounting may be further divided into financial accounting and managerial accounting. **Financial accounting** is the field of accounting that provides economic and financial information for investors, creditors, and other external users. **Managerial accounting** provides economic and financial information for managers and other internal users. Financial accounting is covered in Chapters 1–19 of this text. Managerial accounting is discussed in Chapters 20–27.

ACCOUNTING IN ACTION  e Business Insight

E-business involves much more than simply selling goods over the Internet. According to Lou Gerstner, **IBM**'s CEO, "e-business is all about cycle time, speed, globalization, enhanced productivity, reaching new customers, and sharing knowledge across institutions for competitive advantage." Many accountants are involved in designing and implementing computer systems, including systems for e-business. In fact, in recent years e-business consulting has been one of the largest areas of growth for large accounting firms.

E-Business Insight examples show how e-business technology has expanded the services provided by accountants.

Accounting and You

One question frequently asked by students of accounting is, "How will the study of accounting help me?" It should help you a great deal, because a working knowledge of accounting is desirable for virtually every field of endeavor. Some examples of how accounting is used in other careers include:

- **General management**: Imagine running **General Motors**, a major hospital, a school, a **McDonald's** franchise, a bike shop. All general managers need to understand accounting data in order to make wise business decisions.

- **Marketing**: A marketing specialist develops strategies to help the sales force be successful. But making a sale is meaningless unless it is a profitable sale. Marketing people must be sensitive to costs and benefits, which accounting helps them quantify and understand.

- **Finance**: Do you want to be a banker, an investment analyst, a stock broker? These fields rely heavily on accounting. In all of them you will regularly examine and analyze financial statements. In fact, it is difficult to get a good job in a finance function without two or three courses in accounting.

- **Real estate**: The most prevalent career in real estate is that of a broker, a person who sells real estate. Because a third party—the bank—is almost always involved in financing a real estate transaction, brokers must understand the numbers involved: Can the buyer afford to make the payments to the bank? Does the cash flow from an industrial property justify the purchase price? What are the tax benefits of the purchase?

Accounting is useful even for occupations you might think completely unrelated. If you become a doctor, a lawyer, a social worker, a teacher, an engineer, an architect, or an entrepreneur—you name it—a working knowledge of accounting is relevant. You will need to understand financial reports in any enterprise you are associated with.

Before You Go On questions at the end of major text sections offer an opportunity to stop and reexamine the key points you have studied.

BEFORE YOU GO ON...

Review It

1. What is accounting?
2. What is meant by analysis and interpretation?
3. Who uses accounting information? Identify specific internal and external users of accounting information.

4. To whom are the origins of accounting generally attributed?

5. What is the difference between bookkeeping and accounting?

6. How can you use your accounting knowledge?

The Building Blocks of Accounting ✳

Every profession develops a body of theory consisting of principles, assumptions, and standards. Accounting is no exception. Just as a doctor follows certain standards in treating a patient's illness, an accountant follows certain standards in reporting financial information. For these standards to work, a fundamental business concept is followed—ethical behavior.

Ethics—A Fundamental Business Concept

Wherever you make your career—whether in accounting, marketing, management, finance, government, or elsewhere—your actions will affect other people and organizations. The standards of conduct by which one's actions are judged as right or wrong, honest or dishonest, fair or not fair, are **ethics**. Imagine trying to carry on a business or invest money if you could not depend on the individuals you deal with to be honest. If managers, customers, investors, co-workers, and creditors all consistently lied, effective communication and economic activity would be impossible. Information would have no credibility.

Fortunately most individuals in business are ethical. Their actions are both legal and responsible, and they consider the organization's interests in their decision making.

To sensitize you to ethical situations and to give you practice at solving ethical dilemmas, we have included in the book three types of ethics materials: (1) marginal notes that provide helpful hints for developing ethical sensitivity, (2) Ethics in Accounting boxes that highlight ethics situations and issues, and (3) at the end of the chapter, an ethics case simulating a business situation. In the process of analyzing these ethics cases and your own ethical experiences, you should apply the three steps outlined in Illustration 1-4.

> **STUDY OBJECTIVE 3**
>
> Understand why ethics is a fundamental business concept.

Illustration 1-4
Steps in analyzing ethics cases

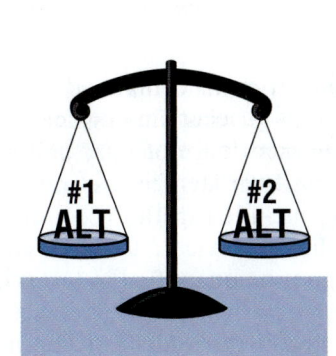

✳ **Solving an Ethical Dilemma**

1. Recognize an ethical situation and the ethical issues involved.

Use your personal ethics to identify ethical situations and issues. Some businesses and professional organizations provide written codes of ethics for guidance in some business situations.

2. Identify and analyze the principal elements in the situation.

Identify the *stakeholders*—persons or groups who may be harmed or benefited. Ask the question: What are the responsibilities and obligations of the parties involved?

3. Identify the alternatives, and weigh the impact of each alternative on various stakeholders.

Select the most ethical alternative, considering all the consequences. Sometimes there will be one right answer. Other situations involve more than one right solution; these situations require an evaluation of each and a selection of the best alternative.

Generally Accepted Accounting Principles

The accounting profession has developed standards that are generally accepted and universally practiced. This common set of standards is called **generally accepted accounting principles (GAAP)**. These standards indicate how to report economic events.

Two organizations are primarily responsible for establishing generally accepted accounting principles. The first is the **Financial Accounting Standards Board (FASB)**. This private organization establishes broad reporting standards of general applicability as well as specific accounting rules. The second standards-setting group is the **Securities and Exchange Commission (SEC)**. The SEC is a governmental agency that requires companies to file financial reports following generally accepted accounting principles. In situations where no principles exist, the SEC often mandates that certain guidelines be used. In general, the FASB and the SEC work hand in hand to assure that timely and useful accounting principles are developed.

One important principle is the **cost principle**, which states that assets should be recorded at their cost. **Cost is the value exchanged at the time something is acquired**. If you buy a house today, the cost is the amount you pay for it, say $200,000. If you sell the house in two years for $230,000, the sales price is its **market value**—the value determined by the market for homes at that time. At the time of acquisition, cost and fair market value are the same. In subsequent periods, cost and fair market value may vary, **but the cost amount continues to be used in the accounting records**.

To see the importance of the cost principle, consider the following example. At one time, **Greyhound Corporation** had 128 bus stations nationwide that cost approximately $200 million. The current market value of the stations is now close to $1 billion. But, until the bus stations are actually sold, estimates of their market values are subjective—they are informed estimates. So, under the cost principle, the bus stations are recorded and reported at $200 million, not $1 billion.

As the Greyhound example indicates, cost has an important advantage over other valuations: Cost is **reliable**. The values exchanged at the time something is acquired generally can be **objectively measured** and can be **verified**. Critics argue that cost is often not relevant and that market values provide more useful information. Despite this shortcoming, cost continues to be used in the financial statements because of its reliability.

Assumptions

In developing generally accepted accounting principles, certain basic assumptions are made. These assumptions provide a foundation for the accounting process. Two main assumptions are the **monetary unit assumption** and the **economic entity assumption**.

Monetary Unit Assumption

The **monetary unit assumption** requires that only transaction data that can be expressed in terms of money be included in the accounting records. This assumption enables accounting to quantify (measure) economic events. The monetary unit assumption is vital to applying the cost principle discussed earlier. This assumption does prevent some relevant information from being included in the accounting records. For example, the health of the owner, the quality of service, and the morale of employees would not be included because they cannot be quantified in terms of money.

An important part of the monetary unit assumption is the added assumption that the unit of measure remains sufficiently constant over time. However, the assumption of a stable monetary unit has been challenged because of the significant decline in the purchasing power of the dollar. For example, what used to cost $1 in 1960 costs over $4 in 2004. In such situations, adding, subtracting, or comparing 1960 dollars with 2004 dollars is highly questionable. The profession has recognized this problem and encourages companies to disclose the effects of changing prices.

Economic Entity Assumption

An economic entity can be any organization or unit in society. It may be a business enterprise (such as **General Electric Company**), a governmental unit (the state of Ohio), a municipality (Seattle), a school district (St. Louis District 48), or a church (Southern Baptist). The **economic entity assumption** requires that the activities of the entity be kept separate and distinct from the activities of its owner and all other economic entities. To illustrate, Sally Rider, owner of Sally's Boutique, should keep her personal living costs separate from the expenses of the Boutique. **PepsiCo**, **Coca-Cola Company**, and **Cadbury-Schweppes** are segregated into separate economic entities for accounting purposes.

We will generally discuss the economic entity assumption in relation to a business enterprise, which may be organized as a proprietorship, partnership, or corporation.

PROPRIETORSHIP.   A business owned by one person is generally a **proprietorship**. The owner is often the manager/operator of the business. Small service-type businesses (plumbing companies, beauty salons, and auto repair shops), farms, and small retail stores (antique shops, clothing stores, and used-book stores) are often sole proprietorships. **Usually only a relatively small amount of money (capital) is necessary to start in business as a proprietorship. The owner (proprietor) receives any profits, suffers any losses, and is personally liable for all debts of the business.** There is no legal distinction between the business as an economic unit and the owner, but the accounting records of the business activities are kept separate from the personal records and activities of the owner.

PARTNERSHIP.   A business owned by two or more persons associated as partners is a **partnership**. In most respects a partnership is like a proprietorship except that more than one owner is involved. Typically a partnership agreement (written or oral) sets forth such terms as initial investment, duties of each partner, division of net income (or net loss), and settlement to be made upon death or withdrawal of a partner. Each partner generally has unlimited personal liability for the debts of the partnership. **Like a proprietorship, for accounting purposes the partnership affairs must be kept separate from the personal activities of the partners.** Partnerships are often used to organize retail and service-type businesses, including professional practices (lawyers, doctors, architects, and certified public accountants).

CORPORATION.   A business organized as a separate legal entity under state corporation law and having ownership divided into transferable shares of stock is a **corporation**. The holders of the shares (stockholders) **enjoy limited liability;** that is, they are not personally liable for the debts of the corporate entity. Stockholders **may transfer all or part of their shares to other investors at any time** (i.e., sell their shares). The ease with which ownership can change adds to the attractiveness of investing in a corporation. Because ownership can be transferred without dissolving the corporation, the corporation **enjoys an unlimited life**.

Although the combined number of proprietorships and partnerships in the United States is more than four times the number of corporations, the revenue produced by corporations is nine times greater. Most of the largest enterprises in the United States—for example, **ExxonMobil**, **General Motors**, **Wal-Mart**, **Citigroup**, and **PepsiCo, Inc.**—are corporations.

> **HELPFUL HINT**
>
> Approximately 70% of U. S. companies are proprietorships; however, they account for only 6.5% of gross revenues. Corporations, on the other hand, are approximately 19% of all companies, but account for 90% of the revenues. Obviously, proprietorships, though numerous, tend to be small.

Basic Accounting Equation

3.4

Other essential building blocks of accounting are the categories into which economic events are classified. The two basic elements of a business are what it owns

> **STUDY OBJECTIVE 6**
>
> State the basic accounting equation, and explain the meaning of assets, liabilities, and owner's equity.

Accounting Cycle Tutorial—
Analyzing Business Transactions

and what it owes. **Assets** are the resources owned by a business. For example, Pep-siCo's competitor **The Coca-Cola Company** has total assets of approximately $24.5 billion. Liabilities and owner's equity are the rights or claims against these resources. Thus, a company such as Coca-Cola Company that has $24.5 billion of assets also has $12.7 billion of claims against those assets. Claims of those to whom money is owed (creditors) are called **liabilities**. Claims of owners are called **owner's equity**. For example, Coca-Cola Company has liabilities of $12.7 billion and owners' equity of $11.8 billion. This relationship of assets, liabilities, and owner's equity can be expressed as an equation as follows.

Illustration 1-5
The basic accounting equation

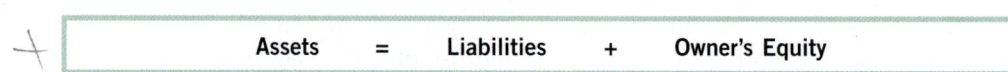

| Assets | = | Liabilities | + | Owner's Equity |

This relationship is referred to as the **basic accounting equation.** Assets must equal the sum of liabilities and owner's equity. Because creditors' claims must be paid before ownership claims if a business is liquidated, liabilities are shown before owner's equity in the basic accounting equation.

The accounting equation applies to all **economic entities** regardless of size, nature of business, or form of business organization. It applies to a small proprietorship such as a corner grocery store as well as to a giant corporation such as **Kellogg** or **General Mills**. The equation provides the **underlying framework** for recording and summarizing the economic events of a business enterprise.

Let's look in more detail at the categories in the basic accounting equation.

Assets

As noted above, **assets** are resources owned by a business. They are used in carrying out such activities as production, consumption, and exchange. The common characteristic possessed by all assets is the capacity to provide future services or benefits. In a business enterprise, that service potential or future economic benefit eventually results in cash inflows (receipts) to the enterprise.

For example, the enterprise Campus Pizza owns a delivery truck that provides economic benefits from its use in delivering pizzas. Other assets of Campus Pizza are tables, chairs, jukebox, cash register, oven, mugs and silverware, and, of course, cash.

Liabilities

Liabilities are claims against assets. That is, **liabilities are existing debts and obligations**. For example, businesses of all sizes usually borrow money and purchase merchandise on credit. Campus Pizza, for instance, purchases cheese, sausage, flour, and beverages on credit from suppliers. These obligations are called **accounts payable**. Campus Pizza also has a **note payable** to First National Bank for the money borrowed to purchase the delivery truck. Campus Pizza may also have **wages payable** to employees and **sales and real estate taxes payable** to the local government. All of these persons or entities to whom Campus Pizza owes money are its **creditors**.

Most claims of creditors attach to the entity's **total** assets rather than to the specific assets provided by the creditor. Creditors may legally force the liquidation of a business that does not pay its debts. In that case, the law requires that creditor claims be paid before ownership claims.

Owner's Equity

The ownership claim on total assets is known as **owner's equity**. It is equal to total assets minus total liabilities. Here is why: The assets of a business are supplied or claimed by either creditors or owners. To find out what belongs to owners, we subtract the creditors' claims (the liabilities) from assets. The remainder is the owner's claim on the assets—the owner's equity. Since the claims of creditors must be paid before ownership claims, owner's equity is often referred to as **residual equity**.

INCREASES IN OWNER'S EQUITY.   In a proprietorship, owner's equity is increased by owner's investments and revenues.

Investments by Owner. **Investments by owner** are the assets the owner puts into the business. These investments increase owner's equity.

Revenues. **Revenues** are the **gross increase in owner's equity resulting from business activities entered into for the purpose of earning income**. Generally, revenues result from the sale of merchandise, the performance of services, the rental of property, and the lending of money.

Revenues usually result in an increase in an asset. They may arise from different sources and are identified by various names depending on the nature of the business. Campus Pizza, for instance, has two categories of sales revenues—pizza sales and beverage sales. Common sources of revenue are: sales, fees, services, commissions, interest, dividends, royalties, and rent.

DECREASES IN OWNER'S EQUITY.   In a proprietorship, owner's equity is decreased by owner's drawings and expenses.

Drawings. An owner may withdraw cash or other assets for personal use. These withdrawals could be recorded as a direct decrease of owner's equity. However, it is generally considered preferable to use a separate classification called **drawings** to determine the total withdrawals for each accounting period. **Drawings decrease owner's equity.**

Expenses. **Expenses** are the cost of assets consumed or services used in the process of earning revenue. They are **decreases in owner's equity that result from operating the business**. Expenses represent actual or expected cash outflows (payments). Like revenues, expenses take many forms and are identified by various names depending on the type of asset consumed or service used. For example, Campus Pizza recognizes the following expenses: cost of ingredients (meat, flour, cheese, tomato paste, mushrooms, etc.); cost of beverages; wages expense; utility expense (electric, gas, and water expense); telephone expense; delivery expense (gasoline, repairs, licenses, etc.); supplies expense (napkins, detergents, aprons, etc.); rent expense; interest expense; and property tax expense.

In summary, owner's equity is increased by an owner's investments and by revenues from business operations. In contrast, owner's equity is decreased by an owner's withdrawals of assets and by expenses. These relationships are shown in Illustration 1-6. **Net income** results when revenues exceed expenses. A **net loss** occurs when expenses exceed revenues.

HELPFUL HINT

In some places we use the term *owner's equity* and in others we use *owners' equity. Owner's* refers to one owner (the case with a sole proprietorship), and *owners'* refers to multiple owners (the case with partnerships or corporations).

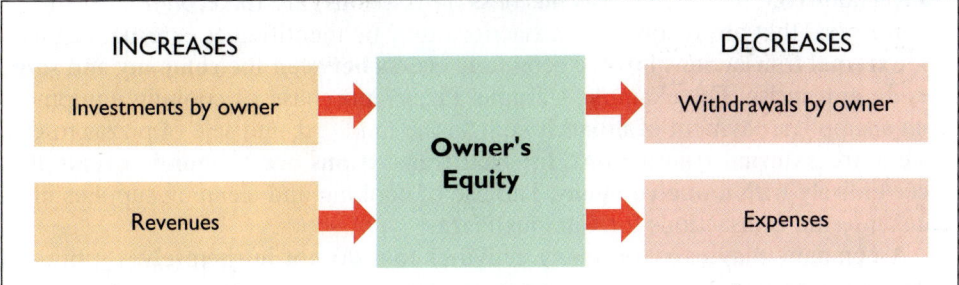

Illustration 1-6
Increases and decreases in owner's equity

Review It questions marked with this icon require that you use PepsiCo's Annual Report.

*Sometimes **Review It** questions stand alone; other times they are accompanied by practice exercises.*
*The **Do It** exercises, like the one here, ask you to put newly acquired knowledge to work. They outline the Action Plan necessary to complete the exercise and show a Solution.*

BEFORE YOU GO ON...

Review It

1. Why is ethics a fundamental business concept?

2. What are generally accepted accounting principles? Give an example.

3. Explain the monetary unit and the economic entity assumptions.

4. The accounting equation is: Assets = Liabilities + Owner's Equity. Replacing the words in that equation with dollar amounts, what is **PepsiCo's** accounting equation at December 28, 2002? (*Hint:* Owner's equity is equivalent to stockholders' equity. The answer to this question is provided on page 42.)

5. What are assets, liabilities, and owner's equity?

Do It

Classify the following items as investment by owner (I), owner's drawings (D), revenues (R), or expenses (E). Then indicate whether the following items increase or decrease owner's equity: (1) rent expense, (2) service revenue, (3) drawings, and (4) salaries expense.

ACTION PLAN

■ Review the rules for changes in owner's equity: Investments and revenues increase owner's equity. Expenses and drawings decrease owner's equity.
■ Understand the sources of revenue: the sale of merchandise, performance of services, rental of property, and lending of money.
■ Understand what causes expenses: the consumption of assets or services.
■ Recognize that drawings are withdrawals of cash or other assets from the business for personal use.

SOLUTION

1. Rent expense is classified as an expense (E); it decreases owner's equity.

2. Service revenue is classified as revenue (R); it increases owner's equity.

3. Drawings is classified as owner's drawings (D); it decreases owner's equity.

4. Salaries expense is classified as an expense (E); it decreases owner's equity.

Related exercise material: BE1-1, BE1-2, BE1-3, BE1-4, BE1-5, BE1-6, BE1-7, BE1-9, E1-1, E1-2, E1-3, E1-4, E1-6, and E1-7.

Using the Building Blocks

STUDY OBJECTIVE 7

Analyze the effects of business transactions on the basic accounting equation.

Transactions (often referred to as business transactions) are the economic events of an enterprise that are recorded. Transactions may be identified as external or internal. **External transactions involve economic events between the company and some outside enterprise.** For example, Campus Pizza's purchase of cooking equipment from a supplier, payment of monthly rent to the landlord, and sale of pizzas to customers are external transactions. **Internal transactions are economic events that occur entirely within one company.** The use of cooking and cleaning supplies illustrates internal transactions for Campus Pizza.

A company may carry on many activities that do not in themselves represent business transactions. Hiring employees, answering the telephone, talking with customers, and placing orders for merchandise are examples. Some of these activities, however, may lead to business transactions: Employees will earn wages, and merchandise will be delivered by suppliers. Each event must be analyzed to find out if it has an effect on the components of the basic accounting equation. If it does, it will be recorded in the accounting process. Illustration 1-7 demonstrates the transaction identification process.

Illustration 1-7
Transaction identification process

The equality of the basic equation must be preserved. Therefore, each transaction must have a dual effect on the equation. For example, if an asset is increased, there must be a corresponding:

1. Decrease in another asset, or
2. Increase in a specific liability, or
3. Increase in owner's equity.

It follows that two or more items could be affected when an asset is increased. For example, as one asset is increased $10,000, another asset could decrease $6,000 and a specific liability could increase $4,000. Any change in a liability or ownership claim is subject to similar analysis.

Transaction Analysis

The following examples are business transactions for a computer programming business during its first month of operations. You will want to study these transactions until you are sure you understand them. They are not difficult, but they are important to your success in this course. The ability to analyze transactions in terms of the basic accounting equation is essential for an understanding of accounting.

TRANSACTION (1). INVESTMENT BY OWNER.   Ray Neal decides to open a computer programming service which he names Softbyte. On September 1, 2005, he invests $15,000 cash in the business. This transaction results in an equal increase in assets and owner's equity. The asset Cash increases $15,000, as does the owner's equity, identified as R. Neal, Capital. The effect of this transaction on the basic equation is:

	Assets	=	Liabilities	+	Owner's Equity	
	Cash	=			R. Neal, Capital	
(1)	+$15,000	=			+$15,000	Investment

Observe that the equality of the basic equation has been maintained. Note also that the source of the increase in owner's equity (Investment) is indicated. Why does this matter? Because investments by the owner do not represent revenues, and they are excluded in determining net income. Therefore it is necessary to make clear that the increase is an investment rather than revenue from operations.

TRANSACTION (2). PURCHASE OF EQUIPMENT FOR CASH. Softbyte purchases computer equipment for $7,000 cash. This transaction results in an equal increase and decrease in total assets, though the composition of assets changes: Cash is decreased $7,000, and the asset Equipment is increased $7,000. The specific effect of this transaction and the cumulative effect of the first two transactions are:

		Assets		=	Liabilities	+	Owner's Equity
		Cash	Equipment	=			R. Neal, Capital
	Old Bal.	$15,000					$15,000
(2)		−7,000	+$7,000				
	New Bal.	$ 8,000	$7,000	=			$15,000
			$15,000				

Observe that total assets are still $15,000, and Neal's equity also remains at $15,000, the amount of his original investment.

TRANSACTION (3). PURCHASE OF SUPPLIES ON CREDIT. Softbyte purchases for $1,600 from Acme Supply Company computer paper and other supplies expected to last several months. Acme agrees to allow Softbyte to pay this bill next month, in October. This transaction is referred to as a purchase on account or a credit purchase. Assets are increased because of the expected future benefits of using the paper and supplies, and liabilities are increased by the amount due Acme Company. The asset Supplies is increased $1,600, and the liability Accounts Payable is increased by the same amount. The effect on the equation is:

		Assets				=	Liabilities	+	Owner's Equity
		Cash	+	Supplies	+ Equipment	=	Accounts Payable	+	R. Neal, Capital
	Old Bal.	$8,000			$7,000				$15,000
(3)				+$1,600			+$1,600		
	New Bal.	$8,000	+	$1,600	+ $7,000	=	$1,600	+	$15,000
				$16,600			$16,600		

Total assets are now $16,600. This total is matched by a $1,600 creditor's claim and a $15,000 ownership claim.

TRANSACTION (4). SERVICES PROVIDED FOR CASH. Softbyte receives $1,200 cash from customers for programming services it has provided. This transaction represents Softbyte's principal revenue-producing activity. Recall that **revenue increases owner's equity**. In this transaction, Cash is increased $1,200, and R. Neal, Capital is increased $1,200. The new balances in the equation are:

		Assets			=	Liabilities	+	Owner's Equity	
		Cash	+ Supplies	+ Equipment	=	Accounts Payable	+	R. Neal, Capital	
	Old Bal.	$8,000	$1,600	$7,000		$1,600		$15,000	
(4)		+$1,200						+1,200	**Service Revenue**
	New Bal.	$9,200	+ $1,600	+ $7,000	=	$1,600	+	$16,200	
			$17,800				$17,800		

The two sides of the equation balance at $17,800. The source of the increase in owner's equity is indicated as Service Revenue. Service revenue is included in determining Softbyte's net income.

TRANSACTION (5). PURCHASE OF ADVERTISING ON CREDIT. Softbyte receives a bill for $250 from the *Daily News* for advertising but postpones payment of the bill until a later date. This transaction results in an increase in liabilities and a decrease in owner's equity. The specific items involved are Accounts Payable and R. Neal, Capital. The effect on the equation is:

		Assets			=	Liabilities	+	Owner's Equity	
		Cash	+ Supplies	+ Equipment	=	Accounts Payable	+	R. Neal, Capital	
	Old Bal.	$9,200	$1,600	$7,000		$1,600		$16,200	
(5)						+250		−250	**Advertising Expense**
	New Bal.	$9,200	+ $1,600	+ $7,000	=	$1,850	+	$15,950	
			$17,800				$17,800		

The two sides of the equation still balance at $17,800. Owner's equity is decreased when the expense is incurred, and the specific cause of the decrease (advertising expense) is noted. Expenses do not have to be paid in cash at the time they are incurred. When payment is made at a later date, the liability Accounts Payable will be decreased and the asset Cash will be decreased [see Transaction (8)]. The cost of advertising is considered an expense, as opposed to an asset, because the benefits have been used. This expense is included in determining net income.

TRANSACTION (6). SERVICES PROVIDED FOR CASH AND CREDIT. Softbyte provides $3,500 of programming services for customers. Cash of $1,500 is received from customers, and the balance of $2,000 is billed on account. This transaction results in an equal increase in assets and owner's equity. Three specific items are affected: Cash is increased $1,500; Accounts Receivable is increased $2,000; and R. Neal, Capital is increased $3,500. The new balances are as follows.

			Assets					=	Liabilities	+	Owner's Equity	
		Cash	+	Accounts Receivable	+ Supplies +	Equipment	=		Accounts Payable	+	R. Neal, Capital	
Old Bal.		$9,200			$1,600	$7,000			$1,850		$15,950	
(6)		+1,500		+$2,000							+3,500	**Service Revenue**
New Bal.		$10,700	+	$2,000	+ $1,600 +	$7,000	=		$1,850	+	$19,450	
					$21,300					$21,300		

Why increase owner's equity $3,500 when only $1,500 has been collected? Because the inflow of assets resulting from the earning of revenues does not have to be in the form of cash. Remember that owner's equity is increased when revenues are earned; in Softbyte's case revenues are earned when the service is provided. When collections on account are received later, Cash will be increased and Accounts Receivable will be decreased [see Transaction (9)].

TRANSACTION (7). PAYMENT OF EXPENSES. Expenses paid in cash for September are store rent $600, salaries of employees $900, and utilities $200. These payments result in an equal decrease in assets and owner's equity. Cash is decreased $1,700, and R. Neal, Capital is decreased by the same amount. The effect of these payments on the equation is:

			Assets					=	Liabilities	+	Owner's Equity	
		Cash	+	Accounts Receivable	+ Supplies +	Equipment	=		Accounts Payable	+	R. Neal, Capital	
Old Bal.		$10,700		$2,000	$1,600	$7,000			$1,850		$19,450	
(7)		−1,700									−600	**Rent Expense**
											−900	**Salaries Expense**
											−200	**Utilities Expense**
New Bal.		$9,000	+	$2,000	+ $1,600 +	$7,000	=		$1,850	+	$17,750	
					$19,600					$19,600		

The two sides of the equation now balance at $19,600. Three lines are required in the analysis to indicate the different types of expenses that have been incurred.

TRANSACTION (8). PAYMENT OF ACCOUNTS PAYABLE. Softbyte pays its $250 *Daily News* advertising bill in cash. Remember that the bill was previously recorded [in Transaction (5)] as an increase in Accounts Payable and a decrease in owner's equity. This payment "on account" decreases the asset Cash by $250 and also decreases the liability Accounts Payable by $250. The effect of this transaction on the equation is:

				Assets				=	Liabilities	+	Owner's Equity
		Cash	+	Accounts Receivable	+ Supplies +	Equipment	=		Accounts Payable	+	R. Neal, Capital
Old Bal.		$9,000		$2,000	$1,600	$7,000			$1,850		$17,750
(8)		−250							−250		
New Bal.		$8,750	+	$2,000	+ $1,600 +	$7,000	=		$1,600	+	$17,750
					$19,350					$19,350	

Observe that the payment of a liability related to an expense that has previously been recorded does not affect owner's equity. The expense was recorded in Transaction (5) and should not be recorded again.

TRANSACTION (9). RECEIPT OF CASH ON ACCOUNT. The sum of $600 in cash is received from customers who have previously been billed for services [in Transaction (6)]. This transaction does not change total assets, but it changes the composition of those assets. Cash is increased $600 and Accounts Receivable is decreased $600. The new balances are:

		Cash	+	Accounts Receivable	+	Supplies	+	Equipment	=	Accounts Payable	+	R. Neal, Capital
				Assets					=	**Liabilities**	+	**Owner's Equity**
	Old Bal.	$8,750		$2,000		$1,600		$7,000		$1,600		$17,750
(9)		+600		−600								
	New Bal.	$9,350	+	$1,400	+	$1,600	+	$7,000	=	$1,600	+	$17,750
					$19,350						$19,350	

Note that a collection on account for services previously billed and recorded does not affect owner's equity. Revenue was already recorded in Transaction (6) and should not be recorded again.

TRANSACTION (10). WITHDRAWAL OF CASH BY OWNER. Ray Neal withdraws $1,300 in cash from the business for his personal use. This transaction results in an equal decrease in assets and owner's equity. Both Cash and R. Neal, Capital are decreased $1,300, as shown below.

		Cash	+	Accounts Receivable	+	Supplies	+	Equipment	=	Accounts Payable	+	R. Neal, Capital	
				Assets					=	**Liabilities**	+	**Owner's Equity**	
	Old Bal.	$9,350		$1,400		$1,600		$7,000		$1,600		$17,750	
(10)		−1,300										−1,300	**Drawings**
	New Bal.	$8,050	+	$1,400	+	$1,600	+	$7,000	=	$1,600	+	$16,450	
					$18,050						$18,050		

Observe that the effect of a cash withdrawal by the owner is the opposite of the effect of an investment by the owner. **Owner's drawings are not expenses.** Like owner's investment, they are excluded in determining net income.

Summary of Transactions

The September transactions of Softbyte are summarized in Illustration 1-8 (page 20). The transaction number, the specific effects of the transaction, and the balances after each transaction are indicated. The illustration demonstrates some significant facts listed below.

1. Each transaction must be analyzed in terms of its effect on:
   (a) the three components of the basic accounting equation.
   (b) specific types (kinds) of items within each component.
2. The two sides of the equation must always be equal.
3. The causes of each change in the owner's claim on assets must be indicated in the owner's equity column.

Illustration 1-8
Tabular summary of Softbyte
transactions

			Assets				=	Liabilities	+	Owner's Equity	
Transaction	Cash	+	Accounts Receivable	+ Supplies +	Equipment	=		Accounts Payable	+	R. Neal, Capital	
(1)	+$15,000									+$15,000	**Investment**
(2)	−7,000				+$7,000						
	8,000			+	7,000	=				15,000	
(3)				+$1,600				+$1,600			
	8,000	+		1,600 +	7,000	=		1,600	+	15,000	
(4)	+1,200									+1,200	**Service Revenue**
	9,200			+ 1,600 +	7,000	=		1,600	+	16,200	
(5)								+250		−250	**Advertising Expense**
	9,200			+ 1,600 +	7,000	=		1,850	+	15,950	
(6)	+1,500		+$2,000							+3,500	**Service Revenue**
	10,700 +		2,000 +	1,600 +	7,000	=		1,850	+	19,450	
(7)	−1,700									−600	**Rent Expense**
										−900	**Salaries Expense**
										−200	**Utilities Expense**
	9,000 +		2,000 +	1,600 +	7,000	=		1,850	+	17,750	
(8)	−250							−250			
	8,750 +		2,000 +	1,600 +	7,000	=		1,600	+	17,750	
(9)	+600		−600								
	9,350 +		1,400 +	1,600 +	7,000	=		1,600	+	17,750	
(10)	−1,300									−1,300	**Drawings**
	$8,050 +		$1,400 +	$1,600 +	$7,000	=		$1,600	+	$16,450	

$18,050 $18,050

There! You made it through transaction analysis. If you feel a bit shaky on any of the transactions, it might be a good idea at this point to get up, take a short break, and come back again for a 10- to 15-minute review of the transactions, to make sure you understand them before you go on to the next section.

BEFORE YOU GO ON...

Review It

1. What is an example of an external transaction? What is an example of an internal transaction?
2. If an asset increases, what are the three possible effects on the basic accounting equation?

Do It

A tabular analysis of the transactions made by Roberta Mendez & Co., a certified public accounting firm, for the month of August is shown on page 21. Each increase and decrease in owner's equity is explained.

	Assets			=	Liabilities	+		Owner's Equity	
	Cash	+	Office Equipment	=	Accounts Payable	+		R. Mendez, Capital	
1.	+$25,000						+25,000	Investment	
2.			+7,000		+7,000				
3.	+8,000						+8,000	Service Revenue	
4.	−850						−850	Rent Expense	

Describe each transaction that occurred for the month.

ACTION PLAN
- Analyze the tabular analysis to determine the nature and effect of each transaction.
- Keep the accounting equation always in balance.
- Remember that a change in an asset will require a change in another asset, a liability, or in owner's equity.

SOLUTION
1. The owner invested $25,000 of cash in the business.

2. The company purchased $7,000 of office equipment on credit.

3. The company received $8,000 of cash in exchange for services performed.

4. The company paid $850 for this month's rent.

Related exercise material: *BE1-4, BE1-5, BE1-6, BE1-7, E1-2, E1-3, E1-4, E1-6,* and *E1-7.*

✓ THE NAVIGATOR

Financial Statements ✳

After transactions are identified, recorded, and summarized, four financial statements are prepared from the summarized accounting data:

1. An **income statement** presents the revenues and expenses and resulting net income or net loss for a specific period of time.

2. An **owner's equity statement** summarizes the changes in owner's equity for a specific period of time.

3. A **balance sheet** reports the assets, liabilities, and owner's equity at a specific date.

4. A **statement of cash flows** summarizes information about the cash inflows (receipts) and outflows (payments) for a specific period of time.

Each statement provides management, owners, and other interested parties with relevant financial data.

The financial statements of Softbyte are shown in Illustration 1-9 (page 22). The statements are interrelated: **(1) Net income of $2,750 shown on the income statement is added to the beginning balance of owner's capital in the owner's equity statement. (2) Owner's capital of $16,450 at the end of the reporting period shown in the owner's equity statement is reported on the balance sheet. (3) Cash of $8,050 on the balance sheet is reported on the statement of cash flows.**

Also, every set of financial statements is accompanied by explanatory notes and supporting schedules that are an integral part of the statements. Examples of these notes and schedules are illustrated in later chapters of this textbook.

STUDY OBJECTIVE 8

Understand what the four financial statements are and how they are prepared.

HELPFUL HINT

The income statement, owner's equity statement, and statement of cash flows are all for a *period* of time, whereas the balance sheet is for a *point* in time.

Illustration 1-9
Financial statements and
their interrelationships

SOFTBYTE
Income Statement
For the Month Ended September 30, 2005

Revenues		
Service revenue		$ 4,700
Expenses		
Salaries expense	$900	
Rent expense	600	
Advertising expense	250	
Utilities expense	200	
Total expenses		1,950
Net income		**$ 2,750**

①

SOFTBYTE
Owner's Equity Statement
For the Month Ended September 30, 2005

R. Neal, Capital September 1		$ –0–
Add: Investments	$15,000	
Net income	**2,750**	17,750
		17,750
Less: Drawings		1,300
R. Neal, Capital, September 30		**$16,450**

②

SOFTBYTE
Balance Sheet
September 30, 2005

Assets

Cash	**$ 8,050**
Accounts receivable	1,400
Supplies	1,600
Equipment	7,000
Total assets	$18,050

Liabilities and Owner's Equity

Liabilities	
Accounts payable	$ 1,600
Owner's equity	
R. Neal, Capital	**16,450**
Total liabilities and owner's equity	$18,050

③

SOFTBYTE
Statement of Cash Flows
For the Month Ended September 30, 2005

Cash flows from operating activities		
Cash receipts from revenues		$ 3,300
Cash payments for expenses		(1,950)
Net cash provided by operating activities		1,350
Cash flows from investing activities		
Purchase of equipment		(7,000)
Cash flows from financing activities		
Investments by owner	$15,000	
Drawings by owner	(1,300)	13,700
Net increase in cash		8,050
Cash at the beginning of the period		0
Cash at the end of the period		**$ 8,050**

Be sure to carefully examine the format and content of each statement. The essential features of each are briefly described in the following sections.

Income Statement

Softbyte's income statement reports the revenues and expenses for a specific period of time (in this "case, "For the Month Ended September 30, 2005"). Its income statement is prepared from the data appearing in the owner's equity column of Illustration 1-8.

On the income statement, revenues are listed first, followed by expenses. Finally net income (or net loss) is determined. Although practice varies, we have chosen in our illustrations and homework solutions to list expenses in order of magnitude. Alternative formats for the income statement will be considered in later chapters.

Note that investment and withdrawal transactions between the owner and the business are not included in the measurement of net income. For example, the withdrawal by Ray Neal of cash from Softbyte was not regarded as a business expense, as explained earlier.

> **ALTERNATIVE TERMINOLOGY**
>
> The income statement is sometimes referred to as the *statement of operations, earnings statement,* or *profit and loss statement.*

Owner's Equity Statement

Softbyte's owner's equity statement reports the changes in owner's equity for a specific period of time. The time period is the same as that covered by the income statement. Data for the preparation of the owner's equity statement are obtained from the owner's equity column of the tabular summary (Illustration 1-8) and from the income statement. The beginning owner's equity amount is shown on the first line of the statement. Then, the owner's investments, net income, and the owner's drawings are identified. The information in this statement indicates the reasons why owner's equity has increased or decreased during the period.

What if Softbyte reported a net loss in its first month? Let's assume that during the month of September 2005, Softbyte lost $10,000. The presentation in the owner's equity statement of a net loss appears in Illustration 1-10.

SOFTBYTE		
Owner's Equity Statement		
For the Month Ended September 30, 2005		
R. Neal, Capital, September 1		$ –0–
Add: Investments		15,000
		15,000
Less: Drawings	$ 1,300	
Net loss	10,000	11,300
R. Neal, Capital, September 30		$ 3,700

Illustration 1-10
Presentation of net loss

Any additional investments are reported as investments in the owner's equity statement.

Balance Sheet

Softbyte's balance sheet reports the assets, liabilities, and owner's equity at a specific date (in this case, September 30, 2005). The balance sheet is prepared from the column headings and the month-end data shown in the last line of the tabular summary (Illustration 1-8).

Observe that the assets are listed at the top, followed by liabilities and owner's equity. Total assets must equal total liabilities and owner's equity. In the Softbyte balance sheet, only one liability, accounts payable, is reported. In most cases, there will be more than one liability. When two or more liabilities are involved, a customary way of listing is as follows.

Illustration 1-11
Presentation of liabilities

Liabilities	
Notes payable	$10,000
Account payable	63,000
Salaries payable	18,000
Total liabilities	$91,000

The balance sheet is like a snapshot of the company's financial condition at a specific moment in time (usually the month-end or year-end).

ACCOUNTING IN ACTION · Business Insight

Why do companies choose the particular year-ends that they do? Not every company uses December 31 as the accounting year-end. Many companies choose to end their accounting year when inventory or operations are at a low. This is advantageous because compiling accounting information requires much time and effort by managers, so they would rather do it when they aren't as busy operating the business. Also, inventory is easier and less costly to count when it is low. Some companies whose year-ends differ from December 31 are **Delta Air Lines**, June 30; **Walt Disney Productions**, September 30; **Kmart Corp.**, January 31; and **Dunkin' Donuts Inc.**, October 31.

Statement of Cash Flows

5.4

HELPFUL HINT

Investing activities pertain to investments made by the company, not investments made by the owner.

Softbyte's statement of cash flows provides information on the cash receipts and payments for a specific period of time. **The statement of cash flows reports (1) the cash effects of a company's operations during a period, (2) its investing transactions, (3) its financing transactions, (4) the net increase or decrease in cash during the period, and (5) the cash amount at the end of the period.**

Reporting the sources, uses, and net increase or decrease in cash is useful because investors, creditors, and others want to know what is happening to a company's most liquid resource. The statement of cash flows, therefore, provides answers to the following simple but important questions.

1. Where did the cash come from during the period?
2. What was the cash used for during the period?
3. What was the change in the cash balance during the period?

Softbyte's statement of cash flows is provided in Illustration 1-9.

As shown in the statement, cash increased $8,050 during the period. Net cash flow provided from operating activities increased cash $1,350. Cash flow from investing transactions decreased cash $7,000. And cash flow from financing transactions increased cash $13,700. At this time, you need not be concerned with how these amounts are determined. Chapter 18 will examine the statement of cash flows in detail.

BEFORE YOU GO ON...

Review It
1. What are the income statement, statement of owner's equity, balance sheet, and statement of cash flows?
2. How are the financial statements interrelated?

THE NAVIGATOR

DEMONSTRATION PROBLEM

Joan Robinson opens her own law office on July 1, 2005. During the first month of operations, the following transactions occurred.

1. Invested $10,000 in cash in the law practice.
2. Paid $800 for July rent on office space.
3. Purchased office equipment on account $3,000.
4. Provided legal services to clients for cash $1,500.
5. Borrowed $700 cash from a bank on a note payable.
6. Performed legal services for client on account $2,000.
7. Paid monthly expenses: salaries $500, utilities $300, and telephone $100.

Instructions

(a) Prepare a tabular summary of the transactions.
(b) Prepare the income statement, owner's equity statement, and balance sheet at July 31 for Joan Robinson, Attorney at Law.

*Demonstration Problems are a final review of the chapter. The **Action Plan** gives tips about how to approach the problem, and the **Solution** demonstrates both the form and content of complete answers.*

SOLUTION TO DEMONSTRATION PROBLEM

(a)

Trans-action		Assets		=	Liabilities	+	Owner's Equity	
	Cash	+ Accounts Receivable	+ Equipment	= Notes Payable	+ Accounts Payable	+	Joan Robinson, Capital	
(1)	+$10,000						+$10,000	Investment
(2)	−800						−800	Rent Expense
	9,200			=			9,200	
(3)			+$3,000		+$3,000			
	9,200	+	3,000 =		3,000	+	9,200	
(4)	+1,500						+1,500	Service Revenue
	10,700	+	3,000 =		3,000	+	10,700	
(5)	+700			+$700				
	11,400	+	3,000 =	700	+ 3,000	+	10,700	
(6)		+$2,000					+2,000	Service Revenue
	11,400 +	2,000	+ 3,000 =	700	+ 3,000	+	12,700	
(7)	−900						−500	Salaries Expense
							−300	Utilities Expense
							−100	Telephone Expense
	$10,500 +	$2,000	+ $3,000 =	$700	+ $3,000	+	$11,800	

ACTION PLAN

- Remember that assets must equal liabilities and owner's equity after each transaction.
- Investments and revenues increase owner's equity.
- Expenses decrease owner's equity.
- The income statement shows revenues and expenses for a period of time.
- The owner's equity statement shows the changes in owner's equity for a period of time.
- The balance sheet reports assets, liabilities, and owner's equity at a specific date.

(b)

JOAN ROBINSON
Attorney at Law
Income Statement
For the Month Ended July 31, 2005

Revenues		
Service revenue		$3,500
Expenses		
Rent expense	$800	
Salaries expense	500	
Utilities expense	300	
Telephone expense	100	
Total expenses		1,700
Net income		$1,800

*This would be a good time to return to the **Student Owner's Manual** at the beginning of the book (or look at it for the first time if you skipped it before) to read about the various types of assignment materials that appear at the end of each chapter. Knowing the purpose of the different assignments will help you appreciate what each contributes to your accounting skills and competencies.*

JOAN ROBINSON
Attorney at Law
Owner's Equity Statement
For the Month Ended July 31, 2005

Joan Robinson, Capital, July 1		$ –0–
Add: Investments	$10,000	
Net income	1,800	11,800
Joan Robinson, Capital, July 31		$11,800

JOAN ROBINSON
Attorney at Law
Balance Sheet
July 31, 2005

Assets

Cash	$10,500
Accounts receivable	2,000
Equipment	3,000
Total assets	$15,500

Liabilities and Owner's Equity

Liabilities		
Notes payable		$ 700
Accounts payable		3,000
Total liabilities		3,700
Owner's equity		
Joan Robinson, Capital		11,800
Total liabilities and owner's equity		$15,500

☑ THE NAVIGATOR

SUMMARY OF STUDY OBJECTIVES

1. **Explain what accounting is.** Accounting is an information system that identifies, records, and communicates the economic events of an organization to interested users.

2. **Identify the users and uses of accounting.** The major users and uses of accounting are: (a) Management uses accounting information in planning, controlling, and evaluating business operations. (b) Investors (owners) decide whether to buy, hold, or sell their financial interests on the basis of accounting data. (c) Creditors (suppliers and bankers) evaluate the risks of granting credit or lending money on the basis of accounting information. Other groups that use accounting information are taxing authorities, regulatory agencies, customers, labor unions, and economic planners.

3. **Understand why ethics is a fundamental business concept.** Ethics are the standards of conduct by which actions are judged as right or wrong. If you cannot depend on the honesty of the individuals you deal with, effective communication and economic activity would be impossible, and information would have no credibility.

4. **Explain the meaning of generally accepted accounting principles and the cost principle.** Generally accepted accounting principles are a common set of standards used by accountants. The cost principle states that assets should be recorded at their cost.

5. **Explain the meaning of the monetary unit assumption and the economic entity assumption.** The monetary unit assumption requires that only transaction data capable of being expressed in terms of money be included in the accounting records. The economic entity assumption requires that the activities of each economic entity be kept separate from the activities of its owner and other economic entities.

6. **State the basic accounting equation, and explain the meaning of assets, liabilities, and owner's equity.** The basic accounting equation is:

$$\text{Assets} = \text{Liabilities} + \text{Owner's Equity}$$

Assets are resources owned by a business. Liabilities are creditorship claims on total assets. Owner's equity is the ownership claim on total assets.

7. **Analyze the effects of business transactions on the basic accounting equation.** Each business transaction must have a dual effect on the accounting equation. For example, if an individual asset is increased, there must be a corre-

sponding (1) decrease in another asset, or (2) increase in a specific liability, or (3) increase in owner's equity.

8. **Understand what the four financial statements are and how they are prepared.** An income statement presents the revenues and expenses of a company for a specified period of time. An owner's equity statement summarizes the changes in owner's equity that have occurred for a specific period of time. A balance sheet reports the assets, liabilities, and owner's equity of a business at a specific date. A statement of cash flows summarizes information about the cash inflows (receipts) and outflows (payments) for a specific period of time.

Web icons next to end-of-chapter materials indicate that you can find additional study resources on the book's Web site.

GLOSSARY

Accounting The information system that identifies, records, and communicates the economic events of an organization to interested users. (p. 4).

Assets Resources owned by a business. (p. 12).

Balance sheet A financial statement that reports the assets, liabilities, and owner's equity at a specific date. (p. 21).

Basic accounting equation Assets = Liabilities + Owner's Equity. (p. 12).

Bookkeeping A part of accounting that involves only the recording of economic events. (p. 7).

Corporation A business organized as a separate legal entity under state corporation law, having ownership divided into transferable shares of stock. (p. 11).

Cost principle An accounting principle that states that assets should be recorded at their cost. (p. 10).

Drawings Withdrawal of cash or other assets from an unincorporated business for the personal use of the owner(s). (p. 13).

Economic entity assumption An assumption that requires that the activities of the entity be kept separate and distinct from the activities of its owner and all other economic entities. (p. 11).

Ethics The standards of conduct by which one's actions are judged as right or wrong, honest or dishonest, fair or not fair. (p. 9).

Expenses The cost of assets consumed or services used in the process of earning revenue. (p. 13).

Financial accounting The field of accounting that provides economic and financial information for investors, creditors, and other external users. (p. 7).

Financial Accounting Standards Board (FASB) A private organization that establishes generally accepted accounting principles. (p. 10).

Generally accepted accounting principles (GAAP) Common standards that indicate how to report economic events. (p. 9).

Income statement A financial statement that presents the revenues and expenses and resulting net income or net loss of a company for a specific period of time. (p. 21).

Investments by owner The assets put into the business by the owner. (p. 13).

Liabilities Creditorship claims on total assets. (p. 12).

Managerial accounting The field of accounting that provides economic and financial information for managers and other internal users. (p. 7).

Monetary unit assumption An assumption stating that only transaction data that can be expressed in terms of money be included in the accounting records. (p. 10).

Net income The amount by which revenues exceed expenses. (p. 13).

Net loss The amount by which expenses exceed revenues. (p. 13).

Owner's equity The ownership claim on total assets. (p. 12).

Owner's equity statement A financial statement that summarizes the changes in owner's equity for a specific period of time. (p. 21).

Partnership An association of two or more persons to carry on as co-owners of a business for profit. (p. 11).

Proprietorship A business owned by one person. (p. 11).

Revenues The gross increase in owner's equity resulting from business activities entered into for the purpose of earning income. (p. 13).

Securities and Exchange Commission (SEC) A governmental agency that requires companies to file financial reports in accordance with generally accepted accounting principles. (p. 10).

Statement of cash flows A financial statement that summarizes information about the cash inflows (receipts) and cash outflows (payments) for a specific period of time. (p. 21).

Transactions The economic events of an enterprise that are recorded by accountants. (p. 14).

APPENDIX THE ACCOUNTING PROFESSION

The Accounting Profession

Careers in Accounting

What would you do if you join the accounting profession? You probably would work in one of three major fields—public accounting, private accounting, or not-for-profit accounting.

Public Accounting

STUDY OBJECTIVE 9

Identify the three major fields of the accounting profession and potential accounting careers.

In **public accounting**, you would offer expert service to the general public in much the same way that a doctor serves patients and a lawyer serves clients. A major portion of public accounting involves **auditing**. In this area, a certified public accountant (CPA) examines the financial statements of companies and expresses an opinion as to the fairness of presentation. When the presentation is fair, users consider the statements to be **reliable**. For example, **PepsiCo** investors would demand audited financial statements before extending it financing.

Taxation is another major area of public accounting. The work performed by tax specialists includes tax advice and planning, preparing tax returns, and representing clients before governmental agencies such as the Internal Revenue Service.

A third area in public accounting is **management consulting**. It ranges from the installing of basic accounting systems to helping companies determine whether they should use the space shuttle for high-tech research and development projects.

Private Accounting

Instead of working in public accounting, you might choose to be an employee of a business enterprise. In **private** (or **managerial**) **accounting**, you would be involved in one of the following activities.

1. **General accounting**—recording daily transactions and preparing financial statements and related information.
2. **Cost accounting**—determining the cost of producing specific products.
3. **Budgeting**—assisting management in quantifying goals concerning revenues, costs of goods sold, and operating expenses.
4. **Accounting information systems**—designing both manual and computerized data processing systems.
5. **Tax accounting**—preparing tax returns and doing tax planning for the company.
6. **Internal auditing**—reviewing the company's operations to see if they comply with management policies and evaluating the efficiency of operations.

You can see that within a specific company, private accountants perform as wide a variety of duties as the public accountant.

Illustration 1A-1 (page 29) presents the general career paths in public and private accounting.

Not-for-Profit Accounting

Like businesses that exist to make a profit, not-for-profit organizations also need sound financial reporting and control. Donors to such organizations as the **United Way**, the **Ford Foundation**, and the **Red Cross** want information about how well the organization has met its financial objectives and whether continued support is justified. Hospitals, colleges, and universities must make decisions about allocating funds.

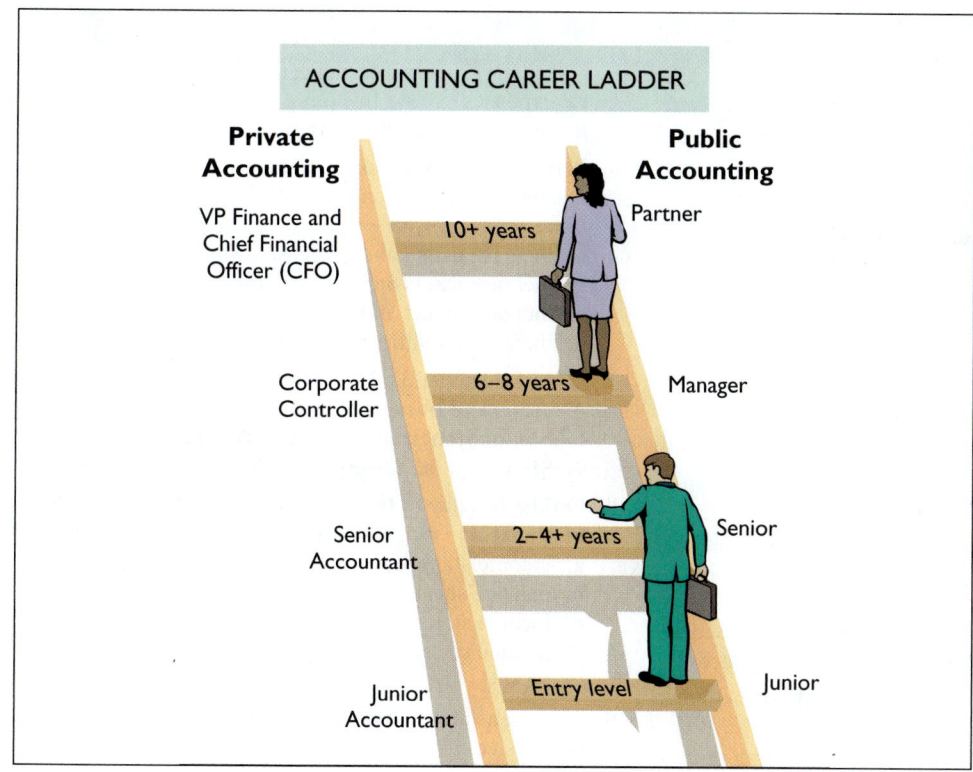

Another area of not-for-profit accounting is government accounting. Local, state, and federal governmental units provide financial information to legislators, citizens, employees, and creditors. At the federal level, the largest employers of accountants are the **Internal Revenue Service**, the **General Accounting Office**, the **Federal Bureau of Investigation**, and the **Securities and Exchange Commission**.

SUMMARY OF STUDY OBJECTIVE FOR APPENDIX

9. **Identify the three major fields of the accounting profession and potential accounting careers.** The accounting profession is comprised of three major fields: public accounting, private accounting, and not-for-profit accounting. In public accounting one may pursue a career in auditing, taxation, or management consulting. In private or managerial accounting, one may pursue a career in cost accounting, budgeting, general accounting, accounting information systems, tax accounting, or internal auditing. In not-for-profit accounting one may pursue a career at hospitals, universities, and foundations, or in local, state, and federal governmental units.

GLOSSARY FOR APPENDIX

Auditing The examination of financial statements by a certified public accountant in order to express an opinion as to the fairness of presentation. (p. 28).

Management consulting An area of public accounting involving financial planning and control and the development of accounting and computer systems. (p. 28).

Private (or managerial) accounting An area of accounting within a company that involves such activities as cost accounting, budgeting, and accounting information systems. (p. 28).

Public accounting An area of accounting in which the accountant offers expert service to the general public. (p. 28).

Taxation An area of public accounting involving tax advice, tax planning, and preparation of tax returns. (p. 28).

SELF-STUDY QUESTIONS

Answers are at the end of the chapter.

(SO 1) **1.** Which of the following is *not* a step in the accounting process?
    a. identification.   **c.** recording.
    b. verification.   **d.** communication.

(SO 2) **2.** Which of the following statements about users of accounting information is *incorrect*?
    a. Management is an internal user.
    b. Taxing authorities are external users.
    c. Present creditors are external users.
    d. Regulatory authorities are internal users.

(SO 4) **3.** The cost principle states that:
    a. assets should be initially recorded at cost and adjusted when the market value changes.
    b. activities of an entity are to be kept separate and distinct from its owner.
    c. assets should be recorded at their cost.
    d. only transaction data capable of being expressed in terms of money be included in the accounting records.

(SO 5) **4.** Which of the following statements about basic assumptions is *incorrect*?
    a. Basic assumptions are the same as accounting principles.
    b. The economic entity assumption states that there should be a particular unit of accountability.
    c. The monetary unit assumption enables accounting to measure economic events.
    d. An important part of the monetary unit assumption is the stable monetary unit assumption.

(SO 6) **5.** Net income will result during a time period when:
    a. assets exceed liabilities.
    b. assets exceed revenues.
    c. expenses exceed revenues.
    d. revenues exceed expenses.

6. Performing services on account will have the following (SO effects on the components of the basic accounting equation:
    a. increase assets and decrease owner's equity.
    b. increase assets and increase owner's equity.
    c. increase assets and increase liabilities.
    d. increase liabilities and increase owner's equity.

7. As of December 31, 2005, Stoneland Company has assets (SO of $3,500 and owner's equity of $2,000. What are the liabilities for Stoneland Company as of December 31, 2005?
    a. $1,500.   **b.** $1,000.   **c.** $2,500.   **d.** $2,000.

8. On the last day of the period, Jim Otto Company buys a (SO $900 machine on credit. This transaction will affect the:
    a. income statement only.
    b. balance sheet only.
    c. income statement and owner's equity statement only.
    d. income statement, owner's equity statement, and balance sheet.

9. The financial statement that reports assets, liabilities, and (SO owner's equity is the:
    a. income statement.
    b. owner's equity statement.
    c. balance sheet.
    d. statement of cash flow.

*__**10.**__ Services provided by a public accountant include: (SO
    a. auditing, taxation, and management consulting.
    b. auditing, budgeting, and management consulting.
    c. auditing, budgeting, and cost accounting.
    d. internal auditing, budgeting, and management consulting.

QUESTIONS

1. "Accounting is ingrained in our society and it is vital to our economic system." Do you agree? Explain.

2. Identify and describe the steps in the accounting process.

3. (a) Who are internal users of accounting data?(b) How does accounting provide relevant data to these users?

4. What uses of financial accounting information are made by (a) investors and (b) creditors?

5. "Bookkeeping and accounting are the same." Do you agree? Explain.

6. Jackie Remmers Travel Agency purchased land for $85,000 cash on December 10, 2005. At December 31, 2005, the land's value has increased to $93,000. What amount should be reported for land on Jackie Remmers' balance sheet at December 31, 2005? Explain.

7. What is the monetary unit assumption? What impact does inflation have on the monetary unit assumption?

8. What is the economic entity assumption?

9. What are the three basic forms of business organizations for profit-oriented enterprises?

10. Teresa Alvarez is the owner of a successful printing shop. Recently her business has been increasing, and Teresa has been thinking about changing the organization of her business from a proprietorship to a corporation. Discuss some of the advantages Teresa would enjoy if she were to incorporate her business.

11. What is the basic accounting equation?

12. (a) Define the terms assets, liabilities, and owner's equity.
    (b) What items affect owner's equity?

13. Which of the following items are liabilities of Design Jewelry Stores?
(a) Cash.
(b) Accounts payable.
(c) Drawings.
(d) Accounts receivable.
(e) Supplies.
(f) Equipment.
(g) Salaries payable.
(h) Service revenue.
(i) Rent expense.

14. Can a business enter into a transaction in which only the left side of the basic accounting equation is affected? If so, give an example.

15. Are the following events recorded in the accounting records? Explain your answer in each case.
(a) The owner of the company dies.
(b) Supplies are purchased on account.
(c) An employee is fired.
(d) The owner of the business withdraws cash from the business for personal use.

16. Indicate how the following business transactions affect the basic accounting equation.
(a) Paid cash for janitorial services.
(b) Purchased equipment for cash.
(c) Invested cash in the business.
(d) Paid accounts payable in full.

17. Listed below are some items found in the financial statements of Frank B. Robinson Co. Indicate in which financial statement(s) the following items would appear.
(a) Service revenue.
(b) Equipment.
(c) Advertising expense.
(d) Accounts receivable.
(e) Frank B. Robinson, Capital.
(f) Wages payable.

18. In February 2005, Erica Shin invested an additional $10,000 in her business, Shin's Pharmacy, which is organized as a proprietorship. Shin's accountant, Lance Jones, recorded this receipt as an increase in cash and revenues. Is this treatment appropriate? Why or why not?

19. "A company's net income appears directly on the income statement and the owner's equity statement, and it is included indirectly in the company's balance sheet." Do you agree? Explain.

20. Jardine Enterprises had a capital balance of $158,000 at the beginning of the period. At the end of the accounting period, the capital balance was $198,000.
(a) Assuming no additional investment or withdrawals during the period, what is the net income for the period?
(b) Assuming an additional investment of $13,000 but no withdrawals during the period, what is the net income for the period?

21. Summarized operations for H. J. Oslo Co. for the month of July are as follows.

Revenues earned: for cash $30,000; on account $70,000.

Expenses incurred: for cash $26,000; on account $40,000.

Indicate for H. J. Oslo Co. (a) the total revenues, (b) the total expenses, and (c) net income for the month of July.

BRIEF EXERCISES

BE1-1 Presented below is the basic accounting equation. Determine the missing amounts.

Use basic accounting equation.
(SO 6)

	Assets	=	Liabilities	+	Owner's Equity
(a)	$90,000		$50,000		?
(b)	?		$45,000		$70,000
(c)	$94,000		?		$65,000

BE1-2 Given the accounting equation, answer each of the following questions.

Use basic accounting equation.
(SO 6)

(a) The liabilities of Shumway Company are $100,000 and the owner's equity is $232,000. What is the amount of Shumway Company's total assets?
(b) The total assets of Company are $190,000 and its owner's equity is $80,000. What is the amount of its total liabilities?
(c) The total assets of Norris Co. are $600,000 and its liabilities are equal to one half of its total assets. What is the amount of Norris Co.'s owner's equity?

BE1-3 At the beginning of the year, Gonzales Company had total assets of $870,000 and total liabilities of $500,000. Answer the following questions.

Use basic accounting equation.
(SO 6)

(a) If total assets increased $150,000 during the year and total liabilities decreased $80,000, what is the amount of owner's equity at the end of the year?
(b) During the year, total liabilities increased $100,000 and owner's equity decreased $70,000. What is the amount of total assets at the end of the year?
(c) If total assets decreased $80,000 and owner's equity increased $120,000 during the year, what is the amount of total liabilities at the end of the year?

Determine effect of transactions on basic accounting equation.
(SO 7)

BE1-4 Presented below are three business transactions. On a sheet of paper, list the letters (a), (b), (c) with columns for assets, liabilities, and owner's equity. For each column, indicate whether the transactions increased (+), decreased (−), or had no effect (NE) on assets, liabilities, and owner's equity.

(a) Purchased supplies on account.

(b) Received cash for providing a service.

(c) Paid expenses in cash.

Determine effect of transactions on basic accounting equation.

(SO 7)

BE1-5 Follow the same format as BE1-4 above. Determine the effect on assets, liabilities, and owner's equity of the following three transactions.

(a) Invested cash in the business.

(b) Withdrawal of cash by owner.

(c) Received cash from a customer who had previously been billed for services provided.

Determine effect of transactions on owner's equity.

(SO 7)

BE1-6 Classify each of the following items as owner's drawing (D), revenue (R), or expense (E).

_____(a) Advertising expense

_____(b) Commission revenue

_____(c) Insurance expense

_____(d) Salaries expense

_____(e) Carland, Drawing

_____(f) Rent revenue

_____(g) Utilities expense

Determine effect of transactions on basic owner's equity.

(SO 7)

BE1-7 Presented below are three transactions. Mark each transaction as affecting owner's investment (I), owner's drawings (D), revenue (R), expense (E), or not affecting owner's equity (NOE).

_____(a) Received cash for services performed

_____(b) Paid cash to purchase equipment

_____(c) Paid employee salaries.

Prepare a balance sheet.

(SO 8)

BE1-8 In alphabetical order below are balance sheet items for Gomez Company at December 31, 2005. Kim Gomez is the owner of Gomez Company. Prepare a balance sheet, following the format of Illustration 1-9.

Accounts payable	$85,000
Accounts receivable	$72,500
Cash	$44,000
Kim Gomez, Capital	$31,500

Identify assets, liabilities, and owner's equity.

(SO 6)

BE1-9 Indicate whether each of the following items is an asset (A), liability (L), or part of owner's equity (OE).

_____(a) Accounts receivable

_____(b) Salaries payable

_____(c) Equipment

_____(d) Office supplies

_____(e) Owner's investment

_____(f) Notes payable

Determine where items appear on financial statements.

(SO 8)

BE1-10 Indicate whether the following items would appear on the income statement (IS), balance sheet (BS), or owner's equity statement (OE).

_____(a) Notes payable

_____(b) Advertising expense

_____(c) Morgan M. Sondgeroth, Capital

_____(d) Cash

_____(e) Service revenue

EXERCISES

Classify accounts as assets, liabilities, and owner's equity.

(SO 6)

E1-1 Robinson Cleaners has the following balance sheet items.

Accounts payable	Accounts receivable
Cash	Notes Payable
Cleaning equipment	Salaries payable
Cleaning supplies	Karin Robinson, Capital

Instructions

Classify each item as an asset, liability, or owner's equity.

Analyze the effect of transactions.

(SO 6, 7)

E1-2 Selected transactions for Green Acres Lawn Care Company are listed below.

1. Made cash investment to start business.

2. Paid monthly rent.

3. Purchased equipment on account.
4. Billed customers for services performed.
5. Withdrew cash for owner's personal use.
6. Received cash from customers billed in (4).
7. Incurred advertising expense on account.
8. Purchased additional equipment for cash.
9. Received cash from customers when service was performed.

Instructions
List the numbers of the above transactions and describe the effect of each transaction on assets, liabilities, and owner's equity. For example, the first answer is: (1) Increase in assets and increase in owner's equity.

E1-3 Rollins Computer Timeshare Company entered into the following transactions during May 2005.

Analyze the effect of transactions on assets, liabilities, and owner's equity.

(SO 6, 7)

1. Purchased computer terminals for $21,500 from Digital Equipment on account.
2. Paid $4,000 cash for May rent on storage space.
3. Received $15,000 cash from customers for contracts billed in April.
4. Provided computer services to Fisher Construction Company for $3,000 cash.
5. Paid Northern States Power Co. $11,000 cash for energy usage in May.
6. Rollins invested an additional $32,000 in the business.
7. Paid Digital Equipment for the terminals purchased in (1) above.
8. Incurred advertising expense for May of $1,200 on account.

Instructions
Indicate with the appropriate letter whether each of the transactions above results in:

(a) an increase in assets and a decrease in assets.
(b) an increase in assets and an increase in owner's equity.
(c) an increase in assets and an increase in liabilities.
(d) a decrease in assets and a decrease in owner's equity.
(e) a decrease in assets and a decrease in liabilities.
(f) an increase in liabilities and a decrease in owner's equity.
(g) an increase in owner's equity and a decrease in liabilities.

E1-4 An analysis of the transactions made by J. L. Kang & Co., a certified public accounting firm, for the month of August is shown below. Each increase and decrease in owner's equity is explained.

Analyze transactions and compute net income.

(SO 7)

	Cash	+	Accounts Receivable	+	Supplies	+	Office Equipment	=	Accounts Payable	+	Owner's Equity J. L. Kang, Capital	
1.	+$15,000										+$15,000	Investment
2.	−2,000						+$5,000		+$3,000			
3.	−750				+$750							
4.	+2,600		+$3,700								+6,300	Service Revenue
5.	−1,500								−1,500			
6.	−2,000										−2,000	Drawings
7.	−650										−650	Rent Expense
8.	+450		−450									
9.	−3,900										−3,900	Salaries Expense
10.									+500		−500	Utilities Expense

Instructions
(a) Describe each transaction that occurred for the month.
(b) Determine how much owner's equity increased for the month.
(c) Compute the amount of net income for the month.

E1–5 An analysis of transactions for J. L. Kang & Co. was presented in E1–4.

Prepare an income statement and owner's equity statement.

(SO 8)

Instructions
Prepare an income statement and an owner's equity statement for August and a balance sheet at August 31, 2005.

E1-6 The Kimm Company had the following assets and liabilities on the dates indicated.

December 31	Total Assets	Total Liabilities
2005	$380,000	$250,000
2006	$460,000	$310,000
2007	$590,000	$400,000

Kimm began business on January 1, 2005, with an investment of $100,000.

Instructions
From an analysis of the change in owner's equity during the year, compute the net income (or loss) for:

(a) 2005, assuming Kimm's drawings were $15,000 for the year.

(b) 2006, assuming Kimm made an additional investment of $50,000 and had no drawings in 2006.

(c) 2007, assuming Kimm made an additional investment of $15,000 and had drawings of $30,000 in 2007.

E1-7 Two items are omitted from each of the following summaries of balance sheet and income statement data for two proprietorships for the year 2005, Craig Stevens and Holly Enterprises.

	Craig Stevens	Holly Enterprises
Beginning of year:		
Total assets	$ 97,000	$129,000
Total liabilities	85,000	(c)
Total owner's equity	(a)	75,000
End of year:		
Total assets	160,000	180,000
Total liabilities	120,000	50,000
Total owner's equity	40,000	130,000
Changes during year in owner's equity:		
Additional investment	(b)	25,000
Drawings	24,000	(d)
Total revenues	215,000	100,000
Total expenses	175,000	55,000

Instructions
Determine the missing amounts.

E1-8 The following information relates to Karin Weigel Co. for the year 2005.

Karin Weigel, Capital, January 1, 2005	$ 48,000	Advertising expense	$ 1,800
Karin Weigel, Drawing during 2005	5,000	Rent expense	10,400
Service revenue	62,500	Utilities expense	3,100
Salaries expense	28,000		

Instructions
After analyzing the data, prepare an income statement and an owner's equity statement for the year ending December 31, 2005

E1-9 Lynn Close is the bookkeeper for Sanculi Company. Lynn has been trying to get the balance sheet of Sanculi Company to balance. Sanculi's balance sheet is as follows.

SANCULI COMPANY
Balance Sheet
December 31, 2005

Assets		Liabilities	
Cash	$16,500	Accounts payable	$20,000
Supplies	8,000	Accounts receivable	(8,500)
Equipment	46,000	Sanculi, Capital	67,500
Sanculi, Drawing	8,500	Total liabilities and	
Total assets	$79,000	owner's equity	$79,000

Instructions
Prepare a correct balance sheet.

E1–10 Jan Way is the sole owner of Bear Park, a public camping ground near the Lake Mead National Recreation Area. Jan has compiled the following financial information as of December 31, 2005.

Compute net income and prepare a balance sheet. (SO 8)

Revenues during 2005—camping fees	$140,000	Market value of equipment	$140,000
Revenues during 2005—general store	47,000	Notes payable	60,000
Accounts payable	11,000	Expenses during 2005	150,000
Cash on hand	20,000	Supplies on hand	2,500
Original cost of equipment	105,500		

Instructions
(a) Determine Jan Way's net income from Bear Park for 2005.
(b) Prepare a balance sheet for Bear Park as of December 31, 2005.

E1–11 Presented below is financial information related to the 2005 operations of Debra-Joan Cruise Company.

Prepare an income statement. (SO 8)

Maintenance expense	$ 97,000
Property tax expense (on dock facilities)	10,000
Salaries expense	142,000
Advertising expense	3,500
Ticket revenue	335,000

Instructions
Prepare the 2005 income statement for Debra-Joan Cruise Company.

E1–12 Presented below is information related to the sole proprietorship of Douglas William, attorney.

Pepare an owner's equity statement. (SO 8)

Legal service revenue—2005	$340,000
Total expenses—2005	211,000
Assets, January 1, 2005	85,000
Liabilities, January 1, 2005	62,000
Assets, December 31, 2005	168,000
Liabilities, December 31, 2005	80,000
Drawings—2005	?

Instructions
Prepare the 2005 owner's equity statement for Douglas William's legal practice.

PROBLEMS: SET A

P1-1A On April 1, Holly Palmer established Matrix Travel Agency. The following transactions were completed during the month.

Analyze transactions and compute net income. (SO 6, 7)

1. Invested $10,000 cash to start the agency.
2. Paid $400 cash for April office rent.
3. Purchased office equipment for $2,500 cash.
4. Incurred $300 of advertising costs in the *Chicago Tribune,* on account.
5. Paid $600 cash for office supplies.
6. Earned $7,500 for services rendered: $1,000 cash is received from customers, and the balance of $6,500 is billed to customers on account.
7. Withdrew $200 cash for personal use.
8. Paid *Chicago Tribune* amount due in transaction (4).
9. Paid employees' salaries $2,200.
10. Received $5,000 in cash from customers who have previously been billed in transaction (6).

Instructions
(a) Prepare a tabular analysis of the transactions using the following column headings: Cash, Accounts Receivable, Supplies, Office Equipment, Accounts Payable, and Holly Palmer, Capital.

(a) Ending capital $14,400

(b) Net income $4,600

(b) From an analysis of the column Holly Palmer, Capital, compute the net income or net loss for April.

Analyze transactions and prepare income statement, owner's equity statement, and balance sheet.
(SO 6, 7, 8)

P1-2A Mandy Arnold opened a law office, Mandy Arnold, Attorney at Law, on July 1, 2005. On July 31, the balance sheet showed Cash $4,000, Accounts Receivable $1,500, Supplies $500, Office Equipment $5,000, Accounts Payable $4,200, and Mandy Arnold, Capital $6,800. During August the following transactions occurred.

1. Collected $1,400 of accounts receivable.
2. Paid $2,700 cash on accounts payable.
3. Earned revenue of $7,500 of which $3,000 is collected in cash and the balance is due in September.
4. Purchased additional office equipment for $1,000, paying $400 in cash and the balance on account.
5. Paid salaries $3,000, rent for August $900, and advertising expenses $350.
6. Withdrew $550 in cash for personal use.
7. Received $2,000 from Standard Federal Bank—money borrowed on a note payable.
8. Incurred utility expenses for month on account $250.

Instructions

(a) Ending capital $9,250

(a) Prepare a tabular analysis of the August transactions beginning with July 31 balances. The column headings should be as follows: Cash + Accounts Receivable + Supplies + Office Equipment = Notes Payable + Accounts Payable + Mandy Arnold, Capital.

(b) Net income $3,000
    Total assets $13,600

(b) Prepare an income statement for August, an owner's equity statement for August, and a balance sheet at August 31.

Prepare income statement, owner's equity statement, and balance sheet.
(SO 8)

P1-3A On June 1, Jennifer Garner started Divine Cosmetics Co., a company that provides individual skin care treatment, by investing $26,200 cash in the business. Following are the assets and liabilities of the company at June 30 and the revenues and expenses for the month of June.

Cash	$10,000	Notes Payable	$13,000
Accounts Receivable	4,000	Accounts Payable	1,200
Service Revenue	5,500	Supplies Expense	1,600
Cosmetic Supplies	2,000	Gas and Oil Expense	800
Advertising Expense	500	Utilities Expense	300
Equipment	25,000		

Jennifer made no additional investment in June, but withdrew $1,700 in cash for personal use during the month.

Instructions

(a) Net income $2,300
    Owner's equity $26,800
    Total assets $41,000

(a) Prepare an income statement and owner's equity statement for the month of June and a balance sheet at June 30, 2005.

(b) Net income $3,000
    Owner's equity $27,500

(b) Prepare an income statement and owner's equity statement for June assuming the following data are not included above: (1) $800 of revenue was earned and billed but not collected at June 30, and (2) $100 of gas and oil expense was incurred but not paid.

Analyze transactions and prepare financial statements.
(SO 7, 8)

P1-4A Laura Stiner started her own consulting firm, Stiner Consulting, on May 1, 2005. The following transactions occurred during the month of May.

May	1	Stiner invested $8,000 cash in the business.
	2	Paid $800 for office rent for the month.
	3	Purchased $500 of supplies on account.
	5	Paid $50 to advertise in the *County News*.
	9	Received $3,000 cash for services provided.
	12	Withdrew $700 cash for personal use.
	15	Performed $3,300 of services on account.
	17	Paid $3,000 for employee salaries.
	20	Paid for the supplies purchased on account on May 3.
	23	Received a cash payment of $2,000 for services provided on account on May 15.
	26	Borrowed $5,000 from the bank on a note payable.
	29	Purchased office equipment for $2,400 on account.
	30	Paid $150 for utilities.

Instructions

(a) Show the effects of the previous transactions on the accounting equation using the following format.

(a) Ending capital $9,600

		Assets				Liabilities			Owner's Equity
Date	Cash	+ Accounts Receivable	+ Supplies	+ Office Equipment	=	Notes Payable	+ Accounts Payable	+	L. Stiner Capital

Include explanations for any changes in the L. Stiner, Capital account in your analysis.

(b) Prepare an income statement for the month of May.
(c) Prepare a balance sheet at May 31, 2005.

(b) Net income $2,300
(c) Cash $12,800

P1-5A Financial statement information about four different companies is as follows.

Determine financial statement amounts and prepare owner's equity statement.
(SO 7, 8)

	Winger Company	Selara Company	Delta Company	Hindi Company
January 1, 2005				
Assets	$ 75,000	$90,000	(g)	$150,000
Liabilities	50,000	(d)	75,000	(j)
Owner's equity	(a)	50,000	54,000	100,000
December 31, 2005				
Assets	(b)	117,000	180,000	(k)
Liabilities	55,000	62,000	(h)	80,000
Owner's equity	40,000	(e)	100,000	140,000
Owner's equity changes in year				
Additional investment	(c)	8,000	10,000	15,000
Drawings	10,000	(f)	12,000	10,000
Total revenues	350,000	400,000	(i)	500,000
Total expenses	335,000	385,000	360,000	(l)

Instructions

(a) Determine the missing amounts. (*Hint:* For example, to solve for (a), Assets – Liabilities = Owner's equity = $25,000.)
(b) Prepare the owner's equity statement for Winger Company.
(c)  Write a memorandum explaining the sequence for preparing financial statements and the interrelationship of the owner's equity statement to the income statement and balance sheet.

PROBLEMS: SET B

P1-1B McInnes's Repair Shop was started on May 1 by Jane McInnes. A summary of May transactions is presented below.

Analyze transactions and compute net income.
(SO 6, 7)

1. Invested $10,000 cash to start the repair shop.
2. Purchased equipment for $5,000 cash.
3. Paid $400 cash for May office rent.
4. Paid $500 cash for supplies.
5. Incurred $250 of advertising costs in the *Beacon News* on account.
6. Received $3,100 in cash from customers for repair service.
7. Withdrew $1,000 cash for personal use.
8. Paid part-time employee salaries $1,000.
9. Paid utility bills $140.
10. Provided repair service on account to customers $850.
11. Collected cash of $120 for services billed in transaction (10).

Instructions

(a) Prepare a tabular analysis of the transactions, using the following column headings: Cash, Accounts Receivable, Supplies, Equipment, Accounts Payable, and Jane McInnes, Capital. Revenue is called Service Revenue.

(a) Ending capital $11,160

(b) Net income $2,160

(b) From an analysis of the column Jane McInnes, Capital, compute the net income or net loss for May.

Analyze transactions and prepare income statement, owner's equity statement, and balance sheet.
(SO 6, 7, 8)

P1-2B Patricia Perez opened a veterinary business in Nashville, Tennessee, on August 1. On August 31, the balance sheet showed Cash $9,000, Accounts Receivable $1,700, Supplies $600, Office Equipment $6,000, Accounts Payable $3,600, and P. Perez, Capital $13,700. During September the following transactions occurred.

1. Paid $2,900 cash on accounts payable.
2. Collected $1,300 of accounts receivable.
3. Purchased additional office equipment for $2,100, paying $800 in cash and the balance on account.
4. Earned revenue of $6,300, of which $2,500 is paid in cash and the balance is due in October.
5. Withdrew $600 cash for personal use.
6. Paid salaries $1,700, rent for September $900, and advertising expense $300.
7. Incurred utilities expense for month on account $170.
8. Received $10,000 from Capital Bank—money borrowed on a note payable.

Instructions

(a) Ending capital $16,330

(a) Prepare a tabular analysis of the September transactions beginning with August 31 balances. The column headings should be as follows: Cash + Accounts Receivable + Supplies + Office Equipment = Notes Payable + Accounts Payable + P. Perez, Capital.

(b) Net income $3,230
  Total assets $28,500

(b) Prepare an income statement for September, an owner's equity statement for September, and a balance sheet at September 30.

Prepare income statement, owner's equity statement, and balance sheet.
(SO 8)

P1-3B On May 1, Jacob Bablad started Skyward Flying School, a company that provides flying lessons, by investing $45,000 cash in the business. Following are the assets and liabilities of the company on May 31, 2005, and the revenues and expenses for the month of May.

Cash	$ 4,500	Notes Payable	$30,000
Accounts Receivable	7,200	Rent Expense	1,200
Equipment	64,000	Repair Expense	400
Lesson Revenue	6,600	Fuel Expense	2,500
Advertising Expense	500	Insurance Expense	400
		Accounts Payable	800

Jacob Bablad made no additional investment in May, but he withdrew $1,700 in cash for personal use.

Instructions

(a) Net income $1,600
  Owner's equity $44,900
  Total assets $75,700
(b) Net income $1,000
  Owner's equity $44,300

(a) Prepare an income statement and owner's equity statement for the month of May and a balance sheet at May 31.
(b) Prepare an income statement and owner's equity statement for May assuming the following data are not included above: (1) $900 of revenue was earned and billed but not collected at May 31, and (2) $1,500 of fuel expense was incurred but not paid.

Analyze transactions and prepare financial statements.
(SO 7, 8)

P1-4B Pat Donahue started his own delivery service, Donahue Deliveries, on June 1, 2005. The following transactions occurred during the month of June.

June 1 Pat invested $10,000 cash in the business.
     2 Purchased a used van for deliveries for $10,000. Pat paid $2,000 cash and signed a note payable for the remaining balance.
     3 Paid $500 for office rent for the month.
     5 Performed $2,400 of services on account.
     9 Withdrew $200 cash for personal use.
   12 Purchased supplies for $150 on account.
   15 Received a cash payment of $750 for services provided on June 5.
   17 Purchased gasoline for $100 on account.
   20 Received a cash payment of $1,500 for services provided.
   23 Made a cash payment of $500 on the note payable.
   26 Paid $250 for utilities.
   29 Paid for the gasoline purchased on account on June 17.
   30 Paid $1,000 for employee salaries.

Instructions

(a) Show the effects of the previous transactions on the accounting equation using the following format.

(a) Ending capital $11,850

		Assets					**Liabilities**			**Owner's Equity**
Date	Cash +	Accounts Receivable	+ Supplies +	Delivery Van	=	Notes Payable	+	Accounts Payable	+	P. Donahue Capital

Include explanations for any changes in the P. Donahue, Capital account in your analysis.

(b) Prepare an income statement for the month of June.
(c) Prepare a balance sheet at June 30, 2005.

(b) Net income $2,050
(c) Cash $7,700

P1–5B Financial statement information about four different companies is as follows.

Determine financial statement amounts and prepare owner's equity statement.
(SO 7, 8)

	Karma Company	Molly Company	McCain Company	Bodie Company
January 1, 2005				
Assets	$ 89,000	$110,000	(g)	$170,000
Liabilities	50,000	(d)	75,000	(f)
Owner's equity	(a)	60,000	40,000	90,000
December 31, 2005				
Assets	(b)	147,000	200,000	(k)
Liabilities	55,000	75,000	(h)	80,000
Owner's equity	60,000	(e)	130,000	160,000
Owner's equity changes in year				
Additional investment	(c)	15,000	10,000	15,000
Drawings	25,000	(f)	14,000	20,000
Total revenues	350,000	420,000	(i)	520,000
Total expenses	320,000	385,000	342,000	(l)

Instructions

(a) Determine the missing amounts.
(b) Prepare the owner's equity statement for Molly Company.
(c) ▭▭▭▭▷ Write a memorandum explaining the sequence for preparing financial statements and the interrelationship of the owner's equity statement to the income statement and balance sheet.

Financial Reporting and Analysis

■ **FINANCIAL REPORTING PROBLEM: PepsiCo**

BYP1-1 The actual financial statements of **PepsiCo**, as presented in the company's 2002 Annual Report, are contained in Appendix A (at the back of the textbook).

Instructions
Refer to PepsiCo's financial statements and answer the following questions.

(a) What were PepsiCo's total assets at December 28, 2002? At December 29, 2001?
(b) How much cash (and cash equivalents) did have on December 28, 2002?
(c) What amount of accounts payable did PepsiCo report on December 28, 2002? On December 29, 2001?
(d) What were PepsiCo net sales in 2000? In 2001? In 2002?
(e) What is the amount of the change in PepsiCo's net income from 2001 to 2002?

■ **COMPARATIVE ANALYSIS PROBLEM: PepsiCo vs. Coca-Cola**

BYP1-2 **PepsiCo**'s financial statements are presented in Appendix A. **Coca-Cola**'s financial statements are presented in Appendix B.

Instructions

(a) Based on the information contained in these financial statements, determine the following for each company.

(1) Total assets at December 28, 2002, for PepsiCo, and for Coca-Cola at December 31, 2002.

(2) Accounts (notes) receivable, net at December 28, 2002, for PepsiCo and at December 31, 2002, for Coca-Cola.

(3) Net sales for year ended in 2002.

(4) Net income for year ended in 2002.

(b) What conclusions concerning the two companies can be drawn from these data?

■ **INTERPRETING FINANCIAL STATEMENTS: A Global Focus**

BYP1-3 Today companies must compete in a global economy. **Nestlé**, a Swiss company, is the largest food company in the world. If you were interested in broadening your investment portfolio, you might consider investing in Nestlé. However, investing in international companies can pose some additional challenges. Consider the following excerpts from the notes to Nestlé's financial statements.

NESTLÉ
Notes to the Financial Statements (partial)

(a) The Group accounts comply with International Accounting Standards (IAS) issued by the International Accounting Standards Committee (IASC) and with the Standards Interpretations issued by the Standards Interpretation Committee of the IASC (SIC).

(b) The accounts have been prepared under the historical cost convention and on an accrual basis. All significant consolidated companies have a 31st December accounting year end. All disclosures required by the 4th and 7th European Union company law directives are provided.

(c) On consolidation, assets and liabilities of Group companies denominated in foreign currencies are translated into Swiss francs at year-end rates. Income and expense items are translated into Swiss francs at the annual average rates of exchange or, where known or determinable, at the rate on the date of the transaction for significant items.

Instructions

Discuss the implications of each of these items in terms of the effect it might have (positive or negative) on your ability to compare Nestlé to a U.S. food company such as Tootsie Roll or Hershey Foods. (*Hint:* In preparing your answer review the discussion of principles and assumptions in financial reporting on pages 10 and 11.)

■ **EXPLORING THE WEB**

BYP1-4 This exercise will familiarize you with skill requirements, job descriptions, and salaries for accounting careers.

Address: www.careers-in-accounting.com, or go to www.wiley.com/college/weygandt

Instructions
Go to the site shown above. Answer the following questions.

(a) What are the three broad areas of accounting (from "Skills and Talents Required")?
(b) List eight skills required in accounting.
(c) How do the three accounting areas differ in terms of these eight required skills?
(d) Explain one of the key job functions in accounting.
(e) Based on the *Smart Money* survey, what is the salary range for a junior staff accountant with Deloitte & Touche?

Critical Thinking

■ GROUP DECISION CASE

BYP1-5 Lucy and Nick Lars, local golf stars, opened the Chip-Shot Driving Range on March 1, 2005, by investing $20,000 of their cash savings in the business. A caddy shack was constructed for cash at a cost of $6,000, and $800 was spent on golf balls and golf clubs. The Lars leased five acres of land at a cost of $1,000 per month and paid the first month's rent. During the first month, advertising costs totaled $750, of which $150 was unpaid at March 31, and $400 was paid to members of the high-school golf team for retrieving golf balls. All revenues from customers were deposited in the company's bank account. On March 15, Lucy and Nick withdrew a total of $800 in cash for personal living expenses. A $100 utility bill was received on March 31 but was not paid. On March 31, the balance in the company's bank account was $15,100.

Lucy and Nick thought they had a pretty good first month of operations. But, their estimates of profitability ranged from a loss of $4,900 to net income of $1,650.

Instructions
With the class divided into groups, answer the following.

(a) How could the Lars have concluded that the business operated at a loss of $4,900? Was this a valid basis on which to determine net income?
(b) How could the Lars have concluded that the business operated at a net income of $1,650? (*Hint:* Prepare a balance sheet at March 31.) Was this a valid basis on which to determine net income?
(c) Without preparing an income statement, determine the actual net income for March.
(d) What was the revenue earned in March?

■ COMMUNICATION ACTIVITY

BYP1-6 Erin Danielle, the bookkeeper for New York Company, has been trying to get the balance sheet to balance. The company's balance sheet is as follows.

NEW YORK COMPANY
Balance Sheet
For the Month Ended December 31, 2005

Assets		Liabilities	
Equipment	$22,500	Cole William, Capital	$23,000
Cash	9,000	Accounts receivable	(6,000)
Supplies	2,000	Cole William, Drawing	(2,000)
Accounts payable	(8,000)	Notes payable	10,500
	$25,500		$25,500

Instructions
Explain to Erin Danielle in a memo why the original balance sheet is incorrect, and what should be done to correct it.

■ ETHICS CASE

BYP1-7   After numerous campus interviews, Jeff Hunter, a senior at Great Northern College, received two office interview invitations from the Baltimore offices of two large firms. Both firms offered to cover his out-of-pocket expenses (travel, hotel, and meals). He scheduled the interviews for both firms on the same day, one in the morning and one in the afternoon. At the conclusion of each interview, he submitted to both firms his total out-of-pocket expenses for the trip to Baltimore: mileage $98 (280 miles at $0.35), hotel $130, meals $36, parking and tolls $18, for a total of $282. He believes this approach is appropriate. If he had made two trips, his cost would have been two times $282. He is also certain that neither firm knew he had visited the other on that same trip. Within ten days Jeff received two checks in the mail, each in the amount of $282.

Instructions
(a) Who are the stakeholders (affected parties) in this situation?
(b) What are the ethical issues in this case?
(c) What would you do in this situation?

Answers to Self-Study Questions
1. b   **2.** d   **3.** c   **4.** a   **5.** d   **6.** b   **7.** a   **8.** b   **9.** c   **10.** a

Answer to PepsiCo Review It Question 4, p. 14
PepsiCo's accounting equation is:

Assets	=	Liabilities	+	Owners' (Stockholders') Equity
$23,474,000,000	=	$14,183,000,000	+	$9,291,000,000

(Owners' equity includes preferred stock.)

 ☑ **REMEMBER** to go back to the Navigator box on the chapter-opening page and check off your completed work.

The Recording Process

CONCEPTS FOR REVIEW

Before studying this chapter, you should know or, if necessary, review:

■ What are assets, liabilities, owner's capital, owner's drawings, revenues, and expenses.
(Ch. 1, pp. 12–13)

■ Why assets equal liabilities plus owner's equity.
(Ch. 1, p. 12)

■ What transactions are and how they affect the basic accounting equation.
(Ch. 1, pp. 14–20)

THE
NAVIGATOR

No Such Thing as a Perfect World

When she got a job doing the accounting for Forster's Restaurants, Tanis Anderson had almost finished her business administration degree at Simon Fraser University. But even after Tanis completed her degree requirements, her education still continued—this time, in the real world.

Tanis's responsibilities include paying the bills, tracking food and labor costs, and managing the payroll for The Mug and Musket, a popular destination restaurant in Surrey, British Columbia. "My title is Director of Finance," she laughs, "but really that means I take care of whatever needs doing!"

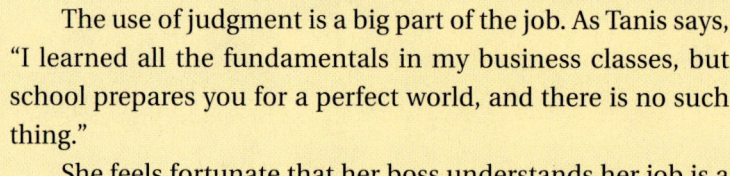

The use of judgment is a big part of the job. As Tanis says, "I learned all the fundamentals in my business classes, but school prepares you for a perfect world, and there is no such thing."

She feels fortunate that her boss understands her job is a learning experience as well as a responsibility. "Sometimes he's let me do something he knew perfectly well was a mistake so I can learn something through experience," she admits.

To help others gain the benefits of her real-world learning, Tanis is always happy to help students in the area who want to use Forster's as the subject of a project or report. "It's the least I can do," she says.

THE NAVIGATOR

After studying this chapter, you should be able to:

1. Explain what an account is and how it helps in the recording process.
2. Define debits and credits and explain how they are used to record business transactions.
3. Identify the basic steps in the recording process.
4. Explain what a journal is and how it helps in the recording process.
5. Explain what a ledger is and how it helps in the recording process.
6. Explain what posting is and how it helps in the recording process.
7. Prepare a trial balance and explain its purposes.

THE NAVIGATOR

In Chapter 1, we analyzed business transactions in terms of the accounting equation. The cumulative effects of these transactions were presented in tabular form. Imagine a restaurant and gift shop such as The Mug and Musket using the same tabular format as Softbyte to keep track of every one of its transactions. In a single day, this restaurant and gift shop engages in hundreds of business transactions. To record each transaction this way would be impractical, expensive, and unnecessary. Instead, a set of procedures and records are used to keep track of transaction data more easily.

This chapter introduces and illustrates these basic procedures and records. The content and organization of Chapter 2 are as follows.

THE RECORDING PROCESS

The Account	Steps in the Recording Process	The Recording Process Illustrated	The Trial Balance
• Debit and credits • Expansion of basic equation	• Journal • Ledger	• Summary illustration of journalizing and posting	• Limitations of a trial balance • Locating errors • Use of dollar signs

☑ THE NAVIGATOR

The Account

An **account** is an individual accounting record of increases and decreases in a specific asset, liability, or owner's equity item. For example, Softbyte (the company discussed in Chapter 1) would have separate accounts for Cash, Accounts Receivable, Accounts Payable, Service Revenue, Salaries Expense, and so on. In its simplest form, an account consists of three parts: (1) the title of the account, (2) a left or debit side, and (3) a right or credit side. Because the alignment of these parts of an account resembles the letter T, it is referred to as a **T account**. The basic form of an account is shown in Illustration 2-1.

STUDY OBJECTIVE 1

Explain what an account is and how it helps in the recording process.

Illustration 2-1
Basic form of account

Title of Account	
Left or debit side	Right or credit side
Debit balance	Credit balance

← T-account

Accounting Cycle Tutorial—
Recording Business Transactions

The T account is a standard shorthand in accounting that helps make clear the effects of transactions on individual accounts. We will use it often throughout this book to explain basic accounting relationships. (Note that when we are referring to a specific account, we capitalize its name.)

Debits and Credits

Today, the term **debit** indicates left, and **credit** indicates right. They are commonly abbreviated as Dr. for debit and Cr. for credit.[1] These terms come from Latin words that originally meant "debtor" and "creditor." Today they are directional signals: They indicate which side of a T account a number will be recorded on. Entering an amount on the left side of an account is called **debiting** the account; making an entry on the right side is **crediting** the account.

The procedure of having debits on the left and credits on the right is an accounting custom, or rule (like the custom of driving on the right-hand side of the road in the United States). **This rule applies to all accounts.** When the totals of the two sides are compared, an account will have a **debit balance** if the total of the debit amounts exceeds the credits. An account will have a **credit balance** if the credit amounts exceed the debits.

The recording of debits and credits in an account is shown in Illustration 2-2 for the cash transactions of Softbyte. The data are taken from the cash column of the tabular summary in Illustration 1-8.

Illustration 2-2
Tabular summary compared to account form

Tabular Summary		Account Form			
Cash		**Cash**			
$15,000		**(Debits)**	15,000	**(Credits)**	7,000
−7,000			1,200		1,700
1,200			1,500		250
1,500			600		1,300
−1,700		Balance	8,050		
−250		**(Debit)**			
600					
−1,300					
$ 8,050					

In the tabular summary every positive item represents a receipt of cash; every negative amount represents a payment of cash. Notice that in the account form the increases in cash are recorded as debits, and the decreases in cash are recorded as credits. Having increases on one side and decreases on the other helps in determining the total of each side of the account as well as the overall balance in the account. The account balance, a debit of $8,050, indicates that Softbyte has had $8,050 more increases than decreases in cash.

Debit and Credit Procedure

In Chapter 1 you learned the effect of a transaction on the basic accounting equation. Remember that each transaction must affect two or more accounts to keep the basic accounting equation in balance. In other words, for each transaction debits must equal credits in the accounts. The equality of debits and credits provides the basis for the **double-entry system** of recording transactions.

Under the double-entry system the dual (two-sided) effect of each transaction is recorded in appropriate accounts. This universally used system provides a logical

---

[1]These terms and their abbreviations come from the Latin words *debere* (Dr.) and *credere* (Cr.).

method for recording transactions. It also offers a means of proving the accuracy of the recorded amounts. If every transaction is recorded with equal debits and credits, then the sum of all the debits to the accounts must equal the sum of all the credits.

The double-entry system for determining the equality of the accounting equation is much more efficient than the plus/minus procedure used in Chapter 1. There, it was necessary after each transaction to compare total assets with total liabilities and owner's equity to determine the equality of the two sides of the accounting equation.

ASSETS AND LIABILITIES.   We know that both sides of the basic equation (Assets = Liabilities + Owner's equity) must be equal. It follows that increases and decreases in assets and liabilities must be recorded opposite from each other. In Illustration 2-2, increases in cash—an asset—were entered on the left side, and decreases in cash were entered on the right side. Therefore, increases in liabilities must be entered on the right or credit side, and decreases in liabilities must be entered on the left or debit side. The effects that debits and credits have on assets and liabilities are summarized as follows.

COPY

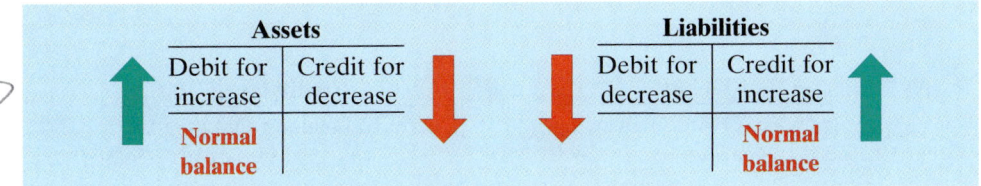

Debits	Credits
Increase assets	Decrease assets
Decrease liabilities	Increase liabilities

Illustration 2-3
Debit and credit effects—
assets and liabilities

Debits to a specific asset account should exceed the credits to that account. Credits to a liability account should exceed debits to that account. **The normal balance of an account is on the side where an increase in the account is recorded.** Thus, asset accounts normally show debit balances, and liability accounts normally show credit balances. The normal balances can be diagrammed as follows.

Assets		Liabilities	
Debit for increase	Credit for decrease	Debit for decrease	Credit for increase
Normal balance			**Normal balance**

Illustration 2-4
Normal balances—assets
and liabilities

Knowing the normal balance in an account may help you trace errors. For example, a credit balance in an asset account such as Land or a debit balance in a liability account such as Wages Payable would indicate recording errors. Occasionally, an abnormal balance may be correct. The Cash account, for example, will have a credit balance when a company has overdrawn its bank balance (i.e., written a "bad" check).

OWNER'S EQUITY.   As indicated in Chapter 1, owner's equity is increased by owner's investments and by revenues. It is decreased by owner's drawings and by expenses. In a double-entry system, accounts are kept for each of these types of transactions, as explained below.

Owner's Capital. Investments by owners are credited to the Owner's Capital account. Credits increase this account and debits decrease it. For example, when cash is invested in the business, Cash is debited (increased) and Owner's Capital is credited (increased). When the owner's investment in the business is reduced, Owner's Capital is debited (decreased).

The rules of debit and credit for the Owner's Capital account are stated as follows.

Illustration 2-5
Debit and credit effects—
Owner's Capital

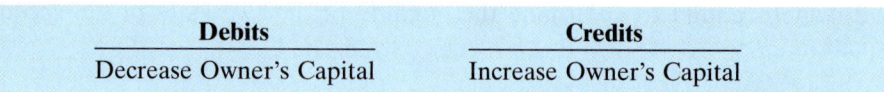

Debits	Credits
Decrease Owner's Capital	Increase Owner's Capital

The normal balance in this account can be diagrammed as follows.

Illustration 2-6
Normal balance—
Owner's Capital

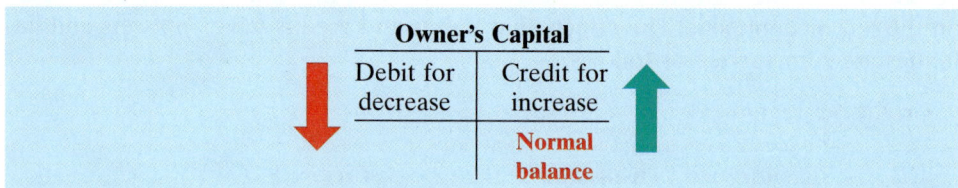

Owner's Drawing. An owner may withdraw cash or other assets for personal use. Withdrawals could be debited directly to Owner's Capital to indicate a decrease in owner's equity. However, it is preferable to establish a separate account, called the Owner's Drawing account. This separate account makes it easier to determine total withdrawals for each accounting period. **The drawing account decreases owner's equity. It is not an income statement account like revenues and expenses.** Owner's Drawing is increased by debits and decreased by credits. Normally, the drawing account will have a debit balance.

The rules of debit and credit for the drawing account are stated as follows.

Illustration 2-7
Debit and credit effects—
Owner's Drawing

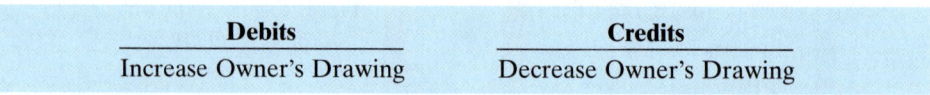

Debits	Credits
Increase Owner's Drawing	Decrease Owner's Drawing

The normal balance can be diagrammed as follows.

Illustration 2-8
Normal balance—
Owner's Drawing

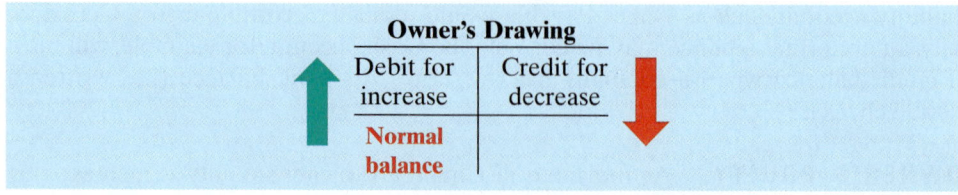

Revenues and Expenses. Remember that the ultimate purpose of earning revenues is to benefit the owner(s) of the business. When revenues are earned, owner's equity is increased. Therefore, **the effect of debits and credits on revenue accounts is the same as their effect on Owner's Capital**. Revenue accounts are increased by credits and decreased by debits.

Expenses have the opposite effect: expenses decrease owner's equity. Since expenses are the negative factor in computing net income, and revenues are the positive factor, it is logical that the increase and decrease sides of expense accounts should be the reverse of revenue accounts. Thus, expense accounts are increased by debits and decreased by credits.

The effect of debits and credits on revenues and expenses can be stated as follows.

Debits	Credits
Decrease revenues	Increase revenues
Increase expenses	Decrease expenses

Illustration 2-9
Debit and credit effects—revenues and expenses

Credits to revenue accounts should exceed debits, and debits to expense accounts should exceed credits. Thus, revenue accounts normally show credit balances and expense accounts normally show debit balances. The normal balances can be diagrammed as follows.

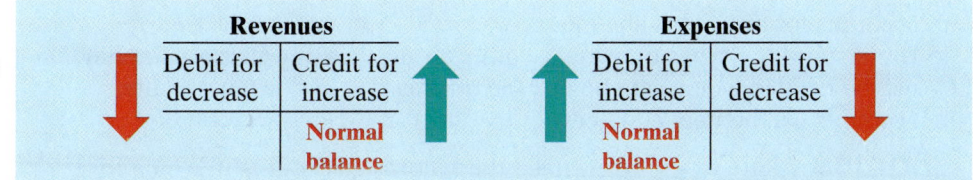

Illustration 2-10
Normal balances—revenues and expenses

Expansion of the Basic Equation

You have already learned the basic accounting equation. Illustration 2-11 expands this equation to show the accounts that comprise owner's equity. In addition, the debit/credit rules and effects on each type of account are illustrated. Study this diagram carefully. It will help you understand the fundamentals of the double-entry system. Like the basic equation, the expanded basic equation must be in balance (total debits equal total credits).

Illustration 2-11
Expanded basic equation and debit/credit rules and effects

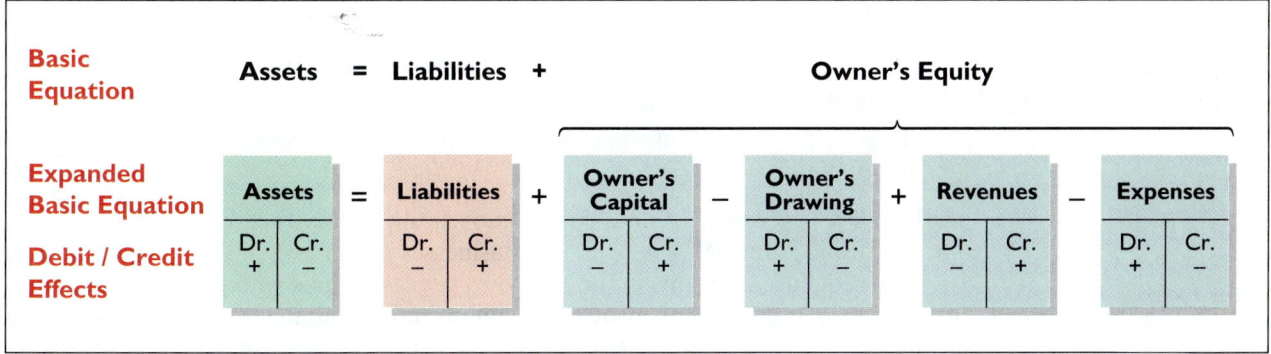

BEFORE YOU GO ON...

Review It

1. What do the terms debit and credit mean?
2. What are the debit and credit effects on assets, liabilities, and owner's capital?
3. What are the debit and credit effects on revenues, expenses, and owner's drawing?
4. What are the normal balances for **PepsiCo**'s Cash, Accounts Payable, and Interest Expense accounts? The answers to this question are provided on page 85.

Do It

Kate Browne has just rented space in a shopping mall in which she will open a beauty salon, to be called "Hair It Is." Long before opening day and before purchasing equipment, hiring employees, and remodeling the space, Kate has been advised to set up a double-entry set of accounting records in which to record all of her business transactions.

Identify the balance sheet accounts that Kate will likely need to record the transactions needed to open her business. Indicate whether the normal balance of each account is a debit or a credit.

ACTION PLAN

- Determine the types of accounts needed: Kate will need asset accounts for each different type of asset she invests in the business, and liability accounts for any debts she incurs.
- Understand the types of owner's equity accounts: Only Owner's Capital will be needed when Kate begins the business. Other owner's equity accounts will be needed later.

SOLUTION   Kate would likely need the following accounts in which to record the transactions necessary to ready her beauty salon for opening day: Cash (debit balance); Equipment (debit balance); Supplies (debit balance); Accounts Payable (credit balance); if she borrows money, Notes payable (credit balance); K. Browne, Capital (credit balance).

Related exercise material: BE2-1, BE2-2, E2-1, E2-3, and E2-10.

Steps in the Recording Process

STUDY OBJECTIVE 3

Identify the basic steps in the recording process.

In practically every business, the basic steps in the recording process are:

1. Analyze each transaction for its effects on the accounts.
2. Enter the transaction information in a journal (book of original entry).
3. Transfer the journal information to the appropriate accounts in the ledger (book of accounts).

Although it is possible to enter transaction information directly into the accounts without using a journal or ledger, few businesses do so.

The sequence of events in the recording process begins with the transaction. Evidence of the transaction is provided by a **business document**, such as a sales slip, a check, a bill, or a cash register tape. This evidence is analyzed to determine the effects of the transaction on specific accounts. The transaction is then entered in the journal. Finally, the journal entry is transferred to the designated accounts in the ledger. The sequence of events in the recording process is shown in Illustration 2-12.

Illustration 2-12
The recording process

The Recording Process

Analyze each transaction

Enter transaction in a journal

Transfer journal information to ledger accounts

The basic steps in the recording process occur repeatedly. The analysis of transactions was illustrated in Chapter 1. Further examples will be given in this and later chapters. The other steps in the recording process are explained in the next sections.

ACCOUNTING IN ACTION Business Insight

While most companies record transactions very carefully, the reality is that sometimes even the most careful companies make mistakes in their accounting records. For example, **Hanover Compressor** at one time announced that it was restating its financial results for an error that had been made in each of the previous five years. It had accidentally omitted the cost of compressors manufactured at one of its plants, causing the cost of its inventory to be misstated. **Bank One Corporation** was fined $1.8 million by banking regulators because regulators felt that its accounting system was unreliable and caused the bank to violate certain minimum banking requirements. Finally, before a major overhaul of its accounting system, the financial records of **Waste Management Company** were in such disarray that of the company's 57,000 employees, 10,000 were receiving pay slips that were in error.

The Journal

Transactions are initially recorded in chronological order in **journals** before being transferred to the accounts. Thus, the journal is referred to as the book of original entry. For each transaction the journal shows the debit and credit effects on specific accounts. (In a computerized system, "journals" are now kept as files, and "accounts" are recorded in computer databases.)

STUDY OBJECTIVE 4

Explain what a journal is and how it helps in the recording process.

Companies may use various kinds of journals, but every company has the most basic form of journal, a **general journal.** Typically, a general journal has spaces for dates, account titles and explanations, references, and two amount columns. Whenever we use the term journal in this textbook without a modifying adjective, we mean the general journal.

The journal makes several significant contributions to the recording process:

1. It discloses in one place the complete effects of a transaction.

2. It provides a chronological record of transactions.

3. It helps to prevent or locate errors because the debit and credit amounts for each entry can be readily compared.

Journalizing

Entering transaction data in the journal is known as **journalizing**. Separate journal entries are made for each transaction. A complete entry consists of: (1) the date of the transaction, (2) the accounts and amounts to be debited and credited, and (3) a brief explanation of the transaction.

Illustration 2-13 shows the technique of journalizing, using the first two transactions of Softbyte. These transactions were: September 1, Ray Neal invested $15,000 cash in the business, and computer equipment was purchased for $7,000 cash. The numbered J1 indicates that these two entries are recorded on the first page of the journal. The standard form and content of journal entries are as follows.

Illustration 2-13
Technique of journalizing

GENERAL JOURNAL				J1
Date	**Account Titles and Explanation**	**Ref.**	**Debit**	**Credit**
2005				
Sept. 1	Cash		15,000	
	R. Neal, Capital			15,000
	(Owner's investment of cash in business)			
1	Computer Equipment		7,000	
	Cash			7,000
	(Purchase of equipment for cash)			

1. The date of the transaction is entered in the Date column. The date recorded should include the year, month, and day of the transaction.
2. The debit account title (that is, the account to be debited) is entered first at the extreme left margin of the column headed "Account Titles and Explanation," and the amount of the debit is recorded in the Debit column.
3. The credit account title (that is, the account to be credited) is indented and entered on the next line in the column headed "Account Titles and Explanation," and the amount of the credit is recorded in the Credit column.
4. A brief explanation of the transaction is given on the line below the credit account title.
5. A space is left between journal entries. The blank space separates individual journal entries and makes the entire journal easier to read.
6. The column titled Ref. (which stands for reference) is left blank when the journal entry is made. This column is used later when the journal entries are transferred to the ledger accounts. At that time, the ledger account number is placed in the Reference column to indicate where the amount in the journal entry was transferred.

It is important to use correct and specific account titles in journalizing. Since most accounts appear later in the financial statements, wrong account titles lead to incorrect financial statements. Some flexibility exists initially in selecting account titles. The main criterion is that each title must appropriately describe the content of the account. For example, the account title used for the cost of delivery trucks may be Delivery Equipment, Delivery Trucks, or Trucks. Once a company chooses the specific title to use, all later transactions involving the account should be recorded under that account title.[2]

If an entry involves only two accounts, one debit and one credit, it is considered a **simple entry**. Some transactions, however, require more than two accounts in jour-

---

[2]In homework problems, when specific account titles are given, they should be used. When account titles are not given, you may select account titles that identify the nature and content of each account. The account titles used in journalizing should not contain explanations such as Cash Paid or Cash Received.

nalizing. When three or more accounts are required in one journal entry, the entry is referred to as a **compound entry**. To illustrate, assume that on July 1, Butler Company purchases a delivery truck costing $14,000 by paying $8,000 cash and the balance on account (to be paid later). The compound entry is as follows.

GENERAL JOURNAL				J1
Date	**Account Titles and Explanation**	**Ref.**	**Debit**	**Credit**
2005 July 1	Delivery Equipment		14,000	
	Cash			8,000
	Accounts Payable			6,000
	(Purchased truck for cash with balance on account)			

Illustration 2-14
Compound journal entry

In a compound entry, the total debit and credit amounts must be equal. Also, the standard format requires that all debits be listed before the credits.

BEFORE YOU GO ON...

Review It

1. What is the sequence of the steps in the recording process?
2. What contribution does the journal make to the recording process?
3. What is the standard form and content of a journal entry made in the general journal?

Do It

In establishing her beauty salon, Hair It Is, Kate Browne engaged in the following activities:

1. Opened a bank account in the name of Hair It Is and deposited $20,000 of her own money in this account as her initial investment.
2. Purchased equipment on account (to be paid in 30 days) for a total cost of $4,800.
3. Interviewed three persons for the position of beautician.

In what form (type of record) should Kate record these three activities? Prepare the entries to record the transactions.

ACTION PLAN

- Understand which activities need to be recorded and which do not. Any that have economic effects should be recorded in a journal.
- Analyze the effects of transactions on asset, liability, and owner's equity accounts.

SOLUTION   Each transaction that is recorded is entered in the general journal. The three activities would be recorded as follows.

1. Cash		20,000	
K. Browne, Capital			20,000
(Owner's investment of cash in business)			
2. Equipment		4,800	
Accounts Payable			4,800
(Purchase of equipment on account)			
3. No entry because no transaction has occurred.			

Related exercise material: BE2-3, BE2-5, BE2-6, E2-2, E2-4, E2-6, E2-7, and E2-8.

✓ THE
NAVIGATOR

The Ledger

STUDY OBJECTIVE 5

Explain what a ledger is and how it helps in the recording process.

The entire group of accounts maintained by a company is called the **ledger**. The ledger keeps in one place all the information about changes in specific account balances.

Companies may use various kinds of ledgers, but every company has a general ledger. A **general ledger** contains all the assets, liabilities, and owner's equity accounts, as shown in Illustration 2-15. A business can use a looseleaf binder or card file for the ledger. Each account is kept on a separate sheet or card. Whenever we use the term ledger in this textbook without a modifying adjective, we mean the general ledger.

Illustration 2-15
The general ledger

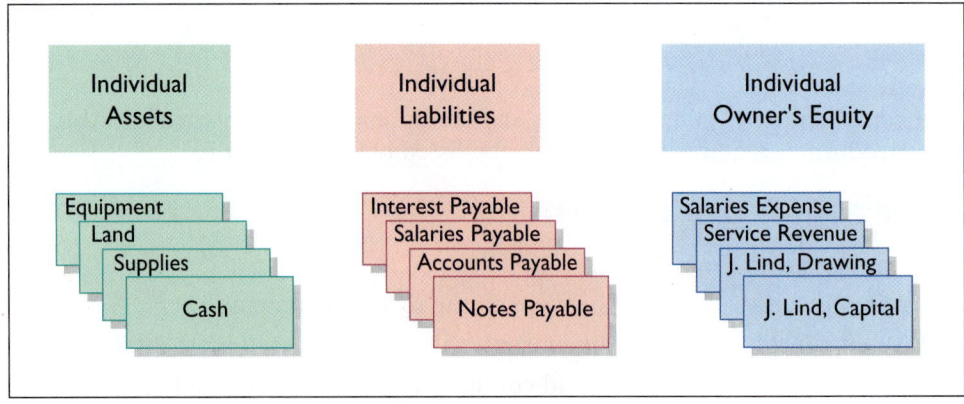

The ledger should be arranged in the order in which accounts are presented in the financial statements, beginning with the balance sheet accounts. First in order are the asset accounts, followed by liability accounts, owner's capital, owner's drawing, revenues, and expenses. Each account is numbered for easier identification.

The ledger provides management with the balances in various accounts. For example, the Cash account shows the amount of cash that is available to meet current obligations. Amounts due from customers can be found by examining Accounts Receivable, and amounts owed to creditors can be found by examining Accounts Payable.

ACCOUNTING IN ACTION **Business Insight**

In his autobiography Sam Walton described the double-entry accounting system he began the **WalMart** empire with: "We kept a little pigeonhole on the wall for the cash receipts and paperwork of each [Wal-Mart] store. I had a blue binder ledger book for each store. When we added a store, we added a pigeonhole. We did this at least up to twenty stores. Then once a month, the bookkeeper and I would enter the merchandise, enter the sales, enter the cash, and balance it."

Source: Sam Walton, *Made in America* (New York: Doubleday, 1992), p. 53.

Standard Form of Account

The simple T-account form used in accounting textbooks is often very useful for illustration purposes. However, in practice, the account forms used in ledgers are much more structured. A widely used form is shown in Illustration 2-16, using assumed data from a cash account.

Illustration 2-16
Three-column form of account

CASH						No. 101
Date	**Explanation**	**Ref.**	**Debit**	**Credit**		**Balance**
2005						
June 1			25,000			25,000
2				8,000		17,000
3			4,200			21,200
9			7,500			28,700
17				11,700		17,000
20				250		16,750
30				7,300		9,450

This form is often called the **three-column form of account** because it has three money columns—debit, credit, and balance. The balance in the account is determined after each transaction. Note that the explanation space and reference columns are used to provide special information about the transaction.

Posting

The procedure of transferring journal entries to the ledger accounts is called **posting**. Posting involves the following steps.

1. In the ledger, enter in the appropriate columns of the account(s) debited the date, journal page, and debit amount shown in the journal.
2. In the reference column of the journal, write the account number to which the debit amount was posted.
3. In the ledger, enter in the appropriate columns of the account(s) credited the date, journal page, and credit amount shown in the journal.
4. In the reference column of the journal, write the account number to which the credit amount was posted.

These four steps are diagrammed in Illustration 2-17 (on page 56) using the first journal entry of Softbyte. The boxed numbers indicate the sequence of the steps.

Posting should be performed in chronological order. That is, all the debits and credits of one journal entry should be posted before proceeding to the next journal entry. Postings should be made on a timely basis to ensure that the ledger is up to date.[3]

The reference column **in the journal** serves several purposes. The numbers in this column indicate the entries that have been posted. After the last entry has been posted, this column should be scanned to see that all postings have been made.

The reference column **of a ledger** account indicates the journal page from which the transaction was posted. The explanation space of the ledger account is used

---

[3]In homework problems, it will be permissible to journalize all transactions before posting any of the journal entries.

infrequently because an explanation already appears in the journal. It generally is used only when detailed analysis of account activity is required.

Illustration 2-17
Posting a journal entry

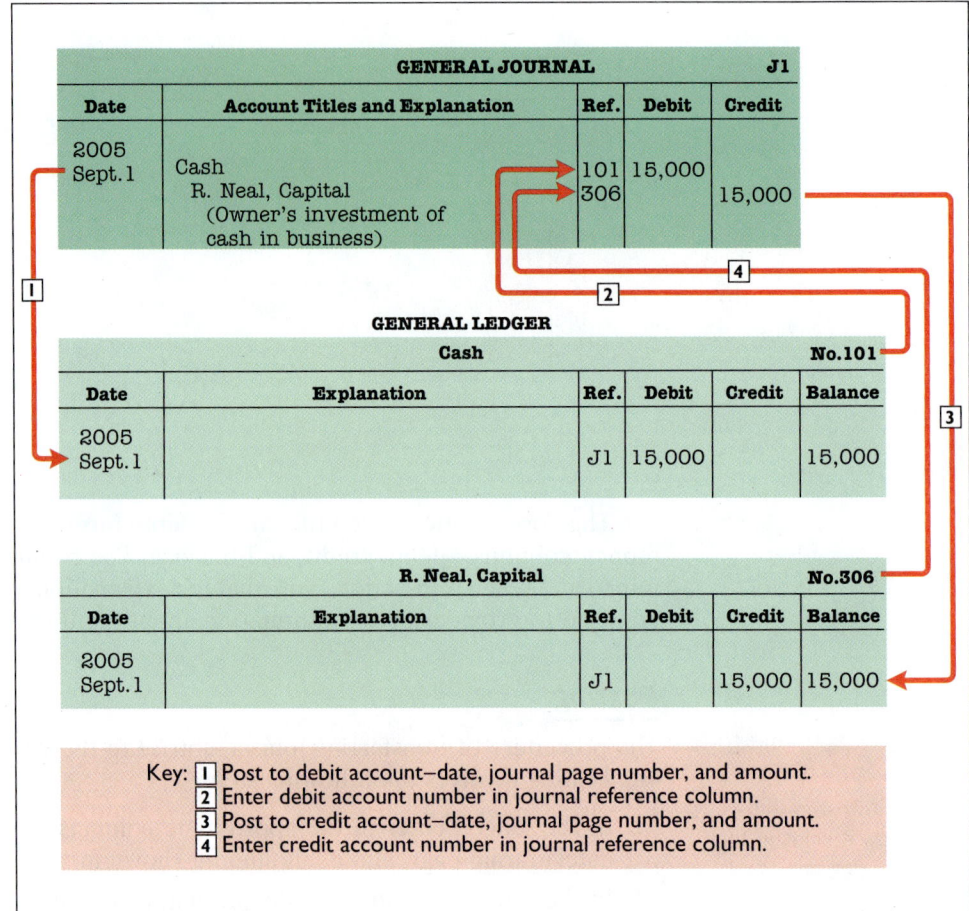

Key: 1 Post to debit account—date, journal page number, and amount.
2 Enter debit account number in journal reference column.
3 Post to credit account—date, journal page number, and amount.
4 Enter credit account number in journal reference column.

Chart of Accounts

The number and type of accounts used differ for each enterprise. The number of accounts depends on the amount of detail desired by management. For example, the management of one company may want one account for all types of utility expense. Another may keep separate expense accounts for each type of utility, such as gas, electricity, and water. Similarly, a single proprietorship like Softbyte will have fewer accounts than a corporate giant like **Ford Motor Company**. Softbyte may be able to manage and report its activities in twenty to thirty accounts, while Ford requires thousands of accounts to keep track of its worldwide activities.

Most companies have a **chart of accounts** that lists the accounts and the account numbers that identify their location in the ledger. The numbering system used to identify the accounts usually starts with the balance sheet accounts and follows with the income statement accounts.

In this and the next two chapters, we will be explaining the accounting for the proprietorship Pioneer Advertising Agency (a service enterprise). Accounts 101–199 indicate asset accounts; 200–299 indicate liabilities; 301–350 indicate owner's equity accounts; 400–499, revenues; 601–799, expenses; 800–899, other revenues; and 900–999, other expenses.

The chart of accounts for Pioneer Advertising Agency (C. R. Byrd, owner) is shown in Illustration 2-18. Accounts shown in red are used in this chapter; accounts shown in black are explained in later chapters.

Illustration 2-18
Chart of accounts

PIONEER ADVERTISING AGENCY
Chart of Accounts

Assets	Owner's Equity
101 Cash	301 C. R. Byrd, Capital
112 Accounts Receivable	306 C. R. Byrd, Drawing
126 Advertising Supplies	350 Income Summary
130 Prepaid Insurance	
157 Office Equipment	**Revenues**
158 Accumulated Depreciation—Office Equipment	400 Service Revenue
Liabilities	**Expenses**
200 Notes Payable	631 Advertising Supplies Expense
201 Accounts Payable	711 Depreciation Expense
209 Unearned Revenue	722 Insurance Expense
212 Salaries Payable	726 Salaries Expense
230 Interest Payable	729 Rent Expense
	905 Interest Expense

You will notice that there are gaps in the numbering system of the chart of accounts for Pioneer Advertising. Gaps are left to permit the insertion of new accounts as needed during the life of the business.

The Recording Process Illustrated

Illustrations 2-19 through 2-28 show the basic steps in the recording process, using the October transactions of the Pioneer Advertising Agency. Its accounting period is a month. A basic analysis and a debit-credit analysis precede the journalizing and posting of each transaction. For simplicity, the T-account form is used in the illustrations instead of the standard account form.

Study the transaction analyses in Illustrations 2-19 through 2-28 carefully. **The purpose of transaction analysis is first to identify the type of account involved, and then to determine whether a debit or a credit to the account is required.** You should always perform this type of analysis before preparing a journal entry. Doing so will help you understand the journal entries discussed in this chapter as well as more complex journal entries to be described in later chapters.

Keep in mind that every journal entry affects one or more of the following items: assets, liabilities, owner's capital, owner's drawing, revenues, or expenses. By becoming skilled at transaction analysis, you will be able to recognize quickly the impact of any transaction on these six items.

Illustration 2-19
Investment of cash by owner

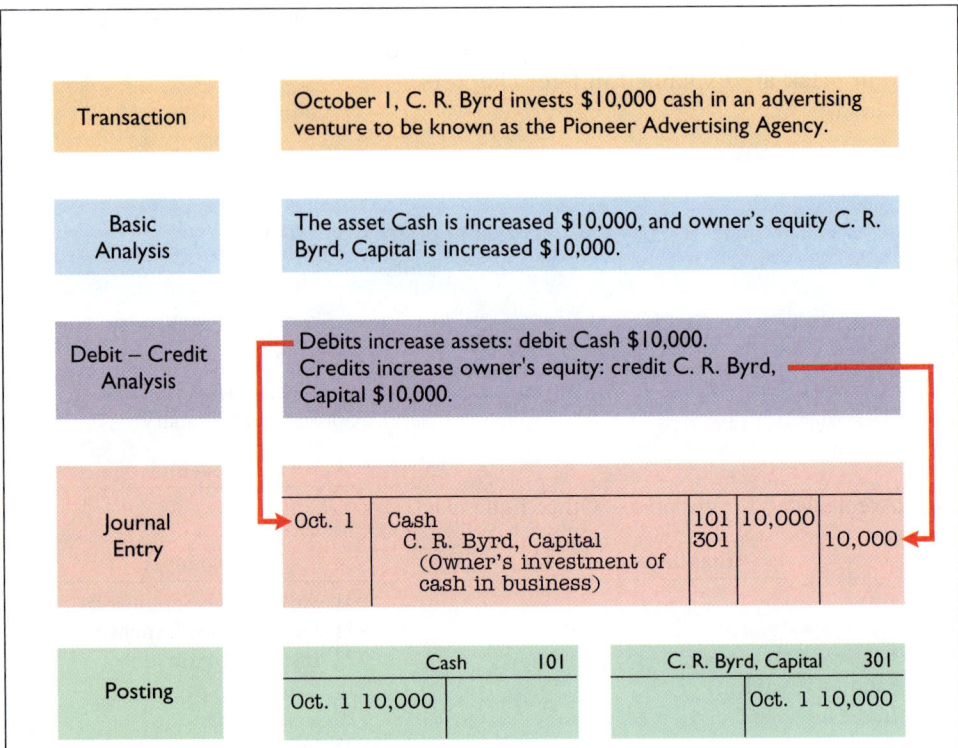

Illustration 2-20
Purchase of office equipment

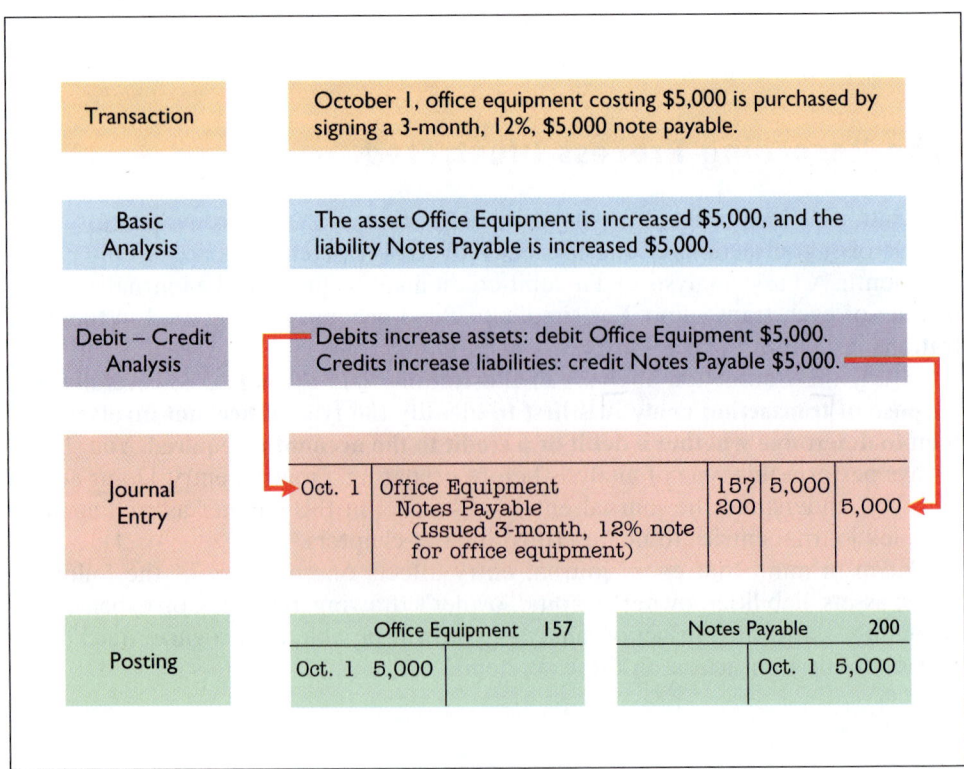

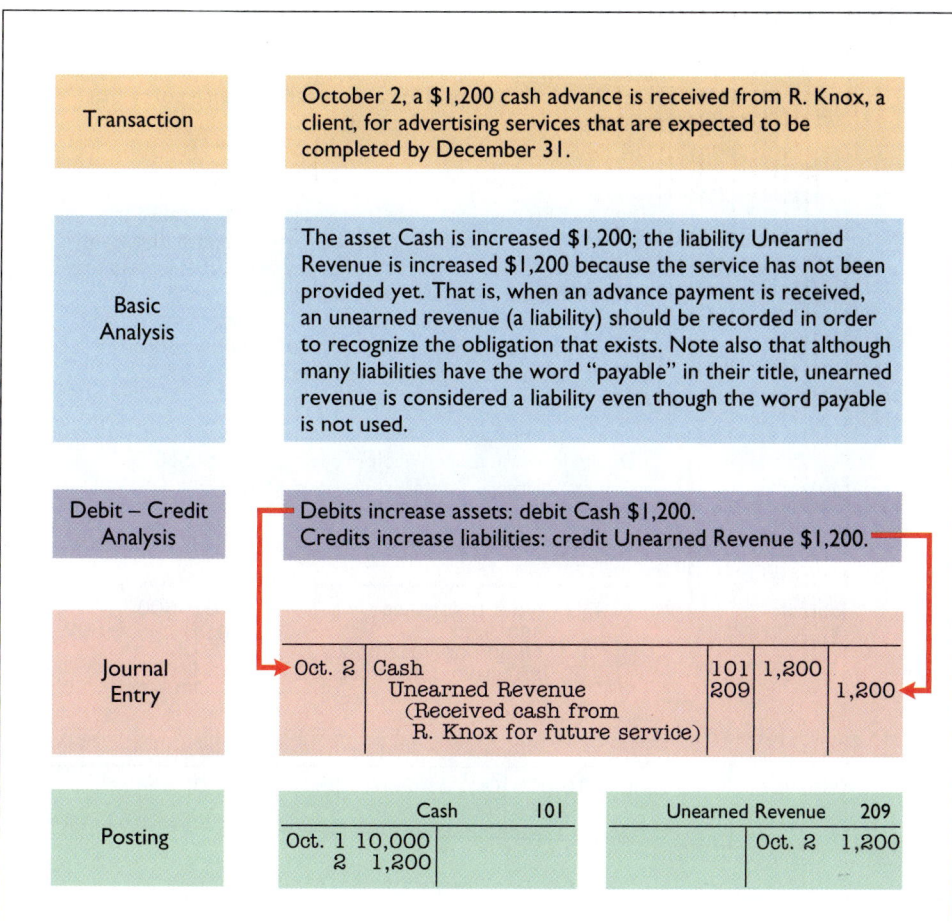

Illustration 2-21
Receipt of cash for future service

| Transaction | October 2, a $1,200 cash advance is received from R. Knox, a client, for advertising services that are expected to be completed by December 31. |

| Basic Analysis | The asset Cash is increased $1,200; the liability Unearned Revenue is increased $1,200 because the service has not been provided yet. That is, when an advance payment is received, an unearned revenue (a liability) should be recorded in order to recognize the obligation that exists. Note also that although many liabilities have the word "payable" in their title, unearned revenue is considered a liability even though the word payable is not used. |

| Debit – Credit Analysis | Debits increase assets: debit Cash $1,200.
Credits increase liabilities: credit Unearned Revenue $1,200. |

Journal Entry

Oct. 2	Cash	101	1,200	
	Unearned Revenue	209		1,200
	(Received cash from			
	R. Knox for future service)			

Posting

Cash		101
Oct. 1 10,000		
2 1,200		

| Unearned Revenue | | 209 |
| | Oct. 2 | 1,200 |

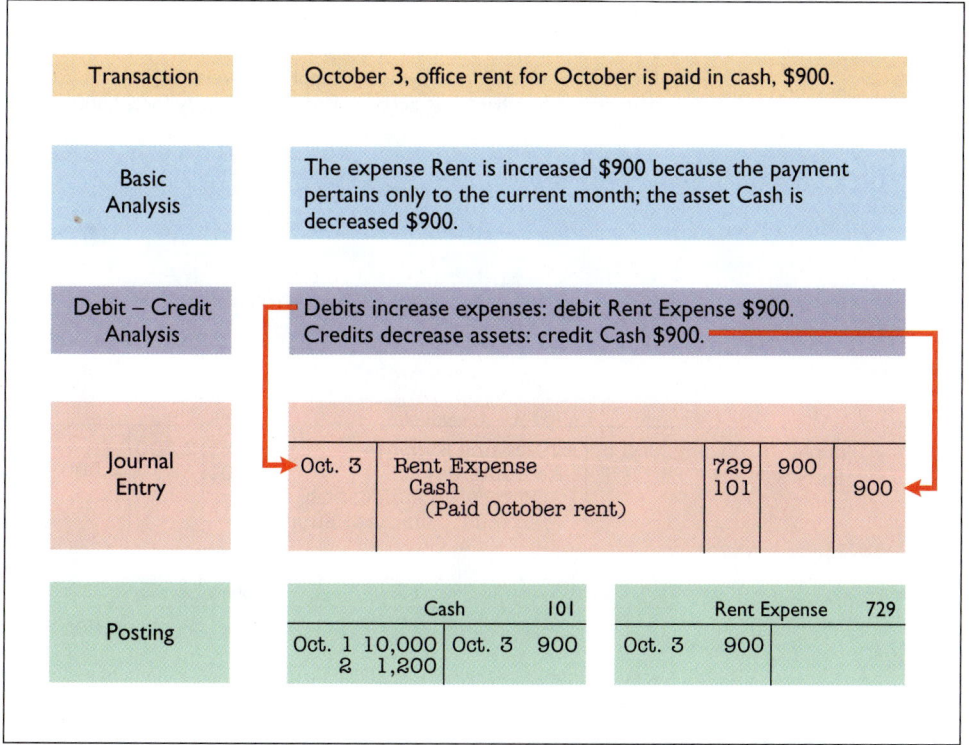

Illustration 2-22
Payment of monthly rent

| Transaction | October 3, office rent for October is paid in cash, $900. |

| Basic Analysis | The expense Rent is increased $900 because the payment pertains only to the current month; the asset Cash is decreased $900. |

| Debit – Credit Analysis | Debits increase expenses: debit Rent Expense $900.
Credits decrease assets: credit Cash $900. |

Journal Entry

Oct. 3	Rent Expense	729	900	
	Cash	101		900
	(Paid October rent)			

Posting

Cash		101
Oct. 1 10,000	Oct. 3	900
2 1,200		

| Rent Expense | | 729 |
| Oct. 3 900 | | |

Illustration 2-23
Payment for insurance

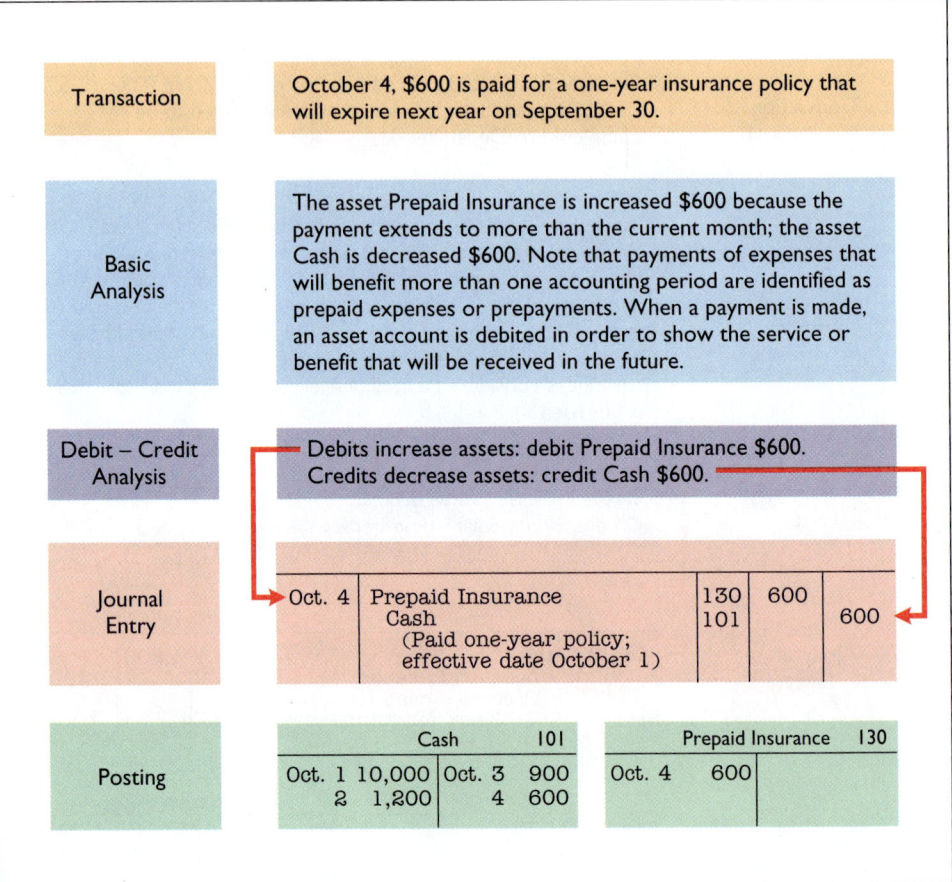

Illustration 2-24
Purchase of supplies on credit

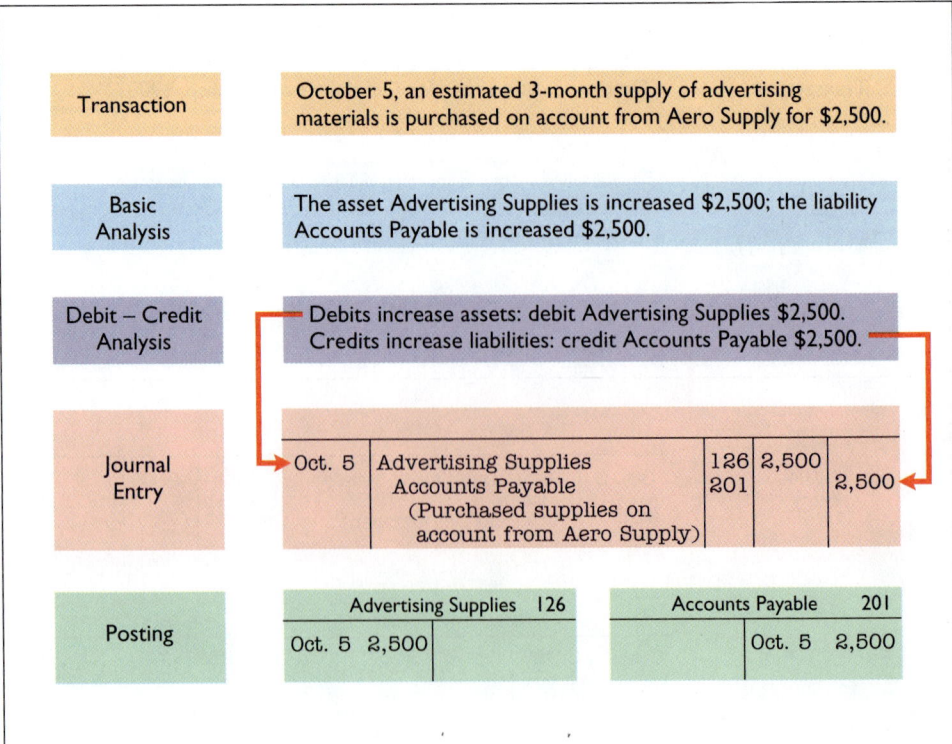

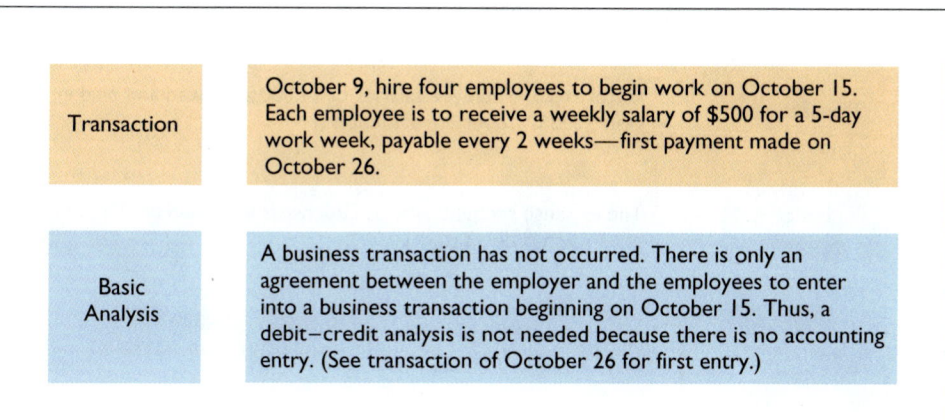

Illustration 2-25
Hiring of employees

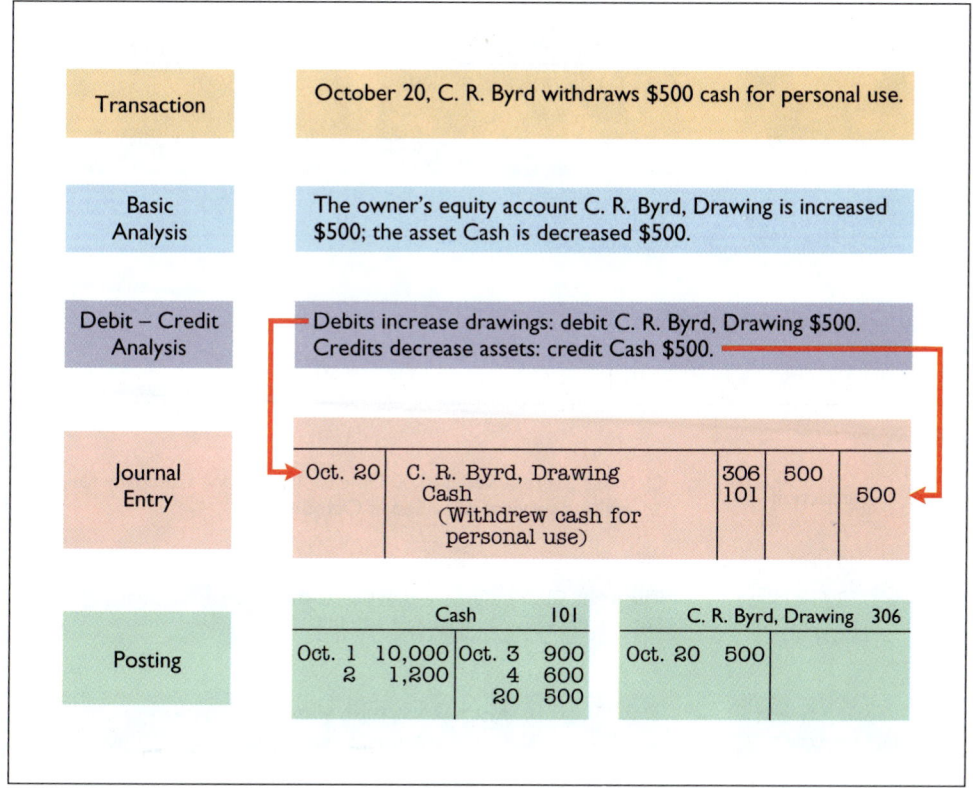

Illustration 2-26
Withdrawal of cash by owner

Illustration 2-27
Payment of salaries

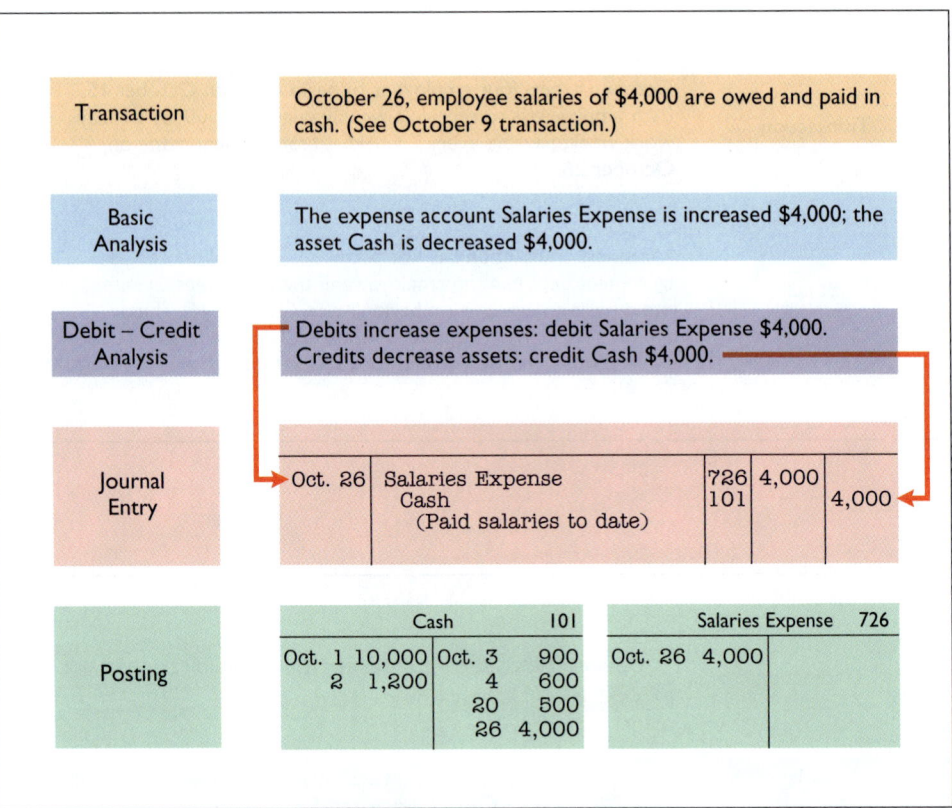

Illustration 2-28
Receipt of cash for services
provided

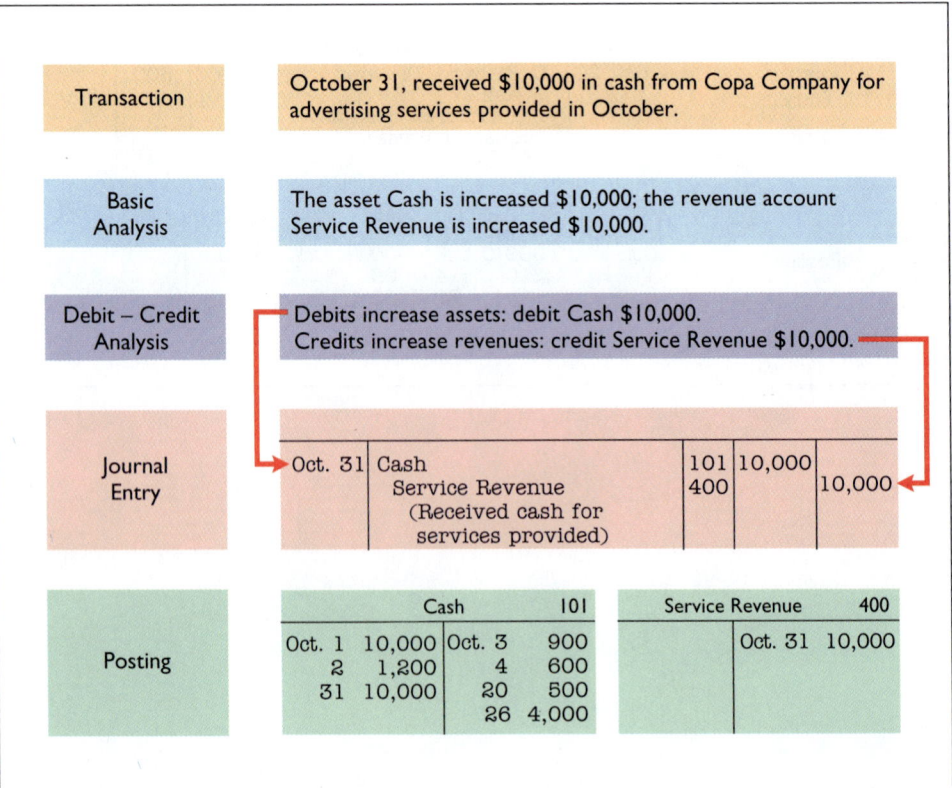

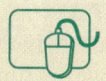 

ACCOUNTING IN ACTION   **Business Insight**

E-business is having a tremendous impact on how companies share information within the company, and with people outside the company, such as suppliers, creditors, and investors. A new type of software, Extensible Markup Language (XML), is enabling the creation of a universal way to exchange data.

An organization called XBRL.org is using XML to develop an internationally accepted reporting format called the Extensible Business Reporting Language (XBRL). The organization is comprised of representatives from industry, accounting firms, investment houses, bankers, regulators, and others. The goal of this organization is to establish a framework that "the global business information supply chain will use to create, exchange, and analyze financial reporting information including, but not limited to, regulatory filings such as annual and quarterly financial statements, general ledger information, and audit schedules."

Source: www.XBRL.org.

BEFORE YOU GO ON...

Review It

1. How does journalizing differ from posting?
2. What is the purpose of (a) the ledger and (b) a chart of accounts?

Do It

Kate Brown recorded the following transactions in a general journal during the month of March.

Cash	2,280	
Service Revenue		2,280
Wages Expense	400	
Cash		400
Utilities Expense	92	
Cash		92

Post these entries to the Cash account of the general ledger to determine the ending balance in cash. The beginning balance in cash on March 1 was $600.

ACTION PLAN

- Recall that posting involves transferring the journalized debits and credits to specific accounts in the ledger.
- Determine the ending balance by netting the total debits and credits.

SOLUTION

Cash

3/1	600	400	
	2,280	92	
3/31 Bal.	2,388		

Related exercise material: *BE2-7, BE2-8, E2-5, and E2-8.*

✔ THE NAVIGATOR

Summary Illustration of Journalizing and Posting

The journal for Pioneer Advertising Agency for October is shown in Illustration 2-29. The ledger is shown in Illustration 2-30, on page 65, with all balances in color.

Illustration 2-29
General journal entries

	GENERAL JOURNAL			Page J1
Date	**Account Titles and Explanation**	**Ref.**	**Debit**	**Credit**
2005				
Oct. 1	Cash	101	10,000	
	C. R. Byrd, Capital	301		10,000
	(Owner's investment of cash in business)			
1	Office Equipment	157	5,000	
	Notes Payable	200		5,000
	(Issued 3-month, 12% note for office equipment)			
2	Cash	101	1,200	
	Unearned Revenue	209		1,200
	(Received cash for future services)			
3	Rent Expense	729	900	
	Cash	101		900
	(Paid October rent)			
4	Prepaid Insurance	130	600	
	Cash	101		600
	(Paid one-year policy; effective date October 1)			
5	Advertising Supplies	126	2,500	
	Accounts Payable	201		2,500
	(Purchased supplies on account from Aero Supply)			
20	C. R. Byrd, Drawing	306	500	
	Cash	101		500
	(Withdrew cash for personal use)			
26	Salaries Expense	726	4,000	
	Cash	101		4,000
	(Paid salaries to date)			
31	Cash	101	10,000	
	Service Revenue	400		10,000
	(Received cash for services provided)			

Illustration 2-30
General ledger

GENERAL JOURNAL

Cash					**No. 101**
Date	Explanation	Ref.	Debit	Credit	Balance
2005					
Oct. 1		J1	10,000		10,000
2		J1	1,200		11,200
3		J1		900	10,300
4		J1		600	9,700
20		J1		500	9,200
26		J1		4,000	5,200
31		J1	10,000		**15,200**

Advertising Supplies					**No. 126**
Date	Explanation	Ref.	Debit	Credit	Balance
2005					
Oct. 5		J1	2,500		**2,500**

Prepaid Insurance					**No. 130**
Date	Explanation	Ref.	Debit	Credit	Balance
2005					
Oct. 4		J1	600		**600**

Office Equipment					**No. 157**
Date	Explanation	Ref.	Debit	Credit	Balance
2005					
Oct. 1		J1	5,000		**5,000**

Notes Payable					**No. 200**
Date	Explanation	Ref.	Debit	Credit	Balance
2005					
Oct. 1		J1		5,000	**5,000**

Accounts Payable					**No. 201**
Date	Explanation	Ref.	Debit	Credit	Balance
2005					
Oct. 5		J1		2,500	**2,500**

Unearned Revenue					**No. 209**
Date	Explanation	Ref.	Debit	Credit	Balance
2005					
Oct. 2		J1		1,200	**1,200**

C.R. Byrd, Capital					**No. 301**
Date	Explanation	Ref.	Debit	Credit	Balance
2005					
Oct. 1		J1		10,000	**10,000**

C.R. Byrd, Drawing					**No. 306**
Date	Explanation	Ref.	Debit	Credit	Balance
2005					
Oct. 20		J1	500		**500**

Service Revenue					**No. 400**
Date	Explanation	Ref.	Debit	Credit	Balance
2005					
Oct. 31		J1		10,000	**10,000**

Salaries Expense					**No. 726**
Date	Explanation	Ref.	Debit	Credit	Balance
2005					
Oct. 26		J1	4,000		**4,000**

Rent Expense					**No. 729**
Date	Explanation	Ref.	Debit	Credit	Balance
2005					
Oct. 3		J1	900		**900**

The Trial Balance

A trial balance is a list of accounts and their balances at a given time. Customarily, a trial balance is prepared at the end of an accounting period. The accounts are listed in the order in which they appear in the ledger; debit balances are listed in the left column and credit balances in the right column.

The primary purpose of a trial balance is to prove (check) that the debits equal the credits after posting. In other words, the sum of the debit account balances in the trial balance should equal the sum of the credit account balances. **If the debits and credits do not agree, the trial balance can be used to uncover errors in journalizing and posting. In addition, it is useful in the preparation of financial statements,** as will be explained in the next two chapters.

The steps for preparing a trial balance are:

1. List the account titles and their balances.
2. Total the debit and credit columns.
3. Prove the equality of the two columns.

The trial balance prepared from Pioneer Advertising's ledger is shown below.

Illustration 2-31
A trial balance

PIONEER ADVERTISING AGENCY
Trial Balance
October 31, 2005

	Debit	Credit
Cash	$15,200	
Advertising Supplies	2,500	
Prepaid Insurance	600	
Office Equipment	5,000	
Notes Payable		$ 5,000
Accounts Payable		2,500
Unearned Revenue		1,200
C. R. Byrd, Capital		10,000
C. R. Byrd, Drawing	500	
Service Revenue		10,000
Salaries Expense	4,000	
Rent Expense	900	
	$28,700	**$28,700**

Note that the total debits ($28,700) equal the total credits ($28,700). Account numbers are sometimes shown to the left of the account titles in the trial balance.

A trial balance is a necessary checkpoint for uncovering certain types of errors before you proceed to other steps in the accounting process. For example, if only the debit portion of a journal entry has been posted, the trial balance would bring this error to light.

Limitations of a Trial Balance

A trial balance does not guarantee freedom from recording errors, however. **It does not prove that all transactions have been recorded or that the ledger is correct.** Numerous errors may exist even though the trial balance columns agree. For example, the trial balance may balance even when (1) a transaction is not journalized, (2) a correct journal entry is not posted, (3) a journal entry is posted twice, (4) incorrect accounts are used in journalizing or posting, or (5) offsetting errors are made in recording the amount of a transaction. In other words, as long as equal debits and credits are posted, even to the wrong account or in the wrong amount, the total debits will equal the total credits.

Locating Errors

The procedure for preparing a trial balance is relatively simple. However, if the trial balance does not balance, locating an error in a manual system can be timeconsuming, tedious, and frustrating. Errors generally result from mathematical mistakes, incorrect postings, or simply transcribing data incorrectly.

What do you do if you are faced with a trial balance that does not balance? First determine the amount of the difference between the two columns of the trial balance. After this amount is known, the following steps are often helpful:

ETHICS NOTE

Auditors are required to differentiate *errors* from *irregularities*. An *error* is the result of an unintentional mistake; it is neither ethical nor unethical. An *irregularity* is an intentional misstatement, which *is* viewed as unethical.

1. If the error is $1, $10, $100, or $1,000, re-add the trial balance columns and re-compute the account balances.

2. If the error is divisible by 2, scan the trial balance to see whether a balance equal to half the error has been entered in the wrong column.

3. If the error is divisible by 9, retrace the account balances on the trial balance to see whether they are incorrectly copied from the ledger. For example, if a balance was $12 and it was listed as $21, a $9 error has been made. Reversing the order of numbers is called a transposition error.

4. If the error is not divisible by 2 or 9 (for example, $365), scan the ledger to see whether an account balance of $365 has been omitted from the trial balance, and scan the journal to see whether a $365 posting has been omitted.

Use of Dollar Signs

Note that dollar signs do not appear in the journals or ledgers. Dollar signs are usually used only in the trial balance and the financial statements. Generally, a dollar sign is shown only for the first item in the column and for the total of that column. A single line is placed under the column of figures to be added or subtracted; the total amount is double underlined to indicate the final sum.

BEFORE YOU GO ON...

Review It

1. What is a trial balance and what is its primary purpose?
2. How is a trial balance prepared?
3. What are the limitations of a trial balance?

✓ THE NAVIGATOR

DEMONSTRATION PROBLEM

Bob Sample opened the Campus Laundromat on September 1, 2005. During the first month of operations the following transactions occurred.

Sept.	1	Invested $20,000 cash in the business.
	2	Paid $1,000 cash for store rent for the month of September.
	3	Purchased washers and dryers for $25,000, paying $10,000 in cash and signing a $15,000, 6-month, 12% note payable.
	4	Paid $1,200 for one-year accident insurance policy.
	10	Received bill from the *Daily News* for advertising the opening of the laundromat $200.
	20	Withdrew $700 cash for personal use.
	30	Determined that cash receipts for laundry services for the month were $6,200.

The chart of accounts for the company is the same as in Pioneer Advertising Agency except for the following: No. 154 Laundry Equipment and No. 610 Advertising Expense.

Instructions

(a) Journalize the September transactions. (Use J1 for the journal page number.)
(b) Open ledger accounts and post the September transactions.
(c) Prepare a trial balance at September 30, 2005.

SOLUTION TO DEMONSTRATION PROBLEM

(a)

	GENERAL JOURNAL			J1

Date	Account Titles and Explanation	Ref.	Debit	Credit
2005				
Sept. 1	Cash	101	20,000	
	Bob Sample, Capital	301		20,000
	(Owner's investment of cash in business)			
2	Rent Expense	729	1,000	
	Cash	101		1,000
	(Paid September rent)			
3	Laundry Equipment	154	25,000	
	Cash	101		10,000
	Notes Payable	200		15,000
	(Purchased laundry equipment for cash and 6-month, 12% note payable)			
4	Prepaid Insurance	130	1,200	
	Cash	101		1,200
	(Paid one-year insurance policy)			
10	Advertising Expense	610	200	
	Accounts Payable	201		200
	(Received bill from *Daily News* for advertising)			
20	Bob Sample, Drawing	306	700	
	Cash	101		700
	(Withdrew cash for personal use)			
30	Cash	101	6,200	
	Service Revenue	400		6,200
	(Received cash for services provided)			

(b)

GENERAL LEDGER

Cash   **No. 101**

Date	Explanation	Ref.	Debit	Credit	Balance
2005					
Sept. 1		J1	20,000		20,000
2		J1		1,000	19,000
3		J1		10,000	9,000
4		J1		1,200	7,800
20		J1		700	7,100
30		J1	6,200		13,300

Notes Payable   **No. 200**

Date	Explanation	Ref.	Debit	Credit	Balance
2005					
Sept. 3		J1		15,000	15,000

Accounts Payable   **No. 201**

Date	Explanation	Ref.	Debit	Credit	Balance
2005					
Sept. 10		J1		200	200

Prepaid Insurance   **No. 130**

Date	Explanation	Ref.	Debit	Credit	Balance
2005					
Sept. 4		J1	1,200		1,200

Bob Sample, Capital   **No. 301**

Date	Explanation	Ref.	Debit	Credit	Balance
2005					
Sept. 1		J1		20,000	20,000

Laundry Equipment   **No. 154**

Date	Explanation	Ref.	Debit	Credit	Balance
2005					
Sept. 3		J1	25,000		25,000

Bob Sample, Drawing   **No. 306**

Date	Explanation	Ref.	Debit	Credit	Balance
2005					
Sept. 20		J1	700		700

Service Revenue					No. 400
Date	Explanation	Ref.	Debit	Credit	Balance
2005					
Sept. 30		J1		6,200	6,200

Advertising Expense					No. 610
Date	Explanation	Ref.	Debit	Credit	Balance
2005					
Sept. 10		J1	200		200

Rent Expense					No. 729
Date	Explanation	Ref.	Debit	Credit	Balance
2005					
Sept. 2		J1	1,000		1,000

(c)

CAMPUS LAUNDROMAT
Trial Balance
September 30, 2005

	Debit	Credit
Cash	$13,300	
Prepaid Insurance	1,200	
Laundry Equipment	25,000	
Notes Payable		$15,000
Accounts Payable		200
Bob Sample, Capital		20,000
Bob Sample, Drawing	700	
Service Revenue		6,200
Advertising Expense	200	
Rent Expense	1,000	
	$41,400	$41,400

THE NAVIGATOR

SUMMARY OF STUDY OBJECTIVES

1. **Explain what an account is and how it helps in the recording process.** An account is a record of increases and decreases in specific asset, liability, and owner's equity items.

2. **Define debits and credits and explain how they are used to record business transactions.** The terms debit and credit are synonymous with left and right. Assets, drawings, and expenses are increased by debits and decreased by credits. Liabilities, owner's capital, and revenues are increased by credits and decreased by debits.

3. **Identify the basic steps in the recording process.** The basic steps in the recording process are: (a) analyze each transaction in terms of its effects on the accounts, (b) enter the transaction information in a journal, (c) transfer the journal information to the appropriate accounts in the ledger.

4. **Explain what a journal is and how it helps in the recording process.** The initial accounting record of a transaction is entered in a journal before the data are entered in the accounts. A journal (a) discloses in one place the complete effects of a transaction, (b) provides a chronological record of transactions, and (c) prevents or locates errors because

the debit and credit amounts for each entry can be readily compared.

5. **Explain what a ledger is and how it helps in the recording process.** The entire group of accounts maintained by a company is referred to as the ledger. The ledger keeps in one place all the information about changes in specific account balances.

6. **Explain what posting is and how it helps in the recording process.** Posting is the procedure of transferring journal entries to the ledger accounts. This phase of the recording process accumulates the effects of journalized transactions in the individual accounts.

7. **Prepare a trial balance and explain its purposes.** A trial balance is a list of accounts and their balances at a given time. Its primary purpose is to prove the equality of debits and credits after posting. A trial balance also uncovers errors in journalizing and posting and is useful in preparing financial statements.

THE NAVIGATOR

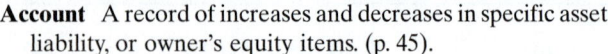

GLOSSARY

Account   A record of increases and decreases in specific asset, liability, or owner's equity items. (p. 45).

Chart of accounts   A list of accounts and the account numbers that identify their location in the ledger. (p. 56).

Compound entry   A journal entry that involves three or more accounts. (p. 53).

Credit   The right side of an account. (p. 46).

Debit   The left side of an account. (p. 46).

Double-entry system   A system that records in appropriate accounts the dual effect of each transaction. (p. 46).

General journal   The most basic form of journal. (p. 51).

General ledger   A ledger that contains all asset, liability, and owner's equity accounts. (p. 54).

Journal   An accounting record in which transactions are initially recorded in chronological order. (p. 51).

Journalizing   The entering of transaction data in the journal. (p. 52).

Ledger   The entire group of accounts maintained by a company. (p. 54).

Posting   The procedure of transferring journal entries to the ledger accounts. (p. 55).

Simple entry   A journal entry that involves only two accounts. (p. 52).

T account   The basic form of an account. (p. 45).

Three-column form of account   A form with columns for debit, credit, and balance amounts in an account. (p. 55).

Trial balance   A list of accounts and their balances at a given time. (p. 65).

SELF-STUDY QUESTIONS

Self-Study/Self-Test

Answers are at the end of the chapter.

(SO 1)   **1.** Which of the following statements about an account is true?
  a. In its simplest form, an account consists of two parts.
  b. An account is an individual accounting record of increases and decreases in specific asset, liability, and owner's equity items.
  c. There are separate accounts for specific assets and liabilities but only one account for owner's equity items.
  d. The left side of an account is the credit or decrease side.

(SO 2)   **2.** Debits:
  a. increase both assets and liabilities.
  b. decrease both assets and liabilities.
  c. increase assets and decrease liabilities.
  d. decrease assets and increase liabilities.

(SO 2)   **3.** A revenue account:
  a. is increased by debits.
  b. is decreased by credits.
  c. has a normal balance of a debit.
  d. is increased by credits.

(SO 2)   **4.** Accounts that normally have debit balances are:
  a. assets, expenses, and revenues.
  b. assets, expenses, and owner's capital.
  c. assets, liabilities, and owner's drawings.
  d. assets, owner's drawings, and expenses.

(SO 3)   **5.** Which of the following is *not* part of the recording process?
  a. Analyzing transactions.
  b. Preparing a trial balance.
  c. Entering transactions in a journal.
  d. Posting transactions.

(SO 4)   **6.** Which of the following statements about a journal is false?

  a. It is not a book of original entry.
  b. It provides a chronological record of transactions.
  c. It helps to locate errors because the debit and credit amounts for each entry can be readily compared.
  d. It discloses in one place the complete effect of a transaction.

7. A ledger: (SO 5)
  a. contains only asset and liability accounts.
  b. should show accounts in alphabetical order.
  c. is a collection of the entire group of accounts maintained by a company.
  d. is a book of original entry.

8. Posting: (SO 6)
  a. normally occurs before journalizing.
  b. transfers ledger transaction data to the journal.
  c. is an optional step in the recording process.
  d. transfers journal entries to ledger accounts.

9. A trial balance: (SO 7)
  a. is a list of accounts with their balances at a given time.
  b. proves the mathematical accuracy of journalized transactions.
  c. will not balance if a correct journal entry is posted twice.
  d. proves that all transactions have been recorded.

10. A trial balance will not balance if: (SO 7)
  a. a correct journal entry is posted twice.
  b. the purchase of supplies on account is debited to Supplies and credited to Cash.
  c. a $100 cash drawing by the owner is debited to Owner's Drawing for $1,000 and credited to Cash for $100.
  d. a $450 payment on account is debited to Accounts Payable for $45 and credited to Cash for $45.

✔ THE NAVIGATOR

QUESTIONS

1. Describe the parts of a T account.

2. "The terms *debit* and *credit* mean increase and decrease, respectively." Do you agree? Explain.

3. John Alcorn, a fellow student, contends that the double-entry system means each transaction must be recorded twice. Is John correct? Explain.

4. Kathy Mendosa, a beginning accounting student, believes debit balances are favorable and credit balances are unfavorable. Is Kathy correct? Discuss.

5. State the rules of debit and credit as applied to (a) asset accounts, (b) liability accounts, and (c) the owner's equity accounts (revenue, expenses, owner's drawing, and owner's capital).

6. What is the normal balance for each of the following accounts? (a) Accounts Receivable. (b) Cash. (c) Owner's Drawing. (d) Accounts Payable. (e) Service Revenue. (f) Salaries Expense. (g) Owner's Capital.

7. Indicate whether each of the following accounts is an asset, a liability, or an owner's equity account and whether it has a normal debit or credit balance: (a) Accounts Receivable, (b) Accounts Payable, (c) Equipment, (d) Owner's Drawing, (e) Supplies.

8. For the following transactions, indicate the account debited and the account credited.
   (a) Supplies are purchased on account.
   (b) Cash is received on signing a note payable.
   (c) Employees are paid salaries in cash.

9. Indicate whether the following accounts generally will have (a) debit entries only, (b) credit entries only, or (c) both debit and credit entries.
   (1) Cash.
   (2) Accounts Receivable.
   (3) Owner's Drawing.
   (4) Accounts Payable.
   (5) Salaries Expense.
   (6) Service Revenue.

10. What are the basic steps in the recording process?

11. What are the advantages of using a journal in the recording process?

12. (a) When entering a transaction in the journal, should the debit or credit be written first?
    (b) Which should be indented, the debit or credit?

13. Describe a compound entry, and provide an example.

14. (a) Should business transaction debits and credits be recorded directly in the ledger accounts?
    (b) What are the advantages of first recording transactions in the journal and then posting to the ledger?

15. The account number is entered as the last step in posting the amounts from the journal to the ledger. What is the advantage of this step?

16. Journalize the following business transactions.
    (a) Alberto Rivera invests $7,000 cash in the business.
    (b) Insurance of $800 is paid for the year.
    (c) Supplies of $1,000 are purchased on account.
    (d) Cash of $7,500 is received for services rendered.

17. (a) What is a ledger?
    (b) What is a chart of accounts and why is it important?

18. What is a trial balance and what are its purposes?

19. Joe Kirby is confused about how accounting information flows through the accounting system. He believes the flow of information is as follows.
    (a) Debits and credits posted to the ledger.
    (b) Business transaction occurs.
    (c) Information entered in the journal.
    (d) Financial statements are prepared.
    (e) Trial balance is prepared.

    Is Joe correct? If not, indicate to Joe the proper flow of the information.

20. Two students are discussing the use of a trial balance. They wonder whether the following errors, each considered separately, would prevent the trial balance from balancing.
    (a) The bookkeeper debited Cash for $600 and credited Wages Expense for $600 for payment of wages.
    (b) Cash collected on account was debited to Cash for $900 and Service Revenue was credited for $90.

    What would you tell them?

BRIEF EXERCISES

BE2-1 For each of the following accounts indicate the effects of (a) a debit and (b) a credit on the accounts and (c) the normal balance of the account.

Indicate debit and credit effects and normal balance.

(SO 2)

1. Accounts Payable.
2. Advertising Expense.
3. Service Revenue.
4. Accounts Receivable.
5. B. C. King, Capital.
6. B. C. King, Drawing.

Identify accounts to be debited and credited.

(SO 2)

BE2-2 Transactions for the Kaustav Sen Company for the month of June are presented below. Identify the accounts to be debited and credited for each transaction.

June 1   Kaustav Sen invests $4,000 cash in a small welding business of which he is the sole proprietor.
     2   Purchases equipment on account for $900.
     3   $800 cash is paid to landlord for June rent.
   12   Bills J. Kronsnoble $300 for welding work done on account.

Journalize transactions.

(SO 4)

BE2-3 Using the data in BE2-2, journalize the transactions. (You may omit explanations.)

Identify and explain steps in recording process.

(SO 3)

BE2-4 ✏ Tim Weber, a fellow student, is unclear about the basic steps in the recording process. Identify and briefly explain the steps in the order in which they occur.

Indicate basic and debit-credit analysis.

(SO 2)

BE2-5 J. A. Motzek has the following transactions during August of the current year. Indicate (a) the effect on the accounting equation and (b) the debit-credit analysis illustrated on pages 58–62 of the text.

Aug. 1   Opens an office as a financial advisor, investing $5,000 in cash.
     4   Pays insurance in advance for 6 months, $1,800 cash.
   16   Receives $800 from clients for services provided.
   27   Pays secretary $1,000 salary.

Journalize transactions.

(SO 4)

BE2-6 Using the data in BE2-5, journalize the transactions. (You may omit explanations.)

Post journal entries to T accounts.

(SO 6)

BE2-7 Selected transactions for the Gilles Company are presented in journal form below. Post the transactions to T accounts. Make one T account for each item and determine each account's ending balance.

J1

Date	Account Titles and Explanation	Ref.	Debit	Credit
May 5	Accounts Receivable		6,000	
	Service Revenue			6,000
	(Billed for services provided)			
12	Cash		2,400	
	Accounts Receivable			2,400
	(Received cash in payment of account)			
15	Cash		3,000	
	Service Revenue			3,000
	(Received cash for services provided)			

Post journal entries to standard form of account.

(SO 6)

BE2-8 Selected journal entries for the Gilles Company are presented in BE2-7. Post the transactions using the standard form of account.

Prepare a trial balance.

(SO 7)

BE2-9 From the ledger balances given below, prepare a trial balance for the P. J. Farve Company at June 30, 2005. List the accounts in the order shown on page 57 of the text. All account balances are normal.

Accounts Payable $9,000, Cash $6,800, P. J. Farve, Capital $20,000, P. J. Farve, Drawing $1,200, Equipment $17,000, Service Revenue $6,000, Accounts Receivable $3,000, Salaries Expense $6,000, and Rent Expense $1,000.

Prepare a correct trial balance.

(SO 7)

BE2-10 An inexperienced bookkeeper prepared the following trial balance. Prepare a correct trial balance, assuming all account balances are normal.

CHENG COMPANY
Trial Balance
December 31, 2005

	Debit	Credit
Cash	$16,800	
Prepaid Insurance		$3,500
Accounts Payable		3,000
Unearned Revenue	4,200	
P. Cheng, Capital		13,000
P. Cheng, Drawing		4,500
Service Revenue		25,600
Salaries Expense	18,600	
Rent Expense		2,400
	$39,600	$52,000

EXERCISES

E2-1 Selected transactions for H. Burns, an interior decorator, in her first month of business, are as follows.

Jan. 2 Invested $15,000 cash in business.
  3 Purchased used car for $4,000 cash for use in business.
  9 Purchased supplies on account for $500.
  11 Billed customers $1,800 for services performed.
  16 Paid $200 cash for advertising.
  20 Received $700 cash from customers billed on January 11.
  23 Paid creditor $300 cash on balance owed.
  28 Withdrew $2,000 cash for personal use of owner.

Identify debits, credits, and normal balances.

(SO 2)

Instructions
For each transaction indicate the following.

(a) The basic type of account debited and credited (asset, liability, owner's equity).
(b) The specific account debited and credited (cash, rent expense, service revenue, etc.).
(c) Whether the specific account is increased or decreased.
(d) The normal balance of the specific account.

Use the following format, in which the January 2 transaction is given as an example.

	Account Debited				Account Credited			
Date	(a) Basic Type	(b) Specific Account	(c) Effect	(d) Normal Balance	(a) Basic Type	(b) Specific Account	(c) Effect	(d) Normal Balance
Jan. 2	Asset	Cash	Increase	Debit	Owner's Equity	H. Burns, Capital	Increase	Credit

E2-2 Data for H. Burns, interior decorator, are presented in E2-1.

Journalize transactions.

(SO 4)

Instructions
Journalize the transactions using journal page J1. (You may omit explanations.)

E2-3 Presented below is information related to Robbins Real Estate Agency.

Oct. 1 Lynn Robbins begins business as a real estate agent with a cash investment of $20,000.
  2 Hires an administrative assistant.
  3 Purchases office furniture for $1,900, on account.
  6 Sells a house and lot for B. Kidman; bills B. Kidman $3,200 for realty services provided.
  27 Pays $700 on the balance related to the transaction of October 3.
  30 Pays the administrative assistant $2,000 in salary for October.

Analyze transactions and determine their effect on accounts.

(SO 2)

Instructions
Prepare the debit-credit analysis for each transaction as illustrated on pages 58–62.

Journalize transactions.

(SO 4)

E2-4 Transaction data for Robbins Real Estate Agency are presented in E2-3.

Instructions

Journalize the transactions. (You may omit explanations.)

Post journal entries and prepare a trial balance.

(SO 6, 7)

E2-5 Selected transactions from the journal of Roberta Mendez, investment broker, are presented below.

Date	Account Titles and Explanation	Ref.	Debit	Credit
Aug. 1	Cash		3,000	
	Roberta Mendez, Capital			3,000
	(Owner's investment of cash in business)			
10	Cash		2,400	
	Service Revenue			2,400
	(Received cash for services provided)			
12	Office Equipment		5,000	
	Cash			1,000
	Notes Payable			4,000
	(Purchased office equipment for cash and notes payable)			
25	Accounts Receivable		1,600	
	Service Revenue			1,600
	(Billed for services provided)			
31	Cash		900	
	Accounts Receivable			900
	(Receipt of cash on account)			

Instructions

(a) Post the transactions to T accounts.

(b) Prepare a trial balance at August 31, 2005.

Journalize transactions from account data and prepare a trial balance.

(SO 4, 7)

E2-6 The T accounts below summarize the ledger of Padre Landscaping Company at the end of the first month of operations.

Cash			No. 101
4/1	10,000	4/15	600
4/12	900	4/25	1,500
4/29	400		
4/30	1,000		

Unearned Revenue		No. 205
	4/30	1,000

Accounts Receivable			No. 112
4/7	3,200	4/29	400

J. Padre, Capital		No. 301
	4/1	10,000

Supplies		No. 126
4/4	1,800	

Service Revenue		No. 400
	4/7	3,200
	4/12	900

Accounts Payable			No. 201
4/25	1,500	4/4	1,800

Salaries Expense		No. 726
4/15	600	

Instructions

(a) Prepare the complete general journal (including explanations) from which the postings to Cash were made.

(b) Prepare a trial balance at April 30, 2005.

E2-7 Presented below is the ledger for Maxim Co.

Journalize transactions from account data and prepare a trial balance.

(SO 4, 7)

Cash			No. 101
10/1	5,000	10/4	400
10/10	650	10/12	1,500
10/10	3,000	10/15	250
10/20	500	10/30	300
10/25	2,000	10/31	500

Accounts Receivable			No. 112
10/6	800	10/20	500
10/20	940		

Supplies		No. 126
10/4	400	

Furniture		No. 149
10/3	2,000	

Notes Payable		No. 200
	10/10	3,000

Accounts Payable			No. 201
10/12	1,500	10/3	2,000

Maxim, Capital		No. 301
	10/1	5,000
	10/25	2,000

Maxim, Drawing		No. 306
10/30	300	

Service Revenue		No. 407
	10/6	800
	10/10	650
	10/20	940

Store Wages Expense		No. 628
10/31	500	

Rent Expense		No. 729
10/15	250	

Instructions

(a) Reproduce the journal entries for the transactions that occurred on October 1, 10, and 20, and provide explanations for each.

(b) Determine the October 31 balance for each of the accounts above, and prepare a trial balance at October 31, 2005.

E2-8 Selected transactions for Neve Campbell Company during its first month in business are presented below.

Prepare journal entries and post using standard account form.

(SO 4, 6)

Sept. 1 Invested $10,000 cash in the business.
　　5 Purchased equipment for $12,000 paying $6,000 in cash and the balance on account.
　　25 Paid $3,000 cash on balance owed for equipment.
　　30 Withdrew $500 cash for personal use.

Campbell's chart of accounts shows: No. 101 Cash, No. 157 Equipment, No. 201 Accounts Payable, No. 301 Neve Campbell, Capital, No. 306 Neve Campbell, Drawing.

Instructions

(a) Journalize the transactions on page J1 of the journal.

(b) Post the transactions using the standard account form.

E2-9 The bookkeeper for Stan Tucci Equipment Repair made a number of errors in journalizing and posting, as described below.

Analyze errors and their effects on trial balance.

(SO 7)

1. A credit posting of $400 to Accounts Receivable was omitted.

2. A debit posting of $750 for Prepaid Insurance was debited to Insurance Expense.

3. A collection from a customer of $100 in payment of its account owed was journalized and posted as a debit to Cash $100 and a credit to Service Revenue $100.

4. A credit posting of $300 to Property Taxes Payable was made twice.

5. A cash purchase of supplies for $250 was journalized and posted as a debit to Supplies $25 and a credit to Cash $25.

6. A debit of $495 to Advertising Expense was posted as $459.

Instructions

For each error:

(a) Indicate whether the trial balance will balance.

(b) If the trial balance will not balance, indicate the amount of the difference.

(c) Indicate the trial balance column that will have the larger total.

Consider each error separately. Use the following form, in which error (1) is given as an example.

Error	(a) In Balance	(b) Difference	(c) Larger Column
(1)	No	$400	debit

Prepare a trial balance.

(SO 2, 7)

E2-10 The accounts in the ledger of Speedy Delivery Service contain the following balances on July 31, 2005.

Accounts Receivable	$10,642	Prepaid Insurance	$1,968
Accounts Payable	8,396	Repair Expense	961
Cash	?	Service Revenue	10,610
Delivery Equipment	49,360	I. M. Speedy, Drawing	700
Gas and Oil Expense	758	I. M. Speedy, Capital	44,636
Insurance Expense	523	Salaries Expense	4,428
Notes Payable	26,450	Salaries Payable	815

Instructions

Prepare a trial balance with the accounts arranged as illustrated in the chapter and fill in the missing amount for Cash.

PROBLEMS: SET A

Journalize a series of transactions.

(SO 2, 4)

P2-1A Surepar Miniature Golf and Driving Range was opened on March 1 by Bill Affleck. The following selected events and transactions occurred during March:

Mar. 1 Invested $60,000 cash in the business.

3 Purchased Lee's Golf Land for $38,000 cash. The price consists of land $23,000, building $9,000, and equipment $6,000. (Make one compound entry.)

5 Advertised the opening of the driving range and miniature golf course, paying advertising expenses of $1,600.

6 Paid cash $1,480 for a one-year insurance policy.

10 Purchased golf clubs and other equipment for $2,600 from Parton Company payable in 30 days.

18 Received $800 in cash for golf fees earned.

19 Sold 100 coupon books for $15 each. Each book contains 10 coupons that enable the holder to play one round of miniature golf or to hit one bucket of golf balls.

25 Withdrew $1,000 cash for personal use.

30 Paid salaries of $600.

30 Paid Parton Company in full.

31 Received $500 cash for fees earned.

Bill Affleck uses the following accounts: Cash; Prepaid Insurance; Land; Buildings; Equipment; Accounts Payable; Unearned Revenue; Bill Affleck, Capital; Bill Affleck, Drawing; Golf Revenue; Advertising Expense; and Salaries Expense.

Instructions

Journalize the March transactions.

Journalize transactions, post, and prepare a trial balance.

(SO 2, 4, 6, 7)

P2-2A Judi Dench is a licensed architect. During the first month of the operation of her business, the following events and transactions occurred.

April 1 Invested $25,000 cash.

1 Hired a secretary-receptionist at a salary of $300 per week payable monthly.

2 Paid office rent for the month $800.

3 Purchased architectural supplies on account from Halo Company $1,500.

10 Completed blueprints on a carport and billed client $900 for services.
11 Received $500 cash advance from R. Welk for the design of a new home.
20 Received $1,500 cash for services completed and delivered to P. Donahue.
30 Paid secretary-receptionist for the month $1,500.
30 Paid $600 to Halo Company for accounts payable due.

Judi uses the following chart of accounts: No. 101 Cash, No. 112 Accounts Receivable, No. 126 Supplies, No. 201 Accounts Payable, No. 205 Unearned Revenue, No. 301 Judi Dench, Capital, No. 400 Service Revenue, No. 726 Salaries Expense, and No. 729 Rent Expense.

Instructions

(a) Journalize the transactions.

(b) Post to the ledger accounts.

(c) Prepare a trial balance on April 30, 2005.

Trial balance totals $28,800

P2-3A Chambers Brokerage Services was formed on May 1, 2005. The following transactions took place during the first month.

Journalize transactions, post, and prepare a trial balance and financial statements.

(SO 2, 4, 6, 7)

Transactions on May 1:

1. Dennis Chambers invested $120,000 cash in the company, as its sole owner.
2. Hired two employees to work in the warehouse. They will each be paid a salary of $2,000 per month.
3. Signed a 2-year rental agreement on a warehouse; paid $36,000 cash in advance for the first year. (*Hint:* The portion of the cost related to May 2005 is an expense for this month.)
4. Purchased furniture and equipment costing $70,000. A cash payment of $20,000 was made immediately; the remainder will be paid in 6 months.
5. Paid $3,000 cash for a one-year insurance policy on the furniture and equipment. (*Hint:* The portion of the cost related to May 2005 is an expense for this month.)

Transactions during the remainder of the month:

6. Purchased basic office supplies for $1,000 cash.
7. Purchased more office supplies for $3,000 on account.
8. Total revenues earned were $30,000—$10,000 cash and $20,000 on account.
9. Paid $800 to suppliers for accounts payable due.
10. Received $5,000 from customers in payment of accounts receivable.
11. Received utility bills in the amount of $400, to be paid next month.
12. Paid the monthly salaries of the two employees, totalling $4,000.

Instructions

(a) Prepare journal entries to record each of the events listed.

(b) Post the journal entries to T accounts.

(c) Prepare a trial balance as of May 31, 2005.

(d) Prepare an income statement and a statement of owner's equity for Chambers Brokerage Services for the month ended May 31, 2005, and a balance sheet as of May 31, 2005.

Trial balance totals $202,600

P2-4A The trial balance of Ron Salem Co. shown below does not balance.

Prepare a correct trial balance.

(SO 7)

RON SALEM CO.
Trial Balance
June 30, 2005

	Debit	Credit
Cash		$ 3,840
Accounts Receivable	$ 3,231	
Supplies	800	
Equipment	3,000	
Accounts Payable		2,666
Unearned Revenue	2,200	
R. Salem, Capital		9,000
R. Salem, Drawing	800	
Service Revenue		2,380
Salaries Expense	3,400	
Office Expense	910	
	$14,341	$17,886

Each of the listed accounts has a normal balance per the general ledger. An examination of the ledger and journal reveals the following errors.

1. Cash received from a customer in payment of its account was debited for $570, and Accounts Receivable was credited for the same amount. The actual collection was for $750.
2. The purchase of a typewriter on account for $340 was recorded as a debit to Supplies for $340 and a credit to Accounts Payable for $340.
3. Services were performed on account for a client for $890. Accounts Receivable was debited for $890, and Service Revenue was credited for $89.
4. A debit posting to Salaries Expense of $367 was omitted.
5. A payment of a balance due for $309 was credited to Cash for $309 and credited to Accounts Payable for $390.
6. The withdrawal of $500 cash for Salem's personal use was debited to Salaries Expense for $500 and credited to Cash for $500.

Instructions

Trial balance totals $16,348

Prepare a correct trial balance. (*Hint:* It helps to prepare the correct journal entry for the transaction described and compare it to the mistake made).

Journalize transactions, post, and prepare a trial balance.

(SO 2, 4, 6, 7)

P2-5A   The Russo Theater, owned by Alan Russo, will begin operations in March. The Russo will be unique in that it will show only triple features of sequential theme movies. As of March 1, the ledger of Russo showed: No. 101 Cash $16,000; No. 140 Land $42,000; No. 145 Buildings (concession stand, projection room, ticket booth, and screen) $18,000; No. 157 Equipment $16,000; No. 201 Accounts Payable $12,000; and No. 301 A. Russo, Capital $80,000. During the month of March the following events and transactions occurred.

Mar. 2   Rented the three *Star Wars* movies (*Star Wars, The Empire Strikes Back,* and *The Return of the Jedi*) to be shown for the first 3 weeks of March. The film rental was $9,000; $3,000 was paid in cash and $6,000 will be paid on March 10.
       3   Ordered the first three *Star Trek* movies to be shown the last 10 days of March. It will cost $300 per night.
       9   Received $6,500 cash from admissions.
      10   Paid balance due on *Star Wars* movies rental and $3,000 on March 1 accounts payable.
      11   Russo Theater contracted with M. Brewer Company to operate the concession stand. Brewer is to pay 10% of gross concession receipts (payable monthly) for the right to operate the concession stand.
      12   Paid advertising expenses $800.
      20   Received $7,200 cash from customers for admissions.
      20   Received the *Star Trek* movies and paid the rental fee of $3,000.
      31   Paid salaries of $4,800.
      31   Received statement from M. Brewer showing gross receipts from concessions of $8,000 and the balance due to Russo Theater of $800 ($8,000 × 10%) for March. Brewer paid one-half the balance due and will remit the remainder on April 5.
      31   Received $12,000 cash from customers for admissions.

In addition to the accounts identified above, the chart of accounts includes: No. 112 Accounts Receivable, No. 405 Admission Revenue, No. 406 Concession Revenue, No. 610 Advertising Expense, No. 632 Film Rental Expense, and No. 726 Salaries Expense.

Instructions
(a) Enter the beginning balances in the ledger. Insert a check mark (✓) in the reference column of the ledger for the beginning balance.
(b) Journalize the March transactions.
(c) Post the March journal entries to the ledger. Assume that all entries are posted from page 1 of the journal.

Trial balance totals $115,500

(d) Prepare a trial balance on March 31, 2005.

PROBLEMS: SET B

P2-1B Frontier Park was started on April 1 by C. J. Amaro. The following selected events and transactions occurred during April.

Journalize a series of transactions.

(SO 2, 4)

Apr. 1 Amaro invested $50,000 cash in the business.
      4 Purchased land costing $30,000 for cash.
      8 Incurred advertising expense of $1,800 on account.
     11 Paid salaries to employees $1,500.
     12 Hired park manager at a salary of $4,000 per month, effective May 1.
     13 Paid $1,500 cash for a one-year insurance policy.
     17 Withdrew $600 cash for personal use.
     20 Received $5,700 in cash for admission fees.
     25 Sold 100 coupon books for $25 each. Each book contains 10 coupons that entitle the holder to one admission to the park.
     30 Received $8,900 in cash admission fees.
     30 Paid $900 on balance owed for advertising incurred on April 8.

Amaro uses the following accounts: Cash; Prepaid Insurance; Land; Accounts Payable; Unearned Admission Revenue; C. J. Amaro, Capital; C. J. Amaro, Drawing; Admission Revenue; Advertising Expense; and Salaries Expense.

Instructions
Journalize the April transactions.

P2-2B Kara Shin is a licensed CPA. During the first month of operations of her business, the following events and transactions occurred.

Journalize transactions, post, and prepare a trial balance.

(SO 2, 4, 6, 7)

May 1 Shin invested $20,000 cash.
     2 Hired a secretary-receptionist at a salary of $1,000 per month.
     3 Purchased $1,500 of supplies on account from Read Supply Company.
     7 Paid office rent of $900 cash for the month.
    11 Completed a tax assignment and billed client $2,100 for services provided.
    12 Received $3,500 advance on a management consulting engagement.
    17 Received cash of $1,200 for services completed for H. Arnold Co.
    31 Paid secretary-receptionist $1,000 salary for the month.
    31 Paid 40% of balance due Read Supply Company.

Kara uses the following chart of accounts: No. 101 Cash, No. 112 Accounts Receivable, No. 126 Supplies, No. 201 Accounts Payable, No. 205 Unearned Revenue, No. 301 Kara Shin, Capital, No. 400 Service Revenue, No. 726 Salaries Expense, and No. 729 Rent Expense.

Instructions
(a) Journalize the transactions.
(b) Post to the ledger accounts.
(c) Prepare a trial balance on May 31, 2005.

Trial balance totals $27,700

P2-3B Mark Hockenberry owns and manages a computer repair service, which had the following trial balance on December 31, 2004 (the end of its fiscal year).

Journalize and post transactions, prepare a trial balance, and determine elements of financial statements.

(SO 2, 4, 6, 7)

BYTE REPAIR SERVICE
Trial Balance
December 31, 2004

Cash	$ 8,000	
Accounts Receivable	15,000	
Parts Inventory	13,000	
Prepaid Rent	3,000	
Shop Equipment	21,000	
Accounts Payable		$19,000
Mark Hockenberry, Capital		41,000
	$60,000	$60,000

Summarized transactions for January 2005 were as follows:

1. Advertising costs, paid in cash, $1,000.
2. Additional repair parts inventory acquired on account $4,000.
3. Miscellaneous expenses, paid in cash, $2,000.
4. Cash collected from customers in payment of accounts receivable $13,000.
5. Cash paid to creditors for accounts payable due $15,000.
6. Repair parts used during January $4,000. (*Hint*: Debit this to Repair Parts Expense.)
7. Repair services performed during January: for cash $5,000; on account $9,000.
8. Wages for January, paid in cash, $3,000.
9. Rent expense for January recorded. However, no cash was paid out for rent during January. A rent payment had been made for 4 months, in advance, on December 1, 2004, in the amount of $4,000.
10. Mark's drawings during January were $2,000.

Instructions

(a) Explain why the December 31, 2004, balance in the Prepaid Rent account is $3,000. (Refer to the Trial Balance and item (9) above.)
(b) Open T accounts for each of the accounts listed in the trial balance, and enter the opening balances for 2005.
(c) Prepare journal entries to record each of the January transactions.
(d) Post the journal entries to the accounts in the ledger. (Add accounts as needed.)
(e) Prepare a trial balance as of January 31, 2005.
(f) Determine the total assets as of January 31, 2005. (It is not necessary to prepare a balance sheet. Simply list the relevant amounts from the trial balance and calculate the total.)

Trial balance totals $63,000

(g) Determine the net income or loss for the month of January 2005. (It is not necessary to prepare an income statement. Simply list the relevant amounts from the trial balance, and calculate the amount of the net income or loss.)

Prepare a correct trial balance.
(SO 7)

P2-4B The trial balance of the Garland Company shown below does not balance.

GARLAND COMPANY
Trial Balance
May 31, 2005

	Debit	Credit
Cash	$3,850	
Accounts Receivable		$2,750
Prepaid Insurance	700	
Equipment	12,000	
Accounts Payable		4,500
Property Taxes Payable	560	
M. Garland, Capital		11,700
Service Revenue	8,690	
Salaries Expense	4,200	
Advertising Expense		1,100
Property Tax Expense	800	
	$30,800	$20,050

Your review of the ledger reveals that each account has a normal balance. You also discover the following errors.

1. The totals of the debit sides of Prepaid Insurance, Accounts Payable, and Property Tax Expense were each understated $100.
2. Transposition errors were made in Accounts Receivable and Service Revenue. Based on postings made, the correct balances were $2,570 and $8,960, respectively.
3. A debit posting to Salaries Expense of $200 was omitted.
4. A $1,000 cash drawing by the owner was debited to M. Garland, Capital for $1,000 and credited to Cash for $1,000.
5. A $520 purchase of supplies on account was debited to Equipment for $520 and credited to Cash for $520.

6. A cash payment of $450 for advertising was debited to Advertising Expense for $45 and credited to Cash for $45.

7. A collection from a customer for $420 was debited to Cash for $420 and credited to Accounts Payable for $420.

Instructions

Prepare a correct trial balance. Note that the chart of accounts includes the following: M. Garland, Drawing, and Supplies. (*Hint:* It helps to prepare the correct journal entry for the transaction described and compare it to the mistake made.)

Trial balance totals $26,720

P2-5B The Lake Theater is owned by Alvin Wasicko. All facilities were completed on March 31. At this time, the ledger showed: No. 101 Cash $6,000; No. 140 Land $10,000; No. 145 Buildings (concession stand, projection room, ticket booth, and screen) $8,000; No. 157 Equipment $6,000; No. 201 Accounts Payable $2,000; No. 275 Mortgage Payable $8,000; and No. 301 Alvin Wasicko, Capital $20,000. During April, the following events and transactions occurred.

Journalize transactions, post, and prepare a trial balance.

(SO 2, 4, 6, 7)

  Peachtree

Apr. 2 Paid film rental of $800 on first movie.
    3 Ordered two additional films at $1,000 each.
    9 Received $1,800 cash from admissions.
   10 Made $2,000 payment on mortgage and $1,000 for accounts payable due.
   11 Lake Theater contracted with R. Zarle Company to operate the concession stand. Zarle is to pay 17% of gross concession receipts (payable monthly) for the right to operate the concession stand.
   12 Paid advertising expenses $300.
   20 Received one of the films ordered on April 3 and was billed $1,000. The film will be shown in April.
   25 Received $5,200 cash from admissions.
   29 Paid salaries $1,600.
   30 Received statement from R. Zarle showing gross concession receipts of $1,000 and the balance due to The Lake Theater of $170 ($1,000 × 17%) for April. Zarle paid one-half of the balance due and will remit the remainder on May 5.
   30 Prepaid $900 rental on special film to be run in May.

In addition to the accounts identified above, the chart of accounts shows: No. 112 Accounts Receivable, No. 136 Prepaid Rentals, No. 405 Admission Revenue, No. 406 Concession Revenue, No. 610 Advertising Expense, No. 632 Film Rental Expense, and No. 726 Salaries Expense.

Instructions

Trial balance totals $35,170

(a) Enter the beginning balances in the ledger as of April 1. Insert a check mark (✓) in the reference column of the ledger for the beginning balance.

(b) Journalize the April transactions.

(c) Post the April journal entries to the ledger. Assume that all entries are posted from page 1 of the journal.

(d) Prepare a trial balance on April 30, 2005.

BROADENING YOUR PERSPECTIVE

Financial Reporting and Analysis

■ **FINANCIAL REPORTING PROBLEM: PepsiCo**

BYP2-1 The financial statements of **PepsiCo** are presented in Appendix A. The notes accompanying the statements contain the following selected accounts, stated in millions of dollars.

Accounts Payable	$4,998	Income Taxes Payable	$ 492
Accounts Receivable	2,531	Interest Expense	178
Property, Plant, and Equipment	7,390	Inventory	1,342

Instructions

(a) Answer the following questions.

    (1) What is the increase and decrease side for each account?

    (2) What is the normal balance for each account?

(b) Identify the probable other account in the transaction and the effect on that account when:

    (1) Accounts Receivable is decreased.

    (2) Accounts Payable is decreased.

    (3) Inventory is increased.

(c) Identify the other account(s) that ordinarily would be involved when:

    (1) Interest Expense is increased.

    (2) Property, Plant, and Equipment is increased.

■ COMPARATIVE ANALYSIS PROBLEM: PepsiCo vs. Coca-Cola

BYP2-2 PepsiCo's financial statements are presented in Appendix A. **Coca-Cola**'s financial statements are presented in Appendix B.

Instructions

(a) Based on the information contained in the financial statements, determine the normal balance of the listed accounts for each company.

PepsiCo	Coca-Cola
1. Inventory	**1.** Accounts Receivable
2. Property, Plant, and Equipment	**2.** Cash and Cash Equivalents
3. Accounts Payable	**3.** Cost of Goods Sold
4. Interest Expense	**4.** Sales (revenue)

(b) Identify the other account ordinarily involved when:

    (1) Accounts Receivable is increased.

    (2) Wages Payable is decreased.

    (3) Property, Plant, and Equipment is increased.

    (4) Interest Expense is increased.

■ INTERPRETING FINANCIAL STATEMENTS: A Global Focus

BYP2-3 Doman Industries Ltd., whose products are sold in 30 countries worldwide, is an integrated Canadian forest products company.

Doman sells the majority of its lumber products in the United States and a significant amount of its pulp products in Asia. Doman also has loans from other countries. For example, the Company borrowed US$160 million at an annual interest rate of 12%. Doman must repay this loan, and interest, in U.S. dollars.

One of the challenges global companies face is to make themselves attractive to investors from other countries. This is difficult to do when different accounting rules in different countries blur the real impact of earnings. For example, in 1998 Doman reported a loss of $2.3 million, using Canadian accounting rules. Had it reported under U.S. accounting rules, its loss would have been $12.1 million.

Many companies that want to be more easily compared with U.S. and other global competitors have switched to U.S. accounting principles. **Canadian National Railway**, **Corel**, **Cott**, **Inco**, and the **Thomson Corporation** are but a few examples of large Canadian companies whose financial statements are now presented in U.S. dollars, which adhere to U.S. GAAP, or are reconciled to U.S. GAAP.

Instructions

(a) Identify advantages and disadvantages that companies should consider when switching to U.S. reporting standards.

(b) Suppose you wish to compare Doman Industries to a U.S.-based competitor. Do you believe the use of country-specific accounting policies would hinder your comparison? If so, explain how.

(c) Suppose you wish to compare Doman Industries to a Canadian-based competitior. If the companies chose to apply generally acceptable Canadian accounting policies differently, how could this affect your comparison of their financial results?

(d) Do you see any significant distinction between comparing statements prepared using generally accepted accounting principles of different countries and comparing statements prepared using generally accepted accounting principles of the same country (e.g., U.S.) but that apply the principles differently?

■ EXPLORING THE WEB

BYP2-4 Much information about specific companies is available on the World Wide Web. Such information includes basic descriptions of the company's location, activities, industry, financial health, and financial performance.

Address: biz.yahoo.com/i, or go to www.wiley.com/college/weygandt

Steps

1. Type in a company name, or use index to find company name.
2. Choose **Profile**. Perform instructions (a)–(c) below.
3. Click on the company's specific industry to identify competitors. Perform instructions (d)–(g) below.

Instructions
Answer the following questions.

(a) What is the company's industry?
(b) What was the company's total sales?
(c) What was the company's net income?
(d) What are the names of four of the company's competitors?
(e) Choose one of these competitors.
(f) What is this competitor's name? What were its sales? What was its net income?
(g) Which of these two companies is larger by size of sales? Which one reported higher net income?

Critical Thinking

■ GROUP DECISION CASE

BYP2-5 Amy Torbert operates Hollins Riding Academy. The academy's primary sources of revenue are riding fees and lesson fees, which are paid on a cash basis. Amy also boards horses for owners, who are billed monthly for boarding fees. In a few cases, boarders pay in advance of expected use. For its revenue transactions, the academy maintains the following accounts: No. 1 Cash, No. 5 Boarding Accounts Receivable, No. 27 Unearned Boarding Revenue, No. 51 Riding Revenue, No. 52 Lesson Revenue, and No. 53 Boarding Revenue.

The academy owns 10 horses, a stable, a riding corral, riding equipment, and office equipment. These assets are accounted for in accounts No. 11 Horses, No. 12 Building No. 13 Riding Corral, No. 14 Riding Equipment, and No. 15 Office Equipment.

For its expenses, the academy maintains the following accounts: No. 6 Hay and Feed Supplies, No. 7 Prepaid Insurance, No. 21 Accounts Payable, No. 60 Salaries Expense, No. 61 Advertising Expense, No. 62 Utilities Expense, No. 63 Veterinary Expense, No. 64 Hay and Feed Expense, and No. 65 Insurance Expense.

Amy makes periodic withdrawals of cash for personal living expenses. To record Amy's equity in the business and her drawings, two accounts are maintained: No. 50 Amy Torbert, Capital, and No. 51 Amy Torbert, Drawing.

During the first month of operations an inexperienced bookkeeper was employed. Amy Torbert asks you to review the following eight entries of the 50 entries made during the month. In each case, the explanation for the entry is correct.

May 1	Cash		18,000	
	Amy Torbert, Capital			18,000
	(Invested $18,000 cash in business)			
5	Cash		250	
	Riding Revenue			250
	(Received $250 cash for lessons provided)			
7	Cash		500	
	Boarding Revenue			500
	(Received $500 for boarding of horses beginning June 1)			

(*continued from p. 83*)

14	Riding Equipment	80	
	Cash		800
	(Purchased desk and other office equipment for $800 cash)		
15	Salaries Expense	400	
	Cash		400
	(Issued check to Amy Torbert for personal use)		
20	Cash	148	
	Riding Revenue		184
	(Received $184 cash for riding fees)		
30	Veterinary Expense	75	
	Accounts Payable		75
	(Received bill of $75 from veterinarian for services rendered)		
31	Hay and Feed Expense	1,500	
	Cash		1,500
	(Purchased an estimated 2 months' supply of feed and hay for $1,500 on account)		

Instructions

With the class divided into groups, answer the following.

(a) Identify each journal entry that is correct. For each journal entry that is incorrect, prepare the entry that should have been made by the bookkeeper.
(b) Which of the incorrect entries would prevent the trial balance from balancing?
(c) What was the correct net income for May, assuming the bookkeeper reported net income of $4,500 after posting all 50 entries?
(d) What was the correct cash balance at May 31, assuming the bookkeeper reported a balance of $12,475 after posting all 50 entries (and the only errors occurred in the items listed above)?

■ COMMUNICATION ACTIVITY

BYP2-6 Shandler's Maid Company offers home cleaning service. Two recurring transactions for the company are billing customers for services rendered and paying employee salaries. For example, on March 15, bills totaling $5,000 were sent to customers and $2,000 was paid in salaries to employees.

Instructions

Write a memo to your instructor that explains and illustrates the steps in the recording process for each of the March 15 transactions. Use the format illustrated in the text under the heading, "The Recording Process Illustrated" (p. 57).

■ ETHICS CASE

BYP2-7 Sara Rankin is the assistant chief accountant at Hokey Company, a manufacturer of computer chips and cellular phones. The company presently has total sales of $20 million. It is the end of the first quarter. Sara is hurriedly trying to prepare a general ledger trial balance so that quarterly financial statements can be prepared and released to management and the regulatory agencies. The total credits on the trial balance exceed the debits by $1,000. In order to meet the 4 p.m. deadline, Sara decides to force the debits and credits into balance by adding the amount of the difference to the Equipment account. She chose Equipment because it is one of the larger account balances; percentage-wise, it will be the least misstated. Sara "plugs" the difference! She believes that the difference will not affect anyone's decisions. She wishes that she had another few days to find the error but realizes that the financial statements are already late.

Instructions

(a) Who are the stakeholders in this situation?
(b) What are the ethical issues involved in this case?
(c) What are Sara's alternatives?

Answers to Self-Study Questions
1. b   **2.** c   **3.** d   **4.** d   **5.** b   **6.** a   **7.** c   **8.** d   **9.** a   **10.** c

Answer to PepsiCo Review It Question 4, p. 50

Normal balances for **PepsiCo** (or any company) are: Cash—debit; Accounts Payable—credit; Interest Expense—debit.

Adjusting
the Accounts

THE NAVIGATOR ✓

Understand **Concepts for Review** ☐

Read **Feature Story** ☐

Scan **Study Objectives** ☐

Read **Preview** ☐

Read text and answer **Before You Go On**
p. 92 ☐   p. 99 ☐   p. 104 ☐   p. 109 ☐

Work **Demonstration Problem** ☐

Review **Summary of Study Objectives** ☐

Answer **Self-Study Questions** ☐

Complete **Assignments** ☐

CONCEPTS FOR REVIEW

Before studying this chapter, you should know or, if necessary, review:

What a double-entry system is.
(Ch. 2, p. 46)

How to increase or decrease assets, liabilities, and owner's equity using debit and
credit procedures.   (Ch. 2, pp. 46–49)

How to journalize a transaction.
(Ch. 2, pp. 51–53)

How to post a transaction.
(Ch. 2, pp. 55–56)

How to prepare a trial balance.
(Ch. 2, pp. 65–66)

THE NAVIGATOR

Timing Is Everything

In Chapter 1 you learned a neat little formula: Net income = Revenues − Expenses. And in Chapter 2 you learned some nice, orderly rules for recording corporate revenue and expense transactions. Guess what? Things are not really that nice and neat. In fact, it is often difficult to determine in what time period some revenues and expenses should be reported. And, in measuring net income, timing is everything.

There are rules that give guidance on these issues. But occasionally these rules are overlooked, misinterpreted, or even intentionally ignored. Consider the following examples.

- **McKesson HBOC**, one of the largest prescription drug distributors, at one time restated its first-quarter earnings because $26.2 million included in healthcare software sales weren't final and should not have been recorded. This negative surprise caused McKesson's share price to plummet 48 percent overnight, from $65.75 to $34.50, wiping out $9 billion in the market value of its stock.
- **Cambridge Biotech Corp.**, which develops vaccines and diagnostic tests for humans and animals, said that it reported revenue from transactions that "don't appear to be bona fide."
- **Media Vision Technology Inc.**, a maker of sound and animation equipment for computers, was accused of operating a "phantom" warehouse to hide inventory for returned products already recorded as sales.
- **Penguin USA**, a book publisher, said that it understated expenses in a number of years because it failed to report expenses for discounts given to customers for paying early.

In each case, accrual accounting concepts were violated. That is, revenues or expenses were not recorded in the proper period, which had a substantial impact on reported income. Their timing was off!

☑ THE NAVIGATOR

After studying this chapter, you should be able to:

1. Explain the time period assumption.
2. Explain the accrual basis of accounting.
3. Explain why adjusting entries are needed.
4. Identify the major types of adjusting entries.
5. Prepare adjusting entries for prepayments.
6. Prepare adjusting entries for accruals.
7. Describe the nature and purpose of an adjusted trial balance.

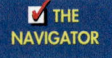

☑ THE NAVIGATOR

In Chapter 2 we examined the recording process through the preparation of the trial balance. Before we will be ready to prepare financial statements from the trial balance, additional steps need to be taken. The timing mismatch between revenues and expenses of the four companies mentioned in our Feature Story illustrates the types of situations that make these additional steps necessary. For example, long-lived assets purchased or constructed in prior accounting years are being used to produce goods and provide services in the current year. What portion of these assets' costs, if any, should be recognized as an expense of the current period? Before financial statements can be prepared, this and other questions relating to the recognition of revenues and expenses must be answered. With the answers in hand, we can then adjust the relevant account balances.

The content and organization of Chapter 3 are as follows.

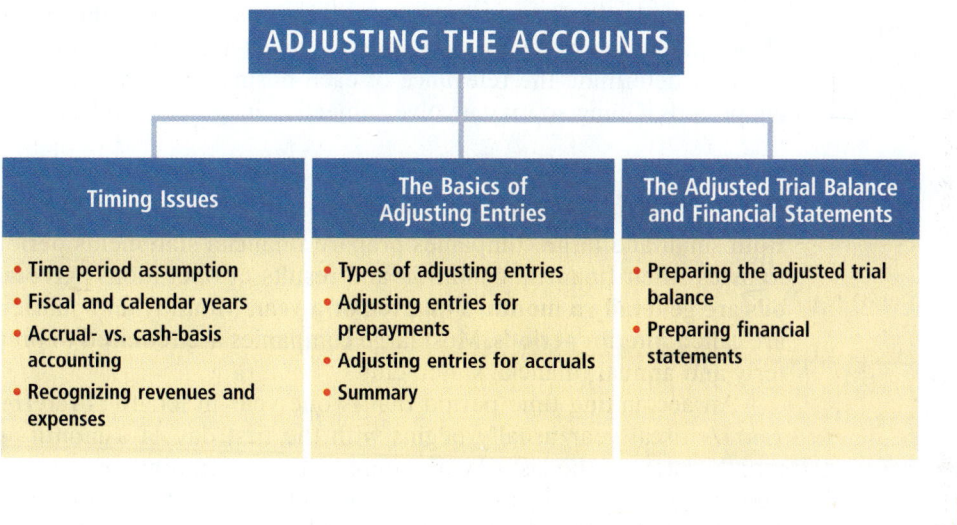

Timing Issues

No adjustments would be necessary if we could wait to prepare financial statements until a company ended its operations. At that point, we could easily determine its final balance sheet and the amount of lifetime income it earned. The following anecdote illustrates one way to compute lifetime income.

STUDY OBJECTIVE 1

Explain the time period assumption.

> A grocery store owner from the old country kept his accounts payable on a spindle, accounts receivable on a note pad, and cash in a cigar box. His daughter, having just passed the CPA exam, chided the father: "I don't understand how you can run your business this way. How do you know what your profits are?"
>
> "Well," the father replied, "when I got off the boat 40 years ago, I had nothing but the pants I was wearing. Today your brother is a doctor, your sister is a college professor, and you are a CPA. Your mother and I have a nice car, a

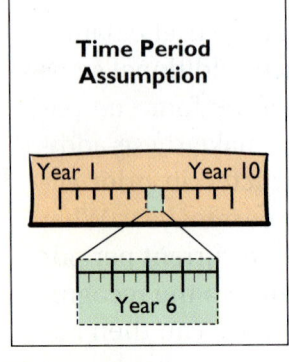

Time Period Assumption

Year 1   Year 10

Year 6

well-furnished house, and a lake home. We have a good business, and everything is paid for. So, you add all that together, subtract the pants, and there's your profit."

Selecting an Accounting Time Period

Although the old grocer may be correct in his evaluation, it is impractical to wait so long for the results of operations. All entities, from the corner grocery, to a global company like **Kellogg**, to your college or university, find it desirable and necessary to report the results of their activities more frequently. For example, management usually wants monthly financial statements, and the Internal Revenue Service requires all businesses to file annual tax returns. Therefore, **accountants divide the economic life of a business into artificial time periods**. This convenient assumption is referred to as the **time period assumption**.

Many business transactions affect more than one of these arbitrary time periods. For example, Farmer Brown's milking machine bought in 2001 and the airplanes purchased by **Delta Air Lines** five years ago are still in use today. Therefore we must determine the relevance of each business transaction to specific accounting periods. Doing so may involve subjective judgments and estimates.

Fiscal and Calendar Years

Both small and large companies prepare financial statements periodically in order to assess their financial condition and results of operations. **Accounting time periods are generally a month, a quarter, or a year.** Monthly and quarterly time periods are called **interim periods**. Most large companies are required to prepare both quarterly and annual financial statements.

An accounting time period that is one year in length is referred to as a **fiscal year.** A fiscal year usually begins with the first day of a month and ends twelve months later on the last day of a month. The accounting period used by most businesses coincides with the **calendar year** (January 1 to December 31). Companies whose fiscal year differs from the calendar year include **Delta Air Lines**, June 30; **Walt Disney Productions**, September 30; and **Kmart Corp.**, January 31. Sometimes a company's year-end will vary from year to year. For example, **PepsiCo**'s fiscal year ends on the Friday closest to December 31, which was December 29 in 2001 and December 28 in 2002.

Accrual- vs. Cash-Basis Accounting

What you will learn in this chapter is **accrual-basis accounting**. Under the accrual basis, transactions that change a company's financial statements are recorded **in the periods in which the events occur.** For example, using the accrual basis to determine net income means recognizing revenues when earned (rather than when the cash is received). It also means recognizing expenses when incurred (rather than when paid). Information presented on an accrual basis reveals relationships likely to be important in predicting future results. Under accrual accounting, revenues are recognized when services are performed, so trends in revenues are thus more meaningful for decision-making.

An alternative to the accrual basis is the cash basis. Under **cash-basis accounting**, revenue is recorded when cash is received, and an expense is recorded when cash is paid. The cash basis often leads to misleading financial statements. It fails to record revenue that has been earned but for which the cash has not been received. Also, expenses are not matched with earned revenues. **Cash-basis accounting is not in accordance with generally accepted accounting principles (GAAP).**

Most companies use accrual-basis accounting. Individuals and some small companies use cash-basis accounting. The cash basis is justified for small businesses because they often have few receivables and payables. Accountants are sometimes asked to convert cash-basis records to the accrual basis. As you might expect, extensive adjusting entries are required for this task.

Recognizing Revenues and Expenses

Determining the amount of revenues and expenses to be reported in a given accounting period can be difficult. To help in this task, accountants have developed two principles as part of generally accepted accounting principles (GAAP): the revenue recognition principle and the matching principle.

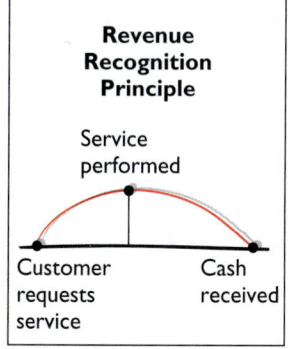

Revenue Recognition Principle

The **revenue recognition principle** dictates that revenue be recognized in the accounting period in which it is earned. *recorded* **In a service enterprise, revenue is considered to be earned at the time the service is performed.** To illustrate, assume that a dry cleaning business cleans clothing on June 30 but customers do not claim and pay for their clothes until the first week of July. Under the revenue recognition principle, revenue is earned in June when the service is performed, rather than in July when the cash is received. At June 30, the dry cleaner would report a receivable on its balance sheet and revenue in its income statement for the service performed.

Accountants follow the approach of "let expenses follow revenues." That is, expense recognition is tied to revenue recognition. In the preceding example, this principle means that the salary expense incurred in performing the cleaning service on June 30 should be reported in the income statement for the same period in which the service revenue is recognized. The critical issue in expense recognition is when the expense makes its contribution to revenue. This may or may not be the same period in which the expense is paid. If the salary incurred on June 30 is not paid until July, the dry cleaner would report salaries payable on its June 30 balance sheet. The practice of expense recognition is referred to as the **matching principle** because it dictates that efforts (expenses) be matched with accomplishments (revenues).

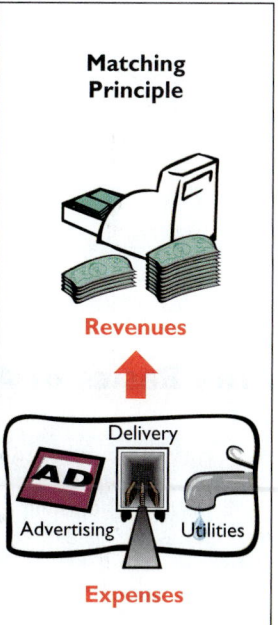

Once the economic life of a business has been divided into artificial time periods, the revenue recognition and matching principles can be applied. This one assumption and two principles thus provide guidelines as to when revenues and expenses should be reported. These relationships are shown in Illustration 3-1 (page 92).

ACCOUNTING IN ACTION   **Business Insight**

Suppose you are a filmmaker like George Lucas and spend $11 million to produce a film such as *Star Wars*. Over what period should the cost be expensed? It should be expensed over the economic life of the film. But what is its economic life? The filmmaker must estimate how much revenue will be earned from box office sales, video sales, television, and games and toys—a period that could be less than a year or more than 20 years, as is the case for **Twentieth Century Fox**'s *Star Wars*. Originally released in 1977, and rereleased in 1997, domestic revenues total nearly $500 million for *Star Wars* and continue to grow. This situation demonstrates the difficulty of properly matching expenses to revenues.

Source: Star Trek Newsletter, 22.

Illustration 3-1
GAAP relationships in revenue and expense recognition

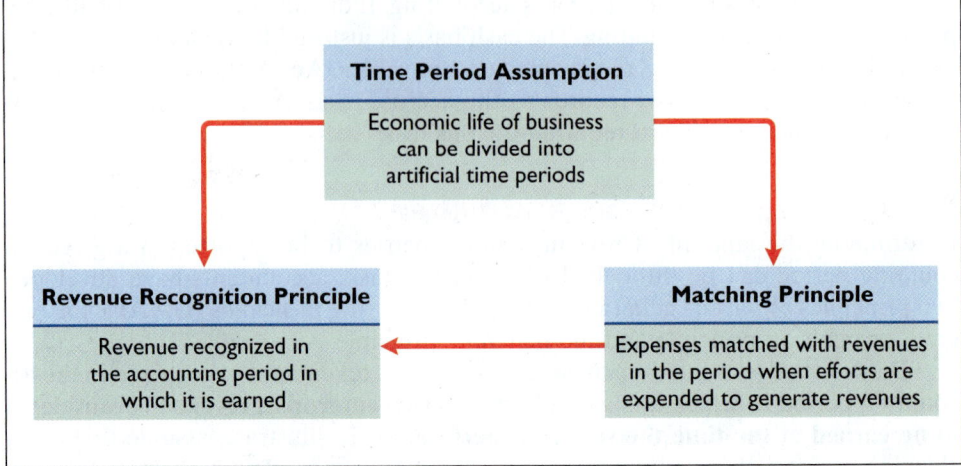

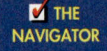

BEFORE YOU GO ON...

Review It

1. What is the relevance of the time period assumption to accounting?
2. What are the revenue recognition and matching principles?

The Basics of Adjusting Entries

STUDY OBJECTIVE 3

Explain why adjusting entries are needed.

Accounting Cycle Tutorial—
Making Adjusting Entries

In order for revenues to be recorded in the period in which they are earned, and for expenses to be recognized in the period in which they are incurred, adjusting entries are made at the end of the accounting period. In short, **adjusting entries are needed to ensure that the revenue recognition and matching principles are followed**.

Adjusting entries make it possible to report on the balance sheet the appropriate assets, liabilities, and owner's equity at the statement date and to report on the income statement the proper net income (or loss) for the period. However, the trial balance—the first pulling together of the transaction data—may not contain up-to-date and complete data. This is true for the following reasons.

1. Some events are not journalized daily because it is inexpedient to do so. Examples are the consumption of supplies and the earning of wages by employees.
2. Some costs are not journalized during the accounting period because they expire with the passage of time rather than through recurring daily transactions. Examples are equipment deterioration, and rent and insurance.
3. Some items may be unrecorded. An example is a utility service bill that will not be received until the next accounting period.

Adjusting entries are required every time financial statements are prepared. The starting point is an analysis of each account in the trial balance to determine whether it is complete and up-to-date. The analysis requires a thorough understanding of the company's operations and the interrelationship of accounts. Preparing adjusting entries is often an involved process. The company may need to make inventory counts of supplies and repair parts. It may need to prepare supporting schedules of insurance policies, rental agreements, and other contractual commitments. Adjustments are often prepared after the balance sheet date. However, the adjusting entries are dated as of the balance sheet date.

HELPFUL HINT

Adjusting entries are needed to enable financial statements to be in conformity with GAAP.

Types of Adjusting Entries

Adjusting entries can be classified as either prepayments or accruals. Each of these classes has two subcategories as shown in Illustration 3-2.

Prepayments
1. **Prepaid Expenses.** Expenses paid in cash and recorded as assets before they are used or consumed.
2. **Unearned Revenues.** Cash received and recorded as liabilities before revenue is earned.

Accruals
1. **Accrued Revenues.** Revenues earned but not yet received in cash or recorded.
2. **Accrued Expenses.** Expenses incurred but not yet paid in cash or recorded.

Illustration 3-2
Categories of adjusting entries

Specific examples and explanations of each type of adjustment are given on the following pages. Each example is based on the October 31 trial balance of Pioneer Advertising Agency, from Chapter 2, reproduced in Illustration 3-3.

Illustration 3-3
Trial balance

PIONEER ADVERTISING AGENCY
Trial Balance
October 31, 2005

	Debit	Credit
Cash	$15,200	
Advertising Supplies	2,500	
Prepaid Insurance	600	
Office Equipment	5,000	
Notes Payable		$ 5,000
Accounts Payable		2,500
Unearned Revenue		1,200
C. R. Byrd, Capital		10,000
C. R. Byrd, Drawing	500	
Service Revenue		10,000
Salaries Expense	4,000	
Rent Expense	900	
	$28,700	$28,700

We assume that Pioneer Advertising uses an accounting period of one month. Thus, monthly adjusting entries will be made. The entries will be dated October 31.

Adjusting Entries for Prepayments

As indicated earlier, prepayments are either prepaid expenses or unearned revenues. Adjusting entries for prepayments are required to record the portion of the prepayment that represents the **expense incurred or the revenue earned** in the current accounting period.

If an adjustment is needed for prepayments, the asset and liability are overstated and the related expense and revenue are understated before the adjustment. For example, in the trial balance, the balance in the asset Advertising Supplies shows only supplies purchased. This balance is overstated; a related expense account, Advertising Supplies Expense, is understated because the cost of supplies used has not been recognized. Thus the adjusting entry for prepayments will **decrease a balance sheet account** (Advertising Supplies) and **increase an income statement account** (Advertising Supplies Expense).

Prepaid Expenses

As stated on page 93, expenses paid in cash and recorded as assets before they are used or consumed are called **prepaid expenses** or **prepayments**. When a cost is prepaid, an asset account is debited to show the service or benefit that will be received in the future. Prepayments often occur in regard to insurance, supplies, advertising, and rent. In addition, prepayments are made when buildings and equipment are purchased.

Prepaid expenses expire either with the passage of time (e.g., rent and insurance) or through use and consumption (e.g., supplies). The expiration of these costs does not require daily journal entries, which would be unnecessary and impractical. Instead, it is customary to postpone recognizing cost expirations until financial statements are prepared. At each statement date, adjusting entries are made for two purposes: (1) to record the expenses that apply to the current accounting period, and (2) to show the unexpired costs in the asset accounts.

Prior to adjustment, assets are overstated and expenses are understated. Therefore, as shown in Illustration 3-4, **an adjusting entry for prepaid expense results in an increase (debit) to an expense account and a decrease (credit) to an asset account**.

Illustration 3-4
Adjusting entries for prepaid expenses

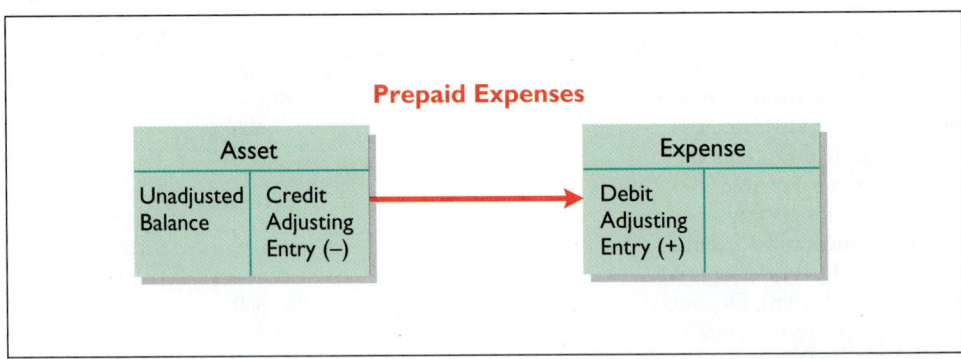

SUPPLIES. Businesses use various types of supplies. For example, a CPA firm will have **office supplies** such as stationery, envelopes, and accounting paper. An advertising firm will have **advertising supplies** such as graph paper, video film, and poster paper. Supplies are generally debited to an asset account when they are acquired. In the course of operations, supplies are depleted, but recognition of supplies used is deferred until the adjustment process. At that point, a physical inventory (count) of supplies is taken. The difference between the balance in the Supplies (asset) account and the cost of supplies on hand represents the supplies used (expense) for the period.

Pioneer Advertising Agency purchased advertising supplies costing $2,500 on October 5. A debit (increase) was made to the asset Advertising Supplies. This account shows a balance of $2,500 in the October 31 trial balance. An inventory count at the close of business on October 31 reveals that $1,000 of supplies are still on hand. Thus, the cost of supplies used is $1,500 ($2,500–$1,000), and the following adjusting entry is made.

Oct. 31	Advertising Supplies Expense	1,500	
	Advertising Supplies		1,500
	(To record supplies used)		

After the adjusting entry is posted, the two supplies accounts show:

Illustration 3-5
Supplies accounts after adjustment

Advertising Supplies				Advertising Supplies Expense		
10/5	2,500	10/31 **Adj.**	**1,500**	10/31 **Adj.**	**1,500**	
10/31 Bal.	1,000					

The asset account Advertising Supplies now shows a balance of $1,000, which is the cost of supplies on hand at the statement date. In addition, Advertising Supplies Expense shows a balance of $1,500, which equals the cost of supplies used in October. **If the adjusting entry is not made, October expenses will be understated and net income overstated by $1,500. Also, both assets and owner's equity will be overstated by $1,500 on the October 31 balance sheet.**

ACCOUNTING IN ACTION Business Insight

In the past, the costs of media advertising for burgers, bleaches, athletic shoes, and such products were sometimes recorded as assets and expensed in subsequent periods as sales took place. The reasoning behind this treatment was that long ad campaigns provided benefits over multiple accounting periods. Today this treatment is no longer allowed because it was decided that the benefits were too difficult to measure. Instead, advertising costs must be expensed when the advertising takes place. The issue is important because the outlays for advertising can be substantial. Recent (2001) big spenders: **Coca-Cola** spent $2 billion, **PepsiCo., Inc.** $1.7 billion, **Campbell Soup Company** $1.7 billion, and **JCPenney Company** $947 million.

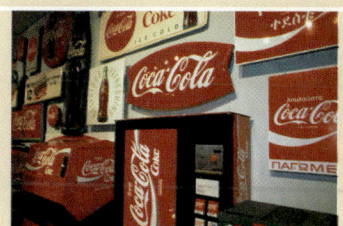

INSURANCE.   Most companies have fire and theft insurance on merchandise and equipment, personal liability insurance for accidents suffered by customers, and automobile insurance on company cars and trucks. The cost of insurance protection is determined by the payment of insurance premiums. The minimum term of coverage is usually one year, but three- to five-year terms are available and offer lower annual premiums. Insurance premiums normally are charged to the asset account Prepaid Insurance when paid. At the financial statement date it is necessary to debit (increase) Insurance Expense and credit (decrease) Prepaid Insurance for the cost that has expired during the period.

On October 4, Pioneer Advertising Agency paid $600 for a one-year fire insurance policy. The effective date of coverage was October 1. The premium was charged to Prepaid Insurance when it was paid, and this account shows a balance of $600 in the October 31 trial balance. Analysis reveals that $50 ($600 ÷ 12) of insurance expires each month. Thus, the following adjusting entry is made.

Insurance

Oct.4
  Insurance purchased; record asset

Insurance Policy			
Oct	Nov	Dec	Jan
$50	$50	$50	$50
Feb	March	April	May
$50	$50	$50	$50
June	July	Aug	Sept
$50	$50	$50	$50
1 YEAR $600			

A = L + OE
−50   −50 Exp

Cash Flows
no effect

Oct.31
  Insurance expired; record insurance expense

Oct. 31	Insurance Expense	50	
	Prepaid Insurance		50
	(To record insurance expired)		

After the adjusting entry is posted, the accounts show:

Illustration 3-6
Insurance accounts after
adjustment

Prepaid Insurance				Insurance Expense		
10/4	600	10/31 **Adj.**	50	10/31 **Adj.**	50	
10/31 Bal.	550					

The asset Prepaid Insurance shows a balance of $550. This amount represents the unexpired cost for the remaining eleven months of coverage. The $50 balance in Insurance Expense is equal to the insurance cost that has expired in October. **If this adjustment is not made, October expenses will be understated by $50 and net income overstated by $50. Also, both assets and owner's equity will be overstated by $50 on the October 31 balance sheet**.

DEPRECIATION.   A business enterprise typically owns productive facilities such as buildings, equipment, and vehicles. Because these assets provide service for a number of years, each is recorded as an asset, rather than an expense, in the year it is acquired. As explained in Chapter 1, such assets are recorded at cost, as required by the cost principle. The term of service is referred to as the **useful life**.

According to the matching principle, a portion of the cost of a long-lived asset should be reported as an expense during each period of the asset's useful life. **Depreciation** is the allocation of the cost of an asset to expense over its useful life in a rational and systematic manner.

Depreciation

Oct.2

Office equipment purchased;
record asset

Office Equipment			
Oct	Nov	Dec	Jan
$40	$40	$40	$40
Feb	March	April	May
$40	$40	$40	$40
June	July	Aug	Sept
$40	$40	$40	$40
Depreciation = $480/year			

Oct.31
Depreciation recognized;
record depreciation expense

Need for Depreciation Adjustment. From an accounting standpoint, acquiring productive facilities is viewed essentially as a long-term prepayment for services. The need for periodic adjusting entries for depreciation is, therefore, the same as that for other prepaid expenses: to recognize the cost that has expired (expense) during the period and to report the unexpired cost (asset) at the end of the period.

At the time an asset is acquired, its useful life cannot be known with certainty. The asset may be useful for a longer or shorter time than expected, depending on such factors as actual use, deterioration due to the elements, or obsolescence. Thus, you should recognize that **depreciation is an estimate** rather than a factual measurement of the cost that has expired. A common procedure in computing depreciation expense is to divide the cost of the asset by its useful life. For example, if cost is $10,000 and useful life is expected to be 10 years, annual depreciation is $1,000.[1]

For Pioneer Advertising, depreciation on the office equipment is estimated to be $480 a year, or $40 per month. Accordingly, depreciation for October is recognized by the following adjusting entry.

A	=	L	+	OE
−40				−40 Exp

Cash Flows
no effect

Oct. 31	Depreciation Expense	40	
	Accumulated Depreciation—Office Equipment		40
	(To record monthly depreciation)		

After the adjusting entry is posted, the accounts show:

Illustration 3-7
Accounts after adjustment
for depreciation

Office Equipment	
10/1	5,000

Accumulated Depreciation—Office Equipment		Depreciation Expense	
	10/31 **Adj.** 40	10/31 **Adj.** 40	

[1]Additional consideration is given to computing depreciation expense in Chapter 10.

The balance in the accumulated depreciation account will increase $40 each month. After journalizing and posting the adjusting entry at November 30, the balance will be $80; at December 31, $120; and so on.

Statement Presentation. Accumulated Depreciation—Office Equipment is a contra asset account. A **contra asset account** is one that is offset against an asset account on the balance sheet. This accumulated depreciation account appears just after Office Equipment on the balance sheet. Its normal balance is a credit. An alternative would be to credit (decrease) Office Equipment directly for the depreciation each month. But use of the contra account provides disclosure of **both the original cost** of the equipment **and the total cost that has expired to date**. In the balance sheet, Accumulated Depreciation—Office Equipment is deducted from the related asset account as follows.

| Office equipment | $5,000 | |
| Less: Accumulated depreciation—office equipment | 40 | **$4,960** |

Illustration 3-8
Balance sheet presentation of accumulated depreciation

The difference between the cost of any depreciable asset and its related accumulated depreciation is referred to as the **book value** of that asset. In Illustration 3-8, the book value of the equipment at the balance sheet date is $4,960. You should realize that the book value is generally different from the market value (the price at which the asset could be sold in the marketplace). The reason the two are different is that depreciation is a means of cost allocation, not a matter of valuation.

Depreciation expense also identifies that portion of the asset's cost that has expired in October. As in the case of other prepaid adjustments, the omission of this adjusting entry would cause total assets, total owner's equity, and net income to be overstated and depreciation expense to be understated.

If the company owns additional equipment, such as delivery or store equipment, or if it has buildings, depreciation expense is recorded on each of those items. Related accumulated depreciation accounts also are established, such as: Accumulated Depreciation—Delivery Equipment; Accumulated Depreciation—Store Equipment; and Accumulated Depreciation—Buildings.

Unearned Revenues

As stated on page 93, cash received and recorded as liabilities before revenue is earned is called **unearned revenues**. Such items as rent, magazine subscriptions, and customer deposits for future service may result in unearned revenues. Airlines such as **United**, **American**, and **Delta** treat receipts from the sale of tickets as unearned revenue until the flight service is provided. Similarly, college tuition received prior to the start of a semester is considered unearned revenue. Unearned revenues are the opposite of prepaid expenses. Indeed, unearned revenue on the books of one company is likely to be a prepayment on the books of the company that has made the advance payment. For example, if identical accounting periods are assumed, a landlord will have unearned rent revenue when a tenant has prepaid rent.

When the payment is received for services to be provided in a future accounting period, an unearned revenue account (a liability) should be credited (increased) to recognize the obligation that exists. Later, unearned revenues are earned by providing service to a customer. It may not be practical to make daily journal entries as the revenue is earned. In such cases, recognition of earned revenue is delayed until the end of the period. Then an adjusting entry is made to record the revenue that has been earned and to show the liability that remains. Typically, prior to adjustment, liabilities are overstated and revenues are understated. Therefore, as shown in Illustration 3-9 (page 98), **the adjusting entry for unearned revenues results in a decrease (a debit) to a liability account and an increase (a credit) to a revenue account**.

Unearned Revenues

Oct.2 — Thank you in advance for your work

I will finish by Dec. 31

$1,200

Cash is received in advance; liability is recorded

Oct.31
Service is provided; revenue is recorded.

Illustration 3-9
Adjusting entries for
unearned revenues

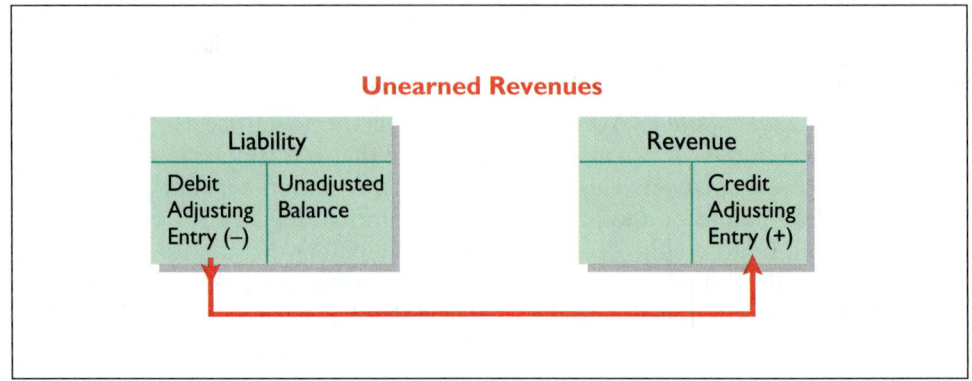

Unearned Revenues

Liability	
Debit Adjusting Entry (−)	Unadjusted Balance

Revenue
Credit Adjusting Entry (+)

A	=	L	+	OE
		−400		+400 Rev

Cash Flows
no effect

Pioneer Advertising Agency received $1,200 on October 2 from R. Knox for advertising services expected to be completed by December 31. The payment was credited to Unearned Revenue; this account shows a balance of $1,200 in the October 31 trial balance. Analysis reveals that $400 of those fees was earned in October. The following adjusting entry is made.

Oct. 31	Unearned Revenue	400	
	Service Revenue		400
	(To record revenue for services provided)		

After the adjusting entry is posted, the accounts show:

Illustration 3-10
Revenue accounts after prepayments adjustment

Unearned Revenue				**Service Revenue**	
10/31 **Adj.** 400	10/2	1,200		10/31 Bal.	10,000
	10/31 Bal.	800		31 **Adj.**	400

The liability Unearned Revenue now shows a balance of $800. This amount represents the remaining prepaid advertising services to be performed in the future. At the same time, Service Revenue shows total revenue of $10,400 earned in October. **If this adjustment were not made, revenues and net income would be understated by $400 in the income statement. Also, liabilities would be overstated and owner's equity would be understated by $400 on the October 31 balance sheet.**

 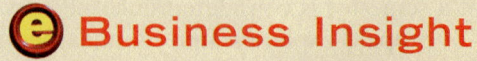

ACCOUNTING IN ACTION **e Business Insight**

Many early dot-com investors focused almost entirely on revenue growth instead of net income. Many early dot-com companies earned most of their revenue from selling advertising space on their Web sites. To boost reported revenue, some sites began swapping ad space. Company A would put an ad for its Web site on company B's Web site, and company B would put an ad for its Web site on company A's Web site. No money ever changed hands, but each company recorded revenue (for the value of the space that it gave up on its site) and expense (for the value of its ad that it placed on the other company's site). This practice did little to boost net income and resulted in no additional cash inflow—but it did boost *reported* revenue. This practice was quickly put to an end because it did not meet the criteria of the revenue recognition principle.

BEFORE YOU GO ON...

Review It

1. What are the four types of adjusting entries?

2. What is the effect on assets, owner's equity, expenses, and net income if a prepaid expense adjusting entry is not made?

3. What is the effect on liabilities, owner's equity, revenues, and net income if an unearned revenue adjusting entry is not made?

4. Using **PepsiCo**'s Consolidated Statement of Income, what was the amount of depreciation expense for 2002 and 2001? (See Note 4 to the financial statements.) The answer to this question is provided on page 131.

Do It

The ledger of Hammond, Inc. on March 31, 2005, includes the following selected accounts before adjusting entries.

	Debit	Credit
Prepaid Insurance	3,600	
Office Supplies	2,800	
Office Equipment	25,000	
Accumulated Depreciation—Office Equipment		5,000
Unearned Revenue		9,200

An analysis of the accounts shows the following.

1. Insurance expires at the rate of $100 per month.

2. Supplies on hand total $800.

3. The office equipment depreciates $200 a month.

4. One-half of the unearned revenue was earned in March.

Prepare the adjusting entries for the month of March.

ACTION PLAN

■ Make adjusting entries at the end of the period for revenues earned and expenses incurred in the period.

■ Don't forget to make adjusting entries for prepayments. Failure to adjust for prepayments leads to overstatement of the asset or liability and related understatement of the expense or revenue.

SOLUTION

		Debit	Credit
1.	Insurance Expense	100	
	Prepaid Insurance		100
	(To record insurance expired)		
2.	Office Supplies Expense	2,000	
	Office Supplies		2,000
	(To record supplies used)		
3.	Depreciation Expense	200	
	Accumulated Depreciation—Office Equipment		200
	(To record monthly depreciation)		
4.	Unearned Revenue	4,600	
	Service Revenue		4,600
	(To record revenue for services provided)		

Related exercise material: *BE3-3, BE3-4, BE3-5, BE3-6, E3-2, E3-3, E3-4, E3-5, E3-6, E3-7, E3-8, and E3-9.*

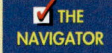

STUDY OBJECTIVE 6

Prepare adjusting entries for accruals.

Adjusting Entries for Accruals

The second category of adjusting entries is **accruals**. Adjusting entries for accruals are required to record revenues earned and expenses incurred in the current accounting period that have not been recognized through daily entries.

An accrual adjustment is needed when various accounts are understated: the revenue account and the related asset account, and/or the expense account and the related liability account. Thus, the adjusting entry for accruals will **increase both a balance sheet and an income statement account**.

Accrued Revenues

Oct.31

My fee is $200

Revenue and receivable are recorded for unbilled services

Nov.

Cash is received; receivable is reduced

Accrued Revenues

As explained on page 93, revenues earned but not yet received in cash or recorded at the statement date are accrued revenues. Accrued revenues may accumulate (accrue) with the passing of time, as in the case of interest revenue and rent revenue. Or they may result from services that have been performed but are neither billed nor collected, as in the case of commissions and fees. The former are unrecorded because the earning of interest and rent does not involve daily transactions. The latter may be unrecorded because only a portion of the total service has been provided.

An adjusting entry is required for two purposes: (1) to show the receivable that exists at the balance sheet date, and (2) to record the revenue that has been earned during the period. Prior to adjustment both assets and revenues are understated. Therefore, as shown in Illustration 3-11, **an adjusting entry for accrued revenues results in an increase (a debit) to an asset account and an increase (a credit) to a revenue account**.

Illustration 3-11
Adjusting entries for accrued revenues

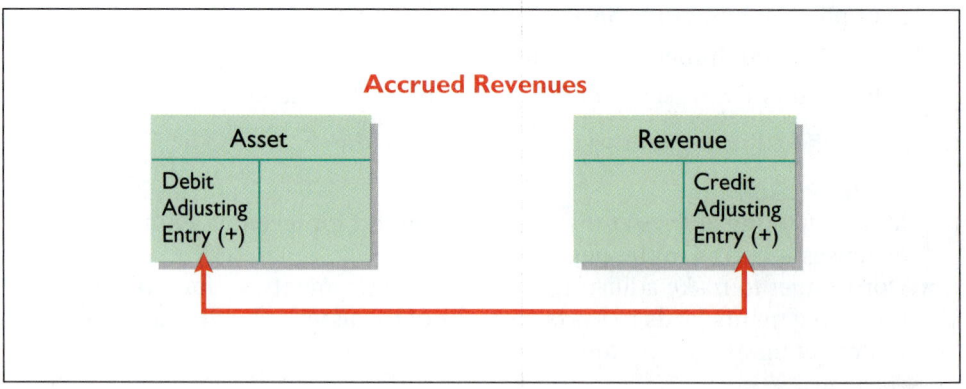

In October Pioneer Advertising Agency earned $200 for advertising services that have not been recorded. The following adjusting entry is made on October 31.

A	=	L	+	OE
+200				+200 Rev

Cash Flows
no effect

Oct. 31	Accounts Receivable	200	
	Service Revenue		200
	(To record revenue for services provided)		

After the adjusting entry is posted, the accounts show:

Illustration 3-12
Receivable and revenue accounts after accrual adjustment

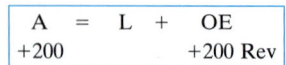
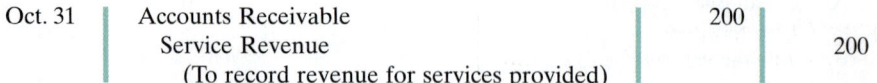

Accounts Receivable		Service Revenue	
10/31 **Adj.** 200		10/31 10,000	
		31 400	
		31 **Adj.** 200	
		10/31 Bal. 10,600	

The asset Accounts Receivable shows that $200 is owed by clients at the balance sheet date. The balance of $10,600 in Service Revenue represents the total revenue earned during the month ($10,000 + $400 + $200). **If the adjusting entry is not made, the following will all be understated: assets and owner's equity on the balance sheet, and revenues and net income on the income statement.**

On November 10, Pioneer receives cash of $200 for the services performed in October. Thus, the following entry is made.

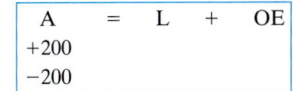

Nov. 10	Cash	200	
	Accounts Receivable		200
	(To record cash collected on account)		

```
  A    =  L  +  OE
+200
-200
```

Cash Flows
+200

The subsequent collection of revenue from clients will be recorded with a debit (increase) to Cash and a credit (decrease) to Accounts Receivable.

Accrued Expenses

As indicated on page 93, expenses incurred but not yet paid or recorded at the statement date are called **accrued expenses**. Interest, rent, taxes, and salaries can be accrued expenses. Accrued expenses result from the same causes as accrued revenues. In fact, an accrued expense on the books of one company is an accrued revenue to another company. For example, the $200 accrual of fees by Pioneer is an accrued expense to the client that received the service.

Adjustments for accrued expenses are needed for two purposes: (1) to record the obligations that exist at the balance sheet date, and (2) to recognize the expenses that apply to the current accounting period. Prior to adjustment, both liabilities and expenses are understated. Therefore, as shown in Illustration 3-13, **an adjusting entry for accrued expenses results in an increase (a debit) to an expense account and an increase (a credit) to a liability account.**

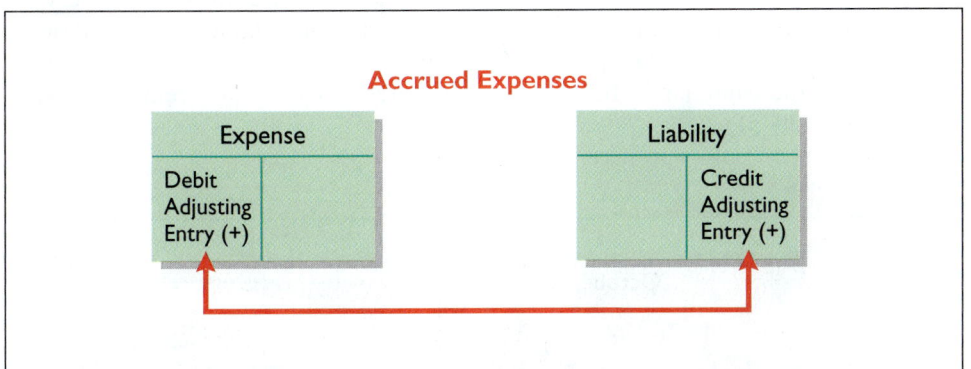

Illustration 3-13
Adjusting entries for accrued expenses

ACCRUED INTEREST. Pioneer Advertising Agency signed a $5,000, 3-month note payable on October 1. The note requires interest at an annual rate of 12%. The amount of the interest accumulation is determined by three factors: (1) the face value of the note, (2) the interest rate, which is always expressed as an annual rate, and (3) the length of time the note is outstanding. In this instance, the total interest due on the $5,000 note at its due date 3 months hence is $150 ($5,000 × 12% × 3/12), or $50 for one month. The formula for computing interest and its application to Pioneer Advertising Agency for the month of October[2] are shown in Illustration 3-14 (page 102). Note that the time period is expressed as a fraction of a year.

---

[2]The computation of interest will be considered in more depth in later chapters.

Illustration 3-14
Formula for computing interest

Face Value of Note	×	Annual Interest Rate	×	Time in Terms of One Year	=	Interest
$5,000	×	12%	×	1/12	=	**$50**

The accrued expense adjusting entry at October 31 is:

A	=	L	+	OE
		+50		−50 Exp

Cash Flows
no effect

Oct. 31	Interest Expense	50	
	Interest Payable		50
	(To record interest on notes payable)		

After this adjusting entry is posted, the accounts show:

Illustration 3-15
Interest accounts after adjustment

Interest Expense		Interest Payable	
10/31 **Adj.** 50			10/31 **Adj.** 50

Interest Expense shows the interest charges for the month. The amount of interest owed at the statement date is shown in Interest Payable. It will not be paid until the note comes due at the end of 3 months. The Interest Payable account is used instead of crediting (increasing) Notes Payable. The reason for using the two accounts is to disclose the two types of obligations (interest and principal) in the accounts and statements. **If this adjusting entry is not made, liabilities and interest expense will be understated, and net income and owner's equity will be overstated.**

ACCRUED SALARIES. Some types of expenses are paid for after the services have been performed. Examples are employee salaries and commissions. At Pioneer Advertising, salaries were last paid on October 26; the next payday is November 9. As shown in the calendar in Illustration 3-16, three working days remain in October (October 29–31).

Illustration 3-16
Calendar showing Pioneer's pay periods

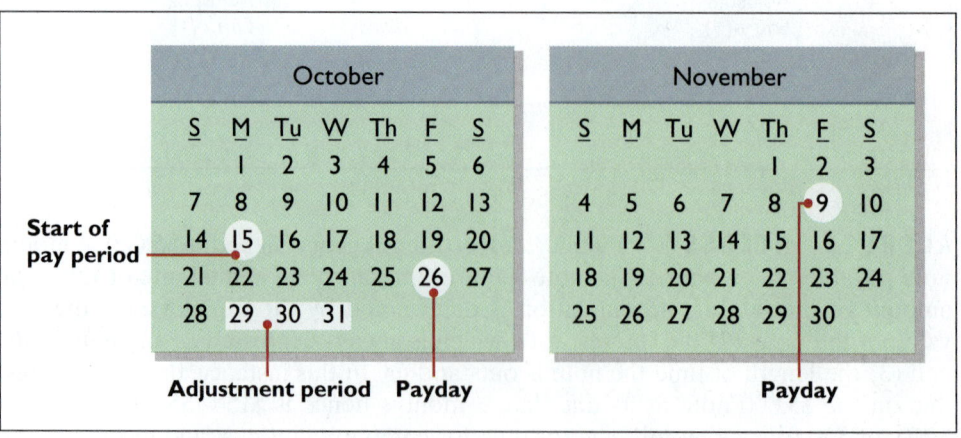

At October 31, the salaries for the last three days of the month represent an accrued expense and a related liability. The employees receive total salaries of $2,000

for a five-day work week, or $400 per day. Thus, accrued salaries at October 31 are $1,200 ($400 × 3). The adjusting entry is:

Oct. 31	Salaries Expense	1,200	
	Salaries Payable		1,200
	(To record accrued salaries)		

A	=	L	+	OE
		+1,200		−1,200 Exp

Cash Flows
no effect

After this adjusting entry is posted, the accounts show:

Salaries Expense		Salaries Payable	
10/26 4,000			10/31 **Adj.** **1,200**
31 **Adj.** **1,200**			
10/31 Bal. 5,200			

Illustration 3-17
Salary accounts after adjustment

After this adjustment, the balance in Salaries Expense of $5,200 (13 days × $400) is the actual salary expense for October. (The employees started work on October 15.) The balance in Salaries Payable of $1,200 is the amount of the liability for salaries owed as of October 31. **If the $1,200 adjustment for salaries is not recorded, Pioneer's expenses will be understated $1,200, and its liabilities will be understated $1,200.**

At Pioneer Advertising, salaries are payable every two weeks. The next payday is November 9, when total salaries of $4,000 will again be paid. The payment will consist of $1,200 of salaries payable at October 31 plus $2,800 of salaries expense for November (seven working days as shown in the November calendar × $400). Therefore, the following entry is made on November 9.

Nov. 9	Salaries Payable	1,200	
	Salaries Expense	2,800	
	Cash		4,000
	(To record November 9 payroll)		

A	=	L	+	OE
−4,000		−1,200		−2,800 Exp

Cash Flows
−4,000

This entry does two things: (1) It eliminates the liability for Salaries Payable that was recorded in the October 31 adjusting entry. (2) It records the proper amount of Salaries Expense for the period between November 1 and November 9.

ACCOUNTING IN ACTION   ⊜ Business Insight

In many computer systems, the adjusting process is handled like any other transaction, with the accountant inputting the adjustment at the time required. The main difference between adjusting entries and regular transactions is that with adjusting entries, one part of the computer system may perform the required calculation for such items as depreciation or interest and then "feed" these figures to the journalizing process.

Such systems are also able to display information before and after changes are made. Management may be interested in such information to highlight the impact that adjustments have on the various accounts and financial statements.

BEFORE YOU GO ON...

Review It

1. If an accrued revenue adjusting entry is not made, what is the effect on assets, owner's equity, revenues, and net income?

2. If an accrued expense adjusting entry is not made, what is the effect on liabilities, owner's equity, and interest expense?

Do It

Calvin and Hobbs are the new owners of Micro Computer Services. At the end of August 2005, their first month of ownership, Calvin and Hobbs are trying to prepare monthly financial statements. They have the following information for the month.

1. At August 31, Calvin and Hobbs owed employees $800 in salaries that will be paid on September 1.

2. On August 1, Calvin and Hobbs borrowed $30,000 from a local bank on a 15-year note. The annual interest rate is 10%.

3. Service revenue unrecorded in August totaled $1,100.

Prepare the adjusting entries needed at August 31, 2005.

ACTION PLAN

■ Make adjusting entries at the end of the period for revenues earned and expenses incurred in the period.

■ Don't forget to make adjusting entries for accruals. Adjusting entries for accruals will increase both a balance sheet and an income statement account.

SOLUTION

1. Salaries Expense	800	
Salaries Payable		800
(To record accrued salaries)		
2. Interest Expense	250	
Interest Payable		250
(To record interest)		
($30,000 × 10% × 1/12 = $250)		
3. Accounts Receivable	1,100	
Service Revenue		1,100
(To record revenue for services provided)		

Related exercise material: *BE3-7, E3-2, E3-3, E3-4, E3-5, E3-6, E3-7, E3-8, and E3-9.*

 THE NAVIGATOR

Summary of Basic Relationships

The four basic types of adjusting entries are summarized in Illustration 3-18. Take some time to study and analyze the adjusting entries shown in the summary. Be sure to note that **each adjusting entry affects one balance sheet account and one income statement account**.

Illustration 3-18
Summary of adjusting entries

Type of Adjustment	Reason for Adjustment	Accounts before Adjustment	Adjusting Entry
1. Prepaid expenses	Prepaid expenses originally recorded in asset accounts have been used.	Assets overstated Expenses understated	Dr. Expenses Cr. Assets
2. Unearned revenues	Unearned revenues initially recorded in liability accounts have been earned.	Liabilities overstated Revenues understated	Dr. Liabilities Cr. Revenues
3. Accrued revenues	Revenues have been earned but not yet received in cash or recorded.	Assets understated Revenues understated	Dr. Assets Cr. Revenues
4. Accrued expenses	Expenses have been incurred but not yet paid in cash or recorded.	Expenses understated Liabilities understated	Dr. Expenses Cr. Liabilities

The journalizing and posting of adjusting entries for Pioneer Advertising Agency on October 31 are shown in Illustrations 3-19 and 3-20. All adjustments are identified in the ledger by the reference J2 because they have been journalized on page 2 of the general journal. A center caption entitled "Adjusting Entries" may be inserted between the last transaction entry and the first adjusting entry to identify these entries. When reviewing the general ledger in Illustration 3-20, note that the adjustments are highlighted in color.

Illustration 3-19
General journal showing adjusting entries

	GENERAL JOURNAL			J2
Date	**Account Titles and Explanation**	**Ref.**	**Debit**	**Credit**
2005	Adjusting Entries			
Oct. 31	Advertising Supplies Expense	631	1,500	
	Advertising Supplies	126		1,500
	(To record supplies used)			
31	Insurance Expense	722	50	
	Prepaid Insurance	130		50
	(To record insurance expired)			
31	Depreciation Expense	711	40	
	Accumulated Depreciation—Office Equipment	158		40
	(To record monthly depreciation)			
31	Unearned Revenue	209	400	
	Service Revenue	400		400
	(To record revenue for services provided)			
31	Accounts Receivable	112	200	
	Service Revenue	400		200
	(To record revenue for services provided)			
31	Interest Expense	905	50	
	Interest Payable	230		50
	(To record interest on notes payable)			
31	Salaries Expense	726	1,200	
	Salaries Payable	212		1,200
	(To record accrued salaries)			

HELPFUL HINT

(1) Adjusting entries should not involve debits or credits to cash.

(2) Evaluate whether the adjustment makes sense. For example, an adjustment to recognize supplies used should increase supplies expense.

(3) Double-check all computations.

Illustration 3-20
General ledger after adjustment

GENERAL LEDGER

Cash — No. 101

Date	Explanation	Ref.	Debit	Credit	Balance
2005					
Oct. 1		J1	10,000		10,000
2		J1	1,200		11,200
3		J1		900	10,300
4		J1		600	9,700
20		J1		500	9,200
26		J1		4,000	5,200
31		J1	10,000		15,200

Accounts Receivable — No. 112

Date	Explanation	Ref.	Debit	Credit	Balance
2005					
Oct. 31	Adj. entry	J2	200		200

Advertising Supplies — No. 126

Date	Explanation	Ref.	Debit	Credit	Balance
2005					
Oct. 5		J1	2,500		2,500
31	Adj. entry	J2		1,500	1,000

Prepaid Insurance — No. 130

Date	Explanation	Ref.	Debit	Credit	Balance
2005					
Oct. 4		J1	600		600
31	Adj. entry	J2		50	550

Office Equipment — No. 157

Date	Explanation	Ref.	Debit	Credit	Balance
2005					
Oct. 1		J1	5,000		5,000

Accumulated Depreciation—Office Equipment — No. 158

Date	Explanation	Ref.	Debit	Credit	Balance
2005					
Oct. 31	Adj. entry	J2		40	40

Notes Payable — No. 200

Date	Explanation	Ref.	Debit	Credit	Balance
2005					
Oct. 1		J1		5,000	5,000

Accounts Payable — No. 201

Date	Explanation	Ref.	Debit	Credit	Balance
2005					
Oct. 5		J1		2,500	2,500

Unearned Revenue — No. 209

Date	Explanation	Ref.	Debit	Credit	Balance
2005					
Oct. 2		J1		1,200	1,200
31	Adj. entry	J2	400		800

Salaries Payable — No. 212

Date	Explanation	Ref.	Debit	Credit	Balance
2005					
Oct. 31	Adj. entry	J2		1,200	1,200

Interest Payable — No. 230

Date	Explanation	Ref.	Debit	Credit	Balance
2005					
Oct. 31	Adj. entry	J2		50	50

C. R. Byrd, Capital — No. 301

Date	Explanation	Ref.	Debit	Credit	Balance
2005					
Oct. 1		J1		10,000	10,000

C. R. Byrd, Drawing — No. 306

Date	Explanation	Ref.	Debit	Credit	Balance
2005					
Oct. 20		J1	500		500

Service Revenue — No. 400

Date	Explanation	Ref.	Debit	Credit	Balance
2005					
Oct. 31		J1		10,000	10,000
31	Adj. entry	J2		400	10,400
31	Adj. entry	J2		200	10,600

Advertising Supplies Expense — No. 631

Date	Explanation	Ref.	Debit	Credit	Balance
2005					
Oct. 31	Adj. entry	J2	1,500		1,500

Depreciation Expense — No. 711

Date	Explanation	Ref.	Debit	Credit	Balance
2005					
Oct. 31	Adj. entry	J2	40		40

Insurance Expense — No. 722

Date	Explanation	Ref.	Debit	Credit	Balance
2005					
Oct. 31	Adj. entry	J2	50		50

Salaries Expense — No. 726

Date	Explanation	Ref.	Debit	Credit	Balance
2005					
Oct. 26		J1	4,000		4,000
31	Adj. entry	J2	1,200		5,200

Rent Expense — No. 729

Date	Explanation	Ref.	Debit	Credit	Balance
2005					
Oct. 3		J1	900		900

Interest Expense — No. 905

Date	Explanation	Ref.	Debit	Credit	Balance
2005					
Oct. 31	Adj. entry	J2	50		50

The Adjusted Trial Balance and Financial Statements

After all adjusting entries have been journalized and posted, another trial balance is prepared from the ledger accounts. This is called an adjusted trial balance. Its purpose is to **prove the equality** of the total debit balances and the total credit balances in the ledger after all adjustments have been made. The accounts in the adjusted trial balance contain all data that are needed for the preparation of financial statements.

Preparing the Adjusted Trial Balance

The adjusted trial balance for Pioneer Advertising Agency is presented in Illustration 3-21. It has been prepared from the ledger accounts in Illustration 3-20. The amounts affected by the adjusting entries are highlighted in color. Compare these amounts to those in the unadjusted trial balance in Illustration 3-3 on page 93.

Illustration 3-21
Adjusted trial balance

PIONEER ADVERTISING AGENCY
Adjusted Trial Balance
October 31, 2005

	Dr.	Cr.
Cash	$15,200	
Accounts Receivable	200	
Advertising Supplies	1,000	
Prepaid Insurance	550	
Office Equipment	5,000	
Accumulated Depreciation—Office Equipment		$ 40
Notes Payable		5,000
Accounts Payable		2,500
Unearned Revenue		800
Salaries Payable		1,200
Interest Payable		50
C. R. Byrd, Capital		10,000
C. R. Byrd, Drawing	500	
Service Revenue		10,600
Salaries Expense	5,200	
Advertising Supplies Expense	1,500	
Rent Expense	900	
Insurance Expense	50	
Interest Expense	50	
Depreciation Expense	40	
	$30,190	$30,190

Preparing Financial Statements

Financial statements can be prepared directly from the adjusted trial balance. Illustrations 3-22 and 3-23 show the interrelationships of data in the adjusted trial balance and the financial statements.

As shown in Illustration 3-22, the income statement is first prepared from the revenue and expense accounts. The owner's equity statement is derived from the owner's capital and drawing accounts and the net income (or net loss) from the income statement. As shown in Illustration 3-23, the balance sheet is then prepared from the asset and liability accounts and the ending owner's capital balance as reported in the owner's equity statement.

Illustration 3-22

Preparation of the income statement and owner's equity statement from the adjusted trial balance

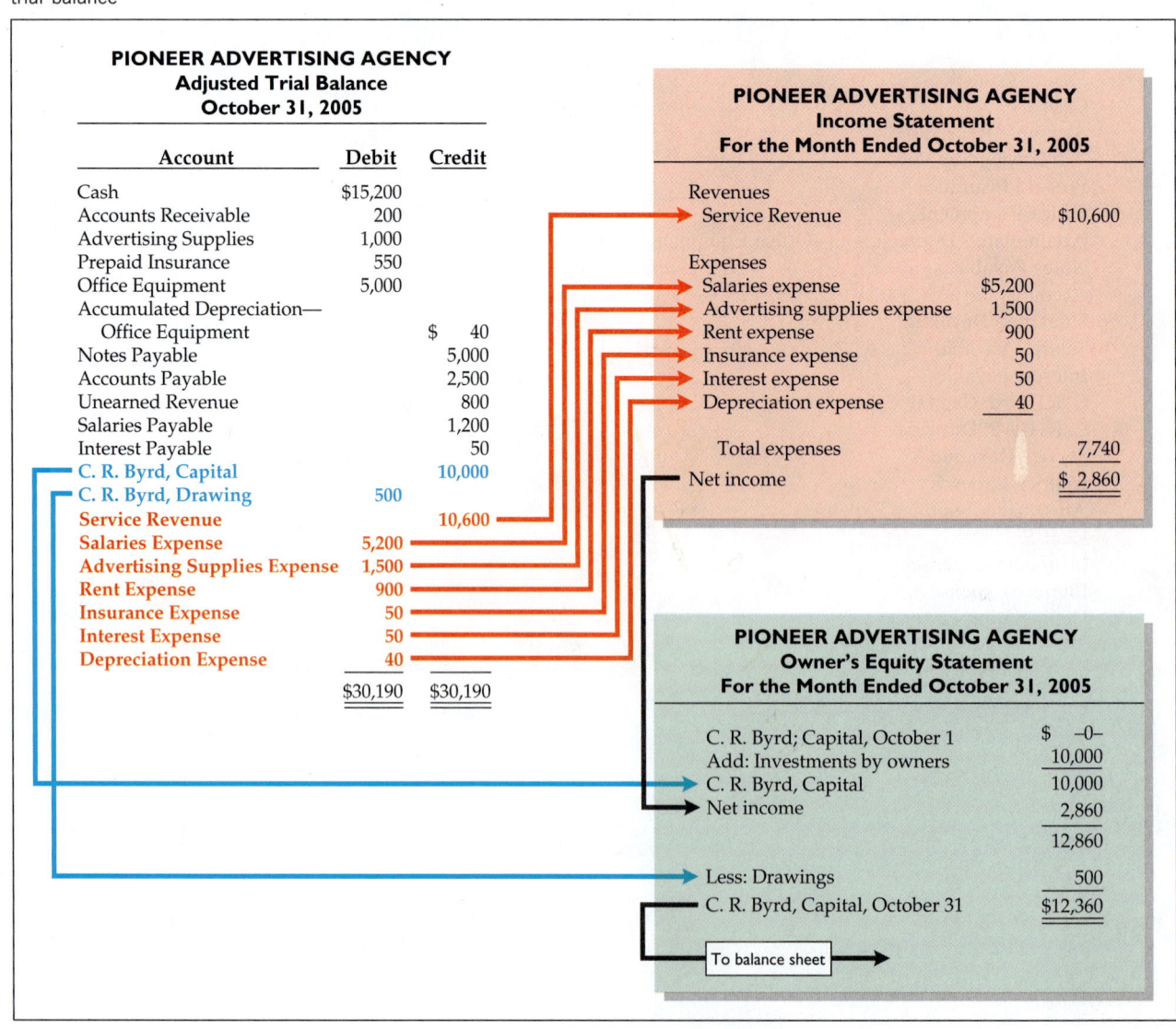

Illustration 3-23
Preparation of the balance sheet from the adjusted trial balance

PIONEER ADVERTISING AGENCY
Adjusted Trial Balance
October 31, 2005

Account	Debit	Credit
Cash	$15,200	
Accounts Receivable	200	
Advertising Supplies	1,000	
Prepaid Insurance	550	
Office Equipment	5,000	
Accumulated Depreciation— Office Equipment		$ 40
Notes Payable		5,000
Accounts Payable		2,500
Unearned Revenue		800
Salaries Payable		1,200
Interest Payable		50
C. R. Byrd, Capital		10,000
C. R. Byrd, Drawing	500	
Service Revenue		10,600
Salaries Expense	5,200	
Advertising Supplies Expense	1,500	
Rent Expense	900	
Insurance Expense	50	
Interest Expense	50	
Depreciation Expense	40	
	$30,190	$30,190

PIONEER ADVERTISING AGENCY
Balance Sheet
October 31, 2005

Assets

Cash		$15,200
Accounts receivable		200
Advertising supplies		1,000
Prepaid insurance		550
Office equipment	$5,000	
Less: Accumulated depreciation	40	4,960
Total assets		$21,910

Liabilities and Owner's Equity

Liabilities		
Notes payable		$ 5,000
Accounts payable		2,500
Unearned revenue		800
Salaries payable		1,200
Interest payable		50
Total liabilities		9,550
Owner's equity		
C. R. Byrd, Capital		12,360
Total liabilities and owner's equity		$21,910

Capital Balance at Oct. 31 from Owner's Equity Statement in Illustration 3-22

BEFORE YOU GO ON...

Review It

1. What is the purpose of an adjusted trial balance?
2. How is an adjusted trial balance prepared?

DEMONSTRATION PROBLEM

Terry Thomas opens the Green Thumb Lawn Care Company on April 1. At April 30, the trial balance shows the following balances for selected accounts.

Prepaid Insurance	$ 3,600
Equipment	28,000
Notes Payable	20,000
Unearned Revenue	4,200
Service Revenue	1,800

Analysis reveals the following additional data.

1. Prepaid insurance is the cost of a 2-year insurance policy, effective April 1.
2. Depreciation on the equipment is $500 per month.

3. The note payable is dated April 1. It is a 6-month, 12% note.
4. Seven customers paid for the company's 6 months' lawn service package of $600 beginning in April. These customers were serviced in April.
5. Lawn services provided other customers but not recorded at April 30 totaled $1,500.

Instructions

Prepare the adjusting entries for the month of April. Show computations.

SOLUTION TO DEMONSTRATION PROBLEM

ACTION PLAN

- Note that adjustments are being made for one month.
- Make computations carefully.
- Select account titles carefully.
- Make sure debits are made first and credits are indented.
- Check that debits equal credits for each entry.

GENERAL JOURNAL J1

Date	Account Titles and Explanation	Ref.	Debit	Credit
	Adjusting Entries			
Apr. 30	Insurance Expense		150	
	Prepaid Insurance			150
	(To record insurance expired: $3,600 ÷ 24 = $150 per month)			
30	Depreciation Expense		500	
	Accumulated Depreciation—Equipment			500
	(To record monthly depreciation)			
30	Interest Expense		200	
	Interest Payable			200
	(To record interest on notes payable: $20,000 × 12% × 1/12 = $200)			
30	Unearned Revenue		700	
	Service Revenue			700
	(To record service revenue: $600 ÷ 6 = $100; $100 per month × 7 = $700)			
30	Accounts Receivable		1,500	
	Service Revenue			1,500
	(To record revenue for services provided)			

☑ THE NAVIGATOR

SUMMARY OF STUDY OBJECTIVES

1. **Explain the time period assumption.** The time period assumption assumes that the economic life of a business can be divided into artificial time periods.

2. **Explain the accrual basis of accounting.** Accrual-basis accounting means that events that change a company's financial statements are recorded in the periods in which the events occur, rather than in the periods in which the company receives or pays cash.

3. **Explain why adjusting entries are needed.** Adjusting entries are made at the end of an accounting period. They ensure that revenues are recorded in the period in which they are earned and that expenses are recognized in the period in which they are incurred.

4. **Identify the major types of adjusting entries.** The major types of adjusting entries are prepaid expenses, unearned revenues, accrued revenues, and accrued expenses.

5. **Prepare adjusting entries for prepayments.** Prepayments are either prepaid expenses or unearned revenues. Adjusting entries for prepayments are required at the statement date to record the portion of the prepayment that represents the expense incurred or the revenue earned in the current accounting period.

6. **Prepare adjusting entries for accruals.** Accruals are either accrued revenues or accrued expenses. Adjusting entries for accruals are required to record revenues earned and expenses incurred in the current accounting period that have not been recognized through daily entries.

7. **Describe the nature and purpose of an adjusted trial balance.** An adjusted trial balance shows the balances of all accounts, including those that have been adjusted, at the end of an accounting period. Its purpose is to show the effects of all financial events that have occurred during the accounting period.

☑ THE NAVIGATOR

GLOSSARY

Accrual-basis accounting Accounting basis in which transactions that change a company's financial statements are recorded in the periods in which the events occur. (p. 90).

Accrued expenses Expenses incurred but not yet paid in cash or recorded. (p. 101).

Accrued revenues Revenues earned but not yet received in cash or recorded. (p. 100).

Adjusted trial balance A list of accounts and their balances after all adjustments have been made. (p. 107).

Adjusting entries Entries made at the end of an accounting period to ensure that the revenue recognition and matching principles are followed. (p. 92).

Book value The difference between the cost of a depreciable asset and its related accumulated depreciation. (p. 97).

Calendar year An accounting period that extends from January 1 to December 31. (p. 90).

Cash-basis accounting Accounting basis in which revenue is recorded when cash is received and an expense is recorded when cash is paid. (p. 90).

Contra asset account An account that is offset against an asset account on the balance sheet. (p. 97).

Depreciation The allocation of the cost of an asset to expense over its useful life in a rational and systematic manner. (p. 96).

Fiscal year An accounting period that is one year in length. (p. 90).

Interim periods Monthly or quarterly accounting time periods. (p. 90).

Matching principle The principle that efforts (expenses) be matched with accomplishments (revenues). (p. 91).

Prepaid expenses Expenses paid in cash and recorded as assets before they are used or consumed. (p. 94).

Revenue recognition principle The principle that revenue be recognized in the accounting period in which it is earned. (p. 91).

Time period assumption An assumption that the economic life of a business can be divided into artificial time periods. (p. 90).

Unearned revenues Cash received and recorded as liabilities before revenue is earned. (p. 97).

Useful life The length of service of a productive facility. (p. 96).

Appendix ALTERNATIVE TREATMENT OF PREPAID EXPENSES AND UNEARNED REVENUES

In our discussion of adjusting entries for prepaid expenses and unearned revenues, we illustrated transactions for which the initial entries were made to balance sheet accounts. In the case of prepaid expenses, the prepayment was debited to an asset account. In the case of unearned revenue, the cash received was credited to a liability account. Some businesses use an alternative treatment: (1) At the time an expense is prepaid, it is debited to an expense account. (2) At the time of a receipt for future services, it is credited to a revenue account. The circumstances that justify such entries and the different adjusting entries that may be required are described below. The alternative treatment of prepaid expenses and unearned revenues has the same effect on the financial statements as the procedures described in the chapter.

> **STUDY OBJECTIVE 8**
>
> Prepare adjusting entries for the alternative treatment of prepayments.

Prepaid Expenses

Prepaid expenses become expired costs either through the passage of time (e.g., insurance) or through consumption (e.g., advertising supplies). If, at the time of purchase, the company expects to consume the supplies before the next financial statement date, **it may be more convenient initially to debit (increase) an expense account rather than an asset account**.

Assume that Pioneer Advertising expects that all of the supplies purchased on October 5 will be used before the end of the month. A debit of $2,500 to Advertising Supplies Expense (rather than to the asset account Advertising Supplies) on October 5 will eliminate the need for an adjusting entry on October 31, if all the supplies are used. At October 31, the Advertising Supplies Expense account will show a balance of $2,500, which is the cost of supplies used between October 5 and October 31.

But what if the company does not use all the supplies, and an inventory of $1,000 of advertising supplies remains on October 31? Obviously, an adjusting entry is needed. Prior to adjustment, the expense account Advertising Supplies Expense is overstated $1,000, and the asset account Advertising Supplies is understated $1,000. Thus the following adjusting entry is made.

A	=	L	+	OE
+1,000				+1,000 Exp

Cash Flows
no effect

Oct. 31	Advertising Supplies	1,000	
	Advertising Supplies Expense		1,000
	(To record supplies inventory)		

After posting the adjusting entry, the accounts show:

Illustration 3A-1
Prepaid expenses accounts after adjustment

Advertising Supplies			Advertising Supplies Expense			
10/31 **Adj.** **1,000**			10/5	2,500	10/31 **Adj.**	**1,000**
			10/31 **Bal.**	**1,500**		

After adjustment, the asset account Advertising Supplies shows a balance of $1,000, which is equal to the cost of supplies on hand at October 31. In addition, Advertising Supplies Expense shows a balance of $1,500, which is equal to the cost of supplies used between October 5 and October 31. If the adjusting entry is not made, expenses will be overstated and net income will be understated by $1,000 in the October income statement. Also, both assets and owner's equity will be understated by $1,000 on the October 31 balance sheet.

A comparison of the entries and accounts for advertising supplies is shown in Illustration 3A-2.

Illustration 3A-2
Adjustment approaches—a comparison

Prepayment Initially Debited to Asset Account (per chapter)			Prepayment Initially Debited to Expense Account (per appendix)		
Oct. 5	Advertising Supplies	2,500	Oct. 5	Advertising Supplies Expense	2,500
	Accounts Payable	2,500		Accounts Payable	2,500
Oct. 31	Advertising Supplies		Oct. 31	Advertising Supplies	1,000
	Expense	1,500		Advertising Supplies Expense	1,000
	Advertising Supplies	1,500			

After posting the entries, the accounts appear as follows.

Illustration 3A-3
Comparison of accounts

(per chapter) Advertising Supplies				(per appendix) Advertising Supplies		
10/5	2,500	10/31 **Adj.**	**1,500**	10/31 **Adj.** **1,000**		
10/31 **Bal.**	**1,000**					

Advertising Supplies Expense			Advertising Supplies Expense			
10/31 **Adj.** **1,500**			10/5	2,500	10/31 **Adj.**	**1,000**
			10/31 **Bal.**	**1,500**		

Note that the account balances under each alternative are the same at October 31: Advertising Supplies $1,000, and Advertising Supplies Expense $1,500.

Unearned Revenues

Unearned revenues become earned either through the passage of time (e.g., unearned rent) or through providing the service (e.g., unearned fees). Similar to the case for prepaid expenses, a revenue account may be credited (increased) when cash is received for future services.

To illustrate, assume that Pioneer Advertising received $1,200 for future services on October 2. The services were expected to be performed before October 31.[3] In such a case, Service Revenue is credited. If revenue is in fact earned before October 31, no adjustment is needed.

However, if at the statement date $800 of the services have not been performed, an adjusting entry is required. The revenue account Service Revenue is overstated $800, and the liability account Unearned Revenue is understated $800. Thus, the following adjusting entry is made.

> **HELPFUL HINT**
>
> The required adjusted balances here are Service Revenue $400 and Unearned Revenue $800.

Oct. 31	Service Revenue	800	
	Unearned Revenue		800
	(To record unearned revenue)		

A	=	L	+	OE
		+800		−800 Rev

Cash Flows
no effect

After posting the adjusting entry, the accounts show:

Unearned Revenue			Service Revenue			
	10/31 **Adj.**	**800**	10/31 **Adj.**	**800**	10/2	1,200
					10/31 **Bal.**	**400**

Illustration 3A-4
Unearned revenue accounts after adjustment

The liability account Unearned Revenue shows a balance of $800. This is equal to the services that will be provided in the future. In addition, the balance in Service Revenue equals the services provided in October. If the adjusting entry is not made, both revenues and net income will be overstated by $800 in the October income statement. Also, liabilities will be understated by $800, and owner's equity will be overstated by $800 on the October 31 balance sheet.

A comparison of the entries and accounts for service revenue earned and unearned is shown in Illustration 3A-5.

Illustration 3A-5
Adjustment approaches—a comparison

Unearned Revenue Initially Credited to Liability Account (per chapter)			Unearned Revenue Initially Credited to Revenue Account (per appendix)		
Oct. 2 Cash	1,200		Oct. 2 Cash	1,200	
Unearned Revenue		1,200	Service Revenue		1,200
Oct. 31 Unearned Revenue	400		Oct. 31 Service Revenue	800	
Service Revenue		400	Unearned Revenue		800

---

[3]This example focuses only on the alternative treatment of unearned revenues. In the interest of simplicity, the entries to Service Revenue pertaining to the immediate earning of revenue ($10,000) and the adjusting entry for accrued revenue ($200) have been ignored.

After posting the entries, the accounts appear as follows.

Illustration 3A-6
Comparison of accounts

	(per chapter) Unearned Revenue			(per appendix) Unearned Revenue	
10/31 **Adj.** 400	10/2 1,200			10/31 **Adj.** 800	
	10/31 **Bal.** 800				

	(per chapter) Service Revenue			(per appendix) Service Revenue	
	10/31 **Adj.** 400		10/31 **Adj.** 800	10/2 1,200	
				10/31 **Bal.** 400	

Note that the balances in the accounts are the same under the two alternatives: Unearned Revenue $800, and Service Revenue $400.

Summary of Additional Adjustment Relationships

The use of alternative adjusting entries requires additions to the summary of basic relationships presented earlier in Illustration 3-18. The additions are shown in color in Illustration 3A-7.

Alternative adjusting entries **do not apply** to accrued revenues and accrued expenses because **no entries occur before these types of adjusting entries are made**. Therefore, the entries in Illustration 3-18 for these two types of adjustments remain unchanged.

Illustration 3A-7
Summary of basic relationships for prepayments

Type of Adjustment	Reason for Adjustment	Account Balances before Adjustment	Adjusting Entry
1. Prepaid expenses	(a) Prepaid expenses initially recorded in asset accounts have been used.	Assets overstated Expenses understated	Dr. Expenses Cr. Assets
	(b) Prepaid expenses initially recorded in expense accounts have not been used.	**Assets understated Expenses overstated**	**Dr. Assets Cr. Expenses**
2. Unearned revenues	(a) Unearned revenues initially recorded in liability accounts have been earned.	Liabilities overstated Revenues understated	Dr. Liabilities Cr. Revenues
	(b) Unearned revenues initially recorded in revenue accounts have not been earned.	**Liabilities understated Revenues overstated**	**Dr. Revenues Cr. Liabilities**

SUMMARY OF STUDY OBJECTIVE FOR APPENDIX

8. **Prepare adjusting entries for the alternative treatment of prepayments.** Prepayments may be initially debited to an expense account. Unearned revenues may be credited to a revenue account. At the end of the period, these accounts may be overstated. The adjusting entries for prepaid expenses are a debit to an asset account and a credit to an expense account. Adjusting entries for unearned revenues are a debit to a revenue account and a credit to a liability account.

*Note: All asterisked Questions, Exercises, and Problems relate to material in the appendix to the chapter.

SELF-STUDY QUESTIONS

Answers are at the end of the chapter.

(SO 1) **1.** The time period assumption states that:
  a. revenue should be recognized in the accounting period in which it is earned.
  b. expenses should be matched with revenues.
  c. the economic life of a business can be divided into artificial time periods.
  d. the fiscal year should correspond with the calendar year.

(SO 2) **2.** The principle or assumption dictating that efforts (expenses) be matched with accomplishments (revenues) is the:
  a. matching principle.
  b. cost assumption.
  c. periodicity principle.
  d. revenue recognition principle.

(SO 2) **3.** One of the following statements about the accrual basis of accounting is *false*. That statement is:
  a. Events that change a company's financial statements are recorded in the periods in which the events occur.
  b. Revenue is recognized in the period in which it is earned.
  c. This basis is in accord with generally accepted accounting principles.
  d. Revenue is recorded only when cash is received, and expense is recorded only when cash is paid.

(SO 3) **4.** Adjusting entries are made to ensure that:
  a. expenses are recognized in the period in which they are incurred.
  b. revenues are recorded in the period in which they are earned.
  c. balance sheet and income statement accounts have correct balances at the end of an accounting period.
  d. all of the above.

(SO 4) **5.** Each of the following is a major type (or category) of adjusting entries *except:*
  a. prepaid expenses.
  b. accrued revenues.
  c. accrued expenses.
  d. earned revenues.

(SO 5) **6.** The trial balance shows Supplies $1,350 and Supplies Expense $0. If $600 of supplies are on hand at the end of the period, the adjusting entry is:
  a. Supplies   600
       Supplies Expense   600
  b. Supplies   750
       Supplies Expense   750

  c. Supplies Expense   750
       Supplies   750
  d. Supplies Expense   600
       Supplies   600

7. Adjustments for unearned revenues: (SO 5)
  a. decrease liabilities and increase revenues.
  b. have an assets and revenues account relationship.
  c. increase assets and increase revenues.
  d. decrease revenues and decrease assets.

8. Adjustments for accrued revenues: (SO 6)
  a. have a liabilities and revenues account relationship.
  b. have an assets and revenues account relationship.
  c. decrease assets and revenues.
  d. decrease liabilities and increase revenues.

9. Kathy Siska earned a salary of $400 for the last week of (SO 6) September. She will be paid on October 1. The adjusting entry for Kathy's employer at September 30 is:
  a. No entry is required.
  b. Salaries Expense   400
       Salaries Payable   400
  c. Salaries Expense   400
       Cash   400
  d. Salaries Payable   400
       Cash   400

10. Which of the following statements is *incorrect* concern- (SO 7) ing the adjusted trial balance?
  a. An adjusted trial balance proves the equality of the total debit balances and the total credit balances in the ledger after all adjustments are made.
  b. The adjusted trial balance provides the primary basis for the preparation of financial statements.
  c. The adjusted trial balance lists the account balances segregated by assets and liabilities.
  d. The adjusted trial balance is prepared after the adjusting entries have been journalized and posted.

*****11.** The trial balance shows Supplies $0 and Supplies Ex- (SO 8) pense $1,500. If $800 of supplies are on hand at the end of the period, the adjusting entry is:
  a. Debit Supplies $800 and credit Supplies Expense $800.
  b. Debit Supplies Expense $800 and credit Supplies $800.
  c. Debit Supplies $700 and credit Supplies Expense $700.
  d. Debit Supplies Expense $700 and credit Supplies $700.

QUESTIONS

1. (a) How does the time period assumption affect an accountant's analysis of business transactions?
  (b) Explain the terms *fiscal year, calendar year,* and *interim periods.*

2. State two generally accepted accounting principles that relate to adjusting the accounts.

3. Joe Thomas, a lawyer, accepts a legal engagement in March, performs the work in April, and is paid in May. If

Thomas's law firm prepares monthly financial statements, when should it recognize revenue from this engagement? Why?

4. Why do accrual-basis financial statements provide more useful information than cash-basis statements?

5. In completing the engagement in (3) above, Thomas incurs $4,500 of expenses in March, which are paid in April. How much expense should be deducted from revenues in the month the revenue is recognized? Why?

6. "Adjusting entries are required by the cost principle of accounting." Do you agree? Explain.

7. Why may a trial balance not contain up-to-date and complete financial information?

8. Distinguish between the two categories of adjusting entries, and identify the types of adjustments applicable to each category.

9. What is the debit/credit effect of a prepaid expense adjusting entry?

10. "Depreciation is a valuation process that results in the reporting of the fair market value of the asset." Do you agree? Explain.

11. Explain the differences between depreciation expense and accumulated depreciation.

12. Corts Company purchased equipment for $18,000. By the current balance sheet date, $7,000 had been depreciated. Indicate the balance sheet presentation of the data.

13. What is the debit/credit effect of an unearned revenue adjusting entry?

14. A company fails to recognize revenue earned but not yet received. Which of the following accounts are involved in the adjusting entry: (a) asset, (b) liability, (c) revenue, or (d) expense? For the accounts selected, indicate whether they would be debited or credited in the entry.

15. A company fails to recognize an expense incurred but not paid. Indicate which of the following accounts is debited and which is credited in the adjusting entry: (a) asset, (b) liability, (c) revenue, or (d) expense.

16. A company makes an accrued revenue adjusting entry for $900 and an accrued expense adjusting entry for $600. How much was net income understated prior to these entries? Explain.

17. On January 9, a company pays $6,000 for salaries, of which $2,000 was reported as Salaries Payable on December 31. Give the entry to record the payment.

18. For each of the following items before adjustment, indicate the type of adjusting entry (prepaid expense, unearned revenue, accrued revenue, and accrued expense) that is needed to correct the misstatement. If an item could result in more than one type of adjusting entry, indicate each of the types.
(a) Assets are understated.
(b) Liabilities are overstated.
(c) Liabilities are understated.
(d) Expenses are understated.
(e) Assets are overstated.
(f) Revenue is understated.

19. One-half of the adjusting entry is given below. Indicate the account title for the other half of the entry.
(a) Salaries Expense is debited.
(b) Depreciation Expense is debited.
(c) Interest Payable is credited.
(d) Supplies is credited.
(e) Accounts Receivable is debited.
(f) Unearned Service Revenue is debited.

20. "An adjusting entry may affect more than one balance sheet or income statement account." Do you agree? Why or why not?

21. Why is it possible to prepare financial statements directly from an adjusted trial balance?

*22. Moon Company debits Supplies Expense for all purchases of supplies and credits Rent Revenue for all advanced rentals. For each type of adjustment, give the adjusting entry.

BRIEF EXERCISES

Indicate why adjusting entries are needed.
(SO 3)

BE3-1 The ledger of Lim Company includes the following accounts. Explain why each account may require adjustment.
(a) Prepaid Insurance
(b) Depreciation Expense
(c) Unearned Revenue
(d) Interest Payable

Identify the major types of adjusting entries.
(SO 4)

BE3-2 Lopez Company accumulates the following adjustment data at December 31. Indicate (a) the type of adjustment (prepaid expense, accrued revenues and so on), and (b) the accounts before adjustment (overstated or understated).
1. Supplies of $100 are on hand.
2. Services provided but not recorded total $900.
3. Interest of $200 has accumulated on a note payable.
4. Rent collected in advance totaling $800 has been earned.

Prepare adjusting entry for supplies.
(SO 5)

BE3-3 Gleason Advertising Company's trial balance at December 31 shows Advertising Supplies $6,700 and Advertising Supplies Expense $0. On December 31, there are $1,700 of supplies on hand. Prepare the adjusting entry at December 31, and using T accounts, enter the balances in the accounts, post the adjusting entry, and indicate the adjusted balance in each account.

BE3-4 At the end of its first year, the trial balance of Easton Company shows Equipment $30,000 and zero balances in Accumulated Depreciation—Equipment and Depreciation Expense. Depreciation for the year is estimated to be $6,000. Prepare the adjusting entry for depreciation at December 31, post the adjustments to T accounts, and indicate the balance sheet presentation of the equipment at December 31.

Prepare adjusting entry for depreciation.
(SO 5)

BE3-5 On July 1, 2005, Orlow Co. pays $12,000 to Pizner Insurance Co. for a 3-year insurance contract. Both companies have fiscal years ending December 31. For Orlow Co., journalize and post the entry on July 1 and the adjusting entry on December 31.

Prepare adjusting entry for prepaid expense.
(SO 5)

BE3-6 Using the data in BE3-5, journalize and post the entry on July 1 and the adjusting entry on December 31 for Pizner Insurance Co. Pizner uses the accounts Unearned Insurance Revenue and Insurance Revenue.

Prepare adjusting entry for unearned revenue.
(SO 5)

BE3-7 The bookeeper for Wooster Company asks you to prepare the following accrued adjusting entries at December 31.

Prepare adjusting entries for accruals.
(SO 6)

1. Interest on notes payable of $400 is accrued.
2. Services provided but not recorded total $1,250.
3. Salaries earned by employees of $900 have not been recorded.

Use the following account titles: Service Revenue, Accounts Receivable, Interest Expense, Interest Payable, Salaries Expense, and Salaries Payable.

BE3-8 The trial balance of Wow Company includes the following balance sheet accounts. Identify the accounts that require adjustment. For each account that requires adjustment, indicate **(a)** the type of adjusting entry (prepaid expenses, unearned revenues, accrued revenues, and accrued expenses) and **(b)** the related account in the adjusting entry.

Analyze accounts in an unadjusted trial balance.
(SO 4)

        Accounts Receivable   Interest Payable
        Prepaid Insurance   Unearned Service Revenue
        Accumulated Depreciation—Equipment

BE3-9 The adjusted trial balance of Lucille Company at December 31, 2005, includes the following accounts: S. Lucille, Capital $15,600; S. Lucille, Drawing $6,000; Service Revenue $38,400; Salaries Expense $16,000; Insurance Expense $2,000; Rent Expense $4,000; Supplies Expense $1,500; and Depreciation Expense $1,300. Prepare an income statement for the year.

Prepare an income statement from an adjusted trial balance.
(SO 7)

BE3-10 Partial adjusted trial balance data for Lucille Company is presented in BE3-9. The balance in S. Lucille, Capital is the balance as of January 1. Prepare an owner's equity statement for the year assuming net income is $13,600 for the year.

Prepare an owner's equity statement from an adjusted trial balance.
(SO 7)

*BE3-11 Basler Company records all prepayments in income statement accounts. At April 30, the trial balance shows Supplies Expense $2,800, Service Revenue $9,200, and zero balances in related balance sheet accounts. Prepare the adjusting entries at April 30 assuming **(a)** $1,000 of supplies on hand and **(b)** $2,000 of service revenue should be reported as unearned.

Prepare adjusting entries under alternative treatment of prepayments.
(SO 8)

EXERCISES

E3-1 On numerous occasions, proposals have surfaced to put the federal government on the accrual basis of accounting. This is no small issue. If this basis were used, it would mean that billions in unrecorded liabilities would have to be booked, and the federal deficit would increase substantially.

Distinguish between cash and accrual basis of accounting.
(SO 2)

Instructions

(a) What is the difference between accrual-basis accounting and cash-basis accounting?
(b) Why would politicians prefer the cash basis over the accrual basis?
(c) Write a letter to your senator explaining why the federal government should adopt the accrual basis of accounting.

Identify types of adjustments and account relationships.

(SO 4, 5, 6)

E3-2 Shumway Company accumulates the following adjustment data at December 31.

1. Services provided but not recorded total $750.
2. Store supplies of $300 have been used.
3. Utility expenses of $225 are unpaid.
4. Unearned revenue of $260 has been earned.
5. Salaries of $900 are unpaid.
6. Prepaid insurance totaling $350 has expired.

Instructions

For each of the above items indicate the following.

(a) The type of adjustment (prepaid expense, unearned revenue, accrued revenue, or accrued expense).

(b) The accounts before adjustment (overstatement or understatement).

Prepare adjusting entries from selected account data.

(SO 5, 6, 7)

E3-3 The ledger of Welch Rental Agency on March 31 of the current year includes the following selected accounts before adjusting entries have been prepared.

	Debit	**Credit**
Prepaid Insurance	$ 3,600	
Supplies	2,800	
Equipment	25,000	
Accumulated		
Depreciation—Equipment		$ 8,400
Notes Payable		20,000
Unearned Rent		9,900
Rent Revenue		60,000
Interest Expense	–0–	
Wages Expense	14,000	

An analysis of the accounts shows the following.

1. The equipment depreciates $300 per month.
2. One-third of the unearned rent was earned during the quarter.
3. Interest of $500 is accrued on the notes payable.
4. Supplies on hand total $900.
5. Insurance expires at the rate of $200 per month.

Instructions

Prepare the adjusting entries at March 31, assuming that adjusting entries are made quarterly. Additional accounts are: Depreciation Expense, Insurance Expense, Interest Payable, and Supplies Expense.

Prepare adjusting entries.

(SO 5, 6, 7)

E3-4 Greg Mabasa, D.D.S., opened a dental practice on January 1, 2005. During the first month of operations the following transactions occurred.

1. Performed services for patients who had dental plan insurance. At January 31, $875 of such services was earned but not yet recorded.
2. Utility expenses incurred but not paid prior to January 31 totaled $520.
3. Purchased dental equipment on January 1 for $80,000, paying $20,000 in cash and signing a $60,000, 3-year note payable. The equipment depreciates $400 per month. Interest is $500 per month.
4. Purchased a one-year malpractice insurance policy on January 1 for $18,000.
5. Purchased $1,600 of dental supplies. On January 31, determined that $600 of supplies were on hand.

Instructions

Prepare the adjusting entries on January 31. Account titles are: Accumulated Depreciation—Dental Equipment, Depreciation Expense, Service Revenue, Accounts Receivable, Insurance Expense, Interest Expense, Interest Payable, Prepaid Insurance, Supplies, Supplies Expense, Utilities Expense, and Utilities Payable.

Prepare adjusting entries.

(SO 5, 6, 7)

E3-5 The trial balance for Pioneer Advertising Agency is shown in Illustration 3-3, p. 93. In lieu of the adjusting entries shown in the text at October 31, assume the following adjustment data.

1. Advertising supplies on hand at October 31 total $1,000.
2. Expired insurance for the month is $100.
3. Depreciation for the month is $50.
4. Unearned revenue earned in October totals $600.
5. Services provided but not recorded at October 31 are $300.
6. Interest accrued at October 31 is $70.
7. Accrued salaries at October 31 are $1,200.

Instructions
Prepare the adjusting entries for the items above.

E3-6 The income statement of Olympic Co. for the month of July shows net income of $1,400 based on Service Revenue $5,500, Wages Expense $2,300, Supplies Expense $1,200, and Utilities Expense $600. In reviewing the statement, you discover the following.

Prepare correct income statement.

(SO 2, 5, 6, 7)

1. Insurance expired during July of $400 was omitted.
2. Supplies expense includes $300 of supplies that are still on hand at July 31.
3. Depreciation on equipment of $150 was omitted.
4. Accrued but unpaid wages at July 31 of $300 were not included.
5. Services provided but unrecorded totaled $1,000.

Instructions
Prepare a correct income statement for July 2005.

E3-7 A partial adjusted trial balance of Ruiz Company at January 31, 2005, shows the following.

Analyze adjusted data.

(SO 4, 5, 6, 7)

RUIZ COMPANY
Adjusted Trial Balance
January 31, 2005

	Debit	Credit
Supplies	$ 850	
Prepaid Insurance	2,400	
Salaries Payable		$ 800
Unearned Revenue		750
Supplies Expense	950	
Insurance Expense	400	
Salaries Expense	1,800	
Service Revenue		2,000

Instructions
Answer the following questions, assuming the year begins January 1.

(a) If the amount in Supplies Expense is the January 31 adjusting entry, and $650 of supplies was purchased in January, what was the balance in Supplies on January 1?
(b) If the amount in Insurance Expense is the January 31 adjusting entry, and the original insurance premium was for one year, what was the total premium and when was the policy purchased?
(c) If $3,000 of salaries was paid in January, what was the balance in Salaries Payable at December 31, 2004?
(d) If $1,600 was received in January for services performed in January, what was the balance in Unearned Revenue at December 31, 2004?

E3-8 Selected accounts of Engle Company are shown below.

Journalize basic transactions and adjusting entries.

(SO 5, 6, 7)

Supplies Expense	
7/31 800	

	Supplies		
7/1 Bal.	1,100	7/31	800
7/10	200		

Salaries Payable	
	7/31 1,200

(continued from p. 119)

Accounts Receivable		
7/31	500	

Unearned Revenue		
7/31	900	7/1 Bal. 1,500
		7/20 750

Salaries Expense		
7/15	1,200	
7/31	1,200	

Service Revenue		
		7/14 2,000
		7/31 900
		7/31 500

Instructions

After analyzing the accounts, journalize **(a)** the July transactions and **(b)** the adjusting entries that were made on July 31. (*Hint:* July transactions were for cash.)

Prepare adjusting entries from analysis of trial balances.

(SO 5, 6, 7)

E3-9 The trial balances before and after adjustment for Villa Company at the end of its fiscal year are presented below.

VILLA COMPANY
Trial Balance
August 31, 2004

	Before Adjustment		After Adjustment	
	Dr.	**Cr.**	**Dr.**	**Cr.**
Cash	$10,400		$10,400	
Accounts Receivable	8,800		9,400	
Office Supplies	2,300		700	
Prepaid Insurance	4,000		2,500	
Office Equipment	14,000		14,000	
Accumulated Depreciation—Office Equipment		$ 3,600		$ 4,900
Accounts Payable		5,800		5,800
Salaries Payable		–0–		1,100
Unearned Rent		1,500		600
T. Villa, Capital		15,600		15,600
Service Revenue		34,000		34,600
Rent Revenue		11,000		11,900
Salaries Expense	17,000		18,100	
Office Supplies Expense	–0–		1,600	
Rent Expense	15,000		15,000	
Insurance Expense	–0–		1,500	
Depreciation Expense	–0–		1,300	
	$71,500	$71,500	$74,500	$74,500

Instructions

Prepare the adjusting entries that were made.

Prepare financial statements from adjusted trial balance.

(SO 7)

E3-10 The adjusted trial balance for Villa Company is given in E3-9.

Instructions

Prepare the income and owner's equity statements for the year and the balance sheet at August 31.

Record transactions on accrual basis; convert revenue to cash receipts.

(SO 5, 6)

E3-11 The following data are taken from the comparative balance sheets of Midway Billiards Club, which prepares its financial statements using the accrual basis of accounting.

December 31	**2005**	**2004**
Fees receivable from members	$12,000	$ 9,000
Unearned fees revenue	17,000	20,000

Fees are billed to members based upon their use of the club's facilities. Unearned fees arise from the sale of gift certificates, which members can apply to their future use of club facilities.

The 2005 income statement for the club showed that fees revenue of $153,000 was earned during the year.

Instructions

(*Hint:* You will probably find it helpful to use T accounts to analyze these data.)

(a) Prepare journal entries for each of the following events that took place during 2005.

(1) Fees receivable from 2004 were all collected.

(2) Gift certificates outstanding at the end of 2004 were all redeemed.

(3) An additional $35,000 worth of gift certificates were sold during 2005. A portion of these was used by the recipients during the year; the remainder was still outstanding at the end of 2005.

(4) Fees for 2005 for services provided to members were billed to members.

(5) Fees receivable for 2005 (i.e., those billed in item [4] above) were partially collected.

(b) Determine the amount of cash received by the club, with respect to fees, during 2005.

*E3-12 At Concord Company, prepayments are debited to expense when paid, and unearned revenues are credited to revenue when received. During January of the current year, the following transactions occurred.

Journalize transactions and adjusting entries using appendix.

(SO 8)

Jan. 2   Paid $2,400 for fire insurance protection for the year.
     10   Paid $1,700 for supplies.
     15   Received $6,100 for services to be performed in the future.

On January 31, it is determined that $1,500 of the services fees have been earned and that there are $800 of supplies on hand.

Instructions

(a) Journalize and post the January transactions. (Use T accounts.)

(b) Journalize and post the adjusting entries at January 31.

(c) Determine the ending balance in each of the accounts.

PROBLEMS: SET A

P3-1A Lindy Rig started her own consulting firm, Vektek Consulting, on May 1, 2005. The trial balance at May 31 is as follows.

Prepare adjusting entries, post to ledger accounts, and prepare an adjusted trial balance.

(SO 5, 6, 7)

VEKTEK CONSULTING
Trial Balance
May 31, 2005

Account Number		Debit	Credit
101	Cash	$ 7,700	
110	Accounts Receivable	4,000	
120	Prepaid Insurance	2,400	
130	Supplies	1,500	
135	Office Furniture	12,000	
200	Accounts Payable		$ 3,500
230	Unearned Service Revenue		3,000
300	L. Rig, Capital		19,100
400	Service Revenue		6,000
510	Salaries Expense	3,000	
520	Rent Expense	1,000	
		$31,600	$31,600

In addition to those accounts listed on the trial balance, the chart of accounts for Vektek Consulting also contains the following accounts and account numbers: No. 136 Accumulated Depreciation—Office Furniture, No. 210 Travel Payable, No. 220 Salaries Payable, No. 530 Depreciation Expense, No. 540 Insurance Expense, No. 550 Travel Expense, and No. 560 Supplies Expense.

Other data:

1. $500 of supplies have been used during the month.
2. Travel expense incurred but not paid on May 31, 2004, $200.
3. The insurance policy is for 2 years.
4. $1,000 of the balance in the unearned service revenue account remains unearned at the end of the month.
5. May 31 is a Wednesday, and employees are paid on Fridays. Vektek Consulting has two employees, who are paid $500 each for a 5-day work week.
6. The office furniture has a 5-year life with no salvage value. It is being depreciated at $200 per month for 60 months.
7. Invoices representing $1,000 of services performed during the month have not been recorded as of May 31.

Instructions

(a) Prepare the adjusting entries for the month of May. Use J4 as the page number for your journal.
(b) Post the adjusting entries to the ledger accounts. Enter the totals from the trial balance as beginning account balances and place a check mark in the posting reference column.
(c) Prepare an adjusted trial balance at May 31, 2005.

(c) Adj. trial balance $33,600

Prepare adjusting entries, post, and prepare adjusted trial balance, and financial statements.

(SO 5, 6, 7)

P3-2A The Thayer Motel opened for business on May 1, 2005. Its trial balance before adjustment on May 31 is as follows.

THAYER MOTEL
Trial Balance
May 31, 2005

Account Number		Debit	Credit
101	Cash	$ 2,500	
126	Supplies	1,900	
130	Prepaid Insurance	2,400	
140	Land	15,000	
141	Lodge	70,000	
149	Furniture	16,800	
201	Accounts Payable		$ 5,300
208	Unearned Rent		3,600
275	Mortgage Payable		35,000
301	Sue Phillips, Capital		60,000
429	Rent Revenue		9,200
610	Advertising Expense	500	
726	Salaries Expense	3,000	
732	Utilities Expense	1,000	
		$113,100	$113,100

In addition to those accounts listed on the trial balance, the chart of accounts for Thayer Motel also contains the following accounts and account numbers: No. 142 Accumulated Depreciation—Lodge, No. 150 Accumulated Depreciation—Furniture, No. 212 Salaries Payable, No. 230 Interest Payable, No. 619 Depreciation Expense—Lodge, No. 621 Depreciation Expense—Furniture, No. 631 Supplies Expense, No. 718 Interest Expense, and No. 722 Insurance Expense.

Other data:

1. Insurance expires at the rate of $200 per month.
2. A count of supplies shows $900 of unused supplies on May 31.
3. Annual depreciation is $2,400 on the lodge and $3,000 on furniture.
4. The mortgage interest rate is 12%. (The mortgage was taken out on May 1.)
5. Unearned rent of $2,500 has been earned.
6. Salaries of $800 are accrued and unpaid at May 31.

Instructions

(a) Journalize the adjusting entries on May 31.
(b) Prepare a ledger using the three-column form of account. Enter the trial balance amounts and post the adjusting entries. (Use J1 as the posting reference.)
(c) Prepare an adjusted trial balance on May 31.
(d) Prepare an income statement and an owner's equity statement for the month of May and a balance sheet at May 31.

(c) Adj. trial balance
$114,700
(d) Net income $4,400
Ending capital balance
$64,400
Total assets $106,950

P3-3A Mendoza Co. was organized on July 1, 2005. Quarterly financial statements are prepared. The unadjusted and adjusted trial balances as of September 30 are shown below.

Prepare adjusting entries and financial statements.
(SO 5, 6, 7)

MENDOZA CO.
Trial Balance
September 30, 2005

	Unadjusted Dr.	Unadjusted Cr.	Adjusted Dr.	Adjusted Cr.
Cash	$ 6,700		$ 6,700	
Accounts Receivable	400		600	
Prepaid Rent	1,500		900	
Supplies	1,200		1,000	
Equipment	15,000		15,000	
Accumulated Depreciation—Equipment				$ 850
Notes Payable		$ 5,000		5,000
Accounts Payable		1,510		1,510
Salaries Payable				400
Interest Payable				50
Unearned Rent		900		500
Jose Mendoza, Capital		14,000		14,000
Jose Mendoza, Drawing	600		600	
Commission Revenue		14,000		14,200
Rent Revenue		400		800
Salaries Expense	9,000		9,400	
Rent Expense	900		1,500	
Depreciation Expense			850	
Supplies Expense			200	
Utilities Expense	510		510	
Interest Expense			50	
	$35,810	$35,810	$37,310	$37,310

Instructions

(a) Journalize the adjusting entries that were made.
(b) Prepare an income statement and an owner's equity statement for the 3 months ending September 30 and a balance sheet at September 30.
(c) If the note bears interest at 12%, how many months has it been outstanding?

(b) Net income $2,490
Ending capital $15,890
Total assets $23,350

P3-4A A review of the ledger of Khan Company at December 31, 2005, produces the following data pertaining to the preparation of annual adjusting entries.

Prepare adjusting entries
(SO 5, 6)

1. Prepaid Insurance $9,800. The company has separate insurance policies on its buildings and its motor vehicles. Policy B4564 on the building was purchased on July 1, 2004, for $6,000. The policy has a term of 3 years. Policy A2958 on the vehicles was purchased on January 1, 2005, for $4,800. This policy has a term of 2 years.
2. Unearned Subscriptions $49,000. The company began selling magazine subscriptions in 2005 on an annual basis. The magazine is published monthly. The selling price of a subscription is $50. A review of subscription contracts reveals the following.

1. Insurance expense $4,400

2. Subscription revenue
$7,000

Subscription Date	Number of Subscriptions
October 1	200
November 1	300
December 1	480
	980

3. Interest expense $1,200

4. Salaries expense $2,940

3. Notes Payable $40,000. This balance consists of a note for 6 months at an annual interest rate of 9%, dated September 1.

4. Salaries Payable $0. There are eight salaried employees. Salaries are paid every Friday for the current week. Five employees receive a salary of $500 each per week, and three employees earn $800 each per week. December 31 is a Wednesday. Employees do not work weekends. All employees worked the last 3 days of December.

Instructions
Prepare the adjusting entries at December 31, 2005.

Journalize transactions and follow through accounting cycle to preparation of financial statements.

(SO 5, 6, 7)

P3-5A On November 1, 2005, the account balances of Samone Equipment Repair were as follows.

No.	Debits		No.	Credits	
101	Cash	$ 2,790	154	Accumulated Depreciation	$ 500
112	Accounts Receivable	2,510	201	Accounts Payable	2,100
126	Supplies	2,000	209	Unearned Service Revenue	1,400
153	Store Equipment	10,000	212	Salaries Payable	500
			301	P. Samone, Capital	12,800
		$17,300			$17,300

During November the following summary transactions were completed.

Nov. 8 Paid $1,100 for salaries due employees, of which $600 is for November.
10 Received $1,200 cash from customers on account.
12 Received $1,400 cash for services performed in November.
15 Purchased store equipment on account $3,000.
17 Purchased supplies on account $500.
20 Paid creditors on account $2,500.
22 Paid November rent $300.
25 Paid salaries $1,000.
27 Performed services on account and billed customers for services provided $700.
29 Received $550 from customers for future service.

Adjustment data consist of:

1. Supplies on hand $1,000.
2. Accrued salaries payable $500.
3. Depreciation for the month is $120.
4. Unearned service revenue of $1,150 is earned.

Instructions

(a) Enter the November 1 balances in the ledger accounts.
(b) Journalize the November transactions.
(c) Post to the ledger accounts. Use J1 for the posting reference. Use the following accounts: No. 407 Service Revenue, No. 615 Depreciation Expense, No. 631 Supplies Expense, No. 726 Salaries Expense, and No. 729 Rent Expense.

(d) Trial balance $20,450
(f) Adj. trial balance $21,070
(g) Net loss $770; Ending capital $12,030; Total assets $16,430

(d) Prepare a trial balance at November 30.
(e) Journalize and post adjusting entries.
(f) Prepare an adjusted trial balance.
(g) Prepare an income statement and an owner's equity statement for November and a balance sheet at November 30.

*P3-6A Salzer Graphics Company was organized on January 1, 2005, by Jill Salzer. At the end of the first 6 months of operations, the trial balance contained the following accounts.

Prepare adjusting entries, adjusted trial balance, and financial statements using appendix.
(SO 5, 6, 7, 8)

Debits		Credits	
Cash	$ 9,500	Notes Payable	$ 20,000
Accounts Receivable	14,000	Accounts Payable	9,000
Equipment	45,000	Jill Salzer, Capital	22,000
Insurance Expense	1,800	Graphic Revenue	52,100
Salaries Expense	30,000	Consulting Revenue	6,000
Supplies Expense	3,700		
Advertising Expense	1,900		
Rent Expense	1,500		
Utilities Expense	1,700		
	$109,100		$109,100

Analysis reveals the following additional data.

1. The $3,700 balance in Supplies Expense represents supplies purchased in January. At June 30, $1,300 of supplies was on hand.
2. The note payable was issued on February 1. It is a 12%, 6-month note.
3. The balance in Insurance Expense is the premium on a one-year policy, dated March 1, 2005.
4. Consulting fees are credited to revenue when received. At June 30, consulting fees of $1,100 are unearned.
5. Graphic revenue earned but unrecorded at June 30 totals $2,000.
6. Depreciation is $3,000 per year.

Instructions

(a) Journalize the adjusting entries at June 30. (Assume adjustments are recorded every 6 months.)
(b) Prepare an adjusted trial balance.
(c) Prepare an income statement and owner's equity statement for the 6 months ended June 30 and a balance sheet at June 30.

(b) Adj. trial balance
    $113,600
(c) Net income $18,400
    Ending capital $40,400
    Total assets $71,500

PROBLEMS: SET B

P3-1B Joey Cuono started his own consulting firm, Cuono Company, on June 1, 2005. The trial balance at June 30 is as follows.

Prepare adjusting entries, post to ledger accounts, and prepare adjusted trial balance.
(SO 5, 6, 7)

CUONO COMPANY
Trial Balance
June 30, 2005

Account Number		Debit	Credit
100	Cash	$ 7,150	
110	Accounts Receivable	6,000	
120	Prepaid Insurance	3,000	
130	Supplies	2,000	
135	Office Equipment	15,000	
200	Accounts Payable		$ 4,500
230	Unearned Service Revenue		4,000
300	J. Cuono, Capital		21,750
400	Service Revenue		7,900
510	Salaries Expense	4,000	
520	Rent Expense	1,000	
		$38,150	$38,150

In addition to those accounts listed on the trial balance, the chart of accounts for Cuono Company also contains the following accounts and account numbers: No. 136 Accumulated Depreciation—Office Equipment, No. 210 Utilities Payable, No. 220 Salaries Payable, No. 530 Depreciation Expense, No. 540 Insurance Expense, No. 550 Utilities Expense, and No. 560 Supplies Expense.

Other data:

1. Supplies on hand at June 30 are $1,100.
2. A utility bill for $150 has not been recorded and will not be paid until next month.
3. The insurance policy is for a year.
4. $2,500 of unearned service revenue has been earned at the end of the month.
5. Salaries of $1,500 are accrued at June 30.
6. The office equipment has a 5-year life with no salvage value. It is being depreciated at $250 per month for 60 months.
7. Invoices representing $2,000 of services performed during the month have not been recorded as of June 30.

Instructions

(a) Prepare the adjusting entries for the month of June. Use J3 as the page number for your journal.
(b) Post the adjusting entries to the ledger accounts. Enter the totals from the trial balance as beginning account balances and place a check mark in the posting reference column.
(c) Prepare an adjusted trial balance at June 30, 2005.

(c) Adj. trial balance
$42,050

Prepare adjusting entries, post, and prepare adjusted trial balance, and financial statements.

(SO 5, 6, 7)

P3-2B Spring River Resort opened for business on June 1 with eight air-conditioned units. Its trial balance before adjustment on August 31 is as follows.

SPRING RIVER RESORT
Trial Balance
August 31, 2005

Account Number		Debit	Credit
101	Cash	$ 19,600	
126	Supplies	3,300	
130	Prepaid Insurance	6,000	
140	Land	25,000	
143	Cottages	125,000	
149	Furniture	26,000	
201	Accounts Payable		$ 6,500
208	Unearned Rent		7,400
275	Mortgage Payable		80,000
301	P. Orbis, Capital		100,000
306	P. Orbis, Drawing	5,000	
429	Rent Revenue		80,000
622	Repair Expense	3,600	
726	Salaries Expense	51,000	
732	Utilities Expense	9,400	
		$273,900	$273,900

In addition to those accounts listed on the trial balance, the chart of accounts for Spring River Resort also contains the following accounts and account numbers: No. 112 Accounts Receivable, No. 144 Accumulated Depreciation—Cottages, No. 150 Accumulated Depreciation—Furniture, No. 212 Salaries Payable, No. 230 Interest Payable, No. 620 Depreciation Expense—Cottages, No. 621 Depreciation Expense—Furniture, No. 631 Supplies Expense, No. 718 Interest Expense, and No. 722 Insurance Expense.

Other data:

1. Insurance expires at the rate of $400 per month.
2. A count on August 31 shows $900 of supplies on hand.
3. Annual depreciation is $3,600 on cottages and $2,400 on furniture.
4. Unearned rent of $4,100 was earned prior to August 31.

5. Salaries of $400 were unpaid at August 31.

6. Rentals of $800 were due from tenants at August 31. (Use Accounts Receivable.)

7. The mortgage interest rate is 9% per year. (The mortgage was taken out on August 1.)

Instructions

(a) Journalize the adjusting entries on August 31 for the 3-month period June 1–August 31.

(b) Prepare a ledger using the three-column form of account. Enter the trial balance amounts and post the adjusting entries. (Use J1 as the posting reference.)

(c) Prepare an adjusted trial balance on August 31.

(d) Prepare an income statement and an owner's equity statement for the 3 months ending August 31 and a balance sheet as of August 31.

(c) Adj. trial balance
$277,200
(d) Net income $14,800
Ending capital balance
$109,800
Total assets $200,600

P3-3B Costello Advertising Agency was founded by John Costello in January of 2004. Presented on the next page are both the adjusted and unadjusted trial balances as of December 31, 2005.

Prepare adjusting entries and financial statements.

(SO 5, 6, 7)

COSTELLO ADVERTISING AGENCY
Trial Balance
December 31, 2005

	Unadjusted		Adjusted	
	Dr.	**Cr.**	**Dr.**	**Cr.**
Cash	$ 11,000		$ 11,000	
Accounts Receivable	20,000		23,500	
Art Supplies	8,600		5,000	
Prepaid Insurance	3,350		2,500	
Printing Equipment	60,000		60,000	
Accumulated Depreciation		$ 28,000		$ 33,000
Accounts Payable		5,000		5,000
Interest Payable		–0–		150
Notes Payable		5,000		5,000
Unearned Advertising Fees		7,200		5,600
Salaries Payable		–0–		1,300
J. Costello, Capital		25,500		25,500
J. Costello, Drawing	12,000		12,000	
Advertising Revenue		58,600		63,700
Salaries Expense	10,000		11,300	
Insurance Expense			850	
Interest Expense	350		500	
Depreciation Expense			5,000	
Art Supplies Expense			3,600	
Rent Expense	4,000		4,000	
	$129,300	$129,300	$139,250	$139,250

Instructions

(a) Journalize the annual adjusting entries that were made.

(b) Prepare an income statement and a statement of owner's equity for the year ending December 31, 2005, and a balance sheet at December 31.

(c) Answer the following questions.

(1) If the note has been outstanding 6 months, what is the annual interest rate on that note?

(2) If the company paid $14,500 in salaries in 2005, what was the balance in Salaries Payable on December 31, 2004?

(b) Net income $38,450
Ending capital $51,950
Total assets $69,000
(c) (1) 6%
(2) $4,500

P3-4B A review of the ledger of Bellingham Company at December 31, 2005, produces the following data pertaining to the preparation of annual adjusting entries.

Preparing adjusting entries.

(SO 5, 6)

1. Salaries Payable $0. There are eight salaried employees. Salaries are paid every Friday for the current week. Five employees receive a salary of $800 each per week, and three employees earn $500 each per week. December 31 is a Tuesday. Employees do not work weekends. All employees worked the last 2 days of December.

1. Salaries expense $2,200

2. Rent revenue $74,000

2. Unearned Rent $324,000. The company began subleasing office space in its new building on November 1. At December 31, the company had the following rental contracts that are paid in full for the entire term of the lease.

Date	Term (in months)	Monthly Rent	Number of Leases
Nov. 1	6	$4,000	5
Dec. 1	6	$8,500	4

3. Advertising expense $5,200

3. Prepaid Advertising $15,600. This balance consists of payments on two advertising contracts. The contracts provide for monthly advertising in two trade magazines. The terms of the contracts are as follows.

Contract	Date	Amount	Number of Magazine Issue
A650	May 1	$6,000	12
B974	Oct. 1	9,600	24

The first advertisement runs in the month in which the contract is signed.

4. Interest expense $5,250

4. Notes Payable $100,000. This balance consists of a note for one year at an annual interest rate of 9%, dated June 1.

Instructions

Prepare the adjusting entries at December 31, 2005. (Show all computations.)

Journalize transactions and follow through accounting cycle to preparation of financial statements.

(SO 5, 6, 7)

P3-5B On September 1, 2005, the account balances of Beck Equipment Repair were as follows.

No.	Debits		No.	Credits	
101	Cash	$ 4,880	154	Accumulated Depreciation	$ 1,500
112	Accounts Receivable	3,520	201	Accounts Payable	3,400
126	Supplies	2,000	209	Unearned Service Revenue	1,400
153	Store Equipment	15,000	212	Salaries Payable	500
			301	J. Beck, Capital	18,600
		$25,400			$25,400

During September the following summary transactions were completed.

Sept. 8 Paid $1,400 for salaries due employees, of which $900 is for September.
10 Received $1,200 cash from customers on account.
12 Received $3,400 cash for services performed in September.
15 Purchased store equipment on account $3,000.
17 Purchased supplies on account $1,200.
20 Paid creditors $4,500 on account.
22 Paid September rent $500.
25 Paid salaries $1,050.
27 Performed services on account and billed customers for services provided $1,200.
29 Received $650 from customers for future service.

Adjustment data consist of:

1. Supplies on hand $1,700.
2. Accrued salaries payable $400.
3. Depreciation is $200 per month.
4. Unearned service revenue of $1,450 is earned.

Instructions

(a) Enter the September 1 balances in the ledger accounts.
(b) Journalize the September transactions.
(c) Post to the ledger accounts. Use J1 for the posting reference. Use the following accounts: No. 407 Service Revenue, No. 615 Depreciation Expense, No. 631 Supplies Expense, No. 726 Salaries Expense, and No. 729 Rent Expense.

(d) Prepare a trial balance at September 30.
(e) Journalize and post adjusting entries.
(f) Prepare an adjusted trial balance.
(g) Prepare an income statement and an owner's equity statement for September and a balance sheet at September 30.

(d) Trial balance $29,850
(f) Adj. trial balance $30,450
(g) Net income $1,500
    Ending capital $20,100
    Total assets $24,200

BROADENING YOUR PERSPECTIVE

Financial Reporting and Analysis

■ FINANCIAL REPORTING PROBLEM: PepsiCo

BYP3-1 The financial statements of **PepsiCo** are presented in Appendix A at the end of this textbook.

Instructions
(a) Using the consolidated financial statements and related information, identify items that may result in adjusting entries for prepayments.
(b) Using the consolidated financial statements and related information, identify items that may result in adjusting entries for accruals.
(c) Using the Selected Financial Data and 5-Year Summary, what has been the trend since 1998 for net income?

■ COMPARATIVE ANALYSIS PROBLEM: PepsiCo vs. Coca-Cola

BYP3-2 **PepsiCo**'s financial statements are presented in Appendix A. **Coca-Cola**'s financial statements are presented in Appendix B.

Instructions
Based on information contained in these financial statements, determine the following for each company.

(a) Net increase (decrease) in property, plant, and equipment (net) from 2001 to 2002.
(b) Increase (decrease) in selling, general, and administrative expenses from 2001 to 2002.
(c) Increase (decrease) in long-term debt (obligations) from 2001 to 2002.
(d) Increase (decrease) in net income from 2001 to 2002.
(e) Increase (decrease) in cash and cash equivalents from 2001 to 2002.

■ INTERPRETING FINANCIAL STATEMENTS: A Global Focus

BYP3-3 **Hoescht Marion Roussel (HMR)** is one of the world's largest research-based pharmaceutical companies. It is headquartered in Frankfurt, Germany. It conducts research in Germany, France, and the United States. Its financial statements are based on the International Accounting Standards of the International Accounting Standards Committee.

Instructions
Answer each of the following questions.

(a) The statement of cash flows reports interest paid during 1998 of $344 million, while the income statement reports interest expense of $721 million. What might explain this difference? Give an example of the journal entry that you would expect to see that would cause this difference (ignore amounts).
(b) Among its liabilities, the company reports provisions for litigation and environmental protection. What types of litigation and environmental protection costs might this company incur? What are the possible points in time that litigation costs might be expensed? At what point do you think these costs should be expensed on the income statement in order to provide proper matching of revenues and expenses? What challenges to matching does litigation present?

(c) The notes to the company's financial statements state that the company records revenues "at the time of shipment of products or performance of services." Is this consistent with the revenue recognition practices described in this chapter? What considerations might you want to take into account in determining whether this is the appropriate approach to recognize revenues?

■ EXPLORING THE WEB

BYP3-4 A wealth of accounting-related information is available via the Internet. For example the Rutgers Accounting Web offers access to a great variety of sources.

Address: www.rutgers.edu/accounting/raw, or go to www.wiley.com/college/weygandt

Steps: Click on **Accounting Resources**, or click on **RAW's Features**. (*Note:* Once on this page, you may have to click on the **text only** box to access the available information.)

Instructions
(a) List the categories of information available through the **Accounting Resources** page.
(b) Select any one of these categories and briefly describe the types of information available.

Critical Thinking

■ GROUP DECISION CASE

BYP3-5. The Happy Travel Court was organized on April 1, 2004, by Alice Henry. Alice is a good manager but a poor accountant. From the trial balance prepared by a part-time bookkeeper, Alice prepared the following income statement for the quarter that ended March 31, 2005.

HAPPY TRAVEL COURT
Income Statement
For the Quarter Ended March 31, 2005

Revenues		
Travel court rental revenue		$90,000
Operating expenses		
Advertising	$ 5,200	
Wages	29,800	
Utilities	900	
Depreciation	800	
Repairs	4,000	
Total operating expenses		40,700
Net income		$49,300

Alice knew that something was wrong with the statement because net income had never exceeded $20,000 in any one quarter. Knowing that you are an experienced accountant, she asks you to review the income statement and other data.

You first look at the trial balance. In addition to the account balances reported above in the income statement, the ledger contains the following additional selected balances at March 31, 2005.

Supplies	$ 6,200
Prepaid Insurance	7,200
Notes Payable	12,000

You then make inquiries and discover the following.

1. Travel court rental fees include advanced rentals for summer month occupancy $20,000.
2. There were $1,300 of supplies on hand at March 31.
3. Prepaid insurance resulted from the payment of a one-year policy on January 1, 2005.
4. The mail on April 1, 2005, brought the following bills: advertising for week of March 24, $110; repairs made March 10, $260; and utilities, $180.

5. There are four employees, who receive wages totaling $350 per day. At March 31, 2 days' wages have been incurred but not paid.

6. The note payable is a 3-month, 10% note dated January 1, 2005.

Instructions

With the class divided into groups, answer the following.

(a) Prepare a correct income statement for the quarter ended March 31, 2005.

(b) Explain to Alice the generally accepted accounting principles that she did not recognize in preparing her income statement and their effect on her results.

■ COMMUNICATION ACTIVITY

BYP3-6 In reviewing the accounts of Karibeth Co. at the end of the year, you discover that adjusting entries have not been made.

Instructions

Write a memo to Kari Beth Renfro, the owner of Karibeth Co., that explains the following: the nature and purpose of adjusting entries, why adjusting entries are needed, and the types of adjusting entries that may be made.

■ ETHICS CASE

BYP3-7 Santa Fe Company is a pesticide manufacturer. Its sales declined greatly this year due to the passage of legislation outlawing the sale of several of Santa Fe's chemical pesticides. In the coming year, Santa Fe will have environmentally safe and competitive chemicals to replace these discontinued products. Sales in the next year are expected to greatly exceed any prior year's. The decline in sales and profits appears to be a one-year aberration. But even so, the company president fears a large dip in the current year's profits. He believes that such a dip could cause a significant drop in the market price of Santa Fe's stock and make the company a takeover target.

To avoid this possibility, the company president calls in Diane Leno, controller, to discuss this period's year-end adjusting entries. He urges her to accrue every possible revenue and to defer as many expenses as possible. He says to Diane, "We need the revenues this year, and next year can easily absorb expenses deferred from this year. We can't let our stock price be hammered down!" Diane didn't get around to recording the adjusting entries until January 17, but she dated the entries December 31 as if they were recorded then. Diane also made every effort to comply with the president's request.

Instructions

(a) Who are the stakeholders in this situation?

(b) What are the ethical considerations of (1) the president's request and (2) Diane's dating the adjusting entries December 31?

(c) Can Diane accrue revenues and defer expenses and still be ethical?

Answers to Self-Study Questions

1. c   **2.** a   **3.** d   **4.** d   **5.** d   **6.** c   **7.** a   **8.** b   **9.** b   **10.** c   ***11.** a

Answer to PepsiCo Review It Question 4, p. 99

Per Note 4, **PepsiCo**'s 2002 depreciation expense is $929 million; 2001 depreciation expense is $843 million.

 ✓ REMEMBER to go back to the Navigator box on the chapter-opening page and check off your completed work.

Completion of the Accounting Cycle

THE NAVIGATOR ✓

Understand **Concepts for Review**	❏
Read **Feature Story**	❏
Scan **Study Objectives**	❏
Read **Preview**	❏
Read text and answer **Before You Go On**	
p. 141 ❏ p. 151 ❏ p. 158 ❏	
Work **Demonstration Problem**	❏
Review **Summary of Study Objectives**	❏
Answer **Self-Study Questions**	❏
Complete **Assignments**	❏

CONCEPTS FOR REVIEW

Before studying this chapter, you should know or, if necessary, review:

How to apply the revenue recognition and matching principles.
(Ch. 3, pp. 91–92)

How to make adjusting entries.
(Ch. 3, pp. 92–103)

How to prepare an adjusted trial balance.
(Ch. 3, p. 107)

How to prepare a balance sheet, income statement, and owner's equity statement.
(Ch. 3, pp. 108–109)

☑ THE NAVIGATOR

Everyone Likes to Win

When Ted Castle was a hockey coach at the University of Vermont, his players were self-motivated by their desire to win. Hockey was a game you either won or lost. But at **Rhino Foods, Inc.**, a specialty-bakery-foods company he founded in Burlington, Vermont, he discovered that manufacturing-line workers were not so self-motivated. Ted thought, what if he turned the food-making business into a game, with rules, strategies, and trophies?

Ted knew that in a game knowing the score is all-important. He felt that only if the employees know the score—know exactly how the business is doing daily, weekly, monthly—could he turn food-making into a game. But Rhino is a closely held, family-owned business, and its financial statements and profits were confidential. Should Ted open Rhino's books to the employees?

A consultant he was working with put Ted's concerns in perspective. The consultant said, "Imagine you're playing touch football. You play for an hour or two, and the whole time I'm sitting there with a book, keeping score. All of a sudden I blow the whistle, and I say, 'OK, that's it. Everybody go home.' I close my book and walk away. How would you feel?" Ted opened his books and revealed the financial statements to his employees.

The next step was to teach employees the rules and strategies of how to win at making food. The first lesson: "Your opponent at Rhino is expenses. You must cut and control expenses." Ted and his staff distilled those lessons into daily scorecards (production reports and income statements) that keep Rhino's employees up-to-date on the game. At noon each day, Ted posts the previous day's results at the entrance to the production room. Everyone checks whether they made or lost money on what they produced the day before. And it's not just an academic exercise; there's a bonus check for each employee at the end of every four-week "game" that meets profitability guidelines. Everyone can be a winner!

Rhino has flourished since the first game. Employment has increased from 20 to 130 people, while both revenues and profits have grown dramatically.

After studying this chapter, you should be able to:

1. Prepare a work sheet.
2. Explain the process of closing the books.
3. Describe the content and purpose of a post-closing trial balance.
4. State the required steps in the accounting cycle.
5. Explain the approaches to preparing correcting entries.
6. Identify the sections of a classified balance sheet.

As was true at **Rhino Foods, Inc.**, financial statements can help employees understand what is happening in the business. In Chapter 3, we prepared financial statements directly from the adjusted trial balance. However, with so many details involved in the end-of-period accounting procedures, it is easy to make errors. Locating and correcting errors can cost much time and effort. One way to minimize errors in the records and to simplify the end-of-period procedures is to use a work sheet.

In this chapter we will explain the role of the work sheet in accounting as well as the remaining steps in the accounting cycle, especially the closing process, again using Pioneer Advertising Agency as an example. Then we will consider (1) correcting entries and (2) classified balance sheets. The content and organization of Chapter 4 are as follows.

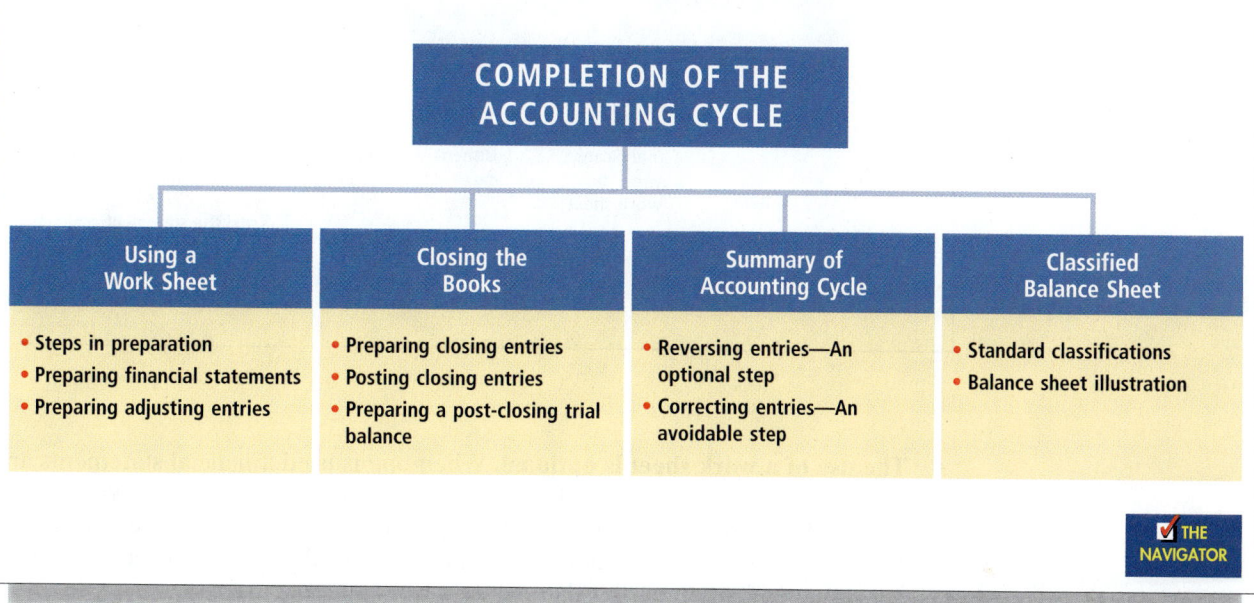

COMPLETION OF THE ACCOUNTING CYCLE

Using a Work Sheet
- Steps in preparation
- Preparing financial statements
- Preparing adjusting entries

Closing the Books
- Preparing closing entries
- Posting closing entries
- Preparing a post-closing trial balance

Summary of Accounting Cycle
- Reversing entries—An optional step
- Correcting entries—An avoidable step

Classified Balance Sheet
- Standard classifications
- Balance sheet illustration

☑ THE NAVIGATOR

Using a Work Sheet

A **work sheet** is a multiple-column form that may be used in the adjustment process and in preparing financial statements. As its name suggests, the work sheet is a working tool. **A work sheet is not a permanent accounting record**; it is neither a journal nor a part of the general ledger. The work sheet is merely a device used to make it easier to prepare adjusting entries and the financial statements. In small companies with relatively few accounts and adjustments, a work sheet may not be needed. In large companies with numerous accounts and many adjustments, it is almost indispensable.

The basic form of a work sheet and the procedure (five steps) for preparing it are shown in Illustration 4-1 (page 136). Each step must be performed in the prescribed sequence.

STUDY OBJECTIVE 1

Prepare a work sheet.

Illustration 4-1
Form and procedure for a
work sheet

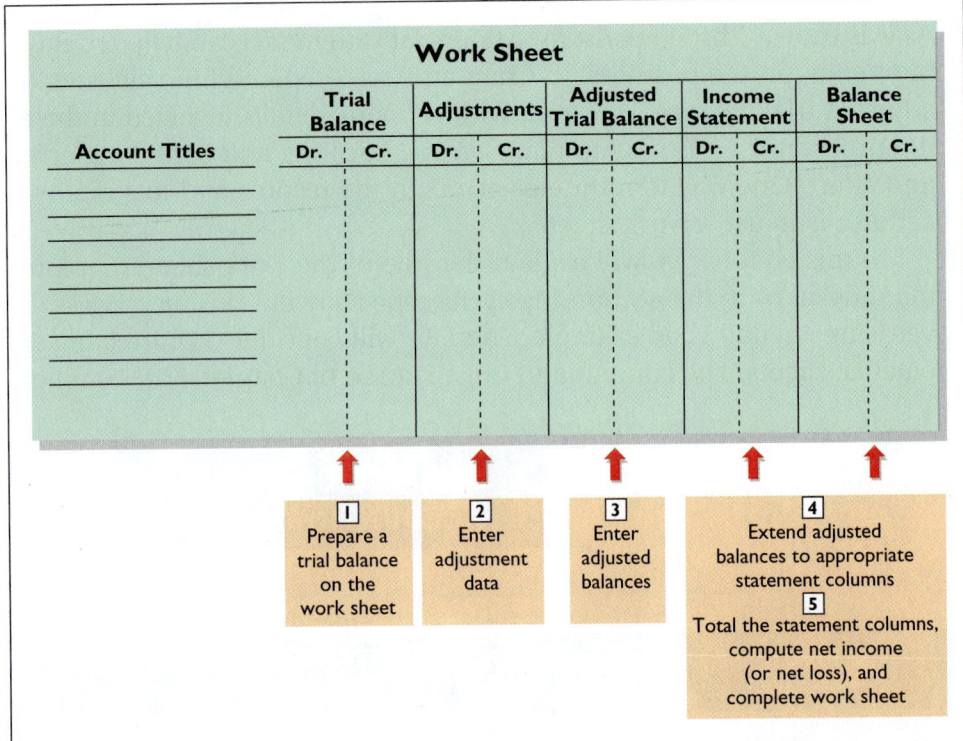

The use of a work sheet is optional. When one is used, financial statements are prepared from the work sheet. The adjustments are entered in the work sheet columns and are then journalized and posted after the financial statements have been prepared. Thus, management and other interested parties can receive the financial statements at an earlier date when a work sheet is used.

Steps in Preparing a Work Sheet

We will use the October 31 trial balance and adjustment data of Pioneer Advertising in Chapter 3 to illustrate the preparation of a work sheet. Each step of the process is described below and demonstrated in Illustrations 4-2 and 4-3A, B, C, and D following page 137.

Step 1. Prepare a Trial Balance on the Work Sheet

All ledger accounts with balances are entered in the account titles space. Debit and credit amounts from the ledger are entered in the trial balance columns. The work sheet trial balance for Pioneer Advertising Agency is shown in Illustration 4-2 on page 138.

Step 2. Enter the Adjustments in the Adjustments Columns

Turn over the first transparency, Illustration 4-3A. When a work sheet is used, all adjustments are entered in the adjustments columns. In entering the adjustments, applicable trial balance accounts should be used. If additional accounts are needed, they are inserted on the lines immediately below the trial balance totals. Each adjustment is indexed and keyed; this practice facilitates the journalizing of the adjusting entry in the general journal. **The adjustments are not journalized until after the work sheet is completed and the financial statements have been prepared.**

The adjustments for Pioneer Advertising Agency are the same as the adjustments illustrated on page 105. They are keyed in the adjustments columns of the work sheet as follows.

(a) An additional account Advertising Supplies Expense is debited $1,500 for the cost of supplies used, and Advertising Supplies is credited $1,500.

(b) An additional account Insurance Expense is debited $50 for the insurance that has expired, and Prepaid Insurance is credited $50.

(c) Two additional depreciation accounts are needed. Depreciation Expense is debited $40 for the month's depreciation, and Accumulated Depreciation—Office Equipment is credited $40.

(d) Unearned Revenue is debited $400 for services provided, and Service Revenue is credited $400.

(e) An additional account Accounts Receivable is debited $200 for services provided but not billed, and Service Revenue is credited $200.

(f) Two additional accounts relating to interest are needed. Interest Expense is debited $50 for accrued interest, and Interest Payable is credited $50.

(g) Salaries Expense is debited $1,200 for accrued salaries, and an additional account Salaries Payable is credited $1,200.

Note in the illustration that after all the adjustments have been entered, the adjustments columns are totaled and the equality of the column totals is proved.

Step 3. Enter Adjusted Balances in the Adjusted Trial Balance Columns

Turn over the second transparency, Illustration 4-3B. The adjusted balance of an account is obtained by combining the amounts entered in the first four columns of the work sheet for each account. For example, the Prepaid Insurance account in the trial balance columns has a $600 debit balance and a $50 credit in the adjustments columns. The result is a $550 debit balance recorded in the adjusted trial balance columns. **For each account on the work sheet, the amount in the adjusted trial balance columns is the account balance that will appear in the ledger after the adjusting entries have been journalized and posted.** The balances in these columns are the same as those in the adjusted trial balance in Illustration 3-21 (page 107).

After all account balances have been entered in the adjusted trial balance columns, the columns are totaled and their equality is proved. The agreement of the column totals facilitates the completion of the work sheet. If these columns are not in agreement, the financial statement columns will not balance and the financial statements will be incorrect.

Step 4. Extend Adjusted Trial Balance Amounts to Appropriate Financial Statement Columns

Turn over the third transparency, Illustration 4-3C. The fourth step is to extend adjusted trial balance amounts to the income statement and balance sheet columns of the work sheet. Balance sheet accounts are entered in the appropriate balance sheet debit and credit columns. For instance, Cash is entered in the balance sheet debit column, and Notes Payable is entered in the credit column. Accumulated Depreciation is extended to the balance sheet credit column. The reason is that accumulated depreciation is a contra-asset account with a credit balance.

Because the work sheet does not have columns for the owner's equity statement, the balance in owner's capital is extended to the balance sheet credit column. In addition, the balance in owner's drawing is extended to the balance sheet debit column because it is an owner's equity account with a debit balance.

HELPFUL HINT

Every adjusted trial balance amount must be extended to one of the four statement columns.

(**Note:** Text continues on page 139, following acetate overlays.)

Illustration 4-2
Preparing a trial balance

PIONEER ADVERTISING AGENCY												
Work Sheet												
For the Month Ended October 31, 2005												
Account Titles	Trial Balance		Adjustments		Adjusted Trial Balance		Income Statement		Balance Sheet			
	Dr.	Cr.	Dr.	Cr.	Dr.	Cr.	Dr.	Cr.	Dr.	Cr.		
Cash	15,200											
Advertising Supplies	2,500											
Prepaid Insurance	600											
Office Equipment	5,000											
Notes Payable		5,000										
Accounts Payable		2,500										
Unearned Revenue		1,200										
C. R. Byrd, Capital		10,000										
C. R. Byrd, Drawing	500											
Service Revenue		10,000										
Salaries Expense	4,000											
Rent Expense	900											
Totals	28,700	28,700										

Include all accounts with balances from ledger.

Trial balance amounts are taken directly from ledger accounts.

The expense and revenue accounts such as Salaries Expense and Service Revenue are entered in the appropriate income statement columns.

All of these extensions are shown in Illustration 4-3C.

Step 5. Total the Statement Columns, Compute the Net Income (or Net Loss), and Complete the Work Sheet

Turn over the fourth transparency, Illustration 4-3D. Each of the financial statement columns must be totaled. The net income or loss for the period is then found by computing the difference between the totals of the two income statement columns. If total credits exceed total debits, net income has resulted. In such a case, as shown in Illustration 4-3D, the words "Net Income" are inserted in the account titles space. The amount then is entered in the income statement debit column and the balance sheet credit column. **The debit amount balances the income statement columns, and the credit amount balances the balance sheet columns.** In addition, the credit in the balance sheet column indicates the increase in owner's equity resulting from net income.

If, instead, total debits in the income statement columns exceed total credits, a net loss has occurred. The amount of the net loss is entered in the income statement credit column and the balance sheet debit column.

After the net income or net loss has been entered, new column totals are determined. The totals shown in the debit and credit income statement columns will match. The totals shown in the debit and credit balance sheet columns will also match. If either the income statement columns or the balance sheet columns are not equal after the net income or net loss has been entered, an error has been made in the work sheet. The completed work sheet for Pioneer Advertising Agency is shown in Illustration 4-3D.

ACCOUNTING IN ACTION  **e Business Insight**

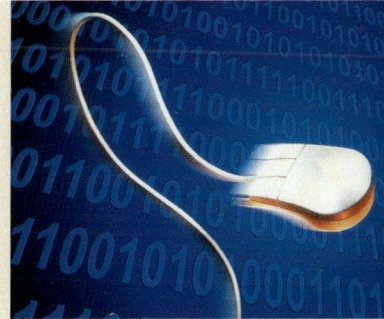

The work sheet can be computerized using an electronic spreadsheet program. The Excel supplement for this textbook is one of the most popular versions of such spreadsheet packages. With a program like Excel, you can produce any type of work sheet (accounting or otherwise) that you could produce with paper and pencil on a columnar pad. The tremendous advantage of an electronic work sheet over the paper-and-pencil version is the ability to change selected data easily. When data are changed, the computer updates the balance of your computations instantly. More specific applications of electronic spreadsheets will be noted as we proceed.

Preparing Financial Statements from a Work Sheet

After a work sheet has been completed, all the data that are required for the preparation of financial statements are at hand. The income statement is prepared from the income statement columns. The balance sheet and owner's equity statement are prepared from the balance sheet columns. The financial statements prepared from the work sheet for Pioneer Advertising Agency are shown in Illustration 4-4 (page 140). At this point, adjusting entries have not been journalized and posted. Therefore, the ledger does not support all financial statement amounts.

Accounting Cycle Tutorial—
Preparing Financial Statements
and Closing the Books

The amount shown for owner's capital on the work sheet is the account balance **before considering drawings and net income (or loss).** When there have been no

Illustration 4-4
Financial statements from a
work sheet

PIONEER ADVERTISING AGENCY
Income Statement
For the Month Ended October 31, 2005

Revenues		
Service revenue		$10,600
Expenses		
Salaries expense	$5,200	
Advertising supplies expense	1,500	
Rent expense	900	
Insurance expense	50	
Interest expense	50	
Depreciation expense	40	
Total expenses		7,740
Net income		$ 2,860

PIONEER ADVERTISING AGENCY
Owner's Equity Statement
For the Month Ended October 31, 2005

C. R. Byrd, Capital, October 1		$ –0–
Add: Investments	$10,000	
Net income	2,860	12,860
		12,860
Less: Drawings		500
C. R. Byrd, Capital, October 31		$12,360

PIONEER ADVERTISING AGENCY
Balance Sheet
October 31, 2005

Assets

Cash		$15,200
Accounts receivable		200
Advertising supplies		1,000
Prepaid insurance		550
Office equipment	$5,000	
Less: Accumulated depreciation	40	4,960
Total assets		$21,910

Liabilities and Owner's Equity

Liabilities		
Notes payable		$ 5,000
Accounts payable		2,500
Interest payable		50
Unearned revenue		800
Salaries payable		1,200
Total liabilities		9,550
Owner's equity		
C. R. Byrd, Capital		12,360
Total liabilities and owner's equity		$21,910

additional investments of capital by the owner during the period, this amount is the balance at the beginning of the period.

Using a work sheet, financial statements can be prepared before adjusting entries are journalized and posted. **However, the completed work sheet is not a substitute for formal financial statements.** Data in the financial statement columns of the work sheet are not properly arranged for statement purposes. Also, as noted above, the financial statement presentation for some accounts differs from their statement columns on the work sheet. **A work sheet is essentially a working tool of the accountant; it is not distributed to management and other parties.**

Preparing Adjusting Entries from a Work Sheet

A work sheet is not a journal, and it cannot be used as a basis for posting to ledger accounts. To adjust the accounts, it is necessary to journalize the adjustments and post them to the ledger. **The adjusting entries are prepared from the adjustments columns of the work sheet.** The reference letters in the adjustments columns and the explanations of the adjustments at the bottom of the work sheet help identify the adjusting entries. However, writing the explanation to the adjustments at the bottom of the work sheet is not required. As indicated previously, the journalizing and posting of adjusting entries **follows** the preparation of financial statements when a work sheet is used. The adjusting entries on October 31 for Pioneer Advertising Agency are the same as those shown in Illustration 3-19 (page 105).

BEFORE YOU GO ON...

Review It

1. What are the five steps in preparing a work sheet?
2. How is net income or net loss shown in a work sheet?
3. How does a work sheet relate to preparing financial statements and adjusting entries?

Do It

Susan Elbe is preparing a work sheet. Explain to Susan how the following adjusted trial balance accounts should be extended to the financial statement columns of the work sheet: Cash; Accumulated Depreciation; Accounts Payable; Julie Kerr, Drawing; Service Revenue; and Salaries Expense.

ACTION PLAN

- Extend asset balances to the balance sheet debit column. Extend liability balances to the balance sheet credit column. Extend accumulated depreciation to the balance sheet credit column.
- Extend the drawing account to the balance sheet debit column.
- Extend expenses to the income statement debit column.
- Extend revenue accounts to the income statement credit column.

SOLUTION

Income statement debit column—Salaries Expense
Income statement credit column—Service Revenue
Balance sheet debit column—Cash; Julie Kerr, Drawing
Balance sheet credit column—Accumulated Depreciation; Accounts Payable

As indicated in the e-Business box on page 139, the work sheet is an ideal application for electronic spreadsheet software like Microsoft Excel and LOTUS 1–2–3.

Related exercise material: *BE4-1, BE4-2, BE4-3, E4-1, E4-2, E4-4, and E4-5.*

☑ THE NAVIGATOR

Closing the Books

STUDY OBJECTIVE 2

Explain the process of closing the books.

At the end of the accounting period, the accounts are made ready for the next period. This is called **closing the books**. In closing the books, it is necessary to distinguish between temporary and permanent accounts. **Temporary** or **nominal accounts** relate only to a given accounting period. They include all income statement accounts and owner's drawing. All temporary accounts are closed. In contrast, **permanent** or **real accounts** relate to one or more future accounting periods. They consist of all balance sheet accounts, including owner's capital. Permanent accounts are not closed. Instead, their balances are carried forward into the next accounting period. Illustration 4-5 identifies the accounts in each category.

Illustration 4-5
Temporary versus permanent accounts

HELPFUL HINT

A contra asset account, such as accumulated depreciation, is a permanent account also.

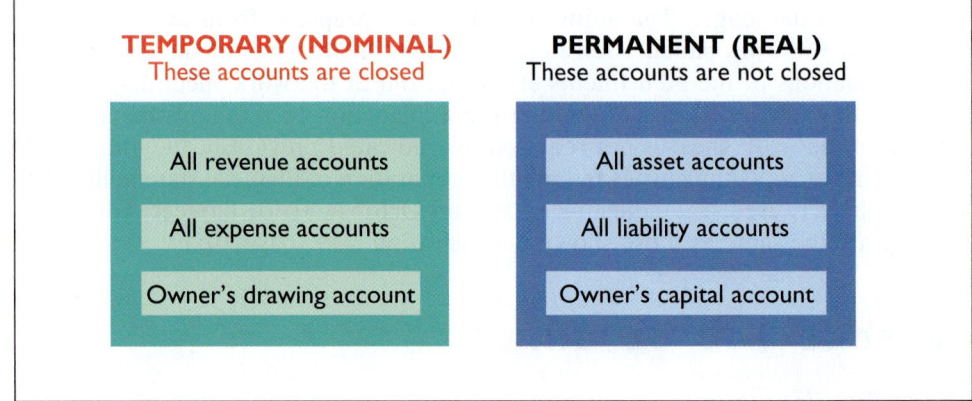

TEMPORARY (NOMINAL) These accounts are closed	PERMANENT (REAL) These accounts are not closed
All revenue accounts	All asset accounts
All expense accounts	All liability accounts
Owner's drawing account	Owner's capital account

Preparing Closing Entries

At the end of the accounting period, the temporary account balances are transferred to the permanent owner's equity account, owner's capital, through the preparation of closing entries.[1] **Closing entries** formally recognize in the ledger the transfer of net income (or net loss) and owner's drawing to owner's capital. The results of these entries are shown in the owner's equity statement. **These entries also produce a zero balance in each temporary account. These accounts are then ready to accumulate data in the next accounting period separate from the data of prior periods.** Permanent accounts are not closed.

Journalizing and posting closing entries is a required step in the accounting cycle. (See Illustration 4-12 on page 149.) This step is performed after financial statements have been prepared. In contrast to the steps in the cycle that you have already studied, closing entries are generally journalized and posted **only at the end of a company's annual accounting period**. This practice facilitates the preparation of annual financial statements because all temporary accounts will contain data for the entire year.

In preparing closing entries, each income statement account could be closed directly to owner's capital. However, to do so would result in excessive detail in the permanent owner's capital account. Instead, the revenue and expense accounts are closed to another temporary account, **Income Summary**; only the net income or net loss is transferred from this account to owner's capital.

Closing entries are journalized in the general journal. A center caption entitled Closing Entries, inserted in the journal between the last adjusting entry and the first closing entry, identifies these entries. Then the closing entries are posted to the ledger accounts.

---

[1]Closing entries for a partnership and for a corporation are explained in Chapters 13 and 14, respectively.

Closing entries may be prepared directly from the adjusted balances in the ledger, from the income statement and balance sheet columns of the work sheet, or from the income and owner's equity statements. Separate closing entries could be prepared for each nominal account, but the following four entries accomplish the desired result more efficiently:

1. Debit each revenue account for its balance, and credit Income Summary for total revenues.

2. Debit Income Summary for total expenses, and credit each expense account for its balance.

3. Debit Income Summary and credit Owner's Capital for the amount of net income.

4. Debit Owner's Capital for the balance in the Owner's Drawing account, and credit Owner's Drawing for the same amount.

The four entries are referenced in the diagram of the closing process shown in Illustration 4-6 and in the journal entries in Illustration 4-7 (page 144). The posting of closing entries is shown in Illustration 4-8 (page 145).

HELPFUL HINT

Owner's Drawing is closed directly to Capital and *not* to Income Summary because Owner's Drawing is not an expense.

Illustration 4-6
Diagram of closing process—proprietorship

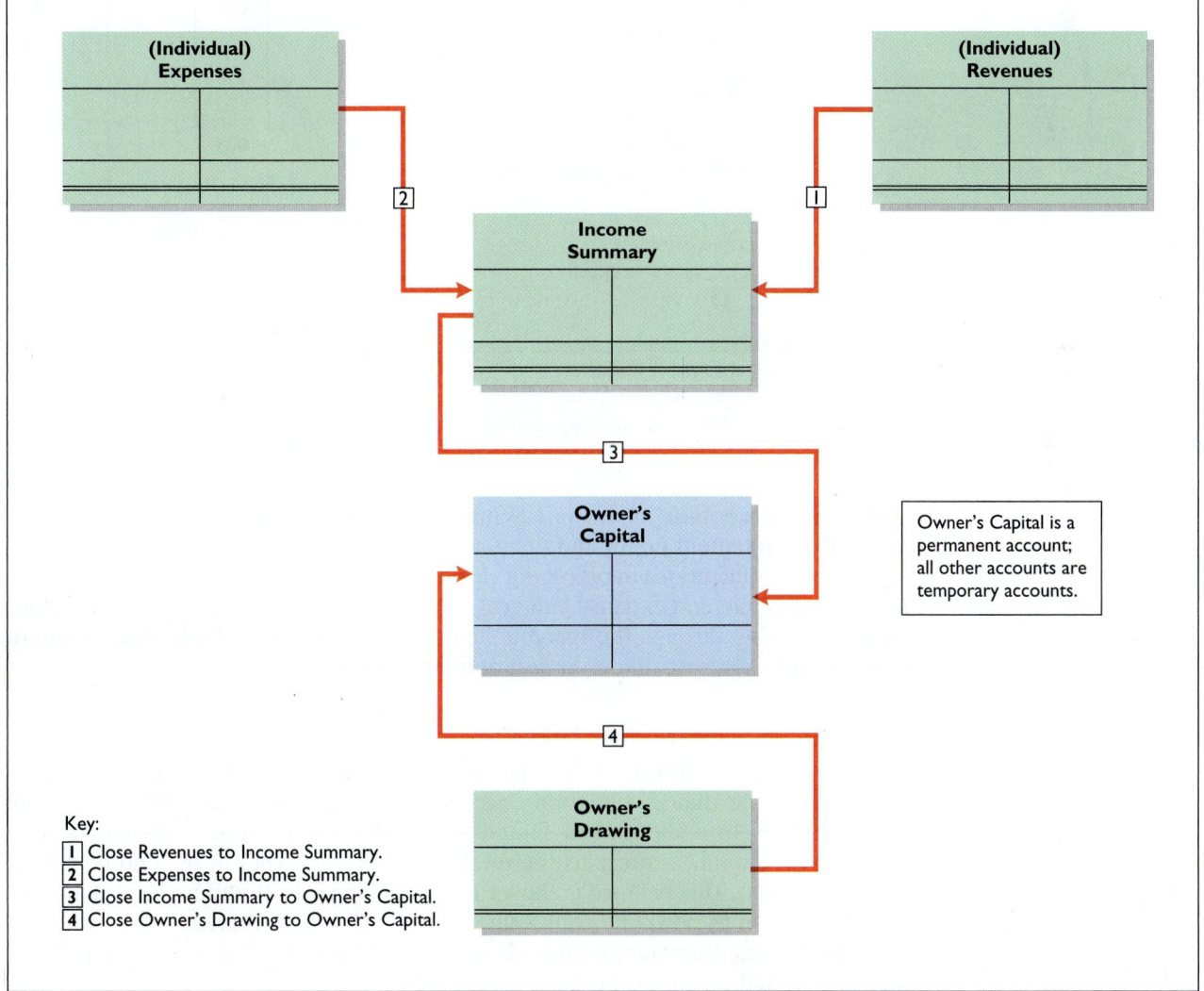

Key:
1. Close Revenues to Income Summary.
2. Close Expenses to Income Summary.
3. Close Income Summary to Owner's Capital.
4. Close Owner's Drawing to Owner's Capital.

Owner's Capital is a permanent account; all other accounts are temporary accounts.

If there were a net loss because expenses exceeded revenues, entry 3 in Illustration 4-6 would be reversed: Credit Income Summary and debit Owner's Capital.

Closing Entries Illustrated

In practice, closing entries are generally prepared only at the end of the annual accounting period. However, to illustrate the journalizing and posting of closing entries, we will assume that Pioneer Advertising Agency closes its books monthly. The closing entries at October 31 are shown in Illustration 4-7.

Illustration 4-7
Closing entries journalized

GENERAL JOURNAL					J3
Date	**Account Titles and Explanation**	**Ref.**	**Debit**		**Credit**
	Closing Entries				
	(1)				
2005					
Oct. 31	Service Revenue	400	10,600		
	Income Summary	350			10,600
	(To close revenue account)				
	(2)				
31	Income Summary	350	7,740		
	Advertising Supplies Expense	631			1,500
	Depreciation Expense	711			40
	Insurance Expense	722			50
	Salaries Expense	726			5,200
	Rent Expense	729			900
	Interest Expense	905			50
	(To close expense accounts)				
	(3)				
31	Income Summary	350	2,860		
	C. R. Byrd, Capital	301			2,860
	(To close net income to capital)				
	(4)				
31	C. R. Byrd, Capital	301	500		
	C. R. Byrd, Drawing	306			500
	(To close drawings to capital)				

Note that the amounts for Income Summary in entries (1) and (2) are the totals of the income statement credit and debit columns, respectively, in the work sheet.

A couple of cautions in preparing closing entries: (1) Avoid unintentionally doubling the revenue and expense balances rather than zeroing them. (2) Do not close owner's drawing through the Income Summary account. **Owner's drawing is not an expense, and it is not a factor in determining net income.**

Posting Closing Entries

The posting of the closing entries and the ruling of the accounts are shown in Illustration 4-8. Note that all temporary accounts have zero balances after posting the closing entries. In addition, you should realize that the balance in owner's capital (C. R. Byrd, Capital) represents the total equity of the owner at the end of the accounting period. This balance is shown on the balance sheet and is the ending capital reported on the owner's equity statement, as shown in Illustration 4-4 on page 140. **The Income Summary account is used only in closing.** No entries are journalized and posted to this account during the year.

As part of the closing process, the **temporary accounts** (revenues, expenses, and owner's drawing) in T-account form are totaled, balanced, and double-ruled as shown in Illustration 4-8. The **permanent accounts** (assets, liabilities, and owner's capital) are not closed: A single rule is drawn beneath the current period entries, and the account balance carried forward to the next period is entered below the single rule. (For example, see C. R. Byrd, Capital.)

Illustration 4-8
Posting of closing entries

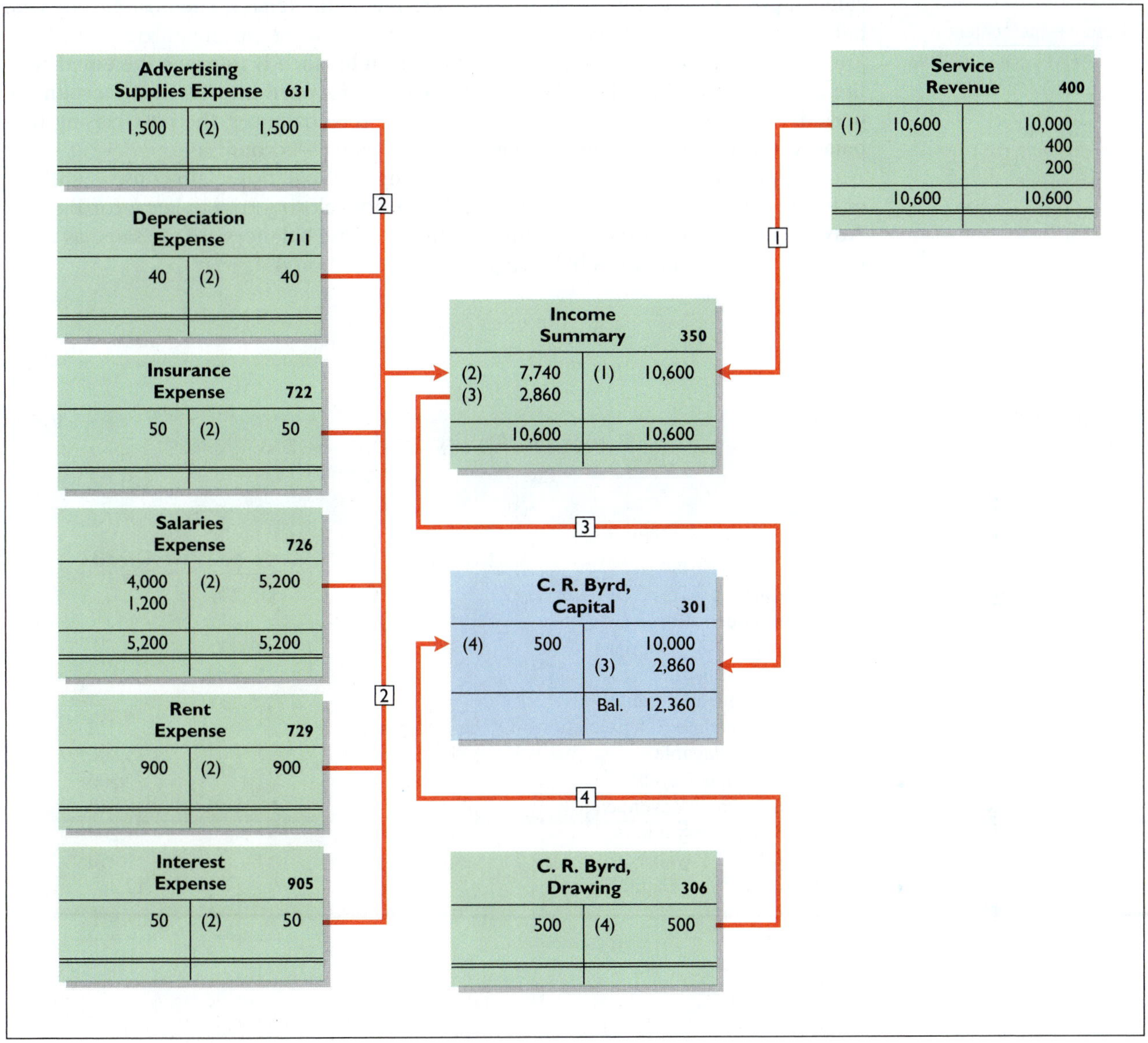
Advertising Supplies Expense 631
1,500
(2) 1,500
Depreciation Expense 711
40
(2) 40
Insurance Expense 722
50
(2) 50
Salaries Expense 726
4,000
1,200
(2) 5,200
5,200
5,200
Rent Expense 729
900
(2) 900
Interest Expense 905
50
(2) 50
Service Revenue 400
(1) 10,600
10,000
400
200
10,600
10,600
Income Summary 350
(2) 7,740
(3) 2,860
(1) 10,600
10,600
10,600
C. R. Byrd, Capital 301
(4) 500
10,000
(3) 2,860
Bal. 12,360
C. R. Byrd, Drawing 306
500
(4) 500
1
2
3
4

Accounting in Action — e Business Insight

Technology has dramatically changed the accounting process. When Larry Carter became chief financial officer of **Cisco Systems**, closing the quarterly accounts would take up to ten days. Within four years he got it down to two days and halved the cost of finance, to 1 percent of sales. Now he is aiming to be able to do a "virtual close"—closing within a day on any day in the quarter.

This is not just showing off. Knowing exactly where you are all of the time, says Mr. Carter, allows you to respond faster than your competitors. But it also means that the 600 people who used to spend 10 days a quarter tracking transactions can now be more usefully employed on things such as mining data for business intelligence.

Source: Excerpted from "Business and the Internet," *The Economist*, June 26, 1999, p. 12.

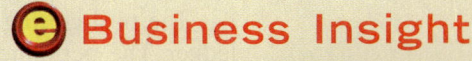

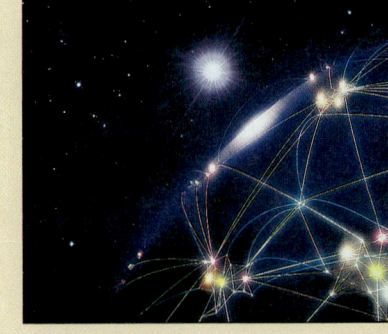

Preparing a Post-Closing Trial Balance

STUDY OBJECTIVE 3

Describe the content and purpose of a post-closing trial balance.

After all closing entries have been journalized and posted, another trial balance, called a **post-closing trial balance**, is prepared from the ledger. The post-closing trial balance lists permanent accounts and their balances after closing entries have been journalized and posted. **The purpose of this trial balance is to prove the equality of the permanent account balances that are carried forward into the next accounting period.** Since all temporary accounts will have zero balances, **the post-closing trial balance will contain only permanent—balance sheet—accounts**.

The procedure for preparing a post-closing trial balance again consists entirely of listing the accounts and their balances. The post-closing trial balance for Pioneer Advertising Agency is shown in Illustration 4-9. These balances are the same as those reported in the company's balance sheet in Illustration 4-4.

Illustration 4-9
Post-closing trial balance

PIONEER ADVERTISING AGENCY
Post-Closing Trial Balance
October 31, 2005

	Debit	Credit
Cash	$15,200	
Accounts Receivable	200	
Advertising Supplies	1,000	
Prepaid Insurance	550	
Office Equipment	5,000	
Accumulated Depreciation—Office Equipment		$ 40
Notes Payable		5,000
Accounts Payable		2,500
Unearned Revenue		800
Salaries Payable		1,200
Interest Payable		50
C. R. Byrd, Capital		12,360
	$21,950	$21,950

The post-closing trial balance is prepared from the permanent accounts in the ledger. The permanent accounts of Pioneer Advertising are shown in the general ledger in Illustration 4-10 on page 147. Remember that the balance of each permanent account is computed after every posting. Therefore, no additional work on these accounts is needed as part of the closing process.

A post-closing trial balance provides evidence that the journalizing and posting of closing entries have been properly completed. It also shows that the accounting equation is in balance at the end of the accounting period. However, like the trial balance, it does not prove that all transactions have been recorded or that the ledger is correct. For example, the post-closing trial balance will balance if a transaction is not journalized and posted or if a transaction is journalized and posted twice.

The remaining accounts in the general ledger are temporary accounts (shown in Illustration 4-11 on page 148). After the closing entries are correctly posted, each temporary account has a zero balance. These accounts are double-ruled to finalize the closing process.

Illustration 4-10
General ledger, permanent accounts

(Permanent Accounts Only)

GENERAL LEDGER

	Cash				No. 101
Date	Explanation	Ref.	Debit	Credit	Balance
2005					
Oct. 1		J1	10,000		10,000
2		J1	1,200		11,200
3		J1		900	10,300
4		J1		600	9,700
20		J1		500	9,200
26		J1		4,000	5,200
31		J1	10,000		**15,200**

	Accounts Receivable				No. 112
Date	Explanation	Ref.	Debit	Credit	Balance
2005					
Oct. 31	Adj. entry	J2	**200**		**200**

	Advertising Supplies				No. 126
Date	Explanation	Ref.	Debit	Credit	Balance
2005					
Oct. 5		J1	2,500		2,500
31	Adj. entry	J2		**1,500**	**1,000**

	Prepaid Insurance				No. 130
Date	Explanation	Ref.	Debit	Credit	Balance
2005					
Oct. 4		J1	600		600
31	Adj. entry	J2		**50**	**550**

	Office Equipment				No. 157
Date	Explanation	Ref.	Debit	Credit	Balance
2005					
Oct. 1		J1	5,000		**5,000**

	Accumulated Depreciation—Office Equipment				No. 158
Date	Explanation	Ref.	Debit	Credit	Balance
2005					
Oct. 31	Adj. entry	J2		**40**	**40**

	Notes Payable				No. 200
Date	Explanation	Ref.	Debit	Credit	Balance
2005					
Oct. 1		J1		5,000	**5,000**

	Accounts Payable				No. 201
Date	Explanation	Ref.	Debit	Credit	Balance
2005					
Oct. 5		J1		2,500	**2,500**

	Unearned Revenue				No. 209
Date	Explanation	Ref.	Debit	Credit	Balance
2005					
Oct. 2		J1		1,200	1,200
31	Adj. entry	J2	400		**800**

	Salaries Payable				No. 212
Date	Explanation	Ref.	Debit	Credit	Balance
2005					
Oct. 31	Adj. entry	J2		**1,200**	**1,200**

	Interest Payable				No. 230
Date	Explanation	Ref.	Debit	Credit	Balance
2005					
Oct. 31	Adj. entry	J2		**50**	**50**

	C. R. Byrd, Capital				No. 301
Date	Explanation	Ref.	Debit	Credit	Balance
2005					
Oct. 1		J1		10,000	10,000
31	**Closing entry**	**J3**		**2,860**	**12,860**
31	**Closing entry**	**J3**	**500**		**12,360**

Note: The permanent accounts for Pioneer Advertising Agency are shown here; the temporary accounts are shown in Illustration 4-11. Both permanent and temporary accounts are part of the general ledger; they are segregated here to aid in learning.

Summary of the Accounting Cycle

The steps in the accounting cycle are shown in Illustration 4-12 on page 149. From the graphic you can see that the cycle begins with the analysis of business transactions and ends with the preparation of a post-closing trial balance. The steps in the cycle are performed in sequence and are repeated in each accounting period.

STUDY OBJECTIVE 4

State the required steps in the accounting cycle.

Illustration 4-11
General ledger, temporary
accounts

(Temporary Accounts Only)

GENERAL LEDGER

C. R. Byrd, Drawing   No. 306

Date	Explanation	Ref.	Debit	Credit	Balance
2005					
Oct. 20		J1	500		500
31	Closing entry	J3		500	–0–

Income Summary   No. 350

Date	Explanation	Ref.	Debit	Credit	Balance
2005					
Oct. 31	Closing entry	J3		10,600	10,600
31	Closing entry	J3	7,740		2,860
31	Closing entry	J3	2,860		–0–

Service Revenue   No. 400

Date	Explanation	Ref.	Debit	Credit	Balance
2005					
Oct. 31		J1		10,000	10,000
31	Adj. entry	J2		400	10,400
31	Adj. entry	J2		200	10,600
31	Closing entry	J3	10,600		–0–

Advertising Supplies Expense   No. 631

Date	Explanation	Ref.	Debit	Credit	Balance
2005					
Oct. 31	Adj. entry	J2	1,500		1,500
31	Closing entry	J3		1,500	–0–

Depreciation Expense   No. 711

Date	Explanation	Ref.	Debit	Credit	Balance
2005					
Oct. 31	Adj. entry	J2	40		40
31	Closing entry	J3		40	–0–

Insurance Expense   No. 722

Date	Explanation	Ref.	Debit	Credit	Balance
2005					
Oct. 31	Adj. entry	J2	50		50
31	Closing entry	J3		50	–0–

Salaries Expense   No. 726

Date	Explanation	Ref.	Debit	Credit	Balance
2005					
Oct. 26		J1	4,000		4,000
31	Adj. entry	J2	1,200		5,200
31	Closing entry	J3		5,200	–0–

Rent Expense   No. 729

Date	Explanation	Ref.	Debit	Credit	Balance
2005					
Oct. 3		J1	900		900
31	Closing entry	J3		900	–0–

Interest Expense   No. 905

Date	Explanation	Ref.	Debit	Credit	Balance
2005					
Oct. 31	Adj. entry	J2	50		50
31	Closing entry	J3		50	–0–

Note: The temporary accounts for Pioneer Advertising Agency are shown here; the permanent accounts are shown in Illustration 4-10. Both permanent and temporary accounts are part of the general ledger; they are segregated here to aid in learning.

Steps 1–3 may occur daily during the accounting period, as explained in Chapter 2. Steps 4–7 are performed on a periodic basis, such as monthly, quarterly, or annually. Steps 8 and 9, closing entries, and a post-closing trial balance, are usually prepared only at the end of a company's **annual** accounting period.

There are also two optional steps in the accounting cycle. As you have seen, a work sheet may be used in preparing adjusting entries and financial statements. In addition, reversing entries may be used as explained below.

Reversing Entries—An Optional Step

Some accountants prefer to reverse certain adjusting entries at the beginning of a new accounting period. A **reversing entry** is made at the beginning of the next accounting period. It is the exact opposite of the adjusting entry made in the previous period. **The preparation of reversing entries is an optional bookkeeping procedure that is not a required step in the accounting cycle.** Accordingly, we have chosen to cover this topic in an appendix at the end of the chapter.

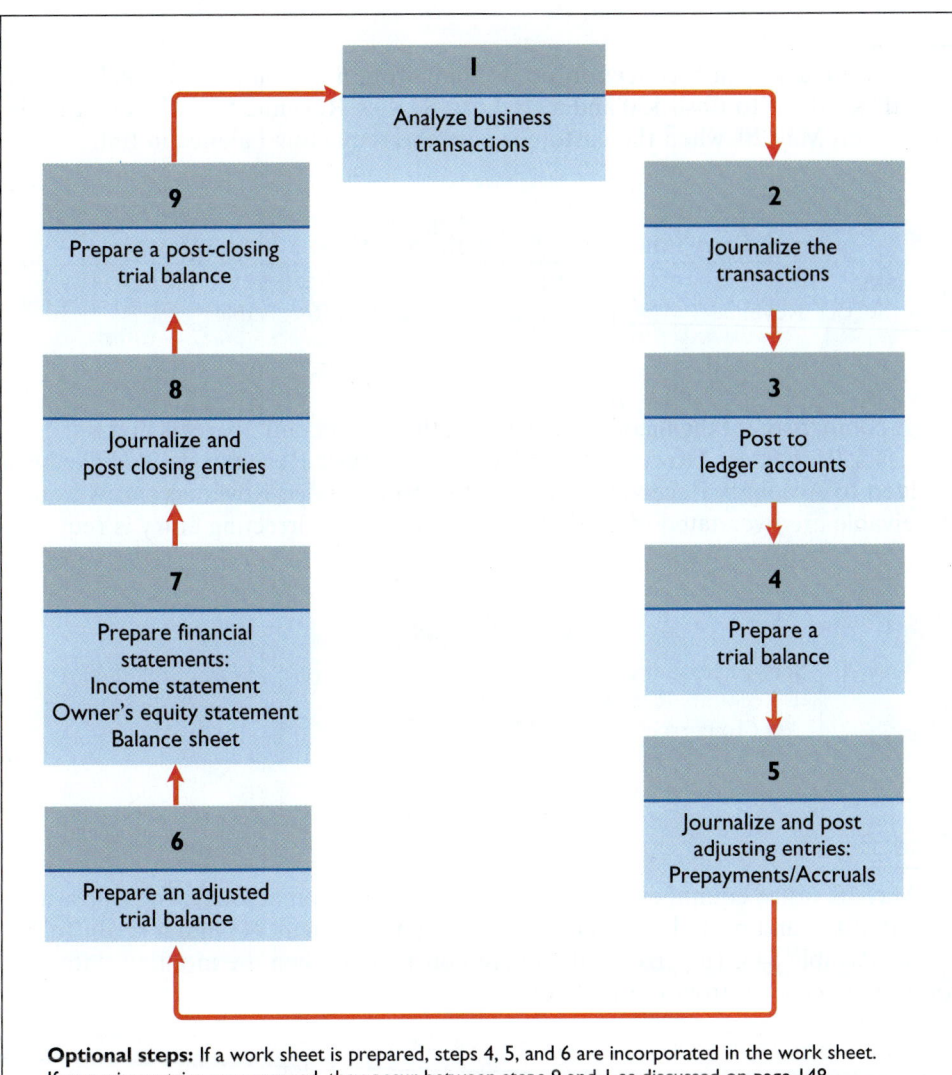

Illustration 4-12
Steps in the accounting cycle

Steps in the accounting cycle:

1 — Analyze business transactions
2 — Journalize the transactions
3 — Post to ledger accounts
4 — Prepare a trial balance
5 — Journalize and post adjusting entries: Prepayments/Accruals
6 — Prepare an adjusted trial balance
7 — Prepare financial statements: Income statement, Owner's equity statement, Balance sheet
8 — Journalize and post closing entries
9 — Prepare a post-closing trial balance

Optional steps: If a work sheet is prepared, steps 4, 5, and 6 are incorporated in the work sheet. If reversing entries are prepared, they occur between steps 9 and 1 as discussed on page 148.

Correcting Entries—An Avoidable Step

Unfortunately, errors may occur in the recording process. Errors should be corrected **as soon as they are discovered** by journalizing and posting correcting entries. If the accounting records are free of errors, no correcting entries are necessary.

You should recognize several differences between correcting entries and adjusting entries. First, adjusting entries are an integral part of the accounting cycle. Correcting entries, on the other hand, are unnecessary if the records are free of errors. Second, **adjustments are journalized and posted only at the end of an accounting period. In contrast, correcting entries are made whenever an error is discovered.** Finally, adjusting entries always affect at least one balance sheet account and one income statement account. In contrast, correcting entries may involve any combination of accounts in need of correction. **Correcting entries must be posted before closing entries.**

To determine the correcting entry, it is useful to compare the incorrect entry with the correct entry. Doing so helps identify the accounts and amounts that should—and should not—be corrected. After comparison, a correcting entry is made to correct the accounts. This approach is illustrated in the following two cases.

STUDY OBJECTIVE 5

Explain the approaches to preparing correcting entries.

ETHICS NOTE

Citigroup once reported a correcting entry reducing reported revenue by $23 million, while firing 11 employees. Company officials did not specify why the employees had apparently intentionally inflated the revenue figures, although it was noted that their bonuses were tied to their unit's performance.

Case 1

On May 10, a $50 cash collection on account from a customer is journalized and posted as a debit to Cash $50 and a credit to Service Revenue $50. The error is discovered on May 20, when the customer pays the remaining balance in full.

Illustration 4-13
Comparison of entries

Incorrect Entry (May 10)			Correct Entry (May 10)		
Cash	50		Cash	50	
Service Revenue		50	Accounts Receivable		50

A comparison of the incorrect entry with the correct entry reveals that the debit to Cash $50 is correct. However, the $50 credit to Service Revenue should have been credited to Accounts Receivable. As a result, both Service Revenue and Accounts Receivable are overstated in the ledger. The following correcting entry is required.

Illustration 4-14
Correcting entry

A	=	L	+	OE
−50				−50 Rev

Cash Flows
no effect

	Correcting Entry		
May 20	Service Revenue	50	
	Accounts Receivable		50
	(To correct entry of May 10)		

Case 2

On May 18, office equipment costing $450 is purchased on account. The transaction is journalized and posted as a debit to Delivery Equipment $45 and a credit to Accounts Payable $45. The error is discovered on June 3, when the monthly statement for May is received from the creditor.

Illustration 4-15
Comparison of entries

Incorrect Entry (May 18)			Correct Entry (May 18)		
Delivery Equipment	45		Office Equipment	450	
Accounts Payable		45	Accounts Payable		450

A comparison of the two entries shows that three accounts are incorrect. Delivery Equipment is overstated $45; Office Equipment is understated $450; and Accounts Payable is understated $405. The correcting entry is:

Illustration 4-16
Correcting entry

A	=	L	+	OE
+450				
−45		+405		

Cash Flows
no effect

	Correcting Entry		
June 3	Office Equipment	450	
	Delivery Equipment		45
	Accounts Payable		405
	(To correct entry of May 18)		

Instead of preparing a correcting entry, **it is possible to reverse the incorrect entry and then prepare the correct entry**. This approach will result in more entries and postings than a correcting entry, but it will accomplish the desired result.

ACCOUNTING IN ACTION Business Insight

Yale Express, a short-haul trucking firm, turned over much of its cargo to local truckers for delivery completion. Yale collected the entire delivery charge and, when billed by the local trucker, sent payment for the final phase to the local trucker. Yale used a cutoff period of 20 days into the next accounting period in making its adjusting entries for accrued liabilities. That is, it waited 20 days to receive the local truckers' bills to determine the amount of the unpaid but incurred delivery charges as of the balance sheet date.

On the other hand, **Republic Carloading**, a nationwide, long-distance freight forwarder, frequently did not receive transportation bills from truckers to whom it passed on cargo until months after the year-end. In making its year-end adjusting entries, Republic waited for months in order to include all of these outstanding transportation bills.

When Yale Express merged with Republic Carloading, Yale's vice president employed the 20-day cutoff procedure for both firms. As a result, millions of dollars of Republic's accrued transportation bills went unrecorded. When the erroneous procedure was detected and correcting entries were made, these and other errors changed a reported profit of $1.14 million into a loss of $1.88 million!

BEFORE YOU GO ON...

Review It

1. How do permanent accounts differ from temporary accounts?
2. What four different types of entries are required in closing the books?
3. What are the content and purpose of a post-closing trial balance?
4. What are the required and optional steps in the accounting cycle?

Do It

The work sheet for Hancock Company shows the following in the financial statement columns: R. Hancock, Drawing $15,000, R. Hancock, Capital $42,000, and net income $18,000. Prepare the closing entries at December 31 that affect owner's capital.

ACTION PLAN

- Remember to make closing entries in the correct sequence.
- Make the first two entries to close revenues and expenses.
- Make the third entry to close net income to owner's capital.
- Make the final entry to close owner's drawing to owner's capital.

SOLUTION

Dec. 31	Income Summary	18,000	
	R. Hancock, Capital		18,000
	(To close net income to capital)		
31	R. Hancock, Capital	15,000	
	R. Hancock, Drawing		15,000
	(To close drawings to capital)		

Related exercise material: *BE4-4, BE4-5, BE4-6, BE4-8, E4-3, E4-6, E4-8, and E4-9.*

☑ THE NAVIGATOR

Classified Balance Sheet

STUDY OBJECTIVE 6

Identify the sections of a classified balance sheet.

The financial statements illustrated up to this point were purposely kept simple. We classified items as assets, liabilities, and owner's equity in the balance sheet, and as revenues and expenses in the income statement. **Financial statements, however, become more useful to management, creditors, and potential investors when the elements are classified into significant subgroups.** In the remainder of this chapter, we will introduce you to the primary balance sheet classifications. The classified income statement will be presented in Chapter 5. The classified financial statements are what Ted Castle, owner of **Rhino Foods, Inc.**, gave to his employees to understand what was happening in the business.

Standard Classifications

A **classified balance sheet** usually contains these standard classifications:

Illustration 4-17
Standard balance sheet classifications

Assets	Liabilities and Owner's Equity
Current assets	Current liabilities
Long-term investments	Long-term liabilities
Property, plant, and equipment	Owner's (Stockholders') equity
Intangible assets	

These sections help the financial statement user determine such matters as (1) the availability of assets to meet debts as they come due and (2) the claims of short- and long-term creditors on total assets. A classified balance sheet also makes it easier to compare companies in the same industry, such as **GM**, **Ford**, and **DaimlerChrysler** in the automobile industry. Each of the sections is explained next.

A complete set of specimen financial statements for **PepsiCo, Inc.** is shown in Appendix A at the back of the book.

Current Assets

Current assets are cash and other resources that are reasonably expected to be realized in cash or sold or consumed in the business within one year of the balance sheet date or the company's operating cycle, whichever is longer. For example, accounts receivable are current assets because they will be realized in cash through collection within one year. A prepayment such as supplies is a current asset because of its expected use or consumption in the business within one year.

The **operating cycle** of a company is the average time that is required to go from cash to cash in producing revenues. The term "cycle" suggests a circular flow, which in this case, starts and ends with cash. For example, in municipal transit companies, the operating cycle would tend to be short since services are provided entirely on a cash basis. On the other hand, the operating cycle in manufacturing companies is longer: they purchase goods and materials, manufacture and sell products, bill customers, and collect cash. This is a cash to cash cycle that may extend for several months. Most companies have operating cycles of less than one year. More will be said about operating cycles in later chapters.

In a service enterprise, it is customary to recognize four types of current assets: (1) cash, (2) short-term investments such as U.S. government bonds, (3) receivables (notes receivable, accounts receivable, and interest receivable), and (4) prepaid expenses (insurance and supplies). **These items are listed in the order of liquidity.** That is, they are listed in the order in which they are expected to be converted into cash. This arrangement is illustrated below in the presentation of **UAL, Inc. (United Airlines)**.

UAL, INC, (UNITED AIRLINES) Balance Sheet (partial) (in millions)	
Current assets	
Cash	$1,348
Short-term investments	388
Receivables	788
Aircraft fuel, spare parts, and supplies	310
Prepaid expenses	219
Other current assets	326
Total current assets	$3,379

Illustration 4-18
Current assets section

A company's current assets are important in assessing the company's short-term debt-paying ability, as explained later in the chapter.

Long-Term Investments

Like current assets, **long-term investments** are resources that can be realized in cash. However, the conversion into cash is not expected within one year or the operating cycle, whichever is longer. In addition, long-term investments are not intended for use or consumption within the business. This category, often just called "investments," normally includes stocks and bonds of other corporations. **Yahoo! Inc.** reported the following in its balance sheet.

HELPFUL HINT

Long-term investments are investments *made* by the business—not investments by the owner *in* the business. Investments by the owner in the business are reported as part of owner's (stockholders') equity (see p. 156).

YAHOO! INC. Balance Sheet (partial)	
Long-term investments	
Long-term investments in marketable securities	$763,408

Illustration 4-19
Long-term investments section

Property, Plant, and Equipment

Property, plant, and equipment are tangible resources of a relatively permanent nature that are used in the business and not intended for sale. This category includes land, buildings, machinery and equipment, delivery equipment, and furniture and fixtures. Assets subject to depreciation should be reported at cost less accumulated

ALTERNATIVE TERMINOLOGY

Property, plant, and equipment are sometimes referred to as *plant assets* or *fixed assets*.

depreciation. This practice is illustrated in the following presentation of **Delta Air Lines**.

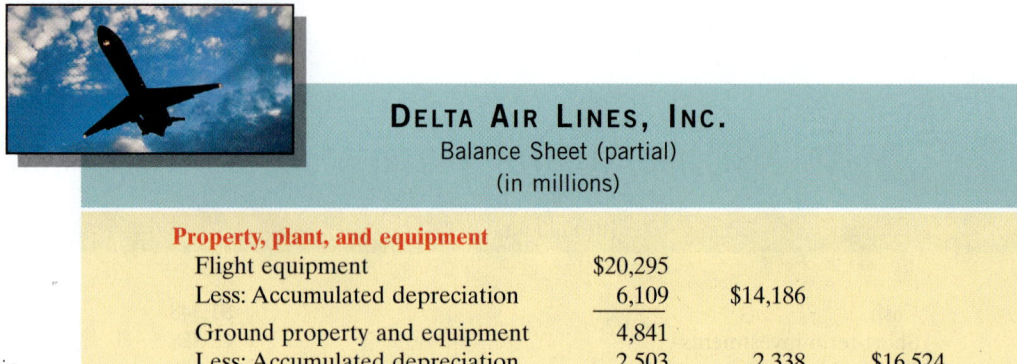

DELTA AIR LINES, INC.
Balance Sheet (partial)
(in millions)

Property, plant, and equipment

Flight equipment	$20,295		
Less: Accumulated depreciation	6,109	$14,186	
Ground property and equipment	4,841		
Less: Accumulated depreciation	2,503	2,338	$16,524

Illustration 4-20
Property, plant, and equipment section

Intangible Assets

Intangible assets are noncurrent resources that do not have physical substance. They are recorded at cost, and this cost is expensed over the useful life of the intangible asset. Intangible assets include patents, copyrights, and trademarks or trade names that give the holder **exclusive right** of use for a specified period of time. Their value to a company is generally derived from the rights or privileges granted by governmental authority.

In its balance sheet, **The Walt Disney Company** reported the following.

THE WALT DISNEY COMPANY
Balance Sheet (partial)
(in millions)

Intangible assets

Patents, trademarks, and other intangibles	$ 2,776	
Goodwill	17,083	19,859

Illustration 4-21
Intangible assets section

Current Liabilities

Listed first in the liabilities and owner's equity section of the balance sheet are current liabilities. **Current liabilities** are obligations that are reasonably expected to be paid from existing current assets or through the creation of other current liabilities. As in the case of current assets, the time period for payment is one year or the operating cycle, whichever is longer. Current liabilities include (1) debts related to the operating cycle, such as accounts payable and wages and salaries payable, and (2) other short-term debts, such as bank loans payable, interest payable, taxes payable, and current maturities of long-term obligations (payments to be made within the next year on long-term obligations).

The arrangement of items within the current liabilities section has evolved through custom rather than from a prescribed rule. Notes payable is usually listed first, followed by accounts payable. Other items are then listed in any order. The current liabilities section adapted from the balance sheet of **Deckers Outdoor Corporation** is as follows.

Illustration 4-22
Current liabilities section

DECKERS OUTDOOR CORPORATION
Balance Sheet (partial)
(in thousands)

Current liabilities	
Notes payable	$ 3,951,000
Accounts payable	12,916,000
Allowance for returns	1,255,000
Salaries and commissions payable	2,342,000
Taxes payable	732,000
Other current liabilities	912,000
Total current liabilities	$22,108,000

Users of financial statements look closely at the relationship between current assets and current liabilities. This relationship is important in evaluating a company's **liquidity**—its ability to pay obligations that are expected to become due within the next year or operating cycle. When current assets exceed current liabilities at the balance sheet date, the likelihood for paying the liabilities is favorable. When the reverse is true, short-term creditors may not be paid, and the company may ultimately be forced into bankruptcy.

Long-Term Liabilities

Obligations expected to be paid after one year or an operating cycle, whichever is longer, are classified as **long-term liabilities**. Liabilities in this category include bonds payable, mortgages payable, long-term notes payable, lease liabilities, and obligations under employee pension plans. Many companies report long-term debt maturing after one year as a single amount in the balance sheet. They then show the details of the debt in the notes that accompany the financial statements. Others list the various sources of long-term liabilities. In its balance sheet, **Brunswick Corporation** reported the following.

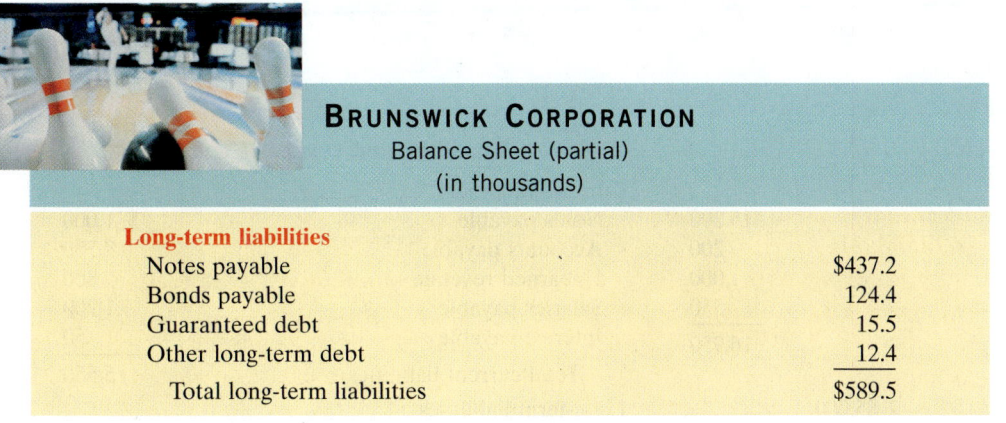

BRUNSWICK CORPORATION
Balance Sheet (partial)
(in thousands)

Long-term liabilities	
Notes payable	$437.2
Bonds payable	124.4
Guaranteed debt	15.5
Other long-term debt	12.4
Total long-term liabilities	$589.5

Illustration 4-23
Long-term liabilities section

Owner's Equity

The content of the owner's equity section varies with the form of business organization. In a proprietorship, there is one capital account. In a partnership, there is a capital account for each partner. For a corporation, owners' equity is divided into two accounts—Capital Stock and Retained Earnings. Investments of assets in the business by the stockholders are recorded by debiting an asset account and crediting the Capital Stock account. Income retained for use in the business is recorded in the Retained Earnings account. The Capital Stock and Retained Earnings accounts are combined and reported as stockholders' equity on the balance sheet. (We'll learn more about these corporation accounts in later chapters.)

In its balance sheet, **Dell Computer Corporation** recently reported its owners' (stockholders') equity section as follows.

Illustration 4-24
Stockholders' equity section

DELL	DELL COMPUTER CORPORATION	
	($ in millions)	
Stockholders' equity		
Common stock, 2,681,000,000 shares		$1,479
Retained earnings		3,394
Total stockholders' equity		$4,873

Classified Balance Sheet, Illustrated

An unclassified, report form balance sheet of Pioneer Advertising Agency was presented in Illustration 3-23 on page 109. Using the same adjusted trial balance accounts at October 31, 2005, we can prepare the classified balance sheet shown in Illustration 4-25. For illustrative purposes, assume that $1,000 of the notes payable is due currently and $4,000 is long-term.

The balance sheet is most often presented in **report form**, with assets listed above liabilities and owner's equity. The balance sheet may also be presented in **account form**: the assets section is placed on the left and the liabilities and owner's equity sections on the right, as shown in Illustration 4-25.

Illustration 4-25
Classified balance sheet in account form

PIONEER ADVERTISING AGENCY
Balance Sheet
October 31, 2005

Assets			Liabilities and Owner's Equity		
Current assets			Current liabilities		
Cash		$15,200	Notes payable		$ 1,000
Accounts receivable		200	Accounts payable		2,500
Advertising supplies		1,000	Unearned revenue		800
Prepaid insurance		550	Salaries payable		1,200
Total current assets		16,950	Interest payable		50
Property, plant, and equipment			Total current liabilities		5,550
Office equipment	$5,000		Long-term liabilities		
Less: Accumulated depreciation	40	4,960	Notes payable		4,000
Total assets		$21,910	Total liabilities		9,550
			Owner's equity		
			C. R. Byrd, Capital		12,360
			Total liabilities and owner's equity		$21,910

Another, more complete example of a classified balance sheet is presented in report form in Illustration 4-26.

Illustration 4-26
Classified balance sheet in report form

FRANKLIN CORPORATION
Balance Sheet
October 31, 2005

Assets

Current assets			
Cash		$ 6,600	
Short-term investments		2,000	
Accounts receivable		7,000	
Inventories		4,000	
Supplies		2,100	
Prepaid insurance		400	
Total current assets			$22,100
Long-term investments			
Investment in stock of Walters Corp.		5,200	
Investment in real estate		2,000	7,200
Property, plant, and equipment			
Land		10,000	
Office equipment	$ 24,000		
Less: Accumulated depreciation	5,000	19,000	29,000
Intangible assets			
Patents			3,100
Total assets			$61,400

Liabilities and Owner's Equity

Current liabilities			
Notes payable		$11,000	
Accounts payable		2,100	
Salaries payable		1,600	
Unearned revenue		900	
Interest payable		450	
Total current liabilities			$16,050
Long-term liabilities			
Notes payable		1,300	
Mortgage payable		10,000	
Total long-term liabilities			11,300
Total liabilities			27,350
Owner's equity			
B. Franklin, Capital			34,050
Total liabilities and owner's equity			$61,400

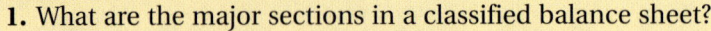

BEFORE YOU GO ON...

Review It

1. What are the major sections in a classified balance sheet?

2. Using the **PepsiCo, Inc.** annual report, determine its current liabilities at December 28, 2002, and December 29, 2001. Were current liabilities higher or lower than current assets in these two years? The answer to this question is provided on page 180.

3. What is the difference between the report form and the account form of the classified balance sheet?

THE NAVIGATOR

DEMONSTRATION PROBLEM

At the end of its first month of operations, Watson Answering Service has the following unadjusted trial balance.

WATSON ANSWERING SERVICE
August 31, 2005
Trial Balance

	Debit	Credit
Cash	$ 5,400	
Accounts Receivable	2,800	
Prepaid Insurance	2,400	
Supplies	1,300	
Equipment	60,000	
Notes Payable		$40,000
Accounts Payable		2,400
Ray Watson, Capital		30,000
Ray Watson, Drawing	1,000	
Service Revenue		4,900
Salaries Expense	3,200	
Utilities Expense	800	
Advertising Expense	400	
	$77,300	$77,300

Other data consist of the following:

1. Insurance expires at the rate of $200 per month.
2. There are $1,000 of supplies on hand at August 31.
3. Monthly depreciation on the equipment is $900.
4. Interest of $500 on the notes payable has accrued during August.

Instructions

(a) Prepare a work sheet.

(b) Prepare a classified balance sheet assuming $35,000 of the notes payable are long-term.

(c) Journalize the closing entries.

ACTION PLAN

■ In completing the work sheet, be sure to (a) key the adjustments, (b) start at the top of the adjusted trial balance columns and extend adjusted balances to the correct statement columns, and (c) enter net income (or net loss) in the proper columns.

■ In preparing a classified balance sheet, know the contents of each of the sections.

■ In journalizing closing entries, remember that there are only four entries and that owner's drawing is closed to owner's capital.

SOLUTION TO DEMONSTRATION PROBLEM

(a)

WATSON ANSWERING SERVICE
Work Sheet
For the Month Ended August 31, 2005

Account Titles	Trial Balance Dr.	Trial Balance Cr.	Adjustments Dr.	Adjustments Cr.	Adjusted Trial Balance Dr.	Adjusted Trial Balance Cr.	Income Statement Dr.	Income Statement Cr.	Balance Sheet Dr.	Balance Sheet Cr.
Cash	5,400				5,400				5,400	
Accounts Receivable	2,800				2,800				2,800	
Prepaid Insurance	2,400			(a) 200	2,200				2,200	
Supplies	1,300			(b) 300	1,000				1,000	
Equipment	60,000				60,000				60,000	
Notes Payable		40,000				40,000				40,000
Accounts Payable		2,400				2,400				2,400
Ray Watson, Capital		30,000				30,000				30,000
Ray Watson, Drawing	1,000				1,000				1,000	
Service Revenue		4,900				4,900		4,900		
Salaries Expense	3,200				3,200		3,200			
Utilities Expense	800				800		800			
Advertising Expense	400				400		400			
Totals	77,300	77,300								
Insurance Expense			(a) 200		200		200			
Supplies Expense			(b) 300		300		300			
Depreciation Expense			(c) 900		900		900			
Accumulated Depreciation— Equipment				(c) 900		900				900
Interest Expense			(d) 500		500		500			
Interest Payable				(d) 500		500				500
Totals			1,900	1,900	78,700	78,700	6,300	4,900	72,400	73,800
Net Loss								1,400	1,400	
Totals							6,300	6,300	73,800	73,800

Explanation: (a) Insurance expired, (b) Supplies used, (c) Depreciation expensed, (d) Interest accrued.

(b)

WATSON ANSWERING SERVICE
Balance Sheet
August 31, 2005

Assets

Current assets		
Cash		$ 5,400
Accounts receivable		2,800
Prepaid insurance		2,200
Supplies		1,000
Total current assets		11,400
Property, plant, and equipment		
Equipment	$60,000	
Less: Accumulated depreciation—equipment	900	59,100
Total assets		$70,500

Liabilities and Owner's Equity

Current liabilities		
Notes payable		$ 5,000
Accounts payable		2,400
Interest payable		500
Total current liabilities		7,900
Long-term liabilities		
Notes payable		35,000
Total liabilities		42,900
Owner's equity		
Ray Watson, Capital		27,600*
Total liabilities and owner's equity		$70,500

*Ray Watson, Capital, $30,000 less drawings $1,000 and net loss $1,400.

(c)

Aug. 31	Service Revenue	4,900	
	Income Summary		4,900
	(To close revenue account)		
31	Income Summary	6,300	
	Salaries Expense		3,200
	Depreciation Expense		900
	Utilities Expense		800
	Interest Expense		500
	Advertising Expense		400
	Supplies Expense		300
	Insurance Expense		200
	(To close expense accounts)		
31	Ray Watson, Capital	1,400	
	Income Summary		1,400
	(To close net loss to capital)		
31	Ray Watson, Capital	1,000	
	Ray Watson, Drawing		1,000
	(To close drawings to capital)		

✓ THE NAVIGATOR

SUMMARY OF STUDY OBJECTIVES

1. **Prepare a work sheet.** The steps in preparing a work sheet are: (a) prepare a trial balance on the work sheet, (b) enter the adjustments in the adjustments columns, (c) enter adjusted balances in the adjusted trial balance columns, (d) extend adjusted trial balance amounts to appropriate financial statement columns, and (e) total the statement columns, compute net income (or net loss), and complete the work sheet.

2. **Explain the process of closing the books.** Closing the books occurs at the end of an accounting period. The process is to journalize and post closing entries and then rule and balance all accounts. In closing the books, separate entries are made to close revenues and expenses to Income Summary, Income Summary to Owner's Capital, and Owner's Drawings to Owner's Capital. Only temporary accounts are closed.

3. **Describe the content and purpose of a post-closing trial balance.** A post-closing trial balance contains the balances in permanent accounts that are carried forward to the next accounting period. The purpose of this trial balance is to prove the equality of these balances.

4. **State the required steps in the accounting cycle.** The required steps in the accounting cycle are: (a) analyze business transactions, (b) journalize the transactions, (c) post to ledger accounts, (d) prepare a trial balance, (e) journalize and post adjusting entries, (f) prepare an adjusted trial balance, (g) prepare financial statements, (h) journalize and post closing entries, and (i) prepare a post-closing trial balance.

5. **Explain the approaches to preparing correcting entries.** One approach for determining the correcting entry is to

compare the incorrect entry with the correct entry. After comparison, a correcting entry is made to correct the accounts. An alternative to a correcting entry is to reverse the incorrect entry and then prepare the correct entry.

6. **Identify the sections of a classified balance sheet.** In a classified balance sheet, assets are classified as current assets;

long-term investments; property, plant, and equipment; and intangibles. Liabilities are classified as either current or long-term. There is also an owner's equity section, which varies with the form of business organization.

GLOSSARY

Classified balance sheet A balance sheet that contains a number of standard classifications or sections. (p. 152).

Closing entries Entries made at the end of an accounting period to transfer the balances of temporary accounts to a permanent owner's equity account, Owner's Capital. (p. 142).

Correcting entries Entries to correct errors made in recording transactions. (p. 149).

Current assets Cash and other resources that are reasonably expected to be realized in cash or sold or consumed in the business within one year or the operating cycle, whichever is longer. (p. 152).

Current liabilities Obligations reasonably expected to be paid from existing current assets or through the creation of other current liabilities within the next year or operating cycle, whichever is longer. (p. 154).

Income Summary A temporary account used in closing revenue and expense accounts. (p. 142).

Intangible assets Noncurrent resources that do not have physical substance. (p. 154).

Liquidity The ability of a company to pay obligations that are expected to become due within the next year or operating cycle. (p. 155).

Long-term investments Resources not expected to be realized in cash within the next year or operating cycle. (p. 153).

Long-term liabilities Obligations expected to be paid after one year. (p. 155).

Operating cycle The average time required to go from cash to cash in producing revenues. (p. 152).

Permanent (real) accounts Balance sheet accounts whose balances are carried forward to the next accounting period. (p. 142).

Post-closing trial balance A list of permanent accounts and their balances after closing entries have been journalized and posted. (p. 146).

Property, plant, and equipment Assets of a relatively permanent nature that are being used in the business and not intended for sale. (p. 153).

Reversing entry An entry made at the beginning of the next accounting period that is the exact opposite of the adjusting entry made in the previous period. (p. 148).

Stockholders' equity The ownership claim of shareholders on total assets. It is to a corporation what owner's equity is to a proprietorship. (p. 156).

Temporary (nominal) accounts Revenue, expense, and drawing accounts whose balances are transferred to owner's capital at the end of an accounting period. (p. 142).

Work sheet A multiple-column form that may be used in the adjustment process and in preparing financial statements. (p. 135).

APPENDIX REVERSING ENTRIES

After the financial statements are prepared and the books are closed, it is often helpful to reverse some of the adjusting entries before recording the regular transactions of the next period. Such entries are called reversing entries. **A reversing entry is made at the beginning of the next accounting period and is the exact opposite of the adjusting entry made in the previous period.** The recording of reversing entries is an **optional** step in the accounting cycle.

STUDY OBJECTIVE 7

Prepare reversing entries.

The purpose of reversing entries is to simplify the recording of a subsequent transaction related to an adjusting entry. In Chapter 3, you may recall, the payment of salaries after an adjusting entry resulted in two debits: one to Salaries Payable and the other to Salaries Expense. With reversing entries, the entire subsequent payment can be debited to Salaries Expense. **The use of reversing entries does not change the amounts reported in the financial statements. What it does is simplify the recording of subsequent transactions.**

Illustration of Reversing Entries

Reversing entries are most often used to reverse two types of adjusting entries: accrued revenues and accrued expenses. They are seldom made for prepaid expenses and unearned revenues. To illustrate the optional use of reversing entries for accrued expenses, we will use the salaries expense transactions for Pioneer Advertising Agency. The transaction and adjustment data are as follows.

1. October 26 (initial salary entry): $4,000 of salaries earned between October 15 and October 26 are paid.
2. October 31 (adjusting entry): Salaries earned between October 29 and October 31 are $1,200. These will be paid in the November 9 payroll.
3. November 9 (subsequent salary entry): Salaries paid are $4,000. Of this amount, $1,200 applied to accrued wages payable and $2,800 was earned between November 1 and November 9.

The comparative entries with and without reversing entries are shown in Illustration 4A-1.

Illustration 4A-1
Comparative entries—not reversing vs. reversing

When Reversing Entries Are Not Used (per chapter)				When Reversing Entries Are Used (per appendix)			
	Initial Salary Entry				**Initial Salary Entry**		
Oct. 26	Salaries Expense	4,000		Oct. 26	Salaries Expense	4,000	
	Cash		4,000		Cash		4,000
	Adjusting Entry				**Adjusting Entry**		
Oct. 31	Salaries Expense	1,200		Oct. 31	Salaries Expense	1,200	
	Salaries Payable		1,200		Salaries Payable		1,200
	Closing Entry				**Closing Entry**		
Oct. 31	Income Summary	5,200		Oct. 31	Income Summary	5,200	
	Salaries Expense		5,200		Salaries Expense		5,200
	Reversing Entry				**Reversing Entry**		
Nov. 1	No reversing entry is made.			Nov. 1	Salaries Payable	1,200	
					Salaries Expense		1,200
	Subsequent Salary Entry				**Subsequent Salary Entry**		
Nov. 9	Salaries Payable	1,200		Nov. 9	Salaries Expense	4,000	
	Salaries Expense	2,800			Cash		4,000
	Cash		4,000				

The first three entries are the same whether or not reversing entries are used. The last two entries are different. The November 1 **reversing entry** eliminates the $1,200 balance in Salaries Payable that was created by the October 31 adjusting entry. The reversing entry also creates a $1,200 credit balance in the Salaries Expense account. As you know, it is unusual for an expense account to have a credit balance. The balance is correct in this instance, though, because it anticipates that the entire amount of the first salary payment in the new accounting period will be debited to Salaries Expense. This debit will eliminate the credit balance, and the resulting debit balance in the expense account will equal the salaries expense incurred in the new accounting period ($2,800 in this example).

When reversing entries are made, all cash payments of expenses can be debited to the expense account. This means that on November 9 (and every payday) Salaries Expense can be debited for the amount paid without regard to any accrued salaries payable. Being able to make the same entry each time simplifies the recording process: Subsequent transactions can be recorded as if the related adjusting entry had never been made.

The posting of the entries with reversing entries is shown in Illustration 4A-2.

Illustration 4A-2
Postings with reversing entries

Salaries Expense					Salaries Payable			
10/26 Paid	4,000	10/31 Closing	5,200	11/1 **Reversing**	**1,200**	10/31 Adjusting	1,200
31 Adjusting	1,200						
	5,200		5,200				
11/9 Paid	4,000	11/1 **Reversing**	**1,200**				

Reversing entries may also be made for accrued revenue adjusting entries. For Pioneer Advertising, the adjusting entry was: Accounts Receivable (Dr.) $200 and Service Revenue (Cr.) $200. Thus, the reversing entry on November 1 is:

Nov. 1	Service Revenue	200	
	Accounts Receivable		200
	(To reverse October 31 adjusting entry)		

A	=	L	+	OE
−200				−200 Rev

Cash Flows
no effect

When the accrued fees are collected, Cash is debited and Service Revenue is credited.

SUMMARY OF STUDY OBJECTIVE FOR APPENDIX

7. Prepare reversing entries. Reversing entries are the opposite of the adjusting entries made in the preceding period. They are made at the beginning of a new accounting period to simplify the recording of later transactions related to the adjusting entries. In most cases, only accrued adjusting entries are reversed.

*__Note:__ All asterisked Questions, Exercises, and Problems relate to material in the appendix to the chapter.

SELF-STUDY QUESTIONS

Self-Study/Self-Test

Answers are at the end of the chapter.

1) **1.** Which of the following statements is *incorrect* concerning the work sheet?
   a. The work sheet is essentially a working tool of the accountant.
   b. The work sheet is distributed to management and other interested parties.
   c. The work sheet cannot be used as a basis for posting to ledger accounts.
   d. Financial statements can be prepared directly from the work sheet before journalizing and posting the adjusting entries.

2. In a work sheet, net income is entered in the following (SO 1) columns:
   a. income statement (Dr) and balance sheet (Dr).
   b. income statement (Cr) and balance sheet (Dr).
   c. income statement (Dr) and balance sheet (Cr).
   d. income statement (Cr) and balance sheet (Cr).

3. An account that will have a zero balance after closing en- (SO 2) tries have been journalized and posted is:
   a. Service Revenue.
   b. Advertising Supplies.
   c. Prepaid Insurance.
   d. Accumulated Depreciation.

(SO 2)   **4.** When a net loss has occurred, Income Summary is:
   a. debited and Owner's Capital is credited.
   b. credited and Owner's Capital is debited.
   c. debited and Owner's Drawing is credited.
   d. credited and Owner's Drawing is debited.

(SO 2)   **5.** The closing process involves separate entries to close (1) expenses, (2) drawings, (3) revenues, and (4) income summary. The correct sequencing of the entries is:
   a. (4), (3), (2), (1)
   b. (1), (2), (3), (4)
   c. (3), (1), (4), (2)
   d. (3), (2), (1), (4)

(SO 3)   **6.** Which types of accounts will appear in the post-closing trial balance?
   a. Permanent (real) accounts.
   b. Temporary (nominal) accounts.
   c. Accounts shown in the income statement columns of a work sheet.
   d. None of the above.

(SO 4)   **7.** All of the following are required steps in the accounting cycle *except*:
   a. journalizing and posting closing entries.
   b. preparing financial statements.
   c. journalizing the transactions.
   d. preparing a work sheet.

(SO 5)   **8.** Cash of $100 received at the time the service was provided was journalized and posted as a debit to Cash $100 and a credit to Accounts Receivable $100. Assuming the incorrect entry is not reversed, the correcting entry is:
   a. debit Service Revenue $100 and credit Accounts Receivable $100.
   b. debit Accounts Receivable $100 and credit Service Revenue $100.
   c. debit Cash $100 and credit Service Revenue $100.
   d. debit Accounts Receivable $100 and credit Cash $100.

9. In a classified balance sheet, assets are usually classified   (SO
using the following categories:
   a. current assets; long-term assets; property, plant, and equipment; and intangible assets.
   b. current assets; long-term investments; property, plant, and equipment; and other assets.
   c. current assets; long-term investments; tangible assets; and intangible assets.
   d. current assets; long-term investments; property, plant, and equipment; and intangible assets.

10. Current assets are listed: (SO
   a. by liquidity.
   b. by importance.
   c. by longevity.
   d. alphabetically.

*****11.** On December 31, Frank Voris Company correctly made   (SO
an adjusting entry to recognize $2,000 of accrued salaries payable. On January 8 of the next year, total salaries of $3,400 were paid. Assuming the correct reversing entry was made on January 1, the entry on January 8 will result in a credit to Cash $3,400 and the following debit(s):
   a. Salaries Payable $1,400, and Salaries Expense $2,000.
   b. Salaries Payable $2,000 and Salaries Expense $1,400.
   c. Salaries Expense $3,400.
   d. Salaries Payable $3,400.

QUESTIONS

1. "A work sheet is a permanent accounting record and its use is required in the accounting cycle." Do you agree? Explain.

2. Explain the purpose of the work sheet.

3. What is the relationship, if any, between the amount shown in the adjusted trial balance column for an account and that account's ledger balance?

4. If a company's revenues are $125,000 and its expenses are $113,000, in which financial statement columns of the work sheet will the net income of $12,000 appear? When expenses exceed revenues, in which columns will the difference appear?

5. Why is it necessary to prepare formal financial statements if all of the data are in the statement columns of the work sheet?

6. Identify the account(s) debited and credited in each of the four closing entries, assuming the company has net income for the year.

7. Describe the nature of the Income Summary account and identify the types of summary data that may be posted to this account.

8. What are the content and purpose of a post-closing trial balance?

9. Which of the following accounts would not appear in the post-closing trial balance? Interest Payable; Equipment; Depreciation Expense; Elizabeth Sherrick, Drawing; Unearned Revenue; Accumulated Depreciation—Equipment; and Service Revenue.

10. Distinguish between a reversing entry and an adjusting entry. Are reversing entries required?

11. Indicate, in the sequence in which they are made, the three required steps in the accounting cycle that involve journalizing.

12. Identify, in the sequence in which they are prepared, the three trial balances that are often used to report financial information about a company.

13. How do correcting entries differ from adjusting entries?

14. What standard classifications are used in preparing a classified balance sheet?

15. What is meant by the term "operating cycle?"

16. Define current assets. What basis is used for arranging individual items within the current assets section?

17. Distinguish between long-term investments and property, plant, and equipment.

18. How do current liabilities differ from long-term liabilities?

19. (a) What is the term used to describe the owner's equity section of a corporation? (b) Identify the two owner's equity accounts in a corporation and indicate the purpose of each.

20. How does a report form balance sheet differ from an account form balance sheet?

*21. Sang Nam Company prepares reversing entries. If the adjusting entry for interest payable is reversed, what type of an account balance, if any, will there be in Interest Payable and Interest Expense after the reversing entry is posted?

*22. At December 31, accrued salaries payable totaled $4,500. On January 10, total salaries of $8,000 are paid. (a) Assume that reversing entries are made at January 1. Give the January 10 entry, and indicate the Salaries Expense account balance after the entry is posted. (b) Repeat part (a) assuming reversing entries are not made.

BRIEF EXERCISES

BE4-1 The steps in using a work sheet are presented in random order below. List the steps in the proper order by placing numbers 1–5 in the blank spaces.

List the steps in preparing a work sheet.

(SO 1)

(a) _____ Prepare a trial balance on the work sheet.
(b) _____ Enter adjusted balances.
(c) _____ Extend adjusted balances to appropriate statement columns.
(d) _____ Total the statement columns, compute net income (loss), and complete the work sheet.
(e) _____ Enter adjustment data.

BE4-2 The ledger of Keo Company includes the following unadjusted balances: Prepaid Insurance $4,000, Service Revenue $58,000, and Salaries Expense $25,000. Adjusting entries are required for **(a)** expired insurance $1,200; **(b)** services provided $1,100, but unbilled and uncollected; and **(c)** accrued salaries payable $800. Enter the unadjusted balances and adjustments into a work sheet and complete the work sheet for all accounts. *Note:* You will need to add the following accounts: Accounts Receivable, Salaries Payable, and Insurance Expense.

Prepare partial work sheet.

(SO 1)

BE4-3 The following selected accounts appear in the adjusted trial balance columns of the work sheet for Cesar Company: Accumulated Depreciation; Depreciation Expense; N. Cesar, Capital; N. Cesar, Drawing; Service Revenue; Supplies; and Accounts Payable. Indicate the financial statement column (income statement Dr., balance sheet Cr., etc.) to which each balance should be extended.

Identify work sheet columns for selected accounts.

(SO 1)

BE4-4 The ledger of Rowen Company contains the following balances: D. Rowen, Capital $30,000; D. Rowen, Drawing $2,000; Service Revenue $50,000; Salaries Expense $23,000; and Supplies Expense $4,000. Prepare the closing entries at December 31.

Prepare closing entries from ledger balances.

(SO 2)

BE4-5 Using the data in BE4-4, enter the balances in T accounts, post the closing entries, and rule and balance the accounts.

Post closing entries; rule and balance T accounts.

(SO 2)

BE4-6 The income statement for Mosquera Golf Club for the month ending July 31 shows Green Fee Revenue $14,600, Salaries Expense $8,200, Maintenance Expense $2,500, and Net Income $3,900. Prepare the entries to close the revenue and expense accounts. Post the entries to the revenue and expense accounts, and complete the closing process for these accounts using the three-column form of account.

Journalize and post closing entries using the three-column form of account.

(SO 2)

BE4-7 Using the data in BE4-3, identify the accounts that would be included in a post-closing trial balance.

Identify post-closing trial balance accounts.

(SO 3)

BE4-8 The steps in the accounting cycle are listed in random order below. List the steps in proper sequence, assuming no work sheet is prepared, by placing numbers 1–9 in the blank spaces.

List the required steps in the accounting cycle in sequence.

(SO 4)

(a) _____ Prepare a trial balance.
(b) _____ Journalize the transactions.
(c) _____ Journalize and post closing entries.
(d) _____ Prepare financial statements.
(e) _____ Journalize and post adjusting entries.
(f) _____ Post to ledger accounts.
(g) _____ Prepare a post-closing trial balance.
(h) _____ Prepare an adjusted trial balance.
(i) _____ Analyze business transactions.

Prepare correcting entries.
(SO 5)

BE4-9 At Rafeul Huda Company, the following errors were discovered after the transactions had been journalized and posted. Prepare the correcting entries.

1. A collection on account from a customer for $780 was recorded as a debit to Cash $780 and a credit to Service Revenue $780.
2. The purchase of store supplies on account for $1,580 was recorded as a debit to Store Supplies $1,850 and a credit to Accounts Payable $1,850.

Prepare the current assets section of a balance sheet.
(SO 6)

BE4-10 The balance sheet debit column of the work sheet for Kren Company includes the following accounts: Accounts Receivable $12,500; Prepaid Insurance $3,600; Cash $18,400; Supplies $5,200, and Short-term Investments $6,700. Prepare the current assets section of the balance sheet, listing the accounts in proper sequence.

Prepare reversing entries.
(SO 7)

*BE4-11** At October 31, Prasad Company made an accrued expense adjusting entry of $1,200 for salaries. Prepare the reversing entry on November 1, and indicate the balances in Salaries Payable and Salaries Expense after posting the reversing entry.

EXERCISES

Complete work sheet
(SO 1)

E4-1 The adjusted trial balance columns of the work sheet for Cajon Company are as follows.

CAJON COMPANY
Work Sheet (partial)
For the Month Ended April 30, 2005

Account Titles	Adjusted Trial Balance		Income Statement		Balance Sheet	
	Dr.	Cr.	Dr.	Cr.	Dr.	Cr.
Cash	14,752					
Accounts Receivable	7,840					
Prepaid Rent	2,280					
Equipment	23,050					
Accumulated Depreciation		4,921				
Notes Payable		5,700				
Accounts Payable		5,672				
P. Cajon, Capital		33,960				
P. Cajon, Drawing	3,650					
Service Revenue		12,590				
Salaries Expense	9,840					
Rent Expense	760					
Depreciation Expense	671					
Interest Expense	57					
Interest Payable		57				
Totals	62,900	62,900				

Instructions
Complete the work sheet.

Prepare financial statements from work sheet.
(SO 1, 6)

E4-2 Work sheet data for Cajon Company are presented in E4-1. The owner did not make any additional investments in the business in April.

Instructions
Prepare an income statement, an owner's equity statement, and a classified balance sheet.

Journalize and post closing entries and prepare a post-closing trial balance
(SO 2, 3)

E4-3 Work sheet data for Cajon Company are presented in E4-1.

Instructions
(a) Journalize the closing entries at April 30.
(b) Post the closing entries to Income Summary and P. Cajon, Capital. Use T accounts.
(c) Prepare a post-closing trial balance at April 30.

E4-4 The adjustments columns of the work sheet for Munoz Company are shown below.

Prepare adjusting entries from a work sheet and extend balance to work sheet columns.

(SO 1)

	Adjustments	
Account Titles	**Debit**	**Credit**
Accounts Receivable	600	
Prepaid Insurance		400
Accumulated Depreciation		900
Salaries Payable		500
Service Revenue		600
Salaries Expense	500	
Insurance Expense	400	
Depreciation Expense	900	
	2,400	2,400

Instructions
(a) Prepare the adjusting entries.
(b) Assuming the adjusted trial balance amount for each account is normal, indicate the financial statement column to which each balance should be extended.

E4-5 Selected work sheet data for Jane Freeman Company are presented below.

Derive adjusting entries from work sheet data.

(SO 1)

Account Titles	Trial Balance		Adjusted Trial Balance	
	Dr.	**Cr.**	**Dr.**	**Cr.**
Accounts Receivable	?		34,000	
Prepaid Insurance	26,000		18,000	
Supplies	7,000		?	
Accumulated Depreciation		12,000		?
Salaries Payable		?		5,000
Service Revenue		88,000		95,000
Insurance Expense			?	
Depreciation Expense			10,000	
Supplies Expense			4,000	
Salaries Expense	?		49,000	

Instructions
(a) Fill in the missing amounts.
(b) Prepare the adjusting entries that were made.

E4-6 The adjusted trial balance of Lanza Company at the end of its fiscal year is:

Journalize and post closing entries and prepare a post-closing trial balance.

(SO 2, 3)

LANZA COMPANY
Adjusted Trial Balance
July 31, 2005

No.	Account Titles	Debits	Credits
101	Cash	$ 14,840	
112	Accounts Receivable	8,780	
157	Equipment	15,900	
167	Accumulated Depreciation		$ 5,400
201	Accounts Payable		4,220
208	Unearned Rent Revenue		1,800
301	C. J. Lanza, Capital		45,200
306	C. J. Lanza, Drawing	16,000	
404	Commission Revenue		67,000
429	Rent Revenue		6,500
711	Depreciation Expense	4,000	
720	Salaries Expense	55,700	
732	Utilities Expense	14,900	
		$130,120	$130,120

Instructions

(a) Prepare the closing entries using page J15.

(b) Post to C. J. Lanza, Capital and No. 350 Income Summary accounts. (Use the three-column form.)

(c) Prepare a post-closing trial balance at July 31.

Prepare financial statements.
(SO 6)

E4-7 The adjusted trial balance for Lanza Company is presented in E4-6.

Instructions

(a) Prepare an income statement and an owner's equity statement for the year. Lanza did not make any capital investments during the year.

(b) Prepare a classified balance sheet at July 31.

Prepare closing entries and an owner's equity statement.
(SO 2)

E4-8 Selected accounts for Roth Salon are presented below. All June 30 postings are from closing entries.

Salaries Expense			
6/10	3,200	6/30	8,800
6/28	5,600		

Service Revenue			
6/30	16,100	6/15	7,700
		6/24	8,400

Jamie Roth, Capital			
6/30	2,500	6/1	12,000
		6/30	3,000
		Bal.	12,500

Supplies Expense			
6/12	600	6/30	1,300
6/24	700		

Rent Expense			
6/1	3,000	6/30	3,000

Jamie Roth, Drawing			
6/13	1,000	6/30	2,500
6/25	1,500		

Instructions

(a) Prepare the closing entries that were made.

(b) Post the closing entries to Income Summary.

Prepare correcting entries.
(SO 5)

E4-9 Kogan Company has an inexperienced accountant. During the first 2 weeks on the job, the accountant made the following errors in journalizing transactions. All entries were posted as made.

1. A payment on account of $830 to a creditor was debited to Accounts Payable $380 and credited to Cash $380.

2. The purchase of supplies on account for $560 was debited to Equipment $56 and credited to Accounts Payable $56.

3. A $400 withdrawal of cash for M. Kogan's personal use was debited to Salaries Expense $400 and credited to Cash $400.

Instructions

Prepare the correcting entries.

Prepare a classified balance sheet.
(SO 6)

E4-10 The adjusted trial balance for Rego Bowling Alley at December 31, 2005, contains the following accounts.

Debits		Credits	
Building	$128,800	Ann Rego, Capital	$115,000
Accounts Receivable	14,520	Accumulated Depreciation—Building	45,600
Prepaid Insurance	4,680	Accounts Payable	12,300
Cash	18,040	Mortgage Payable	94,780
Equipment	62,400	Accumulated Depreciation—Equipment	18,720
Land	64,000	Interest Payable	2,600
Insurance Expense	780	Bowling Revenues	14,180
Depreciation Expense	7,360		$303,180
Interest Expense	2,600		
	$303,180		

Instructions

(a) Prepare a classified balance sheet; assume that $13,600 of the mortgage payable will be paid in 2006.

(b)  Comment on the liquidity of the company.

*E4-11 On December 31, the adjusted trial balance of Garg Employment Agency shows the following selected data.

Prepare closing and reversing entries.

(SO 2, 4, 7)

Accounts Receivable	$24,000	Commission Revenue	$92,000
Interest Expense	7,800	Interest Payable	1,500

Analysis shows that adjusting entries were made to (1) accrue $4,200 of commission revenue and (2) accrue $1,500 interest expense.

Instructions

(a) Prepare the closing entries for the temporary accounts at December 31.

(b) Prepare the reversing entries on January 1.

(c) Post the entries in (a) and (b). Rule and balance the accounts. (Use T accounts.)

(d) Prepare the entries to record (1) the collection of the accrued commissions on January 10 and (2) the payment of all interest due ($2,700) on January 15.

(e) Post the entries in (d) to the temporary accounts.

PROBLEMS: SET A

P4-1A The trial balance columns of the work sheet for Undercover Roofing at March 31, 2005, are as follows.

Prepare a work sheet, financial statements, and adjusting and closing entries.

(SO 1, 2, 3, 6)

UNDERCOVER ROOFING
Work Sheet
For the Month Ended March 31, 2005

Account Titles	Trial Balance Dr.	Trial Balance Cr.
Cash	2,500	
Accounts Receivable	1,800	
Roofing Supplies	1,100	
Equipment	6,000	
Accumulated Depreciation—Equipment		1,200
Accounts Payable		1,400
Unearned Revenue		300
I. Spy, Capital		7,000
I. Spy, Drawing	600	
Service Revenue		3,000
Salaries Expense	700	
Miscellaneous Expense	200	
	12,900	12,900

Other data:

1. A physical count reveals only $140 of roofing supplies on hand.

2. Depreciation for March is $200.

3. Unearned revenue amounted to $130 after adjustment on March 31.

4. Accrued salaries are $350.

Instructions

(a) Enter the trial balance on a work sheet and complete the work sheet.

(b) Prepare an income statement and owner's equity statement for the month of March and a classified balance sheet at March 31. I. Spy did not make any additional investments in the business in March.

(c) Journalize the adjusting entries from the adjustments columns of the work sheet.

(d) Journalize the closing entries from the financial statement columns of the work sheet.

(a) Adjusted trial balance
  $13,450

(b) Net income $ 760
  Total assets $9,040

Complete work sheet; prepare financial statements, closing entries, and post-closing trial balance.

(SO 1, 2, 3, 6)

P4-2A The adjusted trial balance columns of the work sheet for Eagle Company, owned by Alfred Eagle, are as follows.

EAGLE COMPANY
Work Sheet
For the Year Ended December 31, 2005

Account No.	Account Titles	Adjusted Trial Balance Dr.	Cr.
101	Cash	13,600	
112	Accounts Receivable	15,400	
126	Supplies	2,000	
130	Prepaid Insurance	2,800	
151	Office Equipment	34,000	
152	Accumulated Depreciation—Office Equipment		8,000
200	Notes Payable		20,000
201	Accounts Payable		6,000
212	Salaries Payable		3,500
230	Interest Payable		800
301	A. Eagle, Capital		25,000
306	A. Eagle, Drawing	10,000	
400	Service Revenue		88,000
610	Advertising Expense	12,000	
631	Supplies Expense	5,700	
711	Depreciation Expense	8,000	
722	Insurance Expense	5,000	
726	Salaries Expense	42,000	
905	Interest Expense	800	
	Totals	151,300	151,300

Instructions

(a) Net income $14,500

(b) Current assets $33,800;
Current liabilities
$20,300

(e) Post-closing trial balance
$67,800

(a) Complete the work sheet by extending the balances to the financial statement columns.

(b) Prepare an income statement, owner's equity statement, and a classified balance sheet. (*Note:* $10,000 of the notes payable become due in 2006.) Alfred Eagle did not make any additional investments in the business during the year.

(c) Prepare the closing entries. Use J14 for the journal page.

(d) Post the closing entries. Use the three-column form of account. Income Summary is No. 350.

(e) Prepare a post-closing trial balance.

Prepare financial statements, closing entries, and post-closing trial balance.

(SO 1, 2, 3, 6)

P4-3A The completed financial statement columns of the work sheet for Lathrop Company are shown below and on the next page.

LATHROP COMPANY
Work Sheet
For the Year Ended December 31, 2005

Account No.	Account Titles	Income Statement Dr.	Cr.	Balance Sheet Dr.	Cr.
101	Cash			17,400	
112	Accounts Receivable			13,500	
130	Prepaid Insurance			3,500	
157	Equipment			26,000	
167	Accumulated Depreciation				5,600
201	Accounts Payable				11,300
212	Salaries Payable				3,000
301	Sue Lathrop, Capital				36,000
306	Sue Lathrop, Drawing			14,000	
400	Service Revenue		64,000		
622	Repair Expense	2,000			
711	Depreciation Expense	2,600			
722	Insurance Expense	2,200			

Account No.	Account Titles	Income Statement Dr.	Income Statement Cr.	Balance Sheet Dr.	Balance Sheet Cr.
726	Salaries Expense	37,000			
732	Utilities Expense	1,700			
	Totals	45,500	64,000	74,400	55,900
	Net Income	18,500			18,500
		64,000	64,000	74,400	74,400

Instructions

(a) Prepare an income statement, owner's equity statement, and a classified balance sheet.

(b) Prepare the closing entries. Sue did not make any additional investments during the year.

(c) Post the closing entries and rule and balance the accounts. Use T accounts. Income Summary is account No. 350.

(d) Prepare a post-closing trial balance.

(a) Ending capital $40,500; Total current assets $34,400

(d) Post-closing trial balance $60,400

P4-4A Nish Kumar Management Services began business on January 1, 2005, with a capital investment of $120,000. The company manages condominiums for owners (Service Revenue) and rents space in its own office building (Rent Revenue). The trial balance and adjusted trial balance columns of the work sheet at the end of the first year are as follows.

Complete work sheet; prepare classified balance sheet, entries, and post-closing trial balance.

(SO 1, 2, 3, 6)

NISH KUMAR MANAGEMENT SERVICES
Work Sheet
For the Year Ended December 31, 2005

Account Titles	Trial Balance Dr.	Trial Balance Cr.	Adjusted Trial Balance Dr.	Adjusted Trial Balance Cr.
Cash	14,500		14,500	
Accounts Receivable	23,600		23,600	
Prepaid Insurance	3,100		1,400	
Land	56,000		56,000	
Building	106,000		106,000	
Equipment	49,000		49,000	
Accounts Payable		10,400		10,400
Unearned Rent Revenue		5,000		2,800
Mortgage Payable		100,000		100,000
N. Kumar, Capital		120,000		120,000
N. Kumar, Drawing	20,000		20,000	
Service Revenue		75,600		75,600
Rent Revenue		24,000		26,200
Salaries Expense	30,000		30,000	
Advertising Expense	17,000		17,000	
Utilities Expense	15,800		15,800	
Totals	335,000	335,000		
Insurance Expense			1,700	
Depreciation Expense—Building			2,500	
Accumulated Depreciation—Building				2,500
Depreciation Expense—Equipment			3,900	
Accumulated Depreciation—Equipment				3,900
Interest Expense			9,000	
Interest Payable				9,000
Totals			350,400	350,400

Instructions

(a) Prepare a complete work sheet.

(b) Prepare a classified balance sheet. (*Note*: $10,000 of the mortgage payable is due for payment next year.)

(c) Journalize the adjusting entries.

(d) Journalize the closing entries.

(e) Prepare a post-closing trial balance.

(a) Net income $21,900

(b) Total current assets $39,500

(e) Post-closing trial balance $250,500

Complete all steps in accounting cycle.

(SO 1, 2, 3, 4, 6)

P4-5A Eve Tsai opened Tsai's Window Washing on July 1, 2005. During July the following transactions were completed.

July 1   Tsai invested $12,000 cash in the business.
       1   Purchased used truck for $6,000, paying $3,000 cash and the balance on account.
       3   Purchased cleaning supplies for $1,300 on account.
       5   Paid $1,200 cash on one-year insurance policy effective July 1.
      12   Billed customers $2,500 for cleaning services.
      18   Paid $1,000 cash on amount owed on truck and $800 on amount owed on cleaning supplies.
      20   Paid $1,200 cash for employee salaries.
      21   Collected $1,400 cash from customers billed on July 12.
      25   Billed customers $3,000 for cleaning services.
      31   Paid gas and oil for month on truck $200.
      31   Withdrew $900 cash for personal use.

The chart of accounts for Tsai's Window Washing contains the following accounts: No. 101 Cash, No. 112 Accounts Receivable, No. 128 Cleaning Supplies, No. 130 Prepaid Insurance, No. 157 Equipment, No. 158 Accumulated Depreciation—Equipment, No. 201 Accounts Payable, No. 212 Salaries Payable, No. 301 Eve Tsai, Capital, No. 306 Eve Tsai, Drawing, No. 350 Income Summary, No. 400 Service Revenue, No. 633 Gas & Oil Expense, No. 634 Cleaning Supplies Expense, No. 711 Depreciation Expense, No. 722 Insurance Expense, and No. 726 Salaries Expense.

Instructions

(a) Journalize and post the July transactions. Use page J1 for the journal and the three-column form of account.

(b) Trial balance $20,000

(b) Prepare a trial balance at July 31 on a work sheet.

(c) Adjusted trial balance $22,300

(c) Enter the following adjustments on the work sheet and complete the work sheet.
    (1) Services provided but unbilled and uncollected at July 31 were $1,500.
    (2) Depreciation on equipment for the month was $200.
    (3) One-twelfth of the insurance expired.
    (4) An inventory count shows $600 of cleaning supplies on hand at July 31.
    (5) Accrued but unpaid employee salaries were $600.

(d) Net income $4,000; Total assets $18,200

(d) Prepare the income statement and owner's equity statement for July and a classified balance sheet at July 31.

(e) Journalize and post adjusting entries. Use page J2 for the journal.

(f) Journalize and post closing entries and complete the closing process. Use page J3 for the journal.

(g) Post-closing trial balance $18,400

(g) Prepare a post-closing trial balance at July 31.

Analyze errors and prepare correcting entries and trial balance.

(SO 5)

P4-6A Tom Brennan, CPA, was retained by 24/7 Cable to prepare financial statements for April 2005. Brennan accumulated all the ledger balances per 24/7's records and found the following.

24/7 CABLE
Trial Balance
April 30, 2005

	Debit	Credit
Cash	$ 4,100	
Accounts Receivable	3,200	
Supplies	800	
Equipment	10,600	
Accumulated Depreciation		$ 1,350
Accounts Payable		2,100
Salaries Payable		500
Unearned Revenue		890
A. Manion, Capital		12,900
Service Revenue		5,450
Salaries Expense	3,300	
Advertising Expense	400	
Miscellaneous Expense	290	
Depreciation Expense	500	
	$23,190	$23,190

Tom Brennan reviewed the records and found the following errors.

1. Cash received from a customer on account was recorded as $870 instead of $780.
2. A payment of $65 for advertising expense was entered as a debit to Miscellaneous Expense $65 and a credit to Cash $65.
3. The first salary payment this month was for $1,900, which included $500 of salaries payable on March 31. The payment was recorded as a debit to Salaries Expense $1,900 and a credit to Cash $1,900. (No reversing entries were made on April 1.)
4. The purchase on account of a printer costing $290 was recorded as a debit to Supplies and a credit to Accounts Payable for $290.
5. A cash payment of repair expense on equipment for $95 was recorded as a debit to Equipment $59 and a credit to Cash $59.

Instructions
(a) Prepare an analysis of each error showing (1) the incorrect entry, (2) the correct entry, and (3) the correcting entry. Items 4 and 5 occurred on April 30, 2005.
(b) Prepare a correct trial balance.

Trial balance $22,690

PROBLEMS: SET B

P4-1B Sherlock Holmes began operations as a private investigator on January 1, 2005. The trial balance columns of the work sheet for Sherlock Holmes P.I. at March 31 are as follows.

Prepare work sheet, financial statements, and adjusting and closing entries.

(SO 1, 2, 3, 6)

SHERLOCK HOLMES P.I.
Work Sheet
For the Quarter Ended March 31, 2005

	Trial Balance	
Account Titles	**Dr.**	**Cr.**
Cash	11,400	
Accounts Receivable	5,620	
Supplies	1,050	
Prepaid Insurance	2,400	
Equipment	30,000	
Notes Payable		10,000
Accounts Payable		12,350
S. Holmes, Capital		20,000
S. Holmes, Drawing	600	
Service Revenue		13,620
Salaries Expense	2,200	
Travel Expense	1,300	
Rent Expense	1,200	
Miscellaneous Expense	200	
	55,970	55,970

Other data:
1. Supplies on hand total $680.
2. Depreciation is $1,000 per quarter.
3. Interest accrued on 6-month note payable, issued January 1, $300.
4. Insurance expires at the rate of $200 per month.
5. Services provided but unbilled at March 31 total $830.

Instructions
(a) Enter the trial balance on a work sheet and complete the work sheet.
(b) Prepare an income statement and owner's equity statement for the quarter and a classified balance sheet at March 31. S. Holmes did not make any additional investments in the business during the quarter ended March 31, 2005.
(c) Journalize the adjusting entries from the adjustments columns of the work sheet.
(d) Journalize the closing entries from the financial statement columns of the work sheet.

(a) Adjusted trial balance
$58,100
(b) Net income $ 7,280
Total assets $49,330

Complete work sheet; prepare financial statements, closing entries, and post-closing trial balance.

(SO 1, 2, 3, 6)

P4-2B The adjusted trial balance columns of the work sheet for Mr. Watson Company is as follows.

MR. WATSON COMPANY
Work Sheet
For the Year Ended December 31, 2005

Account No.	Account Titles	Adjusted Trial Balance Dr.	Cr.
101	Cash	20,800	
112	Accounts Receivable	16,200	
126	Supplies	2,300	
130	Prepaid Insurance	4,400	
151	Office Equipment	44,000	
152	Accumulated Depreciation—Office Equipment		18,000
200	Notes Payable		20,000
201	Accounts Payable		8,000
212	Salaries Payable		2,600
230	Interest Payable		1,000
301	M. Watson, Capital		36,000
306	M. Watson, Drawing	12,000	
400	Service Revenue		79,800
610	Advertising Expense	12,000	
631	Supplies Expense	3,700	
711	Depreciation Expense	6,000	
722	Insurance Expense	4,000	
726	Salaries Expense	39,000	
905	Interest Expense	1,000	
	Totals	165,400	165,400

Instructions

(a) Net income $14,100

(b) Current assets $43,700
Current liabilities $21,600

(e) Post-closing trial balance $87,700

(a) Complete the work sheet by extending the balances to the financial statement columns.

(b) Prepare an income statement, owner's equity statement, and a classified balance sheet. $10,000 of the notes payable become due in 2006. M. Watson did not make any additional investments in the business during 2005.

(c) Prepare the closing entries. Use J14 for the journal page.

(d) Post the closing entries. Use the three-column form of account. Income Summary is account No. 350.

(e) Prepare a post-closing trial balance.

Prepare financial statements, closing entries, and post-closing trial balance.

(SO 1, 2, 3, 6)

P4-3B The completed financial statement columns of the work sheet for Hubbs Company are shown below and on page 175.

HUBBS COMPANY
Work Sheet
For the Year Ended December 31, 2005

Account No.	Account Titles	Income Statement Dr.	Cr.	Balance Sheet Dr.	Cr.
101	Cash			10,200	
112	Accounts Receivable			7,500	
130	Prepaid Insurance			1,800	
157	Equipment			28,000	
167	Accumulated Depreciation				8,600
201	Accounts Payable				11,700
212	Salaries Payable				3,000
301	D. Hubbs, Capital				34,000
306	D. Hubbs, Drawing			7,200	

Account No.	Account Titles	Income Statement Dr.	Income Statement Cr.	Balance Sheet Dr.	Balance Sheet Cr.
400	Service Revenue		44,000		
622	Repair Expense	3,400			
711	Depreciation Expense	2,800			
722	Insurance Expense	1,200			
726	Salaries Expense	35,200			
732	Utilities Expense	4,000			
	Totals	46,600	44,000	54,700	57,300
	Net Loss		2,600	2,600	
		46,600	46,600	57,300	57,300

Instructions

(a) Prepare an income statement, owner's equity statement, and a classified balance sheet. D. Hubbs made an additional investment in the business of $4,000 during 2005.

(b) Prepare the closing entries.

(c) Post the closing entries and rule and balance the accounts. Use T accounts. Income Summary is account No. 350.

(d) Prepare a post-closing trial balance.

(a) Net loss $2,600
Ending capital $24,200
Total assets $38,900

(d) Post-closing trial balance $47,500

P4-4B London Amusement Park has a fiscal year ending on September 30. Selected data from the September 30 work sheet are presented below.

Complete work sheet; prepare classified balance sheet, entries, and post-closing trial balance.

(SO 1, 2, 3, 6)

LONDON AMUSEMENT PARK
Work Sheet
For the Year Ended September 30, 2005

	Trial Balance Dr.	Trial Balance Cr.	Adjusted Trial Balance Dr.	Adjusted Trial Balance Cr.
Cash	41,400		41,400	
Supplies	18,600		1,200	
Prepaid Insurance	31,900		3,900	
Land	80,000		80,000	
Equipment	120,000		120,000	
Accumulated Depreciation		36,200		42,200
Accounts Payable		14,600		14,600
Unearned Admissions Revenue		3,700		1,000
Mortgage Payable		50,000		50,000
J. London, Capital		109,700		109,700
J. London, Drawing	14,000		14,000	
Admissions Revenue		277,500		280,200
Salaries Expense	105,000		105,000	
Repair Expense	30,500		30,500	
Advertising Expense	9,400		9,400	
Utilities Expense	16,900		16,900	
Property Taxes Expense	18,000		21,000	
Interest Expense	6,000		10,000	
Totals	491,700	491,700		
Insurance Expense			28,000	
Supplies Expense			17,400	
Interest Payable				4,000
Depreciation Expense			6,000	
Property Taxes Payable				3,000
Totals			504,700	504,700

(a) Net income $36,000

(b) Total current assets
$46,500

(e) Post-closing trial balance
$246,500

Instructions

(a) Prepare a complete work sheet.

(b) Prepare a classified balance sheet. (*Note*: $10,000 of the mortgage payable is due for payment in the next fiscal year.)

(c) Journalize the adjusting entries using the work sheet as a basis.

(d) Journalize the closing entries using the work sheet as a basis.

(e) Prepare a post-closing trial balance.

Complete all steps in accounting cycle.

(SO 1, 2, 3, 4, 6)

P4-5B Mike Young opened Young's Carpet Cleaners on March 1. During March, the following transactions were completed.

Mar. 1 Invested $10,000 cash in the business.
 1 Purchased used truck for $6,000, paying $3,000 cash and the balance on account.
 3 Purchased cleaning supplies for $1,200 on account.
 5 Paid $1,800 cash on one-year insurance policy effective March 1.
 14 Billed customers $2,800 for cleaning services.
 18 Paid $1,500 cash on amount owed on truck and $500 on amount owed on cleaning supplies.
 20 Paid $1,800 cash for employee salaries.
 21 Collected $1,400 cash from customers billed on March 14.
 28 Billed customers $2,500 for cleaning services.
 31 Paid gas and oil for month on truck $200.
 31 Withdrew $700 cash for personal use.

The chart of accounts for Young's Carpet Cleaners contains the following accounts: No. 101 Cash, No. 112 Accounts Receivable, No. 128 Cleaning Supplies, No. 130 Prepaid Insurance, No. 157 Equipment, No. 158 Accumulated Depreciation—Equipment, No. 201 Accounts Payable, No. 212 Salaries Payable, No. 301 M. Young, Capital, No. 306, M. Young, Drawing, No. 350 Income Summary, No. 400 Service Revenue, No. 633 Gas & Oil Expense, No. 634 Cleaning Supplies Expense, No. 711 Depreciation Expense, No. 722 Insurance Expense, and No. 726 Salaries Expense.

Instructions

(a) Journalize and post the March transactions. Use page J1 for the journal and the three-column form of account.

(b) Trial balance $17,500
(c) Adjusted trial balance
$18,950

(b) Prepare a trial balance at March 31 on a work sheet.

(c) Enter the following adjustments on the work sheet and complete the work sheet.
   (1) Earned but unbilled revenue at March 31 was $700.
   (2) Depreciation on equipment for the month was $250.
   (3) One-twelfth of the insurance expired.
   (4) An inventory count shows $600 of cleaning supplies on hand at March 31.
   (5) Accrued but unpaid employee salaries were $500.

(d) Net income $2,500
Total assets $14,500

(d) Prepare the income statement and owner's equity statement for March and a classified balance sheet at March 31.

(e) Journalize and post adjusting entries. Use page J2 for the journal.

(f) Journalize and post closing entries and complete the closing process. Use page J3 for the journal.

(g) Post-closing trial balance
$14,750

(g) Prepare a post-closing trial balance at March 31.

COMPREHENSIVE PROBLEM: CHAPTERS 2 TO 4

Mary Coleman opened Mary's Maids Cleaning Service on July 1, 2005. During July, the following transactions were completed.

July 1 Invested $14,000 cash in the business.
 1 Purchased a used truck for $10,000, paying $3,000 cash and the balance on account.
 3 Purchased cleaning supplies for $800 on account.
 5 Paid $2,400 on a one-year insurance policy, effective July 1.

12 Billed customers $3,800 for cleaning services.
18 Paid $1,000 of amount owed on truck, and $400 of amount owed on cleaning supplies.
20 Paid $1,600 for employee salaries.
21 Collected $1,400 from customers billed on July 12.
25 Billed customers $2,500 for cleaning services.
31 Paid gas and oil for the month on the truck, $400.
31 Withdrew $600 cash for personal use.

The chart of accounts for Mary's Maids Cleaning Service contains the following accounts: No. 101 Cash, No. 112 Accounts Receivable, No. 128 Cleaning Supplies, No. 130 Prepaid Insurance, No. 157 Equipment, No. 158 Accumulated Depreciation—Equipment, No. 201 Accounts Payable, No. 212 Salaries Payable, No. 301, Mary Coleman, Capital, No. 306 Mary Coleman, Drawing, No. 350 Income Summary, No. 400 Service Revenue, No. 633 Gas & Oil Expense, No. 634 Cleaning Supplies Expense, No. 711 Depreciation Expense, No. 722 Insurance Expense, and No. 726 Salaries Expense.

Instructions

(a) Journalize and post the July transactions. Use page J1 for the journal.
(b) Prepare a trial balance at July 31 on a work sheet.
(c) Enter the following adjustments on the work sheet, and complete the work sheet.
   (1) Earned but unbilled fees at July 31 were $1,300.
   (2) Depreciation on equipment for the month was $200.
   (3) One-twelfth of the insurance expired.
   (4) An inventory count shows $300 of cleaning supplies on hand at July 31.
   (5) Accrued but unpaid employee salaries were $500.
(d) Prepare the income statement and statement of owner's equity for July, and a classified balance sheet at July 31, 2005.
(e) Journalize and post the adjusting entries. Use page J2 for the journal.
(f) Journalize and post the closing entries, and complete the closing process. Use page J3 for the journal.
(g) Prepare a post-closing trial balance at July 31.

(b) Trial balance totals $26,700

(d) Net income $4,200
Total assets $24,500

(g) Trial balance totals $24,700

BROADENING YOUR PERSPECTIVE

Financial Reporting and Analysis

■ FINANCIAL REPORTING PROBLEM: PepsiCo

BYP4-1 The financial statements of **PepsiCo, Inc.** are presented in Appendix A at the end of this textbook.

Instructions
Answer the following questions using the Consolidated Balance Sheet and the Notes to Consolidated Financial Statements section.

(a) What were PepsiCo's total current assets at December 28, 2002 and December 29, 2001?
(b) Are assets that PepsiCo included under current assets listed in proper order? Explain.
(c) How are PepsiCo's assets classified?
(d) What are "cash equivalents"?
(e) What were PepsiCo's total current liabilities at December 28, 2002 and December 29, 2001?

■ COMPARATIVE ANALYSIS PROBLEM: PepsiCo vs. Coca-Cola

BYP4-2 **PepsiCo**'s financial statements are presented in Appendix A. **Coca-Cola**'s financial statements are presented in Appendix B.

Instructions

(a) Based on the information contained in these financial statements, determine each of the following for PepsiCo at December 28, 2002, and for Coca-Cola at December 31, 2002.
　　(1) Total current assets.
　　(2) Net amount of property, plant, and equipment (land, buildings, and equipment).
　　(3) Total current liabilities.
　　(4) Total stockholders' (shareholders') equity.
(b) What conclusions concerning the companies' respective financial positions can be drawn?

■ **INTERPRETING FINANCIAL STATEMENTS: A Global Focus**

BYP4-3　**Lign Multiwood** is a Swedish forest products company. Its statements conform with the standards of the Swedish Standards Board. Its financial statements are presented to have minimal difference in methods with member countries of the European Union. The balance sheet presented on page 179 is from its 2000 annual report.

Instructions

List all differences that you notice between Lign Multiwood's balance sheet presentation (format and terminology) and the presentation of U.S. companies shown in the chapter: For differences in terminology, list the corresponding terminology used by U.S. companies.

■ **EXPLORING THE WEB**

BYP4-4　Numerous companies have established home pages on the Internet, e.g., **Boston Beer Company** (www.samadams.com) and **Kodak** (www.kodak.com).

Instructions

Examine the home pages of any two companies and answer the following questions.

(a) What type of information is available?
(b) Is any accounting-related information presented?
(c) Would you describe the home page as informative, promotional, or both? Why?

Critical Thinking

■ **GROUP DECISION CASE**

BYP4-5　Everclean Janitorial Service was started 2 years ago by Laurie Merar. Because business has been exceptionally good, Laurie decided on July 1, 2005, to expand operations by acquiring an additional truck and hiring two more assistants. To finance the expansion, Laurie obtained on July 1, 2005, a $25,000, 10% bank loan, payable $10,000 on July 1, 2006, and the balance on July 1, 2007. The terms of the loan require the borrower to have $10,000 more current assets than current liabilities at December 31, 2005. If these terms are not met, the bank loan will be refinanced at 15% interest. At December 31, 2005, the accountant for Everclean Janitorial Service Inc. prepared the balance sheet shown at the top of page 180.

　　Laurie presented the balance sheet to the bank's loan officer on January 2, 2006, confident that the company had met the terms of the loan. The loan officer was not impressed. She said, "We need financial statements audited by a CPA." A CPA was hired and immediately realized that the balance sheet had been prepared from a trial balance and not from an adjusted trial balance. The adjustment data at the balance sheet date consisted of the following.

(1) Earned but unbilled janitorial services were $5,700.
(2) Janitorial supplies on hand were $2,800.
(3) Prepaid insurance was a 3-year policy dated January 1, 2005.
(4) December expenses incurred but unpaid at December 31, $700.
(5) Interest on the bank loan was not recorded.
(6) The amounts for property, plant, and equipment presented in the balance sheet were reported net of accumulated depreciation (cost less accumulated depreciation). These amounts were $4,000 for cleaning equipment and $5,000 for delivery trucks as of January 1, 2005. Depreciation for 2005 was $2,000 for cleaning equipment and $5,000 for delivery trucks.

LIGN MULTIWOOD
Balance Sheet
at December 31
(Swedish kronor)

ASSETS	2000	1999
Fixed assets		
Intangible fixed assets		
Balanced expenses for development work	28 407 064	12 056 864
Licence rights	1 200 000	600 000
	29 607 064	12 656 864
Material fixed assets		
Machinery and other technical plant	33 608 189	34 606 812
Fittings & fixtures, tools and installations	564 952	163 020
	34 173 141	34 769 832
Financial fixed assets		
Other long-term securities holdings	165 000	165 000
Deferred tax claim	3 042 000	1 129 000
	3 207 000	1 294 000
Total fixed assets	66 987 205	48 720 696
Current assets		
Stocks held, etc.		
Stocks of test materials	554 000	116 924
	554 000	116 924
Short-term receivables		
Customer receivables	727 159	652 662
Other receivables	1 099 197	711 979
Prepaid costs and accrued income	2 479 411	1 620 467
	4 305 767	2 985 108
Cash in hand and on deposit	17 965 269	40 755 806
Total current assets	22 825 036	43 857 838
TOTAL ASSETS	89 812 241	92 578 534
EQUITY CAPITAL AND LIABILITIES		
Equity capital		
Tied equity capital		
Share capital	2 825 740	2 825 740
Tied reserves	56 745 410	56 745 410
	59 571 150	59 571 150
Accumulated loss		
Balanced loss	−2 801 000	− 598 000
Year's profit/loss	−4 933 000	−2 203 000
	−7 734 000	−2 801 000
	51 837 150	56 770 150
Minority interest	40 000	40 000
Long-term liabilities		
Other liabilities	33 619 451	34 162 457
	33 619 451	34 162 457
Short-term liabilities		
Accounts payable	2 151 435	1 232 505
Other liabilities	959 044	64 099
Accrued costs and prepaid income	1 205 161	309 323
	4 315 640	1 605 927
TOTAL EQUITY CAPITAL AND LIABILITIES	89 812 241	92 578 534

EVERCLEAN JANITORIAL SERVICE
Balance Sheet
December 31, 2005

Assets		
Current assets		
Cash		$ 6,500
Accounts receivable		9,000
Janitorial supplies		5,200
Prepaid insurance		4,800
Total current assets		25,500
Property, plant, and equipment		
Cleaning equipment (net)		22,000
Delivery trucks (net)		34,000
Total property, plant, and equipment		56,000
Total assets		$81,500

Liabilities and Owner's Equity		
Current liabilities		
Notes payable		$10,000
Accounts payable		2,500
Total current liabilities		12,500
Long-term liability		
Notes payable		15,000
Total liabilities		27,500
Owner's equity		
Laurie Merar, Capital		54,000
Total liabilities and owner's equity		$81,500

Instructions

With the class divided into groups, answer the following.

(a) Prepare a correct balance sheet.
(b) Were the terms of the bank loan met? Explain.

■ COMMUNICATION ACTIVITY

BYP4-6   The accounting cycle is important in understanding the accounting process.

Instructions

Write a memo to your instructor that lists the steps of the accounting cycle in the order they should be completed. End with a paragraph that explains the optional steps in the cycle.

■ ETHICS CASE

BYP4-7   As the controller of Take No Prisoners Perfume Company, you discover a misstatement that overstated net income in the prior year's financial statements. The misleading financial statements appear in the company's annual report which was issued to banks and other creditors less than a month ago. After much thought about the consequences of telling the president, Rocky Balboa, about this misstatement, you gather your courage to inform him. Rocky says, "Hey! What they don't know won't hurt them. But, just so we set the record straight, we'll adjust this year's financial statements for last year's misstatement. We can absorb that misstatement better in this year than in last year anyway! Just don't make such a mistake again."

Instructions

(a) Who are the stakeholders in this situation?
(b) What are the ethical issues in this situation?
(c) What would you do as a controller in this situation?

Answers to Self-Study Questions
1. b   **2.** c   **3.** a   **4.** b   **5.** c   **6.** a   **7.** d   **8.** b   **9.** d   **10.** a   **11.** c

Answers to PepsiCo Review It Question 2, p. 158
PepsiCo's current liabilities in 2002 were $6,052,000. Current liabilities in 2001 were $4,998,000. In both 2002 and 2001, current liabilities were less than current assets.

 ☑ **REMEMBER** to go back to the Navigator box on the chapter-opening page and check off your completed work.

Accounting for Merchandising Operations

THE NAVIGATOR ✓

Understand **Concepts for Review** ❑

Read **Feature Story** ❑

Scan **Study Objectives** ❑

Read **Preview** ❑

Read text and answer **Before You Go On**
p. 192 ❑   p. 195 ❑   p. 200 ❑   p. 201 ❑

Work **Demonstration Problem** ❑

Review **Summary of Study Objectives** ❑

Answer **Self-Study Questions** ❑

Complete **Assignments** ❑

CONCEPTS FOR REVIEW

Before studying this chapter, you should know or, if necessary, review:

■ How to close revenue, expense, and drawing accounts.
(Ch. 4, pp. 142–145)

■ The steps in the accounting cycle.
(Ch. 4, pp. 147–149)

THE NAVIGATOR

Selling Dollars for 85 Cents

For most of the last decade **Wal-Mart** has set the rules of the retail game. Entrepreneur Scott Blum, founder and CEO of **Buy.com**, has a different game plan. He is selling consumer products at or below cost. Buy.com is trying to create an outlet synonymous with low prices—in the hope of becoming the leading e-commerce portal on the Internet. He plans to make up the losses from sales by selling advertising on the company's Web site and a magazine to be mailed to Buy.com customers.

As if the idea of selling below cost weren't unusual enough, Blum has added another twist to merchandising: Unlike **Amazon.com**, he doesn't want to handle inventory. So he has wholesalers and distributors ship the products directly to his Web site customers.

Buy.com's slogan, "The lowest prices on earth," may be the most eye-catching sales pitch ever. The company is ruthlessly committed to being the price leader—even if it means losing money on every sale. Its own computers search competitors' Web sites to make sure that Buy.com has the lowest prices on the Internet. When Amazon.com, in June 2002, reduced its minimum-purchase order for free shipping to $49 (from $99), Buy.com one-upped that move a day later by offering free shipping with no minimum purchase.

Etoys, la Pets.com, and **Cyberian Outpost** all went under during the dot-com wreck of 2000–2001, and Amazon.com, after seven years, had yet to turn a profit. Only **eBay**, an auction site, is consistently profitable. Still, Scott Blum stretches for a bigger portion of a $50 billion online sales market by being the low-cost e-tailer.

Consider the implications if Buy.com is successful: Buy.com's success could change the very way wholesalers and distributors view their businesses. Its success may have an impact on all kinds of retailers—starting with Buy.com itself. If Buy.com proves that the ad space on a product order form—its Web site—is almost as valuable as the product being ordered, another virtual reseller is sure to enter the market with even lower prices.

Of course, there is one big winner if Buy.com succeeds: you. It has never been a better time to be a customer.

www.buy.com

Source: Quentin Hardy, "The Death and Life of Buy.com," *Forbes,* January 21, 2002, pp. 86–89.

☑ THE NAVIGATOR

After studying this chapter, you should be able to:

1. Identify the differences between a service enterprise and a merchandiser.
2. Explain the entries for purchases under a perpetual inventory system.
3. Explain the entries for sales revenues under a perpetual inventory system.
4. Explain the steps in the accounting cycle for a merchandiser.
5. Distinguish between a multiple-step and a single-step income statement.
6. Explain the computation and importance of gross profit.
7. Determine cost of goods sold under a periodic system.

☑ THE NAVIGATOR

As indicated in the Feature Story, Wal-Mart is a gigantic merchandiser with over a 60% share of the retail sales market. Like traditional merchandisers such as Sears Roebuck, it generates revenues by selling goods to customers rather than performing services. Merchandisers that purchase and sell directly to consumers—such as Kmart, Safeway, and Toys "R" Us—are called **retailers**. In contrast, merchandisers that sell to retailers are known as **wholesalers**. For example, retailer Walgreens might buy goods from wholesaler McKesson; Office Depot might buy office supplies from wholesaler United Stationers.

The steps in the accounting cycle for a merchandiser are the same as the steps for a service enterprise. But merchandisers use additional accounts and entries that are required in recording merchandising transactions.

The content and organization of Chapter 5 are as follows.

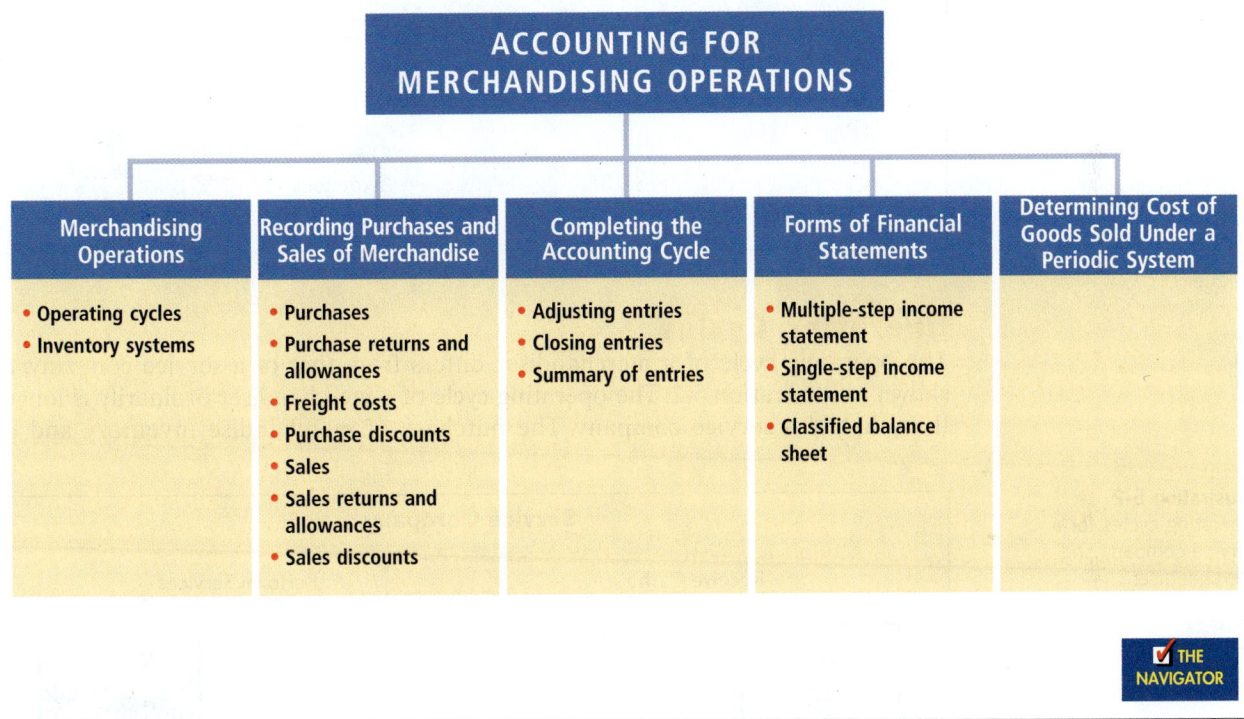

ACCOUNTING FOR MERCHANDISING OPERATIONS

Merchandising Operations	Recording Purchases and Sales of Merchandise	Completing the Accounting Cycle	Forms of Financial Statements	Determining Cost of Goods Sold Under a Periodic System
• Operating cycles • Inventory systems	• Purchases • Purchase returns and allowances • Freight costs • Purchase discounts • Sales • Sales returns and allowances • Sales discounts	• Adjusting entries • Closing entries • Summary of entries	• Multiple-step income statement • Single-step income statement • Classified balance sheet	

☑ THE NAVIGATOR

Merchandising Operations

Measuring net income for a merchandiser is conceptually the same as for a service enterprise. That is, net income (or loss) results from the matching of expenses with revenues. For a merchandiser, the primary source of revenues is the sale of merchandise. This revenue source is often referred to as **sales revenue** or **sales**. Unlike expenses for a service company, expenses for a merchandiser are divided into two categories: (1) the cost of goods sold and (2) operating expenses.

The **cost of goods sold** is the total cost of merchandise sold during the period. This expense is directly related to the revenue recognized from the sale of the goods. Sales revenue less cost of goods sold is called **gross profit** on sales. For example, when a calculator costing $15 is sold for $25, the gross profit is $10. Merchandisers report gross profit on sales in the income statement.

STUDY OBJECTIVE 1

Identify the differences between a service enterprise and a merchandiser.

After gross profit is calculated, operating expenses are deducted to determine net income (or net loss). **Operating expenses** are expenses incurred in the process of earning sales revenue. Examples of operating expenses are sales salaries, advertising expense, and insurance expense. The operating expenses of a merchandiser include many of the expenses found in a service company.

The income measurement process for a merchandiser is diagrammed in Illustration 5-1. The items in the three blue boxes are peculiar to a merchandiser. They are not used by a service company.

Illustration 5-1
Income measurement process for a merchandiser

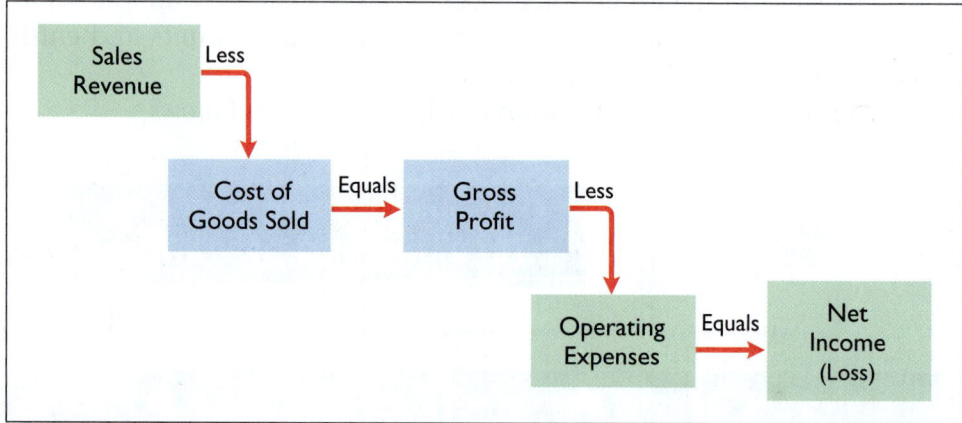

Operating Cycles

The operating cycle of a merchandiser differs from that of a service company, as shown in Illustration 5-2. The operating cycle of a merchandiser ordinarily is longer than that of a service company. The purchase of merchandise inventory and its

Illustration 5-2
Operating cycles for a service company and a merchandiser

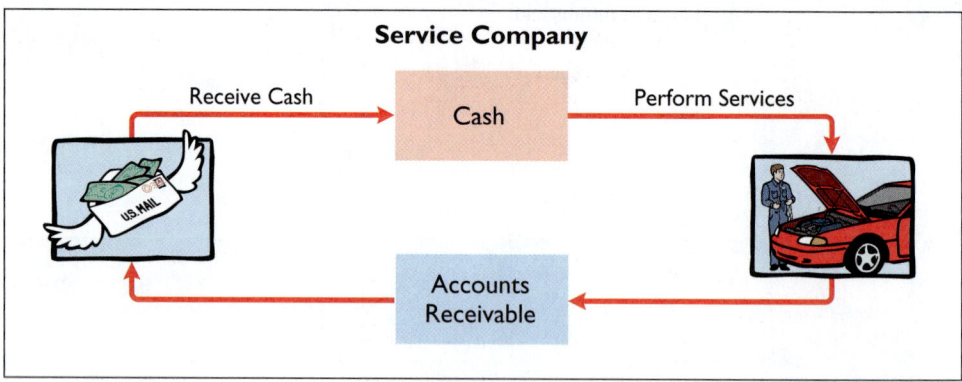

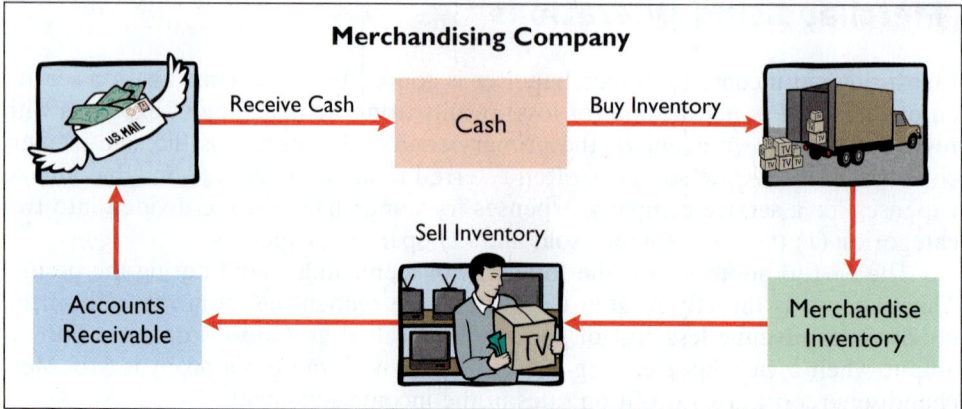

eventual sale lengthen the cycle. Note that the added asset account for a merchandising company is an **inventory** account. It is usually entitled Merchandise Inventory. Merchandise inventory is reported as a current asset on the balance sheet.

Inventory Systems

A merchandiser keeps track of its inventory to determine what is available for sale and what has been sold. One of two systems is used to account for inventory: a **perpetual inventory system** or a **periodic inventory system**.

Perpetual System

In a **perpetual inventory system**, detailed records of the cost of each inventory purchase and sale are maintained. This system continuously—perpetually—shows the inventory that should be on hand for every item. For example, a **Ford** dealership has separate inventory records for each automobile, truck, and van on its lot. With the use of bar codes and optical scanners, a grocery store can keep a daily running record of every box of cereal and every jar of jelly that it buys and sells. Under a perpetual inventory system, the cost of goods sold is **determined each time a sale occurs**.

> **HELPFUL HINT**
>
> For control purposes a physical inventory count is taken under the perpetual system, even though it is not needed to determine cost of goods sold.

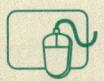 

ACCOUNTING IN ACTION — e Business Insight

What's in a bar code? First, the bar code usually doesn't contain descriptive data (just as your Social Security number or car's license plate number doesn't have anything about your name or where you live). For example, the bar codes found on food items at grocery stores don't contain the price or description of the food item. Instead, the bar code has a 12-digit "product number" in it. When read by a bar code reader and transmitted to the computer, the computer finds the disk file item record(s) associated with that item number. In the disk file is the price, vendor name, quantity on-hand, description, and so on. The computer does a "price lookup" by reading the bar code, and then it creates a register of the items and adds the price to the subtotal of the groceries sold. It also subtracts the quantity from the "on-hand" total.

Periodic System

In a **periodic inventory system**, detailed inventory records of the goods on hand are not kept throughout the period. The cost of goods sold is **determined only at the end of the accounting period**—that is, periodically. At that time, a physical inventory count is taken to determine the cost of goods on hand (Merchandise Inventory). To determine the cost of goods sold under a periodic inventory system, you must (1) determine the cost of goods on hand at the beginning of the accounting period, (2) add to it the cost of goods purchased, and (3) subtract the cost of goods on hand at the end of the accounting period.

Illustration 5-3 graphically compares the sequence of activities and the timing of the cost of goods sold computation under the two inventory systems.

Illustration 5-3
Comparing perpetual and
periodic inventory systems

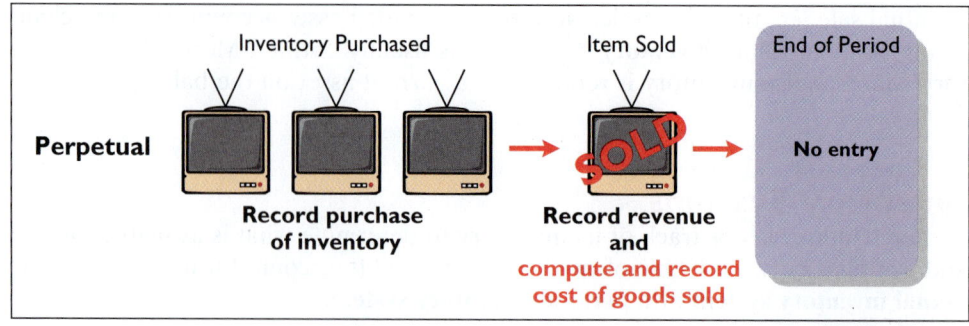

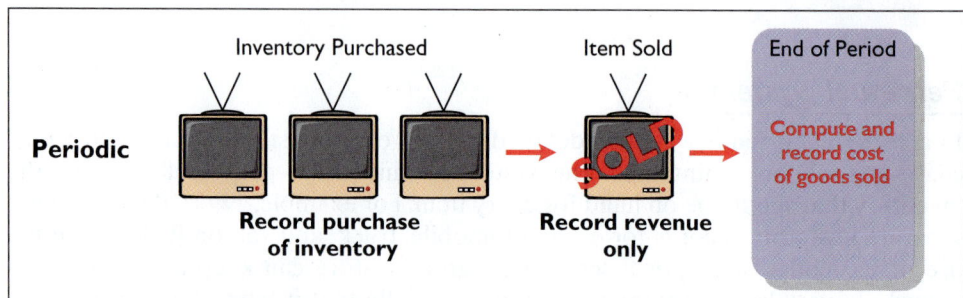

Additional Considerations

Perpetual systems have traditionally been used by companies that sell merchandise with high unit values. Examples are automobiles, furniture, and major home appliances. The widespread use of computers and electronic scanners now enables many more companies to install perpetual inventory systems. The perpetual inventory system is so named because the accounting records continuously—perpetually—show the quantity and cost of the inventory that should be on hand at any time.

A perpetual inventory system provides better control over inventories than a periodic system. The inventory records show the quantities that should be on hand. So, the goods can be counted at any time to see whether the amount of goods actually on hand agrees with the inventory records. Any shortages uncovered can be investigated immediately. A perpetual inventory system does require additional clerical work and additional cost to maintain the subsidiary records. But a computerized system can minimize this cost. Much of **Wal-Mart**'s success is attributed to its sophisticated perpetual inventory system. When snowboard maker **Morrow Snowboards Inc.** issued shares of stock to the public for the first time, some investors expressed reluctance to invest in Morrow. They were concerned about a number of accounting control problems. To reduce investor concerns, Morrow implemented a perpetual inventory system to improve its control over inventory.

Because the perpetual inventory system is growing in popularity and use, we illustrate it in this chapter. The periodic system, still widely used, is described in an appendix to this chapter.

Recording Purchases and Sales of Merchandise

Purchases

STUDY OBJECTIVE 2

Explain the entries for purchases under a perpetual inventory system.

Purchases of inventory may be made for cash or on account (credit). Purchases are normally recorded when the goods are received from the seller. Every purchase should be supported by business documents that provide written evidence of the transaction. Each cash purchase should be supported by a canceled check or a cash register receipt indicating the items purchased and amounts paid. Cash purchases are recorded by an increase in Merchandise Inventory and a decrease in Cash.

Each credit purchase should be supported by a **purchase invoice**. This document indicates the total purchase price and other relevant information. But the purchaser does not prepare a separate purchase invoice. Instead, the copy of the sales invoice sent by the seller is used by the buyer as a purchase invoice. In Illustration 5-4, for example, the sales invoice prepared by Sellers Electronix (the seller) is used as a purchase invoice by Beyer Video (the buyer).

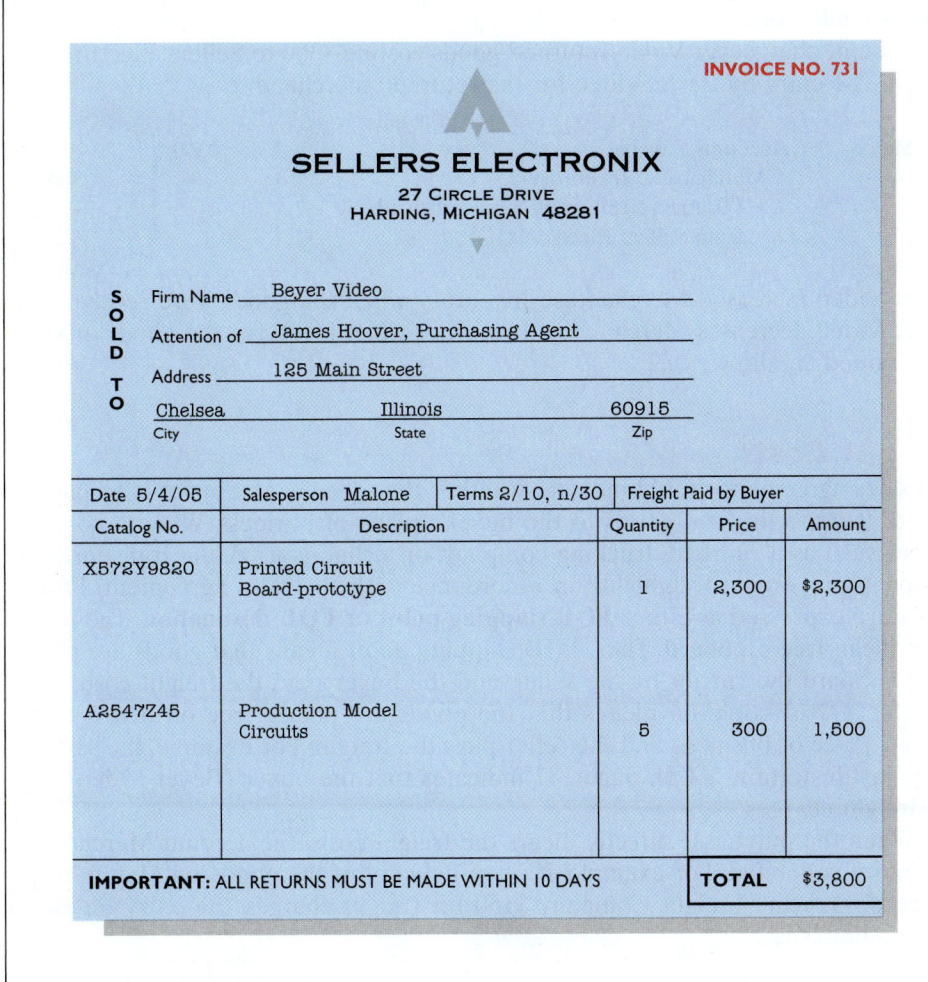

Illustration 5-4
Sales invoice used as purchase invoice by Beyer Video

HELPFUL HINT

To better understand the contents of this invoice, identify these items:
1. Seller
2. Invoice date
3. Purchaser
4. Salesperson
5. Credit terms
6. Freight terms
7. Goods sold: catalog number, description, quantity, price per unit
8. Total invoice amount

The associated entry for Beyer Video for the invoice from Sellers Electronix is:

May 4	Merchandise Inventory	3,800	
	Accounts Payable		3,800
	(To record goods purchased on account		
	from Sellers Electronix)		

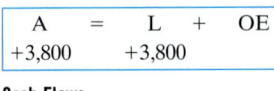

A	=	L	+	OE
+3,800		+3,800		

Cash Flows
no effect

Under the perpetual inventory system, purchases of merchandise for sale are recorded in the Merchandise Inventory account. Thus, a retailer of general merchandise such as **Wal-Mart** would debit Merchandise Inventory for clothing, sporting goods, and anything else purchased for resale to customers.

Not all purchases are debited to Merchandise Inventory, however. Purchases of assets acquired for use and not for resale (such as supplies, equipment, and similar items) are recorded as increases to specific asset accounts rather than to Merchandise Inventory. Wal-Mart would increase Supplies to record the purchase of materials used to make shelf signs or for cash register receipt paper.

Purchase Returns and Allowances

A purchaser may be dissatisfied with the merchandise received. The goods may be damaged or defective, of inferior quality, or perhaps they do not meet the purchaser's specifications. In such cases, the purchaser may return the goods to the seller. The purchaser is granted credit if the sale was made on credit, or a cash refund if the purchase was for cash. This transaction is known as a **purchase return**. Or the purchaser may choose to keep the merchandise if the seller is willing to grant an allowance (deduction) from the purchase price. This transaction is known as a **purchase allowance**.

Assume that Beyer Video returned goods costing $300 to Sellers Electronix on May 8. The entry by Beyer Video for the returned merchandise is:

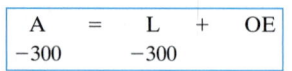

Cash Flows
no effect

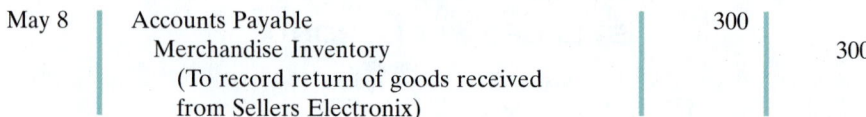

May 8	Accounts Payable	300	
	Merchandise Inventory		300
	(To record return of goods received		
	from Sellers Electronix)		

Beyer Video increased Merchandise Inventory when the goods were received. So, Beyer Video decreases Merchandise Inventory when it returns the goods or when it is granted an allowance.

Freight Costs

The sales agreement should indicate whether the seller or the buyer is to pay the cost of transporting the goods to the buyer's place of business. When a common carrier such as a railroad, trucking company, or airline is used, the transportation company prepares a freight bill in accordance with the sales agreement. Freight terms are expressed as either **FOB shipping point** or **FOB destination**. The letters FOB mean **free on board**. Thus, **FOB shipping point** means that goods are placed free on board the carrier by the seller, and the buyer pays the freight costs. Conversely, **FOB destination** means that the goods are placed free on board to the buyer's place of business, and the seller pays the freight. For example, the sales invoice in Illustration 5-4 on page 187 indicates that the buyer (Beyer Video) pays the freight charges.

When the purchaser directly incurs the freight costs, the account Merchandise Inventory is debited. For example, if upon delivery of the goods on May 6, Beyer Video pays Acme Freight Company $150 for freight charges, the entry on Beyer Video's books is:

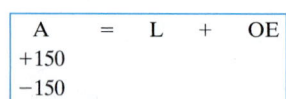

Cash Flows
−150

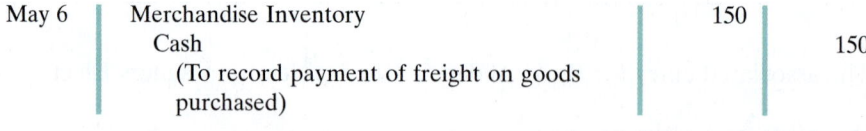

May 6	Merchandise Inventory	150	
	Cash		150
	(To record payment of freight on goods		
	purchased)		

In contrast, **freight costs incurred by the seller on outgoing merchandise are an operating expense to the seller**. These costs increase an expense account titled Freight-out or Delivery Expense. If the freight terms on the invoice in Illustration 5-4 had required that Sellers Electronix pay the $150 freight charges, the entry by Sellers Electronix would have been:

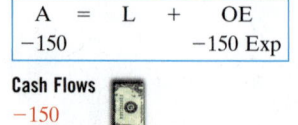

Cash Flows
−150

May 4	Freight-out (or Delivery Expense)	150	
	Cash		150
	(To record payment of freight on		
	goods sold)		

When the freight charges are paid by the seller, the seller will usually establish a higher invoice price for the goods to cover the expense of shipping.

 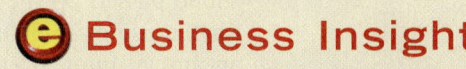

Purchase Discounts

The credit terms of a purchase on account may permit the buyer to claim a cash discount for prompt payment. The buyer calls this cash discount a **purchase discount**. This incentive offers advantages to both parties: The purchaser saves money, and the seller is able to shorten the operating cycle by converting the accounts receivable into cash earlier.

The **credit terms** specify the amount of the cash discount and time period during which it is offered. They also indicate the length of time in which the purchaser is expected to pay the full invoice price. In the sales invoice in Illustration 5-4, credit terms are 2/10, n/30. This is read "two-ten, net thirty." It means that a 2 percent cash discount may be taken on the invoice price, less any returns or allowances, if payment is made within 10 days of the invoice date (the **discount period**). If payment is not made in that time, the invoice price, less any returns or allowances, is due 30 days from the invoice date. Or, the discount period may extend to a specified number of days after the month in which the sale occurs. For example, 1/10 EOM (end of month) means that a 1 percent discount is available if the invoice is paid within the first 10 days of the next month.

The seller may elect not to offer a cash discount for prompt payment. In that case, credit terms will specify only the maximum time period for paying the balance due. For example, the time period may be stated as n/30, n/60, or n/10 EOM. These mean, respectively, that the net amount must be paid in 30 days, 60 days, or within the first 10 days of the next month.

When an invoice is paid within the discount period, the amount of the discount decreases Merchandise Inventory. Inventory is recorded at its cost and, by paying within the discount period, the merchandiser has reduced its cost. To illustrate, assume Beyer Video pays the balance due of $3,500 (gross invoice price of $3,800 less purchase returns and allowances of $300) on May 14, the last day of the discount period. The cash discount is $70 ($3,500 × 2%), and the amount of cash paid by Beyer Video is $3,430 ($3,500 − $70). The entry to record the May 14 payment by Beyer Video is:

May 14	Accounts Payable	3,500	
	Cash		3,430
	Merchandise Inventory		70
	(To record payment within discount period)		

A	=	L	+	OE
−3,430		−3,500		
−70				

Cash Flows
−3,430

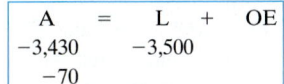

If Beyer Video failed to take the discount and instead made full payment on June 3, Beyer Video's entry would be:

June 3	Accounts Payable	3,500	
	Cash		3,500
	(To record payment with no discount taken)		

A	=	L	+	OE
−3,500		−3,500		

Cash Flows
−3,500

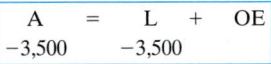

A merchandiser usually should take all available discounts. Passing up the discount may be viewed as **paying interest** for use of the money. For example, if Beyer

Video passed up the discount, it would be like paying an interest rate of 2 percent for the use of $3,500 for 20 days (30 days minus 10 days). This is the equivalent of an annual interest rate of approximately 36.5 percent (2% × 365/20). Obviously, it would be better for Beyer Video to borrow at prevailing bank interest rates of 8 percent to 12 percent than to lose the discount.

Sales

STUDY OBJECTIVE 3

Explain the entries for sales revenues under a perpetual inventory system.

Sales revenues, like service revenues, are recorded when earned. This is done in accord with the revenue recognition principle. Typically, sales revenues are earned when the goods are transferred from the seller to the buyer. At this point the sales transaction is completed, and the sales price has been established.

Sales may be made on credit or for cash. Every sales transaction should be supported by a **business document** that provides written evidence of the sale. **Cash register tapes** provide evidence of cash sales. A sales invoice, like the one that was shown in Illustration 5-4 (page 187), provides support for a credit sale. The original copy of the invoice goes to the customer. A copy is kept by the seller for use in recording the sale. The invoice shows the date of sale, customer name, total sales price, and other relevant information.

Two entries are made for each sale. The first entry records the sale: Cash (or Accounts Receivable, if a credit sale) is increased by a debit, and Sales is increased by a credit at the selling (invoice) price of the goods. The second entry records the cost of the merchandise sold: Cost of Goods Sold is increased by a debit, and Merchandise Inventory is decreased by a credit for the cost of those goods. As a result, the Merchandise Inventory account will show at all times the amount of inventory that should be on hand.

To illustrate a credit sales transaction, Sellers Electronix's sale of $3,800 on May 4 to Beyer Video (see Illustration 5-4, page 187) is recorded as follows. (Assume the merchandise cost Sellers Electronix $2,400.)

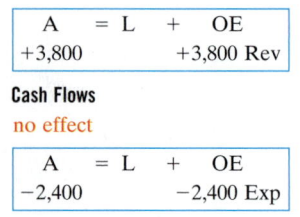

A	= L	+	OE	
+3,800			+3,800 Rev	

Cash Flows
no effect

A	= L	+	OE	
−2,400			−2,400 Exp	

Cash Flows
no effect

May 4	Accounts Receivable	3,800	
	Sales		3,800
	(To record credit sale to Beyer Video per		
	invoice #731)		
4	Cost of Goods Sold	2,400	
	Merchandise Inventory		2,400
	(To record cost of merchandise sold on		
	invoice #731 to Beyer Video)		

For internal decision-making purposes, merchandisers may use more than one sales account. For example, Sellers Electronix may keep separate sales accounts for its TV sets, videocassette recorders, and microwave ovens. By using separate sales accounts for major product lines, company management can monitor sales trends more closely and respond more strategically to changes in sales patterns. For example, if TV sales are increasing while microwave oven sales are decreasing, the company could reevaluate its advertising and pricing policies on each of these items.

HELPFUL HINT

The Sales account is credited only for sales of goods held for resale. Sales of assets not held for resale (such as equipment or land) are credited directly to the asset account.

However, on its income statement presented to outside investors, a merchandiser would normally provide only a single sales figure—the sum of all of its individual sales accounts. This is done for two reasons. First, providing detail on individual sales accounts would add length to the income statement. Second, companies do not want their competitors to know the details of their operating results.

Sales Returns and Allowances

We now look at the "flipside" of purchase returns and allowances, which are **sales returns and allowances** recorded on the books of the seller. Sellers Electronix's entries to record credit for returned goods involve two entries: (1) The first is an increase in Sales Returns and Allowances and a decrease in Accounts Receivable at the $300 selling price. (2) The second is an increase in Merchandise Inventory (assume a $140 cost) and a decrease in Cost of Goods Sold. The entries are as follows.

May 8	Sales Returns and Allowances	300	
	Accounts Receivable		300
	(To record credit granted to Beyer Video		
	for returned goods)		
8	Merchandise Inventory	140	
	Cost of Goods Sold		140
	(To record cost of goods returned)		

A	=	L	+	OE
−300				−300 Rev

Cash Flows
no effect

A	=	L	+	OE
+140				+140 Exp

Cash Flows
no effect

If goods are returned because they are damaged or defective, then the entry to Merchandise Inventory and Cost of Goods Sold should be for the estimated value of the returned goods, rather than their cost. For example, if the goods returned to Sellers Electronix were defective and had a scrap value of $50, Merchandise Inventory would be debited for $50, and Cost of Goods Sold would be credited for $50.

Sales Returns and Allowances is a **contra revenue account** to Sales. The normal balance of Sales Returns and Allowances is a debit. A contra account is used, instead of debiting Sales, to disclose in the accounts the amount of sales returns and allowances. This information is important to management. Excessive returns and allowances suggest inferior merchandise, inefficiencies in filling orders, errors in billing customers, and mistakes in delivery or shipment of goods. Also, a debit recorded directly to Sales could distort comparisons between total sales in different accounting periods.

> **HELPFUL HINT**
>
> Remember that the increases, decreases, and normal balances of contra accounts are the opposite of the accounts to which they correspond.

ACCOUNTING IN ACTION Ethics Insight

How high is too high? Returns can become so high that it is questionable whether sales revenue should have been recognized in the first place. An example of high returns is **Florafax International Inc.**, a floral supply company, which was alleged to have shipped its product without customer authorization on ten holiday occasions, including 8,562 shipments of flowers to customers for Mother's Day and 6,575 for Secretary's Day. The return rate on these shipments went as high as 69% of sales. As one employee noted: "Products went out the front door and came in the back door."

Sales Discounts

As mentioned in our discussion of purchase transactions, the seller may offer the customer a cash discount for the prompt payment of the balance due. From the seller's point of view, this is called a **sales discount**. Like a purchase discount, a sales discount is based on the invoice price less returns and allowances, if any. The Sales Discounts account is debited for discounts that are taken. The entry by Sellers Electronix to record the cash receipt on May 14 from Beyer Video within the discount period is:

May 14	Cash	3,430	
	Sales Discounts	70	
	Accounts Receivable		3,500
	(To record collection within 2/10, n/30		
	discount period from Beyer Video)		

A	=	L	+	OE
+3,430				−70 Rev
−3,500				

Cash Flows
+3,430

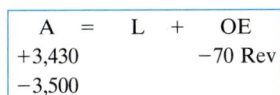

Like Sales Returns and Allowances, Sales Discounts is a **contra revenue account** to Sales. Its normal balance is a debit. This account is used, instead of debiting Sales, to disclose cash discounts taken by customers. If the discount is not taken, Sellers Electronix debits Cash for $3,500 and credits Accounts Receivable for the same amount at the date of collection.

BEFORE YOU GO ON...

Review It

1. How does the measurement of net income in a merchandising company differ from that in a service enterprise?
2. In what ways is a perpetual inventory system different from a periodic system?
3. Under the perpetual inventory system, what entries are made to record purchases, purchase returns and allowances, purchase discounts, and freight costs?
4. Under a perpetual inventory system, what are the two entries that must be recorded at the time of each sale?
5. Why is it important to use the Sales Returns and Allowances account, rather than simply reducing the Sales account, when goods are returned?

Do It

On September 5, NewIdea Company buys merchandise on account from Janet Diaz Company. The selling price of the goods is $1,500, and the cost to Diaz Company was $800. On September 8 defective goods with a selling price of $200 and a scrap value of $80 are returned. Record the transactions on the books of both companies.

ACTION PLAN

- Purchaser: Record purchases of inventory at its cost and directly reduce the Merchandise Inventory account for returned goods.
- Seller: Record both the sale and the cost of goods sold at the time of the sale. Record returns in a contra account, Sales Returns and Allowances.

SOLUTION

NewIdea Company

Sept. 5	Merchandise Inventory	1,500	
	Accounts Payable		1,500
	(To record goods purchased on account)		
8	Accounts Payable	200	
	Merchandise Inventory		200
	(To record return of defective goods)		

Janet Diaz Company

Sept. 5	Accounts Receivable	1,500	
	Sales		1,500
	(To record credit sale)		
5	Cost of Goods Sold	800	
	Merchandise Inventory		800
	(To record cost of goods sold on account)		
8	Sales Returns and Allowances	200	
	Accounts Receivable		200
	(To record credit granted for receipt of returned goods)		
8	Merchandise Inventory	80	
	Cost of Goods Sold		80
	(To record scrap value of goods returned)		

Related exercise material: *BE5-1, BE5-2, BE5-3, BE5-4, E5-1, E5-2, E5-3, and E5-4.*

✔ THE NAVIGATOR

Completing the Accounting Cycle

Up to this point, we have illustrated the basic entries in recording transactions relating to purchases and sales in a perpetual inventory system. Now we consider the remaining steps in the accounting cycle for a merchandiser. Each of the required steps described in Chapter 4 for a service company applies to a merchandising company. Use of a worksheet by a merchandiser (an optional step) is shown in the appendix to this chapter.

STUDY OBJECTIVE 4

Explain the steps in the accounting cycle for a merchandiser.

Adjusting Entries

A merchandiser generally has the same types of adjusting entries as a service company. But a merchandiser using a perpetual system will require one additional adjustment to make the records agree with the actual inventory on hand. Here's why: At the end of each period, a merchandiser using a perpetual system will take a physical count of its goods on hand for control purposes. A company's unadjusted balance in Merchandise Inventory will usually not agree with the actual amount of inventory on hand at year-end. The perpetual inventory records may be incorrect due to a variety of causes such as recording errors, theft, or waste. As a result, the perpetual records need adjustment to ensure that the recorded inventory amount agrees with the actual inventory on hand. **This involves adjusting Merchandise Inventory and Cost of Goods Sold.**

For example, suppose that the records of Sellers Electronix report an unadjusted balance in Merchandise Inventory of $40,500. Through a physical count, the company determines that its actual merchandise inventory on hand at year-end is $40,000. The adjusting entry would be to debit Cost of Goods Sold for $500 and to credit Merchandise Inventory for $500.

HELPFUL HINT

The steps required to determine the actual inventory on hand are discussed in Chapter 6.

Closing Entries

For a merchandiser, like a service enterprise, all accounts that affect the determination of net income are closed to Income Summary. In journalizing, all temporary accounts with debit balances are credited, and all temporary accounts with credit balances are debited, as shown below for Sellers Electronix. Note that cost of goods sold must be closed to Income Summary.

Date	Account	Debit	Credit
Dec. 31	Sales	480,000	
	Income Summary		480,000
	(To close income statement accounts with credit balances)		
31	Income Summary	450,000	
	Sales Returns and Allowances		12,000
	Sales Discounts		8,000
	Cost of Goods Sold		316,000
	Store Salaries Expense		45,000
	Administrative Salaries Expense		19,000
	Freight-out		7,000
	Advertising Expense		16,000
	Utilities Expense		17,000
	Depreciation Expense		8,000
	Insurance Expense		2,000
	(To close income statement accounts with debit balances)		
31	Income Summary	30,000	
	R.A. Lamb, Capital		30,000
	(To close net income to capital)		

HELPFUL HINT

The easiest way to prepare the first two closing entries is to identify the temporary accounts by their balances and then prepare one entry for the credits and one for the debits.

(*continued from p. 195*)

31	R.A. Lamb, Capital	15,000	
	R.A. Lamb, Drawing		15,000
	(To close drawings to capital)		

After the closing entries are posted, all temporary accounts have zero balances. In addition, R.A. Lamb, Capital has a credit balance of $98,000: beginning balance + net income − drawings ($83,000 + $30,000 − $15,000).

Summary of Merchandising Entries

The entries for the merchandising accounts using a perpetual inventory system are summarized in Illustration 5-5.

Illustration 5-5
Daily recurring and adjusting and closing entries

Transactions	Daily Recurring Entries	Dr.	Cr.
Sales Transactions			
Selling merchandise to customers.	Cash or Accounts Receivable	XX	
	Sales		XX
	Cost of Goods Sold	XX	
	Merchandise Inventory		XX
Granting sales returns or allowances to customers.	Sales Returns and Allowances	XX	
	Cash or Accounts Receivable		XX
	Merchandise Inventory	XX	
	Cost of Goods Sold		XX
Paying freight costs on sales; FOB destination.	Freight-out	XX	
	Cash		XX
Receiving payment from customers within discount period.	Cash	XX	
	Sales Discounts	XX	
	Accounts Receivable		XX
Purchase Transactions			
Purchasing merchandise for resale.	Merchandise Inventory	XX	
	Cash or Accounts Payable		XX
Paying freight costs on merchandise purchased; FOB shipping point.	Merchandise Inventory	XX	
	Cash		XX
Receiving purchase returns or allowances from suppliers.	Cash or Accounts Payable	XX	
	Merchandise Inventory		XX
Paying suppliers within discount period.	Accounts Payable	XX	
	Merchandise Inventory		XX
	Cash		XX

Events	Adjusting and Closing Entries		
Adjust because book amount is higher than the inventory amount determined to be on hand.	Cost of Goods Sold	XX	
	Merchandise Inventory		XX
Closing temporary accounts with credit balances.	Sales	XX	
	Income Summary		XX
Closing temporary accounts with debit balances.	Income Summary	XX	
	Sales Returns and Allowances		XX
	Sales Discounts		XX
	Cost of Goods Sold		XX
	Freight-out		XX
	Expenses		XX

Review It

1. Why is an adjustment to the Merchandise Inventory account usually needed?
2. What merchandising account(s) will appear in the post-closing trial balance?

Do It

The trial balance of Celine's Sports Wear Shop at December 31 shows Merchandise Inventory $25,000, Sales $162,400, Sales Returns and Allowances $4,800, Sales Discounts $3,600, Cost of Goods Sold $110,000, Rental Revenue $6,000, Freight-out $1,800, Rent Expense $8,800, and Salaries and Wages Expense $22,000. Prepare the closing entries for the above accounts.

ACTION PLAN

- Close all temporary accounts with credit balances to Income Summary by debiting these accounts.
- Close all temporary accounts with debit balances to Income Summary by crediting these accounts.

SOLUTION   The two closing entries are:

Dec. 31	Sales	162,400	
	Rental Revenue	6,000	
	Income Summary		168,400
	(To close accounts with credit balances)		
Dec. 31	Income Summary	151,000	
	Cost of Goods Sold		110,000
	Sales Returns and Allowances		4,800
	Sales Discounts		3,600
	Freight-out		1,800
	Rent Expense		8,800
	Salaries and Wages Expense		22,000
	(To close accounts with debit balances)		

Related exercise material: *BE5-7, E5-5, and E5-6.*

✓ THE NAVIGATOR

Forms of Financial Statements

Two forms of the income statement are widely used by merchandisers. Also, merchandisers use the classified balance sheet, introduced in Chapter 4. The use of these financial statements by merchandisers is explained below.

Multiple-Step Income Statement

The **multiple-step income statement** is so named because it shows the steps in determining net income (or net loss). It shows two main steps: (1) Cost of goods sold is subtracted from net sales, to determine gross profit. (2) Operating expenses are deducted from gross profit, to determine net income. These steps relate to the company's principal operating activities. A multiple-step statement also distinguishes between **operating** and **non-operating activities**. This distinction provides users with more information about a company's income performance. The statement also high-lights intermediate components of income and shows subgroupings of expenses.

Income Statement Presentation of Sales

The multiple-step income statement begins by presenting sales revenue. As contra revenue accounts, sales returns and allowances, and sales discounts are deducted from sales to arrive at **net sales**. The sales revenues section for Sellers Electronix, using assumed data, is as follows.

Illustration 5-6
Computation of net sales

SELLERS ELECTRONIX Income Statement (partial)		
Sales revenues		
Sales		$480,000
Less: Sales returns and allowances	$12,000	
Sales discounts	8,000	20,000
Net sales		**$460,000**

This presentation discloses the key aspects of the company's principal revenue-producing activities.

Gross Profit

STUDY OBJECTIVE 6

Explain the computation and importance of gross profit.

From Illustration 5-1, you learned that cost of goods sold is deducted from sales revenue to determine **gross profit**. Sales revenue used for this computation is **net sales**. On the basis of the sales data presented in Illustration 5-6 (net sales of $460,000) and the cost of goods sold under the perpetual inventory system (assume $316,000), the gross profit for Sellers Electronix is $144,000, computed as follows.

Illustration 5-7
Computation of gross profit

Net sales	$460,000
Cost of goods sold	316,000
Gross profit	**$144,000**

A company's gross profit may also be expressed as a percentage. This is done by dividing the amount of gross profit by net sales. For Sellers Electronix the **gross profit rate** is 31.3 percent, computed as follows.

Illustration 5-8
Gross profit rate formula and computation

Gross Profit	÷	Net Sales	=	Gross Profit Rate
$144,000	÷	$460,000	=	**31.3%**

The gross profit rate is generally considered to be more useful than the gross profit amount. The rate expresses a more meaningful (qualitative) relationship between net sales and gross profit. For example, a gross profit of $1,000,000 may be impressive. But, if it is the result of a gross profit rate of only 7 percent, it is not so impressive. The gross profit rate tells how many cents of each sales dollar go to gross profit.

Gross profit represents the **merchandising profit** of a company. It is not a measure of the overall profitability, because operating expenses have not been deducted. But the amount and trend of gross profit is closely watched by management and other interested parties. They compare current gross profit with amounts reported in past periods. They also compare the company's gross profit rate with rates of competitors and with industry averages. Such comparisons provide information about the effectiveness of a company's purchasing function and the soundness of its pricing policies.

Operating Expenses and Net Income

Operating expenses are the third component in measuring net income for a merchandiser. As indicated earlier, these expenses are similar in merchandising and service enterprises. At Sellers Electronix, operating expenses were $114,000. The firm's net income is determined by subtracting operating expenses from gross profit. Thus, net income is $30,000, as shown below.

Gross profit	$144,000
Operating expenses	**114,000**
Net income	$ 30,000

Illustration 5-9
Operating expenses in computing net income

The net income amount is the "bottom line" of a company's income statement.

Nonoperating Activities

Nonoperating activities consist of (1) revenues and expenses from auxiliary operations and (2) gains and losses that are unrelated to the company's operations. The results of nonoperating activities are shown in two sections: "**Other revenues and gains**" and "**Other expenses and losses**." For a merchandiser, these sections will typically include the following items.

Nonoperating Activities	
Other revenues and gains	**Other expenses and losses**
Interest revenue from notes receivable and marketable securities	Interest expense on notes and loans payable
Dividend revenue from investments in capital stock	Casualty losses from recurring causes such as vandalism and accidents
Rent revenue from subleasing a portion of the store	Loss from the sale or abandonment of property, plant, and equipment
Gain from the sale of property, plant, and equipment	Loss from strikes by employees and suppliers

Illustration 5-10
Items reported in nonoperating sections

The nonoperating activities are reported in the income statement immediately after the company's primary operating activities. These sections are shown in Illustration 5-11, using assumed data for Sellers Electronix.

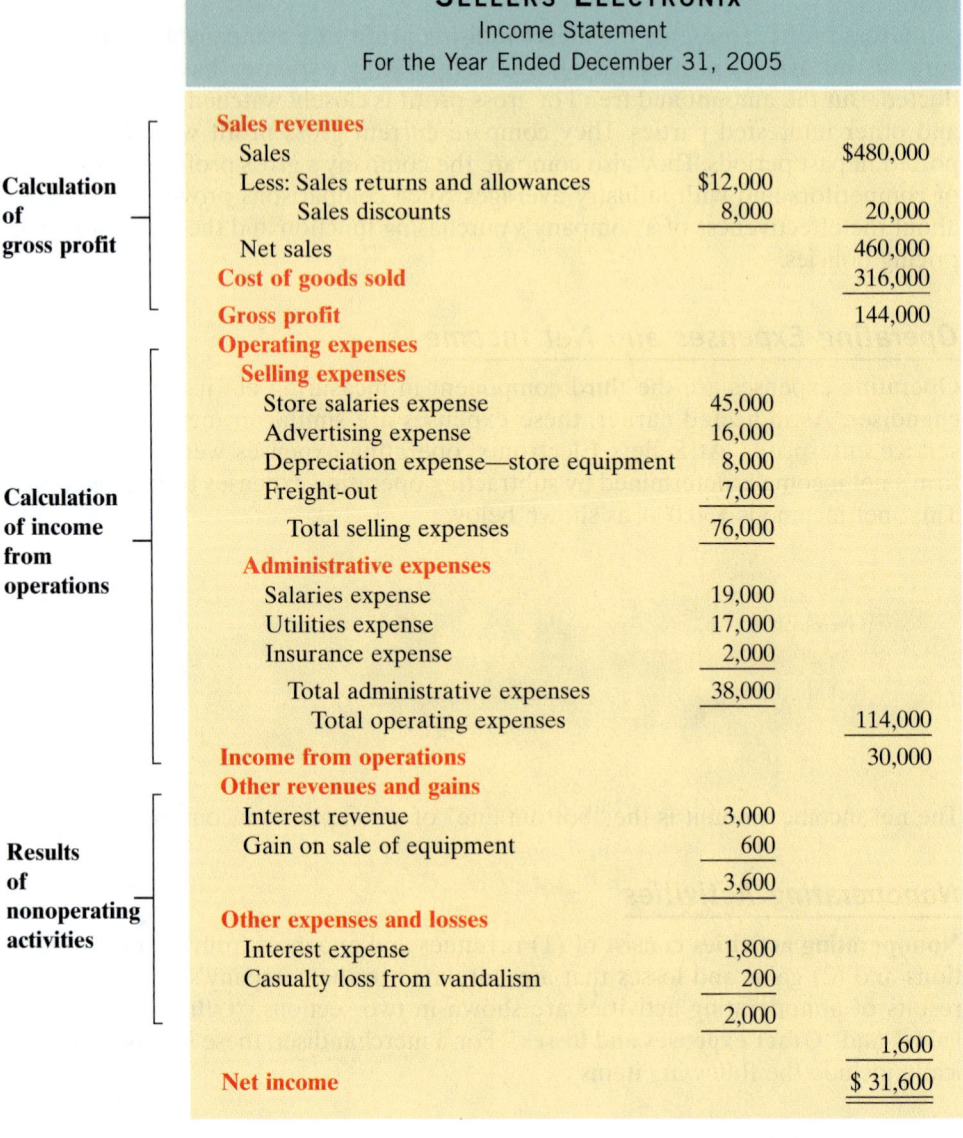

SELLERS ELECTRONIX
Income Statement
For the Year Ended December 31, 2005

Sales revenues			
Sales			$480,000
Less: Sales returns and allowances		$12,000	
Sales discounts		8,000	20,000
Net sales			460,000
Cost of goods sold			316,000
Gross profit			144,000
Operating expenses			
Selling expenses			
Store salaries expense		45,000	
Advertising expense		16,000	
Depreciation expense—store equipment		8,000	
Freight-out		7,000	
Total selling expenses		76,000	
Administrative expenses			
Salaries expense		19,000	
Utilities expense		17,000	
Insurance expense		2,000	
Total administrative expenses		38,000	
Total operating expenses			114,000
Income from operations			30,000
Other revenues and gains			
Interest revenue		3,000	
Gain on sale of equipment		600	
		3,600	
Other expenses and losses			
Interest expense		1,800	
Casualty loss from vandalism		200	
		2,000	
			1,600
Net income			$ 31,600

Calculation of gross profit

Calculation of income from operations

Results of nonoperating activities

When the two nonoperating sections are included, the label "**Income from operations**" (or Operating income) precedes them. It clearly identifies the results of the company's normal operations. Income from operations is determined by subtracting cost of goods sold and operating expenses from net sales.

In the nonoperating activities sections, items are generally reported at the net amount. Thus, if a company received a $2,500 insurance settlement on vandalism losses of $2,700, the loss is reported at $200. Note, too, that the results of the two nonoperating sections are netted. The difference is added to or subtracted from income from operations to determine net income. It is not uncommon for companies to combine these two nonoperating sections into a single "Other revenues and expenses" section.

Subgrouping of Operating Expenses

In larger companies, operating expenses are often subdivided into selling expenses and administrative expenses, as illustrated in Illustration 5-11. **Selling expenses** are those associated with making sales. They include expenses for sales promotion as well as expenses of completing the sale, such as delivery and shipping. **Administrative expenses** (sometimes called general expenses) relate to general operating activities such as personnel management, accounting, and store security.

When subgroupings are made, some expenses may have to be prorated (e.g., 70% to selling and 30% to administrative expenses). For example, if a store building is used for both selling and general functions, building expenses such as depreciation, utilities, and property taxes will need to be allocated.

Any reasonable classification of expenses that serves to inform those who use the statement is satisfactory. The present tendency in statements prepared for management's internal use is to present in considerable detail expense data grouped along lines of responsibility.

Single-Step Income Statement

Another income statement format is the **single-step income statement**. The statement is so named because only one step, subtracting total expenses from total revenues, is required in determining net income (or net loss).

In a single-step statement, all data are classified under two categories: (1) revenues and (2) expenses. The **revenues** category includes both operating revenues and other revenues and gains. The **expenses** category includes cost of goods sold, operating expenses, and other expenses and losses. A condensed single-step statement for Sellers Electronix is shown in Illustration 5-12.

Illustration 5-12
Single-step income statement

SELLERS ELECTRONIX
Income Statement
For the Year Ended December 31, 2005

Revenues		
Net sales		$460,000
Interest revenue		3,000
Gain on sale of equipment		600
Total revenues		463,600
Expenses		
Cost of goods sold	$316,000	
Selling expenses	76,000	
Administrative expenses	38,000	
Interest expense	1,800	
Casualty loss from vandalism	200	
Total expenses		432,000
Net income		$ 31,600

There are two primary reasons for using the single-step format: (1) A company does not realize any type of profit or income until total revenues exceed total expenses, so it makes sense to divide the statement into these two categories. (2) The format is simpler and easier to read than the multiple-step format. But for homework problems, the single-step format should be used only when it is specifically requested.

Classified Balance Sheet

In the balance sheet, merchandise inventory is reported as a current asset immediately below accounts receivable. Recall from Chapter 4 that items are listed under current assets in their order of liquidity. Merchandise inventory is less liquid than accounts receivable because the goods must first be sold and then collection must be made from the customer. Illustration 5-13 presents the assets section of a classified balance sheet for Sellers Electronix.

Illustration 5-13
Assets section of a classified balance sheet (partial)

SELLERS ELECTRONIX
Balance Sheet (Partial)
December 31, 2005

Assets

Current assets		
Cash		$ 9,500
Accounts receivable		16,100
Merchandise inventory		**40,000**
Prepaid insurance		1,800
Total current assets		67,400
Property, plant, and equipment		
Store equipment	$80,000	
Less: Accumulated depreciation—store equipment	24,000	56,000
Total assets		$123,400

HELPFUL HINT

The $40,000 is the cost of the inventory on hand, not its expected selling price.

BEFORE YOU GO ON...

Review It

1. Determine **PepsiCo**'s gross profit rate for 2002 and 2001. Indicate whether it increased or decreased from 2001 to 2002. The answer to this question is provided on page 226.

2. What are nonoperating activities, and how are they reported in the income statement?

3. How does a single-step income statement differ from a multiple-step income statement?

Determining Cost of Goods Sold Under a Periodic System

STUDY OBJECTIVE 7

Determine cost of goods sold under a periodic system.

The determination of cost of goods sold is different under the periodic system than under the perpetual system. When a company uses a perpetual inventory system, all transactions affecting inventory (such as freight costs, returns, and discounts) are recorded directly to the Merchandise Inventory account. In addition, at the time of each sale the perpetual system requires a reduction in Merchandise Inventory and an increase in Cost of Goods Sold. But under a periodic system separate accounts are used to record freight costs, returns, and discounts. In addition, a running account of changes in inventory is not maintained. Instead, the balance in ending inventory, as well as the cost of goods sold for the period, is calculated at the end of the period. The determination of cost of goods sold for Sellers Electronix, using a periodic inventory system, is shown in Illustration 5-14.

SELLERS ELECTRONIX
Cost of Goods Sold
For the Year Ended December 31, 2005

Cost of goods sold			
Inventory, January 1			$36,000
Purchases		$325,000	
Less: Purchase returns and			
allowances	$10,400		
Purchase discounts	6,800	17,200	
Net purchases		307,800	
Add: Freight-in		12,200	
Cost of goods purchased			320,000
Cost of goods available for sale			356,000
Inventory, December 31			40,000
Cost of goods sold			316,000

HELPFUL HINT

The second column from the right identifies the primary items that make up cost of goods sold of $316,000. The third column explains cost of goods purchased of $320,000. The fourth column reports contra purchase items of $17,200.

The use of the periodic inventory system does not affect the content of the balance sheet. As under the perpetual system, merchandise inventory is reported at the same amount in the current assets section.

Further detail on the use of the periodic system is provided in the appendix to this chapter.

BEFORE YOU GO ON...

Review It
1. Name two basic systems of accounting for inventory.
2. What accounts are used in determining the cost of goods purchased?
3. What is included in cost of goods available for sale?

Do It
Aerosmith Company's accounting records show the following at year-end: Purchase Discounts $3,400; Freight-in $6,100; Sales $240,000; Purchases $162,500; Beginning Inventory $18,000; Ending Inventory $20,000; Sales Discounts $10,000; Purchase Returns $5,200; and Operating Expenses $57,000. Compute the following amounts for Aerosmith Company: net sales, cost of goods purchased, cost of goods sold, gross profit, and net income.

ACTION PLAN
- Understand the relationships of the cost components in measuring net income for a merchandising company.
- Compute net sales.
- Compute cost of goods purchased.
- Compute cost of goods sold.
- Compute gross profit.
- Compute net income.

SOLUTION

Net sales:

Sales − Sales discounts = Net sales

$240,000 − $10,000 = $230,000

Cost of goods purchased:

Purchases − Purchase returns − Purchase discounts + Freight-in = Cost of goods purchased

$162,500 − $5,200 − $3,400 + $6,100 = $160,000

Cost of goods sold:

Beginning inventory + Cost of goods purchased − Ending inventory = Cost of goods sold

$18,000 + $160,000 − $20,000 = $158,000

Gross profit:

Net sales − Cost of goods sold = Gross profit

$230,000 − $158,000 = $72,000

Net income:

Gross profit − Operating expenses = Net income

$72,000 − $57,000 = $15,000

Related exercise material: *BE5-10, BE5-11, E5-10, and E5-11.*

☑ THE
NAVIGATOR

DEMONSTRATION PROBLEM

The adjusted trial balance columns of the work sheet for the year ended December 31, 2005, for Falcetto Company are as follows.

Debit		Credit	
Cash	14,500	Accumulated Depreciation	18,000
Accounts Receivable	11,100	Notes Payable	25,000
Merchandise Inventory	29,000	Accounts Payable	10,600
Prepaid Insurance	2,500	Larry Falcetto, Capital	81,000
Store Equipment	95,000	Sales	536,800
Larry Falcetto, Drawing	12,000	Interest Revenue	2,500
Sales Returns and Allowances	6,700		673,900
Sales Discounts	5,000		
Cost of Goods Sold	363,400		
Freight-out	7,600		
Advertising Expense	12,000		
Store Salaries Expense	56,000		
Utilities Expense	18,000		
Rent Expense	24,000		
Depreciation Expense	9,000		
Insurance Expense	4,500		
Interest Expense	3,600		
	673,900		

Instructions

Prepare an income statement assuming Falcetto Company does not use subgroupings for operating expenses.

SOLUTION TO DEMONSTRATION PROBLEM

FALCETTO COMPANY
Income Statement
For the Year Ended December 31, 2005

Sales revenues			
Sales			$536,800
Less: Sales returns and allowances		$6,700	
Sales discounts		5,000	11,700
Net sales			525,100
Cost of goods sold			363,400
Gross profit			161,700
Operating expenses			
Store salaries expense		56,000	
Rent expense		24,000	
Utilities expense		18,000	
Advertising expense		12,000	
Depreciation expense		9,000	
Freight-out		7,600	
Insurance expense		4,500	
Total operating expenses			131,100
Income from operations			30,600
Other revenues and gains			
Interest revenue		2,500	
Other expenses and losses			
Interest expense		3,600	1,100
Net income			$ 29,500

THE NAVIGATOR

SUMMARY OF STUDY OBJECTIVES

1. **Identify the differences between a service enterprise and a merchandiser.** Because of inventory, a merchandiser has sales revenue, cost of goods sold, and gross profit. To account for inventory, a merchandiser must choose between a perpetual inventory system and a periodic inventory system.

2. **Explain the entries for purchases under a perpetual inventory system.** The Merchandise Inventory account is debited for all purchases of merchandise, freight-in, and other costs, and it is credited for purchase discounts and purchase returns and allowances.

3. **Explain the entries for sales revenues under a perpetual inventory system.** When inventory is sold, Accounts Receivable (or Cash) is debited, and Sales is credited for the **selling price** of the merchandise. At the same time, Cost of Goods Sold is debited, and Merchandise Inventory is credited for the **cost** of the inventory items sold.

4. **Explain the steps in the accounting cycle for a merchandiser.** Each of the required steps in the accounting cycle for a service enterprise applies to a merchandiser. A work sheet is again an optional step. Under a perpetual inven-

tory system, the Merchandise Inventory account must be adjusted to agree with the physical count.

5. **Distinguish between a multiple-step and a single-step income statement.** A multiple-step income statement shows numerous steps in determining net income, including nonoperating activities sections. In a single-step income statement all data are classified under two categories, revenues or expenses, and net income is determined by one step.

6. **Explain the computation and importance of gross profit.** Gross profit is computed by subtracting cost of goods sold from net sales. Gross profit represents the merchandising profit of a company. The amount and trend of gross profit are closely watched by management and other interested parties.

7. **Determine cost of goods sold under a periodic inventory system.** The steps in determining cost of goods sold are (a) record the purchases of merchandise, (b) determine the cost of goods purchased, and (c) determine the cost of goods on hand at the beginning and end of the accounting period.

THE NAVIGATOR

GLOSSARY

Administrative expenses Expenses relating to general operating activities such as personnel management, accounting, and store security. (p. 199).

Contra revenue account An account that is offset against a revenue account on the income statement. (p. 191).

Cost of goods sold The total cost of merchandise sold during the period. (p. 183).

FOB destination Freight terms indicating that the goods will be placed free on board at the buyer's place of business, and the seller pays the freight costs. (p. 188).

FOB shipping point Freight terms indicating that goods are placed free on board the carrier by the seller, and the buyer pays the freight costs. (p. 188).

Gross profit The excess of net sales over the cost of goods sold. (p. 183).

Income from operations Income from a company's principal operating activity; determined by subtracting cost of goods sold and operating expenses from net sales. (p. 198).

Multiple-step income statement An income statement that shows numerous steps in determining net income (or net loss). (p. 195).

Net sales Sales less sales returns and allowances and sales discounts. (p. 196).

Operating expenses Expenses incurred in the process of earning sales revenues that are deducted from gross profit in the income statement. (p. 184).

Other expenses and losses A nonoperating activities section of the income statement that shows expenses from auxil-

iary operations and losses unrelated to the company's operations. (p. 197).

Other revenues and gains A nonoperating activities section of the income statement that shows revenues from auxiliary operations and gains unrelated to the company's operations. (p. 197).

Periodic inventory system An inventory system in which detailed records are not maintained throughout the accounting period and the cost of goods sold is determined only at the end of an accounting period. (p. 185).

Perpetual inventory system An inventory system in which the cost of each inventory item is maintained throughout the accounting period and detailed records continuously show the inventory that should be on hand. (p. 185).

Purchase discount A cash discount claimed by a buyer for prompt payment of a balance due. (p. 189).

Purchase invoice A document that supports each credit purchase. (p. 187).

Sales discount A reduction given by a seller for prompt payment of a credit sale. (p. 191).

Sales invoice A document that supports each credit sale. (p. 190).

Sales revenue (sales) Primary source of revenue in a merchandising company. (p. 183).

Selling expenses Expenses associated with making sales. (p. 198).

Single-step income statement An income statement that shows only one step in determining net income (or net loss). (p. 199).

APPENDIX 5A PERIODIC INVENTORY SYSTEM

STUDY OBJECTIVE 8

Prepare the entries for purchases and sales of inventory under a periodic inventory system.

In a **periodic inventory system**, revenues from the sale of merchandise are recorded when sales are made, in the same way as in a perpetual system. But, no attempt is made on the date of sale to record the cost of the merchandise sold. Instead, a physical inventory count is taken at the end of the period. This count determines (1) the cost of the merchandise on hand and (2) the cost of the goods sold during the period. There is another key difference: Under a periodic system, purchases of merchandise are recorded in a Purchases account rather than a Merchandise Inventory account. Also, under a periodic system, it is customary to record the following in separate accounts: purchase returns and allowances, purchase discounts, and freight-in on purchases. That way, accumulated amounts for each are known.

Recording Transactions Under a Periodic Inventory System

To illustrate the recording of merchandise transactions under a periodic inventory system, we will use the purchase/sale transactions between Sellers Electronix and Beyer Video discussed in this chapter.

Recording Purchases of Merchandise

On the basis of the sales invoice (Illustration 5-4 shown on page 187) and receipt of the merchandise ordered from Sellers Electronix, Beyer Video records the $3,800 purchase as follows.

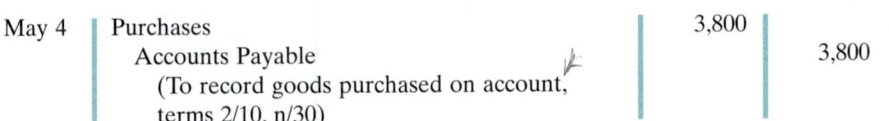

May 4	Purchases	3,800	
	Accounts Payable		3,800
	(To record goods purchased on account, terms 2/10, n/30)		

Purchases is a temporary account whose normal balance is a debit.

A	=	L	+	OE
		+3,800		−3,800 Exp

Cash Flows
no effect

Purchase Returns and Allowances

Some of the merchandise received from Sellers Electronix is defective. Beyer Video returns $300 worth of the goods and prepares the following entry to recognize the purchase return.

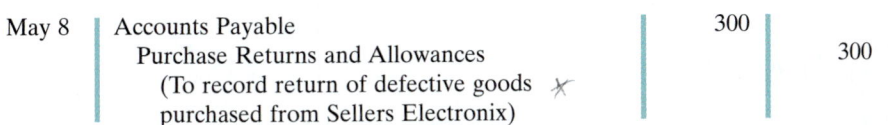

May 8	Accounts Payable	300	
	Purchase Returns and Allowances		300
	(To record return of defective goods purchased from Sellers Electronix)		

Purchase Returns and Allowances is a temporary account whose normal balance is a credit.

A	=	L	+	OE
		−300		+300 Exp

Cash Flows
no effect

Freight Costs

When the purchaser directly incurs the freight costs, the account Freight-in is debited. For example, upon delivery of the goods on May 6, Beyer pays Acme Freight Company $150 for freight charges on its purchase from Sellers Electronix. The entry on Beyer's books is:

May 9	Freight-in	150	
	Cash		150
	(To record payment of freight, terms FOB shipping point)		

Like Purchases, Freight-in is a temporary account whose normal balance is a debit. **Freight-in is part of cost of goods purchased**. In accordance with the cost principle, cost of goods purchased should include any freight charges necessary to bring the goods to the purchaser. Freight costs are not subject to a purchase discount. Purchase discounts apply only on the invoice cost of the merchandise.

A	=	L	+	OE
−150				−150 Exp

Cash Flows
−150

Purchase Discounts

On May 14 Beyer Video pays the balance due on account to Sellers Electronix. Beyer takes the 2% cash discount allowed by Sellers for payment within 10 days. The payment and discount are recorded by Beyer Video as follows.

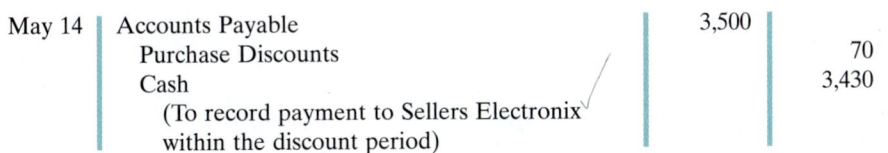

May 14	Accounts Payable	3,500	
	Purchase Discounts		70
	Cash		3,430
	(To record payment to Sellers Electronix within the discount period)		

Purchase Discounts is a temporary account whose normal balance is a credit.

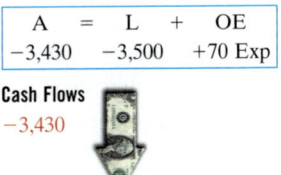

A	=	L	+	OE
−3,430		−3,500		+70 Exp

Cash Flows
−3,430

Recording Sales of Merchandise

The sale of $3,800 of merchandise to Beyer Video on May 4 (sales invoice No. 731, Illustration 5-4 on page 187) is recorded by Sellers Electronix as follows.

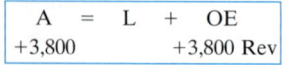

Cash Flows
no effect

May 4	Accounts Receivable		3,800	
	Sales			3,800
	(To record credit sales per invoice #731 to Beyer Video)			

Sales Returns and Allowances

Based on the receipt of returned goods from Beyer Video on May 8, Sellers Electronix records the $300 sales return as follows.

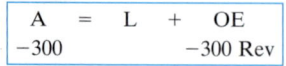

Cash Flows
no effect

May 8	Sales Returns and Allowances		300	
	Accounts Receivable			300
	(To record return of goods from Beyer Video)			

Sales Discounts

On May 15, Sellers Electronix receives payment of $3,430 on account from Beyer Video. Sellers honors the 2% cash discount and records the payment of Beyer's account receivable in full as follows.

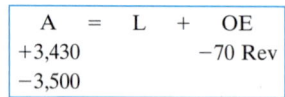

Cash Flows
+3,430

May 15	Cash		3,430	
	Sales Discounts		70	
	Accounts Receivable			3,500
	(To record collection from Beyer Video within 2/10, n/30 discount period)			

Comparison of Entries—Perpetual vs. Periodic

The periodic inventory system entries shown in this appendix are reproduced in the righthand column of Illustration 5A-1. (They are printed in red.) In the middle column (printed in blue) are the entries from Chapter 5 (pages 187–191) for the perpetual inventory system for both Sellers Electronix and Beyer Video. Having these entries side-by-side should help you compare the differences. The entries that are different in the two inventory systems are highlighted.

Illustration 5A-1
Comparison of journal entries under perpetual and periodic inventory systems

	Transaction	Perpetual Inventory System			Periodic Inventory System		
	Entries on Beyer Video's Books						
May 4	Purchase of merchandise on credit.	Merchandise Inventory	3,800		Purchases	3,800	
		Accounts Payable		3,800	Accounts Payable		3,800
May 8	Purchase returns and allowances.	Accounts Payable	300		Accounts Payable	300	
		Merchandise Inventory		300	Purchase Returns and Allowances		300
May 9	Freight costs on purchase.	Merchandise Inventory	150		Freight-in	150	
		Cash		150	Cash		150
May 14	Payment on account with a discount.	Accounts Payable	3,500		Accounts Payable	3,500	
		Cash		3,430	Cash		3,430
		Merchandise Inventory		70	Purchase Discounts		70

Illustration 5A-1
(*continued from p. 206*)

ENTRIES ON SELLERS ELECTRONIX'S BOOKS

Transaction	Perpetual Inventory System		Periodic Inventory System	
May 4 Sale of merchandise on credit.	Accounts Receivable 3,800 Sales	3,800	Accounts Receivable 3,800 Sales	3,800
	Cost of Goods Sold 2,400 Merchandise Inventory	2,400	No entry for cost of goods sold	
May 8 Return of merchandise sold.	Sales Returns and Allowances 300 Accounts Receivable	300	Sales Returns and Allowances 300 Accounts Receivable	300
	Merchandise Inventory 140 Cost of Goods Sold	140	No entry	
May 15 Cash received on account with a discount.	Cash 3,430 Sales Discounts 70 Accounts Receivable	3,500	Cash 3,430 Sales Discounts 70 Accounts Receivable	3,500

SUMMARY OF STUDY OBJECTIVE FOR APPENDIX 5A

8. Prepare the entries for purchases and sales of inventory under a periodic inventory system. In recording purchases, entries are required for (a) cash and credit purchases, (b) purchase returns and allowances, (c) purchase discounts, and (d) freight costs. In recording sales, entries are required for (a) cash and credit sales, (b) sales returns and allowances, and (c) sales discounts.

APPENDIX 5B WORK SHEET FOR A MERCHANDISER

Using a Work Sheet

As indicated in Chapter 4, a work sheet enables financial statements to be prepared before the adjusting entries are journalized and posted. The steps in preparing a work sheet for a merchandiser are the same as they are for a service enterprise (see page 136). The work sheet for Sellers Electronix is shown in Illustration 5B-1 (on page 208). The unique accounts for a merchandiser using a perpetual inventory system are shown in capital letters in red.

STUDY OBJECTIVE 9

Prepare a work sheet for a merchandiser.

Trial Balance Columns

Data for the trial balance are obtained from the ledger balances of Sellers Electronix at December 31. The amount shown for Merchandise Inventory, $40,500, is the year-end inventory amount from the perpetual inventory system.

Illustration 5B-1
Work sheet for merchandiser

SELLERS ELECTRONIX
Work Sheet
For the Year Ended December 31, 2005

	Trial Balance Dr.	Trial Balance Cr.	Adjustments Dr.	Adjustments Cr.	Adjusted Trial Balance Dr.	Adjusted Trial Balance Cr.	Income Statement Dr.	Income Statement Cr.	Balance Sheet Dr.	Balance Sheet Cr.
Cash	9,500				9,500				9,500	
Accounts Receivable	16,100				16,100				16,100	
MERCHANDISE INVENTORY	40,500			(a) 500	40,000				40,000	
Prepaid Insurance	3,800			(b) 2,000	1,800				1,800	
Store Equipment	80,000				80,000				80,000	
Accumulated Depreciation		16,000		(c) 8,000		24,000				24,000
Accounts Payable		20,400				20,400				20,400
R.A. Lamb, Capital		83,000				83,000				83,000
R.A. Lamb, Drawing	15,000				15,000				15,000	
SALES		480,000				480,000		480,000		
SALES RETURNS AND ALLOWANCES	12,000				12,000		12,000			
SALES DISCOUNTS	8,000				8,000		8,000			
COST OF GOODS SOLD	315,500		(a) 500		316,000		316,000			
Freight-out	7,000				7,000		7,000			
Advertising Expense	16,000				16,000		16,000			
Admin. Sal. Exp.	19,000				19,000		19,000			
Store Salaries Expense	40,000		(d) 5,000		45,000		45,000			
Utilities Expense	17,000				17,000		17,000			
Totals	599,400	599,400								
Insurance Expense			(b) 2,000		2,000		2,000			
Depreciation Expense			(c) 8,000		8,000		8,000			
Salaries Payable				(d) 5,000		5,000				5,000
Totals			15,500	15,500	612,400	612,400	450,000	480,000	162,400	132,400
Net Income							30,000			30,000
Totals							480,000	480,000	162,400	162,400

Key: (a) Adjustment to inventory on hand, (b) Insurance expired, (c) Depreciation expense, (d) Salaries accrued.

Adjustments Columns

A merchandiser generally has the same types of adjustments as a service company. As you see in the work sheet, adjustments (b), (c), and (d) are for insurance, depreciation, and salaries. These adjustments were also required for Pioneer Advertising Agency, as illustrated in Chapters 3 and 4. Adjustment (a) was required to adjust the perpetual inventory carrying amount to the actual count.

After all adjustments data are entered on the work sheet, the equality of the adjustments column totals is established. The balances in all accounts are then extended to the adjusted trial balance columns.

Adjusted Trial Balance

The adjusted trial balance shows the balance of all accounts after adjustment at the end of the accounting period.

Income Statement Columns

The accounts and balances that affect the income statement are transferred from the adjusted trial balance columns to the income statement columns. For Sellers Electronix, Sales of $480,000 is shown in the credit column. The contra revenue accounts Sales Returns and Allowances $12,000 and Sales Discounts $8,000 are shown in the debit column. The difference of $460,000 is the net sales shown on the income statement (Illustration 5-11).

Finally, all the credits in the income statement column should be totaled and compared to the total of the debits in the income statement column. If the credits exceed the debits, the company has net income. In Sellers Electronix's case there was net income of $30,000. If the debits exceed the credits, the company would report a net loss.

Balance Sheet Columns

The major difference between the balance sheets of a service company and a merchandiser is inventory. For Sellers Electronix, the ending inventory amount of $40,000 is shown in the balance sheet debit column. The information to prepare the owner's equity statement is also found in these columns. That is, the capital account of R. A. Lamb is $83,000. The drawings for R. A. Lamb are $15,000. Net income results when the total of the debit column exceeds the total of the credit column in the balance sheet columns. A net loss results when the total of the credits exceeds the total of the debit balances.

SUMMARY OF STUDY OBJECTIVE

9. **Prepare a work sheet for a merchandiser.** The steps in preparing a work sheet for a merchandiser are the same as they are for a service company. The unique accounts for a merchandiser are Merchandise Inventory, Sales, Sales Returns and Allowances, Sales Discounts, and Cost of Goods Sold.

Note: All **asterisked Questions, Exercises, and Problems relate to material in the appendixes to the chapter.*

SELF-STUDY QUESTIONS

Self-Study/Self-Test

Answers are at the end of the chapter.

(SO 1) **1.** Gross profit will result if:
   a. operating expenses are less than net income.
   b. sales revenues are greater than operating expenses.
   c. sales revenues are greater than cost of goods sold.
   d. operating expenses are greater than cost of goods sold.

(SO 2) **2.** Under a perpetual inventory system, when goods are purchased for resale by a company:
   a. purchases on account are debited to Merchandise Inventory.
   b. purchases on account are debited to Purchases.
   c. purchase returns are debited to Purchase Returns and Allowances.
   d. freight costs are debited to Freight-out.

(SO 3) **3.** The sales accounts that normally have a debit balance are:

   a. Sales Discounts.
   b. Sales Returns and Allowances.
   c. both (a) and (b).
   d. neither (a) nor (b).

(SO 3) **4.** A credit sale of $750 is made on June 13, terms 2/10, net/30. A return of $50 is granted on June 16. The amount received as payment in full on June 23 is:
   a. $700.
   b. $686.
   c. $685.
   d. $650.

(SO 2) **5.** Which of the following accounts will normally appear in the ledger of a merchandising company that uses a perpetual inventory system?
   a. Purchases.
   b. Freight-in.
   c. Cost of Goods Sold.
   d. Purchase Discounts.

(SO 5) **6.** The multiple-step income statement for a merchandiser shows each of the following features *except*:
 a. gross profit.
 b. cost of goods sold.
 c. a sales revenue section.
 d. investing activities section.

(SO 6) **7.** If sales revenues are $400,000, cost of goods sold is $310,000, and operating expenses are $60,000, the gross profit is:
 a. $30,000.
 b. $90,000.
 c. $340,000.
 d. $400,000.

(SO 5) **8.** In a single-step income statement:
 a. gross profit is reported.
 b. cost of goods sold is not reported.
 c. sales revenues and "other revenues and gains" are reported in the revenues section of the income statement.
 d. operating income is separately reported.

(SO 5) **9.** Which of the following appears on both a single-step and a multiple-step income statement?
 a. merchandise inventory.
 b. gross profit.
 c. income from operations.
 d. cost of goods sold.

(SO 7) **10.** In determining cost of goods sold:
 a. purchase discounts are deducted from net purchases.
 b. freight-out is added to net purchases.

 c. purchase returns and allowances are deducted from net purchases.
 d. freight-in is added to net purchases.

11. If beginning inventory is $60,000, cost of goods purchased is $380,000, and ending inventory is $50,000, cost of goods sold is: (SO
 a. $390,000.
 b. $370,000.
 c. $330,000.
 d. $420,000.

*12. When goods are purchased for resale by a company using (SO a periodic inventory system:
 a. purchases on account are debited to Merchandise Inventory.
 b. purchases on account are debited to Purchases.
 c. purchase returns are debited to Purchase Returns and Allowances.
 d. freight costs are debited to Purchases.

*13. In a work sheet, Merchandise Inventory is shown in the (SO following columns:
 a. Adjusted trial balance debit and balance sheet debit.
 b. Income statement debit and balance sheet debit.
 c. Income statement credit and balance sheet debit.
 d. Income statement credit and adjusted trial balance debit.

---

1. (a) "The steps in the accounting cycle for a merchandising company are different from the accounting cycle for a service enterprise." Do you agree or disagree? (b) Is the measurement of net income for a merchandiser conceptually the same as for a service enterprise? Explain.

2. Why is the normal operating cycle for a merchandiser likely to be longer than for a service company?

3. (a) How do the components of revenues and expenses differ between a merchandiser and a service enterprise? (b) Explain the income measurement process in a merchandising company.

4. How does income measurement differ between a merchandiser and a service company?

5. When is cost of goods sold determined in a perpetual inventory system?

6. Distinguish between FOB shipping point and FOB destination. Identify the freight terms that will result in a debit to Merchandise Inventory by the purchaser and a debit to Freight-out by the seller.

7. Explain the meaning of the credit terms 2/10, n/30.

8. Goods costing $2,500 are purchased on account on July 15 with credit terms of 2/10, n/30. On July 18 a $200 credit memo is received from the supplier for damaged goods. Give the journal entry on July 24 to record payment of

the balance due within the discount period using a perpetual inventory system.

9. Karen Lloyd believes revenues from credit sales may be earned before they are collected in cash. Do you agree? Explain.

10. (a) What is the primary source document for recording (1) cash sales, (2) credit sales, and (3) sales returns and allowances? (b) Using XXs for amounts, give the journal entry for each of the transactions in part (a).

11. A credit sale is made on July 10 for $700, terms 2/10, n/30. On July 12, $100 of goods are returned for credit. Give the journal entry on July 19 to record the receipt of the balance due within the discount period.

12. Explain why the Merchandise Inventory account will usually require adjustment at year-end.

13. Prepare the closing entries for the Sales account, assuming a balance of $200,000 and the Cost of Goods Sold account with a $145,000 balance.

14. What merchandising account(s) will appear in the post-closing trial balance?

15. Regis Co. has sales revenue of $109,000, cost of goods sold of $70,000, and operating expenses of $20,000. What is its gross profit?

16. Kathy Ho Company reports net sales of $800,000, gross profit of $570,000, and net income of $240,000. What are its operating expenses?

17. Identify the distinguishing features of an income statement for a merchandising company.

18. Identify the sections of a multiple-step income statement that relate to (a) operating activities, and (b) nonoperating activities.

19. Distinguish between the types of functional groupings of operating expenses. What problem is created by these groupings?

20. How does the single-step form of income statement differ from the multiple-step form?

21. Identify the accounts that are added to or deducted from Purchases to determine the cost of goods purchased. For each account, indicate whether it is added or deducted.

*22. Goods costing $2,000 are purchased on account on July 15 with credit terms of 2/10, n/30. On July 18 a $200 credit memo is received from the supplier for damaged goods. Give the journal entry on July 24 to record payment of the balance due within the discount period, assuming a periodic inventory system.

*23. Indicate the columns of the work sheet in which (a) merchandise inventory and (b) cost of goods sold will be shown.

BRIEF EXERCISES

BE5-1 Presented below are the components in Clearwater Company's income statement. Determine the missing amounts.

Compute missing amounts in determining net income.

(SO 1)

	Sales	Cost of Goods Sold	Gross Profit	Operating Expenses	Net Income
(a)	$75,000	?	$28,600	?	$10,800
(b)	$108,000	$70,000	?	?	$29,500
(c)	?	$71,900	$99,600	$39,500	?

BE5-2 Giovanni Company buys merchandise on account from Gordon Company. The selling price of the goods is $780, and the cost of the goods is $560. Both companies use perpetual inventory systems. Journalize the transaction on the books of both companies.

Journalize perpetual inventory entries.

(SO 2, 3)

BE5-3 Prepare the journal entries to record the following transactions on Benson Company's books using a perpetual inventory system.

Journalize sales transactions.

(SO 3)

(a) On March 2, Benson Company sold $800,000 of merchandise to Edgebrook Company, terms 2/10, n/30. The cost of the merchandise sold was $620,000.

(b) On March 6, Edgebrook Company returned $120,000 of the merchandise purchased on March 2 because it was defective. The cost of the returned merchandise was $90,000.

(c) On March 12, Benson Company received the balance due from Edgebrook Company.

BE5-4 From the information in BE5-3, prepare the journal entries to record these transactions on Edgebrook Company's books under a perpetual inventory system.

Journalize purchase transactions.

(SO 2)

BE5-5 Piccola Company provides the following information for the month ended October 31, 2005: Sales on credit $280,000, cash sales $100,000 sales discounts $13,000, sales returns and allowances $21,000. Prepare the sales revenues section of the income statement based on this information.

Prepare sales revenues section of income statement.

(SO 3)

BE5-6 At year-end the perpetual inventory records of Salsa Company showed merchandise inventory of $98,000. The company determined, however, that its actual inventory on hand was $96,800. Record the necessary adjusting entry.

Prepare adjusting entry for merchandise inventory.

(SO 4)

BE5-7 Orlaida Company has the following merchandise account balances: Sales $192,000, Sales Discounts $2,000, Cost of Goods Sold $105,000, and Merchandise Inventory $40,000. Prepare the entries to record the closing of these items to Income Summary.

Prepare closing entries for merchandise accounts.

(SO 4)

BE5-8 ✏ Explain where each of the following items would appear on (1) a multiple-step income statement, and on (2) a single-step income statement: (a) gain on sale of equipment, (b) casualty loss from vandalism, and (c) cost of goods sold.

Contrast presentation in multiple-step and single-step income statements.

(SO 5)

BE5-9 Assume Jose Company has the following account balances: Sales $506,000, Sales Returns and Allowances $15,000, Cost of Goods Sold $350,000, Selling Expenses $70,000, and Administrative Expenses $40,000. Compute the following: (a) net sales, (b) gross profit, and (c) income from operations.

Compute net sales, gross profit, and income from operations.

(SO 3, 5, 6)

Compute net purchases and cost of goods purchased.

(SO 7)

BE5-10 Assume that E. Guard Company uses a periodic inventory system and has these account balances: Purchases $400,000; Purchase Returns and Allowances $11,000; Purchase Discounts $8,000; and Freight-in $16,000. Determine net purchases and cost of goods purchased.

Compute cost of goods sold and gross profit.

(SO 7)

BE5-11 Assume the same information as in BE5-10 and also that E. Guard Company has beginning inventory of $60,000, ending inventory of $90,000, and net sales of $630,000. Determine the amounts to be reported for cost of goods sold and gross profit.

Journalize purchase transactions.

(SO, 8)

*BE5-12 Prepare the journal entries to record these transactions on H. Hunt Company's books using a periodic inventory system.

(a) On March 2, H. Hunt Company purchased $900,000 of merchandise from B. Streisand Company, terms 2/10, n/30.

(b) On March 6 H. Hunt Company returned $130,000 of the merchandise purchased on March 2 because it was defective.

(c) On March 12 H. Hunt Company paid the balance due to B. Streisand Company.

Identify work sheet columns for selected accounts.

(SO 9)

*BE5-13 Presented below is the format of the work sheet presented in the chapter.

Trial Balance		Adjustments		Adjusted Trial Balance		Income Statement		Balance Sheet	
Dr.	Cr.	Dr.	Cr.	Dr.	Cr.	Dr.	Cr.	Dr.	Cr.

Indicate where the following items will appear on the work sheet: **(a)** Cash, **(b)** Merchandise Inventory, **(c)** Sales, **(d)** Cost of goods sold.

Example:

Cash: Trial balance debit column; Adjusted trial balance debit column; and Balance sheet debit column.

EXERCISES

Journalize purchases transactions.

(SO 2)

E5-1 Information related to Gilberto Co. is presented below.

1. On April 5, purchased merchandise from Allman Company for $20,000 terms 2/10, net/30, FOB shipping point.
2. On April 6 paid freight costs of $900 on merchandise purchased from Allman.
3. On April 7, purchased equipment on account for $26,000.
4. On April 8, returned damaged merchandise to Allman Company and was granted a $4,000 allowance for returned merchandise.
5. On April 15 paid the amount due to Allman Company in full.

Instructions

(a) Prepare the journal entries to record these transactions on the books of Gilberto Co. under a perpetual inventory system.

(b) Assume that Gilberto Co. paid the balance due to Allman Company on May 4 instead of April 15. Prepare the journal entry to record this payment.

Journalize perpetual inventory entries.

(SO 2, 3)

E5-2 On September 1, Eden Office Supply had an inventory of 30 pocket calculators at a cost of $18 each. The company uses a perpetual inventory system. During September, the following transactions occurred.

Sept. 6   Purchased 80 calculators at $17 each from Mozart Co. for cash.
    9   Paid freight of $80 on calculators purchased from Mozart Co.
    10   Returned 2 calculators to Mozart Co. for $36 credit (including freight) because they did not meet specifications.
    12   Sold 26 calculators costing $18 (including freight) for $31 each to Mega Book Store, terms n/30.
    14   Granted credit of $31 to Mega Book Store for the return of one calculator that was not ordered.
    20   Sold 30 calculators costing $18 for $31 each to Barbara's Card Shop, terms n/30.

Instructions

Journalize the September transactions.

E5-3 On June 10, Lippizan Company purchased $6,000 of merchandise from Bristol Company FOB shipping point, terms 2/10, n/30. Lippizan pays the freight costs of $400 on June 11. Damaged goods totaling $300 are returned to Bristol for credit on June 12. The scrap value of these goods is $150. On June 19, Lippizan pays Bristol Company in full, less the purchase discount. Both companies use a perpetual inventory system.

Prepare purchase and sale entries.

(SO 2, 3)

Instructions
(a) Prepare separate entries for each transaction on the books of Lippizan Company.
(b) Prepare separate entries for each transaction for Bristol Company. The merchandise purchased by Lippizan on June 10 had cost Bristol $3,000.

E5-4 Presented below are transactions related to Rebecca Company.

Journalize sales transactions.

(SO 3)

1. On December 3, Rebecca Company sold $480,000 of merchandise to Simonis Co., terms 2/10, n/30, FOB shipping point. The cost of the merchandise sold was $350,000.
2. On December 8, Simonis Co. was granted an allowance of $27,000 for merchandise purchased on December 3.
3. On December 13, Rebecca Company received the balance due from Simonis Co.

Instructions
(a) Prepare the journal entries to record these transactions on the books of Rebecca Company using a perpetual inventory system.
(b) Assume that Rebecca Company received the balance due from Simonis Co. on January 2 of the following year instead of December 13. Prepare the journal entry to record the receipt of payment on January 2.

E5-5 The adjusted trial balance of Schinzer Company shows the following data pertaining to sales at the end of its fiscal year October 31, 2005: Sales $800,000, Freight-out $16,000, Sales Returns and Allowances $20,000, and Sales Discounts $15,000.

Prepare sales revenues section and closing entries.

(SO 3, 4)

Instructions
(a) Prepare the sales revenues section of the income statement.
(b) Prepare separate closing entries for (1) sales, and (2) the contra accounts to sales.

E5-6 Presented is information related to Taylor Co. for the month of January 2005.

Prepare adjusting and closing entries.

(SO 4)

Ending inventory per		Salary expense	$ 61,000
perpetual records	$ 21,600	Sales discounts	10,000
Ending inventory actually		Sales returns and allowances	13,000
on hand	21,000	Sales	350,000
Cost of goods sold	208,000		
Freight-out	7,000		
Insurance expense	12,000		
Rent expense	20,000		

Instructions
(a) Prepare the necessary adjusting entry for inventory.
(b) Prepare the necessary closing entries.

E5-7 In its income statement for the year ended December 31, 2005, Bach Company reported the following condensed data.

Prepare multiple-step and single-step income statements.

(SO 5)

Administrative expenses	$ 435,000	Selling expenses	$ 490,000
Cost of goods sold	1,289,000	Loss on sale of equipment	10,000
Interest expense	70,000	Net sales	2,342,000
Interest revenue	28,000		

Instructions
(a) Prepare a multiple-step income statement.
(b) Prepare a single-step income statement.

E5-8 An inexperienced accountant for Gulliver Company made the following errors in recording merchandising transactions.

Prepare correcting entries for sales and purchases.

(SO 2, 3)

1. A $175 refund to a customer for faulty merchandise was debited to Sales $175 and credited to Cash $175.
2. A $160 credit purchase of supplies was debited to Merchandise Inventory $160 and credited to Cash $160.

3. A $110 sales discount was debited to Sales.

4. A cash payment of $30 for freight on merchandise purchases was debited to Freight-out $300 and credited to Cash $300.

Instructions

Prepare separate correcting entries for each error, assuming that the incorrect entry is not reversed. (Omit explanations.)

Compute missing amounts.

(SO 5, 6)

E5-9 Presented below is financial information for two different companies.

	Lee Company	Chan Company
Sales	$90,000	(d)
Sales returns	(a)	$ 5,000
Net sales	81,000	95,000
Cost of goods sold	56,000	(e)
Gross profit	(b)	41,500
Operating expenses	15,000	(f)
Net income	(c)	15,000

Instructions

Determine the missing amounts.

Prepare cost of goods sold section.

(SO 7)

E5-10 The trial balance of J. Harlow Company at the end of its fiscal year, August 31, 2005, includes these accounts: Merchandise Inventory $17,200; Purchases $144,000; Sales $190,000; Freight-in $4,000; Sales Returns and Allowances $3,000; Freight-out $1,000; and Purchase Returns and Allowances $2,000. The ending merchandise inventory is $25,000.

Instructions

Prepare a cost of goods sold section for the year ending August 31 (periodic inventory).

Prepare cost of goods sold section.

(SO 7)

E5-11 Below is a series of cost of goods sold sections for companies X, F, L, and S.

	X	F	L	S
Beginning inventory	$ 250	$ 120	$1,000	$ (j)
Purchases	1,500	1,080	(g)	43,590
Purchase returns and allowances	40	(d)	290	(k)
Net purchases	(a)	1,030	7,210	42,090
Freight-in	110	(e)	(h)	2,240
Cost of goods purchased	(b)	1,230	7,940	(l)
Cost of goods available for sale	1,820	1,350	(i)	49,530
Ending inventory	310	(f)	1,450	6,230
Cost of goods sold	(c)	1,230	7,490	43,300

Instructions

Fill in the lettered blanks to complete the cost of goods sold sections.

Journalize purchase transactions.

(SO 8)

*E5-12 This information relates to Hans Olaf Co.

1. On April 5 purchased merchandise from D. DeVito Company for $18,000, terms 2/10, net/30, FOB shipping point.

2. On April 6 paid freight costs of $900 on merchandise purchased from D. DeVito Company.

3. On April 7 purchased equipment on account for $26,000.

4. On April 8 returned some of April 5 merchandise to D. DeVito Company which cost $2,800.

5. On April 15 paid the amount due to D. DeVito Company in full.

Instructions

(a) Prepare the journal entries to record these transactions on the books of Hans Olaf Co. using a periodic inventory system.

(b) Assume that Hans Olaf Co. paid the balance due to D. DeVito Company on May 4 instead of April 15. Prepare the journal entry to record this payment.

Journalize purchase transactions.

(SO 8)

*E5-13 Presented below is the following information related to Argentina Co.

1. On April 5, purchased merchandise from Chile Company for $18,000, terms 2/10, net/30, FOB shipping point.

2. On April 6, paid freight costs of $800 on merchandise purchased from Chile.
3. On April 7, purchased equipment on account from Wayne Higley Mfg. Co. for $26,000.
4. On April 8, returned damaged merchandise to Chile Company and was granted a $4,000 allowance.
5. On April 15, paid the amount due to Chile Company in full.

Instructions
(a) Prepare the journal entries to record these transactions on the books of Argentina Co. using a periodic inventory system.
(b) Assume that Argentina Co. paid the balance due to Chile Company on May 4 instead of April 15. Prepare the journal entry to record this payment.

E5-14 Presented below are selected accounts for Streisand Company as reported in the work sheet at the end of May 2005.

Complete work sheet.
(SO 9)

Accounts	Adjusted Trial Balance		Income Statement		Balance Sheet	
	Dr.	Cr.	Dr.	Cr.	Dr.	Cr.
Cash	9,000					
Merchandise Inventory	76,000					
Sales		450,000				
Sales Returns and Allowances	10,000					
Sales Discounts	9,000					
Cost of Goods Sold	250,000					

Instructions
Complete the work sheet by extending amounts reported in the adjusted trial balance to the appropriate columns in the work sheet. Do not total individual columns.

PROBLEMS: SET A

P5-1A Phantom Book Warehouse distributes hardback books to retail stores and extends credit terms of 2/10, n/30 to all of its customers. At the end of May, Phantom's inventory consisted of 240 books purchased at $1,200. During the month of June the following merchandising transactions occurred.

Journalize purchase and sales transactions under a perpetual inventory system.
(SO 2, 3)

June 1 Purchased 160 books on account for $5 each from Ex Libris Publishers, FOB destination, terms 2/10, n/30. The appropriate party also made a cash payment of $50 for the freight on this date.
    3 Sold 120 books on account to Readers-R-Us for $10 each.
    6 Received $50 credit for 10 books returned to Ex Libris Publishers.
    9 Paid Ex Libris Publishers in full, less discount.
    15 Received payment in full from Readers-R-Us.
    17 Sold 120 books on account to Bargain Books for $10 each.
    20 Purchased 110 books on account for $5 each from Bookem Publishers, FOB destination, terms 2/15, n/30. The appropriate party also made a cash payment of $50 for the freight on this date.
    24 Received payment in full from Bargain Books.
    26 Paid Bookem Publishers in full, less discount.
    28 Sold 110 books on account to Read-n-Weep Bookstore for $10 each.
    30 Granted Read-n-Weep Bookstore $150 credit for 15 books returned costing $75.

Phantom Book Warehouse's chart of accounts includes the following: No. 101 Cash, No. 112 Accounts Receivable, No. 120 Merchandise Inventory, No. 201 Accounts Payable, No. 401 Sales, No. 412 Sales Returns and Allowances, No. 414 Sales Discounts, No. 505 Cost of Goods Sold.

Instructions
Journalize the transactions for the month of June for Phantom Book Warehouse using a perpetual inventory system.

Journalize, post, and prepare a partial income statement.

(SO 2, 3, 5, 6)

P5-2A Copple Hardware Store completed the following merchandising transactions in the month of May. At the beginning of May, the ledger of Copple showed Cash of $5,000 and Brad Copple, Capital of $5,000.

May 1 Purchased merchandise on account from Nute Wholesale Supply $6,000, terms 2/10, n/30.

2 Sold merchandise on account $5,000, terms 1/10, n/30. The cost of the merchandise sold was $3,100.

5 Received credit from Nute Wholesale Supply for merchandise returned $600.

9 Received collections in full, less discounts, from customers billed on sales of $5,000 on May 2.

10 Paid Nute Wholesale Supply in full, less discount.

11 Purchased supplies for cash $900.

12 Purchased merchandise for cash $2,700.

15 Received refund for poor quality merchandise from supplier on cash purchase $230.

17 Purchased merchandise from Sherrick Distributors $1,900, FOB shipping point, terms 2/10, n/30.

19 Paid freight on May 17 purchase $250.

24 Sold merchandise for cash $6,200. The merchandise sold had a cost of $4,600.

25 Purchased merchandise from Duffy Inc. $1,000, FOB destination, terms 2/10, n/30.

27 Paid Sherrick Distributors in full, less discount.

29 Made refunds to cash customers for defective merchandise $100. The returned merchandise had a scrap value of $20.

31 Sold merchandise on account $1,600, terms n/30. The cost of the merchandise sold was $1,120.

Copple Hardware's chart of accounts includes the following: No. 101 Cash, No. 112 Accounts Receivable, No. 120 Merchandise Inventory, No. 126 Supplies, No. 201 Accounts Payable, No. 301 Brad Copple, Capital, No. 401 Sales, No. 412 Sales Returns and Allowances, No. 414 Sales Discounts, No. 505 Cost of Goods Sold.

Instructions

(a) Journalize the transactions using a perpetual inventory system.

(b) Enter the beginning cash and capital balances and post the transactions. (Use J1 for the journal reference.)

(c) Gross profit $3,850

(c) Prepare an income statement through gross profit for the month of May 2005.

Prepare financial statements and adjusting and closing entries.

(SO 4, 5)

P5-3A Moulton Department Store is located in midtown Metropolis. During the past several years, net income has been declining because of suburban shopping centers. At the end of the company's fiscal year on November 30, 2005, the following accounts appeared in two of its trial balances.

	Unadjusted	Adjusted		Unadjusted	Adjusted
Accounts Payable	$ 47,310	$ 47,310	Interest Revenue	$ 5,000	$ 5,000
Accounts Receivable	11,770	11,770	Merchandise Inventory	36,200	36,200
Accumulated Depr.—Delivery Equip.	15,680	18,816	Notes Payable	46,000	46,000
Accumulated Depr.—Store Equip.	32,300	41,800	Prepaid Insurance	13,500	3,000
Cash	8,000	8,000	Property Tax Expense		3,500
M. Moulton, Capital	84,200	84,200	Property Taxes Payable		3,500
Cost of Goods Sold	633,220	633,220	Rent Expense	19,000	19,000
Delivery Expense	8,200	8,200	Salaries Expense	120,000	120,000
Delivery Equipment	57,000	57,000	Sales	850,000	850,000
Depr. Expense—Delivery Equip.		3,136	Sales Commissions Expense	8,000	10,500
Depr. Expense—Store Equip.		9,500	Sales Commissions Payable		2,500
M. Moulton, Drawing	12,000	12,000	Sales Returns and Allowances	10,000	10,000
Insurance Expense		10,500	Store Equip.	125,000	125,000
Interest Expense	8,000	8,000	Utilities Expense	10,600	10,600

Analysis reveals the following additional data.

1. Salaries expense is 75% selling and 25% administrative.

2. Insurance expense is 50% selling and 50% administrative.

3. Rent expense, utilities expense, and property tax expense are administrative expenses.
4. Notes payable are due in 2008.

Instructions

(a) Prepare a multiple-step income statement, an owner's equity statement, and a classified balance sheet.
(b) Journalize the adjusting entries that were made.
(c) Journalize the closing entries that are necessary.

(a) Net income $8,844
Capital $81,044
Total assets $180,354

P5-4A Bill Kokott, a former professional golf star, operates Bill's Pro Shop at Bay Golf Course. At the beginning of the current season on April 1, the ledger of Bill's Pro Shop showed Cash $2,500, Merchandise Inventory $3,500, and B. Kokott, Capital $6,000. The following transactions were completed during April.

Journalize, post, and prepare a trial balance.
(SO 2, 3, 4)

Apr. 5 Purchased golf bags, clubs, and balls on account from Ellis Co. $1,800, FOB shipping point, terms 2/10, n/60.
       7 Paid freight on Ellis purchase $80.
       9 Received credit from Ellis Co. for merchandise returned $100.
      10 Sold merchandise on account to members $1,200, terms n/30. The merchandise sold had a cost of $810.
      12 Purchased golf shoes, sweaters, and other accessories on account from Penguin Sportswear $660, terms 1/10, n/30.
      14 Paid Ellis Co. in full, less discount.
      17 Received credit from Penguin Sportswear for merchandise returned $60.
      20 Made sales on account to members $700, terms n/30. The cost of the merchandise sold was $490.
      21 Paid Penguin Sportswear in full, less discount.
      27 Granted an allowance to members for clothing that did not fit properly $40.
      30 Received payments on account from members $1,000.

The chart of accounts for the pro shop includes the following: No. 101 Cash, No. 112 Accounts Receivable, No. 120 Merchandise Inventory, No. 201 Accounts Payable, No. 301 B. Kokott, Capital, No. 401 Sales, No. 412 Sales Returns and Allowances, No. 505 Cost of Goods Sold.

Instructions

(a) Journalize the April transactions using a perpetual inventory system.
(b) Enter the beginning balances in the ledger accounts and post the April transactions. (Use J1 for the journal reference.)
(c) Prepare a trial balance on April 30, 2005.

(c) Total debits $7,900

P5-5A At the end of Stampfer Department Store's fiscal year on November 30, 2005, these accounts appeared in its adjusted trial balance.

Determine cost of goods sold and gross profit under periodic approach.
(SO 6, 7)

Freight-in	$ 5,060
Merchandise Inventory	44,360
Purchases	630,000
Purchase Discounts	7,000
Purchase Returns and Allowances	3,000
Sales	910,000
Sales Returns and Allowances	20,000

Additional facts:

1. Merchandise inventory on November 30, 2005, is $36,200.
2. Note that Stampfer Department Store uses a periodic system.

Instructions

Prepare an income statement through gross profit for the year ended November 30, 2005.

Gross profit $256,780

Calculate missing amounts and assess profitability.

(SO 6, 7)

P5-6A Psang Inc. operates a retail operation that purchases and sells snowmobiles, amongst other outdoor products. The company purchases all merchandise inventory on credit and uses a perpetual inventory system. The accounts payable account is used for recording inventory purchases only; all other current liabilities are accrued in separate accounts. You are provided with the following selected information for the fiscal years 2003 through 2006, inclusive.

	2003	2004	2005	2006
Income Statement Data				
Sales		$96,850	$ (e)	$82,220
Cost of goods sold		(a)	27,140	26,550
Gross profit		69,260	61,540	(i)
Operating expenses		63,500	(f)	52,060
Net income		$ (b)	$ 4,570	$ (j)
Balance Sheet Data				
Merchandise inventory	$13,000	$ (c)	$14,700	$ (k)
Accounts payable	5,000	6,500	4,600	(l)
Additional Information				
Purchases of merchandise inventory on account		$25,890	$ (g)	$24,050
Cash payments to suppliers		(d)	(h)	24,650

Instructions

(c) $11,300
(g) $30,540
(i) $ 4,000

(a) Calculate the missing amounts.
(b) Sales declined over the 3-year fiscal period, 2004–2006. Does that mean that profitability necessarily also declined? Explain, computing the gross profit rate and the profit margin ratio for each fiscal year to help support your answer.

Journalize, post, and prepare trial balance and partial income statement using periodic approach.

(SO 7, 8)

*P5-7A At the beginning of the current season on April 1, the ledger of Tri-State Pro Shop showed Cash $2,500; Merchandise Inventory $3,500; and Tiger Woods, Capital $6,000. These transactions occured during April 2005.

Apr. 5 Purchased golf bags, clubs, and balls on account from Balata Co. $1,700, FOB shipping point, terms 2/10, n/60.
    7 Paid freight on Balata Co. purchases $80.
    9 Received credit from Balata Co. for merchandise returned $200.
    10 Sold merchandise on account to members $950, terms n/30.
    12 Purchased golf shoes, sweaters, and other accessories on account from Arrow Sportswear $660, terms 1/10, n/30.
    14 Paid Balata Co. in full.
    17 Received credit from Arrow Sportswear for merchandise returned $60.
    20 Made sales on account to members $700, terms n/30.
    21 Paid Arrow Sportswear in full.
    27 Granted credit to members for clothing that did not fit properly $75.
    30 Received payments on account from members $1,100.

The chart of accounts for the pro shop includes Cash; Accounts Receivable, Merchandise Inventory; Accounts Payable; Tiger Woods, Capital; Sales; Sales Returns and Allowances; Purchases; Purchase Returns and Allowances; Purchase Discounts, and Freight-in.

Instructions

(c) Tot. trial
    balance $7,946
  Gross profit $ 455

(a) Journalize the April transactions using a periodic inventory system.
(b) Using T accounts, enter the beginning balances in the ledger accounts and post the April transactions.
(c) Prepare a trial balance on April 30, 2005.
(d) Prepare an income statement through gross profit, assuming merchandise inventory on hand at April 30 is $4,524.

*P5-8A The trial balance of Loren Foelske Wholesale Company contained the following accounts at December 31, the end of the company's fiscal year.

Complete accounting cycle beginning with a work sheet.

(SO 4, 5, 6, 9)

LOREN FOELSKE WHOLESALE COMPANY
Trial Balance
December 31, 2005

	Debit	Credit
Cash	$ 25,400	
Accounts Receivable	37,600	
Merchandise Inventory	90,000	
Land	92,000	
Buildings	197,000	
Accumulated Depreciation—Buildings		$ 54,000
Equipment	83,500	
Accumulated Depreciation—Equipment		42,400
Notes Payable		50,000
Accounts Payable		39,000
L. Foelske, Capital		267,800
L. Foelske, Drawing	10,000	
Sales		904,100
Sales Discounts	6,100	
Cost of Goods Sold	709,900	
Salaries Expense	69,800	
Utilities Expense	19,400	
Repair Expense	5,900	
Gas and Oil Expense	7,200	
Insurance Expense	3,500	
Totals	$1,357,300	$1,357,300

Adjustment data:

1. Depreciation is $10,000 on buildings and $9,000 on equipment. (Both are administrative expenses.)
2. Interest of $5,000 is due and unpaid on notes payable at December 31.
3. Merchandise inventory actually on hand is $88,900.

Other data:

1. Salaries are 80% selling and 20% administrative.
2. Utilities expense, repair expense, and insurance expense are 100% administrative.
3. $10,000 of the notes payable are payable next year.
4. Gas and oil expense is a selling expense.

Instructions
(a) Enter the trial balance on a work sheet, and complete the work sheet.
(b) Prepare a multiple-step income statement and an owner's equity statement for the year, and a classified balance sheet at December 31, 2005.
(c) Journalize the adjusting entries.
(d) Journalize the closing entries.
(e) Prepare a post-closing trial balance.

(a) Adj. trial balance total
$1,381,300
Net income $57,200
(b) Gross profit $187,000
Total assets $409,000
(e) Total debits $524,400

PROBLEMS: SET B

P5-1B Ready-Set-Go distributes suitcases to retail stores and extends credit terms of 1/10, n/30 to all of its customers. At the end of July, R-S-G's inventory consisted of 40 suitcases purchased at $30 each. During the month of July the following merchandising transactions occurred.

Journalize purchase and sales transactions under a perpetual inventory system.

(SO 2, 3)

July 1 Purchased 50 suitcases on account for $30 each from Trunk Manufacturers, FOB destination, terms 2/10, n/30. The appropriate party also made a cash payment of $100 for freight on this date.
     3 Sold 40 suitcases on account to Satchel World for $55 each.

    9   Paid Trunk Manufacturers in full.

  12   Received payment in full from Satchel World.

  17   Sold 30 suitcases on account to The Going Concern for $55 each.

  18   Purchased 60 suitcases on account for $1,700 from Holiday Manufacturers, FOB shipping point, terms 1/10, n/30. The appropriate party also made a cash payment of $100 for freight on this date.

  20   Received $300 credit (including freight) for 10 suitcases returned to Holiday Manufacturers.

  21   Received payment in full from The Going Concern.

  22   Sold 45 suitcases on account to Fly-By-Night for $55 each.

  30   Paid Holiday Manufacturers in full.

  31   Granted Fly-By-Night $220 credit for 4 suitcases returned costing $120.

Ready-Set-Go's chart of accounts includes the following: No. 101 Cash, No. 112 Accounts Receivable, No. 120 Merchandise Inventory, No. 201 Accounts Payable, No. 401 Sales, No. 412 Sales Returns and Allowances, No. 414 Sales Discounts, No. 505 Cost of Goods Sold.

Instructions

Journalize the transactions for the month of July for Ready-Set-Go using a perpetual inventory system.

Journalize, post, and prepare a partial income statement.

(SO 2, 3, 5, 6)

P5-2B Shmi Distributing Company completed the following merchandising transactions in the month of April. At the beginning of April, the ledger of Shmi showed Cash of $9,000 and O. Shmi, Capital of $9,000.

Apr. 2   Purchased merchandise on account from Wookie Supply Co. $5,900, terms 1/10, n/30.

    4   Sold merchandise on account $5,200, FOB destination, terms 1/10, n/30. The cost of the merchandise sold was $4,100.

    5   Paid $240 freight on April 4 sale.

    6   Received credit from Wookie Supply Co. for merchandise returned $500.

  11   Paid Wookie Supply Co. in full, less discount.

  13   Received collections in full, less discounts, from customers billed on April 4.

  14   Purchased merchandise for cash $3,800.

  16   Received refund from supplier for returned goods on cash purchase of April 14, $500.

  18   Purchased merchandise from Skywalker Distributors $4,200, FOB shipping point, terms 2/10, n/30.

  20   Paid freight on April 18 purchase $100.

  23   Sold merchandise for cash $6,400. The merchandise sold had a cost of $5,120.

  26   Purchased merchandise for cash $2,300.

  27   Paid Skywalker Distributors in full, less discount.

  29   Made refunds to cash customers for defective merchandise $90. The returned merchandise had a scrap value of $30.

  30   Sold merchandise on account $3,700, terms n/30. The cost of the merchandise sold was $2,800.

Shmi Company's chart of accounts includes the following: No. 101 Cash, No. 112 Accounts Receivable, No. 120 Merchandise Inventory, No. 201 Accounts Payable, No. 301 O. Shmi, Capital, No. 401 Sales, No. 412 Sales Returns and Allowances, No. 414 Sales Discounts, No. 505 Cost of Goods Sold, and No. 644 Freight-out.

Instructions

(a) Journalize the transactions using a perpetual inventory system.

(b) Enter the beginning cash and capital balances, and post the transactions. (Use J1 for the journal reference.)

(c) Gross profit $3,168

(c) Prepare the income statement through gross profit for the month of April 2005.

Prepare financial statements and adjusting and closing entries.

(SO 4, 5)

P5-3B Starz Department Store is located near the Village Shopping Mall. At the end of the company's fiscal year on December 31, 2005, the following accounts appeared in two of its trial balances.

	Unadjusted	Adjusted		Unadjusted	Adjusted
Accounts Payable	$ 78,700	$ 78,700	Interest Payable		$ 5,000
Accounts Receivable	50,300	50,300	Interest Revenue	$ 4,000	4,000
Accumulated Depr.—Building	42,100	52,500	Merchandise Inventory	75,000	75,000
Accumulated Depr.—Equipment	30,200	42,900	Mortgage Payable	80,000	80,000
Building	190,000	190,000	Office Salaries Expense	32,000	32,000
Cash	20,800	20,800	Prepaid Insurance	9,600	2,400
H. Ford, Capital	176,600	176,600	Property Taxes Expense		4,800
Cost of Goods Sold	412,700	412,700	Property Taxes Payable		4,800
Depr. Expense—Building		10,400	Sales Salaries Expense	76,000	76,000
Depr. Expense—Equipment		12,700	Sales	628,000	628,000
H. Ford, Drawing	28,000	28,000	Sales Commissions Expense	10,200	15,500
Equipment	110,000	110,000	Sales Commissions Payable		5,300
Insurance Expense		7,200	Sales Returns and Allowances	8,000	8,000
Interest Expense	6,000	11,000	Utilities Expense	11,000	12,000
			Utilities Expense Payable		1,000

Analysis reveals the following additional data.

1. Insurance expense and utilities expense are 60% selling and 40% administrative.
2. $20,000 of the mortgage payable is due for payment next year.
3. Depreciation on the building and property tax expense are administrative expenses; depreciation on the equipment is a selling expense.

Instructions

(a) Prepare a multiple-step income statement, an owner's equity statement, and a classified balance sheet.
(b) Journalize the adjusting entries that were made.
(c) Journalize the closing entries that are necessary.

(a) Net income $29,700
Capital $178,300
Total assets $353,100

P5-4B J. Ackbar, a former professional tennis star, operates Ackbar's Tennis Shop at the Miller Lake Resort. At the beginning of the current season, the ledger of Ackbar's Tennis Shop showed Cash $2,500, Merchandise Inventory $1,700, and J. Ackbar, Capital $4,200. The following transactions were completed during April.

Journalize, post, and prepare a trial balance.

(SO 2, 3, 4)

Apr. 4 Purchased racquets and balls from Jay-Mac Co. $640, FOB shipping point, terms 2/10, n/30.
6 Paid freight on purchase from Jay-Mac Co. $40.
8 Sold merchandise to members $1,150, terms n/30. The merchandise sold had a cost of $790.
10 Received credit of $40 from Jay-Mac Co. for a damaged racquet that was returned.
11 Purchased tennis shoes from Venus Sports for cash, $420.
13 Paid Jay-Mac Co. in full.
14 Purchased tennis shirts and shorts from Serena's Sportswear $700, FOB shipping point, terms 3/10, n/60.
15 Received cash refund of $50 from Venus Sports for damaged merchandise that was returned.
17 Paid freight on Serena's Sportswear purchase $30.
18 Sold merchandise to members $760, terms n/30. The cost of the merchandise sold was $530.
20 Received $500 in cash from members in settlement of their accounts.
21 Paid Serena's Sportswear in full.
27 Granted an allowance of $30 to members for tennis clothing that did not fit properly.
30 Received cash payments on account from members, $660.

The chart of accounts for the tennis shop includes the following: No. 101 Cash, No. 112 Accounts Receivable, No. 120 Merchandise Inventory, No. 201 Accounts Payable, No. 301 J. Ackbar, Capital, No. 401 Sales, No. 412 Sales Returns and Allowances, No. 505 Cost of Goods Sold.

Instructions

(a) Journalize the April transactions using a perpetual inventory system.
(b) Enter the beginning balances in the ledger accounts and post the April transactions. (Use J1 for the journal reference.)
(c) Prepare a trial balance on April 30, 2005.

(c) Total debits $6,110

Determine cost of goods sold and gross profit under periodic approach.

(SO 6, 7)

P5-5B At the end of High-Point Department Store's fiscal year on December 31, 2005, these accounts appeared in its adjusted trial balance.

Freight-in	$5,600
Merchandise Inventory	40,500
Purchases	442,000
Purchase Discounts	12,000
Purchase Returns and Allowances	6,400
Sales	718,000
Sales Returns and Allowances	8,000

Additional facts:

1. Merchandise inventory on December 31, 2005, is $75,000.
2. Note that High-Point Department Store uses a periodic system.

Instructions

Gross profit $315,300

Prepare an income statement through gross profit for the year ended December 31, 2005.

Calculate missing amounts and assess profitability.

(SO 6, 7)

P5-6B Danielle MacLean operates a retail clothing operation. She purchases all merchandise inventory on credit and uses a perpetual inventory system. The accounts payable account is used for recording inventory purchases only; all other current liabilities are accrued in separate accounts. You are provided with the following selected information for the fiscal years 2003, 2004, 2005, and 2006.

	2003	2004	2005	2006
Inventory (ending)	$ 13,000	$ 11,300	$ 14,700	$ 12,200
Accounts payable (ending)	20,000			
Sales		225,700	227,600	219,500
Purchases of merchandise inventory on account		141,000	150,000	132,000
Cash payments to suppliers		135,000	161,000	127,000

Instructions

(a) 2005 $146,600

(a) Calculate cost of goods sold for each of the 2004, 2005, and 2006 fiscal years.
(b) Calculate the gross profit for each of the 2004, 2005, and 2006 fiscal years.

(c) 2005 Ending accts payable $15,000

(c) Calculate the ending balance of accounts payable for each of the 2004, 2005, and 2006 fiscal years.
(d) Sales declined in fiscal 2006. Does that mean that profitability, as measured by the gross profit rate, necessarily also declined? Explain, calculating the gross profit rate for each fiscal year to help support your answer.

Journalize, post, and prepare trial balance and partial income statement using periodic approach.

(SO 7, 8)

*P5-7B At the beginning of the current season, the ledger of Village Tennis Shop showed Cash $2,500; Merchandise Inventory $1,700; and Althea Gibson, Capital $4,200. The following transactions were completed during April.

Apr. 4	Purchased racquets and balls from Robert Co. $840, terms 3/10, n/30.
6	Paid freight on Robert Co. purchase $60.
8	Sold merchandise to members $900, terms n/30.
10	Received credit of $40 from Robert Co. for a damaged racquet that was returned.
11	Purchased tennis shoes from Newbee Sports for cash $300.
13	Paid Robert Co. in full.
14	Purchased tennis shirts and shorts from Venus's Sportswear $500, terms 2/10, n/60.
15	Received cash refund of $50 from Newbee Sports for damaged merchandise that was returned.
17	Paid freight on Venus's Sportswear purchase $30.
18	Sold merchandise to members $800, terms n/30.
20	Received $500 in cash from members in settlement of their accounts.
21	Paid Venus's Sportswear in full.
27	Granted an allowance of $30 to members for tennis clothing that did not fit properly.
30	Received cash payments on account from members $500.

The chart of accounts for the tennis shop includes Cash; Accounts Receivable; Merchandise Inventory; Accounts Payable; Althea Gibson, Capital; Sales; Sales Returns and Allowances; Purchases; Purchase Returns and Allowances; Purchase Discounts; and Freight-in.

Instructions

(a) Journalize the April transactions using a periodic inventory system.
(b) Using T accounts, enter the beginning balances in the ledger accounts and post the April transactions.
(c) Prepare a trial balance on April 30, 2005.
(d) Prepare an income statement through gross profit, assuming merchandise inventory on hand at April 30 is $2,296.

(c) Tot. trial balance $6,024
(d) Gross profit $ 660

*P5-8B The trial balance of Kevin Poorten Fashion Center contained the following accounts at November 30, the end of the company's fiscal year.

Complete accounting cycle beginning with a work sheet.
(SO 4, 5, 6, 9)

KEVIN POORTEN FASHION CENTER
Trial Balance
November 30, 2005

	Debit	Credit
Cash	$ 26,700	
Accounts Receivable	30,700	
Merchandise Inventory	44,700	
Store Supplies	6,200	
Store Equipment	85,000	
Accumulated Depreciation—Store Equipment		$ 18,000
Delivery Equipment	48,000	
Accumulated Depreciation—Delivery Equipment		6,000
Notes Payable		51,000
Accounts Payable		48,500
Kevin Poorten, Capital		110,000
Kevin Poorten, Drawing	12,000	
Sales		759,200
Sales Returns and Allowances	8,800	
Cost of Goods Sold	497,400	
Salaries Expense	140,000	
Advertising Expense	26,400	
Utilities Expense	14,000	
Repair Expense	12,100	
Delivery Expense	16,700	
Rent Expense	24,000	
Totals	$992,700	$992,700

Adjustment data:

1. Store supplies on hand totaled $3,500.
2. Depreciation is $9,000 on the store equipment and $6,000 on the delivery equipment.
3. Interest of $4,080 is accrued on notes payable at November 30.
4. Merchandise inventory actually on hand is $44,400.

Other data:

1. Salaries expense is 70% selling and 30% administrative.
2. Rent expense and utilities expense are 80% selling and 20% administrative.
3. $30,000 of notes payable are due for payment next year.
4. Repair expense is 100% administrative.

Instructions

(a) Enter the trial balance on a work sheet, and complete the work sheet.
(b) Prepare a multiple-step income statement and an owner's equity statement for the year, and a classified balance sheet as of November 30, 2005.
(c) Journalize the adjusting entries.
(d) Journalize the closing entries.
(e) Prepare a post-closing trial balance.

(a) Adj. trial balance
* $1,011,780*
* Net loss $2,280*
(b) Gross profit $252,700
* Total assets $199,300*

BROADENING YOUR PERSPECTIVE

Financial Reporting and Analysis

■ **FINANCIAL REPORTING PROBLEM: PepsiCo, Inc.**

BYP5-1 The financial statements of **PepsiCo, Inc.** are presented in Appendix A at the end of this textbook.

Instructions
Answer the following questions using the Consolidated Statement of Income.

(a) What was the percentage change in (1) sales and in (2) net income from 2000 to 2001 and from 2001 to 2002?

(b) What was the company's gross profit rate in 2000, 2001, and 2002?

(c) What was the company's percentage of net income to net sales in 2000, 2001, and 2002? Comment on any trend in this percentage.

■ **COMPARATIVE ANALYSIS PROBLEM: PepsiCo vs. Coca-Cola**

BYP5-2 **PepsiCo**'s financial statements are presented in Appendix A. **The Coca-Cola Company**'s financial statements are presented in Appendix B.

Instructions
(a) Based on the information contained in these financial statements, determine each of the following for each company.
  (1) Gross profit for 2002.
  (2) Gross profit rate for 2002.
  (3) Operating income for 2002.
  (4) Percent change in operating income from 2001 to 2002.

(b) What conclusions concerning the relative profitability of the two companies can be drawn from these data?

■ **INTERPRETING FINANCIAL STATEMENTS: A Global Focus**

BYP5-3 Recently it was announced that two giant French retailers, **Carrefour SA** and **Promodes SA**, would merge. A headline in the *Wall Street Journal* blared, "French Retailers Create New Wal-Mart Rival." While **Wal-Mart**'s total sales would still exceed those of the combined company, Wal-Mart's international sales are far less than those of the combined company. This is a serious concern for Wal-Mart, since its primary opportunity for future growth lies outside of the United States.

Below are basic financial data for the combined corporation (in French francs) and Wal-Mart (in U.S. dollars). Even though their results are presented in different currencies, by employing ratios we can make some basic comparisons.

	Carrefour/ Promodes (in billions)	Wal-Mart (in billions)
Sales	Fr 298.0	$137.6
Cost of goods sold	274.0	108.7
Operating expenses	9.6	22.4
Net income	5.5	4.4
Total assets	155.0	50.0
Average total assets	140.4	47.7
Current assets	63.5	21.1
Current liabilities	85.8	16.8
Total liabilities	114.2	28.9

Instructions
Compare the two companies by answering the following.

(a) Calculate the gross profit rate for each of the companies, and discuss their relative abilities to control cost of goods sold.

(b) Calculate the operating expense to sales ratio (operating expenses ÷ sales), and discuss the companies' relative abilities to control operating expenses.

(c) What concerns might you have in relying on this comparison?

■ EXPLORING THE WEB

BYP5-4 No financial decision maker should ever rely solely on the financial information reported in the annual report to make decisions. It is important to keep abreast of financial news. This activity demonstrates how to search for financial news on the Web.

Address: biz.yahoo.com/i, or go to www.wiley.com/college/weygandt

Steps:

1. Type in either PepsiCo or Coca-Cola.
2. Choose **News**.
3. Select an article that sounds interesting to you.

Instructions

(a) What was the source of the article? (For example, Reuters, Businesswire, PR Newswire.)

(b) Pretend that you are a personal financial planner and that one of your clients owns stock in the company. Write a brief memo to your client, summarizing the article and explaining the implications of the article for their investment.

Critical Thinking

■ GROUP DECISION CASE

BYP5-5 Three years ago, Debbie Sells and her brother-in-law Mike Mooney opened FedCo Department Store. For the first two years, business was good, but the following condensed income results for 2004 were disappointing.

FEDCO DEPARTMENT STORE
Income Statement
For the Year Ended December 31, 2004

Net sales		$700,000
Cost of goods sold		560,000
Gross profit		140,000
Operating expenses		
Selling expenses	$100,000	
Administrative expenses	20,000	120,000
Net income		$ 20,000

Debbie believes the problem lies in the relatively low gross profit rate (gross profit divided by net sales) of 20%. Mike believes the problem is that operating expenses are too high.

Debbie thinks the gross profit rate can be improved by making both of the following changes:

1. Increase average selling prices by 17%. This increase is expected to lower sales volume so that total sales will increase only 8%.
2. Buy merchandise in larger quantities and take all purchase discounts. These changes are expected to increase the gross profit rate by 3%.

Debbie does not anticipate that these changes will have any effect on operating expenses.

Mike thinks expenses can be cut by making both of the following changes.

1. Cut 2004 sales salaries of $60,000 in half and give sales personnel a commission of 2% of net sales.
2. Reduce store deliveries to one day per week rather than twice a week; this change will reduce 2004 delivery expenses of $40,000 by 40%.

Mike feels that these changes will not have any effect on net sales.

Debbie and Mike come to you for help in deciding the best way to improve net income.

Instructions

With the class divided into groups, answer the following.

(a) Prepare a condensed income statement for 2005 assuming (1) Debbie's changes are implemented and (2) Mike's ideas are adopted.
(b) What is your recommendation to Debbie and Mike?
(c) Prepare a condensed income statement for 2005 assuming both sets of proposed changes are made.

■ COMMUNICATION ACTIVITY

BYP5-6 The following situation is in chronological order.

1. Dexter decides to buy a surfboard.
2. He calls Surfing USA Co. to inquire about their surfboards.
3. Two days later he requests Surfing USA Co. to make him a surfboard.
4. Three days later, Surfing USA Co. sends him a purchase order to fill out.
5. He sends back the purchase order.
6. Surfing USA Co. receives the completed purchase order.
7. Surfing USA Co. completes the surfboard.
8. Dexter picks up the surfboard.
9. Surfing USA Co. bills Dexter.
10. Surfing USA Co. receives payment from Dexter.

Instructions

In a memo to the president of Surfing USA Co., answer the following.

(a) When should Surfing USA Co. record the sale?
(b) Suppose that with his purchase order, Dexter is required to make a down payment. Would that change your answer?

■ ETHICS CASE

BYP5-7 Anita Zurbrugg was just hired as the assistant treasurer of Dorchester Stores. The company is a specialty chain store with nine retail stores concentrated in one metropolitan area. Among other things, the payment of all invoices is centralized in one of the departments Anita will manage. Her primary responsibility is to maintain the company's high credit rating by paying all bills when due and to take advantage of all cash discounts.

Chris Dadian, the former assistant treasurer who has been promoted to treasurer, is training Anita in her new duties. He instructs Anita that she is to continue the practice of preparing all checks "net of discount" and dating the checks the last day of the discount period. "But," Chris continues, "we always hold the checks at least 4 days beyond the discount period before mailing them. That way we get another 4 days of interest on our money. Most of our creditors need our business and don't complain. And, if they scream about our missing the discount period, we blame it on the mail room or the post office. We've only lost one discount out of every hundred we take that way. I think everybody does it. By the way, welcome to our team!"

Instructions

(a) What are the ethical considerations in this case?
(b) Who are the stakeholders that are harmed or benefitted in this situation?
(c) Should Anita continue the practice started by Chris? Does she have any choice?

Answers to Self-Study Questions
1. c **2.** a **3.** c **4.** b **5.** c **6.** d **7.** b **8.** c **9.** d **10.** d **11.** a ***12.** b ***13.** a

Answer to PepsiCo Review It Question 1, p. 200
For **PepsiCo**, the 2002 gross profit rate is 54.2% ($13,615 ÷ $25,112). The 2001 gross profit rate was 54.3% ($12,762 ÷ $23,512). The rate therefore decreased by 0.1% from 2001 to 2002.

☑ **REMEMBER** to go back to the Navigator box on the chapter-opening page and check off your completed work.

Inventories

THE NAVIGATOR ✓

Understand **Concepts for Review**	❑
Read **Feature Story**	❑
Scan **Study Objectives**	❑
Read **Preview**	❑
Read text and answer **Before You Go On** p. 233 ❑ p. 241 ❑ p. 246 ❑	
Work **Demonstration Problems**	❑
Review **Summary of Study Objectives**	❑
Answer **Self-Study Questions**	❑
Complete **Assignments**	❑

CONCEPTS FOR REVIEW

Before studying this chapter, you should know or, if necessary, review:

The cost principle (Ch. 1, p. 10) and matching principle of accounting. (Ch. 3, p. 91)

How to record purchases, sales, and cost of goods sold under a perpetual inventory system. (Ch. 5, pp. 186–191)

How to prepare financial statements for a merchandiser. (Ch. 5, pp. 195–201)

☑ THE NAVIGATOR

Taking Stock—from Backpacks to Bicycles

Backpacks and jackets sporting the jagged peaks of the Mountain Equipment Co-op (MEC) logo are a familiar sight on hiking trails and campuses. Sales of these popular items help the Vancouver-based co-op to finance its primary goal: to provide members with products and services for wilderness recreational activities at a reasonable cost.

MEC has five retail stores across Canada and a huge market in catalog and online sales around the world. It ships everything from climbing ropes, kayaks, and bike helmets to destinations as far away as Japan and South America.

Keeping financial track of the flow of these items is a responsibility of Fara Jumani, a member of the inventory costing group at MEC and a part-time college student. "We have tens of thousands of items in inventory, and we are adding new ones all the time," says Ms. Jumani. "Because we make a lot of our own clothing goods, we also have a lot of in-house inventory—fabric and supplies that will be used to make products."

MEC tracks the cost of its inventory using the average cost of the various items in inventory, weighted by the number purchased at each different unit cost. (This procedure is called the weighted average cost method.) "Because costs tend to fluctuate," explains Ms. Jumani, "that method best captures our overall costs."

Unlike most retail operations, MEC is not out to make a profit. As a co-op, it exists to serve its members. "But we have to stay fiscally healthy to do that," points out Ms. Jumani. "If we go bankrupt, we won't be serving anyone." Accounting for inventory—from backpacks to bicycles—is an important part of MEC's fiscal fitness routine.

☑ THE NAVIGATOR

After studying this chapter, you should be able to:

1. Describe the steps in determining inventory quantities.
2. Explain the basis of accounting for inventories, and describe the inventory cost flow methods.
3. Explain the financial statement and tax effects of each of the inventory cost flow methods.
4. Explain the lower of cost or market basis of accounting for inventories.
5. Indicate the effects of inventory errors on the financial statements.
6. Compute and interpret inventory turnover.

☑ THE NAVIGATOR

As indicated in the opening story about Mountain Equipment Co-op, careful accounting for inventory is necessary to stay in business. In this chapter we will explain the methods used in determining the cost of inventory on hand at the balance sheet date. We also will discuss differences in perpetual and periodic inventory systems, and the effects of inventory errors on a company's financial statements.

The content and organization of Chapter 6 are as follows.

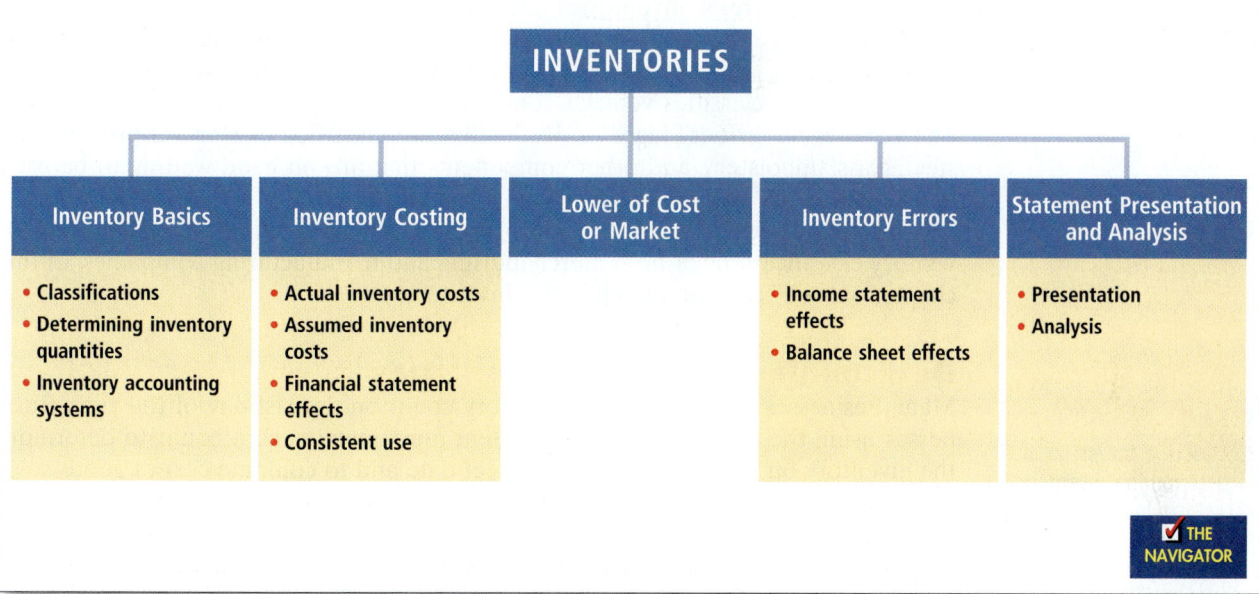

Inventory Basics

In our economy, inventories are an important barometer of business activity. The U.S. Commerce Department publishes monthly inventory data for retailers, wholesalers, and manufacturers. The amount of inventories and the time required to sell the goods on hand are two closely watched indicators. During downturns in the economy, there is an initial buildup of inventories, as it takes longer to sell existing quantities. Inventories generally decrease with an upturn in business activity. A delicate balance must be maintained between too little inventory and too much. A company with too little inventory to meet demand will have dissatisfied customers and sales personnel. One with too much inventory will be burdened with unnecessary carrying costs.

Inventories affect both the balance sheet and the income statement. In the **balance sheet** of merchandising companies, inventory is frequently the most significant current asset. Of course, its amount and relative importance can vary, even for companies in the same industry. For example, Wal-Mart reported inventory of $23 billion, representing 80% of total current assets. For the same period, J.C. Penney Company reported $5 billion of inventory, representing 57% of total current assets. In the **income statement**, inventory is vital in determining the results of operations for a particular period. The income statement for a merchandiser, as shown in Chapter 5, contains three features not found in the income statement of a service enterprise. These features are: (1) a sales revenue section, (2) cost of goods sold, and (3) gross profit. Gross profit (net sales less cost of goods sold) is closely watched by management, owners, and other interested parties.

Classifying Inventory

How a company classifies its inventory depends on whether the firm is a merchandiser or a manufacturer. A **merchandiser's** inventory consists of many different items. For example, in a grocery store, canned goods, dairy products, meats, and produce are just a few of the inventory items on hand. These items have two common characteristics: (1) They are owned by the company, and (2) they are in a form ready for sale in the ordinary course of business. Only one inventory classification, **merchandise inventory**, is needed to describe the many different items in inventory.

A **manufacturer's** inventories are also owned by the company, but some goods may not yet be ready for sale. As a result, inventory is usually classified into three categories: finished goods, work in process, and raw materials. For example, **General Motors** classifies vehicles completed and ready for sale as **finished goods**. The vehicles in various stages of production are classified as **work in process**. The steel, glass, upholstery, and other components that are on hand waiting to be used in production are **raw materials**.

The accounting principles and concepts discussed in this chapter apply to inventory classifications of both merchandising and manufacturing companies. In this chapter we will focus on merchandise inventory.

Determining Inventory Quantities

Many businesses take a physical inventory count on the last day of the year. Businesses using the periodic inventory system **must** make such a count to determine the inventory on hand at the balance sheet date and to compute cost of goods sold. Even businesses using a perpetual inventory system must take a physical inventory at some time during the year.

Determining inventory quantities consists of two steps: (1) taking a physical inventory of goods on hand, and (2) determining the ownership of goods.

Taking a Physical Inventory

Taking a physical inventory involves actually counting, weighing, or measuring each kind of inventory on hand. In many companies, taking an inventory is a formidable task, even with the current widespread use of bar codes and scanning equipment. Retailers such as **Kmart**, **The Home Depot**, or your favorite music store have thousands of different inventory items. An inventory count is generally more accurate when goods are not being sold or received during the counting. So, companies often "take inventory" when the business is closed or when business is slow. Many retailers, for example, close early on a chosen day in January—after the holiday sales and returns—to count inventory.

To minimize errors in taking the inventory, a company should adhere to **internal control** principles and practices that safeguard inventory:

1. The counting should be done by employees who do not have custodial responsibility for the inventory.
2. Each counter should establish the authenticity of each inventory item. For example, does each box contain a 25-inch television set? Does each storage tank contain gasoline?
3. There should be a second count by another employee.
4. Prenumbered inventory tags (or scanning equipment) should be used. All inventory tags should be accounted for.
5. At the end of the count, a supervisor should check that all inventory items are tagged or scanned and that no items have been doubled-counted.

After the physical inventory is taken, the quantity of each kind of inventory is listed on **inventory summary sheets**. To ensure accuracy, the listing should be verified by a second employee. Later, unit costs will be applied to the quantities in order to determine a total cost of the inventory—which is the topic of later sections.[1]

Determining Ownership of Goods

Before we can begin to calculate the cost of inventory, we need to consider the ownership of goods. Specifically, we need to be sure that we have not included in the inventory any goods that do not belong to the company.

GOODS IN TRANSIT.   Goods are considered **in transit** when they are in the hands of a public carrier (such as a railroad, trucking, or airline company) at the statement date. Goods in transit should be included in the inventory of the party that has legal title to the goods. Legal title is determined by the terms of sale, as shown in Illustration 6-1 and described on the next page.

Illustration 6-1
Terms of sale

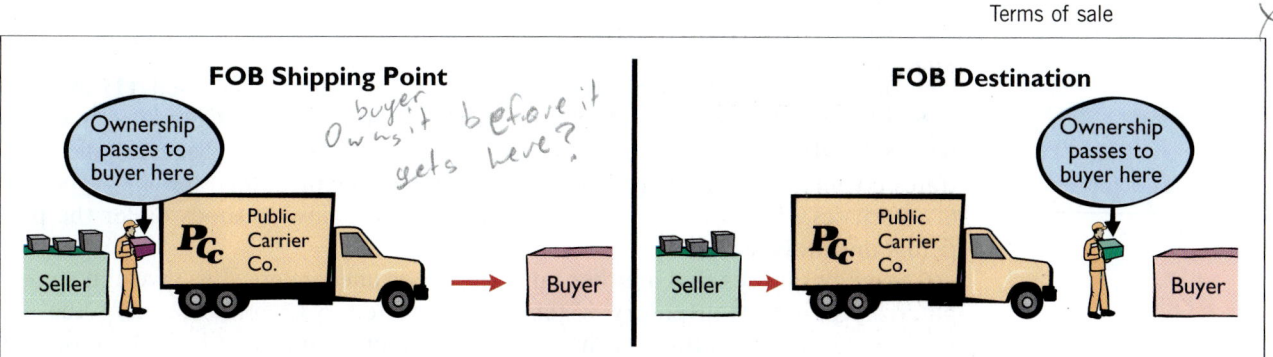

[1]To estimate the cost of inventory when a physical inventory cannot be taken (the inventory is destroyed) or when it is inconvenient (during interim periods), estimating methods are applied. These methods (gross profit method and retail inventory method) are discussed in Appendix 6B.

Goods in transit

1. **FOB (free on board) shipping point:** Ownership of the goods passes to the buyer when the public carrier accepts the goods from the seller.

2. **FOB destination:** Legal title to the goods remains with the seller until the goods reach the buyer.

Inventory quantities may be seriously miscounted if goods in transit at the statement date are ignored. Assume that Hargrove Company has 20,000 units of inventory on hand on December 31. It also has the following goods in transit: (1) **sales** of 1,500 units shipped December 31 FOB destination, and (2) **purchases** of 2,500 units shipped FOB shipping point by the seller on December 31. Hargrove has legal title to both the units sold and the units purchased. If units in transit are ignored, inventory quantities would be understated by 4,000 units (1,500 + 2,500). As we will see later in the chapter, inaccurate inventory counts affect not only the inventory amount shown on the balance sheet but also the cost of goods sold calculation on the income statement.

ACCOUNTING IN ACTION **Business Insight**

Many companies have invested large amounts of time and money in automated inventory systems. One of the most sophisticated is **Federal Express**'s Digitally Assisted Dispatch System (DADS). It uses hand-held "SuperTrackers" to transmit data about the packages and documents to the firm's computer system. Based on bar codes, the system allows the firm to know where any package is at any time to prevent losses and to fulfill the firm's delivery commitments. More recently, FedEx's software enables customers to track shipments on their own PCs.

CONSIGNED GOODS. In some lines of business, it is customary to acquire merchandise on consignment. Under such an arrangement, the holder of the goods (the *consignee*) does not own the goods. Ownership remains with the shipper of the goods (the *consignor*) until the goods are actually sold to a customer. Because **consigned goods** are not owned by the consignee, they should not be included in the consignee's physical inventory count. But, the consignor should include merchandise held by the consignee as part of its inventory.

Inventory Accounting Systems

One of two basic systems of accounting for inventories may be used: **(1) the perpetual inventory system,** or **(2) the periodic inventory system.** Chapter 5 and Appendix 5A discussed and illustrated both systems. This chapter discusses and illustrates inventory cost flow methods under the periodic inventory system. Appendix 6A discusses and illustrates the same inventory cost flow methods under the perpetual inventory system.

Some businesses find it either unnecessary or uneconomical to invest in a computerized perpetual inventory system. As illustrated in Chapter 5, a perpetual inventory system keeps track of inventory in number of units **and** in dollar costs per unit. Many small merchandising business managers still feel that a perpetual inventory system costs more than it is worth. These managers can control merchandise and manage day-to-day operations either without detailed inventory records or with a perpetual **units only** inventory system.

BEFORE YOU GO ON...

Review It

1. What steps are involved in determining inventory quantities?
2. How is ownership determined for goods in transit at the balance sheet date?
3. Who has title to consigned goods?

Do It

Hasbeen Company completed its inventory count. It arrived at a total inventory value of $200,000. You have been informed of the information listed below. Discuss how this information affects the reported cost of inventory.

1. Goods held on consignment for Falls Co., costing $15,000, were included in the inventory.
2. Purchased goods of $10,000 which were in transit (terms: FOB shipping point) were not included in the count.
3. Sold inventory with a cost of $12,000 which was in transit (terms: FOB shipping point) was not included in the count.

ACTION PLAN

- Apply the rules of ownership to goods held on consignment.
- Apply the rules of ownership to goods in transit FOB shipping point.

SOLUTION   The goods of $15,000 held on consignment should be deducted from the inventory count. The goods of $10,000 purchased FOB shipping point should be added to the inventory count. Sold goods of $12,000 which were in transit FOB shipping point should not be included in the ending inventory. Thus, inventory should be carried at $195,000.

Related exercise material: *BE6-1, E6-1, and E6-2.*

☑ THE NAVIGATOR

Inventoriable Cost = beginning Inv + Purchases

Inventory Costing Under a Periodic Inventory System

All expenditures needed to acquire goods and to make them ready for sale are included as inventoriable costs. **Inventoriable costs** may be regarded as a pool of costs that consists of two elements: (1) the cost of the beginning inventory and (2) the cost of goods purchased during the year. The sum of these two equals the cost of goods available for sale.

Conceptually, the costs of the purchasing, receiving, and warehousing departments (whose efforts make the goods available for sale) should also be included in inventoriable costs. But, there are practical difficulties in allocating these costs to inventory. So these costs are generally accounted for as **operating expenses** in the period in which they are incurred.

Inventoriable costs are allocated either to ending inventory or to cost of goods sold. Under a **periodic inventory system**, the allocation is made at the end of the accounting period. First, the costs for the ending inventory are determined. Next, the cost of the ending inventory is subtracted from the cost of goods available for sale, to determine the cost of goods sold.

To illustrate, assume that General Suppliers has a cost of goods available for sale of $120,000. This amount is based on a beginning inventory of $20,000 and cost of goods purchased of $100,000. The physical inventory indicates that 5,000 units are

STUDY OBJECTIVE 2

Explain the basis of accounting for inventories, and describe the inventory cost flow methods.

on hand. The costs applicable to the units are $3.00 per unit. The allocation of the pool of costs is shown in Illustration 6-2. As shown, the $120,000 of goods available for sale are allocated $15,000 to ending inventory (5,000 × $3.00) and $105,000 to cost of goods sold.

Illustration 6-2
Allocation (matching) of pool of costs

Pool of Costs Cost of Goods Available for Sale				
Beginning inventory				$ 20,000
Cost of goods purchased				100,000
Cost of goods available for sale				**$120,000**

Step 1 Ending Inventory			Step 2 Cost of Goods Sold	
Units	Unit Cost	Total Cost	Cost of goods available for sale	$120,000
			Less: Ending inventory	15,000
5,000	$3.00	**$15,000**	Cost of goods sold	**$105,000**

Using Actual Physical Flow Costing—Specific Identification

Costing of the inventory is complicated because specific items of inventory on hand may have been purchased at different prices. For example, a company may experience several increases in the cost of identical goods within a given year. Or, unit costs may decline. Under such circumstances, how should different unit costs be allocated between the ending inventory and cost of goods sold?

One answer is to use **specific identification** of the units purchased. This method tracks the **actual physical flow** of the goods. **Each item of inventory is marked, tagged, or coded with its "specific" unit cost.** At the end of the year the specific costs of items still in inventory make up the total cost of the ending inventory. Assume, for example, that Southland Music Company purchases three 46-inch television sets at costs of $700, $750, and $800, respectively. During the year, two sets are sold at $1,200 each. At December 31, the $750 set is still on hand. The ending inventory is $750, and the cost of goods sold is $1,500 ($700 + $800). This is shown graphically in Illustration 6-3.

Illustration 6-3
Specific identification method

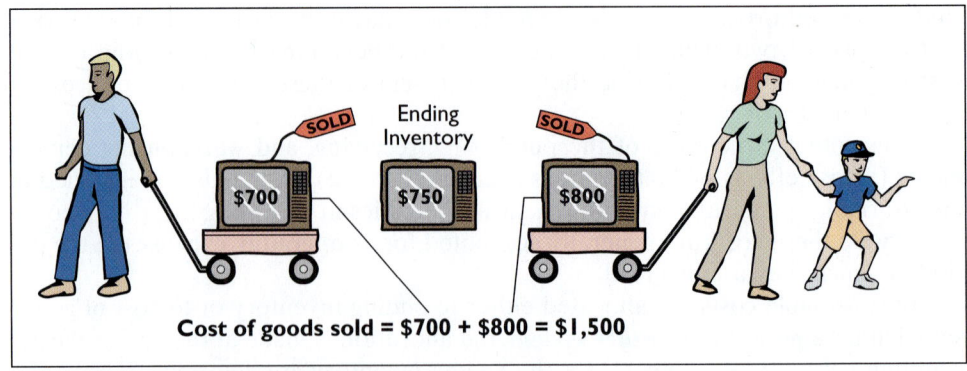

Cost of goods sold = $700 + $800 = $1,500

Specific identification is possible when a company sells a limited variety of high-unit-cost items that can be clearly identified from purchase through sale. Examples are automobile dealerships (cars, trucks, and vans), music stores (pianos and organs), and antique shops (tables and cabinets).

But what if we cannot specifically identify particular inventory items? For example, drug, grocery, and hardware stores sell thousands of relatively low-unit-cost items of inventory. These are often indistinguishable from one another. It may be impossible or impractical to track each item's cost. In that case (as the next section will show), we must make assumptions about which units were sold.

The general rule is this: <u>When feasible, specific identification is the ideal method of allocating cost of goods available for sale</u>. It reports ending inventory at actual cost and matches the actual cost of goods sold against sales revenue.

However, specific identification may enable management to manipulate net income. To see how, assume that a music store has three identical Steinway grand pianos, purchased at different costs. When selling one piano, management could maximize net income by selecting the piano with the lowest cost to match against revenues. Or, it could minimize net income (and lower its taxes) by selecting the highest-cost piano.

Using Assumed Cost Flow Methods—FIFO, LIFO, and Average Cost

Because specific identification is often impractical, other cost flow methods are allowed. These assume flows of costs that may be unrelated to the physical flow of goods. For this reason we call them **assumed cost flow methods** or **cost flow assumptions**. They are:

1. First-in, first-out (FIFO).
2. Last-in, first-out (LIFO).
3. Average cost.

To illustrate these three inventory cost flow methods, we will assume that Bow Valley Electronics uses a **periodic inventory system**.[2] The information shown in Illustration 6-4 relates to its Z202 Astro Condenser.

Illustration 6-4
Inventoriable units and costs for Bow Valley Electronics

BOW VALLEY ELECTRONICS
Z202 Astro Condensers

Date	Explanation	Units	Unit Cost	Total Cost
1/1	Beginning inventory	100	$10	$ 1,000
4/15	Purchase	200	11	2,200
8/24	Purchase	300	12	3,600
11/27	Purchase	400	13	5,200
	Total	1,000		$12,000

During the year, 550 units were sold, and 450 units are on hand at 12/31.

There is no accounting requirement that the cost flow assumption be consistent with the physical movement of the goods. Management selects the appropriate cost

[2]We have chosen to use the periodic approach for a number of reasons. First, many companies that use a perpetual inventory system use it to keep track of units on hand, but then determine cost of goods sold at the end of the period using one of the three cost flow approaches applied under essentially a periodic approach. Second, because of the complexity, few companies use average cost on a perpetual basis. Third, most companies that use perpetual LIFO employ dollar-value LIFO, which is presented in more advanced texts. Fourth, FIFO gives the same results under either perpetual or periodic. And finally, it is easier to demonstrate the cost flow assumptions under the periodic system, which makes it more pedagogically appropriate.

flow method. Even in the same industry, different companies may reach different conclusions as to the most appropriate method.

First-in, First-out (FIFO)

The **FIFO method** assumes that the **earliest goods** purchased are the first to be sold. FIFO often parallels the actual physical flow of merchandise because it generally is good business practice to sell the earliest units first. Under the FIFO method, the **costs** of the earliest goods purchased are the first to be recognized as cost of goods sold. (Note that this does not necessarily mean that the earliest units *are* sold first, but that the costs of the earliest units are recognized first. In a bin of picture hangers at the hardware store, for example, no one really knows, nor would it matter, which hangers are sold first.) The allocation of the cost of goods available for sale at Bow Valley Electronics under FIFO is shown in Illustrations 6-5 and 6-6.

Illustration 6-5
Allocation of costs—FIFO method

		Pool of Costs Cost of Goods Available for Sale			
Date	**Explanation**		**Units**	**Unit Cost**	**Total Cost**
1/1	Beginning inventory		100	$10	$ 1,000
4/15	Purchase		200	11	2,200
8/24	Purchase		300	12	3,600
11/27	Purchase		400	13	5,200
	Total		1,000		**$12,000**

		Step 1 Ending Inventory		Step 2 Cost of Goods Sold	
Date	**Units**	**Unit Cost**	**Total Cost**		
11/27	400	$13	$5,200	Cost of goods available for sale	$12,000
8/24	50	12	600	Less: Ending inventory	5,800
Total	450		**$5,800**	Cost of goods sold	**$ 6,200**

HELPFUL HINT

Note the sequencing of the allocation: (1) Compute ending inventory. (2) Determine cost of goods sold.

Illustration 6-6
FIFO—First costs in are first costs out in computing cost of goods sold

Note that the ending inventory is based on the latest units purchased. That is, **under FIFO, the cost of the ending inventory is found by taking the unit cost of the most recent purchase and working backward until all units of inventory are costed.**

We can verify the accuracy of the cost of goods sold by recognizing that the **first units acquired are the first units sold**. The computations for the 550 units sold are shown in Illustration 6-7.

Illustration 6-7
Proof of cost of goods sold

Date	Units		Unit Cost		Total Cost
1/1	100	×	$10	=	$1,000
4/15	200	×	11	=	2,200
8/24	250	×	12	=	3,000
Total	550				**$6,200**

Last-in, First-out (LIFO)

The **LIFO method** assumes that the **latest goods** purchased are the first to be sold. LIFO seldom coincides with the actual physical flow of inventory. Only for goods in piles, such as hay, coal, or produce at the grocery store would LIFO match the physical flow of inventory. Under the LIFO method, the **costs** of the latest goods purchased are the first to be assigned to cost of goods sold. The allocation of the cost of goods available for sale at Bow Valley Electronics under LIFO is shown in Illustration 6-8.

Illustration 6-8
Allocation of costs—LIFO method

Pool of Costs
Cost of Goods Available for Sale

Date	Explanation	Units	Unit Cost	Total Cost
1/1	Beginning inventory	100	$10	$ 1,000
4/15	Purchase	200	11	2,200
8/24	Purchase	300	12	3,600
11/27	Purchase	400	13	5,200
	Total	1,000		**$12,000**

Step 1
Ending Inventory

Step 2
Cost of Goods Sold

Date	Units	Unit Cost	Total Cost
1/1	100	$10	$1,000
4/15	200	11	2,200
8/24	150	12	1,800
Total	450		**$5,000**

Cost of goods available for sale	$12,000
Less: Ending inventory	5,000
Cost of goods sold	**$ 7,000**

HELPFUL HINT

The costs allocated to ending inventory ($5,000) plus the costs allocated to CGS ($7,000) must equal CGAS ($12,000).

Illustration 6-9 (page 238) graphically displays the LIFO cost flow.

Under the LIFO method, **the cost of the ending inventory is found by taking the unit cost of the oldest goods and working forward until all units of inventory are costed**. As a result, the first costs assigned to ending inventory are the costs of the beginning inventory. Proof of the costs allocated to cost of goods sold is shown in Illustration 6-10 (page 238).

Under a periodic inventory system, **all goods purchased during the period are assumed to be available for the first sale, regardless of the date of purchase**.

Illustration 6-9
LIFO—Last costs in are first costs out in computing cost of goods sold

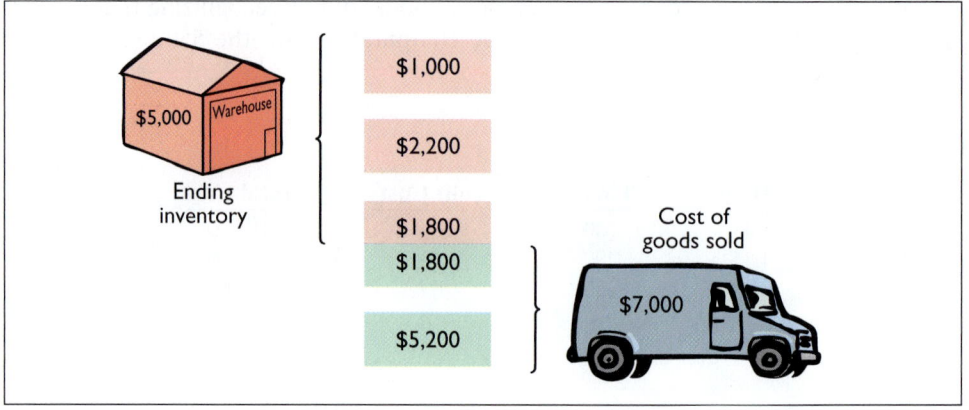

Illustration 6-10
Proof of cost of goods sold

Date	Units		Unit Cost		Total Cost
11/27	400	×	$13	=	$5,200
8/24	150	×	12	=	1,800
Total	550				**$7,000**

Average Cost

The **average cost method** assumes that the goods available for sale have the same (average) cost per unit. Generally such goods are identical. Under this method, the cost of goods available for sale is allocated on the basis of the **weighted-average unit cost**. The formula and a sample computation of the weighted-average unit cost are as follows.

Illustration 6-11
Formula for weighted-average unit cost

Cost of Goods Available for Sale	÷	Total Units Available for Sale	=	Weighted-Average Unit Cost
$12,000	÷	1,000	=	**$12.00**

The weighted-average unit cost is then applied to the units on hand. This computation determines the cost of the ending inventory. The allocation of the cost of goods available for sale at Bow Valley Electronics using average cost is shown in Illustrations 6-12 and 6-13 (below and on the next page).

To verify the cost of goods sold data in Illustration 6-12, multiply the units sold by the weighted-average unit cost (550 × $12 = $6,600). Note that this method does not use the average of the **unit costs**. That average is $11.50 ($10 + $11 + $12 + $13 = $46; $46 ÷ 4). Instead, the average cost method uses the average **weighted** by the quantities purchased at each unit cost.

Illustration 6-12
Allocation of costs—average cost method

Pool of Costs				
Cost of Goods Available for Sale				
Date	Explanation	Units	Unit Cost	Total Cost
1/1	Beginning inventory	100	$10	$ 1,000
4/15	Purchase	200	11	2,200
8/24	Purchase	300	12	3,600
11/27	Purchase	400	13	5,200
	Total	1,000		**$12,000**

Illustration 6-12
(continued from p. 236)

Step 1 Ending Inventory				Step 2 Cost of Goods Sold	
$12,000	÷	1,000	=	$12.00	Cost of goods available for sale	$12,000
		Unit		Total	Less: Ending inventory	5,400
Units		Cost		Cost	Cost of goods sold	**$ 6,600**
450	×	$12.00	=	**$5,400**		

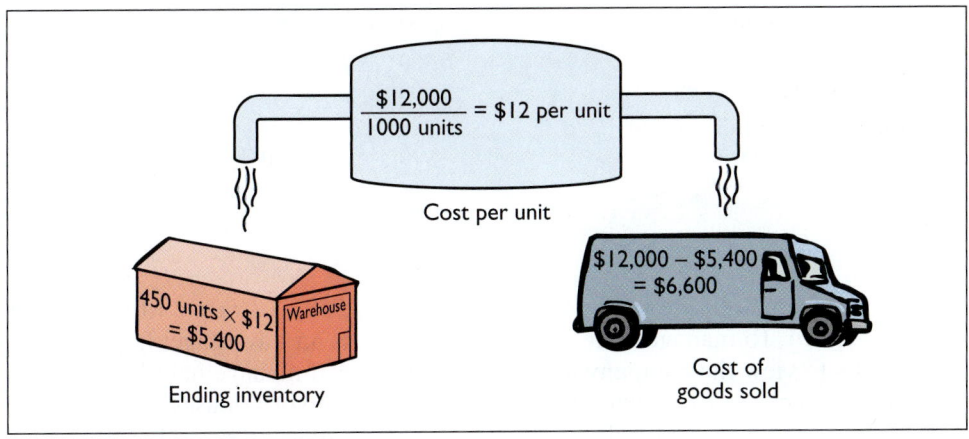

Illustration 6-13
Average cost—the average cost of the goods available for sale during the period is the cost used to compute cost of goods sold

$$\frac{\$12,000}{1000\ units} = \$12\ per\ unit$$

Cost per unit

450 units × $12 = $5,400
Warehouse
Ending inventory

$12,000 − $5,400 = $6,600
Cost of goods sold

Financial Statement Effects of Cost Flow Methods

Each of the three cost flow methods is acceptable. For example, **Black and Decker Manufacturing Company** and **Wendy's International** currently use the FIFO method. **Campbell Soup Company**, **Kroger Co.**, and **Walgreen Drugs** use LIFO. **Bristol-Myers-Squibb Co.** and **Motorola, Inc.** use the average cost method. A company may also use more than one cost flow method at the same time. **Del Monte Corporation** uses LIFO for domestic inventories and FIFO for foreign inventories. Illustration 6-14 shows the use of the three methods in the 600 largest U.S. companies. Companies adopt different inventory cost flow methods for various reasons. Usually, one of the following factors is involved:

1. Income statement effects.
2. Balance sheet effects.
3. Tax effects.

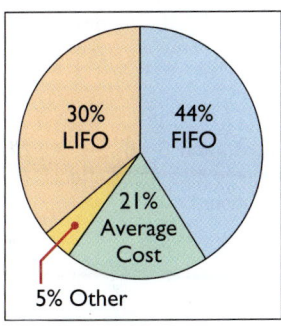

30% LIFO
44% FIFO
21% Average Cost
5% Other

Illustration 6-14
Use of cost flow methods in major U.S. companies

Income Statement Effects

To understand why companies might choose a particular cost flow method, let's compare their effects on the financial statements of Bow Valley Electronics. The condensed income statements in Illustration 6-15 (page 240) assume that Bow Valley sold its 550 units for $11,500, and its operating expenses were $2,000. Its income tax rate is 30%.

The cost of goods available for sale ($12,000) is the same under each of the three inventory cost flow methods. But the ending inventory is different in each method, and this difference affects cost of goods sold. Each dollar of difference in ending inventory therefore results in a corresponding dollar difference in income before income taxes. For Bow Valley, there is an $800 difference between FIFO and LIFO.

In a period of rising prices, FIFO produces a higher net income. This happens because the expenses matched against revenues are the lower unit costs of the first units purchased. In a period of rising prices (as is the case here), FIFO reports the

STUDY OBJECTIVE 3

Explain the financial statement and tax effects of each of the inventory cost flow methods.

Illustration 6-15
Comparative effects of cost
flow methods

BOW VALLEY ELECTRONICS Condensed Income Statements			
	FIFO	**LIFO**	**Average Cost**
Sales	$11,500	$11,500	$11,500
Beginning inventory	1,000	1,000	1,000
Purchases	11,000	11,000	11,000
Cost of goods available for sale	12,000	12,000	12,000
Ending inventory	5,800	5,000	5,400
Cost of goods sold	6,200	7,000	6,600
Gross profit	5,300	4,500	4,900
Operating expenses	2,000	2,000	2,000
Income before income taxes[3]	3,300	2,500	2,900
Income tax expense (30%)	990	750	870
Net income	**$ 2,310**	**$ 1,750**	**$ 2,030**

HELPFUL HINT

If prices are falling, the
results from the use of
FIFO and LIFO are
reversed: FIFO will report
the lowest net income and
LIFO the highest.

highest net income ($2,310) and LIFO the lowest ($1,750); average cost falls in the middle ($2,030). To management, higher net income is an advantage: It causes external users to view the company more favorably. Also, if management bonuses are based on net income, FIFO will provide the basis for higher bonuses.

Some argue that the use of LIFO in a period of rising prices enables the company to avoid reporting **paper or phantom profit** as economic gain. To illustrate, assume that Kralik Company buys 200 XR492s at $20 per unit on January 10. It buys 200 more on December 31 at $24 each. During the year, it sells 200 units at $30 each. The results under FIFO and LIFO are shown in Illustration 6-16.

Illustration 6-16
Income statement effects
compared

	FIFO	**LIFO**
Sales (200 × $30)	$6,000	$6,000
Cost of goods sold	**4,000** (200 × $20)	**4,800** (200 × $24)
Gross profit	$2,000	$1,200

Under LIFO, the company has recovered the current replacement cost ($4,800) of the units sold. The gross profit in economic terms under LIFO is real. Under FIFO, the company has recovered only the January 10 cost ($4,000). To replace the units sold, it must reinvest $800 (200 × $4) of the gross profit. Thus, $800 of the gross profit under FIFO is phantom, or illusory. As a result, reported net income under FIFO is also overstated in real terms.

Balance Sheet Effects

A major advantage of FIFO is that in a period of rising prices, the costs allocated to ending inventory will be close to their current cost. For Bow Valley, for example, 400 of the 450 units in the ending inventory are costed at the November 27 unit cost of $13.

A major shortcoming of LIFO is that in a period of rising prices, the costs allocated to ending inventory may be understated in terms of current cost. This is true

---

[3]It is assumed that Bow Valley is a corporation, and corporations are required to pay income taxes.

for Bow Valley: The cost of the ending inventory includes the $10 unit cost of the beginning inventory. The understatement becomes even greater if the inventory includes goods purchased in one or more prior accounting periods.

Tax Effects

We have seen that both inventory on the balance sheet and net income on the income statement are higher when FIFO is used in a period of rising prices. Why, then, would a company use LIFO? The reason is that LIFO results in the lowest income taxes during times of rising prices. The lower net income reported by LIFO translates to a lower tax liability. For example, at Bow Valley Electronics, income taxes are $750 under LIFO, compared to $990 under FIFO. The tax saving of $240 makes more cash available for use in the business.

Using Inventory Cost Flow Methods Consistently

Whatever cost flow method a company chooses, it should be used consistently from one period to another. Consistent application makes financial statements more comparable over successive time periods. In contrast, using FIFO in one year and LIFO in the next would make it difficult to compare the net incomes of the two years.

Although consistent application is preferred, a company may change its method of inventory costing. Such a change and its effects on net income should be disclosed in the financial statements. A typical disclosure is shown in Illustration 6-17, using information from recent financial statements of **Quaker Oats Company**.

QUAKER OATS COMPANY
Notes to the Financial Statements

Note 1   Effective July 1, the Company adopted the LIFO cost flow assumption for valuing the majority of U.S. Grocery Products inventories. The Company believes that the use of the LIFO method better matches current costs with current revenues. The effect of this change on the current year was to decrease net income by $16.0 million.

Illustration 6-17
Disclosure of change in cost flow method

BEFORE YOU GO ON...

Review It
1. How do the cost and matching principles apply to inventoriable costs?
2. How are the three assumed cost flow methods applied in allocating inventoriable costs?
3. What factors should be considered by management in selecting an inventory cost flow method?
4. Which inventory cost flow method produces (a) the highest net income in a period of rising prices, and (b) the lowest income taxes?
5. What amount is reported by **PepsiCo, Inc.** in its 2002 Annual Report as inventories at December 28, 2002? Which inventory cost flow method does PepsiCo use? (See Note 14.) The answer to this question is provided on p. 274.

(*continued from p. 241*)

Do It

The accounting records of Wayne E. Weather Company show the following data.

Beginning inventory	4,000 units at $3
Purchases	6,000 units at $4
Sales	5,000 units at $8

Determine the cost of goods sold during the period under a periodic inventory system using (a) the FIFO method, (b) the LIFO method, and (c) the average cost method.

ACTION PLAN

- Understand the periodic inventory system.
- Compute the cost of goods sold under the periodic inventory system using the FIFO cost flow method.
- Compute the cost of goods sold under the periodic inventory system using the LIFO cost flow method.
- Compute the cost of goods sold under the periodic inventory system using the average cost method.

SOLUTION

(a) FIFO: (4,000 @ $3) + (1,000 @ $4) = $12,000 + $4,000 = $16,000.
(b) LIFO: 5,000 @ $4 = $20,000.
(c) Average cost: [(4,000 @ $3) + (6,000 @ $4)] ÷ $10,000 = ($12,000 + $24,000) ÷ 10,000 = $3.60 per unit; 5,000 @ $3.60 = $18,000.

Related exercise material: *BE6-3, BE6-4, BE6-5, BE6-6, E6-3, E6-4, E6-5, E6-6, and E6-7.*

THE NAVIGATOR

Valuing Inventory at the Lower of Cost or Market (LCM)

Inventory values sometimes fall due to changes in technology or in fashion. When the value of inventory is lower than its cost, the inventory is written down to its market value. This is done by valuing the inventory at the **lower of cost or market (LCM)** in the period in which the decline occurs. LCM is an example of the **conservatism** constraint: When choosing among alternatives, the best choice is the method that is least likely to overstate assets and net income.

Under the LCM basis, "market" is defined as **current replacement cost**, not selling price. For a merchandiser, "market" is the cost of purchasing the same goods at the present time from the usual suppliers in the usual quantities.

Assume that Ken Tuckie TV has the following lines of merchandise with costs and market values as indicated. LCM produces the following result.

Illustration 6-18
Computation of lower of cost or market

	Cost	Market	Lower of Cost or Market
Television sets			
Consoles	$ 60,000	$ 55,000	$ 55,000
Portables	45,000	52,000	45,000
Total	105,000	107,000	
Video equipment			
Recorders	48,000	45,000	45,000
Movies	15,000	14,000	14,000
Total	63,000	59,000	
Total inventory	$168,000	$166,000	$159,000

The amount entered in the final column is the lower of the cost or market amount for **each item**. LCM is applied to the items in inventory after one of the costing methods (specific identification, FIFO, LIFO, or average cost) has been applied to determine cost.

Inventory Errors

Unfortunately, errors occasionally occur in taking or costing inventory. Some errors are caused by counting or pricing the inventory incorrectly. Others occur because of improper recognition of the transfer of legal title to goods in transit. When errors occur, they affect both the income statement and the balance sheet.

STUDY OBJECTIVE 5

Indicate the effects of inventory errors on the financial statements.

Income Statement Effects
Remember that both the beginning and ending inventories are used to determine cost of goods sold in a periodic system. The ending inventory of one period automatically becomes the beginning inventory of the next period. Inventory errors thus affect the determination of cost of goods sold and net income.

The effects on cost of goods sold can be determined by using the following formula. First enter the incorrect data in the formula. Then substitute the correct data, and find the difference between the two CGS amounts.

$$\text{Beginning Inventory} + \text{Cost of Goods Purchased} - \text{Ending Inventory} = \text{Cost of Goods Sold}$$

Illustration 6-19
Formula for cost of goods sold

If beginning inventory is understated, cost of goods sold will be understated. If ending inventory is understated, cost of goods sold will be overstated. The effects of inventory errors on the current year's income statement are shown in Illustration 6-20.

Inventory Error	Cost of Goods Sold	Net Income
Beginning inventory understated	Understated	Overstated
Beginning inventory overstated	Overstated	Understated
Ending inventory understated	Overstated	Understated
Ending inventory overstated	Understated	Overstated

Illustration 6-20
Effects of inventory errors on current year's income statement

An error in ending inventory in the current period will have a **reverse effect on net income of the next period**. This is shown in Illustration 6-21 on the next page. Note that understating ending inventory in 2005 understates beginning inventory in 2006 and overstates net income in 2006.

Over the two years, total net income is correct. The errors offset one another. Notice that for 2005 and 2006 total income using incorrect data is $35,000 ($22,000 + $13,000). This is the same as the total income of $35,000 ($25,000 + $10,000) using correct data. Also note in this example that an error in the beginning inventory does not result in a corresponding error in the ending inventory. The correctness of the ending inventory depends entirely on the accuracy of taking and costing the inventory at the balance sheet date.

ETHICS NOTE

Inventory fraud includes costing inventory at amounts in excess of their actual value, or claiming to have inventory when no inventory exists. Inventory fraud is usually done to overstate ending inventory, which understates cost of goods sold and creates higher income.

Illustration 6-21
Effects of inventory errors
on two years' income
statements

	Condensed Income Statement							
	2005				**2006**			
	Incorrect		**Correct**		**Incorrect**		**Correct**	
Sales		$80,000		$80,000		$90,000		$90,000
Beginning inventory	$20,000		$20,000		**$12,000**		**$15,000**	
Cost of goods purchased	40,000		40,000		68,000		68,000	
Cost of goods available for sale	60,000		60,000		80,000		83,000	
Ending inventory	**12,000**		**15,000**		23,000		23,000	
Cost of goods sold		48,000		45,000		57,000		60,000
Gross profit		32,000		35,000		33,000		30,000
Operating expenses		10,000		10,000		20,000		20,000
Net income		$22,000		$25,000		$13,000		$10,000

($3,000)
Net income
understated

$3,000
Net income
overstated

**The total combined income for
the 2 years is correct.**

Balance Sheet Effects

The effect of ending-inventory errors on the balance sheet can be determined by the basic accounting equation: Assets = Liabilities + Owner's equity. Errors in the ending inventory have the following effects on these components.

Illustration 6-22
Ending inventory error—
balance sheet effects

Ending Inventory Error	Assets	Liabilities	Owner's Equity
Overstated	Overstated	None	Overstated
Understated	Understated	None	Understated

The effect of an error in ending inventory on the next period was shown in Illustration 6-21. If the error is not corrected, total net income for the two periods would be correct. Thus, total owner's equity reported on the balance sheet at the end of the next period will also be correct.

Statement Presentation and Analysis

Presentation

As indicated in Chapter 5, inventory is classified as a current asset after receivables in the balance sheet. In a multiple-step income statement, cost of goods sold is subtracted from sales. There also should be disclosure of (1) the major inventory classifications, (2) the basis of accounting (cost, or lower of cost or market), and (3) the costing method (FIFO, LIFO, or average).

Wal-Mart, for example, in its January 31, 2002, balance sheet reported inventories of $22,614 million under current assets. The accompanying notes to the financial statements, as shown in Illustration 6-23, disclosed the following information.

Illustration 6-23
Inventory disclosures by
Wal-Mart

WAL★MART

WAL-MART STORES, INC.
Notes to the Financial Statements

Note 1. Summary of accounting policies

Inventories

The Company uses the retail last-in, first-out (LIFO) method for the Wal-Mart Stores segment, cost LIFO for the SAM'S CLUB segment, and other cost methods, including the retail first-in, first-out (FIFO) and average cost methods, for the International segment. Inventories are not recorded in excess of market value.

As indicated in this note, Wal-Mart values its inventories at the lower of cost or market using all three inventory costing methods—LIFO, FIFO, and average cost.

Analysis

The amount of inventory carried by a company has significant economic consequences. And inventory management is a double-edged sword that requires constant attention. On the one hand, management wants to have a great variety and quantity on hand so that customers have a wide selection and items are always in stock. But such a policy may incur high carrying costs (e.g., investment, storage, insurance, obsolescence, and damage). On the other hand, low inventory levels lead to stockouts and lost sales.

Common ratios used to manage and evaluate inventory levels are inventory turnover and a related measure, average days to sell the inventory.

Inventory turnover measures the number of times on average the inventory is sold during the period. Its purpose is to measure the liquidity of the inventory. The inventory turnover is computed by dividing cost of goods sold by the average inventory during the period. Unless seasonal factors are significant, average inventory can be computed from the beginning and ending inventory balances. For example, **Wal-Mart** reported in its 2002 Annual Report a beginning inventory of $21,442 million, an ending inventory of $22,614 million, and cost of goods sold for the year ended January 31, 2002, of $171,562 million. The inventory turnover formula and computation for Wal-Mart are shown below.

STUDY OBJECTIVE 6

Compute and interpret inventory turnover.

Illustration 6-24
Inventory turnover formula and computation for
Wal-Mart

Cost of Goods Sold	÷	Average Inventory	=	Inventory Turnover
$171,562	÷	$\dfrac{\$21{,}442 + \$22{,}614}{2}$	=	7.79 times

A variant of the inventory turnover ratio is the **average days to sell inventory**. For example, the inventory turnover for Wal-Mart of 7.8 times divided into 365 is approximately 47 days. This is the approximate age of the inventory.

There are typical levels of inventory in every industry. Companies that are able to keep their inventory at lower levels and higher turnovers and still satisfy customer needs are the most successful.

BEFORE YOU GO ON...

Review It

1. Why is it appropriate to report inventories at the lower of cost or market?
2. How do inventory errors affect financial statements?
3. What does inventory turnover reveal?

DEMONSTRATION PROBLEM 1

Gerald D. Englehart Company has the following inventory, purchases, and sales data for the month of March.

Inventory:	March 1	200 units @ $4.00	$ 800
Purchases:			
	March 10	500 units @ $4.50	2,250
	March 20	400 units @ $4.75	1,900
	March 30	300 units @ $5.00	1,500
Sales:			
	March 15	500 units	
	March 25	400 units	

The physical inventory count on March 31 shows 500 units on hand.

Instructions

Under a **periodic inventory system**, determine the cost of inventory on hand at March 31 and the cost of goods sold for March under the (a) first-in, first-out (FIFO) method, (b) last-in, first-out (LIFO) method, and (c) average cost method.

ACTION PLAN

- Compute the cost of inventory under the periodic FIFO method by allocating to the units on hand the **latest costs**.
- Compute the cost of inventory under the periodic LIFO method by allocating to the units on hand the **earliest costs**.
- Compute the cost of inventory under the periodic average cost method by allocating to the units on hand a **weighted-average cost**.

SOLUTION TO DEMONSTRATION PROBLEM 1

The cost of goods available for sale is $6,450, as follows.

Inventory:		200 units @ $4.00	$ 800
Purchases:			
	March 10	500 units @ $4.50	2,250
	March 20	400 units @ $4.75	1,900
	March 30	300 units @ $5.00	1,500
Total cost of goods available for sale			$6,450

Under a **periodic inventory system**, the cost of goods sold under each cost flow method is as follows.

FIFO Method

Ending inventory:

Date	Units	Unit Cost	Total Cost	
March 30	300	$5.00	$1,500	
March 20	200	4.75	950	$2,450

Cost of goods sold: $6,450 − $2,450 = $4,000

LIFO Method

Ending inventory:

Date	Units	Unit Cost	Total Cost	
March 1	200	$4.00	$ 800	
March 10	300	4.50	1,350	$2,150

Cost of goods sold: $6,450 − $2,150 = $4,300

Average Cost Method

Average unit cost: $6,450 ÷ 1,400 = $4.607
Ending inventory: 500 × $4.607 = $2,303.50

Cost of goods sold: $6,450 − $2,303.50 = $4,146.50

SUMMARY OF STUDY OBJECTIVES

1. **Describe the steps in determining inventory quantities.** The steps in determining inventory quantities are (1) taking a physical inventory of goods on hand and (2) determining the ownership of goods in transit.

2. **Explain the basis of accounting for inventories, and describe the inventory cost flow methods.** The primary basis of accounting for inventories is cost. Cost includes all expenditures necessary to acquire goods and to make them ready for sale. Inventoriable costs include (1) the cost of beginning inventory and (2) the cost of goods purchased. The inventory cost flow methods are: specific identification, FIFO, LIFO, and average cost.

3. **Explain the financial statement and tax effects of each of the inventory cost flow methods.** The cost of goods available for sale may be allocated to cost of goods sold and ending inventory by specific identification or by a method based on an assumed cost flow. These methods have different effects on financial statements during periods of changing prices. When prices are rising, FIFO results in lower cost of goods sold and higher net income than the average cost and the LIFO methods. LIFO results in the lowest income taxes (because of lower net income). In the balance sheet, FIFO results in an ending inventory that is closest to current value. The inventory under LIFO is the farthest from current value.

4. **Explain the lower of cost or market basis of accounting for inventories.** The lower of cost or market (LCM) basis is used when the current replacement cost (market) is less than cost. Under LCM, the loss is recognized in the period in which the price decline occurs.

5. **Indicate the effects of inventory errors on the financial statements.** In the income statement of the current year: (a) An error in beginning inventory will have a reverse effect on net income (overstatement of inventory results in understatement of net income); and (b) an error in ending inventory will have a similar effect on net income (overstatement of inventory results in overstatement of net income). If ending inventory errors are not corrected in the next period, their effect on net income for that period is reversed, and total net income for the two years will be correct. In the balance sheet, ending inventory errors will have the same effect on total assets and total owner's equity and no effect on liabilities.

6. **Compute and interpret inventory turnover.** Inventory turnover is calculated as cost of goods sold divided by average inventory. It can be converted to average days in inventory by dividing 365 days by the inventory turnover ratio. A higher turnover or lower average days in inventory suggests that management is trying to keep inventory levels low relative to sales.

GLOSSARY

Average cost method Inventory costing method that assumes that the goods available for sale have the same (average) cost per unit; generally the goods are identical. (p. 238).

Consigned goods Goods shipped by a consignor, who retains ownership, to another party called the consignee. (p. 232).

Current replacement cost The amount that would be paid at the present time to acquire an identical item. (p. 242).

First-in, first-out (FIFO) method Inventory costing method that assumes that the costs of the earliest goods acquired are the first to be recognized as cost of goods sold. (p. 236).

Inventoriable costs The pool of costs that consists of two elements: (1) the cost of the beginning inventory and (2) the cost of goods purchased during the period. (p. 233).

Inventory turnover A measure of the number of times on average the inventory is sold during the period; computed by dividing cost of goods sold by the average inventory during the period. (p. 245).

Last-in, first-out (LIFO) method Inventory costing method that assumes that the costs of the latest units purchased are the first to be allocated to cost of goods sold. (p. 237).

Lower of cost or market (LCM) basis Method of valuing inventory that recognizes the decline in the value when the current purchase price (market) is less than cost. (p. 242).

Periodic inventory system An inventory system in which inventoriable costs are allocated to ending inventory and cost of goods sold at the end of the period. Cost of goods sold is computed at the end of the period by subtracting the ending inventory (costs are assigned based on a physical count of items on hand) from the cost of goods available for sale. (p. 233).

Specific identification method An actual, physical flow inventory costing method in which items still in inventory are specifically costed to arrive at the total cost of the ending inventory. (p. 234).

APPENDIX 6A INVENTORY COST FLOW METHODS IN PERPETUAL INVENTORY SYSTEMS

Each of the inventory cost flow methods described in the chapter for a periodic inventory system can be used in a perpetual inventory system. To illustrate the application of the three assumed cost flow methods (FIFO, LIFO, and average cost), we will use the data shown below and in this chapter for Bow Valley Electronics' product Z202 Astro Condenser.

STUDY OBJECTIVE 7

Apply the inventory cost flow methods to perpetual inventory records.

Illustration 6A-1
Inventoriable units and costs

BOW VALLEY ELECTRONICS					
Z202 Astro Condensers					
Date	**Explanation**	**Units**	**Unit Cost**	**Total Cost**	**Balance in Units**
1/1	Beginning inventory	100	$10	$ 1,000	100
4/15	Purchases	200	11	2,200	300
8/24	Purchases	300	12	3,600	600
9/10	Sales	550			50
11/27	Purchases	400	13	5,200	450
				$12,000	

First-In, First-Out (FIFO)

Under FIFO, the cost of the earliest goods on hand prior to each sale is charged to cost of goods sold. The cost of goods sold on September 10 consists of the units on hand January 1 and the units purchased April 15 and August 24. The inventory on a FIFO method perpetual system is shown in Illustration 6A-2.

Date	Purchases		Sales	Balance	
January 1				(100 @ $10)	$1,000
April 15	(200 @ $11)	$2,200		(100 @ $10) (200 @ $11) }	$3,200
August 24	(300 @ $12)	$3,600		(100 @ $10) (200 @ $11) } (300 @ $12)	$6,800
September 10			(100 @ $10) (200 @ $11) (250 @ $12)	(50 @ $12)	$ 600
			$6,200		
November 27	(400 @ $13)	$5,200		(50 @ $12) (400 @ $13) }	**$5,800**

Illustration 6A-2
Perpetual system—FIFO

The ending inventory in this situation is $5,800. The cost of goods sold is $6,200 [(100 @ $10) + (200 @ $11) + (250 @ $12)].

The results under FIFO in a perpetual system are the **same as in a periodic system**. See Illustration 6-5 on page 236. There, similarly, the ending inventory is $5,800 and cost of goods sold is $6,200. Regardless of the system, the first costs in are the costs assigned to cost of goods sold.

Last-In, First-Out (LIFO)

Under the LIFO method using a perpetual system, the cost of the most recent purchase prior to sale is allocated to the units sold. The cost of the goods sold on September 10 consists of all the units from the August 24 and April 15 purchases and 50 of the units in beginning inventory. The ending inventory on a LIFO method is computed in Illustration 6A-3.

Date	Purchases		Sales	Balance	
January 1				(100 @ $10)	$1,000
April 15	(200 @ $11)	$2,200		(100 @ $10) (200 @ $11) }	$3,200
August 24	(300 @ $12)	$3,600		(100 @ $10) (200 @ $11) } (300 @ $12)	$6,800
September 10			(300 @ $12) (200 @ $11) (50 @ $10)	(50 @ $10)	$ 500
			$6,300		
November 27	(400 @ $13)	$5,200		(50 @ $10) (400 @ $13) }	**$5,700**

Illustration 6A-3
Perpetual system—LIFO

The use of LIFO in a perpetual system will usually produce cost allocations that differ from using LIFO in a periodic system. In a perpetual system, the latest units incurred **prior to each sale** are allocated to cost of goods sold. In contrast, in a periodic system, the latest units incurred **during the period** are allocated to cost of goods sold. Thus, when a purchase is made after the last sale, the LIFO periodic system will apply this purchase to the previous sale. See Illustration 6-10 on page 238. There, the proof shows the 400 units @ $13 purchased on November 27 applied to the sale of 550 units on September 10. As shown above under the LIFO perpetual system, the 400 units @ $13 purchased on November 27 are all applied to the ending inventory.

The ending inventory in this LIFO perpetual example is $5,700 and cost of goods sold is $6,300. Compare these amounts to the LIFO periodic illustration where the ending inventory is $5,000 and cost of goods sold is $7,000.

Average Cost

The average cost method in a perpetual inventory system is called the **moving-average method**. Under this method a new average is computed **after each purchase**. The average cost is computed by dividing the cost of goods available for sale by the units on hand. The average cost is then applied to: (1) the units sold, to determine the cost of goods sold, and (2) the remaining units on hand, to determine the ending inventory amount. The application of the average cost method by Bow Valley Electronics is shown in Illustration 6A-4.

Illustration 6A-4
Perpetual system—average cost method

Date	Purchases	Sales	Balance	
January 1			(100 @ $10)	$1,000
April 15	(200 @ $11) $2,200		(300 @ $10.667)	$3,200
August 24	(300 @ $12) $3,600		(600 @ $11.333)	$6,800
September 10		(550 @ $11.333)	(50 @ $11.333)	$ 567
		($6,233)		
November 27	(400 @ $13) $5,200		(450 @ $12.816)	$5,767

As indicated above, **a new average is computed each time a purchase is made**. On April 15, after 200 units are purchased for $2,200, a total of 300 units costing $3,200 ($1,000 + $2,200) are on hand. The average unit cost is $10.667 ($3,200 ÷ 300). On August 24, after 300 units are purchased for $3,600, a total of 600 units costing $6,800 ($1,000 + $2,200 + $3,600) are on hand at an average cost per unit of $11.333 ($6,800 ÷ 600). This unit cost of $11.333 is used in costing sales until another purchase is made, when a new unit cost is computed. Thus, the unit cost of the 550 units sold on September 10 is $11.333, and the total cost of goods sold is $6,233. On November 27, following the purchase of 400 units for $5,200, there are 450 units on hand costing $5,767 ($567 + $5,200), with a new average cost of $12.816 ($5,767 ÷ 450).

Compare this moving-average cost under the perpetual inventory system to Illustration 6-12 (on page 239) showing the average cost method under a periodic inventory system.

DEMONSTRATION PROBLEM 2

Demonstration Problem 1 on pages 246–247 showed cost of goods sold computations under a periodic inventory system. Now let's assume that Gerald D. Englehart Company uses a perpetual inventory system. The company has the same inventory, purchases, and sales data for the month of March as shown earlier.

Inventory:	March 1	200 units @ $4.00	$ 800
Purchases:	March 10	500 units @ $4.50	2,250
	March 20	400 units @ $4.75	1,900
	March 30	300 units @ $5.00	1,500
Sales:	March 15	500 units	
	March 25	400 units	

The physical inventory count on March 31 shows 500 units on hand.

Instructions

Under a **perpetual inventory system**, determine the cost of inventory on hand at March 31 and the cost of goods sold for March under the (a) first-in, first-out (FIFO) method, (b) last-in, first-out (LIFO) method, and (c) average cost method.

SOLUTION TO DEMONSTRATION PROBLEM 2

The cost of goods available for sale is $6,450, as follows.

Inventory:		200 units @ $4.00	$ 800
Purchases:	March 10	500 units @ $4.50	2,250
	March 20	400 units @ $4.75	1,900
	March 30	300 units @ $5.00	1,500
Total cost of goods available for sale			$6,450

Under a **perpetual inventory system**, the cost of goods sold under each cost flow method is as follows.

FIFO Method

Date	Purchases	Sales	Balance
March 1			(200 @ $4.00) $ 800
March 10	(500 @ $4.50) $2,250		(200 @ $4.00) ⎫ $3,050 (500 @ $4.50) ⎭
March 15		(200 @ $4.00) (300 @ $4.50) ⎱ $2,150	(200 @ $4.50) $ 900
March 20	(400 @ $4.75) $1,900		(200 @ $4.50) ⎫ $2,800 (400 @ $4.75) ⎭
March 25		(200 @ $4.50) (200 @ $4.75) ⎱ $1,850	(200 @ $4.75) $ 950
March 30	(300 @ $5.00) $1,500		(200 @ $4.75) ⎫ $2,450 (300 @ $5.00) ⎭

Ending inventory, $2,450   Cost of goods sold: $6,450 − $2,450 = $4,000

ACTION PLAN

- Compute the cost of goods sold under the perpetual FIFO method by allocating to the goods sold the **earliest** cost of goods purchased.
- Compute the cost of goods sold under the perpetual LIFO method by allocating to the goods sold the **latest** cost of goods purchased.
- Compute the cost of goods sold under the perpetual average cost method by allocating to the goods sold a **moving-average** cost.

LIFO Method

Date	Purchases	Sales	Balance
March 1			(200 @ $4.00) $ 800
March 10	(500 @ $4.50) $2,250		(200 @ $4.00) }$3,050 (500 @ $4.50)
March 15		(500 @ $4.50) $2,250	(200 @ $4.00) $ 800
March 20	(400 @ $4.75) $1,900		(200 @ $4.00) }$2,700 (400 @ $4.75)
March 25		(400 @ $4.75) $1,900	(200 @ $4.00) $ 800
March 30	(300 @ $5.00) $1,500		(200 @ $4.00) }$2,300 (300 @ $5.00)

Ending inventory, $2,300   Cost of goods sold: $6,450 − $2,300 = $4,150

Moving-Average Cost Method

Date	Purchases	Sales	Balance
March 1			(200 @ $ 4.00) $ 800
March 10	(500 @ $4.50) $2,250		(700 @ $4.357) $3,050
March 15		(500 @ $4.357) $2,179	(200 @ $4.357) $ 871
March 20	(400 @ $4.75) $1,900		(600 @ $4.618) $2,771
March 25		(400 @ $4.618) $1,847	(200 @ $4.618) $ 924
March 30	(300 @ $5.00) $1,500		(500 @ $4.848) $2,424

Ending inventory, $2,424   Cost of goods sold: $6,450 − $2,424 = $4,026

☑ THE NAVIGATOR

SUMMARY OF STUDY OBJECTIVE FOR APPENDIX 6A

7. Apply the inventory cost flow methods to perpetual inventory records. Under FIFO, the cost of the earliest goods on hand prior to each sale is charged to cost of goods sold. Under LIFO, the cost of the most recent purchase prior to sale is charged to cost of goods sold. Under the average cost method, a new average cost is computed after each purchase.

APPENDIX 6B ESTIMATING INVENTORIES

STUDY OBJECTIVE 8

Describe the two methods of estimating inventories.

We assumed in the chapter that a company would be able to physically count its inventory. But what if it cannot? What if the inventory were destroyed by fire, for example? In that case, we would use an estimate.

Two circumstances explain why inventories are sometimes estimated. First, management may want monthly or quarterly financial statements, but a physical inventory is taken only annually. Second, a casualty such as fire, flood, or earthquake may make it impossible to take a physical inventory. The need for estimating inventories is associated primarily with a periodic inventory system because of the absence of detailed inventory records.

There are two widely used methods of estimating inventories: (1) the gross profit method and (2) the retail inventory method.

Gross Profit Method

The **gross profit method** estimates the cost of ending inventory by applying a gross profit rate to net sales. It is used in preparing monthly financial statements under a periodic system. This method is relatively simple but effective. It will detect large errors. Accountants, auditors, and managers frequently use the gross profit method to test the reasonableness of the ending inventory amount.

To use this method, a company needs to know its net sales, cost of goods available for sale, and gross profit rate. With the gross profit rate, the company can estimate its gross profit for the period. The formulas for using the gross profit method are given in Illustration 6B-1.

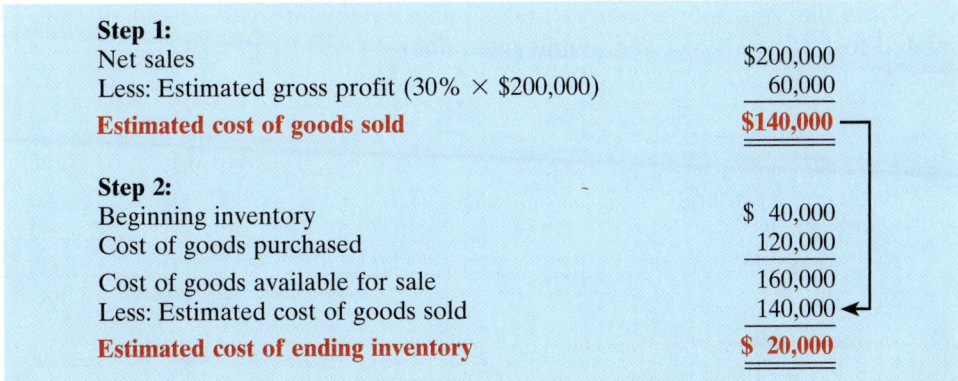

Illustration 6B-1
Gross profit method formulas

To illustrate, assume that Kishwaukee Company wishes to prepare an income statement for the month of January. Its records show net sales $200,000, beginning inventory $40,000, and cost of goods purchased $120,000. In the preceding year, the company realized a 30% gross profit rate. It expects to earn the same rate this year. Given these facts and assumptions, the estimated cost of the ending inventory at January 31 can be computed under the gross profit method as follows.

Step 1:	
Net sales	$200,000
Less: Estimated gross profit (30% × $200,000)	60,000
Estimated cost of goods sold	**$140,000**
Step 2:	
Beginning inventory	$ 40,000
Cost of goods purchased	120,000
Cost of goods available for sale	160,000
Less: Estimated cost of goods sold	140,000
Estimated cost of ending inventory	**$ 20,000**

Illustration 6B-2
Example of gross profit method

The gross profit method is based on the assumption that the gross profit rate will remain constant. But it may not remain constant, because of a change in merchandising policies or in market conditions. In such cases, the rate should be adjusted to reflect current operating conditions. In some cases, a more accurate estimate can be obtained by applying this method on a department or product-line basis.

The gross profit method should not be used in preparing a company's financial statements at the end of the year. These statements should be based on a physical inventory count.

Retail Inventory Method

A retail store such as **Kmart**, **Ace Hardware**, or **Wal-Mart** has thousands of different types of merchandise at low unit costs. In such cases it is difficult and time-consuming to apply unit costs to inventory quantities. An alternative is to use the **retail inventory method** to estimate the cost of inventory. In most retail concerns, a relationship between cost and sales price can be established. The cost-to-retail percentage is then applied to the ending inventory at retail prices to determine inventory at cost.

To use the retail inventory method, a company's records must show both the cost and retail value of the goods available for sale. The formulas for using the retail inventory method are presented in Illustration 6B-3.

Illustration 6B-3
Retail inventory method formulas

		Goods Available for Sale at Retail	−	Net Sales	=	Ending Inventory at Retail
Step 1:						

		Goods Available for Sale at Cost	÷	Goods Available for Sale at Retail	=	Cost-to-Retail Ratio
Step 2:						

		Ending Inventory at Retail	×	Cost-to-Retail Ratio	=	Estimated Cost of Ending Inventory
Step 3:						

The logic of the retail method can be demonstrated by using unit-cost data. Assume that 10 units purchased at $7 each are marked to sell for $10 per unit. Thus, the cost-to-retail ratio is 70% ($70 ÷ $100). If 4 units remain unsold, their retail value is $40 (4 × $10), and their cost is $28 ($40 × 70%). This amount agrees with the total cost of goods on hand on a per unit basis (4 × $7).

The application of the retail method for Valley West Co. is shown in Illustration 6B-4. Note that it is not necessary to take a physical inventory to determine the estimated cost of goods on hand at any given time.

Illustration 6B-4
Example of retail inventory method

	At Cost	At Retail
Beginning inventory	$14,000	$ 21,500
Goods purchased	61,000	78,500
Goods available for sale	$75,000	100,000
Net sales		70,000
(1) Ending inventory at retail		**$ 30,000**
(2) Cost-to-retail ratio = ($75,000 ÷ $100,000) = 75%		
(3) Estimated cost of ending inventory = ($30,000 × 75%)	**$22,500**	

The retail inventory method also facilitates taking a physical inventory at the end of the year. The goods on hand can be valued at the prices marked on the merchandise. The cost-to-retail ratio is then applied to the goods on hand at retail to determine the ending inventory at cost.

The major disadvantage of the retail method is that it is an averaging technique. It may produce an incorrect inventory valuation if the mix of the ending inventory is not representative of the mix in the goods available for sale. Assume, for example, that the cost-to-retail ratio of 75% for Valley West Co. consists of equal proportions of inventory items that have cost-to-retail ratios of 70%, 75%, and 80%. If the ending inventory contains only items with a 70% ratio, an incorrect inventory cost will result. This problem can be minimized by applying the retail method on a department or product-line basis.

SUMMARY OF STUDY OBJECTIVE FOR APPENDIX 6B

8. Describe the two methods of estimating inventories. The two methods of estimating inventories are the gross profit method and the retail inventory method. Under the gross profit method, a gross profit rate is applied to net sales to determine estimated cost of goods sold. Estimated cost of goods sold is then subtracted from cost of goods available for sale to determine the estimated cost of the ending inventory.

Under the retail inventory method, a cost-to-retail ratio is computed by dividing the cost of goods available for sale by the retail value of the goods available for sale. This ratio is then applied to the ending inventory at retail to determine the estimated cost of the ending inventory.

GLOSSARY FOR APPENDIX 6B

Gross profit method A method for estimating the cost of the ending inventory by applying a gross profit rate to net sales. (p. 252).

Retail inventory method A method used to estimate the cost of the ending inventory by applying a cost-to-retail ratio to the ending inventory at retail. (p. 254).

Note: All **asterisked Questions, Exercises, and Problems relate to material in the appendixes to the chapter.*

SELF-STUDY QUESTIONS

Self-Study/Self-Test

Answers are at the end of the chapter.

(SO 1) **1.** Which of the following should *not* be included in the physical inventory of a company?
  a. Goods held on consignment from another company.
  b. Goods shipped on consignment to another company.
  c. Goods in transit from another company shipped FOB shipping point.
  d. None of the above.

(SO 2) **2.** Inventoriable costs consist of two elements: beginning inventory and
  a. ending inventory.
  b. cost of goods purchased.
  c. cost of goods sold.
  d. cost of goods available for sale.

(SO 2) **3.** Tinker Bell Company has the following:

	Units	Unit Cost
Inventory, Jan. 1	8,000	$11
Purchase, June 19	13,000	12
Purchase, Nov. 8	5,000	13

If 9,000 units are on hand at December 31, the cost of the ending inventory under FIFO is:
  a. $99,000.   **c.** $113,000.
  b. $108,000.   **d.** $117,000.

(SO 2) **4.** Using the data in (3) above, the cost of the ending inventory under LIFO is:
  a. $113,000.   **c.** $99,000.
  b. $108,000.   **d.** $100,000.

(SO 3) **5.** In periods of rising prices, LIFO will produce:
  a. higher net income than FIFO.
  b. the same net income as FIFO.

  c. lower net income than FIFO.
  d. higher net income than average costing.

(SO 3) **6.** Factors that affect the selection of an inventory costing method do *not* include:
  a. tax effects.
  b. balance sheet effects.
  c. income statement effects.
  d. perpetual vs. periodic inventory system.

(SO 4) **7.** Rickety Company purchased 1,000 widgets and has 200 widgets in its ending inventory at a cost of $91 each and a current replacement cost of $80 each. The ending inventory under lower of cost or market is:
  a. $91,000.
  b. $80,000.
  c. $18,200.
  d. $16,000.

(SO 5) **8.** Atlantis Company's ending inventory is understated $4,000. The effects of this error on the current year's cost of goods sold and net income, respectively, are:
  a. understated, overstated.
  b. overstated, understated.
  c. overstated, overstated.
  d. understated, understated.

(SO 6) **9.** Which of these would cause the inventory turnover ratio to increase the most?
  a. Increasing the amount of inventory on hand.
  b. Keeping the amount of inventory on hand constant but increasing sales.
  c. Keeping the amount of inventory on hand constant but decreasing sales.
  d. Decreasing the amount of inventory on hand and increasing sales.

(SO 8)*10. Songbird Company has sales of $150,000 and cost of goods available for sale of $135,000. If the gross profit rate is 30%, the estimated cost of the ending inventory under the gross profit method is:
   a. $15,000.
   b. $30,000.
   c. $45,000.
   d. $75,000.

*11. In a perpetual inventory system,   (SO
   a. LIFO cost of goods sold will be the same as in a periodic inventory system.
   b. average costs are based entirely on unit cost averages.
   c. a new average is computed under the average cost method after each sale.
   d. FIFO cost of goods sold will be the same as in a periodic inventory system.

QUESTIONS

1. "The key to successful business operations is effective inventory management." Do you agree? Explain.

2. An item must possess two characteristics to be classified as inventory by a merchandiser. What are these two characteristics?

3. Your friend Art Mega has been hired to help take the physical inventory in Hawkeye Hardware Store. Explain to Art Mega what this job will entail.

4. (a) Hansen Company ships merchandise to Fox Company on December 30. The merchandise reaches the buyer on January 6. Indicate the terms of sale that will result in the goods being included in (1) Hansen's December 31 inventory, and (2) Fox's December 31 inventory.
   (b) Under what circumstances should Hansen Company include consigned goods in its inventory?

5. Topp Hat Shop received a shipment of hats for which it paid the wholesaler $2,970. The price of the hats was $3,000 but Topp was given a $30 cash discount and required to pay freight charges of $80. In addition, Topp paid $130 to cover the travel expenses of an employee who negotiated the purchase of the hats. What amount will Topp record for inventory? Why?

6. What is the primary basis of accounting for inventories? What is the major objective in accounting for inventories? What accounting principles are involved here?

7. Identify the distinguishing features of an income statement for a merchandiser.

8. Jason Bradley believes that the allocation of inventoriable costs should be based on the actual physical flow of the goods. Explain to Jason why this may be both impractical and inappropriate.

9. What is a major advantage and a major disadvantage of the specific identification method of inventory costing?

10. "The selection of an inventory cost flow method is a decision made by accountants." Do you agree? Explain. Once a method has been selected, what accounting requirement applies?

11. Which assumed inventory cost flow method:
   (a) usually parallels the actual physical flow of merchandise?
   (b) assumes that goods available for sale during an accounting period are identical?

   (c) assumes that the latest units purchased are the first to be sold?

12. In a period of rising prices, the inventory reported in Barto Company's balance sheet is close to the current cost of the inventory. Cecil Company's inventory is considerably below its current cost. Identify the inventory cost flow method being used by each company. Which company has probably been reporting the higher gross profit?

13. Olsen Company has been using the FIFO cost flow method during a prolonged period of rising prices. During the same time period, Olsen has been paying out all of its net income as dividends. What adverse effects may result from this policy?

14. Steve Kerns is studying for the next accounting mid-term examination. What should Steve know about (a) departing from the cost basis of accounting for inventories and (b) the meaning of "market" in the lower of cost or market method?

15. Steering Music Center has 5 CD players on hand at the balance sheet date. Each cost $400. The current replacement cost is $360 per unit. Under the lower of cost or market basis of accounting for inventories, what value should be reported for the CD players on the balance sheet? Why?

16. Maggie Stores has 20 toasters on hand at the balance sheet data. Each cost $28. The current replacement cost is $30 per unit. Under the lower of cost or market basis of accounting for inventories, what value should be reported for the toasters on the balnce sheet? Why?

17. Cohen Company discovers in 2005 that its ending inventory at December 31, 2004, was $7,000 understated. What effect will this error have on (a) 2004 net income, (b) 2005 net income, and (c) the combined net income for the 2 years?

18. Yin & Yang Company's balance sheet shows Inventories $162,800. What additional disclosures should be made?

19. Under what circumstances might inventory turnover be too high? That is, what possible negative consequences might occur?

*20. "When perpetual inventory records are kept, the results under the FIFO and LIFO methods are the same as they would be in a periodic inventory system." Do you agree? Explain.

*21. How does the average cost method of inventory costing differ between a perpetual inventory system and a periodic inventory system?

*22. When is it necessary to estimate inventories?

*23. Both the gross profit method and the retail inventory method are based on averages. For each method, indicate the average used, how it is determined, and how it is applied.

*24. Edmonds Company has net sales of $400,000 and cost of goods available for sale of $300,000. If the gross profit rate is 40%, what is the estimated cost of the ending inventory? Show computations.

*25. Park Shoe Shop had goods available for sale in 2005 with a retail price of $120,000. The cost of these goods was $84,000. If sales during the period were $90,000, what is the ending inventory at cost using the retail inventory method?

BRIEF EXERCISES

Identify items to be included in taking a physical inventory.
(SO 1)

BE6-1 Dayne Company identifies the following items for possible inclusion in the taking of a physical inventory. Indicate whether each item should be included or excluded from the inventory taking.

(a) Goods shipped on consignment by Dayne to another company.
(b) Goods in transit from a supplier shipped FOB destination.
(c) Goods sold but being held for customer pickup.
(d) Goods held on consignment from another company.

Identify the components of inventoriable costs.
(SO 2)

BE6-2 The ledger of Perez Company includes the following items: (a) Freight-in, (b) Purchase Returns and Allowances, (c) Purchases, (d) Sales Discounts, (e) Purchase Discounts. Identify which items are included in inventoriable costs.

Compute ending inventory using FIFO and LIFO.
(SO 2)

BE6-3 In its first month of operations, Rusch Company made three purchases of merchandise in the following sequence: (1) 300 units at $6, (2) 400 units at $7, and (3) 200 units at $8. Assuming there are 450 units on hand, compute the cost of the ending inventory under the (a) FIFO method and (b) LIFO method. Rusch uses a periodic inventory system.

Compute the ending inventory using average cost.
(SO 2)

BE6-4 Data for Rusch Company are presented in BE6-3. Compute the cost of the ending inventory under the average cost method, assuming there are 450 units on hand.

Explain the financial statement effect of inventory cost flow assumptions.
(SO 3)

BE6-5 The management of Muni Corp. is considering the effects of various inventory-costing methods on its financial statements and its income tax expense. Assuming that the price the company pays for inventory is increasing, which method will:

(a) provide the highest net income?
(b) provide the highest ending inventory?
(c) result in the lowest income tax expense?
(d) result in the most stable earnings over a number of years?

Explain the financial statement effect of inventory cost flow assumptions.
(SO 3)

BE6-6 In its first month of operation, Marquette Company purchased 100 units of inventory for $6, then 200 units for $7, and finally 150 units for $8. At the end of the month, 200 units remained. Compute the amount of phantom profit that would result if the company used FIFO rather than LIFO. Explain why this amount is referred to as phantom profit. The company uses the periodic method.

Determine the LCM valuation using inventory categories.
(SO 4)

BE6-7 Pena Appliance Center accumulates the following cost and market data at December 31.

Inventory Categories	Cost Data	Market Data
Cameras	$12,000	$12,100
Camcorders	9,000	9,700
VCRs	14,000	12,800

Compute the lower of cost or market valuation for the company's total inventory.

Determine correct income statement amounts.
(SO 5)

BE6-8 Farr Company reports net income of $90,000 in 2005. However, ending inventory was understated $5,000. What is the correct net income for 2005? What effect, if any, will this error have on total assets as reported in the balance sheet at December 31, 2005?

Compute inventory turnover and days in inventory.
(SO 6)

BE6-9 At December 31, 2005, the following information was available for J. Simon Company: ending inventory $40,000, beginning inventory $60,000, cost of goods sold $300,000, and sales revenue $380,000. Calculate inventory turnover and days in inventory for J. Simon Company.

Apply cost flow methods to perpetual inventory records.
(SO 7)

*****BE6-10** Abbott's Department Store uses a perpetual inventory system. Data for product E2-D2 include the following purchases.

Date	Number of Units	Unit Price
May 7	50	$10
July 28	30	13

On June 1 Abbott's sold 30 units, and on August 27, 35 more units. Prepare the perpetual inventory card for the above transactions using (1) FIFO, (2) LIFO, and (3) average cost.

Apply the gross profit method.
(SO 8)

*****BE6-11** At May 31, Stuart Company has net sales of $330,000 and cost of goods available for sale of $230,000. Compute the estimated cost of the ending inventory, assuming the gross profit rate is 40%.

Apply the retail inventory method.
(SO 8)

*****BE6-12** On June 30, Dusto Fabrics has the following data pertaining to the retail inventory method: Goods available for sale: at cost $35,000, at retail $50,000; net sales $42,000, and ending inventory at retail $8,000. Compute the estimated cost of the ending inventory using the retail inventory method.

EXERCISES

Determine the correct inventory amount.
(SO 1)

E6-1 Premier Bank and Trust is considering giving Alou Company a loan. Before doing so, they decide that further discussions with Alou's accountant may be desirable. One area of particular concern is the inventory account, which has a year-end balance of $297,000. Discussions with the accountant reveal the following.

1. Alou sold goods costing $38,000 to Comerica Company, FOB shipping point, on December 28. The goods are not expected to arrive at Comerica until January 12. The goods were not included in the physical inventory because they were not in the warehouse.
2. The physical count of the inventory did not include goods costing $95,000 that were shipped to Alou FOB destination on December 27 and were still in transit at year-end.
3. Alou received goods costing $17,000 on January 2. The goods were shipped FOB shipping point on December 26 by Galant Co. The goods were not included in the physical count.
4. Alou sold goods costing $35,000 to Emerick Co., FOB destination, on December 30. The goods were received at Emerick on January 8. They were not included in Alou's physical inventory.
5. Alou received goods costing $44,000 on January 2 that were shipped FOB destination on December 29. The shipment was a rush order that was supposed to arrive December 31. This purchase was included in the ending inventory of $297,000.

Instructions
Determine the correct inventory amount on December 31.

Determine the correct inventory amount.
(SO 1)

E6-2 Kale Thompson, an auditor with Sneed CPAs, is performing a review of Platinum Company's inventory account. Platinum did not have a good year and top management is under pressure to boost reported income. According to its records, the inventory balance at year-end was $740,000. However, the following information was not considered when determining that amount.

1. Included in the company's count were goods with a cost of $250,000 that the company is holding on consignment. The goods belong to Superior Corporation.
2. The physical count did not include goods purchased by Platinum with a cost of $40,000 that were shipped FOB destination on December 28 and did not arrive at Platinum's werehouse until January 3.
3. Included in the inventory account was $17,000 of office supplies that were stored in the warehouse and were to be used by the company's supervisors and managers during the coming year.
4. The company received an order on December 29 that was boxed and was sitting on the loading dock awaiting pick-up on December 31. The shipper picked up the goods on January 1

and delivered them on January 6. The shipping terms were FOB shipping point. The goods had a selling price of $40,000 and a cost of $30,000. The goods were not included in the count because they were sitting on the dock.

5. On December 29 Platinum shipped goods with a selling price of $80,000 and a cost of $60,000 to District Sales Corporation FOB shipping point. The goods arrived on January 3. District Sales had only ordered goods with a selling price of $10,000 and a cost of $8,000. However, a sales manager at Platinum had authorized the shipment and said that if District wanted to ship the goods back next week, it could.

6. Included in the count was $50,000 of goods that were parts for a machine that the company no longer made. Given the high-tech nature of Platinum's products, it was unlikely that these obsolete parts had any other use. However, management would prefer to keep them on the books at cost, "since that is what we paid for them, after all."

Instructions
Prepare a schedule to determine the correct inventory amount. Provide explanations for each item above, saying why you did or did not make an adjustment for each item.

E6-3 On December 1, Discount Electronics Ltd. has three DVD players left in stock. All are identical, all are priced to sell at $750. One of the three DVD players left in stock, with serial #1012, was purchased on June 1 at a cost of $500. Another, with serial #1045, was purchased on November 1 for $450. The last player, serial #1056, was purchased on November 30 for $400.

Calculate cost of goods sold using specific identification and FIFO.

(SO 2, 3)

Instructions
(a) Calculate the cost of goods sold using the FIFO periodic inventory method assuming that two of the three players were sold by the end of December, Discount Electronic's year-end.
(b) If Discount Electronics used the specific identification method instead of the FIFO method, how might it alter its earnings by "selectively choosing" which particular players to sell to the two customers? What would Discount's cost of goods sold be if the company wished to minimize earnings? Maximize earnings?
(c) Which inventory method do you recommend that Discount use? Explain why.

E6-4 Sherpers sells a snowboard, Xpert, that is popular with snowboard enthusiasts. Below is information relating to Sherpers's purchases of Xpert snowboards during September. During the same month, 124 Xpert snowboards were sold. Sherpers uses a periodic inventory system.

Compute inventory and cost of goods sold using FIFO and LIFO.

(SO 2)

Date	Explanation	Units	Unit Cost	Total Cost
Sept. 1	Inventory	26	$ 97	$ 2,522
Sept. 12	Purchases	45	102	4,590
Sept. 19	Purchases	20	104	2,080
Sept. 26	Purchases	50	105	5,250
	Totals	141		$14,442

Instructions
(a) Compute the ending inventory at September 30 using the FIFO and LIFO methods. Prove the amount allocated to cost of goods sold under each method.
(b) For both FIFO and LIFO, calculate the sum of ending inventory and cost of goods sold. What do you notice about the answers you found for each method?

E6-5 Zambia Co. uses a periodic inventory system. Its records show the following for the month of May, in which 70 units were sold.

Compute inventory and cost of goods sold using FIFO and LIFO.

(SO 2)

		Units	Unit Cost	Total Cost
May 1	Inventory	30	$ 8	$240
15	Purchases	25	11	275
24	Purchases	35	12	420
	Totals	90		$935

Instructions
Compute the ending inventory at May 31 using the FIFO and LIFO methods. Prove the amount allocated to cost of goods sold under each method.

Compute inventory and cost of goods sold using FIFO and LIFO.
(SO 2, 3)

E6-6 In June, Zambia Company reports the following for the month of June.

		Units	Unit Cost	Total Cost
June 1	Inventory	200	$5	$1,000
12	Purchase	300	6	1,800
23	Purchase	500	7	3,500
30	Inventory	160		

Instructions
(a) Compute the cost of the ending inventory and the cost of goods sold under (1) FIFO and (2) LIFO.
(b) Which costing method gives the higher ending inventory? Why?
(c) Which method results in the higher cost of goods sold? Why?

Compute inventory and cost of goods sold using average costs.
(SO 2, 3)

E6-7 Inventory data for Zambia Company are presented in E6-6.

Instructions
(a) Compute the cost of the ending inventory and the cost of goods sold using the average cost method.
(b) Will the results in (a) be higher or lower than the results under (1) FIFO and (2) LIFO?
(c) Why is the average unit cost not $6?

Determine ending inventory under lower of cost or market inventory method.
(SO 4)

E6-8 Kinshasa Camera Shop uses the lower of cost or market basis for its inventory. The following data are available at December 31.

Item	Units	Unit Cost	Market
Cameras:			
Minolta	5	$170	$156
Canon	6	150	152
Light Meters:			
Vivitar	12	125	110
Kodak	14	115	135

Instructions
Determine the amount of the ending inventory by applying the lower of cost or market basis.

Determine effects of inventory errors.
(SO 5)

E6-9 Delhi Hardware reported cost of goods sold as follows.

	2005	2006
Beginning inventory	$ 20,000	$ 30,000
Cost of goods purchased	150,000	175,000
Cost of goods available for sale	170,000	205,000
Ending inventory	30,000	35,000
Cost of goods sold	$140,000	$170,000

Delhi made two errors: (1) 2005 ending inventory was overstated $2,000, and (2) 2006 ending inventory was understated $6,000.

Instructions
Compute the correct cost of goods sold for each year.

Prepare correct income statements.
(SO 5)

E6-10 Horner Watch Company reported the following income statement data for a 2-year period.

	2005	2006
Sales	$210,000	$250,000
Cost of goods sold		
Beginning inventory	32,000	44,000
Cost of goods purchased	173,000	202,000
Cost of goods available for sale	205,000	246,000
Ending inventory	44,000	52,000
Cost of goods sold	161,000	194,000
Gross profit	$ 49,000	$ 56,000

Horner uses a periodic inventory system. The inventories at January 1, 2005, and December 31, 2006, are correct. However, the ending inventory at December 31, 2005, was overstated $3,000.

Instructions
(a) Prepare correct income statement data for the 2 years.
(b) What is the cumulative effect of the inventory error on total gross profit for the 2 years?
(c) ▭▬▭▶ Explain in a letter to the president of Horner Company what has happened—i.e., the nature of the error and its effect on the financial statements.

E6-11 This information is available for Tella's Photo Corporation for 2003, 2004, and 2005.

Compute inventory turnover, days in inventory, and gross profit rate.

(SO 6, 8)

	2003	2004	2005
Beginning inventory	$ 100,000	$ 300,000	$ 400,000
Ending inventory	300,000	400,000	480,000
Cost of goods sold	850,000	1,120,000	1,200,000
Sales	1,200,000	1,600,000	1,900,000

Instructions
Calculate inventory turnover, days in inventory, and gross profit rate (from Chapter 5) for Tella's Photo Corporation for 2003, 2004, 2005. Comment on any trends.

*E6-12 Simpson Appliance uses a perpetual inventory system. For its flat-screen television sets, the January 1 inventory was 3 sets at $600 each. On January 10, Alpine purchased 6 units at $660 each. The company sold 2 units on January 8 and 5 units on January 15.

Apply cost flow methods to perpetual records.

(SO 7)

Instructions
Compute the ending inventory under (1) FIFO, (2) LIFO, and (3) average cost.

*E6-13 Newport Company reports the following for the month of June.

Calculate inventory and cost of goods sold using three cost flow methods in a perpetual inventory system.

(SO 7)

Date	Explanation	Units	Unit Cost	Total Cost
June 1	Inventory	200	$5	$1,000
12	Purchase	300	6	1,800
23	Purchase	500	7	3,500
30	Inventory	160		

Instructions
(a) Calculate the cost of the ending inventory and the cost of goods sold for each cost flow assumption, using a perpetual inventory system. Assume a sale of 400 units occurred on June 15 for a selling price of $8 and a sale of 440 units on June 27 for $9.
(b) How do the results differ from E6-6 and E6-7?
(c) Why is the average unit cost not $6 [($5 + $6 + $7) ÷ 3 = $6]?

*E6-14 Information about Sherpers is presented in E6-4. Additional data regarding Sherpers's sales of Xpert snowboards are provided below. Assume that Sherpers uses a perpetual inventory system.

Apply cost flow methods to perpetual records.

(SO 7)

Date		Units	Unit Price	Total Cost
Sept. 5	Sale	12	$199	$ 2,388
Sept. 16	Sale	50	199	9,950
Sept. 29	Sale	62	209	12,958
	Totals	124		$25,296

Instructions
(a) Compute ending inventory at September 30 using FIFO, LIFO, and average cost.
(b) Compare ending inventory using a perpetual inventory system to ending inventory using a periodic inventory system (from E6-4).
(c) Which inventory cost flow method (FIFO, LIFO) gives the same ending inventory value under both periodic and perpetual? Which method gives different ending inventory values?

Determine merchandise lost using the gross profit method of estimating inventory.

(SO 8)

*E6-15 The inventory of Lemon Company was destroyed by fire on March 1. From an examination of the accounting records, the following data for the first 2 months of the year are obtained: Sales $51,000, Sales Returns and Allowances $1,000, Purchases $31,200, Freight-in $1,200, and Purchase Returns and Allowances $1,400.

Instructions

Determine the merchandise lost by fire, assuming:

(a) A beginning inventory of $20,000 and a gross profit rate of 30% on net sales.

(b) A beginning inventory of $30,000 and a gross profit rate of 25% on net sales.

Determine ending inventory at cost using retail method.

(SO 8)

*E6-16 Peacock Shoe Store uses the retail inventory method for its two departments, Women's Shoes and Men's Shoes. The following information for each department is obtained.

Item	Women's Department	Men's Department
Beginning inventory at cost	$ 32,000	$ 45,000
Cost of goods purchased at cost	148,000	137,300
Net sales	177,000	185,000
Beginning inventory at retail	45,000	60,000
Cost of goods purchased at retail	179,000	185,000

Instructions

Compute the estimated cost of the ending inventory for each department under the retail inventory method.

PROBLEMS: SET A

Determine items and amounts to be recorded in inventory.

(SO 1)

Peachtree

P6-1A Kananaskis Country Limited is trying to determine the value of its ending inventory as of February 28, 2004, the company's year-end. The following transactions occurred, and the accountant asked your help in determining whether they should be recorded or not.

(a) On February 26, Kananaskis shipped goods costing $800 to a customer and charged the customer $1,000. The goods were shipped with terms FOB destination and the receiving report indicates that the customer received the goods on March 2.

(b) On February 26, Seller Inc. shipped goods to Kananaskis under terms FOB shipping point. The invoice price was $350 plus $25 for freight. The receiving report indicates that the goods were received by Kananaskis on March 2.

(c) Kananaskis had $500 of inventory isolated in the warehouse. The inventory is designated for a customer who has requested that the goods be shipped on March 10.

(d) Also included in Kananaskis' warehouse is $400 of inventory that Craft Producers shipped to Kananaskis on consignment.

(e) On February 26, Kananaskis issued a purchase order to acquire goods costing $750. The goods were shipped with terms FOB destination on February 27. Kananaskis received the goods on March 2.

(f) On February 26, Kananaskis shipped goods to a customer under terms FOB shipping point. The invoice price was $350 plus $25 for freight; the cost of the items was $280. The receiving report indicates that the goods were received by the customer on March 2.

Instructions

For each of the above transactions, specify whether the item in question should be included in ending inventory, and if so, at what amount.

Determine cost of goods sold and ending inventory using FIFO, LIFO, and average cost with analysis.

(SO 2, 3)

P6-2A Breathless Distribution markets CDs of the performing artist Christina Spears. At the beginning of October, Breathless had in beginning inventory 1,000 Spears CDs with a unit cost of $5. During October Breathless made the following purchases of Spears CDs.

Oct. 3	3,500 @ $6	Oct. 19	2,000 @ $8
Oct. 9	4,000 @ $7	Oct. 25	2,000 @ $9

During October 10,000 units were sold. Breathless uses a periodic inventory system.

Instructions

(a) Determine the cost of goods available for sale.

(b) Determine (1) the ending inventory and (2) the cost of goods sold under each of the assumed cost flow methods (FIFO, LIFO, and average cost). Prove the accuracy of the cost of goods sold under the FIFO and LIFO methods.

(c) Which cost flow method results in (1) the highest inventory amount for the balance sheet and (2) the highest cost of goods sold for the income statement?

(b)(2) Cost of goods sold:
FIFO $66,000
LIFO $74,000
Average $70,400

P6-3A Milokimball Company had a beginning inventory on January 1 of 100 units of Product WD-44 at a cost of $21 per unit. During the year, the following purchases were made.

Determine cost of goods sold and ending inventory, using FIFO, LIFO, and average cost with analysis.
(SO 2, 3)

Mar. 15	300 units at $24	Sept. 4	300 units at $28
July 20	200 units at $25	Dec. 2	100 units at $30

700 units were sold. Milokimball Company uses a periodic inventory system.

Instructions

(a) Determine the cost of goods available for sale.

(b) Determine (1) the ending inventory, and (2) the cost of goods sold under each of the assumed cost flow methods (FIFO, LIFO, and average cost). Prove the accuracy of the cost of goods sold under the FIFO and LIFO methods.

(c) Which cost flow method results in (1) the highest inventory amount for the balance sheet, and (2) the highest cost of goods sold for the income statement?

(b)(2) Cost of goods sold:
FIFO $17,100
LIFO $18,800
Average $17,990

P6-4A The management of Red Robin Inc. is reevaluating the appropriateness of using its present inventory cost flow method, which is average cost. The company requests your help in determining the results of operations for 2005 if either the FIFO or the LIFO method had been used. For 2005 the accounting records show these data:

Compute ending inventory, prepare income statements, and answer questions using FIFO and LIFO.
(SO 2, 3)

Inventories		Purchases and Sales	
Beginning (10,000 units)	$22,800	Total net sales (225,000 units)	$865,000
Ending (15,000 units)		Total cost of goods purchased	
		(230,000 units)	578,500

Purchases were made quarterly as follows.

Quarter	Units	Unit Cost	Total Cost
1	60,000	$2.30	$138,000
2	50,000	2.50	125,000
3	50,000	2.60	130,000
4	70,000	2.65	185,500
	230,000		$578,500

Operating expenses were $147,000, and the company's income tax rate is 32%.

Instructions

(a) Prepare comparative condensed income statements for 2005 under FIFO and LIFO. (Show computations of ending inventory.)

(b) ▭▭▭▭▷ Answer the following questions for management in business-letter form.

(1) Which cost flow method (FIFO or LIFO) produces the more meaningful inventory amount for the balance sheet? Why?

(2) Which cost flow method (FIFO or LIFO) produces the more meaningful net income? Why?

(3) Which cost flow method (FIFO or LIFO) is more likely to approximate the actual physical flow of goods? Why?

(4) How much more cash will be available for management under LIFO than under FIFO? Why?

(5) Will gross profit under the average cost method be higher or lower than FIFO? Than LIFO? (*Note*: It is not necessary to quantify your answer.)

(a) Gross profit:
FIFO $303,450
LIFO $298,000

P6-5A You are provided with the following information for Danielle Inc. for the month ended June 30, 2005. Danielle uses the periodic method for inventory.

Date	Description	Quantity	Unit Cost or Selling Price
June 1	Beginning inventory	25	$60
June 4	Purchase	85	64
June 10	Sale	70	90
June 11	Sale return	10	90
June 18	Purchase	35	68
June 18	Purchase return	5	68
June 25	Sale	50	95
June 28	Purchase	20	72

Instructions

(a) Calculate (i) ending inventory, (ii) cost of goods sold, (iii) gross profit, and (iv) gross profit rate under each of the following methods.
   (1) LIFO.   **(2)** FIFO.   **(3)** Average cost.
(b) Compare results for the three cost flow assumptions.

P6-6A You are provided with the following information for Gas Guzzlers. Gas Guzzlers uses the periodic method of accounting for its inventory transactions.

March 1   Beginning inventory 1,500 litres at a cost of 40¢ per litre.
March 3   Purchased 2,000 litres at a cost of 45¢ per litre.
March 5   Sold 1,800 litres for 60¢ per litre.
March 10 Purchased 3,500 litres at a cost of 49¢ per litre.
March 20 Purchased 2,000 litres at a cost of 55¢ per litre.
March 30 Sold 5,000 litres for 70¢ per litre.

Instructions

(a) Prepare partial income statements through gross profit, and calculate the value of ending inventory that would be reported on the balance sheet, under each of the following cost flow assumptions.

   (1) Specific identification method assuming:
      (i) the March 5 sale consisted of 900 litres from the March 1 beginning inventory and 900 litres from the March 3 purchase; and
      (ii) the March 30 sale consisted of the following number of units sold from each purchase: 400 litres from March 1; 500 litres from March 3; 2,600 litres from March 10; 1,500 litres from March 20.

   (2) FIFO.
   (3) LIFO.
(b) How can companies use a cost flow method to justify price increases? Which cost flow method would best support an argument to increase prices?

P6-7A The management of Creek Co. asks your help in determining the comparative effects of the FIFO and LIFO inventory cost flow methods. For 2005, the accounting records show the following data.

Inventory, January 1 (10,000 units)	$ 37,000
Cost of 110,000 units purchased	479,000
Selling price of 95,000 units sold	665,000
Operating expenses	120,000

Units purchased consisted of 40,000 units at $4.20 on May 10; 50,000 units at $4.40 on August 15; and 20,000 units at $4.55 on November 20. Income taxes are 30%.

Instructions

(a) Prepare comparative condensed income statements for 2005 under FIFO and LIFO. (Show computations of ending inventory.)
(b) ▭▭▭▷ Answer the following questions for management in the form of a business letter.
   (1) Which inventory cost flow method produces the most meaningful inventory amount for the balance sheet? Why?

(2) Which inventory cost flow method produces the most meaningful net income? Why?

(3) Which inventory cost flow method is most likely to approximate actual physical flow of the goods? Why?

(4) How much additional cash will be available for management under LIFO than under FIFO? Why?

(5) How much of the gross profit under FIFO is illusory in comparison with the gross profit under LIFO?

*P6-8A Matthew Inc. is a retailer operating in Dartmouth, Nova Scotia. Matthew uses the perpetual inventory method. All sales returns from customers result in the goods being returned to inventory; the inventory is not damaged. Assume that there are no credit transactions; all amounts are settled in cash. You are provided with the following information for Matthew Inc. for the month of January 2005.

Calculate cost of goods sold and ending inventory under LIFO, FIFO, and average cost under the perpetual system; compare gross profit under each assumption.

(SO 3, 7)

Date	Description	Quantity	Unit Cost or Selling Price
January 1	Beginning inventory	50	$12
January 5	Purchase	100	14
January 8	Sale	80	25
January 10	Sale return	10	25
January 15	Purchase	30	18
January 16	Purchase return	5	18
January 20	Sale	90	25
January 25	Purchase	10	20

Instructions

(a) For each of the following cost flow assumptions, calculate (i) cost of goods sold, (ii) ending inventory, and (iii) gross profit.

  (1) LIFO.   **(2)** FIFO.   **(3)** Moving average cost.

(b) Compare results for the three cost flow assumptions.

Gross profit:
LIFO $1,730
FIFO $1,820
Average $1,767

*P6-9A Ramos Co. began operations on July 1. It uses a perpetual inventory system. During July the company had the following purchases and sales.

Determine ending inventory under a perpetual inventory system.

(SO 7)

	Purchases		
Date	Units	Unit Cost	Sales Units
July 1	4	$ 90	
July 6			3
July 11	5	$ 99	
July 14			2
July 21	3	$106	
July 27			3

Instructions

(a) Determine the ending inventory under a perpetual inventory system using (1) FIFO, (2) average cost, and (3) LIFO.

(b) Which costing method produces the highest ending inventory valuation?

(a) Ending inventory
FIFO $417
Avg. $405
LIFO $387

*P6-10A Virginia Company lost all of its inventory in a fire on December 26, 2005. The accounting records showed the following gross profit data for November and December.

Compute gross profit rate and inventory loss using gross profit method.

(SO 8)

	November	December (to 12/26)
Net sales	$500,000	$400,000
Beginning inventory	34,100	31,100
Purchases	319,975	236,000
Purchase returns and allowances	11,800	5,000
Purchase discounts	7,577	6,000
Freight-in	6,402	3,700
Ending inventory	31,100	?

Virginia is fully insured for fire losses but must prepare a report for the insurance company.

Instructions
(a) Compute the gross profit rate for November.
(b) Using the gross profit rate for November, determine the estimated cost of the inventory lost in the fire.

Compute ending inventory using retail method.

(SO 8)

***P6-11A** Hooked on Books uses the retail inventory method to estimate its monthly ending inventories. The following information is available for two of its departments at October 31, 2005.

	Hardcovers		**Paperbacks**	
	Cost	**Retail**	**Cost**	**Retail**
Beginning inventory	$ 256,000	$ 400,000	$ 65,000	$ 90,000
Purchases	1,180,000	1,825,000	266,000	380,000
Freight-in	4,000		2,000	
Purchase discounts	16,000		4,000	
Net sales		1,820,000		368,000

At December 31, Hooked on Books takes a physical inventory at retail. The actual retail values of the inventories in each department are Hardcovers $400,000 and Paperbacks $88,000.

Instructions
(a) Determine the estimated cost of the ending inventory for each department at **October 31**, 2005, using the retail inventory method.
(b) Compute the ending inventory at cost for each department at **December 31**, assuming the cost-to-retail ratios for the year are 65% for hardcovers and 70% for paperbacks.

PROBLEMS: SET B

Determine items and amounts to be recorded in inventory.

(SO 1)

P6-1B Banff Limited is trying to determine the value of its ending inventory at February 28, 2005, the company's year end. The accountant counted everything that was in the warehouse as of February 28, which resulted in an ending inventory valuation of $48,000. However, she didn't know how to treat the following transactions so she didn't record them.
(a) On February 26, Banff shipped to a customer goods costing $800. The goods were shipped FOB shipping point, and the receiving report indicates that the customer received the goods on March 2.
(b) On February 26, Seller Inc. shipped goods to Banff FOB destination. The invoice price was $350. The receiving report indicates that the goods were received by Banff on March 2.
(c) Banff had $500 of inventory at a customer's warehouse "on approval." The customer was going to let Banff know whether it wanted the merchandise by the end of the week, March 4.
(d) Banff also had $400 of inventory at a Jasper craft shop, on consignment from Banff.
(e) On February 26, Banff ordered goods costing $750. The goods were shipped FOB shipping point on February 27. Banff received the goods on March 1.
(f) On February 28, Banff packaged goods and had them ready for shipping to a customer FOB destination. The invoice price was $350; the cost of the items was $280. The receiving report indicates that the goods were received by the customer on March 2.
(g) Banff had damaged goods set aside in the warehouse because they are no longer saleable. These goods originally cost $400 and, originally, Banff expected to sell these items for $600.

Instructions
For each of the above transactions, specify whether the item in question should be included in ending inventory, and if so, at what amount. For each item that is not included in ending inventory, indicate who owns it and what account, if any, it should have been recorded in.

Determine cost of goods sold and ending inventory using FIFO, LIFO, and average cost with analysis.

(SO 2, 3)

P6-2B Doom's Day Distribution markets CDs of the performing artist Harrilyn Hannson. At the beginning of March, Doom's Day had in beginning inventory 1,500 Hannson CDs with a unit cost of $7. During March Doom's Day made the following purchases of Hannson CDs.

March 5	3,000 @ $8	March 21	4,000 @ $10
March 13	5,500 @ $9	March 26	2,000 @ $11

During March 13,500 units were sold. Doom's Day uses a periodic inventory system.

Instructions

(a) Determine the cost of goods available for sale.

(b) Determine (1) the ending inventory and (2) the cost of goods sold under each of the assumed cost flow methods (FIFO, LIFO, and average cost). Prove the accuracy of the cost of goods sold under the FIFO and LIFO methods.

(c) Which cost flow method results in (1) the highest inventory amount for the balance sheet and (2) the highest cost of goods sold for the income statement?

(b)(2) Cost of goods sold:
   FIFO $119,000
   LIFO $127,500
   Average $123,187

P6-3B Collins Company had a beginning inventory of 400 units of Product E2-D2 at a cost of $8.00 per unit. During the year, purchases were:

Determine cost of goods sold and ending inventory, using FIFO, LIFO, and average cost with analysis.

(SO 2, 3)

| Feb. 20 | 600 units at $9.00 | Aug. 12 | 300 units at $11.00 |
| May 5 | 500 units at $10.00 | Dec. 8 | 200 units at $12.00 |

Collins Company uses a periodic inventory system. Sales totaled 1,400 units.

Instructions

(a) Determine the cost of goods available for sale.

(b) Determine (1) the ending inventory, and (2) the cost of goods sold under each of the assumed cost flow methods (FIFO, LIFO, and average). Prove the accuracy of the cost of goods sold under the FIFO and LIFO methods.

(c) Which cost flow method results in (1) the lowest inventory amount for the balance sheet, and (2) the lowest cost of goods sold for the income statement?

(b) Cost of goods sold:
   FIFO $12,600
   LIFO $14,300
   Average $13,510

P6-4B The management of Gilbert Co. is reevaluating the appropriateness of using its present inventory cost flow method, which is average cost. They request your help in determining the results of operations for 2005 if either the FIFO method or the LIFO method had been used. For 2005, the accounting records show the following data.

Compute ending inventory, prepare income statements, and answer questions using FIFO and LIFO.

(SO 2, 3)

Inventories		Purchases and Sales	
Beginning (15,000 units)	$32,000	Total net sales (225,000 units)	$865,000
Ending (20,000 units)		Total cost of goods purchased	
		(230,000 units)	595,000

Purchases were made quarterly as follows.

Quarter	Units	Unit Cost	Total Cost
1	60,000	$2.40	$144,000
2	50,000	2.50	125,000
3	50,000	2.60	130,000
4	70,000	2.80	196,000
	230,000		$595,000

Operating expenses were $147,000, and the company's income tax rate is 34%.

Instructions

(a) Prepare comparative condensed income statements for 2005 under FIFO and LIFO. (Show computations of ending inventory.)

(b) ▭▭▭▷ Answer the following questions for management in the form of a business letter.

  (1) Which cost flow method (FIFO or LIFO) produces the more meaningful inventory amount for the balance sheet? Why?

  (2) Which cost flow method (FIFO or LIFO) produces the more meaningful net income? Why?

  (3) Which cost flow method (FIFO or LIFO) is more likely to approximate actual physical flow of the goods? Why?

  (4) How much additional cash will be available for management under LIFO than under FIFO? Why?

  (5) Will gross profit under the average cost method be higher or lower than (a) FIFO and (b) LIFO? (*Note*: It is not necessary to quantify your answer.)

(a) Net income
   FIFO $97,020
   LIFO $89,100
(b) (4) $4,080

Calculate ending inventory, cost of goods sold, gross profit, and gross profit rate under periodic method; compare results.

(SO 2, 3)

P6-5B You are provided with the following information for Lahti Inc. for the month ended October 31, 2005. Lahti uses a periodic method for inventory.

Date	Description	Units	Unit Cost or Selling Price
October 1	Beginning inventory	60	$25
October 9	Purchase	120	26
October 11	Sale	100	35
October 17	Purchase	70	27
October 22	Sale	60	40
October 25	Purchase	80	28
October 29	Sale	150	40

Instructions
(a) Calculate (i) ending inventory, (ii) cost of goods sold, (iii) gross profit, and (iv) gross profit rate under each of the following methods.
(1) LIFO.
(2) FIFO.
(3) Average cost.
(b) Compare results for the three cost flow assumptions.

(a)(iii) Gross profit:
LIFO $3,650
FIFO $3,710
Average $3,680

Compare specific identification and FIFO under periodic method; use cost flow assumption to influence earnings.

(SO 2, 3)

P6-6B You have the following information for Discount Diamonds. Discount Diamonds uses the periodic method of accounting for its inventory transactions. Discount only carries one brand and size of diamonds—all are identical. Each batch of diamonds purchased is carefully coded and marked with its purchase cost.

March 1 Beginning inventory 150 diamonds at a cost of $300 per diamond.
March 3 Purchased 200 diamonds at a cost of $350 each.
March 5 Sold 180 diamonds for $600 each.
March 10 Purchased 350 diamonds at a cost of $375 each.
March 25 Sold 500 diamonds for $650 each.

Instructions
(a) Assume that Discount Diamonds uses the specific identification cost flow method.
(1) Demonstrate how Discount Diamonds could maximize its gross profit for the month by specifically selecting which diamonds to sell on March 5 and March 25.
(2) Demonstrate how Discount Diamonds could minimize its gross profit for the month by selecting which diamonds to sell on March 5 and March 25.
(b) Assume that Discount Diamonds uses the FIFO cost flow assumption. Calculate cost of goods sold. How much gross profit would Discount Diamonds report under this cost flow assumption?
(c) Assume that Discount Diamonds uses the LIFO cost flow assumption. Calculate cost of goods sold. How much gross profit would the company report under this cost flow assumption?
(d) Which cost flow method should Discount Diamonds select? Explain.

(a) Gross profit:
(1) Maximum $194,250
(2) Minimum $192,750

Compute ending inventory, prepare income statements, and answer questions using FIFO and LIFO.

(SO 2, 3)

P6-7B The management of Zwick Inc. asks your help in determining the comparative effects of the FIFO and LIFO inventory cost flow methods. For 2005 the accounting records show these data.

Inventory, January 1 (10,000 units)	$ 35,000
Cost of 120,000 units purchased	504,500
Selling price of 95,000 units sold	665,000
Operating expenses	120,000

Units purchased consisted of 35,000 units at $4.00 on May 10; 60,000 units at $4.20 on August 15; and 25,000 units at $4.50 on November 20. Income taxes are 28%.

Gross profit:
FIFO $280,000
LIFO $260,500

Instructions
(a) Prepare comparative condensed income statements for 2005 under FIFO and LIFO. (Show computations of ending inventory.)
(b) ▭▭▭▷ Answer the following questions for management in the form of a business letter.
(1) Which inventory cost flow method produces the most meaningful inventory amount for the balance sheet? Why?

(2) Which inventory cost flow method produces the most meaningful net income? Why?

(3) Which inventory cost flow method is most likely to approximate the actual physical flow of the goods? Why?

(4) How much more cash will be available for management under LIFO than under FIFO? Why?

(5) How much of the gross profit under FIFO is illusionary in comparison with the gross profit under LIFO?

*P6-8B Yuan Li Ltd. is a retailer operating in Edmonton, Alberta. Yuan Li uses the perpetual inventory method. All sales returns from customers result in the goods being returned to inventory; the inventory is not damaged. Assume that there are no credit transactions; all amounts are settled in cash. You are provided with the following information for Yuan Li Ltd. for the month of January 2005.

Calculate cost of goods sold and ending inventory for FIFO, average cost, and LIFO under the perpetual system; compare gross profit under each assumption.

(SO 7)

Date	Description	Quantity	Unit Cost or Selling Price
December 31	Ending inventory	150	$17
January 2	Purchase	100	21
January 6	Sale	150	40
January 9	Sale return	10	40
January 9	Purchase	75	24
January 10	Purchase return	15	24
January 10	Sale	50	45
January 23	Purchase	100	28
January 30	Sale	160	50

Instructions

(a) For each of the following cost flow assumptions, calculate (i) cost of goods sold, (ii) ending inventory, and (iii) gross profit.

    (1) LIFO.   **(2)** FIFO.   **(3)** Moving average cost.

(b) Compare results for the three cost flow assumptions.

Gross profit:
LIFO $7,980
FIFO $8,640
Average $8,395

*P6-9B Lemansky Appliance Mart began operations on May 1. It uses a perpetual inventory system. During May the company had the following purchases and sales for its Model 25 Sureshot camera.

Determine ending inventory under a perpetual inventory system.

(SO 7)

Date	Purchases Units	Purchases Unit Cost	Sales Units
May 1	7	$150	
4			4
8	8	$170	
12			5
15	6	$185	
20			3
25			5

Instructions

(a) Determine the ending inventory under a perpetual inventory system using (1) FIFO, (2) average cost, and (3) LIFO.

(b) Which costing method produces (1) the highest ending inventory valuation and (2) the lowest ending inventory valuation?

(a) FIFO $740
Average $699
LIFO $620

*P6-10B Levi Johnson Company lost 70% of its inventory in a fire on March 25, 2005. The accounting records showed the following gross profit data for February and March.

Estimate inventory loss using gross profit method.

(SO 8)

	February	March (to 3/25)
Net sales	$300,000	$260,000
Net purchases	197,800	191,000
Freight-in	2,900	4,000
Beginning inventory	4,500	25,200
Ending inventory	25,200	?

Levi Johnson Company is fully insured for fire losses but must prepare a report for the insurance company.

Instructions

(a) Compute the gross profit rate for the month of February.

(b) Using the gross profit rate for February, determine both the estimated total inventory and inventory lost in the fire in March.

Compute ending inventory and cost of inventory lost using retail method.

(SO 8)

*P6-11B Thai Department Store uses the retail inventory method to estimate its monthly ending inventories. The following information is available for two of its departments at August 31, 2005.

	Sporting Goods		Jewelry and Cosmetics	
	Cost	Retail	Cost	Retail
Net sales		$1,010,000		$1,150,000
Purchases	$675,000	1,066,000	$741,000	1,158,000
Purchase returns	(26,000)	(40,000)	(12,000)	(20,000)
Purchase discounts	(12,360)	—	(2,440)	—
Freight-in	9,000	—	14,000	—
Beginning inventory	47,360	74,000	39,440	62,000

At December 31, Thai Department Store takes a physical inventory at retail. The actual retail values of the inventories in each department are Sporting Goods $85,000, and Jewelry and Cosmetics $54,000.

Instructions

(a) Determine the estimated cost of the ending inventory for each department on **August 31**, 2005, using the retail inventory method.

(b) Compute the ending inventory at cost for each department at **December 31**, assuming the cost-to-retail ratios are 60% for Sporting Goods and 64% for Jewelry and Cosmetics.

BROADENING YOUR PERSPECTIVE

Financial Reporting and Analysis

■ **FINANCIAL REPORTING PROBLEM: PepsiCo**

BYP6-1 The notes that accompany a company's financial statements provide informative details that would clutter the amounts and descriptions presented in the statements. Refer to the financial statements of **PepsiCo, Inc.** and the Notes to Consolidated Financial Statements in Appendix A.

Instructions

Answer the following questions. Complete the requirements in millions of dollars, as shown in PepsiCo's annual report.

(a) What did PepsiCo report for the amount of inventories in its Consolidated Balance Sheet at December 28, 2002? At December 29, 2001?

(b) Compute the dollar amount of change and the percentage change in inventories between 2001 and 2002. Compute inventory as a percentage of current assets at December, 28, 2002.

(c) How does PepsiCo value its inventories? Which inventory cost flow method does PepsiCo use? (See Notes to the Financial Statements.)

(d) What is the cost of sales (cost of goods sold) reported by PepsiCo for 2002, 2001, and 2000? Compute the percentage of cost of sales to net sales in 2002.

■ **COMPARATIVE ANALYSIS PROBLEM: PepsiCo vs. Coca-Cola**

BYP6-2 **PepsiCo**'s financial statements are presented in Appendix A. **Coca-Cola**'s financial statements are presented in Appendix B.

Instructions

(a) Based on the information contained in these financial statements, compute the following 2002 ratios for each company.

(1) Inventory turnover ratio

(2) Average days to sell inventory

(b) What conclusions concerning the management of the inventory can be drawn from these data?

■ INTERPRETING FINANCIAL STATEMENTS: A Global Focus

BYP6-3 Fuji Photo Film Co., Ltd. is a Japanese manufacturer of photographic products. Its U.S. counterpart, and arch rival, is **Eastman Kodak Company**. Together the two dominate the global market for film. The information below and on the next page was extracted from the financial statements of the two companies.

FUJI PHOTO FILM CO., LTD.
Notes to the Financial Statements

Summary of significant accounting policies

The Company and its domestic subsidiaries maintain their records and prepare their financial statements in accordance with accounting practices generally accepted in Japan. Certain reclassifications and adjustments have been incorporated in the consolidated financial statements to conform them to accounting principles generally accepted in the United States of America.

Inventories

Inventories are valued at the lower of cost or market with cost being determined principally by the moving-average method.

Note 6. Inventories

Inventories at March 31, 2002 and 2001, consisted of the following:

	(millions of yen)		(thousands of U.S. dollars)
	2002	**2001**	**2002**
Finished goods	¥222,523	¥218,507	$1,673,105
Work in process	65,714	67,399	494,090
Raw materials and supplies	70,266	68,415	528,316
	¥358,503	¥354,321	$2,695,511

EASTMAN KODAK COMPANY
Notes to the Financial Statements

Note: Significant accounting policies

Inventories

Inventories are stated at the lower of cost or market. The cost of most inventories in the U.S. is determined by the "last-in, first-out" (LIFO) method.

The cost of all of the Company's remaining inventories in and outside the U.S. is determined by the first-in, first-out (FIFO) or average cost method, which approximates current cost.

Note 3. Inventories

	(in millions)	
	2002	**2001**
At FIFO or average cost (approximates current cost)		
Finished goods	$ 831	$ 851
Work in process	322	318
Raw materials and supplies	301	346
	1,454	1,515
LIFO reserve	(392)	(444)
Total at LIFO	$1,062	$1,071

Inventories valued on the LIFO method are approximately 47% and 48% of total inventories in 2002 and 2001, respectively.

Additional information:

	Fuji Photo Film (yen)	**Eastman Kodak (dollars)**
2002 Cost of goods sold (millions)	1,268,521	8,225

Instructions

Answer each of the following questions.

(a) Why do you suppose that Fuji makes adjustments to its accounts so that they conform with U.S. accounting principles when it reports its results?

(b) What are the 2002 inventory turnover ratios and average days in inventory of the two companies (use inventory at FIFO, that is, before the LIFO reserve).

(c) What are the 2002 inventory turnover and average days in inventory of the two companies, adjusting for the LIFO reserve, if given? Do you encounter any problems when making this comparison?

(d) Calculate as a percentage of total inventory the portion that each of the components of 2002 inventory (raw materials, work in process, and finished goods) represents. Comment on your findings. (Use FIFO for Kodak.)

■ EXPLORING THE WEB

BYP6-4 A company's annual report usually will identify the inventory method used. Knowing that, you can analyze the effects of the inventory method on the income statement and balance sheet.

Address: www.cisco.com, or go to www.wiley.com/college/weygandt

Instructions

Answer the following questions based on the current year's Annual Report on Cisco's Web site.

(a) At Cisco's fiscal year-end, what was the net inventory on the balance sheet?

(b) How has this changed from the previous fiscal year-end?

(c) How much of the inventory was finished goods?

(d) What inventory method does Cisco use?

Critical Thinking

■ GROUP DECISION CASE

BYP6-5 On April 10, 2004, fire damaged the office and warehouse of Ehlert Company. Most of the accounting records were destroyed, but the following account balances were determined as of March 31, 2004: Merchandise Inventory, January 1, 2004, $80,000; Sales (January 1–March 31, 2004), $180,000; Purchases (January 1–March 31, 2004) $94,000.

The company's fiscal year ends on December 31. It uses a periodic inventory system.

From an analysis of the April bank statement, you discover cancelled checks of $4,200 for cash purchases during the period April 1–10. Deposits during the same period totaled $18,500. Of that amount, 60% were collections on accounts receivable, and the balance was cash sales.

Correspondence with the company's principal suppliers revealed $12,400 of purchases on account from April 1 to April 10. Of that amount, $1,600 was for merchandise in transit on April 10 that was shipped FOB destination.

Correspondence with the company's principal customers produced acknowledgments of credit sales totaling $28,000 from April 1 to April 10. It was estimated that $5,100 of credit sales will never be acknowledged or recovered from customers.

Ehlert Company reached an agreement with the insurance company that its fire-loss claim should be based on the average of the gross profit rates for the preceding 2 years. The financial statements for 2002 and 2003 showed the following data.

	2003	2002
Net sales	$600,000	$480,000
Cost of goods purchased	416,000	356,000
Beginning inventory	60,000	40,000
Ending inventory	80,000	60,000

Inventory with a cost of $17,000 was salvaged from the fire.

Instructions

With the class divided into groups, answer the following.

(a) Determine the balances in (1) Sales and (2) Purchases at April 10.

*(b) Determine the average profit rate for the years 2002 and 2003. (*Hint*: Find the gross profit rate for each year and divide the sum by 2.)

*(c) Determine the inventory loss as a result of the fire, using the gross profit method.

■ COMMUNICATION ACTIVITY

BYP6-6 You are the controller of Small Toys Inc. Denise Ramos, the president, recently mentioned to you that she found an error in the 2004 financial statements which she believes has corrected itself. She determined, in discussions with the Purchasing Department, that 2004 ending inventory was overstated by $1 million. Denise says that the 2005 ending inventory is correct. Thus she assumes that 2005 income is correct. Denise says to you, "What happened has happened—there's no point in worrying about it anymore."

Instructions

You conclude that Denise is incorrect. Write a brief, tactful memo to Denise, clarifying the situation.

■ ETHICS CASE

BYP6-7 S. R. Marsh Wholesale Corp. uses the LIFO method of inventory costing. In the current year, profit at S. R. Marsh is running unusually high. The corporate tax rate is also high this year, but it is scheduled to decline significantly next year. In an effort to lower the current year's net income and to take advantage of the changing income tax rate, the president of S. R. Marsh Wholesale instructs the plant accountant to recommend to the purchasing department a large purchase of inventory for delivery 3 days before the end of the year. The price of the inventory to be purchased has doubled during the year, and the purchase will represent a major portion of the ending inventory value.

Instructions
(a) What is the effect of this transaction on this year's and next year's income statement and income tax expense? Why?
(b) If S. R. Marsh Wholesale had been using the FIFO method of inventory costing, would the president give the same directive?
(c) Should the plant accountant order the inventory purchase to lower income? What are the ethical implications of this order?

Answers to Self-Study Questions
1. a   **2.** b   **3.** c   **4.** d   **5.** c   **6.** d   **7.** d   **8.** b   **9.** d   *10. b   *11. d

Answer to PepsiCo Review It Question 5, p. 241
PepsiCo reported inventories of $1,342 million in its balance sheet of December 28, 2002. On page 54 in its Note 14 to the financial statements, PepsiCo reported a breakdown of this total as follows: Raw materials, $525 million; Work in process, $214 million; and Finished goods, $603 million. Note 14 contains the following paragraph revealing the inventory cost flow methods used by PepsiCo:

> **(c)** Inventories are valued at the lower of cost or market. Cost is determined using the average, first-in, first-out (FIFO) or last-in, first-out (LIFO) methods. Approximately 19% in 2002 and 20% in 2001 of the inventory cost was computed using the LIFO method. The differences between LIFO and FIFO methods of valuing these inventories are not material.

Accounting Information Systems

THE NAVIGATOR ✓

Understand **Concepts for Review**	❏
Read **Feature Story**	❏
Scan **Study Objectives**	❏
Read **Preview**	❏
Read text and answer **Before You Go On** p. 282 ❏ p. 295 ❏	
Work **Demonstration Problem**	❏
Review **Summary of Study Objectives**	❏
Answer **Self-Study Questions**	❏
Complete **Assignments**	❏

CONCEPTS FOR REVIEW

Before studying this chapter, you should know or, if necessary, review:

- How to perform each of the steps in the accounting cycle.
  (Ch. 4, pp. 147–149)
- How to record transactions for a merchandiser.
  (Ch. 5, pp. 186–195)
- How to prepare financial statements for a merchandiser.
  (Ch. 5, pp. 195–200)

☑ THE NAVIGATOR

Accidents Happen

How organized are you financially? Take a short quiz.

- Is your wallet jammed full of gas station receipts from places you don't remember ever going?
- Is your wallet such a mess that it is often faster to fish for money in the crack of your car seat than to dig around in your wallet?
- Have you ever been tempted to burn down your house so you don't have to look for the receipts and records that you need to fill out your tax returns?

If you think it is hard to keep track of the many transactions that make up *your* life, imagine what it is like for a major corporation like **Fidelity Investments**. As the largest mutual fund management firm in the world, Fidelity manages more than $400 billion of investments.

Millions of individuals have the bulk of their life savings invested in mutual funds. If you had your savings invested at Fidelity, you might be just slightly displeased if, when you called to find out your balance, the representative said, "You know, I kind of remember someone with a name like yours sending us some money—now what did we do with that?"

To ensure the accuracy of your balance and the security of your funds, Fidelity Investments, like all other companies large and small, relies on a sophisticated accounting information system. That's not to say that Fidelity or anybody else is error-free. In fact, if you've ever really messed up your checkbook register, you may take some comfort from one accountant's mistake at Fidelity Investments. The accountant failed to include a minus sign while doing a calculation, making what was actually a $1.3 billion loss look like a $1.3 billion gain! Fortunately, like most accounting errors, it was detected before any real harm was done.

No one expects that kind of mistake at a firm like Fidelity, which has sophisticated computer systems and top investment managers. In explaining the mistake to shareholders, a spokesperson wrote: "Some people have asked how, in this age of technology, such a mistake could be made. While many of our processes are computerized, accounting systems are complex and dictate that some steps must be handled manually by our managers and accountants, and people can make mistakes."

www.fidelity.com

THE NAVIGATOR

STUDY OBJECTIVES

After studying this chapter, you should be able to:

1. Identify the basic principles of accounting information systems.
2. Explain the major phases in the development of an accounting system.
3. Describe the nature and purpose of a subsidiary ledger.
4. Explain how special journals are used in journalizing.
5. Indicate how a multi-column journal is posted.

THE NAVIGATOR

As you see from the Feature Story, a reliable information system is a necessity for any company. Whether you use pen, pencil, or computers in maintaining accounting records, certain principles and procedures apply. The purpose of this chapter is to explain and illustrate these features.

The content and organization of Chapter 7 are as follows.

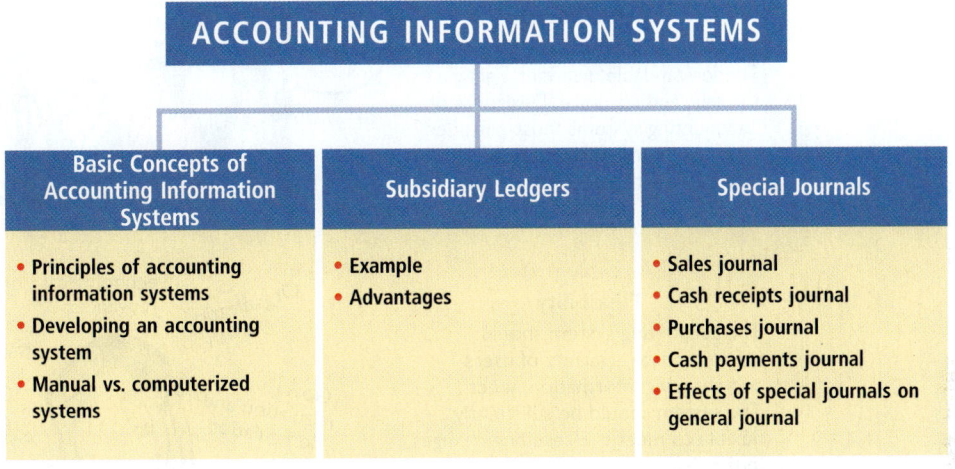

Basic Concepts of Accounting Information Systems

The system that collects and processes transaction data and disseminates financial information to interested parties is known as the **accounting information system**. It includes each of the steps in the accounting cycle that you have studied in earlier chapters. It also includes the documents that provide evidence of the transactions and events, and the records, trial balances, work sheets, and financial statements that result. An accounting information system may be either manual or electronic (computerized).

In this chapter, we explore the basic concepts that underlie accounting information systems, which from here on we will often refer to simply as **accounting systems**.

Principles of Accounting Information Systems

Efficient and effective accounting information systems are based on certain basic principles. These principles are: (1) cost effectiveness, (2) usefulness, and (3) flexibility, as described in Illustration 7-1 (page 278). If the accounting system is cost effective, provides useful output, and has the flexibility to meet future needs, it can contribute to both individual and organizational goals.

STUDY OBJECTIVE 1

Identify the basic principles of accounting information systems.

Cost Effectiveness

The accounting system must be cost effective. Benefits of information must outweigh the cost of providing it.

Useful Output

To be useful, information must be understandable, relevant, reliable, timely, and accurate. Designers of accounting systems must consider the needs and knowledge of various users.

Flexibility

The accounting system should accommodate a variety of users and changing information needs. The system should be sufficiently flexible to meet the resulting changes in the demands made upon it.

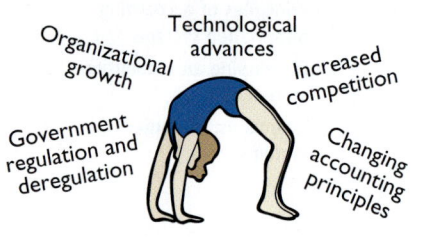

Developing an Accounting System

Good accounting systems do not just happen. They are carefully planned, designed, installed, managed, and refined. Generally, an accounting system is developed in the following four phases.

1. **Analysis.** The starting point is to determine the information needs of internal and external users. The system analyst then identifies the sources of the needed information and the records and procedures for collecting and reporting the data. If an existing system is being analyzed, its strengths and weaknesses must be identified.

2. **Design.** A new system must be built from the ground up: forms and documents designed, methods and procedures selected, job descriptions prepared, controls integrated, reports formatted, and equipment selected. Redesigning an existing system may involve only minor changes or a complete overhaul.

3. **Implementation.** Implementation of new or revised systems requires that documents, procedures, and processing equipment be installed and made operational. Also, personnel must be trained and closely supervised through a start-up period.

4. **Follow-up.** After the system is up and running, it must be monitored for weaknesses or breakdowns. Also, its effectiveness must be compared to design and organizational objectives. Changes in design or implementation may be necessary.

Illustration 7-2 highlights the relationship of these four phases in the life cycle of the accounting system.

These phases represent the life cycle of an accounting system. They suggest that few systems remain the same forever. As experience and knowledge are obtained, and as technological and organizational changes occur, the accounting system may also have to grow and change.

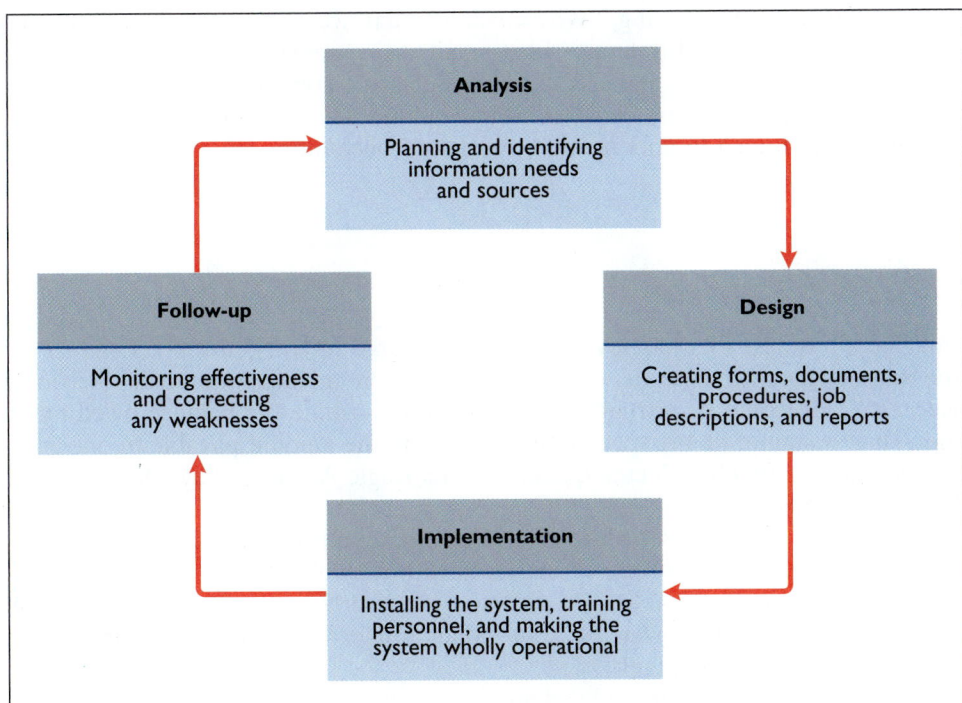

Illustration 7-2
Phases in the development
of an accounting system

The accounting system represented in the first six chapters is satisfactory in a company where the volume of transactions is extremely low. However, in most companies, it is necessary to add additional ledgers and journals to the accounting system to record transaction data efficiently.

Manual vs. Computerized Systems

In a **manual accounting system**, each of the steps in the accounting cycle is performed by hand. For example, each accounting transaction is entered manually in the journal; each is posted manually to the ledger. Other manual computations must be made to obtain ledger account balances and to prepare a trial balance and financial statements.

In a computerized accounting system, there are programs for performing the steps in the accounting cycle, such as journalizing, posting, and preparing a trial balance. In computerized systems, journals and ledgers are recorded in computer databases. In addition, there is software for business functions such as billing customers, preparing the payroll, and budgeting.

ACCOUNTING IN ACTION   **e Business Insight**

Accounting software companies have recognized the tremendous opportunities that result from making the accounting system an integral part of a comprehensive e-business package. For example, **Great Plains** recently published a story about an online art gallery called Art.com that uses two Great Plains e-business packages, eEnterprise™ and e.Commerce™ to meet the information needs of every aspect of its business. eEnterprise provides financial, distribution, purchasing, and manufacturing applications. e.Commerce provides real-time product information and on-the-fly customer data collection, reducing the need for order-desk staff because the customer keys in the order. This feature eliminates data re-entry errors.

Source: www.greatplains.com/ebusiness

You might be wondering, "Why cover manual accounting systems if the real world uses computerized systems?" First, small businesses still abound. Most of them begin operations with manual accounting systems and convert to computerized systems as the business grows. Second, to understand what computerized accounting systems do, you need to understand how manual accounting systems work.

Subsidiary Ledgers

STUDY OBJECTIVE 3

Describe the nature and purpose of a subsidiary ledger.

Imagine a business that has several thousand charge (credit) customers and shows the transactions with these customers in only one general ledger account—Accounts Receivable. It would be virtually impossible to determine the balance owed by an individual customer at any specific time. Similarly, the amount payable to one creditor would be difficult to locate quickly from a single Accounts Payable account in the general ledger.

Instead, companies use subsidiary ledgers to keep track of individual balances. A **subsidiary ledger** is a group of accounts with a common characteristic (for example, all accounts receivable). The subsidiary ledger frees the general ledger from the details of individual balances. A subsidiary ledger is an addition to, and an expansion of, the general ledger.

Two common subsidiary ledgers are:

1. The **accounts receivable** (or **customers'**) **subsidiary ledger**, which collects transaction data of individual customers.

2. The **accounts payable** (or **creditors'**) **subsidiary ledger**, which collects transaction data of individual creditors.

In each of these subsidiary ledgers, individual accounts are usually arranged in alphabetical order.

The detailed data from a subsidiary ledger are summarized in a general ledger account. For example, the detailed data from the accounts receivable subsidiary ledger are summarized in Accounts Receivable in the general ledger. The general ledger account that summarizes subsidiary ledger data is called a **control account**. An overview of the relationship of subsidiary ledgers to the general ledger is shown in Illustration 7-3. The general ledger control accounts and subsidiary ledger accounts are shown in green color. Note that cash and owner's capital in this illustration are not control accounts because there are no subsidiary ledger accounts related to these accounts.

Each general ledger control account balance must equal the composite balance of the individual accounts in the related subsidiary ledger at the end of an accounting period. For example, the balance in Accounts Payable in Illustration 7-3 must equal the total of the subsidiary balances of Creditors X + Y + Z.

Illustration 7-3
Relationship of general ledger and subsidiary ledgers

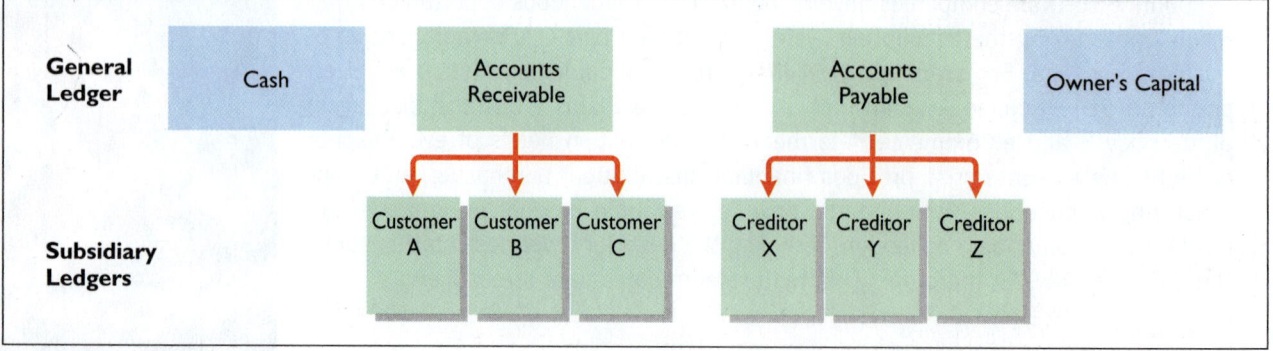

Example

An example of a control account and subsidiary ledger for Larson Enterprises is provided in Illustration 7-4. (The explanation column in these accounts is not shown in this and subsequent illustrations due to space considerations.)

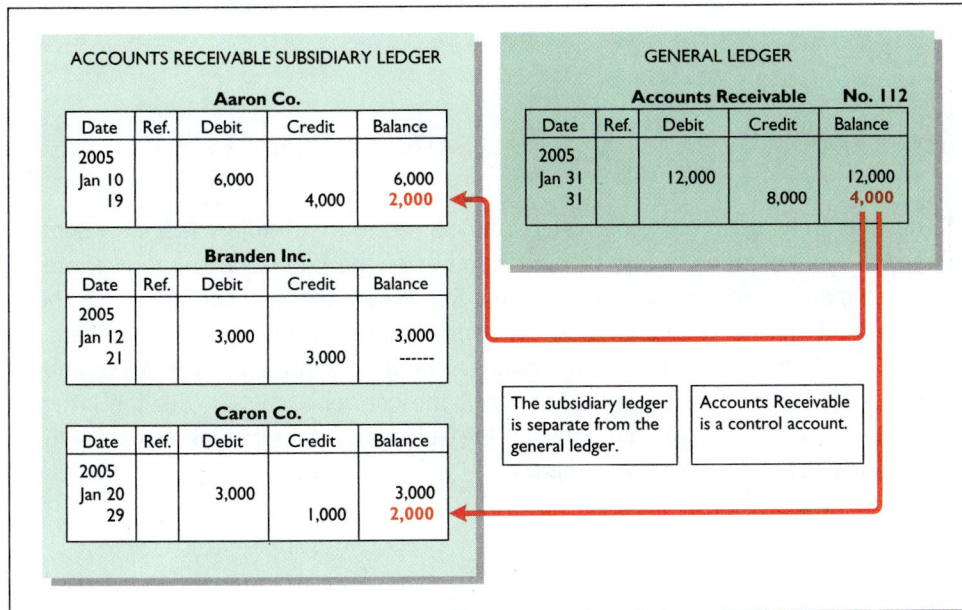

Illustration 7-4
Relationship between general and subsidiary ledgers

The example is based on the transactions listed below.

Illustration 7-5
Sales and collection transactions

Credit Sales			Collections on Account		
Jan. 10	Aaron Co.	$ 6,000	Jan. 19	Aaron Co.	$ 4,000
12	Branden Inc.	3,000	21	Branden Inc.	3,000
20	Caron Co.	3,000	29	Caron Co.	1,000
		$12,000			$ 8,000

The total debits ($12,000) and credits ($8,000) in Accounts Receivable in the general ledger are reconcilable to the detailed debits and credits in the subsidiary accounts. Also, the balance of $4,000 in the control account agrees with the total of the balances in the individual accounts (Aaron Co. $2,000 + Branden Inc. $0 + Caron Co. $2,000) in the subsidiary ledger.

As shown, postings are made monthly to the control accounts in the general ledger. This practice allows monthly financial statements to be prepared. Postings to the individual accounts in the subsidiary ledger are made daily. Daily posting ensures that account information is current. This enables the company to monitor credit limits, bill customers, and answer inquiries from customers about their account balances.

Advantages of Subsidiary Ledgers

Subsidiary ledgers have several advantages. They:

1. **Show transactions affecting one customer or one creditor in a single account**, thus providing up-to-date information on specific account balances.

2. **Free the general ledger of excessive details.** As a result, a trial balance of the general ledger does not contain vast numbers of individual account balances.

3. **Help locate errors in individual accounts** by reducing the number of accounts in one ledger and by using control accounts.

4. **Make possible a division of labor** in posting. One employee can post to the general ledger while someone else posts to the subsidiary ledgers.

ACCOUNTING IN ACTION

Rather than relying on customer or creditor names in a subsidiary ledger, a computerized system expands the account number of the control account in a pre-specified manner. For example, if Accounts Receivable was numbered 10010, the first account in the accounts receivable subsidiary ledger might be numbered 10010–0001. Most systems allow inquiries about specific accounts in the subsidiary ledger (by account number) or about the control account. With the latter, the system would automatically total all the subsidiary accounts whenever an inquiry to the control account was made.

BEFORE YOU GO ON...

Review It

1. What basic principles are followed in designing and developing an effective accounting information system?

2. What are the major phases in the development of an accounting information system?

3. What is a subsidiary ledger, and what purpose does it serve?

Do It

Presented below is information related to Sims Company for its first month of operations. Determine the balances that appear in the accounts payable subsidiary ledger. What Accounts Payable balance appears in the general ledger at the end of January?

Credit Purchases			Cash Paid		
Jan. 5	Devon Co.	$11,000	Jan. 9	Devon Co.	$7,000
11	Shelby Co.	7,000	14	Shelby Co.	2,000
22	Taylor Co.	14,000	27	Taylor Co.	9,000

ACTION PLAN

■ Subtract cash paid from credit purchases to determine the balances in the accounts payable subsidiary ledger.

■ Sum the individual balances to determine the Accounts Payable balance.

SOLUTION Subsidiary ledger balances: Devon Co. $4,000 ($11,000 − $7,000); Shelby Co. $5,000 ($7,000 − $2,000); Taylor Co. $5,000 ($14,000 − $9,000). General ledger Accounts Payable balance: $14,000 ($4,000 + $5,000 + $5,000).

Related exercise material: *BE7-3, BE7-4, E7-1, E7-2, E7-3, E7-4, E7-5, and E7-9.*

Special Journals

So far you have learned to journalize transactions in a two-column general journal and post each entry to the general ledger. This procedure is satisfactory in only the very smallest companies. To expedite journalizing and posting, most companies use special journals **in addition to the general journal**.

A special journal is used to record similar types of transactions. Examples would be all sales of merchandise on account, or all cash receipts. What special journals a company uses depends largely on the types of transactions that occur frequently. Most merchandising enterprises use the journals shown in Illustration 7-6 to record transactions daily.

STUDY OBJECTIVE 4

Explain how special journals are used in journalizing.

Illustration 7-6
Use of special journals and the general journal

Sales Journal	Cash Receipts Journal	Purchases Journal	Cash Payments Journal	General Journal
Used for: All sales of merchandise on account	Used for: All cash received (including cash sales)	Used for: All purchases of merchandise on account	Used for: All cash paid (including cash purchases)	Used for: Transactions that cannot be entered in a special journal, including correcting, adjusting, and closing entries

If a transaction cannot be recorded in a special journal, it is recorded in the general journal. For example, if you had special journals only for the four types of transactions listed above, purchase returns and allowances would be recorded in the general journal. So would sales returns and allowances. Similarly, **correcting, adjusting, and closing entries are recorded in the general journal.** Other types of special journals may sometimes be used in some situations. For example, when sales returns and allowances are frequent, special journals may be used to record these transactions.

Special journals **permit greater division of labor** because several people can record entries in different journals at the same time. For example, one employee may journalize all cash receipts, and another may journalize all credit sales. Also, the use of special journals **reduces the time needed to complete the posting process.** With special journals, some accounts may be posted monthly, instead of daily, as will be illustrated later in the chapter.

Sales Journal

The sales journal is used to record sales of merchandise on account. Cash sales of merchandise are entered in the cash receipts journal. Credit sales of assets other than merchandise are entered in the general journal.

Journalizing Credit Sales

Karns Wholesale Supply uses a **perpetual inventory** system. Under this system, each entry in the sales journal results in one entry **at selling price** and another entry at cost—a debit to Accounts Receivable (a control account) and a credit of equal amount to Sales. The entry **at cost** is a debit to Cost of Goods Sold and a credit of equal amount to Merchandise Inventory (a control account). A sales journal with two amount columns can show on only one line a sales transaction at both selling price and cost. The two-column sales journal of Karns Wholesale Supply is shown

HELPFUL HINT

Postings are also made daily to individual ledger accounts in the inventory subsidiary ledger to maintain a perpetual inventory.

Illustration 7-7
Journalizing the sales journal—perpetual inventory system

in Illustration 7-7, using assumed credit sales transactions (for sales invoices 101–107).

				Accts. Receivable Dr.	Cost of Goods Sold Dr.
	Karns Wholesale Supply				
	SALES JOURNAL				S1
Date	Account Debited	Invoice No.	Ref.	Accts. Receivable Dr. Sales Cr.	Cost of Goods Sold Dr. Merchandise Inventory Cr.
2005					
May 3	Abbot Sisters	101		10,600	6,360
7	Babson Co.	102		11,350	7,370
14	Carson Bros.	103		7,800	5,070
19	Deli Co.	104		9,300	6,510
21	Abbot Sisters	105		15,400	10,780
24	Deli Co.	106		21,210	15,900
27	Babson Co.	107		14,570	10,200
				90,230	62,190

The reference (Ref.) column is not used in journalizing. It is used in posting the sales journal, as explained in the next section. Also, note that, unlike the general journal, an explanation is not required for each entry in a special journal. Finally, note that each invoice is prenumbered to ensure that all invoices are journalized.

Posting the Sales Journal

Postings from the sales journal are made **daily to the individual accounts receivable** in the subsidiary ledger. Posting **to the general ledger** is made **monthly**. Illustration 7-8 (on page 285) shows both the daily and monthly postings.

A check mark (✓) is inserted in the reference posting column to indicate that the daily posting to the customer's account has been made. A check mark (✓) is used in this illustration because the subsidiary ledger accounts are not numbered. At the end of the month, the column totals of the sales journal are posted to the general ledger. Here, the column totals are a debit of $90,230 to Accounts Receivable (account No. 112), a credit of $90,230 to Sales (account No. 401), a debit of $62,190 to Cost of Goods Sold (account No. 505), and a credit of $62,190 to Merchandise Inventory (account No. 120). Insertion of the account numbers below the column total indicates that the postings have been made. In both the general ledger and subsidiary ledger accounts, the reference **S1** indicates that the posting came from page 1 of the sales journal.

Proving the Ledgers

The next step is to "prove" the ledgers. To do so, we must determine two things: (1) The total of the general ledger debit balances must equal the total of the general ledger credit balances. (2) The sum of the subsidiary ledger balances must equal the balance in the control account. The proof of the postings from the sales journal to the general and subsidiary ledger is shown in Illustration 7-9 (on page 286).

Advantages of the Sales Journal

The use of a special journal to record sales on account has a number of advantages. First, the one-line entry for each sales transaction **saves time**. In the sales journal, it is not necessary to write out the four account titles for each transaction. Second,

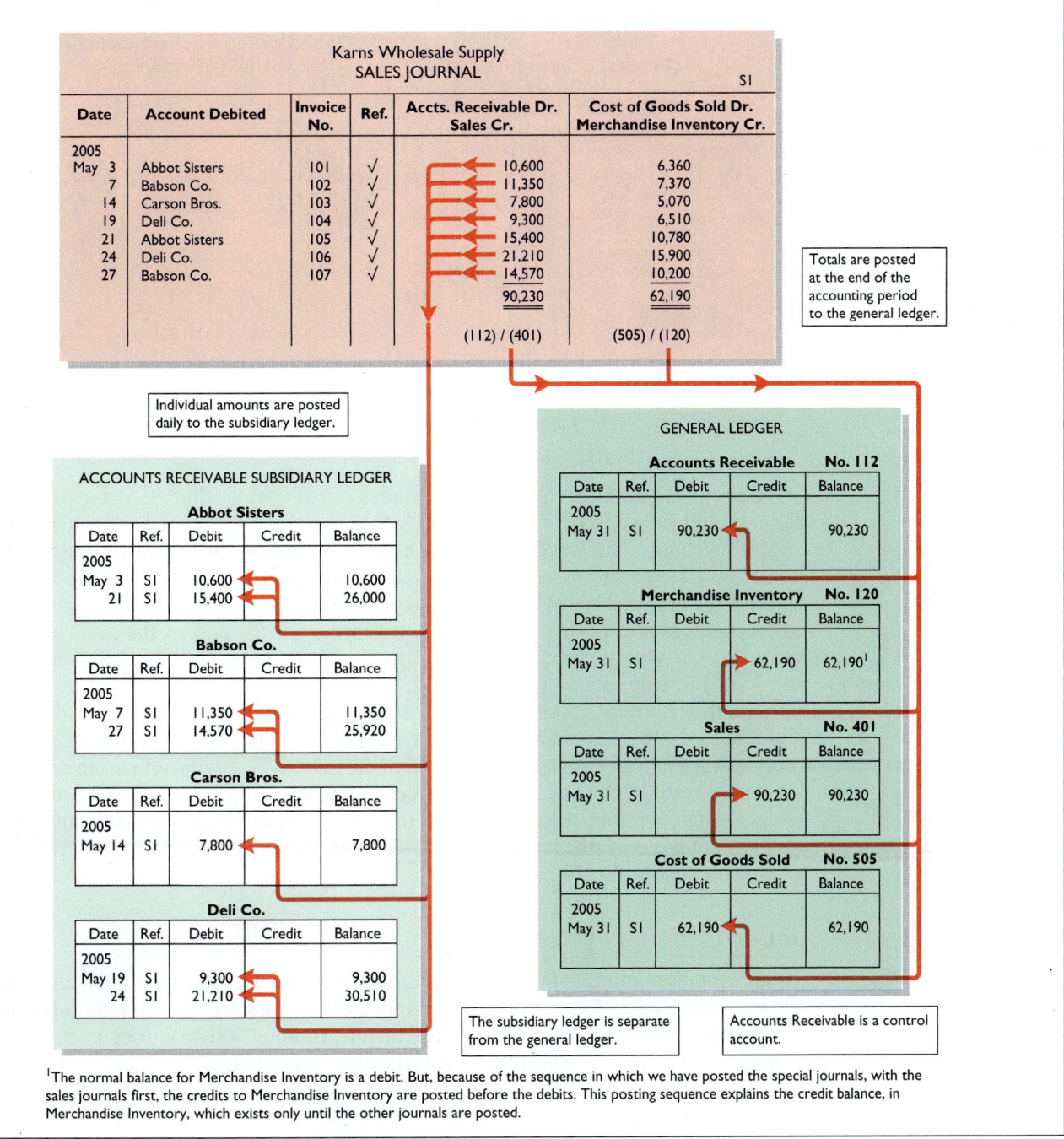

Illustration 7-8
Posting the sales journal

only totals, rather than individual entries, are posted to the general ledger. This **saves posting time and reduces the possibilities of errors in posting.** Finally, **a division of labor results,** because one individual can take responsibility for the sales journal.

Cash Receipts Journal

All receipts of cash are recorded in the cash receipts journal. The most common types of cash receipts are cash sales of merchandise and collections of accounts receivable. Many other possibilities exist, such as receipt of money from bank loans and cash proceeds from disposal of equipment. A one- or two-column cash receipts journal would not have space enough for all possible cash receipt transactions. Therefore, a multiple-column cash receipts journal is used.

Illustration 7-9
Proving the equality of the postings from the sales journal

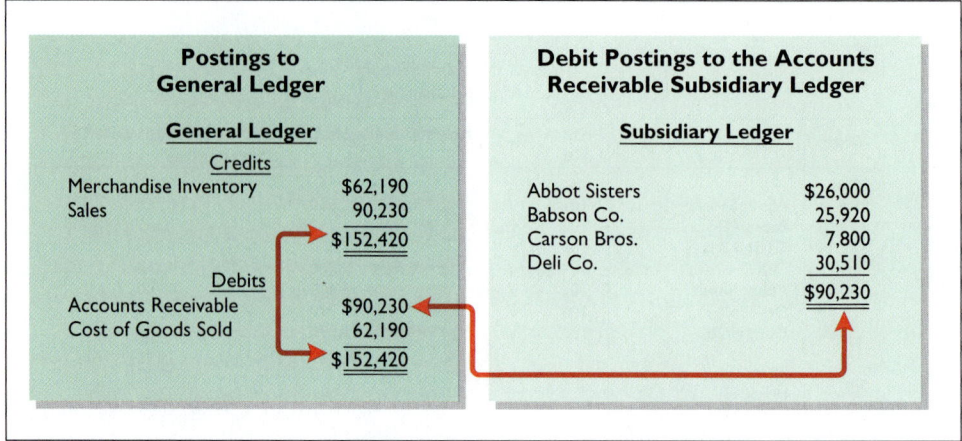

Generally, a cash receipts journal includes the following columns: debit columns for cash and sales discounts; and credit columns for accounts receivable, sales, and "other" accounts. The Other Accounts category is used when the cash receipt does not involve a cash sale or a collection of accounts receivable. Under a perpetual inventory system, each sales entry is accompanied by another entry that debits Cost of Goods Sold and credits Merchandise Inventory for the cost of the merchandise sold. This entry may be recorded separately. A six-column cash receipts journal is shown in Illustration 7-10 (on page 287).

Additional credit columns may be used if they significantly reduce postings to a specific account. For example, a loan company, such as **Household International**, receives thousands of cash collections from customers. A significant saving in posting would result from using separate credit columns for Loans Receivable and Interest Revenue, rather than using the Other Accounts credit column. In contrast, a retailer that has only one interest collection a month would not find it useful to have a separate column for Interest Revenue.

Journalizing Cash Receipts Transactions

To illustrate the journalizing of cash receipts transactions, we will continue with the May transactions of Karns Wholesale Supply. Collections from customers relate to the entries recorded in the sales journal in Illustration 7-7. The entries in the cash receipts journal are based on the following cash receipts.

May 1   D. A. Karns makes an investment of $5,000 in the business.
     7   Cash sales of merchandise total $1,900 (cost, $1,240).
  10   A check for $10,388 is received from Abbot Sisters in payment of invoice No. 101 for $10,600 less a 2% discount.
  12   Cash sales of merchandise total $2,600 (cost, $1,690).
  17   A check for $11,123 is received from Babson Co. in payment of invoice No. 102 for $11,350 less a 2% discount.
  22   Cash is received by signing a note for $6,000.
  23   A check for $7,644 is received from Carson Bros. in full for invoice No. 103 for $7,800 less a 2% discount.
  28   A check for $9,114 is received from Deli Co. in full for invoice No. 104 for $9,300 less a 2% discount.

Further information about the columns in the cash receipts journal (see Illustration 7-10) is listed on page 288.

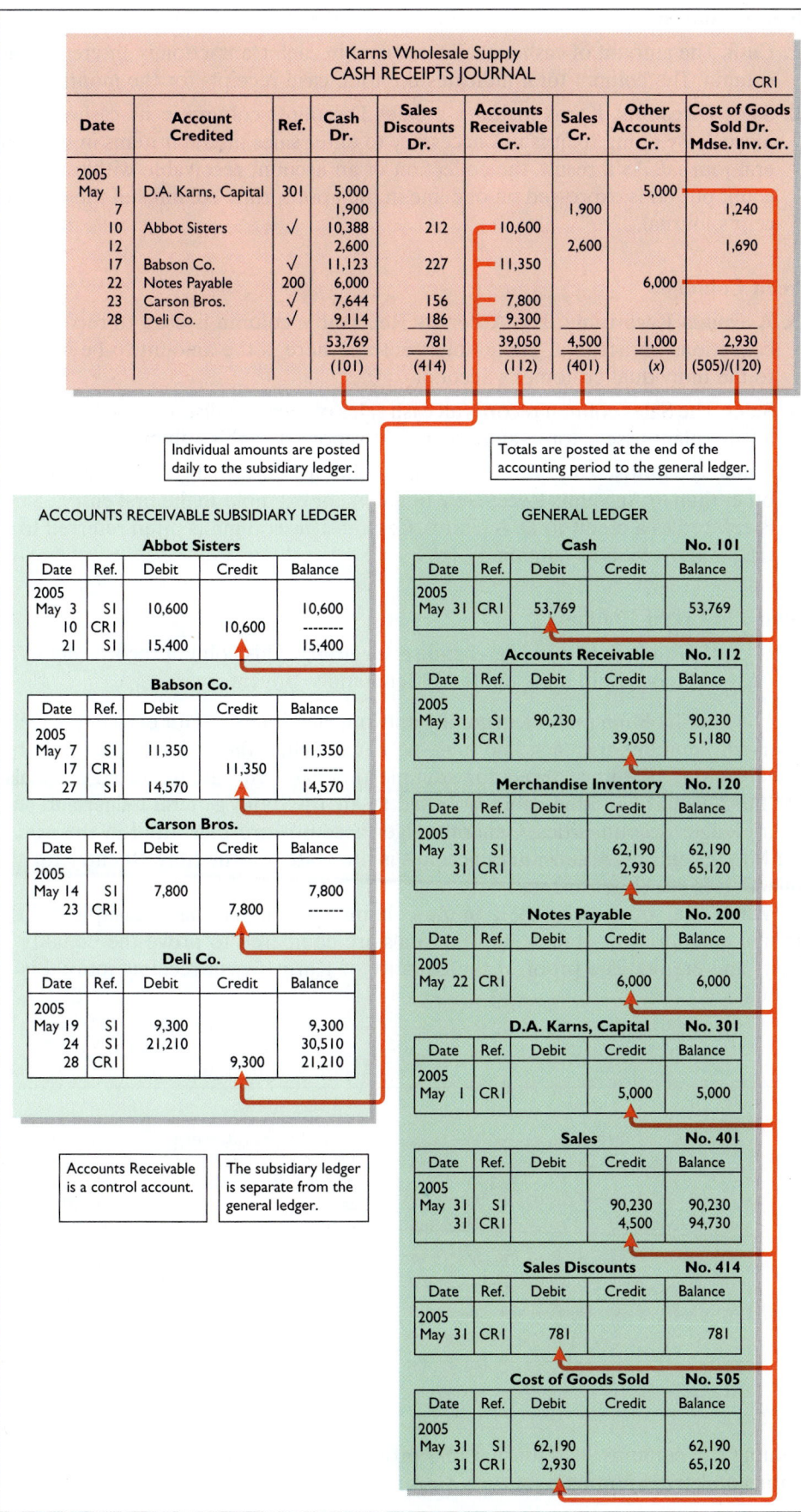

Illustration 7-10
Journalizing and posting the
cash receipts journal

Debit Columns:

1. **Cash.** The amount of cash actually received in each transaction is entered in this column. The column total indicates the total cash receipts for the month.

2. **Sales Discounts.** Karns includes a Sales Discounts column in its cash receipts journal. By doing so, it is not necessary to enter sales discount items in the general journal. As a result, the collection of an account receivable within the discount period is expressed on one line in the appropriate columns of the cash receipts journal.

Credit Columns:

3. **Accounts Receivable.** The Accounts Receivable column is used to record cash collections on account. The amount entered here is the amount to be credited to the individual customer's account.

4. **Sales.** The Sales column records all cash sales of merchandise. Cash sales of other assets (plant assets, for example) are not reported in this column.

5. **Other Accounts.** The Other Accounts column is used whenever the credit is other than to Accounts Receivable or Sales. For example, in the first entry, $5,000 is entered as a credit to D. A. Karns, Capital. This column is often referred to as the sundry accounts column.

Debit and Credit Column:

6. **Cost of Goods Sold and Merchandise Inventory.** This column records debits to Cost of Goods Sold and credits to Merchandise Inventory.

In a multi-column journal, generally only one line is needed for each entry. Debit and credit amounts for each line must be equal. When the collection from Abbot Sisters on May 10 is journalized, for example, three amounts are indicated. Note also that the Account Credited column is used to identify both general ledger and subsidiary ledger account titles. General ledger accounts are illustrated in the May 1 and May 22 entries. A subsidiary account is illustrated in the May 10 entry for the collection from Abbot Sisters.

When the journalizing of a multi-column journal has been completed, the amount columns are totaled, and the totals are compared to prove the equality of debits and credits. The proof of the equality of Karns's cash receipts journal is as follows.

HELPFUL HINT

When is an account title entered in the "Account Credited" column of the cash receipts journal? Answer: A *subsidiary ledger* title is entered there whenever the entry involves a collection of accounts receivable. A *general ledger* account title is entered there whenever the entry involves an account that is not the subject of a special column (and an amount must be entered in the Other Accounts column). No account title is entered there if neither of the foregoing applies.

Illustration 7-11
Proving the equality of the cash receipts journal

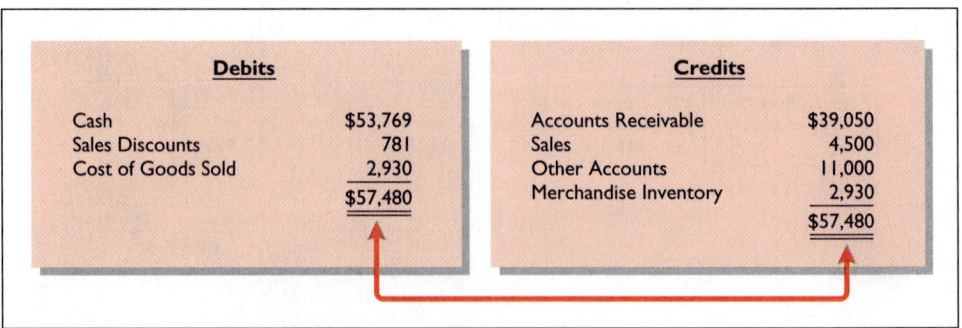

Debits		Credits	
Cash	$53,769	Accounts Receivable	$39,050
Sales Discounts	781	Sales	4,500
Cost of Goods Sold	2,930	Other Accounts	11,000
	$57,480	Merchandise Inventory	2,930
			$57,480

Totaling the columns of a journal and proving the equality of the totals is called **footing** and **cross-footing** a journal.

Posting the Cash Receipts Journal

Posting a multi-column journal involves the following steps.

1. All column totals except for the Other Accounts total are posted **once at the end of the month** to the account title(s) specified in the column heading (such as Cash or Accounts Receivable). Account numbers are entered below the column totals to show that they have been posted. Cash is posted to account No. 101, accounts receivable to account No. 112, merchandise inventory to account No. 120, sales to account No. 401, sales discounts to account No. 414, and cost of goods sold to account No. 505.

2. The **individual amounts comprising the Other Accounts total are posted separately** to the general ledger accounts specified in the Account Credited column. See, for example, the credit posting to D. A. Karns, Capital. The total amount of this column is not posted. The symbol (X) is inserted below the total to this column to indicate that the amount has not been posted.

3. The individual amounts in a column, posted in total to a control account (Accounts Receivable, in this case), are posted **daily to the subsidiary ledger** account specified in the Account Credited column. See, for example, the credit posting of $10,600 to Abbot Sisters.

The symbol **CR** is used in both the subsidiary and general ledgers to identify postings from the cash receipts journal.

Proving the Ledgers

After posting of the cash receipts journal is completed, it is necessary to prove the ledgers. As shown in Illustration 7-12, the general ledger totals are in agreement. Also, the sum of the subsidiary ledger balances equals the control account balance.

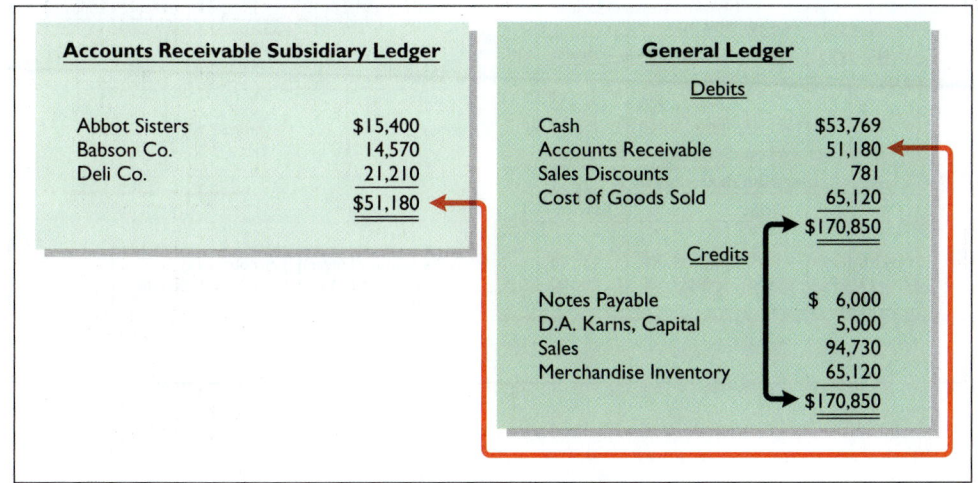

Illustration 7-12
Proving the ledgers after posting the sales and the cash receipts journals

Purchases Journal

All purchases of merchandise on account are recorded in the **purchases journal**. Each entry in this journal results in a debit to Merchandise Inventory and a credit to Accounts Payable. When a one-column purchases journal is used (as in Illustration 7-13, on page 290), other types of purchases on account and cash purchases cannot be journalized in it. For example, credit purchases of equipment or supplies must be recorded in the general journal. Likewise, all cash purchases are entered in the cash payments journal. As illustrated later, where credit purchases for items other than merchandise are numerous, the purchases journal is often expanded to a multi-column format. The purchases journal for Karns Wholesale Supply is shown in Illustration 7-13.

Illustration 7-13
Journalizing and posting the purchases journal

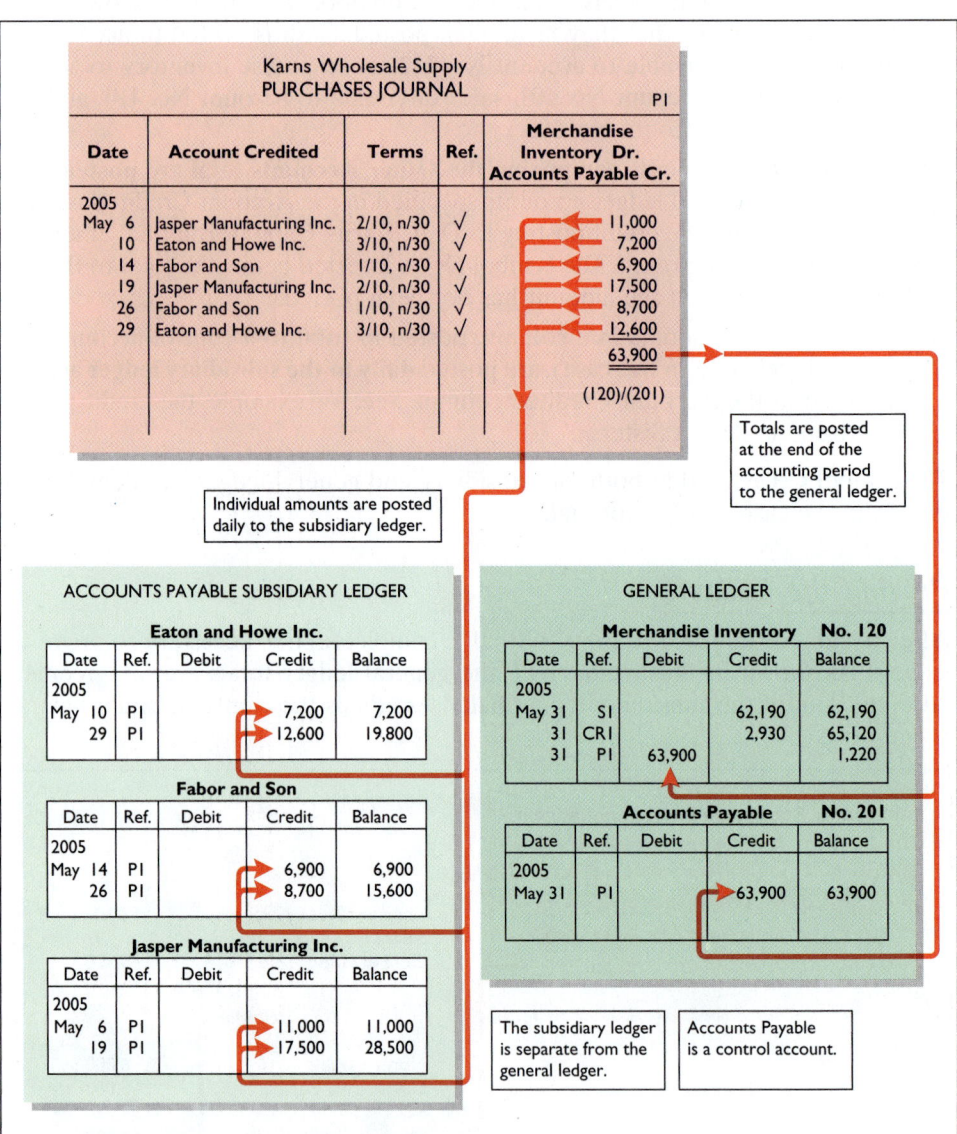

Journalizing Credit Purchases of Merchandise

Entries in the purchases journal are made from purchase invoices. The journalizing procedure is similar to that for a sales journal. In contrast to the sales journal, the purchases journal may not have an invoice number column, because invoices received from different suppliers will not be in numerical sequence. To assure that all purchase invoices are recorded, some companies consecutively number each invoice upon receipt and then use an internal document number column in the purchases journal.

The entries for Karns Wholesale Supply are based on the following assumed credit purchases.

Date	Supplier	Amount
5/6	Jasper Manufacturing Inc.	$11,000
5/10	Eaton and Howe Inc.	7,200
5/14	Fabor and Son	6,900
5/19	Jasper Manufacturing Inc.	17,500
5/26	Fabor and Son	8,700
5/29	Eaton and Howe Inc.	12,600

Illustration 7-14
Credit purchases transactions

Posting the Purchases Journal

The procedures for posting the purchases journal are similar to those for the sales journal. In this case, postings are made **daily** to the **accounts payable ledger** and **monthly** to Merchandise Inventory and Accounts Payable in the general ledger. In both ledgers, P1 is used in the reference column to show that the postings are from page 1 of the purchases journal.

Proof of the equality of the postings from the purchases journal to both ledgers is shown by the following.

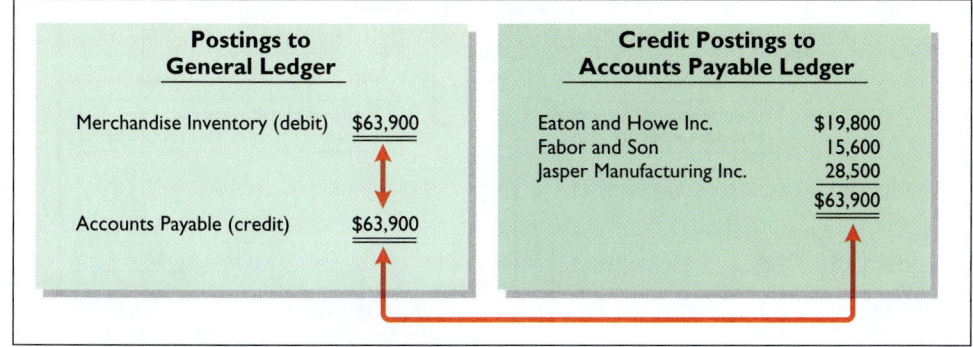

Illustration 7-15
Proving the equality of the purchases journal

Expanding the Purchases Journal

Some companies expand the purchases journal to include all types of purchases on account. Instead of one column for merchandise inventory and accounts payable, they use a multiple-column format. The multi-column format usually includes a credit column for accounts payable and debit columns for purchases of merchandise, of office supplies, of store supplies, and other accounts. Illustration 7-16 is an example of a multi-column purchases journal for Hanover Co. The posting procedures are similar to those illustrated earlier for posting the cash receipts journal.

Illustration 7-16
Columnar purchases journal

Hanover Co.
PURCHASES JOURNAL
P1

Date	Account Credited	Ref.	Account Payable Cr.	Merchandise Inventory Dr.	Office Supplies Dr.	Store Supplies Dr.	Other Accounts Dr. Account	Other Accounts Dr. Ref.	Other Accounts Dr. Amount
2005									
June 1	Signe Audio	✓	2,000		2,000				
3	Wight Co.	✓	1,500	1,500					
5	Orange Tree Co.	✓	2,600				Equipment	157	2,600
30	Sue's Business Forms	✓	800			800			
			56,600	43,000	7,500	1,200			4,900

ALTERNATIVE TERMINOLOGY

The cash payments journal is sometimes called the *cash disbursements journal.*

Cash Payments Journal

All disbursements of cash are entered in a **cash payments journal**. Entries are made from prenumbered checks. Because cash payments are made for various purposes, the cash payments journal has multiple columns. A four-column journal is shown in Illustration 7-17.

Illustration 7-17
Journalizing and posting the cash payments journal

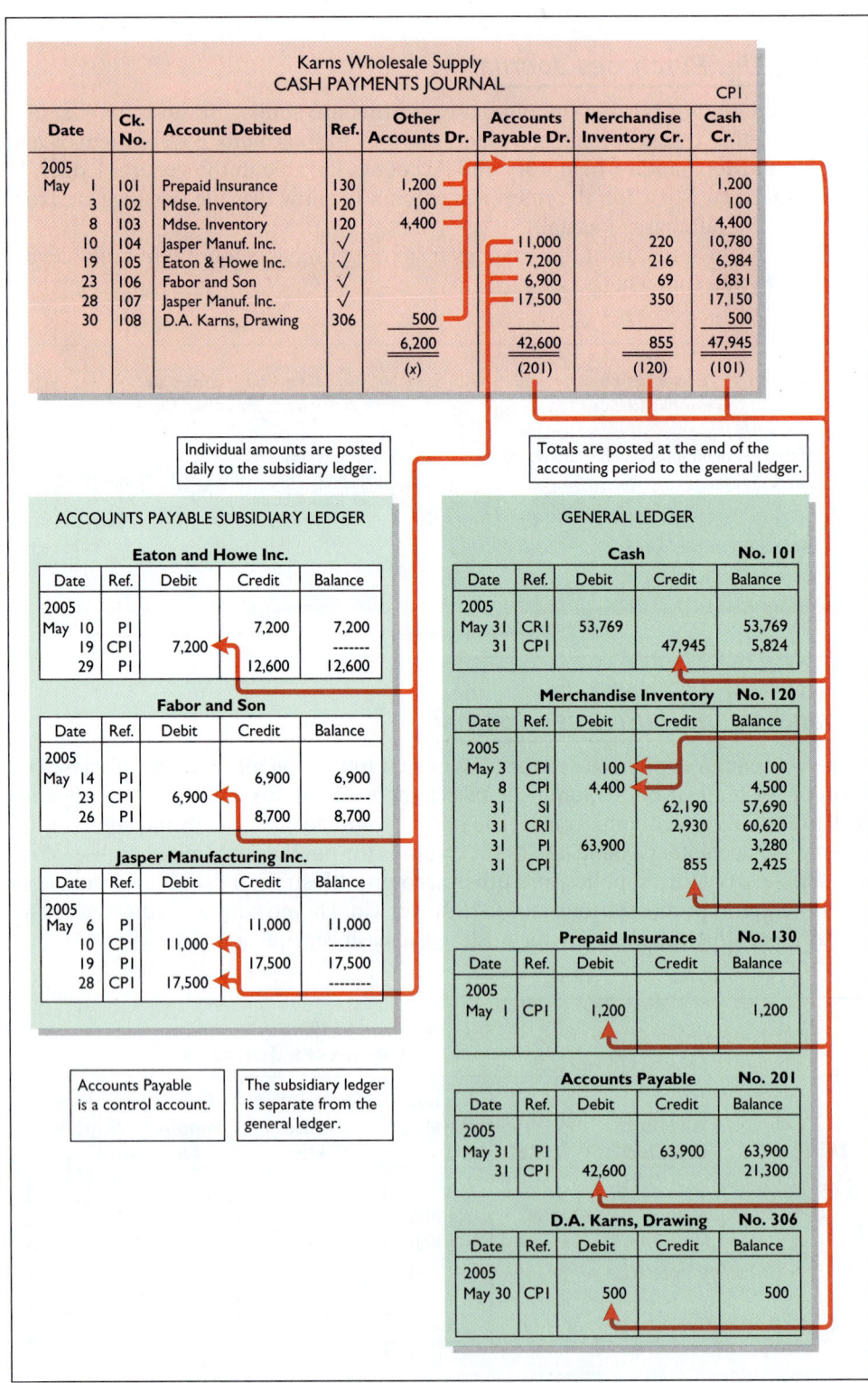

Journalizing Cash Payments Transactions

The procedures for journalizing transactions in this journal are similar to those described earlier for the cash receipts journal. Each transaction is entered on one line, and for each line there must be equal debit and credit amounts. The entries in the cash payments journal in Illustration 7-17 are based on the following transactions for Karns Wholesale Supply.

May 1 Check No. 101 for $1,200 issued for the annual premium on a fire insurance policy.

 3 Check No. 102 for $100 issued in payment of freight when terms were FOB shipping point.

 8 Check No. 103 for $4,400 issued for the purchase of merchandise.

 10 Check No. 104 for $10,780 sent to Jasper Manufacturing Inc. in payment of May 6 invoice for $11,000 less a 2% discount.

 19 Check No. 105 for $6,984 mailed to Eaton and Howe Inc. in payment of May 10 invoice for $7,200 less a 3% discount.

 23 Check No. 106 for $6,831 sent to Fabor and Son in payment of May 14 invoice for $6,900 less a 1% discount.

 28 Check No. 107 for $17,150 sent to Jasper Manufacturing Inc. in payment of May 19 invoice for $17,500 less a 2% discount.

 30 Check No. 108 for $500 issued to D. A. Karns as a cash withdrawal for personal use.

Note that whenever an amount is entered in the Other Accounts column, a specific general ledger account must be identified in the Account Debited column. The entries for checks No. 101, 102, and 103 illustrate this situation. Similarly, a subsidiary account must be identified in the Account Debited column whenever an amount is entered in the Accounts Payable column. See, for example, the entry for check No. 104.

After the cash payments journal has been journalized, the columns are totaled. The totals are then balanced to prove the equality of debits and credits.

Posting the Cash Payments Journal

The procedures for posting the cash payments journal are similar to those for the cash receipts journal. The amounts recorded in the Accounts Payable column are posted individually to the subsidiary ledger and in total to the control account. Merchandise Inventory and Cash are posted only in total at the end of the month. Transactions in the Other Accounts column are posted individually to the appropriate account(s) affected. No totals are posted for this column.

The posting of the cash payments journal is shown in Illustration 7-17. Note that the symbol **CP** is used as the posting reference. After postings are completed, the equality of the debit and credit balances in the general ledger should be determined. In addition, the control account balances should agree with the subsidiary ledger total balance. The agreement of these balances is shown in Illustration 7-18 (page 294).

Effects of Special Journals on General Journal

Special journals for sales, purchases, and cash substantially reduce the number of entries that are made in the general journal. **Only transactions that cannot be entered in a special journal are recorded in the general journal.** For example, the general journal may be used to record such transactions as granting of credit to a customer for a sales return or allowance, granting of credit from a supplier for purchases returned, acceptance of a note receivable from a customer, and purchase of equipment by issuing a note payable. Also, correcting, adjusting, and closing entries are made in the general journal.

Illustration 7-18
Proving the ledgers after postings from the sales, cash receipts, purchases, and cash payments journals

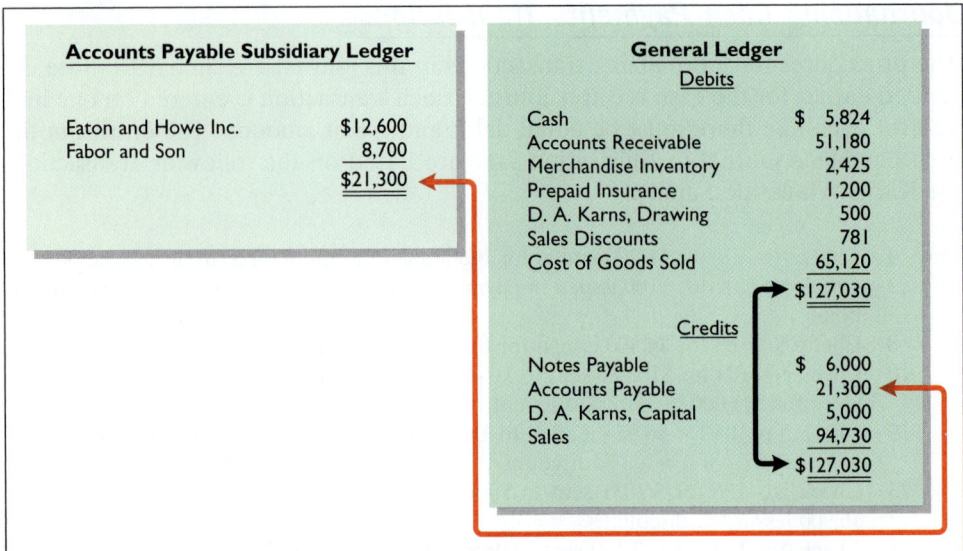

The general journal has columns for date, account title and explanation, reference, and debit and credit amounts. When control and subsidiary accounts are not involved, the procedures for journalizing and posting of transactions are the same as those described in earlier chapters. When control and subsidiary accounts are involved, two changes from the earlier procedures are required:

1. In **journalizing**, both the control and the subsidiary accounts must be identified.
2. In **posting**, there must be a **dual posting**: once to the control account and once to the subsidiary account.

Illustration 7-19
Journalizing and posting the general journal

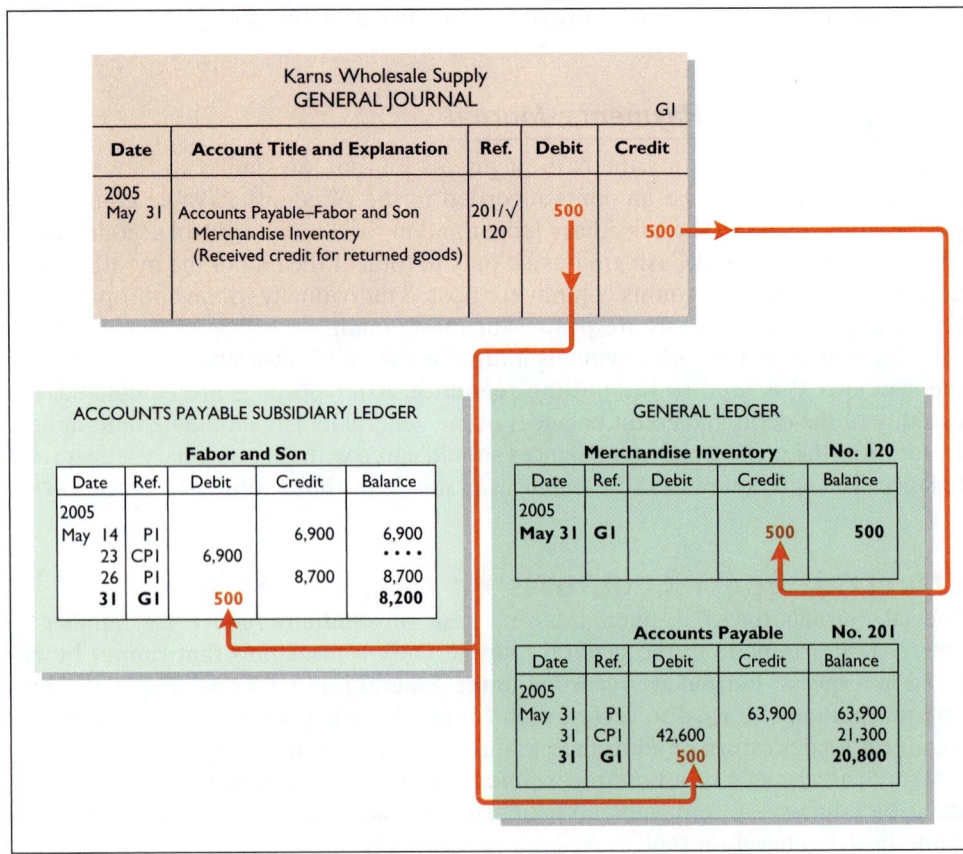

To illustrate, assume that on May 31, Karns Wholesale Supply returns $500 of merchandise for credit to Fabor and Son. The entry in the general journal and the posting of the entry are shown in Illustration 7-19. Note that if cash is received instead of credit granted on this return, then the transaction is recorded in the cash receipts journal.

Observe in the journal that two accounts are indicated for the debit, and two postings ("201/✓") are indicated in the reference column. One amount is posted to the control account and the other to the creditor's account in the subsidiary ledger.

BEFORE YOU GO ON...

Review It

1. What types of special journals are frequently used to record transactions? Why are special journals used?

2. Explain how transactions recorded in the sales journal and the cash receipts journal are posted.

3. Indicate the types of transactions that are recorded in the general journal when special journals are used.

✓ THE NAVIGATOR

DEMONSTRATION PROBLEM

Celine Dion Company uses a six-column cash receipts journal with the following columns: Cash (Dr.), Sales Discounts (Dr.), Accounts Receivable (Cr.), Sales (Cr.), Other Accounts (Cr.), and Cost of Goods Sold (Dr.) and Merchandise Inventory (Cr.). Cash receipts transactions for the month of July 2005 are as follows.

July 3   Cash sales total $5,800 (cost, $3,480).
    5   A check for $6,370 is received from Jeltz Company in payment of an invoice dated June 26 for $6,500, terms 2/10, n/30.
    9   An additional investment of $5,000 in cash is made in the business by Celine Dion, the proprietor.
   10   Cash sales total $12,519 (cost, $7,511).
   12   A check for $7,275 is received from R. Eliot & Co. in payment of a $7,500 invoice dated July 3, terms 3/10, n/30.
   15   A customer advance of $700 cash is received for future sales.
   20   Cash sales total $15,472 (cost, $9,283).
   22   A check for $5,880 is received from Beck Company in payment of $6,000 invoice dated July 13, terms 2/10, n/30.
   29   Cash sales total $17,660 (cost, $10,596).
   31   Cash of $200 is received on interest earned for July.

Instructions

(a) Journalize the transactions in the cash receipts journal.
(b) Contrast the posting of the Accounts Receivable and Other Accounts columns.

ACTION PLAN

■ Record all cash receipts in the cash receipts journal.

■ The "account credited" indicates items posted individually to the subsidiary ledger or general ledger.

■ Record cash sales in the cash receipts journal—not in the sales journal.

■ The total debits must equal the total credits.

(continued from p. 295)

SOLUTION TO DEMONSTRATION PROBLEM

(a)

Celine Dion Company
CASH RECEIPTS JOURNAL   **CR1**

Date	Account Credited	Ref.	Cash Dr.	Sales Discounts Dr.	Accounts Receivable Cr.	Sales Cr.	Other Accounts Cr.	Cost of Goods Sold Dr. Mdse. Inv. Cr.
2005								
7/3			5,800			5,800		3,480
5	Jeltz Company		6,370	130	6,500			
9	Celine Dion, Capital		5,000				5,000	
10			12,519			12,519		7,511
12	R. Eliot & Co.		7,275	225	7,500			
15	Unearned Revenue		700				700	
20			15,472			15,472		9,283
22	Beck Company		5,880	120	6,000			
29			17,660			17,660		10,596
31	Interest Revenue		200				200	
			76,876	475	20,000	51,451	5,900	30,870

(b) The Accounts Receivable column is posted as a credit to Accounts Receivable. The individual amounts are credited to the customers' accounts identified in the Account Credited column, which are maintained in the accounts receivable subsidiary ledger.

    The amounts in the Other Accounts column are only posted individually. They are credited to the account titles identified in the Account Credited column.

SUMMARY OF STUDY OBJECTIVES

1. **Identify the basic principles of accounting information systems.** The basic principles in developing an accounting information system are cost effectiveness, useful output, and flexibility.

2. **Explain the major phases in the development of an accounting system.** The major phases in the development of an accounting system are analysis, design, implementation, and follow-up.

3. **Describe the nature and purpose of a subsidiary ledger.** A subsidiary ledger is a group of accounts with a common characteristic. It facilitates the recording process by freeing the general ledger from details of individual balances.

4. **Explain how special journals are used in journalizing.** A special journal is used to group similar types of transac-

tions. In a special journal, generally only one line is used to record a complete transaction.

5. **Indicate how a multi-column journal is posted.** In posting a multi-column journal:
   (a) All column totals except for the Other Accounts column are posted once at the end of the month to the account title specified in the column heading.
   (b) The total of the Other Accounts column is not posted. Instead, the individual amounts comprising the total are posted separately to the general ledger accounts specified in the Account Credited (Debited) column.
   (c) The individual amounts in a column posted in total to a control account are posted daily to the subsidiary ledger accounts specified in the Account Credited (Debited) column.

GLOSSARY

Accounting information system A system that collects and processes transaction data, and disseminates financial information to interested parties. (p. 277).

Accounts payable (creditors') subsidiary ledger A subsidiary ledger that contains accounts of individual creditors. (p. 280).

Accounts receivable (customers') subsidiary ledger A subsidiary ledger that contains individual customer accounts. (p. 280).

Cash payments journal A special journal used to record all cash paid. (p. 292).

Cash receipts journal A special journal used to record all cash received. (p. 285).

Control account An account in the general ledger that controls a subsidiary ledger. (p. 280).

Manual accounting system A system in which each of the steps in the accounting cycle is performed by hand. (p. 279).

Purchases journal A special journal used to record all purchases of merchandise on account. (p. 289).

Sales journal A special journal used to record all sales of merchandise on account. (p. 283).

Special journal A journal that is used to record similar types of transactions, such as all credit sales. (p. 283).

Subsidiary ledger A group of accounts with a common characteristic. (p. 280).

SELF-STUDY QUESTIONS

Answers are at the end of the chapter.

(SO 1) **1.** The basic principles of an accounting information system include all of the following *except*:
  a. cost effectiveness.
  b. flexibility.
  c. useful output.
  d. periodicity.

(SO 2) **2.** Which of the following is *not* a major phase in the development of an accounting information system?
  a. Design.
  b. Responsiveness.
  c. Implementation.
  d. Follow-up.

(SO 3) **3.** Which of the following is *incorrect* concerning subsidiary ledgers?
  a. The purchases ledger is a common subsidiary ledger for creditor accounts.
  b. The accounts receivable ledger is a subsidiary ledger.
  c. A subsidiary ledger is a group of accounts with a common characteristic.
  d. An advantage of the subsidiary ledger is that it permits a division of labor in posting.

(SO 4) **4.** A sales journal will be used for:

	Credit Sales	Cash Sales	Sales Discounts
a.	no	yes	yes
b.	yes	no	yes
c.	yes	no	no
d.	yes	yes	no

(SO 5) **5.** Which of the following statements is correct?
  a. The sales discount column is included in the cash receipts journal.
  b. The purchases journal records all purchases of merchandise whether for cash or on account.
  c. The cash receipts journal records sales on account.
  d. Merchandise returned by the buyer is recorded by the seller in the purchases journal.

(SO 5) **6.** Which of the following is *incorrect* concerning the posting of the cash receipts journal?
  a. The total of the Other Accounts column is not posted.
  b. All column totals except the total for the Other Accounts column are posted once at the end of the month to the account title(s) specified in the column heading.
  c. The totals of all columns are posted daily to the accounts specified in the column heading.
  d. The individual amounts in a column posted in total to a control account are posted daily to the subsidiary ledger account specified in the Account Credited column.

(SO 5) **7.** Postings from the purchases journal to the subsidiary ledger are generally made:
  a. yearly.
  b. monthly.
  c. weekly.
  d. daily.

(SO 4) **8.** Which statement is *incorrect* regarding the general journal?
  a. Only transactions that cannot be entered in a special journal are recorded in the general journal.
  b. Dual postings are always required in the general journal.
  c. The general journal may be used to record acceptance of a note receivable in payment of an account receivable.
  d. Correcting, adjusting, and closing entries are made in the general journal.

(SO 4) **9.** When special journals are used:
  a. all purchase transactions are recorded in the purchases journal.
  b. all cash received, except from cash sales, is recorded in the cash receipts journal.
  c. all cash disbursements are recorded in the cash payments journal.
  d. a general journal is not necessary.

(SO 4) **10.** If a customer returns goods for credit, an entry is normally made in the:
  a. cash payments journal.
  b. sales journal.
  c. general journal.
  d. cash receipts journal.

QUESTIONS

1. (a) What is an accounting information system? (b) "An accounting information system applies only to a manual system." Do you agree? Explain.

2. Certain principles should be followed in the development of an accounting information system. Identify and explain each of the principles.

3. Kikujiro Company might change its accounting system for accounts receivable billing. At present, the procedure is performed manually by three clerks. A consultant has recommended that a new computer and related software be purchased for $1,000,000. What basic principle of designing and developing an effective accounting system might be violated by this proposal?

4. There are four phases in the life cycle of an accounting system. Identify and briefly explain each phase.

5. What are the advantages of using subsidiary ledgers?

6. (a) When are postings normally made to (1) the subsidiary accounts and (2) the general ledger control accounts? (b) Describe the relationship between a control account and a subsidiary ledger.

7. Identify and explain the four special journals discussed in the chapter. List an advantage of using each of these journals rather than using only a general journal.

8. Tom Wetzel Company uses special journals. A sale made on account to R. Janine for $435 was recorded in a sales journal. A few days later, R. Janine returns $70 worth of merchandise for credit. Where should Tom Wetzel Company record the sales return? Why?

9. A $500 purchase of merchandise on account from Brim Company was properly recorded in the purchases journal. When posted, however, the amount recorded in the subsidiary ledger was $50. How might this error be discovered?

10. Why would special journals used in different businesses not be identical in format? Can you think of a business that would maintain a cash receipts journal but not include a column for accounts receivable?

11. The cash and the accounts receivable columns in the cash receipts journal were mistakenly overadded by $4,000 at the end of the month. (a) Will the customers' ledger agree with the Accounts Receivable control account? (b) Assuming no other errors, will the trial balance totals be equal?

12. One column total of a special journal is posted at month-end to only two general ledger accounts. One of these two accounts is Accounts Receivable. What is the name of this special journal? What is the other general ledger account to which that same month-end total is posted?

13. In what journal would the following transactions be recorded? (Assume that a two-column sales journal and a single-column purchases journal are used.)
    (a) Recording of depreciation expense for the year.
    (b) Credit given to a customer for merchandise purchased on credit and returned.
    (c) Sales of merchandise for cash.
    (d) Sales of merchandise on account.
    (e) Collection of cash on account from a customer.
    (f) Purchase of office supplies on account.

14. In what journal would the following transactions be recorded? (Assume that a two-column sales journal and a single-column purchases journal are used.)
    (a) Cash received from signing a note payable.
    (b) Investment of cash by the owner of the business.
    (c) Closing of the expense accounts at the end of the year.
    (d) Purchase of merchandise on account.
    (e) Credit received for merchandise purchased and returned to supplier.
    (f) Payment of cash on account due a supplier.

15. What transactions might be included in a multiple-column purchases journal that would not be included in a single-column purchases journal?

16. Give an example of a transaction in the general journal that causes an entry to be posted twice (i.e., to two accounts), one in the general ledger, the other in the subsidiary ledger. Does this affect the debit/credit equality of the general ledger?

17. Give some examples of appropriate general journal transactions for an organization using special journals.

BRIEF EXERCISES

Identify basic principles of accounting information system development.

(SO 1)

BE7-1 Indicate whether each of the following statements is true or false.
1. When designing an accounting system, we need to think about the needs and knowledge of both the top management and various other users.
2. When the environment changes as a result of technological advances, increased competition, or government regulation, an accounting system does not have to be sufficiently flexible to meet the changes in order to save money.
3. In developing an accounting system, cost is relevant. The system must be cost-effective. That is, the benefits obtained from the information disseminated must outweigh the cost of providing it.

BE7-2 The development of an accounting system involves four phases: analysis, design, implementation, and follow-up. Identify the statement that best describes each of these four phases.

Identify major phases in accounting system development.

(SO 2)

1. Determining internal and external information needs, identifying information sources and the needs for controls, and studying alternatives.
2. Evaluation and monitoring of effectiveness and efficiency, and correction of weaknesses, implementation, and design.
3. Creation of forms and documents, selection of procedures, and preparation of job descriptions.
4. Implementing new or revised documents, procedures, reports, and processing equipment; hiring and training personnel through a start-up or transition period.

BE7-3 Presented below is information related to Holloway Company for its first month of operations. Identify the balances that appear in the accounts receivable subsidiary ledger and the accounts receivable balance that appears in the general ledger at the end of January.

Identify subsidiary ledger balances.

(SO 3)

Credit Sales			Cash Collections		
Jan. 7	Duffy Co.	$8,000	Jan. 17	Duffy Co.	$7,000
15	Hanson Co.	6,000	24	Hanson Co.	4,000
23	Lewis Co.	9,000	29	Lewis Co.	9,000

BE7-4 Identify in what ledger (general or subsidiary) each of the following accounts is shown.

Identify subsidiary ledger accounts.

(SO 3)

1. Rent Expense
2. Accounts Receivable—Char
3. Notes Payable
4. Accounts Payable—Thebeau

BE7-5 Identify the journal in which each of the following transactions is recorded.

Identify special journals.

(SO 4)

1. Cash sales
2. Owner withdrawal of cash
3. Cash purchase of land
4. Credit sales
5. Purchase of merchandise on account
6. Receipt of cash for services performed

BE7-6 Indicate whether each of the following debits and credits is included in the cash receipts journal. (Use "Yes" or "No" to answer this question.)

Identify entries to cash receipts journal.

(SO 4)

1. Debit to Sales
2. Credit to Merchandise Inventory
3. Credit to Accounts Receivable
4. Debit to Accounts Payable

BE7-7 Henning Computer Components Inc. uses a multi-column cash receipts journal. Indicate which column(s) is/are posted only in total, only daily, or both in total and daily.

Indicate postings to cash receipts journal.

(SO 5)

1. Accounts Receivable
2. Sales Discounts
3. Cash
4. Other Accounts

BE7-8 Hitache Co. uses special journals and a general journal. Identify the journal in which each of the following transactions is recorded.

Identify transactions for special journals.

(SO 4)

(a) Purchased equipment on account.
(b) Purchased merchandise on account.
(c) Paid utility expense in cash.
(d) Sold merchandise on account.

BE7-9 Identify the special journal(s) in which the following column headings appear.

Identify transactions for special journals.

(SO 4)

1. Sales Discounts Dr.
2. Accounts Receivable Cr.
3. Cash Dr.
4. Sales Cr.
5. Merchandise Inventory Dr.

EXERCISES

E7-1 Maureen Company uses both special journals and a general journal as described in this chapter. On June 30, after all monthly postings had been completed, the Accounts Receivable control account in the general ledger had a debit balance of $320,000; the Accounts Payable control account had a credit balance of $87,000.

Determine control account balances, and explain posting of special journals.

(SO 3, 5)

The July transactions recorded in the special journals are summarized below. No entries affecting accounts receivable and accounts payable were recorded in the general journal for July.

Sales journal	Total sales $161,400
Purchases journal	Total purchases $56,400
Cash receipts journal	Accounts receivable column total $141,000
Cash payments journal	Accounts payable column total $47,500

Instructions

(a) What is the balance of the Accounts Receivable control account after the monthly postings on July 31?

(b) What is the balance of the Accounts Payable control account after the monthly postings on July 31?

(c) To what account(s) is the column total of $161,400 in the sales journal posted?

(d) To what account(s) is the accounts receivable column total of $141,000 in the cash receipts journal posted?

Explain postings to subsidiary ledger.

(SO 3)

E7-2 Presented below is the subsidiary accounts receivable account of Nathan Ross.

Date	Ref.	Debit	Credit	Balance
2005				
Sept. 2	S31	61,000		61,000
9	G4		14,000	47,000
27	CR8		47,000	—

Instructions

✏️ Write a memo to Barb Murphy that explains each transaction.

Post various journals to control and subsidiary accounts.

(SO 3, 5)

E7-3 On September 1 the balance of the Accounts Receivable control account in the general ledger of Welter Company was $11,960. The customers' subsidiary ledger contained account balances as follows: Jana $2,440, Kingston $2,640, Cavanaugh $2,060, Bickford $4,820. At the end of September the various journals contained the following information.

Sales journal: Sales to Bickford $800; to Jana $1,260; to Iman $1,030; to Cavanaugh $1,100.
Cash receipts journal: Cash received from Cavanaugh $1,310; from Bickford $2,300; from Iman $380; from Kingston $1,800; from Jana $1,240.
General journal: An allowance is granted to Bickford $220.

Instructions

(a) Set up control and subsidiary accounts and enter the beginning balances. Do not construct the journals.

(b) Post the various journals. Post the items as individual items or as totals, whichever would be the appropriate procedure. (No sales discounts given.)

(c) Prepare a list of customers and prove the agreement of the controlling account with the subsidiary ledger at September 30, 2005.

Record transactions in sales and purchases journal.

(SO 3, 4)

E7-4 Sing Tao Company uses special journals and a general journal. The following transactions occurred during September 2005.

Sept. 2 Sold merchandise on account to T. Mephisto, invoice no. 101, $520, terms n/30. The cost of the merchandise sold was $300.

10 Purchased merchandise on account from L. Fantasia $600, terms 2/10, n/30.

12 Purchased office equipment on account from R. Press $6,500.

21 Sold merchandise on account to P. Shinhan, invoice no. 102 for $800, terms 2/10, n/30. The cost of the merchandise sold was $480.

25 Purchased merchandise on account from W. Manion $810, terms n/30.

27 Sold merchandise to S. Miller for $700 cash. The cost of the merchandise sold was $400.

Instructions

(a) Draw a sales journal (see Illustration 7-8) and a single-column purchase journal (see Illustration 7-13). (Use page 1 for each journal.)

(b) Record the transaction(s) for September that should be journalized in the sales journal and the purchases journal.

E7-5 Svenska Co. uses special journals and a general journal. The following transactions occurred during May 2005.

*Record transactions in cash
receipts and cash payments
journal.*

(SO 3, 4)

May 1 I. Svenska invested $60,000 cash in the business.
2 Sold merchandise to B. Sherrick for $6,300 cash. The cost of the merchandise sold was
   $4,200.
3 Purchased merchandise for $8,200 from J. Rome using check no. 101.
14 Paid salary to H. Potter $700 by issuing check no. 102.
16 Sold merchandise on account to K. Denmark for $900, terms n/30. The cost of the
   merchandise sold was $630.
22 A check of $9,000 is received from M. Irish in full for invoice 101; no discount given.

Instructions
(a) Draw a multiple-column cash receipts journal (see Illustration 7-10) and a multiple-column
cash payments journal (see Illustration 7-17). (Use page 1 for each journal.)
(b) Record the transaction(s) for May that should be journalized in the cash receipts journal
and cash payments journal.

E7-6 Dodi Company uses the columnar cash journals illustrated in the textbook. In April, the
following selected cash transactions occurred.

*Explain journalizing in cash
journals.*

(SO 4)

1. Made a refund to a customer for the return of damaged goods.
2. Received collection from customer within the 3% discount period.
3. Purchased merchandise for cash.
4. Paid a creditor within the 3% discount period.
5. Received collection from customer after the 3% discount period had expired.
6. Paid freight on merchandise purchased.
7. Paid cash for office equipment.
8. Received cash refund from supplier for merchandise returned.
9. Withdrew cash for personal use of owner.
10. Made cash sales.

Instructions
Indicate (a) the journal, and (b) the columns in the journal that should be used in recording
each transaction.

E7-7 Argentina Company has the following selected transactions during March.

*Journalize transactions in
general journal and post.*

(SO 3, 5)

Mar. 2 Purchased equipment costing $7,400 from Chile Company on account.
5 Received credit memorandum for $410 from Lyden Company for merchan-
   dise damaged in shipment to Argentina.
7 Issued a credit memorandum for $400 to Higley Company for merchandise
   the customer returned. The returned merchandise had a cost of $260.

Argentina Company uses a one-column purchases journal, a sales journal, the columnar cash
journals used in the text, and a general journal.

Instructions
(a) Journalize the transactions in the general journal.
(b) ▭▭▭▷ In a brief memo to the president of Argentina Company, explain the postings
to the control and subsidiary accounts from each type of journal.

E7-8 Below are some typical transactions incurred by Peru Company.

*Indicate journalizing in special
journals.*

(SO 4)

1. Payment of creditors on account.
2. Return of merchandise sold for credit.
3. Collection on account from customers.
4. Sale of land for cash.
5. Sale of merchandise on account.
6. Sale of merchandise for cash.
7. Received credit for merchandise
   purchased on credit.
8. Sales discount taken on goods sold.
9. Payment of employee wages.
10. Income summary closed to owner's capital.
11. Depreciation on building.
12. Purchase of office supplies for cash.
13. Purchase of merchandise on account.

Instructions
For each transaction, indicate whether it would normally be recorded in a cash receipts journal, cash payments journal, sales journal, single-column purchases journal, or general journal.

Explain posting to control account and subsidiary ledger.

(SO 3, 5)

E7-9 The general ledger of Bolivia Company contained the following Accounts Payable control account (in T-account form). Also shown is the related subsidiary ledger.

GENERAL LEDGER

Accounts Payable

Feb. 15 General journal	1,400	Feb. 1 Balance	26,025
28 ?	?	5 General journal	265
		11 General journal	550
		28 Purchases	13,900
		Feb. 28 Balance	10,200

ACCOUNTS PAYABLE LEDGER

Perez

Feb. 28	Bal. 4,600

Fernando

Feb. 28	Bal. ?

Lucia

Feb. 28	Bal. 2,300

Instructions

(a) Indicate the missing posting reference and amount in the control account, and the missing ending balance in the subsidiary ledger.

(b) Indicate the amounts in the control account that were dual-posted (i.e., posted to the control account and the subsidiary accounts).

Prepare purchases and general journals.

(SO 3, 4)

E7-10 Selected accounts from the ledgers of Rockford Company at July 31 showed the following.

GENERAL LEDGER

Store Equipment   No. 153

Date	Explanation	Ref.	Debit	Credit	Balance
July 1		G1	3,900		3,900

Accounts Payable   No. 201

Date	Explanation	Ref.	Debit	Credit	Balance
July 1		G1		3,900	3,900
15		G1		400	4,300
18		G1	100		4,200
25		G1	200		4,000
31		P1		8,800	12,800

Merchandise Inventory   No. 120

Date	Explanation	Ref.	Debit	Credit	Balance
July 15		G1	400		400
18		G1		100	300
25		G1		200	100
31		P1	8,800		8,900

ACCOUNTS PAYABLE LEDGER

Adam Equipment Co.

Date	Explanation	Ref.	Debit	Credit	Balance
July 1		G1		3,900	3,900

Dan Co.

Date	Explanation	Ref.	Debit	Credit	Balance
July 14		P1		1,100	1,100
25		G1	200		900

Brian Co.

Date	Explanation	Ref.	Debit	Credit	Balance
July 3		P1		2,400	2,400
20		P1		700	3,100

Erik Co.

Date	Explanation	Ref.	Debit	Credit	Balance
July 12		P1		500	500
21		P1		600	1,100

Colleen Corp

Date	Explanation	Ref.	Debit	Credit	Balance
July 17		P1		1,400	1,400
18		G1	100		1,300
29		P1		2,100	3,400

Grace Inc.

Date	Explanation	Ref.	Debit	Credit	Balance
July 15		G1		400	400

Instructions
From the data prepare:
(a) the single-column purchases journal for July.
(b) the general journal entries for July.

*(a) Purchases journal total
$8,800*

E7-11   Canada Products uses both special journals and a general journal as described in this chapter. Canada also posts customers' accounts in the accounts receivable subsidiary ledger. The postings for the most recent month are included in the subsidiary T accounts below.

*Determine correct posting
amount to control account.*

(SO 5)

	Brynn				Marcus	
Bal.	340	250		Bal.	150	150
	200				290	

	Carol				Paul	
Bal.	–0–	145		Bal.	120	120
	145				190	
					150	

Instructions
Determine the correct amount of the end-of-month posting from the sales journal to the Accounts Receivable control account.

PROBLEMS: SET A

P7-1A   Lewis Company's chart of accounts includes the following selected accounts.

101 Cash	401 Sales
112 Accounts Receivable	414 Sales Discounts
120 Merchandise Inventory	505 Cost of Goods Sold
301 J. Lewis, Capital	

*Journalize transactions in cash
receipts journal; post to
control account and subsidiary
ledger.*

(SO 3, 4, 5)

On June 1 the accounts receivable ledger of Lewis Company showed the following balances: Bernard & Son $3,500, Farley Co. $1,900, Grinnell Bros. $1,600, and Maquoketa Co. $1,300. The June transactions involving the receipt of cash were as follows.

June   1   The owner, J. Lewis, invested additional cash in the business $10,000.
   3   Received check in full from Maquoketa Co. less 2% cash discount.
   6   Received check in full from Farley Co. less 2% cash discount.
   7   Made cash sales of merchandise totaling $6,135. The cost of the merchandise sold was $4,090.
   9   Received check in full from Bernard & Son less 2% cash discount.
   11   Received cash refund from a supplier for damaged merchandise $320.
   15   Made cash sales of merchandise totaling $4,800. The cost of the merchandise sold was $3,200.
   20   Received check in full from Grinnell Bros. $1,600.

Instructions
(a) Journalize the transactions above in a six-column cash receipts journal with columns for Cash Dr., Sales Discounts Dr., Accounts Receivable Cr., Sales Cr., Other Accounts Cr., and Cost of Goods Sold Dr./Merchandise Inventory Cr. Foot and crossfoot the journal.
(b) Insert the beginning balances in the Accounts Receivable control and subsidiary accounts, and post the June transactions to these accounts.
(c) Prove the agreement of the control account and subsidiary account balances.

(a) Balancing totals $29,555

(c) Accounts Receivable $0

P7-2A   Congo Company's chart of accounts includes the following selected accounts.

101 Cash	157 Equipment
120 Merchandise Inventory	201 Accounts Payable
130 Prepaid Insurance	306 B. Congo, Drawing

*Journalize transactions in cash
payments journal; post to the
general and subsidiary ledgers.*

(SO 3, 4, 5)

On November 1 the accounts payable ledger of Congo Company showed the following balances: A. Hess & Co. $4,500, C. Pillsbury $2,350, G. Saeman $1,000, and Wex Bros. $1,900. The November transactions involving the payment of cash were as follows.

Nov. 1 Purchased merchandise, check no. 11, $1,140.
     3 Purchased store equipment, check no. 12, $1,700.
     5 Paid Wex Bros. balance due of $1,900, less 1% discount, check no. 13, $1,881.
    11 Purchased merchandise, check no. 14, $2,000.
    15 Paid G. Saeman balance due of $1,000, less 3% discount, check no. 15, $970.
    16 B. Congo, the owner, withdrew $500 cash for own use, check no. 16.
    19 Paid C. Pillsbury in full for invoice no. 1245, $1,150 less 2% discount, check no. 17, $1,127.
    25 Paid premium due on one-year insurance policy, check no. 18, $3,000.
    30 Paid A. Hess & Co. in full for invoice no. 832, $2,800, check no. 19.

Instructions

(a) Balancing totals $15,190

(a) Journalize the transactions above in a four-column cash payments journal with columns for Other Accounts Dr., Accounts Payable Dr., Merchandise Inventory Cr., and Cash Cr. Foot and crossfoot the journal.

(b) Insert the beginning balances in the Accounts Payable control and subsidiary accounts, and post the November transactions to these accounts.

(c) Accounts Payable $2,900

(c) Prove the agreement of the control account and the subsidiary account balances.

Journalize transactions in multi-column purchases journal; post to the general and subsidiary ledgers.

(SO 3, 4, 5)

P7-3A The chart of accounts of Dutch Company includes the following selected accounts.

112 Accounts Receivable	401 Sales
120 Merchandise Inventory	412 Sales Returns and Allowances
126 Supplies	505 Cost of Goods Sold
157 Equipment	610 Advertising Expense
201 Accounts Payable	

In May the following selected transactions were completed. All purchases and sales were on account except as indicated. The cost of all merchandise sold was 65% of the sales price.

May 2 Purchased merchandise from Van Houk Company $9,500.
    3 Received freight bill from Ruden Freight on Van Houk purchase $360.
    5 Sales were made to Ellie Company $1,980, Cornelis Bros. $2,700, and Jan Company $1,500.
    8 Purchased merchandise from Tulip Company $8,000 and Zeider Company $8,700.
   10 Received credit on merchandise returned to Zeider Company $500.
   15 Purchased supplies from Sandvoort Supply $900.
   16 Purchased merchandise from Van Houk Company $4,500, and Tulip Company $7,200.
   17 Returned supplies to Sandvoort Supply, receiving credit $100. (*Hint:* Credit Supplies.)
   18 Received freight bills on May 16 purchases from Ruden Freight $500.
   20 Returned merchandise to Van Houk Company receiving credit $300.
   23 Made sales to Cornelis Bros. $2,400 and to Jan Company $3,100.
   25 Received bill for advertising from Amster Advertising $900.
   26 Granted allowance to Jan Company for merchandise damaged in shipment $200.
   28 Purchased equipment from Sandvoort Supply $250.

Instructions

(a) Purchases journal—
Accounts Payable, Cr.
$40,810
Sales journal total
$11,680

(c) Accounts Receivable
$11,480
Accounts Payable
$39,910

(a) Journalize the transactions above in a purchases journal, a sales journal, and a general journal. The purchases journal should have the following column headings: Date, Accounts Credited (Debited), Ref., Merchandise Inventory Dr., Accounts Payable Cr., and Other Accounts Dr.

(b) Post to both the general and subsidiary ledger accounts. (Assume that all accounts have zero beginning balances.)

(c) Prove the agreement of the control and subsidiary accounts.

P7-4A Selected accounts from the chart of accounts of Jolie Company are shown below.

Journalize transactions in special journals.
(SO 3, 4, 5)

101 Cash	201 Accounts Payable
112 Accounts Receivable	401 Sales
120 Merchandise Inventory	414 Sales Discounts
126 Supplies	505 Cost of Goods Sold
140 Land	610 Advertising Expense
145 Buildings	

The cost of all merchandise sold was 70% of the sales price. During October, Jolie Company completed the following transactions.

Oct. 2 Purchased merchandise on account from Angelina Company $18,500.
   4 Sold merchandise on account to Drew Co. $8,700. Invoice no. 204, terms 2/10, n/30.
   5 Purchased supplies for cash $80.
   7 Made cash sales for the week totaling $9,160.
   9 Paid in full the amount owed Angelina Company less a 2% discount.
   10 Purchased merchandise on account from Diez Corp. $3,500.
   12 Received payment from Drew Co. for invoice no. 204.
   13 Issued a debit memorandum to Diez Corp. and returned $210 worth of damaged goods.
   14 Made cash sales for the week totaling $8,180.
   16 Sold a parcel of land for $27,000 cash, the land's book value.
   17 Sold merchandise on account to G. Paltrow & Co. $5,350, invoice no. 205, terms 2/10, n/30.
   18 Purchased merchandise for cash $2,125.
   21 Made cash sales for the week totaling $8,200.
   23 Paid in full the amount owed Diez Corp. for the goods kept (no discount).
   25 Purchased supplies on account from Robinson Co. $260.
   25 Sold merchandise on account to Hunt Corp. $5,220, invoice no. 206, terms 2/10, n/30.
   25 Received payment from G. Paltrow & Co. for invoice no. 205.
   26 Purchased for cash a small parcel of land and a building on the land to use as a storage facility. The total cost of $35,000 was allocated $21,000 to the land and $14,000 to the building.
   27 Purchased merchandise on account from Kudro Co. $8,500.
   28 Made cash sales for the week totaling $8,540.
   30 Purchased merchandise on account from Angelina Company $14,000.
   30 Paid advertising bill for the month from the *Gazette*, $400.
   30 Sold merchandise on account to G. Paltrow & Co. $4,600, invoice no. 207, terms 2/10, n/30.

Jolie Company uses the following journals.

1. Sales journal.
2. Single-column purchases journal.
3. Cash receipts journal with columns for Cash Dr., Sales Discounts Dr., Accounts Receivable Cr., Sales Cr., Other Accounts Cr., and Cost of Goods Sold Dr./Merchandise Inventory Cr.
4. Cash payments journal with columns for Other Accounts Dr., Accounts Payable Dr., Merchandise Inventory Cr., and Cash Cr.
5. General journal.

Instructions

Using the selected accounts provided:
(a) Record the October transactions in the appropriate journals.
(b) Foot and crossfoot all special journals.
(c) Show how postings would be made by placing ledger account numbers and check marks as needed in the journals. (Actual posting to ledger accounts is not required.)

(b) Sales journal $23,870
Purchases journal $44,500
Cash receipts journal—
    Cash, Dr. $74,849
Cash payments journal,
    Cash, Cr. $59,025

Journalize in purchases and cash payments journals; post; prepare a trial balance; prove control to subsidiary; prepare adjusting entries; prepare an adjusted trial balance.

(SO 3, 4, 5)

P7-5A Presented below are the sales and cash receipts journals for Zamtel Co. for its first month of operations.

SALES JOURNAL S1

Date	Account Debited	Ref.	Accounts Receivable Dr. Sales Cr.	Cost of Goods Sold Dr. Merchandise Inventory Cr.
Feb. 3	S. Appel		5,500	3,630
9	C. Boyd		6,500	4,290
12	F. Catt		8,000	5,280
26	M. Dogg		6,000	3,960
			26,000	17,160

CASH RECEIPTS JOURNAL CR1

Date	Account Credited	Ref.	Cash Dr.	Sales Discounts Dr.	Accounts Receivable Cr.	Sales Cr.	Other Accounts Cr.	Cost of Goods Sold Dr. Merchandise Inventory Cr.
Feb. 1	A. Zamtel, Capital		30,000				30,000	
2			6,500			6,500		4,290
13	S. Appel		5,445	55	5,500			
18	Merchandise Inventory		150				150	
26	C. Boyd		6,500		6,500			
			48,595	55	12,000	6,500	30,150	4,290

In addition, the following transactions have not been journalized for February 2005.

Feb. 2 Purchased merchandise on account from J. Zea for $4,600, terms 2/10, n/30.
7 Purchased merchandise on account from P. Kneiser for $30,000, terms 1/10, n/30.
9 Paid cash of $1,250 for purchase of supplies.
12 Paid $4,508 to J. Zea in payment for $4,600 invoice, less 2% discount.
15 Purchased equipment for $8,000 cash.
16 Purchased merchandise on account from J. Lakota $2,400, terms 2/10, n/30.
17 Paid $29,700 to P. Kneiser in payment of $30,000 invoice, less 1% discount.
20 A. Zamtel withdrew cash of $1,100 from business for personal use.
21 Purchased merchandise on account from G. Reedy for $5,800, terms 1/10, n/30.
28 Paid $2,400 to J. Lakota in payment of $2,400 invoice.

Instructions

(a) Open the following accounts in the general ledger.

101 Cash	301 A. Zamtel, Capital
112 Accounts Receivable	306 A. Zamtel, Drawing
120 Merchandise Inventory	401 Sales
126 Supplies	414 Sales Discounts
157 Equipment	505 Cost of Goods Sold
158 Accumulated Depreciation—Equipment	631 Supplies Expense
201 Accounts Payable	711 Depreciation Expense

(b) Journalize the transactions that have not been journalized in a one-column purchases journal and the cash payments journal (see Illustration 7-17).

(c) Post to the accounts receivable and accounts payable subsidiary ledgers. Follow the sequence of transactions as shown in the problem.

(d) Post the individual entries and totals to the general ledger.

(e) Prepare a trial balance at February 28, 2005.

(f) Determine that the subsidiary ledgers agree with the control accounts in the general ledger.

(g) The following adjustments at the end of February are necessary.
    (1) A count of supplies indicates that $300 is still on hand.
    (2) Depreciation on equipment for February is $200.
    Prepare the adjusting entries and then post the adjusting entries to the general ledger.
(h) Prepare an adjusted trial balance at February 28, 2005.

(h) Totals $68,500

P7-6A The post-closing trial balance for Bedazzle Co. is as follows.

Journalize in special journals; post; prepare a trial balance.

(SO 3, 4, 5)

BEDAZZLE CO.
Post-Closing Trial Balance
December 31, 2005

	Debit	Credit
Cash	$ 41,500	
Accounts Receivable	15,000	
Notes Receivable	45,000	
Merchandise Inventory	23,000	
Equipment	6,450	
Accumulated Depreciation—Equipment		$ 1,500
Accounts Payable		43,000
B. Dazzle, Capital		86,450
	$130,950	$130,950

The subsidiary ledgers contain the following information: (1) accounts receivable—J. Balton $2,500, F. Cone $7,500, T. Dudley $5,000; (2) accounts payable—J. Feeney $10,000, D. Goodman $18,000, and K. Hollis $15,000. The cost of all merchandise sold was 60% of the sales price.

The transactions for January 2006 are as follows.

Jan. 3 Sell merchandise to M. Sanford $4,000, terms 2/10, n/30.
    5 Purchase merchandise from E. Westphal $3,000, terms 2/10, n/30.
    7 Receive a check from T. Dudley $3,500.
  11 Pay freight on merchandise purchased $300.
  12 Pay rent of $1,000 for January.
  13 Receive payment in full from M. Sanford.
  14 Post all entries to the subsidiary ledgers. Issue a credit memo to acknowledge receipt of damaged merchandise of $500 returned by J. Balton.
  15 Send K. Hollis a check for $14,850 in full payment of account, discount $150.
  17 Purchase merchandise from G. Louis $1,600, terms 2/10, n/30.
  18 Pay sales salaries of $2,800 and office salaries $1,500.
  20 Give D. Goodman a 60-day note for $18,000 in full payment of account payable.
  23 Total cash sales amount to $9,100.
  24 Post all entries to the subsidiary ledgers. Sell merchandise on account to F. Cone $7,400, terms 1/10, n/30.
  27 Send E. Westphal a check for $950.
  29 Receive payment on a note of $40,000 from B. Lemke.
  30 Return merchandise of $500 to G. Louis for credit.

Post all journals to the subsidiary ledger.

Instructions
(a) Open general and subsidiary ledger accounts for the following.

101 Cash	301 B. Dazzle, Capital
112 Accounts Receivable	401 Sales
115 Notes Receivable	412 Sales Returns and Allowances
120 Merchandise Inventory	414 Sales Discounts
157 Equipment	505 Cost of Goods Sold
158 Accumulated Depreciation—Equipment	726 Sales Salaries Expense
200 Notes Payable	727 Office Salaries Expense
201 Accounts Payable	729 Rent Expense

(b) Record the January transactions in a sales journal, a single-column purchases journal, a cash receipts journal (see Illustration 7-10), a cash payments journal (see Illustration 7-17), and a general journal.

(c) Post the appropriate amounts to the general ledger.

(d) Prepare a trial balance at January 31, 2006.

(e) Determine whether the subsidiary ledgers agree with controlling accounts in the general ledger.

PROBLEMS: SET B

Journalize transactions in cash receipts journal; post to control account and subsidiary ledger.

(SO 3, 4, 5)

Peachtree

P7-1B Iqbal Company's chart of accounts includes the following selected accounts.

101 Cash	401 Sales
112 Accounts Receivable	414 Sales Discounts
120 Merchandise Inventory	505 Cost of Goods Sold
301 O. Iqbal, Capital	

On April 1 the accounts receivable ledger of Iqbal Company showed the following balances: Naper $1,550, Chelsea $1,200, Finlandia Co. $2,900, and Baez $1,400. The April transactions involving the receipt of cash were as follows.

Apr. 1 The owner, O. Iqbal, invested additional cash in the business $7,200.
  4 Received check for payment of account from Baez less 2% cash discount.
  5 Received check for $620 in payment of invoice no. 307 from Finlandia Co.
  8 Made cash sales of merchandise totaling $7,245. The cost of the merchandise sold was $4,347.
  10 Received check for $600 in payment of invoice no. 309 from Naper.
  11 Received cash refund from a supplier for damaged merchandise $740.
  23 Received check for $1,500 in payment of invoice no. 310 from Finlandia Co.
  29 Received check for payment of account from Chelsea.

Instructions

(a) Balancing totals $20,505

(a) Journalize the transactions above in a six-column cash receipts journal with columns for Cash Dr., Sales Discounts Dr., Accounts Receivable Cr., Sales Cr., Other Accounts Cr., and Cost of Goods Sold Dr./Merchandise Inventory Cr. Foot and crossfoot the journal.

(b) Insert the beginning balances in the Accounts Receivable control and subsidiary accounts, and post the April transactions to these accounts.

(c) Accounts Receivable $1,730

(c) Prove the agreement of the control account and subsidiary account balances.

Journalize transactions in cash payments journal; post to control account and subsidiary ledgers.

(SO 3, 4, 5)

P7-2B Mann Company's chart of accounts includes the following selected accounts.

101 Cash	201 Accounts Payable
120 Merchandise Inventory	306 T. Mann, Drawing
130 Prepaid Insurance	505 Cost of Goods Sold
157 Equipment	

On October 1 the accounts payable ledger of Mann Company showed the following balances: Bovary Company $1,700, Magic Co. $2,500, Pyron Co. $1,800, and Tess Company $3,700. The October transactions involving the payment of cash were as follows.

Oct. 1 Purchased merchandise, check no. 63, $300.
  3 Purchased equipment, check no. 64, $800.
  5 Paid Bovary Company balance due of $1,700, less 2% discount, check no. 65, $1,666.
  10 Purchased merchandise, check no. 66, $2,250.
  15 Paid Pyron Co. balance due of $1,800, check no. 67.
  16 T. Mann, the owner, pays his personal insurance premium of $400, check no. 68.
  19 Paid Magic Co. in full for invoice no. 610, $1,600 less 2% cash discount, check no. 69, $1,568.
  29 Paid Tess Company in full for invoice no. 264, $3,100, check no. 70.

Instructions

(a) Journalize the transactions above in a four-column cash payments journal with columns for Other Accounts Dr., Accounts Payable Dr., Merchandise Inventory Cr., and Cash Cr. Foot and crossfoot the journal.

(b) Insert the beginning balances in the Accounts Payable control and subsidiary accounts, and post the October transactions to these accounts.

(c) Prove the agreement of the control account and the subsidiary account balances.

(a) Balancing totals $11,950

(c) Accounts Payable $1,500

P7-3B The chart of accounts of Odeon Company includes the following selected accounts.

112 Accounts Receivable	401 Sales
120 Merchandise Inventory	412 Sales Returns and Allowances
126 Supplies	505 Cost of Goods Sold
157 Equipment	610 Advertising Expense
201 Accounts Payable	

Journalize transactions in multi-column purchases journal; post to the general and subsidiary ledgers.

(SO 3, 4, 5)

In July the following selected transactions were completed. All purchases and sales were on account. The cost of all merchandise sold was 70% of the sales price.

July 1 Purchased merchandise from Gucci Company $5,000.
    2 Received freight bill from Wayward Shipping on Gucci purchase $400.
    3 Made sales to Marion Company $1,300, and to Wayne Bros. $1,500.
    5 Purchased merchandise from Lee Company $3,200.
    8 Received credit on merchandise returned to Lee Company $300.
  13 Purchased store supplies from Boyd Supply $720.
  15 Purchased merchandise from Gucci Company $3,600 and from Anton Company $3,300.
  16 Made sales to Rowen Company $3,450 and to Wayne Bros. $1,570.
  18 Received bill for advertising from Lynda Advertisements $600.
  21 Sales were made to Marion Company $310 and to Haddad Company $2,300.
  22 Granted allowance to Marion Company for merchandise damaged in shipment $40.
  24 Purchased merchandise from Lee Company $3,000.
  26 Purchased equipment from Boyd Supply $600.
  28 Received freight bill from Wayward Shipping on Lee purchase of July 24, $380.
  30 Sales were made to Rowen Company $5,600.

Instructions

(a) Journalize the transactions above in a purchases journal, a sales journal, and a general journal. The purchases journal should have the following column headings: Date, Account Credited (Debited), Ref., Merchandise Inventory Dr., Accounts Payable Cr., and Other Accounts Dr.

(b) Post to both the general and subsidiary ledger accounts. (Assume that all accounts have zero beginning balances.)

(c) Prove the agreement of the control and subsidiary accounts.

(a) Purchases journal—
Accounts Payable
$20,800
Sales journal $16,030
(c) Accounts Receivable
$15,990
Accounts Payable
$20,500

P7-4B Selected accounts from the chart of accounts of Alpine Company are shown below.

101 Cash	401 Sales
112 Accounts Receivable	412 Sales Returns and Allowances
120 Merchandise Inventory	414 Sales Discounts
126 Supplies	505 Cost of Goods Sold
157 Equipment	726 Salaries Expense
201 Accounts Payable	

Journalize transactions in special journals.

(SO 3, 4, 5)

The cost of all merchandise sold was 60% of the sales price. During January, Alpine completed the following transactions.

Jan. 3 Purchased merchandise on account from Vanessa Co. $12,000.
    4 Purchased supplies for cash $80.
    4 Sold merchandise on account to Niki $7,250, invoice no. 371, terms 1/10, n/30.
    5 Issued a debit memorandum to Vanessa Co. and returned $300 worth of damaged goods.
    6 Made cash sales for the week totaling $3,150.
    8 Purchased merchandise on account from Marti Co. $4,500.
    9 Sold merchandise on account to Connor Corp. $6,400, invoice no. 372, terms 1/10, n/30.

11 Purchased merchandise on account from Betz Co. $3,700.
13 Paid in full Vanessa Co. on account less a 2% discount.
13 Made cash sales for the week totaling $6,260.
15 Received payment from Connor Corp. for invoice no. 372.
15 Paid semi-monthly salaries of $14,300 to employees.
17 Received payment from Niki for invoice no. 371.
17 Sold merchandise on account to Andrews Co. $1,200, invoice no. 373, terms 1/10, n/30.
19 Purchased equipment on account from Murphy Corp. $5,500.
20 Cash sales for the week totaled $3,200.
20 Paid in full Marti Co. on account less a 2% discount.
23 Purchased merchandise on account from Vanessa Co. $7,800.
24 Purchased merchandise on account from Forgetta Corp. $5,100.
27 Made cash sales for the week totaling $3,730.
30 Received payment from Andrews Co. for invoice no. 373.
31 Paid semi-monthly salaries of $13,200 to employees.
31 Sold merchandise on account to Niki $9,330, invoice no. 374, terms 1/10, n/30.

Anton Company uses the following journals.

1. Sales journal.
2. Single-column purchases journal.
3. Cash receipts journal with columns for Cash Dr., Sales Discounts Dr., Accounts Receivable Cr., Sales Cr., Other Accounts Cr., and Cost of Goods Sold Dr./Merchandise Inventory Cr.
4. Cash payments journal with columns for Other Accounts Dr., Accounts Payable Dr., Merchandise Inventory Cr., and Cash Cr.
5. General journal.

Instructions

(a) Sales journal $24,180
Purchases journal $33,100
Cash receipts journal balancing total $31,190
Cash payments journal balancing total $43,780

Using the selected accounts provided:
(a) Record the January transactions in the appropriate journal noted.
(b) Foot and crossfoot all special journals.
(c) Show how postings would be made by placing ledger account numbers and checkmarks as needed in the journals. (Actual posting to ledger accounts is not required.)

Journalize in sales and cash receipts journals; post; prepare a trial balance; prove control to subsidiary; prepare adjusting entries; prepare an adjusted trial balance.

(SO 3, 4, 5)

P7-5B Presented below are the purchases and cash payments journals for Scott Co. for its first month of operations.

	PURCHASES JOURNAL		P1
Date	**Account Credited**	**Ref.**	**Merchandise Inventory Dr. Accounts Payable Cr.**
July 4	G. Bashful		6,800
5	A. Doc		8,100
11	J. Happy		3,920
13	C. Sleepy		15,300
20	M. Sneezy		7,900
			42,020

	CASH PAYMENTS JOURNAL					CP1
Date	**Account Debited**	**Ref.**	**Other Accounts Dr.**	**Accounts Payable Dr.**	**Merchandise Inventory Cr.**	**Cash Cr.**
July 4	Store Supplies		600			600
10	A. Doc			8,100	81	8,019
11	Prepaid Rent		6,000			6,000
15	G. Bashful			6,800		6,800
19	Scott, Drawing		2,500			2,500
21	C. Sleepy			15,300	153	15,147
			9,100	30,200	234	39,066

In addition, the following transactions have not been journalized for July. The cost of all merchandise sold was 65% of the sales price.

July 1 The founder, D. Scott, invests $80,000 in cash.
      6 Sell merchandise on account to Dopey Co. $6,200 terms 1/10, n/30.
      7 Make cash sales totaling $4,000.
      8 Sell merchandise on account to S. Beauty $3,600, terms 1/10, n/30.
     10 Sell merchandise on account to W. Queen $4,900, terms 1/10, n/30.
     13 Receive payment in full from S. Beauty.
     16 Receive payment in full from W. Queen.
     20 Receive payment in full from Dopey Co.
     21 Sell merchandise on account to H. Prince $4,000, terms 1/10, n/30.
     29 Returned damaged goods to G. Bashful and received cash refund of $420.

Instructions

(a) Open the following accounts in the general ledger.

101 Cash	306 Scott, Drawing
112 Accounts Receivable	401 Sales
120 Merchandise Inventory	414 Sales Discounts
127 Store Supplies	505 Cost of Goods Sold
131 Prepaid Rent	631 Supplies Expense
201 Accounts Payable	729 Rent Expense
301 Scott, Capital	

(b) Journalize the transactions that have not been journalized in the sales journal, the cash receipts journal (see Illustration 7-10), and the general journal.

(c) Post to the accounts receivable and accounts payable subsidiary ledgers. Follow the sequence of transactions as shown in the problem.

(d) Post the individual entries and totals to the general ledger.

(e) Prepare a trial balance at July 31, 2005.

(f) Determine whether the subsidiary ledgers agree with the control accounts in the general ledger.

(g) The following adjustments at the end of July are necessary.
   (1) A count of supplies indicates that $140 is still on hand.
   (2) Recognize rent expense for July, $500.
   Prepare the necessary entries in the general journal. Post the entries to the general ledger.

(h) Prepare an adjusted trial balance at July 31, 2005.

(b) Sales journal total
$18,700
Cash receipts journal
balancing totals $99,120

(e) Totals $114,520
(f) Accounts Receivable
$4,000
Accounts Payable $11,820

(h) Totals $114,520

COMPREHENSIVE PROBLEM: CHAPTERS 3 TO 7

Raymond Company has the following opening account balances in its general and subsidiary ledgers on January 1 and uses the periodic inventory system. All accounts have normal debit and credit balances.

General Ledger

Account Number	Account Title	January 1 Opening Balance
101	Cash	$33,750
112	Accounts Receivable	13,000
115	Notes Receivable	39,000
120	Merchandise Inventory	20,000
125	Office Supplies	1,000
130	Prepaid Insurance	2,000
157	Equipment	6,450
158	Accumulated Depreciation	1,500
201	Accounts Payable	35,000
301	Raymond, Capital	78,700

Accounts Receivable Subsidiary Ledger			Accounts Payable Subsidiary Ledger	
Customer	**January 1 Opening Balance**		**Creditor**	**January 1 Opening Balance**
R. Draves	$1,500		S. Liazuk	$ 9,000
B. Jacovetti	7,500		R. Mikush	15,000
S. Kysely	4,000		D. Nguyen	11,000

Jan. 3   Sell merchandise on credit to B. Soto $3,100, invoice no. 510, and J. Ebel $1,800, invoice no. 511.

5   Purchase merchandise from S. Welz $3,000 and D. Laux $2,700.

7   Receive checks for $4,000 from S. Kysely and $2,000 from B. Jacovetti.

8   Pay freight on merchandise purchased $180.

9   Send checks to S. Liazuk for $9,000 and D. Nguyen for $11,000.

9   Issue credit memo for $300 to J. Ebel for merchandise returned.

10   Summary cash sales total $15,500.

11   Sell merchandise on credit to R. Draves for $1,900, invoice no. 512, and to S. Kysely $900, invoice no. 513.

      Post all entries to the subsidiary ledgers.

12   Pay rent of $1,000 for January.

13   Receive payment in full from B. Soto and J. Ebel.

15   Withdraw $800 cash by I. Raymond for personal use.

16   Purchase merchandise from D. Nguyen for $15,000, from S. Liazuk for $13,900, and from S. Welz for $1,500.

17   Pay $400 cash for office supplies.

18   Return $200 of merchandise to S. Liazuk and receive credit.

20   Summary cash sales total $17,500.

21   Issue $15,000 note to R. Mikush in payment of balance due.

21   Receive payment in full from S. Kysely.

      Post all entries to the subsidiary ledgers.

22   Sell merchandise on credit to B. Soto for $1,700, invoice no. 514, and to R. Draves for $800, invoice no. 515.

23   Send checks to D. Nguyen and S. Liazuk in full payment.

25   Sell merchandise on credit to B. Jacovetti for $3,500, invoice no. 516, and to J. Ebel for $6,100, invoice no. 517.

27   Purchase merchandise from D. Nguyen for $14,500, from D. Laux for $1,200, and from S. Welz for $2,800.

28   Pay $200 cash for office supplies.

31   Summary cash sales total $19,920.

31   Pay sales salaries of $4,300 and office salaries of $2,600.

Instructions

(a) Record the January transactions in the appropriate journal—sales, purchases, cash receipts, cash payments, and general.

(b) Post the journals to the general and subsidiary ledgers. New accounts should be added and numbered in an orderly fashion as needed.

(c) Prepare a trial balance at January 31, 2005, using a work sheet. Complete the work sheet using the following additional information.

(1) Office supplies at January 31 total $700.

(2) Insurance coverage expires on October 31, 2005.

(3) Annual depreciation on the equipment is $1,500.

(4) Interest of $30 has accrued on the note payable.

(5) Merchandise inventory at January 31 is $16,000.

(d) Prepare a multiple-step income statement and a statement of owner's equity for January and a classified balance sheet at the end of January.

(e) Prepare and post the adjusting and closing entries.

(f) Prepare a post-closing trial balance, and determine whether the subsidiary ledgers agree with the control accounts in the general ledger.

(c) Trial balance totals
$193,820;
Adj. T/B totals $193,975

(d) Net income $4,685
Total assets $123,315

(f) Post-closing T/B totals
$124,940

BROADENING YOUR PERSPECTIVE

Financial Reporting and Analysis

■ FINANCIAL REPORTING PROBLEM—Mini Practice Set

Peachtree

BYP7-1 (The working papers that accompany this textbook are needed in order to work this mini practice set.)

Cedzo Co. uses a perpetual inventory system and both an accounts receivable and an accounts payable subsidiary ledger. Balances related to both the general ledger and the subsidiary ledger for Cedzo are indicated in the working papers. Presented below are a series of transactions for Cedzo Co. for the month of January. Credit sales terms are 2/10, n/30. The cost of all merchandise sold was 60% of the sales price.

Jan.	3	Sell merchandise on credit to B. Stahre $4,100, invoice no. 510, and to J. Eppler $1,800, invoice no. 511.
	5	Purchase merchandise from S. Wong $3,000 and D. Lynch $2,200, terms n/30.
	7	Receive checks from S. LaDew $4,000 and B. Garcia $2,000 after discount period has lapsed.
	8	Pay freight on merchandise purchased $235.
	9	Send checks to S. Jung for $9,000 less 2% cash discount, and to D. Norby for $11,000 less 1% cash discount.
	9	Issue credit memo for $300 to J. Eppler for merchandise returned.
	10	Summary daily cash sales total $15,500.
	11	Sell merchandise on credit to R. Dvorak $1,600, invoice no. 512, and to S. LaDew $900, invoice no. 513.
	12	Pay rent of $1,000 for January.
	13	Receive payment in full from B. Stahre and J. Eppler less cash discounts.
	15	Withdraw $800 cash by M. Cedzo for personal use.
	15	Post all entries to the subsidiary ledgers.
	16	Purchase merchandise from D. Norby $16,000, terms 1/10, n/30; S. Jung $14,200, terms 2/10, n/30; and S. Wong $1,500, terms n/30.
	17	Pay $400 cash for office supplies.
	18	Return $200 of merchandise to S. Jung and receive credit.
	20	Summary daily cash sales total $18,100.
	21	Issue $15,000 note to R. Moses in payment of balance due.
	21	Receive payment in full from S. LaDew less cash discount.
	22	Sell merchandise on credit to S. Stahre $2,700, invoice no. 514, and to R. Dvorak $800, invoice no. 515.
	22	Post all entries to the subsidiary ledgers.
	23	Send checks to D. Norby and S. Jung in full payment less cash discounts.
	25	Sell merchandise on credit to B. Garcia $3,500, invoice no. 516, and to J. Eppler $6,100, invoice no. 517.
	27	Purchase merchandise from D. Norby $14,500, terms 1/10, n/30; D. Lynch $1,200, terms n/30; and S. Wong $5,400, terms n/30.
	27	Post all entries to the subsidiary ledgers.
	28	Pay $200 cash for office supplies.
	31	Summary daily cash sales total $21,300.
	31	Pay sales salaries $4,300 and office salaries $2,800.

Instructions

(a) Record the January transactions in a sales journal, a single-column purchases journal, a cash receipts journal as shown on page 287, a cash payments journal as shown on page 292, and a two-column general journal.

(b) Post the journals to the general ledger.

(c) Prepare a trial balance at January 31, 2005, in the trial balance columns of the work sheet. Complete the work sheet using the following additional information.

    (1) Office supplies at January 31 total $900.

    (2) Insurance coverage expires on October 31, 2005.

(3) Annual depreciation on the equipment is $1,500.

(4) Interest of $50 has accrued on the note payable.

(d) Prepare a multiple-step income statement and an owner's equity statement for January and a classified balance sheet at the end of January.

(e) Prepare and post adjusting and closing entries.

(f) Prepare a post-closing trial balance, and determine whether the subsidiary ledgers agree with the control accounts in the general ledger.

■ EXPLORING THE WEB

BYP7-2 Great Plains' Accounting is one of the leading accounting software packages. Information related to this package is found at its Web site.

Address: www.microsoft.com/businesssolutions/great%20plains/demos.mspx, or go to www.wiley.com/college/weygandt

Steps

1. Go to the site shown above.

2. Choose **General Ledger**. Perform instruction (a) below.

3. Choose **Accounts Payable**. Perform instruction (b) below.

Instructions

(a) What are three key features of the general ledger module highlighted by the company?

(b) What are three key features of the payables management module highlighted by the company?

Critical Thinking

■ GROUP DECISION CASE

BYP7-3 Manion & Roben is a wholesaler of small appliances and parts. Manion & Roben is operated by two owners, Andy Manion and Lorelei Roben. In addition, the company has one employee, a repair specialist, who is on a fixed salary. Revenues are earned through the sale of appliances to retailers (approximately 75% of total revenues), appliance parts to do-it-yourselfers (10%), and the repair of appliances brought to the store (15%). Appliance sales are made on both a credit and cash basis. Customers are billed on prenumbered sales invoices. Credit terms are always net/30 days. All parts sales and repair work are cash only.

Merchandise is purchased on account from the manufacturers of both the appliances and the parts. Practically all suppliers offer cash discounts for prompt payments, and it is company policy to take all discounts. Most cash payments are made by check. Checks are most frequently issued to suppliers, to trucking companies for freight on merchandise purchases, and to newspapers, radio, and TV stations for advertising. All advertising bills are paid as received. Andy and Lorelei each make a monthly drawing in cash for personal living expenses. The salaried repairman is paid twice monthly. Manion & Roben currently has a manual accounting system.

Instructions

With the class divided into groups, answer the following.

(a) Identify the special journals that Manion & Roben should have in its manual system. List the column headings appropriate for each of the special journals.

(b) What control and subsidiary accounts should be included in Manion & Roben manual system? Why?

■ COMMUNICATION ACTIVITY

BYP7-4 Kris Leask, a classmate, has a part-time bookkeeping job. She is concerned about the inefficiencies in journalizing and posting transactions. Jon Breiwa is the owner of the company where Kris works. In response to numerous complaints from Kris and others, Jon hired two additional bookkeepers a month ago. However, the inefficiencies have continued at an even higher rate. The accounting information system for the company has only a general journal and a general ledger. Jon refuses to install an electronic accounting system.

Instructions

Now that Kris is an expert in manual accounting information systems, she decides to send a letter to Jon Breiwa explaining (1) why the additional personnel did not help and (2) what changes should be made to improve the efficiency of the accounting department. Write the letter that you think Kris should send.

■ ETHICS CASE

BYP7-5   Teofilo Products Company operates three divisions, each with its own manufacturing plant and marketing/sales force. The corporate headquarters and central accounting office are in Teofilo, and the plants are in Freeport, Rockport, and Bayport, all within 50 miles of Teofilo. Corporate management treats each division as an independent profit center and encourages competition among them. They each have similar but different product lines. As a competitive incentive, bonuses are awarded each year to the employees of the fastest growing and most profitable division.

Ismael Soto is the manager of Teofilo centralized computer accounting operation that keyboards the sales transactions and maintains the accounts receivable for all three divisions. Ismael came up in the accounting ranks from the Bayport division where his wife, several relatives, and many friends still work.

As sales documents are keyboarded into the computer, the originating division is identified by code. Most sales documents (95%) are coded, but some (5%) are not coded or are coded incorrectly. As the manager, Ismael has instructed the keyboard operators to assign the Bayport code to all uncoded and incorrectly coded sales documents. This is done he says, "in order to expedite processing and to keep the computer files current since they are updated daily." All receivables and cash collections for all three divisions are handled by Teofilo as one subsidiary accounts receivable ledger.

Instructions

(a) Who are the stakeholders in this situation?

(b) What are the ethical issues in this case?

(c) How might the system be improved to prevent this situation?

Answers to Self-Study Questions

1. d   **2.** b   **3.** a   **4.** c   **5.** a   **6.** c   **7.** d   **8.** b   **9.** c   **10.** c

✓ **REMEMBER** to go back to the Navigator box on the chapter-opening page and check off your completed work.

Internal Control and Cash

THE NAVIGATOR ✓

Understand **Concepts for Review**	❏
Read **Feature Story**	❏
Scan **Study Objectives**	❏
Read **Preview**	❏
Read text and answer **Before You Go On** p. 325 ❏ p. 333 ❏ p. 341 ❏ p. 342 ❏	
Work **Demonstration Problem**	❏
Review **Summary of Study Objectives**	❏
Answer **Self-Study Questions**	❏
Complete **Assignments**	❏

CONCEPTS FOR REVIEW

Before studying this chapter, you should know or, if necessary, review:

How cash transactions are recorded.
(Ch. 2, pp. 50–62)

How cash is classified on a balance sheet.
(Ch. 4, pp. 152–153)

The role ethics plays in proper financial reporting.
(Ch. 1, p. 9)

Minding the Money in Moose Jaw

If you're ever looking for a cappuccino in Moose Jaw, Saskatchewan, stop by **Stephanie's Gourmet Coffee and More**, located on Main Street. Staff there serve, on average, 646 cups of coffee a day—including both regular and specialty coffees—not to mention soups, Italian sandwiches, and a wide assortment of gourmet cheesecakes.

"We've got high school students who come here, and students from the community college," says owner/manager Stephanie Mintenko, who has run the place since opening it in 1995. "We have customers who are retired, and others who are working people and have only 30 minutes for lunch. We have to be pretty quick."

That means that the cashiers have to be efficient. Like most businesses where purchases are low-cost and high-volume, cash control has to be simple.

"We have an electronic cash register, but it's not the fancy new kind where you just punch in the item," explains Ms. Mintenko. "You have to punch in the prices." The machine does keep track of sales in several categories, however. Cashiers punch a button to indicate whether each item is a beverage, a meal, or a charge for the cafe's Internet connections. All transactions are recorded on an internal tape in the machine; the customer receives a receipt only upon request.

There is only one cash register. "Up to three of us might operate it on any given shift, including myself," says Ms. Mintenko.

She and her staff do two "cashouts" each day—one with the shift change at 5:00, and one when the shop closes at 10:00. The cash in the register drawer is counted. That amount, minus the cash change carried forward (the float), should match the shift total on the register tape. If there's a discrepancy, they do another count. Then, if necessary, "we go through the whole tape to find the mistake," she explains. "It usually turns out to be someone who punched in $18 instead of $1.80, or something like that."

Ms. Mintenko sends all the cash tapes and float totals to a bookkeeper, who double checks everything and provides regular reports. "We try to keep the accounting simple, so we can concentrate on making great coffee and food."

THE NAVIGATOR

After studying this chapter, you should be able to:

1. Define internal control.
2. Identify the principles of internal control.
3. Explain the applications of internal control principles to cash receipts.
4. Explain the applications of internal control principles to cash disbursements.
5. Describe the operation of a petty cash fund.
6. Indicate the control features of a bank account.
7. Prepare a bank reconciliation.
8. Explain the reporting of cash.

THE NAVIGATOR

PREVIEW OF CHAPTER 8

As the story about recording cash sales at Stephanie's Gourmet Coffee and More indicates, control of cash is important. Controls are also needed to safeguard other types of assets. For example, Stephanie's undoubtedly has controls to prevent the theft of food and supplies, and controls to prevent the theft of silverware and dishes from its kitchen.

In this chapter, we explain the essential features of an internal control system and then describe how those controls apply to cash. The applications include some controls with which you may be already familiar. Toward the end of the chapter, we describe the use of a bank and explain how cash is reported on the balance sheet.

The content and organization of Chapter 8 are as follows.

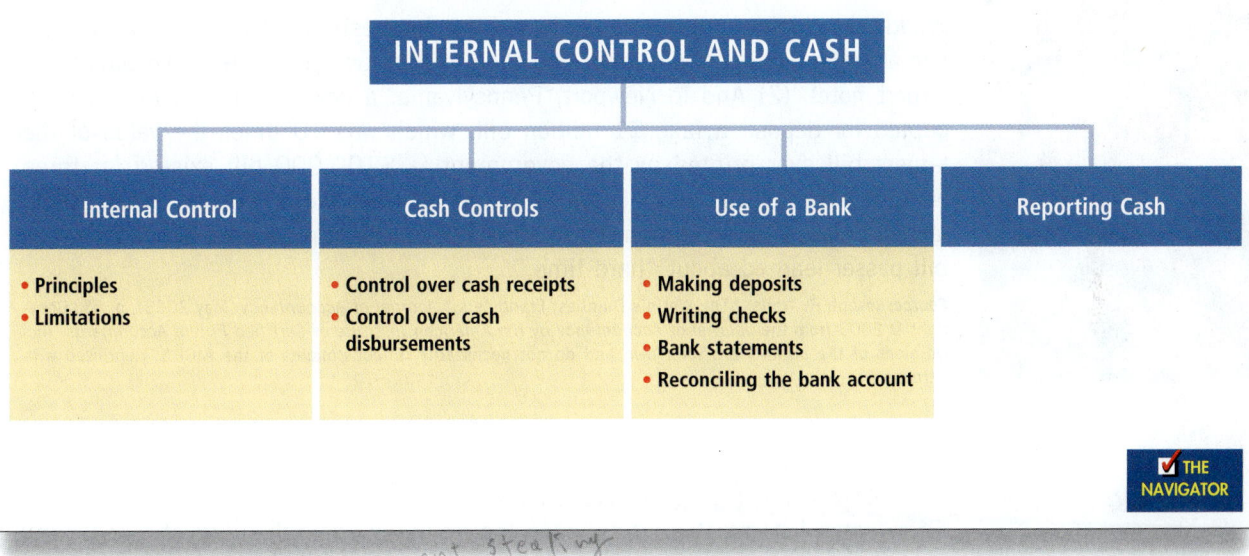

INTERNAL CONTROL AND CASH

Internal Control	Cash Controls	Use of a Bank	Reporting Cash
• Principles • Limitations	• Control over cash receipts • Control over cash disbursements	• Making deposits • Writing checks • Bank statements • Reconciling the bank account	

☑ THE NAVIGATOR

Prevent stealing

Internal Control

Could there be dishonest employees where you work? Unfortunately, the answer sometimes is Yes. For example, in addition to the highly publicized frauds at **Enron**, **WorldCom**, **Tyco**, and **Global Crossing**, the financial press recently reported the following.

A bookkeeper in a small company diverted $750,000 of bill payments to a personal bank account over a 3-year period.

A shipping clerk with 28 years of service shipped $125,000 of merchandise to himself.

A computer operator embezzled $21 million from **Wells Fargo Bank** over a 2-year period.

A church treasurer "borrowed" $150,000 of church funds to finance a friend's business dealings.

These situations emphasize the need for a good system of internal control.

Internal control consists of the plan of organization and all the related methods and measures adopted within a business to:

1. **Safeguard its assets** from employee theft, robbery, and unauthorized use.
2. **Enhance the accuracy and reliability of its accounting records.** This is done by reducing the risk of **errors** (unintentional mistakes) and **irregularities** (intentional mistakes and misrepresentations) in the accounting process.

STUDY OBJECTIVE 1.

Define internal control.

1. Safeguard asset
2. Accuracy & reliability

319

The Foreign Corrupt Practices Act of 1977 and more recently, the Sarbanes-Oxley Act of 2002 require all major U.S. corporations to maintain an adequate system of internal control. Companies that fail to comply are subject to fines, and company officers may be imprisoned. Also, the National Commission on Fraudulent Financial Reporting concluded that all companies whose stock is publicly traded should maintain internal controls that can provide reasonable assurance that fraudulent financial reporting will be prevented or subject to early detection.

ACCOUNTING IN ACTION — Ethics Insight

Fraud takes many forms. Here are two of the dumbest: (1) In Wichita, Kansas, police arrested a 22-year-old male who tried to pass two counterfeit $16 bills at an airport hotel. (2) And in Newport, Pennsylvania, a new-accounts bank clerk accepted for deposit a fake $1 million bill, which was 10 times the value of the largest bill ever printed by the government (a $100,000 bill existed for three weeks in the 1930s) and 10,000 times larger than the $100 bill, which is the largest bill now in circulation. While the bank clerk learned a hard lesson, the fake bill passer learned about "hard time."

Source: Joseph R. Wells, "The World's Dumbest Fraudsters," *Journal of Accountancy* (May 2003), p. 55. Copyright © 2003 from the *Journal of Accountancy* by the American Institute of Certified Public Accountants, *Inc.* Opinions of the authors are their own and do not necessarily reflect policies of the AICPA. Reprinted with permission.

STUDY OBJECTIVE 2

Identify the principles of internal control.

Principles of Internal Control

To safeguard its assets and enhance the accuracy and reliability of its accounting records, a company follows specific control principles. Of course, internal control measures vary with the size and nature of the business and with management's control philosophy. The six principles listed in Illustration 8-1 apply to most enterprises. Each principle is explained in the following sections.

Illustration 8-1
Principles of internal control

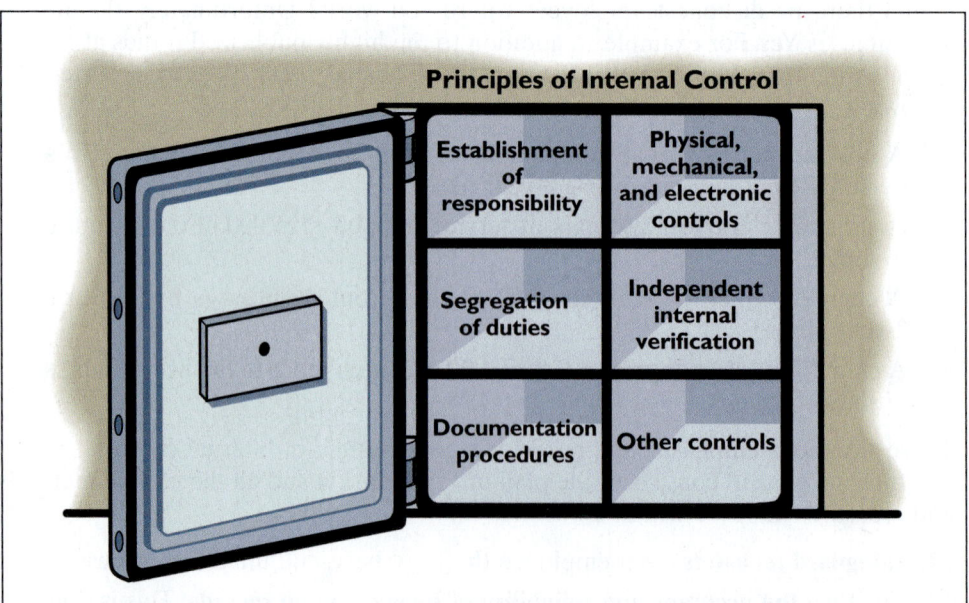

Establishment of Responsibility

An essential characteristic of internal control is the assignment of responsibility to specific employees. **Control is most effective when only one person is responsible for a given task.** To illustrate, assume that the cash on hand at the end of the day in a **Safeway** supermarket is $10 short of the cash rung up on the cash register. If only one person has operated the register, responsibility for the shortage can be assessed quickly. If two or more individuals have worked the register, it may be impossible to determine who is responsible for the error unless each person is assigned a separate cash drawer and register key. The principle of establishing responsibility does not appear to be strictly applied by **Stephanie's** (in the Feature Story) since three people operate the cash register on any given shift. To identify any shortages quickly at Stephanie's, two cashouts are performed each day.

Establishing responsibility includes the authorization and approval of transactions. For example, the vice president of sales should have the authority to establish policies for making credit sales. The policies ordinarily will require written credit department approval of credit sales.

It's your shift now. I'm turning in my cash drawer and heading home.

Transfer of cash drawers

Segregation of Duties

Segregation of duties (also called separation of functions or division of work) is indispensable in a system of internal control. There are two common applications of this principle:

1. Related activities should be assigned to different individuals.
2. Establishing the accountability (keeping the records) for an asset should be separate from the physical custody of that asset.

The rationale for segregation of duties is this: **The work of one employee should, without a duplication of effort, provide a reliable basis for evaluating the work of another employee.**

RELATED ACTIVITIES. Related activities that should be assigned to different individuals arise in both purchasing and selling. **When one individual is responsible for all of the related activities, the potential for errors and irregularities is increased.** Related purchasing activities include ordering merchandise, receiving the goods, and paying (or authorizing payment) for the merchandise. In purchasing, for example, orders could be placed with friends or with suppliers who give kickbacks. Or, only a cursory count and inspection could be made upon receiving the goods, which could lead to errors and poor-quality merchandise. Payment might be authorized without a careful review of the invoice. Even worse, fictitious invoices might be approved for payment. When the ordering, receiving, and paying are assigned to different individuals, the risk of such abuses is minimized.

Similarly, related sales activities should be assigned to different individuals. Related selling activities include making a sale, shipping (or delivering) the goods to the customer, billing the customer, and receiving payment. When one person handles related sales transactions, a salesperson could make sales at unauthorized prices to increase sales commissions; a shipping clerk could ship goods to himself; a billing clerk could understate the amount billed for sales made to friends and relatives. These abuses are reduced by dividing the sales tasks: the salespersons make the sale; the shipping department ships the goods on the basis of the sales order; and the billing department prepares the sales invoice after comparing the sales order with the report of goods shipped.

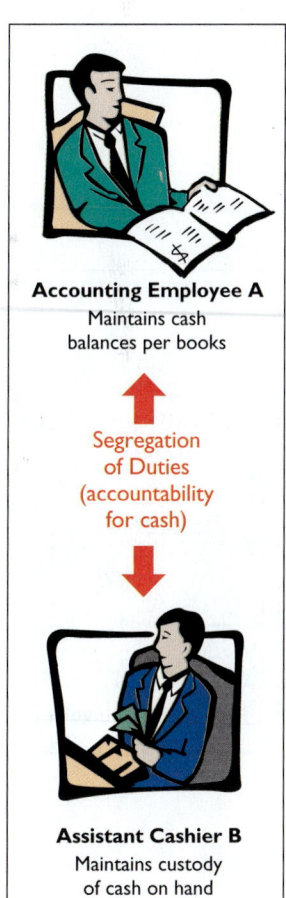

Accounting Employee A
Maintains cash balances per books

Segregation of Duties (accountability for cash)

Assistant Cashier B
Maintains custody of cash on hand

It's said that accountants' predecessors were the scribes of ancient Egypt, who kept the pharaohs' books. They inventoried grain, gold, and other assets. Unfortunately, some fell victim to temptation and stole from their leader, as did other employees of the king. The solution was to have two scribes independently record each transaction (the first internal control). As long as the scribes' totals agreed exactly, there was no problem. But if the totals were materially different, both scribes would be put to death. That proved to be a great incentive for them to carefully check all the numbers and make sure the help wasn't stealing. In fact, fraud prevention and detection became the royal accountants' main duty.

Source: Joseph T. Wells, "So That's Why It's Called a Pyramid Scheme," *Journal of Accountancy* (October 2000), p. 91. Copyright © 2000 from the *Journal of Accountancy by the American Institute of Certified Public Accountants, Inc.* Opinions of the authors are their own and do not necessarily reflect policies of the AICPA. Reprinted with permission.

ACCOUNTABILITY FOR ASSETS.   To provide a valid basis of accountability for an asset, the accountant should have neither physical custody of the asset nor access to it. Likewise, the custodian of the asset should not maintain or have access to the accounting records. **When one employee maintains the record of the asset that should be on hand, and a different employee has physical custody of the asset, the custodian of the asset is not likely to convert the asset to personal use.** The separation of accounting responsibility from the custody of assets is especially important for cash and inventories because these assets are very vulnerable to unauthorized use or misappropriation.

Documentation Procedures

Documents provide evidence that transactions and events have occurred. At **Stephanie's Gourmet Coffee and More**, the cash register tape was the restaurant's documentation for the sale and the amount of cash received. Similarly, the shipping document indicates that the goods have been shipped, and the sales invoice indicates that the customer has been billed for the goods. By adding signatures (or initials) to the documents, the individual(s) responsible for the transaction or event can be identified. Documentation of transactions should be made when the transaction occurs. Documentation of events, such as those leading to adjusting entries, is generally developed when the adjustments are made.

Several procedures should be established for documents. First, whenever possible, **documents should be prenumbered, and all documents should be accounted for**. Prenumbering helps to prevent a transaction from being recorded more than once. It also helps to prevent the transactions from not being recorded. Second, documents that are **source documents for accounting entries should be promptly forwarded to the accounting department**. **This control measure helps to ensure timely recording of the transaction** and contributes directly to the accuracy and reliability of the accounting records.

Prenumbered invoices

Physical, Mechanical, and Electronic Controls

Use of physical, mechanical, and electronic controls is essential. Physical controls relate primarily to the safeguarding of assets. Mechanical and electronic controls also safeguard assets; some enhance the accuracy and reliability of the accounting records. Examples of these controls are shown in Illustration 8-2.

Illustration 8-2
Physical, mechanical, and electronic controls

Physical Controls

Safes, vaults, and safety deposit boxes for cash and business papers

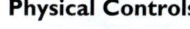

Locked warehouses and storage cabinets for inventories and records

Computer facilities with pass key access or fingerprint or eyeball scans

Mechanical and Electronic Controls

Alarms to prevent break-ins

Television monitors and garment sensors to deter theft

Time clocks for recording time worked

Independent Internal Verification

Most internal control systems provide for **independent internal verification**. This principle involves the review, comparison, and reconciliation of data prepared by other employees. To obtain maximum benefit from independent internal verification:

1. The verification should be made periodically or on a surprise basis.
2. The verification should be done by someone who is independent of the employee responsible for the information. *(Int Aud)*
3. Discrepancies and exceptions should be reported to a management level that can take appropriate corrective action.

Independent internal verification is especially useful in comparing recorded accountability with existing assets. The reconciliation of the cash register tape with the cash in the register at **Stephanie's Gourmet Coffee and More** is an example of this internal control principle. Another common example is the reconciliation by an independent person of the cash balance per books with the cash balance per bank. The relationship between this principle and the segregation of duties principle is shown graphically in Illustration 8-3 (page 324).

In large companies, independent internal verification is often assigned to internal auditors. **Internal auditors** are company employees who evaluate on a continuous basis the effectiveness of the company's system of internal control. They periodically review the activities of departments and individuals to determine whether prescribed internal controls are being followed. They also recommend improvements when needed. The importance of this function is illustrated by the fact that most fraud is discovered by the company through internal mechanisms, such as existing internal controls and internal audits. The recent alleged fraud at **WorldCom** involving billions of dollars, for example, was uncovered by an internal auditor.

Illustration 8-3
Comparison of segregation of duties principle with independent internal verification principle

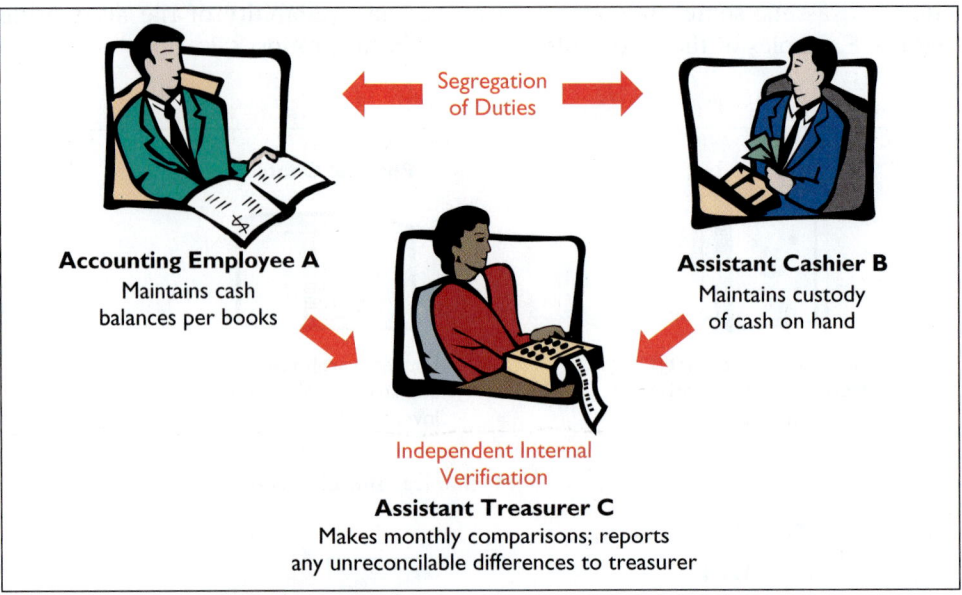

Other Controls

Other control measures include the following.

1. **Bonding of employees who handle cash.** Bonding involves obtaining insurance protection against misappropriation of assets by dishonest employees. This measure contributes to the safeguarding of cash in two ways: First, the insurance company carefully screens all individuals before adding them to the policy and may reject risky applicants. Second, bonded employees know that the insurance company will vigorously prosecute all offenders.

2. **Rotating employees' duties and requiring employees to take vacations.** These measures are designed to deter employees from attempting any thefts since they will not be able to permanently conceal their improper actions. Many bank embezzlements, for example, were discovered when the perpetrator was on vacation or assigned to a new position.

Limitations of Internal Control

A company's system of internal control is generally designed to provide **reasonable assurance** that assets are properly safeguarded and that the accounting records are reliable. **The concept of reasonable assurance rests on the premise that the costs of establishing control procedures should not exceed their expected benefit.** To illustrate, consider shoplifting losses in retail stores. Such losses could be eliminated by having a security guard stop and search customers as they leave the store. But, store managers have concluded that the negative effects of adopting such a procedure cannot be justified. Instead, stores have attempted to "control" shoplifting losses by less costly procedures such as: (1) posting signs saying, "We reserve the right to inspect all packages," and "All shoplifters will be prosecuted," (2) using hidden TV cameras and store detectives to monitor customer activity, and (3) using sensoring equipment at exits.

The **human element** is an important factor in every system of internal control. A good system can become ineffective as a result of employee fatigue, carelessness, or indifference. For example, a receiving clerk may not bother to count goods received or may just "fudge" the counts. Occasionally, two or more individuals may work together to get around prescribed controls. Such **collusion** can significantly impair the effectiveness of a system, eliminating the protection offered by segregation of duties. If a supervisor and a cashier collaborate to understate cash receipts, the system of internal control may be negated (at least in the short run). No system of internal control is perfect.

The size of the business also may impose limitations on internal control. In a small company, for example, it may be difficult to segregate duties or to provide for independent internal verification.

ACCOUNTING IN ACTION  e Business Insight

Unfortunately, computer-related frauds have become a major concern. The average computer fraud loss is $650,000, compared with an average loss of only $19,000 resulting from other types of white-collar crime.

Computer fraud can be perpetrated almost invisibly and done with electronic speed. Psychologically, stealing with impersonal computer tools can seem far less criminal to some people. Therefore, the moral threshold to commit computer fraud is lower than fraud involving person-to-person contact.

Preventing and detecting computer fraud represents a major challenge. One of the best ways for a company to minimize the likelihood of computer fraud is to have a good system of internal control that allows the benefits of computerization to be gained without opening the possibility for rampant fraud.

BEFORE YOU GO ON...

Review It

1. What are the two primary objectives of internal control?
2. Identify and describe the principles of internal control.
3. What are the limitations of internal control?

Do It

Li Song owns a small retail store. Li wants to establish good internal control procedures but is confused about the difference between segregation of duties and independent internal verification. Explain the differences to Li.

ACTION PLAN

■ Understand and explain the differences between (1) segregation of duties and (2) independent internal verification.

SOLUTION   Segregation of duties involves assigning responsibility so that the work of one employee evaluates the work of another employee. Segregation of duties occurs daily in executing and recording transactions. In contrast, independent internal verification involves reviewing, comparing, and reconciling data prepared by one or several employees. Independent internal verification occurs after the fact, as in the case of reconciling cash register totals at the end of the day with cash on hand.

Related exercise material: *BE8-1, BE8-2,* and *E8-1.*

Cash Controls

Just as cash is the beginning of a company's operating cycle, it is also usually the starting point for a company's system of internal control. Cash is the one asset that is readily convertible into any other type of asset. It is easily concealed and transported, and it is highly desired. Because of these characteristics, **cash is the asset most susceptible to improper diversion and use**. Moreover, because of the large volume of cash transactions, numerous errors may occur in executing and recording them. To safeguard cash and to ensure the accuracy of the accounting records for cash, effective internal control over cash is imperative.

Cash consists of coins, currency (paper money), checks, money orders, and money on hand or on deposit in a bank or similar depository. The general rule is that if the bank will accept it for deposit, it is cash. Items such as postage stamps and postdated checks (checks payable in the future) are not cash. Stamps are a prepaid expense; the postdated checks are accounts receivable. In the following sections we explain the application of internal control principles to cash receipts and cash disbursements.

Internal Control over Cash Receipts

STUDY OBJECTIVE 3

Explain the applications of internal control principles to cash receipts.

Cash receipts come from a variety of sources: cash sales; collections on account from customers; the receipt of interest, rent, and dividends; investments by owners; bank loans; and proceeds from the sale of noncurrent assets. Illustration 8-4 (page 327) shows how the internal control principles explained earlier apply to cash receipts transactions.

As might be expected, companies vary considerably in how they apply these principles. To illustrate internal control over cash receipts, we will examine control measures for a retail store with both over-the-counter and mail receipts.

Over-the-Counter Receipts

Control of over-the-counter receipts in retail businesses is centered on cash registers that are visible to customers. In supermarkets and in variety stores such as **Kmart**, cash registers are placed in check-out lines near the exit. In stores such as **Sears, Roebuck & Co.** and **J. C. Penney**, each department has its own cash register. A cash sale is "rung up" on a cash register **with the amount clearly visible to the customer**. This measure prevents the cashier from ringing up a lower amount and pocketing the difference. The customer receives an itemized cash register receipt slip and is expected to count the change received. A cash register tape is locked into the register until removed by a supervisor or manager. This tape accumulates the daily transactions and totals. When the tape is removed, the supervisor compares the total with the amount of cash in the register. The tape should show all registered receipts accounted for. The supervisor's findings are reported on a cash count sheet which is signed by both the cashier and supervisor. The cash count sheet used by Alrite Food Mart is shown in Illustration 8-5 (page 327).

The count sheets, register tapes, and cash are then given to the head cashier. This individual prepares a daily cash summary showing the total cash received and the amount from each source, such as cash sales and collections on account. The head cashier sends one copy of the summary to the accounting department for entry into the cash receipts journal. The other copy goes to the treasurer's office for later comparison with the daily bank deposit.

Next, the head cashier prepares a deposit slip (see Illustration 8-9 on page 334) and makes the bank deposit. The total amount deposited should be equal to the total receipts on the daily cash summary. This will ensure that all receipts have been placed in the custody of the bank. In accepting the bank deposit, the bank stamps (authenticates) the duplicate deposit slip and sends it to the company treasurer, who makes the comparison with the daily cash summary.

Illustration 8-4
Application of internal
control principles to cash
receipts

Internal Control over Cash Receipts

**Establishment of
Responsibility**

Only designated
personnel are
authorized to
handle cash receipts
(cashiers)

**Physical,
Mechanical, and
Electronic Controls**

Store cash in safes
and bank vaults;
limit access to
storage areas; use
cash registers

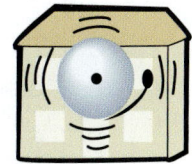

**Segregation
of Duties**

Different individuals
receive cash, record
cash receipts, and
hold the cash

**Independent
Internal
Verification**

Supervisors count
cash receipts daily;
treasurer compares
total receipts to
bank deposits daily

**Documentation
Procedures**

Use remittance
advice (mail
receipts), cash
register tapes, and
deposit slips

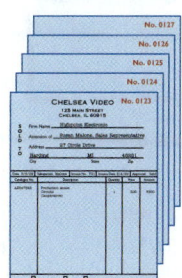

Other Controls

Bond personnel
who handle cash;
require employees
to take vacations;
deposit all cash
in bank daily

Illustration 8-5
Cash count sheet

Store No. ___8___	Date March 8, 2005
1. Opening cash balance	$ 50.00
2. Cash sales per tape (attached)	6,956.20
3. Total cash to be accounted for	7,006.20
4. Cash on hand (see list)	6,996.10
5. Cash (short) or over	$ (10.10)
6. Ending cash balance	$ 50.00
7. Cash for deposit (Line 4 – Line 6)	$6,946.10

Cashier *J. Cruse*   Supervisor *M. Braun*

These measures for cash sales are graphically presented in Illustration 8-6. The activities of the sales department are shown separately from those of the cashier's department to indicate the segregation of duties in handling cash.

Illustration 8-6
Executing over-the-counter cash sales

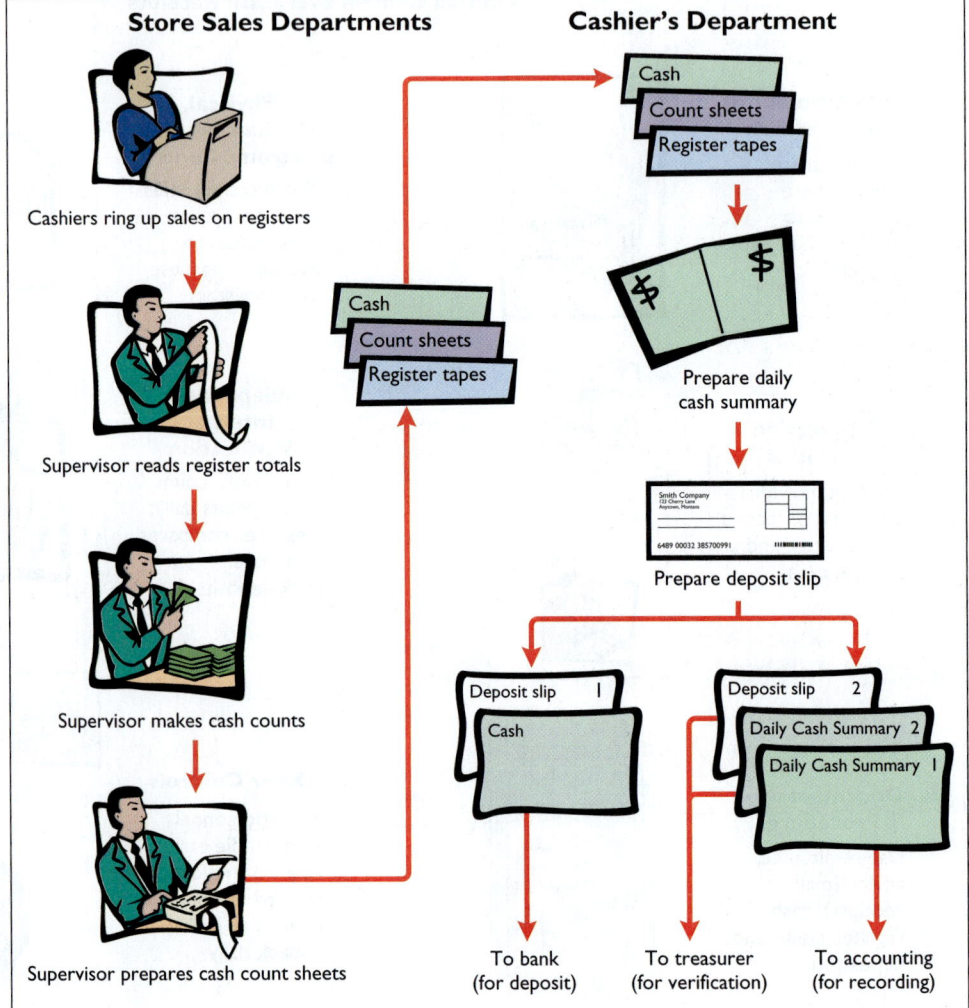

Mail Receipts

As an individual customer, you may be more familiar with over-the-counter receipts than with mail receipts. However, mail receipts resulting from billings and credit sales are by far the most common way cash is received by businesses. Think, for example, of the number of checks received through the mail daily by a national retailer such as **J. Crew** or **Abercrombie & Fitch**.

All mail receipts should be opened in the presence of two mail clerks. These receipts are generally in the form of checks or money orders. They frequently are accompanied by a remittance advice stating the purpose of the check (sometimes attached to the check, but often a part of the bill that the customer tears off and returns). Each check should be promptly endorsed "For Deposit Only" by use of a company stamp. This **restrictive endorsement** reduces the likelihood that the check will be diverted to personal use. Banks will not give an individual any cash under this type of endorsement.

A list of the checks received each day should be prepared in duplicate. This list shows the name of the issuer of the check, the purpose of the payment, and the

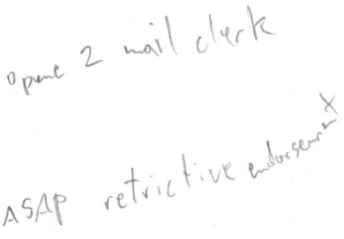

amount of the check. Each mail clerk should sign the list to establish responsibility for the data. The original copy of the list, along with the checks and remittance advices, are then sent to the cashier's department. There they are added to over-the-counter receipts (if any) in preparing the daily cash summary and in making the daily bank deposit. Also, a copy of the list is sent to the treasurer's office for comparison with the total mail receipts shown on the daily cash summary. This copy ensures that all mail receipts have been included.

Internal Control over Cash Disbursements

Cash may be disbursed for a variety of reasons, such as to pay expenses and liabilities, or to purchase assets. **Generally, internal control over cash disbursements is more effective when payments are made by check, rather than by cash.** One exception is **for incidental amounts that are paid out of petty cash.**[1] Payment by check generally occurs only after specified control procedures have been followed. In addition, the "paid" check provides proof of payment. Illustration 8-7 shows how principles of internal control apply to cash disbursements.

STUDY OBJECTIVE 4

Explain the applications of internal control principles to cash disbursements.

Illustration 8-7
Application of internal control principles to cash disbursements

---

Internal Control over Cash Disbursements

Establishment of Responsibility

Only designated personnel are authorized to sign checks (treasurer)

Physical, Mechanical, and Electronic Controls

Store blank checks in safes, with limited access; print check amounts by machine in indelible ink

Segregation of Duties

Different individuals approve and make payments; check signers do not record disbursements

Independent Internal Verification

Compare checks to invoices; reconcile bank statement monthly

Documentation Procedures

Use prenumbered checks and account for them in sequence; each check must have approved invoice

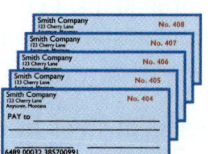

Other Controls

Stamp invoices PAID

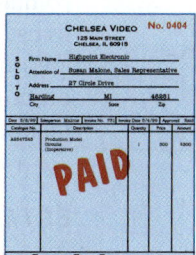

---

[1]The operation of a petty cash fund is explained on pages 330–332.

Voucher System

Most medium and large companies use vouchers as part of their internal control over cash disbursements. A **voucher system** is a network of approvals by authorized individuals acting independently to ensure that all disbursements by check are proper.

The system begins with the authorization to incur a cost or expense. It ends with the issuance of a check for the liability incurred. A **voucher** is an authorization form prepared for each expenditure. Vouchers are required for all types of cash disbursements except those from petty cash. The voucher generally is prepared in the accounts payable department.

The starting point in preparing a voucher is to fill in the appropriate information about the liability on the face of the voucher. The vendor's invoice provides most of the needed information. Then, the voucher must be recorded (in the journal called a **voucher register**) and filed according to the date on which it is to be paid. A check is sent on that date, the voucher is stamped "paid," and the paid voucher is sent to the accounting department for recording (in a journal called the **check register**). A voucher system involves two journal entries, one to issue the voucher and a second to pay the voucher.

Electronic Funds Transfer (EFT) System

Accounting for and controlling cash is an expensive and time-consuming process. The cost to process a check through a bank system is about $1.00 per check and is increasing. It is not surprising, therefore, that new approaches are being developed to transfer funds among parties without the use of paper (deposit tickets, checks, etc.). Such procedures, called **electronic funds transfers (EFT)**, are disbursement systems that use wire, telephone, or computers to transfer cash from one location to another. Use of EFT is quite common. For example, many employees receive no formal payroll checks from their employers, which instead send electronic depository information to the appropriate banks. Regular payments such as those for house, car, and utilities are frequently made by EFT.

Petty Cash Fund

STUDY OBJECTIVE 5

Describe the operation of a petty cash fund.

As you learned earlier in the chapter, better internal control over cash disbursements is possible when payments are made by check. However, using checks to pay small amounts is both impractical and a nuisance. For instance, a company would not want to write checks to pay for postage due, employee lunches, or taxi fares. A common way of handling such payments, while maintaining satisfactory control, is to use a petty cash fund. A **petty cash fund** is a cash fund used to pay relatively small amounts but still maintain satisfactory control. The operation of a petty cash fund, often called an **imprest system**, involves three steps: (1) establishing the fund, (2) making payments from the fund, and (3) replenishing the fund.[2]

ESTABLISHING THE FUND. Two essential steps in establishing a petty cash fund are (1) appointing a petty cash custodian who will be responsible for the fund and (2) determining the size of the fund. Ordinarily, the amount is expected to cover anticipated disbursements for a 3- to 4-week period. To establish the fund, a check

---

[2]The term "imprest" means an advance of money for a designated purpose.

payable to the petty cash custodian is issued for the stipulated amount. If the Laird Company decides to establish a $100 fund on March 1, the entry in general journal form is:

Mar. 1	Petty Cash	100	
	Cash		100
	(To establish a petty cash fund)		

A	=	L	+	OE
+100				
−100				

Cash Flows
no effect

The custodian cashes the check and places the proceeds in a locked petty cash box or drawer. Most petty cash funds are established on a fixed-amount basis. No additional entries will be made to the Petty Cash account unless management changes the stipulated amount of the fund. For example, if Laird Company decides on July 1 to increase the size of the fund to $250, it would debit Petty Cash $150 and credit Cash $150.

MAKING PAYMENTS FROM THE FUND.   The custodian of the petty cash fund has the authority to make payments from the fund that conform to prescribed management policies. Usually, management limits the size of expenditures that may be made. Likewise, it may not permit use of the fund for certain types of transactions (such as making short-term loans to employees). Each payment from the fund must be documented on a prenumbered petty cash receipt (or petty cash voucher), as shown in Illustration 8-8. Note that the signatures of both the custodian and the person receiving payment are required on the receipt. If other supporting documents such as a freight bill or invoice are available, they should be attached to the petty cash receipt.

Illustration 8-8
Petty cash receipt

> No. 7   W. A. LAIRD COMPANY
>   Petty Cash Receipt
>
> Date   3/6/05
>
> Paid to   Acme Express Agency   Amount $18.00
>
> For   Collect Express Charges
>
> CHARGE TO   Freight-in
>
> Approved   Received Payment
>
> *L. A. Bird* Custodian   *R. E. Meins*

The receipts are kept in the petty cash box until the fund runs low and needs to be replenished. The sum of the petty cash receipts and money in the fund should equal the established total at all times. Surprise counts can be made at any time by an independent person, such as an internal auditor, to determine whether the fund is being maintained intact.

No accounting entry is made to record a payment at the time it is made from petty cash. It is considered unnecessary to do so. Instead, the accounting effects of each payment are recognized when the fund is replenished.

REPLENISHING THE FUND. When the money in the petty cash fund reaches a minimum level, the fund is replenished. The request for reimbursement is initiated by the petty cash custodian. This individual prepares a schedule (or summary) of the payments that have been made and sends the schedule, supported by petty cash receipts and other documentation, to the treasurer's office. The receipts and supporting documents are examined in the treasurer's office to verify that they were proper payments from the fund. The treasurer then approves the request and a check is prepared to restore the fund to its established amount. At the same time, all supporting documentation is stamped "paid" so that it cannot be submitted again for payment.

To illustrate, assume that on March 15 the petty cash custodian requests a check for $87. The fund contains $13 cash and petty cash receipts for postage $44, freight-out $38, and miscellaneous expenses $5. The general journal entry to record the check is:

```
A   =   L   +   OE
−87            −44 Exp
               −38 Exp
               −5 Exp
```

Cash Flows
−87

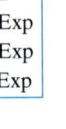

Mar. 15	Postage Expense	44	
	Freight-out	38	
	Miscellaneous Expense	5	
	Cash		87
	(To replenish petty cash fund)		

Note that the Petty Cash account is not affected by the reimbursement entry. Replenishment changes the composition of the fund by replacing the petty cash receipts with cash. It does not change the balance in the fund.

It may be necessary in replenishing a petty cash fund to recognize a cash shortage or overage. This results when the cash plus receipts in the petty cash box do not equal the established amount of the petty cash fund. To illustrate, assume in the example on the preceding page that the custodian had only $12 in cash in the fund plus the receipts as listed. The request for reimbursement would, therefore, have been for $88. The following entry would be made:

```
A   =   L   +   OE
−88            −44 Exp
               −38 Exp
               −5 Exp
               −1 Exp
```

Cash Flows
−88

Mar. 15	Postage Expense	44	
	Freight-out	38	
	Miscellaneous Expense	5	
	Cash Over and Short	1	
	Cash		88
	(To replenish petty cash fund)		

If the custodian had $14 in cash, the reimbursement request would have been for $86 and Cash Over and Short would have been credited for $1 (overage). A debit balance in Cash Over and Short is reported in the income statement as miscellaneous expense. A credit balance in the account is reported as miscellaneous revenue. Cash Over and Short is closed to Income Summary at the end of the year.

A petty cash fund should be replenished at the end of the accounting period regardless of the cash in the fund. Replenishment at this time is necessary in order to recognize the effects of the petty cash payments on the financial statements.

Internal control over a petty cash fund is strengthened by (1) having a supervisor make surprise counts of the fund to ascertain whether the paid vouchers and fund cash equal the imprest amount and (2) canceling or mutilating the paid vouchers so they cannot be resubmitted for reimbursement.

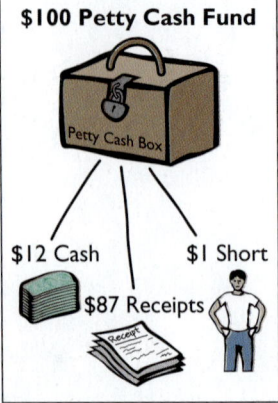

$100 Petty Cash Fund

Petty Cash Box

$12 Cash $1 Short

$87 Receipts

Use of a Bank

STUDY OBJECTIVE 6

Indicate the control features of a bank account.

The use of a bank contributes significantly to good internal control over cash. A company can safeguard its cash by using a bank as a depository and as a clearing house for checks received and checks written. Use of a bank minimizes the amount of currency that must be kept on hand. Also, the use of a bank facilitates the control of cash because it creates a double record of all bank transactions—one by the business and the other by the bank. The asset account Cash maintained by the depositor is the reciprocal of the bank's liability account for each depositor. It should be possible to **reconcile these accounts** (make them agree) at any time.

Opening a bank checking account is a relatively simple procedure. Typically, the bank makes a credit check on the new customer and the depositor is required to sign a **signature card**. The card contains the signatures of each person authorized to sign checks on the account. The signature card is used by bank employees to validate signatures on the checks.

Soon after an account is opened, the bank provides the depositor with serially numbered checks and deposit slips imprinted with the depositor's name and address. Each check and deposit slip is imprinted with both a bank and a depositor identification number. This number, printed in magnetic ink, permits computer processing of transactions.

Many companies have more than one bank account. For efficiency of operations and better control, national retailers like **Wal-Mart** and **Kmart** may have regional bank accounts. A company such as **Intel** with more than 70,000 employees may have a payroll bank account, as well as one or more general bank accounts. Also, a company may maintain several bank accounts in order to have more than one source for short-term loans when needed.

Making Bank Deposits

Bank deposits should be made by an authorized employee, such as the head cashier. Each deposit must be documented by a deposit slip (ticket), as shown in Illustration 8-9.

Illustration 8-9
Deposit slip

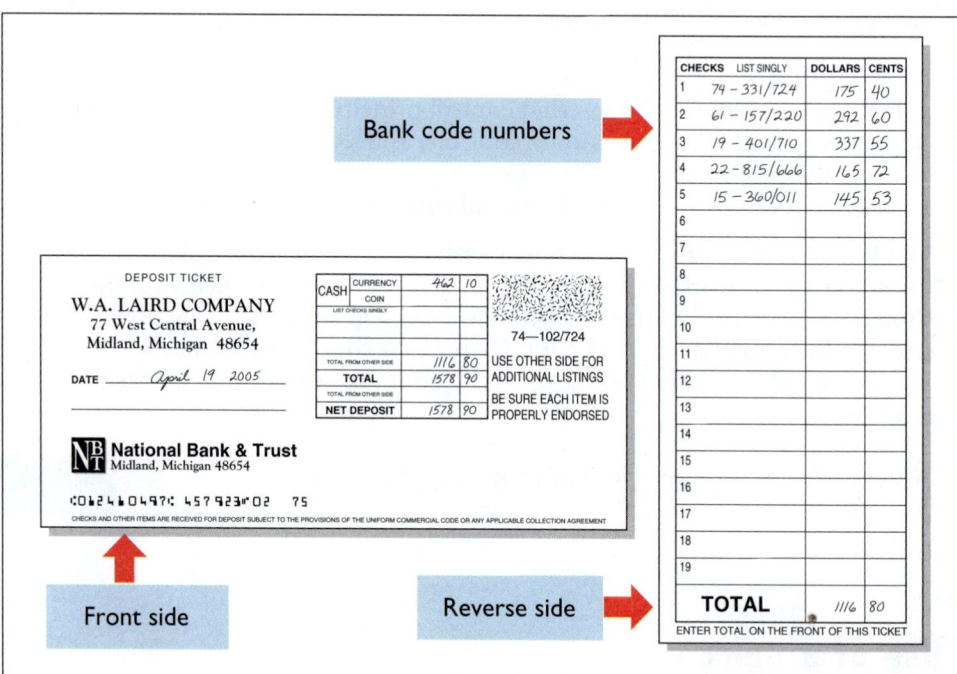

Deposit slips are prepared in duplicate. The original is retained by the bank; the duplicate, machine-stamped by the bank to establish its authenticity, is retained by the depositor.

Writing Checks

A **check** is a written order signed by the depositor directing the bank to pay a specified sum of money to a designated recipient. There are three parties to a check: (1) the **maker** (or drawer) who issues the check; (2) the **bank** (or payer) on which the check is drawn; and (3) the **payee** to whom the check is payable. A check is a **negotiable instrument** that can be transferred to another party by endorsement. Each check should be accompanied by an explanation of its purposes. In many businesses, this is done by a remittance advice attached to the check, as shown in Illustration 8-10 (page 335).

It is important to know the balance in the checking account at all times. To keep the balance current, each deposit and check should be entered on running balance memorandum forms provided by the bank or on the check stubs contained in the checkbook.

[Handwritten margin notes: 3 Parties to check (1) Maker (2) Bank (3) Payee Negotiable Instrument Remittance advice as evidence]

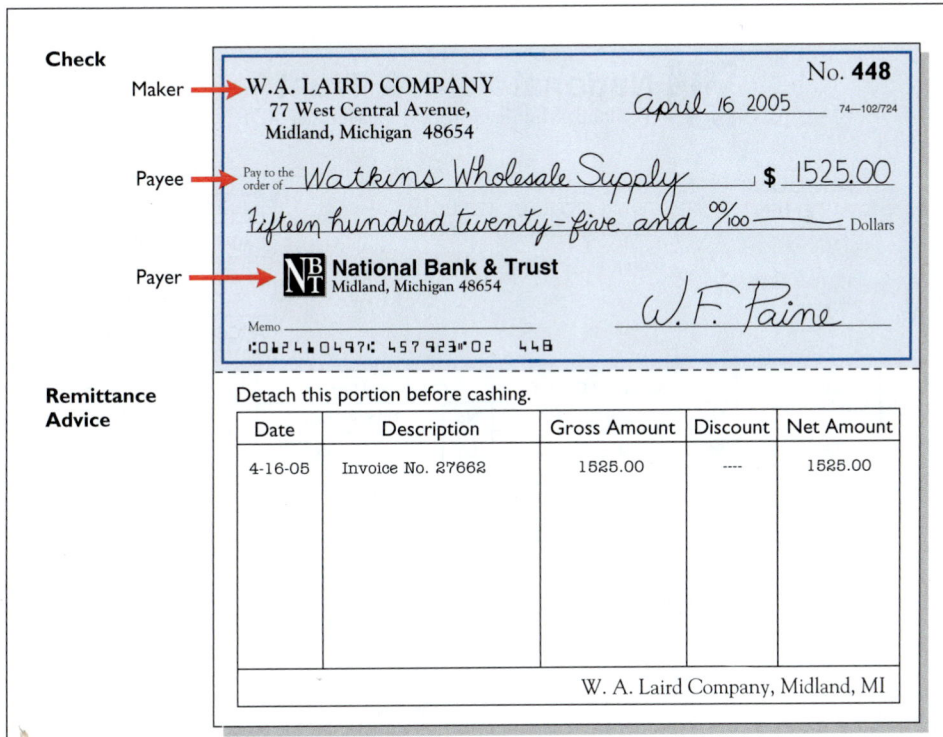

Illustration 8-10
Check with remittance
advice

ACCOUNTING IN ACTION      ℮ Business Insight

Cash is virtually obsolete. Today, many people use debit cards and credit cards to pay for most of their purchases. But debit cards are usable only at specified locations, and credit cards are cumbersome for small transactions. They are no good for transferring cash between individuals or to small companies that do not want to pay credit card fees. Digital cash is the next online wave.

There are many digital-cash companies. One of the most flexible appears to be **PayPal** (*www.paypal.com*). PayPal became popular with users of the auction site **eBay**, because it allows them to transfer funds to each other as easily as sending e-mail. (PayPal is now owned by eBay, though it is operated as an independent site.)

Source: Mathew Ingram, "Will Digital Cash Work This Time?" *The Globe and Mail,* March 18, 2000, p. N4.

Bank Statements

Each month, the depositor receives a bank statement from the bank. A **bank statement** shows the depositor's bank transactions and balances.[3] A typical statement is presented in Illustration 8-11 (page 336). It shows (1) checks paid and other debits that reduce the balance in the depositor's account, (2) deposits and other credits that increase the balance in the depositor's account, and (3) the account balance after each day's transactions.

HELPFUL HINT

Essentially, the bank statement is a copy of the bank's records sent to the customer for periodic review.

---

[3]Our presentation assumes that all adjustments are made at the end of the month. In practice, a company may also make journal entries during the month as it receives information from the bank regarding its account.

Illustration 8-11
Bank statement

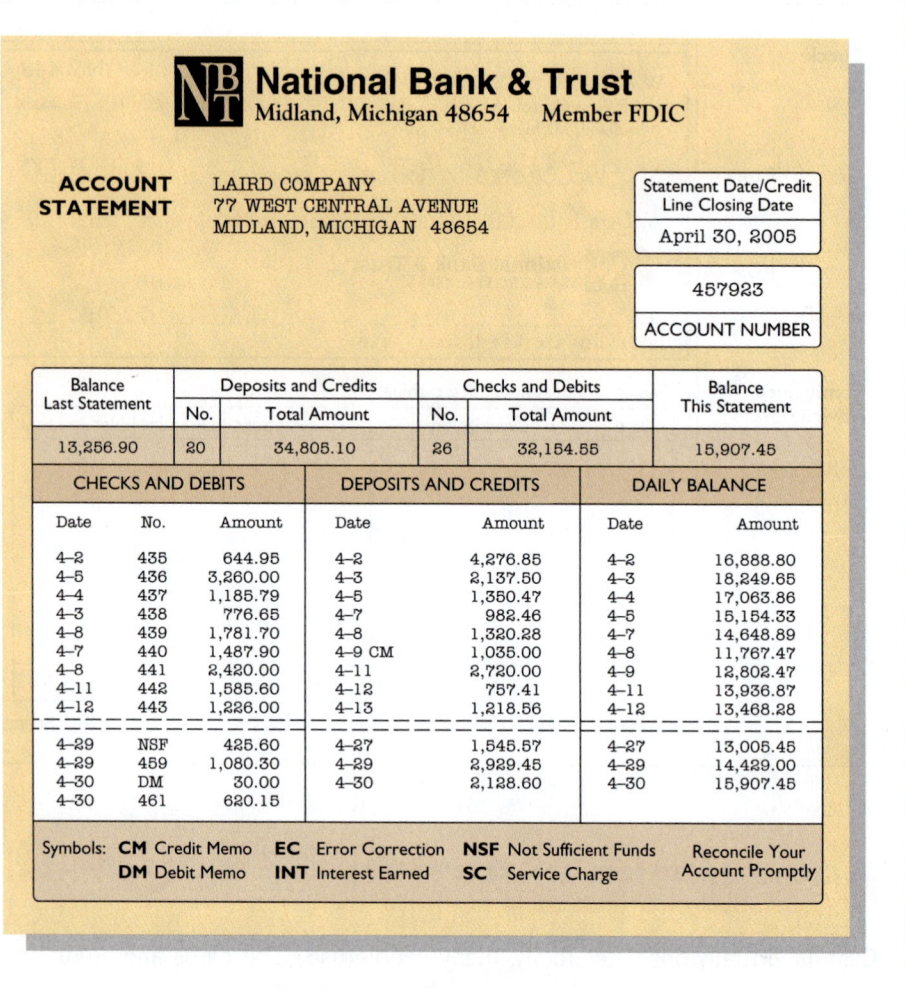

National Bank & Trust
Midland, Michigan 48654 Member FDIC

ACCOUNT STATEMENT

LAIRD COMPANY
77 WEST CENTRAL AVENUE
MIDLAND, MICHIGAN 48654

Statement Date/Credit Line Closing Date
April 30, 2005

457923
ACCOUNT NUMBER

Balance Last Statement	Deposits and Credits		Checks and Debits		Balance This Statement
	No.	Total Amount	No.	Total Amount	
13,256.90	20	34,805.10	26	32,154.55	15,907.45

CHECKS AND DEBITS			DEPOSITS AND CREDITS		DAILY BALANCE	
Date	No.	Amount	Date	Amount	Date	Amount
4-2	435	644.95	4-2	4,276.85	4-2	16,888.80
4-5	436	3,260.00	4-3	2,137.50	4-3	18,249.65
4-4	437	1,185.79	4-5	1,350.47	4-4	17,063.86
4-3	438	776.65	4-7	982.46	4-5	15,154.33
4-8	439	1,781.70	4-8	1,320.28	4-7	14,648.89
4-7	440	1,487.90	4-9 CM	1,035.00	4-8	11,767.47
4-8	441	2,420.00	4-11	2,720.00	4-9	12,802.47
4-11	442	1,585.60	4-12	757.41	4-11	13,936.87
4-12	443	1,226.00	4-13	1,218.56	4-12	13,468.28
4-29	NSF	425.60	4-27	1,545.57	4-27	13,005.45
4-29	459	1,080.30	4-29	2,929.45	4-29	14,429.00
4-30	DM	30.00	4-30	2,128.60	4-30	15,907.45
4-30	461	620.15				

Symbols: **CM** Credit Memo **EC** Error Correction **NSF** Not Sufficient Funds
DM Debit Memo **INT** Interest Earned **SC** Service Charge

Reconcile Your Account Promptly

All "paid" checks are listed in numerical sequence on the bank statement along with the date the check was paid and its amount. Upon paying a check, the bank stamps the check "paid"; a paid check is sometimes referred to as a **canceled** check. Most banks offer depositors the option of receiving "paid" checks with their bank statements. For those who decline, the bank keeps a record of each check on microfilm.

The bank also includes on the bank statement memoranda explaining other debits and credits made by the bank to the depositor's account.

Debit Memorandum

Banks charge a monthly fee for their services. Often the fee is charged only when the average monthly balance in a checking account falls below a specified amount. The fee, called a **bank service charge**, is identified on the bank statement by a code symbol such as SC. A debit memorandum explaining the charge is included with the bank statement and noted on the statement. Separate debit memoranda may also be issued for other bank services such as the cost of printing checks, issuing traveler's checks, and wiring funds to other locations. The symbol DM is often used for such charges.

A debit memorandum is also used by the bank when a deposited check from a customer "bounces" because of insufficient funds. In such a case, the check is marked

NSF (not sufficient funds) by the customer's bank and is returned to the depositor's bank. The bank then debits the depositor's account, as shown by the symbol NSF on the bank statement in Illustration 8-11 (on page 336). The bank sends the NSF check and debit memorandum to the depositor as notification of the charge. The NSF check creates an account receivable (from the bad check writer) for the depositor and reduces cash in the bank account.

Credit Memorandum   *Bank Plus*

A depositor may ask the bank to collect its notes receivable. In such a case, the bank will credit the depositor's account for the cash proceeds of the note. This is illustrated on the W. A. Laird Company bank statement by the symbol CM. The bank will issue a credit memorandum which is sent with the statement to explain the entry. Many banks also offer interest on checking accounts. The interest earned may be indicated on the bank statement by the symbol CM or INT.

Reconciling the Bank Account

The bank and the depositor maintain independent records of the depositor's checking account. If you've never had a checking account, you might assume that the respective balances will always agree. In fact, the two balances are seldom the same at any given time. It is therefore necessary to make the balance per books agree with the balance per bank—a process called **reconciling the bank account**. The lack of agreement between the two balances is due to:

> STUDY OBJECTIVE 7
>
> Prepare a bank reconciliation.

1. **Time lags** that prevent one of the parties from recording the transaction in the same period.
2. **Errors** by either party in recording transactions.

Time lags occur frequently. For example, several days may elapse between the time a check is mailed to a payee and the date the check is paid by the bank. Similarly, when the depositor uses the bank's night depository to make its deposits, there will be a difference of at least one day between the time the receipts are recorded by the depositor and the time they are recorded by the bank. A time lag also occurs whenever the bank mails a debit or credit memorandum to the depositor.

Also, errors sometimes occur. The incidence of errors depends on the effectiveness of the internal controls of the depositor and the bank. Bank errors are infrequent. However, either party could accidentally record a $450 check as $45 or $540. In addition, the bank might mistakenly charge a check drawn by C. D. Berg to the account of C. D. Burg.

Reconciliation Procedure

To obtain maximum benefit from a bank reconciliation, the reconciliation should be prepared by an employee who has no other responsibilities pertaining to cash. When the internal control principle of independent internal verification is not followed in preparing the reconciliation, cash embezzlements may go unnoticed. For example, a cashier who prepares the reconciliation can embezzle cash and conceal the embezzlement by misstating the reconciliation. Thus, the bank accounts would reconcile, and the embezzlement would not be detected.

In reconciling the bank account, it is customary to reconcile the balance per books and balance per bank to their adjusted (correct or true) cash balances. The reconciliation schedule is divided into two sections. The starting point in preparing the reconciliation is to enter the balance per bank statement and balance per books on the schedule. Adjustments are then made to each section, as shown in

Illustration 8-12. The steps listed below and on the next page should reveal all the reconciling items that cause the difference between the two balances.

Illustration 8-12
Bank reconciliation procedures

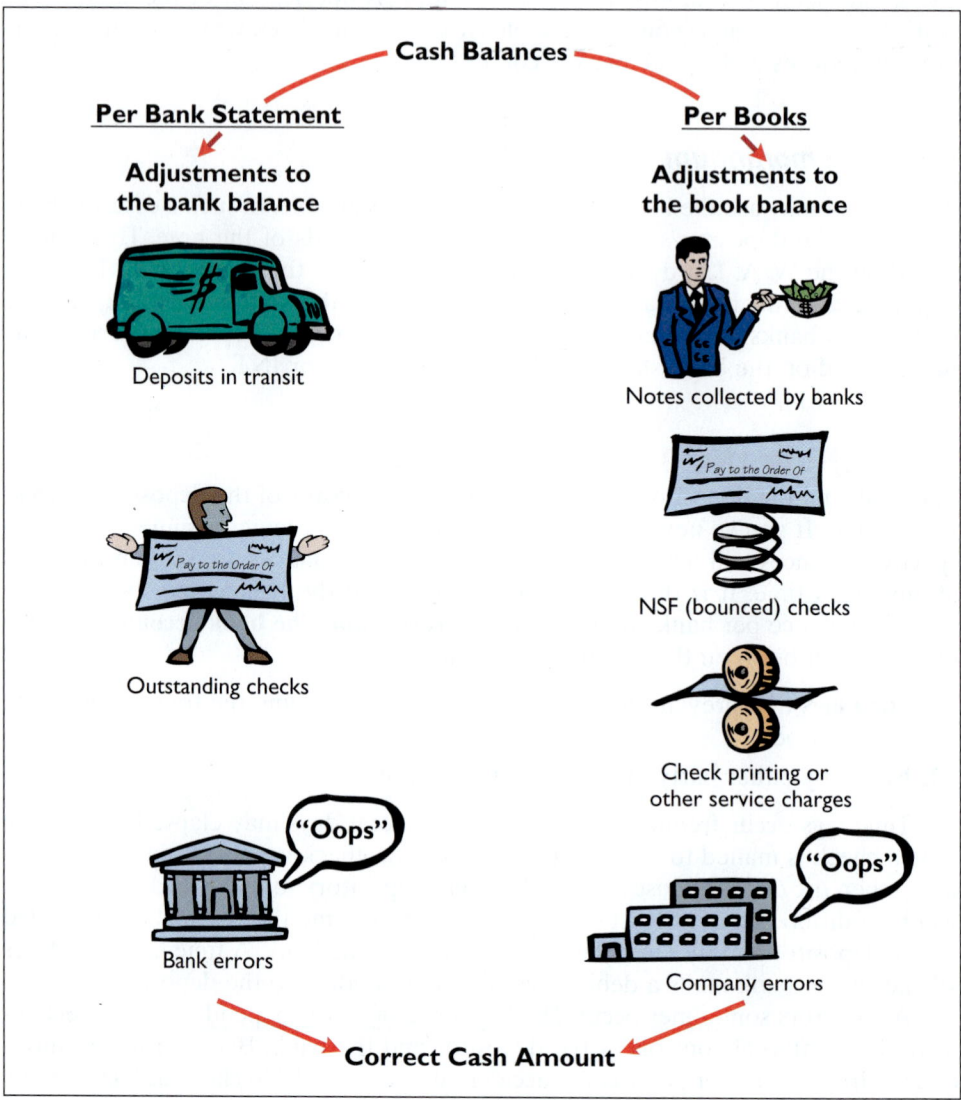

Steps in the Reconciliation Procedure

1. **Deposits in transit.** Compare the individual deposits on the bank statement with deposits in transit from the preceding bank reconciliation and with the deposits per company records or duplicate deposit slips. Deposits recorded by the depositor that have not been recorded by the bank represent **deposits in transit.** They are added to the balance per bank.

2. **Outstanding checks.** Compare the paid checks shown on the bank statement or the paid checks returned with the bank statement with (a) checks outstanding from the preceding bank reconciliation, and (b) checks issued by the company as recorded in the cash payments journal. Issued checks recorded by the company that have not been paid by the bank represent **outstanding checks.** They are deducted from the balance per the bank.

3. **Errors.** Note any **errors** discovered in the foregoing steps. List them in the appropriate section of the reconciliation schedule. For example, if a paid check correctly written by the company for $195 was mistakenly recorded by the com-

pany for $159, the error of $36 is deducted from the balance per books. All errors made by the depositor are reconciling items in determining the adjusted cash balance per books. In contrast, all errors made by the bank are reconciling items in determining the adjusted cash balance per the bank.

4. **Bank memoranda.** Trace **bank memoranda** to the depositor's records. Any unrecorded memoranda should be listed in the appropriate section of the reconciliation schedule. For example, a $5 debit memorandum for bank service charges is deducted from the balance per books, and $32 of interest earned is added to the balance per books.

Bank Reconciliation Illustrated

The bank statement for Laird Company was shown in Illustration 8-11. It shows a balance per bank of $15,907.45 on April 30, 2005. On this date the balance of cash per books is $11,589.45. From the foregoing steps, the following reconciling items are determined.

> **HELPFUL HINT**
>
> Note in the bank statement that checks no. 459 and 461 have been paid but check no. 460 is not listed. Thus, this check is outstanding. If a complete bank statement were provided, checks no. 453 and 457 would also not be listed. The amounts for these three checks are obtained from the company's cash payments records.

1. **Deposits in transit:** April 30 deposit (received by bank on May 1). — $2,201.40

2. **Outstanding checks:** No. 453, $3,000.00; no. 457, $1,401.30; no. 460, $1,502.70. — 5,904.00

3. **Errors:** Check no. 443 was correctly written by Laird for $1,226.00 and was correctly paid by the bank. However, it was recorded for $1,262.00 by Laird Company. — 36.00

4. **Bank memoranda:**
   a. Debit—NSF check from J. R. Baron for $425.60 — 425.60
   b. Debit—Printing company checks charge $30.00 — 30.00
   c. Credit—Collection of note receivable for $1,000 plus interest earned $50, less bank collection fee $15.00 — 1,035.00

The bank reconciliation is shown in Illustration 8-13.

Illustration 8-13
Bank reconciliation

W. A. LAIRD COMPANY
Bank Reconciliation
April 30, 2005

Cash balance per bank statement		$15,907.45
Add: Deposits in transit		2,201.40
		18,108.85
Less: Outstanding checks		
No. 453	$3,000.00	
No. 457	1,401.30	
No. 460	1,502.70	5,904.00
Adjusted cash balance per bank		**$12,204.85**
Cash balance per books		$11,589.45
Add: Collection of note receivable $1,000, plus interest		
earned $50, less collection fee $15	$1,035.00	
Error in recording check no. 443	36.00	1,071.00
		12,660.45
Less: NSF check	425.60	
Bank service charge	30.00	455.60
Adjusted cash balance per books		**$12,204.85**

> **ALTERNATIVE TERMINOLOGY**
>
> The terms *adjusted balance, true cash balance,* and *correct cash balance* may be used interchangeably.

Entries from Bank Reconciliation

Each reconciling item in determining the **adjusted cash balance per books** should be recorded by the depositor. **If these items are not journalized and posted, the Cash account will not show the correct balance.** The entries for W. A. Laird Company on April 30 are as follows.

COLLECTION OF NOTE RECEIVABLE. This entry involves four accounts. Assuming that the interest of $50 has not been accrued and the collection fee is charged to Miscellaneous Expense, the entry is:

A	=	L	+	OE
+1,035				−15 Exp
−1,000				+50 Rev

Cash Flows
+1,035

Apr. 30	Cash	1,035.00	
	Miscellaneous Expense	15.00	
	Notes Receivable		1,000.00
	Interest Revenue		50.00
	(To record collection of note		
	receivable by bank)		

BOOK ERROR. The cash disbursements journal shows that check no. 443 was a payment on account to Andrea Company, a supplier. The correcting entry is:

A	=	L	+	OE
+36		+36		

Cash Flows
+36

Apr. 30	Cash	36.00	
	Accounts Payable—Andrea Company		36.00
	(To correct error in recording check		
	no. 443)		

NSF CHECK. As indicated earlier, an NSF check becomes an account receivable to the depositor. The entry is:

A	=	L	+	OE
+425.60				
−425.60				

Cash Flows
−425.60

Apr. 30	Accounts Receivable—J. R. Baron	425.60	
	Cash		425.60
	(To record NSF check)		

BANK SERVICE CHARGES. Check printing charges (DM) and other bank service charges (SC) are debited to Miscellaneous Expense. They are usually nominal in amount. The entry is:

A	=	L	+	OE
−30				−30 Exp

Cash Flows
−30

Apr. 30	Miscellaneous Expense	30.00	
	Cash		30.00
	(To record charge for printing company		
	checks)		

The foregoing four entries could also be combined into one compound entry. After the entries are posted, the cash account will show the following.

Illustration 8-14
Adjusted balance in cash account

Cash				
Apr. 30 Bal.	11,589.45	Apr. 30		425.60
30	1,035.00	30		30.00
30	36.00			
Apr. 30 Bal.	**12,204.85**			

The adjusted cash balance in the ledger should agree with the adjusted cash balance per books in the bank reconciliation in Illustration 8-13.

What entries does the bank make? If any bank errors are discovered in preparing the reconciliation, the bank should be notified. It then can make the necessary corrections on its records. The bank does not make any entries for deposits in transit or outstanding checks. Only when these items reach the bank will the bank record these items.

Reporting Cash

Cash on hand, cash in banks, and petty cash are often combined and reported simply as **Cash.** Because it is the most liquid asset owned by a company, cash is listed first in the current assets section of the balance sheet. Some companies use the term "Cash and cash equivalents" in reporting cash, as illustrated by the following.

STUDY OBJECTIVE 8

Explain the reporting of cash.

EASTMAN KODAK COMPANY
Balance Sheets (partial)

	2002	2001
Current assets (in millions)		
Cash and cash equivalents	$569	$448

Illustration 8-15
Presentation of cash and cash equivalents

Cash equivalents are highly liquid investments that can be converted into a specific amount of cash. They typically have maturities of three months or less when purchased. They include money market funds, money market savings certificates, bank certificates of deposit, and U.S. Treasury bills and notes.

A company may have cash that is restricted for a special purpose. An example is a payroll bank account for paying salaries and wages. Another would be a plant expansion cash fund for financing new construction. If the restricted cash is expected to be used **within the next year**, the amount should be reported as a current asset. When the restricted funds will not be used in that time, they should be reported as a noncurrent asset. Since a payroll bank account will be used as early as the next payday, it is reported as a current asset. In contrast, unless the new construction will begin within the next year, plant expansion fund cash is classified as a noncurrent asset (long-term investment).

In making loans to depositors, banks commonly require borrowers to maintain minimum cash balances. These minimum balances, called **compensating balances**, provide the bank with support for the loans. They are a restriction on the use of cash that may affect a company's liquidity. Thus, compensating balances should be disclosed in the financial statements.

BEFORE YOU GO ON...

Review It

1. What is generally reported as cash on a company's balance sheet?
2. What is meant by cash equivalents and compensating balances?
3. At what amount does **PepsiCo** report cash and cash equivalents in its 2002 consolidated balance sheet? The answer to this question is provided on page 359.

☑ **THE NAVIGATOR**

DEMONSTRATION PROBLEM

K. Poorten Company's bank statement for May 2005 shows the following data.

Balance 5/1	$12,650	Balance 5/31	$14,280
Debit memorandum:		Credit memorandum:	
NSF check	$175	Collection of note receivable	$505

The cash balance per books at May 31 is $13,319. Your review of the data reveals the following.

1. The NSF check was from Copple Co., a customer.
2. The note collected by the bank was a $500, 3-month, 12% note. The bank charged a $10 collection fee. No interest has been accrued.
3. Outstanding checks at May 31 total $2,410.
4. Deposits in transit at May 31 total $1,752.
5. A K. Poorten Company check for $352 dated May 10 cleared the bank on May 25. This check, which was a payment on account, was journalized for $325.

Instructions

(a) Prepare a bank reconciliation at May 31.
(b) Journalize the entries required by the reconciliation.

SOLUTION TO DEMONSTRATION PROBLEM

(a)

K. POORTEN COMPANY
Bank Reconciliation
May 31, 2005

Cash balance per bank statement		$14,280
Add: Deposits in transit		1,752
		16,032
Less: Outstanding checks		2,410
Adjusted cash balance per bank		$13,622
Cash balance per books		$13,319
Add: Collection of note receivable $500, plus $15 interest, less collection fee $10		505
		13,824
Less: NSF check	$175	
Error in recording check	27	202
Adjusted cash balance per books		$13,622

(b)

May 31	Cash	505	
	Miscellaneous Expense	10	
	Notes Receivable		500
	Interest Revenue		15
	(To record collection of note by bank)		
31	Accounts Receivable—Copple Co.	175	
	Cash		175
	(To record NSF check from Copple Co.)		
31	Accounts Payable	27	
	Cash		27
	(To correct error in recording check)		

✓ THE NAVIGATOR

ACTION PLAN

- Follow the four steps in the reconciliation procedure. (p. 338–339).
- Work carefully to minimize mathematical errors in the reconciliation.
- Prepare adjusting entries from reconciling items per books.
- Make sure the cash ledger balance after posting the reconciling entries agrees with the adjusted cash balance per books.

SUMMARY OF STUDY OBJECTIVES

1. **Define internal control.** Internal control is the plan of organization and related methods and procedures adopted within a business to safeguard its assets and to enhance the accuracy and reliability of its accounting records.

2. **Identify the principles of internal control.** The principles of internal control are: establishment of responsibility; segregation of duties; documentation procedures; physical, mechanical, and electronic controls; independent internal verification; and other controls.

3. **Explain the applications of internal control principles to cash receipts.** Internal controls over cash receipts include: (a) designating only personnel such as cashiers to handle cash; (b) assigning the duties of receiving cash, recording cash, and custody of cash to different individuals; (c) obtaining remittance advices for mail receipts, cash register tapes for over-the-counter receipts, and deposit slips for bank deposits; (d) using company safes and bank vaults to store cash with access limited to authorized personnel, and using cash registers in executing over-the-counter receipts; (e) making independent daily counts of register receipts and daily comparisons of total receipts with total deposits; and (f) bonding personnel that handle cash and requiring them to take vacations.

4. **Explain the applications of internal control principles to cash disbursements.** Internal controls over cash disbursements include: (a) having only specified individuals such as the treasurer authorized to sign checks; (b) assigning the duties of approving items for payment, paying the items, and recording the payment to different individuals; (c) using prenumbered checks and accounting for all checks, with each check supported by an approved invoice; (d) storing blank checks in a safe or vault with access restricted to authorized personnel, and using a checkwriter to imprint amounts on checks; (e) comparing each check with

the approved invoice before issuing the check, and making monthly reconciliations of bank and book balances; and (f) after payment, stamping each approved invoice "paid."

5. **Describe the operation of a petty cash fund.** In operating a petty cash fund, it is necessary to establish the fund, make payments from the fund, and replenish the fund.

6. **Indicate the control features of a bank account.** A bank account contributes to good internal control by providing physical controls for the storage of cash. It minimizes the amount of currency that must be kept on hand, and it creates a double record of a depositor's bank transactions.

7. **Prepare a bank reconciliation.** It is customary to reconcile the balance per books and balance per bank to their ad-

justed balances. The steps in determining the reconciling items are to ascertain deposits in transit, outstanding checks, errors by the depositor or the bank, and unrecorded bank memoranda.

8. **Explain the reporting of cash.** Cash is listed first in the current assets section of the balance sheet. In some cases, cash is reported together with cash equivalents. Cash restricted for a special purpose is reported separately as a current asset or as a noncurrent asset, depending on when the cash is expected to be used.

✓ THE NAVIGATOR

GLOSSARY

Bank service charge A fee charged by a bank for the use of its services. (p. 336).

Bank statement A statement received monthly from the bank that shows the depositor's bank transactions and balances. (p. 335).

Cash Resources that consist of coins, currency, checks, money orders, and money on hand or on deposit in a bank or similar depository. (p. 326).

Cash equivalents Highly liquid investments, with maturities of three months or less when purchased, that can be converted to a specific amount of cash. (p. 341).

Check A written order signed by the depositor directing the bank to pay a specified sum of money to a designated recipient. (p. 334).

Compensating balances Minimum cash balances required by a bank in support of bank loans. (p. 342).

Deposits in transit Deposits recorded by the depositor that have not been recorded by the bank. (p. 338).

Electronic funds transfer (EFT) A disbursement system that uses wire, telephone, telegraph, or computer to transfer cash from one location to another. (p. 330).

Internal auditors Company employees who evaluate on a continuous basis the effectiveness of the company's system of internal control. (p. 323).

Internal control The plan of organization and all the related methods and measures adopted within a business to safeguard its assets and enhance the accuracy and reliability of its accounting records. (p. 319).

NSF check A check that is not paid by a bank because of insufficient funds in a customer's bank account. (p. 337).

Outstanding checks Checks issued and recorded by a company that have not been paid by the bank. (p. 338).

Petty cash fund A cash fund used to pay relatively small amounts. (p. 330).

Voucher An authorization form prepared for each payment by check in a voucher system. (p. 330).

Voucher system A network of approvals by authorized individuals acting independently to ensure that all disbursements by check are proper. (p. 330).

SELF-STUDY QUESTIONS

Self-Study/Self-Test

Answers are at the end of the chapter.

(SO 1) 1. Internal control is used in a business to enhance the accuracy and reliability of its accounting records and to:
    a. safeguard its assets.
    b. prevent fraud.
    c. produce correct financial statements.
    d. deter employee dishonesty.

(SO 2) 2. The principles of internal control do not include:
    a. establishment of responsibility.
    b. documentation procedures.
    c. management responsibility.
    d. independent internal verification.

3. Physical controls do *not* include: (SO
    a. safes and vaults to store cash.
    b. independent bank reconciliations.
    c. locked warehouses for inventories.
    d. bank safety deposit boxes for important papers.

4. Which of the following items in a cash drawer at No- (SO vember 30 is *not* cash?
    a. Money orders.
    b. Coins and currency.
    c. A customer check dated December 1.
    d. A customer check dated November 28.

O 3) **5.** Permitting only designated personnel to handle cash receipts is an application of the principle of:
  a. segregation of duties.
  b. establishment of responsibility.
  c. independent check.
  d. other controls.

O 4) **6.** The use of prenumbered checks in disbursing cash is an application of the principle of:
  a. establishment of responsibility.
  b. segregation of duties.
  c. physical, mechanical, and electronic controls.
  d. documentation procedures.

O 5) **7.** A check is written to replenish a $100 petty cash fund when the fund contains receipts of $94 and $3 in cash. In recording the check,
  a. Cash Over and Short should be debited for $3.
  b. Petty Cash should be debited for $94.
  c. Cash should be credited for $94.
  d. Petty Cash should be credited for $3.

O 6) **8.** The control features of a bank account do *not* include:
  a. having bank auditors verify the correctness of the bank balance per books.
  b. minimizing the amount of cash that must be kept on hand.

  c. providing a double record of all bank transactions.
  d. safeguarding cash by using a bank as a depository.

9. In a bank reconciliation, deposits in transit are: (SO 7)
  a. deducted from the book balance.
  b. added to the book balance.
  c. added to the bank balance.
  d. deducted from the bank balance.

10. The reconciling item in a bank reconciliation that will re-   (SO 7) sult in an adjusting entry by the depositor is:
  a. outstanding checks.
  b. deposit in transit.
  c. a bank error.
  d. bank service charges.

11. The statement that correctly describes the reporting of   (SO 8) cash is:
  a. Cash cannot be combined with cash equivalents.
  b. Restricted cash funds may be combined with Cash.
  c. Cash is listed first in the current assets section.
  d. Restricted cash funds cannot be reported as a current asset.

QUESTIONS

1. "Internal control is concerned only with enhancing the accuracy of the accounting records." Do you agree? Explain.

2. What principles of internal control apply to most business enterprises?

3. At the corner grocery store, all sales clerks make change out of one cash register drawer. Is this a violation of internal control? Why?

4. Pam Duffy is reviewing the principle of segregation of duties. What are the two common applications of this principle?

5. How do documentation procedures contribute to good internal control?

6. What internal control objectives are met by physical, mechanical, and electronic controls?

7. (a) Explain the control principle of independent internal verification. (b) What practices are important in applying this principle?

8. The management of Yaeger Company asks you, as the company accountant, to explain (a) the concept of reasonable assurance in internal control and (b) the importance of the human factor in internal control.

9. Yorkville Fertilizer Co. owns the following assets at the balance sheet date.

Cash in bank savings account	$ 6,000
Cash on hand	850
Cash refund due from the IRS	1,000
Checking account balance	12,000
Postdated checks	500

What amount should be reported as cash in the balance sheet?

10. What principle(s) of internal control is (are) involved in making daily cash counts of over-the-counter receipts?

11. Aurora Department Stores has just installed new electronic cash registers in its stores. How do cash registers improve internal control over cash receipts?

12. At Oswego Wholesale Company, two mail clerks open all mail receipts. How does this strengthen internal control?

13. "To have maximum effective internal control over cash disbursements, all payments should be made by check." Is this true? Explain.

14. Ted Rampolla Company's internal controls over cash disbursements provide for the treasurer to sign checks imprinted by a checkwriter after comparing the check with the approved invoice. Identify the internal control principles that are present in these controls.

15. How do the principles of (a) physical, mechanical, and electronic controls and (b) other controls apply to cash disbursements?

16. (a) What is a voucher system? (b) What principles of internal control apply to a voucher system?

17. What is the essential feature of an electronic funds transfer (EFT) procedure?

18. (a) Identify the three activities that pertain to a petty cash fund, and indicate an internal control principle that is applicable to each activity. (b) When are journal entries required in the operation of a petty cash fund?

19. "The use of a bank contributes significantly to good internal control over cash." Is this true? Why or why not?

20. Faye Uhlik is confused about the lack of agreement between the cash balance per books and the balance per the bank. Explain the causes for the lack of agreement to Faye, and give an example of each cause.

21. What are the four steps involved in finding differences between the balance per books and balance per bank?

22. Pauline Duch asks your help concerning an NSF check. Explain to Pauline (a) what an NSF check is, (b) how it is treated in a bank reconciliation, and (c) whether it will require an adjusting entry.

23. (a) "Cash equivalents are the same as cash." Do you agree? Explain. (b) How should restricted cash funds be reported on the balance sheet?

BRIEF EXERCISES

Explain the importance of internal control.
(SO 1)

BE8-1 Bridget Harrard is the new owner of Essex Parking. She has heard about internal control but is not clear about its importance for her business. Explain to Bridget the two purposes of internal control and give her one application of each purpose for Essex Parking.

Identify internal control principles.
(SO 2)

BE8-2 The internal control procedures in Naperville Company provide that:

(a) Employees who have physical custody of assets do not have access to the accounting records.

(b) Each month the assets on hand are compared to the accounting records by an internal auditor.

(c) A prenumbered shipping document is prepared for each shipment of goods to customers.

Identify the principles of internal control that are being followed.

Identify the internal control principles applicable to cash receipts.
(SO 3)

BE8-3 Sycamore Company has the following internal control procedures over cash receipts. Identify the internal control principle that is applicable to each procedure.

1. All over-the-counter receipts are registered on cash registers.
2. All cashiers are bonded.
3. Daily cash counts are made by cashier department supervisors.
4. The duties of receiving cash, recording cash, and custody of cash are assigned to different individuals.
5. Only cashiers may operate cash registers.

Identify the internal control principles applicable to cash disbursements.
(SO 4)

BE8-4 Helen Hunt Company has the following internal control procedures over cash disbursements. Identify the internal control principle that is applicable to each procedure.

1. Company checks are prenumbered.
2. The bank statement is reconciled monthly by an internal auditor.
3. Blank checks are stored in a safe in the treasurer's office.
4. Only the treasurer or assistant treasurer may sign checks.
5. Check signers are not allowed to record cash disbursement transactions.

Prepare entry to replenish a petty cash fund.
(SO 5)

BE8-5 On March 20, Batavia's petty cash fund of $100 is replenished when the fund contains $9 in cash and receipts for postage $52, freight-out $26, and travel expense $10. Prepare the journal entry to record the replenishment of the petty cash fund.

Identify the control features of a bank account.
(SO 6)

BE8-6 Louis St. Pierre is uncertain about the control features of a bank account. Explain the control benefits of (a) a signature card, (b) a check, and (c) a bank statement.

Indicate location of reconciling items in a bank reconciliation.
(SO 7)

BE8-7 The following reconciling items are applicable to the bank reconciliation for Hinckley Company: (1) outstanding checks, (2) bank debit memorandum for service charge, (3) bank credit memorandum for collecting a note for the depositor, (4) deposits in transit. Indicate how each item should be shown on a bank reconciliation.

Identify reconciling items that require adjusting entries.
(SO 7)

BE8-8 Using the data in BE8-7, indicate (a) the items that will result in an adjustment to the depositor's records and (b) why the other items do not require adjustment.

Prepare partial bank reconciliation.
(SO 7)

BE8-9 At July 31, Shabbona Company has the following bank information: cash balance per bank $7,420, outstanding checks $762, deposits in transit $1,620, and a bank service charge $20. Determine the adjusted cash balance per bank at July 31.

BE8-10 At August 31, DeKalb Company has a cash balance per books of $8,900 and the following additional data from the bank statement: charge for printing DeKalb Company checks $35, interest earned on checking account balance $40, and outstanding checks $800. Determine the adjusted cash balance per books at August 31.

Prepare partial bank reconciliation.

(SO 7)

BE8-11 Plano Company has the following cash balances: Cash in Bank $15,742, Payroll Bank Account $6,000, and Plant Expansion Fund Cash $25,000. Explain how each balance should be reported on the balance sheet.

Explain the statement presentation of cash balances.

(SO 8)

EXERCISES

E8-1 Sue Ernesto is the owner of Ernesto's Pizza. Ernesto's is operated strictly on a carryout basis. Customers pick up their orders at a counter where a clerk exchanges the pizza for cash. While at the counter, the customer can see other employees making the pizzas and the large ovens in which the pizzas are baked.

Identify the principles of internal control.

(SO 2)

Instructions
Identify the six principles of internal control and give an example of each principle that you might observe when picking up your pizza. (*Note*: It may not be possible to observe all the principles.)

E8-2 The following control procedures are used at Sandwich Company for over-the-counter cash receipts.

Identify internal control weaknesses over cash receipts and suggest improvements.

(SO 2, 3)

1. To minimize the risk of robbery, cash in excess of $100 is stored in an unlocked attaché case in the stock room until it is deposited in the bank.
2. All over-the-counter receipts are registered by three clerks who use a cash register with a single cash drawer.
3. The company accountant makes the bank deposit and then records the day's receipts.
4. At the end of each day, the total receipts are counted by the cashier on duty and reconciled to the cash register total.
5. Cashiers are experienced; they are not bonded.

Instructions
(a) For each procedure, explain the weakness in internal control, and identify the control principle that is violated.
(b) For each weakness, suggest a change in procedure that will result in good internal control.

E8-3 The following control procedures are used in Morgan's Boutique Shoppe for cash disbursements.

Identify internal control weaknesses over cash disbursements and suggest improvements.

(SO 2, 4)

1. The company accountant prepares the bank reconciliation and reports any discrepancies to the owner.
2. The store manager personally approves all payments before signing and issuing checks.
3. Each week, Morgan leaves 100 company checks in an unmarked envelope on a shelf behind the cash register.
4. After payment, bills are filed in a paid invoice folder.
5. The company checks are unnumbered.

Instructions
(a) For each procedure, explain the weakness in internal control, and identify the internal control principle that is violated.
(b) For each weakness, suggest a change in the procedure that will result in good internal control.

E8-4 At Teresa Speck Company, checks are not prenumbered because both the purchasing agent and the treasurer are authorized to issue checks. Each signer has access to unissued checks kept in an unlocked file cabinet. The purchasing agent pays all bills pertaining to goods purchased for resale. Prior to payment, the purchasing agent determines that the goods have been received and verifies the mathematical accuracy of the vendor's invoice. After payment, the invoice is filed by vendor, and the purchasing agent records the payment in the cash disbursements journal. The treasurer pays all other bills following approval by authorized employees. After payment, the treasurer stamps all bills PAID, files them by payment date, and

Identify internal control weaknesses for cash disbursements and suggest improvements.

(SO 4)

records the checks in the cash disbursements journal. Teresa Speck Company maintains one checking account that is reconciled by the treasurer.

Instructions
(a) List the weaknesses in internal control over cash disbursements.
(b) ▭▭▭▷ Write a memo to the company treasurer indicating your recommendations for improvement.

Prepare journal entries for a petty cash fund.
(SO 5)

E8-5 LaSalle-Peru Company uses an imprest petty cash system. The fund was established on March 1 with a balance of $100. During March the following petty cash receipts were found in the petty cash box.

Date	Receipt No.	For	Amount
3/5	1	Stamp Inventory	$39
7	2	Freight-out	19
9	3	Miscellaneous Expense	6
11	4	Travel Expense	24
14	5	Miscellaneous Expense	5

The fund was replenished on March 15 when the fund contained $4 in cash. On March 20, the amount in the fund was increased to $150.

Instructions
Journalize the entries in March that pertain to the operation of the petty cash fund.

Prepare bank reconciliation and adjusting entries.
(SO 7)

E8-6 Lisa Ceja is unable to reconcile the bank balance at January 31. Lisa's reconciliation is as follows.

Cash balance per bank	$3,660.20
Add: NSF check	590.00
Less: Bank service charge	25.00
Adjusted balance per bank	$4,225.20
Cash balance per books	$3,875.20
Less: Deposits in transit	530.00
Add: Outstanding checks	930.00
Adjusted balance per books	$4,275.20

Instructions
(a) Prepare a correct bank reconciliation.
(b) Journalize the entries required by the reconciliation.

Determine outstanding checks.
(SO 7)

E8-7 On April 30, the bank reconciliation of Ottawa Company shows three outstanding checks: no. 254, $650, no. 255, $720, and no. 257, $410. The May bank statement and the May cash payments journal show the following.

Bank Statement			**Cash Payments Journal**		
Checks Paid			**Checks Issued**		
Date	Check No.	Amount	Date	Check No.	Amount
5/4	254	650	5/2	258	159
5/2	257	410	5/5	259	275
5/17	258	159	5/10	260	790
5/12	259	275	5/15	261	500
5/20	261	500	5/22	262	750
5/29	263	480	5/24	263	480
5/30	262	750	5/29	264	560

Instructions
Using step 2 in the reconciliation procedure, list the outstanding checks at May 31.

E8-8 The following information pertains to Worthy Video Company.

Prepare bank reconciliation and adjusting entries.

(SO 7)

1. Cash balance per bank, July 31, $7,263.
2. July bank service charge not recorded by the depositor $28.
3. Cash balance per books, July 31, $7,284.
4. Deposits in transit, July 31, $1,500.
5. Bank collected $800 note for Worthy in July, plus interest $36, less fee $20. The collection has not been recorded by Worthy, and no interest has been accrued.
6. Outstanding checks, July 31, $691.

Instructions
(a) Prepare a bank reconciliation at July 31.
(b) Journalize the adjusting entries at July 31 on the books of Worthy Video Company.

E8-9 The information below relates to the Cash account in the ledger of Dick Wasson Company.

Prepare bank reconciliation and adjusting entries.

(SO 7)

 Balance September 1—$17,150; Cash deposited—$64,000.
 Balance September 30—$17,404; Checks written—$63,746.

The September bank statement shows a balance of $16,422 on September 30 and the following memoranda.

Credits		Debits	
Collection of $1,500 note plus interest $30	$1,530	NSF check: J. E. Hoover	$725
Interest earned on checking account	$45	Safety deposit box rent	$65

At September 30, deposits in transit were $4,150, and outstanding checks totaled $2,383.

Instructions
(a) Prepare the bank reconciliation at September 30.
(b) Prepare the adjusting entries at September 30, assuming (1) the NSF check was from a customer on account, and (2) no interest had been accrued on the note.

E8-10 The cash records of Satter Company show the following four situations.

Compute deposits in transit and outstanding checks for two bank reconciliations.

(SO 7)

1. The June 30 bank reconciliation indicated that deposits in transit total $920. During July the general ledger account Cash shows deposits of $15,750, but the bank statement indicates that only $15,600 in deposits were received during the month.
2. The June 30 bank reconciliation also reported outstanding checks of $880. During the month of July, Satter Company books show that $17,200 of checks were issued. The bank statement showed that $16,400 of checks cleared the bank in July.
3. In September, deposits per the bank statement totaled $26,700, deposits per books were $25,400, and deposits in transit at September 30 were $2,600.
4. In September, cash disbursements per books were $23,700, checks clearing the bank were $24,000, and outstanding checks at September 30 were $2,100.

There were no bank debit or credit memoranda. No errors were made by either the bank or Satter Company.

Instructions
Answer the following questions.

(a) In situation (1), what were the deposits in transit at July 31?
(b) In situation (2), what were the outstanding checks at July 31?
(c) In situation (3), what were the deposits in transit at August 31?
(d) In situation (4), what were the outstanding checks at August 31?

PROBLEMS: SET A

P8-1A Anita Theater is located in the Zurbrugg Mall. A cashier's booth is located near the entrance to the theater. Two cashiers are employed. One works from 1–5 P.M., the other from 5–9 P.M. Each cashier is bonded. The cashiers receive cash from customers and operate a machine that ejects serially numbered tickets. The rolls of tickets are inserted and locked into the machine by the theater manager at the beginning of each cashier's shift.

Identify internal control weaknesses over cash receipts.

(SO 2, 3)

After purchasing a ticket, the customer takes the ticket to an usher stationed at the entrance of the theater lobby some 60 feet from the cashier's booth. The usher tears the ticket in half, admits the customer, and returns the ticket stub to the customer. The other half of the ticket is dropped into a locked box by the usher.

At the end of each cashier's shift, the theater manager removes the ticket rolls from the machine and makes a cash count. The cash count sheet is initialed by the cashier. At the end of the day, the manager deposits the receipts in total in a bank night deposit vault located in the mall. The manager also sends copies of the deposit slip and the initialed cash count sheets to the theater company treasurer for verification and to the company's accounting department. Receipts from the first shift are stored in a safe located in the manager's office.

Instructions

(a) Identify the internal control principles and their application to the cash receipts transactions of the Anita Theater.

(b) If the usher and cashier decide to collaborate to misappropriate cash, what actions might they take?

Journalize and post petty cash fund transactions.

(SO 5)

P8-2A M.L. McArtor Company maintains a petty cash fund for small expenditures. The following transactions occurred over a 2-month period.

July 1 Established petty cash fund by writing a check on Landmark Bank for $200.
     15 Replenished the petty cash fund by writing a check for $196.30. On this date the fund consisted of $3.70 in cash and the following petty cash receipts: freight-out $94.00, postage expense $42.40, entertainment expense $45.90, and miscellaneous expense $10.70.
     31 Replenished the petty cash fund by writing a check for $192.00. At this date, the fund consisted of $8.00 in cash and the following petty cash receipts: freight-out $82.10, charitable contributions expense $30.00, postage expense $47.80, and miscellaneous expense $32.10.

Aug. 15 Replenished the petty cash fund by writing a check for $188.00. On this date, the fund consisted of $12.00 in cash and the following petty cash receipts: freight-out $74.40, entertainment expense $41.50, postage expense $33.00, and miscellaneous expense $38.00.
     16 Increased the amount of the petty cash fund to $300 by writing a check for $100.
     31 Replenished petty cash fund by writing a check for $283.00. On this date, the fund consisted of $17 in cash and the following petty cash receipts: postage expense $145.00, entertainment expense $90.60, and freight-out $46.00.

Instructions

(a) July 15 Cash short $3.30
(b) Aug. 31 balance $300

(a) Journalize the petty cash transactions.
(b) Post to the Petty Cash account.
(c) What internal control features exist in a petty cash fund?

Prepare a bank reconciliation and adjusting entries.

(SO 7)

P8-3A Agricultural Genetics Company of Lawrence, Kansas, spreads herbicides and applies liquid fertilizer for local farmers. On May 31, 2005, the company's cash account per its general ledger showed the following balance.

		CASH				No. 101
Date	**Explanation**	**Ref.**	**Debit**	**Credit**	**Balance**
May 31	Balance				6,781.50

The bank statement from Lawrence State Bank on that date showed the following balance.

LAWRENCE STATE BANK

Checks and Debits	**Deposits and Credits**	**Daily Balance**	
XXX	XXX	5/31	6,804.60

A comparison of the details on the bank statement with the details in the cash account revealed the following facts.

1. The statement included a debit memo of $40 for the printing of additional company checks.
2. Cash sales of $836.15 on May 12 were deposited in the bank. The cash receipts journal entry and the deposit slip were incorrectly made for $846.15. The bank credited Agricultural Genetics Company for the correct amount.

3. Outstanding checks at May 31 totaled $315.25, and deposits in transit were $936.15.
4. On May 18, the company issued check no. 1181 for $685 to M. Datz, on account. The check, which cleared the bank in May, was incorrectly journalized and posted by Agricultural Genetics Company for $658.
5. A $2,000 note receivable was collected by the bank for Agricultural Genetics Company on May 31 plus $80 interest. The bank charged a collection fee of $25. No interest has been accrued on the note.
6. Included with the cancelled checks was a check issued by Bohr Company to Fred Mertz for $600 that was incorrectly charged to Agricultural Genetics Company by the bank.
7. On May 31, the bank statement showed an NSF charge of $734 for a check issued by Tyler Gricius, a customer, to Agricultural Genetics Company on account.

Instructions
(a) Prepare the bank reconciliation at May 31, 2005.
(b) Prepare the necessary adjusting entries for Agricultural Genetics Company at May 31, 2005.

(a) Adj. cash bal. $8,025.50

P8-4A The bank portion of the bank reconciliation for Mooney Company at October 31, 2005 was as follows.

Prepare a bank reconciliation and adjusting entries from detailed data.

(SO 7)

MOONEY COMPANY
Bank Reconciliation
October 31, 2005

Cash balance per bank		$12,444.70
Add: Deposits in transit		1,530.20
		13,974.90
Less: Outstanding checks		

Check Number	Check Amount	
2451	$1,260.40	
2470	720.10	
2471	844.50	
2472	503.60	
2474	1,050.00	4,378.60
Adjusted cash balance per bank		$ 9,596.30

The adjusted cash balance per bank agreed with the cash balance per books at October 31.
The November bank statement showed the following checks and deposits:

	Bank Statement			
Checks			**Deposits**	
Date	Number	Amount	Date	Amount
11-1	2470	$ 720.10	11-1	$ 1,530.20
11-2	2471	844.50	11-4	1,211.60
11-5	2474	1,050.00	11-8	990.10
11-4	2475	1,640.70	11-13	2,575.00
11-8	2476	2,830.00	11-18	1,472.70
11-10	2477	600.00	11-21	2,945.00
11-15	2479	1,750.00	11-25	2,567.30
11-18	2480	1,330.00	11-28	1,650.00
11-27	2481	695.40	11-30	1,186.00
11-30	2483	575.50	Total	$16,127.90
11-29	2486	900.00		
	Total	$12,936.20		

The cash records per books for November showed the following.

	Cash Payments Journal						Cash Receipts Journal	
Date	**Number**	**Amount**	**Date**	**Number**	**Amount**		**Date**	**Amount**
11-1	2475	$1,640.70	11-20	2483	$ 575.50		11-3	$ 1,211.60
11-2	2476	2,830.00	11-22	2484	829.50		11-7	990.10
11-2	2477	600.00	11-23	2485	974.80		11-12	2,575.00
11-4	2478	538.20	11-24	2486	900.00		11-17	1,472.70
11-8	2479	1,570.00	11-29	2487	398.00		11-20	2,954.00
11-10	2480	1,330.00	11-30	2488	1,200.00		11-24	2,567.30
11-15	2481	695.40	Total		$14,694.10		11-27	1,650.00
11-18	2482	612.00					11-29	1,186.00
							11-30	1,338.00
							Total	$15,944.70

The bank statement contained two bank memoranda:

1. A credit of $1,505.00 for the collection of a $1,400 note for Mooney Company plus interest of $120 and less a collection fee of $15. Mooney Company has not accrued any interest on the note.
2. A debit for the printing of additional company checks $72.00.

At November 30, the cash balance per books was $10,846.90, and the cash balance per the bank statement was $17,069.40. The bank did not make any errors, but two errors were made by Mooney Company.

Instructions

(a) Adjusted cash balance per bank $12,090.90

(a) Using the four steps in the reconciliation procedure described on page 338, prepare a bank reconciliation at November 30.
(b) Prepare the adjusting entries based on the reconciliation. (*Hint*: The correction of any errors pertaining to recording checks should be made to Accounts Payable. The correction of any errors relating to recording cash receipts should be made to Accounts Receivable).

Prepare a bank reconciliation and adjusting entries.

(SO 7)

P8-5A Mario Tizani Company's bank statement from Last National Bank at August 31, 2005, shows the following information.

Balance, August 1	$17,400	Bank credit memoranda:	
August deposits	73,110	Collection of note	
Checks cleared in August	69,660	receivable plus $90	
Balance, August 31	25,932	interest	$5,090
		Interest earned	32
		Bank debit memorandum:	
		Safety deposit box rent	40

A summary of the Cash account in the ledger for August shows: Balance, August 1, $16,900; receipts $77,000; disbursements $73,570; and balance, August 31, $20,330. Analysis reveals that the only reconciling items on the July 31 bank reconciliation were a deposit in transit for $4,000 and outstanding checks of $4,500. The deposit in transit was the first deposit recorded by the bank in August. In addition, you determine that there were two errors involving company checks drawn in August: (1) A check for $400 to a creditor on account that cleared the bank in August was journalized and posted for $420. (2) A salary check to an employee for $275 was recorded by the bank for $278.

Instructions

(a) Adjusted balance per books $25,432

(a) Prepare a bank reconciliation at August 31.
(b) Journalize the adjusting entries to be made by Mario Tizani Company at August 31. Assume the interest on the note has been accrued by the company.

Prepare comprehensive bank reconciliation with theft and internal control deficiencies.

(SO 2, 3, 4, 7)

P8-6A Stupendous Company is a very profitable small business. It has not, however, given much consideration to internal control. For example, in an attempt to keep clerical and office expenses to a minimum, the company has combined the jobs of cashier and bookkeeper. As a result, Jake Stickyfingers handles all cash receipts, keeps the accounting records, and prepares the monthly bank reconciliations.

The balance per the bank statement on October 31, 2005, was $18,280. Outstanding checks were: no. 62 for $326.75, no. 183 for $150, no. 284 for $253.25, no. 862 for $190.71, no. 863 for $226.80, and no. 864 for $165.28. Included with the statement was a credit memorandum of $300 indicating the collection of a note receivable for Stupendous Company by the bank on October 25. This memorandum has not been recorded by Stupendous Company.

The company's ledger showed one cash account with a balance of $21,892.72. The balance included undeposited cash on hand. Because of the lack of internal controls, Stickyfingers took for personal use all of the undeposited receipts in excess of $3,795.51. He then prepared the following bank reconciliation in an effort to conceal his theft of cash.

BANK RECONCILIATION

Cash balance per books, October 31		$21,892.72
Add: Outstanding checks		
No. 862	$190.71	
No. 863	226.80	
No. 864	165.28	482.79
		22,375.51
Less: Undeposited receipts		3,795.51
Unadjusted balance per bank, October 31		18,580.00
Less: Bank credit memorandum		300.00
Cash balance per bank statement, October 31		$18,280.00

Instructions

(a) Prepare a correct bank reconciliation. (*Hint*: Deduct the amount of the theft from the adjusted balance per books.)

(b) Indicate the three ways that Stickyfingers attempted to conceal the theft and the dollar amount pertaining to each method.

(c) What principles of internal control were violated in this case?

(a) Adjusted balance per books $20,762.72

PROBLEMS: SET B

P8-1B Gore Office Supply Company recently changed its system of internal control over cash disbursements. The system includes the following features.

Instead of being unnumbered and manually prepared, all checks must now be prenumbered and written by using the new checkwriter purchased by the company. Before a check can be issued, each invoice must have the approval of Sally Morgan, the purchasing agent, and John Countryman, the receiving department supervisor. Checks must be signed by either Ann Lynn, the treasurer, or Bob Skabo, the assistant treasurer. Before signing a check, the signer is expected to compare the amount of the check with the amount on the invoice.

After signing a check, the signer stamps the invoice PAID and inserts within the stamp, the date, check number, and amount of the check. The "paid" invoice is then sent to the accounting department for recording.

Blank checks are stored in a safe in the treasurer's office. The combination to the safe is known only by the treasurer and assistant treasurer. Each month, the bank statement is reconciled with the bank balance per books by the assistant chief accountant.

Identify internal control principles over cash disbursements.

(SO 2, 4)

Instructions

Identify the internal control principles and their application to cash disbursements of Gore Office Supply Company.

P8-2B Sammy Sosa Company maintains a petty cash fund for small expenditures. The following transactions occurred over a 2-month period.

July 1   Established petty cash fund by writing a check on Cubs Bank for $200.
     15   Replenished the petty cash fund by writing a check for $198.00. On this date the fund consisted of $2.00 in cash and the following petty cash receipts: freight-out $94.00, postage expense $42.40, entertainment expense $46.60, and miscellaneous expense $11.20.

Journalize and post petty cash fund transactions.

(SO 5)

Peachtree

31 Replenished the petty cash fund by writing a check for $192.00. At this date, the fund consisted of $8.00 in cash and the following petty cash receipts: freight-out $82.10, charitable contributions expense $45.00, postage expense $25.50, and miscellaneous expense $39.40.

Aug. 15 Replenished the petty cash fund by writing a check for $187.00. On this date, the fund consisted of $13.00 in cash and the following petty cash receipts: freight-out $74.60, entertainment expense $43.00, postage expense $33.00, and miscellaneous expense $37.00.

16 Increased the amount of the petty cash fund to $300 by writing a check for $100.

31 Replenished petty cash fund by writing a check for $284.00. On this date, the fund consisted of $16 in cash and the following petty cash receipts: postage expense $140.00, travel expense $95.60, and freight-out $47.10.

Instructions

(a) July 15, Cash short $3.80
(b) Aug. 31 balance $300

(a) Journalize the petty cash transactions.
(b) Post to the Petty Cash account.
(c) What internal control features exist in a petty cash fund?

Prepare a bank reconciliation and adjusting entries.

(SO 7)

P8-3B On May 31, 2005, Terry Duffy Company had a cash balance per books of $6,781.50. The bank statement from Farmers State Bank on that date showed a balance of $6,804.60. A comparison of the statement with the cash account revealed the following facts.

1. The statement included a debit memo of $40 for the printing of additional company checks.
2. Cash sales of $836.15 on May 12 were deposited in the bank. The cash receipts journal entry and the deposit slip were incorrectly made for $886.15. The bank credited Duffy Company for the correct amount.
3. Outstanding checks at May 31 totaled $276.25. Deposits in transit were $1,916.15.
4. On May 18, the company issued check No. 1181 for $685 to Barry Trest, on account. The check, which cleared the bank in May, was incorrectly journalized and posted by Duffy Company for $658.
5. A $3,000 note receivable was collected by the bank for Duffy Company on May 31 plus $80 interest. The bank charged a collection fee of $20. No interest has been accrued on the note.
6. Included with the cancelled checks was a check issued by Bridgetown Company to Tom Lujak for $600 that was incorrectly charged to Duffy Company by the bank.
7. On May 31, the bank statement showed an NSF charge of $680 for a check issued by Sandy Grifton, a customer, to Duffy Company on account.

Instructions

(a) Adjusted cash balance per bank $9,044.50

(a) Prepare the bank reconciliation at May 31, 2005.
(b) Prepare the necessary adjusting entries for Duffy Company at May 31, 2005.

Prepare a bank reconciliation and adjusting entries from detailed data.

(SO 7)

P8-4B The bank portion of the bank reconciliation for Heinisch Company at November 30, 2005, was as follows.

HEINISCH COMPANY
Bank Reconciliation
November 30, 2005

Cash balance per bank		$14,367.90
Add: Deposits in transit		2,530.20
		16,898.10
Less: Outstanding checks		
Check Number	Check Amount	
3451	$2,260.40	
3470	720.10	
3471	844.50	
3472	1,426.80	
3474	1,050.00	6,301.80
Adjusted cash balance per bank		$10,596.30

The adjusted cash balance per bank agreed with the cash balance per books at November 30.

The December bank statement showed the following checks and deposits.

Bank Statement				
Checks			**Deposits**	
Date	**Number**	**Amount**	**Date**	**Amount**
12-1	3451	$ 2,260.40	12-1	$ 2,530.20
12-2	3471	844.50	12-4	1,211.60
12-7	3472	1,426.80	12-8	2,365.10
12-4	3475	1,640.70	12-16	2,672.70
12-8	3476	1,300.00	12-21	2,945.00
12-10	3477	2,130.00	12-26	2,567.30
12-15	3479	3,080.00	12-29	2,836.00
12-27	3480	600.00	12-30	1,025.00
12-30	3482	475.50	Total	$18,152.90
12-29	3483	1,140.00		
12-31	3485	540.80		
	Total	$15,438.70		

The cash records per books for December showed the following.

Cash Payments Journal							Cash Receipts Journal	
Date	**Number**	**Amount**	**Date**	**Number**	**Amount**		**Date**	**Amount**
12-1	3475	$1,640.70	12-20	3482	$ 475.50		12-3	$ 1,211.60
12-2	3476	1,300.00	12-22	3483	1,140.00		12-7	2,365.10
12-2	3477	2,130.00	12-23	3484	798.00		12-15	2,672.70
12-4	3478	621.30	12-24	3485	450.80		12-20	2,954.00
12-8	3479	3,080.00	12-30	3486	1,889.50		12-25	2,567.30
12-10	3480	600.00	Total		$14,933.20		12-28	2,836.00
12-17	3481	807.40					12-30	1,025.00
							12-31	1,190.40
							Total	$16,822.10

The bank statement contained two memoranda:

1. A credit of $3,645 for the collection of a $3,500 note for Heinisch Company plus interest of $160 and less a collection fee of $15.00. Heinisch Company has not accrued any interest on the note.
2. A debit of $572.80 for an NSF check written by D. Chagnon, a customer. At December 31, the check had not been redeposited in the bank.

At December 31 the cash balance per books was $12,485.20, and the cash balance per the bank statement was $20,154.30. The bank did not make any errors, but two errors were made by Heinisch Company.

Instructions

(a) Using the four steps in the reconciliation procedure, prepare a bank reconciliation at December 31.

(b) Prepare the adjusting entries based on the reconciliation. (*Hint:* The correction of any errors pertaining to recording checks should be made to Accounts Payable. The correction of any errors relating to recording cash receipts should be made to Accounts Receivable.)

(a) Adjusted balance per books $15,458.40

Prepare a bank reconciliation and adjusting entries.

(SO 7)

P8-5B Cell Ten Company maintains a checking account at the Commerce Bank. At July 31, selected data from the ledger balance and the bank statement are as follows.

Peachtree

| | Cash in Bank | |
	Per Books	**Per Bank**
Balance, July 1	$17,600	$18,800
July receipts	81,400	
July credits		80,470
July disbursements	77,150	
July debits		74,756
Balance, July 31	$21,850	$24,514

Analysis of the bank data reveals that the credits consist of $79,000 of July deposits and a credit memorandum of $1,470 for the collection of a $1,400 note plus interest revenue of $70. The July debits per bank consist of checks cleared $74,700 and a debit memorandum of $56 for printing additional company checks.

You also discover the following errors involving July checks: (1) A check for $230 to a creditor on account that cleared the bank in July was journalized and posted as $320. (2) A salary check to an employee for $255 was recorded by the bank for $155.

The June 30 bank reconciliation contained only two reconciling items: deposits in transit $5,000 and outstanding checks of $6,200.

Instructions

(a) Prepare a bank reconciliation at July 31.

(b) Journalize the adjusting entries to be made by Cell Ten Company at July 31, 2005. Assume that the interest on the note has been accrued.

(a) Adjusted balance per books $23,354

Identify internal control weaknesses in cash receipts and cash disbursements.

(SO 2, 3, 4)

P8-6B Anamosa Middle School wants to raise money for a new sound system for its auditorium. The primary fund-raising event is a dance at which the famous disc jockey Obnoxious Al will play classic and not-so-classic dance tunes. Rob Drexler, the music and theater instructor, has been given the responsibility for coordinating the fund-raising efforts. This is Rob's first experience with fund-raising. He decides to put the eighth-grade choir in charge of the event; he will be a relatively passive observer.

Rob had 500 unnumbered tickets printed for the dance. He left the tickets in a box on his desk and told the choir students to take as many tickets as they thought they could sell for $5 each. In order to ensure that no extra tickets would be floating around, he told them to dispose of any unsold tickets. When the students received payment for the tickets, they were to bring the cash back to Rob, and he would put it in a locked box in his desk drawer.

Some of the students were responsible for decorating the gymnasium for the dance. Rob gave each of them a key to the money box and told them that if they took money out to purchase materials, they should put a note in the box saying how much they took and what it was used for. After 2 weeks the money box appeared to be getting full, so Rob asked Erik Radley to count the money, prepare a deposit slip, and deposit the money in a bank account Rob had opened.

The day of the dance, Rob wrote a check from the account to pay the DJ. Obnoxious Al, however, said that he accepted only cash and did not give receipts. So Rob took $200 out of the cash box and gave it to Al. At the dance Rob had Mel Harris working at the entrance to the gymnasium, collecting tickets from students and selling tickets to those who had not prepurchased them. Rob estimated that 400 students attended the dance.

The following day Rob closed out the bank account, which had $250 in it, and gave that amount plus the $180 in the cash box to Principal Foran. Principal Foran seemed surprised that, after generating roughly $2,000 in sales, the dance netted only $430 in cash. Rob did not know how to respond.

Instructions

Identify as many internal control weaknesses as you can in this scenario, and suggest how each could be addressed.

BROADENING YOUR PERSPECTIVE

Financial Reporting and Analysis

■ **FINANCIAL REPORTING PROBLEM: PepsiCo**

BYP8-1 The financial statements of **PepsiCo, Inc.** are presented in Appendix A at the end of this textbook.

Instructions
(a) What comments, if any, are made about cash in the report of the independent auditors?
(b) What data about cash and cash equivalents are shown in the consolidated balance sheet?
(c) In its notes to Consolidated Financial Statements, how does PepsiCo, Inc. define cash equivalents?
(d) In management's letter that assumes "Responsibility for Financial Statements," what does PepsiCo's management say about internal control? (See page 55 of its 2002 Annual Report.)

■ **COMPARATIVE ANALYSIS PROBLEM: PepsiCo vs. Coca-Cola**

BYP8-2 **PepsiCo**'s financial statements are presented in Appendix A. **Coca-Cola Company**'s financial statements are presented in Appendix B.

Instructions
(a) Based on the information contained in these financial statements, determine each of the following for each company:
  (1) Cash and cash equivalents balance at December 28, 2002, for PepsiCo and at December 31, 2002, for Coca-Cola.
  (2) Increase (decrease) in cash and cash equivalents from 2001 to 2002.
  (3) Cash provided by operating activities during the year ended December 2002 (from Statement of Cash Flows).
(b) What conclusions concerning the management of cash can be drawn from these data?

■ **INTERPRETING FINANCIAL STATEMENTS: A Global Focus**

BYP8-3 The international accounting firm **KPMG** recently performed a global survey on e-fraud. Included in its virtual library, at its Web site, **www.kpmg.com**, is a March 29, 2001, article entitled "E-fraud: Is Technology Running Unchecked?" that summarizes the findings of that global survey.

Address: www.kpmg.com/about/press.asp?cid=469, or go to www.wiley.com/college/weygandt

Instructions
Read the article at the Web site, and answer the following questions.

(a) What do most senior managers in corporations believe to be the most likely perpetrator of a breach of their network systems, and in fact, what is the actual greatest threat?
(b) What percentage of firms perform security audits of their e-commerce systems?
(c) What is the problem with fixing a security breach immediately upon learning that a breach of the system has occurred?
(d) What percentage of the companies had experienced a security breach in the last year? In these instances, what percentage did not take legal action against the perpetrator of the breach?
(e) How did the findings of the survey vary across countries and across other geographic distinctions?

■ **EXPLORING THE WEB**

BYP8-4 All organizations should have systems of internal control. Universities are no exception. This site discusses the basics of internal control in a university setting.

Address: www.bc.edu/offices/audit/controls, or go to www.wiley.com/college/weygandt

Steps: Go to the site shown above.

Instructions

The front page of this site provides links to pages that answer six critical questions. Use these links to answer the following questions.

(a) In a university setting who has responsibility for evaluating the adequacy of the system of internal control?

(b) What do reconciliations ensure in the university setting? Who should review the reconciliation?

(c) What are some examples of physical controls?

(d) What are two ways to accomplish inventory counts?

Critical Thinking

■ **GROUP DECISION CASE**

BYP8-5 The board of trustees of a local church is concerned about the internal accounting controls for the offering collections made at weekly services. The trustees ask you to serve on a three-person audit team with the internal auditor of a local college and a CPA who has just joined the church.

At a meeting of the audit team and the board of trustees you learn the following.

1. The church's board of trustees has delegated responsibility for the financial management and audit of the financial records to the finance committee. This group prepares the annual budget and approves major disbursements. It is not involved in collections or record keeping. No audit has been made in recent years because the same trusted employee has kept church records and served as financial secretary for 15 years. The church does not carry any fidelity insurance.

2. The collection at the weekly service is taken by a team of ushers who volunteer to serve one month. The ushers take the collection plates to a basement office at the rear of the church. They hand their plates to the head usher and return to the church service. After all plates have been turned in, the head usher counts the cash received. The head usher then places the cash in the church safe along with a notation of the amount counted. The head usher volunteers to serve for 3 months.

3. The next morning the financial secretary opens the safe and recounts the collection. The secretary withholds $150–$200 in cash, depending on the cash expenditures expected for the week, and deposits the remainder of the collections in the bank. To facilitate the deposit, church members who contribute by check are asked to make their checks payable to "Cash."

4. Each month, the financial secretary reconciles the bank statement and submits a copy of the reconciliation to the board of trustees. The reconciliations have rarely contained any bank errors and have never shown any errors per books.

Instructions

With the class divided into groups, answer the following.

(a) Indicate the weaknesses in internal accounting control over the handling of collections.

(b) List the improvements in internal control procedures that you plan to make at the next meeting of the audit team for (1) the ushers, (2) the head usher, (3) the financial secretary, and (4) the finance committee.

(c) What church policies should be changed to improve internal control?

■ **COMMUNICATION ACTIVITY**

BYP8-6 As a new auditor for the CPA firm of Croix, Marais, and Kale, you have been assigned to review the internal controls over mail cash receipts of Stillwater Company. Your review reveals the following: Checks are promptly endorsed "For Deposit Only," but no list of the checks is prepared by the person opening the mail. The mail is opened either by the cashier or by the employee who maintains the accounts receivable records. Mail receipts are deposited in the bank weekly by the cashier.

Instructions

Write a letter to M. R. Lynn, owner of the Stillwater Company, explaining the weaknesses in internal control and your recommendations for improving the system.

■ ETHICS CASE

BYP8-7 You are the assistant controller in charge of general ledger accounting at Springtime Bottling Company. Your company has a large loan from an insurance company. The loan agreement requires that the company's cash account balance be maintained at $200,000 or more, as reported monthly.

At June 30 the cash balance is $80,000, which you report to Anne Shirley, the financial vice president. Anne excitedly instructs you to keep the cash receipts book open for one additional day for purposes of the June 30 report to the insurance company. Anne says, "If we don't get that cash balance over $200,000, we'll default on our loan agreement. They could close us down, put us all out of our jobs!" Anne continues, "I talked to Oconto Distributors (one of Springtime's largest customers) this morning. They said they sent us a check for $150,000 yesterday. We should receive it tomorrow. If we include just that one check in our cash balance, we'll be in the clear. It's in the mail!"

Instructions

(a) Who will suffer negative effects if you do not comply with Anne Shirley's instructions? Who will suffer if you do comply?

(b) What are the ethical considerations in this case?

(c) What alternatives do you have?

BYP8-8 **Fraud Bureau** is a free service, established to alert consumers and investors about prior complaints relating to online vendors, including sellers at online auctions, and to provide consumers, investors, and users with information and news. One of the services it provides is a collection of online educational articles related to fraud.

Address: www.fraudbureau.com/articles/, or go to www.wiley.com/college/weygandt

Instructions

Go to this site and choose an article of interest to you. Write a short summary of your findings.

Answers to Self-Study Questions

1. a **2.** c **3.** b **4.** c **5.** b **6.** d **7.** a **8.** a **9.** c **10.** d **11.** c

Answer to PepsiCo Review It Question 3, p. 342

PepsiCo reports cash and cash equivalents on its balance sheet for 2002 of $1,638 million.

 REMEMBER to go back to the Navigator box on the chapter-opening page and check off your completed work.

Accounting for Receivables

THE NAVIGATOR ✓

Understand **Concepts for Review** ❑

Read **Feature Story** ❑

Scan **Study Objectives** ❑

Read **Preview** ❑

Read text and answer **Before You Go On**
p. 371 ❑   p. 374 ❑   p. 379 ❑   p. 381 ❑

Work **Demonstration Problem** ❑

Review **Summary of Study Objectives** ❑

Answer **Self-Study Questions** ❑

Complete **Assignments** ❑

CONCEPTS FOR REVIEW

Before studying this chapter, you should know or, if necessary, review:

How to record sales transactions.
(Ch. 5, pp. 190–192)

Why adjusting entries are made.
(Ch. 3, p. 92)

How to compute interest.
(Ch. 3, pp. 101–102)

How Do You Spell Relief?

Fred Tarter believes that in every problem lies an opportunity—and sometimes that opportunity can mean a big profit. For example, today fewer people pay cash for their prescriptions. Instead, pharmacies bill a customer's health plan for some or all of the prescription's cost. As a result, pharmacies must spend a lot of time and energy collecting cash from these health plans. This procedure is a headache for pharmacies because there are 4,500 different health plans in the United States. Also, it often leaves pharmacies with too many receivables and not enough cash. Their suppliers want to be paid within 15 days, but their receivables are outstanding for 30 and often 60 days.

Enter Fred Tarter. Having recently sold his advertising agency, Fred had some spare time and money on his hands. While reading a pharmacy trade journal, he learned of the pharmacies' headache. To Fred this problem spelled opportunity.

Fred found out that 56,000 pharmacies are connected by computer to a claims-processing business. Fred's idea was this: Using this network, he would purchase pharmacy receivables, charging a fee of 1.4–2 percent. Pharmacies would be willing to pay this fee because they would get their cash sooner and would be spared the headache of having to collect the accounts. Fred would then use the receivables as backing to raise new money so he could buy more receivables.

Based on this idea, Fred started a company called the Pharmacy Fund. Over 500 small pharmacies sell their receivables to his company. By means of a computer link with each pharmacy, the Pharmacy Fund buys the receivables at the end of each day and credits the pharmacy's account immediately. Rather than having to wait weeks to receive its cash from insurance companies, the pharmacy gets its cash the same day as the sale. The Pharmacy Fund's customers say that this has solved their cash-flow problems. It also has reduced their overhead costs and allowed them to automate their billing and record-keeping.

Fred Tarter has already identified his next opportunity—a target some would say is a "natural" for him: dentistry receivables. (Get it? Tarter—dentistry. We'll stick to accounting jokes from now on!)

THE NAVIGATOR

STUDY OBJECTIVES

After studying this chapter, you should be able to:

1. Identify the different types of receivables.
2. Explain how accounts receivable are recognized in the accounts.
3. Distinguish between the methods and bases used to value accounts receivable.
4. Describe the entries to record the disposition of accounts receivable.
5. Compute the maturity date of and interest on notes receivable.
6. Explain how notes receivable are recognized in the accounts.
7. Describe how notes receivable are valued.
8. Describe the entries to record the disposition of notes receivable.
9. Explain the statement presentation and analysis of receivables.

THE NAVIGATOR

As indicated in the Feature Story, receivables are a significant asset on the books of many pharmacies. Receivables are significant to companies in other industries as well, because a significant portion of sales are done on credit in the United States. As a consequence, companies must pay close attention to their receivables and manage them carefully. In this chapter you will learn what journal entries companies make when products are sold, when cash is collected from those sales, and when accounts that cannot be collected are written off.

The content and organization of the chapter are as follows.

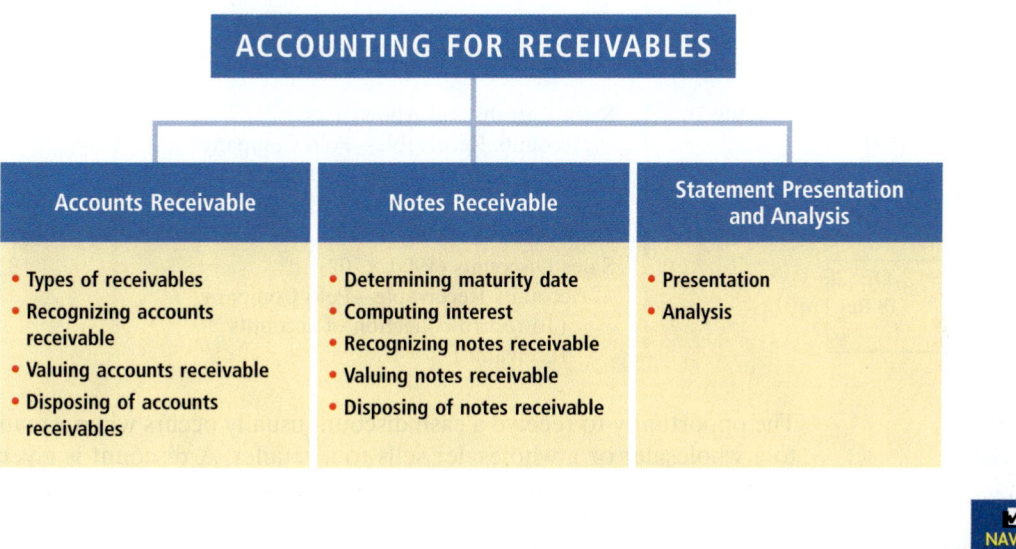

ACCOUNTING FOR RECEIVABLES

Accounts Receivable	Notes Receivable	Statement Presentation and Analysis
• Types of receivables • Recognizing accounts receivable • Valuing accounts receivable • Disposing of accounts receivables	• Determining maturity date • Computing interest • Recognizing notes receivable • Valuing notes receivable • Disposing of notes receivable	• Presentation • Analysis

THE NAVIGATOR

Accounts Receivable

Types of Receivables

The term "receivables" refers to amounts due from individuals and other companies. They are claims that are expected to be collected in cash. Receivables are frequently classified as (1) accounts, (2) notes, and (3) other.

Accounts receivable are amounts owed by customers on account. They result from the sale of goods and services. These receivables generally are expected to be collected within 30 to 60 days. They are the most significant type of claim held by a company.

Notes receivable are claims for which formal instruments of credit are issued as proof of the debt. A note receivable normally extends for time periods of 60–90 days or longer and requires the debtor to pay interest. Notes and accounts receivable that result from sales transactions are often called **trade receivables**.

Other receivables include nontrade receivables. Examples are interest receivable, loans to company officers, advances to employees, and income taxes refundable. These do not generally result from the operations of the business. Therefore they are generally classified and reported as separate items in the balance sheet.

Three primary accounting issues are associated with accounts receivable.

1. **Recognizing** accounts receivable.
2. **Valuing** accounts receivable.
3. **Disposing of** accounts receivable.

Recognizing Accounts Receivable

STUDY OBJECTIVE 2

Explain how accounts receivable are recognized in the accounts.

Recognizing accounts receivable is relatively straightforward. In Chapter 5 we saw how accounts receivable are affected by the sale of merchandise. To illustrate, assume that Jordache Co. on July 1, 2005, sells merchandise on account to Polo Company for $1,000 terms 2/10, n/30. On July 5, Polo returns merchandise worth $100 to Jordache Co. On July 11, Jordache receives payment from Polo Company for the balance due. The journal entries to record these transactions on the books of Jordache Co. are as follows.

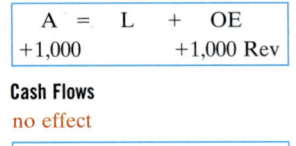

A = L + OE	
+1,000	+1,000 Rev

Cash Flows
no effect

A = L + OE	
−100	−100 Rev

Cash Flows
no effect

A = L + OE	
+882	−18 Rev
−900	

Cash Flows
+882

July 1	Accounts Receivable—Polo Company	1,000	
	Sales		1,000
	(To record sales on account)		
July 5	Sales Returns and Allowances	100	
	Accounts Receivable—Polo Company		100
	(To record merchandise returned)		
July 11	Cash ($900−$18)	882	
	Sales Discounts ($900 × .02)	18	
	Accounts Receivable—Polo Company		900
	(To record collection of accounts receivable)		

The opportunity to receive a cash discount usually occurs when a manufacturer sells to a wholesaler or a wholesaler sells to a retailer. A discount is given in these situations either to encourage prompt payment or for competitive reasons.

Retailers rarely grant cash discounts to customers. We would be surprised if you ever received a cash discount in purchasing goods from any well-known retailer, such as **Sears**, **Target**, or **Wal-Mart**. In fact, when you use a retailer's credit card (Sears, for example), instead of giving a discount, the retailer charges interest on the balance due if not paid within a specified period (usually 25–30 days).

To illustrate, assume that you use your **JCPenney Co.** credit card to purchase an outfit with a sales price of $300. JCPenney will make the following entry at the date of sale.

HELPFUL HINT

The preceding entries are the same as those described in Chapter 5. For simplicity, inventory and cost of goods sold are omitted from this set of journal entries and from end-of-chapter material.

A = L + OE	
+300	+300 Rev

Cash Flows
no effect

Accounts Receivable	300	
Sales		300
(To record sale of merchandise)		

JCPenney will send you a monthly statement of this transaction and any others that have occurred during the month. If you do not pay in full within 30 days, JCPenney adds an interest (financing) charge to the balance due. Although interest rates vary by region and over time, a common rate for retailers is 18% per year (1.5% per month).

When financing charges are added, the seller recognizes interest revenue. Assuming that you owe $300 at the end of the month, and JCPenney charges 1.5% per month on the balance due, the adjusting entry to record interest revenue of $4.50 ($300 × 1.5%) is as follows.

A = L + OE	
+4.50	+4.50 Rev

Cash Flows
no effect

Accounts Receivable	4.50	
Interest Revenue		4.50
(To record interest on amount due)		

Interest revenue is often substantial for many retailers.

ACCOUNTING IN ACTION **Business Insight**

Interest rates on most credit cards are quite high, sometimes 18 percent or higher. As a result, consumers often look for companies that charge lower rates. Be careful—some companies offer lower interest rates but have eliminated the standard 25-day grace period before finance charges are incurred. Other companies encourage consumers to get more in debt by advertising that only a $1 minimum payment is due on a $1,000 account balance. The less you pay off, the more interest they earn! One bank markets a credit card that allows cardholders to skip a payment twice a year. However, the outstanding balance continues to incur interest. Other credit card companies calculate finance charges initially on two-month, rather than one-month, averages, a practice which often translates into higher interest charges. In short, read the fine print.

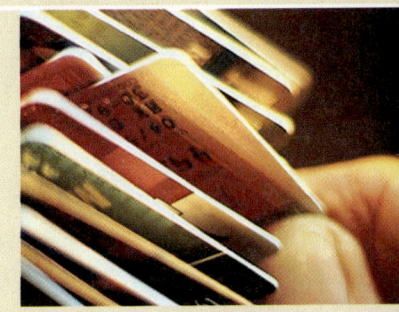

Not yet paid

Valuing Accounts Receivable

Once receivables are recorded in the accounts, the next question is: How should receivables be reported in the financial statements? They are reported on the balance sheet as an asset. But determining the **amount** to report is sometimes difficult because some receivables will become uncollectible.

Each customer must satisfy the credit requirements of the seller before the credit sale is approved. Inevitably, though, some accounts receivable become uncollectible. For example, one of your customers may not be able to pay because of a decline in sales due to a downturn in the economy. Similarly, individuals may be laid off from their jobs or be faced with unexpected hospital bills. Credit losses are recorded as debits to **Bad Debts Expense** (or Uncollectible Accounts Expense). Such losses are considered a normal and necessary risk of doing business on a credit basis.

Two methods are used in accounting for uncollectible accounts: (1) the direct write-off method and (2) the allowance method. These methods are explained in the following sections.

> **STUDY OBJECTIVE 3**
>
> Distinquish between the methods and bases used to value accounts receivable.

Direct Write-off Method for Uncollectible Accounts

Under the **direct write-off method**, when a particular account is determined to be uncollectible, the loss is charged to Bad Debts Expense. Assume, for example, that Warden Co. writes off M. E. Doran's $200 balance as uncollectible on December 12. The entry is:

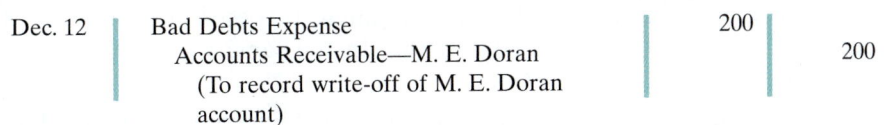

Dec. 12	Bad Debts Expense	200	
	Accounts Receivable—M. E. Doran		200
	(To record write-off of M. E. Doran account)		

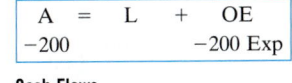

A	=	L	+	OE
−200				−200 Exp

Cash Flows
no effect

When this method is used, bad debts expense will show only **actual losses** from uncollectibles. Accounts receivable will be reported at its gross amount.

Although this method is simple, its use can reduce the usefulness of both the income statement and balance sheet. Consider the following example. Assume that in 2005, Quick Buck Computer Company decided it could increase its revenues by offering computers to college students without requiring any money down and with no credit-approval process. On campuses across the country it distributed 1,000,000 computers with a selling price of $800 each. This increased Quick Buck's revenues and receivables by $800,000,000. The promotion was a huge success! The 2005 balance sheet and income statement looked great. Unfortunately, during 2006, nearly 40 percent of the college student customers defaulted on their loans. This made the 2006 income statement and balance sheet look terrible. Illustration 9-1 shows the effect of these events on the financial statements if the direct write-off method is used.

Illustration 9-1
Effects of direct write-off method

Under the direct write-off method, bad debts expense is often recorded in a period different from the period in which the revenue was recorded. No attempt is made to match bad debts expense to sales revenues in the income statement. Nor does the direct write-off method show accounts receivable in the balance sheet at the amount actually expected to be received. **Consequently, unless bad debts losses are insignificant, the direct write-off method is not acceptable for financial reporting purposes.**

Allowance Method for Uncollectible Accounts

The **allowance method** of accounting for bad debts involves estimating uncollectible accounts at the end of each period. This provides better matching on the income statement and ensures that receivables are stated at their cash (net) realizable value on the balance sheet. **Cash (net) realizable value** is the net amount expected to be received in cash. It excludes amounts that the company estimates it will not collect. Receivables are therefore reduced by estimated uncollectible receivables in the balance sheet through use of this method.

The allowance method is required for financial reporting purposes when bad debts are material in amount. It has three essential features:

1. Uncollectible accounts receivable are **estimated**. This estimate is treated as an expense and is **matched against revenues** in the same accounting period in which the revenues are recorded.

2. Estimated uncollectibles are debited to Bad Debts Expense and are credited to Allowance for Doubtful Accounts (a contra asset account) through an adjusting entry at the end of each period.

3. When a specific account is written off, actual uncollectibles are debited to Allowance for Doubtful Accounts and credited to Accounts Receivable.

RECORDING ESTIMATED UNCOLLECTIBLES. To illustrate the allowance method, assume that Hampson Furniture has credit sales of $1,200,000 in 2005. Of this amount, $200,000 remains uncollected at December 31. The credit manager estimates that $12,000 of these sales will be uncollectible. The adjusting entry to record the estimated uncollectibles is:

Dec. 31	Bad Debts Expense	12,000	
	Allowance for Doubtful Accounts		12,000
	(To record estimate of uncollectible accounts)		

A	=	L	+	OE
−12,000				−12,000 Exp

Cash Flows
no effect

Bad Debts Expense is reported in the income statement as an operating expense (usually as a selling expense). Thus, the estimated uncollectibles are matched with sales in 2005. The expense is recorded in the same year the sales are made.

Allowance for Doubtful Accounts shows the estimated amount of claims on customers that are expected to become uncollectible in the future. This contra account is used instead of a direct credit to Accounts Receivable because we do not know which customers will not pay. The credit balance in the allowance account will absorb the specific write-offs when they occur. It is deducted from accounts receivable in the current assets section of the balance sheet as shown in Illustration 9-2.

Illustration 9-2
Presentation of allowance for doubtful accounts

HAMPSON FURNITURE		
Balance Sheet (partial)		
Current assets		
Cash		$ 14,800
Accounts receivable	$200,000	
Less: Allowance for doubtful accounts	12,000	188,000
Merchandise inventory		310,000
Prepaid expense		25,000
Total current assets		$537,800

The amount of $188,000 in Illustration 9-2 represents the expected **cash realizable value** of the accounts receivable at the statement date. **Allowance for Doubtful Accounts is not closed at the end of the fiscal year.**

RECORDING THE WRITE-OFF OF AN UNCOLLECTIBLE ACCOUNT. Companies use various methods of collecting past-due accounts, such as letters, calls, and legal action. When all means of collecting a past-due account have been exhausted and collection appears impossible, the account should be written off. In the credit card industry, for example, it is standard practice to write off accounts that are 210 days past due. To prevent premature or unauthorized write-offs, each write-off should be formally approved in writing by management. To maintain good internal control, authorization to write off accounts should not be given to someone who also has daily responsibilities related to cash or receivables.

To illustrate a receivables write-off, assume that the vice-president of finance of Hampson Furniture authorizes a write-off of the $500 balance owed by R. A. Ware on March 1, 2006. The entry to record the write-off is:

Mar. 1	Allowance for Doubtful Accounts	500	
	Accounts Receivable—R. A. Ware		500
	(Write-off of R. A. Ware account)		

A	=	L	+	OE
+500				
−500				

Cash Flows
no effect

Bad Debts Expense is not increased when the write-off occurs. **Under the allowance method, every bad debt write-off is debited to the allowance account rather than to**

Bad Debts Expense. A debit to Bad Debts Expense would be incorrect because the expense has already been recognized when the adjusting entry was made for estimated bad debts. Instead, the entry to record the write-off of an uncollectible account reduces both Accounts Receivable and the Allowance for Doubtful Accounts. After posting, the general ledger accounts will appear as in Illustration 9-3.

Illustration 9-3
General ledger balances after write-off

Accounts Receivable				Allowance for Doubtful Accounts			
Jan. 1 Bal. 200,000	Mar. 1		500	Mar. 1	500	Jan. 1 Bal. 12,000	
Mar. 1 Bal. 199,500						Mar. 1 Bal. 11,500	

A write-off affects only balance sheet accounts—not income statement accounts. The write-off of the account reduces both Accounts Receivable and Allowance for Doubtful Accounts. Cash realizable value in the balance sheet, therefore, remains the same, as shown in Illustration 9-4.

Illustration 9-4
Cash realizable value comparison

	Before Write-off	After Write-off
Accounts receivable	$200,000	$199,500
Allowance for doubtful accounts	12,000	11,500
Cash realizable value	**$188,000**	**$188,000**

RECOVERY OF AN UNCOLLECTIBLE ACCOUNT. Occasionally, a company collects from a customer after the account has been written off. Two entries are required to record the recovery of a bad debt: (1) The entry made in writing off the account is reversed to reinstate the customer's account. (2) The collection is journalized in the usual manner.

To illustrate, assume that on July 1, R. A. Ware pays the $500 amount that had been written off on March 1. These are the entries:

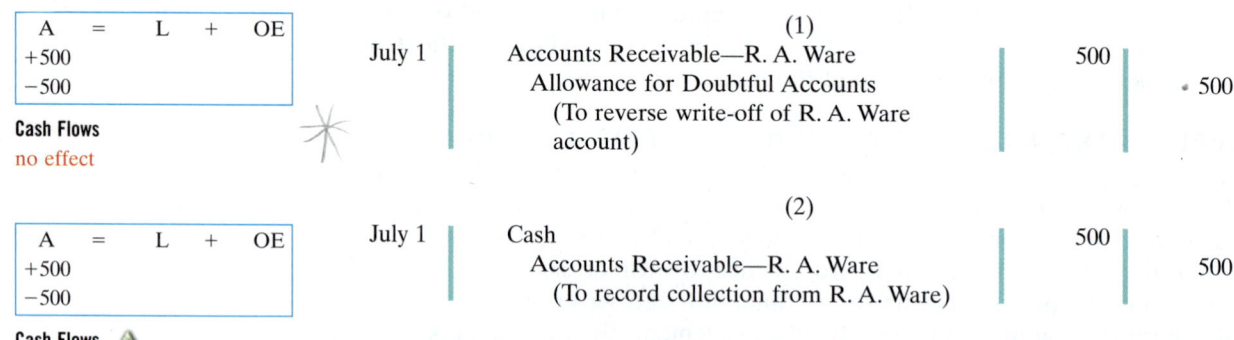

A	=	L	+	OE
+500				
−500				

Cash Flows
no effect

A	=	L	+	OE
+500				
−500				

Cash Flows
+500

	(1)		
July 1	Accounts Receivable—R. A. Ware	500	
	Allowance for Doubtful Accounts		500
	(To reverse write-off of R. A. Ware account)		
	(2)		
July 1	Cash	500	
	Accounts Receivable—R. A. Ware		500
	(To record collection from R. A. Ware)		

Note that the recovery of a bad debt, like the write-off of a bad debt, affects only balance sheet accounts. The net effect of the two entries above is a debit to Cash and a credit to Allowance for Doubtful Accounts for $500. Accounts Receivable is debited and the Allowance for Doubtful Accounts is credited in entry (1) for two reasons: First, the company made an error in judgment when it wrote off the account receivable. Second, after R. A. Ware did pay, Accounts Receivable in the general ledger and Ware's account in the subsidiary ledger should show the collection for possible future credit purposes.

BASES USED FOR ALLOWANCE METHOD. To simplify the preceding explanation, we assumed we knew the amount of the expected uncollectibles. In "real life," companies must estimate that amount if they use the allowance method. Two bases are used to determine this amount: **(1) percentage of sales**, and **(2) percentage of receivables**. Both bases are generally accepted. The choice is a management decision. It depends on the relative emphasis that management wishes to give to expenses and revenues on the one hand or to cash realizable value of the accounts receivable on the other. The choice is whether to emphasize income statement or balance sheet relationships. Illustration 9-5 compares the two bases.

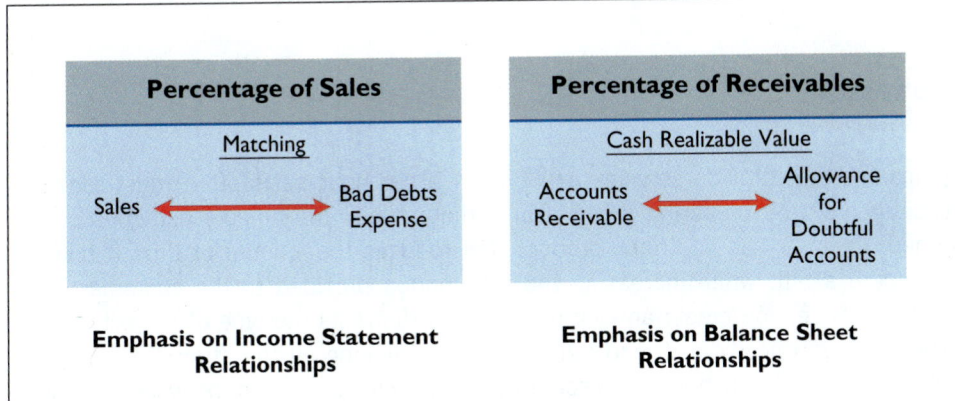

Illustration 9-5
Comparison of bases for estimating uncollectibles

The percentage of sales basis results in a better matching of expenses with revenues—an income statement viewpoint. The percentage of receivables basis produces the better estimate of cash realizable value—a balance sheet viewpoint. Under both bases, it is necessary to determine the company's past experience with bad debt losses.

Percentage of Sales. In the **percentage of sales basis**, management estimates what percentage of credit sales will be uncollectible. This percentage is based on past experience and anticipated credit policy.

The percentage is applied to either total credit sales or net credit sales of the current year. To illustrate, assume that Gonzalez Company elects to use the percentage of sales basis. It concludes that 1 percent of net credit sales will become uncollectible. If net credit sales for 2005 are $800,000, the estimated bad debts expense is $8,000 (1% × $800,000). The adjusting entry is:

Dec. 31	Bad Debts Expense	8,000	
	Allowance for Doubtful Accounts		8,000
	(To record estimated bad debts for year)		

A	=	L	+	OE
−8,000				−8,000 Exp

Cash Flows
no effect

After the adjusting entry is posted, assuming the allowance account already has a credit balance of $1,723, the accounts of Gonzalez Company will show:

Illustration 9-6
Bad debts accounts after posting

Bad Debts Expense		Allowance for Doubtful Accounts	
Dec. 31 Adj. **8,000**		Jan. 1 Bal. 1,723	
		Dec. 31 Adj. **8,000**	
		Dec. 31 Bal. 9,723	

This basis of estimating uncollectibles emphasizes the matching of expenses with revenues. As a result, Bad Debts Expense will show a direct percentage relationship to the sales base on which it is computed. **When the adjusting entry is made, the existing balance in Allowance for Doubtful Accounts is disregarded.** The adjusted balance in this account should be a reasonable approximation of the realizable value of the receivables. If actual write-offs differ significantly from the amount estimated, the percentage for future years should be modified.

Percentage of Receivables. Under the **percentage of receivables basis**, management estimates what percentage of receivables will result in losses from uncollectible accounts. An **aging schedule** is prepared, in which customer balances are classified by the length of time they have been unpaid. Because of its emphasis on time, the analysis is often called **aging the accounts receivable**.

ACCOUNTING IN ACTION   e Business Insight

Companies that provide services and bill on a per hour basis often must spend considerable time preparing detailed bills that specify the billable activities performed. **Open Air** has an online product that reduces the amount of time it takes to prepare a bill, while increasing the information provided to the customer. To use the service, you create an electronic record that lists the type of project, customer name, project dates, and billing rate. By clicking on the "timer" function, you can automatically track time spent on a particular project as the work is being performed. Open Air's software will either mail or e-mail invoices to customers, and keep track of collections, including providing an aging schedule.

After the accounts are aged, the expected bad debt losses are determined. This is done by applying percentages based on past experience to the totals in each category. The longer a receivable is past due, the less likely it is to be collected. So, the estimated percentage of uncollectible debts increases as the number of days past due increases. An aging schedule for Dart Company is shown in Illustration 9-7. Note the increasing percentages from 2 to 40 percent.

Illustration 9-7
Aging schedule

| Customer | Total | Not Yet Due | Number of Days Past Due ||||
			1–30	31–60	61–90	Over 90
T. E. Adert	$ 600		$ 300		$ 200	$ 100
R. C. Bortz	300	$ 300				
B. A. Carl	450		200	$ 250		
O. L. Diker	700	500			200	
T. O. Ebbet	600			300		300
Others	36,950	26,200	5,200	2,450	1,600	1,500
	$39,600	$27,000	$5,700	$3,000	$2,000	$1,900
Estimated Percentage Uncollectible		2%	4%	10%	20%	40%
Total Estimated Bad Debts	$ 2,228	$ 540	$ 228	$ 300	$ 400	$ 760

HELPFUL HINT

The higher percentages are used for the older categories because the longer an account is past due, the less likely it is to be collected.

Total estimated bad debts for Dart Company ($2,228) represent the amount of existing customer claims expected to become uncollectible in the future. This amount represents the **required balance** in Allowance for Doubtful Accounts at the balance sheet date. **The amount of the bad debt adjusting entry is the difference between the required balance and the existing balance in the allowance account.** If the trial balance shows Allowance for Doubtful Accounts with a credit balance of $528, an adjusting entry for $1,700 ($2,228−$528) is necessary, as shown on page 371.

Dec. 31	Bad Debts Expense	1,700	
	Allowance for Doubtful Accounts		1,700
	(To adjust allowance account to total estimated uncollectibles)		

A	=	L	+	OE
−1,700				−1,700 Exp

Cash Flows
no effect

After the adjusting entry is posted, the accounts of the Dart Company will show:

Bad Debts Expense		Allowance for Doubtful Accounts	
Dec. 31 Adj. **1,700**		Bal. 528	
		Dec. 31 Adj. **1,700**	
		Bal. 2,228	

Illustration 9-8
Bad debts accounts after posting

Occasionally the allowance account will have a **debit balance** prior to adjustment. This occurs when write-offs during the year have exceeded previous provisions for bad debts. In such a case **the debit balance is added to the required balance** when the adjusting entry is made. Thus, if there had been a $500 debit balance in the allowance account before adjustment, the adjusting entry would have been for $2,728 ($2,228 + $500) to arrive at a credit balance of $2,228.

The percentage of receivables method will normally result in the better approximation of cash realizable value. But it will not result in the better matching of expenses with revenues if some customers' accounts are more than one year past due. In such a case, bad debts expense for the current period would include amounts related to the sales of a prior year.

ACCOUNTING IN ACTION   **Ethics Insight**

Nearly half of the goods sold by **Sears, Roebuck & Co.** are purchased with a Sears credit card. This means that how Sears accounts for its uncollectible accounts can have a very significant effect on Sears's net income. In one quarter in a recent year Sears reduced its bad debts expense by 61 percent compared to the same quarter in the previous year. In so doing, Sears was able to report earnings that slightly exceeded analysts' forecasts. Some analysts expressed concern that, because the number of delinquent accounts receivable had actually increased, Sears should probably have *increased* its bad debts expense, rather than reduced it. While Sears management defended its actions, analysts appeared to be unimpressed, and Sears's stock price declined on the news.

BEFORE YOU GO ON...

Review It

1. What is the primary criticism of the direct write-off method?
2. Explain the difference between the percentage of sales and the percentage of receivables methods.
3. What percentage does **PepsiCo**'s allowance for doubtful accounts represent as a percent of its gross receivables? (*Hint:* See PepsiCo's Note 14.) The answer to this question is provided on page 397.

(continued from p. 371)

Do It

Brule Co. has been in business 5 years. The ledger at the end of the current year shows: Accounts Receivable $30,000, Sales $180,000, and Allowance for Doubtful Accounts with a debit balance of $2,000. Bad debts are estimated to be 10% of receivables. Prepare the entry to adjust the Allowance for Doubtful Accounts.

ACTION PLAN

- Report receivables at their cash (net) realizable value.
- Estimate the amount the company does not expect to collect.
- Consider the existing balance in the allowance account when using the percentage of receivables basis.

SOLUTION   The following entry should be made to bring the balance in the Allowance for Doubtful Accounts up to a balance of $3,000 (0.1 × $30,000):

Bad Debts Expense	5,000	
Allowance for Doubtful Accounts		5,000
(To record estimate of uncollectible accounts)		

Related exercise material: *BE9-3, BE9-4, BE9-5, BE9-6, BE9-7, E9-2, E9-3, and E9-4.*

✓ THE NAVIGATOR

Disposing of Accounts Receivable

STUDY OBJECTIVE 4

Describe the entries to record the disposition of accounts receivable.

In the normal course of events, accounts receivable are collected in cash and removed from the books. However, as credit sales and receivables have grown in significance, their "normal course of events" has changed. As indicated in our Feature Story, companies now frequently sell their receivables to another company for cash, thereby shortening the cash-to-cash operating cycle.

Receivables are sold for two major reasons. First, **receivables may be sold because they may be the only reasonable source of cash**. When money is tight, companies may not be able to borrow money in the usual credit markets. Or, if money is available, the cost of borrowing may be prohibitive.

A second reason for selling receivables is that **billing and collection are often time consuming and costly**. It is often easier for a retailer to sell the receivables to another party with expertise in billing and collection matters. Credit card companies such as **MasterCard**, **VISA**, **American Express**, and **Diners Club** specialize in billing and collecting accounts receivable.

Sale of Receivables

A common sale of receivables is a sale to a factor. A **factor** is a finance company or bank that buys receivables from businesses and then collects the payments directly from the customers. Factoring is a multibillion dollar business. For example, **Sears, Roebuck and Co.** recently sold $14.8 billion of customer accounts receivable to a factor.

Factoring arrangements vary widely. Typically the factor charges a commission to the company that is selling the receivables. This fee ranges from 1–3 percent of the amount of receivables purchased. To illustrate, assume that Hendredon Furniture factors $600,000 of receivables to Federal Factors. Federal Factors assesses a service charge of 2 percent of the amount of receivables sold. The journal entry to record the sale by Hendredon Furniture is as follows.

Cash	588,000	
Service Charge Expense (2% × $600,000)	12,000	
Accounts Receivable		600,000
(To record the sale of accounts receivable)		

A	=	L	+	OE
+588,000				−12,000 Exp
−600,000				

Cash Flows
+588,000

If the company often sells its receivables, the service charge expense (such as that incurred by Hendredon) is recorded as selling expense. If receivables are sold infrequently, this amount may be reported in the "other expenses and losses" section of the income statement.

Credit Card Sales

One billion credit cards were estimated to be in use recently—more than three credit cards for every man, woman, and child in this country. Companies such as VISA, MasterCard, Discover, American Express, and Diners Club offer national credit cards. Three parties are involved when national credit cards are used in making retail sales: (1) the credit card issuer, who is independent of the retailer, (2) the retailer, and (3) the customer. A retailer's acceptance of a national credit card is another form of selling (factoring) the receivable.

The major advantages of these national credit cards to the retailer are shown in Illustration 9-9. In exchange for these advantages, the retailer pays the credit card issuer a fee of 2–6 percent of the invoice price for its services.

Illustration 9-9
Advantages of credit cards to the retailer

CASH SALES: VISA AND MASTERCARD.   Sales resulting from the use of **VISA** and **MasterCard** are considered cash sales by the retailer. These cards are issued by banks. Upon receipt of credit card sales slips from a retailer, the bank immediately adds the amount to the seller's bank balance, deducting a fee of 2–4 percent of the credit card sales slips for this service. These credit card sales slips are recorded in the same manner as checks deposited from a cash sale.

To illustrate, Anita Ferreri purchases $1,000 of compact discs for her restaurant from Karen Kerr Music Co., using her VISA First Bank Card. The service fee that First Bank charges is 3 percent. The entry to record this transaction by Karen Kerr Music is as follows.

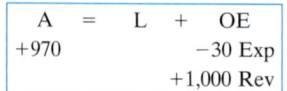

A = L + OE
+970   −30 Exp
            +1,000 Rev

Cash Flows
+970

Cash	970	
Service Charge Expense	30	
Sales		1,000
(To record VISA credit card sales)		

CREDIT SALES: AMERICAN EXPRESS AND DINERS CLUB. Sales using **American Express** and **Diners Club** cards are reported as credit sales, not cash sales. Conversion into cash does not occur until these companies remit the net amount to the seller. To illustrate, assume that Four Seasons restaurant accepts an American Express card for a $300 bill. The entry for the sale by Four Seasons, assuming a 5 percent service fee, is:

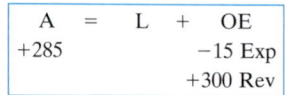

A = L + OE
+285   −15 Exp
            +300 Rev

Cash Flows
no effect

Accounts Receivable—American Express	285	
Service Charge Expense	15	
Sales		300
(To record American Express credit card sales)		

American Express will subsequently pay the restaurant $285. The restaurant will record this payment as follows.

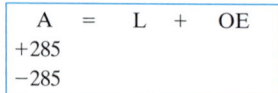

A = L + OE
+285
−285

Cash Flows
+285

Cash	285	
Accounts Receivable—American Express		285
(To record redemption of credit card billings)		

Service Charge Expense is reported by the restaurant as a selling expense in the income statement.

BEFORE YOU GO ON...

Review It

1. Why do companies sell their receivables?
2. What is the journal entry when a company sells its receivables to a factor?
3. How are sales using a VISA or MasterCard reported? Is a sale using an American Express card recorded differently? Explain.

Do It

Peter M. Dell Wholesalers Co. has been expanding faster than it can raise capital. According to its local banker, the company has reached its debt ceiling. Dell's customers are slow in paying (60–90 days), but its suppliers (creditors) are demanding 30-day payment. Dell has a cash flow problem.

Dell needs $120,000 in cash to safely cover next Friday's employee payroll. Its balance of outstanding receivables totals $750,000. What might Dell do to alleviate this cash crunch? Record the entry that Dell would make when it raises the needed cash.

ACTION PLAN

- To speed up the collection of cash, sell receivables to a factor.
- Calculate service charge expense as a percentage of the factored receivables.

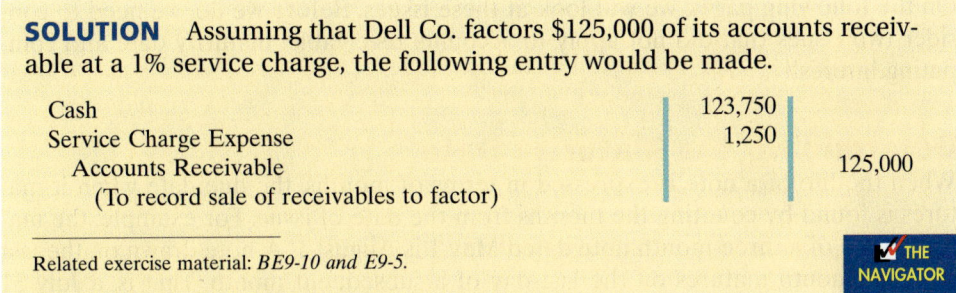

SOLUTION   Assuming that Dell Co. factors $125,000 of its accounts receivable at a 1% service charge, the following entry would be made.

Cash	123,750	
Service Charge Expense	1,250	
Accounts Receivable		125,000
(To record sale of receivables to factor)		

Related exercise material: *BE9-10* and *E9-5.*

☑ **THE NAVIGATOR**

Notes Receivable

Credit may also be granted in exchange for a promissory note. A **promissory note** is a written promise to pay a specified amount of money on demand or at a definite time. Promissory notes may be used (1) when individuals and companies lend or borrow money; (2) when the amount of the transaction and the credit period exceed normal limits; or (3) in settlement of accounts receivable.

In a promissory note, the party making the promise to pay is called the **maker**. The party to whom payment is to be made is called the **payee**. The payee may be specifically identified by name or may be designated simply as the bearer of the note. In the note shown in Illustration 9-10, Brent Company is the maker, Wilma Company is the payee. To Wilma Company, the promissory note is a note receivable; to Brent Company, it is a note payable.

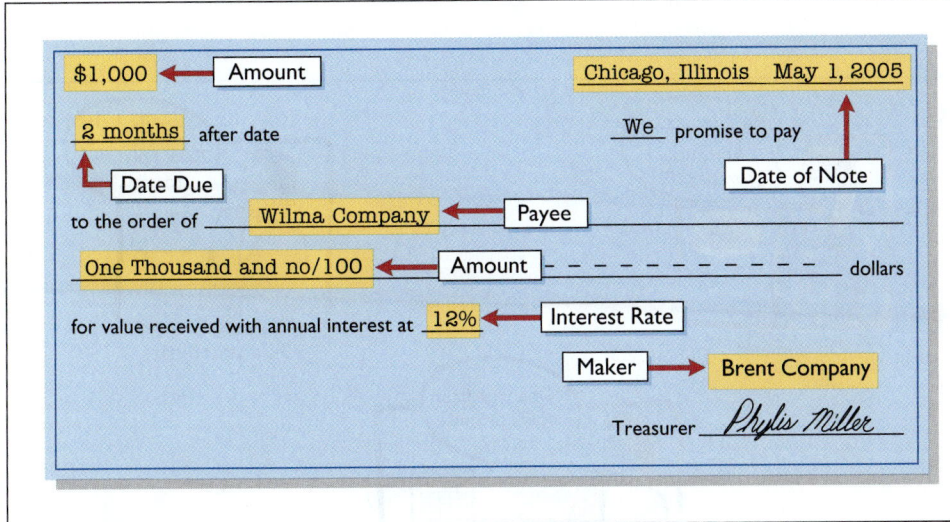

Illustration 9-10
Promissory note

HELPFUL HINT

Who are the two key parties to a note, and what entry does each party make when the note is issued?

Answer:

1. The maker, Brent Company, credits Notes Payable.
2. The payee, Wilma Company, debits Notes Receivable.

Notes receivable give the payee a stronger legal claim to assets than accounts receivable. Like accounts receivable, notes receivable can be readily sold to another party. Promissory notes are negotiable instruments (as are checks), which means that they can be transferred to another party by endorsement.

Notes receivable are frequently accepted from customers who need to extend the payment of an account receivable. They are often required from high-risk customers. In some industries (such as the pleasure boat industry), all credit sales are supported by notes. The majority of notes originate from loans. The basic issues in accounting for notes receivable are the same as those for accounts receivable:

1. **Recognizing** notes receivable.
2. **Valuing** notes receivable.
3. **Disposing of** notes receivable.

On the following pages, we will look at these issues. Before we do, we need to consider two issues that did not apply to accounts receivable: maturity date and computing interest.

Determining the Maturity Date

when is the maturity date if the Date of a 2-mo note starts on Dec 30

When the life of a note is expressed in terms of months, the due date when it matures is found by counting the months from the date of issue. For example, the maturity date of a three-month note dated May 1 is August 1. A note drawn on the last day of a month matures on the last day of a subsequent month. That is, a July 31 note due in two months matures on September 30. When the due date is stated in terms of days, you need to count the exact number of days to determine the maturity date. In counting, **the date the note is issued is omitted but the due date is included**. For example, the maturity date of a 60-day note dated July 17 is September 15, computed as follows.

Illustration 9-11
Computation of maturity date

Term of note		60 days
July (31−17)	14	
August	31	45
Maturity date: September		**15**

The due date (maturity date) of a promissory note may be stated in one of three ways, as shown in Illustration 9-12.

Illustration 9-12
Maturity date of different notes

Computing Interest

As indicated in Chapter 3, the basic formula for computing interest on an interest-bearing note is:

Illustration 9-13
Formula for computing interest

Face Value of Note	×	Annual Interest Rate	×	Time in Terms of One Year	=	Interest

The interest rate specified in a note is an **annual** rate of interest. The time factor in the formula in Illustration 9-13 expresses the fraction of a year that the note is outstanding. When the maturity date is stated in days, the time factor is often the number of days divided by 360. When the due date is stated in months, the time factor is the number of months divided by 12. Computation of interest for various time periods is shown in Illustration 9-14.

Terms of Note	Interest Computation
	Face × Rate × Time = Interest
$ 730, 18%, 120 days	$ 730 × 18% × 120/360 = $ 43.80
$1,000, 15%, 6 months	$1,000 × 15% × 6/12 = $ 75.00
$2,000, 12%, 1 year	$2,000 × 12% × 1/1 = $240.00

Illustration 9-14
Computation of interest

There are many different ways to calculate interest. The computation above assumed 360 days for the length of the year. Financial instruments actually use 365 days. In order to simplify calculations in our illustrations, we have assumed 360 days. For homework problems, assume 360 days.

Recognizing Notes Receivable

To illustrate the basic entry for notes receivable, we will use the $1,000, 2-month, 12% promissory note on page 375. Assuming that the note was written to settle an open account, the entry for the receipt of the note by Wilma Company is:

STUDY OBJECTIVE 6

Explain how notes receivable are recognized in the accounts.

May 1	Notes Receivable	1,000	
	Accounts Receivable—Brent Company		1,000
	(To record acceptance of Brent Company note)		

A	=	L	+	OE
+1,000				
−1,000				

Cash Flows
no effect

Observe that the note receivable is recorded at its **face value**, the value shown on the face of the note. No interest revenue is reported when the note is accepted because the revenue recognition principle does not recognize revenue until earned. Interest is earned (accrued) as time passes.

If a note is exchanged for cash, the entry is a debit to Notes Receivable and a credit to Cash in the amount of the loan.

Valuing Notes Receivable

Valuing short-term notes receivable is the same as valuing accounts receivable. Like accounts receivable, short-term notes receivable are reported at their **cash (net) realizable value**. The notes receivable allowance account is Allowance for Doubtful Accounts. The estimations involved in determining cash realizable value and in recording bad debts expense and related allowance are similar.

STUDY OBJECTIVE 7

Describe how notes receivable are valued.

Disposing of Notes Receivable

Notes may be held to their maturity date, at which time the face value plus accrued interest is due. Sometimes the maker of the note defaults and an adjustment to the accounts must be made. At other times the holder of the note speeds up the conversion to cash by selling the note. The entries for honoring and dishonoring notes are illustrated below.

STUDY OBJECTIVE 8

Describe the entries to record the disposition of notes receivable.

Honor of Notes Receivable

A note is **honored** when it is paid in full at its maturity date. For an interest-bearing note, the amount due at maturity is the face value of the note plus interest for the length of time specified on the note.

To illustrate, assume that Betty Co. lends Wayne Higley Inc. $10,000 on June 1, accepting a 5-month, 9% interest note. Interest will be $375 ($10,000 × 9% × 5/12). The amount due, the maturity value, will be $10,375. To obtain payment, Betty Co. (the payee) must present the note either to Wayne Higley Inc. (the maker) or to the maker's duly appointed agent, such as a bank. Assuming that Betty Co. presents the note to Wayne Higley Inc. on the maturity date, the entry by Betty Co. to record the collection is:

A	=	L	+	OE
+10,375				+375 Rev
−10,000				

Cash Flows
+10,375

Nov. 1	Cash	10,375	
	Notes Receivable		10,000
	Interest Revenue		375
	(To record collection of Higley Inc. note)		

If Betty Co. prepares financial statements as of September 30, it would be necessary to accrue interest. In this case, the adjusting entry by Betty Co. would be to record 4 months' interest ($300), as shown below.

A	=	L	+	OE
+300				+300 Rev

Cash Flows
no effect

Sept. 30	Interest Receivable ($10,000 × 9% × 4/12)	300	
	Interest Revenue		300
	(To accrue 4 months' interest)		

When interest has been accrued, at maturity it is necessary to credit Interest Receivable. In addition, since an additional month has passed, one month of interest revenue is recorded. The entry by Betty Co. to record the honoring of the Wayne Higley Inc. note on November 1 is:

A	=	L	+	OE
+10,375				+75 Rev
−10,000				
−300				

Cash Flows
+10,375

Nov. 1	Cash	10,375	
	Notes Receivable		10,000
	Interest Receivable		300
	Interest Revenue ($10,000 × 9% × 1/12)		75
	(To record collection of note at maturity)		

In this case, Interest Receivable is credited because the receivable was established in the adjusting entry.

Dishonor of Notes Receivable

A **dishonored note** is a note that is not paid in full at maturity. A dishonored note receivable is no longer negotiable. However, the payee still has a claim against the maker of the note. Therefore the Notes Receivable account is usually transferred to an Account Receivable.

To illustrate, assume that Wayne Higley Inc. on November 1 indicates that it cannot pay at the present time. The entry to record the dishonor of the note depends on whether eventual collection is expected. If Betty Co. expects eventual collection, the amount due (face value and interest) on the note is debited to Accounts Receivable. Betty Co. would make the following entry at the time the note is dishonored (assuming no previous accrual of interest).

A	=	L	+	OE
+10,375				+375 Rev
−10,000				

Cash Flows
no effect

Nov. 1	Accounts Receivable—Wayne Higley Inc.	10,375	
	Notes Receivable		10,000
	Interest Revenue		375
	(To record the dishonor of Higley Inc. note)		

If there is no hope of collection, the face value of the note would be written off by debiting the Allowance for Doubtful Accounts. No interest revenue would be recorded because collection will not occur.

ACCOUNTING IN ACTION   Business Insight

In the weeks prior to **Kmart**'s decision in early 2002 to file for Chapter 11 bankruptcy protection, many of its suppliers were taking concrete steps to protect themselves. For example, the garden supply company **The Scotts Company**, which in the previous year sold Kmart $175 million in goods, decided to quit shipping to Kmart until its survival plans were more clear. This was a big decision for Scotts, since Kmart represented 10% of its sales in the previous year: One consultant said that in an informal survey of Kmart suppliers, one-third weren't shipping to Kmart, one-third were holding back shipments until they learned more, and one-third were doing business as usual. Many of those that were shipping were demanding cash on delivery (rather than extending credit). All of this meant that Kmart had a lot of empty shelves, at a time when it was hard pressed for cash.

Source: Amy Merrick, "Kmart Suppliers Limit Risk in Case of Chapter 11 Filing," *Wall Street Journal Online* (January 21, 2002).

Sale of Notes Receivable

The accounting for the sale of notes receivable is recorded similarly to the sale of accounts receivable. The accounting entries for the sale of notes receivable are left for a more advanced course.

BEFORE YOU GO ON...

Review It

1. What is the basic formula for computing interest?
2. At what value are notes receivable reported on the balance sheet?
3. Explain the difference between honoring and dishonoring a note receivable.

Do It

Gambit Stores accepts from Leonard Co. a $3,400, 90-day, 12% note dated May 10 in settlement of Leonard's overdue account. What is the maturity date of the note? What is the entry made by Gambit at the maturity date, assuming Leonard pays the note and interest in full at that time?

ACTION PLAN

- Count the exact number of days to determine the maturity date. Omit the date the note is issued, but include the due date.
- Determine whether interest was accrued. The entry here assumes that no interest has been previously accrued on this note.

SOLUTION   The maturity date is August 8, computed as follows.

Term of note:		90 days
May (31−10)	21	
June	30	
July	31	82
Maturity date: August		8

The interest payable at maturity date is $102, computed as follows.

$$\text{Face} \times \text{Rate} \times \text{Time} = \text{Interest}$$
$$\$3,400 \times 12\% \times 90/360 = \$102$$

(continued from p. 379)

The entry recorded by Gambit Stores at the maturity date is:

Cash	3,502	
Notes Receivable		3,400
Interest Revenue		102
(To record collection of Leonard note)		

Related exercise material: *BE9-8, BE9-9, E9-8, E9-9, and E9-10.*

✔ THE NAVIGATOR

Statement Presentation and Analysis

Presentation

STUDY OBJECTIVE 9

Explain the statement presentation and analysis of receivables.

Each of the major types of receivables should be identified in the balance sheet or in the notes to the financial statements. Short-term receivables are reported in the current assets section of the balance sheet, below short-term investments. Short-term investments appear before receivables, because short-term investments are more liquid (nearer to cash). Both the gross amount of receivables and the allowance for doubtful accounts should be reported.

In a multiple-step income statement, bad debts expense and service charge expense are reported as selling expenses in the operating expenses section. Interest revenue is shown under "other revenues and gains" in the nonoperating activities section of the income statement.

Analysis

Financial ratios are frequently computed to evaluate the liquidity of a company's accounts receivable. The **accounts receivable turnover ratio** is used to assess the liquidity of the receivables. This ratio measures the number of times, on average, accounts receivable are collected during the period. It is computed by dividing net credit sales (net sales less cash sales) by the average gross accounts receivable during the year. Unless seasonal factors are significant, average gross accounts receivable outstanding can be computed from the beginning and ending balances of gross accounts receivable.

For example, in 2002 **Cisco Systems** had net sales of $18,915 million for the year. It had a beginning accounts receivable (net) balance of $1,466 million and an ending accounts receivable (net) balance of $1,105 million. Assuming that Cisco's sales were all on credit, its accounts receivable turnover ratio is computed as follows.

Illustration 9-15
Accounts receivable turnover ratio and computation

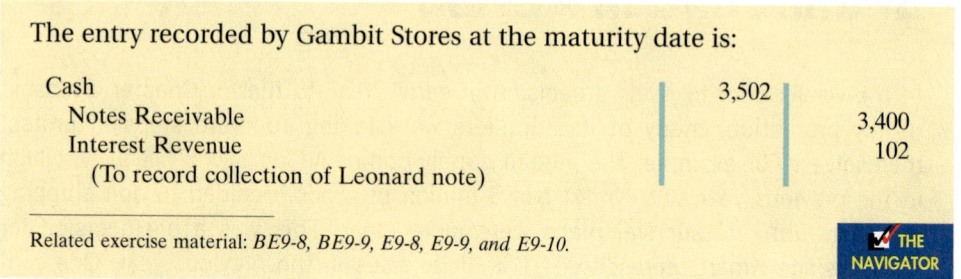

Net Credit Sales	÷	Average Net Accounts Receivable	=	Accounts Receivable Turnover
$18,915	÷	$\dfrac{\$1,466 + \$1,105}{2}$	=	**14.7 times**

The result indicates an accounts receivable turnover ratio of 14.7 times per year. The higher the turnover ratio the more liquid the company's receivables.

A variant of the accounts receivable turnover ratio that makes the liquidity even more evident is the conversion of it into an **average collection period** in terms of days. This is done by dividing the turnover ratio into 365 days. For example, Cisco's turnover of 14.7 times is divided into 365 days, as shown in Illustration 9-16, to obtain approximately 24.8 days.

Days in Year	÷	Accounts Receivable Turnover	=	Average Collection Period in Days
365 days	÷	14.7 times	=	**24.8 days**

Illustration 9-16
Average collection period for receivables formula and computation

This means that it takes Cisco about 25 days to collect its accounts receivable.

The average collection period is frequently used to assess the effectiveness of a company's credit and collection policies. The general rule is that the collection period should not greatly exceed the credit term period (i.e., the time allowed for payment).

BEFORE YOU GO ON...

Review It

1. Explain where accounts and notes receivable are reported on the balance sheet.
2. Where are bad debts expense, service charge expense, and interest revenue reported on the multiple-step income statement?

DEMONSTRATION PROBLEM

The following selected transactions relate to Falcetto Company.

Mar. 1 Sold $20,000 of merchandise to Potter Company, terms 2/10, n/30.

11 Received payment in full from Potter Company for balance due.

12 Accepted Juno Company's $20,000, 6-month, 12% note for balance due.

13 Made Falcetto Company credit card sales for $13,200.

15 Made American Express credit sales totaling $6,700. A 5% service fee is charged by American Express.

30 Received payment in full from American Express Company.

Apr. 11 Sold accounts receivable of $8,000 to Harcot Factor. Harcot Factor assesses a service charge of 2% of the amount of receivables sold.

13 Received collections of $8,200 on Falcetto Company credit card sales and added finance charges of 1.5% to the remaining balances.

May 10 Wrote off as uncollectible $16,000 of accounts receivable. Falcetto uses the percentage of sales basis to estimate bad debts.

June 30 Credit sales for the first 6 months total $2,000,000. The bad debt percentage is 1% of credit sales. At June 30, the balance in the allowance account is $3,500.

July 16 One of the accounts receivable written off in May was from J. Simon, who pays the amount due, $4,000, in full.

Instructions

Prepare the journal entries for the transactions.

ACTION PLAN

- Generally, record accounts receivable at invoice price.
- Recognize that sales returns and allowances and cash discounts reduce the amount received on accounts receivable.
- Record a service charge expense on the seller's books when accounts receivable are sold.
- Prepare an adjusting entry for bad debts expense.
- Ignore any balance in the allowance account under the percentage of sales basis. Recognize the balance in the allowance account under the percentage of receivables basis.
- Record write-offs of accounts receivable only in balance sheet accounts.

SOLUTION TO DEMONSTRATION PROBLEM

Mar. 1	Accounts Receivable–Potter	20,000	
	Sales		20,000
	(To record sales on account)		
Mar. 11	Cash	19,600	
	Sales Discounts (2% × $20,000)	400	
	Accounts Receivable—Potter		20,000
	(To record collection of accounts receivable)		
Mar. 12	Notes Receivable	20,000	
	Accounts Receivable—Juno		20,000
	(To record acceptance of Juno Company note)		
Mar. 13	Accounts Receivable	13,200	
	Sales		13,200
	(To record company credit card sales)		
Mar. 15	Accounts Receivable—American Express	6,365	
	Service Charge Expense (5% × $6,700)	335	
	Sales		6,700
	(To record credit card sales)		
Mar. 30	Cash	6,365	
	Accounts Receivable—American Express		6,365
	(To record redemption of credit card billings)		
Apr. 11	Cash	7,840	
	Service Charge Expense (2% × $8,000)	160	
	Accounts Receivable		8,000
	(To record sale of receivables to factor)		
Apr. 13	Cash	8,200	
	Accounts Receivable		8,200
	(To record collection of accounts receivable)		
	Accounts Receivable [($13,200 − $8,200) × 1.5%]	75	
	Interest Revenue		75
	(To record interest on amount due)		
May 10	Allowance for Doubtful Accounts	16,000	
	Accounts Receivable		16,000
	(To record write-off of accounts receivable)		
June 30	Bad Debts Expense ($2,000,000 × 1%)	20,000	
	Allowance for Doubtful Accounts		20,000
	(To record estimate of uncollectible accounts)		
July 16	Accounts Receivable—J. Simon	4,000	
	Allowance for Doubtful Accounts		4,000
	(To reverse write-off of accounts receivable)		
	Cash	4,000	
	Accounts Receivable—J. Simon		4,000
	(To record collection of accounts receivable)		

SUMMARY OF STUDY OBJECTIVES

1. **Identify the different types of receivables.** Receivables are frequently classified as (1) accounts, (2) notes, and (3) other. Accounts receivable are amounts owed by customers on account. Notes receivable are claims for which formal instruments of credit are issued as proof of the debt. Other receivables include nontrade receivables such as interest receivable, loans to company officers, advances to employees, and income taxes refundable.

2. **Explain how accounts receivable are recognized in the accounts.** Accounts receivable are recorded at invoice price. They are reduced by Sales Returns and Allowances. Cash discounts reduce the amount received on accounts receivable. When interest is charged on a past due receivable, this interest is added to the accounts receivable balance and is recognized as interest revenue.

3. **Distinguish between the methods and bases used to value accounts receivable.** There are two methods of accounting for uncollectible accounts: (1) the allowance method and (2) the direct write-off method. Either the percentage of sales or the percentage of receivables basis may be used to estimate uncollectible accounts using the allowance method. The percentage of sales basis emphasizes the matching principle. The percentage of receivables basis emphasizes the cash realizable value of the accounts receivable. An aging schedule is often used with this basis.

4. **Describe the entries to record the disposition of accounts receivable.** When an account receivable is collected, Accounts Receivable is credited. When an account receivable is sold, a service charge expense is charged which reduces the amount collected.

5. **Compute the maturity date of and interest on notes receivable.** The maturity date of a note must be computed unless the due date is specified or the note is payable on demand. For a note stated in months, the maturity date is found by counting the months from the date of issue. For a note stated in days, the number of days is counted, omit-ting the issue date and counting the due date. The formula for computing interest is face value × interest rate × time.

6. **Explain how notes receivable are recognized in the accounts.** Notes receivable are recorded at face value. In some cases, it is necessary to accrue interest prior to maturity. In this case, Interest Receivable is debited and Interest Revenue is credited.

7. **Describe how notes receivable are valued.** Like accounts receivable, notes receivable are reported at their cash (net) realizable value. The notes receivable allowance account is the Allowance for Doubtful Accounts. The computation and estimations involved in valuing notes receivable at cash realizable value, and in recording the proper amount of bad debts expense and related allowance are similar to those for accounts receivable.

8. **Describe the entries to record the disposition of notes receivable.** Notes can be held to maturity. At that time the face value plus accrued interest is due, and the note is removed from the accounts. In many cases, the holder of the note speeds up the conversion by selling the receivable to another party. In some situations, the maker of the note dishonors the note (defaults), and the note is written off.

9. **Explain the statement presentation and analysis of receivables.** Each major type of receivable should be identified in the balance sheet or in the notes to the financial statements. Short-term receivables are considered current assets. The gross amount of receivables and the allowance for doubtful accounts should be reported. Bad debts and service charge expenses are reported in the multiple-step income statement as operating (selling) expenses; interest revenue is shown as other revenues and gains in the nonoperating activities section of the statement. Accounts receivable may be evaluated for liquidity by computing a turnover ratio and an average collection period.

GLOSSARY

Accounts receivable turnover ratio A measure of the liquidity of accounts receivable; computed by dividing net credit sales by average net accounts receivable. (p. 380).

Aging of accounts receivable The analysis of customer balances by the length of time they have been unpaid. (p. 370).

Allowance method A method of accounting for bad debts that involves estimating uncollectible accounts at the end of each period. (p. 366).

Average collection period The average amount of time that a receivable is outstanding; calculated by dividing 365 days by the receivables turnover ratio. (p. 380).

Bad Debts Expense An expense account to record uncollectible receivables. (p. 365).

Cash (net) realizable value The net amount expected to be received in cash. (p. 366).

Direct write-off method A method of accounting for bad debts that involves expensing accounts at the time they are determined to be uncollectible. (p. 365).

Dishonored note A note that is not paid in full at maturity. (p. 378).

Factor A finance company or bank that buys receivables from businesses and then collects the payments directly from the customers. (p. 372).

Maker The party in a promissory note who is making the promise to pay. (p. 375).

Payee The party to whom payment of a promissory note is to be made. (p. 375).

Percentage of receivables basis Management establishes a percentage relationship between the amount of receivables and the expected losses from uncollectible accounts. (p. 370).

Percentage of sales basis Management establishes a percentage relationship between the amount of credit sales and expected losses from uncollectible accounts. (p. 369).

Promissory note A written promise to pay a specified amount of money on demand or at a definite time. (p. 375).

Trade receivables Notes and accounts receivable that result from sales transactions. (p. 363).

SELF-STUDY QUESTIONS

Answers are at the end of the chapter.

(SO 2) **1.** Buehler Company on June 15 sells merchandise on account to Chaz Co. for $1,000, terms 2/10, n/30. On June 20, Chaz Co. returns merchandise worth $300 to Buehler Company. On June 24, payment is received from Chaz Co. for the balance due. What is the amount of cash received?
  a. $700.
  b. $680.
  c. $686.
  d. None of the above.

(SO 3) **2.** Which of the following approaches for bad debts is best described as a balance sheet method?
  a. Percentage of receivables basis.
  b. Direct write-off method.
  c. Percentage of sales basis.
  d. Both a and b.

(SO 3) **3.** Net sales for the month are $800,000, and bad debts are expected to be 1.5% of net sales. The company uses the percentage of sales basis. If the Allowance for Doubtful Accounts has a credit balance of $15,000 before adjustment, what is the balance after adjustment?
  a. $15,000.
  b. $27,000.
  c. $23,000.
  d. $31,000.

(SO 3) **4.** In 2005, Roso Carlson Company had net credit sales of $750,000. On January 1, 2005, Allowance for Doubtful Accounts had a credit balance of $18,000. During 2005, $30,000 of uncollectible accounts receivable were written off. Past experience indicates that 3% of net credit sales become uncollectible. What should be the adjusted balance of Allowance for Doubtful Accounts at December 31, 2005?
  a. $10,050.
  b. $10,500.
  c. $22,500.
  d. $40,500.

(SO 3) **5.** An analysis and aging of the accounts receivable of Prince Company at December 31 reveals the following data.

Accounts receivable	$800,000
Allowance for doubtful accounts per books before adjustment	50,000
Amounts expected to become uncollectible	65,000

The cash realizable value of the accounts receivable at December 31, after adjustment, is:
  a. $685,000.
  b. $750,000.
  c. $800,000.
  d. $735,000.

6. One of the following statements about promissory notes (SO is incorrect. The *incorrect* statement is:
  a. The party making the promise to pay is called the maker.
  b. The party to whom payment is to be made is called the payee.
  c. A promissory note is not a negotiable instrument.
  d. A promissory note is more liquid than an account receivable.

7. Which of the following statements about VISA credit (SO card sales is *incorrect*?
  a. The credit card issuer makes the credit investigation of the customer.
  b. The retailer is not involved in the collection process.
  c. Two parties are involved.
  d. The retailer receives cash more quickly than it would from individual customers on account.

8. Blinka Retailers accepted $50,000 of Citibank VISA (SO credit card charges for merchandise sold on July 1. Citibank charges 4% for its credit card use. The entry to record this transaction by Blinka Retailers will include a credit to Sales of $50,000 and a debit(s) to:

a. Cash	$48,000
and Service Charge Expense	2,000
b. Accounts Receivable	$48,000
and Service Charge Expense	$2,000
c. Cash	$50,000
d. Accounts Receivable	$50,000

9. Foti Co. accepts a $1,000, 3-month, 12% promissory note (SO in settlement of an account with Bartelt Co. The entry to record this transaction is as follows.

a. Notes Receivable	1,030	
Accounts Receivable		1,030
b. Notes Receivable	1,000	
Accounts Receivable		1,000
c. Notes Receivable	1,000	
Sales		1,000
d. Notes Receivable	1,020	
Accounts Receivable		1,020

(SO 8) **10.** Ginter Co. holds Kolar Inc.'s $10,000, 120-day, 9% note. The entry made by Ginter Co. when the note is collected, assuming no interest has been previously accrued, is:

a. Cash | 10,300 |
    Notes Receivable | | 10,300

b. Cash | 10,000 |
    Notes Receivable | | 10,000

c. Accounts Receivable | 10,300 |
    Notes Receivable | | 10,000
    Interest Revenue | | 300

d. Cash | 10,300 |
    Notes Receivable | | 10,000
    Interest Revenue | | 300

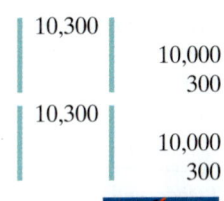

THE NAVIGATOR

QUESTIONS

1. What is the difference between an account receivable and a note receivable?

2. What are some common types of receivables other than accounts receivable and notes receivable?

3. Texaco Oil Company issues its own credit cards. Assume that Texaco charges you $40 on an unpaid balance. Prepare the journal entry that Texaco makes to record this revenue.

4. What are the essential features of the allowance method of accounting for bad debts?

5. Roger Holloway cannot understand why cash realizable value does not decrease when an uncollectible account is written off under the allowance method. Clarify this point for Roger Holloway.

6. Distinguish between the two bases that may be used in estimating uncollectible accounts.

7. Borke Company has a credit balance of $3,200 in Allowance for Doubtful Accounts. The estimated bad debts expense under the percentage of sales basis is $4,100. The total estimated uncollectibles under the percentage of receivables basis is $5,800. Prepare the adjusting entry under each basis.

8. How are bad debts accounted for under the direct write-off method? What are the disadvantages of this method?

9. Freida Company accepts both its own credit cards and national credit cards. What are the advantages of accepting both types of cards?

10. An article recently appeared in the *Wall Street Journal* indicating that companies are selling their receivables at a record rate. Why are companies selling their receivables?

11. WestSide Textiles decides to sell $800,000 of its accounts receivable to First Factors Inc. First Factors assesses a service charge of 3% of the amount of receivables sold. Prepare the journal entry that WestSide Textiles makes to record this sale.

12. Your roommate is uncertain about the advantages of a promissory note. Compare the advantages of a note receivable with those of an account receivable.

13. How may the maturity date of a promissory note be stated?

14. Indicate the maturity date of each of the following promissory notes:

Date of Note	Terms
(a) March 13	one year after date of note
(b) May 4	3 months after date
(c) June 20	30 days after date
(d) July 1	60 days after date

15. Compute the missing amounts for each of the following notes.

	Principal	Annual Interest Rate	Time	Total Interest
(a)	?	9%	120 days	$ 450
(b)	$30,000	10%	3 years	?
(c)	$60,000	?	5 months	$3,000
(d)	$45,000	8%	?	$1,200

16. In determining interest revenue, some financial institutions use 365 days per year and others use 360 days. Why might a financial institution use 360 days?

17. Jana Company dishonors a note at maturity. What actions by Jana may occur with the dishonoring of the note?

18. **General Motors Corporation** has accounts receivable and notes receivable. How should the receivables be reported on the balance sheet?

19. The accounts receivable turnover ratio is 8.14, and average net receivables during the period are $300,000. What is the amount of net credit sales for the period?

BRIEF EXERCISES

Identify different types of receivables.

(SO 1)

BE9-1 Presented below are three receivables transactions. Indicate whether these receivables are reported as accounts receivable, notes receivable, or other receivables on a balance sheet.

(a) Sold merchandise on account for $64,000 to a customer.
(b) Received a promissory note of $57,000 for services performed.
(c) Advanced $10,000 to an employee.

Record basic accounts receivable transactions.

(SO 2)

BE9-2 Record the following transactions on the books of Galaxy Co.

(a) On July 1, Galaxy Co. sold merchandise on account to Kingston Inc. for $17,200, terms 2/10, n/30.
(b) On July 8, Kingston Inc. returned merchandise worth $3,800 to Galaxy Co.
(c) On July 11, Kingston Inc. paid for the merchandise.

Prepare entry for allowance method and partial balance sheet.

(SO 3, 9)

BE9-3 During its first year of operations, Energy Company had credit sales of $3,000,000; $600,000 remained uncollected at year-end. The credit manager estimates that $32,000 of these receivables will become uncollectible.

(a) Prepare the journal entry to record the estimated uncollectibles.
(b) Prepare the current assets section of the balance sheet for Energy Company. Assume that in addition to the receivables it has cash of $90,000, merchandise inventory of $130,000, and prepaid expenses of $7,500.

Prepare entry for write-off; determine cash realizable value.

(SO 3)

BE9-4 At the end of 2005, Endrun Co. has accounts receivable of $700,000 and an allowance for doubtful accounts of $54,000. On January 24, 2006, the company learns that its receivable from Oswego Inc. is not collectible, and management authorizes a write-off of $6,400.

(a) Prepare the journal entry to record the write-off.
(b) What is the cash realizable value of the accounts receivable (1) before the write-off and (2) after the write-off?

Prepare entries for collection of bad debts write-off.

(SO 3)

BE9-5 Assume the same information as BE9-4. On March 4, 2006, Endrun Co. receives payment of $6,400 in full from Oswego Inc. Prepare the journal entries to record this transaction.

Prepare entry using percentage of sales method.

(SO 3)

BE9-6 Elgin Co. elects to use the percentage of sales basis in 2005 to record bad debts expense. It estimates that 2% of net credit sales will become uncollectible. Sales are $800,000 for 2005, sales returns and allowances are $37,000, and the allowance for doubtful accounts has a credit balance of $9,000. Prepare the adjusting entry to record bad debts expense in 2005.

Prepare entry using percentage of receivables method.

(SO 3)

BE9-7 Gleason Co. uses the percentage of accounts receivable basis to record bad debts expense. It estimates that 1% of accounts receivable will become uncollectible. Accounts receivable are $400,000 at the end of the year, and the allowance for doubtful accounts has a credit balance of $1,500.

(a) Prepare the adjusting journal entry to record bad debts expense for the year.
(b) If the allowance for doubtful accounts had a debit balance of $800 instead of a credit balance of $1,500, determine the amount to be reported for bad debts expense.

Compute interest and determine maturity dates on notes.

(SO 5)

BE9-8 Compute interest and find the maturity date for the following notes.

	Date of Note	Principal	Interest Rate (%)	Terms
(a)	June 10	$100,000	6%	60 days
(b)	July 14	$ 50,000	$7\frac{1}{2}$%	90 days
(c)	April 27	$ 12,000	8%	75 days

Determine maturity dates and compute interest and rates on notes.

(SO 5)

BE9-9 Presented below are data on three promissory notes. Determine the missing amounts.

	Date of Note	Terms	Maturity Date	Principal	Annual Interest Rate	Total Interest
(a) April 1		60 days	?	$900,000	9%	?
(b) July 2		30 days	?	90,000	?	$600
(c) March 7		6 months	?	120,000	11%	?

Prepare entries to dispose of accounts receivable.

(SO 4)

BE9-10 Presented below are two independent transactions.

(a) St. Charles Restaurant accepted a VISA card in payment of a $200 lunch bill. The bank charges a 4% fee. What entry should St. Charles make?
(b) Marge Company sold its accounts receivable of $80,000. What entry should Marge make, given a service charge of 3% on the amount of receivables sold?

Prepare entry for notes receivable exchanged for account receivable.

(SO 6)

BE9-11 On January 10, 2005, Batavia Co. sold merchandise on account to Dustin Eola for $11,600, n/30. On February 9, Dustin Eola gave Batavia Co. a 10% promissory note in settlement of this account. Prepare the journal entry to record the sale and the settlement of the account receivable.

BE9-12 The financial statements of **Minnesota Mining and Manufacturing Company (3M)** report net sales of $15.0 billion. Accounts receivable (net) are $2.5 billion at the beginning of the year and $2.8 billion at the end of the year. Compute 3M's receivables turnover ratio. Compute 3M's average collection period for accounts receivable in days.

Compute ratios to analyze receivables.

(SO 9)

EXERCISES

E9-1 Presented below are two independent situations.

(a) On January 6, Bennett Co. sells merchandise on account to Jackie, Inc. for $7,000, terms 2/10, n/30. On January 16, Jackie Inc. pays the amount due. Prepare the entries on Bennett's books to record the sale and related collection.

(b) On January 10, Erin Bybee uses her Sheridan Co. credit card to purchase merchandise from Sheridan Co. for $9,000. On February 10, Bybee is billed for the amount due of $9,000. On February 12, Bybee pays $6,000 on the balance due. On March 10, Bybee is billed for the amount due, including interest at 2% per month on the unpaid balance as of February 12. Prepare the entries on Sheridan Co.'s books related to the transactions that occurred on January 10, February 12, and March 10.

Journalize entries for recognizing accounts receivable.

(SO 2)

E9-2 The ledger of Elburn Company at the end of the current year shows Accounts Receivable $110,000, Sales $840,000, and Sales Returns and Allowances $28,000.

Instructions

(a) If Elburn uses the direct write-off method to account for uncollectible accounts, journalize the adjusting entry at December 31, assuming Elburn determines that Copp's $1,400 balance is uncollectible.

(b) If Allowance for Doubtful Accounts has a credit balance of $2,100 in the trial balance, journalize the adjusting entry at December 31, assuming bad debts are expected to be (1) 1% of net sales, and (2) 10% of accounts receivable.

(c) If Allowance for Doubtful Accounts has a debit balance of $200 in the trial balance, journalize the adjusting entry at December 31, assuming bad debts are expected to be (1) 0.75% of net sales and (2) 6% of accounts receivable.

Journalize entries to record allowance for doubtful accounts using two different bases.

(SO 3)

E9-3 Leland Company has accounts receivable of $98,100 at March 31. An analysis of the accounts shows the following.

Month of Sale	Balance, March 31
March	$65,000
February	17,600
January	8,500
Prior to January	7,000
	$98,100

Determine bad debts expense; prepare the adjusting entry for bad debts expense.

(SO 3)

Credit terms are 2/10, n/30. At March 31, Allowance for Doubtful Accounts has a credit balance of $1,200 prior to adjustment. The company uses the percentage of receivables basis for estimating uncollectible accounts. The company's estimate of bad debts is as follows.

Age of Accounts	Estimated Percentage Uncollectible
1–30 days	2.0%
30–60 days	5.0%
60–90 days	30.0%
Over 90 days	50.0%

Instructions

(a) Determine the total estimated uncollectibles.

(b) Prepare the adjusting entry at March 31 to record bad debts expense.

E9-4 On December 31, 2005, Crawford Co. estimated that 1.5% of its net sales of $400,000 will become uncollectible. The company recorded this amount as an addition to Allowance for Doubtful Accounts. On May 11, 2006, Crawford Co. determined that Kevin Hayes' account was uncollectible and wrote off $1,100. On June 12, 2006, Hayes' paid the amount previously written off.

Journalize percentage of sales basis, write-off, recovery.

(SO 3)

Instructions
Prepare the journal entries on December 31, 2005, May 11, 2006, and June 12, 2006.

Journalize entries for the sale of accounts receivable.

(SO 4)

E9-5 Presented below are two independent situations.

(a) On March 3, Hinckley Appliances sells $580,000 of its receivables to Marsh Factors Inc. Marsh Factors assesses a finance charge of 3% of the amount of receivables sold. Prepare the entry on Hinckley Appliances' books to record the sale of the receivables.

(b) On May 10, Cody Company sold merchandise for $3,800 and accepted the customer's Allstar Bank MasterCard. At the end of the day, the Allstar Bank MasterCard receipts were deposited in the company's bank account. Allstar Bank charges a 4% service charge for credit card sales. Prepare the entry on Cody Company's books to record the sale of merchandise.

Journalize entries for credit card sales.

(SO 4)

E9-6 Presented below are two independent situations.

(a) On April 2, Julie Keiser uses her J. C. Penney Company credit card to purchase merchandise from a J. C. Penney store for $1,800. On May 1, Keiser is billed for the $1,800 amount due. Keiser pays $700 on the balance due on May 3. On June 1, Keiser receives a bill for the amount due, including interest at 1.0% per month on the unpaid balance as of May 3. Prepare the entries on J. C. Penney Co.'s books related to the transactions that occurred on April 2, May 3, and June 1.

(b) On July 4, Newark's Restaurant accepts an American Express card for a $350 dinner bill. American Express charges a 4% service fee. On July 10, American Express pays Newark $336. Prepare the entries on Newark books related to the transactions.

Journalize credit card sales, and indicate the statement presentation of financing charges and service charge expense.

(SO 4)

E9-7 Ottawa Stores accepts both its own and national credit cards. During the year the following selected summary transactions occurred.

Jan. 15   Made Ottawa credit card sales totaling $18,000. (There were no balances prior to January 15.)

    20   Made American Express credit card sales (service charge fee 5%) totaling $4,100.

    30   Received payment in full from American Express less the 5% service charge.

Feb. 10   Collected $12,000 on Ottawa credit card sales.

    15   Added finance charges of 1% to Ottawa credit card balance.

Instructions
(a) Journalize the transactions for Ottawa Stores.
(b) Indicate the statement presentation of the financing charges and the credit card service charge expense for Ottawa Stores.

Journalize entries for notes receivable transactions.

(SO 5, 6)

E9-8 Mexico Supply Co. has the following transactions related to notes receivable during the last 2 months of 2005.

Nov. 1   Loaned $18,000 cash to Norma Hanson on a 1-year, 10% note.

Dec. 11   Sold goods to John Countryman, Inc., receiving a $6,750, 90-day, 8% note.

    16   Received a $4,000, 6-month, 9% note in exchange for Bob Shabo's outstanding accounts receivable.

    31   Accrued interest revenue on all notes receivable.

Instructions
(a) Journalize the transactions for Mexico Supply Co.
(b) Record the collection of the Hanson note at its maturity in 2006.

Journalize entries for notes receivable.

(SO 5, 6)

E9-9 Record the following transactions for Sandwich Co. in the general journal.

2005

May 1   Received an $8,700, 1-year, 10% note in exchange for Linda Anderson's outstanding accounts receivable.

Dec. 31   Accrued interest on the Anderson note.

Dec. 31   Closed the interest revenue account.

2006

May 1   Received principal plus interest on the Anderson note. (No interest has been accrued in 2006.)

Journalize entries for dishonor of notes receivable.

(SO 5, 8)

E9-10 On May 2, Maple Park Company lends $6,600 to Cortland, Inc., issuing a 6-month, 9% note. At the maturity date, November 2, Cortland indicates that it cannot pay.

Instructions

(a) Prepare the entry to record the issuance of the note.

(b) Prepare the entry to record the dishonor of the note, assuming that Maple Park Company expects collection will occur.

(c) Prepare the entry to record the dishonor of the note, assuming that Maple Park Company does not expect collection in the future.

E9-11 The following information pertains to Sosa Merchandising Company.

Determine missing amounts related to sales and accounts receivable.

(SO 2, 4, 9)

Merchandise inventory at end of year	$33,000
Accounts receivable at beginning of year	24,000
Cash sales made during the year	18,000
Gross profit on sales	25,000
Accounts receivable written off during the year	1,000
Purchases made during the year	60,000
Accounts receivable collected during the year	78,000
Merchandise inventory at beginning of year	36,000

Instructions

(a) Calculate the amount of credit sales made during the year. (*Hint:* You will need to use income statement relationships—introduced in Chapter 5—in order to determine this.)

(b) Calculate the balance of accounts receivable at the end of the year.

PROBLEMS: SET A

P9-1A At December 31, 2005, Sycamore Imports reported the following information on its balance sheet.

Prepare journal entries related to bad debts expense.

(SO 2, 3, 9)

Accounts receivable	$1,020,000
Less: Allowance for doubtful accounts	60,000

During 2006, the company had the following transactions related to receivables.

1. Sales on account	$2,670,000
2. Sales returns and allowances	40,000
3. Collections of accounts receivable	2,300,000
4. Write-offs of accounts receivable deemed uncollectible	65,000
5. Recovery of bad debts previously written off as uncollectible	20,000

Instructions

(a) Prepare the journal entries to record each of these five transactions. Assume that no cash discounts were taken on the collections of accounts receivable.

(b) Enter the January 1, 2006, balances in Accounts Receivable and Allowance for Doubtful Accounts. Post the entries to the two accounts (use T accounts), and determine the balances.

(c) Prepare the journal entry to record bad debts expense for 2006, assuming that an aging of accounts receivable indicates that estimated bad debts are $95,000.

(d) Compute the accounts receivable turnover ratio for the year 2006.

(b) Accounts receivable
$1,285,000
ADA $15,000

(c) Bad debts expense
$80,000

P9-2A Information related to DeKalb Company for 2005 is summarized below.

Compute bad debts amounts.

(SO 3)

Total credit sales	$1,640,000
Accounts receivable at December 31	620,000
Bad debts written off	26,000

Instructions

(a) What amount of bad debts expense will DeKalb Company report if it uses the direct write-off method of accounting for bad debts?

(b) Assume that DeKalb Company decides to estimate its bad debts expense to be 2% of credit sales. What amount of bad debts expense will DeKalb record if Allowance for Doubtful Accounts has a credit balance of $3,000?

(c) Assume that DeKalb Company decides to estimate its bad debts expense based on 5% of accounts receivable. What amount of bad debts expense will DeKalb Company record if Allowance for Doubtful Accounts has a credit balance of $4,000?

(d) Assume the same facts as in (c), except that there is a $2,000 debit balance in Allowance for Doubtful Accounts. What amount of bad debts expense will DeKalb record?

(e)  What is the weakness of the direct write-off method of reporting bad debts expense?

Journalize entries to record transactions related to bad debts.

(SO 2, 3)

P9-3A Presented below is an aging schedule for Emporia Company.

Customer	Total	Not Yet Due	Number of Days Past Due			
			1–30	**31–60**	**61–90**	**Over 90**
Anders	$ 20,000		$ 9,000	$11,000		
Baietto	30,000	$ 30,000				
Cyrs	50,000	15,000	5,000		$30,000	
DeJong	38,000					$38,000
Others	126,000	92,000	15,000	13,000		6,000
	$264,000	$137,000	$29,000	$24,000	$30,000	$44,000
Estimated Percentage Uncollectible		2%	5%	10%	24%	50%
Total Estimated Bad Debts	$ 35,790	$ 2,740	$ 1,450	$ 2,400	$ 7,200	$22,000

At December 31, 2005, the unadjusted balance in Allowance for Doubtful Accounts is a credit of $8,000.

Instructions

(a) Bad debts expense $27,790

(a) Journalize and post the adjusting entry for bad debts at December 31, 2005.

(b) Journalize and post to the allowance account the following events and transactions in the year 2006.

    (1) March 1, an $1,100 customer balance originating in 2005 is judged uncollectible.

    (2) May 1, a check for $1,100 is received from the customer whose account was written off as uncollectible on March 1.

(c) Bad debts expense $32,500

(c) Journalize the adjusting entry for bad debts on December 31, 2006. Assume that the unadjusted balance in Allowance for Doubtful Accounts is a debit of $1,200, and the aging schedule indicates that total estimated bad debts will be $31,300.

Journalize transactions related to bad debts.

(SO 2, 3)

P9-4A The following represents selected information taken from a company's aging schedule to estimate uncollectible accounts receivable at year end.

	Total	Number of Days Outstanding				
		0–30	**31–60**	**61–90**	**91–120**	**Over 120**
Accounts receivable	$260,000	$100,000	$60,000	$50,000	$30,000	$20,000
% uncollectible		1%	5%	7.5%	10%	12%
Estimated bad debts						

Instructions

(a) Tot. est. bad debts $13,150

(a) Calculate the total estimated bad debts based on the above information.

(b) Prepare the year-end adjusting journal entry to record the bad debts using the allowance method and the aged uncollectible accounts receivable determined in (a). Assume the opening balance in the Allowance for Doubtful Accounts account is a $10,000 credit.

(c) Of the above accounts, $2,000 is determined to be specifically uncollectible. Prepare the journal entry to write off the uncollectible accounts.

(d) The company subsequently collects $1,000 on a specific account that had previously been determined to be uncollectible in (c). Prepare the journal entry(ies) necessary to restore the account and record the cash collection.

(e) Explain how establishing an allowance account satisfies the matching principle.

P9-5A At December 31, 2005, the trial balance of Larry Falcetto Company contained the following amounts before adjustment.

Journalize entries to record transactions related to bad debts.

(SO 3)

	Debits	Credits
Accounts Receivable	$350,000	
Allowance for Doubtful Accounts		$ 1,300
Sales		880,000

Instructions

(a) Prepare the adjusting entry at December 31, 2005, to record bad debts expense under each of the following independent assumptions.

(a) (2) $17,600

  (1) An aging schedule indicates that $17,550 of accounts receivable will be uncollectible.

  (2) The company estimates that 2% of sales will be uncollectible.

(b) Repeat part (a) assuming that instead of a credit balance, there is a $1,300 debit balance in Allowance for Doubtful Accounts.

(c) During the next month, January 2006, a $4,500 account receivable is written off as uncollectible. Prepare the journal entry to record the write-off.

(d) Repeat part (c) assuming that Larry Falcetto Company uses the direct write-off method instead of the allowance method in accounting for uncollectible accounts receivable.

(e) ▭▭▭▭▷ What are the advantages of using the allowance method in accounting for uncollectible accounts as compared to the direct write-off method?

P9-6A Rochelle Graves Co. closes its books monthly. On June 30, selected ledger account balances are:

Prepare entries for various notes receivable transactions.

(SO 2, 4, 5, 8, 9)

Notes Receivable	$30,000
Interest Receivable	$ 240

Notes Receivable include the following.

Date	Maker	Face	Term	Interest
May 16	Alexis Inc.	$ 6,000	60 days	10%
May 25	Domino Co.	15,000	60 days	11%
June 30	ERV Corp.	9,000	6 months	8%

During July, the following transactions were completed.

July	5	Made sales of $6,200 on Rochelle Graves Co. credit cards.
	14	Made sales of $700 on VISA credit cards. The credit card service charge is 4%.
	14	Added $440 to Rochelle Graves Co. credit card customer balances for finance charges on unpaid balances.
	15	Received payment in full from Alexis Inc. on the amount due.
	25	Received notice that the Domino Co. note has been dishonored. (Assume that Domino Co. is expected to pay in the future.)

Instructions

(a) Journalize the July transactions and the July 31 adjusting entry for accrued interest receivable. (Interest is computed using 360 days.)

(b) Enter the balances at July 1 in the receivable accounts. Post the entries to all of the receivable accounts.

(b) Accounts receivable
$21,915

(c) Show the balance sheet presentation of the receivable accounts at July 31.

(c) Total receivables $30,975

P9-7A On January 1, 2005, Bettendorf Company had Accounts Receivable $56,900 and Allowance for Doubtful Accounts $4,700. Bettendorf Company prepares financial statements annually. During the year the following selected transactions occurred.

Prepare entries for various receivables transactions.

(SO 2, 4, 5, 6, 7, 8)

Jan.	5	Sold $6,900 of merchandise to John Yockey Company, terms n/30.
Feb.	2	Accepted a $6,900, 4-month, 10% promissory note from John Yockey Company for the balance due.
	12	Sold $7,800 of merchandise to Skosey Company and accepted Skosey's $7,800, 2-month, 10% note for the balance due.
	26	Sold $3,000 of merchandise to Platz Co., terms n/10.
Apr.	5	Accepted a $3,000, 3-month, 8% note from Platz Co. for the balance due.
	12	Collected Skosey Company note in full.
June	2	Collected John Yockey Company note in full.

July 5 Platz Co. dishonors its note of April 5. It is expected that Platz will eventually pay the amount owed.

    15 Sold $7,000 of merchandise to King Co. and accepted King's $7,000, 3-month, 12% note for the amount due.

Oct. 15 King Co.'s note was dishonored. King Co. is bankrupt, and there is no hope of future settlement.

Instructions

Journalize the transactions.

PROBLEMS: SET B

Prepare journal entries related to bad debts expense.

(SO 2, 3, 9)

P9-1B At December 31, 2005, Hilo Co. reported the following information on its balance sheet.

Accounts receivable	$960,000
Less: Allowance for doubtful accounts	70,000

During 2006, the company had the following transactions related to receivables.

1. Sales on account	$3,315,000
2. Sales returns and allowances	50,000
3. Collections of accounts receivable	2,810,000
4. Write-offs of accounts receivable deemed uncollectible	90,000
5. Recovery of bad debts previously written off as uncollectible	29,000

Instructions

(a) Prepare the journal entries to record each of these five transactions. Assume that no cash discounts were taken on the collections of accounts receivable.

(b) Accounts receivable
$1,325,000
ADA $9,000

(b) Enter the January 1, 2006, balances in Accounts Receivable and Allowance for Doubtful Accounts, post the entries to the two accounts (use T accounts), and determine the balances.

(c) Bad debts expense
$116,000

(c) Prepare the journal entry to record bad debts expense for 2006, assuming that an aging of accounts receivable indicates that expected bad debts are $125,000.

(d) Compute the accounts receivable turnover ratio for 2006.

Compute bad debts amounts.

(SO 3)

P9-2B Information related to Kap Shin Company for 2005 is summarized below.

Total credit sales	$2,100,000
Accounts receivable at December 31	837,000
Bad debts written off	33,000

Instructions

(a) What amount of bad debts expense will Kap Shin Company report if it uses the direct write-off method of accounting for bad debts?

(b) Assume that Kap Shin Company estimates its bad debts expense to be 2% of credit sales. What amount of bad debts expense will Kap Shin record if it has an Allowance for Doubtful Accounts credit balance of $4,000?

(c) Assume that Kap Shin Company estimates its bad debts expense based on 6% of accounts receivable. What amount of bad debts expense will Kap Shin record if it has an Allowance for Doubtful Accounts credit balance of $3,000?

(d) Assume the same facts as in (c), except that there is a $3,000 debit balance in Allowance for Doubtful Accounts. What amount of bad debts expense will Kap Shin record?

(e) What is the weakness of the direct write-off method of reporting bad debts expense?

P9-3B Presented below is an aging schedule for Yee Chow Company.

Journalize entries to record transactions related to bad debts.

(SO 2, 3)

Customer	Total	Not Yet Due	Number of Days Past Due			
			1–30	31–60	61–90	Over 90
Arndt	$ 22,000		$10,000	$12,000		
Blair	40,000	$ 40,000				
Chase	57,000	16,000	6,000		$35,000	
Drea	34,000					$34,000
Others	132,000	96,000	16,000	14,000		6,000
	$285,000	$152,000	$32,000	$26,000	$35,000	$40,000
Estimated Percentage Uncollectible		3%	6%	13%	25%	60%
Total Estimated Bad Debts	$ 42,610	$ 4,560	$ 1,920	$ 3,380	$ 8,750	$24,000

At December 31, 2005, the unadjusted balance in Allowance for Doubtful Accounts is a credit of $9,000.

Instructions
(a) Journalize and post the adjusting entry for bad debts at December 31, 2005.
(b) Journalize and post to the allowance account the following events and transactions in the year 2006.
    (1) On March 31, a $1,000 customer balance originating in 2005 is judged uncollectible.
    (2) On May 31, a check for $1,000 is received from the customer whose account was written off as uncollectible on March 31.
(c) Journalize the adjusting entry for bad debts on December 31, 2006, assuming that the unadjusted balance in Allowance for Doubtful Accounts is a debit of $800 and the aging schedule indicates that total estimated bad debts will be $31,600.

(a) Bad debts expense
    $33,610

(c) Bad debts expense
    $32,400

P9-4B Image.com uses the allowance method to estimate uncollectible accounts receivable. The company produced the following aging of the accounts receivable at year end.

Journalize transactions related to bad debts.

(SO 2, 3)

	Total	Number of Days Outstanding				
		0–30	31–60	61–90	91–120	Over 120
Accounts receivable	$375,000	$220,000	$90,000	$40,000	$10,000	$15,000
% uncollectible		1%	4%	5%	6%	10%
Estimated bad debts						

Instructions
(a) Calculate the total estimated bad debts based on the above information.
(b) Prepare the year-end adjusting journal entry to record the bad debts using the aged uncollectible accounts receivable determined in (a). Assume the opening balance in Allowance for Doubtful Accounts is a $10,000 debit.
(c) Of the above accounts, $5,000 is determined to be specifically uncollectible. Prepare the journal entry to write off the uncollectible account.
(d) The company collects $5,000 subsequently on a specific account that had previously been determined to be uncollectible in (c). Prepare the journal entry(ies) necessary to restore the account and record the cash collection.
(e) Comment on how your answers to (a)–(d) would change if Image.com used 3% of *total* accounts receivable, rather than aging the accounts receivable. What are the advantages to the company of aging the accounts receivable rather than applying a percentage to total accounts receivable?

(a) Tot. est.
    bad debts $9,900

Journalize entries to record transactions related to bad debts.

(SO 3)

P9-5B At December 31, 2005, the trial balance of Videosoft Company contained the following amounts before adjustment.

	Debits	Credits
Accounts Receivable	$385,000	
Allowance for Doubtful Accounts		$ 800
Sales		918,000

Instructions

(a) Based on the information given, which method of accounting for bad debts is Videosoft Company using—the direct write-off method or the allowance method? How can you tell?

(b) (2) $9,180

(b) Prepare the adjusting entry at December 31, 2005, for bad debts expense under each of the following independent assumptions.

   (1) An aging schedule indicates that $11,750 of accounts receivable will be uncollectible.

   (2) The company estimates that 1% of sales will be uncollectible.

(c) Repeat part (b) assuming that instead of a credit balance there is an $800 debit balance in Allowance for Doubtful Accounts.

(d) During the next month, January 2006, a $3,000 account receivable is written off as uncollectible. Prepare the journal entry to record the write-off.

(e) Repeat part (d) assuming that Videosoft uses the direct write-off method instead of the allowance method in accounting for uncollectible accounts receivable.

(f) ▱▱▱▱▱▱ What type of account is Allowance for Doubtful Accounts? How does it affect how accounts receivable is reported on the balance sheet at the end of the accounting period?

Prepare entries for various notes receivable transactions.

(SO 2, 4, 5, 8, 9)

Peachtree

P9-6B Derek Lu Company closes its books monthly. On September 30, selected ledger account balances are:

Notes Receivable	$29,000
Interest Receivable	$ 210

Notes Receivable include the following.

Date	Maker	Face	Term	Interest
Aug. 16	Demaster Inc.	$ 8,000	60 days	12%
Aug. 25	Almer Co.	9,000	60 days	10%
Sept. 30	Skinner Corp.	12,000	6 months	9%

Interest is computed using a 360-day year. During October, the following transactions were completed.

Oct. 7 Made sales of $6,900 on Derek Lu credit cards.
   12 Made sales of $800 on MasterCard credit cards. The credit card service charge is 3%.
   15 Added $460 to Derek Lu customer balance for finance charges on unpaid balances.
   15 Received payment in full from Demaster Inc. on the amount due.
   24 Received notice that the Almer note has been dishonored. (Assume that Almer is expected to pay in the future.)

Instructions

(a) Journalize the October transactions and the October 31 adjusting entry for accrued interest receivable.

(b) Accounts receivable $16,510

(c) Total receivables $28,600

(b) Enter the balances at October 1 in the receivable accounts. Post the entries to all of the receivable accounts.

(c) Show the balance sheet presentation of the receivable accounts at October 31.

Prepare entries for various receivable transactions.

(SO 2, 4, 5, 6, 7, 8)

P9-7B On January 1, 2005, Cedar Grove Company had Accounts Receivable $139,000, Notes Receivable $15,000, and Allowance for Doubtful Accounts $13,200. The note receivable is from Sara Rogers Company. It is a 4-month, 12% note dated December 31, 2004. Cedar Grove Company prepares financial statements annually. During the year the following selected transactions occurred.

Jan. 5 Sold $16,000 of merchandise to Billings Company, terms n/15.
   20 Accepted Billings Company's $16,000, 3-month, 9% note for balance due.
Feb. 18 Sold $8,000 of merchandise to Grania Company and accepted Grania's $8,000, 6-month, 9% note for the amount due.

Apr. 20 Collected Billings Company note in full.

30 Received payment in full from Sara Rogers Company on the amount due.

May 25 Accepted Fiona Inc.'s $6,000, 3-month, 7% note in settlement of a past-due balance on account.

Aug. 18 Received payment in full from Grania Company on note due.

25 The Fiona Inc. note was dishonored. Fiona Inc. is not bankrupt; future payment is anticipated.

Sept. 1 Sold $12,000 of merchandise to Lena Torme Company and accepted a $12,000, 6-month, 10% note for the amount due.

Instructions

Journalize the transactions.

BROADENING YOUR PERSPECTIVE

Financial Reporting and Analysis

■ FINANCIAL REPORTING PROBLEM: CAF Company

BYP9-1 CAF Company sells office equipment and supplies to many organizations in the city and surrounding area on contract terms of 2/10, n/30. In the past, over 75% of the credit customers have taken advantage of the discount by paying within 10 days of the invoice date.

The number of customers taking the full 30 days to pay has increased within the last year. Current indications are that less than 60% of the customers are now taking the discount. Bad debts as a percentage of gross credit sales have risen from the 2.5% provided in past years to about 4.5% in the current year.

The company's Finance Committee has requested more information on the collections of accounts receivable. The controller responded to this request with the report reproduced below.

CAF COMPANY
Accounts Receivable Collections
May 31, 2005

The fact that some credit accounts will prove uncollectible is normal. Annual bad debts write-offs have been 2.5% of gross credit sales over the past 5 years. During the last fiscal year, this percentage increased to slightly less than 4.5%. The current Accounts Receivable balance is $1,400,000. The condition of this balance in terms of age and probability of collection is as follows.

Proportion of Total	Age Categories	Probability of Collection
60%	not yet due	98%
22%	less than 30 days past due	96%
9%	30 to 60 days past due	94%
5%	61 to 120 days past due	91%
$2\frac{1}{2}$%	121 to 180 days past due	75%
$1\frac{1}{2}$%	over 180 days past due	30%

The Allowance for Doubtful Accounts had a credit balance of $29,500 on June 1, 2004. CAF has provided for a monthly bad debts expense accrual during the current fiscal year based on the assumption that 4.5% of gross credit sales will be uncollectible. Total gross credit sales for the 2004–05 fiscal year amounted to $2,800,000. Write-offs of bad accounts during the year totaled $102,000.

Instructions

(a) Prepare an accounts receivable aging schedule for CAF Company using the age categories identified in the controller's report to the Finance Committee showing the following.

(1) The amount of accounts receivable outstanding for each age category and in total.

(2) The estimated amount that is uncollectible for each category and in total.

(b) Compute the amount of the year-end adjustment necessary to bring Allowance for Doubtful Accounts to the balance indicated by the age analysis. Then prepare the necessary journal entry to adjust the accounting records.

(c) In a recessionary environment with tight credit and high interest rates:

   (1) Identify steps CAF Company might consider to improve the accounts receivable situation.

   (2) Then evaluate each step identified in terms of the risks and costs involved.

■ COMPARATIVE ANALYSIS PROBLEM: PepsiCo vs. Coca-Cola

BYP9-2 **PepsiCo**'s financial statements are presented in Appendix A. **Coca-Cola**'s financial statements are presented in Appendix B.

Instructions

(a) Based on the information contained in these financial statements, compute the following 2002 ratios for each company. (Assume all sales are credit sales. See PepsiCo's Note 14 for some information.)

   (1) Accounts receivable turnover ratio.

   (2) Average collection period for receivables.

(b) What conclusions concerning the management of accounts receivable can be drawn from these data?

■ INTERPRETING FINANCIAL STATEMENTS: A Global Focus

BYP9-3 **Art World Industries, Inc.** was incorporated in 1986 in Delaware, and is located in Los Angeles. The company prints, publishes, and sells limited-edition graphics and reproduction prints in the wholesale market.

The company's balance sheet at the end of a recent year showed an allowance for doubtful accounts of $175,477. The allowance was set up against certain Japanese accounts receivable that average more than one year in age. The Japanese acknowledge the amount due, but with the slow economy in Japan lack the resources to pay at this time.

Instructions

(a) Which method of accounting for uncollectible accounts does Art World Industries use?

(b) Explain the difference between the direct write-off and percentage of receivables methods. Based on Art World's disclosure above, what important factor would you have to consider in arriving at appropriate percentages to apply for the percentage of receivables method?

(c) What are the implications for a company's receivables management of selling its products internationally?

■ EXPLORING THE WEB

BYP9-4 **Purpose:** To learn more about factoring from the Web site of a company that provides factoring services.

Address: www.invoicefinancial.com, or go to www.wiley.com/college/weygandt

Steps: Go to the Web site and answer the following questions.

(a) What are some of the benefits of factoring?

(b) What is the range of the percentages of the typical discount rate?

(c) If a company factors its receivables, what percentage of the value of the receivables can it expect to receive from the factor in the form of cash, and how quickly will it receive the cash?

Critical Thinking

■ GROUP DECISION CASE

BYP9-5 Hilda and Jan Piwek own Campus Fashions. From its inception Campus Fashions has sold merchandise on either a cash or credit basis, but no credit cards have been accepted. During the past several months, the Piweks have begun to question their sales policies. First, they have lost some sales because of refusing to accept credit cards. Second, representatives of two metropolitan banks have been persuasive in almost convincing them to accept their national credit cards. One bank, City National Bank, has stated that its credit card fee is 4%.

The Piweks decide that they should determine the cost of carrying their own credit sales. From the accounting records of the past 3 years they accumulate the following data.

	2005	2004	2003
Net credit sales	$530,000	$650,000	$400,000
Collection agency fees for slow-paying			
customers	2,450	2,500	2,400
Salary of part-time accounts receivable clerk	4,100	4,100	4,100

Credit and collection expenses as a percentage of net credit sales are: uncollectible accounts 1.6%, billing and mailing costs 0.5%, and credit investigation fee on new customers 0.15%.

Hilda and Jan also determine that the average accounts receivable balance outstanding during the year is 5% of net credit sales. The Piweks estimate that they could earn an average of 8% annually on cash invested in other business opportunities.

Instructions

With the class divided into groups, answer the following.

(a) Prepare a table showing, for each year, total credit and collection expenses in dollars and as a percentage of net credit sales.
(b) Determine the net credit and collection expense in dollars and as a percentage of sales after considering the revenue not earned from other investment opportunities.
(c) Discuss both the financial and nonfinancial factors that are relevant to the decision.

■ COMMUNICATION ACTIVITY

BYP9-6 Lily Pao, a friend of yours, overheard a discussion at work about changes her employer wants to make in accounting for uncollectible accounts. Lily knows little about accounting, and she asks you to help make sense of what she heard. Specifically, she asks you to explain the differences between the percentage of sales, percentage of receivables, and the direct write-off methods for uncollectible accounts.

Instructions

In a letter of one page (or less), explain to Lily the three methods of accounting for uncollectibles. Be sure to discuss differences among these methods.

■ ETHICS CASE

BYP 9-7 The controller of Vest Co. believes that the yearly allowance for doubtful accounts for Shirt Co. should be 2% of net credit sales. The president of Vest Co., nervous that the stockholders might expect the company to sustain its 10% growth rate, suggests that the controller increase the allowance for doubtful accounts to 4%. The president thinks that the lower net income, which reflects a 6% growth rate, will be a more sustainable rate for Vest Co.

Instructions

(a) Who are the stakeholders in this case?
(b) Does the president's request pose an ethical dilemma for the controller?
(c) Should the controller be concerned with Vest Co.'s growth rate in estimating the allowance? Explain your answer.

Answers to Self-Study Questions
1. c   **2.** a   **3.** b   **4.** b   **5.** d   **6.** c   **7.** c   **8.** a   **9.** b   **10.** d

Answer to PepsiCo Review It Question 3, p. 371
According to Note 14, **PepsiCo**'s gross receivables were $2,647 million. Its allowance for doubtful accounts was $116 million. Therefore, the allowance is 4.4% of the gross receivables balance.

Plant Assets, Natural Resources, and Intangible Assets

CONCEPTS FOR REVIEW

Before studying this chapter, you should know or, if necessary, review:

- The time period assumption.
  (Ch. 3, p. 90)

- The cost principle (Ch. 1, p. 10) and the matching principle.
  (Ch. 3, p. 91)

- What is depreciation?
  (Ch. 3, p. 96)

- How to make adjustments for depreciation.
  (Ch. 3, pp. 96–97)

THE NAVIGATOR

How Much for a Ride to the Beach?

It's spring break. Your plane has landed, you've finally found your bags, and you're dying to hit the beach—but first you need a "vehicular unit" to get you there. As you turn away from baggage claim you see a long row of rental agency booths. Many are names you are familiar with—Hertz, Avis, and Budget. But a booth at the far end catches your eye—Rent-A-Wreck. Now there's a company making a clear statement!

Any company that relies on equipment to generate revenues must make decisions about what kind of equipment to buy, how long to keep it, and how vigorously to maintain it. Rent-

A-Wreck has decided to rent used rather than new cars and trucks. It rents these vehicles across the United States, Europe, and Asia. While the big-name agencies push vehicles with that "new car smell," Rent-A-Wreck competes on price. The message is simple: Rent a used car and save some cash. It's not a message that appeals to everyone. If you're a marketing executive wanting to impress a big client, you probably don't want to pull up in a Rent-A-Wreck car. But if you want to get from point A to point B for the minimum cash per mile, then they are playing your tune. The company's message seems to be getting across to the right clientele. Revenues have increased from $29.9 million in 1996 to $51.7 million in 2000.

When you rent a car from Rent-A-Wreck, you are renting from an independent business person who has paid a "franchise fee" for the right to use the Rent-A-Wreck name. In order to gain a franchise, he or she must meet financial and other criteria, and must agree to run the rental agency according to rules prescribed by Rent-A-Wreck. Some of these rules require that each franchise maintain its cars in a reasonable fashion. This ensures that, though you won't be cruising down Daytona Beach's Atlantic Avenue in a Mercedes convertible, you can be reasonably assured that you won't be calling a towtruck.

www.rent-a-wreck.com

THE NAVIGATOR

STUDY OBJECTIVES

After studying this chapter, you should be able to:

1. Describe how the cost principle applies to plant assets.
2. Explain the concept of depreciation.
3. Compute periodic depreciation using different methods.
4. Describe the procedure for revising periodic depreciation.
5. Distinguish between revenue and capital expenditures, and explain the entries for these expenditures.
6. Explain how to account for the disposal of a plant asset.
7. Compute periodic depletion of natural resources.
8. Explain the basic issues related to accounting for intangible assets.
9. Indicate how plant assets, natural resources, and intangible assets are reported and analyzed.

THE NAVIGATOR

The accounting for long-term assets has important implications for a company's reported results. In this chapter, we explain the application of the cost principle of accounting to property, plant, and equipment, such as Rent-A-Wreck vehicles, as well as to natural resources and intangible assets such as the "Rent-A-Wreck" trademark. We also describe the methods that may be used to allocate an asset's cost over its useful life. In addition, the accounting for expenditures incurred during the useful life of assets, such as the cost of replacing tires and brake pads on rental cars, is discussed.

The content and organization of Chapter 10 are as follows.

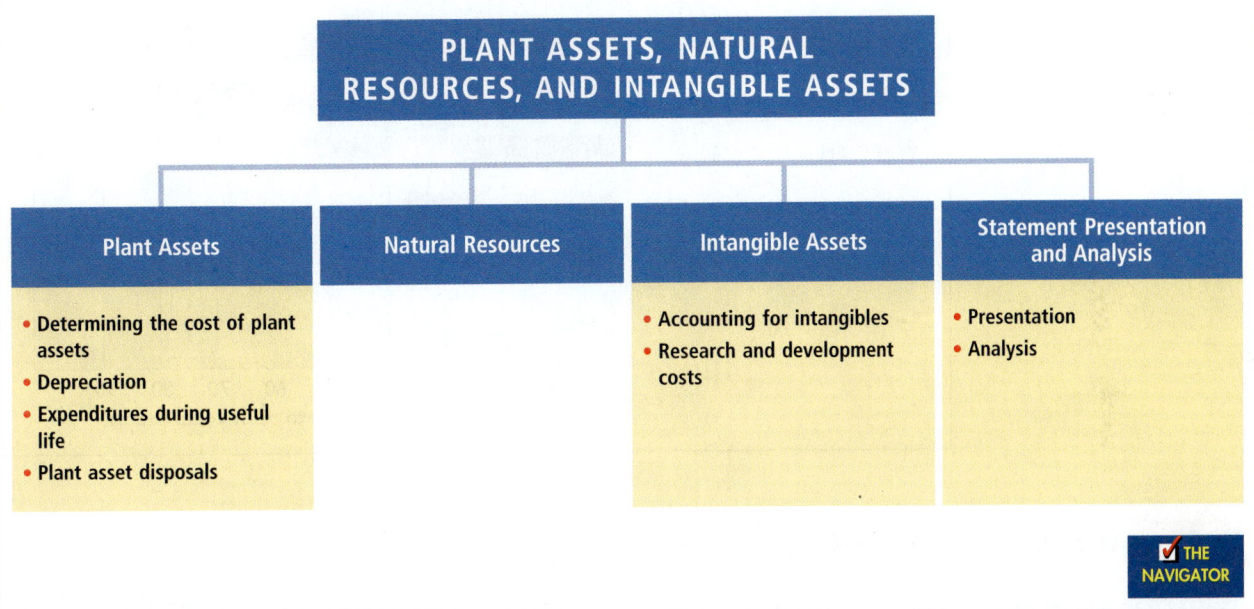

PLANT ASSETS, NATURAL RESOURCES, AND INTANGIBLE ASSETS

Plant Assets	Natural Resources	Intangible Assets	Statement Presentation and Analysis
• Determining the cost of plant assets • Depreciation • Expenditures during useful life • Plant asset disposals		• Accounting for intangibles • Research and development costs	• Presentation • Analysis

☑ THE NAVIGATOR

SECTION 1 PLANT ASSETS

Plant assets are resources that have three characteristics: they have a physical substance (a definite size and shape), are used in the operations of a business, and are not intended for sale to customers. They are also called **property, plant, and equipment; plant and equipment;** or **fixed assets**. These assets are expected to provide services to the company for a number of years. Except for land, plant assets decline in service potential over their useful lives.

It is important for a business to keep plant assets in good operating condition, replace worn-out or outdated plant assets, and expand its productive resources as needed. The decline of rail travel in the United States can be traced in part to the failure of railroad companies to meet the first two conditions. The growth of U.S. air travel is due in part to airlines having generally met these conditions.

Many companies have substantial investments in plant assets. Illustration 10-1 shows the percentages of plant assets in relation to total assets of companies in a number of industries.

Illustration 10-1
Percentages of plant assets in relation to total assets

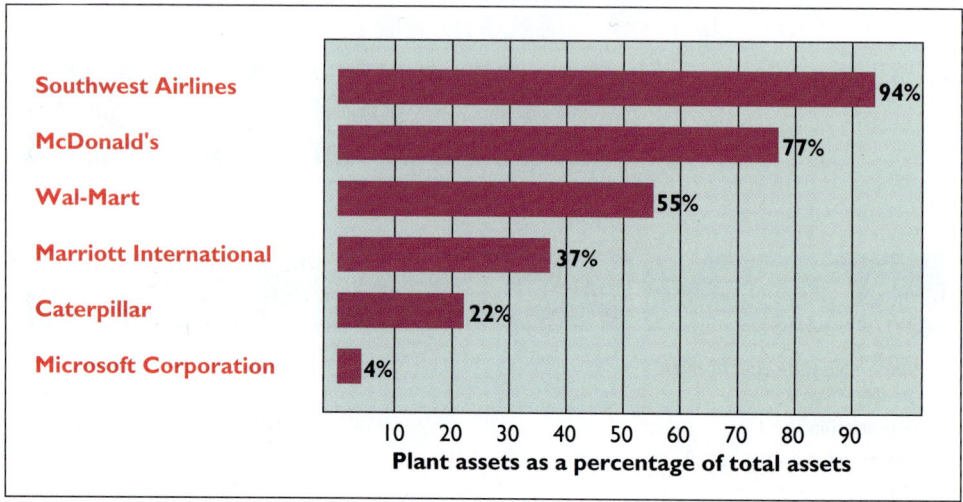

Determining the Cost of Plant Assets

The cost principle requires that plant assets be recorded at cost. Thus the vehicles at **Rent-A-Wreck** are recorded at cost. Cost consists of **all expenditures necessary to acquire the asset and make it ready for its intended use**. For example, the cost of factory machinery includes the purchase price, freight costs paid by the purchaser, and installation costs. Once cost is established, it becomes the basis of accounting for the plant asset over its useful life. Current market or replacement values are not used after acquisition.

The application of the cost principle to each of the major classes of plant assets is explained in the following sections.

Land

Land is often used as a building site for a manufacturing plant or office site. The cost of land includes (1) the cash purchase price, (2) closing costs such as title and attorney's fees, (3) real estate brokers' commissions, and (4) accrued property taxes and other liens on the land assumed by the purchaser. For example, if the cash price is $50,000 and the purchaser agrees to pay accrued taxes of $5,000, the cost of the land is $55,000.

All necessary costs incurred to make land **ready for its intended use** are debited to the Land account. When vacant land is acquired, these costs include expenditures for clearing, draining, filling, and grading. Sometimes the land has a building on it that must be removed before construction of a new building. In this case, all demolition and removal costs, less any proceeds from salvaged materials, are debited to the Land account.

To illustrate, assume that Hayes Manufacturing Company acquires real estate at a cash cost of $100,000. The property contains an old warehouse that is razed at a net cost of $6,000 ($7,500 in costs less $1,500 proceeds from salvaged materials). Additional expenditures are the attorney's fee, $1,000, and the real estate broker's commission, $8,000. The cost of the land is $115,000, computed as follows.

Illustration 10-2
Computation of cost of land

Land	
Cash price of property	$100,000
Net removal cost of warehouse	6,000
Attorney's fee	1,000
Real estate broker's commission	8,000
Cost of land	**$115,000**

When the acquisition is recorded, Land is debited for $115,000 and Cash is credited for $115,000.

Land Improvements

Land improvements are structural additions made to land, such as driveways, parking lots, fences, landscaping, and underground sprinklers. The cost of land improvements includes all expenditures necessary to make the improvements ready for their intended use. For example, the cost of a new company parking lot includes the amount paid for paving, fencing, and lighting; thus the total of all of these costs would be debited to Land Improvements. Land improvements have limited useful lives, and their maintenance and replacement are the responsibility of the company. Because of their limited useful life, the cost of land improvements are expensed (depreciated) over their useful life.

Buildings

Buildings are facilities used in operations, such as stores, offices, factories, warehouses, and airplane hangars. All necessary expenditures related to the purchase or construction of a building are debited to the Buildings account. When a building is **purchased**, such costs include the purchase price, closing costs (attorney's fees, title insurance, etc.) and real estate broker's commission. Costs to make the building ready for its intended use include expenditures for remodeling and replacing or repairing the roof, floors, electrical wiring, and plumbing.

When a new building is **constructed**, cost consists of the contract price plus payments for architects' fees, building permits, and excavation costs. In addition, interest costs incurred to finance the project are included when a significant period of time is required to get the building ready for use. In these circumstances, interest costs are considered as necessary as materials and labor. However, the inclusion of interest costs in the cost of a constructed building is **limited to the construction period**. When construction has been completed, subsequent interest payments on funds borrowed to finance the construction are debited to Interest Expense.

Equipment

Equipment includes assets used in operations, such as store check-out counters, office furniture, factory machinery, delivery trucks and airplanes. The cost of equipment, such as **Rent-A-Wreck** vehicles, consists of the **cash purchase price**, **sales taxes**, **freight charges**, **and insurance during transit paid by the purchaser**. It also includes expenditures required in assembling, installing, and testing the unit. However, motor vehicle licenses and accident insurance on company trucks and cars are not included in the cost of equipment. They are treated as expenses as they are incurred. They represent annual recurring expenditures and do not benefit future periods.

To illustrate, assume Merten Company purchases factory machinery at a cash price of $50,000. Related expenditures are for sales taxes $3,000, insurance during shipping $500, and installation and testing $1,000. The cost of the factory machinery is $54,500, computed as follows.

Illustration 10-3
Computation of cost of factory machinery

Factory Machinery	
Cash price	$50,000
Sales taxes	3,000
Insurance during shipping	500
Installation and testing	1,000
Cost of factory machinery	**$54,500**

The summary entry to record the purchase and related expenditures is:

A	=	L	+	OE
+54,500				
−54,500				

Cash Flows
−54,500

Factory Machinery	54,500	
Cash		54,500
(To record purchase of factory machine)		

For another example, assume that Lenard Company purchases a delivery truck at a cash price of $22,000. Related expenditures consist of sales taxes $1,320, painting and lettering $500, motor vehicle license $80, and a 3-year accident insurance policy $1,600. The cost of the delivery truck is $23,820, computed as follows.

Illustration 10-4
Computation of cost of delivery truck

Delivery Truck	
Cash price	$22,000
Sales taxes	1,320
Painting and lettering	500
Cost of delivery truck	**$23,820**

The cost of the motor vehicle license is treated as an expense, and the cost of the insurance policy is considered a prepaid asset. Thus, the entry to record the purchase of the truck and related expenditures is:

A	=	L	+	OE
+23,820				−80 Exp
+1,600				
−25,500				

Cash Flows
−25,500

Delivery Truck	23,820	
License Expense	80	
Prepaid Insurance	1,600	
Cash		25,500
(To record purchase of delivery truck and related expenditures)		

BEFORE YOU GO ON...

Review It

1. What are plant assets? What are the major classes of plant assets? How is the cost principle applied to accounting for plant assets?

2. What classifications and amounts are shown in **PepsiCo**'s Note 4 to explain its total property, plant, and equipment (net) of $7,390,000,000? The answer to this question is provided on p. 444.

Do It

Assume that a delivery truck is purchased for $15,000 cash, plus sales taxes of $900 and delivery costs to the dealer of $500. The buyer also pays $200 for painting and lettering, $600 for an annual insurance policy, and $80 for a motor vehicle license. Explain how each of these costs would be accounted for.

ACTION PLAN

- Identify expenditures made in order to get delivery equipment ready for its intended use.
- Treat operating costs as expenses.

SOLUTION   The first four payments ($15,000, $900, $500, and $200) are considered to be expenditures necessary to make the truck ready for its intended use. Thus, the cost of the truck is $16,600. The payments for insurance and the license are considered to be operating costs and therefore are expensed.

Related exercise material: *BE10-1, BE10-2, E10-1, and E10-2.*

☑ **THE NAVIGATOR**

Depreciation

As explained in Chapter 3, **depreciation is the allocation of the cost of a plant asset to expense over its useful (service) life in a rational and systematic manner**. Cost allocation provides for the proper matching of expenses with revenues in accordance with the matching principle (see Illustration 10-5).

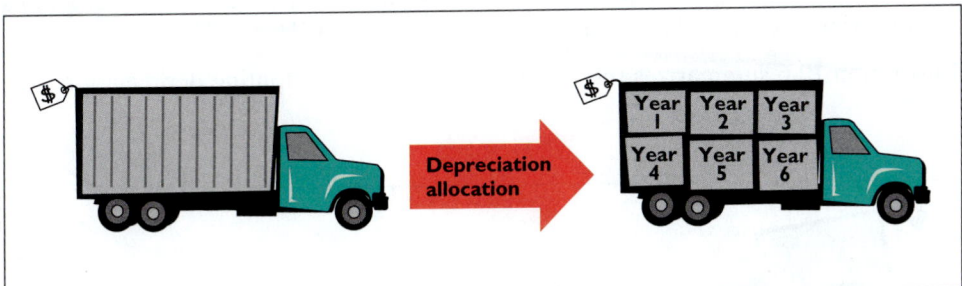

Illustration 10-5
Depreciation as an allocation concept

Depreciation is a process of cost allocation, not a process of asset valuation. The change in an asset's market value is not measured during ownership because plant assets are not held for resale. So, the **book value** (cost less accumulated depreciation) of a plant asset may be quite different from its market value.
Depreciation applies to three classes of plant assets: land improvements, buildings, and equipment. Each asset in these classes is considered to be a **depreciable asset**. Why? Because the usefulness to the company and revenue-producing ability of each asset will decline over the asset's useful life. Depreciation does not apply to land because its usefulness and revenue-producing ability generally remain intact over time. In fact, in many cases, the usefulness of land is greater over time because of the scarcity of good land sites. Thus, **land is not a depreciable asset**.

During a depreciable asset's useful life its revenue-producing ability will decline because of **wear and tear**. A delivery truck that has been driven 100,000 miles will be less useful to a company than one driven only 800 miles. Trucks and planes exposed to snow and salt will deteriorate faster than equipment that is not exposed to these elements.

Revenue-producing ability may also decline because of **obsolescence**. Obsolescence is the process of becoming out of date before the asset physically wears out. Major airlines were re-routed from Chicago's Midway Airport to Chicago-O'Hare International Airport because Midway's runways were too short for jumbo jets, for example.

It is important to understand that **recognizing depreciation on an asset does not result in an accumulation of cash for replacement of the asset**. The balance in Accumulated Depreciation represents the total cost that has been charged to expense. It is not a cash fund.

Factors in Computing Depreciation

Three factors affect the computation of depreciation:

1. **Cost.** Issues affecting the cost of a depreciable asset were explained earlier in this chapter. Recall that plant assets are recorded at cost, in accordance with the cost principle.

2. **Useful life.** Useful life is an estimate of the expected productive life, also called service life, of the asset. Useful life may be expressed in terms of time, units of activity (such as machine hours), or units of output. Useful life is an estimate. In making the estimate, management considers such factors as the intended use of the asset, its expected repair and maintenance, and its vulnerability to obsolescence. Past experience with similar assets is often helpful in deciding on expected useful life. We might reasonably expect the estimated useful life used by **Rent-A-Wreck** to differ from that used by **Avis**.

3. **Salvage value.** Salvage value is an estimate of the asset's value at the end of its useful life. This value may be based on the asset's worth as scrap or on its expected trade-in value. Like useful life, salvage value is an estimate. In making the estimate, management considers how it plans to dispose of the asset and its experience with similar assets.

Illustration 10-6 summarizes the three factors used in computing depreciation.

**ALTERNATIVE
TERMINOLOGY**

Another term sometimes used for salvage value is *residual value*.

Illustration 10-6
Three factors in computing depreciation

HELPFUL HINT

Depreciation expense is reported on the income statement, and accumulated depreciation is reported as a deduction from plant assets on the balance sheet.

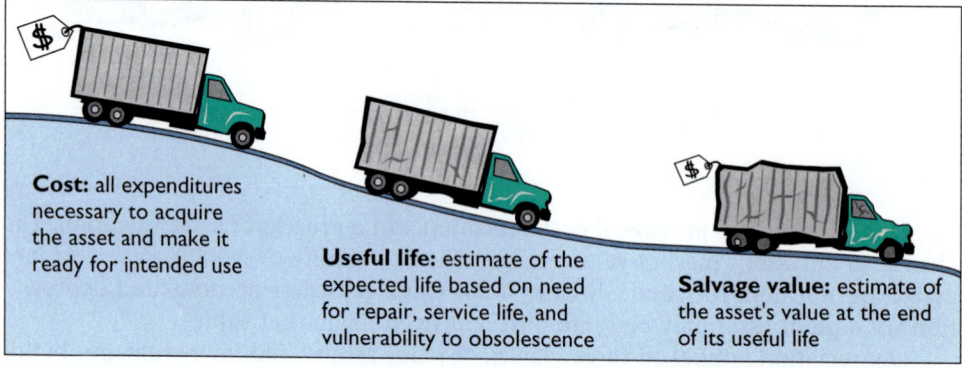

Cost: all expenditures necessary to acquire the asset and make it ready for intended use

Useful life: estimate of the expected life based on need for repair, service life, and vulnerability to obsolescence

Salvage value: estimate of the asset's value at the end of its useful life

Willamette Industries, Inc., of Portland, Oregon, recently changed its accounting estimates relating to depreciation of certain assets. The vertically integrated forest products company said the changes were due to advances in technology that have increased the service life on its equipment an extra five years. Willamette expected the accounting changes to increase its full-year earnings by about $57 million, or $0.52 a share. Its prior-year earnings were $89 million, or $0.80 a share. Imagine a 65 percent improvement in earnings per share from a mere change in the estimated life of equipment!

Depreciation Methods

Depreciation is generally computed using one of the following methods:

1. Straight-line
2. Units-of-activity
3. Declining-balance

Each method is acceptable under generally accepted accounting principles. Management selects the method(s) it believes to be appropriate. The objective is to select the method that best measures an asset's contribution to revenue over its useful life. Once a method is chosen, it should be applied consistently over the useful life of the asset. Consistency enhances the comparability of financial statements.

We will compare the three depreciation methods using the following data for a small delivery truck purchased by Barb's Florists on January 1, 2005.

Cost	$13,000
Expected salvage value	$ 1,000
Estimated useful life in years	5
Estimated useful life in miles	100,000

Illustration 10-7
Delivery truck data

Depreciation affects the balance sheet through accumulated depreciation and the income statement through depreciation expense. Illustration 10-8 (in the margin) shows the use of the different depreciation methods in 600 of the largest companies in the United States.

Straight-Line

Under the **straight-line method**, depreciation is the same for each year of the asset's useful life. It is measured solely by the passage of time.

In order to compute depreciation expense under the straight-line method, it is necessary to determine depreciable cost. **Depreciable cost** is the cost of the asset less its salvage value. It represents the total amount subject to depreciation. Under the straight-line method, depreciable cost is divided by the asset's useful life to determine annual depreciation expense. The computation of depreciation expense in the first year for Barb's Florists is shown in Illustration 10-9 (on page 408).

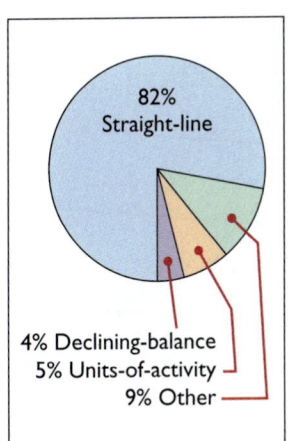

Illustration 10-8
Use of depreciation methods in 600 large U.S. companies

Illustration 10-9
Formula for straight-line method

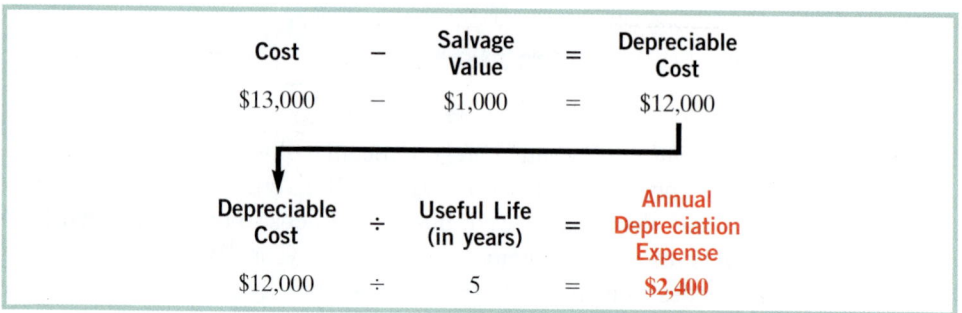

Alternatively, we also can compute an **annual rate of depreciation**. In this case, the rate is 20% (100% ÷ 5 years). When an annual straight-line rate is used, the percentage rate is applied to the depreciable cost of the asset. The use of an annual rate is shown in the following **depreciation schedule**.

Illustration 10-10
Straight-line depreciation schedule

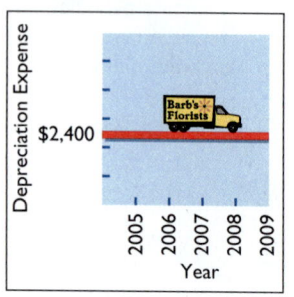

	BARB'S FLORISTS				
	Computation		**Annual**	**End of Year**	
Year	**Depreciable Cost**	**× Depreciation Rate**	**= Depreciation Expense**	**Accumulated Depreciation**	**Book Value**
2005	$12,000	20%	$2,400	$ 2,400	$10,600*
2006	12,000	20	2,400	4,800	8,200
2007	12,000	20	2,400	7,200	5,800
2008	12,000	20	2,400	9,600	3,400
2009	12,000	20	2,400	12,000	1,000

*($13,000 − $2,400).

Note that the depreciation expense of $2,400 is the same each year. The book value at the end of the useful life is equal to the estimated $1,000 salvage value.

What happens when an asset is purchased **during** the year, rather than on January 1, as in our example? In that case, it is necessary to **prorate the annual depreciation** on a time basis. If Barb's Florists had purchased the delivery truck on April 1, 2005, the depreciation for 2005 would be $1,800 ($12,000 × 20% × 9/12 of a year).

The straight-line method predominates in practice. Such large companies as **Campbell Soup**, **Marriott Corporation**, and **General Mills** use the straight-line method. It is simple to apply, and it matches expenses with revenues when the use of the asset is reasonably uniform throughout the service life. In the Feature Story, for simplicity **Rent-A-Wreck** is probably using the straight-line method of depreciation for its vehicles.

Units-of-Activity

Under the **units-of-activity method**, useful life is expressed in terms of the total units of production or use expected from the asset, rather than as a time period. The units-of-activity method is ideally suited to factory machinery. Production can be measured in units of output or in machine hours. This method can also be used for such assets as delivery equipment (miles driven) and airplanes (hours in use). The units-of-activity method is generally not suitable for buildings or furniture, because depreciation for these assets is more a function of time than of use.

To use this method, the total units of activity for the entire useful life are estimated, and these units are divided into depreciable cost. The resulting number represents the depreciation cost per unit. The depreciation cost per unit is then applied to the units of activity during the year to determine the annual depreciation expense.

To illustrate, assume that Barb's Florists' delivery truck is driven 15,000 miles in the first year. The computation of depreciation expense in the first year is:

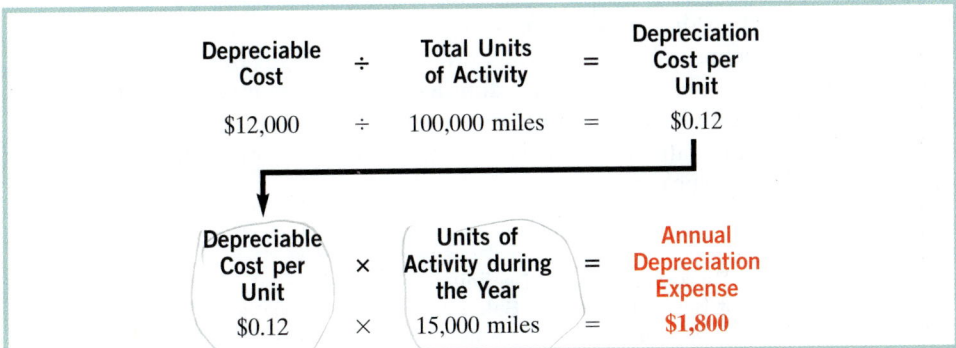

Illustration 10-11
Formula for units-of-activity method

The units-of-activity depreciation schedule, using assumed mileage, is as follows.

Illustration 10-12
Units-of-activity depreciation schedule

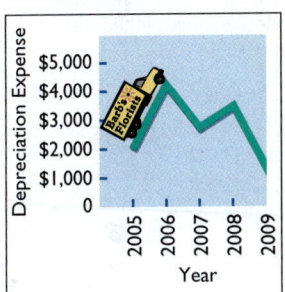

| | Computation | | | Annual | End of Year | |
Year	Units of Activity	× Depreciation Cost/Unit	=	Depreciation Expense	Accumulated Depreciation	Book Value
2005	15,000	$0.12		$1,800	$ 1,800	$11,200*
2006	30,000	0.12		3,600	5,400	7,600
2007	20,000	0.12		2,400	7,800	5,200
2008	25,000	0.12		3,000	10,800	2,200
2009	10,000	0.12		1,200	12,000	1,000

BARB'S FLORISTS

*($13,000 − $1,800).

This method is easy to apply when assets are purchased mid-year. In such a case, the productivity of the asset for the partial year is used in computing the depreciation.

The units-of-activity method is not nearly as popular as the straight-line method (see Illustration 10-8), primarily because it is often difficult to make a reasonable estimate of total activity. However, this method is used by some very large companies, such as **Chevron Oil** and **Boise Cascade Corporation** (a forestry company). When the productivity of an asset varies significantly from one period to another, the units-of-activity method results in the best matching of expenses with revenues.

Declining-Balance

The **declining-balance method** produces a decreasing annual depreciation expense over the asset's useful life. The method is so named because the periodic depreciation is based on a **declining book value** (cost less accumulated depreciation) of the asset. Annual depreciation expense is computed by multiplying the book value at the beginning of the year by the declining-balance depreciation rate. **The depreciation rate remains constant from year to year, but the book value to which the rate is applied declines each year.**

Book value at the beginning of the first year is the cost of the asset. This is so because the balance in accumulated depreciation at the beginning of the asset's useful life is zero. In subsequent years, book value is the difference between cost and accumulated depreciation to date. Unlike the other depreciation methods, the declining-balance method does not use depreciable cost. That is, **salvage value is ignored in determining the amount to which the declining-balance rate is applied**. Salvage value, however, does limit the total depreciation that can be taken. Depreciation stops when the asset's book value equals expected salvage value.

A common declining-balance rate is double the straight-line rate. As a result, the method is often referred to as the **double-declining-balance method**. If Barb's Florists uses the double-declining-balance method, the depreciation rate is 40% (2 × the straight-line rate of 20%). The computation of depreciation for the first year on the delivery truck is:

Illustration 10-13
Formula for declining-balance method

Book Value at Beginning of Year	×	Declining-Balance Rate	=	Annual Depreciation Expense
$13,000	×	40%	=	**$5,200**

The depreciation schedule under this method is as follows.

Illustration 10-14
Double-declining-balance depreciation schedule

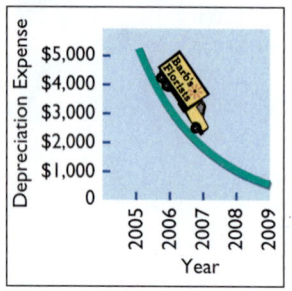

BARB'S FLORISTS

	Computation			Annual	End of Year	
Year	Book Value Beginning of Year	× Depreciation Rate	=	Depreciation Expense	Accumulated Depreciation	Book Value
2005	$13,000	40%		**$5,200**	$ 5,200	$7,800
2006	7,800	40		**3,120**	8,320	4,680
2007	4,680	40		**1,872**	10,192	2,808
2008	2,808	40		**1,123**	11,315	1,685
2009	1,685	40		**685***	12,000	**1,000**

*Computation of $674 ($1,685 × 40%) is adjusted to $685 in order for book value to equal salvage value.

You can see that the delivery equipment is 69% depreciated ($8,320 ÷ $12,000) at the end of the second year. Under the straight-line method it would be depreciated 40% ($4,800 ÷ $12,000) at that time. Because the declining-balance method produces higher depreciation expense in the early years than in the later years, it is considered an **accelerated-depreciation method**. The declining-balance method is compatible with the matching principle. The higher depreciation expense in early years is matched with the higher benefits received in these years. On the other hand, lower depreciation expense is recognized in later years when the asset's contribution to revenue is less. Also, some assets lose usefulness rapidly because of obsolescence. In these cases, the declining-balance method provides a more appropriate depreciation amount.

When an asset is purchased during the year, the first year's declining-balance depreciation must be prorated on a time basis. For example, if Barb's Florists had purchased the truck on April 1, 2005, depreciation for 2005 would become $3,900 ($13,000 × 40% × 9/12). The book value at the beginning of 2006 is then $9,100 ($13,000 − $3,900), and the 2006 depreciation is $3,640 ($9,100 × 40%). Subsequent computations would follow from those amounts.

Comparison of Methods

A comparison of annual and total depreciation expense under each of the three methods is shown for Barb's Florists in Illustration 10-15.

Most tax friendly

Easiest *Most Accurate*

Year	Straight-Line	Units-of-Activity	Declining-Balance
2005	$ 2,400	$ 1,800	$ 5,200
2006	2,400	3,600	3,120
2007	2,400	2,400	1,872
2008	2,400	3,000	1,123
2009	2,400	1,200	685
	$12,000	**$12,000**	**$12,000**

Illustration 10-15
Comparison of depreciation methods

Observe that annual depreciation varies considerably among the methods. But total depreciation is the same for the 5-year period under all three methods. Each method is acceptable in accounting, because each recognizes the decline in service potential of the asset in a rational and systematic manner. The depreciation expense pattern under each method is presented graphically in Illustration 10-16.

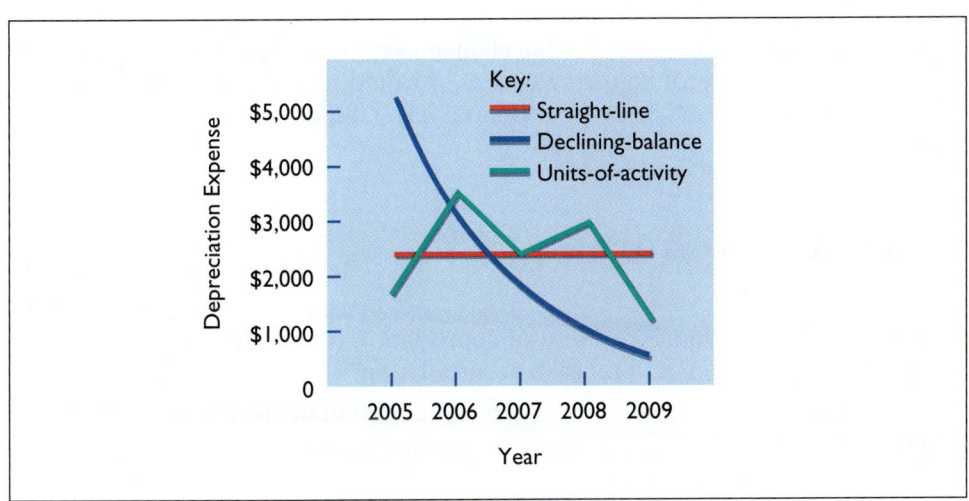

Illustration 10-16
Patterns of depreciation

Depreciation and Income Taxes

The Internal Revenue Service (IRS) allows corporate taxpayers to deduct depreciation expense when they compute taxable income. However, the IRS does not require the taxpayer to use the same depreciation method on the tax return that is used in preparing financial statements. Many corporations use straight-line in their financial statements to maximize net income. At the same time, they use a special accelerated-depreciation method on their tax returns to minimize their income taxes. Taxpayers must use on their tax returns either the straight-line method or a special accelerated-depreciation method called the **Modified Accelerated Cost Recovery System** (MACRS).

Revising Periodic Depreciation

Depreciation is one example of the use of estimation in the accounting process. Annual depreciation expense should be reviewed periodically by management. If wear and tear or obsolescence indicate that annual depreciation estimates are inadequate or excessive, a change should be made.

STUDY OBJECTIVE 4

Describe the procedure for revising periodic depreciation.

When a change in an estimate is required, the change is made in **current and future years**. It is not made retroactively **to prior periods**. Thus, there is no correction of previously recorded depreciation expense. Instead, depreciation expense for current and future years is revised. The rationale is that continual restatement of prior periods would adversely affect confidence in financial statements.

To determine the new annual depreciation expense, we first compute the asset's depreciable cost at the time of the revision. We then allocate the revised depreciable cost to the remaining useful life. To illustrate, assume that Barb's Florists decides on January 1, 2008, to extend the useful life of the truck one year because of its excellent condition. The company has used the straight-line method to depreciate the asset to date, and book value is $5,800 ($13,000 − $7,200). The new annual depreciation is $1,600, computed as follows.

Illustration 10-17
Revised depreciation computation

Book value, 1/1/08	$5,800
Less: Salvage value	1,000
Depreciable cost	$4,800
Remaining useful life	3 years (2008–2010)
Revised annual depreciation ($4,800 ÷ 3)	**$1,600**

Barb's Florists makes no entry for the change in estimate. On December 31, 2008, during the preparation of adjusting entries, it would record depreciation expense of $1,600. Significant changes in estimates must be described in the financial statements.

BEFORE YOU GO ON...

Review It

1. What is the relationship, if any, of depreciation to (a) cost allocation, (b) asset valuation, and (c) cash accumulation?

2. Explain the factors that affect the computation of depreciation.

3. What are the formulas for computing annual depreciation under each of the depreciation methods?

4. How do the methods differ in terms of their effects on annual depreciation over the useful life of the asset?

5. Are revisions of periodic depreciation made to prior periods? Explain.

Do It

On January 1, 2005, Iron Mountain Ski Corporation purchased a new snow-grooming machine for $50,000. The machine is estimated to have a 10-year life with a $2,000 salvage value. What journal entry would Iron Mountain Ski Corporation make at December 31, 2005, if it uses the straight-line method of depreciation?

ACTION PLAN

■ Calculate depreciable cost (Cost − Salvage value).
■ Divide the depreciable cost by the estimated useful life.

SOLUTION

$$\text{Depreciation expense} = \frac{\text{Cost} - \text{Salvage value}}{\text{Useful life}} = \frac{\$50,000 - \$2,000}{10} = \$4,800$$

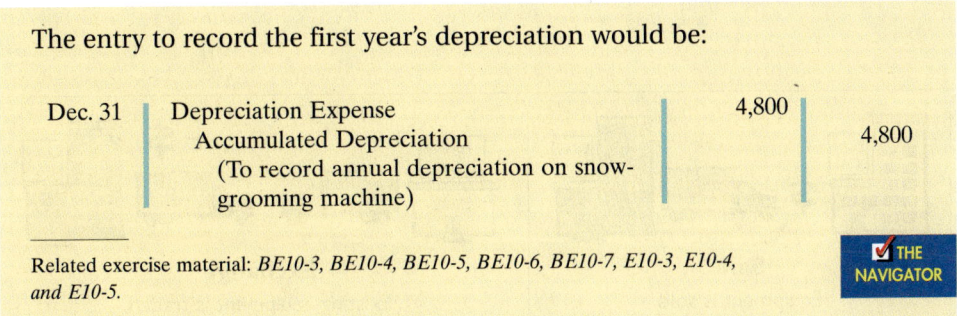

The entry to record the first year's depreciation would be:

Dec. 31	Depreciation Expense	4,800	
	Accumulated Depreciation		4,800
	(To record annual depreciation on snow-grooming machine)		

Related exercise material: *BE10-3, BE10-4, BE10-5, BE10-6, BE10-7, E10-3, E10-4, and E10-5.*

☑ THE NAVIGATOR

Expenditures During Useful Life

During the useful life of a plant asset a company may incur costs for ordinary repairs, additions, or improvements. **Ordinary repairs** are expenditures to maintain the operating efficiency and productive life of the unit. They usually are fairly small amounts that occur frequently. Motor tune-ups and oil changes, the painting of buildings, and the replacing of worn-out gears on machinery are examples. Such repairs are debited to Repair (or Maintenance) Expense as they are incurred. Because they are immediately charged as an expense against revenues, these costs are often referred to as **revenue expenditures**.

    Additions and improvements are costs incurred to increase the operating efficiency, productive capacity, or useful life of a plant asset. They are usually material in amount and occur infrequently. Additions and improvements increase the company's investment in productive facilities and are generally debited to the plant asset affected. They are often referred to as **capital expenditures**. Most major U.S. corporations disclose annual capital expenditures. In a recent year, both **IBM** and **General Motors** reported capital expenditures slightly in excess of $6 billion.

> **STUDY OBJECTIVE 5**
>
> Distinguish between revenue and capital expenditures, and explain the entries for these expenditures.

ACCOUNTING IN ACTION   **Ethics Insight**

In what could become one of the largest accounting frauds in history, **WorldCom** announced the discovery of $7 billion in expenses improperly booked as capital expenditures, a gimmick that boosted profit over a recent five-quarter period. If these expenses had been recorded properly, WorldCom, one of the biggest stock market stars of the 1990s, would have reported a net loss for 2001, as well as for the first quarter of 2002. Instead, WorldCom reported a profit of $1.4 billion for 2001 and $130 million for the first quarter of 2002. As a result of these problems, WorldCom declared bankruptcy, to the dismay of its investors and creditors.

Plant Asset Disposals

Plant assets may be disposed of in three ways—retirement, sale, or exchange—as shown in Illustration 10-18 (on page 414). Whatever the method, at the time of disposal it is necessary to determine the book value of the plant asset. As noted earlier, book value is the difference between the cost of a plant asset and the accumulated depreciation to date.

> **STUDY OBJECTIVE 6**
>
> Explain how to account for the disposal of a plant asset.

Illustration 10-18
Methods of plant asset
disposal

At the time of disposal, depreciation for the fraction of the year to the date of disposal must be recorded. The book value is then eliminated by debiting (decreasing) Accumulated Depreciation for the total depreciation to date and crediting (decreasing) the asset account for the cost of the asset. In this chapter we will examine the accounting for the retirement and sale of plant assets. In the appendix to this chapter we will examine and demonstrate the method of accounting for exchanges of plant assets.

Retirement of Plant Assets

To illustrate the retirement of plant assets, assume that Hobart Enterprises retires its computer printers, which cost $32,000. The accumulated depreciation on these printers is $32,000. The equipment, therefore, is fully depreciated (zero book value). The entry to record this retirement is as follows.

A	=	L	+	OE
+32,000				
−32,000				

Cash Flows
no effect

Accumulated Depreciation—Printing Equipment	32,000	
Printing Equipment		32,000
(To record retirement of fully depreciated equipment)		

What happens if a fully depreciated plant asset is still useful to the company? In this case, the asset and its accumulated depreciation continue to be reported on the balance sheet without further depreciation adjustment until the asset is retired. Reporting the asset and related accumulated depreciation on the balance sheet informs the financial statement reader that the asset is still in use. However, once an asset is fully depreciated, even if it is still being used, no additional depreciation should be taken. In no situation can the accumulated depreciation on a plant asset exceed its cost.

If a plant asset is retired before it is fully depreciated, and no cash is received for scrap or salvage value, a loss on disposal occurs. For example, assume that Sunset Company discards delivery equipment that cost $18,000 and has accumulated depreciation of $14,000. The entry is as follows.

A	=	L	+	OE
+14,000				−4,000 Exp
−18,000				

Cash Flows
no effect

Accumulated Depreciation—Delivery Equipment	14,000	
Loss on Disposal	4,000	
Delivery Equipment		18,000
(To record retirement of delivery equipment at a loss)		

The loss on disposal is reported in the "Other expenses and losses" section of the income statement.

Sale of Plant Assets

In a disposal by sale, the book value of the asset is compared with the proceeds received from the sale. **If the proceeds of the sale exceed the book value of the plant asset, a gain on disposal occurs. If the proceeds of the sale are less than the book value of the plant asset sold, a loss on disposal occurs.**

Only by coincidence will the book value and the fair market value of the asset be the same when the asset is sold. Gains and losses on sales of plant assets are therefore quite common. For example, **Delta Airlines** reported a $94,343,000 gain on the sale of five **Boeing** B727-200 aircraft and five **Lockheed** L-1011-1 aircraft.

Gain on Disposal

To illustrate a gain, assume that on July 1, 2005, Wright Company sells office furniture for $16,000 cash. The office furniture originally cost $60,000. As of January 1, 2005, it had accumulated depreciation of $41,000. Depreciation for the first 6 months of 2005 is $8,000. The entry to record depreciation expense and update accumulated depreciation to July 1 is as follows.

July 1	Depreciation Expense	8,000	
	Accumulated Depreciation—Office Furniture		8,000
	(To record depreciation expense for the first 6 months of 2005)		

A	=	L	+	OE
−8,000				−8,000 Exp

Cash Flows
no effect

After the accumulated depreciation balance is updated, a gain on disposal of $5,000 is computed:

Cost of office furniture	$60,000
Less: Accumulated depreciation ($41,000 + $8,000)	49,000
Book value at date of disposal	11,000
Proceeds from sale	16,000
Gain on disposal	**$ 5,000**

Illustration 10-19
Computation of gain on disposal

The entry to record the sale and the gain on disposal is as follows.

July 1	Cash	16,000	
	Accumulated Depreciation—Office Furniture	49,000	
	Office Furniture		60,000
	Gain on Disposal		5,000
	(To record sale of office furniture at a gain)		

A	=	L	+	OE
+16,000				+5,000 Rev
+49,000				
−60,000				

Cash Flows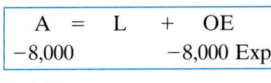
+16,000

The gain on disposal is reported in the "Other revenues and gains" section of the income statement.

Loss on Disposal

Assume that instead of selling the office furniture for $16,000, Wright sells it for $9,000. In this case, a loss of $2,000 is computed:

Cost of office furniture	$60,000
Less: Accumulated depreciation	49,000
Book value at date of disposal	11,000
Proceeds from sale	9,000
Loss on disposal	**$ 2,000**

Illustration 10-20
Computation of loss on disposal

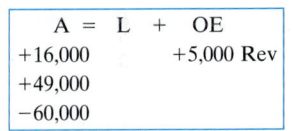

The entry to record the sale and the loss on disposal is as follows.

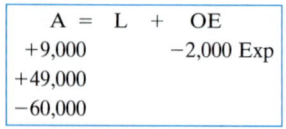

A = L + OE
+9,000   −2,000 Exp
+49,000
−60,000

Cash Flows
+9,000

July 1	Cash	9,000	
	Accumulated Depreciation—Office Furniture	49,000	
	Loss on Disposal	2,000	
	Office Furniture		60,000
	(To record sale of office furniture at a loss)		

The loss on disposal is reported in the "Other expenses and losses" section of the income statement.

BEFORE YOU GO ON...

Review It

1. How does a capital expenditure differ from a revenue expenditure?
2. What is the proper accounting for the retirement and sale of plant assets?

Do It

Overland Trucking has an old truck that cost $30,000. The truck has accumulated depreciation of $16,000 and a fair value of $17,000. Overland has decided to sell the truck for $17,000 cash. What is the entry that Overland Trucking would make to record the sale of the truck? What is the entry that Overland trucking would make to record the sale of the truck, assuming it sold for $10,000 cash?

ACTION PLAN

■ At the time of disposal, determine the book value of the asset.
■ Compare the asset's book value with the proceeds received to determine whether a gain or loss has occurred.

SOLUTION

Sale of truck for cash at a gain:

Cash	17,000	
Accumulated Depreciation—Truck	16,000	
Truck		30,000
Gain on Disposal [$17,000 − ($30,000 − $16,000)]		3,000
(To record sale of truck at a gain)		

Sale of truck for cash at a loss:

Cash	10,000	
Loss on Disposal [$10,000 − ($30,000 − $16,000)]	4,000	
Accumulated Depreciation—Truck	16,000	
Truck		30,000
(To record sale of truck at a loss)		

Related exercise material: *BE10-8, BE10-9, and E10-6.*

 ✓ THE NAVIGATOR

SECTION 2 NATURAL RESOURCES

Natural resources consist of standing timber and underground deposits of oil, gas, and minerals. These long-lived productive assets have two distinguishing characteristics: (1) They are physically extracted in operations (such as mining, cutting, or pumping), and (2) they are replaceable only by an act of nature. The acquisition cost of a natural resource is the price needed to acquire the resource and prepare it for its intended use. For an already discovered resource, such as an existing coal mine, cost is the price paid for the property.

The allocation of the cost of natural resources to expense in a rational and systematic manner over the resource's useful life is called **depletion**. **The units-of-activity method** (learned earlier in the chapter) **is generally used to compute depletion**. The reason it is used is that **depletion generally is a function of the units extracted during the year**.

Under the units-of-activity method, the total cost of the natural resource minus salvage value is divided by the number of units estimated to be in the resource. The result is a depletion cost per unit of product. The depletion cost per unit is then multiplied by the number of units extracted and sold. The result is the annual depletion expense. The formula is as follows.

HELPFUL HINT

On a balance sheet, natural resources may be described more specifically as timberlands, mineral deposits, oil reserves, and so on.

STUDY OBJECTIVE 7

Compute periodic depletion of natural resources.

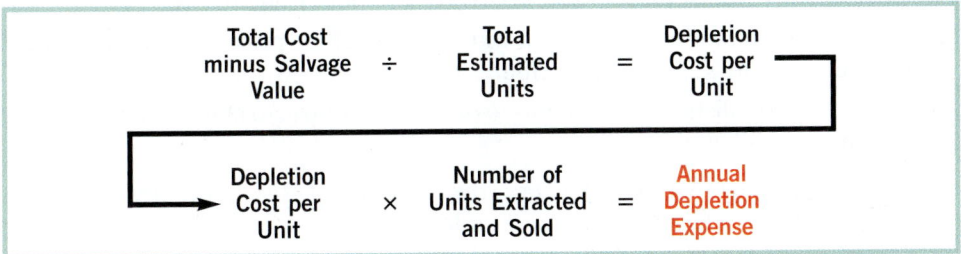

Illustration 10-21
Formula to compute depletion expense

To illustrate, assume that Lane Coal Company invests $5 million in a mine estimated to have 10 million tons of coal and no salvage value. In the first year, 800,000 tons of coal are extracted and sold. Using the formulas above, the computations are as follows:

$$\$5,000,000 \div 10,000,000 = \$0.50 \text{ depletion cost per ton}$$

$$\$0.50 \times 800,000 = \$400,000 \text{ annual depletion expense}$$

The entry to record depletion expense for the first year of operation is as follows.

Dec. 31	Depletion Expense	400,000	
	Accumulated Depletion		400,000
	(To record depletion expense on coal		
	deposits)		

A	=	L	+	OE
−400,000				−400,000 Exp

Cash Flows
no effect

The account Depletion Expense is reported as a part of the cost of producing the product. Accumulated Depletion is a contra asset account similar to accumulated depreciation. It is deducted from the cost of the natural resource in the balance sheet, as shown in Illustration 10-22.

Illustration 10-22
Statement presentation of accumulated depletion

LANE COAL COMPANY		
Balance Sheet (partial)		
Coal mine	$5,000,000	
Less: Accumulated depletion	**400,000**	$4,600,000

However, in many companies an Accumulated Depletion account is not used. In such cases, the amount of depletion is credited directly to the natural resources account.

Sometimes, natural resources extracted in one accounting period will not be sold until a later period. In this case, depletion is not expensed until the resource is sold. The amount not sold is reported in the current assets section as inventory.

SECTION 3 INTANGIBLE ASSETS

Intangible assets are rights, privileges, and competitive advantages that result from the ownership of long-lived assets that do not possess physical substance. Evidence of intangibles may exist in the form of contracts or licenses. Intangibles may arise from:

1. Government grants, such as patents, copyrights, and trademarks.
2. Acquisition of another business, in which the purchase price includes a payment for the company's favorable attributes (called goodwill).
3. Private monopolistic arrangements arising from contractual agreements, such as franchises and leases.

Some widely known intangibles are the patents of **Intel**, the franchises of **McDonald's**, the trade name of Col. Sander's **Kentucky Fried Chicken**, and the trademark **Rent-A-Wreck** in the Feature Story.

Accounting for Intangible Assets

STUDY OBJECTIVE 8

Explain the basic issues related to accounting for intangible assets.

Intangible assets are recorded at cost. The cost of an intangible asset should be allocated over its useful life, assuming the useful life is limited. If the life of the intangible is indefinite, the cost of the intangible should not be allocated. **Indefinite** means that no legal, regulatory, contractual, competitive, economic, or other factors limit the intangible's useful life. At disposal, the book value of the intangible asset is eliminated, and a gain or loss, if any, is recorded.

There are several differences between accounting for intangible assets and accounting for plant assets. First, assuming an intangible has a limited life, the term used to describe the allocation of the cost of an intangible asset to expense is **amortization**, rather than depreciation. Also, to record amortization of an intangible, an amortization expense is debited and the specific intangible asset is credited (rather than crediting a contra account). An alternative is to credit an Accumulated Amortization account, similar to Accumulated Depreciation.

There is also a difference in determining cost. For plant assets, cost includes both the purchase price of the asset and the costs incurred in designing and constructing the asset. In contrast, cost for an intangible asset includes only the purchase price. Any costs incurred in developing an intangible asset are expensed as incurred.

The method of amortizing an intangible asset with a limited life should reflect the pattern in which the asset's economic benefits are used. If such a pattern cannot be reliably determined, a straight-line method of amortization should be used. For homework purposes, use the straight-line method, unless otherwise indicated.

An indefinite-life intangible asset should not be amortized until its life is determined to be limited. At that time, the intangible asset should be amortized.

= 20 yrs

Patents

A **patent** is an exclusive right issued by the U.S. Patent Office that enables the recipient to manufacture, sell, or otherwise control an invention for a period of 20 years from the date of the grant. A patent is nonrenewable. But the legal life of a patent may be extended by obtaining new patents for improvements or other changes in the basic design.

The initial cost of a patent is the cash or cash equivalent price paid to acquire the patent. The saying, "A patent is only as good as the money you're prepared to spend defending it" is very true. Many patents are subject to some type of litigation. For example, in 2003 **Intel** won a patent infringement suit against **Broadcom** in protecting its patent, receiving $60 million in cash. Legal costs an owner incurs in successfully defending a patent in an infringement suit are considered necessary to establish the validity of the patent. **They are added to the Patent account and amortized over the remaining life of the patent.**

The cost of a patent should be amortized over its 20-year legal life or its useful life, whichever is shorter. Obsolescence and inadequacy should be considered in determining useful life. These factors may cause a patent to become economically ineffective before the end of its legal life.

To illustrate the computation of patent expense, assume that National Labs purchases a patent at a cost of $60,000. If the useful life of the patent is 8 years, the annual amortization expense is $7,500 ($60,000 ÷ 8). The entry to record the annual amortization is:

Dec. 31	Amortization Expense—Patents	7,500	
	Patents		7,500
	(To record patent amortization)		

A	=	L	+	OE
−7,500				−7,500 Exp

Cash Flows
no effect

Amortization Expense—Patents is classified as an **operating expense** in the income statement.

Copyrights

Copyrights are grants from the federal government, giving the owner the exclusive right to reproduce and sell an artistic or published work. Copyrights extend for the life of the creator plus 70 years. The cost of a copyright is the **cost of acquiring and defending it**. The cost may be only the small fee paid to the U.S. Copyright Office. Or it may amount to a great deal more if a copyright infringement suit is involved.

The useful life of a copyright generally is significantly shorter than its legal life. Therefore, copyrights usually are amortized over a relatively short period of time.

Trademarks and Trade Names

A **trademark** or **trade name** is a word, phrase, jingle, or symbol that identifies a particular enterprise or product. Trade names like Wheaties, Game Boy, Sunkist, Kleenex, Windows, Coca-Cola, Big Mac, and Jeep create immediate product identification. They also generally enhance the sale of the product. The creator or original user may obtain exclusive legal right to the trademark or trade name by registering it with the U.S. Patent Office. Such registration provides 20 years' protection. The registration may be renewed indefinitely as long as the trademark or trade name is in use.

If the trademark or trade name is **purchased** by the company that will sell the product, its cost is the purchase price. If the trademark or trade name is **developed** by the company itself, the cost includes attorney's fees, registration fees, design costs, successful legal defense costs, and other expenditures directly related to securing it.

Because trademarks and trade names have indefinite lives, they are not amortized.

Domain names are a good example of a trade name. Buying domain names is a hot market these days. While the cost of registration is negligible, if a company has to purchase its name from a cybersquatter—people who register names in the hopes of reselling them for a profit—the cost can rise quickly.

When **eBay Inc.**, the world's largest online auction house, recently tried to register www.ebay.ca in Canada, it discovered that the name had been registered previously by an entrepreneur. eBay then had two options to consider. Since eBay is a registered trademark around the world, the company could take legal action, or it could negotiate to buy the name from the current registrant. In the meantime, eBay is using the domain name www.ebaycanada.ca, which had also been registered previously by a self-described "Internet entrepreneur." This entrepreneur said he hoped to make some quick money when he registered www.ebaycanada.ca last year. He eventually gave up the name without a fight rather than go to court and face huge legal bills.

Franchises and Licenses

When you drive down the street in your RAV4 purchased from a **Toyota** dealer, fill up your tank at the corner **Shell** station, eat lunch at **Taco Bell**, or rent a car from **Rent-A-Wreck**, you are dealing with franchises. A **franchise** is a contractual arrangement under which the franchisor grants the franchisee the right to sell certain products, provide specific services, or use certain trademarks or trade names. The franchise is usually restricted to a designated geographical area.

Another type of franchise is that entered into between a governmental body (commonly municipalities) and a business enterprise. This franchise permits the enterprise to use public property in performing its services. Examples are the use of city streets for a bus line or taxi service, use of public land for telephone and electric lines, and the use of airwaves for radio or TV broadcasting. Such operating rights are referred to as **licenses**.

When costs can be identified with the acquisition of a franchise or license, an intangible asset should be recognized. Franchises and licenses may be granted for a period of time, limited or indefinite. The cost of a limited-life franchise (or license) should be amortized over the useful life. If the life is indefinite, the cost is not amortized. Annual payments made under a franchise agreement are recorded as **operating expenses** in the period in which they are incurred.

Goodwill

Usually, the largest intangible asset that appears on a company's balance sheet is goodwill. **Goodwill** is the value of all favorable attributes that relate to a business enterprise. These include exceptional management, desirable location, good customer relations, skilled employees, high-quality products, and harmonious relations with labor unions. Some view goodwill as expected earnings in excess of normal earnings. Goodwill is therefore unusual: Unlike other assets such as investments and plant assets, which can be sold individually in the marketplace, goodwill can be identified only with the business as a whole.

If goodwill can be identified only with the business as a whole, how can it be determined? One could try to put a dollar value on the factors listed above (exceptional management, desirable location, and so on), but the results would be very subjective. Such subjective valuations would not contribute to the reliability of financial statements. **Therefore, goodwill is recorded only when there is a transaction that involves the purchase of an entire business. In that case, goodwill is the excess of cost over the fair market value of the net assets (assets less liabilities) acquired.**

In recording the purchase of a business, the net assets are debited at their fair market values, cash is credited for the purchase price, and goodwill is debited for the difference. **Goodwill is not amortized** (because it is considered to have an indefinite life), **but it must be written down if its value is determined to have declined** (been permanently impaired). Goodwill is reported in the balance sheet under intangible assets.

HELPFUL HINT

Goodwill is recorded only when it has been purchased along with tangible and identifiable intangible assets of a business.

Research and Development Costs

Research and development costs are expenditures that may lead to patents, copyrights, new processes, and new products. Many companies spend considerable sums of money on research and development (R&D). For example, in a recent year **IBM** spent over $5.2 billion on R&D.

Research and development costs present accounting problems. For one thing, it is sometimes difficult to assign the costs to specific projects. Also, there are uncertainties in identifying the extent and timing of future benefits. As a result, R&D costs are **usually recorded as an expense when incurred**, whether the research and development is successful or not.

To illustrate, assume that Laser Scanner Company spent $3 million on research and development. This expenditure resulted in the development of two highly successful patents obtained with $20,000 in lawyers' fees. The lawyers' fees would be added to the patent account. The R&D costs, however, cannot be included in the cost of the patent. Rather, they are recorded as an expense when incurred.

Many disagree with this accounting approach. They argue that expensing R&D costs leads to understated assets and net income. Others, however, argue that capitalizing these costs will lead to highly speculative assets on the balance sheet. It is difficult to determine who is right. The controversy illustrates how difficult it is to establish proper guidelines for financial reporting.

HELPFUL HINT

Research and development (R&D) costs are not intangible assets. But because they may lead to patents and copyrights, we discuss them in this section.

Statement Presentation and Analysis

Presentation

Usually plant assets and natural resources are combined under "Property, plant, and equipment" in the balance sheet. Intangibles are shown separately. The balances of the major classes of assets, such as land, buildings, and equipment, and accumulated depreciation by major classes or in total should be disclosed in the balance sheet or notes. In addition, the depreciation and amortization methods that were used should be described. Finally, the amount of depreciation and amortization expense for the period should be disclosed.

The financial statement presentation of property, plant, and equipment and intangibles by **The Procter & Gamble Company (P&G)** in its 2002 balance sheet is shown in Illustration 10-23 (on page 422).

STUDY OBJECTIVE 9

Indicate how plant assets, natural resources, and intangible assets are reported and analyzed.

Illustration 10-23
P&G's presentation of property, plant, and equipment, and intangible assets

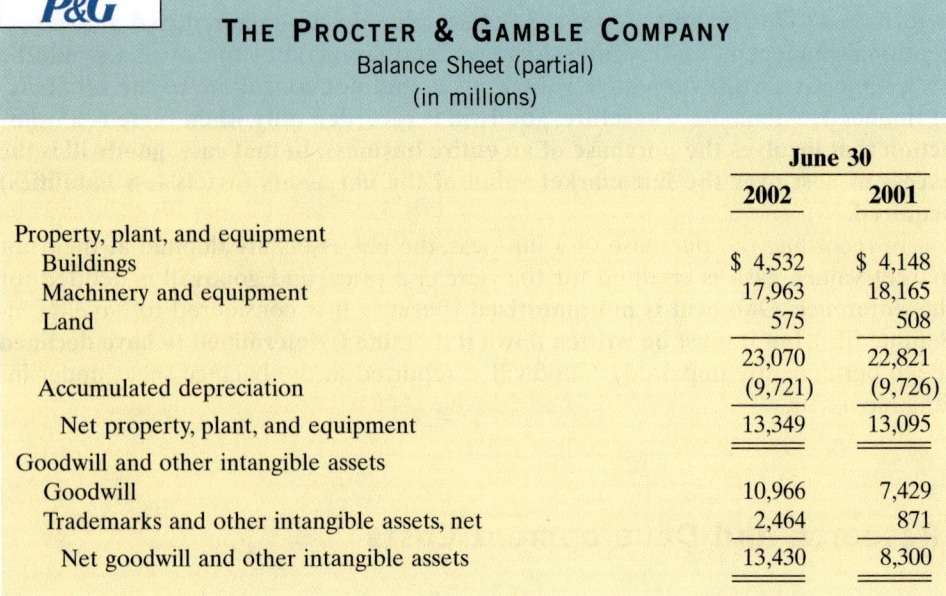

		June 30	
		2002	**2001**
Property, plant, and equipment			
Buildings		$ 4,532	$ 4,148
Machinery and equipment		17,963	18,165
Land		575	508
		23,070	22,821
Accumulated depreciation		(9,721)	(9,726)
Net property, plant, and equipment		13,349	13,095
Goodwill and other intangible assets			
Goodwill		10,966	7,429
Trademarks and other intangible assets, net		2,464	871
Net goodwill and other intangible assets		13,430	8,300

THE PROCTER & GAMBLE COMPANY
Balance Sheet (partial)
(in millions)

The notes to P&G's financial statements present greater details about the accounting for its long-term tangible and intangible assets.

Another comprehensive presentation of property, plant, and equipment, excerpted from the balance sheet of **Owens-Illinois**, is shown in Illustration 10-24.

Illustration 10-24
Owens-Illinois' presentation of property, plant, and equipment, and intangible assets

OWENS-ILLINOIS, INC.
Balance Sheet (partial)
(in millions)

Property, plant, and equipment			
Timberlands, at cost, less accumulated depletion		$ 95.4	
Buildings and equipment, at cost	$2,207.1		
Less: Accumulated depreciation	1,229.0	978.1	
Total property, plant, and equipment			$1,073.5
Intangibles			
Patents			410.0
Total			$1,483.5

The notes to the financial statements of Owens-Illinois identify the major classes of property, plant, and equipment. They also indicate that depreciation is by the straight-line method, depletion is by the units-of-activity method, and amortization is by the straight-line method.

Analysis

We can analyze how efficiently a company uses its assets to generate sales. The **asset turnover ratio** analyzes the productivity of a company's assets. It is computed by dividing net sales by average total assets for the period, as shown in the formula in Illustration 10-25. The computation is for **Proctor & Gamble Company**. Its net sales for 2002 were $40,238 million. Its total ending assets were $40,776 million, and beginning assets were $34,387 million.

Illustration 10-25
Asset turnover formula and computation

Net Sales	÷	Average Total Assets	=	Asset Turnover Ratio
$40,238	÷	$\dfrac{\$40,776 + \$34,387}{2}$	=	**1.07 times**

This ratio shows the dollars of sales produced for each dollar invested in average total assets. Each dollar invested in assets produced $1.07 in sales for P&G. If a company is using its assets efficiently, each dollar of assets will create a high amount of sales. This ratio varies greatly among different industries—from those that are asset intensive (utilities) to those that are not (services).

BEFORE YOU GO ON...

Review It

1. How is depletion expense computed?
2. What are the main differences between accounting for intangible assets and for plant assets?
3. Identify the major types of intangibles and the proper accounting for them.
4. Explain the accounting for research and development costs.
5. What ratio may be computed to analyze property, plant, and equipment?

 THE NAVIGATOR

DEMONSTRATION PROBLEM 1

DuPage Company purchases a factory machine at a cost of $18,000 on January 1, 2005. The machine is expected to have a salvage value of $2,000 at the end of its 4-year useful life.

During its useful life, the machine is expected to be used 160,000 hours. Actual annual hourly use was: 2005, 40,000; 2006, 60,000; 2007, 35,000; and 2008, 25,000.

Instructions

Prepare depreciation schedules for the following methods: (a) the straight-line, (b) units-of-activity, and (c) declining-balance using double the straight-line rate.

SOLUTION TO DEMONSTRATION PROBLEM 1

(a)

Straight-Line Method

	Computation				End of Year	
Year	Depreciable Cost	×	Depreciation Rate	= Annual Depreciation Expense	Accumulated Depreciation	Book Value
2005	$16,000		25%	$4,000	$ 4,000	$14,000*
2006	16,000		25%	4,000	8,000	10,000
2007	16,000		25%	4,000	12,000	6,000
2008	16,000		25%	4,000	16,000	2,000

*$18,000 − $4,000.

(b)

Units-of-Activity Method

| | Computation | | | End of Year | |
| | Units of Activity | × Depreciation Cost/Unit = | Annual Depreciation Expense | Accumulated Depreciation | Book Value |
Year					
2005	40,000	$0.10	$4,000	$ 4,000	$14,000
2006	60,000	0.10	6,000	10,000	8,000
2007	35,000	0.10	3,500	13,500	4,500
2008	25,000	0.10	2,500	16,000	2,000

(c)

Declining-Balance Method

| | Computation | | | End of Year | |
| | Book Value Beginning of Year | × Depreciation Rate = | Annual Depreciation Expense | Accumulated Depreciation | Book Value |
Year					
2005	$18,000	50%	$9,000	$ 9,000	$9,000
2006	9,000	50%	4,500	13,500	4,500
2007	4,500	50%	2,250	15,750	2,250
2008	2,250	50%	250*	16,000	2,000

*Adjusted to $250 because ending book value should not be less than expected salvage value.

✓ THE NAVIGATOR

DEMONSTRATION PROBLEM 2

On January 1, 2003, Skyline Limousine Co. purchased a limo at an acquisition cost of $28,000. The vehicle has been depreciated by the straight-line method using a 4-year service life and a $4,000 salvage value. The company's fiscal year ends on December 31.

Instructions

Prepare the journal entry or entries to record the disposal of the limousine assuming that it was:

(a) Retired and scrapped with no salvage value on January 1, 2007.
(b) Sold for $5,000 on July 1, 2006.

SOLUTION TO DEMONSTRATION PROBLEM 2

ACTION PLAN

- At the time of disposal, determine the book value of the asset.

- Recognize any gain or loss from disposal of the asset.

- Remove the book value of the asset from the records by debiting Accumulated Depreciation for the total depreciation to date of disposal and crediting the asset account for the cost of the asset.

(a)	1/1/07	Accumulated Depreciation—Limousine	24,000	
		Loss on Disposal	4,000	
		Limousine		28,000
		(To record retirement of limousine)		
(b)	7/1/06	Depreciation Expense	3,000	
		Accumulated Depreciation—Limousine		3,000
		(To record depreciation to date of disposal)		
		Cash	5,000	
		Accumulated Depreciation—Limousine	21,000	
		Loss on Disposal	2,000	
		Limousine		28,000
		(To record sale of limousine)		

✓ THE NAVIGATOR

SUMMARY OF STUDY OBJECTIVES

1. **Describe how the cost principle applies to plant assets.** The cost of plant assets includes all expenditures necessary to acquire the asset and make it ready for its intended use. Cost is measured by the cash or cash equivalent price paid.

2. **Explain the concept of depreciation.** Depreciation is the allocation of the cost of a plant asset to expense over its useful (service) life in a rational and systematic manner. Depreciation is not a process of valuation, nor is it a process that results in an accumulation of cash.

3. **Compute periodic depreciation using different methods.** There are three depreciation methods:

Method	Effect on Annual Depreciation	Formula
Straight-line	Constant amount	Depreciable cost ÷ Useful life (in years)
Units-of-activity	Varying amount	Depreciation cost per unit × Units of activity during the year
Declining-balance	Decreasing amount	Book value at beginning of year × Declining-balance rate

4. **Describe the procedure for revising periodic depreciation.** Revisions of periodic depreciation are made in present and future periods, not retroactively. The new annual depreciation is found by dividing the depreciable cost at the time of the revision by the remaining useful life.

5. **Distinguish between revenue and capital expenditures, and explain the entries for these expenditures.** Revenue expenditures are incurred to maintain the operating efficiency and expected productive life of the asset. These expenditures are debited to Repair Expense as incurred. Capital expenditures increase the operating efficiency, productive capacity, or expected useful life of the asset. These expenditures are generally debited to the plant asset affected.

6. **Explain how to account for the disposal of a plant asset.** The accounting for disposal of a plant asset through retirement or sale is as follows:
   (a) Eliminate the book value of the plant asset at the date of disposal.
   (b) Record cash proceeds, if any.
   (c) Account for the difference between the book value and the cash proceeds as a gain or loss on disposal.

7. **Compute periodic depletion of natural resources.** Compute depletion cost per unit by dividing the total cost of the natural resource minus salvage value by the number of units estimated to be in the resource. Then multiply the depletion cost per unit by the number of units extracted and sold.

8. **Explain the basic issues related to accounting for intangible assets.** The accounting for intangible assets and plant assets is much the same. One difference is that the term used to describe the write-off of an intangible asset is amortization, rather than depreciation. The straight-line method is normally used for amortizing intangible assets.

9. **Indicate how plant assets, natural resources, and intangible assets are reported and analyzed.** Usually plant assets and natural resources are combined under property, plant, and equipment; intangibles are shown separately under intangible assets. Either within the balance sheet or in the notes, the balances of the major classes of assets, such as land, buildings, and equipment, and accumulated depreciation by major classes or in total, should be disclosed. Also, the depreciation and amortization methods used should be described, and the amount of depreciation and amortization expense for the period should be disclosed. The asset turnover ratio measures the productivity of a company's assets in generating sales.

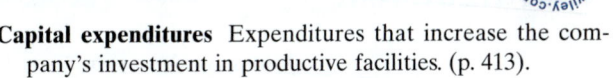

GLOSSARY

Accelerated-depreciation method Depreciation method that produces higher depreciation expense in the early years than in the later years. (p. 410).

Additions and improvements Costs incurred to increase the operating efficiency, productive capacity, or useful life of a plant asset. (p. 413).

Amortization The allocation of the cost of an intangible asset to expense over its useful life in a systematic and rational manner. (p. 418).

Asset turnover ratio A measure of how efficiently a company uses its assets to generate sales; calculated as net sales divided by average total assets. (p. 422).

Capital expenditures Expenditures that increase the company's investment in productive facilities. (p. 413).

Copyright Exclusive grant from the federal government that allows the owner to reproduce and sell an artistic or published work. (p. 419).

Declining-balance method Depreciation method that applies a constant rate to the declining book value of the asset and produces a decreasing annual depreciation expense over the useful life of the asset. (p. 409).

Depletion The allocation of the cost of a natural resource to expense in a rational and systematic manner over the resource's useful life. (p. 417).

Depreciable cost The cost of a plant asset less its salvage value. (p. 407).

Franchise (license) A contractual arrangement under which the franchisor grants the franchisee the right to sell certain products, provide specific services, or use certain trademarks or trade names, usually within a designated geographical area. (p. 420).

Goodwill The value of all favorable attributes that relate to a business enterprise. (p. 420).

Intangible assets Rights, privileges, and competitive advantages that result from the ownership of long-lived assets that do not possess physical substance. (p. 418).

Licenses Operating rights to use public property, granted to a business enterprise by a governmental agency. (p. 420).

Natural resources Assets that consist of standing timber and underground deposits of oil, gas, or minerals. (p. 416).

Ordinary repairs Expenditures to maintain the operating efficiency and productive life of the unit. (p. 413).

Patent An exclusive right issued by the U.S. Patent Office that enables the recipient to manufacture, sell, or otherwise control an invention for a period of 20 years from the date of the grant. (p. 419).

Plant assets Tangible resources that are used in the operations of the business and are not intended for sale to customers. (p. 401).

Research and development (R&D) costs Expenditures that may lead to patents, copyrights, new processes, or new products. (p. 421).

Revenue expenditures Expenditures that are immediately charged against revenues as an expense. (p. 413).

Salvage value An estimate of an asset's value at the end of its useful life. (p. 406).

Straight-line method Depreciation method in which periodic depreciation is the same for each year of the asset's useful life. (p. 407).

Trademark (trade name) A word, phrase, jingle, or symbol that identifies a particular enterprise or product. (p. 419).

Units-of-activity method Depreciation method in which useful life is expressed in terms of the total units of production or use expected from an asset. (p. 408).

Useful life An estimate of the expected productive life, also called service life, of an asset. (p. 406).

APPENDIX EXCHANGE OF PLANT ASSETS

STUDY OBJECTIVE 10

Explain how to account for the exchange of plant assets.

Plant assets may also be disposed of through exchange. Exchanges can be for either similar or dissimilar assets. Because exchanges of similar assets are more common, they are discussed here. An exchange of similar assets occurs, for example, when old office furniture is exchanged for new office furniture. In an exchange of similar assets, the new asset performs the **same function** as the old asset.

In exchanges of similar plant assets, it is necessary to determine two things: (1) the cost of the asset acquired, and (2) the gain or loss on the asset given up. Because a noncash asset is given up in the exchange, cost is the **cash equivalent price** paid. That is, cost is the fair market value of the asset given up plus the cash paid. The gain or loss on disposal is the **difference between the fair market value and the book value of the asset given up**. These determinations are explained and illustrated below.

Loss Treatment

A loss on the exchange of similar assets is recognized immediately. To illustrate, assume that Roland Company exchanged old office equipment for new office equipment. The book value of the old equipment is $26,000 (cost $70,000 less accumulated depreciation $44,000). Its fair market value is $10,000, and cash of $81,000 is paid. The cost of the new office equipment, $91,000, is computed as follows.

Illustration 10A-1
Computation of cost of new office equipment

Fair market value of old office equipment	$10,000
Cash	81,000
Cost of new office equipment	**$91,000**

A loss on disposal of $16,000 on this exchange is incurred. The reason is that the book value is greater than the fair market value of the asset given up. The computation is as follows.

Book value of old office equipment ($70,000 − $44,000)	$26,000
Fair market value of old office equipment	10,000
Loss on disposal	**$16,000**

Illustration 10A-2
Computation of loss on disposal

In recording an exchange at a loss, three steps are required: (1) Eliminate the book value of the asset given up, (2) record the cost of the asset acquired, and (3) recognize the loss on disposal. The entry for Roland Company is as follows.

Office Equipment (new)	91,000	
Accumulated Depreciation—Office Equipment (old)	44,000	
Loss on Disposal	16,000	
Office Equipment (old)		70,000
Cash		81,000
(To record exchange of old office equipment for similar new equipment)		

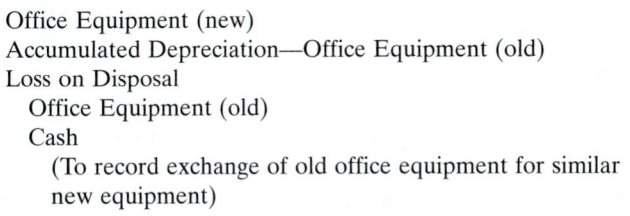

A =	L +	OE
+91,000		−16,000 Exp
+44,000		
−70,000		
−81,000		

Cash Flows
−81,000

Gain Treatment

A gain on the exchange of similar assets is not recognized immediately but, instead, is deferred. This is done by reducing the cost basis of the new asset. In determining the cost of the new asset, compute the **cost before deferral of the gain** and then the **cost after deferral of the gain**.

    To illustrate, assume that Mark's Express Delivery decides to exchange its old delivery equipment plus cash of $3,000 for new delivery equipment. The book value of the old delivery equipment is $12,000 (cost $40,000 less accumulated depreciation $28,000). The fair market value of the old delivery equipment is $19,000.

    The cost of the new asset (before deferral of the gain) is the **fair market value of the old asset exchanged plus any cash (or other consideration given up).** The cost of the new delivery equipment (before deferral of the gain) is $22,000, computed as follows.

Fair market value of old delivery equipment	$19,000
Cash	3,000
Cost of new delivery equipment (before deferral of gain)	**$22,000**

Illustration 10A-3
Cost of new equipment (before deferral of gain)

A gain results when the fair market value is greater than the book value of the asset given up. For Mark's Express, there is a gain of $7,000, computed as follows, on the disposal.

Fair market value of old delivery equipment	$19,000
Book value of old delivery equipment ($40,000 − $28,000)	12,000
Gain on disposal	**$7,000**

Illustration 10A-4
Computation of gain on disposal

The $7,000 gain on disposal is then offset against the $22,000 cost of the new delivery equipment. The result is a $15,000 cost of the new delivery equipment, after deferral of the gain, as shown in Illustration 10A-5.

Illustration 10A-5
Cost of new equipment (after deferral of gain)

Cost of new delivery equipment (before deferral of gain)	$22,000
Less: Gain on disposal	7,000
Cost of new delivery equipment (after deferral of gain)	**$15,000**

The entry to record the exchange is as follows.

A = L + OE
+15,000
+28,000
−40,000
−3,000

Cash Flows
−3,000

Delivery Equipment (new)	15,000	
Accumulated Depreciation—Delivery Equipment (old)	28,000	
Delivery Equipment (old)		40,000
Cash		3,000
(To record exchange of old delivery equipment for similar new delivery equipment)		

This entry does not eliminate the gain; it just postpones or defers it to future periods. The deferred gain of $7,000 reduces the $22,000 cost to $15,000. As a result, net income in future periods increases because depreciation expense on the newly acquired delivery equipment is less by $7,000.

Summarizing, the rules for accounting for exchanges of similar assets are as follows.

Illustration 10A-6
Accounting rules for plant asset exchanges

Type of Event	Recognition
Loss	Recognize immediately by debiting Loss on Disposal
Gain	Defer and reduce cost of new asset

SUMMARY OF STUDY OBJECTIVE FOR APPENDIX

10. Explain how to account for the exchange of plant assets. In accounting for exchanges of similar assets:
  (a) Eliminate the book value of the old asset at the date of the exchange.
  (b) Record the acquisition cost of the new asset.

  (c) Account for the loss or gain, if any, on the old asset:
    (1) If a loss, recognize it immediately.
    (2) If a gain, defer and reduce the cost of the new asset.

*__Note:__ All **asterisked** Questions, Exercises, and Problems relate to material in the appendix to the chapter.

SELF-STUDY QUESTIONS

Self-Study/Self-Test

Answers are at the end of the chapter.

(SO 1) **1.** Erin Danielle Company purchased equipment and incurred the following costs.

Cash price	$24,000
Sales taxes	1,200
Insurance during transit	200
Installation and testing	400
Total costs	$25,800

What amount should be recorded as the cost of the equipment?
  a. $24,000.
  b. $25,200.
  c. $25,400.
  d. $25,800.

2. Depreciation is a process of: (SO
  a. valuation.
  b. cost allocation.

c. cash accumulation.

d. appraisal.

(SO 3) **3.** Micah Bartlett Company purchased equipment on January 1, 2004, at a total invoice cost of $400,000. The equipment has an estimated salvage value of $10,000 and an estimated useful life of 5 years. The amount of accumulated depreciation at December 31, 2005, if the straight-line method of depreciation is used, is:

a. $80,000.

b. $160,000.

c. $78,000.

d. $156,000.

(SO 3) **4.** Ann Torbert purchased a truck for $11,000 on January 1, 2004. The truck will have an estimated salvage value of $1,000 at the end of 5 years. Using the units-of-activity method, the balance in accumulated depreciation at December 31, 2005, can be computed by the following formula:

a. ($11,000 ÷ Total estimated activity) × Units of activity for 2005.

b. ($10,000 ÷ Total estimated activity) × Units of activity for 2005.

c. ($11,000 ÷ Total estimated activity) × Units of activity for 2004 and 2005.

d. ($10,000 ÷ Total estimated activity) × Units of activity for 2004 and 2005.

(SO 4) **5.** When there is a change in estimated depreciation:

a. previous depreciation should be corrected.

b. current and future years' depreciation should be revised.

c. only future years' depreciation should be revised.

d. None of the above.

(SO 5) **6.** Additions to plant assets are:

a. revenue expenditures.

b. debited to a Repair Expense account.

c. debited to a Purchases account.

d. capital expenditures.

(SO 7) **7.** Maggie Sharrer Company expects to extract 20 million tons of coal from a mine that cost $12 million. If no salvage value is expected, and 2 million tons are mined and

sold in the first year, the entry to record depletion will include a:

a. debit to Accumulated Depletion of $2,000,000.

b. credit to Depletion Expense of $1,200,000.

c. debit to Depletion Expense of $1,200,000.

d. credit to Accumulated Depletion of $2,000,000.

(SO 8, 9) **8.** Martha Beyerlein Company incurred $150,000 of research and development costs in its laboratory to develop a patent granted on January 2, 2005. On July 31, 2005, Beyerlein paid $35,000 for legal fees in a successful defense of the patent. The total amount debited to Patents through July 31, 2005, should be:

a. $150,000.

b. $35,000.

c. $185,000.

d. some other amount.

(SO 9) **9.** Indicate which of the following statements is *true*.

a. Since intangible assets lack physical substance, they need be disclosed only in the notes to the financial statements.

b. Goodwill should be reported as a contra-account in the owner's equity section.

c. Totals of major classes of assets can be shown in the balance sheet, with asset details disclosed in the notes to the financial statements.

d. Intangible assets are typically combined with plant assets and natural resources and shown in the property, plant, and equipment section.

(SO 10) *****10.** Schopenhauer Company exchanged an old machine, with a book value of $39,000 and a fair market value of $35,000, and paid $10,000 cash for a similar new machine. At what amount should the machine acquired in the exchange be recorded on Schopenhauer's books?

a. $45,000.   **c.** $49,000.

b. $46,000.   **d.** $50,000.

(SO 10) *****11.** In exchanges of similar assets:

a. neither gains nor losses are recognized immediately.

b. gains, but not losses, are recognized immediately.

c. losses, but not gains, are recognized immediately.

d. both gains and losses are recognized immediately.

QUESTIONS

1. Rick Baden is uncertain about the applicability of the cost principle to plant assets. Explain the principle to Rick.

2. What are some examples of land improvements?

3. Hilo Company acquires the land and building owned by Corrs Company. What types of costs may be incurred to make the asset ready for its intended use if Hilo Company wants to use (a) only the land, and (b) both the land and the building?

4. In a recent newspaper release, the president of Wanzo Company asserted that something has to be done about

depreciation. The president said, "Depreciation does not come close to accumulating the cash needed to replace the asset at the end of its useful life." What is your response to the president?

5. Jeremy is studying for the next accounting examination. He asks your help on two questions: (a) What is salvage value? (b) Is salvage value used in determining periodic depreciation under each depreciation method? Answer Jeremy's questions.

6. Contrast the straight-line method and the units-of-activity method as to (a) useful life, and (b) the pattern of periodic depreciation over useful life.

7. Contrast the effects of the three depreciation methods on annual depreciation expense.

8. In the fourth year of an asset's 5-year useful life, the company decides that the asset will have a 6-year service life. How should the revision of depreciation be recorded? Why?

9. Distinguish between revenue expenditures and capital expenditures during useful life.

10. How is a gain or loss on the sale of a plant asset computed?

11. Garcia Corporation owns a machine that is fully depreciated but is still being used. How should Garcia account for this asset and report it in the financial statements?

12. What are natural resources, and what are their distinguishing characteristics?

13. Explain what depletion is and how it is computed.

14. What are the similarities and differences between the terms depreciation, depletion, and amortization?

15. Teresa Speck Company hires an accounting intern who says that intangible assets should always be amortized over their legal lives. Is the intern correct? Explain.

16. Goodwill has been defined as the value of all favorable attributes that relate to a business enterprise. What types of attributes could result in goodwill?

17. Jerry Sain, a business major, is working on a case problem for one of his classes. In the case problem, the company needs to raise cash to market a new product it developed. Sam Morris, an engineering major, takes one look at the company's balance sheet and says, "This company has an awful lot of goodwill. Why don't you recommend that they sell some of it to raise cash?" How should Jerry respond to Sam?

18. Under what conditions is goodwill recorded?

19. Often research and development costs provide companies with benefits that last a number of years. (For example, these costs can lead to the development of a patent that will increase the company's income for many years.) However, generally accepted accounting principles re-

quire that such costs be recorded as an expense when incurred. Why?

20. **McDonald's Corporation** reports total average assets of $19.0 billion and net sales of $12.4 billion. What is the company's asset turnover ratio?

21. Wanzo Corporation and Cheng Corporation operate in the same industry. Wanzo uses the straight-line method to account for depreciation; Cheng uses an accelerated method. Explain what complications might arise in trying to compare the results of these two companies.

22. Shuey Corporation uses straight-line depreciation for financial reporting purposes but an accelerated method for tax purposes. Is it acceptable to use different methods for the two purposes? What is Shuey's motivation for doing this?

23. You are comparing two companies in the same industry. You have determined that Lam Corp. depreciates its plant assets over a 40-year life, whereas Hoi Corp. depreciates its plant assets over a 20-year life. Discuss the implications this has for comparing the results of the two companies.

24. Zito Company is doing significant work to revitalize its warehouses. It is not sure whether it should capitalize these costs or expense them. What are the implications for current-year net income and future net income of expensing versus capitalizing these costs?

*25. When similar assets are exchanged, how is the gain or loss on disposal computed?

*26. Alpha Refrigeration Company trades in an old machine on a new model when the fair market value of the old machine is greater than its book value. Should Alpha recognize a gain on disposal? If the fair market value of the old machine is less than its book value, should Alpha recognize a loss on disposal?

*27. Riko Company experienced a gain on disposal when exchanging similar machines. In accordance with generally accepted accounting principles, the gain was not recognized. How will Riko's future financial statements be affected by not recognizing the gain?

BRIEF EXERCISES

Determine the cost of land.
(SO 1)

BE10-1 The following expenditures were incurred by Rosenberg Company in purchasing land: cash price $50,000, accrued taxes $3,000, attorneys' fees $2,500, real estate broker's commission $2,000, and clearing and grading $3,500. What is the cost of the land?

Determine the cost of a truck.
(SO 1)

BE10-2 Jawson Company incurs the following expenditures in purchasing a truck: cash price $25,000, accident insurance $2,000, sales taxes $1,500, motor vehicle license $100, and painting and lettering $400. What is the cost of the truck?

Compute straight-line depreciation.
(SO 3)

BE10-3 Weller Company acquires a delivery truck at a cost of $40,000. The truck is expected to have a salvage value of $6,000 at the end of its 4-year useful life. Compute annual depreciation for the first and second years using the straight-line method.

Compute depreciation and evaluate treatment.
(SO 3)

BE10-4 Pioneer Company purchased land and a building on January 1, 2005. Management's best estimate of the value of the land was $100,000 and of the building $200,000. But management told the accounting department to record the land at $180,000 and the building at $120,000. The building is being depreciated on a straight-line basis over 20 years with no salvage value. Why do you suppose management requested this accounting treatment? Is it ethical?

BE10-5 Depreciation information for Weller Company is given in BE10-3. Assuming the declining-balance depreciation rate is double the straight-line rate, compute annual depreciation for the first and second years under the declining-balance method.

Compute declining-balance depreciation.
(SO 3)

BE10-6 Yellow Taxi Service uses the units-of-activity method in computing depreciation on its taxicabs. Each cab is expected to be driven 150,000 miles. Taxi no. 10 cost $30,500 and is expected to have a salvage value of $500. Taxi no. 10 is driven 30,000 miles in year 1 and 20,000 miles in year 2. Compute the depreciation for each year.

Compute depreciation using the units-of-activity method.
(SO 3)

BE10-7 On January 1, 2005, the Vasquez Company ledger shows Equipment $32,000 and Accumulated Depreciation $9,000. The depreciation resulted from using the straight-line method with a useful life of 10 years and salvage value of $2,000. On this date, the company concludes that the equipment has a remaining useful life of only 4 years with the same salvage value. Compute the revised annual depreciation.

Compute revised depreciation.
(SO 4)

BE10-8 Prepare journal entries to record the following.

(a) Perez Company retires its delivery equipment, which cost $41,000. Accumulated depreciation is also $41,000 on this delivery equipment. No salvage value is received.

(b) Assume the same information as (a), except that accumulated depreciation for Perez Company is $37,000, instead of $41,000.

Prepare entries for disposal by retirement.
(SO 6)

BE10-9 Tong Company sells office equipment on September 30, 2005, for $20,000 cash. The office equipment originally cost $72,000 and as of January 1, 2005, had accumulated depreciation of $42,000. Depreciation for the first 9 months of 2005 is $4,500. Prepare the journal entries to **(a)** update depreciation to September 30, 2005, and **(b)** record the sale of the equipment.

Prepare entries for disposal by sale.
(SO 6)

BE10-10 Arma Mining Co. purchased for $7 million a mine that is estimated to have 28 million tons of ore and no salvage value. In the first year, 6 million tons of ore are extracted and sold.

(a) Prepare the journal entry to record depletion expense for the first year.
(b) Show how this mine is reported on the balance sheet at the end of the first year.

Prepare depletion expense entry and balance sheet presentation for natural resources.
(SO 7)

BE10-11 Felipe Company purchases a patent for $150,000 on January 2, 2005. Its estimated useful life is 10 years.

(a) Prepare the journal entry to record patent expense for the first year.
(b) Show how this patent is reported on the balance sheet at the end of the first year.

Prepare patent expense entry and balance sheet presentation for intangibles.
(SO 8)

BE10-12 Information related to plant assets, natural resources, and intangibles at the end of 2005 for Lumas Company is as follows: buildings $1,100,000; accumulated depreciation—buildings $650,000; goodwill $410,000; coal mine $300,000; accumulated depletion—coal mine $108,000. Prepare a partial balance sheet of Lumas Company for these items.

Classify long-lived assets on balance sheet.
(SO 9)

BE10-13 In its 2002 annual report **McDonald's Corporation** reported beginning total assets of $22.5 billion; ending total assets of $24.0 billion; property, plant, and equipment (at cost) of $26.2 billion; and net sales of $15.4 billion. Compute McDonald's asset turnover ratio.

Analyze long-lived assets.
(SO 9)

*BE10-14 Cordero Company exchanges old delivery equipment for similar new delivery equipment. The book value of the old delivery equipment is $31,000 (cost $61,000 less accumulated depreciation $30,000). Its fair market value is $19,000, and cash of $3,000 is paid. Prepare the entry to record the exchange.

Prepare entry for disposal by exchange.
(SO 10)

*BE10-15 Assume the same information as BE10-14, except that the fair market value of the old delivery equipment is $38,000. Prepare the entry to record the exchange.

Prepare entry for disposal by exchange.
(SO 10)

EXERCISES

E10-1 The following expenditures relating to plant assets were made by Devereaux Company during the first 2 months of 2005.

Determine cost of plant acquisitions.
(SO 1)

1. Paid $5,000 of accrued taxes at time plant site was acquired.
2. Paid $200 insurance to cover possible accident loss on new factory machinery while the machinery was in transit.

3. Paid $850 sales taxes on new delivery truck.
4. Paid $17,500 for parking lots and driveways on new plant site.
5. Paid $250 to have company name and advertising slogan painted on new delivery truck.
6. Paid $8,000 for installation of new factory machinery.
7. Paid $900 for one-year accident insurance policy on new delivery truck.
8. Paid $75 motor vehicle license fee on the new truck.

Instructions
(a) Explain the application of the cost principle in determining the acquisition cost of plant assets.
(b) List the numbers of the foregoing transactions, and opposite each indicate the account title to which each expenditure should be debited.

Determine acquisition costs on land.
(SO 1)

E10-2 On March 1, 2005, Tanger Company acquired real estate on which it planned to construct a small office building. The company paid $90,000 in cash. An old warehouse on the property was razed at a cost of $6,600; the salvaged materials were sold for $1,700. Additional expenditures before construction began included $1,100 attorney's fee for work concerning the land purchase, $5,000 real estate broker's fee, $7,800 architect's fee, and $14,000 to put in driveways and a parking lot.

Instructions
(a) Determine the amount to be reported as the cost of the land.
(b) For each cost not used in part (a), indicate the account to be debited.

Compute depreciation under units-of-activity method.
(SO 3)

E10-3 Wheeler Bus Lines uses the units-of-activity method in depreciating its buses. One bus was purchased on January 1, 2005, at a cost of $148,000. Over its 4-year useful life, the bus is expected to be driven 100,000 miles. Salvage value is expected to be $8,000.

Instructions
(a) Compute the depreciation cost per unit.
(b) Prepare a depreciation schedule assuming actual mileage was: 2005, 26,000; 2006, 32,000; 2007, 25,000; and 2008, 17,000.

Determine depreciation for partial periods.
(SO 3)

E10-4 Solo Company purchased a new machine on October 1, 2005, at a cost of $96,000. The company estimated that the machine will have a salvage value of $12,000. The machine is expected to be used for 10,000 working hours during its 5-year life.

Instructions
Compute the depreciation expense under the following methods for the year indicated.
(a) Straight-line for 2005.
(b) Units-of-activity for 2005, assuming machine usage was 1,700 hours.
(c) Declining-balance using double the straight-line rate for 2005 and 2006.

Compute revised annual depreciation.
(SO 4)

E10-5 Steve Grant, the new controller of Greenberg Company, has reviewed the expected useful lives and salvage values of selected depreciable assets at the beginning of 2005. His findings are as follows.

Type of Asset	Date Acquired	Cost	Accumulated Depreciation 1/1/05	Useful Life in Years		Salvage Value	
				Old	Proposed	Old	Proposed
Building	1/1/97	$800,000	$152,000	40	50	$40,000	$18,000
Warehouse	1/1/00	100,000	19,000	25	20	5,000	3,600

All assets are depreciated by the straight-line method. Greenberg Company uses a calendar year in preparing annual financial statements. After discussion, management has agreed to accept Steve's proposed changes.

Instructions
(a) Compute the revised annual depreciation on each asset in 2005. (Show computations.)
(b) Prepare the entry (or entries) to record depreciation on the building in 2005.

Journalize entries for disposal of plant assets.
(SO 6)

E10-6 Presented below are selected transactions at Thomas Company for 2005.

Jan. 1   Retired a piece of machinery that was purchased on January 1, 1995. The machine cost $62,000 on that date. It had a useful life of 10 years with no salvage value.

June 30   Sold a computer that was purchased on January 1, 2002. The computer cost $35,000. It had a useful life of 5 years with no salvage value. The computer was sold for $12,000.

Dec. 31   Discarded a delivery truck that was purchased on January 1, 2001. The truck cost $33,000. It was depreciated based on a 6-year useful life with a $3,000 salvage value.

Instructions
Journalize all entries required on the above dates, including entries to update depreciation, where applicable, on assets disposed of. Thomas Company uses straight-line depreciation. (Assume depreciation is up to date as of December 31, 2004.)

E10-7   On July 1, 2005, Sutton Inc. invested $480,000 in a mine estimated to have 800,000 tons of ore of uniform grade. During the last 6 months of 2005, 100,000 tons of ore were mined and sold.

Journalize entries for natural resources depletion.
(SO 7)

Instructions
(a) Prepare the journal entry to record depletion expense.
(b) Assume that the 100,000 tons of ore were mined, but only 80,000 units were sold. How are the costs applicable to the 20,000 unsold units reported?

E10-8   The following are selected 2005 transactions of Yosuke Corporation.

Prepare adjusting entries for amortization.
(SO 8)

Jan. 1   Purchased a small company and recorded goodwill of $150,000. Its useful life is indefinite.
May 1   Purchased for $60,000 a patent with an estimated useful life of 5 years and a legal life of 20 years.

Instructions
Prepare necessary adjusting entries at December 31 to record amortization required by the events above.

E10-9   Ziegler Company, organized in 2005, has the following transactions related to intangible assets.

Prepare entries to set up appropriate accounts for different intangibles; amortize intangible assets.
(SO 8)

1/2/05	Purchased patent (7-year life)	$420,000
4/1/05	Goodwill purchased (indefinite life)	360,000
7/1/05	10-year franchise; expiration date 7/1/2015	480,000
9/1/05	Research and development costs	185,000

Instructions
Prepare the necessary entries to record these intangibles. All costs incurred were for cash. Make the adjusting entries as of December 31, 2005, recording any necessary amortization and reflecting all balances accurately as of that date.

E10-10   During 2004 Otaki Corporation reported net sales of $4,200,000 and net income of $1,500,000. Its balance sheet reported total assets of $1,400,000.

Calculate asset turnover ratio.
(SO 9)

Instructions
Calculate the asset turnover ratio.

*E10-11   Presented below are two independent transactions.

Journalize entries for exchange of similar assets.
(SO 10)

1. Global Co. exchanged old trucks (cost $64,000 less $22,000 accumulated depreciation) plus cash of $17,000 for new trucks. The old trucks had a fair market value of $38,000.
2. Rijo Inc. trades its used machine (cost $12,000 less $4,000 accumulated depreciation) for a new machine. In addition to exchanging the old machine (which had a fair market value of $9,000), Rijo also paid cash of $2,000.

Instructions
(a) Prepare the entry to record the exchange of similar assets by Global Co.
(b) Prepare the entry to record the exchange of similar assets by Rijo Inc.

*E10-12   Astro Company exchanges similar equipment with Logan Company. Also Jay Company exchanges similar equipment with Moon Company. The following information pertains to these two exchanges.

Journalize entries for the exchange of similar plant assets.
(SO 10)

	Astro Co.	**Jay Co.**
Equipment (cost)	$28,000	$22,000
Accumulated depreciation	21,000	5,000
Fair market value of equipment	12,000	15,000
Cash paid	3,000	–0–
Cash received		3,000

Instructions
Prepare the journal entries to record the exchange on the books of Astro Company and Jay Company.

*E10-13 Brown's Delivery Company and Roether's Express Delivery exchanged similar delivery trucks on January 1, 2005. Brown's truck cost $22,000. It has accumulated depreciation of $13,000 and a fair market value of $4,000. Roether's truck cost $10,000. It has accumulated depreciation of $7,000 and a fair market value of $4,000.

Instructions
(a) Journalize the exchange for Brown's Delivery Company.
(b) Journalize the exchange for Roether's Express Delivery.

PROBLEMS: SET A

P10-1A Ripley Company was organized on January 1. During the first year of operations, the following plant asset expenditures and receipts were recorded in random order.

Debits

1. Accrued real estate taxes paid at time of purchase of real estate	$ 2,000
2. Real estate taxes on land paid for the current year	3,000
3. Full payment to building contractor	600,000
4. Excavation costs for new building	25,000
5. Cost of real estate purchased as a plant site (land $100,000 and building $25,000)	125,000
6. Cost of parking lots and driveways	15,000
7. Architect's fees on building plans	10,000
8. Installation cost of fences around property	4,000
9. Cost of demolishing building to make land suitable for construction of new building	21,000
	$805,000

Credit

10. Proceeds from salvage of demolished building	$ 2,500

Instructions
Analyze the foregoing tranactions using the following column headings. Insert the number of each transaction in the Item space, and insert the amounts in the appropriate columns. For amounts entered in the Other Accounts column, also indicate the account title.

Item	Land	Building	Other Accounts

P10-2A In recent years, Hrubeck Company purchased three machines. Because of heavy turnover in the accounting department, a different accountant was in charge of selecting the depreciation method for each machine, and various methods were selected. Information concerning the machines is summarized below.

Machine	Acquired	Cost	Salvage Value	Useful Life in Years	Depreciation Method
1	1/1/02	$76,000	$ 6,000	10	Straight-line
2	1/1/03	80,000	10,000	8	Declining-balance
3	11/1/05	78,000	6,000	6	Units-of-activity

For the declining-balance method, the company uses the double-declining rate. For the units-of-activity method, total machine hours are expected to be 24,000. Actual hours of use in the first 3 years were: 2005, 1,000; 2006, 4,500; and 2007, 5,000.

Instructions
(a) Compute the amount of accumulated depreciation on each machine at December 31, 2005.
(b) If machine 2 had been purchased on April 1 instead of January 1, what would be the depreciation expense for this machine in (1) 2003 and (2) 2004?

P10-3A On January 1, 2005, Solomon Company purchased the following two machines for use in its production process.

Compute depreciation under different methods.

(SO 3)

Machine A: The cash price of this machine was $38,500. Related expenditures included: sales tax $2,200, shipping costs $175, insurance during shipping $75, installation and testing costs $50, and $90 of oil and lubricants to be used with the machinery during its first year of operation. Solomon estimates that the useful life of the machine is 4 years with a $5,000 salvage value remaining at the end of that time period.

Machine B: The recorded cost of this machine was $100,000. Solomon estimates that the useful life of the machine is 4 years with a $8,000 salvage value remaining at the end of that time period.

Instructions

(a) Prepare the following for Machine A.

(1) The journal entry to record its purchase on January 1, 2005.

(2) The journal entry to record annual depreciation at December 31, 2005, assuming the straight-line method of depreciation is used.

(a) (2) $9,000

(b) Calculate the amount of depreciation expense that Solomon should record for machine B each year of its useful life under the following assumption.

(1) Solomon uses the straight-line method of depreciation.

(2) Solomon uses the declining-balance method. The rate used is twice the straight-line rate.

(3) Solomon uses the units-of-activity method and estimates the useful life of the machine is 25,000 units. Actual usage is as follows: 2005, 6,500 units; 2006, 7,500 units; 2007, 6,000 units; 2008, 5,000 units.

(c) Which method used to calculate depreciation on machine B reports the lowest amount of depreciation expense in year 1 (2005)? The lowest amount in year 4 (2008)? The lowest total amount over the 4-year period?

P10-4A At the beginning of 2003, Bellamy Company acquired equipment costing $60,000. It was estimated that this equipment would have a useful life of 6 years and a residual value of $6,000 at that time. The straight-line method of depreciation was considered the most appropriate to use with this type of equipment. Depreciation is to be recorded at the end of each year.

Calculate revisions to depreciation expense.

(SO 3, 4)

During 2005 (the third year of the equipment's life), the company's engineers reconsidered their expectations, and estimated that the equipment's useful life would probably be 7 years (in total) instead of 6 years. The estimated residual value was not changed at that time. However, during 2008 the estimated residual value was reduced to $3,000.

Instructions

Indicate how much depreciation expense should be recorded for this equipment each year by completing the following table.

Year	Depreciation Expense	Accumulated Depreciation
2003		
2004		
2005		
2006		
2007		
2008		
2009		

2009 depreciation expense, $8,700

P10-5A At December 31, 2005, Walton Company reported the following as plant assets.

Journalize a series of equipment transactions related to purchase, sale, retirement, and depreciation.

(SO 6, 9)

Land		$ 3,000,000
Buildings	$26,500,000	
Less: Accumulated depreciation—buildings	12,100,000	14,400,000
Equipment	40,000,000	
Less: Accumulated depreciation—equipment	5,000,000	35,000,000
Total plant assets		$52,400,000

During 2006, the following selected cash transactions occurred.

April 1 Purchased land for $2,200,000.

May 1 Sold equipment that cost $750,000 when purchased on January 1, 2002. The equipment was sold for $460,000.

June 1   Sold land purchased on June 1, 1996, for $1,800,000. The land cost $300,000.
July 1   Purchased equipment for $2,400,000.
Dec. 31   Retired equipment that cost $500,000 when purchased on December 31, 1996. No salvage value was received.

Instructions

(a) Journalize the above transactions. Walton uses straight-line depreciation for buildings and equipment. The buildings are estimated to have a 50-year useful life and no salvage value. The equipment is estimated to have a 10-year useful life and no salvage value. Update depreciation on assets disposed of at the time of sale or retirement.
(b) Record adjusting entries for depreciation for 2006.
(c) Prepare the plant assets section of Walton's balance sheet at December 31, 2006.

Record disposals.

(SO 6)

P10-6A Yount Co. has delivery equipment that cost $50,000 and that has been depreciated $22,000. Record the disposal under the following assumptions.
(a) It was scrapped as having no value.
(b) It was sold for $31,000.
(c) It was sold for $18,000.

Prepare entries to record transactions related to acquisition and amortization of intangibles; prepare the intangible assets section.

(SO 8, 9)

P10-7A The intangible assets section of Glover Company at December 31, 2005, is presented below.

Patent ($60,000 cost less $6,000 amortization)	$54,000
Copyright ($36,000 cost less $14,400 amortization)	21,600
Total	$75,600

The patent was acquired in January 2005 and has a useful life of 10 years. The copyright was acquired in January 2002 and also has a useful life of 10 years. The following cash transactions may have affected intangible assets during 2006.

Jan. 2   Paid $36,000 legal costs to successfully defend the patent against infringement by another company.
Jan.–June   Developed a new product, incurring $140,000 in research and development costs. A patent was granted for the product on July 1. Its useful life is equal to its legal life.
Sept. 1   Paid $75,000 to a quarterback to appear in commercials advertising the company's products. The commercials will air in September and October.
Oct. 1   Acquired a copyright for $80,000. The copyright has a useful life of 50 years.

Instructions

(a) Prepare journal entries to record the transactions above.
(b) Prepare journal entries to record the 2006 amortization expense for intangible assets.
(c) Prepare the intangible assets section of the balance sheet at December 31, 2006.
(d) Prepare the note to the financials on Glover's intangibles as of December 31, 2006.

Prepare entries to correct errors made in recording and amortizing intangible assets.

(SO 8)

P10-8A Due to rapid turnover in the accounting department, a number of transactions involving intangible assets were improperly recorded by Buek Company in 2005.

1. Buek developed a new manufacturing process, incurring research and development costs of $95,000. The company also purchased a patent for $27,000. In early January, Buek capitalized $122,000 as the cost of the patents. Patent amortization expense of $6,100 was recorded based on a 20-year useful life.
2. On July 1, 2005, Buek purchased a small company and as a result acquired goodwill of $80,000. Buek recorded a half-year's amortization in 2002, based on a 50-year life ($800 amortization). The goodwill has an indefinite life.

Instructions

Prepare all journal entries necessary to correct any errors made during 2005. Assume the books have not yet been closed for 2005.

Calculate and comment on asset turnover ratio.

(SO 9)

P10-9A Dirks Corporation and Hewes Corporation, two corporations of roughly the same size, are both involved in the manufacture of canoes and sea kayaks. Each company depreciates its plant assets using the straight-line approach. An investigation of their financial statements reveals the following information.

	Dirks Corp.	**Hewes Corp.**
Net income	$ 400,000	$ 450,000
Sales	1,200,000	1,140,000
Total assets	2,000,000	1,500,000
Plant assets	1,500,000	800,000

Instructions

(a) For each company, calculate (1) the asset turnover ratio and (2) the return on assets ratio.

(b) ▭▭▭▭▷ Based on your calculations in part (a), comment on the relative effectiveness of the two companies in using their assets to generate sales and produce net income.

(a) (1) Dirks Corp. .60 times

PROBLEMS: SET B

P10-1B Foxx Company was organized on January 1. During the first year of operations, the following plant asset expenditures and receipts were recorded in random order.

Determine acquisition costs of land and building.

(SO 1)

Debits

1. Cost of filling and grading the land	$ 4,000
2. Full payment to building contractor	700,000
3. Real estate taxes on land paid for the current year	5,000
4. Cost of real estate purchased as a plant site (land $100,000 and building $45,000)	145,000
5. Excavation costs for new building	30,000
6. Architect's fees on building plans	10,000
7. Accrued real estate taxes paid at time of purchase of real estate	2,000
8. Cost of parking lots and driveways	14,000
9. Cost of demolishing building to make land suitable for construction of new building	20,000
	$930,000

Credits

10. Proceeds from salvage of demolished building	$ 3,500

Instructions

Analyze the foregoing transactions using the following column headings. Insert the number of each transaction in the Item space, and insert the amounts in the appropriate columns. For amounts entered in the Other Accounts column, also indicate the account titles.

Totals

Land $167,500

Building $740,000

Item	**Land**	**Building**	**Other Accounts**

P10-2B In recent years, Freeman Transportation purchased three used buses. Because of frequent turnover in the accounting department, a different accountant selected the depreciation method for each bus, and various methods were selected. Information concerning the buses is summarized below.

Compute depreciation under different methods.

(SO 3)

Bus	Acquired	Cost	Salvage Value	Useful Life in Years	Depreciation Method
1	1/1/03	$ 96,000	$ 6,000	5	Straight-line
2	1/1/03	140,000	10,000	4	Declining-balance
3	1/1/04	92,000	8,000	5	Units-of-activity

For the declining-balance method, the company uses the double-declining rate. For the units-of-activity method, total miles are expected to be 120,000. Actual miles of use in the first 3 years were: 2004, 24,000; 2005, 34,000; and 2006, 30,000.

Instructions

(a) Compute the amount of accumulated depreciation on each bus at December 31, 2005.

(b) If bus no. 2 was purchased on April 1 instead of January 1, what is the depreciation expense for this bus in (1) 2003 and (2) 2004?

*Compute depreciation under
different methods.*

(SO 3)

P10-3B On January 1, 2005, Thao Company purchased the following two machines for use in its production process.

Machine A: The cash price of this machine was $35,000. Related expenditures included: sales tax $1,700, shipping costs $150, insurance during shipping $80, installation and testing costs $70, and $100 of oil and lubricants to be used with the machinery during its first year of operations. Thao estimates that the useful life of the machine is 5 years with a $5,000 salvage value remaining at the end of that time period. Assume that the straight-line method of depreciation is used.

Machine B: The recorded cost of this machine was $80,000. Thao estimates that the useful life of the machine is 4 years with a $5,000 salvage value remaining at the end of that time period.

Instructions

(a) Prepare the following for Machine A.
   (1) The journal entry to record its purchase on January 1, 2005.
   (2) The journal entry to record annual depreciation at December 31, 2005.

*(b) (2) 2005 DDB
depreciation $40,000*

(b) Calculate the amount of depreciation expense that should record for machine B each year of its useful life under the following assumptions.
   (1) Thao uses the straight-line method of depreciation.
   (2) Thao uses the declining-balance method. The rate used is twice the straight-line rate.
   (3) Thao uses the units-of-activity method and estimates that the useful life of the machine is 125,000 units. Actual usage is as follows: 2005, 45,000 units; 2006, 35,000 units; 2007, 25,000 units; 2008, 20,000 units.

(c) Which method used to calculate depreciation on machine B reports the highest amount of depreciation expense in year 1 (2005)? The highest amount in year 4 (2008)? The highest total amount over the 4-year period?

*Calculate revisions to
depreciation expense.*

(SO 3, 4)

P10-4B At the beginning of 2003, Murphy Company acquired equipment costing $80,000. It was estimated that this equipment would have a useful life of 6 years and a residual value of $8,000 at that time. The straight-line method of depreciation was considered the most appropriate to use with this type of equipment. Depreciation is to be recorded at the end of each year.

During 2005 (the third year of the equipment's life), the company's engineers reconsidered their expectations, and estimated that the equipment's useful life would probably be 7 years (in total) instead of 6 years. The estimated residual value was not changed at that time. However, during 2008 the estimated residual value was reduced to $4,400.

Instructions

Indicate how much depreciation expense should be recorded each year for this equipment, by completing the following table.

Year	Depreciation Expense	Accumulated Depreciation
2003		
2004		
2005		
2006		
2007		
2008		
2009		

*2009 depreciation expense,
$11,400*

*Journalize a series of
equipment transactions related
to purchase, sale, retirement,
and depreciation.*

(SO 6, 9)

P10-5B At December 31, 2005, Angelos Company reported the following as plant assets.

Land		$ 4,000,000
Buildings	$28,500,000	
Less: Accumulated depreciation—buildings	12,100,000	16,400,000
Equipment	48,000,000	
Less: Accumulated depreciation—equipment	5,000,000	43,000,000
Total plant assets		$63,400,000

During 2006, the following selected cash transactions occurred.

April 1   Purchased land for $2,130,000.
May 1   Sold equipment that cost $720,000 when purchased on January 1, 2002. The equipment was sold for $430,000.
June 1   Sold land purchased on June 1, 1996, for $1,500,000. The land cost $200,000.
July 1   Purchased equipment for $3,000,000.
Dec. 31   Retired equipment that cost $500,000 when purchased on December 31, 1996. No salvage value was received.

Instructions
(a) Journalize the above transactions. The company uses straight-line depreciation for buildings and equipment. The buildings are estimated to have a 50-year life and no salvage value. The equipment is estimated to have a 10-year useful life and no salvage value. Update depreciation on assets disposed of at the time of sale or retirement.
(b) Record adjusting entries for depreciation for 2006.
(c) Prepare the plant assets section of Angelos' balance sheet at December 31, 2006.

(b) Depreciation Expense—building $570,000; equipment $4,828,000
(c) Total plant assets $62,450,000

P10-6B Spencer Co. has office furniture that cost $80,000 and that has been depreciated $50,000. Record the disposal under the following assumptions.
(a) It was scrapped as having no value.
(b) It was sold for $21,000.
(c) It was sold for $61,000.

Record disposals.
(SO 6)

P10-7B The intangible assets section of Whitley Company at December 31, 2005, is presented below.

Patent ($70,000 cost less $7,000 amortization)	$63,000
Franchise ($48,000 cost less $19,200 amortization)	28,800
Total	$91,800

Prepare entries to record transactions related to acquisition and amortization of intangibles; prepare the intangible assets section.
(SO 8, 9)

The patent was acquired in January 2005 and has a useful life of 10 years. The franchise was acquired in January 2002 and also has a useful life of 10 years. The following cash transactions may have affected intangible assets during 2006.

Jan. 2   Paid $18,000 legal costs to successfully defend the patent against infringement by another company.
Jan.–June   Developed a new product, incurring $140,000 in research and development costs. A patent was granted for the product on July 1. Its useful life is equal to its legal life.
Sept. 1   Paid $50,000 to an extremely large defensive lineman to appear in commercials advertising the company's products. The commercials will air in September and October.
Oct. 1   Acquired a franchise for $80,000. The franchise has a useful life of 50 years.

Instructions
(a) Prepare journal entries to record the transactions above.
(b) Prepare journal entries to record the 2006 amortization expense.
(c) Prepare the intangible assets section of the balance sheet at December 31, 2006.

(b) Amortization Expense—Patents $9,000
Amortization Expense—Franchise $5,200
(c) Total intangible assets $175,600

P10-8B Due to rapid turnover in the accounting department, a number of transactions involving intangible assets were improperly recorded by the Goslin Company in 2005.
1. Goslin developed a new manufacturing process, incurring research and development costs of $136,000. The company also purchased a patent for $48,000. In early January, Goslin capitalized $184,000 as the cost of the patents. Patent amortization expense of $9,200 was recorded based on a 20-year useful life.
2. On July 1, 2005, Goslin purchased a small company and as a result acquired goodwill of $92,000. Goslin recorded a half-year's amortization in 2005, based on a 50-year life ($920 amortization). The goodwill has an indefinite life.

Prepare entries to correct for errors made in recording and amortizing intangible assets.
(SO 8)

Instructions
Prepare all journal entries necessary to correct any errors made during 2005. Assume the books have not yet been closed for 2005.

1. R&D Exp. $136,000

Calculate and comment on asset turnover ratio.
(SO 9)

P10-9B Nina Company and Vernon Corporation, two corporations of roughly the same size, are both involved in the manufacture of in-line skates. Each company depreciates its plant assets using the straight-line approach. An investigation of their financial statements reveals the following information.

	Nina Co.	Vernon Corp.
Net income	$750,000	$1,000,000
Sales	1,200,000	1,100,000
Total assets	2,500,000	2,000,000
Plant assets	1,800,000	1,000,000

Instructions

(a) For each company, calculate (1) the asset turnover ratio and (2) the return on assets ratio.

(b) ▭▬▭▭▬▶ Based on your calculations in part (a), comment on the relative effectiveness of the two companies in using their assets to generate sales and produce net income.

COMPREHENSIVE PROBLEM: CHAPTERS 3 TO 10

Squarepants Corporation's trial balance at December 31, 2004, is presented below. All 2004 transactions have been recorded except for the items described on page 441.

	Debit	Credit
Cash	$ 28,000	
Accounts Receivable	36,800	
Notes Receivable	10,000	
Interest Receivable	–0–	
Merchandise Inventory	36,200	
Prepaid Insurance	3,600	
Land	20,000	
Building	150,000	
Equipment	60,000	
Patent	9,000	
Allowance for Doubtful Accounts		$ 500
Accumulated Depreciation—Building		50,000
Accumulated Depreciation—Equipment		24,000
Accounts Payable		27,300
Salaries Payable		–0–
Unearned Rent		6,000
Notes Payable (short-term)		11,000
Interest Payable		–0–
Notes Payable (long-term)		35,000
Common Stock		50,000
Retained Earnings		63,600
Dividends	12,000	
Sales		900,000
Interest Revenue		–0–
Rent Revenue		–0–
Gain on Disposal		–0–
Bad Debts Expense	–0–	
Cost of Goods Sold	630,000	
Depreciation Expense—Buildings	–0–	
Depreciation Expense—Equipment	–0–	
Insurance Expense	–0–	
Interest Expense	–0–	
Other Operating Expenses	61,800	
Amortization Expense—Patents	–0–	
Salaries Expense	110,000	
Total	$1,167,400	$1,167,400

Unrecorded transactions

1. On May 1, 2004, Squarepants purchased equipment for $12,000 plus sales taxes of $600 (all paid in cash).
2. On July 1, 2004, Squarepants sold for $3,500 equipment which originally cost $5,000. Accumulated depreciation on this equipment at January 1, 2004, was $1,800; 2004 depreciation prior to the sale of equipment was $450.
3. On December 31, 2004, Squarepants sold for $3,000 on account inventory that cost $2,100.
4. Squarepants estimates that uncollectible accounts receivable at year-end is $4,000.
5. The note receivable is a one-year, 12% note dated April 1, 2004. No interest has been recorded.
6. The balance in prepaid insurance represents payment of a $3,600 6-month premium on September 1, 2004.
7. The building is being depreciated using the straight-line method over 30 years. The salvage value is $30,000.
8. The equipment owned prior to this year is being depreciated using the straight-line method over 5 years. The salvage value is 10% of cost.
9. The equipment purchased on May 1, 2004, is being depreciated using the straight-line method over 5 years, with a salvage value of $1,800.
10. The patent was acquired on January 1, 2004, and has a useful life of 10 years from that date.
11. Unpaid salaries at December 31, 2004, total $2,200.
12. The unearned rent of $6,000 was received on December 1, 2004, for 3 months rent.
13. Both the short-term and long-term notes payable are dated January 1, 2004, and carry a 12% interest rate. All interest is payable in the next 12 months.

Instructions

(a) Prepare journal entries for the transactions listed above.
(b) Prepare an updated December 31, 2004, trial balance.
(c) Prepare a 2004 income statement.
(d) Prepare a December 31, 2004, balance sheet.

BROADENING YOUR PERSPECTIVE

Financial Reporting and Analysis

■ FINANCIAL REPORTING PROBLEM: PepsiCo

BYP10-1 The financial statements and the Notes to Consolidated Financial Statements of **PepsiCo** are presented in Appendix A.

Instructions

Refer to PepsiCo's financial statements and answer the following questions.

(a) What was the total cost and book value of property, plant, and equipment at December 28, 2002?
(b) What method or methods of depreciation are used by the company for financial reporting purposes?
(c) What was the amount of depreciation and amortization expense for each of the three years 2000–2002?
(d) Using the statement of cash flows, what is the amount of capital spending in 2002 and 2001?
(e) Where does the company disclose its intangible assets, and what types of intangibles did it have at December 28, 2002?

■ COMPARATIVE ANALYSIS PROBLEM: PepsiCo vs. Coca-Cola

BYP10-2 **PepsiCo**'s financial statements are presented in Appendix A. **Coca-Cola**'s financial statements are presented in Appendix B.

Instructions

(a) Compute the asset turnover ratio for each company for 2002.
(b) What conclusions concerning the efficiency of assets can be drawn from these data?

■ **INTERPRETING FINANCIAL STATEMENTS: A Global Focus**

BYP10-3   As you can imagine, the accounting for goodwill differs in countries around the world. The following discussion of a change in goodwill accounting practices was taken from the notes to the financial statements of **J Sainsbury Plc**, one of the world's leading retailers. Headquartered in the United Kingdom, it serves 15 million customers a week.

J SAINSBURY PLC
Notes to the Financial Statements

Accounting Policies

Goodwill arising in connection with the acquisition of shares in subsidiaries and associated undertakings is calculated as the excess of the purchase price over the fair value of the net tangible assets acquired. In prior years goodwill has been deducted from reserves in the period of acquisition. FRS 10 is applicable in the current financial year, and in accordance with the standard acquired goodwill is now shown as an asset on the Group's Balance Sheet. As permitted by FRS 10, goodwill written off to reserves in prior periods has not been restated as an asset.

Goodwill is treated as having an indefinite economic life where it is considered that the acquired business has strong customer loyalty built up over a long period of time, based on advantageous store locations and a commitment to maintain the marketing advantage of the retail brand. The carrying value of the goodwill will be reviewed annually for impairment and adjusted to its recoverable amount if required. Where goodwill is considered to have a finite life, amortisation will be applied over that period.

For amounts stated as goodwill which are considered to have indefinite life, no amortisation is charged to the Profit and Loss Account.

Instructions

(a) How does the initial determination and recording of goodwill compare with that in the United States? That is, is goodwill initially recorded in the same circumstances, and is the calculation of the initial amount the same in both the United Kingdom and the United States?

(b) Prior to adoption of the new accounting standard (FRS 10), how did the company account for goodwill? What were the implications for the income statement?

(c) Under the new accounting standard, how does the company account for its goodwill? Is it possible, under the new standard, for a company to avoid charging goodwill amortization to net income?

(d) In what ways is the new standard similar to U.S. standards, and in what ways is it different?

■ **EXPLORING THE WEB**

BYP10-4   A company's annual report identifies the amount of its plant assets and the depreciation method used.

Address: www.reportgallery.com, or go to www.wiley.com/college/weygandt

Steps

1. From Report Gallery Homepage, choose **Library of Annual Reports**.
2. Select a particular company.
3. Choose **Annual Report**.
4. Follow instructions below.

Instructions

(a) What is the name of the company?

(b) At fiscal year-end, what is the net amount of its plant assets?

(c) What is the accumulated depreciation?

(d) Which method of depreciation does the company use?

Critical Thinking

■ GROUP DECISION CASE

BYP10-5 Givens Company and Runge Company are two proprietorships that are similar in many respects. One difference is that Givens Company uses the straight-line method and Runge Company uses the declining-balance method at double the straight-line rate. On January 2, 2003, both companies acquired the following depreciable assets.

Asset	Cost	Salvage Value	Useful Life
Building	$320,000	$20,000	40 years
Equipment	125,000	10,000	10 years

Including the appropriate depreciation charges, annual net income for the companies in the years 2003, 2004, and 2005 and total income for the 3 years were as follows.

	2003	2004	2005	Total
Givens Company	$84,000	$88,400	$100,000	$272,400
Runge Company	68,000	76,000	85,000	229,000

At December 31, 2005, the balance sheets of the two companies are similar except that Runge Company has more cash than Givens Company.

Linda Yanik is interested in buying one of the companies. She comes to you for advice.

Instructions

With the class divided into groups, answer the following.

(a) Determine the annual and total depreciation recorded by each company during the 3 years.

(b) Assuming that Runge Company also uses the straight-line method of depreciation instead of the declining-balance method as in (a), prepare comparative income data for the 3 years.

(c) Which company should Linda Yanik buy? Why?

■ COMMUNICATION ACTIVITY

BYP10-6 The following was published with the financial statements to **American Exploration Company**.

AMERICAN EXPLORATION COMPANY
Notes to the Financial Statements

Property, Plant, and Equipment—The Company accounts for its oil and gas exploration and production activities using the successful efforts method of accounting. Under this method, acquisition costs for proved and unproved properties are capitalized when incurred.... The costs of drilling exploratory wells are capitalized pending determination of whether each well has discovered proved reserves. If proved reserves are not discovered, such drilling costs are charged to expense.... Depletion of the cost of producing oil and gas properties is computed on the units-of-activity method.

Instructions

Write a brief memo to your instructor discussing American Exploration Company's note regarding property, plant, and equipment. Your memo should address what is meant by the "successful efforts method" and "units-of-activity method."

■ ETHICS CASE

BYP10-7 Dieker Container Company is suffering declining sales of its principal product, non-biodegradeable plastic cartons. The president, Edward Mohling, instructs his controller, Betty Fetters, to lengthen asset lives to reduce depreciation expense. A processing line of automated plastic extruding equipment, purchased for $3.5 million in January 2005, was originally estimated to have a useful life of 8 years and a salvage value of $300,000. Depreciation has been recorded for 2 years on that basis. Edward wants the estimated life changed to 12 years total, and the straight-line method continued. Betty is hesitant to make the change, believing it is unethical to increase net income in this manner. Edward says, "Hey, the life is only an estimate, and I've heard that our competition uses a 12-year life on their production equipment."

Instructions
(a) Who are the stakeholders in this situation?
(b) Is the change in asset life unethical, or is it simply a good business practice by an astute president?
(c) What is the effect of Edward Mohling's proposed change on income before taxes in the year of change?

Answers to Self-Study Questions
1. d   **2.** b   **3.** d   **4.** d   **5.** b   **6.** d   **7.** c   **8.** b   **9.** c   **10.** a   **11.** c

Answer to PepsiCo Review It Question 2, p. 404
PepsiCo reports the following categories and amounts under the heading "Property, plant, and equipment (net)": Land and improvements $504,000,000; Buildings and improvements $3,119,000,000; Machinery and equipment, including fleet $9,005,000,000; and Construction in progress $767,000,000. In addition, accumulated depreciation of $6,005,000,000 was deducted.

Current Liabilities and Payroll Accounting

CONCEPTS FOR REVIEW

Before studying this chapter, you should know or, if necessary, review:

The importance of liquidity in evaluating the financial position of a company.
(Ch. 4, p. 155)

How to make adjusting entries related to unearned revenue (Ch. 3, pp. 97–98) and accrued expenses.
(Ch. 3, pp. 101–103)

The principles of internal control.
(Ch. 8, p. 320)

THE NAVIGATOR

Financing His Dreams

What would you do if you had a great idea for a new product, but couldn't come up with the cash to get the business off the ground? Small businesses often can't attract investors, nor can they obtain traditional debt financing through bank loans or bond issuances. Instead, they often resort to unusual, and costly, forms of nontraditional financing.

Such was the case for Wilbert Murdock. Murdock grew up in a New York housing project, and always had great ambitions. This ambitious spirit led him into some business ventures

that failed: a medical diagnostic tool, a device to eliminate carpal-tunnel syndrome, custom sneakers, and a device to keep people from falling asleep while driving.

His latest idea was computerized golf clubs that analyze a golfer's swing and provide immediate feedback. Murdock saw great potential in the idea: Many golfers are willing to shell out considerable sums of money for devices that might improve their game. But Murdock had no cash to develop his product, and banks and other lenders had shied away. Rather than give up, Murdock resorted to credit cards—in a big way. He quickly owed $25,000 to credit card companies.

While funding a business with credit cards might sound unusual, it isn't. A recent study found that one-third of businesses with fewer than 20 employees financed at least part of their operations with credit cards. As Murdock explained, credit cards are an appealing way to finance a start-up because "credit-card companies don't care how the money is spent." But they do care how they are paid. And so Murdock faced high interest charges and a barrage of credit card collection letters.

Murdock's debt forced him to sacrifice nearly everything in order to keep his business afloat. His car stopped running, he barely had enough money to buy food, and he lived and worked out of a dimly lit apartment in his mother's basement. Through it all he tried to maintain a positive spirit, joking that, if he becomes successful, he might some day get to appear in an American Express commercial.

Source: Rodney Ho, "Banking on Plastic: To Finance a Dream, Many Entrepreneurs Binge on Credit Cards," *Wall Street Journal*, March 9, 1998, p. A1.

After studying this chapter, you should be able to:

1. Explain a current liability, and identify the major types of current liabilities.
2. Describe the accounting for notes payable.
3. Explain the accounting for other current liabilities.
4. Explain the financial statement presentation and analysis of current liabilities.
5. Describe the accounting and disclosure requirements for contingent liabilities.
6. Discuss the objectives of internal control for payroll.
7. Compute and record the payroll for a pay period.
8. Describe and record employer payroll taxes.

Inventor-entrepreneur Wilbert Murdock, as you can tell from the Feature Story, has had to use multiple credit cards to finance his business ventures. Murdock's credit card debts would be classified as *current liabilities* because they are due every month. Yet by making minimal payments and paying high interest each month, Murdock uses this credit source long-term. Some credit card balances remain outstanding for years as they accumulate interest.

In Chapter 4, we defined liabilities as creditors' claims on total assets and as existing debts and obligations. These claims, debts, and obligations must be settled or paid at some time **in the future** by the transfer of assets or services. The future date on which they are due or payable (maturity date) is a significant feature of liabilities. This "future date" feature gives rise to two basic classifications of liabilities: (1) current liabilities and (2) long-term liabilities. We will explain current liabilities, along with payroll accounting, in this chapter. We will explain long-term liabilities in Chapter 16.

The content and organization of Chapter 11 are as follows.

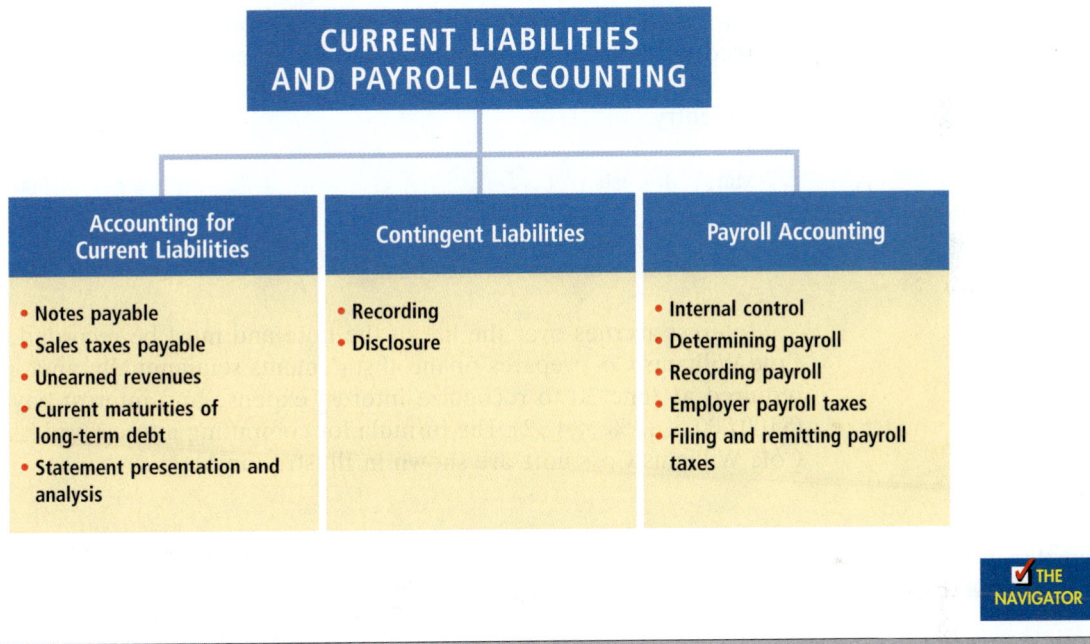

Accounting for Current Liabilities

As explained in Chapter 4, a **current liability** is a debt with two key features: (1) It can reasonably be expected to be paid from existing current assets or through the creation of other current liabilities. And (2) it will be paid within one year or the operating cycle, whichever is longer. Debts that do not meet **both criteria** are classified as long-term liabilities. Most companies pay current liabilities within one year out of current assets, rather than by creating other liabilities.

Companies must carefully monitor the relationship of current liabilities to current assets. This relationship is critical in evaluating a company's short-term debt-paying ability. A company that has more current liabilities than current assets is usually the subject of some concern because the company may not be able to meet its current obligations when they become due.

STUDY OBJECTIVE 1

Explain a current liability, and identify the major types of current liabilities.

Current liabilities include notes payable, accounts payable, and unearned revenues. They also include accrued liabilities such as taxes, salaries and wages, and interest payable. The entries for accounts payable and adjusting entries for some current liabilities have been explained in previous chapters. Other types of current liabilities that are often encountered are discussed in the following sections.

Notes Payable

Obligations in the form of written promissory notes are recorded as **notes payable**. Notes payable are often used instead of accounts payable. Doing so gives the lender formal proof of the obligation in case legal remedies are needed to collect the debt. Notes payable usually require the borrower to pay interest and frequently are issued to meet short-term financing needs.

Notes are issued for varying periods. **Those due for payment within one year of the balance sheet date are usually classified as current liabilities.** Most notes are interest bearing.

To illustrate the accounting for notes payable, assume that First National Bank agrees to lend $100,000 on March 1, 2005, if Cole Williams Co. signs a $100,000, 12%, 4-month note. With an interest-bearing promissory note, the amount of assets received upon issuance of the note generally equals the note's face value. Cole Williams Co. therefore will receive $100,000 cash and will make the following journal entry.

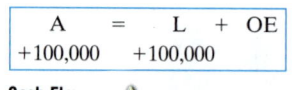

A	=	L	+ OE
+100,000		+100,000	

Cash Flows
+100,000

Mar. 1	Cash	100,000	
	Notes Payable		100,000
	(To record issuance of 12%, 4-month note to First National Bank)		

Interest accrues over the life of the note and must be recorded periodically. If Cole Williams Co. prepares financial statements semiannually, an adjusting entry is required at June 30 to recognize interest expense and interest payable of $4,000 ($100,000 × 12% × 4/12). The formula for computing interest and its application to Cole Williams Co.'s note are shown in Illustration 11-1.

Illustration 11-1
Formula for computing interest

Face Value of Note	×	Annual Interest Rate	×	Time in Terms of One Year	=	Interest
$100,000	×	12%	×	4/12	=	**$4,000**

The adjusting entry is:

A	=	L	+	OE
		+4,000		−4,000 Exp

Cash Flows
no effect

June 30	Interest Expense	4,000	
	Interest Payable		4,000
	(To accrue interest for 4 months on First National Bank note)		

In the June 30 financial statements, the current liabilities section of the balance sheet will show notes payable $100,000 and interest payable $4,000. In addition, interest expense of $4,000 will be reported under "Other expenses and losses" in the income statement. If Cole Williams Co. prepared financial statements monthly, the adjusting entry at the end of each month would have been $1,000 ($100,000 × 12% × 1/12).

At maturity (July 1, 2005), Cole Williams Co. must pay the face value of the note ($100,000) plus $4,000 interest ($100,000 × 12% × 4/12). The entry to record payment of the note and accrued interest is as follows.

July 1	Notes Payable	100,000	
	Interest Payable	4,000	
	Cash		104,000
	(To record payment of First National Bank interest-bearing note and accrued interest at maturity)		

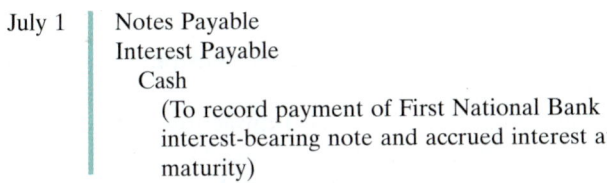

A	=	L	+	OE
−104,000		−100,000		
			−4,000	

Cash Flows
−104,000

Sales Taxes Payable

As a consumer, you know that many of the products you purchase at retail stores are subject to sales taxes. The tax is expressed as a stated percentage of the sales price. The retailer collects the tax from the customer when the sale occurs. Periodically (usually monthly), the retailer remits the collections to the state's department of revenue.

Under most state sales tax laws, the amount of the sale and the amount of the sales tax collected must be rung up separately on the cash register. (Gasoline sales are a major exception.) The cash register readings are then used to credit Sales and Sales Taxes Payable. For example, if the March 25 cash register reading for Cooley Grocery shows sales of $10,000 and sales taxes of $600 (sales tax rate of 6%), the entry is:

Mar. 25	Cash	10,600	
	Sales		10,000
	Sales Taxes Payable		600
	(To record daily sales and sales taxes)		

A	=	L	+	OE
+10,600		+600		+10,000 Rev

Cash Flows
+10,600

When the taxes are remitted to the taxing agency, Sales Taxes Payable is debited and Cash is credited. The company does not report sales taxes as an expense. It simply forwards to the government the amount paid by the customers. Thus, Cooley Grocery serves only as a **collection agent** for the taxing authority.

When sales taxes are not rung up separately on the cash register, they must be extracted from the total receipts. To determine the amount of sales in such cases, divide total receipts by 100% plus the sales tax percentage. To illustrate, assume that in the above example Cooley Grocery rings up total receipts, which are $10,600. The receipts from the sales are equal to the sales price (100%) plus the tax percentage (6% of sales), or 1.06 times the sales total. We can compute the sales amount as follows.

$$\$10,600 \div 1.06 = \$10,000$$

Thus, Cooley Grocery could find the sales tax amount it must remit to the state by subtracting sales from total receipts ($10,600 − $10,000).

ACCOUNTING IN ACTION   e Business Insight

If you buy a book at a bookstore, you pay sales tax. If you buy the same book over the Internet, you don't pay sales tax (in most cases). This is one reason why e-commerce, as it has come to be called, has been growing exponentially and why Web sites like Amazon.com have become so popular. A recent study suggested that Internet sales would fall by 30 percent if sales tax were applied. In December 2001 Congress passed and President Bush signed into law a two-year extension to the ban on sales taxes on Internet purchases. While Internet retailers were pleased, the American Booksellers Association protested the ban, saying it gives online booksellers such as Amazon.com an unfair advantage over brick-and-mortar bookstores.

Source: Edward Nawotka, "Bush Extends Internet Tax Ban," *Publishers Weekly*, December 3, 2001, p. 18.

Unearned Revenues

A magazine publisher, such as **Sports Illustrated**, receives a customer's check when magazines are ordered. An airline company, such as **American Airlines**, receives cash when it sells tickets for future flights. Through these transactions, both companies have incurred unearned revenues—revenues that are received before goods are delivered or services are rendered. How do companies account for unearned revenues?

1. When the advance payment is received, Cash is debited, and a current liability account identifying the source of the unearned revenue is credited.
2. When the revenue is earned, the Unearned Revenue account is debited, and an earned revenue account is credited.

To illustrate, assume that Superior University sells 10,000 season football tickets at $50 each for its five-game home schedule. The entry for the sale of season tickets is:

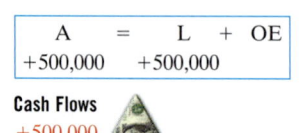

A	=	L	+ OE
+500,000		+500,000	

Cash Flows
+500,000

Aug. 6	Cash	500,000	
	Unearned Football Ticket Revenue		500,000
	(To record sale of 10,000 season tickets)		

As each of the five home games is completed, one-fifth of the revenue is earned. The following entry is made:

A	=	L	+ OE
		−100,000	+100,000 Rev

Cash Flows
no effect

Sept. 7	Unearned Football Ticket Revenue	100,000	
	Football Ticket Revenue		100,000
	(To record football ticket revenue earned)		

Any balance in an unearned revenue account (in Unearned Football Ticket Revenue, for example) is reported as a current liability in the balance sheet. As revenue is earned, a transfer from unearned revenue to earned revenue occurs. Unearned revenue is material for some companies: In the airline industry, for example, tickets sold for future flights represent almost 50% of total current liabilities. At **United Air Lines**, unearned ticket revenue is the largest current liability, recently amounting to over $1 billion.

Illustration 11-2 shows specific unearned and earned revenue accounts used in selected types of businesses.

Illustration 11-2
Unearned and earned revenue accounts

Type of Business	Account Title	
	Unearned Revenue	Earned Revenue
Airline	Unearned Passenger Ticket Revenue	Passenger Revenue
Magazine publisher	Unearned Subscription Revenue	Subscription Revenue
Hotel	Unearned Rental Revenue	Rental Revenue
Insurance company	Unearned Premium Revenue	Premium Revenue

Current Maturities of Long-Term Debt

Companies often have a portion of long-term debt that comes due in the current year. That amount would be considered a current liability. For example, assume that Wendy Construction issues a 5-year interest-bearing $25,000 note on January 1, 2005. Each January 1, starting January 1, 2006, $5,000 of the note is due to be paid. When financial statements are prepared on December 31, 2005, $5,000 should be reported as a current liability. The remaining $20,000 on the note would be reported as a long-term liability. Current maturities of long-term debt are often termed **long-term debt due within one year**.

It is not necessary to prepare an adjusting entry to recognize the current maturity of long-term debt. The proper statement classification of each balance sheet account is recognized when the balance sheet is prepared.

Statement Presentation and Analysis

Presentation

As indicated in Chapter 4, current liabilities are the first category under liabilities on the balance sheet. Each of the principal types of current liabilities is listed separately. In addition, the terms of notes payable and other key information about the individual items are disclosed in the notes to the financial statements.

Current liabilities are seldom listed in the order of maturity. The reason is that varying maturity dates may exist for specific obligations such as notes payable. A more common method of presenting current liabilities is to list them by **order of magnitude**, with the largest ones first. Or, many companies, as a matter of custom, show notes payable and accounts payable first, regardless of amount. The following adapted excerpt from the balance sheet of **Caterpillar Inc.** illustrates its order of presentation.

CATERPILLAR®

CATERPILLAR INC.
Balance Sheet
December 31, 2002
(in millions)

Assets

Current assets	$14,628
Property, plant and equipment (net)	7,046
Other long-term assets	11,177
Total assets	$32,851

Liabilities and Stockholders' Equity

Current liabilities	
Short-term borrowings	$2,175
Accounts payable	2,269
Accrued expenses	1,620
Accrued wages, salaries, and employee benefits	1,178
Dividends payable	120
Deferred and current income taxes payable	70
Long-term debt due within one year	3,912
Total current liabilities	11,344
Noncurrent liabilities	16,035
Total liabilities	27,379
Stockholders' equity	5,472
Total liabilities and stockholders' equity	$32,851

Illustration 11-3
Balance sheet presentation of current liabilities

Analysis

Use of current and noncurrent classifications makes it possible to analyze a company's liquidity. **Liquidity** refers to the ability to pay maturing obligations and meet unexpected needs for cash. The relationship of current assets to current liabilities is critical in analyzing liquidity. This relationship can be expressed as a dollar amount (called working capital) and as a ratio (called the current ratio).

The excess of current assets over current liabilities is **working capital**. The formula for the computation of Caterpillar's working capital is shown in Illustration 11-4 (dollar amounts in millions).

Illustration 11-4
Working capital formula and computation

Current Assets	−	Current Liabilities	=	Working Capital
$14,628	−	$11,344	=	**$3,284**

As an absolute dollar amount, working capital is limited in its informational value. For example, $1 million of working capital may be far more than needed for a small company but be inadequate for a large corporation. And, $1 million of working capital may be adequate for a company at one time but be inadequate at another time.

The **current ratio** permits us to compare the liquidity of different sized companies and of a single company at different times. The current ratio is current assets divided by current liabilities. The formula for this ratio is illustrated below, along with its computation using Caterpillar's current asset and current liability data (dollar amounts in millions).

Illustration 11-5
Current ratio formula and computation

Current Assets	÷	Current Liabilities	=	Current Ratio
$14,628	÷	$11,344	=	**1.29:1**

Historically, a ratio of 2:1 was considered to be the standard for a good credit rating. In recent years, however, many healthy companies have maintained ratios well below 2:1 by improving management of their current assets and liabilities. Caterpillar's ratio of 1.29:1 is adequate but certainly below the standard of 2:1.

Contingent Liabilities

STUDY OBJECTIVE 5

Describe the accounting and disclosure requirements for contingent liabilities.

With notes payable, interest payable, accounts payable, and sales taxes payable, we know that an obligation to make payment exists. But suppose that your company is involved in a dispute with the Internal Revenue Service (IRS) over the amount of its income tax liability. Should you report the disputed amount as a liability on the balance sheet? Or suppose your company is involved in a lawsuit which, if you lose, might result in bankruptcy. How should this major contingency be reported? The answers to these questions are difficult, because these liabilities are dependent—contingent—upon some future event. In other words, a **contingent liability** is a potential liability that may become an actual liability in the future.

How should contingent liabilities be reported? Guidelines have been adopted that help resolve these problems. The guidelines require that:

1. If the contingency is **probable** (if it is likely to occur) **and** the amount can be **reasonably estimated**, the liability should be recorded in the accounts.

2. If the contingency is only **reasonably possible** (if it could happen), then it need be disclosed only in the notes that accompany the financial statements.

3. If the contingency is **remote** (if it is unlikely to occur), it need not be recorded or disclosed.

Contingent liabilities abound in the real world. Consider the following: **Manville Corp**. filed for bankruptcy when it was hit by billions of dollars in asbestos product-liability claims. Companies having multiple toxic waste sites are faced with cleanup costs that average $10 to $30 million and can reach as high as $500 million depending on the type of waste. For life and health insurance companies and their stockholders, the cost of AIDS is like an iceberg: Everyone wonders how big it really is and what damage it might do in the future; according to the U.S. Centers for Disease Control treatment costs could be $8 billion to $16 billion. And frequent-flyer programs are so popular that airlines at one time owed participants more than 3 million round-trip domestic tickets. That's enough to fly at least 5.4 billion miles—free for the passengers, but at what future cost to the airlines?

Recording a Contingent Liability

Product warranties are an example of a contingent liability that should be recorded in the accounts. Warranty contracts result in future costs that may be incurred in replacing defective units or repairing malfunctioning units. Generally, a manufacturer, such as **Black & Decker**, knows that some warranty costs will be incurred. From prior experience with the product, the company usually can reasonably estimate the anticipated cost of servicing (honoring) the warranty.

The accounting for warranty costs is based on the matching principle. **The estimated cost of honoring product warranty contracts should be recognized as an expense in the period in which the sale occurs.** To illustrate, assume that in 2005 Denson Manufacturing Company sells 10,000 washers and dryers at an average price of $600 each. The selling price includes a one-year warranty on parts. It is expected that 500 units (5%) will be defective and that warranty repair costs will average $80 per unit. In 2005, warranty contracts are honored on 300 units at a total cost of $24,000.

At December 31, it is necessary to accrue the estimated warranty costs on the 2005 sales. The computation is as follows.

Number of units sold	10,000	
Estimated rate of defective units	× 5%	
Total estimated defective units	500	
Average warranty repair cost	× $80	
Estimated product warranty liability	**$40,000**	

Illustration 11-6
Computation of estimated product warranty liability

The adjusting entry, therefore, is:

Dec. 31	Warranty Expense	40,000	
	Estimated Warranty Liability		40,000
	(To accrue estimated warranty costs)		

A	=	L	+	OE
		+40,000		−40,000 Exp

Cash Flows
no effect

The entry to record those repair costs incurred in 2005 to honor warranty contracts on 2005 sales is shown below.

Jan. 1–	Estimated Warranty Liability	24,000	
Dec. 31	Repair Parts		24,000
	(To record honoring of 300 warranty		
	contracts on 2005 sales)		

A	=	L	+	OE
−24,000		−24,000		

Cash Flows
no effect

Warranty expense of $40,000 is reported under selling expenses in the income statement. Estimated warranty liability of $16,000 ($40,000 − $24,000) is classified as a current liability on the balance sheet.

In the following year, all expenses incurred in honoring warranty contracts on 2005 sales should be debited to Estimated Warranty Liability. To illustrate, assume that 20 defective units are replaced in January 2006, at an average cost of $80 in parts and labor. The summary entry for the month of January 2006 is:

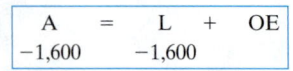

A	=	L	+	OE
−1,600		−1,600		

Cash Flows
no effect

Jan. 31	Estimated Warranty Liability		1,600	
	Repair Parts			1,600
	(To record honoring of 20 warranty			
	contracts on 2002 sales)			

Disclosure of Contingent Liabilities

When it is probable that a contingent liability will be incurred but the amount cannot be reasonably estimated, or when the contingent liability is only reasonably possible, only disclosure of the contingency is required. Examples of contingencies that may require disclosure are pending or threatened lawsuits and assessment of additional income taxes pending an IRS audit of the tax return.

The disclosure should identify the nature of the item and, if known, the amount of the contingency and the expected outcome of the future event. Disclosure is usually accomplished through a note to the financial statements, as illustrated by the following.

Illustration 11-7
Disclosure of contingent liability

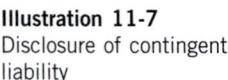

USAIRWAYS
Notes to the Financial Statements

Legal Proceedings

The Company and various subsidiaries have been named as defendants in various suits and proceedings which involve, among other things, environmental concerns about noise and air pollution and employment matters. These suits and proceedings are in various stages of litigation, and the status of the law with respect to several of the issues involved is unsettled. For these reasons the outcome of these suits and proceedings is difficult to predict. In the Company's opinion, however, the disposition of these matters is not likely to have a material adverse effect on its financial condition.

BEFORE YOU GO ON...

Review It

1. What are the two criteria for classifying a debt as a current liability?
2. Identify the liabilities classified as current by **PepsiCo.** The answer to this question is provided on page 486.
3. What entries are made for an interest-bearing note payable?
4. How are sales taxes recorded by a retailer? Identify three unearned revenues.
5. How may the liquidity of a company be analyzed?
6. What are the accounting guidelines for contingent liabilities?

Payroll Accounting

Start here

Payroll and related fringe benefits often make up a large percentage of current liabilities. Employee compensation is often the most significant expense that a company incurs. For example, **General Motors** recently reported total employees of 386,000 and labor costs of $21.6 billion. Add to labor costs such fringe benefits as health insurance, life insurance, disability insurance, and so on, and you can see why proper accounting and control of payroll are so important.

Payroll accounting involves more than paying employees' wages. Companies are required by law to maintain payroll records for each employee, file and pay payroll taxes, and comply with numerous state and federal tax laws related to employee compensation. Accounting for payroll has become much more complex due to these regulations.

The term "payroll" pertains to both salaries and wages. Managerial, administrative, and sales personnel are generally paid **salaries**. Salaries are often expressed in terms of a specified amount per month or per year rather than an hourly rate. For example, the faculty and administrative personnel at the college or university you are attending are paid salaries. In contrast, store clerks, factory employees, and manual laborers are normally paid **wages**. Wages are based on a rate per hour or on a piecework basis (such as per unit of product). Frequently, the terms "salaries" and "wages" are used interchangeably.

The term "payroll" does not apply to payments made for services of professionals such as certified public accountants, attorneys, and architects. Such professionals are independent contractors rather than salaried employees. Payments to them are called **fees**, rather than salaries or wages. This distinction is important because government regulations relating to the payment and reporting of payroll taxes apply only to employees.

Internal Control

Internal control was introduced in Chapter 8. As applied to payrolls, the objectives of internal control are (1) to safeguard company assets against unauthorized payments of payrolls, and (2) to ensure the accuracy and reliability of the accounting records pertaining to payrolls.

STUDY OBJECTIVE 6

Discuss the objectives of internal control for payroll.

Irregularities often result if internal control is lax. Overstating hours, using unauthorized pay rates, adding fictitious employees to the payroll, continuing terminated employees on the payroll, and distributing duplicate payroll checks are all methods of stealing from a company. Moreover, inaccurate records will result in incorrect paychecks, financial statements, and payroll tax returns.

Payroll activities involve four functions: hiring employees, timekeeping, preparing the payroll, and paying the payroll. For effective internal control, these four functions should be assigned to different departments or individuals. To illustrate these functions, we will examine the case of Academy Company and one of its employees, Michael Jordan.

Hiring Employees

Hiring Employees

Human resources

Human Resources department documents and authorizes employment.

The human resources (personnel) department is responsible for posting job openings, screening and interviewing applicants, and hiring employees. From a control standpoint, this department provides significant documentation and authorization. When an employee is hired, the human resources department prepares an authorization form. The one used by Academy Company for Michael Jordan is shown in Illustration 11-8.

The authorization form is sent to the payroll department, where it is used to place the new employee on the payroll. A chief concern of the human resources department is ensuring the accuracy of this form. The reason is quite simple: one of the most common types of payroll frauds is adding fictitious employees to the payroll.

The human resources department is also responsible for authorizing changes in employment status. Specifically, they must authorize (1) changes in pay rates and (2) terminations of employment. Every authorization should be in writing, and a

Illustration 11-8
Authorization form prepared by the human resources department

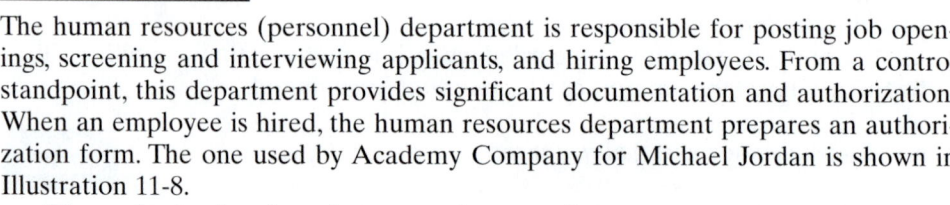

ACADEMY COMPANY

Employee Name __Jordan,__ __Michael__ _____ Starting Date __9/01/03__
LAST FIRST MI

Classification __Skilled-Level 10__ _____ Social Security No. __329-36-9547__

Department __Shipping__ _____ Division __Entertainment__

| **NEW HIRE** | Classification __Clerk__ Salary Grade __Level 10__ Trans. from Temp. ☐ |
| | Rate $__10.00__ per __hour__ Bonus __N/A__ Non-exempt ☒ Exempt ☐ |

RATE CHANGE	New Rate $ __12.00__ Effective Date __9/1/04__
	Present Rate $ __10.00__
	Merit ☒ Promotion ☐ Decrease ☐ Other_____
	Previous Increase Date __None__ Amount $____per____Type____

SEPARATION	Resignation ☐ Discharge ☐ Retirement ☐ Reason_____
	_____
	Leave of absence ☐ From_____ to_____ Type_____
	Last Day Worked_____

APPROVALS	_BEW_ 9/1/04 _EMW_ 9-1-04
	BRANCH OR DEPT. MANAGER DATE DIVISION V.P. DATE
	James E. Speer
	PERSONNEL DEPARTMENT

copy of the change in status should be sent to the payroll department. Notice in Illustration 11-8 that Jordan received a pay increase of $2 per hour.

Timekeeping

Timekeeping

Supervisors monitor hours worked through time cards and time reports.

Another area in which internal control is important is timekeeping. Hourly employees are usually required to record time worked by "punching" a time clock. Times of arrival and departure are automatically recorded by the employee by inserting a time card into the clock. Michael Jordan's time card is shown in Illustration 11-9.

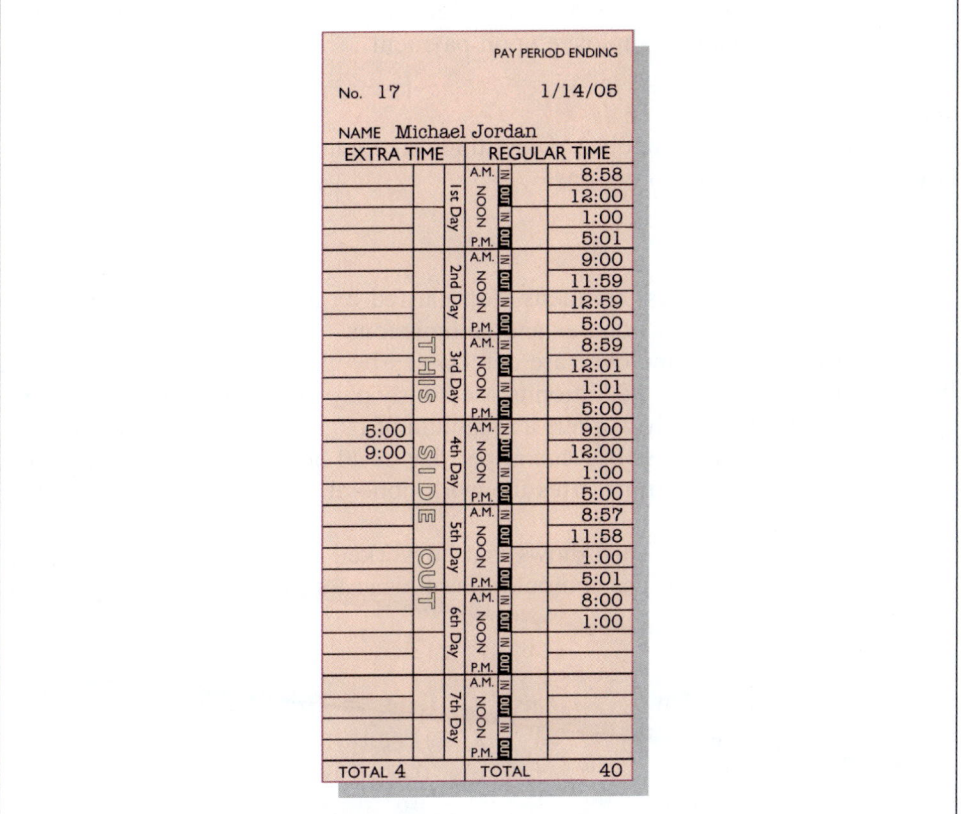

Illustration 11-9
Time card

In large companies, time clock procedures are often monitored by a supervisor or security guard to make sure an employee punches only one card. At the end of the pay period, each employee's supervisor approves the hours shown by signing the time card. When overtime hours are involved, approval by a supervisor is usually mandatory. This guards against unauthorized overtime. The approved time cards are then sent to the payroll department. For salaried employees, a manually prepared weekly or monthly time report kept by a supervisor may be used to record time worked.

Preparing the Payroll

Preparing the Payroll

Two (or more) employees verify payroll amounts; supervisor approves.

The payroll is prepared in the payroll department on the basis of two inputs: (1) human resources department authorizations and (2) approved time cards. Numerous calculations are involved in determining gross wages and payroll deductions. Therefore, a second payroll department employee, working independently, verifies all calculated amounts, and a payroll department supervisor then approves the payroll. The payroll department is also responsible for preparing (but not signing) payroll checks, maintaining payroll records, and preparing payroll tax returns.

Paying the Payroll

Treasurer signs and distributes checks.

Paying the Payroll

The payroll is paid by the treasurer's department. **Payment by check minimizes the risk of loss from theft, and the endorsed check provides proof of payment.** For good internal control, payroll checks should be prenumbered, and all checks should be accounted for. All checks must be signed by the treasurer (or a designated agent). Distribution of the payroll checks to employees should be controlled by the treasurer's department. Many employees have their pay credited electronically to their bank accounts. To control these disbursements, receipts detailing gross pay deductions and net pay are provided to employees.

Occasionally the payroll is paid in currency. In such cases it is customary to have a second person count the cash in each pay envelope. The paymaster should obtain a signed receipt from the employee upon payment.

Determining the Payroll

STUDY OBJECTIVE 7

Compute and record the payroll for a pay period.

Determining the payroll involves computing three amounts: (1) gross earnings, (2) payroll deductions, and (3) net pay.

Gross Earnings

Gross earnings is the total compensation earned by an employee. It consists of wages or salaries, plus any bonuses and commissions.

Total **wages** for an employee are determined by multiplying the hours worked by the hourly rate of pay. In addition to the hourly pay rate, most companies are required by law to pay hourly workers a minimum of $1\frac{1}{2}$ times the regular hourly rate for overtime work in excess of 8 hours per day or 40 hours per week. In addition, many employers pay overtime rates for work done at night, on weekends, and on holidays.

Michael Jordan's time card shows that he worked 44 hours for the weekly pay period ending January 14. The computation of his gross earnings (total wages) is as follows.

Illustration 11-10
Computation of total wages

Type of Pay	Hours	×	Rate	=	Gross Earnings
Regular	40	×	$12.00	=	$480.00
Overtime	4	×	18.00	=	72.00
Total wages					**$552.00**

ETHICS NOTE

Bonuses often reward outstanding individual performance; but successful corporations also need considerable teamwork. A challenge is to motivate individuals while preventing an unethical employee from taking another's idea for his or her own advantage.

This computation assumes that Jordan receives $1\frac{1}{2}$ times his regular hourly rate ($12.00 × 1.5) for his overtime hours. Union contracts often require that overtime rates be as much as twice the regular rates.

The **salary** for an employee is generally based on a monthly or yearly rate. These rates are then prorated to the payroll periods used by the company. Most executive and administrative positions are salaried. Federal law does not require overtime pay for employees in such positions.

Many companies have **bonus** agreements for management personnel and other employees. A recent survey found that over 94% of the largest U.S. manufacturing companies offer annual bonuses to their key executives. Bonus arrangements may be based on such factors as increased sales or net income. Bonuses may be paid in cash and/or by granting executives and employees the opportunity to acquire shares of company stock at favorable prices (called stock option plans).

Payroll Deductions

As anyone who has received a paycheck knows, gross earnings are usually very different from the amount actually received. The difference is due to **payroll deduc-**

tions. Such deductions do not result in payroll tax expense to the employer. The employer is merely a collection agent, and subsequently transfers the amounts deducted to the government and designated recipients. Payroll deductions may be mandatory or voluntary. Mandatory deductions are required by law and consist of FICA taxes and income taxes. Voluntary deductions are at the option of the employee. Illustration 11-11 summarizes the types of payroll deductions.

Illustration 11-11
Payroll deductions

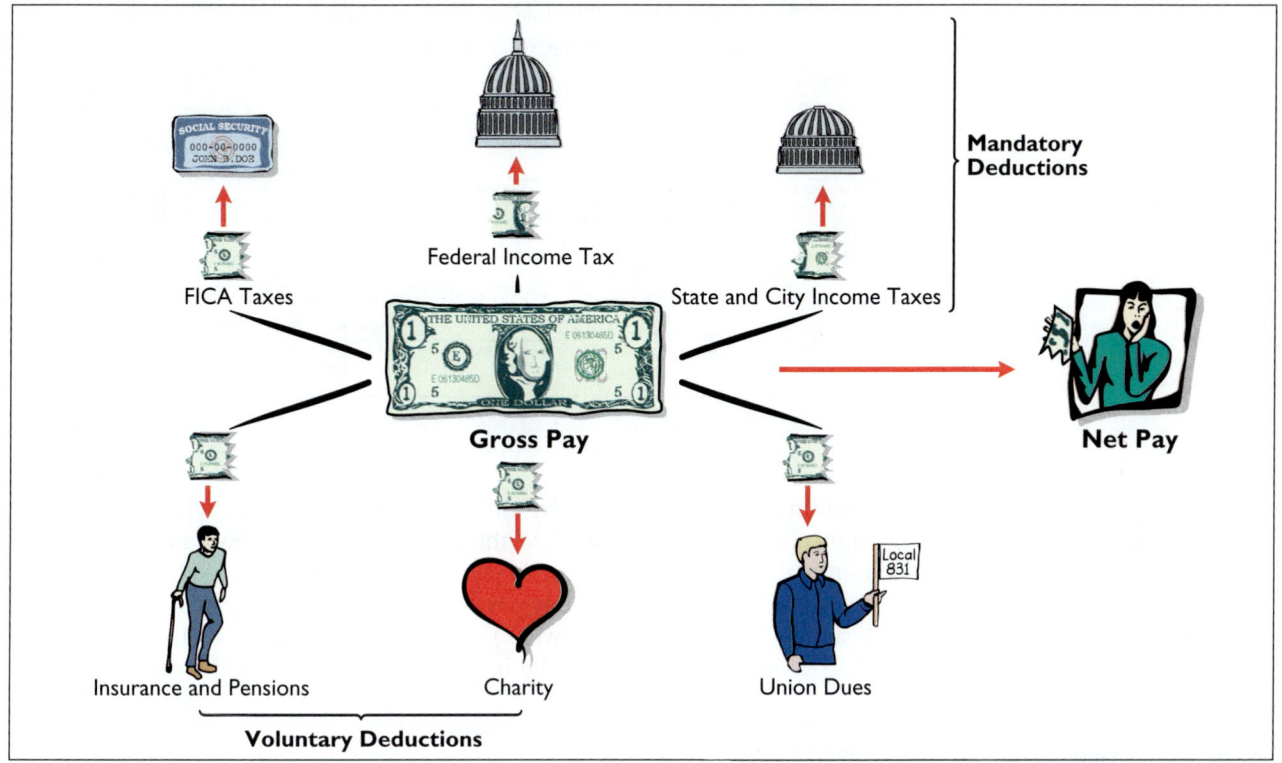

FICA TAXES.

In 1937 Congress enacted the Federal Insurance Contribution Act (FICA). **FICA taxes are designed to provide workers with supplemental retirement, employment disability, and medical benefits.** In 1965, benefits were expanded to include Medicare for individuals over 65 years of age. The benefits are financed by a tax levied on employees' earnings. FICA taxes are commonly referred to as **Social Security taxes**.

The tax rate and the tax base for FICA taxes are set by Congress. When FICA taxes were first imposed, the rate was 1% on the first $3,000 of gross earnings, or a maximum of $30 per year. The rate and base have changed dramatically since that time! In 2003, the rate was 7.65% (6.2% Social Security plus 1.45% Medicare) on the first $87,000 of gross earnings for each employee.[1] For purpose of illustration in this chapter, we will assume a rate of 8% on the first $87,000 of gross earnings, or a maximum of $6,960. Using the 8% rate, the FICA withholding for Jordan for the weekly pay period ending January 14 is $44.16 ($552 × 8%).

INCOME TAXES.

Under the U.S. pay-as-you-go system of federal income taxes, employers are required to withhold income taxes from employees each pay period. The amount to be withheld is determined by three variables: (1) the employee's gross earnings; (2) the number of allowances claimed by the employee; and (3) the

---

[1]The Medicare provision also includes a tax of 1.45% on gross earnings in excess of $87,000. In the interest of simplification, we ignore this 1.45% charge in our end-of-chapter assignment material. We assume zero FICA withholdings on gross earnings above $87,000.

length of the pay period. The number of allowances claimed typically includes the employee, his or her spouse, and other dependents. **To indicate to the Internal Revenue Service the number of allowances claimed, the employee must complete an Employee's Withholding Allowance Certificate (Form W-4).** As shown in Illustration 11-12, Michael Jordan claims two allowances on his W-4.

Illustration 11-12
W-4 form

Withholding tables furnished by the Internal Revenue Service indicate the amount of income tax to be withheld. Withholding amounts are based on gross wages and the number of allowances claimed. Separate tables are provided for weekly, bi-weekly, semimonthly, and monthly pay periods. The withholding tax table for Michael Jordan (assuming he earns $552 per week) is shown in Illustration 11-13. For a weekly salary of $552 with two allowances, the income tax to be withheld is $49.

Illustration 11-13
Withholding tax table

MARRIED Persons — WEEKLY Payroll Period
(For Wages Paid in 2005)

If the wages are — At least	But less than	And the number of withholding allowances claimed is — 0	1	2	3	4	5	6	7	8	9	10
		The amount of income tax to be withheld is —										
490	500	56	48	40	32	24	17	9	1	0	0	0
500	510	57	49	42	34	26	18	10	3	0	0	0
510	520	59	51	43	35	27	20	12	4	0	0	0
520	530	60	52	45	37	29	21	13	6	0	0	0
530	540	62	54	46	38	30	23	15	7	0	0	0
540	550	63	55	48	40	32	24	16	9	1	0	0
550	560	65	57	49	41	33	26	18	10	2	0	0
560	570	66	58	51	43	35	27	19	12	4	0	0
570	580	68	60	52	44	36	29	21	13	5	0	0
580	590	69	61	54	46	38	30	22	15	7	0	0
590	600	71	63	55	47	39	32	24	16	8	1	0
600	610	72	64	57	49	41	33	25	18	10	2	0
610	620	74	66	58	50	42	35	27	19	11	4	0
620	630	75	67	60	52	44	36	28	21	13	5	0
630	640	77	69	61	53	45	38	30	22	14	7	0
640	650	78	70	63	55	47	39	31	24	16	8	0
650	660	80	72	64	56	48	41	33	25	17	10	2
660	670	81	73	66	58	50	42	34	27	19	11	3
670	680	83	75	67	59	51	44	36	28	20	13	5
680	690	84	76	69	61	53	45	37	30	22	14	6

Most states (and some cities) also require **employers** to withhold income taxes from employees' earnings. As a rule, the amounts withheld are a percentage (specified in the state revenue code) of the amount withheld for the federal income tax. Or they may be a specified percentage of the employee's earnings. For the sake of simplicity, we have assumed that Jordan's wages are subject to state income taxes of 2%, or $11.04 (2% × $552) per week.

There is no limit on the amount of gross earnings subject to income tax withholdings. In fact, the higher the earnings, the higher the amount of taxes withheld.

OTHER DEDUCTIONS.   Employees may voluntarily authorize withholdings for charitable, retirement, and other purposes. All voluntary deductions from gross earnings should be authorized in writing by the employee. The authorization(s) may be made individually or as part of a group plan. Deductions for charitable organizations, such as the United Fund, or for financial arrangements, such as U.S. savings bonds and repayment of loans from company credit unions, are made individually. Deductions for union dues, health and life insurance, and pension plans are often made on a group basis. We will assume that Jordan has weekly voluntary deductions of $10 for the United Fund and $5 for union dues.

Net Pay

Net pay is determined by subtracting payroll deductions from gross earnings. For Michael Jordan, net pay for the pay period is $432.80, computed as follows.

Gross earnings		$552.00
Payroll deductions:		
FICA taxes	$44.16	
Federal income taxes	49.00	
State income taxes	11.04	
United Fund	10.00	
Union dues	5.00	119.20
Net pay		**$432.80**

ALTERNATIVE TERMINOLOGY
Net pay is also called *take-home pay*.

Illustration 11-14
Computation of net pay

Assuming that Michael Jordan's wages for each week during the year are $552, total wages for the year are $28,704 (52 × $552). Thus, all of Jordan's wages are subject to FICA tax during the year. Let's assume that Jordan's department head earns $1,800 per week, or $93,600 for the year. Since only the first $87,000 is subject to FICA taxes, the maximum FICA withholdings on the department head's earnings would be $6,960 ($87,000 × 8%).

Recording the Payroll

Recording the payroll involves maintaining payroll department records, recognizing payroll expenses and liabilities, and recording payment of the payroll.

Maintaining Payroll Department Records

To comply with state and federal laws, an employer must keep a cumulative record of each employee's gross earnings, deductions, and net pay during the year. The record that provides this information is the **employee earnings record**. Michael Jordan's employee earnings record is shown in Illustration 11-15 (on page 462).

Illustration 11-15
Employee earnings record

ACADEMY COMPANY
Employee Earnings Record
For the Year 2005

Name	Michael Jordan	**Address**	2345 Mifflin Ave.
Social Security Number	329-36-9547		Hampton, Michigan 48292
Date of Birth	December 24, 1962	**Telephone**	555-238-9051
Date Employed	September 1, 2003	**Date Employment Ended**	
Sex	Male	**Exemptions**	2
Single		**Married** X	

2005 Period Ending	Total Hours	Gross Earnings				Deductions						Payment	
		Regular	Overtime	Total	Cumulative	FICA	Fed. Inc. Tax	State Inc. Tax	United Fund	Union Dues	Total	Net Amount	Check No.
1/7	42	480.00	36.00	516.00	516.00	41.28	43.00	10.32	10.00	5.00	109.60	406.40	974
1/14	**44**	**480.00**	**72.00**	**552.00**	**1,068.00**	**44.16**	**49.00**	**11.04**	**10.00**	**5.00**	**119.20**	**432.80**	**1028**
1/21	43	480.00	54.00	534.00	1,602.00	42.72	46.00	10.68	10.00	5.00	114.40	419.60	1077
1/28	42	480.00	36.00	516.00	2,118.00	41.28	43.00	10.32	10.00	5.00	109.60	406.40	1133
Jan. Total		1,920.00	198.00	2,118.00		169.44	181.00	42.36	40.00	20.00	452.80	1,665.20	

A separate earnings record is kept for each employee. It is updated after each pay period. The cumulative payroll data on the earnings record are used by the employer to: (1) determine when an employee has earned the maximum earnings subject to FICA taxes, (2) file state and federal payroll tax returns (as explained later in the chapter), and (3) provide each employee with a statement of gross earnings and tax withholdings for the year. Illustration 11-19 on page 468 shows this statement.

In addition to employee earnings records, many companies find it useful to prepare a **payroll register**. This record accumulates the gross earnings, deductions, and net pay by employee for each pay period. It provides the documentation for preparing a paycheck for each employee. Academy Company's payroll register is presented in Illustration 11-16. It shows the data for Michael Jordan in the wages section. In this example, Academy Company's total weekly payroll is $17,210, as shown in the gross earnings column.

Note that this record is a listing of each employee's payroll data for the pay period. In some companies, a payroll register is a journal or book of original entry. Postings are made from it directly to ledger accounts. In other companies, the payroll register is a memorandum record that provides the data for a general journal entry and subsequent posting to the ledger accounts. At Academy Company, the latter procedure is followed.

Illustration 11-16
Payroll register

ACADEMY COMPANY
Payroll Register
For the Week Ending January 14, 2005

Employee	Total Hours	Earnings			Deductions						Paid			Accounts Debited	
		Regular	Over-time	Gross	FICA	Federal Income Tax	State Income Tax	United Fund	Union Dues	Total	Net Pay	Check No.	Office Salaries Expense	Wages Expense
Office Salaries														
Arnold, Patricia	40	580.00		580.00	46.40	61.00	11.60	15.00		134.00	446.00	998	580.00	
Canton, Matthew	40	590.00		590.00	47.20	63.00	11.80	20.00		142.00	448.00	999	590.00	
Mueller, William	40	530.00		530.00	42.40	54.00	10.60	11.00		118.00	412.0	1000	530.00	
Subtotal		5,200.00		5,200.00	416.00	1,090.00	104.00	120.00		1,730.00	3,470.00		5,200.00	
Wages														
Bennett, Robin	42	480.00	36.00	516.00	41.28	43.00	10.32	18.00	5.00	117.60	398.40	1025		516.00
Jordan, Michael	**44**	**480.00**	**72.00**	**552.00**	**44.16**	**49.00**	**11.04**	**10.00**	**5.00**	**119.20**	**432.80**	**1028**		**552.00**
Milroy, Lee	43	480.00	54.00	534.00	42.72	46.00	10.68	10.00	5.00	114.40	419.60	1029		534.00
Subtotal		11,000.00	1,010.00	12,010.00	960.80	2,400.00	240.20	301.50	115.00	4,017.50	7,992.50			12,010.00
Total		16,200.00	1,010.00	17,210.00	1,376.80	3,490.00	344.20	421.50	115.00	5,747.50	11,462.50		5,200.00	12,010.00

Recognizing Payroll Expenses and Liabilities

From the payroll register in Illustration 11-16, a journal entry is made to record the payroll. For the week ending January 14 the entry is:

Jan. 14	Office Salaries Expense	5,200.00	
	Wages Expense	12,010.00	
	FICA Taxes Payable		1,376.80
	Federal Income Taxes Payable		3,490.00
	State Income Taxes Payable		344.20
	United Fund Payable		421.50
	Union Dues Payable		115.00
	Salaries and Wages Payable		11,462.50
	(To record payroll for the week ending January 14)		

```
A    =    L    +    OE
    +1,376.80   −5,200.00 Exp
    +3,490.00   −12,010.00 Exp
    +344.20
    +421.50
    +115.00
    +11,472.50
```

Cash Flows
no effect

Specific liability accounts are credited for the mandatory and voluntary deductions made during the pay period. In the example, debits to Office Salaries and Wages Expense are used for gross earnings because office workers are on a salary and other employees are paid on an hourly rate. In other companies, there may be debits to other accounts such as Store Salaries or Sales Salaries. The amount credited to Salaries and Wages Payable is the sum of the individual checks the employees will receive.

Recording Payment of the Payroll

Payment by check is made either from the employer's regular bank account or a payroll bank account. Each paycheck is usually accompanied by a detachable **statement of earnings** document. This shows the employee's gross earnings, payroll deductions, and net pay for the period and for the year-to-date. The Academy Company uses its regular bank account for payroll checks. The paycheck and statement of earnings for Michael Jordan are shown in Illustration 11-17 (on page 464).

Illustration 11-17
Paycheck and statement of earnings

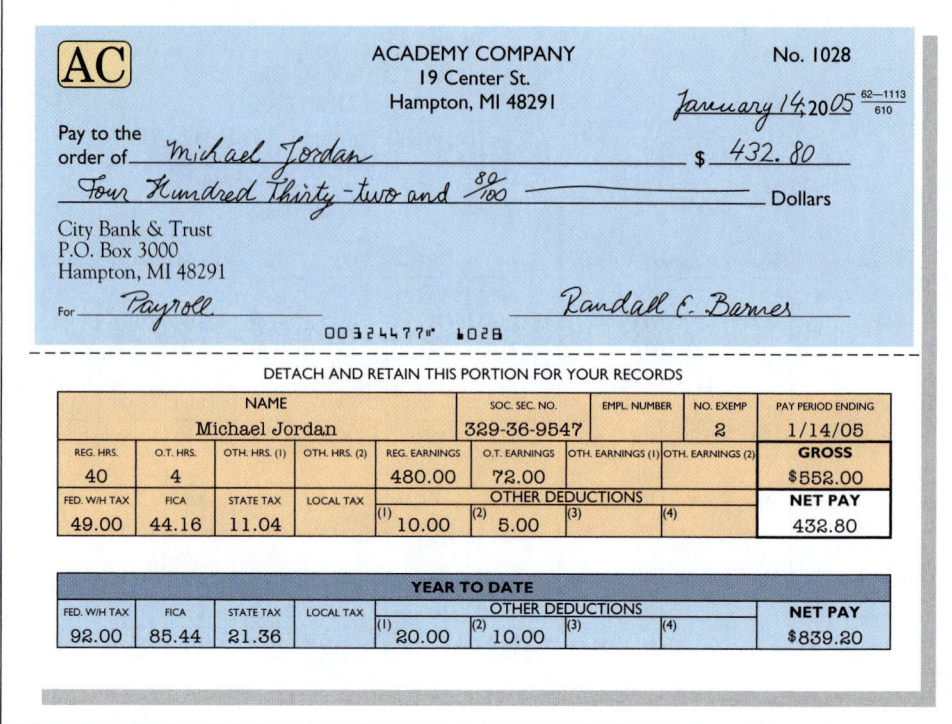

Following payment of the payroll, the check numbers are entered in the payroll register. The entry to record payment of the payroll for Academy Company is as follows.

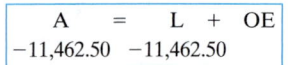

A = L + OE
−11,462.50 −11,462.50

Cash Flows
−11,462.50

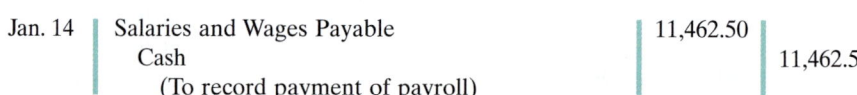

Jan. 14	Salaries and Wages Payable	11,462.50	
	Cash		11,462.50
	(To record payment of payroll)		

When currency is used in payment, one check is prepared for the payroll's total amount of net pay. This check is then cashed, and the coins and currency are inserted in individual pay envelopes for disbursement to individual employees.

BEFORE YOU GO ON...

Review It

1. Identify two internal control procedures that apply to each payroll function.
2. What are the primary sources of gross earnings?
3. What payroll deductions are (a) mandatory and (b) voluntary?
4. What account titles are used in recording a payroll, assuming only mandatory payroll deductions are involved?

Do It

Your cousin Stan is establishing a house-cleaning business and will have a number of employees working for him. He is aware that documentation procedures are an important part of internal control. But he is confused about the difference between an employee earnings record and a payroll register. He asks you to explain the principal differences, because he wants to be sure that he sets up the proper payroll procedures.

Employer Payroll Taxes

Payroll tax expense for businesses results from three taxes **levied on employers** by governmental agencies. These taxes are: (1) FICA, (2) federal unemployment tax, and (3) state unemployment tax. These taxes plus such items as paid vacations and pensions (discussed in the appendix to this chapter) are collectively referred to as **fringe benefits**. As indicated earlier, the cost of fringe benefits in many companies is substantial.

STUDY OBJECTIVE 8

Describe and record employer payroll taxes.

ACCOUNTING IN ACTION **Business Insight**

The battle over fringe benefits has increased as benefits outpace wages and salaries. Growing faster than pay, benefits equaled 38% of wages and salaries in a recent year. While vacations and other forms of paid leave still take the biggest bite of the benefits pie, medical costs are the fastest-growing item.

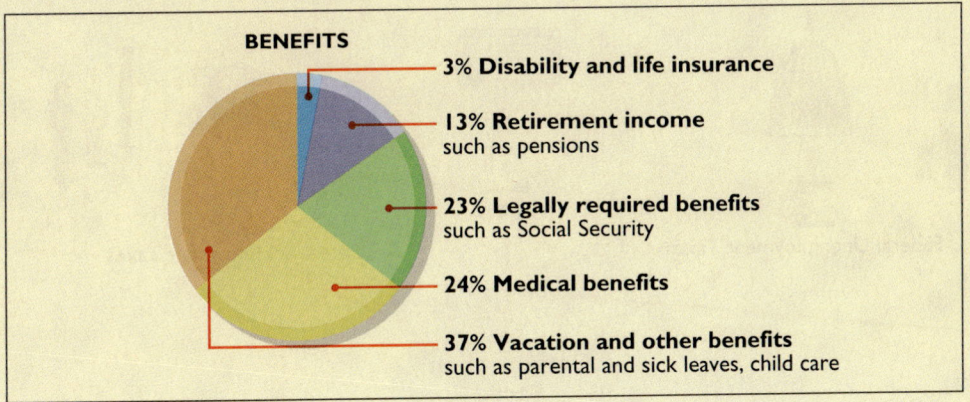

BENEFITS

- 3% Disability and life insurance
- 13% Retirement income such as pensions
- 23% Legally required benefits such as Social Security
- 24% Medical benefits
- 37% Vacation and other benefits such as parental and sick leaves, child care

FICA Taxes

We have seen that each employee must pay FICA taxes. An employer must match each employee's FICA contribution. The matching contribution results in **payroll tax expense** to the employer. The employer's tax is subject to the same rate and maximum earnings applicable to the employee. The account, FICA Taxes Payable, is used for both the employee's and the employer's FICA contributions. For the January 14 payroll, Academy Company's FICA tax contribution is $1,376.80 ($17,210.00 × 8%).

Federal Unemployment Taxes

The Federal Unemployment Tax Act (FUTA) is another feature of the federal Social Security program. **Federal unemployment taxes** provide benefits for a limited period of time to employees who lose their jobs through no fault of their own. Under provisions of the Act, the employer is required to pay a tax of 6.2% on the first $9,000 of gross wages paid to each employee during a calendar year. The law allows the employer a maximum credit of 5.4% on the federal rate for contributions to state unemployment taxes. Because of this provision, state unemployment tax laws generally provide for a 5.4% rate. The effective federal unemployment tax rate thus becomes 0.8% (6.2% − 5.4%). This tax is borne **entirely by the employer**. There is no deduction or withholding from employees.

The account Federal Unemployment Taxes Payable is used to recognize this liability. The federal unemployment tax for Academy Company for the January 14 payroll is $137.68 ($17,210.00 × 0.8%).

> **HELPFUL HINT**
>
> FICA taxes are paid by both the employer and employee. Federal unemployment taxes and (in most states) the state unemployment taxes are borne entirely by the employer.

State Unemployment Taxes

All states have unemployment compensation programs under state unemployment tax acts (SUTA). Like federal unemployment taxes, **state unemployment taxes** provide benefits to employees who lose their jobs. These taxes are levied on employers.[2] The basic rate is usually 5.4% on the first $9,000 of wages paid to an employee during the year. The basic rate is adjusted according to the employer's experience rating: Companies with a history of unstable employment may pay more than the basic rate. Companies with a history of stable employment may pay less than 5.4%. Regardless of the rate paid, the credit on the federal unemployment tax is still 5.4%.

The account State Unemployment Taxes Payable is used for this liability. The state unemployment tax for Academy Company for the January 14 payroll is $929.34 ($17,210.00 × 5.4%).

Illustration 11-18 summarizes the types of employer payroll taxes.

Illustration 11-18
Employer payroll taxes

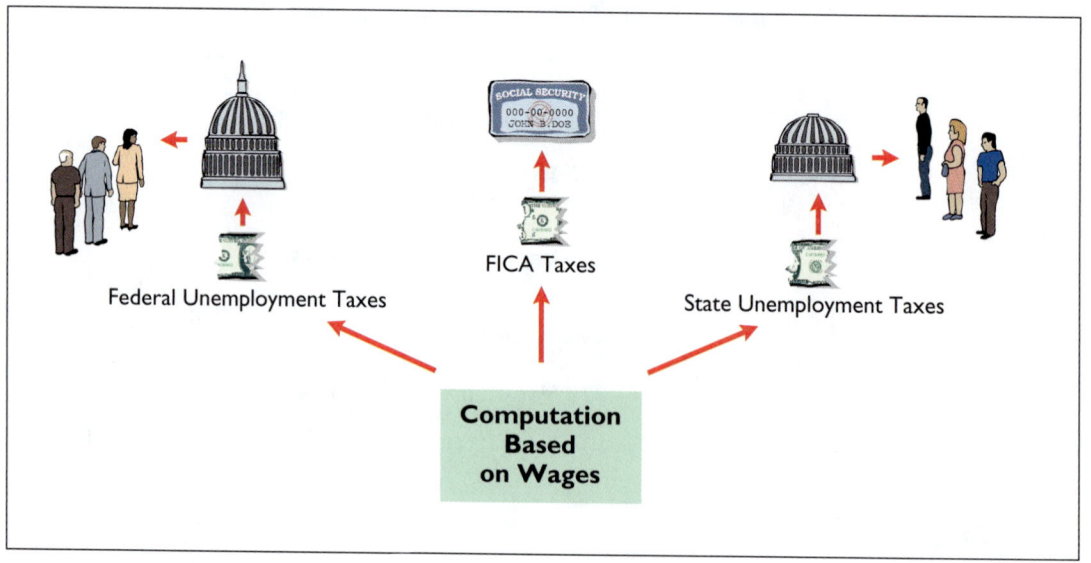

Federal Unemployment Taxes

FICA Taxes

State Unemployment Taxes

Computation Based on Wages

---

[2]In a few states, the employee is also required to make a contribution. In this textbook, including the homework, we will assume that the tax is only on the employer.

Recording Employer Payroll Taxes

Employer payroll taxes are usually recorded at the same time the payroll is journalized. The entire amount of gross pay ($17,210.00) shown in the payroll register in Illustration 11-16 is subject to each of the three taxes mentioned above. Accordingly, the entry to record the payroll tax expense associated with the January 14 payroll is:

Jan. 14	Payroll Tax Expense	2,443.82	
	FICA Taxes Payable		1,376.80
	Federal Unemployment Taxes Payable		137.68
	State Unemployment Taxes Payable		929.34
	(To record employer's payroll taxes on		
	January 14 payroll)		

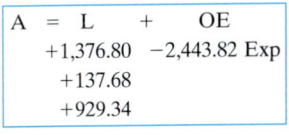

Cash Flows
no effect

Separate liability accounts are used instead of a single credit to Payroll Taxes Payable. Why? Because these liabilities are payable to different taxing authorities at different dates. The liability accounts are classified in the balance sheet as current liabilities since they will be paid within the next year. Payroll Tax Expense is classified on the income statement as an operating expense.

Filing and Remitting Payroll Taxes

Preparation of payroll tax returns is the responsibility of the payroll department. Payment of the taxes is made by the treasurer's department. Much of the information for the returns is obtained from employee earnings records.

For purposes of reporting and remitting to the IRS, FICA taxes and federal income taxes that were withheld are combined. **The taxes must be reported quarterly**, no later than one month following the close of each quarter. The remitting requirements depend on the amount of taxes withheld and the length of the pay period. Remittances are made through deposits in either a Federal Reserve bank or an authorized commercial bank.

Federal unemployment taxes are generally filed and remitted **annually** on or before January 31 of the subsequent year. Earlier payments are required when the tax exceeds a specified amount. State unemployment taxes usually must be filed and paid by the **end of the month following each quarter**. When payroll taxes are paid, payroll liability accounts are debited, and cash is credited.

The employer is also required to provide each employee with a **Wage and Tax Statement (Form W-2)** by January 31 following the end of a calendar year. This statement shows gross earnings, FICA taxes withheld, and income taxes withheld for the year. The required W-2 form for Michael Jordan, using assumed annual data, is shown in Illustration 11-19 (on page 468).

Illustration 11-19
W-2 form

Form **W-2 Wage and Tax Statement**			Calendar Year **2005**

| **1** Control number | | OMB No. 1545-0008 | |

| **2** Employer's name, address and ZIP code | **3** Employer's identification number 36-2167852 | **4** Employer's State number |

Academy Company
19 Center St.
Hampton, MI 48291

| **5** Stat. employee ☐ | Deceased ☐ | Legal rep. ☐ | 942 emp. ☐ | Subtotal ☐ | Void ☐ |

| **6** Allocated tips | **7** Advance EIC payment |

| **8** Employee's social security number 329-36-9547 | **9** Federal income tax withheld $2,248.00 | **10** Wages, tips, other compensation $26,300.00 | **11** Social security tax withheld $2,104.00 |

| **12** Employee's name, address, and ZIP code | **13** Social security wages $26,300.00 | **14** Social security tips |

| | **16** | |

Michael Jordan
2345 Mifflin Ave.
Hampton, MI 48292

| **17** State income tax $526.00 | **18** State wages, tips, etc. | **19** Name of State Michigan |
| **20** Local income tax | **21** Local wages, tips, etc. | **22** Name of locality |

The employer must send a copy of each employee's Wage and Tax Statement (Form W-2) to the Social Security Administration. This agency subsequently furnishes the Internal Revenue Service with the income data required.

BEFORE YOU GO ON...

Review It

1. What payroll taxes are levied on employers?
2. What accounts are involved in accruing employer payroll taxes?

Do It

In January, the payroll supervisor determines that gross earnings in Halo Company are $70,000. All earnings are subject to 8% FICA taxes, 5.4% state unemployment taxes, and 0.8% federal unemployment taxes. You are asked to record the employer's payroll taxes.

ACTION PLAN

■ Compute the employer's payroll taxes on the period's gross earnings.
■ Identify the expense account(s) to be debited.
■ Identify the liability account(s) to be credited.

SOLUTION   The entry to record the employer's payroll taxes is:

Payroll Tax Expense	9,940	
FICA Taxes Payable ($70,000 × 8%)		5,600
Federal Unemployment Taxes Payable ($70,000 × 0.8%)		560
State Unemployment Taxes Payable ($70,000 × 5.4%)		3,780
(To record employer's payroll taxes		
on January payroll)		

Related exercise material: *BE11-10, E11-10, and E11-12.*

☑ THE NAVIGATOR

DEMONSTRATION PROBLEM

Indiana Jones Company had the following selected transactions.

Feb. 1 Signs a $50,000, 6-month, 9%-interest-bearing note payable to CitiBank and receives $50,000 in cash.

10 Cash register sales total $43,200, which includes an 8% sales tax.

28 The payroll for the month consists of Sales Salaries $32,000 and Office Salaries $18,000. All wages are subject to 8% FICA taxes. A total of $8,900 federal income taxes are withheld. The salaries are paid on March 1.

28 The following adjustment data are developed.
1. Interest expense of $375 has been incurred on the note.
2. Employer payroll taxes include 8% FICA taxes, a 5.4% state unemployment tax, and a 0.8% federal unemployment tax.
3. Some sales were made under warranty. Of the units sold under warranty, 350 are expected to become defective. Repair costs are estimated to be $40 per unit.

Instructions

(a) Journalize the February transactions.

(b) Journalize the adjusting entries at February 28.

SOLUTION TO DEMONSTRATION PROBLEM

(a) Feb. 1	Cash	50,000	
	Notes Payable		50,000
	(Issued 6-month, 9%-interest-bearing note to CitiBank)		
10	Cash	43,200	
	Sales ($43,200 ÷ 1.08)		40,000
	Sales Taxes Payable ($40,000 × 8%)		3,200
	(To record sales and sales taxes payable)		
28	Sales Salaries Expense	32,000	
	Office Salaries Expense	18,000	
	FICA Taxes Payable (8% × $50,000)		4,000
	Federal Income Taxes Payable		8,900
	Salaries Payable		37,100
	(To record February salaries)		
(b) Feb. 28	Interest Expense	375	
	Interest Payable		375
	(To record accrued interest for February)		
28	Payroll Tax Expense	7,100	
	FICA Taxes Payable		4,000
	Federal Unemployment Taxes Payable		400
	(0.8% × $50,000)		
	State Unemployment Taxes Payable		2,700
	(5.4% × $50,000)		
	(To record employer's payroll taxes on February payroll)		
28	Warranty Expense (350 × $40)	14,000	
	Estimated Warranty Liability		14,000
	(To record estimated product warranty liability)		

ACTION PLAN

■ To determine sales, divide the cash register total by 100% plus the sales tax percentage.

■ Base payroll taxes on gross earnings.

■ Expense warranty costs in the period in which the sale occurs.

☑ THE NAVIGATOR

SUMMARY OF STUDY OBJECTIVES

1. **Explain a current liability, and identify the major types of current liabilities.** A current liability is a debt that can reasonably be expected to be paid (1) from existing current assets or through the creation of other current liabilities, and (2) within one year or the operating cycle, whichever is longer. The major types of current liabilities are notes payable, accounts payable, sales taxes payable, unearned revenues, and accrued liabilities such as taxes, salaries and wages, and interest payable.

2. **Describe the accounting for notes payable.** When a promissory note is interest-bearing, the amount of assets received upon the issuance of the note is generally equal to the face value of the note. Interest expense is accrued over the life of the note. At maturity, the amount paid is equal to the face value of the note plus accrued interest.

3. **Explain the accounting for other current liabilities.** Sales taxes payable are recorded at the time the related sales occur. The company serves as a collection agent for the taxing authority. Sales taxes are not an expense to the company. Unearned revenues are initially recorded in an unearned revenue account. As the revenue is earned, a transfer from unearned revenue to earned revenue occurs. The current maturities of long-term debt are reported as a current liability in the balance sheet.

4. **Explain the financial statement presentation and analysis of current liabilities.** The nature and amount of each current liability should be reported in the balance sheet or in schedules in the notes accompanying the statements. The liquidity of a company may be analyzed by computing working capital and the current ratio.

5. **Describe the accounting and disclosure requirements for contingent liabilities.** If the contingency is probable (likely to occur) and the amount is reasonably estimable, the liability should be recorded in the accounts. If the contingency is only reasonably possible (it could happen), then it should be disclosed only in the notes to the financial statements. If the possibility that the contingency will happen is remote (unlikely to occur), it need not be recorded or disclosed.

6. **Discuss the objectives of internal control for payroll.** The objectives of internal control for payroll are (1) to safeguard company assets against unauthorized payments of payrolls, and (2) to ensure the accuracy of the accounting records pertaining to payrolls.

7. **Compute and record the payroll for a pay period.** The computation of the payroll involves gross earnings, payroll deductions, and net pay. In recording the payroll, salaries (or wages) expense is debited for gross earnings, individual tax and other liability accounts are credited for payroll deductions, and salaries (wages) payable is credited for net pay. When the payroll is paid, Salaries and Wages Payable is debited, and Cash is credited.

8. **Describe and record employer payroll taxes.** Employer payroll taxes consist of FICA, federal unemployment taxes, and state unemployment taxes. The taxes are usually accrued at the time the payroll is recorded by debiting Payroll Tax Expense and crediting separate liability accounts for each type of tax.

☑ **THE NAVIGATOR**

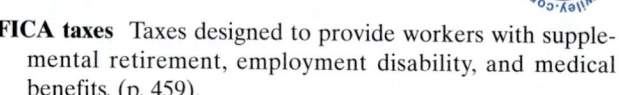

GLOSSARY

Bonus Compensation to management and other personnel, based on factors such as increased sales or the amount of net income. (p. 458).

Contingent liability A potential liability that may become an actual liability in the future. (p. 452).

Current ratio A measure of a company's liquidity; computed as current assets divided by current liabilities. (p. 452).

Employee earnings record A cumulative record of each employee's gross earnings, deductions, and net pay during the year. (p. 461).

Employee's Withholding Allowance Certificate (Form W-4) An Internal Revenue Service form on which the employee indicates the number of allowances claimed for withholding federal income taxes. (p. 460).

Federal unemployment taxes Taxes imposed on the employer by the federal government that provide benefits for a limited time period to employees who lose their jobs through no fault of their own. (p. 466).

FICA taxes Taxes designed to provide workers with supplemental retirement, employment disability, and medical benefits. (p. 459).

Gross earnings Total compensation earned by an employee. (p. 458).

Net pay Gross earnings less payroll deductions. (p. 461).

Notes payable Obligations in the form of written promissory notes. (p. 448).

Payroll deductions Deductions from gross earnings to determine the amount of a paycheck. (p. 458).

Payroll register A payroll record that accumulates the gross earnings, deductions, and net pay by employee for each pay period. (p. 462).

Salaries Employee pay based on a fixed amount rather than an hourly rate. (p. 455).

Statement of earnings A document attached to a paycheck that indicates the employee's gross earnings, payroll deductions, and net pay. (p. 463).

State unemployment taxes Taxes imposed on the employer by states that provide benefits to employees who lose their jobs. (p. 466).

Wage and Tax Statement (Form W-2) A form showing gross earnings, FICA taxes withheld, and income taxes withheld, prepared annually by an employer for each employee. (p. 467).

Wages Amounts paid to employees based on a rate per hour or on a piece-work basis. (p. 455).

Working capital A measure of a company's liquidity; computed as current assets minus current liabilities. (p. 452).

APPENDIX ADDITIONAL FRINGE BENEFITS

In addition to the three payroll tax fringe benefits, employers incur other substantial fringe benefit costs. Two of the most important are paid absences and post-retirement benefits.

> **STUDY OBJECTIVE 9**
>
> Identify additional fringe benefits associated with employee compensation.

Paid Absences

Employees often are given rights to receive compensation for absences when certain conditions of employment are met. The compensation may be for paid vacations, sick pay benefits, and paid holidays. When the payment for such absences is **probable** and the amount can be **reasonably estimated**, a liability should be accrued for paid future absences. When the amount cannot be reasonably estimated, the potential liability should be disclosed. Ordinarily, vacation pay is the only paid absence that is accrued. The other types of paid absences are only disclosed.[3]

To illustrate, assume that Academy Company employees are entitled to one day's vacation for each month worked. If 30 employees earn an average of $110 per day in a given month, the accrual for vacation benefits in one month is $3,300. The liability is recognized at the end of the month by the following adjusting entry.

Jan. 31	Vacation Benefits Expense	3,300	
	Vacation Benefits Payable		3,300
	(To accrue vacation benefits expense)		

A = L + OE
+3,300 −3,300 Exp

Cash Flows
no effect

This accrual is required by the matching principle. Vacation Benefits Expense is reported as an operating expense in the income statement, and Vacation Benefits Payable is reported as a current liability in the balance sheet.

Later, when vacation benefits are paid, Vacation Benefits Payable is debited and Cash is credited. For example, if the above benefits for 10 employees are paid in July, the entry is:

July 31	Vacation Benefits Payable	1,100	
	Cash		1,100
	(To record payment of vacation benefits)		

A = L + OE
−1,100 −1,100

Cash Flows
−1,100

The magnitude of unpaid absences has gained employers' attention. Consider the case of an assistant superintendent of schools who worked for 20 years and rarely took a vacation or sick day. A month or so before she retired, the school district discovered that she was due nearly $30,000 in accrued benefits. Yet the liability had never been accrued.

---

[3]The typical U.S. company provides an average of 12 days of paid vacations for its employees, at an average cost of 5% of gross earnings.

Postretirement Benefits

Postretirement benefits are benefits provided by employers to retired employees for (1) health care and life insurance and (2) pensions. For many years the accounting for postretirement benefits was on a cash basis. Now, both types of postretirement benefits are accounted for on the accrual basis.

Postretirement Health Care and Life Insurance Benefits

Providing medical and related health care benefits for retirees was at one time an inexpensive and highly effective way of generating employee goodwill. This practice has now turned into one of corporate America's most worrisome financial problems. Runaway medical costs, early retirement, and increased longevity are sending the liability for retiree health plans through the roof.

Many companies began offering retiree health care coverage in the form of Medicare supplements in the 1960s. Almost all plans operated on a pay-as-you-go basis. The companies simply paid for the bills as they came in, rather than setting aside funds to meet the cost of future benefits. These plans were accounted for on the cash basis. But, the FASB concluded that shareholders and creditors should know the amount of the employer's obligations. As a result, employers must now use the **accrual basis** in accounting for postretirement health care and life insurance benefits.

Pension Plans

A **pension plan** is an agreement whereby an employer provides benefits (payments) to employees after they retire. Over 50 million workers currently participate in pension plans in the United States. The need for good accounting for pension plans becomes apparent when one appreciates the size of existing pension funds. Most pension plans are subject to the provisions of ERISA (Employee Retirement Income Security Act), a law enacted to curb abuses in the administration and funding of such plans.

Three parties are generally involved in a pension plan. The **employer** (company) sponsors the pension plan. The **plan administrator** receives the contributions from the employer, invests the pension assets, and makes the benefit payments to the **pension recipients** (retired employees). Illustration 11A-1 indicates the flow of cash among the three parties involved in a pension plan.

Illustration 11A-1
Parties in a pension plan

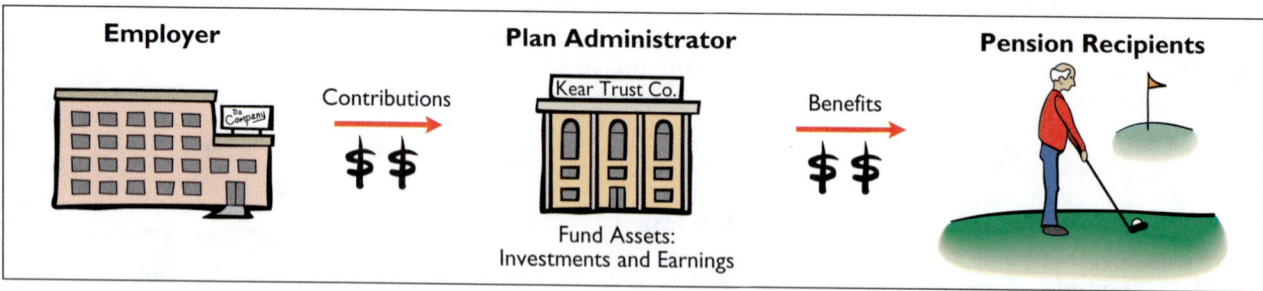

An employer-financed pension is part of the employees' compensation. ERISA establishes the minimum contribution that a company must make each year toward employee pensions. The company records the pension costs as an expense while the employees are working because that is when the company receives benefits from the employees' services. Generally the pension expense is reported as an operating expense in the company's income statement.

Frequently, the amount contributed by the company to the pension plan is different from the amount of the pension expense. A **liability** is recognized when the pension expense to date is **more than** the company's contributions to date. An **asset** is recognized when the pension expense to date is **less than** the company's contributions to date. Further consideration of the accounting for pension plans is left for more advanced courses.

SUMMARY OF STUDY OBJECTIVE FOR APPENDIX

9. **Identify additional fringe benefits associated with employee compensation.** Additional fringe benefits associated with wages are paid absences (paid vacations, sick pay benefits, and paid holidays), and postretirement benefits (health care and life insurance and pensions). Both types of benefits should be accounted for on the accrual basis.

GLOSSARY FOR APPENDIX

Pension plan An agreement whereby an employer provides benefits to employees after they retire. (p. 472).

Postretirement benefits Payments by employers to retired employees for health care, life insurance, and pensions. (p. 472).

*Note: All **asterisked** Questions, Exercises, and Problems relate to material in the appendix to the chapter.

SELF-STUDY QUESTIONS

Self-Study/Self-Test

Answers are at the end of the chapter.

(SO 1) 1. The time period for classifying a liability as current is one year or the operating cycle, whichever is:
   a. longer.
   b. shorter.
   c. probable.
   d. possible.

(SO 1) 2. To be classified as a current liability, a debt must be expected to be paid:
   a. out of existing current assets.
   b. by creating other current liabilities.
   c. within 2 years.
   d. both (a) and (b).

(SO 2) 3. Maggie Sharrer Company borrows $88,500 on September 1, 2005, from Sandwich State Bank by signing an $88,500, 12%, one-year note. What is the accrued interest at December 31, 2005?
   a. $2,655.
   b. $3,540.
   c. $4,425.
   d. $10,620.

(SO 3) 4. Becky Sherrick Company has total proceeds from sales of $4,515. If the proceeds include sales taxes of 5%, the amount to be credited to Sales is:
   a. $4,000.
   b. $4,300.
   c. $4,289.25.
   d. No correct answer given.

(SO 4) 5. Working capital is calculated as:
   a. current assets minus current liabilities.
   b. total assets minus total liabilities.
   c. long-term liabilities minus current liabilities.
   d. both (b) and (c).

(SO 5) 6. A contingent liability should be recorded in the accounts when:
   a. it is probable the contingency will happen, but the amount cannot be reasonably estimated.
   b. it is reasonably possible the contingency will happen, and the amount can be reasonably estimated.
   c. it is probable the contingency will happen, and the amount can be reasonably estimated.
   d. it is reasonably possible the contingency will happen, but the amount cannot be reasonably estimated.

(SO 5) 7. At December 31, Hanes Company prepares an adjusting entry for a product warranty contract. Which of the following accounts is/are included in the entry?
   a. Miscellaneous Expense.
   b. Estimated Warranty Liability.
   c. Repair Parts/Wages Payable.
   d. Both (a) and (b).

(SO 6) 8. The department that should pay the payroll is the:
   a. timekeeping department.
   b. human resources department.
   c. payroll department.
   d. treasurer's department.

(SO 7) **9.** Andy Manion earns $14 per hour for a 40-hour week and $21 per hour for any overtime work. If Manion works 45 hours in a week, gross earnings are:
  a. $560.
  b. $630.
  c. $650.
  d. $665.

(SO 8) **10.** Employer payroll taxes do *not* include:
  a. federal unemployment taxes.
  b. state unemployment taxes.

  c. federal income taxes.
  d. FICA taxes.

*11. Which of the following is *not* an additional fringe benefit? (SO
  a. Postretirement pensions.
  b. Paid absences.
  c. Paid vacations.
  d. Salaries.

QUESTIONS

1. Brad Goebel believes a current liability is a debt that can be expected to be paid in one year. Is Brad correct? Explain.

2. Mark McGwire Company obtains $30,000 in cash by signing a 9%, 6-month, $30,000 note payable to First Bank on July 1. Mark McGwire's fiscal year ends on September 30. What information should be reported for the note payable in the annual financial statements?

3. (a) Your roommate says, "Sales taxes are reported as an expense in the income statement." Do you agree? Explain.
  (b) Planet Hollywood has cash proceeds from sales of $8,400. This amount includes $400 of sales taxes. Give the entry to record the proceeds.

4. Ottawa University sold 10,000 season football tickets at $90 each for its five-game home schedule. What entries should be made (a) when the tickets were sold, and (b) after each game?

5. What is liquidity? What are two measures of liquidity?

6. What is a contingent liability? Give an example of a contingent liability that is usually recorded in the accounts.

7. Under what circumstances is a contingent liability disclosed only in the notes to the financial statements? Under what circumstances is a contingent liability not recorded in the accounts nor disclosed in the notes to the financial statements?

8. You are a newly hired accountant with DeLacey Company. On your first day, the controller asks you to identify the main internal control objectives related to payroll accounting. How would you respond?

9. What are the four functions associated with payroll activities?

10. What is the difference between gross pay and net pay? Which amount should a company record as wages or salaries expense?

11. Which payroll tax is levied on both employers and employees?

12. Are the federal and state income taxes withheld from employee paychecks a payroll tax expense for the employer? Explain your answer.

13. What do the following acronyms stand for: FICA, FUTA, and SUTA?

14. What information is shown in a W-4 statement? In a W-2 statement?

15. Distinguish between the two types of payroll deductions and give examples of each.

16. What are the primary uses of the employee earnings record?

17. (a) Identify the three types of employer payroll taxes.
  (b) How are tax liability accounts and payroll tax expense accounts classified in the financial statements?

*18. Identify three additional types of fringe benefits associated with employees' compensation.

*19. Often during job interviews, the candidate asks the potential employer about the firm's paid absences policy. What are paid absences? How are they accounted for?

*20. What are two types of postretirement benefits? During what years does the FASB advocate expensing the employer's costs of these postretirement benefits?

*21. What basis of accounting for the employer's cost of postretirement health care and life insurance benefits has been used by most companies, and what basis does the FASB now require? Explain the basic difference between these methods in accounting for postretirement benefit costs.

*22. Identify the three parties in a pension plan. What role does each party have in the plan?

BRIEF EXERCISES

Identify whether obligations are current liabilities.

(SO 1)

BE11-1 Cardinal Company has the following obligations at December 31: (a) a note payable for $100,000 due in 2 years, (b) a 10-year mortgage payable of $300,000 payable in ten $30,000 annual payments, (c) interest payable of $15,000 on the mortgage, and (d) accounts payable of $60,000. For each obligation, indicate whether it should be classified as a current liability. (Assume an operating cycle of less than one year.)

BE11-2 Becky Company borrows $60,000 on July 1 from the bank by signing a $60,000, 10%, one-year note payable.
(a) Prepare the journal entry to record the proceeds of the note.
(b) Prepare the journal entry to record accrued interest at December 31, assuming adjusting entries are made only at the end of the year.

Prepare entries for an interest-bearing note payable.

(SO 2)

BE11-3 Goodwin Auto Supply does not segregate sales and sales taxes at the time of sale. The register total for March 16 is $13,440. All sales are subject to a 5% sales tax. Compute sales taxes payable, and make the entry to record sales taxes payable and sales.

Compute and record sales taxes payable.

(SO 3)

BE11-4 Wichita State University sells 4,000 season basketball tickets at $120 each for its 12-game home schedule. Give the entry to record (a) the sale of the season tickets and (b) the revenue earned by playing the first home game.

Prepare entries for unearned revenues.

(SO 3)

BE11-5 **Yahoo! Inc.'s** 2001 financial statements contain the following selected data (in thousands).

Current assets	$1,051,533
Total assets	2,379,346
Current liabilities	358,517
Total liabilities	382,323

Analyze liquidity.

(SO 4)

Compute the following ratios.
(a) Working capital.
(b) Current ratio.

BE11-6 On December 1, Viná Company introduces a new product that includes a one-year warranty on parts. In December, 1,000 units are sold. Management believes that 5% of the units will be defective and that the average warranty costs will be $60 per unit. Prepare the adjusting entry at December 31 to accrue the estimated warranty cost.

Prepare adjusting entry for warranty costs.

(SO 5)

BE11-7 Hernandez Company has the following payroll procedures.

(a) Supervisor approves overtime work.
(b) The human resources department prepares hiring authorization forms for new hires.
(c) A second payroll department employee verifies payroll calculations.
(d) The treasurer's department pays employees.

Identify the payroll function to which each procedure pertains.

Identify payroll functions.

(SO 6)

BE11-8 Sandy Teter's regular hourly wage rate is $16, and she receives an hourly rate of $24 for work in excess of 40 hours. During a January pay period, Sandy works 45 hours. Sandy's federal income tax withholding is $95, and she has no voluntary deductions. Compute Sandy Teter's gross earnings and net pay for the pay period.

Compute gross earnings and net pay.

(SO 7)

BE11-9 Data for Sandy Teter are presented in BE11-8. Prepare the journal entries to record **(a)** Sandy's pay for the period and **(b)** the payment of Sandy's wages. Use January 15 for the end of the pay period and the payment date.

Record a payroll and the payment of wages.

(SO 7)

BE11-10 In January, gross earnings in Yoon Company totaled $90,000. All earnings are subject to 8% FICA taxes, 5.4% state unemployment taxes, and 0.8% federal unemployment taxes. Prepare the entry to record January payroll tax expense.

Record employer payroll taxes.

(SO 8)

*BE11-11 At Alomar Company employees are entitled to one day's vacation for each month worked. In January, 50 employees worked the full month. Record the vacation pay liability for January assuming the average daily pay for each employee is $120.

Record estimated vacation benefits.

(SO 9)

EXERCISES

E11-1 On June 1, Padillio Company borrows $70,000 from First Bank on a 6-month, $70,000, 12% note.

Prepare entries for interest-bearing notes.

(SO 2)

Instructions
(a) Prepare the entry on June 1.
(b) Prepare the adjusting entry on June 30.
(c) Prepare the entry at maturity (December 1), assuming monthly adjusting entries have been made through November 30.
(d) What was the total financing cost (interest expense)?

Journalize sales and related taxes.

(SO 3)

E11-2 In providing accounting services to small businesses, you encounter the following situations pertaining to cash sales.

1. Sue Jackson Company rings up sales and sales taxes separately on its cash register. On April 10, the register totals are sales $25,000 and sales taxes $1,500.
2. Person Company does not segregate sales and sales taxes. Its register total for April 15 is $20,330, which includes a 7% sales tax.

Instructions

Prepare the entry to record the sales transactions and related taxes for each client.

Journalize unearned subscription revenue.

(SO 3)

E11-3 Nevin Company publishes a monthly sports magazine, *Fishing Preview*. Subscriptions to the magazine cost $20 per year. During November 2005, Nevin sells 9,000 subscriptions beginning with the December issue. Nevin prepares financial statements quarterly and recognizes subscription revenue earned at the end of the quarter. The company uses the accounts Unearned Subscriptions and Subscription Revenue.

Instructions

(a) Prepare the entry in November for the receipt of the subscriptions.
(b) Prepare the adjusting entry at December 31, 2005, to record subscription revenue earned in December 2005.
(c) Prepare the adjusting entry at March 31, 2006, to record subscription revenue earned in the first quarter of 2006.

Record estimated liability and expense for warranties.

(SO 5)

E11-4 Boone Company sells automatic can openers under a 75-day warranty for defective merchandise. Based on past experience, Boone estimates that 3% of the units sold will become defective during the warranty period. Management estimates that the average cost of replacing or repairing a defective unit is $15. The units sold and units defective that occurred during the last 2 months of 2005 are as follows.

Month	Units Sold	Units Defective Prior to December 31
November	30,000	600
December	32,000	400

Instructions

(a) Determine the estimated warranty liability at December 31 for the units sold in November and December.
(b) Prepare the journal entries to record the estimated liability for warranties and the costs incurred in honoring 1,000 warranty claims. (Assume actual costs of $15,000.)
(c) Give the entry to record the honoring of 500 warranty contracts in January at an average cost of $15.

Prepare the current liability section of the balance sheet.

(SO 1, 2, 3, 4, 5)

E11-5 Larkin Online Company has the following liability accounts after posting adjusting entries: Accounts Payable $63,000, Unearned Ticket Revenue $24,000, Estimated Warranty Liability $18,000, Interest Payable $8,000, Mortgage Payable $120,000, Notes Payable $80,000, and Sales Taxes Payable $10,000. Assume the company's operating cycle is less than 1 year, ticket revenue will be earned within 1 year, warranty costs are expected to be incurred within 1 year, and the notes mature in 3 years.

Instructions

(a) Prepare the current liabilities section of the balance sheet, assuming $40,000 of the mortgage is payable next year.
(b) Comment on Larkin Online Company's liquidity, assuming total current assets are $300,000.

Calculate liquidity ratios.

(SO 4)

E11-6 **Kroger Co.**'s 2002 financial statements contained the following selected data (in millions).

Current assets	$ 5,512	Accounts receivable	$679
Total assets	19,087	Interest expense	648
Current liabilities	5,485	Income taxes	668
Total liabilities	15,585	Net income	1,043
Cash	161		

Instructions
Compute these values:

(a) Working capital.
(b) Current ratio.

E11-7 The following financial data were reported by **3M Company** for 2000 and 2001 ($ in millions).

Calculate current ratio and working capital before and after paying accounts payable.

(SO 4)

3M COMPANY
Balance Sheets (partial)

	2001	**2000**
Current assets		
Cash and cash equivalents	$ 616	$ 302
Accounts receivable, net	2,482	2,891
Inventories	2,091	2,312
Other current assets	1,107	874
Total current assets	$6,296	$6,379
Current liabilities	$4,509	$4,754

Instructions
(a) Calculate the current ratio and working capital for 3M for 2000 and 2001.
(b) Suppose that at the end of 2001 3M management used $200 million cash to pay off $200 million of accounts payable. How would its current ratio and working capital have changed?

E11-8 Betty Williams' regular hourly wage rate is $14.00, and she receives a wage of 1½ times the regular hourly rate for work in excess of 40 hours. During a March weekly pay period Betty worked 42 hours. Her gross earnings prior to the current week were $6,000. Betty is married and claims three withholding allowances. Her only voluntary deduction is for group hospitalization insurance at $15.00 per week.

Compute net pay and record pay for one employee.

(SO 7)

Instructions
(a) Compute the following amounts for Betty's wages for the current week.
  (1) Gross earnings.
  (2) FICA taxes. (Assume an 8% rate on maximum of $87,000.)
  (3) Federal income taxes withheld. (Use the withholding table in the text, page 460.)
  (4) State income taxes withheld. (Assume a 2.0% rate.)
  (5) Net pay.
(b) Record Betty's pay, assuming she is an office computer operator.

E11-9 Employee earnings records for Brantley Company reveal the following gross earnings for four employees through the pay period of December 15.

Compute maximum FICA deductions.

(SO 7)

C. Mays	$83,500	D. Delgado	$86,100
L. Jeter	$85,600	T. Rolen	$87,000

For the pay period ending December 31, each employee's gross earnings is $3,000. The FICA tax rate is 8% on gross earnings of $87,000.

Instructions
Compute the FICA withholdings that should be made for each employee for the December 31 pay period. (Show computations.)

Prepare payroll register and record payroll and payroll tax expense.

(SO 7, 8)

E11-10 Canseco Company has the following data for the weekly payroll ending January 31.

Employee	\<Hours\> M	T	W	T	F	S	Hourly Rate	Federal Income Tax Withholding	Health Insurance
M. Hindi	8	8	9	8	10	3	$11	$34	$10
E. Benson	8	8	8	8	8	2	13	37	15
K. Estes	9	10	8	8	9	0	14	58	15

Employees are paid 1½ times the regular hourly rate for all hours worked in excess of 40 hours per week. FICA taxes are 8% on the first $87,000 of gross earnings. Canseco Company is subject to 5.4% state unemployment taxes and 0.8% federal unemployment taxes on the first $7,000 of gross earnings.

Instructions
(a) Prepare the payroll register for the weekly payroll.
(b) Prepare the journal entries to record the payroll and Canseco's payroll tax expense.

Compute missing payroll amounts and record payroll.

(SO 7)

E11-11 Selected data from a February payroll register for Landmark Company are presented below. Some amounts are intentionally omitted.

Gross earnings:				
Regular	$8,900	State income taxes	$(3)
Overtime	(1)	Union dues	100
Total	(2)	Total deductions	(4)
Deductions:		Net pay	$7,215
FICA taxes	$ 760	Accounts debited:	
Federal income taxes	1,140	Warehouse wages	(5)
		Store wages	$4,000

FICA taxes are 8%. State income taxes are 3% of gross earnings.

Instructions
(a) Fill in the missing amounts.
(b) Journalize the February payroll and the payment of the payroll.

Determine employer's payroll taxes; record payroll tax expense.

(SO 8)

E11-12 According to a payroll register summary of Cruz Company, the amount of employees' gross pay in December was $850,000, of which $70,000 was not subject to FICA tax and $760,000 was not subject to state and federal unemployment taxes.

Instructions
(a) Determine the employer's payroll tax expense for the month, using the following rates: FICA 8%, state unemployment 5.4%, federal unemployment 0.8%.
(b) Prepare the journal entry to record December payroll tax expense.

Prepare adjusting entries for fringe benefits.

(SO 9)

*E11-13 Bunill Company has two fringe benefit plans for its employees:

1. It grants employees 2 days' vacation for each month worked. Ten employees worked the entire month of March at an average daily wage of $80 per employee.
2. In its pension plan the company recognizes 10% of gross earnings as a pension expense. Gross earnings in March were $30,000. No contribution has been made to the pension fund.

Instructions
Prepare the adjusting entries at March 31.

PROBLEMS: SET A

Prepare current liability entries, adjusting entries, and current liabilities section.

(SO 1, 2, 3, 4, 5)

P11-1A On January 1, 2005, the ledger of Shumway Software Company contains the following liability accounts.

Accounts Payable	$42,500
Sales Taxes Payable	5,800
Unearned Service Revenue	15,000

During January the following selected transactions occurred.

Jan. 1 Borrowed $15,000 in cash from Amsterdam Bank on a 4-month, 8%, $15,000 note.
   5 Sold merchandise for cash totaling $10,400, which includes 4% sales taxes.
   12 Provided services for customers who had made advance payments of $9,000. (Credit Service Revenue.)
   14 Paid state treasurer's department for sales taxes collected in December 2004, $5,800.
   20 Sold 700 units of a new product on credit at $52 per unit, plus 4% sales tax. This new product is subject to a 1-year warranty.
   25 Sold merchandise for cash totaling $12,480, which includes 4% sales taxes.

Instructions
(a) Journalize the January transactions.
(b) Journalize the adjusting entries at January 31 for (1) the outstanding notes payable, and (2) estimated warranty liability, assuming warranty costs are expected to equal 5% of sales of the new product.
(c) Prepare the current liabilities section of the balance sheet at January 31, 2005. Assume no change in accounts payable.

(c) Current liability total $67,756

P11-2A Graves Drug Store has four employees who are paid on an hourly basis plus time-and-a-half for all hours worked in excess of 40 a week. Payroll data for the week ended February 15, 2005, are presented below.

Prepare payroll register and payroll entries.

(SO 7, 8)

Employees	Hours Worked	Hourly Rate	Federal Income Tax Withholdings	United Fund
L. Leiss	39	$14.00	$?	$–0–
S. Bjork	42	$12.00	?	5.00
M. Cape	44	$12.00	61	7.50
L. Wild	48	$12.00	52	5.00

Leiss and Bjork are married. They claim 2 and 4 withholding allowances, respectively. The following tax rates are applicable: FICA 8%, state income taxes 3%, state unemployment taxes 5.4%, and federal unemployment 0.8%. The first three employees are sales clerks (store wages expense). The fourth employee performs administrative duties (office wages expense).

Instructions
(a) Prepare a payroll register for the weekly payroll. (Use the wage-bracket withholding table in the text for federal income tax withholdings.)
(b) Journalize the payroll on February 15, 2005, and the accrual of employer payroll taxes.
(c) Journalize the payment of the payroll on February 16, 2005.
(d) Journalize the deposit in a Federal Reserve bank on February 28, 2005, of the FICA and federal income taxes payable to the government.

(a) Net pay $1,786.32; Store wages expense $1,614.00
(b) Payroll tax expense $317.79
(d) Cash paid $546.08

P11-3A The payroll procedures used by three different companies are described below.

Identify internal control weaknesses and make recommendations for improvement.

(SO 6)

1. In Brewer Company each employee is required to mark on a clock card the hours worked. At the end of each pay period, the employee must have this clock card approved by the department manager. The approved card is then given to the payroll department by the employee. Subsequently, the treasurer's department pays the employee by check.
2. In Hilyard Computer Company clock cards and time clocks are used. At the end of each pay period, the department manager initials the cards, indicates the rates of pay, and sends them to payroll. A payroll register is prepared from the cards by the payroll department. Cash equal to the total net pay in each department is given to the department manager, who pays the employees in cash.
3. In Hyun-chan Company employees are required to record hours worked by "punching" clock cards in a time clock. At the end of each pay period, the clock cards are collected by the department manager. The manager prepares a payroll register in duplicate and forwards the original to payroll. In payroll, the summaries are checked for mathematical accuracy, and a payroll supervisor pays each employee by check.

Instructions

(a) ► Indicate the weakness(es) in internal control in each company.

(b) For each weakness, describe the control procedure(s) that will provide effective internal control. Use the following format for your answer:

(a) Weaknesses **(b) Recommended Procedures**

Journalize payroll transactions and adjusting entries.

(SO 7, 8, 9)

P11-4A The following payroll liability accounts are included in the ledger of Eikleberry Company on January 1, 2005.

FICA Taxes Payable	$ 662.20
Federal Income Taxes Payable	1,254.60
State Income Taxes Payable	102.15
Federal Unemployment Taxes Payable	312.00
State Unemployment Taxes Payable	1,954.40
Union Dues Payable	250.00
U.S. Savings Bonds Payable	350.00

In January, the following transactions occurred.

Jan. 10 Sent check for $250.00 to union treasurer for union dues.
   12 Deposited check for $1,916.80 in Federal Reserve bank for FICA taxes and federal income taxes withheld.
   15 Purchased U.S. Savings Bonds for employees by writing check for $350.00.
   17 Paid state income taxes withheld from employees.
   20 Paid federal and state unemployment taxes.
   31 Completed monthly payroll register, which shows office salaries $17,600, store wages $27,400, FICA taxes withheld $3,600, federal income taxes payable $1,770, state income taxes payable $360, union dues payable $400, United Fund contributions payable $1,800, and net pay $37,070.
   31 Prepared payroll checks for the net pay and distributed checks to employees.

At January 31, the company also makes the following accruals pertaining to employee compensation.

1. Employer payroll taxes: FICA taxes 8%, state unemployment taxes 5.4%, and federal unemployment taxes 0.8%.

*2. Vacation pay: 5% of gross earnings.

(b) Payroll tax expense $6,390.00; Vacation benefits expense $2,250

Instructions

(a) Journalize the January transactions.

(b) Journalize the adjustments pertaining to employee compensation at January 31.

Prepare entries for payroll and payroll taxes; prepare W-2 data.

(SO 7, 8, 9)

P11-5A For the year ended December 31, 2005, R. Visnak Company reports the following summary payroll data.

Gross earnings:	
Administrative salaries	$180,000
Electricians' wages	320,000
Total	$500,000
Deductions:	
FICA taxes	$ 35,200
Federal income taxes withheld	153,000
State income taxes withheld (2.6%)	13,000
United Fund contributions payable	25,000
*Hospital insurance premiums	15,800
Total	$242,000

R. Visnak Company's payroll taxes are: FICA 8%, state unemployment 2.5% (due to a stable employment record), and 0.8% federal unemployment. Gross earnings subject to FICA taxes total $440,000, and unemployment taxes total $110,000.

Instructions

(a) Wages Payable $258,000

(b) Payroll tax expense $38,830

(a) Prepare a summary journal entry at December 31 for the full year's payroll.

(b) Journalize the adjusting entry at December 31 to record the employer's payroll taxes.

(c) The W-2 Wage and Tax Statement requires the dollar data shown on page 481.

Wages, Tips, Other Compensation	Federal Income Tax Withheld	State Income Tax Withheld	FICA Wages	FICA Tax Withheld

Complete the required data for the following employees.

Employee	Gross Earnings	Federal Income Tax Withheld
R. Lopez	$60,000	$27,500
K. Kirk	27,000	11,000

P11-6A The following are selected transactions of Talley Company. Talley prepares financial statements quarterly.

Journalize and post note transactions; show balance sheet presentation.

(SO 2)

Jan.   2   Purchased merchandise on account from Jones Company, $20,000, terms 2/10, n/30.
Feb.   1   Issued a 9%, 2-month, $20,000 note to Jones in payment of account.
Mar. 31   Accrued interest for 2 months on Jones note.
Apr.   1   Paid face value and interest on Jones note.
July   1   Purchased equipment from Seguin Equipment paying $11,000 in cash and signing a 10%, 3-month, $30,000 note.
Sept. 30   Accrued interest for 3 months on Seguin note.
Oct.   1   Paid face value and interest on Seguin note.
Dec.   1   Borrowed $15,000 from the Otago Bank by issuing a 3-month, 8% interest-bearing note with a face value of $15,000.
Dec. 31   Recognized interest expense for 1 month on Otago Bank note.

Instructions
(a) Prepare journal entries for the above transactions and events.
(b) Post to the accounts Notes Payable, Interest Payable, and Interest Expense.
(c) Show the balance sheet presentation of notes payable at December 31.
(d) What is total interest expense for the year?

(d) $1,150

PROBLEMS: SET B

P11-1B On January 1, 2005, the ledger of Zaur Company contains the following liability accounts.

Prepare current liability entries, adjusting entries, and current liabilities section.

(SO 1, 2, 3, 4, 5)

Peachtree

Accounts Payable	$52,000
Sales Taxes Payable	7,700
Unearned Service Revenue	16,000

During January the following selected transactions occurred.

Jan.   5   Sold merchandise for cash totaling $17,280, which includes 8% sales taxes.
       12   Provided services for customers who had made advance payments of $10,000. (Credit Service Revenue.)
       14   Paid state revenue department for sales taxes collected in December 2004 ($7,700).
       20   Sold 600 units of a new product on credit at $50 per unit, plus 8% sales tax. This new product is subject to a 1-year warranty.
       21   Borrowed $18,000 from UCLA Bank on a 3-month, 9%, $18,000 note.
       25   Sold merchandise for cash totaling $12,420, which includes 8% sales taxes.

Instructions
(a) Journalize the January transactions.
(b) Journalize the adjusting entries at January 31 for (1) the outstanding notes payable, and (2) estimated warranty liability, assuming warranty costs are expected to equal 7% of sales of the new product. (*Hint:* Use one-third of a month for the UCLA Bank note.)
(c) Prepare the current liabilities section of the balance sheet at January 31, 2005. Assume no change in accounts payable.

(c) Current liability total $82,745

P11-2B Lee Hardware has four employees who are paid on an hourly basis plus time-and-a half for all hours worked in excess of 40 a week. Payroll data for the week ended March 15, 2005, are presented on page 482.

Prepare payroll register and payroll entries.

(SO 7, 8)

Employee	Hours Worked	Hourly Rate	Federal Income Tax Withholdings	United Fund
Joe Coomer	40	$15.00	$?	$5.00
Mary Walker	42	13.00	?	5.00
Andy Dye	44	13.00	60	8.00
Kim Shen	48	13.00	67	5.00

Coomer and Walker are married. They claim 0 and 4 withholding allowances, respectively. The following tax rates are applicable: FICA 8%, state income taxes 3%, state unemployment taxes 5.4%, and federal unemployment 0.8%. The first three employees are sales clerks (store wages expense). The fourth employee performs administrative duties (office wages expense).

Instructions

(a) Net pay $1,910.37; Store wages expense $1,757

(b) Payroll tax expense $345.48

(d) Cash paid $621.28

(a) Prepare a payroll register for the weekly payroll. (Use the wage-bracket withholding table in the text for federal income tax withholdings.)
(b) Journalize the payroll on March 15, 2005, and the accrual of employer payroll taxes.
(c) Journalize the payment of the payroll on March 16, 2005.
(d) Journalize the deposit in a Federal Reserve bank on March 31, 2005, of the FICA and federal income taxes payable to the government.

Identify internal control weaknesses and make recommendations for improvement.

(SO 6)

P11-3B Selected payroll procedures of Wallace Company are described below.

1. Department managers interview applicants and on the basis of the interview either hire or reject the applicants. When an applicant is hired, the applicant fills out a W-4 form (Employee's Withholding Allowance Certificate). One copy of the form is sent to the human resources department, and one copy is sent to the payroll department as notice that the individual has been hired. On the copy of the W-4 sent to payroll, the managers manually indicate the hourly pay rate for the new hire.
2. The payroll checks are manually signed by the chief accountant and given to the department managers for distribution to employees in their department. The managers are responsible for seeing that any absent employees receive their checks.
3. There are two clerks in the payroll department. The payroll is divided alphabetically; one clerk has employees A to L and the other has employees M to Z. Each clerk computes the gross earnings, deductions, and net pay for employees in the section and posts the data to the employee earnings records.

Instructions

(a) ✏️ Indicate the weaknesses in internal control.
(b) For each weakness, describe the control procedures that will provide effective internal control. Use the following format for your answer:

(a) Weaknesses	**(b) Recommended Procedures**

Journalize payroll transactions and adjusting entries.

(SO 7, 8, 9)

P11-4B The following payroll liability accounts are included in the ledger of Nordlund Company on January 1, 2005.

FICA Taxes Payable	$760.00
Federal Income Taxes Payable	1,204.60
State Income Taxes Payable	108.95
Federal Unemployment Taxes Payable	288.95
State Unemployment Taxes Payable	1,954.40
Union Dues Payable	870.00
U.S. Savings Bonds Payable	360.00

In January, the following transactions occurred.

Jan. 10 Sent check for $870.00 to union treasurer for union dues.
    12 Deposited check for $1,964.60 in Federal Reserve bank for FICA taxes and federal income taxes withheld.
    15 Purchased U.S. Savings Bonds for employees by writing check for $360.00.
    17 Paid state income taxes withheld from employees.
    20 Paid federal and state unemployment taxes.

31 Completed monthly payroll register, which shows office salaries $21,600, store wages $28,400, FICA taxes withheld $4,000, federal income taxes payable $1,958, state income taxes payable $414, union dues payable $400, United Fund contributions payable $1,888, and net pay $41,340.

31 Prepared payroll checks for the net pay and distributed checks to employees.

At January 31, the company also makes the following accrued adjustments pertaining to employee compensation.

1. Employer payroll taxes: FICA taxes 8%, federal unemployment taxes 0.8%, and state unemployment taxes 5.4%.

*__2.__ Vacation pay: 6% of gross earnings.

Instructions

(a) Journalize the January transactions.

(b) Journalize the adjustments pertaining to employee compensation at January 31.

(b) Payroll tax expense $7,100; Vacation benefits expense $3,000

P11-5B For the year ended December 31, 2005, Niehaus Electrical Repair Company reports the following summary payroll data.

Prepare entries for payroll and payroll taxes; prepare W-2 data.

(SO 7, 8, 9)

Gross earnings:	
Administrative salaries	$180,000
Electricians' wages	370,000
Total	$550,000

Deductions:	
FICA taxes	$ 38,000
Federal income taxes withheld	168,000
State income taxes withheld (2.6%)	14,300
United Fund contributions payable	27,500
*Hospital insurance premiums	17,200
Total	$265,000

Niehaus Company's payroll taxes are: FICA 8%, state unemployment 2.5% (due to a stable employment record), and 0.8% federal unemployment. Gross earnings subject to FICA taxes total $475,000, and unemployment taxes total $125,000.

Instructions

(a) Prepare a summary journal entry at December 31 for the full year's payroll.

(b) Journalize the adjusting entry at December 31 to record the employer's payroll taxes.

(c) The W-2 Wage and Tax Statement requires the following dollar data.

(a) Wages Payable $285,000
(b) Payroll tax expense $42,125

Wages, Tips, Other Compensation	Federal Income Tax Withheld	State Income Tax Withheld	FICA Wages	FICA Tax Withheld

Complete the required data for the following employees.

Employee	Gross Earnings	Federal Income Tax Withheld
Anna Hashmi	$59,000	$28,500
Sharon Bishop	26,000	10,200

BROADENING YOUR PERSPECTIVE

Financial Reporting and Analysis

■ FINANCIAL REPORTING PROBLEM: PepsiCo

BYP11-1 The financial statements of **PepsiCo.** and the Notes to Consolidated Financial Statements appear in Appendix A.

Instructions

Refer to PepsiCo's financial statements and answer the following questions about current and contingent liabilities and payroll costs.

(a) What were PepsiCo's total current liabilities at December 28, 2002? What was the increase/decrease in PepsiCo's total current liabilities from the prior year?

(b) In PepsiCo's Note 2 ("Our Significant Accounting Policies"), the company explains the nature of its contingencies. Under what conditions does PepsiCo recognize (record and report) liabilities for contingencies?

(c) What were the components of total current liabilities on December 28, 2002?

■ COMPARATIVE ANALYSIS PROBLEM: PepsiCo vs. Coca-Cola

BYP11-2 **PepsiCo**'s financial statements are presented in Appendix A. **Coca-Cola**'s financial statements are presented in Appendix B.

Instructions

(a) At December 28, 2002, what was PepsiCo's largest current liability account? What were its total current liabilities? At December 31, 2002, what was Coca-Cola's largest current liability account? What were its total current liabilities?

(b) Based on information contained in those financial statements, compute the following 2002 values for each company.
(1) Working capital.
(2) Current ratio.

(c) What conclusions concerning the relative liquidity of these companies can be drawn from these data?

■ INTERPRETING FINANCIAL STATEMENTS: A Global Focus

BYP11-3 Many multinational companies find it beneficial to have their shares listed on stock exchanges in foreign countries. In order to do this, they must comply with the securities laws of those countries. Some of these laws relate to the form of financial disclosure the company must provide, including disclosures related to contingent liabilities. This exercise investigates the **Tokyo Stock Exchange**, the largest stock exchange in Japan.

Address: www.tse.or.jp/ensish/index.shtml, or go to www.wiley.com/college/weygandt

Steps

1. Choose **About TSE** and then **History**. Answer questions (a) and (b).
2. Choose **Listed Companies**.
3. Choose **Disclosure**. Answer questions (c) and (d).

Instructions
Answer the following questions.

(a) When was the first stock exchange opened in Japan? How many exchanges does Japan have today?

(b) What event caused trading to stop for a period of time in Japan?

(c) What are four examples of decisions by corporations that must be disclosed at the time of their occurrence?

(d) What are four examples of "occurrence of material fact" that must be disclosed at the time of their occurrence?

■ EXPLORING THE WEB

BYP11-4 The Internal Revenue Service provides considerable information over the Internet. The following demonstrates how useful one of its sites is in answering payroll tax questions faced by employers.

Address: www.irs.ustreas.gov/formspubs/index.html, or go to www.wiley.com/college/weygandt

Steps

1. Go to the site shown above.
2. Choose **Publications Online**.
3. Choose **Publication 15, Circular E, Employer's Tax Guide**.

Instructions

Answer each of the following questions.

(a) How does the government define "employees"?

(b) What are the special rules for Social Security and Medicare regarding children who are employed by their parents?

(c) How can an employee obtain a Social Security card if he or she doesn't have one?

(d) Must employees report to their employer tips received from customers? If so, what is the process?

(e) Where should the employer deposit Social Security taxes withheld or contributed?

Critical Thinking

■ GROUP DECISION CASE

BYP11-5 Summerville Processing Company provides word-processing services for business clients and students in a university community. The work for business clients is fairly steady throughout the year. The work for students peaks significantly in December and May as a result of term papers, research project reports, and dissertations.

Two years ago, the company attempted to meet the peak demand by hiring part-time help. However, this led to numerous errors and considerable customer dissatisfaction. A year ago, the company hired four experienced employees on a permanent basis instead of using part-time help. This proved to be much better in terms of productivity and customer satisfaction. But, it has caused an increase in annual payroll costs and a significant decline in annual net income.

Recently, Valarie Flynn, a sales representative of Davidson Services Inc., has made a proposal to the company. Under her plan, Davidson Services will provide up to four experienced workers at a daily rate of $80 per person for an 8-hour workday. Davidson workers are not available on an hourly basis. Summerville Processing would have to pay only the daily rate for the workers used.

The owner of Summerville Processing, Nancy Bell, asks you, as the company's accountant, to prepare a report on the expenses that are pertinent to the decision. If the Davidson plan is adopted, Nancy will terminate the employment of two permanent employees and will keep two permanent employees. At the moment, each employee earns an annual income of $22,000. Summerville Processing pays 8% FICA taxes, 0.8% federal unemployment taxes, and 5.4% state unemployment taxes. The unemployment taxes apply to only the first $7,000 of gross earnings. In addition, Summerville Processing pays $40 per month for each employee for medical and dental insurance.

Nancy indicates that if the Davidson Services plan is accepted, her needs for workers will be as follows.

Months	Number	Working Days per Month
January–March	2	20
April–May	3	25
June–October	2	18
November–December	3	23

Instructions

With the class divided into groups, answer the following.

(a) Prepare a report showing the comparative payroll expense of continuing to employ permanent workers compared to adopting the Davidson Services Inc. plan.

(b) What other factors should Nancy consider before finalizing her decision?

■ COMMUNICATION ACTIVITY

BYP11-6 Ivan Blanco, president of the Blue Sky Company, has recently hired a number of additional employees. He recognizes that additional payroll taxes will be due as a result of this hiring, and that the company will serve as the collection agent for other taxes.

Instructions

In a memorandum to Ivan Blanco, explain each of the taxes, and identify the taxes that result in payroll tax expense to Blue Sky Company.

■ ETHICS CASE

BYP11-7   Johnny Fuller owns and manages Johnny's Restaurant, a 24-hour restaurant near the city's medical complex. Johnny employs 9 full-time employees and 16 part-time employees. He pays all of the full-time employees by check, the amounts of which are determined by Johnny's public accountant, Mary Lake. Johnny pays all of his part-time employees in currency. He computes their wages and withdraws the cash directly from his cash register.

Mary has repeatedly urged Johnny to pay all employees by check. But as Johnny has told his competitor and friend, Steve Hill, who owns the Greasy Diner, "First of all, my part-time employees prefer the currency over a check, and secondly I don't withhold or pay any taxes or workmen's compensation insurance on those wages because they go totally unrecorded and unnoticed."

Instructions

(a) Who are the stakeholders in this situation?

(b) What are the legal and ethical considerations regarding Johnny's handling of his payroll?

(c) Mary Lake is aware of Johnny's payment of the part-time payroll in currency. What are her ethical responsibilities in this case?

(d) What internal control principle is violated in this payroll process?

Answers to Self-Study Questions

1. a   **2.** d   **3.** b   **4.** b   **5.** a   **6.** c   **7.** b   **8.** d   **9.** d   **10.** c   **11.** d

Answer to PepsiCo Review It Question 2, p. 454

Under the heading of current liabilities, **PepsiCo** has listed short-term obligations, accounts payable, other current liabilities, and income taxes payable.

Accounting Principles

THE NAVIGATOR ✓

Understand **Concepts for Review** ❑

Read **Feature Story** ❑

Scan **Study Objectives** ❑

Read **Preview** ❑

Read text and answer **Before You Go On**
p. 493 ❑   p. 503 ❑

Work **Demonstration Problems** ❑

Review **Summary of Study Objectives** ❑

Answer **Self-Study Questions** ❑

Complete **Assignments** ❑

CONCEPTS FOR REVIEW

Before studying this chapter, you should know or, if necessary, review:

The two organizations primarily responsible for setting accounting standards.
(Ch. 1, p. 10)

The monetary unit assumption, the economic entity assumption, and the time period assumption.
(Ch. 1, pp. 10–11 and Ch. 3, p. 90)

The cost principle, the revenue recognition principle, and the matching principle.
(Ch. 1, p. 10 and Ch. 3, pp. 90–91)

Certainly Worth Investigating!

It is often difficult to determine in what period some revenues and expenses should be reported. There are rules that give guidance, but occasionally these rules are overlooked, misinterpreted, or even intentionally ignored. Consider the following examples.

- **Policy Management Systems**, which makes insurance software, said that it reported some sales before contracts were signed or products delivered.
- **Sunbeam Corporation**, while under the control of the (in)famous "Chainsaw" Al Dunlap, prematurely booked revenues and recorded overly large restructuring charges. Ultimately the company was forced to restate its net income figures, and Mr. Dunlap lost his job.
- **Rent-Way Inc.**, which owns a large chain of rent-to-own stores, saw its share price plummet from $23.44 down to $5 within a week after it disclosed what the company termed "fictitious" accounting entries on its books. These entries included improper accounting for fixed-asset write-offs, and understating the amount of damaged or missing merchandise.

Often in cases such as these, the company's shareholders sue the company because of the decline in the stock price due to the disclosure of the misinformation. In light of this eventuality, why might management want to report revenues or expenses in the wrong period? Company managers are under intense pressure to report higher earnings every year. If actual performance falls short of expectations, management might be tempted to bend the rules.

One analyst suggests that investors and auditors should be suspicious of sharp increases in monthly sales at the end of each quarter or big jumps in fourth-quarter sales. Such events don't always mean management is cheating, but they are certainly worth investigating.

THE NAVIGATOR

After studying this chapter, you should be able to:

1. Explain the meaning of generally accepted accounting principles and identify the key items of the conceptual framework.
2. Describe the basic objectives of financial reporting.
3. Discuss the qualitative characteristics of accounting information and elements of financial statements.
4. Identify the basic assumptions used by accountants.
5. Identify the basic principles of accounting.
6. Identify the two constraints in accounting.
7. Explain the accounting principles used in international operations.

THE NAVIGATOR

As indicated in the Feature Story, it is important that general guidelines be available to resolve accounting issues. Without these basic guidelines, each enterprise would have to develop its own set of accounting practices. If this happened, we would have to become familiar with every company's peculiar accounting and reporting rules in order to understand their financial statements. It would be difficult, if not impossible, to compare the financial statements of different companies. This chapter explores the basic accounting principles that are followed in developing specific accounting guidelines.

The content and organization of Chapter 12 are as follows.

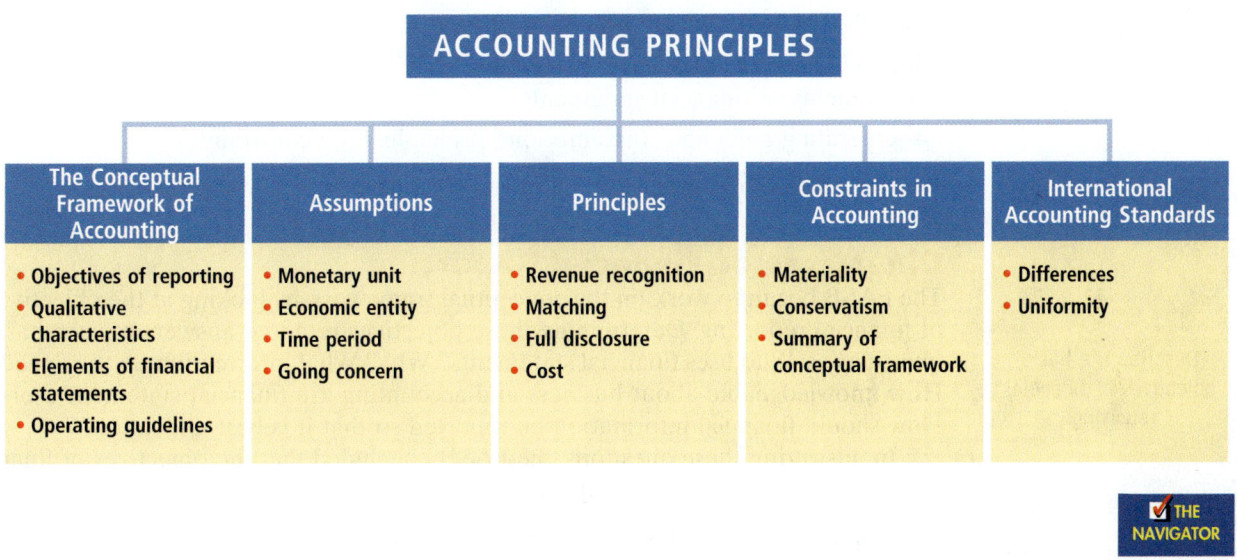

ACCOUNTING PRINCIPLES

The Conceptual Framework of Accounting	Assumptions	Principles	Constraints in Accounting	International Accounting Standards
• Objectives of reporting • Qualitative characteristics • Elements of financial statements • Operating guidelines	• Monetary unit • Economic entity • Time period • Going concern	• Revenue recognition • Matching • Full disclosure • Cost	• Materiality • Conservatism • Summary of conceptual framework	• Differences • Uniformity

THE NAVIGATOR

The Conceptual Framework of Accounting

What you have learned up to this point in the book is a process that leads to the preparation of financial reports about a company. These are the company's financial statements. This area of accounting is called **financial accounting**. The accounting profession has established a set of standards and rules that are recognized as a general guide for financial reporting. This recognized set of standards is called **generally accepted accounting principles (GAAP)**. "Generally accepted" means that these principles must have "substantial authoritative support." Such support usually comes from two standard-setting bodies: the Financial Accounting Standards Board (FASB) and the Securities and Exchange Commission (SEC).[1]

Since the early 1970s the business and governmental communities have given the FASB the responsibility for developing accounting principles in this country. This is an ongoing process; accounting principles change to reflect changes in the business environment and in the needs of users of accounting information.

STUDY OBJECTIVE 1

Explain the meaning of generally accepted accounting principles and identify the key items of the conceptual framework.

---

[1]The SEC is an agency of the U.S. government that was established in 1933 to administer laws and regulations relating to the exchange of securities and the publication of financial information by U.S. businesses. The agency has the authority to mandate generally accepted accounting principles for companies under its jurisdiction. However, throughout its history, the SEC has been willing to accept the principles set forth by the FASB and similar bodies.

Prior to the establishment of the FASB, accounting principles were developed on a problem-by-problem basis. Rule-making bodies developed accounting rules and methods to solve specific problems. Critics charged that the problem-by-problem approach led over time to inconsistent rules and practices. No clearly developed conceptual framework of accounting existed to refer to in solving new problems.

In response to these criticisms, the FASB developed a **conceptual framework**. It serves as the basis for resolving accounting and reporting problems. The FASB spent considerable time and effort on this project. The Board views its conceptual framework as ". . . a constitution, a coherent system of interrelated objectives and fundamentals."[2]

The FASB's conceptual framework consists of the following four items:

1. Objectives of financial reporting.

2. Qualitative characteristics of accounting information.

3. Elements of financial statements.

4. Operating guidelines (assumptions, principles, and constraints).

We will discuss these items on the following pages.

Objectives of Financial Reporting

The FASB began to work on the conceptual framework by looking at the objectives of financial reporting. Determining these objectives required answers to such basic questions as: Who uses financial statements? Why? What information do they need? How knowledgeable about business and accounting are financial statement users? How should financial information be reported so that it is best understood?

In answering these questions, the FASB concluded that the objectives of financial reporting are to provide information that:

1. Is useful to those making investment and credit decisions.

2. Is helpful in assessing future cash flows.

3. Identifies the economic resources (assets), the claims to those resources (liabilities), and the changes in those resources and claims.

The FASB then undertook to describe the characteristics that make accounting information useful.

Qualitative Characteristics of Accounting Information

How does a company like **Microsoft** decide on the amount of financial information to disclose? In what format should its financial information be presented? How should assets, liabilities, revenues, and expenses be measured? The FASB concluded that the overriding criterion for such accounting choices is **decision usefulness**. The accounting practice selected should be the one that generates the most useful financial information for making a decision. To be useful, information should possess the following qualitative characteristics: relevance, reliability, comparability, and consistency.

Relevance

Accounting information has **relevance** if it makes a difference in a decision. Relevant information has either predictive or feedback value or both. **Predictive value**

---

[2]"Conceptual Framework for Financial Accounting and Reporting: Elements of Financial Statements and Their Measurement," *FASB Discussion Memorandum* (Stamford, Conn.: 1976), p. 1.

helps users forecast future events. For example, when **ExxonMobil** issues financial statements, the information in them is considered relevant because it provides a basis for predicting future earnings. **Feedback value** confirms or corrects prior expectations. When ExxonMobil issues financial statements, it confirms or corrects prior expectations about the financial health of the company.

In addition, accounting information has relevance if it is **timely**. It must be available to decision makers before it loses its capacity to influence decisions. If Exxon-Mobil reported its financial information only every five years, the information would be of limited use in decision-making.

Reliability — *Error or bias free*

Reliability of information means that the information is free of error and bias. In short, it can be depended on. To be reliable, accounting information must be **verifiable**: We must be able to prove that it is free of error and bias. It also must be a **faithful representation** of what it purports to be: It must be factual. If **Sears, Roebuck**'s income statement reports sales of $100 billion when it had sales of $51 billion, then the statement is not a faithful representation. Finally, accounting information must be **neutral**: It cannot be selected, prepared, or presented to favor one set of interested users over another. To ensure reliability, certified public accountants audit financial statements.

Comparability

Accounting information about an enterprise is most useful when it can be compared with accounting information about other enterprises. **Comparability** results when different companies use the same accounting principles. For example, **Sears**, **L. L. Bean**, and **The Limited** all use the cost principle in reporting plant assets on the balance sheet. Also, each company uses the revenue recognition and matching principles in determining its net income.

Conceptually, comparability should also extend to the methods used by companies in complying with an accounting principle. Accounting methods include the FIFO and LIFO methods of inventory costing, and various depreciation methods. At this point, comparability of methods is not required, even for companies in the same industry. Thus, **Ford**, **General Motors**, and **DaimlerChrysler** may use different inventory costing and depreciation methods in their financial statements. The only accounting requirement is that each company **must disclose** the accounting methods used. From the disclosures, the external user can determine whether the financial information is comparable.

Consistency

Consistency means that a company uses the same accounting principles and methods from year to year. If a company selects FIFO as the inventory costing method in the first year of operations, it is expected to use FIFO in succeeding years. When financial information has been reported on a consistent basis, the financial statements permit meaningful analysis of trends within a company.

A company *can* change to a new method of accounting. To do so, management must justify that the new method results in more meaningful financial information. In the year in which the change occurs, the change must be disclosed in the notes to the financial statements. Such disclosure makes users of the financial statements aware of the lack of consistency.

The characteristics that make accounting information useful are summarized in Illustration 12-1 (on page 492).

HELPFUL HINT

What makes accounting information relevant? Answer: Relevant accounting information provides feedback, serves as a basis for predictions, and is timely (current).

HELPFUL HINT

What makes accounting information reliable? Answer: Reliable accounting information is free of error and bias, is factual, verifiable, and neutral.

Illustration 12-1
Characteristics of useful information

Relevance
1. Provides a basis for forecasts
2. Confirms or corrects prior expectations
3. Is timely

Reliability
1. Is verifiable
2. Is a faithful representation
3. Is neutral

Comparability
Different companies use similar accounting principles

Consistency
Company uses same accounting methods from year to year

Elements of Financial Statements

An important part of the accounting conceptual framework is a set of definitions that describe the basic terms used in accounting. The FASB refers to this set of definitions as the **elements of financial statements**. They include such terms as assets, liabilities, equity, revenues, and expenses.

Because these elements are so important, it is crucial that they be precisely defined and universally applied. Finding the appropriate definition for many of these elements is not easy. For example, should the value of a company's employees be reported as an asset on a balance sheet? Should the death of the company's president be reported as a loss? A good set of definitions should provide answers to these types of questions. Because you have already encountered most of these definitions in earlier chapters, they are not repeated here.

Operating Guidelines

The objectives of financial reporting, the qualitative characteristics of accounting information, and the elements of financial statements are very broad. Because practicing accountants must solve practical problems, more detailed guidelines are needed. In its conceptual framework, the FASB recognized the need for operating guidelines. We classify these guidelines as assumptions, principles, and constraints. These guidelines are well-established and accepted in accounting.

Assumptions provide a foundation for the accounting process. **Principles** are specific rules that indicate how economic events should be reported in the accounting process. **Constraints** on the accounting process allow for a relaxation of the principles under certain circumstances. Illustration 12-2 provides a road-map of the operating guidelines of accounting. These guidelines (some of which you know from earlier chapters) are discussed in more detail in the following sections.

Illustration 12-2
The operating guidelines of accounting

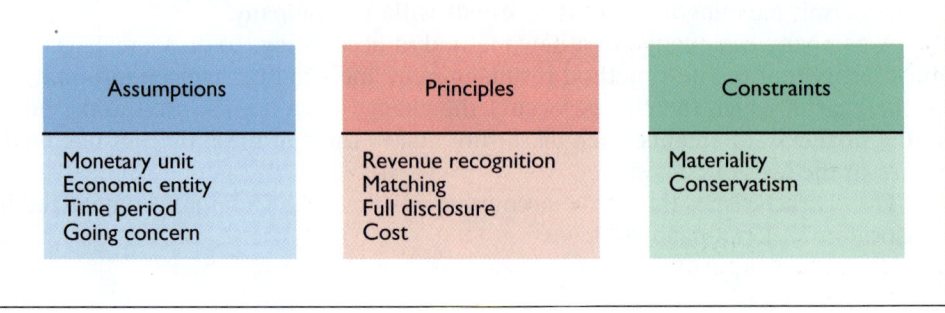

Assumptions	Principles	Constraints
Monetary unit	Revenue recognition	Materiality
Economic entity	Matching	Conservatism
Time period	Full disclosure	
Going concern	Cost	

BEFORE YOU GO ON...

Review It

1. What are generally accepted accounting principles?
2. What is stated about generally accepted accounting principles in the Independent Auditors' Report for **PepsiCo**? The answer to this question appears on page 518.
3. What are the basic objectives of financial information?
4. What are the qualitative characteristics that make accounting information useful? Identify two elements of the financial statements.

 THE NAVIGATOR

Assumptions

As noted above, assumptions provide a foundation for the accounting process. You already know three of the major assumptions—the monetary unit, economic entity, and time period assumptions. The fourth is the going concern assumption.

STUDY OBJECTIVE 4

Identify the basic assumptions used by accountants.

Monetary Unit Assumption

The **monetary unit assumption** states that only transaction data that can be expressed in terms of money be included in the accounting records. For example, the value of a company president is not reported in a company's financial records because it cannot be expressed easily in dollars.

An important corollary to the monetary unit assumption is the assumption that the unit of measure remains relatively constant over time. This point will be discussed in more detail later in this chapter.

ETHICS NOTE

In an action that sent shock waves through the French business community, the CEO of Alcatel-Alsthom was taken into custody for an apparent violation of the economic entity assumption. Allegedly, the executive improperly used company funds to install an expensive security system in his home.

Economic Entity Assumption

The **economic entity assumption** states that the activities of the entity be kept separate and distinct from the activities of the owner and of all other economic entities. For example, it is assumed that the activities of **IBM** can be distinguished from those of other computer companies such as **Apple**, **Dell**, and **Hewlett-Packard**.

Time Period Assumption

The **time period assumption** states that the economic life of a business can be divided into artificial time periods. Thus, it is assumed that the activities of business enterprises such as **General Electric**, **Time Warner**, **ExxonMobil**, or any enterprise can be subdivided into months, quarters, or a year for meaningful financial reporting purposes.

Going Concern Assumption

The **going concern assumption** assumes that the enterprise will continue in operation long enough to carry out its existing objectives. In spite of numerous business failures, companies have a fairly high continuance rate. It has proved useful to adopt a going concern assumption for accounting purposes.

The accounting implications of this assumption are critical. If a going concern assumption is not used, then plant assets should be stated at their liquidation value (selling price less cost of disposal)—not at their cost. In that case, depreciation and amortization of these assets would not be needed. Each period, these assets would simply be reported at their liquidation value. Also, without this assumption, the current–noncurrent classification of assets and liabilities would not matter. Labeling anything as long-term would be difficult to justify.

Acceptance of the going concern assumption gives credibility to the cost principle. Only when liquidation appears imminent is the going concern assumption inapplicable. In that case, assets would be better stated at liquidation value than at cost.

These basic accounting assumptions are illustrated graphically in Illustration 12-3 below.

Illustration 12-3
Assumptions used in accounting

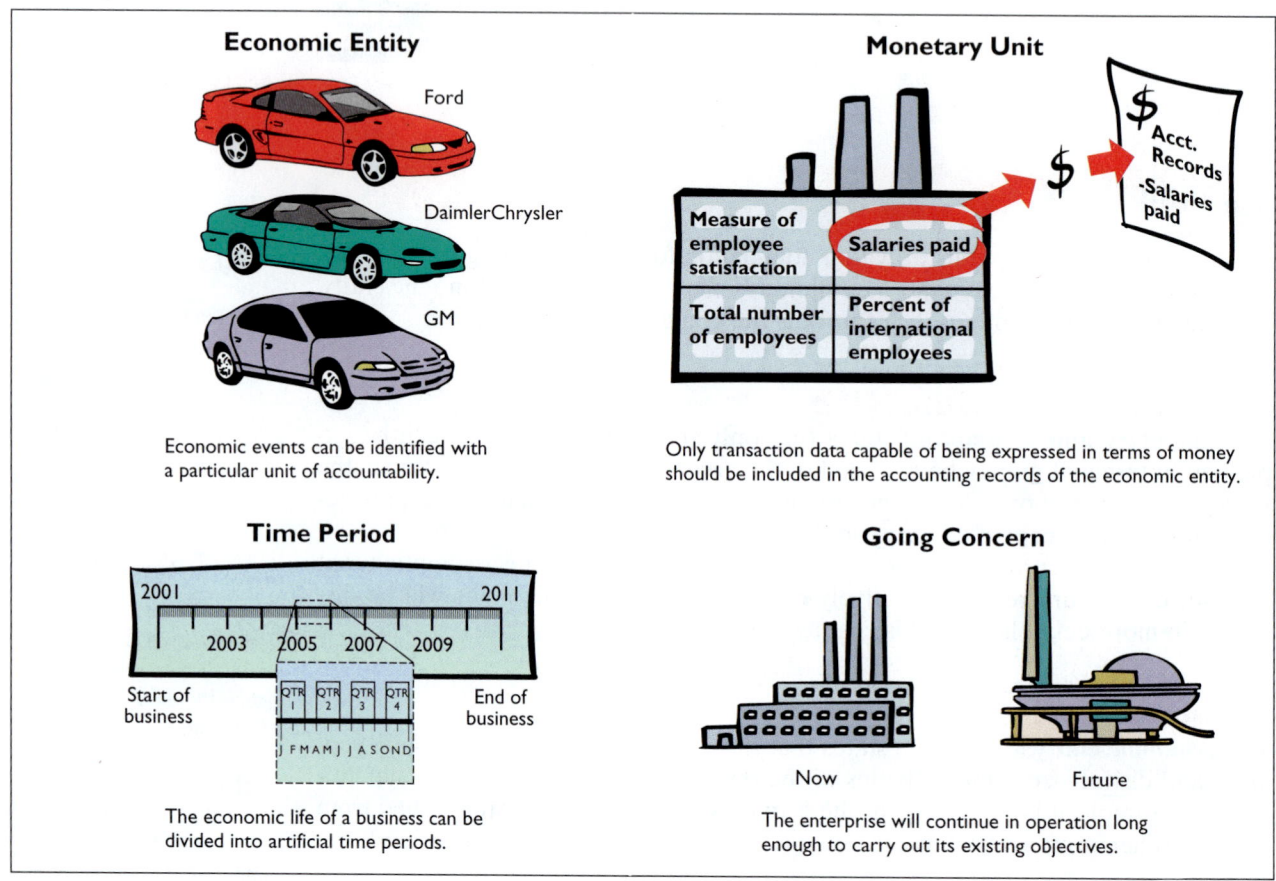

Principles

STUDY OBJECTIVE 5

Identify the basic principles of accounting.

On the basis of the fundamental assumptions of accounting, the accounting profession has developed principles that dictate how economic events should be recorded and reported. In earlier chapters we discussed the cost principle (Chapter 1) and the revenue recognition and matching principles (Chapter 3). Here we now examine a number of reporting issues related to these principles. In addition, we introduce another principle, the full disclosure principle.

Revenue Recognition Principle

The **revenue recognition principle** dictates that revenue should be recognized in the accounting period in which it is earned. But applying this general principle in practice can be difficult. For example, some companies improperly recognize revenue on goods that have not been shipped to customers. Similarly, until recently, financial institutions immediately recorded a large portion of their fees for granting a loan as revenue rather than spreading those fees over the life of the loan.

When a sale is involved, revenue is recognized at the point of sale. This **sales basis** involves an exchange transaction between the seller and buyer. The sales price is an objective measure of the amount of revenue realized. However, there are two exceptions to the sales basis for revenue recognition that have become generally accepted. They are the percentage-of-completion method and the installment method.

Percentage-of-Completion Method

In long-term construction contracts, revenue recognition is usually required before the contract is completed. For example, assume that Warrior Construction Co. had a contract to build a dam for the U.S. Department of the Interior for $400 million. Construction is estimated to take 3 years (starting in 2003) at a cost of $360 million. If Warrior applies the point-of-sale basis, it will report no revenues and no profit in the first two years. In 2005, when completion and sale take place, Warrior will report $400 million in revenues, costs of $360 million, and the entire profit of $40 million. Was Warrior really producing no revenues and earning no profit in 2003 and 2004? Obviously not. Instead, the earning process can be considered substantially completed at various stages. Therefore revenue should be recognized as construction progresses.

In recognizing revenue, Warrior can apply the **percentage-of-completion method**. This method recognizes revenue on a long-term project on the basis of reasonable estimates of progress toward completion. Progress toward completion is measured by comparing the costs incurred in a year to the total estimated costs for the entire project. That percentage is multiplied by the total revenue for the project. The result is then recognized as revenue for the period. The formulas for this method are as follows.

Costs Incurred (Current Period)	÷	Total Estimated Cost	=	Percent Complete (Current Period)
Percent Complete (Current Period)	×	Total Revenue	=	Revenue Recognized (Current Period)

Illustration 12-4
Formula to recognize revenue in the percentage-of-completion method

The costs incurred in the current period are then subtracted from the revenue recognized during the current period to arrive at the gross profit for the current period. This formula is shown in Illustration 12-5.

Revenue Recognized (Current Period)	−	Costs Incurred (Current Period)	=	Gross Profit Recognized (Current Period)

Illustration 12-5
Formula to compute gross profit in current period

Let's look at an illustration of the percentage-of-completion method. Assume that Warrior Construction Co. incurs costs of $54 million in 2003, $180 million in 2004, and $126 million in 2005 on the dam project. The portion of the $400 million of revenue recognized in each of the three years is shown in Illustration 12-6 (page 496).

Illustration 12-6
Revenue recognized—
percentage-of-completion
method

Year	Costs Incurred (Current Period)	÷	Total Estimated Cost	=	Percent Complete (Current Period)	×	Total Revenue	=	Revenue Recognized (Current Period)
2003	$ 54,000,000		$360,000,000		15%		$400,000,000		$ 60,000,000
2004	180,000,000		360,000,000		50%		400,000,000		200,000,000
2005	126,000,000		Balance required to complete the contract						140,000,000
Totals	$360,000,000								$400,000,000

No estimate is made of the percentage of work completed during the final period. In the final period, all remaining revenue is recognized. In this example, the company's cost estimates have been very accurate. The costs incurred in the third year were 35% of the total estimated cost ($126,000 ÷ $360,000).

The gross profit recognized each period is as follows.

Illustration 12-7
Gross profit recognized—
percentage-of-completion
method

Year	Revenue Recognized (Current Period)	–	Actual Cost Incurred (Current Period)	=	Gross Profit Recognized (Current Period)
2003	$ 60,000,000		$ 54,000,000		$ 6,000,000
2004	200,000,000		180,000,000		20,000,000
2005	140,000,000		126,000,000		14,000,000
Totals	$400,000,000		$360,000,000		$40,000,000

Use of the percentage-of-completion method involves some subjectivity. As a result, errors are possible in determining the amount of revenue recognized and gross profit recognized. Yet to wait until completion would seriously distort each period's financial statements. Naturally, **if it is not possible to obtain dependable estimates of costs and progress, then the revenue should be recognized at the completion date** and not by the percentage-of-completion method.

Installment Method

Another basis for revenue recognition is the receipt of cash. The **cash basis** is generally used only when it is difficult to determine the revenue amount at the time of a credit sale because collection is uncertain. One popular revenue recognition approach using the cash basis is the **installment method**.

Under the installment method, each cash collection from a customer consists of (1) a partial recovery of the cost of the goods sold, and (2) partial gross profit from the sale. For example, if the gross profit rate at the date of sale is 40%, each receipt of cash consists of 60% recovery of cost of goods sold and 40% gross profit. The formula to recognize gross profit is as follows.

Illustration 12-8
Gross profit formula—
installment method

Cash Collections from Customer	×	Gross Profit Percentage	=	Gross Profit Recognized during the Period

To illustrate, assume that an Iowa farm machinery dealer in the first year of operations had installment sales of $600,000. Its cost of goods sold on installment was $420,000. Total gross profit is therefore $180,000 ($600,000 − $420,000), and the gross profit percentage is 30% ($180,000 ÷ $600,000). Collections on the installment sales were as follows: first year $280,000 (down payment plus monthly payments), second year $200,000, and third year $120,000. The computation of gross profit recognized is shown in Illustration 12-9. (Interest charges are ignored in this illustration.)

Year	Cash Collected	×	Gross Profit Percentage	=	Gross Profit Recognized
2003	$280,000		30%		$ 84,000
2004	200,000		30%		60,000
2005	120,000		30%		36,000
Total	$600,000				$180,000

Illustration 12-9
Gross profit recognized—installment method

Under the installment method of accounting, gross profit is therefore recognized **in the period in which the cash is collected**.

As indicated earlier, the installment method is used when there is risk of not collecting an account receivable. In that case, the sale itself is not sufficient evidence for revenue to be recognized.

ACCOUNTING IN ACTION **Business Insight**

Datapoint Corp. encouraged its customers to load up with large shipments at the end of the year. This strategy allowed Datapoint to report these shipments as revenues, even though payment hadn't been collected. Unfortunately, some of the customers either went broke or quit before paying for the equipment received. The company had to record substantial bad debts or in some cases reverse previously recorded sales. If Datapoint had used the installment method, this revenue would not have been reported. As a result, revenue recognition practices that are cash-basis oriented, such as the installment method, are becoming more acceptable as it becomes difficult to tell when a sale is a sale.

Matching Principle (Expense Recognition)

Expense recognition is traditionally tied to revenue recognition: "Let the expense follow the revenue." As you learned in Chapter 3, this practice is referred to as the **matching principle**. It dictates that expenses be matched with revenues in the period in which efforts are made to generate revenues. Expenses are not recognized when cash is paid, or when the work is performed, or when the product is produced. Rather, they are recognized when the labor (service) or the product actually makes its contribution to revenue.

But, it is sometimes difficult to determine the accounting period in which the expense contributed to revenues. Several approaches have therefore been devised for matching expenses and revenues on the income statement.

To understand these approaches, you need to understand the nature of expenses. Costs are the source of expenses. Costs that will generate revenues only in the current accounting period are expensed immediately. They are reported as **operating expenses** in the income statement. Examples include costs for advertising, sales salaries, and repairs. These expenses are often called **expired costs**.

HELPFUL HINT

Costs become expenses when they are charged against revenue.

Costs that will generate revenues in future accounting periods are recognized as assets. Examples include merchandise inventory, prepaid expenses, and plant assets. These costs represent **unexpired costs**. Unexpired costs become expenses in two ways:

1. **Cost of goods sold.** Costs carried as merchandise inventory become expenses when the inventory is sold. They are expensed as cost of goods sold in the period when the sale occurs. Thus, there is a direct matching of expenses with revenues.

2. **Operating expenses.** Other unexpired costs become operating expenses through use or consumption (as in the case of store supplies) or through the passage of time (as in the case of prepaid insurance). The costs of plant assets and other long-lived resources are expensed through rational and systematic allocation methods—periodic depreciation or amortization. Operating expenses contribute to the revenues for the period, but their association with revenues is less direct than for cost of goods sold.

These points about expense recognition are illustrated in Illustration 12-10.

Illustration 12-10
Expense recognition pattern

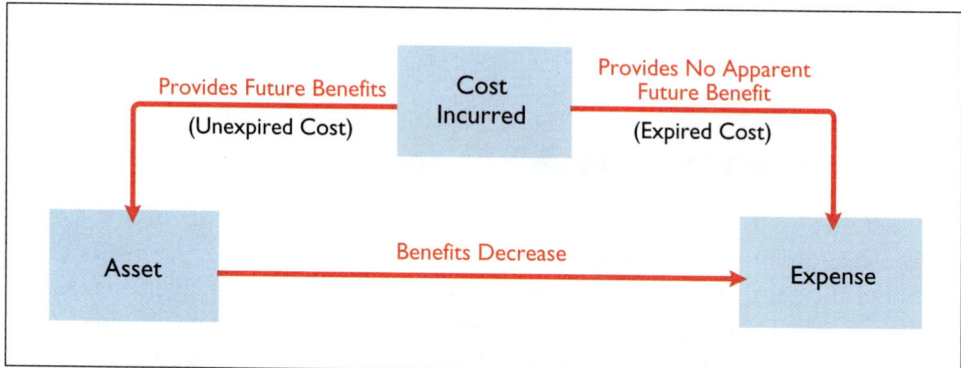

ACCOUNTING IN ACTION Business Insight

Implementing expense recognition guidelines can be difficult. Consider, for example, **Harold's Club** (a gambling casino) in Reno, Nevada. How should it report expenses related to the payoff of its progressive slot machines? Progressive slot machines, which generally have no ceiling on their jackpots, provide a lucky winner with all the money that many losers had previously put in. Payoffs tend to be huge, but infrequent. At Harold's, the progressive slots pay off on average every $4\frac{1}{2}$ months.

The basic accounting question is: Can Harold's deduct the millions of dollars sitting in its progressive slot machines from the revenue recognized at the end of the accounting period? One might argue that no, you cannot deduct the money until the "winning handle pull." However, a winning handle pull might not occur for many months or even years. Although an estimate would have to be used, the better answer is to match these costs with the revenue recognized, assuming that an average $4\frac{1}{2}$ months' payout is well documented. Obviously, the matching principle can be difficult to apply in practice.

Full Disclosure Principle

The **full disclosure principle** requires that circumstances and events that make a difference to financial statement users be disclosed. For example, investors who lost money in **Enron**, **WorldCom**, and **Global Crossing** have complained that the lack of full disclosure regarding some of the companies' transactions caused the financial statements to be misleading. Investors want to be made aware of events that can affect the financial health of a company.

Compliance with the full disclosure principle occurs through the data in the financial statements and the information in the notes that accompany the statements. The first note in most cases is a **summary of significant accounting policies**. It includes, among others, the methods used for inventory costing, depreciation of plant assets, and amortization of intangible assets.

Deciding how much disclosure is enough can be difficult. Accountants could disclose every financial event that occurs and every contingency that exists. But the benefits of providing additional information in some cases may be less than the costs of doing so. Many companies complain of an accounting standards overload. They also object to requirements that force them to disclose confidential information. Determining where to draw the line on disclosure is not easy.

One thing is certain: financial statements were much simpler years ago. In 1930, **General Electric** had no notes to its financial statements. Today it has over 30 pages of notes! Why this change? A major reason is that the objectives of financial statements have changed. In the past, information was generally presented on what the business had done. Today, the objectives of financial reporting are more future-oriented. The goal is to provide information that makes it possible to predict the amounts, timing, and uncertainty of future cash flows.

ACCOUNTING IN ACTION  Business Insight

Some accountants are reconsidering the current means of financial reporting. They propose a database concept of financial reporting. In such a system, all the information from transactions would be stored in a computerized database to be accessed by various user groups. The main benefit of such a system is the ability to tailor the information requested to the needs of each user.

What makes this idea controversial? Discussion currently revolves around access and aggregation issues. Questions abound: "Who should be allowed to make inquiries of the system?" "What is the lowest/smallest level of information to be provided?" "Will such a system necessarily improve on the current means of disclosure?" Such questions must be answered before database financial accounting can be implemented on a large scale.

Cost Principle

As you know, the **cost principle** dictates that assets be recorded at their cost. Cost is used because it is both relevant and reliable. Cost is **relevant** because it represents the price paid, the assets sacrificed, or the commitment made at date of acquisition. Cost is **reliable** because it is objectively measurable, factual, and verifiable. It is the result of an exchange transaction. Cost is the basis used in preparing financial statements.

The cost principle, however, has come under criticism. Some criticize it as irrelevant. After acquisition, the argument goes, the cost of an asset is not equivalent to market value or current value. Also, as the purchasing power of the dollar changes, so does the meaning associated with the dollar used as the basis of measurement. Consider the classic story about the individual who went to sleep and woke up 10 years later. Hurrying to a telephone, he called his broker and asked what his formerly modest stock portfolio was worth. He was told that he was a multi-millionaire. His **General Motors** stock was worth $5 million, and his **Microsoft** stock was up to $10 million. Elated, he was about to inquire about his other holdings, when the telephone operator cut in with "Your time is up. Please deposit $100,000 for the next three minutes."[3]

Despite the inevitability of changing prices due to inflation, the accounting profession still follows the stable monetary unit assumption in preparing the primary financial statements. While admitting that some changes in prices do occur, the profession believes the unit of measure—the dollar—has remained sufficiently constant over time to provide meaningful financial information. Sometimes, the **disclosure of price-level adjusted data is in the form of supplemental information** that accompanies the financial statements.

The basic principles of accounting are summarized in Illustration 12-11.

Illustration 12-11
Basic principles used in accounting

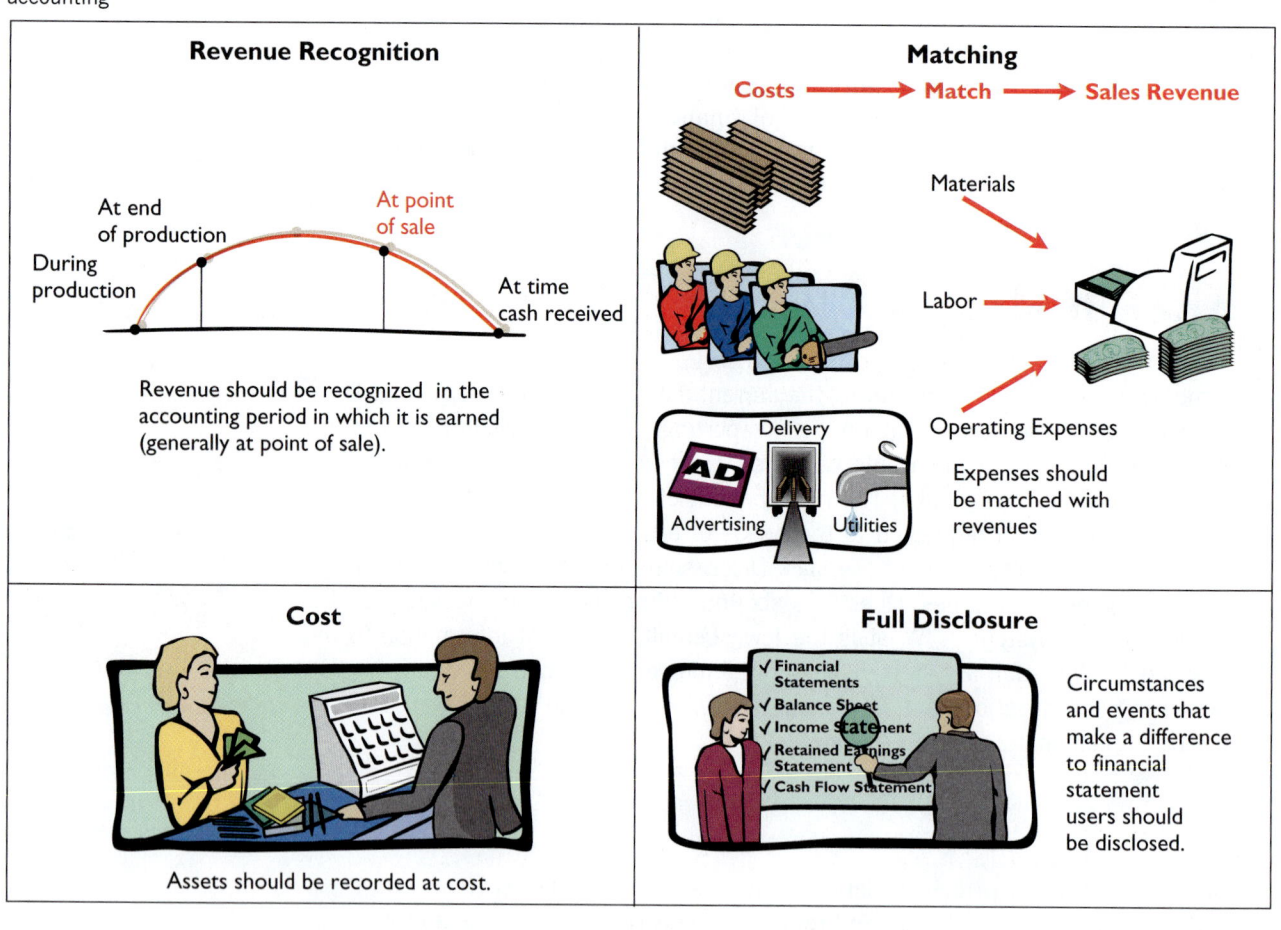

[3]Adapted from *Barron's*, January 28, 1980, p. 27.

Constraints in Accounting

Constraints permit a company to modify generally accepted accounting principles without reducing the usefulness of the reported information. The constraints are materiality and conservatism.

STUDY OBJECTIVE 6

Identify the two constraints in accounting.

Materiality

Materiality relates to an item's impact on a firm's overall financial condition and operations. An item is **material** when it is likely to influence the decision of a reasonably prudent investor or creditor. It is immaterial if its inclusion or omission has no impact on a decision maker. In short, if the item does not make a difference in decision making, GAAP does not have to be followed. To determine the materiality of an amount, the accountant usually compares it with such items as total assets, total liabilities, and net income.

To illustrate how the materiality constraint is applied, assume that Rodriguez Co. purchases a number of low-cost plant assets, such as wastepaper baskets. Although the proper accounting would appear to be to depreciate these wastepaper baskets over their useful life, they are usually expensed immediately. This practice is justified because these costs are considered immaterial. Establishing depreciation schedules for these assets is costly and time-consuming and will not make a material difference on total assets and net income. Another application of the materiality constraint would be the expensing of small tools. Some companies expense any plant assets under a specified dollar amount.

Conservatism

The **conservatism** constraint dictates that when in doubt, choose the method that will be least likely to overstate assets and income. It does **not** mean **understating** assets or income. Conservatism provides a reasonable guide in difficult situations: Do not overstate assets and income.

A common application of the conservatism constraint is the use of the lower of cost or market method for inventories. As indicated in Chapter 6, inventories are reported at market value if market value is below cost. This practice results in a higher cost of goods sold and lower net income. In addition, inventory on the balance sheet is stated at a lower amount.

Other examples of conservatism in accounting are the use of the LIFO method for inventory valuation when prices are rising and the use of accelerated depreciation methods for plant assets. Both these methods result in lower asset carrying values and lower net income than alternative methods.

The two constraints in accounting are graphically depicted in Illustration 12-12.

HELPFUL HINT

In other words, if two methods are otherwise equally appropriate, choose the one that will least likely overstate assets and income.

Illustration 12-12
Constraints in accounting

Materiality	Conservatism
For small amounts, GAAP does not have to be followed.	When in doubt, choose the solution that will be least likely to overstate assets and income.

Summary of Conceptual Framework

As we have seen, the conceptual framework for developing sound reporting practices starts with a set of objectives for financial reporting. It follows with the description of qualities that make information useful. In addition, elements of financial statements are defined. More detailed operating guidelines are then provided. These guidelines take the form of assumptions and principles. The conceptual framework also recognizes that constraints exist on the reporting environment. The conceptual framework is illustrated graphically in Illustration 12-13.

Illustration 12-13
Conceptual framework

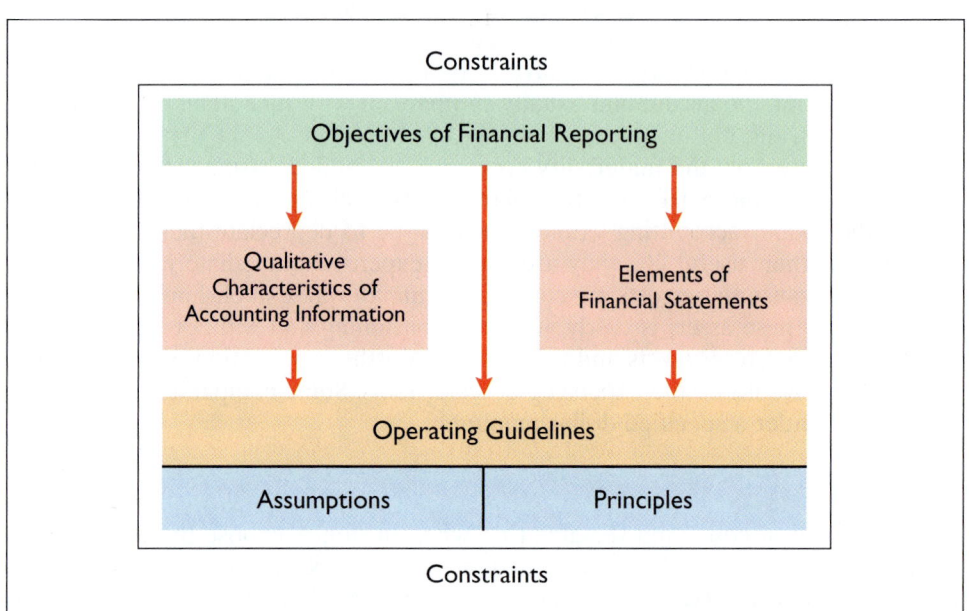

International Accounting Standards

STUDY OBJECTIVE 7

Explain the accounting principles used in international operations.

World markets are becoming increasingly intertwined. Foreigners use American computers, eat American breakfast cereals, read American magazines, listen to American rock music, watch American movies and TV shows, and drink American soda. Americans drive Japanese cars, wear Italian shoes and Scottish woolens, drink Brazilian coffee and Indian tea, eat Swiss chocolate bars, sit on Danish furniture, and use Arabian oil. The variety and volume of exported and imported goods indicates the extensive involvement of U.S. business in international trade. Many U.S. companies consider the world their market.

Firms that conduct operations in more than one country through subsidiaries, divisions, or branches in foreign countries are referred to as **multinational corporations**. The accounting for such corporations is complicated because foreign currencies are involved. These international transactions must be translated into U.S. dollars.

Differences in Standards

In the new global economy many investment and credit decisions require the analysis of foreign financial statements. Unfortunately, accounting standards are not uniform from country to country. This lack of uniformity results from differences in legal systems, in processes for developing accounting standards, in governmental requirements, and in economic environments.

ACCOUNTING IN ACTION   International Insight

Research and development costs are an example of different international accounting standards. Compare how four countries account for research and development (R&D):

Country	Accounting Treatment
United States	Expenditures are expensed.
United Kingdom	Certain expenditures may be capitalized.
Germany	Expenditures are expensed.
Japan	Expenditures may be capitalized and amortized over 5 years.

Thus, an R&D expenditure of $100 million is charged totally to expense in the current period in the United States and Germany. This same expense could range from zero to $100 million in the United Kingdom and from $20 million to $100 million in Japan!

Do you believe that accounting principles should be comparable across countries?

Uniformity in Standards

Recently, the **International Accounting Standards Board (IASB)** has been formed. The board is working toward the development of a single set of high-quality global accounting standards. Its purpose is to formulate international accounting standards and to promote their acceptance worldwide.

At present these standards are not universally applied. However, more international companies are now considering adopting international standards. The foundation has therefore been laid for progress toward greater uniformity in international accounting.

BEFORE YOU GO ON...

Review It

1. What are the monetary unit assumption, the economic entity assumption, the time period assumption, and the going concern assumption?

2. What are the revenue recognition principle, the matching principle, the full disclosure principle, and the cost principle?

3. What are the materiality constraint and the conservatism constraint?

4. What is the purpose of the International Accounting Standards Board?

DEMONSTRATION PROBLEM 1

Carver Construction Company is under contract to build a condominium at a contract price of $2,000,000. The building will take 18 months to complete at an estimated cost of $1,400,000. Construction began in November 2004, and was finished in April 2006. Actual construction costs incurred in each year were: 2004, $140,000; 2005, $910,000; and 2006, $350,000.

Instructions

Compute the gross profit to be recognized in each year.

ACTION PLAN

■ Determine percent complete by dividing costs incurred by total estimated costs.

■ Find revenue recognized by multiplying percent complete by contract price.

■ Calculate gross profit: revenue recognized less actual costs incurred.

■ Under percentage-of-completion method, recognize revenue as the construction occurs. (Revenue is viewed as a series of sales.)

SOLUTION TO DEMONSTRATION PROBLEM 1

Year	Costs Incurred (Current Period)	÷ Total Estimated Cost =	Percent Complete (Current Period)	× Total Revenue =	Revenue Recognized (Current Period)
2004	$ 140,000	$1,400,000	10%	$2,000,000	$ 200,000
2005	910,000	1,400,000	65%	2,000,000	1,300,000
2006	350,000	Balance to complete contract			500,000
	$1,400,000				$2,000,000

Year	Revenue Recognized (Current Period)	−	Actual Costs Incurred (Current Period)	=	Gross Profit Recognized (Current Period)
2004	$ 200,000		$ 140,000		$ 60,000
2005	1,300,000		910,000		390,000
2006	500,000		350,000		150,000
	$2,000,000		$1,400,000		$600,000

THE NAVIGATOR

DEMONSTRATION PROBLEM 2

Valdes Inc. uses the installment method in accounting for its sales. In 2003, its first year of operations, it had installment sales of $900,000 and a cost of goods sold on installments of $600,000. The collections on installment sales were as follows: 2003, $330,000; 2004, $420,000; and 2005, $150,000.

Instructions

Compute the amount of gross profit to be recognized each year.

ACTION PLAN

■ Use the installment method when cash collection is uncertain.

■ Always find gross profit percentage.

■ Recognize gross profit each period by multiplying cash collected times gross profit percentage.

SOLUTION TO DEMONSTRATION PROBLEM 2

Year	Cash Collected	×	Gross Profit Percentage*	=	Gross Profit Recognized
2003	$330,000		33⅓%		$110,000
2004	420,000		33⅓%		140,000
2005	150,000		33⅓%		50,000
	$900,000				$300,000

*$900,000 − $600,000 = $300,000; $300,000 ÷ $900,000 = 33⅓%

THE NAVIGATOR

SUMMARY OF STUDY OBJECTIVES

1. **Explain the meaning of generally accepted accounting principles and identify the key items of the conceptual framework.** Generally accepted accounting principles are a set of rules and practices that are recognized as a general guide for financial reporting purposes. Generally accepted means that these principles must have "substantial authoritative support." The key items of the conceptual framework are: (1) objectives of financial reporting; (2) qualitative characteristics of accounting information; (3) elements of financial statements; and (4) operating guidelines (assumptions, principles, and constraints).

2. **Describe the basic objectives of financial reporting.** The basic objectives of financial reporting are to provide information that is (1) useful to those making investment and credit decisions; (2) helpful in assessing future cash flows; and (3) helpful in identifying economic resources (assets), the claims to those resources (liabilities), and the changes in those resources and claims.

3. **Discuss the qualitative characteristics of accounting information and elements of financial statements.** To be judged useful, information should possess the following qualitative characteristics: relevance, reliability, comparability, and consistency. The elements of financial statements are a set of definitions that can be used to describe the basic terms used in accounting.

4. **Identify the basic assumptions used by accountants.** The major assumptions are: monetary unit, economic entity, time period, and going concern.

5. **Identify the basic principles of accounting.** The major principles are revenue recognition, matching, full disclosure, and cost.

6. **Identify the two constraints in accounting.** The major constraints are materiality and conservatism.

7. **Explain the accounting principles used in international operations.** There are few recognized worldwide accounting standards. The International Accounting Standards Board (IASB) is working to obtain conformity in international accounting practices.

GLOSSARY

Comparability Ability to compare accounting information of different companies because they use the same accounting principles. (p. 491).

Conceptual framework A coherent system of interrelated objectives and fundamentals that can lead to consistent standards. (p. 490).

Conservatism The constraint of choosing an accounting method, when in doubt, that will least likely overstate assets and net income. (p. 501).

Consistency Use of the same accounting principles and methods from year to year within a company. (p. 491).

Cost principle The principle that assets should be recorded at their historical cost. (p. 499).

Economic entity assumption The assumption that the activities of an economic entity be kept separate from the activities of the owner and of all other entities. (p. 493).

Elements of financial statements Definitions of basic terms used in accounting. (p. 492).

Full disclosure principle The principle that circumstances and events that make a difference to financial statement users should be disclosed. (p. 499).

Generally accepted accounting principles (GAAP) A set of rules and practices, having substantial authoritative support, that are recognized as a general guide for financial reporting purposes. (p. 489).

Going concern assumption The assumption that the enterprise will continue in operation long enough to carry out its existing objectives and commitments. (p. 493).

Installment method A method of recognizing revenue using the cash basis; each cash collection consists of a partial re-

covery of cost of goods sold and partial gross profit from the sale. (p. 496).

International Accounting Standards Board (IASB) An accounting organization whose purpose is to formulate and publish international accounting standards and to promote their acceptance worldwide. (p. 503).

Matching principle The principle that expenses should be matched with revenues in the period when efforts are expended to generate revenues. (p. 497).

Materiality The constraint of determining if an item is important enough to likely influence the decision of a reasonably prudent investor or creditor. (p. 501).

Monetary unit assumption The assumption that only transaction data capable of being expressed in monetary terms should be included in accounting records. (p. 493).

Percentage-of-completion method A method of recognizing revenue and income on a construction project on the basis of costs incurred during the period to the total estimated costs for the entire project. (p. 495).

Relevance The quality of information that indicates the information makes a difference in a decision. (p. 490).

Reliability The quality of information that gives assurance that information is free of error and bias. (p. 491).

Revenue recognition principle The principle that revenue should be recognized in the accounting period in which it is earned (generally at the point of sale). (p. 494).

Time period assumption The assumption that the economic life of a business can be divided into artificial time periods. (p. 493).

SELF-STUDY QUESTIONS

Answers are at the end of the chapter.

(SO 1) **1.** Generally accepted accounting principles are:
  a. a set of standards and rules that are recognized as a general guide for financial reporting.
  b. usually established by the Internal Revenue Service.
  c. the guidelines used to resolve ethical dilemmas.
  d. fundamental truths that can be derived from the laws of nature.

(SO 2) **2.** Which of the following is *not* an objective of financial reporting?
  a. Provide information that is useful in investment and credit decisions.
  b. Provide information about economic resources, claims to those resources, and changes in them.
  c. Provide information that is useful in assessing future cash flows.
  d. Provide information on the liquidation value of a business.

(SO 3) **3.** The primary criterion by which accounting information can be judged is:
  a. consistency.
  b. predictive value.
  c. decision-usefulness.
  d. comparability.

(SO 3) **4.** Verifiability is an ingredient of:

	Reliability	Relevance
a.	Yes	Yes
b.	No	No
c.	Yes	No
d.	No	Yes

(SO 4, 5, 6) **5.** Valuing assets at their liquidation value rather than their cost is *inconsistent* with the:
  a. time period assumption.
  b. matching principle.
  c. going concern assumption.
  d. materiality constraint.

(SO 5) **6.** Gonzalez's Construction Company began a long-term construction contract on January 1, 2005. The contract is expected to be completed in 2006 at a total cost of $20,000,000. Gonzalez's revenue for the project is $24,000,000. Gonzalez incurred contract costs of $4,000,000 in 2005. What gross profit should be recognized in 2005?
  a. $800,000.
  b. $1,000,000.
  c. $2,000,000.
  d. $4,000,000.

(SO **7.** Dunlop Company had installment sales of $1,000,000 in its first year of operations. The cost of goods sold on installment was $650,000. Dunlop collected a total of $500,000 on the installment sales. Using the installment method, how much gross profit should be recognized in the first year?
  a. $140,000.
  b. $175,000.
  c. $350,000.
  d. $500,000.

(SO **8.** The full disclosure principle dictates that:
  a. financial statements should disclose all assets at their cost.
  b. financial statements should disclose only those events that can be measured in dollars.
  c. financial statements should disclose all events and circumstances that would matter to users of financial statements.
  d. financial statements should not be relied on unless an auditor has expressed an unqualified opinion on them.

(SO **9.** The accounting constraint that means that when in doubt the accountant should choose the method that will be least likely to overstate assets and income is called:
  a. the matching principle.
  b. materiality.
  c. conservatism.
  d. the monetary unit assumption.

(SO **10.** The organization that issues international accounting standards is the:
  a. Financial Accounting Standards Board.
  b. International Accounting Standards Board.
  c. International Auditing Standards Committee.
  d. None of the above.

QUESTIONS

1. (a) What are generally accepted accounting principles (GAAP)? (b) What bodies provide authoritative support for GAAP?

2. What elements comprise the FASB's conceptual framework?

3. (a) What are the objectives of financial reporting? (b) Identify the qualitative characteristics of accounting information.

4. Jeff Gartner, the president of Verdez Company, is pleased. Verdez substantially increased its net income in 2005 while keeping its unit inventory relatively the same. Jack Borke, chief accountant, cautions Gartner that since Verdez changed from the LIFO to the FIFO method of inventory valuation, there is a consistency problem. It would be difficult to determine if Verdez is better off. Is Jack Borke correct? Why or why not?

5. What is the distinction between comparability and consistency?

6. Why is it necessary for accountants to assume that an economic entity will remain a going concern?

7. When should revenue be recognized? Why has that date been chosen as the point at which to recognize the revenue resulting from the entire producing and selling process?

8. Spartan Construction Company has a $230 million contract to build a bridge. Its total estimated cost for the project is $170 million. Costs incurred in the first year of the project were $34 million. Spartan appropriately uses the percentage-of-completion method. How much revenue and gross profit should Spartan recognize in the first year of the project?

9. Merchandise with a cost of $80,000 was sold during the year for $100,000. Cash collected for the year amounted to $40,000. How much gross profit should be recognized during the year if the company uses the installment method?

10. Distinguish between expired costs and unexpired costs.

11. (a) Where does the accountant disclose information about an entity's financial position, operations, and cash flows? (b) What is the meaning of the full disclosure principle?

12. Mark Sherrick is the president of Mystery Books. He has no accounting background. Sherrick cannot understand why current cost is not used as the basis for accounting measurement and reporting. Explain what basis is used and why.

13. Describe the two constraints inherent in the presentation of accounting information.

14. Your roommate believes that international accounting standards are uniform throughout the world. Is your roommate correct? Explain.

15. What organization establishes international accounting standards?

BRIEF EXERCISES

BE12-1 Indicate whether each of the following statements is true or false.

Identify generally accepted accounting principles.

(SO 1)

(a) ____ "Generally accepted" means that these principles must have "substantial authoritative support."

(b) ____ GAAP is a set of rules and practices established by the accounting profession to serve as a general guide for financial reporting purposes.

(c) ____ Substantial authoritative support for GAAP usually comes from two standard-setting bodies: the FASB and the IRS.

BE12-2 Indicate which of the following items is(are) included in the FASB's conceptual framework. (Use "Yes" or "No" to answer this question.)

Identify items included in conceptual framework.

(SO 1)

(a) ____ Qualitative characteristics of accounting information.

(b) ____ Analysis of financial statement ratios.

(c) ____ Objectives of financial reporting.

BE12-3 According to the FASB's conceptual framework, which of the following are objectives of financial reporting? (Use "Yes" or "No" to answer this question.)

Identify objectives of financial reporting.

(SO 2)

(a) ____ Provide information that identifies the economic resources (assets), the claims to those resources (liabilities), and the changes in those resources and claims.

(b) ____ Provide information that is helpful in assessing past cash flows and stock prices.

(c) ____ Provide information that is useful to those making investment and credit decisions.

BE12-4 Presented below is a chart of the qualitative characteristics of accounting information. Fill in the blanks from (a) to (e).

Identify qualitative characteristics.

(SO 3)

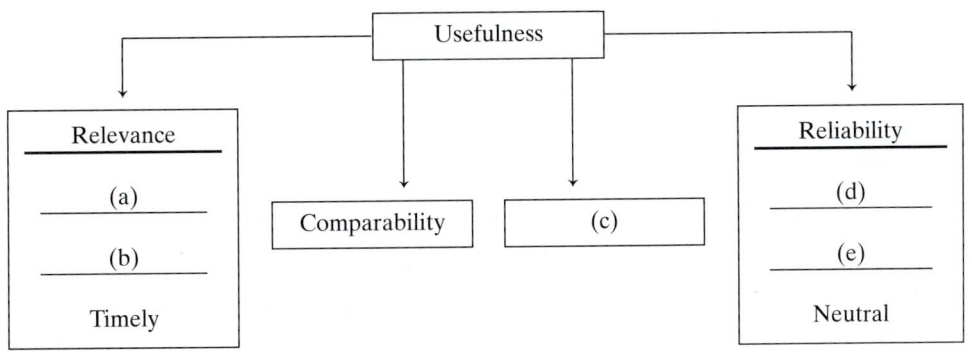

Identify qualitative characteristics.

(SO 3)

BE12-5 Given the *qualitative characteristics* of accounting established by the FASB's conceptual framework, complete each of the following statements.

(a) _____ is the quality of information that gives assurance that it is free of error and bias; it can be depended on.

(b) _____ means using the same accounting principles and methods from year to year within a company.

(c) For information to be _____, it should have predictive or feedback value, and it must be presented on a timely basis.

Identify qualitative characteristics.

(SO 3)

BE12-6 Presented below is a set of qualitative characteristics of accounting information.

1. Predictive value   **3.** Verifiable
2. Neutral   **4.** Timely

Match these qualitative characteristics to the following statements, using the numbers above.

(a) _____Accounting information should help users make predictions about the outcome of future events.

(b) _____Accounting information cannot be selected, prepared, or presented to favor one set of interested users over another.

(c) _____Accounting information must be proved to be free of error and bias.

(d) _____Accounting information must be available to decision makers before it loses its capacity to influence their decisions.

Identify operating guidelines.

(SO 4, 5, 6)

BE12-7 Presented below are four concepts discussed in this chapter.

1. Time period assumption   **3.** Full disclosure principle
2. Cost principle   **4.** Conservatism

Match these concepts to the following accounting practices. Each number can be used only once.

(a) _____Recording inventory at its purchase price.

(b) _____Using notes and supplementary schedules in the financial statements.

(c) _____Preparing financial statements on an annual basis.

(d) _____Using the lower of cost or market method for inventory valuation.

Compute revenue—percentage-of-completion.

(SO 5)

BE12-8 Flynn Construction Company is under contract to build a commercial building at a price of $4,200,000. Construction began in January 2004 and was finished in December 2006. Total estimated construction costs are $2,800,000. Actual construction costs incurred in each year were: 2004, $560,000; 2005, $1,820,000; 2006, $420,000. Compute the revenue to be recognized in each year using the percentage-of-completion method.

Compute gross profit—installment method.

(SO 5)

BE12-9 Gonzalez Co. uses the installment method to determine its net income. In 2005, its first year of operations, it had installment sales of $800,000 and a cost of goods sold of $560,000. The collections on installment sales were as follows: 2005, $360,000; 2006, $440,000. Determine the gross profit recognized for 2005 and 2006.

Identify the constraints that have been violated.

(SO 6)

BE12-10 O'Neill Company uses the following accounting practices.

(a) Small tools are recorded as plant assets and depreciated.

(b) Inventory is reported at cost when market value is lower.

(c) The income statement shows paper clips expense of $10.

(d) Revenue on installment sales is recognized at the time of sale.

Indicate the accounting constraint, if any, that has been violated by each practice.

EXERCISES

Identify the assumption, principle, or constraint that has been violated.

(SO 4, 5, 6)

E12-1 A number of accounting reporting situations are described below.

1. Church Company is in its fifth year of operation and has yet to issue financial statements. (Do not use full disclosure principle.)

2. Leask Company has inventory on hand that cost $400,000. Leask reports inventory on its balance sheet at its current market value of $425,000.

3. Ann Zareena, president of Always Music Company, bought a computer for her personal use. She paid for the computer by using company funds and debited the "computers" account.
4. Mull Company recognizes revenue at the end of the production cycle, but before sale. The price of the product, as well as the amount that can be sold, is not certain.
5. In preparing its financial statements, Rupe Company omitted information concerning its method of accounting for inventories.
6. Martinez Company uses the direct write-off method of accounting for uncollectible accounts.
7. McKane Hospital Supply Corporation reports only current assets and current liabilities on its balance sheet. Property, plant, and equipment are reported as current assets. Bonds payable are reported as current liabilities. Liquidation of the company is unlikely.

Instructions
For each of the above, list the assumption, principle, or constraint that has been violated, if any. List only one term for each case.

E12-2 Presented below are some business transactions that occurred during 2005 for Etheridge Co.

Identify the assumption, principle, or constraint that has been violated; prepare correct entries.

(SO 4, 5, 6)

1. An account receivable has been deemed to be a bad debt. The following entry was made.

Allowance for Doubtful Accounts	10,000	
Accounts Receivable		10,000

2. The president of Etheridge Co., Ben Manion, purchased a truck for personal use and charged it to his expense account. The following entry was made.

Travel Expense	18,000	
Cash		18,000

3. An electric pencil sharpener costing $25 is being depreciated over 5 years. The following entry was made.

Depreciation Expense—Pencil Sharpener	5	
Accumulated Depreciation—Pencil Sharpener		5

4. Equipment worth $90,000 was acquired at a cost of $65,000 from a company that had water damage in a flood. The following entry was made.

Equipment	90,000	
Cash		65,000
Gain		25,000

5. Merchandise inventory with a cost of $208,000 is reported at its market value of $260,000. The following entry was made.

Merchandise Inventory	52,000	
Gain		52,000

Instructions
In each of the situations above, identify the assumption, principle, or constraint that has been violated, if any. Discuss the appropriateness of the journal entries, and give the correct journal entry, if necessary.

E12-3 Presented below are the assumptions, principles, and constraints discussed in this chapter:

Identify accounting assumptions, principles, and constraints.

(SO 4, 5, 6)

1. Economic entity assumption
2. Going concern assumption
3. Monetary unit assumption
4. Time period assumption
5. Cost principle
6. Matching principle
7. Full disclosure principle
8. Revenue recognition principle
9. Materiality
10. Conservatism

Instructions
Identify by number the accounting assumption, principle, or constraint that describes each situation below. Do not use a number more than once.

(a) Requires recognition of expenses in the same period as related revenues.
(b) Indicates that market value changes subsequent to purchase are not recorded in the accounts.

(c) Is the rationale for why plant assets are not reported at liquidation value. (Do not use historical cost principle.)

(d) Indicates that personal and business record keeping should be separately maintained.

(e) Ensures that all relevant financial information is reported.

(f) Assumes that the dollar is the "measuring stick" used to report on financial performance.

(g) Requires that the operational guidelines be followed for all significant items.

(h) Separates financial information into time periods for reporting purposes.

Determine the amount of revenue to be recognized.

(SO 5)

E12-4 Consider the following transactions of Parolini Company for 2005.

1. Leased office space to Easley Supplies for a 1-year period beginning September 1. The rent of $24,000 was paid in advance.

2. Sold a 6-month insurance policy to Orosco Corporation for $8,000 on March 1.

3. Received a sales order for merchandise costing $9,000 and a sales price of $14,000 on December 28 from Gutierrez Company. The goods were shipped FOB shipping point on December 31. Gutierrez received them on January 3, 2006.

4. Signed a long-term contract to construct a building at a total price of $1,600,000. Total estimated cost of construction is $1,200,000. During 2005, the company incurred $300,000 of costs and collected $330,000 in cash. The percentage-of-completion method is used to recognize revenue.

5. Had merchandise inventory on hand at year-end that amounted to $160,000. Parolini Company expects to sell the inventory in 2006 for $190,000.

Instructions

For each item above, indicate the amount of revenue Parolini Company should recognize in calendar year 2005. Explain.

Determine gross profit for construction projects.

(SO 5)

E12-5 Ruiz Construction Company currently has one long-term construction project. The project has a contract price of $140,000,000, with total estimated costs of $100,000,000. Ruiz appropriately uses the percentage-of-completion method. After 2 years of construction, the following costs have been accumulated.

Actual cost incurred, Year 1	$30,000,000
Total estimated cost remaining after Year 1	70,000,000
Actual cost incurred, Year 2	50,000,000
Total estimated cost remaining after Year 2	20,000,000

Instructions

Determine the gross profit for each of the first 2 years of the construction contract.

Determine gross profit using installment sales and point-of-sale bases.

(SO 5)

E12-6 Milton Company sold equipment for $300,000 in 2004. Collections on the sale were as follows: 2004, $70,000; 2005, $190,000; 2006, $40,000. Milton's cost of goods sold is typically 70% of sales.

Instructions

(a) Determine Milton's gross profit for 2004, 2005, and 2006, assuming that Milton recognizes revenue under the installment method.

(b) Determine Milton's gross profit for 2004, 2005, and 2006, assuming that Milton recognizes revenue under the point-of-sale basis.

PROBLEMS: SET A

Analyze transactions to identify accounting principle or assumption violated, and prepare correct entries.

(SO 4, 5)

P12-1A Scott and Quick are accountants for Century Computers. They disagree over the following transactions that occurred during the calendar year 2005.

1. Scott suggests that equipment should be reported on the balance sheet at its liquidation value, which is $15,000 less than its cost.

2. Century bought a custom-made piece of equipment for $36,000. This equipment has a useful life of 6 years. Century depreciates equipment using the straight-line method. "Since the equipment is custom-made, it will have no resale value. Therefore, it shouldn't be depreciated but instead should be expensed immediately," argues Scott. "Besides, it provides for lower net income."

3. Depreciation for the year was $18,000. Since net income is expected to be lower this year, Scott suggests deferring depreciation to a year when there is more net income.

4. Land costing $60,000 was appraised at $90,000. Scott suggests the following journal entry.

Land	30,000	
Gain on Appreciation of Land		30,000

5. Century purchased equipment for $35,000 at a going-out-of-business sale. The equipment was worth $45,000. Scott believes that the following entry should be made.

Equipment	45,000	
Cash		35,000
Gain		10,000

Quick disagrees with Scott on each of the above situations.

Instructions

For each transaction, indicate why Quick disagrees. Identify the accounting principle or assumption that Scott would be violating if his suggestions were used. Prepare the correct journal entry for each transaction, if any.

P12-2A Presented below are a number of business transactions that occurred during the current year for Yerkes, Inc.

Determine the appropriateness of journal entries in terms of generally accepted accounting principles or assumptions.

(SO 4, 5)

1. Because the general level of prices increased during the current year, Yerkes, Inc. determined that there was a $10,000 understatement of depreciation expense on its equipment and decided to record it in its accounts. The following entry was made.

Depreciation Expense	10,000	
Accumulated Depreciation		10,000

2. Because of a "flood sale," equipment obviously worth $250,000 was acquired at a cost of $200,000. The following entry was made.

Equipment	250,000	
Cash		200,000
Gain on Purchase of Equipment		50,000

3. The president of Yerkes, Inc. used his expense account to purchase a new Saab 9000 solely for personal use. The following entry was made.

Miscellaneous Expense	34,000	
Cash		34,000

4. An order for $30,000 has been received from a customer for products on hand. This order is to be shipped on January 9 next year. The following entry was made.

Accounts Receivable	30,000	
Sales		30,000

5. Materials were purchased on March 31 for $65,000. This amount was entered in the Inventory account. On December 31, the materials would have cost $80,000, so the following entry was made.

Inventory	15,000	
Gain on Inventories		15,000

Instructions

▱▭▭▷ In each situation, discuss the appropriateness of the journal entries in terms of generally accepted accounting principles.

Recognize gross profit using the percentage-of-completion method.

(SO 5)

P12-3A McNeil Construction Company is involved in a long-term construction contract to build an office building. The estimated cost is $30 million, and the contract price is $38 million. Additional information follows.

| | Office Building | |
	Cash Collections	Actual Costs Incurred
2004	$ 6,000,000	$ 4,500,000
2005	8,000,000	6,000,000
2006	12,500,000	12,000,000
2007	11,500,000	7,500,000

The project is completed in 2007, and all cash to be received from the contract has been received.

Instructions

2007: $2,000,000

Prepare a schedule to determine the gross profit in each year for the long-term construction contract using the percentage-of-completion method.

Recognize gross profit using the installment method.

(SO 5)

P12-4A Westphal Construction sold to Walker Management Company apartments it had constructed. The sales price was $2.5 million. Westphal's cost to construct the apartments was $1.6 million. Westphal appropriately uses the installment method. Additional information follows.

	Cash Collected
2004	$ 800,000
2005	1,200,000
2006	500,000

(a) 2004: $288,000

(a) Determine the gross profit for each year using the installment method.
(b) Repeat (a) assuming the construction costs were $1.75 million.

Identify accounting assumptions, principles, and constraints.

(SO 4, 5, 6)

P12-5A Presented below are the assumptions, principles, and constraints used in this chapter.

1. Economic entity assumption
2. Going concern assumption
3. Monetary unit assumption
4. Time period assumption
5. Full disclosure principle
6. Revenue recognition principle
7. Matching principle
8. Cost principle
9. Materiality
10. Conservatism

Identify by number the accounting assumption, principle, or constraint that describes each situation below. Do not use a number more than once.

(a) Repair tools are expensed when purchased. These repair tools have a useful life of more than one accounting period. (Do not use conservatism.)
(b) Expenses should be allocated to revenues in proper period.
(c) The dollar is the measuring stick used to report financial information.
(d) Financial information is separated into time periods for reporting purposes.
(e) Market value changes subsequent to purchase are not recorded in the accounts. (Do not use the revenue recognition principle.)
(f) Personal and business record keeping should be separately maintained.
(g) All relevant financial information should be reported.
(h) Lower of cost or market is used to value inventories.

PROBLEMS: SET B

Analyze transactions to identify accounting principle or assumption violated, and prepare correct entries.

(SO 4, 5)

P12-1B Stahl and Cheng are accountants for Chester Printers. They disagree over the following transactions that occurred during the year.

1. Land costing $41,000 was appraised at $49,000. Stahl suggests the following journal entry.

Land	8,000	
Gain on Appreciation of Land		8,000

2. Chester bought equipment for $60,000, including installation costs. The equipment has a useful life of 5 years. Chester depreciates equipment using the straight-line method. "Since the equipment as installed into our system cannot be removed without considerable damage, it will have no resale value. Therefore, it should not be depreciated, but instead should be expensed immediately," argues Stahl. "Besides, it lowers net income."

3. Depreciation for the year was $26,000. Since net income is expected to be lower this year, Stahl suggests deferring depreciation to a year when there is more net income.

4. Chester purchased equipment at a fire sale for $18,000. The equipment was worth $26,000. Stahl believes that the following entry should be made.

Equipment	26,000	
Cash		18,000
Gain		8,000

5. Stahl suggests that Chester should carry equipment on the balance sheet at its liquidation value, which is $20,000 less than its cost.

6. Chester rented office space for 1 year starting October 1, 2005. The total amount of $24,000 was paid in advance. Stahl believes that the following entry should be made on October 1.

Rent Expense	24,000	
Cash		24,000

Cheng disagrees with Stahl on each of the situations above.

Instructions
For each transaction, indicate why Cheng disagrees. Identify the accounting principle or assumption that Stahl would be violating if his suggestions were used. Prepare the correct journal entry for each transaction, if any.

P12-2B Presented below are a number of business transactions that occurred during the current year for Renteria, Inc.

Determine the appropriateness of journal entries in terms of generally accepted accounting principles or assumptions.

(SO 4, 5)

1. Because the general level of prices increased during the current year, Renteria, Inc. determined that there was a $40,000 understatement of depreciation expense on its equipment and decided to record it in its accounts. The following entry was made.

Depreciation Expense	40,000	
Accumulated Depreciation		40,000

2. Because of a "flood sale," equipment obviously worth $300,000 was acquired at a cost of $225,000. The following entry was made.

Equipment	300,000	
Cash		225,000
Gain on Purchase of Equipment		75,000

3. An order for $60,000 has been received from a customer for products on hand. This order is to be shipped on January 9 next year. The following entry was made.

Accounts Receivable	60,000	
Sales		60,000

4. Land was purchased on April 30 for $200,000. This amount was entered in the Land account. On December 31, the land would have cost $240,000, so the following entry was made.

Land	40,000	
Gain on Land		40,000

5. The president of Renteria, Inc. used his expense account to purchase a pre-owned Mercedes-Benz E420 solely for personal use. The following entry was made.

Miscellaneous Expense	54,000	
Cash		54,000

Instructions
In each situation, discuss the appropriateness of the journal entries in terms of generally accepted accounting principles.

Recognize gross profit using the percentage-of-completion method.

(SO 5)

P12-3B Cosky Construction Company is involved in a long-term construction contract to build a shopping center with a total estimated cost of $20 million, and a contract price of $28 million. Additional information follows.

	Shopping Center	
	Cash Collections	**Actual Costs Incurred**
2004	$ 4,500,000	$3,000,000
2005	10,000,000	9,000,000
2006	7,000,000	5,000,000
2007	6,500,000	3,000,000

The project was completed in 2007, and all cash collections related to the contract have been received.

Instructions

2007: $1,200,000

Prepare a schedule to determine the gross profit for each year for the long-term construction contract, using the percentage-of-completion method.

Recognize gross profit using the installment method.

(SO 5)

P12-4B Alicia sold to Lee Management Company condominiums it had constructed. The sales price was $6 million. Alicia's cost to construct the condominiums was $4.2 million. Alicia appropriately uses the installment method. Additional information follows.

	Cash Collected
2004	$ 900,000
2005	3,800,000
2006	1,300,000

Instructions

(a) 2004: $270,000

(a) Prepare a schedule to determine the gross profit for each year using the installment method.
(b) Repeat (a) assuming construction costs were $4.5 million.

Identify accounting assumptions, principles, and constraints.

(SO 4, 5, 6)

P12-5B Presented below are assumptions, principles, and constraints used in this chapter.

1. Economic entity assumption
2. Going concern assumption
3. Monetary unit assumption
4. Time period assumption
5. Full disclosure principle
6. Revenue recognition principle
7. Matching principle
8. Cost principle
9. Materiality
10. Conservatism

Instructions

Identify by number the accounting assumption, principle, or constraint that describes each situation below. Do not use a number more than once.

(a) All important information related to inventories is presented in the financial statements or in the footnotes.
(b) Assets are not stated at their liquidation value. (Do not use the cost principle.)
(c) The death of the president is not recorded in the accounts.
(d) Pencil sharpeners are expensed when purchased.
(e) An allowance for doubtful accounts is established. (Do not use conservatism.)
(f) Each entity is kept as a unit distinct from its owner or owners.
(g) Reporting must be done at defined intervals.
(h) Revenue is recorded at the point of sale.
(i) When in doubt, it is better to understate rather than overstate net income.

COMPREHENSIVE PROBLEM: CHAPTERS 9 TO 12

Paris Company and Troyer Company are competing businesses. Both began operations 6 years ago and are quite similar in most respects. The current balance sheet data for the two companies are as follows.

	Paris Company	Troyer Company
Cash	$ 70,300	$ 48,400
Accounts receivable	309,700	312,500
Allowance for doubtful accounts	(13,600)	–0–
Merchandise inventory	463,900	520,200
Plant and equipment	255,300	257,300
Accumulated depreciation, plant and equipment	(112,650)	(189,850)
Total assets	972,950	$948,550
Current liabilities	$440,200	$436,500
Long-term liabilities	78,000	80,000
Total liabilities	518,200	516,500
Owner's equity	454,750	432,050
Total liabilities and owner's equity	$972,950	$948,550

You have been engaged as a consultant to conduct a review of the two companies. Your goal is to determine which of them is in the stronger financial position.

Your review of their financial statements quickly reveals that the two companies have not followed the same accounting practices. The differences and your conclusions regarding them are summarized below.

1. Paris Company has used the allowance method of accounting for bad debts. A review shows that the amount of its write-offs each year has been quite close to the allowances that have been provided. It therefore seems reasonable to have confidence in its current estimate of bad debts.

   Troyer Company has used the direct write-off method for bad debts, and it has been somewhat slow to write off its uncollectible accounts. Based upon an aging analysis and review of its accounts receivable, it is estimated that $20,000 of its existing accounts will probably prove to be uncollectible.

2. Paris Company has determined the cost of its merchandise inventory on a LIFO basis. The result is that its inventory appears on the balance sheet at an amount that is below its current replacement cost. Based upon a detailed physical examination of its merchandise on hand, the current replacement cost of its inventory is estimated at $517,000.

   Troyer Company has used the FIFO method of valuing its merchandise inventory. Its ending inventory appears on the balance sheet at an amount that quite closely approximates its current replacement cost.

3. Paris Company estimated a useful life of 12 years and a salvage value of $30,000 for its plant and equipment. It has been depreciating them on a straight-line basis.

   Troyer Company has the same type of plant and equipment. However, it estimated a useful life of 10 years and a salvage value of $10,000. It has been depreciating its plant and equipment using the double-declining-balance method.

   Based upon engineering studies of these types of plant and equipment, you conclude that Troyer's estimates and method for calculating depreciation are the more appropriate.

4. Among its current liabilities, Paris has included the portions of long-term liabilities that become due within the next year. Troyer has not done so.

   You find that $16,000 of Troyer's $80,000 of long-term liabilities are due to be repaid in the current year.

Instructions

(a) Revise the balance sheets presented above so that the data are comparable and reflect the current financial position for each of the two companies.

(b) ▭▭▭▷ Prepare a brief report to your client stating your conclusions.

(a) Total assets:
Paris $950,325
Troyer $928,550

BROADENING YOUR PERSPECTIVE

Financial Reporting and Analysis

■ FINANCIAL REPORTING PROBLEM

BYP12-1 Cathy Bishop successfully completed her first accounting course during the spring semester. She is now working as a management trainee for First Arizona Bank during the summer. One of her fellow management trainees, Zane Jones, is taking the same accounting course this summer and has been having a "lot of trouble." On the second exam, for example, Zane became confused about inventory valuation methods. He completely missed all the points on a problem involving LIFO and FIFO.

Zane's instructor recently indicated that the third exam will probably have a number of essay questions dealing with accounting principles issues. Zane is quite concerned about the third exam for two reasons. First, he has never taken an accounting exam in which essay answers were required. Second, Zane feels he must do well on this exam to get an acceptable grade in the course.

Zane has asked Cathy to help him prepare for the next exam. She agrees, and suggests that Zane develop a set of possible questions on the accounting principles material that they might discuss.

Instructions
Answer the following questions that were developed by Zane.

(a) What is a conceptual framework?

(b) Why is there a need for a conceptual framework?

(c) What are the objectives of financial reporting?

(d) If you had to explain generally accepted accounting principles to a nonaccountant, what essential characteristics would you include in your explanation?

(e) What are the qualitative characteristics of accounting? Explain each one.

(f) Identify the basic assumptions used in accounting.

(g) What are two major constraints involved in financial reporting? Explain each of them.

■ EXPLORING THE WEB

BYP12-2 The **Financial Accounting Standards Board (FASB)** is a private organization established to improve accounting standards and financial reporting. The FASB conducts extensive research before issuing a "Statement of Financial Accounting Standards," which represents an authoritative expression of generally accepted accounting principles.

Address: www.rutgers.edu/accounting/raw, or go to www.wiley.com/college/weygandt

Steps
1. Choose **FASB**.
2. Choose **FASB Facts**.

Instructions
Answer the following questions.

(a) What is the mission of the FASB?

(b) How are topics added to the FASB technical agenda?

(c) What characteristics make the FASB's procedures an "open" decision-making process?

Critical Thinking

■ GROUP DECISION CASE

BYP12-3 Werly Industries has two operating divisions—Piper Construction Division and McKenna Securities Division. Each division maintains its own accounting system and method of revenue recognition.

■ PIPER CONSTRUCTION DIVISION

During the fiscal year ended November 30, 2005, Piper Construction Division had one construction project in process. A $33,000,000 contract for construction of a civic center was granted on June 19, 2005, and construction began on August 1, 2005. Estimated costs of completion at the contract date were $26,000,000 over a 2-year time period from the date of the contract. On November 30, 2005, construction costs of $9,000,000 had been incurred. The construction costs to complete the remainder of the project were reviewed on November 30, 2005, and were estimated to amount to only $16,000,000 because of an unexpected decline in raw materials costs. Revenue recognition is based upon a percentage-of-completion method.

■ McKENNA SECURITIES DIVISION

McKenna Securities Division works through manufacturers' agents in various cities. Orders for alarm systems and down payments are forwarded from agents, and the division ships the goods f.o.b. factory directly to customers (usually police departments and security guard companies). Customers are billed directly for the balance due plus actual shipping costs. The firm received orders for $6,000,000 of goods during the fiscal year ended November 30, 2005. Down payments of $600,000 were received and goods with a selling price of $5,250,000 were billed and shipped. Actual freight costs of $100,000 were also billed. Commissions of 10% on product price are paid manufacturing agents after goods are shipped to customers. Such goods are covered under warranty for 90 days after shipment, and warranty returns have been about 1% of sales. Revenue is recognized at the point of sale by this division.

Instructions

With the class divided into groups, answer the following.

(a) There are a variety of methods of revenue recognition. Define and describe each of the following methods of revenue recognition, and indicate whether each is in accordance with generally accepted accounting principles.
  (1) Point of sale.
  (2) Percentage-of-completion.
  (3) Installment contract.
(b) Compute the revenue to be recognized in fiscal year 2005 for both operating divisions of Werly Industries in accordance with generally accepted accounting principles.

■ ETHICS CASE

BYP12-4 When the Financial Accounting Standards Board issues new standards, the required implementation date is usually 12 months or more from the date of issuance, with early implementation encouraged. Andrea Lane, accountant at Ecom Corporation, discusses with her financial vice president the need for early implementation of a recently issued standard that would result in a much fairer presentation of the company's financial condition and earnings. When the financial vice president determines that early implementation of the standard will adversely affect reported net income for the year, he strongly discourages Andrea from implementing the standard until it is required.

Instructions

(a) Who are the stakeholders in this situation?
(b) What, if any, are the ethical considerations in this situation?
(c) What does Andrea have to gain by advocating early implementation? Who might be affected by the decision against early implementation?

Answers to Self-Study Questions

1. a **2.** d **3.** c **4.** c **5.** c **6.** a **7.** b **8.** c **9.** c **10.** b

Answer to PepsiCo Review It Question 2, p. 493
The Independent Auditors' Report indicates that **PepsiCo**'s financial statements (balance sheet, income statement, common stockholders' equity, and cash flows) "present fairly, in all material respects, the financial position of PepsiCo, Inc. . . . and the results of their operations and their cash flows . . . in conformity with accounting principles generally accepted in the United States of America."

Accounting for Partnerships

THE NAVIGATOR ✓

Understand **Concepts for Review**	❑
Read **Feature Story**	❑
Scan **Study Objectives**	❑
Read **Preview**	❑
Read text and answer **Before You Go On** p. 525 ❑ p. 531 ❑ p. 536 ❑	
Work **Demonstration Problem**	❑
Review **Summary of Study Objectives**	❑
Answer **Self-Study Questions**	❑
Complete **Assignments**	❑

CONCEPTS FOR REVIEW

Before studying this chapter, you should know or, if necessary, review:

The cost principle of accounting.
(Ch. 1, p. 10)

The owner's equity statement.
(Ch. 1, pp. 21–23)

How to make closing entries and prepare the post-closing trial balance.
(Ch. 4, pp. 142–146)

The steps in the accounting cycle.
(Ch. 4, p. 149)

The format of classified financial statements.
(Ch. 4, pp. 152–157)

☑ THE NAVIGATOR

From Trials to the Top Ten

In 1990 Cliff Chenfield and Craig Balsam gave up the razors, ties, and six-figure salaries they had become accustomed to as New York lawyers. Instead, they set up a partnership, Razor & Tie Music, in Cliff's living room. Ten years later the label is the only record company in the country that has achieved success by selling music both on television and in the stores. Razor & Tie's entertaining and effective TV commercials have yielded unprecedented sales for multi-artist music compilations. At the same time, its hot young retail label has been behind some of the most recent original, progressive releases.

Razor & Tie's first TV release, *Those Fabulous '70s* (100,000 copies sold), was followed by *Disco Fever* (over 300,000 sold). These albums generated so much publicity that partners Cliff and Craig were guests on dozens of TV interview shows.

After restoring the respectability of the oft-maligned 1970s, the partners forged into the musical '80s with the same zeal that elicited success with their first releases. In July 1993, Razor & Tie released *Totally '80s*, a collection of Top-10 singles from the 1980s that has sold over 450,000 units since its release. Featuring the tag line, "The greatest hits from the decade when communism died and music videos were born," *Totally '80s* was the best-selling direct-response album in the country in 1993.

In 1995, Razor & Tie broke into the contemporary music world with *Living In The '90s*, the most successful record in the history of the company. Featuring a number of songs that were still recurrent hits on the radio at the time the package initially aired, *Living In The '90s* was a blockbuster. It received Gold certification in less than nine months and rewrote the rules on direct-response albums. For the first time, contemporary music was available through an album offered only through direct-response spots.

How has Razor & Tie carved out its sizable piece of the market? Through the complementary talents of the two partners. Their imagination and savvy, along with exciting new releases planned for the coming years, ensure Razor & Tie such continued growth that the partnership form of organization may be challenged to its limits.

www.razorandtie.com

✓ THE NAVIGATOR

STUDY OBJECTIVES

After studying this chapter, you should be able to:

1. Identify the characteristics of the partnership form of business organization.
2. Explain the accounting entries for the formation of a partnership.
3. Identify the bases for dividing net income or net loss.
4. Describe the form and content of partnership financial statements.
5. Explain the effects of the entries to record the liquidation of a partnership.

✓ THE NAVIGATOR

It is not surprising that when Cliff Chenfield and Craig Balsam began **Razor & Tie**, they decided to use the partnership form of organization. Both saw the need for hands-on control of their product and its promotion. In this chapter, we will discuss reasons why the partnership form of organization is often selected. We also will explain the major issues in accounting for partnerships.

The content and organization of Chapter 13 are as follows.

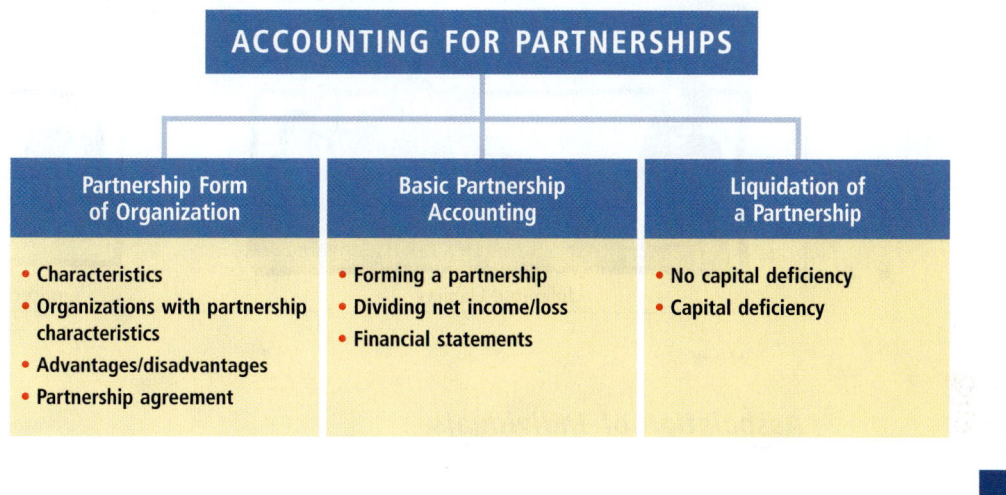

ACCOUNTING FOR PARTNERSHIPS

Partnership Form of Organization	Basic Partnership Accounting	Liquidation of a Partnership
• Characteristics • Organizations with partnership characteristics • Advantages/disadvantages • Partnership agreement	• Forming a partnership • Dividing net income/loss • Financial statements	• No capital deficiency • Capital deficiency

✓ THE NAVIGATOR

Partnership Form of Organization

The Uniform Partnership Act provides the basic rules for the formation and operation of partnerships in more than 90 percent of the states. This act defines a **partnership** as an association of two or more persons to carry on as co-owners of a business for profit. Partnerships are common in retail establishments and in small manufacturing companies. Also, accountants, lawyers, and doctors find it desirable to form partnerships with other professionals in their field. Professional partnerships vary in size from a medical partnership of 3 to 5 doctors, to 150 to 200 partners in a large law firm, to more than 2,000 partners in an international accounting firm.

Characteristics of Partnerships

Partnerships are fairly easy to form. They can be formed simply by a verbal agreement or, more formally, by putting in writing the rights and obligations of the partners. Partners who have not put their agreement in writing sometimes have found that the characteristics of partnerships can lead to later difficulties. The principal characteristics of the partnership form of business organization are shown in Illustration 13-1 (page 522) and explained in the following sections.

STUDY OBJECTIVE 1

Identify the characteristics of the partnership form of business organization.

Illustration 13-1
Partnership characteristics

Association of Individuals

The voluntary association of two or more individuals in a partnership may be based on as simple an act as a handshake. However, it is preferable to state the agreement in writing. Under the Uniform Partnership Act, a partnership is a legal entity for certain purposes. For instance, property (land, buildings, equipment) can be owned in the name of the partnership, and the firm can sue or be sued. **A partnership also is an accounting entity for financial reporting purposes.** Thus, the purely personal assets, liabilities, and transactions of the partners are excluded from the accounting records of the partnership, just as they are in a proprietorship.

The net income of a partnership is not taxed as a separate entity. But, a partnership must file an information tax return showing partnership net income and each partner's share of that net income. Each partner's share is taxable at personal tax rates, regardless of the amount of net income withdrawn from the business during the year.

Mutual Agency

Mutual agency means that each partner acts on behalf of the partnership when engaging in partnership business. The act of any partner is binding on all other partners. This is true even when partners act beyond the scope of their authority, so long as the act appears to be appropriate for the partnership. For example, a partner of a grocery store who purchases a delivery truck creates a binding contract in the name of the partnership, even if the partnership agreement denies this authority. On the other hand, if a partner in a law firm purchased a snowmobile for the partnership, such an act would not be binding on the partnership. The purchase is clearly outside the scope of partnership business.

> **HELPFUL HINT**
>
> Because of mutual agency, an individual should be extremely cautious in selecting partners.

Limited Life

A partnership does not have unlimited life. It may be ended voluntarily at any time through the acceptance of a new partner or the withdrawal of a partner. A partnership may be ended involuntarily by the death or incapacity of a partner. Thus the life of a partnership is indefinite. **Partnership dissolution** occurs whenever a partner withdraws or a new partner is admitted. Dissolution of a partnership does not necessarily mean that the business ends. If the continuing partners agree, operations can continue without interruption by forming a new partnership.

Unlimited Liability

Each partner is **personally and individually liable** for all partnership liabilities. Creditors' claims attach first to partnership assets. If these are insufficient, the claims then attach to the personal resources of any partner, irrespective of that partner's equity in the partnership. Because each partner is responsible for all the debts of the partnership, each partner is said to have **unlimited liability**.

ACCOUNTING IN ACTION   **Business Insight**

The prestigious New York law firm of **Kaye, Scholer, Fierman, Hays, & Handler**, accused of withholding damaging information during a federal investigation of its client **Lincoln Savings & Loan**, settled out of court for $41 million. The firm's liability insurance covered only $25 million of the total. Its 109 partners had to pay the remaining $16 million out of their own pockets.

In a recent year, court damage awards in malpractice suits against U.S. accountants and attorneys was close to $1 billion.

Co-Ownership of Property

Partnership assets are owned jointly by the partners. If the partnership is dissolved, the assets do not legally revert to the original contributor. Each partner has a claim on total assets equal to the balance in his or her respective capital account. This claim does not attach to specific assets that an individual partner contributed to the firm. Similarly, if a partner invests a building in the partnership valued at $100,000 and the building is later sold at a gain of $20,000, that partner does not personally receive the entire gain.

Partnership net income (or net loss) is also co-owned. **If the partnership contract does not specify to the contrary, all net income or net loss is shared equally by the partners.** As you will see later, though, partners may agree to unequal sharing of net income or net loss.

Organizations with Partnership Characteristics

With surprising speed, states are creating special forms of business organizations that have partnership characteristics. These new organizations are being adopted by many small companies. These special forms are: limited partnerships, limited liability partnerships, limited liability companies, and "S" corporations.

Limited Partnerships

In a limited partnership, one or more partners have **unlimited liability** and one or more partners have **limited liability** for the debts of the firm. Those with unlimited liability are called general partners. Those with limited liability are called limited partners. Limited partners are responsible for the debts of the partnership up to the limit of their investment in the firm. This organization is identified in its name with the words "Limited Partnership," or "Ltd.," or "LP." For the privilege of limited liability, the limited partner usually accepts less compensation than a general partner and exercises less influence in the affairs of the firm.

Limited Liability Partnership

Most states allow professionals such as lawyers, doctors, and accountants to form a **limited liability partnership** or "LLP." The LLP is designed to protect innocent partners from malpractice or negligence claims resulting from the acts of another partner. LLPs generally carry large insurance policies in case the partnership is guilty of malpractice.

Limited Liability Companies

A new, hybrid form of business organization with certain features like a corporation and others like a limited partnership is the **limited liability company**, or "LLC" (or "LC"). An LLC usually has a limited life. The owners, called **members**, have limited liability like owners of a corporation. Whereas limited partners do not actively participate in the management of a limited partnership (LP), the members of a limited liability company (LLC) can assume an active management role. For income tax purposes, the IRS usually classifies an LLC as a partnership. For internal accounting purposes, LLCs use the same accounting procedures as those described in this partnership chapter.

"S" Corporations

An **"S" corporation** is a corporation that is taxed in the same way that a partnership is taxed. To qualify as an "S" corporation, the company must have 75 or fewer stockholders, all of whom must be citizens or residents of the United States. The advantage of an "S" corporation (also called a Sub-Chapter "S" corporation) is that, like a partnership and unlike a corporation, it does not pay income taxes.

Advantages and Disadvantages of Partnerships

Why do people choose partnerships? One major advantage of a partnership is that the **skills and resources of two or more individuals can be combined**. For example, a large public accounting firm such as **Ernst & Young** must have expertise in auditing, taxation, and management consulting. In addition, a partnership is **easily formed and is relatively free from governmental regulations and restrictions**. A partnership does not have to contend with the "red tape" that a corporation must face. Also, decisions can be made quickly on substantive matters affecting the firm; there is no board of directors that must be consulted.

On the other hand, partnerships also have some major disadvantages: **mutual agency**, **limited life**, and **unlimited liability**. Unlimited liability is particularly troublesome. Many individuals fear they may lose not only their initial investment but also their personal assets, if those assets are needed to pay partnership creditors. As a result, partnerships often find it difficult to obtain large amounts of investment capital. That is one reason why the largest business enterprises in the United States are corporations, not partnerships.

The advantages and disadvantages of the partnership form of business organization are summarized in Illustration 13-2.

Illustration 13-2
Advantages and disadvantages of a partnership

Advantages	Disadvantages
Combining skills and resources of two or more individuals	Mutual agency
Ease of formation	Limited life
Freedom from governmental regulations and restrictions	Unlimited liability
Ease of decision making	

The Partnership Agreement

Ideally, the agreement of two or more individuals to form a partnership should be expressed in writing. This written contract is often called the **partnership agreement** or **articles of co-partnership**. The partnership agreement contains such basic information as the name and principal location of the firm, the purpose of the business, and date of inception. In addition, relationships among the partners should be specified, such as:

1. Names and capital contributions of partners.
2. Rights and duties of partners.
3. Basis for sharing net income or net loss. *(splitting profit)*
4. Provision for withdrawals of assets.
5. Procedures for submitting disputes to arbitration.
6. Procedures for the withdrawal or addition of a partner.
7. Rights and duties of surviving partners in the event of a partner's death.

[handwritten annotations: Name & place co / Purpose / Date of inception / Partner relationship]

We cannot overemphasize the importance of a written contract. The agreement should be drawn with care and should attempt to anticipate all possible situations, contingencies, and disagreements. The help of a lawyer is highly desirable in preparing the agreement.

> **ETHICS NOTE**
>
> A well-developed partnership agreement reduces ethical conflict among partners. It specifies in clear and concise language the process by which ethical and legal problems will be resolved. This issue is especially significant when the partnership experiences financial distress.

ACCOUNTING IN ACTION  Business Insight

Accounting firms generally use the limited liability (LLP) form. As a consequence, they do not have publicly traded shares of stock. During the dot-com stock market craze of the late 1990s, this proved to be somewhat of a disadvantage for partnerships. The reason: Many dot-com firms lured top high-tech employees to their companies by offering shares of stock. As dot-com stock prices soared, many of these people became very rich—at least for a while. However, when many of these same dot-com companies started to falter and fail, their stock prices plummeted, and they laid off many employees.

BEFORE YOU GO ON...

Review It

1. What are the distinguishing characteristics of a partnership?
2. What are the principal advantages and disadvantages of a partnership? Why is **PepsiCo** not a partnership? The answer to this question is provided on page 555.
3. What are the major items in a partnership agreement?

Basic Partnership Accounting

We now turn to the basic accounting for partnerships. The major accounting issues relate to forming the partnership, dividing income or loss, and preparing financial statements.

How do we look up mrkt value

Forming a Partnership

STUDY OBJECTIVE 2

Explain the accounting entries for the formation of a partnership.

Each partner's initial investment in a partnership is entered in the partnership records. These investments should be recorded at the **fair market value of the assets at the date of their transfer to the partnership**. The values assigned must be agreed to by all of the partners.

To illustrate, assume that A. Rolfe and T. Shea combine their proprietorships to start a partnership named U.S. Software. The firm will specialize in developing financial modeling software packages. Rolfe and Shea have the following assets prior to the formation of the partnership.

Illustration 13-3
Book and market values of assets invested

	Book Value		Market Value	
	A. Rolfe	**T. Shea**	**A. Rolfe**	**T. Shea**
Cash	$ 8,000	$ 9,000	**$ 8,000**	**$ 9,000**
Office equipment	5,000		**4,000**	
Accumulated depreciation	(2,000)			
Accounts receivable		4,000		**4,000**
Allowance for doubtful accounts		(700)		**(1,000)**
	$11,000	$12,300	**$12,000**	**$12,000**

*Items under **owners' equity (OE)** in the marginal accounting equation analyses are not labeled in this partnership chapter. Nearly all affect partners' **capital** accounts.*

A	=	L	+	OE
+8,000				+12,000
+4,000				

Cash Flows
+8,000

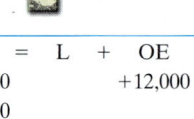

A	=	L	+	OE
+9,000				+12,000
+4,000				
−1,000				

Cash Flows
+9,000

The entries to record the investments are:

Investment of A. Rolfe

Cash	8,000	
Office Equipment	4,000	
A. Rolfe, Capital		12,000
(To record investment of Rolfe)		

Investment of T. Shea

Cash	9,000	
Accounts Receivable	4,000	
Allowance for Doubtful Accounts		1,000
T. Shea, Capital		12,000
(To record investment of Shea)		

How

Note that neither the original cost of the office equipment ($5,000) nor its book value ($5,000 − $2,000) is recorded by the partnership. The equipment is recorded at its fair market value, $4,000. Because the equipment has not been used by the partnership, there is no accumulated depreciation.

In contrast, the gross claims on customers ($4,000) are carried forward to the partnership. The allowance for doubtful accounts is adjusted to $1,000 to arrive at a cash (net) realizable value of $3,000. A partnership may start with an allowance for doubtful accounts because it will continue to collect existing accounts receivable, some of which are expected to be uncollectible. In addition, this procedure maintains the control and subsidiary relationship between Accounts Receivable and the accounts receivable subsidiary ledger.

After the partnership has been formed, the accounting for transactions is similar to any other type of business organization. For example, all transactions with outside parties, such as the purchase or sale of merchandise inventory and the payment or receipt of cash, should be recorded the same for a partnership as for a proprietorship.

The steps in the accounting cycle described in Chapter 4 for a proprietorship also apply to a partnership. For example, the partnership prepares a trial balance and journalizes and posts adjusting entries. A work sheet may be used. There are minor differences in journalizing and posting closing entries and in preparing financial statements, as explained in the following sections. The differences occur because there is more than one owner.

Dividing Net Income or Net Loss

Partnership net income or net loss is shared equally unless the partnership contract indicates otherwise. The same basis of division usually applies to both net income and net loss. It is customary to refer to this basis as the **income ratio**, the **income and loss ratio**, or the **profit and loss (P&L) ratio**. Because of its wide acceptance, we will use the term **income ratio** to identify the basis for dividing net income and net loss. A partner's share of net income or net loss is recognized in the accounts through closing entries.

Closing Entries

As in the case of a proprietorship, four entries are required in preparing closing entries for a partnership. The entries are:

1. Debit each revenue account for its balance, and credit Income Summary for total revenues.

2. Debit Income Summary for total expenses, and credit each expense account for its balance.

3. Debit Income Summary for its balance, and credit each partner's capital account for his or her share of net income. Or, credit Income Summary, and debit each partner's capital account for his or her share of net loss.

4. Debit each partner's capital account for the balance in that partner's drawing account, and credit each partner's drawing account for the same amount.

The first two entries are the same as in a proprietorship. The last two entries are different because (1) there are two or more owners' capital and drawing accounts, and (2) it is necessary to divide net income (or net loss) among the partners.

To illustrate the last two closing entries, assume that AB Company has net income of $32,000 for 2005. The partners, L. Arbor and D. Barnett, share net income and net loss equally. Drawings for the year were Arbor $8,000 and Barnett $6,000. The last two closing entries are:

Dec. 31	Income Summary	32,000	
	L. Arbor, Capital ($32,000 × 50%)		16,000
	D. Barnett, Capital ($32,000 × 50%)		16,000
	(To transfer net income to partners' capital accounts)		

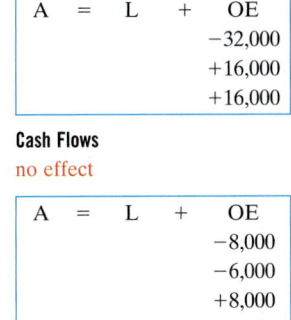

A = L + OE
−32,000
+16,000
+16,000

Cash Flows
no effect

Dec. 31	L. Arbor, Capital	8,000	
	D. Barnett, Capital	6,000	
	L. Arbor, Drawing		8,000
	D. Barnett, Drawing		6,000
	(To close drawing accounts to capital accounts)		

A = L + OE
−8,000
−6,000
+8,000
+6,000

Cash Flows
no effect

Assume that the beginning capital balance is $47,000 for Arbor and $36,000 for Barnett. After posting the closing entries, the capital and drawing accounts will appear as shown in Illustration 13-4 (page 528).

Illustration 13-4
Partners' capital and drawing accounts after closing

L. Arbor, Capital			
12/31 **Clos.** **8,000**	1/1 Bal.	47,000
	12/31 **Clos.**	**16,000**
	12/31 Bal.	55,000

D. Barnett, Capital			
12/31 **Clos.** **6,000**	1/1 Bal.	36,000
	12/31 **Clos.**	**16,000**
	12/31 Bal.	46,000

L. Arbor, Drawing			
12/31 Bal. 8,000	12/31 **Clos.**	**8,000**

D. Barnett, Drawing			
12/31 Bal. 6,000	12/31 **Clos.**	**6,000**

As in a proprietorship, the partners' capital accounts are permanent accounts; their drawing accounts are temporary accounts. Normally, the capital accounts will have credit balances and the drawing accounts will have debit balances. Drawing accounts are debited when partners withdraw cash or other assets from the partnership for personal use.

Income Ratios

STUDY OBJECTIVE 3

Identify the bases for dividing net income or net loss.

As noted earlier, the partnership agreement should specify the basis for sharing net income or net loss. The following are typical income ratios.

1. A fixed ratio, expressed as a proportion (6:4), a percentage (70% and 30%), or a fraction (2/3 and 1/3).
2. A ratio based either on capital balances at the beginning of the year or on average capital balances during the year.
3. Salaries to partners and the remainder on a fixed ratio.
4. Interest on partners' capital balances and the remainder on a fixed ratio.
5. Salaries to partners, interest on partners' capital, and the remainder on a fixed ratio.

The objective is to settle on a basis that will equitably reflect the partners' capital investment and service to the partnership.

A fixed ratio is easy to apply, and it may be an equitable basis in some circumstances. Assume, for example, that Hughes and Lane are partners. Each contributes the same amount of capital, but Hughes expects to work full-time in the partnership and Lane expects to work only half-time. Accordingly, the partners agree to a fixed ratio of 2/3 to Hughes and 1/3 to Lane.

A ratio based on capital balances may be appropriate when the funds invested in the partnership are considered the critical factor. Capital ratios may also be equitable when a manager is hired to run the business and the partners do not plan to take an active role in daily operations.

The three remaining ratios (items 3, 4, and 5) give specific recognition to differences among partners. These ratios provide salary allowances for time worked and interest allowances for capital invested. Then, any remaining net income or net loss is allocated on a fixed ratio. Some caution needs to be exercised in working with these types of income ratios. These ratios pertain exclusively to **the computations that are required in dividing net income or net loss** among the partners.

Salaries to partners and interest on partners' capital are not expenses of the partnership. Therefore, these items do not enter into the matching of expenses with revenues and the determination of net income or net loss. For a partnership, as for other entities, salaries expense pertains to the cost of services performed by employees. Likewise, interest expense relates to the cost of borrowing from creditors. But partners, as owners, are not considered either **employees** or **creditors**. Therefore, when the income ratio includes a salary allowance for partners, some partnership agreements permit the partner to make monthly withdrawals of cash based on their "salary." Such withdrawals are debited to the partner's drawing account.

Salaries, Interest, and Remainder on a Fixed Ratio

Under income ratio (5) in the list above, the provisions for salaries and interest must be applied **before** the remainder is allocated on the specified fixed ratio. **This is true even if the provisions exceed net income. It is also true even if the partnership has suffered a net loss for the year.** Detailed information concerning the division of net income or net loss should be shown below net income on the income statement.

To illustrate this income ratio, assume that Sara King and Ray Lee are co-partners in the Kingslee Company. The partnership agreement provides for: (1) salary allowances of $8,400 to King and $6,000 to Lee, (2) interest allowances of 10% on capital balances at the beginning of the year, and (3) the remainder equally. Capital balances on January 1 were King $28,000, and Lee $24,000. In 2005, partnership net income is $22,000. The division of net income is as follows.

Illustration 13-5
Income statement with division of net income

KINGSLEE COMPANY
Income Statement (partial)
For the Year Ended December 31, 2005

	Sara King	Ray Lee	Total
Sales	$200,000		
Net income	$ 22,000		
Division of Net Income			
Salary allowance	$ 8,400	$6,000	$14,400
Interest allowance on partners' capital			
Sara King ($28,000 × 10%)	2,800		
Ray Lee ($24,000 × 10%)		2,400	
Total interest allowance			5,200
Total salaries and interest	11,200	8,400	19,600
Remaining income, $2,400			
($22,000 − $19,600)			
Sara King ($2,400 × 50%)	1,200		
Ray Lee ($2,400 × 50%)		1,200	
Total remainder			2,400
Total division of net income	**$12,400**	**$9,600**	**$22,000**

The entry to record the division of net income is:

Dec. 31	Income Summary	22,000	
	Sara King, Capital		12,400
	Ray Lee, Capital		9,600
	(To close net income to partners' capital)		

A	=	L	+	OE
				−22,000
				+12,400
				+9,600

Cash Flows
no effect

Now let's look at a situation in which the salary and interest allowances exceed net income. Assume that Kingslee Company's net income is only $18,000. In this case, the salary and interest allowances will create a deficiency of $1,600 ($19,600 − $18,000). The computations of the allowances are the same as those in the preceding example. Beginning with total salaries and interest, we complete the division of net income as shown in Illustration 13-6 (page 530).

Illustration 13-6
Division of net income—
income deficiency

	Sara King	Ray Lee	Total
Total salaries and interest	$11,200	$8,400	$19,600
Remaining deficiency ($1,600)			
($18,000 − $19,600)			
Sara King ($1,600 × 50%)	(800)		
Ray Lee ($1,600 × 50%)		(800)	
Total remainder			(1,600)
Total division	**$10,400**	**$7,600**	**$18,000**

Partnership Financial Statements

STUDY OBJECTIVE 4

Describe the form and content of partnership financial statements.

The financial statements of a partnership are similar to those of a proprietorship. The differences are due to the number of owners involved. The income statement for a partnership is identical to the income statement for a proprietorship except for the division of net income, as shown earlier.

The owners' equity statement for a partnership is called the **partners' capital statement**. Its function is to explain the changes in each partner's capital account and in total partnership capital during the year. The partners' capital statement for Kingslee Company is shown below. It is based on the division of $22,000 of net income in Illustration 13-5. The statement includes assumed data for the additional investment and drawings.

Illustration 13-7
Partners' capital statement

HELPFUL HINT

As in a proprietorship, partners' capital may change due to (1) additional investment, (2) drawings, and (3) net income or net loss.

KINGSLEE COMPANY
Partners' Capital Statement
For the Year Ended December 31, 2005

	Sara King	Ray Lee	Total
Capital, January 1	$28,000	$24,000	$52,000
Add: Additional investment	2,000		2,000
Net income	12,400	9,600	22,000
	42,400	33,600	76,000
Less: Drawings	7,000	5,000	12,000
Capital, December 31	**$35,400**	**$28,600**	**$64,000**

The partners' capital statement is prepared from the income statement and the partners' capital and drawing accounts.

The balance sheet for a partnership is the same as for a proprietorship except for the owner's equity section. In a partnership, the capital balances of each partner are shown in the balance sheet. The owners' equity section for Kingslee Company would show the following.

Illustration 13-8
Owners' equity section of a partnership balance sheet

KINGSLEE COMPANY
Balance Sheet (partial)
December 31, 2005

Total liabilities (assumed amount)		$115,000
Owners' equity		
Sara King, Capital	$35,400	
Ray Lee, Capital	28,600	
Total owners' equity		64,000
Total liabilities and owners' equity		$179,000

BEFORE YOU GO ON...

Review It

1. How should a partner's initial investment of assets be valued?
2. What are the closing entries for a partnership?
3. What income ratios may be used in a partnership?
4. How do partnership financial statements differ from proprietorship financial statements?

Do It

LeeMay Company reports net income of $57,000. The partnership agreement provides for salaries of $15,000 to L. Lee and $12,000 to R. May. The remainder is to be shared on a 60:40 basis (60% to Lee). L. Lee asks your help to divide the net income between the partners and to prepare the closing entry.

ACTION PLAN

■ Compute net income exclusive of any salaries to partners and interest on partners' capital.
■ Deduct salaries to partners from net income.
■ Apply the partners' income ratios to the remaining net income.
■ Prepare the closing entry distributing net income or net loss among the partners' capital accounts.

SOLUTION   The division of net income is as follows.

	L. Lee	R. May	Total
Salary allowance	$15,000	$12,000	$27,000
Remaining income ($57,000 − $27,000)			
L. Lee (60% × $30,000)	18,000		
R. May (40% × $30,000)		12,000	
Total remaining income			30,000
Total division of net income	$33,000	$24,000	$57,000

The closing entry for net income therefore is:

Income Summary	57,000	
L. Lee, Capital		33,000
R. May, Capital		24,000
(To close net income to partners' capital accounts)		

Related exercise material: *BE13-3, BE13-4, BE13-5, and E13-2.*

☑ THE NAVIGATOR

Liquidation of a Partnership

The liquidation of a partnership terminates the business. It involves selling the assets of the firm, paying liabilities, and distributing any remaining assets to the partners. Liquidation may result from the sale of the business by mutual agreement of the partners, from the death of a partner, or from bankruptcy. **Partnership liquidation** ends both the legal and economic life of the entity.

From an accounting standpoint, liquidation should be preceded by completing the accounting cycle for the final operating period. This includes preparing adjusting entries and financial statements. It also involves preparing closing entries and a post-closing trial balance. Thus, only balance sheet accounts should be open as the liquidation process begins.

STUDY OBJECTIVE 5

Explain the effects of the entries to record the liquidation of a partnership.

In liquidation, the sale of noncash assets for cash is called **realization**. Any difference between book value and the cash proceeds is called the **gain or loss on realization**. To liquidate a partnership, it is necessary to:

1. Sell noncash assets for cash and recognize a gain or loss on realization.
2. Allocate gain/loss on realization to the partners based on their income ratios.
3. Pay partnership liabilities in cash.
4. Distribute remaining cash to partners on the basis of their **capital balances**.

Each of the steps must be performed in sequence. Creditors must be paid **before** partners receive any cash distributions. Each step also must be recorded by an accounting entry.

When a partnership is liquidated, all partners may have credit balances in their capital accounts. This situation is called **no capital deficiency**. Or, at least one partner's capital account may have a debit balance. This situation is termed a **capital deficiency**. To illustrate each of these conditions, assume that the Ace Company is liquidated when its ledger shows the following assets, liabilities, and owners' equity accounts.

Illustration 13-9
Account balances prior to liquidation

Assets		Liabilities and Owners' Equity	
Cash	$ 5,000	Notes payable	$15,000
Accounts receivable	15,000	Accounts payable	16,000
Inventory	18,000	R. Arnet, Capital	15,000
Equipment	35,000	P. Carey, Capital	17,800
Accum. depr.—equipment	(8,000)	W. Eaton, Capital	1,200
	$65,000		$65,000

No Capital Deficiency

The partners of Ace Company agree to liquidate the partnership on the following terms: (1) The noncash assets of the partnership will be sold to Jackson Enterprises for $75,000 cash. And (2) the partnership will pay its partnership liabilities. The income ratios of the partners are $3 : 2 : 1$, respectively. The steps in the liquidation process are as follows.

1. The noncash assets (accounts receivable, inventory, and equipment) are sold for $75,000. The book value of these assets is $60,000 ($15,000 + $18,000 + $35,000 − $8,000). Thus a gain of $15,000 is realized on the sale. The entry is:

	A	=	L	+	OE
+75,000					+15,000
+8,000					
−15,000					
−18,000					
−35,000					

Cash Flows
+75,000

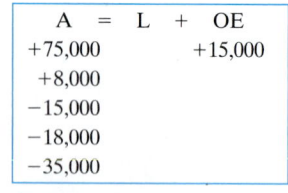

(1)

Cash	75,000	
Accumulated Depreciation–Equipment	8,000	
Accounts Receivable		15,000
Inventory		18,000
Equipment		35,000
Gain on Realization		15,000
(To record realization of noncash assets)		

2. The gain on realization of $15,000 is allocated to the partners on their income ratios, which are 3:2:1. The entry is:

	A	=	L	+	OE
					−15,000
					+7,500
					+5,000
					+2,500

Cash Flows
no effect

(2)

Gain on Realization	15,000	
R. Arnet, Capital ($15,000 × 3/6)		7,500
P. Carey, Capital ($15,000 × 2/6)		5,000
W. Eaton, Capital ($15,000 × 1/6)		2,500
(To allocate gain to partners' capital accounts)		

3. Partnership liabilities consist of Notes Payable $15,000 and Accounts Payable $16,000. Creditors are paid in full by a cash payment of $31,000. The entry is:

(3)

Notes Payable	15,000	
Accounts Payable	16,000	
Cash		31,000
(To record payment of partnership liabilities)		

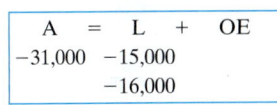

A	=	L	+	OE
−31,000		−15,000		
		−16,000		

Cash Flows
−31,000

4. The remaining cash is distributed to the partners on the basis of **their capital balances.** After the entries in the first three steps are posted, all partnership accounts, including Gain on Realization, will have zero balances except for four accounts: Cash $49,000; R. Arnet, Capital $22,500; P. Carey, Capital $22,800; and W. Eaton, Capital $3,700, as shown below.

Illustration 13-10
Ledger balances before distribution of cash

Cash			R. Arnet, Capital		P. Carey, Capital		W. Eaton, Capital	
Bal. 5,000	(3)	31,000	Bal. 15,000		Bal. 17,800		Bal. 1,200	
(1) 75,000			(2) 7,500		(2) 5,000		(2) 2,500	
Bal. 49,000			**Bal. 22,500**		**Bal. 22,800**		**Bal. 3,700**	

The entry to record the distribution of cash is as follows.

(4)

R. Arnet, Capital	22,500	
P. Carey, Capital	22,800	
W. Eaton, Capital	3,700	
Cash		49,000
(To record distribution of cash to partners)		

A	=	L	+	OE
−49,000				−22,500
				−22,800
				−3,700

Cash Flows
−49,000

After this entry is posted, all partnership accounts will have zero balances.

    A word of caution: **Cash should not be distributed to partners on the basis of their income-sharing ratios.** On this basis, Arnet would receive three-sixths, or $24,500, which would produce an erroneous debit balance of $2,000. The income ratio is the proper basis for allocating net income or loss. **It is not a proper basis for making the final distribution of cash to the partners.**

Schedule of Cash Payments

Some accountants prepare a cash payments schedule to determine the distribution of cash to the partners in the liquidation of a partnership. The **schedule of cash payments** is organized around the basic accounting equation. The schedule for the Ace Company is shown in Illustration 13-11 (page 534). The numbers in parentheses refer to the four required steps in the liquidation of a partnership. They also identify the accounting entries that must be made. The cash payments schedule is especially useful when the liquidation process extends over a period of time.

Illustration 13-11
Schedule of cash payments,
no capital deficiency

ACE COMPANY
Schedule of Cash Payments

Item		Cash	+	Noncash Assets	=	Liabilities	+	R. Arnet Capital	+	P. Carey Capital	+	W. Eaton Capital
Balances before liquidation		5,000	+	60,000	=	31,000	+	15,000	+	17,800	+	1,200
Sales of noncash assets and allocation of gain	(1)&(2)	75,000	+	(60,000)	=			7,500	+	5,000	+	2,500
New balances		80,000	+	–0–	=	31,000	+	22,500	+	22,800	+	3,700
Pay liabilities	(3)	(31,000)			=	(31,000)						
New balances		49,000	+	–0–	=	–0–	+	22,500	+	22,800	+	3,700
Cash distribution to partners	(4)	(49,000)			=			(22,500)	+	(22,800)	+	(3,700)
Final balances		–0–		–0–		–0–		–0–		–0–		–0–

Capital Deficiency

A capital deficiency may be caused by recurring net losses, excessive drawings, or losses from realization suffered during liquidation. To illustrate, assume that Ace Company is on the brink of bankruptcy. The partners decide to liquidate by having a "going-out-of-business" sale. Merchandise is sold at substantial discounts, and the equipment is sold at auction. Cash proceeds from these sales and collections from customers total only $42,000. Thus, the loss from liquidation is $18,000 ($60,000 − $42,000). The steps in the liquidation process are as follows.

1. The entry for the realization of noncash assets is:

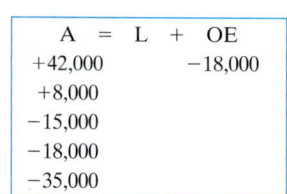

Cash Flows
+42,000

(1)

Cash	42,000	
Accumulated Depreciation—Equipment	8,000	
Loss on Realization	18,000	
Accounts Receivable		15,000
Inventory		18,000
Equipment		35,000
(To record realization of noncash assets)		

A	=	L	+	OE
+42,000				−18,000
+8,000				
−15,000				
−18,000				
−35,000				

2. The loss on realization is allocated to the partners on the basis of their income ratios. The entry is:

Cash Flows
no effect

A	=	L	+	OE
				−9,000
				−6,000
				−3,000
				+18,000

(2)

R. Arnet, Capital ($18,000 × 3/6)	9,000	
P. Carey, Capital ($18,000 × 2/6)	6,000	
W. Eaton, Capital ($18,000 × 1/6)	3,000	
Loss on Realization		18,000
(To allocate loss on realization to partners)		

3. Partnership liabilities are paid. This entry is the same as in the previous example.

Cash Flows
−31,000

A	=	L	+	OE
−31,000		−15,000		
		−16,000		

(3)

Notes payable	15,000	
Accounts Payable	16,000	
Cash		31,000
(To record payment of partnership liabilities)		

4. After posting the three entries, two accounts will have debit balances—Cash $16,000, and W. Eaton, Capital $1,800. Two accounts will have credit balances—R. Arnet, Capital $6,000, and P. Carey, Capital $11,800. All four accounts are shown below.

Illustration 13-12
Ledger balances before distribution of cash

Cash			R. Arnet, Capital			P. Carey, Capital			W. Eaton, Capital		
Bal.	5,000	(3) 31,000	(2)	9,000	Bal. 15,000	(2)	6,000	Bal. 17,800	(2)	3,000	Bal. 1,200
(1)	42,000				Bal. **6,000**			Bal. **11,800**	Bal. **1,800**		
Bal.	**16,000**										

Eaton has a capital deficiency of $1,800, and so owes the partnership $1,800. Arnet and Carey have a legally enforceable claim for that amount against Eaton's personal assets. The distribution of cash is still made on the basis of capital balances. But the amount will vary depending on how Eaton's deficiency is settled. Two alternatives are presented below.

Payment of Deficiency

If the partner with the capital deficiency pays the amount owed the partnership, the deficiency is eliminated. To illustrate, assume that Eaton pays $1,800 to the partnership. The entry is:

A	=	L	+	OE
+1,800				+1,800

(a)

Cash	1,800	
W. Eaton, Capital		1,800
(To record payment of capital deficiency by Eaton)		

Cash Flows
+1,800

After posting this entry, account balances are as follows.

Illustration 13-13
Ledger balances after paying capital deficiency

Cash			R. Arnet, Capital			P. Carey, Capital			W. Eaton, Capital		
Bal.	5,000	(3) 31,000	(2)	9,000	Bal. 15,000	(2)	6,000	Bal. 17,800	(2)	3,000	Bal. 1,200
(1)	42,000				Bal. **6,000**			Bal. **11,800**			(a) 1,800
(a)	1,800										Bal. **–0–**
Bal.	**17,800**										

The cash balance of $17,800 is now equal to the credit balances in the capital accounts (Arnet $6,000 + Carey $11,800). Cash now is distributed on the basis of these balances. The entry is:

A	=	L	+	OE
−17,800				−6,000
				−11,800

R. Arnet, Capital	6,000	
P. Carey, Capital	11,800	
Cash		17,800
(To record distribution of cash to the partners)		

Cash Flows
−17,800

After this entry is posted, all accounts will have zero balances.

Nonpayment of Deficiency

If a partner with a capital deficiency is unable to pay the amount owed to the partnership, the partners with credit balances must absorb the loss. The loss is allocated on the basis of the income ratios that exist between the partners with credit balances.

For example, the income ratios of Arnet and Carey are 3 : 2, or 3/5 and 2/5, respectively. Thus, the following entry would be made to remove Eaton's capital deficiency.

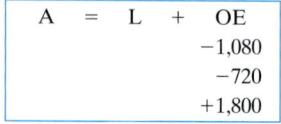

A	=	L	+	OE
−1,080				
−720				
+1,800				

Cash Flows
no effect

(a)

R. Arnet, Capital ($1,800 × 3/5)	1,080	
P. Carey, Capital ($1,800 × 2/5)	720	
W. Eaton, Capital		1,800
(To record write-off of capital deficiency)		

After posting this entry, the cash and capital accounts will have the following balances.

Illustration 13-14
Ledger balances after nonpayment of capital deficiency

	Cash				R. Arnet, Capital				P. Carey, Capital				W. Eaton, Capital		
Bal.	5,000	(3)	31,000	(2)	9,000	Bal.	15,000	(2)	6,000	Bal.	17,800	(2)	3,000	Bal.	1,200
(1)	42,000			(a)	1,080			(a)	720					(a)	1,800
Bal.	**16,000**					**Bal.**	**4,920**			**Bal.**	**11,080**			**Bal.**	**–0–**

The cash balance of $16,000 now equals the sum of the credit balances in the capital accounts (Arnet $4,920 + Carey $11,080). The entry to record the distribution of cash is:

A	=	L	+	OE
−16,000				−4,920
				−11,080

Cash Flows
−16,000

R. Arnet, Capital	4,920	
P. Carey, Capital	11,080	
Cash		16,000
(To record distribution of cash to the partners)		

After this entry is posted, all accounts will have zero balances.

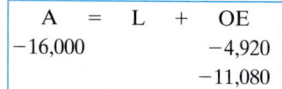

BEFORE YOU GO ON...

Review It

1. What are the steps in liquidating a partnership?
2. What basis is used in making the final distribution of cash to the partners?

☑ THE NAVIGATOR

DEMONSTRATION PROBLEM

On January 1, 2005, the capital balances in Hollingsworth Company are Lois Holly $26,000, and Jim Worth $24,000. In 2005 the partnership reports net income of $30,000. The income ratio provides for salary allowances of $12,000 for Holly and $10,000 to Worth and the remainder equally. Neither partner had any drawings in 2005.

Instructions

(a) Prepare a schedule showing the distribution of net income in 2005.
(b) Journalize the division of 2005 net income to the partners.

SOLUTION TO DEMONSTRATION PROBLEM

ACTION PLAN
- Compute the net income of the partnership.
- Allocate the partners' salaries.
- Divide the remaining net income among the partners, applying the income/loss ratio.
- Journalize the division of net income in a closing entry.

(a) Net income 30,000

Division of Net Income

	Lois Holly	Jim Worth	Total
Salary allowance	$12,000	$10,000	$22,000
Remaining income $8,000 ($30,000 − $22,000)			
Lois Holly ($8,000 × 50%)	4,000		
Jim Worth ($8,000 × 50%)		4,000	
Total remainder			8,000
Total division of net income	$16,000	$14,000	$30,000

(b) 12/31/05

Income Summary	30,000	
Lois Holly, Capital		16,000
Jim Worth, Capital		14,000
(To close net income to partners' capital)		

THE NAVIGATOR

SUMMARY OF STUDY OBJECTIVES

1. **Identify the characteristics of the partnership form of business organization.** The principal characteristics of a partnership are: (a) association of individuals, (b) mutual agency, (c) limited life, (d) unlimited liability, and (e) co-ownership of property.

2. **Explain the accounting entries for the formation of a partnership.** When a partnership is formed, each partner's initial investment should be recorded at the fair market value of the assets at the date of their transfer to the partnership.

3. **Identify the bases for dividing net income or net loss.** Net income or net loss is divided on the basis of the income ratio, which may be (a) a fixed ratio, (b) a ratio based on beginning or average capital balances, (c) salaries to partners and the remainder on a fixed ratio, (d) interest on partners' capital and the remainder on a fixed ratio, and (e) salaries to partners, interest on partners' capital, and the remainder on a fixed ratio.

4. **Describe the form and content of partnership financial statements.** The financial statements of a partnership are similar to those of a proprietorship. The principal differences are: (a) the division of net income is shown on the income statement, (b) the owners' equity statement is called a partners' capital statement, and (c) each partner's capital is reported on the balance sheet.

5. **Explain the effects of the entries to record the liquidation of a partnership.** When a partnership is liquidated, it is necessary to record the (a) sale of noncash assets, (b) allocation of the gain or loss on realization, (c) payment of partnership liabilities, and (d) distribution of cash to the partners on the basis of their capital balances.

THE NAVIGATOR

GLOSSARY

Capital deficiency A debit balance in a partner's capital account after allocation of gain or loss. (p. 532).

General partner A partner who has unlimited liability for the debts of the firm. (p. 523).

Income ratio The basis for dividing net income and net loss in a partnership. (p. 527).

Limited liability company A form of business organization, usually classified as a partnership and usually with limited life, in which partners, who are called *members*, have limited liability. (p. 524).

Limited liability partnership A partnership of professionals in which partners are given limited liability and the public is protected from malpractice by insurance carried by the partnership. (p. 524).

Limited partner A partner who has limited liability for the debts of the firm. (p. 523).

Limited partnership A partnership in which one or more general partners have unlimited liability and one or more partners have limited liability for the obligations of the firm. (p. 523).

No capital deficiency All partners have credit balances after allocation of gain or loss. (p. 532).

Partners' capital statement The owners' equity statement for a partnership which shows the changes in each partner's capital balance and in total partnership capital during the year. (p. 530).

Partnership An association of two or more persons to carry on as co-owners of a business for profit. (p. 521).

Partnership agreement A written contract expressing the voluntary agreement of two or more individuals in a partnership. (p. 525).

Partnership dissolution A change in partners due to withdrawal or admission, which does not necessarily terminate the business. (p. 522).

Partnership liquidation An event that ends both the legal and economic life of a partnership. (p. 531).

"S" corporation Corporation, with 75 or fewer stockholders, that is taxed like a partnership. (p. 524).

Schedule of cash payments A schedule showing the distribution of cash to the partners in a partnership liquidation. (p. 533).

APPENDIX ADMISSION AND WITHDRAWAL OF PARTNERS

The chapter explained how the basic accounting for a partnership works. We now look at how to account for a common occurrence in partnerships—the addition or withdrawal of a partner.

Admission of a Partner

STUDY OBJECTIVE 6

Explain the effects of the entries when a new partner is admitted.

The admission of a new partner results in the **legal dissolution** of the existing partnership and **the beginning of a new one**. From an economic standpoint, the admission of a new partner (or partners) may be of minor significance in the continuity of the business. For example, in large public accounting or law firms, partners are admitted annually without any change in operating policies. **To recognize the economic effects, it is necessary only to open a capital account for each new partner.** In the entries illustrated below, we assume that the accounting records of the predecessor firm will continue to be used by the new partnership.

A new partner may be admitted either by (1) purchasing the interest of an existing partner or (2) investing assets in the partnership, as shown in Illustration 13A-1. The former affects only the capital accounts of the partners who are parties to the transaction. The latter increases both net assets and total capital of the partnership.

Illustration 13A-1
Procedures in adding partners

Admission of Partner through:

1. Purchase of a Partner's Interest

2. Investment of Assets in Partnership

Purchase of a Partner's Interest

The **admission** of a partner **by purchase of an interest** is a personal transaction between one or more existing partners and the new partner. Each party acts as an individual separate from the partnership entity. The price paid is negotiated by the individuals involved. It may be equal to or different from the capital equity acquired. The purchase price passes directly from the new partner to the partners who are giving up part or all of their ownership claims.

Any money or other consideration exchanged is the personal property of the participants and **not** the property of the partnership. Upon purchase of an interest, the new partner acquires each selling partner's capital interest and income ratio.

Accounting for the purchase of an interest is straightforward. In the partnership records, only the realignment of partners' capital is recorded. **Each partner's capital account is debited for the ownership claims that have been relinquished, and the new partner's capital account is credited with the capital equity purchased.** Total assets, total liabilities, and total capital remain unchanged, as do all individual asset and liability accounts.

To illustrate, assume that L. Carson agrees to pay $10,000 each to C. Ames and D. Barker for 33⅓% (one-third) of their interest in the Ames–Barker partnership. At the time of the admission of Carson, each partner has a $30,000 capital balance. Both partners, therefore, give up $10,000 of their capital equity. The entry to record the admission of Carson is:

C. Ames, Capital	10,000	
D. Barker, Capital	10,000	
L. Carson, Capital		20,000
(To record admission of Carson by purchase)		

The effect of this transaction on net assets and partners' capital is shown below.

Illustration 13A-2
Ledger balances after purchase of a partner's interest

Net Assets		C. Ames, Capital		D. Barker, Capital		L. Carson, Capital	
60,000		**10,000**	30,000	**10,000**	30,000		**20,000**
			Bal. 20,000		Bal. 20,000		

Note that net assets remain unchanged at $60,000, and each partner has a $20,000 capital balance. Ames and Barker continue as partners in the firm, but the capital interest of each has changed. The cash paid by Carson goes directly to the individual partners and not to the partnership.

Regardless of the amount paid by Carson for the one-third interest, the entry above would be exactly the same. If Carson pays $12,000 each to Ames and Barker for 33⅓% of the partnership, the foregoing entry is still made.

Investment of Assets in a Partnership

The admission of a partner by an investment of assets is a transaction between the new partner and the partnership. Often referred to simply as **admission by investment**, the transaction **increases both the net assets and total capital of the partnership**. Assume that instead of purchasing an interest, Carson invests $30,000 in cash in the Ames–Barker partnership for a 33⅓% capital interest. In such a case, the entry is:

Cash	30,000	
L. Carson, Capital		30,000
(To record admission of Carson by investment)		

The effects of this transaction on the partnership accounts would be:

Net Assets	C. Ames, Capital	D. Barker, Capital	L. Carson, Capital
60,000	30,000	30,000	30,000
30,000			
Bal. 90,000			

Illustration 13A-3
Ledger balances after investment of assets

Note that both net assets and total capital have increased by $30,000.

Remember that Carson's one-third capital interest might not result in a one-third income ratio. Carson's income ratio should be specified in the new partnership agreement, and it may or may not be equal to the one-third capital interest.

The different effects of the purchase of an interest and admission by investment are shown in the comparison of the net assets and capital balances in Illustration 13A-4.

Illustration 13A-4
Comparison of purchase of an interest and admission by investment

Purchase of an Interest		Admission by Investment	
Net Assets	**$60,000**	**Net Assets**	**$90,000**
Capital		Capital	
C. Ames	$20,000	C. Ames	$30,000
D. Barker	20,000	D. Barker	30,000
L. Carson	20,000	L. Carson	30,000
Total capital	**$60,000**	**Total capital**	**$90,000**

When an interest is purchased, the total net assets and total capital of the partnership do not change. When a partner is admitted by investment, both the total net assets and the total capital change.

In the case of admission by investment, further complications occur when the new partner's investment differs from the capital equity acquired. When those amounts are not the same, the difference is considered a bonus either to (1) the existing (old) partners or (2) the new partner.

Bonus to Old Partners

For both personal and business reasons, the existing partners may be unwilling to admit a new partner without receiving a bonus. In an established firm, existing partners may insist on a bonus as compensation for the work they have put into the company over the years. Two accounting factors underlie the business reason: First, total partners' capital equals the **book value** of the recorded net assets of the partnership. When the new partner is admitted, the fair market values of assets such as land and buildings may be higher than their book values. The bonus will help make up the difference between fair market value and book value. Second, when the partnership has been profitable, goodwill may exist. But, the goodwill will not be recorded or included in total partners' capital. In such cases the new partner is usually willing to pay the bonus to become a partner.

A bonus to old partners results when the new partner's investment in the firm is greater than the capital credit on the date of admittance. The bonus results in **an increase in the capital balances of the old partners**. **It is allocated to them on the basis of their income ratios before the admission of the new partner.**

To illustrate, assume that the Bart–Cohen partnership, owned by Sam Bart and Tom Cohen, has total capital of $120,000. Lea Eden acquires a 25% ownership (capital) interest in the partnership by making a cash investment of $80,000. The procedure for determining Eden's capital credit and the bonus to the old partners is as follows.

1. **Determine the total capital of the new partnership:** Add the new partner's investment to the total capital of the old partnership. In this case the total capital of the new firm is $200,000, computed as follows.

Total capital of existing partnership	$120,000
Investment by new partner, Eden	80,000
Total capital of new partnership	$200,000

2. **Determine the new partner's capital credit:** Multiply the total capital of the new partnership by the new partner's ownership interest. Eden's capital credit is $50,000 ($200,000 × 25%).

3. **Determine the amount of bonus:** Subtract the new partner's capital credit from the new partner's investment. The bonus in this case is $30,000 ($80,000 − $50,000).

4. **Allocate the bonus to the old partners on the basis of their income ratios:** Assuming the ratios are Bart 60%, and Cohen 40%, the allocation is: Bart $18,000 ($30,000 × 60%) and Cohen $12,000 ($30,000 × 40%).

The entry to record the admission of Eden is:

Cash	80,000	
Sam Bart, Capital		18,000
Tom Cohen, Capital		12,000
Lea Eden, Capital		50,000
(To record admission of Eden and bonus to old partners)		

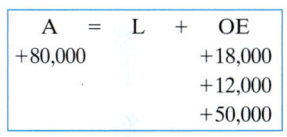

A	=	L	+	OE
+80,000				+18,000
				+12,000
				+50,000

Cash Flows
+80,000

Bonus to New Partner

A bonus to a new partner results when the new partner's investment in the firm is less than his or her capital credit. This may occur when the new partner possesses resources or special attributes that are desired by the partnership. For example, the new partner may be able to supply cash that is urgently needed for expansion or to meet maturing debts. Or the new partner may be a recognized expert or authority in a relevant field. Thus, an engineering firm may be willing to give a renowned engineer a bonus to join the firm. The partners of a restaurant may offer a bonus to a sports celebrity in order to add the athlete's name to the partnership. A bonus to a new partner may also result when recorded book values on the partnership books are higher than their market values.

A bonus to a new partner results in a **decrease in the capital balances of the old partners. The amount of the decrease for each partner is based on their income ratios before the admission of the new partner.** To illustrate, assume that Lea Eden invests $20,000 in cash for a 25% ownership interest in the Bart–Cohen partnership. Using the four procedures described in the preceding section, the computations for Eden's capital credit and the bonus are as follows.

1. Total capital of Bart–Cohen partnership		$120,000
Investment by new partner, Eden		20,000
Total capital of new partnership		$140,000
2. **Eden's capital credit** (25% × $140,000)		**$ 35,000**
3. **Bonus to Eden** ($35,000 − $20,000)		**$ 15,000**
4. Allocation of bonus to old partners:		
Bart ($15,000 × 60%)	$9,000	
Cohen ($15,000 × 40%)	6,000	$ 15,000

Illustration 13A-5
Computation of capital credit and bonus to new partner

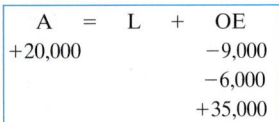

A	=	L	+	OE
+20,000				−9,000
				−6,000
				+35,000

Cash Flows
+20,000

The entry to record the admission of Eden is as follows:

Cash	20,000	
Sam Bart, Capital	9,000	
Tom Cohen, Capital	6,000	
Lea Eden, Capital		35,000
(To record Eden's admission and bonus)		

Withdrawal of a Partner

STUDY OBJECTIVE 7

Describe the effects of the entries when a partner withdraws from the firm.

Now let's look at the opposite situation—the withdrawal of a partner. A partner may withdraw from a partnership **voluntarily**, by selling his or her equity in the firm. Or he or she may withdraw **involuntarily**, by reaching mandatory retirement age or by dying. The withdrawal of a partner, like the admission of a partner, legally dissolves the partnership. The legal effects may be recognized by dissolving the firm. However, it is customary to record only the economic effects of the partner's withdrawal, while the firm continues to operate and reorganizes itself legally.

As indicated earlier, the partnership agreement should specify the terms of withdrawal. The withdrawal of a partner may be accomplished by (1) payment from partners' personal assets or (2) payment from partnership assets, as shown in Illustration 13A-6. The former affects only the partners' capital accounts. The latter decreases total net assets and total capital of the partnership.

Are these the only 2 options?

Illustration 13A-6
Procedures in partnership withdrawal

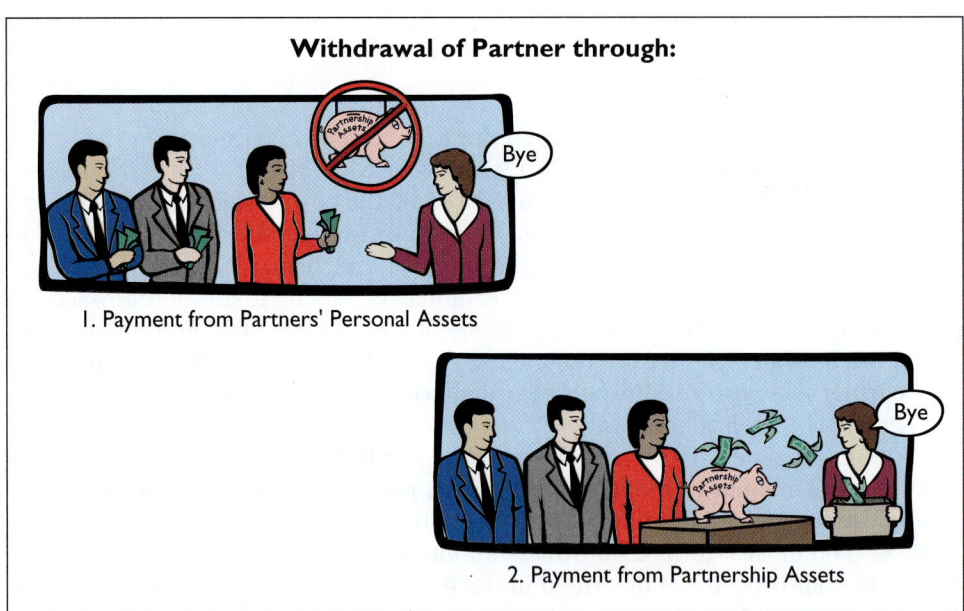

Withdrawal of Partner through:

1. Payment from Partners' Personal Assets

2. Payment from Partnership Assets

Payment from Partners' Personal Assets

Withdrawal by payment from partners' personal assets is a personal transaction between the partners. **It is the direct opposite of admitting a new partner who purchases a partner's interest.** Payment to the retiring partner is made directly from the remaining partners' personal assets. **Partnership assets are not involved in any way, and total capital does not change.** The effect on the partnership is limited to a realignment of the partners' capital balances.

To illustrate, assume that Anne Morz, Mary Nead, and Jill Odom have capital balances of $25,000, $15,000, and $10,000, respectively. Morz and Nead agree to buy out Odom's interest. Each of them agrees to pay Odom $8,000 in exchange for one-half of Odom's total interest of $10,000. The entry to record the withdrawal is:

	A	=	L	+	OE
					−10,000
					+5,000
					+5,000

Jill Odom, Capital		10,000	
Anne Morz, Capital			5,000
Mary Nead, Capital			5,000
(To record purchase of Odom's interest)			

Cash Flows
no effect

The effect of this entry on the partnership accounts is shown below.

Illustration 13A-7
Ledger balances after payment from partners' personal assets

Net Assets		Anne Morz, Capital		Mary Nead, Capital		Jill Odom, Capital	
50, 000			25,000		15,000	**10,000**	10,000
			5,000		**5,000**		Bal. –0–
			Bal. 30,000		Bal. 20,000		

Note that net assets and total capital remain the same at $50,000.

What about the $16,000 paid to Odom? You've probably noted that it is not recorded. Odom's capital is debited only for $10,000, not for the $16,000 that she received. Similarly, both Morz and Nead credit their capital accounts for only $5,000, not for the $8,000 they each paid.

After Odom's withdrawal, Morz and Nead will share net income or net loss equally unless they specifically indicate another income ratio in the partnership agreement.

Payment from Partnership Assets

Withdrawal by payment from partnership assets is a transaction that involves the partnership. **Both partnership net assets and total capital are decreased.** Using partnership assets to pay for a withdrawing partner's interest is the **reverse** of admitting a partner through the investment of assets in the partnership.

Many partnership agreements provide that the amount paid should be based on the fair market value of the assets at the time of the partner's withdrawal. When this basis is required, some maintain that any differences between recorded asset balances and their fair market values should be (1) recorded by an adjusting entry and (2) allocated to all partners on the basis of their income ratios. This position has serious flaws. Recording the revaluations violates the cost principle, which requires that assets be stated at original cost. It also is a departure from the going-concern assumption, which assumes the entity will continue indefinitely. The terms of the partnership contract should not dictate the accounting for this event.

In accounting for a withdrawal by payment from partnership assets, asset revaluations should not be recorded. Any difference between the amount paid and the withdrawing partner's capital balance should be considered a bonus to the retiring partner or a bonus to the remaining partners.

Bonus to Retiring Partner

A bonus may be paid to a retiring partner when:

1. The fair market value of partnership assets is more than their book value,
2. There is unrecorded goodwill resulting from the partnership's superior earnings record, or
3. The remaining partners are anxious to remove the partner from the firm.

The bonus is deducted from the remaining partners' capital balances on the basis of their income ratios at the time of the withdrawal.

To illustrate, assume that the following capital balances exist in the RST partnership: Fred Roman $50,000, Dee Sand $30,000, and Betty Terk $20,000. The partners share income in the ratio of 3 : 2 : 1, respectively. Terk retires from the partnership and receives a cash payment of $25,000 from the firm. The procedure for determining the bonus to the retiring partner and the allocation of the bonus to the remaining partners is as follows.

1. **Determine the amount of the bonus:** Subtract the retiring partner's capital balance from the cash paid by the partnership. The bonus in this case is $5,000 ($25,000 − $20,000).

2. **Allocate the bonus to the remaining partners on the basis of their income ratios:** The ratios of Roman and Sand are 3 : 2. Thus, the allocation of the $5,000 bonus is: Roman $3,000 ($5,000 × 3/5) and Sand $2,000 ($5,000 × 2/5).

HELPFUL HINT

Compare this entry to the one at the top of page 542.

The entry to record the withdrawal of Terk is:

A	=	L	+	OE
−25,000				−20,000
				−3,000
				−2,000

Cash Flows
−25,000

Betty Terk, Capital	20,000	
Fred Roman, Capital	3,000	
Dee Sand, Capital	2,000	
Cash		25,000
(To record withdrawal of and bonus to Terk)		

The remaining partners, Roman and Sand, will recover the bonus given to Terk as the undervalued assets are sold or used.

Bonus to Remaining Partners

The retiring partner may give a bonus to the remaining partners when:

1. Recorded assets are overvalued,
2. The partnership has a poor earnings record, or
3. The partner is anxious to leave the partnership.

In such cases, the cash paid to the retiring partner will be less than the retiring partner's capital balance. **The bonus is allocated (credited) to the capital accounts of the remaining partners on the basis of their income ratios.**

To illustrate, assume (instead of the example above) that Terk is paid only $16,000 for her $20,000 equity when she withdraws from the partnership. In that case:

1. The bonus to remaining partners is $4,000 ($20,000 − $16,000).
2. The allocation of the $4,000 bonus is: Roman $2,400 ($4,000 × 3/5) and Sand $1,600 ($4,000 × 2/5).

A	=	L	+	OE
−16,000				−20,000
				+2,400
				+1,600

Cash Flows
−16,000

The entry to record the withdrawal is:

Betty Terk, Capital	20,000	
Fred Roman, Capital		2,400
Dee Sand, Capital		1,600
Cash		16,000
(To record withdrawal of Terk and bonus to remaining partners)		

HELPFUL HINT

Compare this entry to the one on page 541.

Note that if Sand had withdrawn from the partnership, any bonus would be divided between Roman and Terk on the basis of their income ratio, which is 3 : 1 or 75% and 25%.

Death of a Partner

The death of a partner dissolves the partnership. But provision generally is made for the surviving partners to continue operations. When a partner dies, it usually is necessary to determine the partner's equity at the date of death. This is done by (1) determining the net income or loss for the year to date, (2) closing the books, and (3) preparing financial statements. The partnership agreement may also require an independent audit of the financial statements and a revaluation of assets by an appraisal firm.

The surviving partners may agree to purchase the deceased partner's equity from their personal assets. Or they may use partnership assets to settle with the deceased partner's estate. In both instances, the entries to record the withdrawal of the partner are similar to those presented earlier.

To facilitate payment from partnership assets, some partnerships obtain life insurance policies on each partner. The partnership is named as the beneficiary. The proceeds from the insurance policy on the deceased partner are then used to settle with the estate.

SUMMARY OF STUDY OBJECTIVES FOR APPENDIX

6. Explain the effects of the entries when a new partner is admitted. The entry to record the admittance of a new partner by purchase of a partner's interest affects only partners' capital accounts. The entries to record the admittance by investment of assets in the partnership (a) increase both net assets and total capital and (b) may result in recognition of a bonus to either the old partners or the new partner.

7. Describe the effects of the entries when a partner withdraws from the firm. The entry to record a withdrawal from the firm when payment is made from partners' personal assets affects only partners' capital accounts. The entry to record a withdrawal when payment is made from partnership assets (a) decreases net assets and total capital and (b) may result in recognizing a bonus either to the retiring partner or the remaining partners.

GLOSSARY FOR APPENDIX

Admission by investment Admission of a partner by investing assets in the partnership, causing both partnership net assets and total capital to increase. (p. 539).

Admission by purchase of an interest Admission of a partner in a personal transaction between one or more existing partners and the new partner; does not change total partnership assets or total capital. (p. 539).

Withdrawal by payment from partners' personal assets Withdrawal of a partner in a personal transaction between partners; does not change total partnership assets or total capital. (p. 542).

Withdrawal by payment from partnership assets Withdrawal of a partner in a transaction involving the partnership, causing both partnership net assets and total capital to decrease. (p. 543).

*Note: All **asterisked** Questions, Exercises, and Problems relate to material in the appendix to the chapter.

SELF-STUDY QUESTIONS

Self-Study/Self-Test

Answers are at the end of the chapter.

(SO 1) **1.** Which of the following is *not* a characteristic of a partnership?
   a. Taxable entity
   b. Co-ownership of property
   c. Mutual agency
   d. Limited life

(SO 1) **2.** The advantages of a partnership do *not* include:
   a. ease of formation.
   b. unlimited liability.
   c. freedom from government regulation.
   d. ease of decision making.

3. Upon formation of a partnership, each partner's initial in- (SO 2) vestment of assets should be recorded at their:
   a. book values.
   b. cost.
   c. market values.
   d. appraised values.

(SO 3)   **4.** The NBC Company reports net income of $60,000. If partners N, B, and C have an income ratio of 50%, 30%, and 20%, respectively, C's share of the net income is:
   a. $30,000.
   b. $12,000.
   c. $18,000.
   d. No correct answer is given.

(SO 3)   **5.** Using the data in (4) above, what is B's share of net income if the percentages are applicable after each partner receives a $10,000 salary allowance?
   a. $12,000
   b. $20,000
   c. $19,000
   d. $21,000

(SO 4)   **6.** Which of the following statements about partnership financial statements is true?
   a. Details of the distribution of net income are shown in the owners' equity statement.
   b. The distribution of net income is shown on the balance sheet.
   c. Only the total of all partner capital balances is shown in the balance sheet.
   d. The owners' equity statement is called the partners' capital statement.

(SO 5)   **7.** In the liquidation of a partnership it is necessary to (1) distribute cash to the partners, (2) sell noncash assets, (3) allocate any gain or loss on realization to the partners, and (4) pay liabilities. These steps should be performed in the following order:
   a. (2), (3), (4), (1).
   b. (2), (3), (1), (4).
   c. (3), (2), (1), (4).
   d. (3), (2), (4), (1).

*8. Louisa Santiago purchases 50% of Leo Lemon's capital   (SO interest in the K & L partnership for $22,000. If the capital balance of Kate Kildare and Leo Lemon are $40,000 and $30,000, respectively, Santiago's capital balance following the purchase is:
   a. $22,000.
   b. $35,000.
   c. $20,000.
   d. $15,000.

*9. Capital balances in the MEM partnership are Mary Capital $60,000, Ellen Capital $50,000, and Mills Capital $40,000, and income ratios are 5 : 3 : 2, respectively. The MEMO partnership is formed by admitting Oleg to the firm with a cash investment of $60,000 for a 25% capital interest. The bonus to be credited to Mills Capital in admitting Oleg is:
   a. $10,000.
   b. $7,500.
   c. $3,750.
   d. $1,500.

*10. Capital balances in the MURF partnership are Molly   (SO Capital $50,000, Ursula Capital $40,000, Ray Capital $30,000, and Fred Capital $20,000, and income ratios are 4 : 3 : 2 : 1, respectively. Fred withdraws from the firm following payment of $29,000 in cash from the partnership. Ursula's capital balance after recording the withdrawal of Fred is:
   a. $36,000.
   b. $37,000.
   c. $38,000.
   d. $40,000.

QUESTIONS

1. The characteristics of a partnership include the following: (a) association of individuals, (b) limited life, and (c) co-ownership of property. Explain each of these terms.

2. Eddie Murphy is confused about the partnership characteristics of (a) mutual agency and (b) unlimited liability. Explain these two characteristics for Eddie.

3. Chris Hoett and Paul Sienkiewicz are considering a business venture. They ask you to explain the advantages and disadvantages of the partnership form of organization.

4. Porky Pigg and Daffy Duck form a partnership. Pigg contributes land with a book value of $50,000 and a fair market value of $75,000. Pigg also contributes equipment with a book value of $52,000 and a fair market value of $57,000. The partnership assumes a $20,000 mortgage on the land. What should be the balance in Pigg's capital account upon formation of the partnership?

5. W. Nelson, N. Cash, and W. Jennings have a partnership called Outlaws. A dispute has arisen among the partners. Nelson has invested twice as much in assets as the other two partners, and he believes net income and net losses should be shared in accordance with the capital ratios. The

partnership agreement does not specify the division of profits and losses. How will net income and net loss be divided?

6. Hall and Oats are discussing how income and losses should be divided in a partnership they plan to form. What factors should be considered in determining the division of net income or net loss?

7. M. Marion and R. Hood have partnership capital balances of $40,000 and $80,000, respectively. The partnership agreement indicates that net income or net loss should be shared equally. If net income for the partnership is $24,000, how should the net income be divided?

8. S. Tortoise and F. Hare share net income and net loss equally. (a) Which account(s) is (are) debited and credited to record the division of net income between the partners? (b) If S. Tortoise withdraws $30,000 in cash for personal use in lieu of salary, which account is debited and which is credited?

9. Partners T. Click and R. Clack are provided salary allowances of $30,000 and $25,000, respectively. They divide the remainder of the partnership income in a ratio of

60 : 40. If partnership net income is $50,000, how much is allocated to Click and Clack?

10. Are the financial statements of a partnership similar to those of a proprietorship? Discuss.

11. How does the liquidation of a partnership differ from the dissolution of a partnership?

12. Jerry Lewis and Dean Martin are discussing the liquidation of a partnership. Jerry maintains that all cash should be distributed to partners on the basis of their income ratios. Is he correct? Explain.

13. In continuing their discussion from Question 12, Dean says that even in the case of a capital deficiency, all cash should still be distributed on the basis of capital balances. Is Dean correct? Explain.

14. Murphy, Mooney, and Feeney have income ratios of 5 : 3 : 2 and capital balances of $34,000, $31,000, and $28,000, respectively. Noncash assets are sold at a gain. After creditors are paid, $119,000 of cash is available for distribution to the partners. How much cash should be paid to Mooney?

15. Before the final distribution of cash, account balances are: Cash $25,000; S. Penn, Capital $19,000 (Cr.); L. Dicaprio, Capital $12,000 (Cr.); and M. Damon, Capital $6,000 (Dr.). Damon is unable to pay any of the capital deficiency. If the income-sharing ratios are 5 : 3 : 2, respectively, how much cash should be paid to L. DiCaprio?

*16. Britney Spears decides to pay $50,000 for a one-third interest in an existing partnership. What effect does this transaction have on partnership net assets?

*17. Elton John decides to invest $25,000 in a new partnership for a one-sixth capital interest. How much do the partnership's net assets increase? Does John also acquire a one-sixth income ratio through this investment?

*18. Kate Winslet purchases for $72,000 Stone's interest in the Sharon Stone partnership. Assuming that Stone has a $63,000 capital balance in the partnership, what journal entry is made by the partnership to record this transaction?

*19. Trudy Boesch has a $37,000 capital balance in a partnership. She sells her interest to Kim Bassinger for $45,000 cash. What entry is made by the partnership for this transaction?

*20. Winona Ryder retires from the partnership of Garland, Taylor, and Ryder. She receives $89,000 of partnership assets in settlement of her capital balance of $77,000. Assuming that the income-sharing ratios are 5 : 3 : 2, respectively, how much of Ryder's bonus is debited to Taylor's capital account?

*21. Your roommate argues that partnership assets should be revalued in situations like those in question 20. Why is this generally not done?

*22. How is a deceased partner's equity determined?

BRIEF EXERCISES

BE13-1 Elizabeth Taylor and Richard Burton decide to organize the ALL-Star partnership. Taylor invests $15,000 cash, and Burton contributes $10,000 cash and equipment having a book value of $3,500. Prepare the entry to record Burton's investment in the partnership, assuming the equipment has a fair market value of $9,000

Journalize entries in forming a partnership.
(SO 2)

BE13-2 Adam and Eve decide to merge their proprietorships into a partnership called First Family Company. The balance sheet of Eve Co. shows:

Prepare portion of opening balance sheet for partnership.
(SO 2)

Accounts receivable	$16,000	
Less: Allowance for doubtful accounts	1,200	$14,800
Equipment	20,000	
Less: Accumulated depreciation	7,000	13,000

The partners agree that the net realizable value of the receivables is $12,500 and that the fair market value of the equipment is $11,000. Indicate how the four accounts should appear in the opening balance sheet of the partnership.

BE13-3 Lucy Desi Co. reports net income of $50,000. The income ratios are Lucy 60% and Desi 40%. Indicate the division of net income to each partner, and prepare the entry to distribute the net income.

Journalize the division of net income using fixed income ratios.
(SO 3)

BE13-4 CSN Co. reports net income of $65,000. Partner salary allowances are Crosby $15,000, Stills $5,000, and Nash $5,000. Indicate the division of net income to each partner, assuming the income ratio is 50 : 30 : 20, respectively.

Compute division of net income with a salary allowance and fixed ratios.
(SO 3)

BE13-5 Bob & Ray Co. reports net income of $24,000. Interest allowances are Bob $7,000 and Ray $5,000; salary allowances are Bob $15,000 and Ray $10,000; the remainder is shared equally. Show the distribution of income on the income statement.

Show division of net income when allowances exceed net income.
(SO 3)

Journalize final cash distribution in liquidation.
(SO 5)

BE13-6 After liquidating noncash assets and paying creditors, account balances in the Speedway Co. are Cash $21,000, R Capital (Cr.) $10,000, E Capital (Cr.) $7,000, and O Capital (Cr.) $4,000. The partners share income equally. Journalize the final distribution of cash to the partners.

Journalize admission by purchase of an interest.
(SO 6)

*BE13-7** In Giant Co. capital balances are: Fee $30,000, Fie $25,000, and Foe $22,000. The partners share income equally. Fum is admitted to the firm by purchasing one-half of Foe's interest for $13,000. Journalize the admission of Fum to the partnership.

Journalize admission by investment.
(SO 6)

*BE13-8** In Nelson Co., capital balances are Ozzie $40,000 and Harriet $50,000. The partners share income equally. Ricky is admitted to the firm with a 45% interest by an investment of cash of $42,000. Journalize the admission of Ricky.

Journalize withdrawal paid by personal assets.
(SO 7)

*BE13-9** Capital balances in Jetson Co. are George $40,000, Jane $30,000, and Elroy $20,000. George and Jane each agree to pay Elroy $12,000 from their personal assets. George and Jane each receive 50% of Elroy's equity. The partners share income equally. Journalize the withdrawal of Elroy.

Journalize withdrawal paid by partnership assets.
(SO 7)

*BE13-10** Data pertaining to Jetson Co. are presented in BE13-9. Instead of payment from personal assets, assume that Elroy receives $28,000 from partnership assets in withdrawing from the firm. Journalize the withdrawal of Elroy.

EXERCISES

Journalize entry for formation of a partnership.
(SO 2)

E13-1 Fred Flintstoe has owned and operated a proprietorship for several years. On January 1, he decides to terminate this business and become a partner in the firm of Flintstone and Rubble. Flintstone's investment in the partnership consists of $12,000 in cash, and the following assets of the proprietorship: accounts receivable $14,000 less allowance for doubtful accounts of $2,000, and equipment $20,000 less accumulated depreciation of $4,000. It is agreed that the allowance for doubtful accounts should be $3,000 for the partnership. The fair market value of the equipment is $17,500.

Instructions
Journalize Flintstone's admission to the firm of Rubble and Flintstone.

Prepare schedule showing distribution of net income and closing entry.
(SO 3)

E13-2 F. Astaire and G. Rogers have capital balances on January 1 of $50,000 and $40,000, respectively. The partnership income-sharing agreement provides for (1) annual salaries of $20,000 for Astaire and $12,000 for Rogers, (2) interest at 10% on beginning capital balances, and (3) remaining income or loss to be shared 60% by Astaire and 40% by Rogers.

Instructions
(a) Prepare a schedule showing the distribution of net income, assuming net income is (1) $55,000 and (2) $30,000.
(b) Journalize the allocation of net income in each of the situations above.

Prepare partners' capital statement and partial balance sheet.
(SO 4)

E13-3 For Laugh In Co., beginning capital balances on January 1, 2005, are Dick Rowen $20,000 and Dan Martin $18,000. During the year, drawings were Rowen $8,000 and Martin $5,000. Net income was $32,000, and the partners share income equally.

Instructions
(a) Prepare the partners' capital statement for the year.
(b) Prepare the owners' equity section of the balance sheet at December 31, 2005.

Prepare cash distribution schedule.
(SO 5)

E13-4 The Ares Company at December 31 has cash $20,000, noncash assets $100,000, liabilities $55,000, and the following capital balances: Cassandra $45,000 and Penelope $20,000. The firm is liquidated, and $120,000 in cash is received for the noncash assets. Cassandra and Penelope income ratios are 60% and 40%, respectively.

Instructions
Prepare a cash distribution schedule.

E13-5 Data for The Ares partnership are presented in E13-4.

Journalize transactions in a liquidation.

(SO 5)

Instructions

Prepare the entries to record:

(a) The sale of noncash assets.
(b) The allocation of the gain or loss on liquidation to the partners.
(c) Payment of creditors.
(d) Distribution of cash to the partners.

E13-6 Prior to the distribution of cash to the partners, the accounts in the MPH Company are: Cash $30,000, Mentor Capital (Cr.) $17,000, Poseidon Capital (Cr.) $15,000, and Hermes Capital (Dr.) $2,000. The income ratios are 5 : 3 : 2, respectively.

Journalize transactions with a capital deficiency.

(SO 5)

Instructions

(a) Prepare the entry to record (1) Hermes's payment of $2,000 in cash to the partnership and (2) the distribution of cash to the partners with credit balances.
(b) Prepare the entry to record (1) the absorption of Hermes's capital deficiency by the other partners and (2) the distribution of cash to the partners with credit balances.

*****E13-7** J. Kirk, M. Spock, and F. Scot share income on a 5 : 3 : 2 basis. They have capital balances of $32,000, $26,000, and $15,000, respectively, when Doc Bones is admitted to the partnership.

Journalize admission of a new partner by purchase of an interest.

(SO 6)

Instructions

Prepare the journal entry to record the admission of Doc Bones under each of the following assumptions.

(a) Purchase of 50% of Kirk's equity for $19,000.
(b) Purchase of 50% of Spock's equity for $12,000.
(c) Purchase of 33⅓% of Scot's equity for $9,000.

*****E13-8** G. Zeus and R. Apollo share income on a 6 : 4 basis. They have capital balances of $100,000 and $70,000, respectively, when K. Athena is admitted to the partnership.

Journalize admission of a new partner by investment.

(SO 6)

Instructions

Prepare the journal entry to record the admission of K. Athena under each of the following assumptions.

(a) Investment of $100,000 cash for a 30% ownership interest with bonuses to the existing partners.
(b) Investment of $36,000 cash for a 30% ownership interest with a bonus to the new partner.

*****E13-9** B. Arete, V. Circe, and S. Medusa have capital balances of $50,000, $40,000, and $30,000, respectively. Their income ratios are 5 : 3 : 2. Medusa withdraws from the partnership under each of the following independent conditions.

Journalize withdrawal of a partner with payment from partners' personal assets.

(SO 7)

1. Arete and Circe agree to purchase Medusa's equity by paying $17,000 each from their personal assets. Each purchaser receives 50% of Medusa's equity.
2. Circe agrees to purchase all of Medusa's equity by paying $22,000 cash from her personal assets.
3. Arete agrees to purchase all of Medusa's equity by paying $26,000 cash from her personal assets.

Instructions

Journalize the withdrawal of Medusa under each of the assumptions above.

*****E13-10** H. Achilles, T. Ajax, and R. Calypso have capital balances of $95,000, $75,000, and $60,000, respectively. They share income or loss on a 4 : 3 : 3 basis. Ajax withdraws from the partnership under each of the following conditions.

Journalize withdrawal of a partner with payment from partnership assets.

(SO 7)

1. Ajax is paid $85,500 in cash from partnership assets, and a bonus is granted to the retiring partner.
2. Ajax is paid $68,000 in cash from partnership assets, and bonuses are granted to the remaining partners.

Instructions

Journalize the withdrawal of Ajax under each of the assumptions above.

PROBLEMS: SET A

Prepare entries for formation of a partnership and a balance sheet.

(SO 2, 4)

P13-1A The post-closing trial balances of two proprietorships on January 1, 2005, are presented below.

	Dan Company		John Company	
	Dr.	**Cr.**	**Dr.**	**Cr.**
Cash	$ 9,500		$ 6,000	
Accounts receivable	15,000		23,000	
Allowance for doubtful accounts		$ 2,500		$ 4,000
Merchandise inventory	28,000		17,000	
Equipment	50,000		30,000	
Accumulated depreciation—equipment		24,000		13,000
Notes payable		20,000		
Accounts payable		25,000		37,000
Dan, Capital		31,000		
John, Capital				22,000
	$102,500	$102,500	$76,000	$76,000

Dan and John decide to form a partnership, Blues Brothers Company, with the following agreed upon valuations for noncash assets.

	Dan Company	John Company
Accounts receivable	$15,000	$23,000
Allowance for doubtful accounts	3,500	5,000
Merchandise inventory	32,000	24,000
Equipment	31,000	18,000

All cash will be transferred to the partnership, and the partnership will assume all the liabilities of the two proprietorships. Further, it is agreed that Dan will invest $3,000 in cash, and John will invest $13,000 in cash.

Instructions

(a) Dan, Capital $39,000
John, Capital $29,000

(a) Prepare separate journal entries to record the transfer of each proprietorship's assets and liabilities to the partnership.

(b) Journalize the additional cash investment by each partner.

(c) Total assets $166,000

(c) Prepare a balance sheet for the partnership on January 1, 2005.

Journalize divisions of net income and prepare a partners' capital statement.

(SO 3, 4)

P13-2A At the end of its first year of operations on December 31, 2005, the BBB Company's accounts show the following.

Partner	Drawings	Capital
J. Bach	$12,000	$33,000
L. Beethovan	9,000	20,000
J. Brahms	4,000	10,000

The capital balance represents each partner's initial capital investment. Therefore, net income or net loss for 2005 has not been closed to the partners' capital accounts.

Instructions

(a) (1) Bach $17,000
(2) Bach $14,500
(3) Bach $21,600

(a) Journalize the entry to record the division of net income for 2005 under each of the following independent assumptions.

(1) Net income is $34,000. Income is shared 5:3:2.

(2) Net income is $30,000. Bach and Beethovan are given salary allowances of $11,000 and $8,500, respectively. The remainder is shared equally.

(3) Net income is $25,200. Each partner is allowed interest of 10% on beginning capital balances. Bach is given an $18,000 salary allowance. The remainder is shared equally.

(b) Prepare a schedule showing the division of net income under assumption (3) above.

(c) Bach $42,600

(c) Prepare a partners' capital statement for the year under assumption (3) above.

P13-3A The partners in Musical Company decide to liquidate the firm when the balance sheet shows the following.

Prepare entries and schedule of cash payments in liquidation of a partnership

(SO 5)

MUSICAL COMPANY
Balance Sheet
April 30, 2005

Assets		Liabilities and Owners' Equity	
Cash	$28,000	Notes payable	$14,000
Accounts receivable	19,000	Accounts payable	24,000
Allowance for doubtful accounts	(1,000)	Wages payable	2,000
Merchandise inventory	28,000	Rogers, Capital	25,000
Equipment	17,000	Hammerstein, Capital	11,200
Accumulated depreciation—equipment	(10,000)	Hart, Capital	4,800
Total	$81,000	Total	$81,000

The partners share income and loss 5:3:2. During the process of liquidation, the transactions below were completed in the following sequence.

1. A total of $48,000 was received from converting noncash assets into cash.
2. Liabilities were paid in full.
3. Cash was paid to the partners with credit balances.

Instructions
(a) Prepare a cash distribution schedule.
(b) Prepare the entries to record the transactions.
(c) Post to the cash and capital accounts.

(a) Loss on realization
    $5,000
    Cash paid: to Rogers
    $22,500; to Hart $3,800

*P13-4A At April 30, partners' capital balances in DLM Company are: Donatello $49,000, Leonardo $28,000, and Michaelangelo $20,000. The income-sharing ratios are 5:3:2, respectively. On May 1, the DLMR Company is formed by admitting Rafael to the firm as a partner.

Journalize admission of a partner under different assumptions.

(SO 6)

Instructions
(a) Journalize the admission of Rafael under each of the following independent assumptions.
　(1) Rafael purchases 50% of Michaelanglo's ownership interest by paying Michaelanglo $9,000 in cash.
　(2) Rafael purchases 50% of Leonardo's ownership interest by paying Leonardo $15,000 in cash.
　(3) Rafael invests $38,000 cash in the partnership for a 40% ownership interest that includes a bonus to the new partner.
　(4) Rafael invests $30,000 in the partnership for a 15% ownership interest, and bonuses are given to the old partners.
(b) Michaelangelo's capital balance is $24,000 after admitting Rafael to the partnership by investment. If Michaelangelo's ownership interest is 15% of total partnership capital, what were (1) Rafael's cash investment and (2) the total bonus to the old partners?

(a) (1) Rafael Capital
    $10,000
    (2) Rafael $14,000
    (3) Rafael $54,000
    (4) Rafael $19,050

*P13-5A On December 31, the capital balances and income ratios in the Sesame Company are as follows.

Journalize withdrawal of a partner under different assumptions.

(SO 7)

Partner	Capital Balance	Income Ratio
A. Bert	$70,000	60%
L. Ernie	30,000	30
B. Bird	24,500	10

Instructions
(a) Journalize the withdrawal of Bird under each of the following independent assumptions.
　(1) Each of the remaining partners agrees to pay $13,000 in cash from personal funds to purchase Bird's ownership equity. Each receives 50% of Bird's equity.
　(2) Ernie agrees to purchase Bird's ownership interest for $18,000 in cash.
　(3) From partnership assets, Bird is paid $29,000, which includes a bonus to the retiring partner.
　(4) Bird is paid $14,000 from partnership assets. Bonuses to the remaining partners are recognized.
(b) If Ernie's capital balance after Bird's withdrawal is $33,000, what were (1) the total bonus to the remaining partners and (2) the cash paid by the partnership to Bird?

(a) (1) Ernie, Capital
    $12,250
    (2) Ernie, Capital
    $24,500
    (3) Bonus $4,500
    (4) Bonus $10,500

Prepare entries for formation of a partnership and a balance sheet.

(SO 2, 4)

P13-1B The post-closing trial balances of two proprietorships on January 1, 2005, are presented below.

| | Anthony Company | | Cleopatra Company | |
	Dr.	Cr.	Dr.	Cr.
Cash	$ 14,000		$12,000	
Accounts receivable	17,500		26,000	
Allowance for doubtful accounts		$ 3,000		$ 4,400
Merchandise inventory	26,500		18,400	
Equipment	45,000		29,000	
Accumulated depreciation—equipment		24,000		11,000
Notes payable		20,000		15,000
Accounts payable		20,000		31,000
Anthony, Capital		36,000		
Cleopatra, Capital				24,000
	$103,000	$103,000	$85,400	$85,400

Anthony and Cleopatra decide to form a partnership, Nile Company, with the following agreed upon valuations for noncash assets.

	Anthony Company	Cleopatra Company
Accounts receivable	$17,500	$26,000
Allowance for doubtful accounts	4,500	4,000
Merchandise inventory	30,000	20,000
Equipment	23,000	18,000

All cash will be transferred to the partnership, and the partnership will assume all the liabilities of the two proprietorships. Further, it is agreed that Anthony will invest $5,000 in cash, and Cleopatra will invest $19,000 in cash.

Instructions

(a) Anthony, Capital $40,000
   Cleopatra, Capital
   $26,000

(c) Total assets $176,000

(a) Prepare separate journal entries to record the transfer of each proprietorship's assets and liabilities to the partnership.
(b) Journalize the additional cash investment by each partner.
(c) Prepare a balance sheet for the partnership on January 1, 2005.

Journalize divisions of net income and prepare a partners' capital statement.

(SO 3, 4)

P13-2B At the end of its first year of operations on December 31, 2005, Tara Company's accounts show the following.

Partner	Drawings	Capital
Rhett Butler	$23,000	$48,000
Scarlet O'Hara	14,000	30,000
Ashley Wilkes	10,000	25,000

The capital balance represents each partner's initial capital investment. Therefore, net income or net loss for 2005 has not been closed to the partners' capital accounts.

Instructions

(a) (1) Butler $14,400
   (2) Butler $21,000
   (3) Butler $16,700

(a) Journalize the entry to record the division of net income for the year 2005 under each of the following independent assumptions.
   (1) Net income is $24,000. Income is shared 6 : 3 : 1.
   (2) Net income is $37,000. Butler and O'Hara are given salary allowances of $18,000 and $10,000, respectively. The remainder is shared equally.
   (3) Net income is $22,000. Each partner is allowed interest of 10% on beginning capital balances. Butler is given a $12,000 salary allowance. The remainder is shared equally.
(b) Prepare a schedule showing the division of net income under assumption (3) above.

(c) Butler $41,700

(c) Prepare a partners' capital statement for the year under assumption (3) above.

P13-3B The partners in Road Show Company decide to liquidate the firm when the balance sheet shows the following.

Prepare entries with a capital deficiency in liquidation of a partnership.

(SO 5)

ROAD SHOW COMPANY
Balance Sheet
May 31, 2005

Assets		Liabilities and Owners' Equity	
Cash	$ 27,500	Notes payable	$ 13,500
Accounts receivable	25,000	Accounts payable	27,000
Allowance for doubtful accounts	(1,000)	Wages payable	3,800
Merchandise inventory	34,500	B. Crosby, Capital	33,000
Equipment	21,000	B. Hope, Capital	21,000
Accumulated depreciation—equipment	(5,500)	D. Lamour, Capital	3,200
Total	$101,500	Total	$101,500

The partners share income and loss 5 : 3 : 2. During the process of liquidation, the following transactions were completed in the following sequence.

1. A total of $50,000 was received from converting noncash assets into cash.
2. Liabilities were paid in full.
3. D. Lamour paid his capital deficiency.
4. Cash was paid to the partners with credit balances.

Instructions
(a) Prepare the entries to record the transactions.
(b) Post to the cash and capital accounts.
(c) Assume that Lamour is unable to pay the capital deficiency.
   (1) Prepare the entry to allocate Lamour's debit balance to Crosby and Hope.
   (2) Prepare the entry to record the final distribution of cash.

(a) Loss on realization
$24,000
Cash paid: to Crosby
$21,000; to Hope
$13,800

*P13-4B At April 30, partners' capital balances in RBB Company are: S. Rocky $62,000, X. Bullwinkle $48,000, and T. Boris $14,000. The income sharing ratios are 5:4:1, respectively. On May 1, the RBBN Company is formed by admitting D. Natasha to the firm as a partner.

Journalize admission of a partner under different assumptions.

(SO 6)

Instructions
(a) Journalize the admission of Natasha under each of the following independent assumptions.
   (1) Natasha purchases 50% of Boris's ownership interest by paying Boris $16,000 in cash.
   (2) Natasha purchases 33⅓% of Bullwinkle's ownership interest by paying Bullwinkle $15,000 in cash.
   (3) Natasha invests $75,000 for a 30% ownership interest, and bonuses are given to the old partners.
   (4) Natasha invests $40,000 for a 30% ownership interest, which includes a bonus to the new partner.
(b) Bullwinkle's capital balance is $30,000 after admitting Natasha to the partnership by investment. If Bullwinkle's ownership interest is 20% of total partnership capital, what were (1) Natasha's cash investment and (2) the bonus to the new partner?

(a) (1) Natasha, Capital
$7,000
(2) Natasha $16,000
(3) Natasha $59,700
(4) Natasha $49,200

*P13-5B On December 31, the capital balances and income ratios in Marx Company are as follows.

Journalize withdrawal of a partner under different assumptions.

(SO 7)

Partner	Capital Balance	Income Ratio
J. Harpo	$60,000	50%
P. Chico	40,000	30%
K. Groucho	30,000	20%

Instructions
(a) Journalize the withdrawal of Groucho under each of the following assumptions.
   (1) Each of the continuing partners agrees to pay $18,000 in cash from personal funds to purchase Groucho's ownership equity. Each receives 50% of Groucho's equity.
   (2) Chico agrees to purchase Groucho's ownership interest for $25,000 cash.
   (3) Groucho is paid $36,000 from partnership assets, which includes a bonus to the retiring partner.

(a) (1) Chico, Capital
$15,000
(2) Chico, Capital
$30,000
(3) Bonus $6,000

(4) Bonus $2,000

      (4) Groucho is paid $28,000 from partnership assets, and bonuses to the remaining partners are recognized.

(b) If Chico's capital balance after Groucho's withdrawal is $43,000 what were (1) the total bonus to the remaining partners and (2) the cash paid by the partnership to Groucho?

BROADENING YOUR PERSPECTIVE

Financial Reporting and Analysis

■ **EXPLORING THE WEB**

BYP13-1 This exercise is an introduction to the Big Four Accounting firms, all of which are partnerships.

Addresses

Deloitte & Touche	www.deloitte.com/
Ernst & Young	www.ey.com/
KPMG	www.us.kpmg.com/
PricewaterhouseCoopers	www.pw.com/

      or go to www.wiley.com/college/weygandt

Steps

1. Select a firm that is of interest to you.
2. Go to the firm's homepage.

Instructions

(a) Name two services provided by the firm.
(b) What is the firm's total annual revenue?
(c) How many clients does it service?
(d) How many people are employed by the firm?
(e) How many partners are there in the firm?

Critical Thinking

■ **GROUP DECISION CASE**

BYP13-2 Spencer Tracey and Kate Hepburn, two professionals in the finance area, have worked for Pat Mike Leasing for a number of years. Pat Mike Leasing is a company that leases high-tech medical equipment to hospitals. Spencer and Kate have decided that, with their financial expertise, they might start their own company to provide consulting services to individuals interested in leasing equipment. One form of organization they are considering is a partnership.

    If they start a partnership, each individual plans to contribute $50,000 in cash. In addition, Spencer has a used IBM microcomputer that originally cost $3,700, which he intends to invest in the partnership. The computer has a present market value of $1,500.

    Although both Spencer and Kate are financial wizards, they do not know a great deal about how a partnership operates. As a result, they have come to you for advice.

Instructions

With the class divided into groups, answer the following.

(a) What are the major disadvantages of starting a partnership?
(b) What type of document is needed for a partnership, and what should this document contain?
(c) Both Spencer and Kate plan to work full-time in the new partnership. They believe that net income or net loss should be shared equally. However, they are wondering how they can provide compensation to Spencer Tracey for his additional investment of the microcomputer. What would you tell them?
(d) Spencer is not sure how the computer equipment should be reported on his tax return. What would you tell him?

(e) As indicated above, Spencer and Kate have worked together for a number of years. Spencer's skills complement Kate's and vice versa. If one of them dies, it will be very difficult for the other to maintain the business, not to mention the difficulty of paying the deceased partner's estate for his or her partnership interest. What would you advise them to do?

■ COMMUNICATION ACTIVITY

BYP13-3 You are an expert in the field of forming partnerships. Mickey Rooney and Judy Garland want to establish a partnership to start "Gotta Dance," and they are going to meet with you to discuss their plans. Prior to the meeting you will send them a memo discussing the issues they need to consider before their visit.

Instructions
Write a memo in good form to be sent to Rooney and Garland.

■ ETHICS CASE

BYP13-4 Mary Kate and Ashley operate a beauty salon as partners who share profits and losses equally. The success of their business has exceeded their expectations; the salon is operating quite profitably. Ashley is anxious to maximize profits and schedules appointments from 8 a.m. to 6 p.m. daily, even sacrificing some lunch hours to accommodate regular customers. Mary Kate schedules her appointments from 9 a.m. to 5 p.m. and takes long lunch hours. Mary Kate regularly makes significantly larger withdrawals of cash than Ashley does, but, she says, "Ashley, you needn't worry, I never make a withdrawal without you knowing about it, so it is properly recorded in my drawing account and charged against my capital at the end of the year." Mary Kate's withdrawals to date are double Ashley's.

Instructions
(a) Who are the stakeholders in this situation?
(b) Identify the problems with Mary Kate's actions and discuss the ethical considerations of her actions.
(c) How might the partnership agreement be revised to accommodate the differences in Mary Kate's and Ashley's work and withdrawal habits?

Answers to Self-Study Questions
1. a **2.** b **3.** c **4.** b **5.** c **6.** d **7.** a ***8.** d ***9.** d ***10.** b

Answer to PepsiCo Review It Question 2, p. 525
Mutual agency, limited life, unlimited liability, and co-ownership of property are major characteristics of a partnership. As a company like **PepsiCo** becomes very large, it becomes difficult to remain as a partnership because of these factors. Unlimited liability is particularly troublesome because owners may lose not only their initial investment but also their personal assets, if those assets are needed to pay partnership creditors.

 ☑**REMEMBER** to go back to the Navigator box on the chapter-opening page and check off your completed work.

Corporations: Organization and Capital Stock Transactions

THE NAVIGATOR ✓

Understand **Concepts for Review** ❏

Read **Feature Story** ❏

Scan **Study Objectives** ❏

Read **Preview** ❏

Read text and answer **Before You Go On**
p. 565 ❏   p. 568 ❏   p. 571 ❏   p. 575 ❏
p. 580 ❏

Work **Demonstration Problem** ❏

Review **Summary of Study Objectives** ❏

Answer **Self-Study Questions** ❏

Complete **Assignments** ❏

CONCEPTS FOR REVIEW

Before studying this chapter, you should know or, if necessary, review:

- The content of the owner's equity section of the balance sheet for a proprietorship (Ch. 1, pp. 12–13, Ch. 4, pp. 155–156) and for a partnership. (Ch. 13, p. 530)

- How to prepare closing entries for a proprietorship (Ch. 4, pp. 142–145) and for a partnership. (Ch. 13, pp. 527–528)

✔ THE NAVIGATOR

"Have You Driven a Ford Lately?"

A company that has produced such renowned successes as the Model T and the Mustang, and such a dismal failure as the Edsel, would have some interesting tales to tell. Henry Ford was a defiant visionary from the day **Ford Motor Company** was formed in 1903. His goal from day one was to design a car he could mass-produce and sell at a price that was affordable to the masses. In short order he accomplished this goal. By 1920, 60 percent of all vehicles on U.S. roads were Fords.

Henry Ford was intolerant of anything that stood between him and success. In the early years Ford had issued shares to the public in order to finance the company's exponential growth. In 1916 he decided not to pay a dividend in order to increase the funds available to expand the company.

The shareholders sued. Henry Ford's reaction was swift and direct: If the shareholders didn't see things his way, he would get rid of them. In 1919 the Ford family purchased 100 percent of the outstanding shares of Ford, eliminating any outside "interference." It was over 35 years before shares were again issued to the public.

Ford Motor Company has continued to evolve and grow over the years into one of the largest international corporations. Today there are nearly a billion shares of publicly traded Ford stock outstanding. But some aspects of the company have changed very little. The chairman and chief executive of the company is a member of the Ford family. Also, the Ford family still retains a significant stake in Ford Motor Company. In a move Henry Ford might have supported, top management recently decided to centralize decision making—that is, to have more key decisions made by top management, rather than by division managers. And, reminiscent of Henry Ford's most famous car, the company is attempting to make a "global car"—a mass-produced car that can be sold around the world with only minor changes.

www.ford.com

THE NAVIGATOR

After studying this chapter, you should be able to:

1. Identify the major characteristics of a corporation.
2. Differentiate between paid-in capital and retained earnings.
3. Record the issuance of common stock.
4. Explain the accounting for treasury stock.
5. Differentiate preferred stock from common stock.
6. Prepare a stockholders' equity section.
7. Compute book value per share.

THE NAVIGATOR

Corporations like **Ford Motor Company** have substantial resources. In fact, the corporation is the dominant form of business organization in the United States in terms of dollar volume of sales and earnings, and number of employees. All of the 500 largest companies in the United States are corporations. In this chapter we will explain the essential features of a corporation and the accounting for a corporation's capital stock transactions. In Chapter 15 we will look at other issues related to accounting for corporations.

The content and organization of Chapter 14 are as follows.

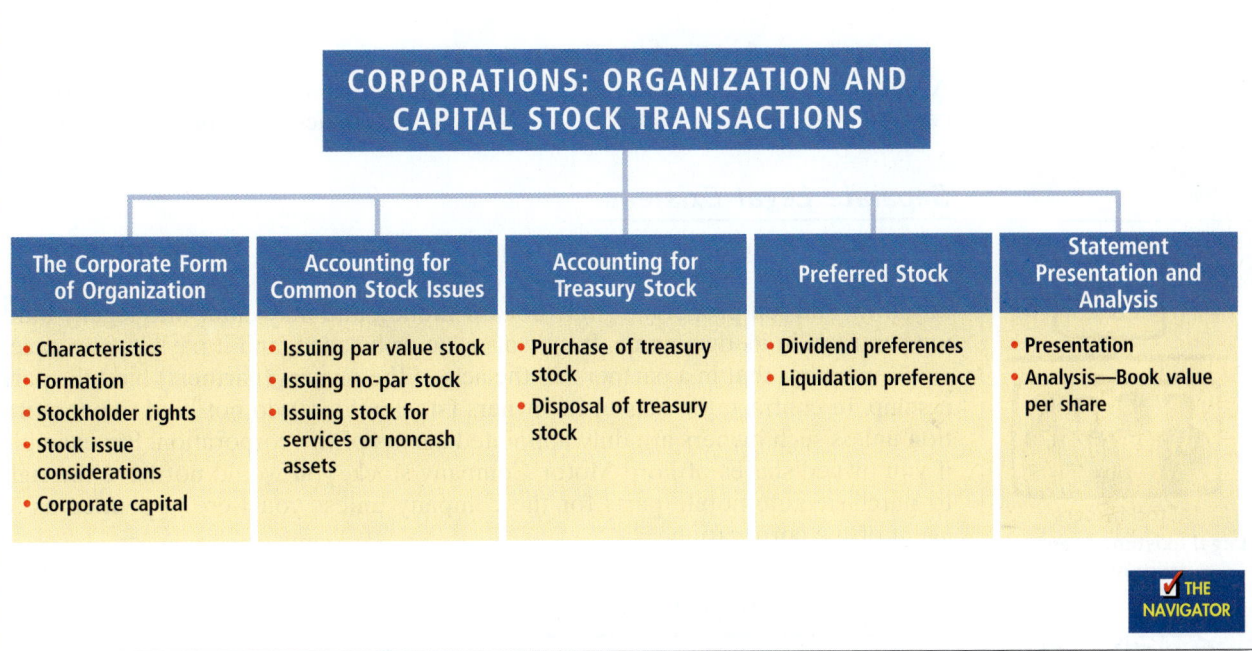

CORPORATIONS: ORGANIZATION AND CAPITAL STOCK TRANSACTIONS

The Corporate Form of Organization	Accounting for Common Stock Issues	Accounting for Treasury Stock	Preferred Stock	Statement Presentation and Analysis
• Characteristics • Formation • Stockholder rights • Stock issue considerations • Corporate capital	• Issuing par value stock • Issuing no-par stock • Issuing stock for services or noncash assets	• Purchase of treasury stock • Disposal of treasury stock	• Dividend preferences • Liquidation preference	• Presentation • Analysis—Book value per share

✓ THE NAVIGATOR

The Corporate Form of Organization

In 1819, Chief Justice John Marshall defined a corporation as "an artificial being, invisible, intangible, and existing only in contemplation of law." This definition is the foundation for the prevailing legal interpretation that a **corporation** is an **entity separate and distinct from its owners**.

A corporation is created by law, and its continued existence depends upon the statutes of the state in which it is incorporated. As a legal entity, a corporation has most of the rights and privileges of a person. The major exceptions relate to privileges that only a living person can exercise, such as the right to vote or to hold public office. A corporation is subject to the same duties and responsibilities as a person. For example, it must abide by the laws and it must pay taxes.

Corporations may be classified in a variety of ways. Two common bases are by purpose and by ownership. A corporation may be organized for the purpose of making a **profit**, or it may be **nonprofit**. Corporations for profit include such well-known companies as **McDonald's**, **Ford Motor Company**, **PepsiCo**, and **Apple Computer**. Nonprofit corporations are organized for charitable, medical, or educational purposes. Examples are the **Salvation Army**, the **American Cancer Society**, and the **Ford Foundation**.

Classification by **ownership** distinguishes between publicly held and privately held corporations. A **publicly held corporation** may have thousands of stockholders.

Its stock is regularly traded on a national securities exchange such as the New York Stock Exchange. Most of the largest U.S. corporations are publicly held. Examples of publicly held corporations are **Intel**, **IBM**, **Caterpillar Inc.**, and **General Electric**. In contrast, a **privately held corporation**, often referred to as a closely held corporation, usually has only a few stockholders, and does not offer its stock for sale to the general public. Privately held companies are generally much smaller than publicly held companies, although some notable exceptions exist. **Cargill Inc.**, a private corporation that trades in grain and other commodities, is one of the largest companies in the United States.

Characteristics of a Corporation

STUDY OBJECTIVE 1

Identify the major characteristics of a corporation.

A number of characteristics distinguish a corporation from proprietorships and partnerships. The most important of these characteristics are explained below.

Separate Legal Existence

Stockholders
Legal existence separate from owners

As an entity separate and distinct from its owners, the corporation acts under its own name rather than in the name of its stockholders. **Ford Motor Company** may buy, own, and sell property. It may borrow money, and may enter into legally binding contracts in its own name. It may also sue or be sued, and it pays its own taxes.

Remember that in a partnership the acts of the owners (partners) bind the partnership. In contrast, the acts of its owners (stockholders) do not bind the corporation unless such owners are duly appointed agents of the corporation. For example, if you owned shares of Ford Motor Company stock, you would not have the right to purchase automobile parts for the company unless you were appointed as an agent of the corporation.

Limited Liability of Stockholders

Stockholders
Limited liability of stockholders

Since a corporation is a separate legal entity, creditors have recourse only to corporate assets to satisfy their claims. The liability of stockholders is normally limited to their investment in the corporation. Creditors have no legal claim on the personal assets of the owners unless fraud has occurred. Even in the event of bankruptcy, stockholders' losses are generally limited to their capital investment in the corporation.

Transferable Ownership Rights

Transferable ownership rights

Ownership of a corporation is held in shares of capital stock. These are transferable units. Stockholders may dispose of part or all of their interest in a corporation simply by selling their stock. Remember that the transfer of an ownership interest in a partnership requires the consent of each owner. In contrast, the transfer of stock is entirely at the discretion of the stockholder. It does not require the approval of either the corporation or other stockholders.

The transfer of ownership rights between stockholders normally has no effect on the operating activities of the corporation. Nor does it affect the corporation's assets, liabilities, and total ownership equity. The transfer of these ownership rights is a transaction between individual owners. The enterprise does not participate in such transfers after it issues the capital stock.

Ability to Acquire Capital

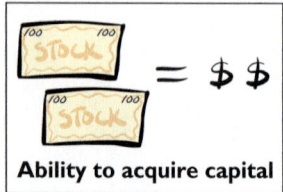

Ability to acquire capital

It is relatively easy for a corporation to obtain capital through the issuance of stock. Buying stock in a corporation is often attractive to an investor because a stockholder has limited liability and shares of stock are readily transferable. Also, numerous individuals can become stockholders by investing small amounts of money. In sum, the ability of a successful corporation to obtain capital is virtually unlimited.

Continuous Life

The life of a corporation is stated in its charter. The life may be perpetual or it may be limited to a specific number of years. If it is limited, the life can be extended through renewal of the charter. Since a corporation is a separate legal entity, its continuance as a going concern is not affected by the withdrawal, death, or incapacity of a stockholder, employee, or officer. As a result, a successful enterprise can have a continuous and perpetual life.

Continuous life

Corporation Management

As in **Ford Motor Company**, stockholders legally own the corporation. But they manage the corporation indirectly through a board of directors they elect. The board, in turn, formulates the operating policies for the company. The board also selects officers, such as a president and one or more vice presidents, to execute policy and to perform daily management functions.

A typical organization chart showing the delegation of responsibility is shown in Illustration 14-1.

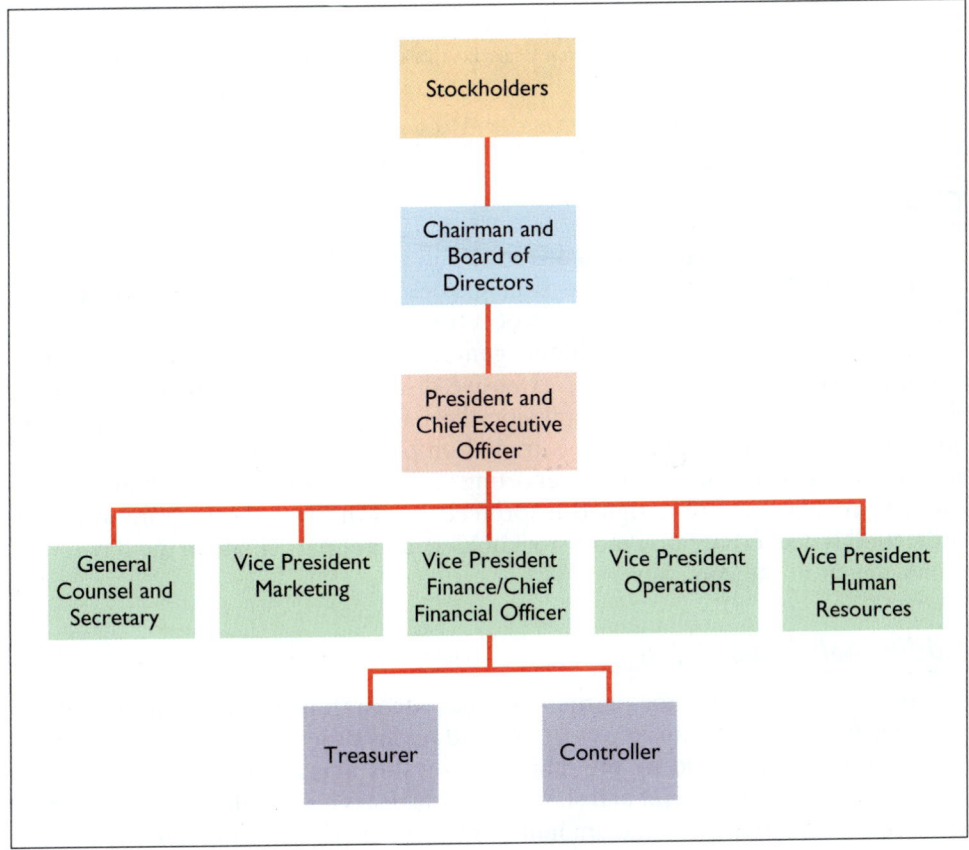

Illustration 14-1
Corporation organization chart

The chief executive officer (CEO) has overall responsibility for managing the business. As the organization chart shows, the CEO delegates responsibility to other officers. The chief accounting officer is the **controller**. The controller's responsibilities include (1) maintaining the accounting records, (2) maintaining an adequate system of internal control, and (3) preparing financial statements, tax returns, and internal reports. The **treasurer** has custody of the corporation's funds and is responsible for maintaining the company's cash position.

The organizational structure of a corporation enables a company to hire professional managers to run the business. On the other hand, the separation of ownership and management prevents owners from having an active role in managing the company, which some owners like to have.

ACCOUNTING IN ACTION   Ethics Perspective

In the wake of **Enron**'s collapse, the members of Enron's board of directors have been questioned and scrutinized to determine what they knew, and when they knew it. A *Wall Street Journal* story reported that Enron's board contends it was "kept in the dark" by management and by Arthur Andersen—Enron's longtime auditors—and didn't learn about the company's troublesome accounting until October 2001. But, the *Wall Street Journal* reported that according to outside attorneys, "directors on at least two occasions waived Enron's ethical code of conduct to approve partnerships between Enron and its chief financial officer. Those partnerships kept significant debt off of Enron's books and masked actual company finances."

Source: Carol Hymowitz, "Serving on a Board Now Means Less Talk, More Accountability," *Wall Street Journal Online* (January 29, 2002).

Government Regulations

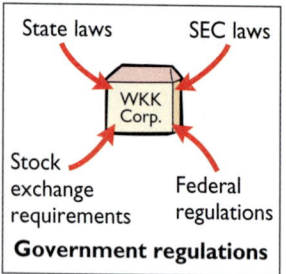

Government regulations

A corporation is subject to numerous state and federal regulations. State laws usually prescribe the requirements for issuing stock, the distributions of earnings permitted to stockholders, and the effects of retiring stock. Federal securities laws govern the sale of capital stock to the general public. Also, most publicly held corporations are required to make extensive disclosure of their financial affairs to the Securities and Exchange Commission through quarterly and annual reports. In addition, when a corporate stock is traded on organized securities exchanges, the corporation must comply with the reporting requirements of these exchanges. Government regulations are designed to protect the owners of the corporation. Such protection is needed because most stockholders do not participate in the day-to-day management of the company.

Additional Taxes

Additional taxes

Neither proprietorships nor partnerships pay income taxes. The owner's share of earnings from these organizations is reported on his or her personal income tax return. Taxes are then paid by the individual on this amount. Corporations, on the other hand, must pay federal and state income taxes as a separate legal entity. These taxes are substantial: They can amount to more than 40 percent of taxable income.

In addition, stockholders are required to pay taxes on cash dividends (pro rata distributions of net income). Thus, many argue that corporate income is **taxed twice (double taxation)**, once at the corporate level, and again at the individual level.

From the foregoing, we can identify the following advantages and disadvantages of a corporation compared to a proprietorship and partnership.

Advantages	Disadvantages
Separate legal existence	Corporation management—separation of
Limited liability of stockholders	ownership and management
Transferable ownership rights	Government regulations
Ability to acquire capital	Additional taxes
Continuous life	
Corporation management—professional	
managers	

Illustration 14-2
Advantages and disadvantages of a corporation

Forming a Corporation

The initial step in forming a corporation is to file an application with the Secretary of State in the state in which incorporation is desired. The application contains such information as: (1) the name and purpose of the proposed corporation; (2) amounts, kinds, and number of shares of capital stock to be authorized; (3) the names of the incorporators; and (4) the shares of stock to which each has subscribed.

After the application is approved, a **charter** is granted. The charter may be an approved copy of the application form or it may be a separate document containing the same basic data. The issuance of the charter creates the corporation. Upon receipt of the charter, the corporation develops its by-laws. The **by-laws** establish the internal rules and procedures for conducting the affairs of the corporation. They also indicate the powers of the stockholders, directors, and officers of the enterprise.[1]

Regardless of the number of states in which a corporation has operating divisions, it is incorporated in only one state. It is to the company's advantage to incorporate in a state whose laws are favorable to the corporate form of business organization. **General Motors**, for example, is incorporated in Delaware, whereas **QUALCOMM** is a New Jersey corporation. Many corporations choose to incorporate in states with rules favorable to existing management. For example, **Gulf Oil** at one time changed its state of incorporation to Delaware to thwart possible unfriendly takeovers. There, certain defensive tactics against takeovers can be approved by the board of directors alone, without a vote by shareholders.

Corporations engaged in interstate commerce must also obtain a license from each state in which they do business. The license subjects the corporation's operating activities to the corporation laws of the state.

Costs incurred in the formation of a corporation are called **organization costs**. These costs include legal and state fees, and promotional expenditures involved in the organization of the business. **Organization costs are expensed as incurred.** To determine the amount and timing of future benefits is so difficult that a conservative approach of expensing these costs immediately is followed.

ALTERNATIVE TERMINOLOGY

The charter is often referred to as the *articles of incorporation*.

Ownership Rights of Stockholders

When chartered, the corporation may begin selling ownership rights in the form of shares of stock. When a corporation has only one class of stock, it is identified as **common stock**. Each share of common stock gives the stockholder the ownership rights pictured in Illustration 14-3 (page 564). The ownership rights of a share of stock are stated in the articles of incorporation or in the by-laws.

[1] Following approval by two-thirds of the stockholders, the by-laws become binding upon all stockholders, directors, and officers. Legally, a corporation is regulated first by the laws of the state, second by its charter, and third by its by-laws. Care must be exercised to ensure that the provisions of the by-laws are not in conflict with either state laws or the charter.

Illustration 14-3
Ownership rights of
stockholders

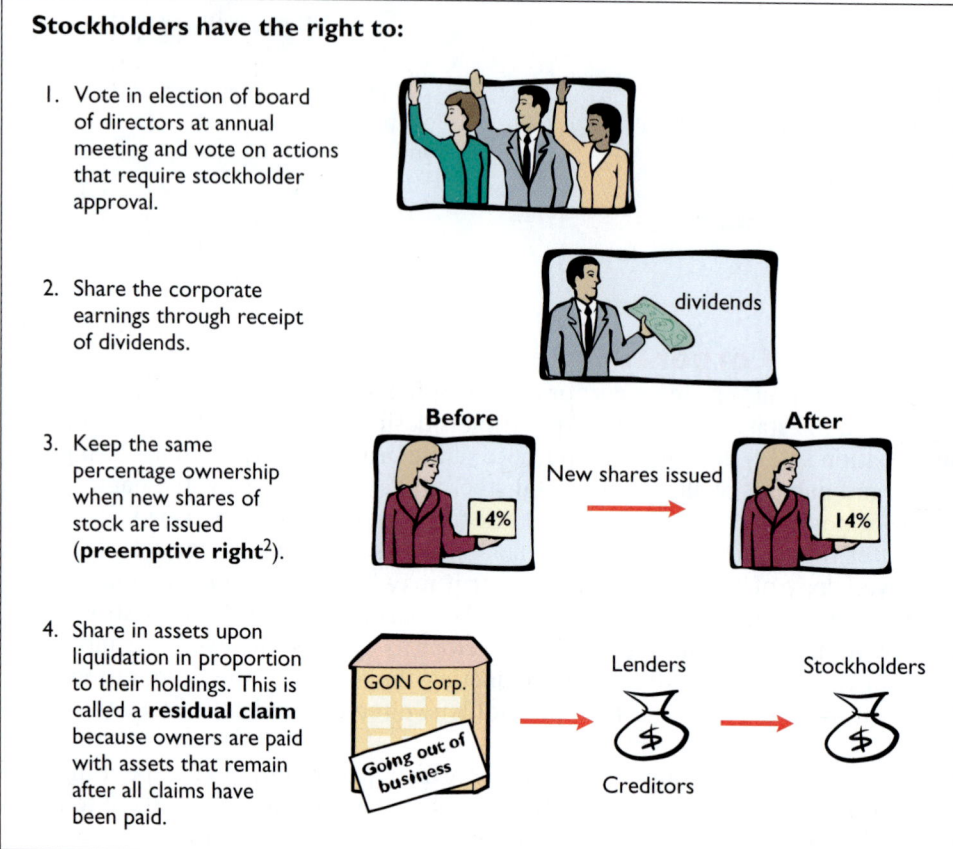

Stockholders have the right to:

1. Vote in election of board of directors at annual meeting and vote on actions that require stockholder approval.

2. Share the corporate earnings through receipt of dividends.

3. Keep the same percentage ownership when new shares of stock are issued (**preemptive right**[2]).

4. Share in assets upon liquidation in proportion to their holdings. This is called a **residual claim** because owners are paid with assets that remain after all claims have been paid.

ACCOUNTING IN ACTION International Insight

In Japan, stockholders are considered to be far less important to a corporation than employees, customers, and suppliers. There, stockholders are rarely asked to vote on an issue, and the notion of bending corporate policy to favor stockholders borders on the heretical. This attitude toward stockholders appears to be slowly changing, however, as influential Japanese are advocating listening to investors, raising the extremely low dividends paid by Japanese corporations, and improving disclosure of financial information.

Proof of stock ownership is evidenced by a form known as a **stock certificate**. As shown in Illustration 14-4, the face of the certificate shows the name of the corporation, the stockholder's name, the class and special features of the stock, the number of shares owned, and the signatures of duly authorized corporate officials. Certificates are prenumbered to facilitate accountability. They may be issued for any quantity of shares.

---

[2]A number of companies have eliminated the preemptive right, because they believe it makes an unnecessary and cumbersome demand on management. For example, by stockholder approval, **IBM** has dropped its preemptive right for stockholders.

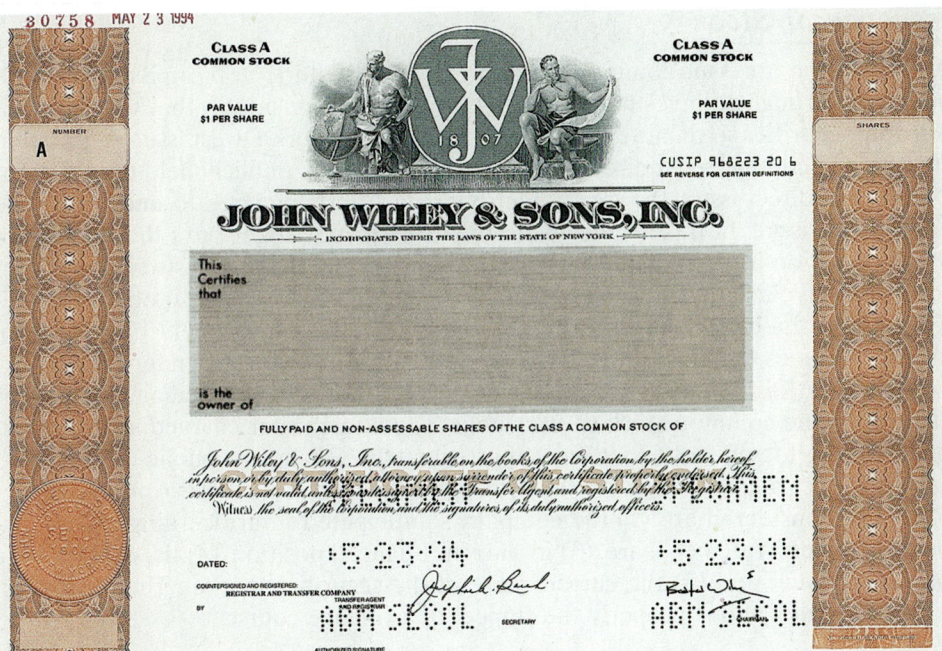

Illustration 14-4
A stock certificate

BEFORE YOU GO ON...

Review It

1. What are the advantages and disadvantages of a corporation compared to a proprietorship and a partnership?
2. Identify the principal steps in forming a corporation.
3. What rights are inherent in owning a share of stock in a corporation?

☑ THE
NAVIGATOR

Stock Issue Considerations

In considering the issuance of stock, a corporation must resolve a number of basic questions: How many shares should be authorized for sale? How should the stock be issued? At what price should the shares be issued? What value should be assigned to the stock? These questions are answered in the following sections.

Authorized Stock

The amount of stock that a corporation is **authorized** to sell is indicated in its charter. The total amount of **authorized stock** at the time of incorporation normally anticipates both initial and subsequent capital needs. As a result, the number of shares authorized generally exceeds the number initially sold. If all authorized stock is sold, a corporation must obtain consent of the state to amend its charter before it can issue additional shares.

The authorization of capital stock does not result in a formal accounting entry. This event has no immediate effect on either corporate assets or stockholders' equity. But, disclosure of the number of authorized shares is often reported in the stockholders' equity section. It is then simple to determine the number of unissued shares that can be issued without amending the charter: subtract the total shares issued from the total authorized. For example, if Advanced Micro was authorized to sell 100,000 shares of common stock and issued 80,000 shares, 20,000 shares would remain unissued.

Indirect Issuance

Issuance of Stock

A corporation can issue common stock **directly** to investors. Or it can issue the stock **indirectly** through an investment banking firm (brokerage house) that specializes in bringing securities to the attention of prospective investors. Direct issue is typical in closely held companies. Indirect issue is customary for a publicly held corporation.

buy & resell

In an indirect issue, the investment banking firm may agree to **underwrite** the entire stock issue. In this arrangement, the investment banker buys the stock from the corporation at a stipulated price and resells the shares to investors. The corporation thus avoids any risk of being unable to sell the shares. Also, it obtains immediate use of the cash received from the underwriter. The investment banking firm, in turn, assumes the risk of reselling the shares in return for an underwriting fee.[3] For example, **Kolff Medical**, maker of the Jarvik artificial heart, used an underwriter to help it issue common stock to the public. The underwriter charged a 6.6 percent underwriting fee on Kolff Medical's approximately $20 million public offering.

How does a corporation set the price for a new issue of stock? Among the factors to be considered are (1) the company's anticipated future earnings, (2) its expected dividend rate per share, (3) its current financial position, (4) the current state of the economy, and (5) the current state of the securities market. The calculation can be complex and is properly the subject of a finance course.

Market Value of Stock

The stock of publicly held companies is traded on organized exchanges. The dollar prices per share are established by the interaction between buyers and sellers. In general, the prices set by the marketplace tend to follow the trend of a company's earnings and dividends. But, factors beyond a company's control, such as an oil embargo, changes in interest rates, and the outcome of a presidential election, may cause day-to-day fluctuations in market prices.

ACCOUNTING IN ACTION   Business Insight

The volume of trading on national and international exchanges is heavy. Shares in excess of a billion are often traded daily on the New York Stock Exchange alone. For each listed stock, the *Wall Street Journal Online* reports the total volume of stock traded for a given day, the high and low price for the day (now in decimals), the closing market price, and the net change for the day. A recent listing for **PepsiCo** is shown below.

Stock	Volume	High	Low	Close	Net Change
PepsiCo	2,942,400	48.88	47.31	47.50	−0.10

These numbers indicate that PepsiCo's trading volume was 2,942,400 shares. The high, low, and closing prices for that date were $48.88, $47.31, and $47.50, respectively. The net change for the day was a decrease of $0.10 per share.

---

[3] Alternatively, the investment banking firm may agree only to enter into a **best efforts** contract with the corporation. In such cases, the banker agrees to sell as many shares as possible at a specified price. The corporation bears the risk of unsold stock. Under a best efforts arrangement, the banking firm is paid a fee or commission for its services.

The trading of capital stock on securities exchanges involves the transfer of **already issued shares** from an existing stockholder to another investor. These transactions have no impact on a corporation's stockholders' equity.

Par and No-Par Value Stocks

Par value stock is capital stock that has been assigned a value per share in the corporate charter. Years ago, par value was used to determine the **legal capital** per share that must be retained in the business for the protection of corporate creditors. That amount is not available for withdrawal by stockholders. Thus, in the past, most states required the corporation to sell its shares at par or above.

However, the usefulness of par value as a protective device to creditors was questionable because par value was often immaterial relative to the value of the company's stock—even at the time of issue. For example, **Reebok**'s par value is $0.01 per share, yet a new issue in 2003 would have sold at a **market value** in the $33 per share range. Thus, par has no relationship with market value and in the vast majority of cases is an immaterial amount. As a consequence, today many states do not require a par value. Instead, other means are used to determine legal capital to protect creditors.

No-par value stock is capital stock that has not been assigned a value in the corporate charter. No-par value stock is quite common today. For example, **Nike**, **Procter & Gamble**, and **North American Van Lines** all have no-par stock. In many states the board of directors is permitted to assign a **stated value** to the no-par shares.

Corporate Capital

Owners' equity is identified as **stockholders' equity**, **shareholders' equity**, or **corporate capital**. The stockholders' equity section of a corporation's balance sheet consists of: (1) paid-in (contributed) capital and (2) retained earnings (earned capital). The distinction between paid-in capital and retained earnings is important from both a legal and a financial point of view. Legally, distributions of earnings (dividends) can be declared out of retained earnings in all states, but in many states they cannot be declared out of paid-in capital. Financially, management, stockholders, and others look to earnings for the continued existence and growth of the corporation.

> **STUDY OBJECTIVE 2**
>
> Differentiate between paid-in capital and retained earnings.

Paid-in Capital

Paid-in capital is the total amount of cash and other assets paid in to the corporation by stockholders in exchange for capital stock. As noted earlier, when a corporation has only one class of stock, it is identified as **common stock**.

Retained Earnings

Retained earnings is net income that is retained in a corporation. Net income is recorded in Retained Earnings by a closing entry in which Income Summary is debited and Retained Earnings is credited. For example, assuming that net income for Delta Robotics in its first year of operations is $130,000, the closing entry is:

Income Summary	130,000	
Retained Earnings		130,000
(To close Income Summary and transfer net income		
to retained earnings)		

A	=	L	+	SE
				−130,000 Inc
				+130,000 RE

Cash Flows
no effect

If Delta Robotics has a balance of $800,000 in common stock at the end of its first year, its stockholders' equity section is as follows.

Illustration 14-5
Stockholders' equity section

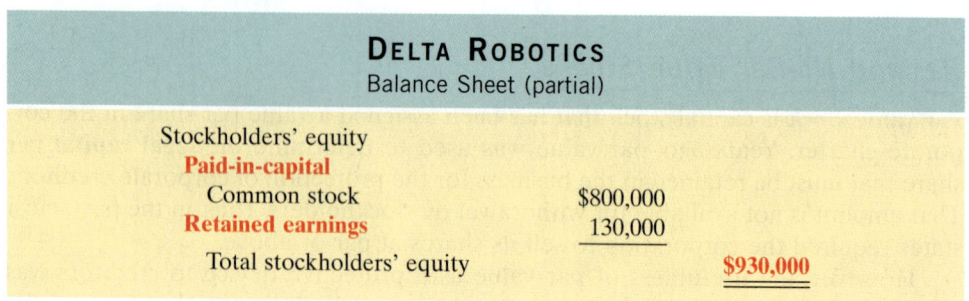

DELTA ROBOTICS Balance Sheet (partial)		
Stockholders' equity		
Paid-in-capital		
Common stock	$800,000	
Retained earnings	130,000	
Total stockholders' equity		**$930,000**

The following illustration compares the owners' equity (stockholders' equity) accounts reported on a balance sheet for a proprietorship, a partnership, and a corporation.

Illustration 14-6
Comparison of owners' equity accounts

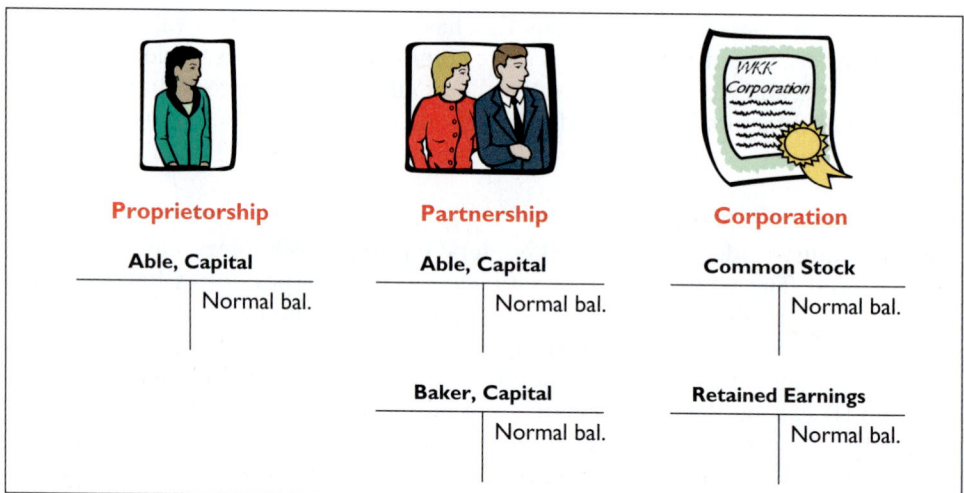

Proprietorship	Partnership	Corporation
Able, Capital	**Able, Capital**	**Common Stock**
Normal bal.	Normal bal.	Normal bal.
	Baker, Capital	**Retained Earnings**
	Normal bal.	Normal bal.

SOLUTION

(a)

Income Summary	122,000	
Retained Earnings		122,000
(To close Income Summary and transfer net		
income to retained earnings)		

(b) Stockholders' equity

Paid-in capital		
Common stock	$750,000	
Retained earnings	122,000	
Total stockholders' equity		$872,000

Related exercise material: *BE14-2, BE14-8, E14-5, and E14-9.*

✓ THE NAVIGATOR

Accounting for Common Stock Issues

Let's now look at how to account for issues of common stock. The primary objectives in accounting for the issuance of common stock are: (1) to identify the specific sources of paid-in capital and (2) to maintain the distinction between paid-in capital and retained earnings. **The issuance of common stock affects only paid-in capital accounts.**

Issuing Par Value Common Stock for Cash

As discussed earlier, par value does not indicate a stock's market value. Therefore, the cash proceeds from issuing par value stock may be equal to, greater than, or less than par value. When the issuance of common stock for cash is recorded, the par value of the shares is credited to Common Stock. The portion of the proceeds that is above or below par value is recorded in a separate paid-in capital account.

To illustrate, assume that Hydro-Slide, Inc. issues 1,000 shares of $1 par value common stock at par for cash. The entry to record this transaction is:

Cash	1,000	
Common Stock		1,000
(To record issuance of 1,000 shares of $1 par common		
stock at par)		

A	=	L	+	SE
+1,000				+1,000 CS

Cash Flows
+1,000

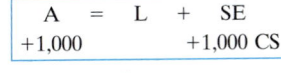

If Hydro-Slide issues an additional 1,000 shares of the $1 par value common stock for cash at $5 per share, the entry is:

Cash	5,000	
Common Stock		1,000
↳ Paid-in Capital in Excess of Par Value		4,000
(To record issuance of 1,000 shares of common stock in		
excess of par)		

ALTERNATIVE TERMINOLOGY

Paid-in Capital in Excess of Par is also called *Premium on Stock.*

A	=	L	+	SE
+5,000				+1,000 CS
				+4,000 CS

Cash Flows
+5,000

The total paid-in capital from these two transactions is $6,000, and the legal capital is $2,000. If Hydro-Slide, Inc. has retained earnings of $27,000, the stockholders' equity section is shown in Illustration 14-7 (page 570).

Illustration 14-7
Stockholders' equity—
paid-in capital in excess of
par value

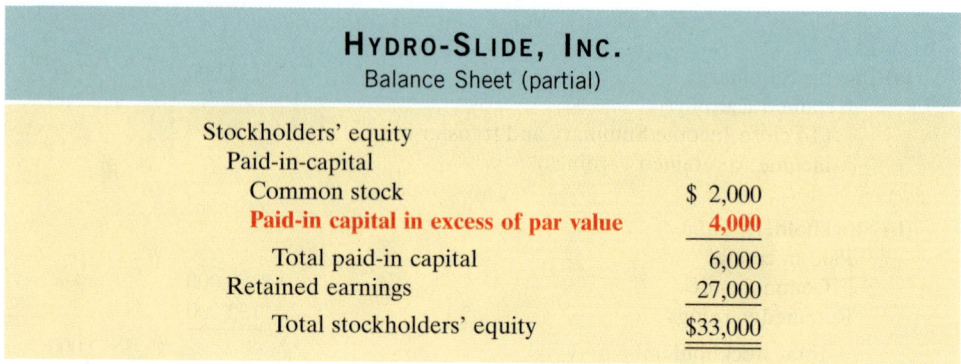

HYDRO-SLIDE, INC.	
Balance Sheet (partial)	
Stockholders' equity	
Paid-in-capital	
Common stock	$ 2,000
Paid-in capital in excess of par value	**4,000**
Total paid-in capital	6,000
Retained earnings	27,000
Total stockholders' equity	$33,000

When stock is issued for less than par value, the account Paid-in Capital in Excess of Par Value is debited, if a credit balance exists in this account. If a credit balance does not exist, then the amount less than par is debited to Retained Earnings. This situation occurs only rarely: The sale of common stock below par value is not permitted in most states, because stockholders may be held personally liable for the difference between the price paid upon original sale and par value.

Issuing No-Par Common Stock for Cash

When no-par common stock has a stated value, the entries are similar to those illustrated for par value stock. The stated value it is credited to Common Stock. Also, when the selling price of no-par stock exceeds stated value, the excess is credited to Paid-in Capital in Excess of Stated Value. For example, assume that instead of $1 par value stock, Hydro-Slide, Inc. has $5 stated value no-par stock and the company issues 5,000 shares at $8 per share for cash. The entry is:

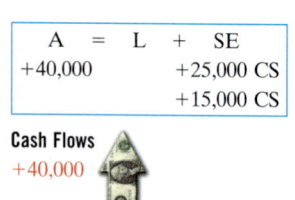

A = L + SE	
+40,000	+25,000 CS
	+15,000 CS

Cash Flows
+40,000

Cash	40,000	
Common Stock		25,000
Paid-in Capital in Excess of Stated Value		15,000
(To record issue of 5,000 shares of $5 stated value no-par stock)		

Paid-in Capital in Excess of Stated Value is reported as part of paid-in capital in the stockholders' equity section.

What happens when no-par stock does not have a stated value? In that case, the entire proceeds are credited to Common Stock. Thus, if Hydro-Slide does not assign a stated value to its no-par stock, the issuance of the 5,000 shares at $8 per share for cash is recorded as follows.

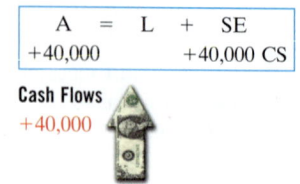

A = L + SE	
+40,000	+40,000 CS

Cash Flows
+40,000

Cash	40,000	
Common Stock		40,000
(To record issue of 5,000 shares of no-par stock)		

Issuing Common Stock for Services or Noncash Assets

Stock may also be issued for services (compensation to attorneys or consultants) or for noncash assets (land, buildings, and equipment). In such cases, what cost should be recognized in the exchange transaction? To comply with the **cost principle**, in a noncash transaction **cost is the cash equivalent price**. Thus, **cost is either the fair market value of the consideration given up**, or the fair market value of the consideration received, whichever is more clearly determinable.

To illustrate, assume that attorneys have helped Jordan Company incorporate. They have billed the company $5,000 for their services. They agree to accept 4,000 shares of $1 par value common stock in payment of their bill. At the time of the exchange, there is no established market price for the stock. In this case, the market value of the consideration received, $5,000, is more clearly evident. Accordingly, the entry is:

Organization Expense	5,000	
Common Stock		4,000
Paid-in Capital in Excess of Par Value		1,000
(To record issuance of 4,000 shares of $1 par value		
stock to attorneys)		

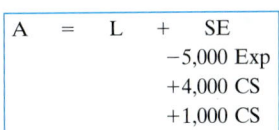

A = L + SE
−5,000 Exp
+4,000 CS
+1,000 CS

Cash Flows
no effect

As explained on page 563, organization costs are expensed as incurred.

In contrast, assume that Athletic Research Inc. is an existing publicly held corporation. Its $5 par value stock is actively traded at $8 per share. The company issues 10,000 shares of stock to acquire land recently advertised for sale at $90,000. The most clearly evident value in this noncash transaction is the market price of the consideration given, $80,000. The transaction is recorded as follows.

Land	80,000	
Common Stock		50,000
Paid-in Capital in Excess of Par Value		30,000
(To record issuance of 10,000 shares of $5 par value		
stock for land)		

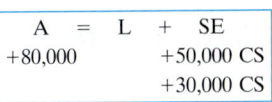

A = L + SE
+80,000   +50,000 CS
+30,000 CS

Cash Flows
no effect

As illustrated in these examples, **the par value of the stock is never a factor in determining the cost of the assets received**. This is also true of the stated value of no-par stock.

BEFORE YOU GO ON...

Review It

1. Explain the accounting for par and no-par common stock issued for cash.
2. Explain the accounting for the issuance of stock for services or noncash assets.
3. What is the par or stated value per share of **PepsiCo**'s common stock? How many shares has PepsiCo issued at December 28, 2002? The answers to these questions are provided on page 593.

Do It

Cayman Corporation begins operations on March 1 by issuing 100,000 shares of $10 par value common stock for cash at $12 per share. On March 15 it issues 5,000 shares of common stock to attorneys in settlement of their bill of $50,000 for organization costs. Journalize the issuance of the shares, assuming the stock is not publicly traded.

ACTION PLAN

■ In issuing shares for cash, credit Common Stock for par value per share.
■ Credit any additional proceeds in excess of par value to a separate paid-in capital account.
■ When stock is issued for services, use the cash equivalent price.
■ For the cash equivalent price use either the fair market value of what is given up or the fair market value of what is received, whichever is more clearly determinable.

SOLUTION

Mar. 1	Cash		1,200,000	
	Common Stock			1,000,000
	Paid-in Capital in Excess of Par Value			200,000
	(To record issuance of 100,000 shares at $12 per share)			
Mar. 15	Organization Expense		50,000	
	Common Stock			50,000
	(To record issuance of 5,000 shares for attorneys' fees)			

Related exercise material: *BE14-3, BE14-4, BE14-5, E14-1, E14-2, E14-3, E14-6, and E14-8.*

☑ THE NAVIGATOR

Accounting for Treasury Stock

STUDY OBJECTIVE 4

Explain the accounting for treasury stock.

Treasury stock is a corporation's own stock that has been issued, fully paid for, and reacquired by the corporation but not retired. A corporation may acquire treasury stock for various reasons:

1. To reissue the shares to officers and employees under bonus and stock compensation plans.
2. To increase trading of the company's stock in the securities market in the hopes of enhancing its market value.
3. To have additional shares available for use in the acquisition of other companies.
4. To reduce the number of shares outstanding and thereby increase earnings per share.
5. To rid the company of disgruntled investors, perhaps to avoid a takeover, as illustrated in the **Ford Motor Company** Feature Story.

HELPFUL HINT

Treasury shares do not have dividend rights or voting rights.

Many corporations have treasury stock. One survey of 600 companies in the United States found that 66 percent have treasury stock.[4] Specifically, **The Gillette Company** recently reported 326 million treasury shares, **The Coca-Cola Company** 1,020 million shares, and **United Airlines** 16.1 million shares.

Purchase of Treasury Stock

Treasury stock is generally accounted for by **the cost method**. This method uses the cost of the shares purchased to value the treasury stock. Under the cost method, **Treasury Stock is debited for the price paid to reacquire the shares**.

The same amount is credited to Treasury Stock when the shares are disposed of. To illustrate, assume that on January 1, 2005, the stockholders' equity section of Mead, Inc. has 100,000 shares of $5 par value common stock outstanding (all issued at par value) and Retained Earnings of $200,000. The stockholders' equity section before purchase of treasury stock is as follows.

---

[4]*Accounting Trends & Techniques 2002* (New York: American Institute of Certified Public Accountants).

Illustration 14-8
Stockholders' equity with no
treasury stock

MEAD, INC.
Balance Sheet (partial)

Stockholders' equity
  Paid-in capital
    Common stock, $5 par value, 100,000 shares
      issued and outstanding $500,000
  Retained earnings   200,000
    Total stockholders' equity $700,000

On February 1, 2005, Mead acquires 4,000 shares of its stock at $8 per share. The entry is:

Feb. 1	Treasury Stock	32,000	
	Cash		32,000
	(To record purchase of 4,000 shares		
	of treasury stock at $8 per share)		

A	=	L	+	SE
−32,000				−32,000 TS

Cash Flows
−32,000

Note that Treasury Stock is debited for the cost of the shares purchased. Is the original paid-in capital account, Common Stock, affected? No, because the number of issued shares does not change. In the stockholders' equity section of the balance sheet, treasury stock is deducted from total paid-in capital and retained earnings. Treasury Stock is a contra stockholders' equity account.

The stockholders' equity section of Mead, Inc. after purchase of treasury stock is as follows.

Illustration 14-9
Stockholders' equity with
treasury stock

MEAD, INC.
Balance Sheet (partial)

Stockholders' equity
  Paid-in capital
    Common stock, $5 par value, 100,000 shares issued
      and 96,000 shares outstanding $500,000
  Retained earnings   200,000
    Total paid-in capital and retained earnings   700,000
    Less: Treasury stock (4,000 shares)   **32,000**
    Total stockholders' equity $668,000

Thus, the acquisition of treasury stock reduces stockholders' equity.

In the balance sheet, both the number of shares issued (100,000) and the number in the treasury (4,000) are disclosed. The difference between these two amounts is the number of shares of stock outstanding (96,000). The term **outstanding stock** means the number of shares of issued stock that are being held by stockholders.

Some maintain that treasury stock should be reported as an asset because it can be sold for cash. Under this reasoning, unissued stock should also be shown as an asset, clearly an erroneous conclusion. Rather than being an asset, treasury stock reduces stockholder claims on corporate assets. This effect is correctly shown by reporting treasury stock as a deduction from total paid-in capital and retained earnings.

ACCOUNTING IN ACTION | Business Insight

In a bold (and some would say risky) move **Reebok** at one time bought back nearly a *third* of its shares. This repurchase of shares dramatically reduced Reebok's available cash. In fact, the company borrowed significant funds to accomplish the repurchase. In a press release, management stated that it was repurchasing the shares because it believed its stock was severely underpriced. The repurchase of so many shares was meant to signal management's belief in good future earnings.

Skeptics, however, suggested that Reebok's management was repurchasing shares to make it less likely that the company would be acquired by another company (in which case Reebok's top managers would likely lose their jobs). By depleting its cash, Reebok became a less likely acquisition target. Acquiring companies like to purchase companies with large cash reserves so they can pay off debt used in the acquisition.

Disposal of Treasury Stock

Treasury stock is usually sold or retired. The accounting for its sale is different when treasury stock is sold above cost than when it is sold below cost.

Sale of Treasury Stock Above Cost

If the selling price of the treasury shares is equal to cost, the sale of the shares is recorded by a debit to Cash and a credit to Treasury Stock. When the selling price of the shares is greater than cost, the difference is credited to Paid-in Capital from Treasury Stock.

To illustrate, assume that 1,000 shares of treasury stock of Mead, Inc., previously acquired at $8 per share, are sold at $10 per share on July 1. The entry is as follows.

July 1	Cash	10,000	
	Treasury Stock		8,000
	Paid-in Capital from Treasury Stock		2,000
	(To record sale of 1,000 shares of treasury stock above cost)		

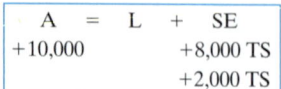

A	=	L	+	SE
+10,000				+8,000 TS
				+2,000 TS

Cash Flows
+10,000

The $2,000 credit in the entry would not be considered a gain on sale of treasury stock for two reasons: (1) Gains on sales occur when **assets** are sold, and treasury stock is not an asset. (2) A corporation does not realize a gain or suffer a loss from stock transactions with its own stockholders. Thus, paid-in capital arising from the sale of treasury stock should not be included in the measurement of net income. Paid-in Capital from Treasury Stock is listed separately on the balance sheet as a part of paid-in capital.

Sale of Treasury Stock Below Cost

When treasury stock is sold below its cost, the excess of cost over selling price is usually debited to Paid-in Capital from Treasury Stock. Thus, if Mead, Inc. sells an additional 800 shares of treasury stock on October 1 at $7 per share, the entry is as follows.

Oct. 1	Cash	5,600	
	Paid-in Capital from Treasury Stock	800	
	Treasury Stock		6,400
	(To record sale of 800 shares of treasury stock below cost)		

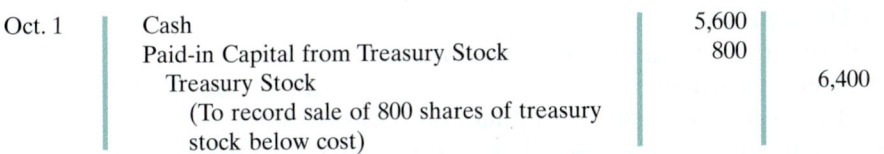

A = L + SE
+5,600   −800 TS
           +6,400 TS

Cash Flows
+5,600

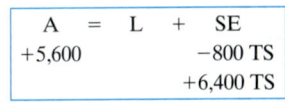

Observe the following from the two sales entries: (1) Treasury Stock is credited at cost in each entry. (2) Paid-in Capital from Treasury Stock is used for the difference between cost and the resale price of the shares. And (3) the original paid-in capital account, Common Stock, is not affected. **The sale of treasury stock increases both total assets and total stockholders' equity.**

After posting the foregoing entries, the treasury stock accounts will show the following balances on October 1.

	Treasury Stock				Paid-in Capital from Treasury Stock			
Feb. 1	32,000	July 1	8,000	Oct. 1	800	July 1	2,000
		Oct. 1	6,400				
						Oct. 1 Bal.	1,200
Oct. 1 Bal.	17,600						

Illustration 14-10
Treasury stock accounts

When the credit balance in Paid-in Capital from Treasury Stock is eliminated, any additional excess of cost over selling price is debited to Retained Earnings. To illustrate, assume that Mead, Inc. sells its remaining 2,200 shares at $7 per share on December 1. The excess of cost over selling price is $2,200 [2,200 × ($8 − $7)]. In this case, $1,200 of the excess is debited to Paid-in Capital from Treasury Stock. The remainder is debited to Retained Earnings. The entry is:

Dec. 1	Cash	15,400	
	Paid-in Capital from Treasury Stock	1,200	
	Retained Earnings	1,000	
	Treasury Stock		17,600
	(To record sale of 2,200 shares of treasury stock at $7 per share)		

A = L + SE
+15,400   −1,200 TS
           −1,000 RE
           +17,600 TS

Cash Flows
+15,400

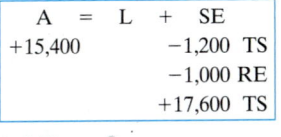

BEFORE YOU GO ON...

Review It

1. What is treasury stock, and why do companies acquire it?
2. How is treasury stock recorded?
3. Where is treasury stock reported in the financial statements? Does a company record gains and losses on treasury stock transactions? Explain.
4. How many shares of treasury stock did **PepsiCo** have at December 28, 2002 and at December 29, 2001? The answer to this question is provided on page 593.

Do It

Santa Anita Inc. purchases 3,000 shares of its $50 par value common stock for $180,000 cash on July 1. The shares are to be held in the treasury until resold. On November 1, the corporation sells 1,000 shares of treasury stock for cash at $70 per share. Journalize the treasury stock transactions.

ACTION PLAN

■ Record the purchase of treasury stock at cost.
■ When treasury stock is sold above its cost, credit the excess of the selling price over cost to Paid-in Capital from Treasury Stock.
■ When treasury stock is sold below its cost, debit the excess of cost over selling price to Paid-in Capital from Treasury Stock.

SOLUTION

July 1	Treasury Stock	180,000	
	Cash		180,000
	(To record the purchase of 3,000 shares at $60 per share)		
Nov. 1	Cash	70,000	
	Treasury Stock		60,000
	Paid-in Capital from Treasury Stock		10,000
	(To record the sale of 1,000 shares at $70 per share)		

Related exercise material: *BE14-6, E14-2, E14-4, E14-6, and E14-8.*

✓ THE NAVIGATOR

Preferred Stock

STUDY OBJECTIVE 5

Differentiate preferred stock from common stock.

To appeal to more potential investors, a corporation may issue an additional class of stock, called preferred stock. **Preferred stock** has contractual provisions that give it a preference or priority over common stock in certain areas. Typically, preferred stockholders have a priority as to (1) distributions of earnings (dividends) and (2) assets in the event of liquidation. However, they generally do not have voting rights.

Like common stock, preferred stock may be issued for cash or for noncash assets. The entries for these transactions are similar to the entries for common stock. When a corporation has more than one class of stock, each paid-in capital account title should identify the stock to which it relates. For example, a company might have the following accounts: Preferred Stock, Common Stock, Paid-in Capital in Excess of Par Value—Preferred Stock, and Paid-in Capital in Excess of Par Value—Common Stock. Assume that Stine Corporation issues 10,000 shares of $10 par value preferred stock for $12 cash per share. The entry to record the issuance is:

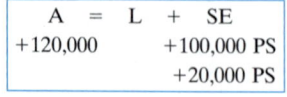

A = L + SE	
+120,000	+100,000 PS
	+20,000 PS

Cash Flows
+120,000

Cash	120,000	
Preferred Stock		100,000
Paid-in Capital in Excess of Par Value–Preferred Stock		20,000
(To record the issuance of 10,000 shares of $10 par value preferred stock)		

Preferred stock may have either a par value or no-par value. In the stockholders' equity section of the balance sheet, preferred stock is shown first because of its dividend and liquidation preferences over common stock.

Various features associated with the issuance of preferred stock, including dividend preferences and liquidation preferences, are discussed on the following pages.

Dividend Preferences

As noted earlier, **preferred stockholders have the right to share in the distribution of corporate income before common stockholders**. For example, if the dividend rate on preferred stock is $5 per share, common shareholders will not receive any dividends in the current year until preferred stockholders have received $5 per share. The first claim to dividends does not, however, guarantee the payment of dividends. Dividends depend on many factors, such as adequate retained earnings and availability of cash.

The per share dividend amount is stated as a percentage of the preferred stock's par value or as a specified amount. For example, at one time **Crane Company** specified a 3¾ percent dividend on its $100 par value preferred ($100 × 3¾% = $3.75 per share). **PepsiCo** has a $5.46 series of no-par preferred stock.

Preferred Common
stockholders stockholders

Dividend Preference

Cumulative Dividend

Preferred stock often contains a **cumulative dividend** feature. This means that preferred stockholders must be paid both current-year dividends and any unpaid prior-year dividends before common stockholders receive dividends. When preferred stock is cumulative, preferred dividends not declared in a given period are called **dividends in arrears**.

To illustrate, assume that Scientific-Leasing has 5,000 shares of 7 percent, $100 par value, cumulative preferred stock outstanding. The annual dividend is $35,000 (5,000 × $7 per share), but dividends are two years in arrears. In this case preferred stockholders are entitled to receive the following dividends in the current year.

Dividends in arrears ($35,000 × 2)	$ 70,000
Current-year dividends	35,000
Total preferred dividends	**$105,000**

Illustration 14-11
Computation of total dividends to preferred stock

No distribution can be made to common stockholders until this entire preferred dividend is paid. In other words, dividends cannot be paid to common stockholders while any preferred stock is in arrears.

Dividends in arrears are not considered a liability. No payment obligation exists until a dividend is declared by the board of directors. However, the amount of dividends in arrears should be disclosed in the notes to the financial statements. Doing so enables investors to assess the potential impact of this commitment on the corporation's financial position.

Companies that are unable to meet their dividend obligations are not looked upon favorably by the investment community. As a financial officer noted in discussing one company's failure to pay its cumulative preferred dividend for a period of time, "Not meeting your obligations on something like that is a major black mark on your record." The accounting entries for preferred stock dividends are explained in Chapter 15.

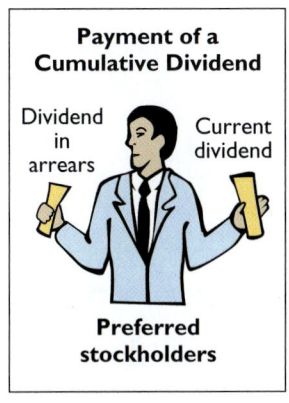

Payment of a Cumulative Dividend

Dividend in arrears   Current dividend

Preferred stockholders

Liquidation Preference

Most preferred stocks also have a preference on corporate assets if the corporation fails. This feature provides security for the preferred stockholder. The preference to assets may be for the par value of the shares or for a specified liquidating value. **EarthLink**'s preferred stock entitles the holders to receive $20.83 per share, plus accrued and unpaid dividends, in the event of involuntary liquidation. The liquidation preference establishes the respective claims of creditors and preferred stockholders.

Statement Presentation and Analysis

In the stockholders' equity section of the balance sheet, paid-in capital and retained earnings are reported. The specific sources of paid-in capital are identified. Within paid-in capital, two classifications are recognized:

1. **Capital stock.** This category consists of preferred and common stock. Preferred stock is shown before common stock because of its preferential rights. Par value, shares authorized, shares issued, and shares outstanding are reported for each class of stock.

2. **Additional paid-in capital.** This includes the excess of amounts paid in over par or stated value and paid-in capital from treasury stock.

Presentation

The stockholders' equity section of Connally Inc. in Illustration 14-12 includes most of the accounts discussed in this chapter. The disclosures pertaining to Connally's common stock indicate that: 400,000 shares are issued; 100,000 shares are unissued (500,000 authorized less 400,000 issued); and 390,000 shares are outstanding (400,000 issued less 10,000 shares in treasury).

Illustration 14-12
Stockholders' equity section

CONNALLY INC. Balance Sheet (partial)		
Stockholders' equity		
Paid-in capital		
Capital stock		
9% preferred stock, $100 par value cumulative, 10,000 shares authorized, 6,000 shares issued and outstanding		$ 600,000
Common stock, no par, $5 stated value, 500,000 shares authorized, 400,000 shares issued, and 390,000 outstanding		2,000,000
Total capital stock		2,600,000
Additional paid-in capital		
In excess of par value—preferred stock	$ 30,000	
In excess of stated value—common stock	860,000	
From treasury stock	140,000	
Total additional paid-in capital		1,030,000
Total paid-in capital		3,630,000
Retained earnings		1,058,000
Total paid-in capital and retained earnings		4,688,000
Less: Treasury stock—common (10,000 shares) (at cost)		(80,000)
Total stockholders' equity		$4,608,000

In published annual reports, the individual sources of additional paid-in capital are often combined and reported as a single amount, as shown in Illustration 14-13. In addition, authorized shares are sometimes not reported.

Illustration 14-13
Published stockholders'
equity section

KELLOGG COMPANY
Balance Sheet (partial)
($ in millions)

Stockholders' equity	
Common stock, $0.25 par value, 1,000,000,000 shares authorized	
Issued: 415,451,198 shares	$ 104.1
Capital in excess of par value	49.9
Retained earnings	1,873.0
Treasury stock, at cost	
7,598,923 shares	(278.2)
Accumulated other comprehensive income	(853.4)
Total stockholders' equity	$ 895.4

In practice, the term ⌈"capital surplus"⌉ is sometimes used in place of additional paid-in capital and ⌈"earned surplus"⌉ in place of retained earnings. The use of the term "surplus" suggests that an excess amount of funds is available. Such is not necessarily the case. Therefore, **the term "surplus" should not be employed in accounting**. Unfortunately, a number of financial statements still do use it.

Analysis—Book Value Per Share

You have learned about a number of per share amounts in this chapter. Another per share amount of some importance is **book value per share**. It represents **the equity a common stockholder has in the net assets of the corporation** from owning one share of stock. Remember that the net assets of a corporation must be equal to total stockholders' equity. Therefore, the formula for computing book value per share when a company has only one class of stock outstanding is:

Illustration 14-14
Book value per share
formula

Total Stockholders' Equity	÷	Number of Common Shares Outstanding	=	Book Value per Share

Thus, if Marlo Corporation has total stockholders' equity of $1,500,000 (common stock $1,000,000 and retained earnings $500,000) and 50,000 shares of common stock outstanding, book value per share is $30 ($1,500,000 ÷ 50,000).[5]

Book Value versus Market Value

Be sure you understand that **book value per share may not equal market value per share**. Book value generally is based on recorded costs. Market value reflects the subjective judgments of thousands of stockholders and prospective investors about a company's potential for future earnings and dividends. Market value per share may exceed book value per share, but that fact does not necessarily mean that the stock is overpriced. The correlation between book value and the annual range of a

---

[5]When a company has both preferred and common stock, the computation of book value is a bit more complex. Since preferred stockholders have a prior claim on net assets over common stockholders, their equity must be deducted from total stockholders' equity.

company's market value per share is often remote, as indicated by the following recent data.

Illustration 14-15
Book and market values compared

Company	Book Value (year-end)	Market Range (for year 2002)
The Limited, Inc.	$8.25	$22.34–$12.53
H. J. Heinz Company	$5.25	$43.48–$29.60
Cisco Systems	$3.92	$21.84–$12.24
Wal-Mart Stores	$9.10	$63.90–$43.70

Book value per share **is useful** in determining the trend of a stockholder's per share equity in a corporation. It is also significant in many contracts and in court cases where the rights of individual parties are based on cost information.

BEFORE YOU GO ON...

Review It

1. Identify the classifications within the paid-in capital section and the totals that are stated in the stockholders' equity section of a balance sheet.
2. What is the method for computing book value per share when only common stock is outstanding?

DEMONSTRATION PROBLEM

The Rolman Corporation is authorized to issue 1,000,000 shares of $5 par value common stock. In its first year, the company has the following stock transactions.

Jan. 10   Issued 400,000 shares of stock at $8 per share.
July 1   Issued 100,000 shares of stock for land. The land had an asking price of $900,000. The stock is currently selling on a national exchange at $8.25 per share.
Sept. 1   Purchased 10,000 shares of common stock for the treasury at $9 per share.
Dec. 1   Sold 4,000 shares of the treasury stock at $10 per share.

Instructions

(a) Journalize the transactions.
(b) Prepare the stockholders' equity section assuming the company had retained earnings of $200,000 at December 31.

ACTION PLAN

- When common stock has a par value, credit Common Stock for par value.
- Use fair market value in a noncash transaction.
- Debit and credit the Treasury Stock account at cost.
- Record differences between the cost and selling price of treasury stock in stockholders' equity accounts, not as gains or losses.

SOLUTION TO DEMONSTRATION PROBLEM

(a) Jan. 10	Cash	3,200,000	
	Common Stock		2,000,000
	Paid-in Capital in Excess of Par Value		1,200,000
	(To record issuance of 400,000 shares of $5 par value stock)		

July 1	Land	825,000	
	Common Stock		500,000
	Paid-in Capital in Excess of Par Value		325,000
	(To record issuance of 100,000 shares of $5 par value stock for land)		

Sept. 1	Treasury Stock	90,000	
	Cash		90,000
	(To record purchase of 10,000 shares of treasury stock at cost)		
Dec. 1	Cash	40,000	
	Treasury Stock		36,000
	Paid-in Capital from Treasury Stock		4,000
	(To record sale of 4,000 shares of treasury stock above cost)		

(b)

ROLMAN CORPORATION
Balance Sheet (partial)

Stockholders' equity		
Paid-in capital		
Capital stock		
Common stock, $5 par value, 1,000,000 shares authorized, 500,000 shares issued, 494,000 shares outstanding		$2,500,000
Additional paid-in capital		
In excess of par value	$1,525,000	
From treasury stock	4,000	
Total additional paid-in capital		1,529,000
Total paid-in capital		4,029,000
Retained earnings		200,000
Total paid-in capital and retained earnings		4,229,000
Less: Treasury stock (6,000 shares)		(54,000)
Total stockholders' equity		$4,175,000

☑ THE NAVIGATOR

SUMMARY OF STUDY OBJECTIVES

1. **Identify the major characteristics of a corporation.** The major characteristics of a corporation are separate legal existence, limited liability of stockholders, transferable ownership rights, ability to acquire capital, continuous life, corporation management, government regulations, and additional taxes.

2. **Differentiate between paid-in capital and retained earnings.** Paid-in capital is the total amount paid in on capital stock. It is often referred to as contributed capital. Retained earnings is net income retained in a corporation. It is often referred to as earned capital.

3. **Record the issuance of common stock.** When the issuance of common stock for cash is recorded, the par value of the shares is credited to Common Stock. The portion of the proceeds that is above or below par value is recorded in a separate paid-in capital account. When no-par common stock has a stated value, the entries are similar to those for par value stock. When no-par stock does not have a stated value, the entire proceeds are credited to Common Stock.

4. **Explain the accounting for treasury stock.** The cost method is generally used in accounting for treasury stock. Under this approach, Treasury Stock is debited at the price paid to reacquire the shares. The same amount is credited to Treasury Stock when the shares are sold. The difference between the sales price and cost is recorded in stockholders' equity accounts, not in income statement accounts.

5. **Differentiate preferred stock from common stock.** Preferred stock has contractual provisions that give it priority over common stock in certain areas. Typically, preferred stockholders have a preference (1) to dividends and (2) to assets in liquidation. They usually do not have voting rights.

6. **Prepare a stockholders' equity section.** In the stockholders' equity section, paid-in capital and retained earnings are reported and specific sources of paid-in capital are identified. Within paid-in capital, two classifications are shown: capital stock and additional paid-in capital. If a corporation has treasury stock, the cost of treasury stock is deducted from total paid-in capital and retained earnings to obtain total stockholders' equity.

7. Compute book value per share. Book value per share represents the equity a common stockholder has in the net assets of a corporation from owning one share of stock. When there is only common stock outstanding, the formula for computing book value is: Total stockholders' equity ÷ Number of common shares outstanding = Book value per share.

GLOSSARY

Authorized stock The amount of stock that a corporation is authorized to sell as indicated in its charter. (p. 565).

Book value per share The equity a common stockholder has in the net assets of the corporation from owning one share of stock. (p. 579).

By-laws The internal rules and procedures for conducting the affairs of a corporation. (p. 563).

Charter A document that creates a corporation. (p. 563).

Corporation A business organized as a legal entity separate and distinct from its owners under state corporation law. (p. 559).

Cumulative dividend A feature of preferred stock entitling the stockholder to receive current and unpaid prior-year dividends before common stockholders receive dividends. (p. 577).

No-par value stock Capital stock that has not been assigned a value in the corporate charter. (p. 567).

Organization costs Costs incurred in the formation of a corporation. (p. 563).

Outstanding stock Capital stock that has been issued and is being held by stockholders. (p. 573).

Paid-in capital Total amount of cash and other assets paid in to the corporation by stockholders in exchange for capital stock. (p. 567).

Par value stock Capital stock that has been assigned a value per share in the corporate charter. (p. 567).

Preferred stock Capital stock that has contractual preferences over common stock in certain areas. (p. 576).

Privately held corporation A corporation that has only a few stockholders and whose stock is not available for sale to the general public. (p. 560).

Publicly held corporation A corporation that may have thousands of stockholders and whose stock is regularly traded on a national securities exchange. (p. 559).

Retained earnings Net income that is retained in the corporation. (p. 567).

Stated value The amount per share assigned by the board of directors to no-par stock that becomes legal capital per share. (p. 567).

Treasury stock A corporation's own stock that has been issued, fully paid for, and reacquired by the corporation but not retired. (p. 572).

SELF-STUDY QUESTIONS

Self-Study/Self-Test

Answers are at the end of the chapter.

(SO 1) **1.** Which of the following is *not* a major advantage of a corporation?
  a. Separate legal existence.
  b. Continuous life.
  c. Government regulations.
  d. Transferable ownership rights.

(SO 1) **2.** A major disadvantage of a corporation is:
  a. limited liability of stockholders.
  b. additional taxes.
  c. transferable ownership rights.
  d. none of the above.

(SO 2) **3.** Which of the following statements is *false*?
  a. Ownership of common stock gives the owner a voting right.
  b. The stockholders' equity section begins with paid-in capital.
  c. The authorization of capital stock does not result in a formal accounting entry.
  d. Legal capital per share applies to par value stock but not to no-par value stock.

4. The account Retained Earnings is: (SO
  a. a subdivision of paid-in capital.
  b. net income retained in the corporation.
  c. reported as an expense in the income statement.
  d. closed to capital stock.

5. ABC Corporation issues 1,000 shares of $10 par value (SO common stock at $12 per share. In recording the transaction, credits are made to:
  a. Common Stock $10,000 and Paid-in Capital in Excess of Stated Value $2,000.
  b. Common Stock $12,000.
  c. Common Stock $10,000 and Paid-in Capital in Excess of Par Value $2,000.
  d. Common Stock $10,000 and Retained Earnings $2,000.

6. XYZ, Inc. sells 100 shares of $5 par value treasury stock (SO at $13 per share. If the cost of acquiring the shares was $10 per share, the entry for the sale should include credits to:
  a. Treasury Stock $1,000 and Paid-in Capital from Treasury Stock $300.

b. Treasury Stock $500 and Paid-in Capital from Treasury Stock $800.

c. Treasury Stock $1,000 and Retained Earnings $300.

d. Treasury Stock $500 and Paid-in Capital in Excess of Par Value $800.

(SO 4)   **7.** In the stockholders' equity section, the cost of treasury stock is deducted from:

a. total paid-in capital and retained earnings.

b. retained earnings.

c. total stockholders' equity.

d. common stock in paid-in capital.

(SO 5)   **8.** Preferred stock may have priority over common stock *except* in:

a. dividends.

b. assets in the event of liquidation.

c. cumulative dividend features.

d. voting.

9. Which of the following is *not* reported under additional (SO 6) paid-in capital?

a. Paid-in capital in excess of par value.

b. Common stock.

c. Paid-in capital in excess of stated value.

d. Paid-in capital from treasury stock.

10. The ledger of JFK, Inc. shows common stock, common (SO 7) treasury stock, and no preferred stock. For this company, the formula for computing book value per share is:

a. Total paid-in capital and retained earnings divided by the number of shares of common stock issued.

b. Common stock divided by the number of shares of common stock issued.

c. Total stockholders' equity divided by the number of shares of common stock outstanding.

d. Total stockholders' equity divided by the number of shares of common stock issued.

QUESTIONS

1. Mike Horn, a student, asks your help in understanding the following characteristics of a corporation: (a) separate legal existence, (b) limited liability of stockholders, and (c) transferable ownership rights. Explain these characteristics to Mike.

2. (a) Your friend Veena Gall cannot understand how the characteristic of corporation management is both an advantage and a disadvantage. Clarify this problem for Veena.

(b) Identify and explain two other disadvantages of a corporation.

3. (a) The following terms pertain to the forming of a corporation: (1) charter, (2) by-laws, and (3) organization costs. Explain the terms.

(b) Marie De Masi believes a corporation must be incorporated in the state in which its headquarters office is located. Is Marie correct? Explain.

4. What are the basic ownership rights of common stockholders in the absence of restrictive provisions?

5. (a) What are the two principal components of stockholders' equity?

(b) What is paid-in capital? Give three examples.

6. How do the financial statements for a corporation differ from the statements for a proprietorship?

7. The corporate charter of Sokol Corporation allows the issuance of a maximum of 100,000 shares of common stock. During its first two years of operations, Sokol sold 80,000 shares to shareholders and reacquired 7,000 of these shares. After these transactions, how many shares are authorized, issued, and outstanding?

8. Which is the better investment—common stock with a par value of $5 per share, or common stock with a par value of $20 per share? Why?

9. What factors help determine the market value of stock?

10. What effect does the issuance of stock at a price above par value have on the issuer's net income? Explain.

11. Why is common stock usually not issued at a price that is less than par value?

12. Land appraised at $80,000 is purchased by issuing 1,000 shares of $20 par value common stock. The market price of the shares at the time of the exchange, based on active trading in the securities market, is $90 per share. Should the land be recorded at $20,000, $80,000, or $90,000? Explain.

13. For what reasons might a company like **IBM** repurchase some of its stock (treasury stock)?

14. Chen, Inc. purchases 1,000 shares of its own previously issued $5 par common stock for $12,000. Assuming the shares are held in the treasury, what effect does this transaction have on (a) net income, (b) total assets, (c) total paid-in capital, and (d) total stockholders' equity?

15. The treasury stock purchased in question 14 is resold by Chen, Inc. for $15,000. What effect does this transaction have on (a) net income, (b) total assets, (c) total paid-in capital, and (d) total stockholders' equity?

16. (a) What are the principal differences between common stock and preferred stock?

(b) Preferred stock may be cumulative. Discuss this feature.

(c) How are dividends in arrears presented in the financial statements?

17. What is the formula for computing book value per share when a corporation has only common stock?

18. Alou Inc.'s common stock has a par value of $1, a book value of $29, and a current market value of $15. Explain why these amounts are all different.

19. Indicate how each of the following accounts should be classified in the stockholders' equity section.
    (a) Common stock
    (b) Paid-in capital in excess of par value
    (c) Retained earnings
    (d) Treasury stock
    (e) Paid-in capital from treasury stock
    (f) Paid-in capital in excess of stated value
    (g) Preferred stock

BRIEF EXERCISES

List the advantages and disadvantages of a corporation.

(SO 1)

BE14-1 Ron Child is studying for his accounting midterm examination. Identify for Ron the advantages and disadvantages of the corporate form of business organization.

Prepare closing entries for a corporation.

(SO 2)

BE14-2 At December 31, Weaner Corporation reports net income of $450,000. Prepare the entry to close net income.

Prepare entries for issuance of par value common stock.

(SO 3)

BE14-3 On May 10, Romano Corporation issues 1,000 shares of $10 par value common stock for cash at $18 per share. Journalize the issuance of the stock.

Prepare entries for issuance of no-par value common stock.

(SO 3)

BE14-4 On June 1, Herrera Inc. issues 3,000 shares of no-par common stock at a cash price of $7 per share. Journalize the issuance of the shares assuming the stock has a stated value of $1 per share.

Prepare entries for issuance of stock in a noncash transaction.

(SO 3)

BE14-5 Tara Inc.'s $10 par value common stock is actively traded at a market value of $16 per share. Tara issues 5,000 shares to purchase land advertised for sale at $85,000. Journalize the issuance of the stock in acquiring the land.

Prepare entries for treasury stock transactions.

(SO 4)

BE14-6 On July 1, Fritz Corporation purchases 500 shares of its $5 par value common stock for the treasury at a cash price of $9 per share. On September 1, it sells 300 shares of the treasury stock for cash at $11 per share. Journalize the two treasury stock transactions.

Prepare entries for issuance of preferred stock.

(SO 5)

BE14-7 Ervay Inc. issues 5,000 shares of $100 par value preferred stock for cash at $120 per share. Journalize the issuance of the preferred stock.

Prepare stockholders' equity section.

(SO 6)

BE14-8 Ingram Corporation has the following accounts at December 31: Common Stock, $10 par, 5,000 shares issued, $50,000; Paid-in Capital in Excess of Par Value $10,000; Retained Earnings $45,000; and Treasury Stock—Common, 500 shares, $11,000. Prepare the stockholders' equity section of the balance sheet.

Compute book value per share.

(SO 7)

BE14-9 The balance sheet for Jimenez Inc. shows the following: total paid-in capital and retained earnings $870,000, total stockholders' equity $810,000, common stock issued 44,000 shares, and common stock outstanding 40,000 shares. Compute the book value per share.

EXERCISES

Journalize issuance of common stock.

(SO 3)

E14-1 During its first year of operations, Klumpe Corporation had the following transactions pertaining to its common stock.

Jan. 10   Issued 70,000 shares for cash at $5 per share.
July   1   Issued 40,000 shares for cash at $8 per share.

Instructions
(a) Journalize the transactions, assuming that the common stock has a par value of $5 per share.
(b) Journalize the transactions, assuming that the common stock is no-par with a stated value of $1 per share.

Journalize issuance of common and preferred stock and purchase of treasury stock.

(SO 3, 4, 5)

E14-2 Garza Co. had the following transactions during the current period.

Mar. 2   Issued 5,000 shares of $1 par value common stock to attorneys in payment of a bill for $30,000 for services provided in helping the company to incorporate.
June 12   Issued 60,000 shares of $1 par value common stock for cash of $375,000.
July 11   Issued 1,000 shares of $100 par value preferred stock for cash at $110 per share.
Nov. 28   Purchased 2,000 shares of treasury stock for $80,000.

Instructions
Journalize the transactions.

E14-3 As an auditor for the CPA firm of Agler and Carl, you encounter the following situations in auditing different clients.

Journalize noncash common stock transactions.

(SO 3)

1. Desi Corporation is a closely held corporation whose stock is not publicly traded. On December 5, the corporation acquired land by issuing 5,000 shares of its $20 par value common stock. The owners' asking price for the land was $120,000, and the fair market value of the land was $110,000.
2. Lucille Corporation is a publicly held corporation whose common stock is traded on the securities markets. On June 1, it acquired land by issuing 20,000 shares of its $10 par value stock. At the time of the exchange, the land was advertised for sale at $250,000. The stock was selling at $11 per share.

Instructions
Prepare the journal entries for each of the situations above.

E14-4 On January 1, 2005, the stockholders' equity section of Rowen Corporation shows: Common stock ($5 par value) $1,500,000; paid-in capital in excess of par value $1,000,000; and retained earnings $1,200,000. During the year, the following treasury stock transactions occurred.

Journalize treasury stock transactions.

(SO 4)

Mar. 1 Purchased 50,000 shares for cash at $16 per share.
July 1 Sold 10,000 treasury shares for cash at $17 per share.
Sept. 1 Sold 8,000 treasury shares for cash at $15 per share.

Instructions
(a) Journalize the treasury stock transactions.
(b) Restate the entry for September 1, assuming the treasury shares were sold at $13 per share.

E14-5 Tinker Corporation is authorized to issue both preferred and common stock. The par value of the preferred is $50. During the first year of operations, the company had the following events and transactions pertaining to its preferred stock.

Journalize preferred stock transactions and indicate statement presentation.

(SO 5, 6)

Feb. 1 Issued 20,000 shares for cash at $51 per share.
July 1 Issued 10,000 shares for cash at $57 per share.

Instructions
(a) Journalize the transactions.
(b) Post to the stockholders' equity accounts.
(c) Indicate the financial statement presentation of the related accounts.

E14-6 Flores Corporation recently hired a new accountant with extensive experience in accounting for partnerships. Because of the pressure of the new job, the accountant was unable to review his textbooks on the topic of corporation accounting. During the first month, the accountant made the following entries for the corporation's capital stock.

Prepare correct entries for capital stock transactions.

(SO 3, 4, 5)

May 2	Cash	120,000	
	Capital Stock		120,000
	(Issued 10,000 shares of $10 par value common stock at $12 per share)		
10	Cash	600,000	
	Capital Stock		600,000
	(Issued 10,000 shares of $50 par value preferred stock at $60 per share)		
15	Capital Stock	14,000	
	Cash		14,000
	(Purchased 1,000 shares of common stock for the treasury at $14 per share)		
31	Cash	8,000	
	Capital Stock		5,000
	Gain on Sale of Stock		3,000
	(Sold 500 shares of treasury stock at $16 per share)		

Instructions
On the basis of the explanation for each entry, prepare the entry that should have been made for the capital stock transactions.

Prepare a stockholders' equity section.

(SO 6)

E14-7 The following stockholders' equity accounts, arranged alphabetically, are in the ledger of Dill Corporation at December 31, 2005.

Common Stock ($5 stated value)	$1,500,000
Paid-in Capital in Excess of Par Value—Preferred Stock	280,000
Paid-in Capital in Excess of Stated Value—Common Stock	900,000
Preferred Stock (8%, $100 par, noncumulative)	500,000
Retained Earnings	1,134,000
Treasury Stock—Common (6,000 shares)	78,000

Instructions

Prepare the stockholders' equity section of the balance sheet at December 31, 2005.

Answer questions about stockholders' equity section.

(SO 3, 4, 5, 6)

E14-8 The stockholders' equity section of Lumley Corporation at December 31 is as follows.

LUMLEY CORPORATION
Balance Sheet (partial)

Paid-in capital	
Preferred stock, cumulative, 10,000 shares authorized, 6,000 shares issued	
and outstanding	$ 600,000
Common stock, no par, 750,000 shares authorized, 600,000 shares issued	1,200,000
Total paid-in capital	1,800,000
Retained earnings	1,858,000
Total paid-in capital and retained earnings	3,658,000
Less: Treasury stock (12,000 common shares)	(64,000)
Total stockholders' equity	$3,594,000

Instructions

From a review of the stockholders' equity section, as chief accountant, write a memo to the president of the company answering the following questions.

(a) How many shares of common stock are outstanding?

(b) Assuming there is a stated value, what is the stated value of the common stock?

(c) What is the par value of the preferred stock?

(d) If the annual dividend on preferred stock is $30,000, what is the dividend rate on preferred stock?

(e) If dividends of $60,000 were in arrears on preferred stock, what would be the balance in Retained Earnings?

Prepare a stockholders' equity section.

(SO 6, 7)

E14-9 In a recent year, the stockholders' equity section of **Aluminum Company of America (Alcoa)** showed the following (in alphabetical order): additional paid-in capital $6,101, common stock $925, preferred stock $55, retained earnings $7,428, and treasury stock 2,828. All dollar data are in millions.

The preferred stock has 557,740 shares authorized, with a par value of $100 and an annual $3.75 per share cumulative dividend preference. At December 31, 557,649 shares of preferred are issued and 546,024 shares are outstanding. There are 1.8 billion shares of $1 par value common stock authorized, of which 924.6 million are issued and 844.8 million are outstanding at December 31.

Instructions

Prepare the stockholders' equity section, including disclosure of all relevant data.

Classify stockholders' equity accounts.

(SO 6)

E14-10 The ledger of O'Dell Corporation contains the following accounts: Common Stock, Preferred Stock, Treasury Stock—Common, Paid-in Capital in Excess of Par Value—Preferred Stock, Paid-in Capital in Excess of Stated Value—Common Stock, Paid-in Capital from Treasury Stock, and Retained Earnings.

Instructions

Classify each account using the following table headings.

	Paid-in Capital			
Account	Capital Stock	Additional	Retained Earnings	Other

E14-11 At December 31, Mayes Corporation has total stockholders' equity of $5,000,000. There are no shares of preferred stock outstanding. At year-end, 250,000 shares of common stock are outstanding and 20,000 shares are in treasury.

Compute book value per share.

(SO 7)

Instructions
Compute the book value per share of common stock.

PROBLEMS: SET A

P14-1A Hayslett Corporation was organized on January 1, 2005. It is authorized to issue 20,000 shares of 6%, $50 par value preferred stock, and 500,000 shares of no-par common stock with a stated value of $2 per share. The following stock transactions were completed during the first year.

Journalize stock transactions, post, and prepare paid-in capital section.

(SO 3, 5, 6)

Jan. 10 Issued 100,000 shares of common stock for cash at $3 per share.
Mar. 1 Issued 10,000 shares of preferred stock for cash at $55 per share.
Apr. 1 Issued 25,000 shares of common stock for land. The asking price of the land was $90,000. The company's estimate of fair market value of the land was $85,000.
May 1 Issued 75,000 shares of common stock for cash at $4 per share.
Aug. 1 Issued 10,000 shares of common stock to attorneys in payment of their bill for $50,000 for services provided in helping the company organize.
Sept. 1 Issued 5,000 shares of common stock for cash at $6 per share.
Nov. 1 Issued 2,000 shares of preferred stock for cash at $58 per share.

Instructions
(a) Journalize the transactions.
(b) Post to the stockholders' equity accounts. (Use J1 as the posting reference.)
(c) Prepare the paid-in capital section of stockholders' equity at December 31, 2005.

(c) Total paid-in capital
    $1,431,000

P14-2A Greeve Corporation had the following stockholders' equity accounts on January 1, 2005: Common Stock ($1 par) $400,000, Paid-in Capital in Excess of Par Value $500,000, and Retained Earnings $100,000. In 2005, the company had the following treasury stock transactions.

Journalize and post treasury stock transactions, and prepare stockholders' equity section.

(SO 4, 6)

Mar. 1 Purchased 5,000 shares at $7 per share.
June 1 Sold 1,000 shares at $10 per share.
Sept. 1 Sold 2,000 shares at $9 per share.
Dec. 1 Sold 1,000 shares at $5 per share.

Greeve Corporation uses the cost method of accounting for treasury stock. In 2005, the company reported net income of $60,000.

Instructions
(a) Journalize the treasury stock transactions, and prepare the closing entry at December 31, 2005, for net income.
(b) Open accounts for (1) Paid-in Capital from Treasury Stock, (2) Treasury Stock, and (3) Retained Earnings. Post to these accounts using J12 as the posting reference.
(c) Prepare the stockholders' equity section for Greeve Corporation at December 31, 2005.

(b) Treasury Stock $7,000
(c) Total stockholders' equity
    $1,058,000

P14-3A The stockholders' equity accounts of Jajoo Corporation on January 1, 2005, were as follows.

Journalize and post transactions, prepare stockholders' equity section.

(SO 2, 3, 4, 5, 6, 7)

Preferred Stock (10%, $100 par noncumulative, 5,000 shares authorized)	$ 300,000
Common Stock ($5 stated value, 300,000 shares authorized)	1,000,000
Paid-in Capital in Excess of Par Value—Preferred Stock	20,000
Paid-in Capital in Excess of Stated Value—Common Stock	425,000
Retained Earnings	488,000
Treasury Stock—Common (5,000 shares)	40,000

During 2005, the corporation had the following transactions and events pertaining to its stockholders' equity.

Feb. 1 Issued 3,000 shares of common stock for $25,000.
Mar. 20 Purchased 1,500 additional shares of common treasury stock at $8 per share.
June 14 Sold 4,000 shares of treasury stock—common for $36,000.

Sept. 3   Issued 2,000 shares of common stock for a patent valued at $17,000.

Dec. 31   Determined that net income for the year was $340,000.

Instructions

(a) Journalize the transactions and the closing entry for net income.

(b) Enter the beginning balances in the accounts and post the journal entries to the stock-holders' equity accounts. (Use J1 as the posting reference.)

(c) Prepare a stockholders' equity section at December 31, 2005.

(c) Total stockholders' equity
$2,599,000

Journalize and post preferred stock transactions, and prepare stockholders' equity section.

(SO 2, 5, 6)

P14-4A Knight Corporation is authorized to issue 10,000 shares of $50 par value, 10% preferred stock and 200,000 shares of $5 par value common stock. On January 1, 2005, the ledger contained the following stockholders' equity balances.

Preferred Stock (4,000 shares)	$200,000
Paid-in Capital in Excess of Par Value—Preferred	60,000
Common Stock (70,000 shares)	350,000
Paid-in Capital in Excess of Par Value—Common	700,000
Retained Earnings	300,000

During 2005, the following transactions occurred.

Feb. 1   Issued 1,000 shares of preferred stock for land having a fair market value of $65,000.

Mar. 1   Issued 1,000 shares of preferred stock for cash at $60 per share.

July 1   Issued 20,000 shares of common stock for cash at $5.80 per share.

Sept. 1   Issued 800 shares of preferred stock for a patent. The asking price of the patent was $60,000. Market values were preferred stock $65 and patent, indeterminable.

Dec. 1   Issued 10,000 shares of common stock for cash at $6 per share.

Dec. 31   Net income for the year was $210,000. No dividends were declared.

Instructions

(a) Journalize the transactions and the closing entry for net income.

(b) Enter the beginning balances in the accounts, and post the journal entries to the stock-holders' equity accounts. (Use J2 as the posting reference.)

(c) Prepare a stockholders' equity section at December 31, 2005.

(c) Total stockholders' equity
$2,173,000

Prepare stockholders' equity section.

(SO 6, 7)

P14-5A The following stockholders' equity accounts arranged alphabetically are in the ledger of McGrath Corporation at December 31, 2005.

Common Stock ($10 stated value)	$1,500,000
Paid-in Capital from Treasury Stock	6,000
Paid-in Capital in Excess of Stated Value—Common Stock	690,000
Paid-in Capital in Excess of Par Value—Preferred Stock	288,400
Preferred Stock (8%, $100 par, noncumulative)	400,000
Retained Earnings	776,000
Treasury Stock—Common (8,000 shares)	88,000

Total stockholders' equity
$3,572,400

Instructions

Prepare a stockholders' equity section at December 31, 2005.

Prepare entries for stock transactions and stockholders' equity section.

(SO 3, 4, 5, 6)

P14-6A Arnold Corporation has been authorized to issue 40,000 shares of $100 par value, 8%, noncumulative preferred stock and 2,000,000 shares of no-par common stock. The corporation assigned a $5 stated value to the common stock. At December 31, 2005, the ledger contained the following balances pertaining to stockholders' equity.

Preferred Stock	$ 240,000
Paid-in Capital in Excess of Par Value—Preferred	56,000
Common Stock	2,000,000
Paid-in Capital in Excess of Stated Value—Common	5,700,000
Treasury Stock—Common (1,000 shares)	22,000
Paid-in Capital from Treasury Stock	3,000
Retained Earnings	560,000

The preferred stock was issued for land having a fair market value of $296,000. All common stock issued was for cash. In November, 1,500 shares of common stock were purchased for the treasury at a per share cost of $22. In December, 500 shares of treasury stock were sold for $28 per share. No dividends were declared in 2005.

Instructions

(a) Prepare the journal entries for the:
   (1) Issuance of preferred stock for land.
   (2) Issuance of common stock for cash.
   (3) Purchase of common treasury stock for cash.
   (4) Sale of treasury stock for cash.
(b) Prepare the stockholders' equity section at December 31, 2005.

(b) Total stockholders' equity
$8,537,000

PROBLEMS: SET B

P14-1B Keeler Corporation was organized on January 1, 2005. It is authorized to issue 10,000 shares of 8%, $100 par value preferred stock, and 500,000 shares of no-par common stock with a stated value of $3 per share. The following stock transactions were completed during the first year.

Journalize stock transactions, post, and prepare paid-in capital section.

(SO 3, 5, 6)

Peachtree

Jan.	10	Issued 80,000 shares of common stock for cash at $4 per share.
Mar.	1	Issued 5,000 shares of preferred stock for cash at $105 per share.
Apr.	1	Issued 24,000 shares of common stock for land. The asking price of the land was $90,000. The fair market value of the land was $85,000.
May	1	Issued 80,000 shares of common stock for cash at $4.50 per share.
Aug.	1	Issued 10,000 shares of common stock to attorneys in payment of their bill of $40,000 for services provided in helping the company organize.
Sept.	1	Issued 10,000 shares of common stock for cash at $5 per share.
Nov.	1	Issued 1,000 shares of preferred stock for cash at $109 per share.

Instructions

(a) Journalize the transactions.
(b) Post to the stockholders' equity accounts. (Use J5 as the posting reference.)
(c) Prepare the paid-in capital section of stockholders' equity at December 31, 2005.

(c) Total paid-in capital
$1,489,000

P14-2B Goldberg Corporation had the following stockholders' equity accounts on January 1, 2005: Common Stock ($5 par) $500,000, Paid-in Capital in Excess of Par Value $200,000, and Retained Earnings $100,000. In 2005, the company had the following treasury stock transactions.

Journalize and post treasury stock transactions, and prepare stockholders' equity section.

(SO 4, 6)

Mar.	1	Purchased 5,000 shares at $8 per share.
June	1	Sold 1,000 shares at $12 per share.
Sept.	1	Sold 2,000 shares at $10 per share.
Dec.	1	Sold 1,000 shares at $6 per share.

Goldberg Corporation uses the cost method of accounting for treasury stock. In 2005, the company reported net income of $40,000.

Instructions

(a) Journalize the treasury stock transactions, and prepare the closing entry at December 31, 2005, for net income.
(b) Open accounts for (1) Paid-in Capital from Treasury Stock, (2) Treasury Stock, and (3) Retained Earnings. Post to these accounts using J10 as the posting reference.
(c) Prepare the stockholders' equity section for Goldberg Corporation at December 31, 2005.

(b) Treasury Stock $8,000
(c) Total stockholders' equity
$838,000

P14-3B The stockholders' equity accounts of Port Corporation on January 1, 2005, were as follows.

Journalize and post transactions, prepare stockholders' equity section.

(SO 2, 3, 4, 5, 6, 7)

Preferred Stock (8%, $50 par cumulative, 10,000 shares authorized)	$ 400,000
Common Stock ($1 stated value, 2,000,000 shares authorized)	1,000,000
Paid-in Capital in Excess of Par Value—Preferred Stock	100,000
Paid-in Capital in Excess of Stated Value—Common Stock	1,450,000
Retained Earnings	1,816,000
Treasury Stock—Common (10,000 shares)	40,000

During 2005, the corporation had the following transactions and events pertaining to its stockholders' equity.

Feb. 1 Issued 25,000 shares of common stock for $100,000.
Apr. 14 Sold 6,000 shares of treasury stock—common for $33,000.
Sept. 3 Issued 5,000 shares of common stock for a patent valued at $30,000.
Nov. 10 Purchased 1,000 shares of common stock for the treasury at a cost of $6,000.
Dec. 31 Determined that net income for the year was $452,000.

No dividends were declared during the year.

Instructions
(a) Journalize the transactions and the closing entry for net income.
(b) Enter the beginning balances in the accounts, and post the journal entries to the stockholders' equity accounts. (Use J5 for the posting reference.)

(c) Total stockholders' equity
$5,335,000

(c) Prepare a stockholders' equity section at December 31, 2005, including the disclosure of the preferred dividends in arrears.

Journalize and post preferred stock transactions, and prepare stockholders' equity section.

(SO 2, 5, 6)

P14-4B Sasser Corporation is authorized to issue 20,000 shares of $50 par value, 10% preferred stock and 125,000 shares of $5 par value common stock. On January 1, 2005, the ledger contained the following stockholders' equity balances.

Preferred Stock (10,000 shares)	$500,000
Paid-in Capital in Excess of Par Value—Preferred	75,000
Common Stock (70,000 shares)	350,000
Paid-in Capital in Excess of Par Value—Common	700,000
Retained Earnings	300,000

During 2005, the following transactions occurred.

Feb. 1 Issued 2,000 shares of preferred stock for land having a fair market value of $125,000.
Mar. 1 Issued 1,000 shares of preferred stock for cash at $65 per share.
July 7 Issued 16,000 shares of common stock for cash at $7 per share.
Sept. 1 Issued 400 shares of preferred stock for a patent. The asking price of the patent was $30,000. Market values were preferred stock $65 and patent indeterminable.
Dec. 1 Issued 8,000 shares of common stock for cash at $7.50 per share.
Dec. 31 Net income for the year was $260,000. No dividends were declared.

Instructions
(a) Journalize the transactions and the closing entry for net income.
(b) Enter the beginning balances in the accounts, and post the journal entries to the stockholders' equity accounts. (Use J2 for the posting reference.)

(c) Total stockholders' equity
$2,573,000

(c) Prepare a stockholders' equity section at December 31, 2005.

Prepare stockholders' equity section.

(SO 6, 7)

P14-5B The following stockholders' equity accounts arranged alphabetically are in the ledger of Rizzo Corporation at December 31, 2005.

Common Stock ($5 stated value)	$2,500,000
Paid-in Capital from Treasury Stock	10,000
Paid-in Capital in Excess of Stated Value—Common Stock	1,600,000
Paid-in Capital in Excess of Par Value—Preferred Stock	679,000
Preferred Stock (8%, $50 par, noncumulative)	800,000
Retained Earnings	1,448,000
Treasury Stock—Common (10,000 shares)	130,000

Total stockholders' equity
$6,907,000

Instructions
Prepare a stockholders' equity section at December 31, 2005.

Prepare entries for stock transactions and stockholders' equity section.

(SO 3, 4, 5, 6)

P14-6B Shields Corporation has been authorized to issue 20,000 shares of $100 par value, 10%, noncumulative preferred stock and 1,000,000 shares of no-par common stock. The corporation assigned a $2.50 stated value to the common stock. At December 31, 2005, the ledger contained the following balances pertaining to stockholders' equity.

Preferred Stock	$120,000
Paid-in Capital in Excess of Par Value—Preferred	20,000
Common Stock	1,000,000
Paid-in Capital in Excess of Stated Value—Common	2,600,000
Treasury Stock—Common (1,000 shares)	12,000

Paid-in Capital from Treasury Stock	1,000	
Retained Earnings	82,000	

The preferred stock was issued for land having a fair market value of $140,000. All common stock issued was for cash. In November, 1,500 shares of common stock were purchased for the treasury at a per share cost of $12. In December, 500 shares of treasury stock were sold for $14 per share. No dividends were declared in 2005.

Instructions
(a) Prepare the journal entries for the:
    (1) Issuance of preferred stock for land.
    (2) Issuance of common stock for cash.
    (3) Purchase of common treasury stock for cash.
    (4) Sale of treasury stock for cash.
(b) Prepare the stockholders' equity section at December 31, 2005.

(b) Total stockholders' equity $3,811,000

BROADENING YOUR PERSPECTIVE

Financial Reporting and Analysis

■ FINANCIAL REPORTING PROBLEM: PepsiCo

BYP14-1 The stockholders' equity section for **PepsiCo, Inc.** is shown in Appendix A. You will also find data relative to this problem on other pages of the appendix.

Instructions
(a) What is the par or stated value per share of PepsiCo's common stock?
(b) What percentage of PepsiCo's authorized common stock was issued at December 28, 2002?
(c) How many shares of common stock were outstanding at December 28, 2002, and at December 29, 2001?
(d) What was book value per share at December 28, 2002, and at December 29, 2001?
(e) What was the high and low market price per share in the fourth quarter of fiscal 2002, as reported under Selected Financial Data?

■ COMPARATIVE ANALYSIS PROBLEM: PepsiCo vs. Coca-Cola

BYP14-2 **PepsiCo**'s financial statements are presented in Appendix A. **Coca-Cola**'s financial statements are presented in Appendix B.

Instructions
(a) Based on the information contained in these financial statements, compute the 2002 book value per share for each company. (*Hint:* Use the value reported for "common shareholders' equity" as the numerator for PepsiCo.)
(b) Compare the market value per share for each company to the book value per share at year-end 2002. Assume that the market value of Coca-Cola's stock was $43.84 at year-end 2002.
(c) Why are book value and market value per share different?

■ INTERPRETING FINANCIAL STATEMENTS: A Global Focus

BYP14-3 American depositary receipts (ADRs) represent a way for U.S. investors to invest in foreign corporations without directly purchasing actual foreign shares of stock. Instead, a U.S. bank purchases the shares in a foreign company and then issues to investors securities (the ADRs) which pass through the risks and rewards of the underlying stock. For example, when the underlying stock pays a dividend the U.S. bank pays a dividend to the holder of the ADR. The March 1, 2001, issue of the *Wall Street Journal* contains an article by Craig Karmin entitled "ADR Holders Find They Retain Unequal Rights" that discusses one potential drawback of this system.

Instructions

Read the article and answer the following questions.

(a) What is the nature of the shareholder resolution that the holders of the **BP Amoco** ADRs are trying to pass?

(b) What do these investors hope to accomplish by getting their resolution on the ballot?

(c) Are ADRs common?

(d) What are some of the advantages of ADRs to U.S. investors as compared to owning local shares?

■ **EXPLORING THE WEB**

BYP 14-4 SEC filings of publicly traded companies are available to view online.

Address: http//biz.yahoo.com/i, or go to www.wiley.com/college/weygandt

Steps

1. Pick a company and type in the company's name.

2. Choose **Quote**.

Instructions

Answer the following questions.

(a) What company did you select?

(b) What is its stock symbol?

(c) What was the stock's trading range today?

(d) What was the stock's trading range for the year?

Critical Thinking

■ **GROUP DECISION CASE**

BYP14-5 The stockholders' meeting for Harris Corporation has been in progress for some time. The chief financial officer for Harris is presently reviewing the company's financial statements and is explaining the items that comprise the stockholders' equity section of the balance sheet for the current year. The stockholders' equity section of Harris Corporation at December 31, 2005, is as follows.

HARRIS CORPORATION
Balance Sheet (partial)
December 31, 2005

Paid in capital		
Capital stock		
Preferred stock, authorized 1,000,000 shares cumulative, $100 par value, $8 per share, 6,000 shares issued and outstanding		$ 600,000
Common stock, authorized 5,000,000 shares, $1 par value, 3,000,000 shares issued, and 2,700,000 outstanding		3,000,000
Total capital stock		3,600,000
Additional paid-in capital		
In excess of par value—preferred stock	$ 50,000	
In excess of par value—common stock	25,000,000	
Total additional paid-in capital		25,050,000
Total paid-in capital		28,650,000
Retained earnings		900,000
Total paid-in capital and retained earnings		29,550,000
Less: Common treasury stock (300,000 shares)		9,300,000
Total stockholders' equity		$20,250,000

At the meeting, stockholders have raised a number of questions regarding the stockholders' equity section.

Instructions

With the class divided into groups, answer the following questions as if you were the chief financial officer for Harris Corporation.

(a) "What does the cumulative provision related to the preferred stock mean?"

(b) "I thought the common stock was presently selling at $29.75, but the company has the stock stated at $1 per share. How can that be?"

(c) "Why is the company buying back its common stock? Furthermore, the treasury stock has a debit balance because it is subtracted from stockholders' equity. Why is treasury stock not reported as an asset if it has a debit balance?"

(d) "Why is it necessary to show additional paid-in capital? Why not just show common stock at the total amount paid in?"

■ COMMUNICATION ACTIVITY

BYP14-6 Sal Greco, your uncle, is an inventor who has decided to incorporate. Uncle Sal knows that you are an accounting major at U.N.O. In a recent letter to you, he ends with the question, "I'm filling out a state incorporation application. Can you tell me the difference in the following terms: (1) authorized stock, (2) issued stock, (3) outstanding stock, (4) preferred stock?"

Instructions

In a brief note, differentiate for Uncle Sal among the four different stock terms. Write the letter to be friendly, yet professional.

■ ETHICS CASE

BYP14-7 The R&D division of Healy Chemical Corp. has just developed a chemical for sterilizing the vicious Brazilian "killer bees" which are invading Mexico and the southern states of the United States. The president of Healy is anxious to get the chemical on the market to boost Healy's profits. He believes his job is in jeopardy because of decreasing sales and profits. Healy has an opportunity to sell this chemical in Central American countries, where the laws are much more relaxed than in the United States.

The director of Healy's R&D division strongly recommends further testing in the laboratory for side-effects of this chemical on other insects, birds, animals, plants, and even humans. He cautions the president, "We could be sued from all sides if the chemical has tragic side-effects that we didn't even test for in the labs." The president answers, "We can't wait an additional year for your lab tests. We can avoid losses from such lawsuits by establishing a separate wholly owned corporation to shield Healy Corp. from such lawsuits. We can't lose any more than our investment in the new corporation, and we'll invest just the patent covering this chemical. We'll reap the benefits if the chemical works and is safe, and avoid the losses from lawsuits if it's a disaster." The following week Healy creates a new wholly owned corporation called Dryden Inc., sells the chemical patent to it for $10, and watches the spraying begin.

Instructions

(a) Who are the stakeholders in this situation?

(b) Are the president's motives and actions ethical?

(c) Can Healy shield itself against losses of Dryden Inc.?

Answers to Self-Study Questions

1. c **2.** b **3.** d **4.** b **5.** c **6.** a **7.** a **8.** d **9.** b **10.** c

Answers to PepsiCo Review It Question 3, p. 571 and Question 4, p. 575

3. The par value of **PepsiCo**'s common stock is $0.0166 per share. On December 28, 2002, PepsiCo had issued 1,782 million shares.

4. Treasury shares held by PepsiCo on December 28, 2002, were 60 million, and on December 29, 2001, were 26 million.

 ✓ REMEMBER to go back to the Navigator box on the chapter-opening page and check off your completed work.

Corporations: Dividends, Retained Earnings, and Income Reporting

CONCEPTS FOR REVIEW

Before studying this chapter, you should know or, if necessary, review:

- Why it is important to distinguish between paid-in capital and retained earnings. (Ch. 14, p. 567)

- The significance of legal capital in accounting for capital stock transactions. (Ch. 14, p. 567)

- The form and content of the stockholders' equity section of the balance sheet. (Ch. 14, pp. 578–579)

- The rights of cumulative preferred stockholders to dividends. (Ch. 14, pp. 576–577)

THE NAVIGATOR

What's Cooking?

What major U.S. corporation got its start over 30 years ago with a waffle iron? Hint: It doesn't sell food. Another hint: Swoosh. Another hint: "Just do it." That's right, Nike. In 1971 Nike cofounder Bill Bowerman put a piece of rubber into a kitchen waffle iron, and the trademark waffle sole was born.

Nike was cofounded by Bowerman and Phil Knight, a member of Bowerman's University of Oregon track team. Each began in the shoe business independently during the early 1960s. Bowerman got his start by making hand-crafted running shoes for his university track team. Knight, after completing graduate school, started a small business importing low-cost, high-quality shoes from Japan. In 1964 the two joined forces. Each contributed $500, and formed Blue Ribbon Sports, a partnership.

At first they marketed Japanese shoes. It wasn't until 1971 that the company began manufacturing its own line of shoes. With the new shoes came a new corporate name—Nike—the Greek goddess of victory. It is hard to imagine that the company that now enlists promoters such as Tiger Woods, Mia Hamm, and Lance Armstrong at one time had part-time employees selling shoes out of car trunks.

By 1980 Nike was sufficiently established that it was able to issue its first stock to the public. In that same year it also created a stock ownership program that allowed its employees to share in the company's success. Since then Nike has enjoyed phenomenal growth. Sales in 2002 were $9.9 billion. Its dividend per share to shareholders increased from 15 cents per share in 1992 to 48 cents per share in 2002.

Nike is not alone in its quest for the top of the sport shoe world. Reebok push Nike every step of the way. It's a race to see who will dominate the sports shoe industry. Currently Nike is outpacing Reebok. But is the race over? Probably not. The shoe market is fickle, with new styles becoming popular almost daily. Whether one of these two giants or another shoe brand does eventually take control of the planet remains to be seen. Meanwhile the shareholders sit anxiously in the stands as this Olympic-size drama unfolds.

www.nike.com
www.reebok.com

After studying this chapter, you should be able to:

1. Prepare the entries for cash dividends and stock dividends.
2. Identify the items that are reported in a retained earnings statement.
3. Prepare and analyze a comprehensive stockholders' equity section.
4. Describe the form and content of corporation income statements.
5. Compute earnings per share.

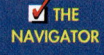

As indicated in the Feature Story, a profitable corporation like **Nike** often distributes substantial portions of corporate income to owners (stockholders), in the form of dividends. In addition, it often reinvests a portion of its earnings in the business. This chapter discusses dividends, retained earnings, corporation income statements, and earnings per share.

The content and organization of Chapter 15 are as follows.

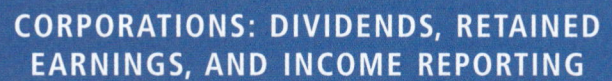

CORPORATIONS: DIVIDENDS, RETAINED EARNINGS, AND INCOME REPORTING

Dividends	Retained Earnings	Corporation Income Statements	Earnings per Share
• Cash dividends • Stock dividends • Stock splits	• Retained earnings restrictions • Prior period adjustments • Retained earnings statement • Statement presentation and analysis		• EPS and preferred stock dividends

☑ THE NAVIGATOR

Dividends

A **dividend** is a distribution by a corporation to its stockholders on a pro rata (proportional) basis. Potential buyers and sellers of stock are very interested in a company's dividend policies and practices. Dividends can take four forms: cash, property, scrip (a promissory note to pay cash), or stock. Cash dividends predominate in practice. Also, stock dividends are declared with some frequency. These two forms of dividends will be the focus of discussion in this chapter.

STUDY OBJECTIVE 1

Prepare the entries for cash dividends and stock dividends.

Dividends may be expressed in two ways: (1) as a percentage of the par or stated value of the stock, or (2) as a dollar amount per share. In the financial press, **dividends are generally reported quarterly as a dollar amount per share**. For example, **Boeing Company**'s quarterly dividend rate is 17 cents a share, **Hershey Foods Corp.**'s is 31.5 cents, and **Nike**'s is 12 cents.

Cash Dividends

A **cash dividend** is a pro rata distribution of cash to stockholders. For a corporation to pay a cash dividend, it must have:

1. **Retained earnings.** The legality of a cash dividend depends on the laws of the state in which the company is incorporated. Payment of cash dividends from retained earnings is legal in all states. In general, cash dividend distributions based only on common stock (legal capital) are illegal. Statutes vary considerably with respect to cash dividends based on paid-in capital in excess of par or stated value. Many states permit such dividends. A dividend declared out of paid-in

capital is termed a **liquidating dividend**. The amount originally paid in by stockholders is being reduced or "liquidated" by such a dividend.

2. **Adequate cash.** The legality of a dividend and the ability to pay a dividend are two different things. For example, **Nike**, with retained earnings of over $3 billion, could legally declare a dividend of at least $3 billion. But Nike's cash balance is only $198 million. In order to pay a $3 billion dividend, Nike would need to raise additional cash through the sale of other assets or through additional financing.

Before declaring a cash dividend, a company's board of directors must carefully consider both current and future demands on the company's cash resources. In some cases, current liabilities may make a cash dividend inappropriate. In other cases, a major plant expansion program may warrant only a relatively small dividend.

3. **A declaration of dividends.** A company does not pay dividends unless its board of directors decides to do so, at which point the board "declares" the dividend. The board of directors has full authority to determine the amount of income to be distributed in the form of a dividend and the amount to be retained in the business. Dividends do not accrue like interest on a note payable, and they are not a liability until declared.

The amount and timing of a dividend are important issues. The payment of a large cash dividend could lead to liquidity problems for the enterprise. On the other hand, a small dividend or a missed dividend may cause unhappiness among stockholders. Many of them expect to receive a reasonable cash payment from the company on a periodic basis. Many companies declare and pay cash dividends quarterly.

ACCOUNTING IN ACTION Business Insight

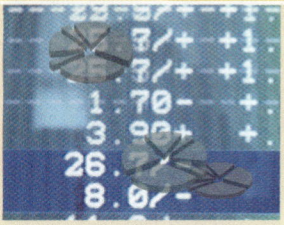

To pay, or not to pay, that seems to be the question. As stock prices fall and the market becomes more volatile, investors become more interested in dividends. And what they found recently was not too pleasing. One article noted that "According to Standard and Poor's, only 72% of companies in its S&P 500 index paid a dividend last year [2001], down from 94% in 1980." However, as a result of new tax regulations reducing the tax on dividends to only 15 percent, many corporate boards increased their dividend in 2003.

Source: "Dividends' End: Should Technology Companies Pay Dividends?" *The Economist* (January 12, 2002), p. 68.

Entries for Cash Dividends

Three dates are important in connection with dividends: (1) the declaration date, (2) the record date, and (3) the payment date. Normally, there are two to four weeks between each date. Accounting entries are required on two of the dates—the declaration date and the payment date.

On the **declaration date**, the board of directors formally declares (authorizes) the cash dividend and announces it to stockholders. Declaration of a cash dividend **commits the corporation to a legal obligation**. The obligation is binding and cannot be rescinded. An entry is required to recognize the decrease in retained earnings and the increase in the liability Dividends Payable. To illustrate, assume that on December 1, 2005, the directors of Media General declare a 50¢ per share cash dividend on 100,000 shares of $10 par value common stock. The dividend is $50,000 (100,000 × 50¢). The entry to record the declaration is:

Declaration Date

Dec. 1	Retained Earnings	50,000	
	Dividends Payable		50,000
	(To record declaration of cash dividend)		

A = L + SE
+50,000 −50,000 Div

Cash Flows
no effect

Dividends Payable is a current liability: it will normally be paid within the next several months.

Instead of debiting Retained Earnings, the account Dividends may be debited. This account provides additional information in the ledger. Also, a company may have separate dividend accounts for each class of stock. When a dividend account is used, its balance is transferred to Retained Earnings at the end of the year by a closing entry. Whichever account is used for the dividend declaration, the effect is the same: retained earnings is decreased and a current liability is increased. For homework problems, you should use the Retained Earnings account for recording dividend declarations.

At the **record date**, ownership of the outstanding shares is determined for dividend purposes. The records maintained by the corporation supply this information. In the interval between the declaration date and the record date, the corporation updates its stock ownership records. For Media General, the record date is December 22. No entry is required on this date because the corporation's liability recognized on the declaration date is unchanged.

HELPFUL HINT

Between the declaration date and record date, the number of shares outstanding should remain the same. The purpose of the record date is to identify the persons or entities that will receive the dividend, not to determine the amount of the dividend liability.

Record Date

| Dec. 22 | | | |
| | No entry necessary | | |

On the **payment date**, dividend checks are mailed to the stockholders and the payment of the dividend is recorded. Assuming that the payment date is January 20 for Media General, the entry on that date is:

Payment Date

Jan. 20	Dividends Payable	50,000	
	Cash		50,000
	(To record payment of cash dividend)		

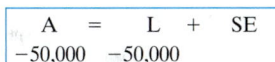

A = L + SE
−50,000 −50,000

Cash Flows
−50,000

Note that payment of the dividend reduces both current assets and current liabilities. It has no effect on stockholders' equity. The **cumulative effect** of the **declaration and payment** of a cash dividend is to **decrease both stockholders' equity and total assets**. Illustration 15-1 summarizes the three important dates associated with dividends.

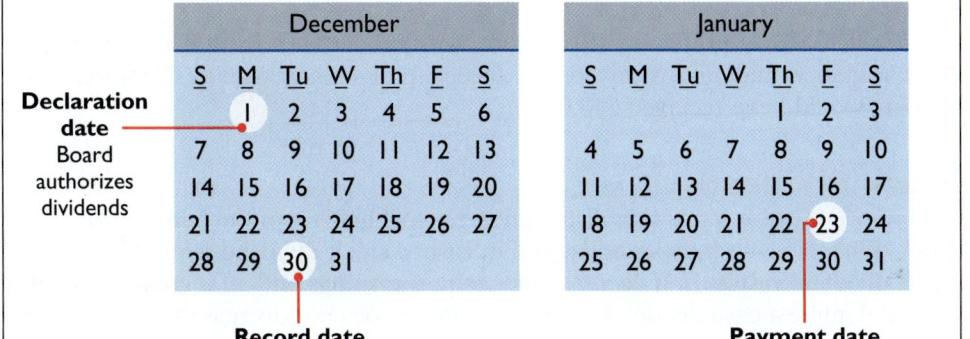

Illustration 15-1
Key dividend dates

Allocating Cash Dividends between Preferred and Common Stock

As explained in Chapter 14, preferred stock has priority over common stock in regard to dividends. Preferred stockholders must be paid any unpaid prior-year dividends before common stockholders receive dividends.

To illustrate, assume that at December 31, 2005, IBR Inc. has 1,000 shares of 8%, $100 par value cumulative preferred stock. It also has 50,000 shares of $10 par value common stock outstanding. The dividend per share for preferred stock is $8 ($100 par value × 8%). The required annual dividend for preferred stock is therefore $8,000 (1,000 × $8). At December 31, 2005, the directors declare a $6,000 cash dividend. In this case, the entire dividend amount goes to preferred stockholders because of their dividend preference. The entry to record the declaration of the dividend is:

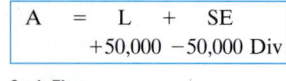

A	=	L	+	SE
		+6,000		−6,000 Div

Cash Flows
no effect

Dec. 31	Retained Earnings	6,000	
	Dividends Payable		6,000
	(To record $6 per share cash dividend to preferred stockholders)		

Because of the cumulative feature, dividends of $2 per share are in arrears on preferred stock for 2005. These dividends must be paid to preferred stockholders before any future dividends can be paid to common stockholders. Dividends in arrears should be disclosed in the financial statements.

At December 31, 2006, IBR declares a $50,000 cash dividend. The allocation of the dividend to the two classes of stock is as follows.

Illustration 15-2
Allocating dividends to preferred and common stock

Total dividend		$50,000
Allocated to preferred stock		
Dividends in arrears, 2005 (1,000 × $2)	**$2,000**	
2006 dividend (1,000 × $8)	**8,000**	10,000
Remainder allocated to common stock		$40,000

The entry to record the declaration of the dividend is:

A	=	L	+	SE
		+50,000		−50,000 Div

Cash Flows
no effect

Dec. 31	Retained Earnings	50,000	
	Dividends Payable		50,000
	(To record declaration of cash dividends of $10,000 to preferred stock and $40,000 to common stock)		

What if IBR's preferred stock were not cumulative? In that case preferred stockholders would have received only $8,000 in dividends in 2006. Common stockholders would have received $42,000.

Stock Dividends

A **stock dividend** is a pro rata distribution to stockholders of the corporation's own stock. Whereas a cash dividend is paid in cash, a stock dividend is paid in stock. **A stock dividend results in a decrease in retained earnings and an increase in paid-in capital.** Unlike a cash dividend, a stock dividend does not decrease total stockholders' equity or total assets.

To illustrate, assume that you have a 2% ownership interest in Cetus Inc.; you own 20 of its 1,000 shares of common stock. If Cetus declares a 10% stock dividend, it would issue 100 shares (1,000 × 10%) of stock. You would receive 2 shares (2% × 100). Would your ownership interest change? No, it would remain at 2% (22 ÷ 1,100). **You now own more shares of stock, but your ownership interest has not changed.** Illustration 15-3 shows the effect of a stock dividend for stockholders.

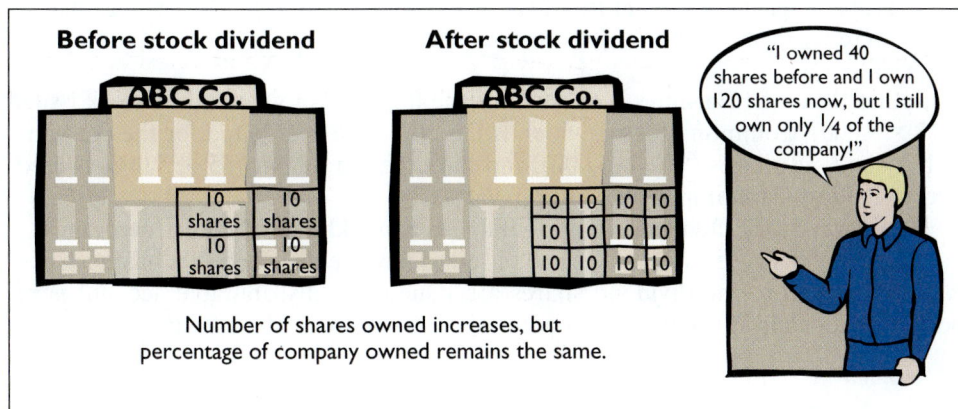

Illustration 15-3
Effect of stock dividend for stockholders

From the company's point of view, no cash has been disbursed, and no liabilities have been assumed by the corporation. What are the purposes and benefits of a stock dividend? Corporations issue stock dividends generally for one or more of the following reasons.

1. To satisfy stockholders' dividend expectations without spending cash.
2. To increase the marketability of the corporation's stock. When the number of shares outstanding increases, the market price per share decreases. Decreasing the market price of the stock makes it easier for smaller investors to purchase the shares.
3. To emphasize that a portion of stockholders' equity has been permanently reinvested in the business (and is unavailable for cash dividends).

The size of the stock dividend and the value to be assigned to each dividend share are determined by the board of directors when the dividend is declared. The per share amount must be at least equal to the par or stated value in order to meet legal requirements.

The accounting profession distinguishes between a **small stock dividend** (less than 20–25% of the corporation's issued stock) and a **large stock dividend** (greater than 20–25%). For small stock dividends, it recommends that the directors assign the **fair market value per share**. This treatment is based on the assumption that a small stock dividend will have little effect on the market price of the outstanding shares. Many stockholders consider small stock dividends to be distributions of earnings equal to the fair market value of the shares distributed. The amount to be assigned for a large stock dividend is not specified by the accounting profession. **Par or stated value per share** is normally assigned. Small stock dividends predominate in practice. Thus, we will illustrate only the entries for small stock dividends.

Entries for Stock Dividends

To illustrate the accounting for small stock dividends, assume that Medland Corporation has a balance of $300,000 in retained earnings. It declares a 10% stock dividend on its 50,000 shares of $10 par value common stock. The current fair market value of its stock is $15 per share. The number of shares to be issued is 5,000

(10% × 50,000). Therefore the total amount to be debited to Retained Earnings is $75,000 (5,000 × $15). The entry to record the declaration of the stock dividend is as follows.

A	=	L	+	SE
				−75,000 Div
				+50,000 CS
				+25,000 CS

Cash Flows
no effect

Retained Earnings	75,000	
Common Stock Dividends Distributable		50,000
Paid-in Capital in Excess of Par Value		25,000
(To record declaration of 10% stock dividend)		

Note that Retained Earnings is debited for the fair market value of the stock issued ($15 × 5,000). Common Stock Dividends Distributable is credited for the par value of the dividend shares ($10 × 5,000), and the excess over par ($5 × 5,000) is credited to Paid-in Capital in Excess of Par Value.

Common Stock Dividends Distributable is a **stockholders' equity account**. It is not a liability because assets will not be used to pay the dividend. If a balance sheet is prepared before the dividend shares are issued, the distributable account is reported under Paid-in capital, as an addition to common stock issued:

Illustration 15-4
Statement presentation of common stock dividends distributable

Paid-in capital		
Common stock	$500,000	
Common stock dividends distributable	**50,000**	$550,000

When the dividend shares are issued, Common Stock Dividends Distributable is debited, and Common Stock is credited as follows.

A	=	L	+	SE
				−50,000 CS
				+50,000 CS

Cash Flows
no effect

Common Stock Dividends Distributable	50,000	
Common Stock		50,000
(To record issuance of 5,000 shares in a stock dividend)		

Effects of Stock Dividends

How do stock dividends affect stockholders' equity? They **change the composition of stockholders' equity**, because a portion of retained earnings is transferred to paid-in capital. However, **total stockholders' equity remains the same**. Stock dividends also have no effect on the par or stated value per share. But the number of shares outstanding increases, and the book value per share decreases. These effects are shown for Medland Corporation in Illustration 15-5.

Illustration 15-5
Stock dividend effects

	Before Dividend	After Dividend
Stockholders' equity		
Paid-in capital		
Common stock, $10 par	$500,000	$550,000
Paid-in capital in excess of par value	—	25,000
Total paid-in capital	500,000	575,000
Retained earnings	300,000	225,000
Total stockholders' equity	**$800,000**	**$800,000**
Outstanding shares	**50,000**	**55,000**
Book value per share	**$16.00**	**$14.55**

In this example, total paid-in capital is increased by $75,000, and retained earnings is decreased by the same amount. Note also that total stockholders' equity remains unchanged at $800,000.

Stock Splits

A **stock split**, like a stock dividend, involves the issuance of additional shares to stockholders according to their percentage ownership. **A stock split results in a reduction in the par or stated value per share.** The purpose of a stock split is to increase the marketability of the stock by lowering its market value per share. A lower market value also makes it easier for the corporation to issue additional stock.

The effect of a split on market value is generally inversely proportional to the size of the split. For example, after a recent 2-for-1 stock split, the market value of **Nike**'s stock fell from $111 to approximately $55. The lower market value stimulated market activity, and within one year the stock was trading above $100 again.

In a stock split, the number of shares is increased in the same proportion that par or stated value per share is decreased. For example, in a 2-for-1 split, one share of $10 par value stock is exchanged for two shares of $5 par value stock. **A stock split does not have any effect on total paid-in capital, retained earnings, or total stockholders' equity.** But the number of shares outstanding increases and book value per share decreases. These effects are shown in Illustration 15-6 for Medland Corporation, assuming that it splits its 50,000 shares of common stock on a 2-for-1 basis.

	Before Stock Split	After Stock Split
Stockholders' equity		
Paid-in capital		
Common stock	$500,000	$500,000
Paid-in capital in excess of par value	–0–	–0–
Total paid-in capital	500,000	500,000
Retained earnings	300,000	300,000
Total stockholders' equity	**$800,000**	**$800,000**
Outstanding shares	**50,000**	**100,000**
Book value per share	**$16.00**	**$8.00**

Illustration 15-6
Stock split effects

A stock split does not affect the balances in any stockholders' equity accounts. Therefore **it is not necessary to journalize a stock split**.

The significant differences between stock splits and stock dividends are shown in Illustration 15-7.

Item	Stock Split	Stock Dividend
Total paid-in capital	No change	Increase
Total retained earnings	No change	Decrease
Total par value (common stock)	No change	Increase
Par value per share	Decrease	No change

Illustration 15-7
Differences between the effects of stock splits and stock dividends

Business Insight

A handful of U.S. companies have no intention of keeping their stock trading in a range accessible to mere mortals. These companies never split their stock, no matter how high their stock price gets. The king is investment company **Berkshire Hathaway**'s Class A stock, which sells for a pricey $74,200—per share! The company's Class B stock is a relative bargain at roughly $2,475 per share.

BEFORE YOU GO ON...

Review It

1. What entries are made for cash dividends on (a) the declaration date, (b) the record date, and (c) the payment date?

2. Distinguish between a small and large stock dividend, and indicate the basis for valuing each kind of dividend.

3. Contrast the effects of a small stock dividend and a 2-for-1 stock split on (a) stockholders' equity, (b) outstanding shares, and (c) book value per share.

4. What were the amounts of the dividends declared per share of common stock by **PepsiCo** during the years 1998 to 2002? Is the trend in dividends consistent with the company's net income trend during that period? The answers to these questions are provided on page 626.

Do It

Sing CD Company has had 5 years of record earnings. Due to this success, the market price of its 500,000 shares of $2 par value common stock has tripled from $15 per share to $45. During this period, paid-in capital remained the same at $2,000,000. Retained earnings increased from $1,500,000 to $10,000,000. President Joan Elbert is considering either (1) a 10% stock dividend or (2) a 2-for-1 stock split. She asks you to show the before-and-after effects of each option on (a) retained earnings and (b) book value per share.

ACTION PLAN

- Calculate the stock dividend's effect on retained earnings by multiplying the number of new shares times the market price of the stock (or par value for a large stock dividend).
- Recall that a stock dividend increases the number of shares without affecting total equity, thus decreasing the book value per share.
- Recall that a stock split only increases the number of shares outstanding and decreases the par value per share.

SOLUTION

(a) (1) The stock dividend amount is $2,250,000 [(500,000 × 10%) × $45]. The new balance in retained earnings is $7,750,000 ($10,000,000 − $2,250,000).

 (2) The retained earnings balance after the stock split would be the same as it was before the split: $10,000,000.

(b) The book value effects are as follows:

	Original Balances	After Dividend	After Split
Paid-in capital	$ 2,000,000	$ 4,250,000	$ 2,000,000
Retained earnings	10,000,000	7,750,000	10,000,000
Total stockholders' equity	$12,000,000	$12,000,000	$12,000,000
Shares outstanding	500,000	550,000	1,000,000
Book value per share	$24	$21.82	$12

Related exercise material: *BE15-2, BE15-3, E15-3, E15-4, E15-5, E15-6, and E15-7.*

☑ THE NAVIGATOR

Retained Earnings

As you learned in Chapter 14, **retained earnings** is net income that is retained in the business. The balance in retained earnings is part of the stockholders' claim on the total assets of the corporation. It does not, though, represent a claim on any specific asset. Nor can the amount of retained earnings be associated with the balance of any asset account. For example, a $100,000 balance in retained earnings does not mean that there should be $100,000 in cash. The reason is that the cash resulting from the excess of revenues over expenses may have been used to purchase buildings, equipment, and other assets. To illustrate that retained earnings and cash may be quite different, Illustration 15-8 shows recent amounts of retained earnings and cash in selected companies.

STUDY OBJECTIVE 2

Identify the items that are reported in a retained earnings statement.

	(in millions)	
Company	Retained Earnings	Cash
Walt Disney Co.	$12,979	$1,239
Intel Corp.	27,847	7,404
Kellogg Co.	1,873	100.6
Amazon.com	(2,861)	540

Illustration 15-8
Retained earnings and cash balances

Remember from Chapter 14 that when a company has net profit, the net income that is retained in the business is recorded in retained earnings by means of a closing entry. This entry debits Income Summary and credits Retained Earnings.

However, when expenses exceed revenues, a **net loss** results. A net loss is debited to Retained Earnings in a closing entry. This is done even if it results in a debit balance in Retained Earnings. **Net losses are not debited to paid-in capital accounts.** To do so would destroy the distinction between paid-in and earned capital. A debit balance in Retained Earnings is identified as a **deficit**. It is reported as a deduction in the stockholders' equity section, as shown below.

HELPFUL HINT

Remember that Retained Earnings is a stockholders' equity account, whose normal balance is a credit.

Illustration 15-9
Stockholders' equity with deficit

Balance Sheet (partial)	
Stockholders' equity	
Paid-in capital	
Common stock	$800,000
Retained earnings (deficit)	**(50,000)**
Total stockholders' equity	$750,000

Retained Earnings Restrictions

The balance in retained earnings is generally available for dividend declarations. Some companies state this fact. For example, in the notes to recent financial statements, **Lockheed Martin Corporation** stated:

Illustration 15-10
Disclosure of unrestricted retained earnings

LOCKHEED MARTIN CORPORATION
Notes to the Financial Statements

At December 31, retained earnings were unrestricted and available for dividend payments.

In some cases, there may be **retained earnings restrictions**. These make a portion of the retained earnings balance currently unavailable for dividends. Restrictions result from one or more of the following causes: legal, contractual, or voluntary.

1. **Legal restrictions.** Many states require a corporation to restrict retained earnings for the cost of treasury stock purchased. The restriction keeps intact the corporation's legal capital that is being temporarily held as treasury stock. When the treasury stock is sold, the restriction is lifted.

2. **Contractual restrictions.** Long-term debt contracts may restrict retained earnings as a condition for the loan. The restriction limits the use of corporate assets for payment of dividends. Thus, it increases the likelihood that the corporation will be able to meet required loan payments.

3. **Voluntary restrictions.** The board of directors may voluntarily create retained earnings restrictions for specific purposes. For example, the board may authorize a restriction for future plant expansion. By reducing the amount of retained earnings available for dividends, more cash may be available for the planned expansion.

Retained earnings restrictions are generally disclosed in the notes to the financial statements. For example, **Tektronix Inc.**, a manufacturer of electronic measurement devices, had total retained earnings of $774 million, but the unrestricted portion was only $223.8 million.

Illustration 15-11
Disclosure of restriction

TEKTRONIX INC.
Notes to the Financial Statements

Certain of the Company's debt agreements require compliance with debt covenants. Management believes that the Company is in compliance with such requirements for the fiscal year ended May 26, 2001. The Company had unrestricted retained earnings of $223.8 million after meeting those requirements.

Prior Period Adjustments

Suppose that a corporation's books have been closed and the financial statements have been issued. The corporation then discovers that a material error has been made in reporting net income of a prior year. How should this situation be recorded in the accounts and reported in the financial statements?

The correction of an error in previously issued financial statements is known as a **prior period adjustment**. The correction is made directly to Retained Earnings because the effect of the error is now in this account: The net income for the prior period has been recorded in retained earnings through the journalizing and posting of closing entries.

To illustrate, assume that General Microwave discovers in 2005 that it understated depreciation expense in 2004 by $300,000 due to computational errors. These errors overstated both net income for 2004 and the current balance in retained earnings. The entry for the prior period adjustment, assuming all tax effects are ignored, is as follows.

Retained Earnings	300,000	
Accumulated Depreciation		300,000
(To adjust for understatement of depreciation in a		
prior period)		

A	=	L	+	SE
−300,000				−300,000 RE

Cash Flows
no effect

A debit to an income statement account in 2005 would be incorrect because the error pertains to a prior year.

Prior period adjustments are reported in the retained earnings statement.[1] They are added (or deducted, as the case may be) from the beginning retained earnings balance. This results in an adjusted beginning balance. Assuming General Microwave has a beginning balance of $800,000 in retained earnings, the prior period adjustment is reported as follows.

GENERAL MICROWAVE	
Retained Earnings Statement (partial)	
Balance, January 1, as reported	$ 800,000
Correction for overstatement of net income	
in prior period (depreciation error)	**(300,000)**
Balance, January 1, as adjusted	$ 500,000

Illustration 15-12
Statement presentation of prior period adjustments

Again, reporting the correction in the current year's income statement would be incorrect because it applies to a prior year's income statement.

Retained Earnings Statement

The **retained earnings statement** shows the changes in retained earnings during the year. The statement is prepared from the Retained Earnings account. Transactions and events that affect retained earnings are tabulated in account form as shown in Illustration 15-13.

Retained Earnings	
1. Net loss	1. Net income
2. Prior period adjustments for overstatement of net income	2. Prior period adjustments for understatement of net income
3. Cash dividends and stock dividends	
4. Some disposals of treasury stock	

Illustration 15-13
Debits and credits to retained earnings

As indicated, net income increases retained earnings, and a net loss decreases retained earnings. Prior period adjustments may either increase or decrease retained earnings. Both cash dividends and stock dividends decrease retained earnings. The

---

[1]A complete retained earnings statement is shown in Illustration 15-14 on the next page.

circumstances under which treasury stock transactions decrease retained earnings are explained in Chapter 14, page 575.

A complete retained earnings statement for Graber Inc., based on assumed data, is as follows.

Illustration 15-14
Retained earnings statement

GRABER INC. Retained Earnings Statement For the Year Ended December 31, 2005		
Balance, January 1, as reported		$ 1,050,000
Correction for understatement of net income in prior period (inventory error)		50,000
Balance, January 1, as adjusted		1,100,000
Add: Net income		360,000
		1,460,000
Less: Cash dividends	$ 100,000	
Stock dividends	200,000	300,000
Balance, December 31		$1,160,000

Statement Presentation and Analysis

STUDY OBJECTIVE 3

Prepare and analyze a comprehensive stockholders' equity section.

Presentation

The stockholders' equity section of Graber Inc.'s balance sheet is presented in Illustration 15-15. Note the following: (1) "Common stock dividends distributable" is shown under "Capital stock," in "Paid-in capital." (2) A retained earnings restriction is disclosed in the notes.

Illustration 15-15
Comprehensive stockholders' equity section

GRABER INC. Balance Sheet (partial)		
Stockholders' equity		
Paid-in capital		
Capital stock		

9% Preferred stock, $100 par value, cumulative,
    callable at $120, 10,000 shares authorized,
    6,000 shares issued and outstanding
		$ 600,000

Common stock, no par, $5 stated value,
    500,000 shares authorized, 400,000 shares issued
    and 390,000 outstanding
	$2,000,000	

Common stock dividends distributable	**50,000**	2,050,000
Total capital stock		2,650,000
Additional paid-in capital		
In excess of par value—preferred stock	30,000	
In excess of stated value—common stock	1,050,000	
Total additional paid-in capital		1,080,000
Total paid-in capital		3,730,000
Retained earnings **(see Note R)**		1,160,000
Total paid-in capital and retained earnings		4,890,000
Less: Treasury stock—common (10,000 shares)		80,000
Total stockholders' equity		$4,810,000

Note R: Retained earnings is restricted for the cost of treasury stock, $80,000.

Instead of presenting a detailed stockholders' equity section in the balance sheet and a retained earnings statement, many companies prepare a **stockholders' equity statement**. This statement shows the changes in each stockholders' equity account and in total that have occurred during the year. An example of a stockholders' equity statement is illustrated in **PepsiCo**'s financial statements in Appendix A.

Analysis

Profitability from the viewpoint of the common stockholder can be measured by the **return on common stockholders' equity**. This ratio shows how many dollars of net income were earned for each dollar invested by the stockholders. It is computed by dividing net income available to common stockholders (which is net income minus preferred stock dividends) by average common stockholders' equity. To illustrate, **Kellogg Company**'s beginning-of-the-year and end-of-the-year common stockholders' equity were $871.5 and $895.1 million respectively. Its net income was $720.9 million, and no preferred stock was outstanding. The return on common stockholders' equity ratio is computed as follows.

Net Income minus Preferred Dividends	÷	Average Common Stockholders' Equity	=	Return on Common Stockholders' Equity
($720.9 − $0)	÷	$\dfrac{($871.5 + $895.1)}{2}$	=	81.6%

Illustration 15-16
Return on common stockholders' equity ratio and computation

As shown above, if a company has preferred stock, the amount of **preferred dividends** is deducted from net income to compute income available to common stockholders. Also, the par value of preferred stock is deducted from total average stockholders' equity to arrive at the amount of common stockholders' equity.

BEFORE YOU GO ON...

Review It

1. How are retained earnings restrictions generally reported?
2. What is a prior period adjustment, and how is it reported?
3. What are the principal sources of debits and credits to Retained Earnings?
4. How are stock dividends distributable reported in the stockholders' equity section?
5. Explain the return on common stockholders' equity ratio.

Do It

Vega Corporation has retained earnings of $5,130,000 on January 1, 2005. During the year, Vega earns $2,000,000 of net income. It declares and pays a $250,000 cash dividend. In 2005, Vega records an adjustment of $180,000 due to the understatement of 2004 depreciation expense from a mathematical error. Prepare a retained earnings statement for 2005.

ACTION PLAN
- Recall that a retained earnings statement begins with retained earnings, as reported at the end of the previous year.
- Add or subtract any prior period adjustments to arrive at the adjusted beginning figure.
- Add net income and subtract dividends declared to arrive at the ending balance in retained earnings.

SOLUTION

VEGA CORPORATION
Retained Earnings Statement
For the Year Ended December 31, 2005

Balance, January 1, as reported	$5,130,000
Correction for overstatement of net income in prior period (depreciation error)	(180,000)
Balance, January 1, as adjusted	4,950,000
Add: Net income	2,000,000
	6,950,000
Less: Cash dividends	250,000
Balance, December 31	$6,700,000

Related exercise material: *BE15-4, BE15-5, BE15-6, BE15-7, and E15-8.*

☑ THE NAVIGATOR

Corporation Income Statements

STUDY OBJECTIVE 4

Describe the form and content of corporation income statements.

Income statements for **corporations are the same as the statements for proprietorships or partnerships except for one thing: the reporting of income taxes**. For income tax purposes, corporations are a separate legal entity. As a result, **income tax expense** is reported in a separate section of the corporation income statement before net income. The condensed income statement for Leads Inc. in Illustration 15-17 shows a typical presentation. Note that the corporation reports income before income taxes as one line item and income tax expense as another.

Illustration 15-17
Income statement with income taxes

LEADS INC.
Income Statement
For the Year Ended December 31, 2005

Sales	$800,000
Cost of goods sold	600,000
Gross profit	200,000
Operating expenses	50,000
Income from operations	150,000
Other revenues and gains	10,000
Other expenses and losses	(4,000)
Income before income taxes	**156,000**
Income tax expense	**46,800**
Net income	$109,200

Income tax expense and the related liability for income taxes payable are recorded as part of the adjusting process. Using the data above for Leads Inc., the adjusting entry for income tax expense at December 31, 2005, would be:

A	=	L	+	SE
		+46,800		−46,800 Exp

Cash Flows
no effect

Income Tax Expense	46,800	
Income Taxes Payable		46,800
(To record income taxes for 2005)		

Another illustration of income taxes is presented in the income statement of **PepsiCo** in Appendix A.

Earnings per Share

Earnings data are frequently reported in the financial press. They are widely used by stockholders and potential investors in evaluating the profitability of a company. A convenient measure of earnings is **earnings per share (EPS)**, which indicates the net income earned by each share of outstanding **common stock**.

> **STUDY OBJECTIVE 5**
>
> Compute earnings per share.

EPS and Preferred Dividends

When a corporation has both preferred and common stock, the current year's dividend declared on preferred stock is subtracted from net income to arrive at **income available to common stockholders**. The formula for computing EPS is:

Net Income minus Preferred Dividends	÷	Weighted Average of Common Shares Outstanding	=	Earnings per Share

Illustration 15-18
Formula for earnings per share

To illustrate, assume that Rally Inc. reports net income of $211,000 on its 102,500 weighted average common shares.[2] During the year it also declares a $6,000 dividend on its preferred stock. Therefore, the amount Rally has available for common stock dividends is $205,000 ($211,000 − $6,000). Earnings per share is $2 ($205,000 ÷ 102,500). If the preferred stock is cumulative, the dividend for the current year is deducted whether or not it is declared. Remember that **earnings per share is reported only for common stock**.

Investors often attempt to link earnings per share to the market price per share of a company's stock.[3] Because of the importance of earnings per share, most companies are required to report it on the face of the income statement. Generally this amount is simply reported below net income on the statement. For Rally Inc. the presentation would be:

RALLY INC. Income Statement (partial)	
Net income	$211,000
Earnings per share	**$2.00**

Illustration 15-19
Basic earnings per share disclosure

---

[2] The calculation of the weighted average of common shares outstanding is discussed in advanced accounting courses.

[3] The ratio of the market price per share to the earnings per share is referred to as the *price/earnings (P/E) ratio*. This ratio is reported in the *Wall Street Journal* and in other newspapers for common stocks listed on major stock exchanges.

ACCOUNTING IN ACTION Business Insight

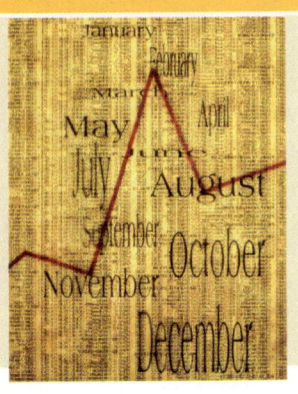

When a company publicly announces its latest earnings per share figure, a change in the company's stock price will often result. The change in stock price will be most pronounced if the company's net income figure differs from what investors were expecting. When **Yahoo!** recently announced earnings per share that exceeded investor expectations, its stock price jumped 14 percent in a single day. When retail giant **Costco Wholesale Corporation** announced earnings per share only 1 cent below analysts' expectations, its stock price fell 22 percent in a single day. To avoid "earnings surprises" and the resultant wide swings in share prices, companies continually try to keep investors informed.

BEFORE YOU GO ON...

Review It

1. What is the unique feature of a corporation income statement?
2. Explain the components of the formula for computing earnings per share when there is only common stock and outstanding shares are unchanged during the year.
3. What effects may preferred stock have on the formula for computing earnings per share?

DEMONSTRATION PROBLEM

On January 1, 2005, Hayslett Corporation had the following stockholders' equity accounts.

Common Stock ($10 par value, 260,000 shares issued and outstanding)	$2,600,000
Paid-in Capital in Excess of Par Value	1,500,000
Retained Earnings	3,200,000

During the year, the following transactions occurred.

April	1	Declared a $1.50 cash dividend per share to stockholders of record on April 15, payable May 1.
May	1	Paid the dividend declared in April.
June	1	Announced a 2-for-1 stock split. Prior to the split, the market price per share was $24.
Aug.	1	Declared a 10% stock dividend to stockholders of record on August 15, distributable August 31. On August 1, the market price of the stock was $10 per share.
	31	Issued the shares for the stock dividend.
Dec.	1	Declared a $1.50 per share dividend to stockholders of record on December 15, payable January 5, 2006.
	31	Determined that net income for the year was $600,000.

Instructions

(a) Journalize the transactions and the closing entry for net income.

(b) Prepare a stockholders' equity section at December 31.

SOLUTION TO DEMONSTRATION PROBLEM

ACTION PLAN

- Award dividends to outstanding shares only.
- Adjust the par value and number of shares for stock splits, but make no journal entry.
- Use market value of stock to determine the value of a stock dividend.
- Close Income Summary to Retained Earnings.

(a)

Apr. 1	Retained Earnings (260,000 × $1.50)	390,000	
	Dividends Payable		390,000
May 1	Dividends Payable	390,000	
	Cash		390,000
June 1	Memo—two-for-one stock split increases number of shares to 520,000 (260,000 × 2) and reduces par value to $5 per share.		
Aug. 1	Retained Earnings (52,000 × $10)	520,000	
	Common Stock Dividends Distributable (52,000 × $5)		260,000
	Paid-in Capital in Excess of Par Value (52,000 × $5)		260,000
31	Common Stock Dividends Distributable	260,000	
	Common Stock		260,000
Dec. 1	Retained Earnings (572,000 × $1.50)	858,000	
	Dividends Payable		858,000
31	Income Summary	600,000	
	Retained Earnings		600,000

(b)

HAYSLETT CORPORATION

Stockholders' equity	
Paid-in capital	
Capital stock	
Common stock, $5 par value, 572,000 shares issued and outstanding	$2,860,000
Additional paid-in capital in excess of par value	1,760,000
Total paid-in capital	4,620,000
Retained earnings	2,032,000
Total stockholders' equity	$6,652,000

THE NAVIGATOR

SUMMARY OF STUDY OBJECTIVES

1. Prepare the entries for cash dividends and stock dividends. Entries for both cash and stock dividends are required at the declaration date and at the payment date. At the declaration date the entries are: cash dividend–debit Retained Earnings, and credit Dividends Payable; small stock dividend–debit Retained Earnings, credit Paid-in Capital in Excess of Par (or Stated) Value, and credit Common Stock Dividends Distributable. At the payment date, the entries for cash and stock dividends are: cash dividend–debit Dividends Payable and credit Cash; small stock dividend–debit Common Stock Dividends Distributable and credit Common Stock.

2. Identify the items that are reported in a retained earnings statement. Each of the individual debits and credits to retained earnings should be reported in the retained earnings statement. Additions consist of net income and prior period adjustments to correct understatements of prior years' net income. Deductions consist of net loss, adjustments to correct overstatements of prior years' net income, cash and stock dividends, and some disposals of treasury stock.

3. Prepare and analyze a comprehensive stockholders' equity section. A comprehensive stockholders' equity section includes all stockholders' equity accounts. It consists of two sections: paid-in capital and retained earnings. It should also include notes to the financial statements that explain any restrictions on retained earnings and any dividends in arrears. One measure of profitability is the return on common stockholders' equity. It is calculated by dividing net income minus preferred stock dividends by average common stockholders' equity.

4. Describe the form and content of corporation income statements. The form and content of corporation income statements are similar to the statements of proprietorships and partnerships with one exception: Income taxes or income tax expense must be reported in a separate section before net income in the corporation's income statement.

5. Compute earnings per share. Earnings per share is computed by dividing net income by the weighted average number of common shares outstanding during the period. When preferred stock dividends exist, they must be deducted from net income in order to calculate EPS.

GLOSSARY

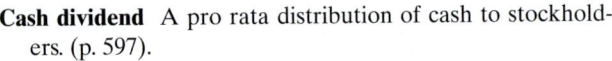

Cash dividend A pro rata distribution of cash to stockholders. (p. 597).

Declaration date The date the board of directors formally declares a dividend and announces it to stockholders. (p. 598).

Deficit A debit balance in retained earnings. (p. 605).

Dividend A distribution by a corporation to its stockholders on a pro rata (proportional) basis. (p. 597).

Earnings per share The net income earned by each share of outstanding common stock. (p 611)

Liquidating dividend A dividend declared out of paid-in capital. (p. 598).

Payment date The date dividend checks are mailed to stockholders. (p. 599).

Prior period adjustment The correction of an error in previously issued financial statements. (p. 606).

Record date The date when ownership of outstanding shares is determined for dividend purposes. (p. 599).

Retained earnings Net income that is retained in the business. (p. 605).

Retained earnings restrictions Circumstances that make a portion of retained earnings currently unavailable for dividends. (p. 606).

Retained earnings statement A financial statement that shows the changes in retained earnings during the year. (p. 607).

Return on common stockholders' equity A measure of profitability that shows how many dollars of net income were earned for each dollar invested by the owners; computed as net income minus preferred dividends divided by average common stockholders' equity. (p. 609).

Stock dividend A pro rata distribution to stockholders of the corporation's own stock. (p. 600).

Stockholders' equity statement A statement that shows the changes in each stockholders' equity account and in total stockholders' equity during the year. (p. 609).

Stock split The issuance of additional shares of stock to stockholders according to their percentage ownership; is accompanied by a reduction in the par or stated value per share. (p. 603).

SELF-STUDY QUESTIONS

Self-Study/Self-Test

Answers are at the end of the chapter.

(SO 1) **1.** Entries for cash dividends are required on the:
   a. declaration date and the payment date.
   b. record date and the payment date.
   c. declaration date, record date, and payment date.
   d. declaration date and the record date.

(SO 1) **2.** Which of the following statements about small stock dividends is true?
   a. A debit to Retained Earnings for the par value of the shares issued should be made.
   b. A small stock dividend decreases total stockholders' equity.
   c. Market value per share should be assigned to the dividend shares.
   d. A small stock dividend ordinarily will have no effect on book value per share of stock.

(SO 1) **3.** Which of the following statements about a 3-for-1 stock split is true?

   a. It will triple the market value of the stock.
   b. It will triple the amount of total stockholders' equity.
   c. It will have no effect on total stockholders' equity.
   d. It requires the company to distribute cash.

4. Which of the following can cause a restriction in retained (SO
   earnings?
   a. State laws regarding treasury stock.
   b. Long-term debt contract terms.
   c. Authorizations by the board of directors in light of planned expansion of corporate facilities.
   d. All of the above.

5. All *but one* of the following is reported in a retained (SO
   earnings statement. The exception is:
   a. cash and stock dividends.
   b. net income and net loss.
   c. some disposals of treasury stock below cost.
   d. sales of treasury stock above cost.

O 2) **6.** A prior period adjustment is:
  a. reported in the income statement as a nontypical item.
  b. a correction of an error that is made directly to retained earnings.
  c. reported directly in the stockholders' equity section.
  d. reported in the retained earnings statement as an adjustment of the ending balance of retained earnings.

O 3) **7.** In the stockholders' equity section, Common Stock Dividends Distributable is reported as a(n):
  a. deduction from total paid-in capital and retained earnings.
  b. addition to additional paid-in capital.
  c. deduction from retained earnings.
  d. addition to capital stock.

O 4) **8.** Corporation income statements may be the same as the income statements for unincorporated companies *except* for:
  a. gross profit.
  b. income tax expense.

  c. operating income.
  d. net sales.

9. The return on common stockholders' equity is defined (SO 3) as:
  a. Net income divided by total assets.
  b. Cash dividends divided by average common stockholders' equity.
  c. Income available to common stockholders divided by average common stockholders' equity.
  d. None of these is correct.

10. The income statement for Nadeen, Inc. shows income be- (SO 5) fore income taxes $700,000, income tax expense $210,000, and net income $490,000. If Nadeen has 100,000 shares of common stock outstanding throughout the year, earnings per share is:
  a. $7.00.
  b. $4.90.
  c. $2.10.
  d. No correct answer is given.

QUESTIONS

1. (a) What is a dividend? (b) "Dividends must be paid in cash." Do you agree? Explain.

2. Lil Carmen maintains that adequate cash is the only requirement for the declaration of a cash dividend. Is Lil correct? Explain.

3. (a) Three dates are important in connection with cash dividends. Identify these dates, and explain their significance to the corporation and its stockholders.
  (b) Identify the accounting entries that are made for a cash dividend and the date of each entry.

4. DeVito Inc. declares a $45,000 cash dividend on December 31, 2005. The required annual dividend on preferred stock is $12,000. Determine the allocation of the dividend to preferred and common stockholders assuming the preferred stock is cumulative and dividends are 1 year in arrears.

5. Contrast the effects of a cash dividend and a stock dividend on a corporation's balance sheet.

6. Mark Federia asks, "Since stock dividends don't change anything, why declare them?" What is your answer to Mark?

7. Fields Corporation has 20,000 shares of $10 par value common stock outstanding when it announces a 2-for-1 stock split. Before the split, the stock had a market price of $120 per share. After the split, how many shares of stock will be outstanding? What will be the approximate market price per share?

8. The board of directors is considering either a stock split or a stock dividend. They understand that total stockholders' equity will remain the same under either action.

However, they are not sure of the different effects of the two types of actions on other aspects of stockholders' equity. Explain the differences to the directors.

9. What is a prior period adjustment, and how is it reported in the financial statements?

10. CBA Corporation has a retained earnings balance of $210,000 on January 1. During the year, a prior period adjustment of $70,000 is recorded because of the understatement of depreciation in the prior period. Show the retained earnings statement presentation of these data.

11. What is the purpose of a retained earnings restriction? Identify the possible causes of retained earnings restrictions.

12. How are retained earnings restrictions generally reported in the financial statements?

13. Identify the events that result in debits and credits to retained earnings.

14. Jose Alzado believes that both the beginning and ending balances in retained earnings are shown in the stockholders' equity section. Is Jose correct? Discuss.

15. Pete Letterman, who owns many investments in common stock, says, "I don't care what a company's net income is. The balance sheet tells me everything I need to know!" How do you respond to Pete?

16. What is the unique feature of a corporation income statement? Illustrate this feature, using assumed data.

17. Why must preferred stock dividends be subtracted from net income in computing earnings per share?

BRIEF EXERCISES

Prepare entries for a cash dividend.

(SO 1)

BE15-1 Chavez Corporation has 50,000 shares of common stock outstanding. It declares a $1 per share cash dividend on November 1 to stockholders of record on December 1. The dividend is paid on December 31. Prepare the entries on the appropriate dates to record the declaration and payment of the cash dividend.

Prepare entries for a stock dividend.

(SO 1)

BE15-2 Walters Corporation has 60,000 shares of $10 par value common stock outstanding. It declares a 10% stock dividend on December 1 when the market value per share is $16. The dividend shares are issued on December 31. Prepare the entries for the declaration and payment of the stock dividend.

Show before and after effects of a stock dividend.

(SO 1)

BE15-3 The stockholders' equity section of Martin Corporation consists of common stock ($10 par) $2,000,000 and retained earnings $300,000. A 10% stock dividend (20,000 shares) is declared when the market value per share is $14. Show the before and after effects of the dividend on the following.
(a) The components of stockholders' equity.
(b) Shares outstanding.
(c) Book value per share.

Prepare a retained earnings statement.

(SO 2)

BE15-4 For the year ending December 31, 2005, Mount Inc. reports net income $120,000 and dividends $85,000. Prepare the retained earnings statement for the year assuming the balance in retained earnings on January 1, 2005, was $220,000.

Prepare a retained earnings statement.

(SO 2)

BE15-5 The balance in retained earnings on January 1, 2005, for Ola Smith Inc, was $800,000. During the year, the corporation paid cash dividends of $90,000 and distributed a stock dividend of $8,000. In addition, the company determined that it had understated its depreciation expense in prior years by $50,000. Net income for 2005 was $150,000. Prepare the retained earnings statements for 2005.

Calculate the return on common stockholders' equity.

(SO 3)

BE15-6 **SUPERVALU,** one of the largest grocery retailers in the United States, is headquartered in Minneapolis. The following financial information (in millions) was taken from the company's 2001 annual report. Net sales $23,194; net income $82; beginning stockholders' equity $1,793; ending stockholders' equity $1,821. Compute the return on common stockholders' equity ratio.

Compute return on common stockholders' equity.

(SO 3)

BE15-7 Henning Corporation reported net income of $190,000, declared dividends on common stock of $50,000, and had an ending balance in retained earnings of $360,000. Stockholders' equity was $700,000 at the beginning of the year and $820,000 at the end of the year. Compute the return on common stockholders' equity.

Prepare a corporate income statement.

(SO 4)

BE15-8 The following information is available for Creek Corporation for the year ended December 31, 2005: Cost of goods sold $105,000; Sales $450,000; Other revenues and gains $50,000; Operating expenses $75,000. Assuming a corporate tax rate of 30%, prepare an income statement for the company.

Compute earnings per share.

(SO 5)

BE15-9 Swartz Corporation reports net income of $320,000 and a weighted average of 200,000 shares of common stock outstanding for the year. Compute the earnings per share of common stock.

Compute earnings per share with cumulative preferred stock.

(SO 5)

BE15-10 Income and common stock data for Swartz Corporation are presented in BE15-9. Assume also that Swartz has cumulative preferred stock dividends for the current year of $20,000 that were declared and paid. Compute the earnings per share of common stock.

EXERCISES

Journalize cash dividends; indicate statement presentation.

(SO 1)

E15-1 On January 1, Armada Corporation had 95,000 shares of no-par common stock issued and outstanding. The stock has a stated value of $5 per share. During the year, the following occurred.

Apr. 1 Issued 15,000 additional shares of common stock for $17 per share.
June 15 Declared a cash dividend of $1 per share to stockholders of record on June 30.
July 10 Paid the $1 cash dividend.

Dec. 1 Issued 2,000 additional shares of common stock for $19 per share.
      15 Declared a cash dividend on outstanding shares of $1.20 per share to stockholders of record on December 31.

Instructions

(a) Prepare the entries, if any, on each of the three dividend dates.

(b) How are dividends and dividends payable reported in the financial statements prepared at December 31?

E15-2 Arnez Corporation was organized on January 1, 2004. During its first year, the corporation issued 2,000 shares of $50 par value preferred stock and 100,000 shares of $10 par value common stock. At December 31, the company declared the following cash dividends: 2004, $6,000, 2005, $12,000, and 2006, $28,000.

Allocate cash dividends to preferred and common stock.

(SO 1)

Instructions

(a) Show the allocation of dividends to each class of stock, assuming the preferred stock dividend is 8% and not cumulative.

(b) Show the allocation of dividends to each class of stock, assuming the preferred stock dividend is 9% and cumulative.

(c) Journalize the declaration of the cash dividend at December 31, 2006, under part (b).

E15-3 On January 1, 2005, Abdella Corporation had $1,000,000 of common stock outstanding that was issued at par. It also had retained earnings of $750,000. The company issued 60,000 shares of common stock at par on July 1 and earned net income of $400,000 for the year.

Journalize stock dividends.

(SO 1)

Instructions

Journalize the declaration of a 15% stock dividend on December 10, 2005, for the following independent assumptions.

1. Par value is $10, and market value is $18.
2. Par value is $5, and market value is $20.

E15-4 On October 31, the stockholders' equity section of Omar Company consists of common stock $600,000 and retained earnings $900,000. Omar is considering the following two courses of action: (1) declaring a 5% stock dividend on the 60,000, $10 par value shares outstanding, or (2) effecting a 2-for-1 stock split that will reduce par value to $5 per share. The current market price is $14 per share.

Compare effects of a stock dividend and a stock split.

(SO 1)

Instructions

Prepare a tabular summary of the effects of the alternative actions on the components of stockholders' equity, outstanding shares, and book value per share. Use the following column headings: Before Action, After Stock Dividend, and After Stock Split.

E15-5 On October 1, Chile Corporation's stockholders' equity is as follows.

Compute book value per share; indicate account balances after a stock dividend.

(SO 1, 3)

Common stock, $5 par value	$200,000
Paid-in capital in excess of par value	25,000
Retained earnings	75,000
Total stockholders' equity	$300,000

On October 1, Chile declares and distributes a 10% stock dividend when the market value of the stock is $15 per share.

Instructions

(a) Compute the book value per share (1) before the stock dividend and (2) after the stock dividend. (Round to two decimals.)

(b) Indicate the balances in the three stockholders' equity accounts after the stock dividend shares have been distributed.

E15-6 During 2005, Gruden Corporation had the following transactions and events.

Indicate the effects on stockholders' equity components.

(SO 1, 2, 3)

1. Declared a cash dividend.
2. Issued par value common stock for cash at par value.
3. Completed a 2-for-1 stock split in which $10 par value stock was changed to $5 par value stock.
4. Declared a small stock dividend when the market value was higher than par value.

5. Made a prior period adjustment for overstatement of net income.
6. Issued the shares of common stock required by the stock dividend declaration in item no. 4 above.
7. Paid the cash dividend in item no. 1 above.
8. Issued par value common stock for cash above par value.

Instructions
Indicate the effect(s) of each of the foregoing items on the subdivisions of stockholders' equity. Present your answer in tabular form with the following columns. Use (I) for increase, (D) for decrease, and (NE) for no effect. Item no. 1 is given as an example.

	Paid-in Capital		
Item	**Capital Stock**	**Additional**	**Retained Earnings**
1	NE	NE	D

Prepare correcting entries for dividends and a stock split.

(SO 1)

E15-7 Before preparing financial statements for the current year, the chief accountant for Springer Company discovered the following errors in the accounts.

1. The declaration and payment of $50,000 cash dividend was recorded as a debit to Interest Expense $50,000 and a credit to Cash $50,000.
2. A 10% stock dividend (1,000 shares) was declared on the $10 par value stock when the market value per share was $16. The only entry made was: Retained Earnings (Dr.) $10,000 and Dividend Payable (Cr.) $10,000. The shares have not been issued.
3. A 4-for-1 stock split involving the issue of 400,000 shares of $5 par value common stock for 100,000 shares of $20 par value common stock was recorded as a debit to Retained Earnings $2,000,000 and a credit to Common Stock $2,000,000.

Instructions
Prepare the correcting entries at December 31.

Prepare a retained earnings statement.

(SO 2)

E15-8 On January 1, 2005, Castle Corporation had retained earnings of $550,000. During the year, Castle had the following selected transactions.

1. Declared cash dividends $120,000.
2. Corrected overstatement of 2004 net income because of depreciation error $30,000.
3. Earned net income $350,000.
4. Declared stock dividends $80,000.

Instructions
Prepare a retained earnings statement for the year.

Prepare a stockholders' equity section.

(SO 3)

E15-9 The following accounts appear in the ledger of Tiger Inc. after the books are closed at December 31.

Common Stock, no par, $1 stated value, 400,000 shares authorized;	
300,000 shares issued	$ 300,000
Common Stock Dividends Distributable	60,000
Paid-in Capital in Excess of Stated Value—Common Stock	1,200,000
Preferred Stock, $5 par value, 8%, 40,000 shares authorized;	
30,000 shares issued	150,000
Retained Earnings	700,000
Treasury Stock (10,000 common shares)	74,000
Paid-in Capital in Excess of Par Value—Preferred Stock	344,000

Instructions
Prepare the stockholders' equity section at December 31, assuming retained earnings is restricted for plant expansion in the amount of $100,000.

Prepare an income statement and compute earnings per share.

(SO 4, 5)

E15-10 The following information is available for Sosa Corporation for the year ended December 31, 2005: Sales $800,000; Other revenues and gains $92,000; Operating expenses $110,000; Cost of goods sold $265,000; Other expenses and losses $28,000; Preferred stock dividends $30,000. The company's tax rate was 20%, and it had 50,000 shares outstanding during the entire year.

Instructions
(a) Prepare a corporate income statement.
(b) Calculate earnings per share.

E15-11 The following financial information is available for Gore Corporation.

Calculate ratios to evaluate earnings performance.

(SO 3, 5)

	2005	2004
Average common stockholders' equity	$1,200,000	$900,000
Dividends paid to common stockholders	50,000	30,000
Dividends paid to preferred stockholders	20,000	20,000
Net income	230,000	155,000
Market price of common stock	20	15

The weighted average number of shares of common stock outstanding was 80,000 for 2004 and 100,000 for 2005.

Instructions
Calculate earnings per share and return on common stockholders' equity for 2005 and 2004.

E15-12 This financial information is available for Begay Corporation.

Calculate ratios to evaluate earnings performance.

(SO 3, 5)

	2005	2004
Average common stockholders' equity	$1,800,000	$1,900,000
Dividends paid to common stockholders	90,000	70,000
Dividends paid to preferred stockholders	20,000	20,000
Net income	260,000	191,000
Market price of common stock	20	25

The weighted number of shares of common stock outstanding was 180,000 for 2004 and 150,000 for 2005.

Instructions
Calculate earnings per share and return on common stockholders' equity for 2005 and 2004.

E15-13 At December 31, 2005, Bush Corporation has 2,000 shares of $100 par value, 8%, preferred stock outstanding and 100,000 shares of $10 par value common stock issued. Bush's net income for the year is $421,000.

Compute earnings per share under different assumptions.

(SO 5)

Instructions
Compute the earnings per share of common stock under the following independent situations. (Round to two decimals.)

(a) The dividend to preferred stockholders was declared. There has been no change in the number of shares of common stock outstanding during the year.
(b) The dividend to preferred stockholders was not declared. The preferred stock is cumulative. Bush held 10,000 shares of common treasury stock throughout the year.

PROBLEMS: SET A

P15-1A On January 1, 2005, Snider Corporation had the following stockholders' equity accounts.

Prepare dividend entries and stockholders' equity section.

(SO 1, 3)

Common Stock ($10 par value, 90,000 shares issued and outstanding)	$900,000
Paid-in Capital in Excess of Par Value	200,000
Retained Earnings	540,000

During the year, the following transactions occurred.

Jan. 15 Declared a $1 cash dividend per share to stockholders of record on January 31, payable February 15.

Feb. 15 Paid the dividend declared in January.

Apr. 15 Declared a 10% stock dividend to stockholders of record on April 30, distributable May 15. On April 15, the market price of the stock was $15 per share.

May 15 Issued the shares for the stock dividend.

July 1 Announced a 2-for-1 stock split. The market price per share prior to the announcement was $17. (The new par value is $5.)

Dec. 1 Declared a $0.50 per share cash dividend to stockholders of record on December 15, payable January 10, 2006.

    31 Determined that net income for the year was $250,000.

Instructions

(a) Journalize the transactions and the closing entry for net income.

(b) Enter the beginning balances, and post the entries to the stockholders' equity accounts. (*Note*: Open additional stockholders' equity accounts as needed.)

(c) Prepare a stockholders' equity section at December 31.

(c) Total stockholders' equity $1,701,000

Journalize and post transactions, and prepare retained earnings statement and stockholders' equity section.

(SO 1, 2, 3)

P15-2A The stockholders' equity accounts of Tracey Inc., at January 1, 2005, are as follows.

Preferred Stock, $100 par, 7%	$500,000
Common Stock, $10 par	900,000
Paid-in Capital in Excess of Par Value—Preferred Stock	100,000
Paid-in Capital in Excess of Par Value—Common Stock	200,000
Retained Earnings	500,000

There were no dividends in arrears on preferred stock. During 2005, the company had the following transactions and events.

July 1 Declared a $0.50 cash dividend on common stock.

Aug. 1 Discovered a $72,000 overstatement of 2004 depreciation. Ignore income taxes.

Sept. 1 Paid the cash dividend declared on July 1.

Dec. 1 Declared a 10% stock dividend on common stock when the market value of the stock was $16 per share.

    15 Declared a 7% cash dividend on preferred stock payable January 31, 2006.

    31 Determined that net income for the year was $380,000.

Instructions

(a) Journalize the transactions and the closing entry for net income.

(b) Enter the beginning balances in the accounts and post to the stockholders' equity accounts. (*Note*: Open additional stockholders' equity accounts as needed.)

(c) Prepare a retained earnings statement for the year.

(d) Prepare a stockholders' equity section at December 31, 2005.

(c) Ending balance $728,000
(d) Total stockholders' equity $2,572,000

Prepare retained earnings statement and stockholders' equity section, and compute earnings per share.

(SO 1, 2, 3, 5)

P15-3A The ledger of Nakona Corporation at December 31, 2005, after the books have been closed, contains the following stockholders' equity accounts.

Preferred Stock (10,000 shares issued)	$1,000,000
Common Stock (400,000 shares issued)	2,000,000
Paid-in Capital in Excess of Par Value—Preferred	200,000
Paid-in Capital in Excess of Stated Value—Common	1,100,000
Common Stock Dividends Distributable	200,000
Retained Earnings	2,365,000

A review of the accounting records reveals the following.

1. No errors have been made in recording 2005 transactions or in preparing the closing entry for net income.

2. Preferred stock is 8%, $100 par value, noncumulative, and callable at $125. Since January 1, 2004, 10,000 shares have been outstanding; 20,000 shares are authorized.

3. Common stock is no-par with a stated value of $5 per share; 600,000 shares are authorized.

4. The January 1 balance in Retained Earnings was $2,450,000.

5. On October 1, 100,000 shares of common stock were sold for cash at $8 per share.

6. A cash dividend of $600,000 was declared and properly allocated to preferred and common stock on November 1. No dividends were paid to preferred stockholders in 2004.

7. On December 31, a 10% common stock dividend was declared out of retained earnings on common stock when the market price per share was $7.

8. Net income for the year was $795,000.
9. On December 31, 2005, the directors authorized disclosure of a $100,000 restriction of retained earnings for plant expansion. (Use Note A.)

Instructions
(a) Reproduce the Retained Earnings account (T-account) for the year.
(b) Prepare a retained earnings statement for the year.
(c) Prepare a stockholders' equity section at December 31.
(d) Compute the earnings per share of common stock using 325,000 as the weighted average shares outstanding for the year.
(e) Compute the allocation of the cash dividend to preferred and common stock.

(b) Retained earnings: $2,365,000
(c) Total stockholders' equity: $6,865,000

P15-4A On January 1, 2005, Casey Corporation had the following stockholders' equity accounts.

Common Stock (no-par value, 120,000 shares issued and	
outstanding)	$2,800,000
Retained Earnings	1,000,000

Prepare the stockholders' equity section, reflecting dividends and stock split.
(SO 1, 2, 3)

During the year, the following transactions occurred.

Feb. 1   Declared a $1 cash dividend per share to stockholders of record on February 15, payable March 1.
Mar. 1   Paid the dividend declared in February.
Apr. 1   Announced a 4-for-1 stock split. Prior to the split, the market price per share was $36.
July 1   Declared a 5% stock dividend to stockholders of record on July 15, distributable July 31. On July 1, the market price of the stock was $13 per share.
    31   Issued the shares for the stock dividend.
Dec. 1   Declared a $0.50 per share dividend to stockholders of record on December 15, payable January 5, 2006.
    31   Determined that net income for the year was $700,000.

Instructions
Prepare the stockholders' equity section of the balance sheet at: (a) March 31, (b) June 30, (c) September 30, and (d) December 31, 2005.

(d) Total, stockholders' equity $4,128,000

P15-5A On January 1, 2005, Andujar Inc. had the following shareholders' equity balances.

Common Stock, no-par value (1,000,000 shares issued)	$3,000,000
Common Stock Dividends Distributable	400,000
Retained Earnings	1,200,000

Prepare the stockholders' equity section, reflecting various events.
(SO 1, 3)

During 2005, the following transactions and events occurred.

1. Issued 100,000 shares of common stock as a result of a 10% stock dividend declared on December 15, 2004.
2. Issued 60,000 shares of common stock for cash at $5 per share.
3. Corrected an error that had understated the net income for 2003 by $140,000.
4. Declared and paid a cash dividend of $200,000.
5. Earned net income of $600,000.

Instructions
Prepare the stockholders' equity section of the balance sheet at December 31, 2005.

Total stockholders' equity $5,440,000

PROBLEMS: SET B

P15-1B On January 1, 2005, Argentina Corporation had the following stockholders' equity accounts.

Common Stock ($20 par value, 75,000 shares issued and	
outstanding)	$1,500,000
Paid-in Capital in Excess of Par Value	200,000
Retained Earnings	600,000

Prepare dividend entries and stockholders' equity section.
(SO 1, 3)

Peachtree

During the year, the following transactions occurred.

Feb. 1 Declared a $1 cash dividend per share to stockholders of record on February 15, payable March 1.

Mar. 1 Paid the dividend declared in February.

Apr. 1 Announced a 2-for-1 stock split. Prior to the split, the market price per share was $36.

July 1 Declared a 10% stock dividend to stockholders of record on July 15, distributable July 31. On July 1, the market price of the stock was $13 per share.

31 Issued the shares for the stock dividend.

Dec. 1 Declared a $0.50 per share dividend to stockholders of record on December 15, payable January 5, 2006.

31 Determined that net income for the year was $350,000.

Instructions

(a) Journalize the transactions and the closing entry for net income.

(b) Enter the beginning balances, and post the entries to the stockholders' equity accounts. (*Note*: Open additional stockholders' equity accounts as needed.)

(c) Total stockholders' equity $2,492,500

(c) Prepare a stockholders' equity section at December 31.

Journalize and post transactions; prepare retained earnings statement and stockholders' equity section.

(SO 1, 2, 3)

Peachtree

P15-2B The stockholders' equity accounts of Hassan Company at January 1, 2005, are as follows.

Preferred Stock, 6%, $50 par	$600,000
Common Stock, $5 par	500,000
Paid-in Capital in Excess of Par Value—Preferred Stock	200,000
Paid-in Capital in Excess of Par Value—Common Stock	300,000
Retained Earnings	800,000

There were no dividends in arrears on preferred stock. During 2005, the company had the following transactions and events.

July 1 Declared a $0.50 cash dividend on common stock.

Aug. 1 Discovered $25,000 understatement of 2004 depreciation. Ignore income taxes.

Sept. 1 Paid the cash dividend declared on July 1.

Dec. 1 Declared a 10% stock dividend on common stock when the market value of the stock was $18 per share.

15 Declared a 6% cash dividend on preferred stock payable January 15, 2006.

31 Determined that net income for the year was $385,000.

31 Recognized a $200,000 restriction of retained earnings for plant expansion.

Instructions

(a) Journalize the transactions, events, and closing entries.

(b) Enter the beginning balances in the accounts, and post to the stockholders' equity accounts. (*Note*: Open additional stockholders' equity accounts as needed.)

(c) Ending balance $894,000
(d) Total stockholders' equity $2,674,000

(c) Prepare a retained earnings statement for the year.

(d) Prepare a stockholders' equity section at December 31, 2005.

Prepare retained earnings statement and stockholders' equity section, and compute earnings per share.

(SO 1, 2, 3, 5)

P15-3B The post-closing trial balance of Chen Corporation at December 31, 2005, contains the following stockholders' equity accounts.

Preferred Stock (15,000 shares issued)	$ 750,000
Common Stock (250,000 shares issued)	2,500,000
Paid-in Capital in Excess of Par Value—Preferred	250,000
Paid-in Capital in Excess of Par Value—Common	400,000
Common Stock Dividends Distributable	250,000
Retained Earnings	902,000

A review of the accounting records reveals the following.

1. No errors have been made in recording 2005 transactions or in preparing the closing entry for net income.

2. Preferred stock is $50 par, 8%, and cumulative; 15,000 shares have been outstanding since January 1, 2004.

3. Authorized stock is 20,000 shares of preferred, 500,000 shares of common with a $10 par value.

4. The January 1 balance in Retained Earnings was $1,170,000.

5. On July 1, 20,000 shares of common stock were sold for cash at $16 per share.
6. On September 1, the company discovered an understatement error of $90,000 in comput-
   ing depreciation in 2004. The net of tax effect of $63,000 was properly debited directly to
   Retained Earnings.
7. A cash dividend of $250,000 was declared and properly allocated to preferred and common
   stock on October 1. No dividends were paid to preferred stockholders in 2004.
8. On December 31, a 10% common stock dividend was declared out of retained earnings on
   common stock when the market price per share was $18.
9. Net income for the year was $495,000.
10. On December 31, 2005, the directors authorized disclosure of a $200,000 restriction of re-
    tained earnings for plant expansion. (Use Note X.)

Instructions
(a) Reproduce the Retained Earnings account for the year.
(b) Prepare a retained earnings statement for the year.   *(b) Retained earnings:*
(c) Prepare a stockholders' equity section at December 31.   *$902,000*
(d) Compute the earnings per share of common stock using 240,000 as the weighted average   *(c) Total stockholders' equity,*
    shares outstanding for the year.   *$5,052,000*
(e) Compute the allocation of the cash dividend to preferred and common stock.

P15-4B On January 1, 2005, Stengel Corporation had the following stockholders' equity   *Prepare the stockholders'*
accounts.   *equity section, reflecting divi-*
                                                                                dends and stock split.

Common Stock (no par value, 60,000 shares issued and outstanding)	$1,400,000
Retained Earnings	500,000

(SO 1, 2, 3)

During the year, the following transactions occurred.

Feb. 1   Declared a $1 cash dividend per share to stockholders of record on February 15,
         payable March 1.
Mar. 1   Paid the dividend declared in February.
Apr. 1   Announced a 4-for-1 stock split. Prior to the split, the market price per share was $36.
July 1   Declared a 5% stock dividend to stockholders of record on July 15, distributable July 31.
         On July 1, the market price of the stock was $13 per share.
    31   Issued the shares for the stock dividend.
Dec. 1   Declared a $0.50 per share dividend to stockholders of record on December 15,
         payable January 5, 2006.
    31   Determined that net income for the year was $350,000.

Instructions
Prepare the stockholders' equity section of the balance sheet at: (a) March 31, (b) June 30, (c)   *(d) Total stockholders' equity*
September 30, and (d) December 31, 2005.   *$2,064,000*

P15-5B On January 1, 2005, Cedeno Inc. had the following stockholders' equity account   *Prepare the stockholders'*
balances.   *equity section, reflecting*
                                                                                various events.

Common Stock, no-par value (500,000 shares issued)	$1,500,000
Common Stock Dividends Distributable	200,000
Retained Earnings	600,000

(SO 1, 3)

During 2005, the following transactions and events occurred.

1. Issued 50,000 shares of common stock as a result of a 10% stock dividend declared on
   December 15, 2004.
2. Issued 30,000 shares of common stock for cash at $5 per share.
3. Corrected an error that had understated the net income for 2003 by $70,000.
4. Declared and paid a cash dividend of $100,000.
5. Earned net income of $300,000.

Instructions
Prepare the stockholders' equity section of the balance sheet at December 31, 2005.   *Total stockholders' equity*
                                                                                $2,720,000

BROADENING YOUR PERSPECTIVE

Financial Reporting and Analysis

■ FINANCIAL REPORTING PROBLEM: PepsiCo

BYP15-1 The financial statements of **PepsiCo** are presented in Appendix A.

Instructions
Refer to PepsiCo's financial statements and answer the following questions.

What amount did PepsiCo declare in dividends on common stock in the year ended December 28, 2002? What is the company's dividend policy? (*Hint:* Read the section entitled "Common Stock Information" in Management's Discussion and Analysis on page A-45.)

■ COMPARATIVE ANALYSIS PROBLEM: PepsiCo vs. Coca-Cola

BYP15-2 **PepsiCo**'s financial statements are presented in Appendix A. **Coca-Cola**'s financial statements are presented in Appendix B.

Instructions
(a) Compute earnings per share and return on common stockholders' equity for both companies for the year ending in January 2002. Assume PepsiCo's weighted average shares were 1,753 million and Coca-Cola's weighted average shares were 2,478 million. Can these measures be used to compare the profitability of the two companies? Why or why not?
(b) What was the total amount of dividends paid by each company in 2002?

■ INTERPRETING FINANCIAL STATEMENTS: A Global Focus

BYP15-3 **Nortel Networks Corporation** is a global leader in telephony, data, wireless, and wireline solutions for the Internet. In July 1999, Nortel announced a stock dividend and a 2-for-1 stock split. In January, and again in May 2000, Nortel announced two more 2-for-1 stock splits. Nortel's common shares now number 3 billion.

From 1999 to 2000, Nortel's revenue grew by 40%. Its share price ranged from $20 to $123. Interestingly, its earnings (loss) per share was only ($0.95) in fiscal 2000 and ($0.15) in fiscal 1999.

Instructions
(a) Explain the different effects that a stock dividend and stock split would have on Nortel's financial position and number of shares.
(b) Why do you think Nortel has split its common shares so often over the past few years?
(c) Nortel reported a loss per share in both 1999 and 2000. Yet its market price per share was positive and increasing. Can you explain why investors might be willing to pay an increasing price for a Nortel share despite its poor operating performance?

■ EXPLORING THE WEB

BYP15-4 Use the stockholders' equity section of an annual report and identify the major components.

Address: www.reportgallery.com, or go to www.wiley.com/college/weygandt

Steps

1. From Report Gallery Homepage, choose Library of Annual Reports.
2. Select a particular company.
3. Choose Annual Report.
4. Follow instructions below.

Instructions
Answer the following questions.

(a) What is the company's name?
(b) What classes of capital stock has the company issued?

(c) For each class of stock:
  (1) How many shares are authorized, issued, and/or outstanding?
  (2) What is the par value?
(d) What are the company's retained earnings?
(e) Has the company acquired treasury stock? How many shares?

Critical Thinking

■ **GROUP DECISION CASE**

BYP15-5 The stockholders' equity accounts of Rodriguez, Inc., at January 1, 2005, are as follows.

Preferred Stock, no par, 4,000 shares issued	$400,000
Common Stock, no par, 180,000 shares issued	900,000
Retained Earnings	500,000

During 2005, the company had the following transactions and events.

July 1 Declared a $0.50 cash dividend on common stock.
Aug. 1 Discovered a $72,000 overstatement of 2004 depreciation expense. (Ignore income taxes.)
Sept. 1 Paid the cash dividend declared on July 1.
Dec. 1 Declared a 10% stock dividend on common stock when the market value of the stock was $12 per share.
  15 Declared a $9 per share cash dividend on preferred stock, payable January 31, 2006.
  31 Determined that net income for the year was $350,000.

Instructions
With the class divided into groups, answer the following questions.

(a) Prepare a retained earnings statement for the year. There are no preferred dividends in arrears.
(b) Discuss why the overstatement of 2004 depreciation expense is not treated as an adjustment of the current year's income.
(c) Discuss the reasons why a company might decide to issue a stock dividend rather than a cash dividend.

■ **COMMUNICATION ACTIVITY**

BYP15-6 In the past year, Battier Corporation declared a 10% stock dividend, and Divac, Inc. announced a 2-for-1 stock split. Your parents own 100 shares of each company's $50 par value common stock. During a recent phone call, your parents ask you, as an accounting student, to explain the differences between the two events.

Instructions
Write a letter to your parents that explains the effects of the two events to them as stockholders and the effects of each event on the financial statements of each corporation.

■ **ETHICS CASE**

BYP15-7 Doleac Corporation has paid 60 consecutive quarterly cash dividends (15 years). The last 6 months, however, have been a cash drain on the company, as profit margins have been greatly narrowed by increasing competition. With a cash balance sufficient to meet only day-to-day operating needs, the president, Tom Duncan, has decided that a stock dividend instead of a cash dividend should be declared. He tells Doleac's financial vice president, Janice Rahn, to issue a press release stating that the company is extending its consecutive dividend record with the issuance of a 5% stock dividend. "Write the press release convincing the stockholders that the stock dividend is just as good as a cash dividend," he orders. "Just watch our stock rise when we announce the stock dividend; it must be a good thing if that happens."

Instructions
(a) Who are the stakeholders in this situation?
(b) Is there anything unethical about Duncan's intentions or actions?

(c) What is the effect of a stock dividend on a corporation's stockholders' equity accounts? Which would you rather receive as a stockholder—a cash dividend or a stock dividend? Why?

Answers to Self-Study Questions
1. a   **2.** c   **3.** c   **4.** d   **5.** d   **6.** b   **7.** d   **8.** b   **9.** c   **10.** b

Answers to PepsiCo Review It Question 4, p. 604
Dividends per share of common stock declared by **PepsiCo** were $0.515 in 1998; $0.535 in 1999; $0.555 in 2000; $0.575 in 2001; and $0.595 in 2002. During this same period net income increased in a similar fashion.

Long-Term Liabilities

CONCEPTS FOR REVIEW

Before studying this chapter, you should know or, if necessary, review:

- What is a current liability? What is a long-term liability?
(Ch. 4, p. 154 and Ch. 4, p. 155)

- How to record adjusting entries for interest expense and interest payable.
(Ch. 3, pp. 101–102)

- How to record entries for the issuance of notes payable and related interest expense.
(Ch. 11, p. 448)

THE NAVIGATOR

UK Builds with Bonds

Every year, hundreds of colleges construct new buildings. Where do most schools get the money for these expensive projects? From long-term bonds, which are obligations in which the issuer of the bond promises to repay the loan amount plus interest on or before a specified date.

The **University of Kentucky** (UK) issued "revenue" bonds to build buildings on the 23,000-student Lexington campus, and on 14 community college campuses throughout the state. These bonds pledged the school's revenues as collateral to guarantee payment of the bonds.

At one time the outstanding debt on the Lexington campus buildings was $137 million. The total debt on the community college buildings equaled $121 million. The bonds generally have maturities ranging from 10 to 20 years.

Additional "guarantees" for bond purchasers are the ratings given the bonds by professional rating agencies. "Our bonds are rated AA– by Standard & Poor's Corp.," says Henry Clay Owen, UK's treasurer. "That's well above investment grade," he says. "We always have a very good market for our bonds. People in Kentucky identify very closely with the university. Even though the bonds are rated AA–, they trade at AAA [the top bond rating] because they're so easy to sell."

One advantage for investors: The bonds' interest revenue is exempt from federal income tax and from state tax for in-state investors. So, an issue offering 6% is the equivalent of 10% to individuals in the top tax bracket. "I would feel very comfortable buying UK bonds because it's inconceivable to me that there would ever be a default," says Owen.

After studying this chapter, you should be able to:

1. Explain why bonds are issued.
2. Prepare the entries for the issuance of bonds and interest expense.
3. Describe the entries when bonds are redeemed or converted.
4. Describe the accounting for long-term notes payable.
5. Contrast the accounting for operating and capital leases.
6. Identify the methods for the presentation and analysis of long-term liabilities.

As you can see from the Feature Story, the **University of Kentucky** has chosen to issue long-term bonds to fund its building projects. The UK bonds are classified as **long-term liabilities** because they are obligations that are expected to be paid after one year. In this chapter we will explain the accounting for the major types of long-term liabilities reported on the balance sheet. These liabilities may be bonds, long-term notes, or lease obligations.

The content and organization of Chapter 16 are as follows.

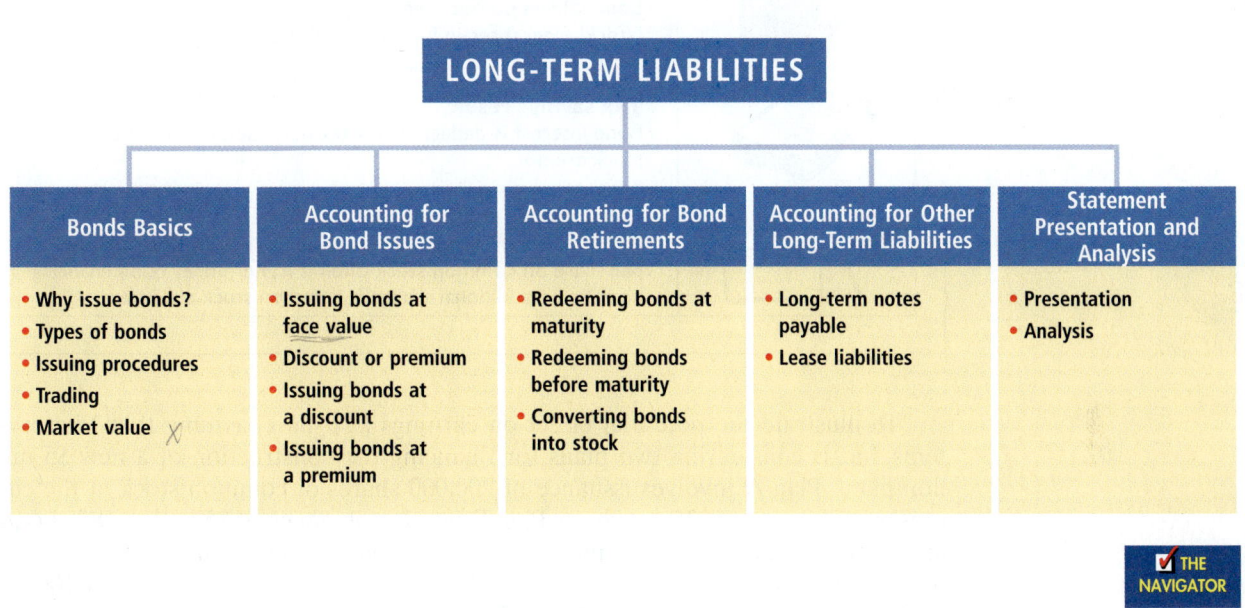

LONG-TERM LIABILITIES

Bonds Basics	Accounting for Bond Issues	Accounting for Bond Retirements	Accounting for Other Long-Term Liabilities	Statement Presentation and Analysis
• Why issue bonds? • Types of bonds • Issuing procedures • Trading • Market value	• Issuing bonds at face value • Discount or premium • Issuing bonds at a discount • Issuing bonds at a premium	• Redeeming bonds at maturity • Redeeming bonds before maturity • Converting bonds into stock	• Long-term notes payable • Lease liabilities	• Presentation • Analysis

☑ THE NAVIGATOR

Bond Basics

Bonds are a form of interest-bearing notes payable. They are issued by corporations, universities, and governmental agencies. Bonds, like common stock, are sold in small denominations (usually a thousand dollars or thousand-dollar multiples). As a result, bonds attract many investors.

Why Issue Bonds?

A corporation may use long-term financing other than bonds, such as notes payable and leasing. These other forms of financing involve finding an individual, a company, or a financial institution willing to supply the needed funds. Notes payable and leasing are therefore seldom sufficient to furnish the funds needed for plant expansion and major projects like new buildings. To obtain **large amounts of long-term capital**, corporate management usually must decide whether to issue common stock (equity financing) or bonds.

STUDY OBJECTIVE 1

Explain why bonds are issued.

From the standpoint of the corporation seeking long-term financing, bonds offer the following advantages over common stock:

Illustration 16-1
Advantages of bond financing over common stock

Bond Financing	Advantages
	1. **Stockholder control is not affected.** Bondholders do not have voting rights, so current owners (stockholders) retain full control of the company.
	2. **Tax savings result.** Bond interest is deductible for tax purposes; dividends on stock are not.
	3. **Earnings per share may be higher.** Although bond interest expense reduces net income, earnings per share on common stock often is higher under bond financing because no additional shares of common stock are issued.

To illustrate the potential effect on earnings per share, assume that Microsystems, Inc. is considering two plans for financing the construction of a new $5 million plant. Plan A involves issuance of 200,000 shares of common stock at the current market price of $25 per share. Plan B involves issuance of $5 million, 8% bonds at face value. Income before interest and taxes on the new plant will be $1.5 million. Income taxes are expected to be 30%. Microsystems currently has 100,000 shares of common stock outstanding. The alternative effects on earnings per share are shown in Illustration 16-2.

Illustration 16-2
Effects on earnings per share—stocks vs. bonds

	Plan A Issue Stock	Plan B Issue Bonds
Income before interest and taxes	$1,500,000	$1,500,000
Interest (8% × $5,000,000)	—	400,000
Income before income taxes	1,500,000	1,100,000
Income tax expense (30%)	450,000	330,000
Net income	$1,050,000	$ 770,000
Outstanding shares	300,000	100,000
Earnings per share	**$3.50**	**$7.70**

Note that net income is $280,000 less ($1,050,000 − $770,000) with long-term debt financing (bonds). However, earnings per share is higher because there are 200,000 fewer shares of common stock outstanding.

The major disadvantages resulting from the use of bonds are that interest must be paid on a periodic basis and the principal (face value) of the bonds must be paid at maturity. A company with fluctuating earnings and a relatively weak cash position may have great difficulty making interest payments when earnings are low.

Types of Bonds

Bonds may have many different features. Types of bonds commonly issued are described on the next page.

[handwritten: outstanding?]

Although bonds are generally secured by solid, substantial assets like land, buildings, and equipment, exceptions occur. **Trans World Airlines Inc.** (TWA) at one time decided to issue $300 million of high-yielding 5-year bonds. TWA's bonds would be secured by a grab bag of assets, including some durable spare parts, but also a lot of disposable items that TWA had in its warehouses, such as light bulbs and gaskets. Some called the planned TWA bonds "light-bulb bonds." As one financial expert noted, "You've got to admit that some security is better than none." Another noted, "They're digging pretty far down in the barrel."

[handwritten: secured bond ex: Mortgag bond, Sinking fund bond. Unsecured, A.K.A Debenture bond]

Secured and Unsecured Bonds *[handwritten: 1]*

Secured bonds have specific assets of the issuer pledged as collateral for the bonds. A bond secured by real estate, for example, is called a **mortgage bond**. A bond secured by specific assets set aside to retire the bonds is called a **sinking fund bond**. **Unsecured bonds** are issued against the general credit of the borrower. These bonds, called **debenture bonds**, are used extensively by large corporations with good credit ratings. For example, in a recent annual report, **DuPont** reported over $2 billion of debenture bonds outstanding.

[handwritten: Term - mature specific. Serial bond installments]

Term and Serial Bonds *[handwritten: 2]*

Bonds that mature (are due for payment) at a single specified future date are called **term bonds**. In contrast, bonds that mature in installments are called **serial bonds**. For example, **Caterpillar Inc.** debentures due in 2007 are term bonds. Caterpillar's debentures due between 2004 and 2007 are serial bonds (maturing annually).

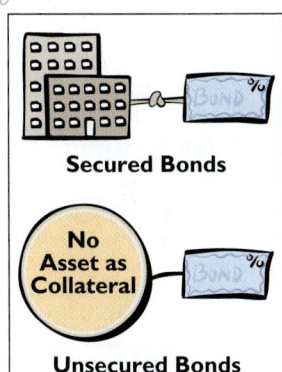

Secured Bonds

No Asset as Collateral

Unsecured Bonds

[handwritten: Reg bond - in name. Bearer (or coupon) bd - send coupon xfer easily]

Registered and Bearer Bonds *[handwritten: 3]*

Bonds issued in the name of the owner are called **registered bonds**. Interest payments on registered bonds are made by check to bondholders of record. Bonds not registered are called **bearer** (or **coupon**) **bonds**. Holders of bearer bonds must send in coupons to receive interest payments. Coupon bonds may be transferred directly to another party. In contrast, the transfer of registered bonds requires cancellation of the bonds by the corporation and the issuance of new bonds. Most bonds issued today are registered bonds.

[handwritten: Cb - to common stock. Callable - prior to maturity]

Convertible and Callable Bonds *[handwritten: 4]*

Bonds that can be converted into common stock at the bondholder's option are called **convertible bonds**. The conversion feature generally is attractive to bond buyers. Bonds subject to retirement at a stated dollar amount prior to maturity at the option of the issuer are known as **callable bonds**. A call feature is included in nearly all corporate bond issues.

[handwritten: Cb - to common stock. cal]

Issuing Procedures

State laws grant corporations the power to issue bonds. Within the corporation, approval by both the board of directors and stockholders is usually required. **In authorizing the bond issue, the board of directors must stipulate the number of bonds to be authorized, total face value, and contractual interest rate.** The total bond

Convertible Bonds

"Hey Harv, Call in those bonds"

Callable Bonds

authorization often exceeds the number of bonds originally issued. This gives the corporation the flexibility it needs to meet future cash requirements.

The **face value** is the amount of principal the issuer must pay at the maturity date. The **contractual interest rate**, often referred to as the **stated rate**, is the rate used to determine the amount of cash interest the borrower pays and the investor receives. Usually the contractual rate is stated as an annual rate. Interest is generally paid semiannually.

The terms of the bond issue are set forth in a legal document called a **bond indenture**. In addition to the terms, the indenture summarizes the rights of the bondholders and their trustees, as well as the obligations of the issuing company. The **trustee** (usually a financial institution) keeps records of each bondholder, maintains custody of unissued bonds, and holds conditional title to pledged property.

After the bond indenture is prepared, **bond certificates** are printed. The indenture and the certificate are separate documents. As shown in Illustration 16-3, a bond certificate provides information such as the following: name of the issuer, face value, contractual interest rate, and maturity date. Bonds are generally sold through an investment company that specializes in selling securities.

Illustration 16-3
Bond certificate

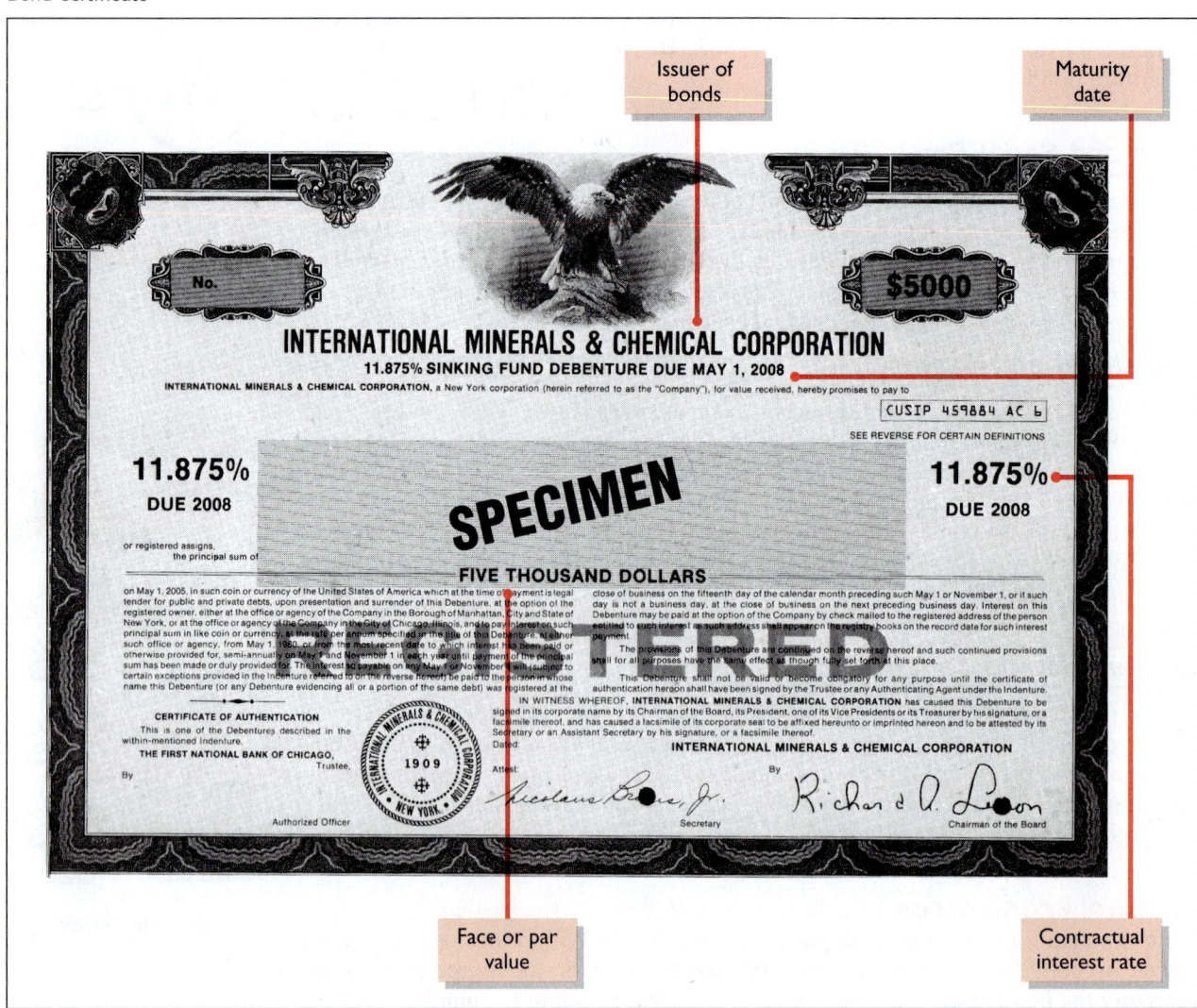

Bond Trading

Corporate bonds, like capital stock, are traded on national securities exchanges. Thus, bondholders have the opportunity to convert their holdings into cash at any time by selling the bonds at the current market price.

Bond prices are quoted as a percentage of the face value of the bond, which is usually $1,000. A $1,000 bond with a quoted price of 97 means that the selling price of the bond is 97% of face value, or $970. Bond prices and trading activity are published daily in newspapers and the financial press, as illustrated by the following.

Bonds	Maturity	Close	Yield	Est. Volume (000)
General Motors 7.2	Jan. 15, 2011	101.110	7.007	62,427

Illustration 16-4
Market information for bonds

This bond listing indicates that **General Motors** has outstanding 7.2%, $1,000 bonds that mature in 2011. They currently yield a 7.007% return. On this day, $62,427,000 of these bonds were traded. At the close of trading, the price was 101.110% of face value, or $1,011.10.

Transactions between a bondholder and other investors **are not journalized by the issuing corporation**. If Tom Smith sells bonds to Faith Jones, the issuing corporation does not journalize the transaction. (The issuer or its trustee does keep records of the names of bondholders in the case of registered bonds.) A corporation makes journal entries **only when it issues or buys back bonds**, and when bondholders convert bonds into common stock.

Determining the Market Value of Bonds

If you were an investor wanting to purchase a bond, how would you determine how much to pay? To be more specific, assume that Coronet, Inc. issues a zero-interest bond (pays no interest) with a face value of $1,000,000 due in 20 years. For this bond, the only cash you receive is a million dollars at the end of 20 years. Would you pay a million dollars for this bond? We hope not! A million dollars received 20 years from now is not the same as a million dollars received today.

The reason you should not pay a million dollars for Coronet's bond relates to what is called the **time value of money**. If you had a million dollars today, you would invest it. From that investment, you would earn interest such that at the end of 20 years, you would have much more than a million dollars. If someone is going to pay you a million dollars 20 years from now, you would want to find its equivalent today. In other words, you would want to determine how much must be invested today at current interest rates to have a million dollars in 20 years. That amount, that must be invested today at a given rate of interest over a specified time, is called **present value**.

The present value of a bond is the value at which it should sell in the marketplace. Market value therefore is a function of the three factors that determine present value: (1) the dollar amounts to be received, (2) the length of time until the amounts are received, and (3) the market rate of interest. The **market interest rate** is the rate investors demand for loaning funds. The process of finding the present value for bonds is discussed in Appendix 16A. Additional material for time value of money computations is also provided in Appendix C near the end of the book.

Same dollars at different times are not equal.

Accounting for Bond Issues

STUDY OBJECTIVE 2

Prepare the entries for the issuance of bonds and interest expense.

Bonds may be issued at face value, below face value (at a discount), or above face value (at a premium).

Issuing Bonds at Face Value

To illustrate the accounting for bonds, assume that on January 1, 2005, Devor Corporation issues 1,000, 10-year, 9%, $1,000 bonds at 100 (100% of face value). The entry to record the sale is:

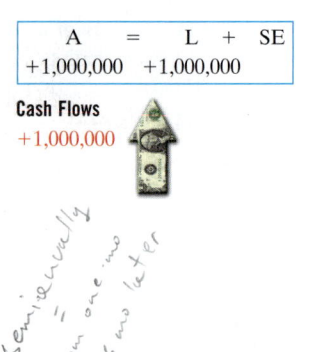

A	=	L	+	SE
+1,000,000		+1,000,000		

Cash Flows
+1,000,000

Jan. 1	Cash	1,000,000	
	Bonds Payable		1,000,000
	(To record sale of bonds at face value)		

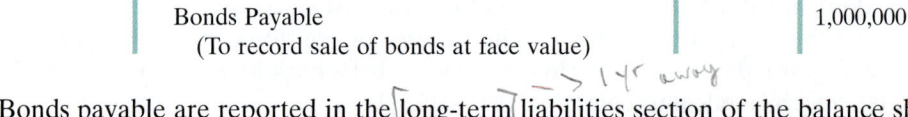

Bonds payable are reported in the long-term liabilities section of the balance sheet because the maturity date is more than one year away.

Over the term (life) of the bonds, entries are required for bond interest. Interest on bonds payable is computed in the same manner as interest on notes payable, as explained in Chapter 11 (page 448). Assume that interest is payable semiannually on January 1 and July 1 on the bonds described above. In that case, interest of $45,000 ($1,000,000 × 9% × 6/12) must be paid on July 1, 2005. The entry for the payment, assuming no previous accrual of interest, is:

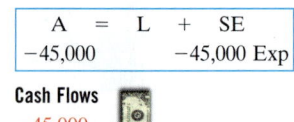

A	=	L	+	SE
−45,000				−45,000 Exp

Cash Flows
−45,000

July 1	Bond Interest Expense	45,000	
	Cash		45,000
	(To record payment of bond interest)		

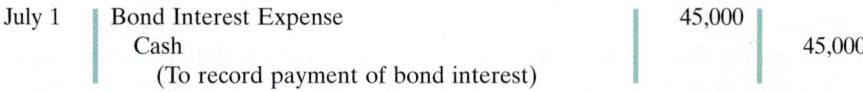

At December 31, an adjusting entry is required to recognize the $45,000 of interest expense incurred since July 1. The entry is:

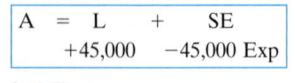

A	=	L	+	SE
		+45,000		−45,000 Exp

Cash Flows
no effect

Dec. 31	Bond Interest Expense	45,000	
	Bond Interest Payable		45,000
	(To accrue bond interest)		

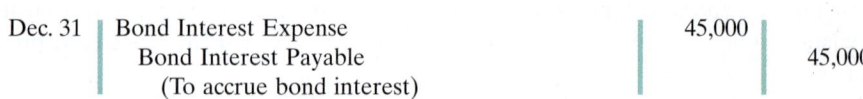

Bond interest payable is classified as a current liability, because it is scheduled for payment within the next year. When the interest is paid on January 1, 2006, Bond Interest Payable is debited and Cash is credited for $45,000.

Discount or Premium on Bonds

In the previous illustrations, we assumed that the contractual (stated) interest rate paid on bonds and the market (effective) interest rate were the same. The contractual interest rate is the rate applied to the face (par) value to arrive at the interest paid in a year. The **market interest rate** is the rate investors demand for loaning funds to the corporation. When the contractual interest rate and the market interest rate are the same, bonds sell at face value, as shown above.

However, market interest rates change daily. They are influenced by the type of bond issued, the state of the economy, current industry conditions, and the company's performance. The contractual and market interest rates often differ. As a result, bonds sell below or above face value.

To illustrate, suppose that investors have one of two options: (1) purchase bonds that have a contractual interest rate of 10%, or (2) purchase bonds that have a contractual interest rate of 8%. If the bonds are of equal risk, investors will select the 10% investment. To make the investments equal, investors will demand a rate of interest higher than the 8% contractual interest rate. But investors cannot change the contractual interest rate. What they can do is to pay less than the face value for the bonds. By paying less for the bonds, investors can obtain the market rate of interest. In these cases, **bonds sell at a discount**.

On the other hand, the market interest rate may be **lower** than the contractual interest rate. In that case investors will have to pay more than face value for the bonds. That is, if the market interest rate is 8% and the contractual interest rate is 9%, the issuer will require more funds from the investor. In these cases, **bonds sell at a premium**. These relationships are shown graphically in Illustration 16-5.

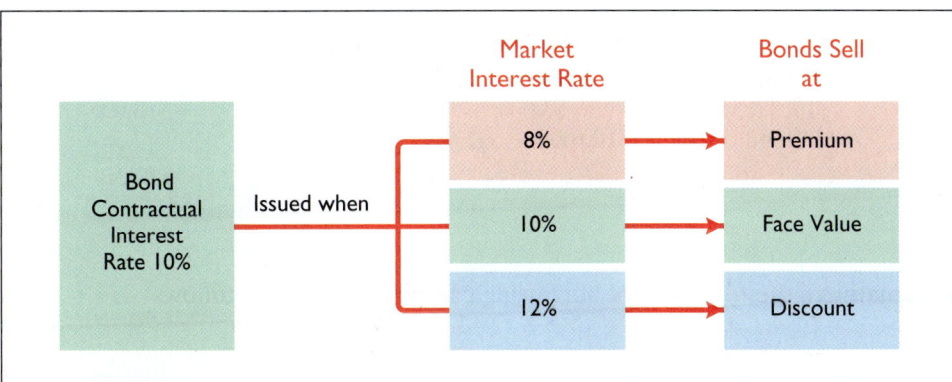

Illustration 16-5
Interest rates and bond prices

Issuing bonds at an amount different from face value is quite common. By the time a company prints the bond certificates and markets the bonds, it will be a coincidence if the market rate and the contractual rate are the same. Thus, the sale of bonds at a discount does not mean that the issuer's financial strength is suspect. Nor does the sale of bonds at a premium indicate exceptional financial strength.

Issuing Bonds at a Discount

To illustrate issuance of bonds at a discount, assume that on January 1, 2005, Candlestick, Inc. sells $100,000, 5-year, 10% bonds for $92,639 (92.639% of face value). Interest is payable on July 1 and January 1. The entry to record the issuance is:

Jan. 1	Cash	92,639	
	Discount on Bonds Payable	7,361	
	Bonds Payable		100,000
	(To record sale of bonds at a discount)		

HELPFUL HINT

Discount on Bonds Payable

Increase	Decrease
Debit	Credit
↓	
Normal	
Balance	

A	=	L	+	SE
+92,639		−7,361		
		+100,000		

Cash Flows
+92,639

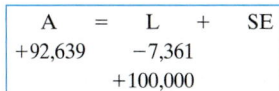

Although Discount on Bonds Payable has a debit balance, **it is not an asset**. Rather, it is a **contra account**. This account is **deducted from bonds payable** on the balance sheet, as illustrated on the next page.

Illustration 16-6
Statement presentation of discount on bonds payable

CANDLESTICK, INC.		
Balance Sheet (partial)		
Long-term liabilities		
Bonds payable	$100,000	
Less: Discount on bonds payable	7,361	$92,639

The $92,639 represents the [carrying (or book) value] of the bonds. On the date of issue this amount equals the market price of the bonds.

The issuance of bonds below face value, at a discount, causes the total cost of borrowing to differ from the bond interest paid. That is, the issuing corporation must pay not only the contractual interest rate over the term of the bonds, but also the face value (rather than the issuance price) at maturity. Therefore, the difference between the issuance price and face value of the bonds—the discount—is an **additional cost of borrowing. This additional cost should be recorded as bond interest expense over the life of the bonds.** The procedures for recording this additional cost are shown in Appendixes 16B and 16C.

The total cost of borrowing $92,639 for Candlestick, Inc. is $57,361, computed as follows.

Illustration 16-7
Total cost of borrowing—bonds issued at a discount

Bonds Issued at a Discount	
Semiannual interest payments	
($100,000 × 10% × ½ = $5,000; $5,000 × 10)	$50,000
Add: Bond discount ($100,000 − $92,639)	7,361
Total cost of borrowing	**$57,361**

Alternatively, the total cost of borrowing can be computed as follows.

Illustration 16-8
Alternative computation of total cost of borrowing—bonds issued at a discount

Face value & carrying

Bonds Issued at a Discount	
Principal at maturity	$100,000
Semiannual interest payments ($5,000 × 10)	50,000
Cash to be paid to bondholders	150,000
Cash received from bondholders	⟨ 92,639 ⟩
Total cost of borrowing	**$ 57,361**

Issuing Bonds at a Premium

To illustrate the issuance of bonds at a premium, we now assume the Candlestick, Inc. bonds described above are sold for $108,111 (108.111% of face value) rather than for $92,639.

The entry to record the sale is:

A	=	L	+	SE
+108,111		+100,000		
		+8,111		

Cash Flows
+108,111

Jan. 1	Cash		108,111	
	Bonds Payable			100,000
	Premium on Bonds Payable			8,111
	(To record sale of bonds at a premium)			

Premium on bonds payable is **added to bonds payable** on the balance sheet, as shown on the following page.

Illustration 16-9
Statement presentation of
bond premium

CANDLESTICK, INC.
Balance Sheet (partial)

Long-term liabilities		
Bonds payable	$100,000	
Add: Premium on bonds payable	**8,111**	$108,111

The sale of bonds above face value causes the total cost of borrowing to be **less than the bond interest paid**. The bond premium is considered to be **a reduction in the cost of borrowing**. It should be credited to Bond Interest Expense over the life of the bonds. The procedures for recording this reduction in the cost of borrowing are shown in Appendixes 16B and 16C. The total cost of borrowing $108,111 for Candlestick, Inc. is computed as follows.

HELPFUL HINT

Premium on Bonds Payable

Decrease	Increase
Debit	Credit
	↓
	Normal
	Balance

Illustration 16-10
Total cost of borrowing—
bonds issued at a premium

Bonds Issued at a Premium

Semiannual interest payments	
($100,000 × 10% × ½ = $5,000; $5,000 × 10)	$50,000
Less: Bond premium ($108,111 − $100,000)	8,111
Total cost of borrowing	**$41,889**

Alternatively, the cost of borrowing can be computed as follows.

Illustration 16-11
Alternative computation of
total cost of borrowing—
bonds issued at a premium

Bonds Issued at a Premium

Principal at maturity	$100,000
Semiannual interest payments ($5,000 × 10)	50,000
Cash to be paid to bondholders	150,000
Cash received from bondholders	< 108,111 >
Total cost of borrowing	**$ 41,889**

BEFORE YOU GO ON...

Review It
1. What entry is made to record the issuance of bonds payable of $1 million at 100? At 96? At 102?
2. Why do bonds sell at a discount? At a premium? At face value?

Related exercise material: *BE16-2, BE16-3, BE16-4, E16-2, E16-3, and E16-4.*

Accounting for Bond Retirements

Bonds may be retired either when they are redeemed by the issuing corporation or when they are converted into common stock by bondholders. The appropriate entries for these transactions are explained in the following sections.

STUDY OBJECTIVE 3

Describe the entries when
bonds are redeemed or
converted.

Redeeming Bonds at Maturity
Regardless of the issue price of bonds, the book value of the bonds at maturity will equal their face value. Assuming that the interest for the last interest period is paid

and recorded separately, the entry to record the redemption of the Candlestick bonds at maturity is:

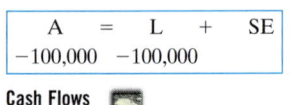

A	=	L	+	SE
−100,000		−100,000		

Cash Flows
−100,000

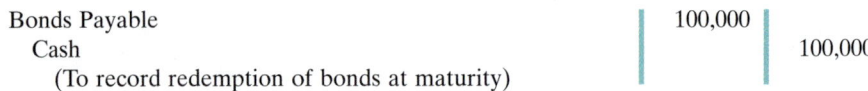

Bonds Payable	100,000	
Cash		100,000
(To record redemption of bonds at maturity)		

Redeeming Bonds before Maturity

Bonds may be redeemed before maturity. A company may decide to retire bonds before maturity to reduce interest cost and remove debt from its balance sheet. A company should retire debt early only if it has sufficient cash resources.

When bonds are retired before maturity, it is necessary to: (1) Eliminate the carrying value of the bonds at the redemption date. (2) Record the cash paid. (3) Recognize the gain or loss on redemption. The carrying value of the bonds is the face value of the bonds less unamortized bond discount or plus unamortized bond premium at the redemption date.

To illustrate, assume that Candlestick, Inc. has sold its bonds at a premium. At the end of the eighth period Candlestick retires these bonds at 103 after paying the semiannual interest. Assume also that the carrying value of the bonds at the redemption date is $101,623. The entry to record the redemption at the end of the eighth interest period (January 1, 2009) is:

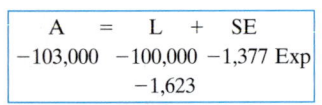

A	=	L	+	SE
−103,000		−100,000		−1,377 Exp
		−1,623		

Cash Flows
−103,000

Jan. 1	Bonds Payable	100,000	
	Premium on Bonds Payable	1,623	
	Loss on Bond Redemption	1,377	
	Cash		103,000
	(To record redemption of bonds at 103)		

Note that the loss of $1,377 is the difference between the cash paid of $103,000 and the carrying value of the bonds of $101,623.

Converting Bonds into Common Stock

Convertible bonds have features that are attractive both to bondholders and to the issuer. The conversion often gives bondholders an opportunity to benefit if the market price of the common stock increases substantially. Until conversion, though, the bondholder receives interest on the bond. For the issuer, the bonds sell at a higher price and pay a lower rate of interest than comparable debt securities without the conversion option. Many corporations, such as **USAir**, **USX Corp.**, and **Daimler-Chrysler Corporation**, have convertible bonds outstanding.

When bonds are converted into common stock and the conversion is recorded, the current market prices of the bonds and the stock are ignored. Instead, the **carrying value** of the bonds is transferred to paid-in capital accounts. **No gain or loss is recognized.** To illustrate, assume that on July 1 Saunders Associates converts $100,000 bonds sold at face value into 2,000 shares of $10 par value common stock. Both the bonds and the common stock have a market value of $130,000. The entry to record the conversion is:

A	=	L	+	SE
		−100,000		+20,000 CS
				+80,000 CS

Cash Flows
no effect

July 1	Bonds Payable	100,000	
	Common Stock		20,000
	Paid-in Capital in Excess of Par Value		80,000
	(To record bond conversion)		

Note that the current market price of the bonds and stock ($130,000) is not considered in making the entry. This method of recording the bond conversion is often referred to as the **carrying (or book) value method**.

BEFORE YOU GO ON...

Review It

1. Explain the accounting for redemption of bonds at maturity, before maturity by payment in cash, and by conversion into common stock.

2. Did **PepsiCo** redeem any of its debt during the fiscal year ended December 28, 2002? (*Hint:* To find information related to this question, examine PepsiCo's statement of cash flows. The answer to this question is provided on page 673.)

Do It

R & B Inc. issued $500,000, 10-year bonds at a premium. Prior to maturity, when the carrying value of the bonds is $508,000, the company retires the bonds at 102. Prepare the entry to record the redemption of the bonds.

ACTION PLAN
- Determine and eliminate the carrying value of the bonds.
- Record the cash paid.
- Compute and record the gain or loss (which is the difference between the first two items).

SOLUTION   There is a loss on redemption: The cash paid, $510,000 ($500,000 × 102%), is greater than the carrying value of $508,000. The entry is:

Bonds Payable	500,000	
Premium on Bonds Payable	8,000	
Loss on Bond Redemption	2,000	
Cash		510,000
(To record redemption of bonds at 102)		

Related exercise material: *BE16-5, E16-4, E16-5, and E16-6.*

✓ **THE NAVIGATOR**

exceed (plural)
exceeds (singular)

Accounting for Other Long-Term Liabilities

Other common types of long-term obligations are notes payable and lease liabilities. The accounting for these liabilities is explained in the following sections.

Long-Term Notes Payable

The use of notes payable in long-term debt financing is quite common. Long-term notes payable are similar to short-term interest-bearing notes payable except that the terms of the notes exceed one year. In periods of unstable interest rates, the interest rate on long-term notes may be tied to changes in the market rate. Examples are the 8.03% adjustable-rate notes issued by **General Motors** and the floating-rate notes issued by **American Express Company**.

A long-term note may be secured by a **mortgage** that pledges title to specific assets as security for a loan. **Mortgage notes payable** are widely used by individuals to purchase homes and by many small and some large companies to acquire plant assets. Approximately 18 percent of **McDonald's** long-term debt relates to mortgage notes on land, buildings, and improvements. Mortgage loan terms may stipulate either a fixed or an adjustable interest rate. Typically, the terms require the borrower to make installment payments over the term of the loan. Each payment consists of (1) interest on the unpaid balance of the loan and (2) a reduction of loan principal.

STUDY OBJECTIVE 4

Describe the accounting for long-term notes payable.

The interest decreases each period, while the portion applied to the loan principal increases.

Mortgage notes payable are recorded initially at face value. Subsequent entries are required for each installment payment. To illustrate, assume that Porter Technology Inc. issues a $500,000, 12%, 20-year mortgage note on December 31, 2005, to obtain needed financing for a new research laboratory. The terms provide for semiannual installment payments of $33,231 (not including real estate taxes and insurance). The installment payment schedule for the first 2 years is as follows.

Illustration 16-12
Mortgage installment payment schedule

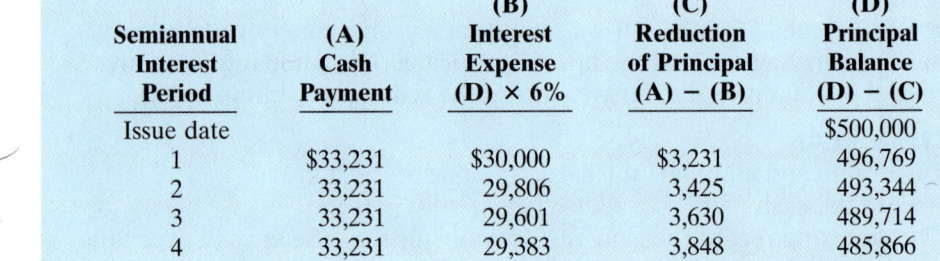

Semiannual Interest Period	(A) Cash Payment	(B) Interest Expense (D) × 6%	(C) Reduction of Principal (A) − (B)	(D) Principal Balance (D) − (C)
Issue date				$500,000
1	$33,231	$30,000	$3,231	496,769
2	33,231	29,806	3,425	493,344
3	33,231	29,601	3,630	489,714
4	33,231	29,383	3,848	485,866

The entries to record the mortgage loan and first installment payment are as follows.

A	=	L	+	SE
+500,000		+500,000		

Cash Flows
+500,000

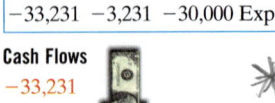

A	=	L	+	SE
−33,231		−3,231		−30,000 Exp

Cash Flows
−33,231

Dec. 31	Cash	500,000	
	Mortgage Notes Payable		500,000
	(To record mortgage loan)		
June 30	Interest Expense	30,000	
	Mortgage Notes Payable	3,231	
	Cash		33,231
	(To record semiannual payment on		
	mortgage)		

In the balance sheet, the reduction in principal for the next year is reported as a current liability. The remaining unpaid principal balance is classified as a long-term liability. At December 31, 2006, the total liability is $493,344. Of that amount, $7,478 ($3,630 + $3,848) is current, and $485,866 ($493,344 − $7,478) is long-term.

ACCOUNTING IN ACTION   **e Business Insight**

Mortgage.com, a pioneer in one of the Web's more promising ideas, exited the online home-lending business and laid off most of its 618 employees. A study of Internet consumers showed that only 4 percent of them have applied online for a mortgage, and fewer than 1 percent have closed a loan. "The fact is, there is still a lot about getting a mortgage that can't be done online," says Dianne Glossman, an analyst with UBS Marburg. Although a recent change in federal law allows people to send their signatures electronically, "in most cases, you still need to sign paper documents, someone to visit the property and appraise it, and these loans still usually need to be closed in person."

Source: Excerpts from Aaron Elstein, "Mortgage.com Plans to Cease Its Lending and Pare Its Staff," *The Wall Street Journal*, November 1, 2000. Reprinted by permission of the Wall Street Journal. © 2000 Dow Jones & Co, Inc. All Rights Reserved Worldwide.

Lease Liabilities

As indicated in Chapter 10, a lease is a contractual arrangement between a lessor (owner of the property) and a lessee (renter of the property). It grants the right to use specific property for a period of time in return for cash payments. Leasing is big business. An estimated $125 billion of capital equipment was leased in a recent year. This represents approximately one-third of equipment financed that year. The two most common types of leases are operating leases and capital leases.

Operating Leases

The renting of an apartment and the rental of a car at an airport are examples of **operating leases**. **In an operating lease the intent is temporary use of the property by the lessee. The lessor continues to own the property.** The lease (or rental) payments are recorded as an expense by the lessee and as revenue by the lessor. For example, assume that a sales representative for Western Inc. leases a car from Hertz Car Rental at the Los Angeles airport and that Hertz charges a total of $275. The entry by the lessee, Western Inc., is:

Car Rental Expense	275	
Cash		275
(To record payment of lease rental charge)		

A	=	L	+	SE
−275				−275 Exp

Cash Flows
−275

The lessee may incur other costs during the lease period. For example, in the case above, the lessee may pay for gas and oil. These costs are also reported as an expense.

Capital Leases
— *rent-to-own*

In most lease contracts, a periodic payment is made by the lessee and is recorded as rent expense in the income statement. But, in some cases, the lease contract transfers substantially all the benefits and risks of ownership to the lessee. Such a lease is in effect a purchase of the property. This type of lease is called a **capital lease**. Its name comes from the fact that the present value of the cash payments for the lease is capitalized and recorded as an asset. Illustration 16-13 indicates the major difference between an operating and a capital lease.

HELPFUL HINT

A capital lease situation is one that, although legally a rental case, is *in substance* an installment purchase by the lessee. Accounting standards require that substance over form be used in such a situation.

Lessor has substantially all of the benefits and risks of ownership

Lessee has substantially all of the benefits and risks of ownership

Illustration 16-13
Types of leases

The lessee must record a lease **as an asset**—that is, as a capital lease—if **any one** of the following conditions exists:

1. **The lease transfers ownership of the property to the lessee.** *Rationale:* If during the lease term the lessee receives ownership of the asset, the leased asset should be reported as an asset on the lessee's books.

2. **The lease contains a bargain purchase option.** *Rationale:* If during the term of the lease the lessee can purchase the asset at a price substantially below its fair market value, the lessee will exercise this option. Thus, the lease should be reported as a leased asset on the lessee's books.

3. **The lease term is equal to 75% or more of the economic life of the leased property.** *Rationale:* If the lease term is for much of the asset's useful life, the asset should be recorded by the lessee.

4. **The present value of the lease payments equals or exceeds 90% of the fair market value of the leased property.** *Rationale:* If the present value of the lease payments is equal to or almost equal to the fair market value of the asset, the lessee has essentially purchased the asset. As a result, the leased asset should be recorded on the books of the lessee.

To illustrate, assume that Gonzalez Company decides to lease new equipment. The lease period is 4 years; the economic life of the leased equipment is estimated to be 5 years. The present value of the lease payments is $190,000, which is equal to the fair market value of the equipment. There is no transfer of ownership during the lease term, nor is there any bargain purchase option.

In this example, Gonzalez has essentially purchased the equipment. Conditions 3 and 4 have been met. First, the lease term is 75% or more of the economic life of the asset. Second, the present value of cash payments is equal to the equipment's fair market value. The entry to record the transaction is as follows.

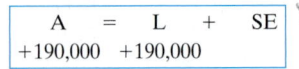

A	=	L	+	SE
+190,000		+190,000		

Cash Flows
no effect

Leased Asset—Equipment	190,000	
Lease Liability		190,000
(To record leased asset and lease liability)		

The leased asset is reported on the balance sheet under plant assets. The lease liability is reported on the balance sheet as a liability. **The portion of the lease liability expected to be paid in the next year is reported as a current liability. The remainder is classified as a long-term liability.**

Most lessees do not like to report leases on their balance sheets. Why? Because the lease liability increases the company's total liabilities. This, in turn, may make it more difficult for the company to obtain needed funds from lenders. As a result, companies attempt to keep leased assets and lease liabilities off the balance sheet by not meeting any of the four conditions mentioned above. The practice of keeping liabilities off the balance sheet is referred to as **off-balance-sheet financing**.

Statement Presentation and Analysis

STUDY OBJECTIVE 6

Identify the methods for the presentation and analysis of long-term liabilities.

Presentation

Long-term liabilities are reported in a separate section of the balance sheet immediately following current liabilities, as shown in Illustration 16-14 on the next page.

Alternatively, summary data may be presented in the balance sheet with detailed data (interest rates, maturity dates, conversion privileges, and assets pledged as collateral) shown in a supporting schedule. The current maturities of long-term debt should be reported under current liabilities if they are to be paid from current assets.

Illustration 16-14
Balance sheet presentation
of long-term liabilities

LAX CORPORATION
Balance Sheet (partial)

Long-term liabilities		
Bonds payable 10% due in 2012	$1,000,000	
Less: Discount on bonds payable	80,000	$ 920,000
Mortgage notes payable, 11%, due		
in 2018 and secured by plant assets		500,000
Lease liability		540,000
Total long-term liabilities		$1,960,000

Analysis

Long-term creditors and stockholders are interested in a company's long-run solvency. Of particular interest is the company's ability to pay interest as it comes due and to repay the face value of the debt at maturity. Debt to total assets and times interest earned are two ratios that provide information about debt-paying ability and long-run solvency.

The **debt to total assets ratio** measures the percentage of the total assets provided by creditors. It is computed, as shown in the formula below, by dividing total debt (both current and long-term liabilities) by total assets. The higher the percentage of debt to total assets, the greater the risk that the company may be unable to meet its maturing obligations.

The **times interest earned ratio** indicates the company's ability to meet interest payments as they come due. It is computed by dividing income before income taxes and interest expense by interest expense.

To illustrate these ratios, we will use data from **Johnson & Johnson**'s 2002 annual report. The company had total liabilities of $17,859 million, total assets of $40,556 million, interest expense of $160 million, income taxes of $2,694 million, and net income of $6,597 million. Johnson & Johnson's debt to total assets ratio and times interest earned ratio are shown below, along with their computations.

Illustration 16-15
Debt to total assets and
times interest earned ratios,
with computations

Total Debt	÷	Total Assets	=	Debt to Total Assets
$17,859	÷	$40,556	=	44%

Income before Income Taxes and Interest Expense	÷	Interest Expense	=	Times Interest Earned
$6,597 + $2,694 + $160	÷	$160	=	59.1 times

Johnson & Johnson has a relatively low debt to total assets percentage of 44%. Its interest coverage of 59.1 times appears extremely safe.

BEFORE YOU GO ON...

Review It

1. Explain the accounting for long-term mortgage notes payable.
2. What is the difference in accounting for an operating lease versus a capital lease? Explain the four conditions used to determine whether the lease contract transfers substantially all the benefits and risks of ownership.
3. What ratios may be computed to analyze a company's long-run solvency?

THE NAVIGATOR

DEMONSTRATION PROBLEM

Snyder Software Inc. has successfully developed a new spreadsheet program. To produce and market the program, the company needed $2.0 million of additional financing. On December 31, 2005, Snyder borrowed money as follows.

1. Snyder issued $500,000, 11%, 10-year convertible bonds. The bonds sold at face value and pay semiannual interest on January 1 and July 1. Each $1,000 bond is convertible into 30 shares of Snyder's $20 par value common stock.
2. Snyder issued $1.0 million, 10%, 10-year bonds at face value. Interest is payable semiannually on January 1 and July 1.
3. Snyder also issued a $500,000, 12%, 15-year mortgage note payable. The terms provide for semiannual installment payments of $36,324 on June 30 and December 31.

Instructions

1. For the convertible bonds, prepare journal entries for:
   (a) The issuance of the bonds on January 1, 2006.
   (b) Interest expense on July 1 and December 31, 2006.
   (c) The payment of interest on January 1, 2007.
   (d) The conversion of all bonds into common stock on January 1, 2007, when the market value of the common stock was $67 per share.
2. For the 10-year, 10% bonds:
   (a) Journalize the issuance of the bonds on January 1, 2006.
   (b) Prepare the journal entries for interest expense in 2006. Assume no accrual of interest on July 1.
   (c) Prepare the entry for the redemption of the bonds at 101 on January 1, 2009, after paying the interest due on this date.
3. For the mortgage note payable:
   (a) Prepare the entry for the issuance of the note on December 31, 2005.
   (b) Prepare a payment schedule for the first four installment payments.
   (c) Indicate the current and noncurrent amounts for the mortgage note payable at December 31, 2006.

SOLUTION TO DEMONSTRATION PROBLEM

ACTION PLAN

- Compute interest semiannually (six months).
- Record the accrual and payment of interest on appropriate dates.
- Record the conversion of the bonds into common stock by removing the book (carrying) value of the bonds from the liability account.

1. (a) 2006

Jan. 1	Cash	500,000	
	Bonds Payable		500,000
	(To record issue of 11%, 10-year		
	convertible bonds at face value)		

(b) 2006

July 1	Bond Interest Expense	27,500	
	Cash ($500,000 × 0.055)		27,500
	(To record payment of semiannual		
	interest)		
Dec. 31	Bond Interest Expense	27,500	
	Bond Interest Payable		27,500
	(To record accrual of semiannual		
	bond interest)		

(c) 2007

Jan. 1	Bond Interest Payable	27,500	
	Cash		27,500
	(To record payment of accrued interest)		

(d) Jan. 1

	Bonds Payable	500,000	
	Common Stock		300,000*
	Paid-in Capital in Excess of Par Value		200,000
	(To record conversion of bonds into common stock)		
	*($500,000 ÷ $1,000 = 500 bonds;		
	500 × 30 = 15,000 shares;		
	15,000 × $20 = $300,000)		

2. (a) 2006

Jan. 1	Cash	1,000,000	
	Bonds Payable		1,000,000
	(To record issuance of bonds)		

(b) 2006

July 1	Bond Interest Expense	50,000	
	Cash		50,000
	(To record payment of semiannual interest)		
Dec. 31	Bond Interest Expense	50,000	
	Bond Interest Payable		50,000
	(To record accrual of semiannual interest)		

(c) 2009

Jan. 1	Bonds Payable	1,000,000	
	Loss on Bond Redemption	10,000*	
	Cash		1,010,000
	(To record redemption of bonds at 101)		
	*($1,010,000 − $1,000,000)		

3. (a) 2005

Dec. 31	Cash	500,000	
	Mortgage Notes Payable		500,000
	(To record issuance of mortgage note payable)		

(b)

Semiannual Interest Period	Cash Payment	Interest Expense	Reduction of Principal	Principal Balance
Issue date				$500,000
1	$36,324	$30,000	$6,324	493,676
2	36,324	29,621	6,703	486,973
3	36,324	29,218	7,106	479,867
4	36,324	28,792	7,532	472,335

(c) Current liability $14,638 ($7,106 + $7,532)
    Long-term liability $472,335

ACTION PLAN

- Record the issuance of the bonds
- Compute interest expense for each period.
- Compute the loss on bond redemption as the excess of the cash paid over the carrying value of the redeemed bonds.

ACTION PLAN

- Compute periodic interest expense on a mortgage note, recognizing that as the principal amount decreases, so does the interest expense.
- Record mortgage payments, recognizing that each payment consists of (1) interest on the unpaid loan balance and (2) a reduction of the loan principal.

☑ **THE NAVIGATOR**

SUMMARY OF STUDY OBJECTIVES

1. **Explain why bonds are issued.** Bonds may be sold to many investors, and they offer the following advantages over common stock: (a) stockholder control is not affected, (b) tax savings result, (c) earnings per share of common stock may be higher.

2. **Prepare the entries for the issuance of bonds and interest expense.** When bonds are issued, Cash is debited for the cash proceeds, and Bonds Payable is credited for the face value of the bonds. The account Premium on Bonds Payable is used to show the bond premium; Discount on Bonds Payable is used to show a bond discount.

3. **Describe the entries when bonds are redeemed or converted.** When bonds are redeemed at maturity, Cash is credited and Bonds Payable is debited for the face value of the bonds. When bonds are redeemed before maturity, it is necessary to (a) eliminate the carrying value of the bonds at the redemption date, (b) record the cash paid, and (c) recognize the gain or loss on redemption. When bonds are converted to common stock, the carrying (or book) value of the bonds is transferred to appropriate paid-in capital accounts; no gain or loss is recognized.

4. **Describe the accounting for long-term notes payable.** Each payment consists of (1) interest on the unpaid balance of the loan and (2) a reduction of loan principal. The interest decreases each period, while the portion applied to the loan principal increases.

5. **Contrast the accounting for operating and capital leases.** For an operating lease, lease (rental) payments are recorded as an expense by the lessee (renter). For a capital lease, the lessee records the asset and related obligation at the present value of the future lease payments.

6. **Identify the methods for the presentation and analysis of long-term liabilities.** The nature and amount of each long-term debt should be reported in the balance sheet or in the notes accompanying the financial statements. Stockholders and long-term creditors are interested in a company's long-run solvency. Debt to total assets and times interest earned are two ratios that provide information about debt-paying ability and long-run solvency.

GLOSSARY

Bearer (coupon) bonds Bonds not registered. (p. 631).

Bond certificate A legal document that indicates the name of the issuer, the face value of the bonds, and such other data as the contractual interest rate and maturity date of the bonds. (p. 632).

Bond indenture A legal document that sets forth the terms of the bond issue. (p. 632).

Bonds A form of interest-bearing notes payable issued by corporations, universities, and governmental entities. (p. 629).

Callable bonds Bonds that are subject to retirement at a stated dollar amount prior to maturity at the option of the issuer. (p. 631).

Capital lease A contractual arrangement that transfers substantially all the benefits and risks of ownership to the lessee so that the lease is in effect a purchase of the property. (p. 641).

Contractual interest rate Rate used to determine the amount of interest the borrower pays and the investor receives. (p. 632).

Convertible bonds Bonds that permit bondholders to convert them into common stock at their option. (p. 631).

Debenture bonds Bonds issued against the general credit of the borrower. Also called unsecured bonds. (p. 631).

Debt to total assets ratio A solvency measure that indicates the percentage of total assets provided by creditors; computed as total debt divided by total assets. (p. 643).

Face value Amount of principal the issuer must pay at the maturity date of the bond. (p. 632).

Long-term liabilities Obligations expected to be paid after one year. (p. 629).

Market interest rate The rate investors demand for loaning funds to the corporation. (p. 633).

Mortgage bond A bond secured by real estate. (p. 631).

Mortgage note payable A long-term note secured by a mortgage that pledges title to specific assets as security for a loan. (p. 639).

Operating lease A contractual arrangement giving the lessee temporary use of the property, with continued ownership of the property by the lessor. (p. 641).

Registered bonds Bonds issued in the name of the owner. (p. 631).

Secured bonds Bonds that have specific assets of the issuer pledged as collateral. (p. 631).

Serial bonds Bonds that mature in installments. (p. 631).

Sinking fund bonds Bonds secured by specific assets set aside to retire them. (p. 631).

Term bonds Bonds that mature at a single specified future date. (p. 631).

Times interest earned ratio A solvency measure that indicates a company's ability to meet interest payments; computed by dividing income before income taxes and interest expense by interest expense. (p. 643).

Unsecured bonds Bonds issued against the general credit of the borrower. Also called debenture bonds. (p. 631).

APPENDIX 16A PRESENT VALUE CONCEPTS RELATED TO BOND PRICING

Congratulations! You have a winning lottery ticket and the state has provided you with three possible options for payment. They are:

1. Receive $10,000,000 in 3 years.
2. Receive $7,000,000 immediately.
3. Receive $3,500,000 at the end of each year for 3 years.

Which of these options would you select? The answer is not easy to determine at a glance. To make a dollar-maximizing choice, you must perform present value computations. A present value computation is based on the concept of time value of money. Time value of money concepts are useful for the lottery situation and for pricing other amounts to be received in the future. This appendix discusses how present value concepts are used to price bonds. It also will tell you how to determine what option you should take as a lottery winner.

Present Value of Face Value

To illustrate present value concepts, assume that you are willing to invest a sum of money that will yield $1,000 at the end of one year. In other words, what amount would you need to invest today to have $1,000 one year from now? If you want to earn 10%, the investment or present value is $909.09 ($1,000 ÷ 1.10). The computation of this amount is shown in Illustration 16A-1.

Present value	×	(1 + Interest rate)	=	Future amount
Present value	×	(1 + 10%)	=	$1,000
Present value			=	$1,000 ÷ 1.10
Present value			=	**$909.09**

Illustration 16A-1
Present value computation—$1,000 discounted at 10% for 1 year

The future amount ($1,000), the interest rate (10%), and the number of periods (1) are known. The variables in this situation can be depicted in the time diagram in Illustration 16A-2.

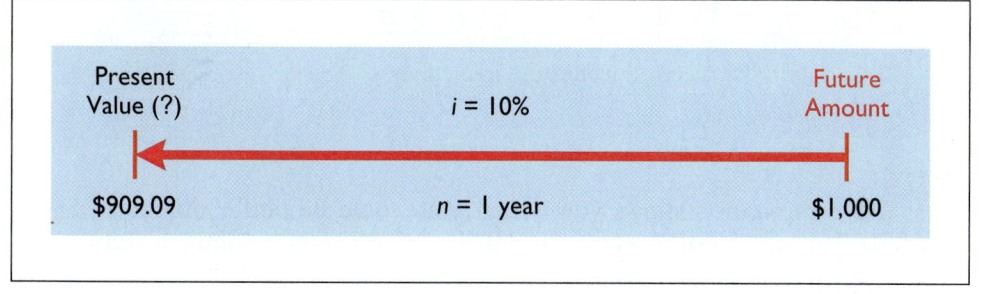

Illustration 16A-2
Finding present value if discounted for one period

If the single future amount of $1,000 is to be received **in 2 years** and discounted at 10%, its present value is $826.45 [($1,000 ÷ 1.10) ÷ 1.10], depicted as follows.

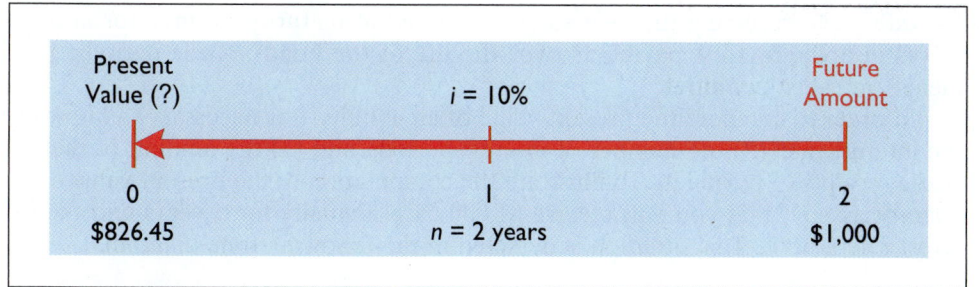

Illustration 16A-3
Finding present value if discounted for two periods

The present value of 1 may also be determined through tables that show the present value of 1 for *n* periods. In Table 16A-1 below, *n* is the number of discounting periods involved. The percentages are the periodic interest rates, and the 5-digit decimal numbers in the respective columns are the factors for the present value of 1.

When Table 16A-1 is used, the future amount is multiplied by the present value factor specified at the intersection of the number of periods and the interest rate. For example, the present value factor for 1 period at an interest rate of 10% is .90909, which equals the $909.09 ($1,000 × .90909) computed in Illustration 16A-1.

TABLE 16A-1
Present Value of 1

(*n*) Periods	4%	5%	6%	8%	9%	10%	11%	12%	15%
1	.96154	.95238	.94340	.92593	.91743	.90909	.90090	.89286	.86957
2	.92456	.90703	.89000	.85734	.84168	.82645	.81162	.79719	.75614
3	.88900	.86384	.83962	.79383	.77218	.75132	.73119	.71178	.65752
4	.85480	.82270	.79209	.73503	.70843	.68301	.65873	.63552	.57175
5	.82193	.78353	.74726	.68058	.64993	.62092	.59345	.56743	.49718
6	.79031	.74622	.70496	.63017	.59627	.56447	.53464	.50663	.43233
7	.75992	.71068	.66506	.58349	.54703	.51316	.48166	.45235	.37594
8	.73069	.67684	.62741	.54027	.50187	.46651	.43393	.40388	.32690
9	.70259	.64461	.59190	.50025	.46043	.42410	.39092	.36061	.28426
10	.67556	.61391	.55839	.46319	.42241	.38554	.35218	.32197	.24719

For 2 periods at an interest rate of 10%, the present value factor is .82645, which equals the $826.45 ($1,000 × .82645) computed previously.

Let's go back to our lottery example now. Given the present value concepts just learned, we can determine whether receiving $10,000,000 in 3 years is better than receiving $7,000,000 today, assuming the appropriate discount rate is 9%. The computation is as follows.

Illustration 16A-4
Present value of $10,000,000 to be received in 3 years

$10,000,000 × PV of 1 due in 3 years at 9% =	
$10,000,000 × .77218 (Table 16A-1)	$7,721,800
Amount to be received from state immediately	7,000,000
Difference	$ 721,800

What this computation shows you is that you would be better off receiving the $10,000,000 at the end of 3 years rather than taking $7,000,000 immediately.

Present Value of Interest Payments (Annuities)

In addition to receiving the face value of a bond at maturity, an investor also receives periodic interest payments over the life of the bonds. These periodic payments are called **annuities**.

In order to compute the present value of an annuity, it is necessary to know (1) the interest rate, (2) the number of interest periods, and (3) the amount of the periodic receipts or payments. To illustrate the computation of the present value of an annuity, assume that you will receive $1,000 cash annually for 3 years and the interest rate is 10%. This situation is depicted in the following time diagram.

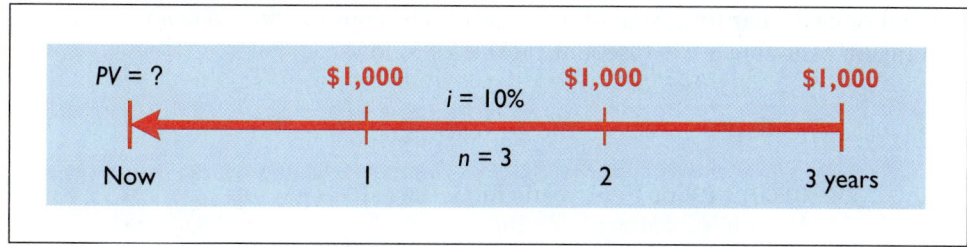

Illustration 16A-5
Time diagram for a 3-year annuity

The present value in this situation may be computed as follows.

Future Amount	×	Present Value of 1 Factor at 10%	=	Present Value
$1,000 (1 year away)		.90909		$ 909.09
1,000 (2 years away)		.82645		826.45
1,000 (3 years away)		.75132		751.32
		2.48686		**$2,486.86**

Illustration 16A-6
Present value of a series of future amounts computation

Annuity tables may also be used to value annuities. As illustrated in Table 16A-2 below, these tables show the present value of 1 to be received periodically for a given number of periods.

TABLE 16A-2
Present Value of an Annuity of 1

(n) Periods	4%	5%	6%	8%	9%	10%	11%	12%	15%
1	.96154	.95238	.94340	.92593	.91743	.90909	.90090	.89286	.86957
2	1.88609	1.85941	1.83339	1.78326	1.75911	1.73554	1.71252	1.69005	1.62571
3	2.77509	2.72325	2.67301	2.57710	2.53130	2.48685	2.44371	2.40183	2.28323
4	3.62990	3.54595	3.46511	3.31213	3.23972	3.16986	3.10245	3.03735	2.85498
5	4.45182	4.32948	4.21236	3.99271	3.88965	3.79079	3.69590	3.60478	3.35216
6	5.24214	5.07569	4.91732	4.62288	4.48592	4.35526	4.23054	4.11141	3.78448
7	6.00205	5.78637	5.58238	5.20637	5.03295	4.86842	4.71220	4.56376	4.16042
8	6.73274	6.46321	6.20979	5.74664	5.53482	5.33493	5.14612	4.96764	4.48732
9	7.43533	7.10782	6.80169	6.24689	5.99525	5.75902	5.53705	5.32825	4.77158
10	8.11090	7.72173	7.36009	6.71008	6.41766	6.14457	5.88923	5.65022	5.01877

From Table 16A-2 you can see that the present value factor of an annuity of 1 for 3 periods at 10% is 2.48685.[1] This present value factor is the total of the three individual present value factors as shown in Illustration 16A-6. Applying this amount to the annual cash flow of $1,000 produces a present value of $2,486.85.

Let's now go back to our lottery example. We determined that you would get more money if you wait and take the $10,000,000 in 3 years rather than take $7,000,000 immediately. But there is still another option—to receive $3,500,000 at

---

[1]The difference of .00001 between 2.48686 and 2.48685 is due to rounding.

the end of **each year** for 3 years (an annuity). The computation to evaluate this option (again assuming a 9% discount rate) is as follows.

Illustration 16A-7
Present value of lottery payments to be received over three years

$3,500,000 × PV of 1 due yearly for 3 years at 9% =	
$3,500,000 × 2.53130 (Table 16A-2)	$8,859,550
Present value of $10,000,000 to be received in 3 years	7,721,800
Difference	$1,137,750

Take the annuity of $3,500,000 for each of 3 years, and you will be $1,137,750 richer as a result.

Time Periods and Discounting

We have used an annual interest rate to determine present value. Present value computations may also be done over shorter periods of time, such as monthly, quarterly, or semiannually. When the time frame is less than one year, it is necessary to convert the annual interest rate to the shorter time frame. Assume, for example, that the investor in Illustration 16A-6 received $500 **semiannually** for 3 years instead of $1,000 annually. In this case, the number of periods becomes 6 (3 × 2), the interest rate is 5% (10% ÷ 2), the present value factor from Table 16A-2 is 5.07569, and the present value of the future cash flows is $2,537.85 (5.07569 × $500). This amount is slightly higher than the $2,486.86 computed in Illustration 16A-6 because interest is computed twice during the same year. That is, interest is earned on the first half year's interest.

Computing the Present Value of a Bond

The present value (or market price) of a bond is a function of three variables: (1) the payment amounts, (2) the length of time until the amounts are paid, and (3) the interest (discount) rate.

The first variable (dollars to be paid) is made up of two elements: (1) a series of interest payments (an annuity) and (2) the principal amount (a single sum). To compute the present value of the bond, both the interest payments and the principal amount must be discounted.

When the investor's interest (discount) rate is equal to the bond's contractual interest rate, the present value of the bonds will equal the face value of the bonds. To illustrate, assume a bond issue of 10%, 5-year bonds with a face value of $100,000 with interest payable **semiannually** on January 1 and July 1. If the discount rate is the same as the contractual rate, the bonds will sell **at face value**. In this case, the investor will receive (1) $100,000 at maturity and (2) a series of ten $5,000 interest payments [($100,000 × 10%) ÷ 2] over the term of the bonds. The length of time is expressed in terms of interest periods (in this case, 10) and the discount rate per interest period (5%). The following time diagram (Illustration 16A-8) depicts the variables involved in this discounting situation.

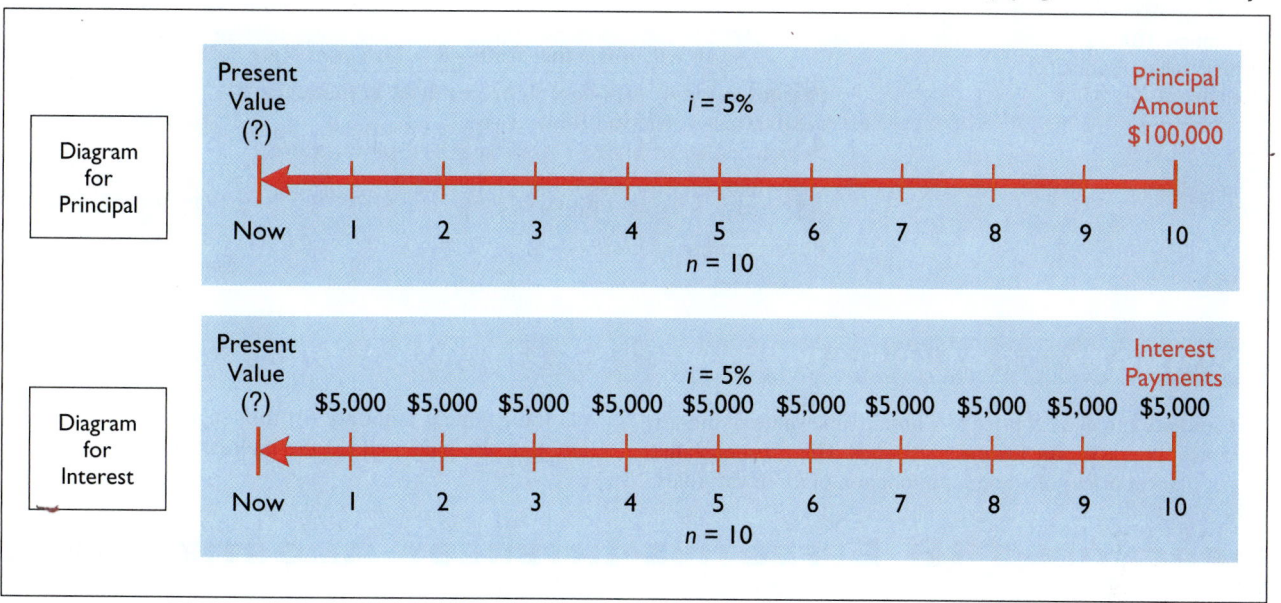

Illustration 16A-8
Time diagram for the present value of a 10%, 5-year bond paying interest semiannually

The computation of the present value of Candlestick's bonds had they been issued at face value (page 635) is shown below.

Illustration 16A-9
Present value of principal and interest (face value)

$$P\left(1 + \frac{r}{n}\right)^{nt}$$

10% Contractual Rate—10% Discount Rate	
Present value of principal to be received at maturity	
$100,000 × PV of 1 due in 10 periods at 5%	
$100,000 × .61391 (Table 16A-1)	$ 61,391
Present value of interest to be received periodically over the term of the bonds	
$5,000 × PV of 1 due periodically for 10 periods at 5%	
$5,000 × 7.72173 (Table 16A-2)	38,609*
Present value of bonds	**$100,000**

*(Rounded).

Now assume that the investor's required rate of return is 12%, not 10%. The future amounts are again $100,000 and $5,000, respectively. But now a discount rate of 6% (12% ÷ 2) must be used. The present value of Candlestick's bonds issued at a discount (page 635) is $92,639 as computed below.

Illustration 16A-10
Present value of principal and interest (discount)

10% Contractual Rate—12% Discount Rate	
Present value of principal to be received at maturity	
$100,000 × .55839 (Table 16A-1)	$55,839
Present value of interest to be received periodically over the term of the bonds	
$5,000 × 7.36009 (Table 16A-2)	36,800
Present value of bonds	**$92,639**

If the discount rate is 8% and the contractual rate is 10%, the present value of Candlestick's bonds issued at a premium (page 636) is $108,111, computed as follows.

Illustration 16A-11
Present value of principal and interest (premium)

10% Contractual Rate—8% Discount Rate	
Present value of principal to be received at maturity	
$100,000 × .67556 (Table 16A-1)	$67,556
Present value of interest to be received periodically over the term of the bonds	
$5,000 × 8.11090 (Table 16A-2)	40.555
Present value of bonds	**$108,111**

SUMMARY OF STUDY OBJECTIVE FOR APPENDIX 16A

7. Compute the market price of a bond. Time value of money concepts are useful for pricing bonds. The present value (or market price) of a bond is a function of three variables: (1) the payment amounts, (2) the length of time until the amounts are paid, and (3) the interest rate.

APPENDIX 16B EFFECTIVE-INTEREST AMORTIZATION —

STUDY OBJECTIVE 8

Apply the effective-interest method of amortizing bond discount and bond premium.

Under the **effective-interest method**, the amortization of bond discount or bond premium results in periodic interest expense equal to a constant percentage of the carrying value of the bonds. The effective-interest method results in varying amounts of amortization and interest expense per period but **a constant percentage rate**.

The following steps are required under the effective-interest method.

1. Compute the **bond interest expense**. To do so, multiply the carrying value of the bonds at the beginning of the interest period by the effective-interest rate.

2. Compute the **bond interest paid** (or accrued). To do so, multiply the face value of the bonds by the contractual interest rate.

3. Compute the **amortization amount**. To do so, determine the difference between the amounts computed in steps (1) and (2).

These steps are depicted in Illustration 16B-1.

Illustration 16B-1
Computation of amortization—effective-interest method

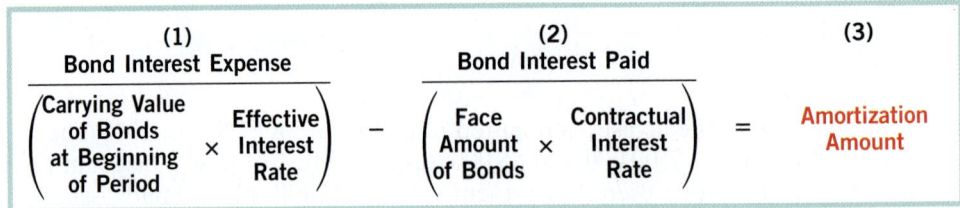

$$\begin{pmatrix} \text{Carrying Value} \\ \text{of Bonds} \\ \text{at Beginning} \\ \text{of Period} \end{pmatrix} \times \begin{matrix}\text{Effective} \\ \text{Interest} \\ \text{Rate}\end{matrix} - \begin{pmatrix} \text{Face} \\ \text{Amount} \\ \text{of Bonds} \end{pmatrix} \times \begin{matrix}\text{Contractual} \\ \text{Interest} \\ \text{Rate}\end{matrix} = \text{Amortization Amount}$$

(1) Bond Interest Expense — (2) Bond Interest Paid = (3) Amortization Amount

When the difference between the straight-line method of amortization (Appendix 16C) and the effective-interest method is material, the use of the effective-interest method is required under generally accepted accounting principles.

Amortizing Bond Discount

To illustrate the effective-interest method of bond discount amortization, assume that Candlestick, Inc. (as per this chapter pages 635–636) issues $100,000 of 10%, 5-year bonds on January 1, 2005, with interest payable each July 1 and January 1. The bonds sell for $92,639 (92.639% of face value). This sales price results in bond discount of $7,361 ($100,000 − $92,639) and an effective-interest rate of 12%. A [bond discount amortization schedule] as shown in Illustration 16B-2 facilitates the recording of interest expense and the discount amortization. Note that interest expense as a percentage of carrying value remains constant at 6%.

Illustration 16B
Bond discount amortization schedule

CANDLESTICK, INC.
Bond Discount Amortization
Effective-Interest Method—Semiannual Interest Payments
10% Bonds Issued at 12%

Semiannual Interest Periods	(A) Interest to Be Paid (5% × $100,000)	(B) Interest Expense to Be Recorded (6% × Preceding Bond Carrying Value)	(C) Discount Amortization (B) − (A)	(D) Unamortized Discount (D) − (C)	(E) Bond Carrying Value ($100,000 − D)
Issue date				$7,361	$ 92,639
1	$ 5,000	$5,558 (6% × $92,639)	$ 558	6,803	93,197
2	5,000	5,592 (6% × $93,197)	592	6,211	93,789
3	5,000	5,627 (6% × $93,789)	627	5,584	94,416
4	5,000	5,665 (6% × $94,416)	665	4,919	95,081
5	5,000	5,705 (6% × $95,081)	705	4,214	95,786
6	5,000	5,747 (6% × $95,786)	747	3,467	96,533
7	5,000	5,792 (6% × $96,533)	792	2,675	97,325
8	5,000	5,840 (6% × $97,325)	840	1,835	98,165
9	5,000	5,890 (6% × $98,165)	890	945	99,055
10	5,000	5,945* (6% × $99,055)	945	–0–	100,000
	$50,000	$57,361	$7,361		

Column **(A)** remains constant because the face value of the bonds ($100,000) is multiplied by the semiannual contractual interest rate (5%) each period.
Column **(B)** is computed as the preceding bond carrying value times the semiannual effective-interest rate (6%).
Column **(C)** indicates the discount amortization each period.
Column **(D)** decreases each period until it reaches zero at maturity.
Column **(E)** increases each period until it equals face value at maturity.

*$2 difference due to rounding.

We have highlighted columns (A), (B), and (C) in the amortization schedule to emphasize their importance. These three columns provide the numbers for each period's journal entries. They are the primary reason for preparing the schedule.

For the first interest period, the computations of bond interest expense and the bond discount amortization are:

Bond interest expense ($92,639 × 6%)	$5,558
Contractual interest ($100,000 × 5%)	5,000
Bond discount amortization	**$ 558**

Illustration 16B-3
Computation of bond discount amortization

The entry to record the payment of interest and amortization of bond discount by Candlestick, Inc. on July 1, 2005, is:

July 1	Bond Interest Expense	5,558	
	Discount on Bonds Payable		558
	Cash		5,000
	(To record payment of bond interest and amortization of bond discount)		

A	=	L	+	SE
−5,000		+558		−5,558 Exp

Cash Flows
−5,000

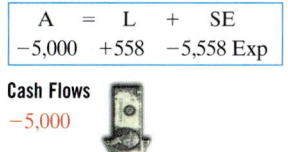

For the second interest period, bond interest expense will be $5,592 ($93,197 × 6%), and the discount amortization will be $592. At December 31, the following adjusting entry is made.

A	=	L	+	SE
		+592		−5,592 Exp
		+5,000		

Cash Flows
no effect

Dec. 31	Bond Interest Expense	5,592	
	Discount on Bonds Payable		592
	Bond Interest Payable		5,000
	(To record accrued interest and		
	amortization of bond discount)		

Total bond interest expense for 2005 is $11,150 ($5,558 + $5,592). On January 1, payment of the interest is recorded by a debit to Bond Interest Payable and a credit to Cash.

Amortizing Bond Premium

HELPFUL HINT

When a bond sells for $108,111, it is quoted as 108.111% of face value. Note that $108,111 can be proven as shown in Appendix 16A.

The amortization of bond premium by the effective-interest method is similar to the procedures described for bond discount. For example, assume that Candlestick, Inc. issues $100,000, 10%, 5-year bonds on January 1, 2005, with interest payable on July 1 and January 1. In this case, the bonds sell for $108,111. This sales price results in bond premium of $8,111 and an effective-interest rate of 8%. The bond premium amortization schedule is shown in Illustration 16B-4.

Illustration 16B-4
Bond premium amortization schedule

CANDLESTICK, INC.
Bond Premium Amortization
Effective-Interest Method—Semiannual Interest Payments
10% Bonds Issued at 8%

Semiannual Interest Periods	(A) Interest to Be Paid (5% × $100,000)	(B) Interest Expense to Be Recorded (4% × Preceding Bond Carrying Value)	(C) Premium Amortization (A) − (B)	(D) Unamortized Premium (D) − (C)	(E) Bond Carrying Value ($100,000 + D)
Issue date				$8,111	$108,111
1	$ 5,000	$ 4,324 (4% × $108,111)	$ 676	7,435	107,435
2	5,000	4,297 (4% × $107,435)	703	6,732	106,732
3	5,000	4,269 (4% × $106,732)	731	6,001	106,001
4	5,000	4,240 (4% × $106,001)	760	5,241	105,241
5	5,000	4,210 (4% × $105,241)	790	4,451	104,451
6	5,000	4,178 (4% × $104,451)	822	3,629	103,629
7	5,000	4,145 (4% × $103,629)	855	2,774	102,774
8	5,000	4,111 (4% × $102,774)	889	1,885	101,885
9	5,000	4,075 (4% × $101,885)	925	960	100,960
10	5,000	4,040* (4% × $100,960)	960	–0–	100,000
	$50,000	$41,889	$8,111		

Column **(A)** remains constant because the face value of the bonds ($100,000) is multiplied by the semiannual contractual interest rate (5%) each period.
Column **(B)** is computed as the carrying value of the bonds times the semiannual effective-interest rate (4%).
Column **(C)** indicates the premium amortization each period.
Column **(D)** decreases each period until it reaches zero at maturity.
Column **(E)** decreases each period until it equals face value at maturity.

---

*$2 difference due to rounding.

For the first interest period, the computations of bond interest expense and the bond premium amortization are:

Bond interest expense ($108,111 × 4%)	$4,324
Contractual interest ($100,000 × 5%)	5,000
Bond premium amortization	**$ 676**

Illustration 16B-5
Computation of bond premium amortization

The entry on the first interest date is:

July 1	Bond Interest Expense	4,324	
	Premium on Bonds Payable	676	
	Cash		5,000
	(To record payment of bond interest and		
	amortization of bond premium)		

A	=	L	+	SE
−5,000		−676		−4,324 Exp

Cash Flows
−5,000

For the second interest period, interest expense will be $4,297, and the premium amortization will be $703. Total bond interest expense for 2005 is $8,621 ($4,324 + $4,297).

DEMONSTRATION PROBLEM FOR APPENDIX 16B

Gardner Corporation issues $1,750,000, 10-year, 12% bonds on January 1, 2005, at $1,820,000 to yield 10%. The bonds pay semiannual interest July 1 and January 1. Gardner uses the effective-interest method of amortization.

Instructions
(a) Prepare the journal entry to record the issuance of the bonds.
(b) Prepare the journal entry to record the payment of interest on July 1, 2005.

ACTION PLAN
- Compute interest expense by multiplying bond carrying value at the beginning of the period by the effective-interest rate.
- Compute credit to cash (or bond interest payable) by multiplying the face value of the bonds by the contractual interest rate.
- Compute bond premium or discount amortization, which is the difference between (1) and (2).
- Interest expense increases when the effective-interest method is used for bonds issued at a discount. The reason is that a constant percentage is applied to an increasing book value to compute interest expense.

SOLUTION TO DEMONSTRATION PROBLEM

(a) 2005

Jan. 1	Cash	1,820,000	
	Bonds Payable		1,750,000
	Premium on Bonds Payable		70,000
	(To record issuance of bonds at a premium)		

(b) 2005

July 1	Bond Interest Expense	91,000*	
	Premium on Bonds Payable	14,000**	
	Cash		105,000
	(To record payment of semiannual interest		
	and amortization of bond premium)		
	*($1,820,000 × 5%)		
	**($105,000 − $91,000)		

☑ THE NAVIGATOR

SUMMARY OF STUDY OBJECTIVE FOR APPENDIX 16B

8. Apply the effective-interest method of amortizing bond discount and bond premium. The effective-interest method results in varying amounts of amortization and interest expense per period but a constant percentage rate of inter- est. When the difference between the straight-line and ef- fective-interest method is material, the use of the effec- tive-interest method is required under GAAP.

GLOSSARY FOR APPENDIX 16B

Effective-interest method of amortization A method of amortizing bond discount or bond premium that results in periodic interest expense equal to a constant percentage of the carrying value of the bonds. (p. 652).

APPENDIX 16C STRAIGHT-LINE AMORTIZATION

Amortizing Bond Discount

To follow the matching principle, bond discount should be allocated systematically to each period in which the bonds are outstanding. The **straight-line method of amortization** allocates the same amount to interest expense in each interest period. The amount is determined using the formula in Illustration 16C-1.

Illustration 16C-1
Formula for straight-line method of bond discount amortization

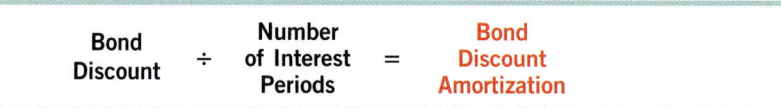

| Bond Discount | ÷ | Number of Interest Periods | = | Bond Discount Amortization |

In the Candlestick, Inc. example (page 635), the company sold $100,000, 5-year, 10% bonds on January 1, 2005, for $92,639. This price resulted in a $7,361 bond discount ($100,000 − $92,639). Interest is payable on July 1 and January 1. The bond discount amortization for each interest period is $736 ($7,361 ÷ 10). The entry to record the payment of bond interest and the amortization of bond discount on the first interest date (July 1, 2005) is:

A	=	L	+	SE
−5,000		+736		−5,736 Exp

Cash Flows
−5,000

July 1	Bond Interest Expense	5,736	
	Discount on Bonds Payable		736
	Cash		5,000
	(To record payment of bond interest and		
	amortization of bond discount)		

At December 31, the adjusting entry is:

A	=	L	+	SE
		+736		−5,736 Exp
		+5,000		

Cash Flows
no effect

Dec. 31	Bond Interest Expense	5,736	
	Discount on Bonds Payable		736
	Bond Interest Payable		5,000
	(To record accrued bond interest and		
	amortization of bond discount)		

Over the term of the bonds, the balance in Discount on Bonds Payable will decrease annually by the same amount until it has a zero balance at the maturity date of the bonds. Thus, the carrying value of the bonds at maturity will be equal to the face value.

Preparing a bond discount amortization schedule as shown in Illustration 16C-2 is useful. The schedule shows interest expense, discount amortization, and the carrying value of the bond for each interest period. As indicated, the interest expense recorded each period for the Candlestick bond is $5,736. Also note that the carrying value of the bond increases $736 each period until it reaches its face value $100,000 at the end of period 10.

CANDLESTICK, INC.
Bond Discount Amortization
Straight-Line Method—Semiannual Interest Payments

Semiannual Interest Periods	(A) Interest to Be Paid (5% × $100,000)	(B) Interest Expense to Be Recorded (A) + (C)	(C) Discount Amortization ($7,361 ÷ 10)	(D) Unamortized Discount (D) − (C)	(E) Bond Carrying Value ($100,000 − D)
Issue date				$7,361	$92,639
1	$ 5,000	$ 5,736	$ 736	6,625	93,375
2	5,000	5,736	736	5,889	94,111
3	5,000	5,736	736	5,153	94,847
4	5,000	5,736	736	4,417	95,583
5	5,000	5,736	736	3,681	96,319
6	5,000	5,736	736	2,945	97,055
7	5,000	5,736	736	2,209	97,791
8	5,000	5,736	736	1,473	98,527
9	5,000	5,736	736	737	99,263
10	5,000	5,737*	737*	–0–	100,000
	$50,000	$57,361	$7,361		

Column **(A)** remains constant because the face value of the bonds ($100,000) is multiplied by the semiannual contractual interest rate (5%) each period.
Column **(B)** is computed as the interest paid (Column A) plus the discount amortization (Column C).
Column **(C)** indicates the discount amortization each period.
Column **(D)** decreases each period by the same amount until it reaches zero at maturity.
Column **(E)** increases each period by the amount of discount amortization until it equals the face value at maturity.

*One dollar difference due to rounding.

We have highlighted columns (A), (B), and (C) in the amortization schedule to emphasize their importance. These three columns provide the numbers for each period's journal entries. They are the primary reason for preparing the schedule. Column (A) provides the amount of the credit to Cash. Column (B) shows the debit to Bond Interest Expense. And column (C) is the credit to Discount on Bonds Payable.

Amortizing Bond Premium

The amortization of bond premium parallels that of bond discount. The formula for determining bond premium amortization under the straight-line method is presented in Illustration 16C-3.

Illustration 16C-3
Formula for straight-line
method of bond premium
amortization

$$\text{Bond Premium} \div \text{Number of Interest Periods} = \text{Bond Premium Amortization}$$

Continuing our example of Candlestick, Inc., assume the bonds described above are sold for $108,111, rather than $92,639. This sale price results in a bond premium of $8,111 ($108,111 − $100,000). The bond premium amortization for each interest period is $811 ($8,111 ÷ 10). The entry to record the first payment of interest on July 1 is:

A	=	L	+	SE
−5,000		−811	−4,189 Exp

Cash Flows
−5,000

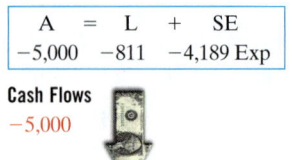

July 1	Bond Interest Expense	4,189	
	Premium on Bonds Payable	811	
	Cash		5,000
	(To record payment of bond interest and		
	amortization of bond premium)		

At December 31, the adjusting entry is:

A	=	L	+	SE
		−811	−4,189 Exp
		+5,000	

Cash Flows
no effect

Dec. 31	Bond Interest Expense	4,189	
	Premium on Bonds Payable	811	
	Bond Interest Payable		5,000
	(To record accrued bond interest and		
	amortization of bond premium)		

Over the term of the bonds, the balance in Premium on Bonds Payable will decrease annually by the same amount until it has a zero balance at maturity.

Preparing a bond premium amortization schedule as shown in Illustration 16C-4 is useful. It shows interest expense, premium amortization, and the carrying value of the bond. The interest expense recorded each period for the Candlestick bond is $4,189. Also note that the carrying value of the bond decreases $811 each period until it reaches its face value $100,000 at the end of period 10.

Illustration 16C-4
Bond premium amortization schedule

CANDLESTICK, INC.
Bond Premium Amortization
Straight-Line Method—Semiannual Interest Payments

Semiannual Interest Periods	(A) Interest to Be Paid (5% × $100,000)	(B) Interest Expense to Be Recorded (A) − (C)	(C) Premium Amortization ($8,111 ÷ 10)	(D) Unamortized Premium (D) − (C)	(E) Bond Carrying Value ($100,000 + D)
Issue date				$8,111	$108,111
1	$ 5,000	$ 4,189	$ 811	7,300	107,300
2	5,000	4,189	811	6,489	106,489
3	5,000	4,189	811	5,678	105,678
4	5,000	4,189	811	4,867	104,867
5	5,000	4,189	811	4,056	104,056
6	5,000	4,189	811	3,245	103,245
7	5,000	4,189	811	2,434	102,434
8	5,000	4,189	811	1,623	101,623
9	5,000	4,189	811	812	100,812
10	5,000	4,188*	812*	–0–	100,000
	$50,000	$41,889	$8,111		

Column **(A)** remains constant because the face value of the bonds ($100,000) is multiplied by the semiannual contractual interest rate (5%) each period.
Column **(B)** is computed as the interest paid (Column A) less the premium amortization (Column C).
Column **(C)** indicates the premium amortization each period.
Column **(D)** decreases each period by the same amount until it reaches zero at maturity.
Column **(E)** decreases each period by the amount of premium amortization until it equals the face value at maturity.

*One dollar difference due to rounding.

DEMONSTRATION PROBLEM FOR APPENDIX 16C

Glenda Corporation issues $1,750,000, 10-year, 12% bonds on January 1, 2005, for $1,820,000 to yield 10%. The bonds pay semiannual interest July 1 and January 1. Glenda uses the straight-line method of amortization.

Instructions

(a) Prepare the journal entry to record the issuance of the bonds.
(b) Prepare the journal entry to record the payment of interest on July 1, 2005.

ACTION PLAN

- Compute credit to cash (or bond interest payable) by multiplying the face value of the bonds by the contractual interest rate.
- Compute bond premium or discount amortization by dividing bond premium or discount by the total number of periods.
- Understand that interest expense is decreased when bonds are issued at a premium. The reason is that the amortization of premium reduces the total cost of borrowing.

SOLUTION TO DEMONSTRATION PROBLEM

(a) 2005

Jan. 1	Cash	1,820,000	
	Bonds Payable		1,750,000
	Premium on Bonds Payable		70,000

(b) 2005

July 1	Bond Interest Expense	101,500**	
	Premium on Bonds Payable	3,500*	
	Cash		105,000

*$70,000 ÷ 20
**$105,000 − $3,500

✓ THE NAVIGATOR

SUMMARY OF STUDY OBJECTIVE FOR APPENDIX 16C

9. **Apply the straight-line method of amortizing bond discount and bond premium.** The straight-line method of amortization results in a constant amount of amortization and interest expense per period.

GLOSSARY FOR APPENDIX 16C

Straight-line method of amortization. A method of amortizing bond discount or bond premium that results in allocating the same amount to interest expense in each interest period. (p. 656)

****Note**: All asterisked Questions, Exercises, and Problems relate to material in the appendixes to the chapter.

SELF-STUDY QUESTIONS

Self-Study/Self-Test

Answers are at the end of the chapter.

(SO 1) 1. The term used for bonds that are unsecured is:
    a. callable bonds.
    b. indenture bonds.
    c. debenture bonds.
    d. bearer bonds.

(SO 2) 2. Karson Inc. issues 10-year bonds with a maturity value of $200,000. If the bonds are issued at a premium, this indicates that:

    a. the contractual interest rate exceeds the market interest rate.
    b. the market interest rate exceeds the contractual interest rate.
    c. the contractual interest rate and the market interest rate are the same.
    d. no relationship exists between the two rates.

3. Gester Corporation retires its $100,000 face value bonds (SO 3) at 105 on January 1, following the payment of semiannual interest. The carrying value of the bonds at the

redemption date is $103,745. The entry to record the redemption will include a:
a. credit of $3,745 to Loss on Bond Redemption.
b. debit of $3,745 to Premium on Bonds Payable.
c. credit of $1,255 to Gain on Bond Redemption.
d. debit of $5,000 to Premium on Bonds Payable.

(SO 3) **4.** Colson Inc. converts $600,000 of bonds sold at face value into 10,000 shares of common stock, par value $1. Both the bonds and the stock have a market value of $760,000. What amount should be credited to Paid-in Capital in Excess of Par as a result of the conversion?
a. $10,000.
b. $160,000.
c. $600,000.
d. $590,000.

(SO 4) **5.** Andrews Inc. issues a $497,000, 10% 3-year mortgage note on January 1. The note will be paid in three annual installments of $200,000, each payable at the end of the year. What is the amount of interest expense that should be recognized by Andrews Inc. in the second year?
a. $16,567.
b. $49,740.
c. $34,670.
d. $347,600.

(SO 5) **6.** Lease A does not contain a bargain purchase option, but the lease term is equal to 90 percent of the estimated economic life of the leased property. Lease B does not transfer ownership of the property to the lessee by the end of the lease term, but the lease term is equal to 75 percent of the estimated economic life of the leased property. How should the lessee classify these leases?

	Lease A	**Lease B**
a.	Operating lease	Capital lease
b.	Operating lease	Operating lease
c.	Capital lease	Operating lease
d.	Capital lease	Capital lease

*7. On January 1, Besalius Inc. issued $1,000,000, 9% bonds (SO for $939,000. The market rate of interest for these bonds is 10%. Interest is payable annually on December 31. Besalius uses the effective-interest method of amortizing bond discount. At the end of the first year, Besalius should report unamortized bond discount of:
a. $54,900.
b. $57,100.
c. $51,610.
d. $51,000.

*8. On January 1, Dias Corporation issued $1,000,000, 14%, (SO 5-year bonds with interest payable on July 1 and January 1. The bonds sold for $1,098,540. The market rate of interest for these bonds was 12%. On the first interest date, using the effective-interest method, the debit entry to Bond Interest Expense is for:
a. $60,000.
b. $76,898.
c. $65,912.
d. $131,825.

*9. On January 1, Hurley Corporation issues $500,000, 5- (SO year, 12% bonds at 96 with interest payable on July 1 and January 1. The entry on July 1 to record payment of bond interest and the amortization of bond discount using the straight-line method will include a:
a. debit to Interest Expense $30,000.
b. debit to Interest Expense $60,000.
c. credit to Discount on Bonds Payable $4,000.
d. credit to Discount on Bonds Payable $2,000.

*10. For the bonds issued in question 9, above, what is the car- (SO rying value of the bonds at the end of the third interest period?
a. $486,000.
b. $488,000.
c. $472,000.
d. $464,000.

QUESTIONS

1. (a) What are long-term liabilities? Give three examples. (b) What is a bond?

2. (a) As a source of long-term financing, what are the major advantages of bonds over common stock? (b) What are the major disadvantages in using bonds for long-term financing?

3. Contrast the following types of bonds: (a) secured and unsecured, (b) term and serial, (c) registered and bearer, and (d) convertible and callable.

4. The following terms are important in issuing bonds: (a) face value, (b) contractual interest rate, (c) bond indenture, and (d) bond certificate. Explain each of these terms.

5. Describe the two major obligations incurred by a company when bonds are issued.

6. Assume that Bedazzled Inc. sold bonds with a par value of $100,000 for $104,000. Was the market interest rate equal to, less than, or greater than the bonds' contractual interest rate? Explain.

7. If a 9%, 10-year, $800,000 bond is issued at par and interest is paid semiannually, what is the amount of the interest payment at the end of the first semiannual period?

8. If the Bonds Payable account has a balance of $900,000 and the Discount on Bonds Payable account has a balance of $60,000, what is the carrying value of the bonds?

9. Which accounts are debited and which are credited if a bond issue originally sold at a premium is redeemed before maturity at 97 immediately following the payment of interest?

10. Karistad Corporation is considering issuing a convertible bond. What is a convertible bond? Discuss the advantages of a convertible bond from the standpoint of (a) the bondholders and (b) the issuing corporation.

11. Roy Brown, a friend of yours, has recently purchased a home for $125,000, paying $25,000 down and the remainder financed by a 10.5%, 20-year mortgage, payable at $998.38 per month. At the end of the first month, Roy receives a statement from the bank indicating that only $123.38 of principal was paid during the month. At this rate, he calculates that it will take over 67 years to pay off the mortgage. Is he right? Discuss.

12. (a) What is a lease agreement? (b) What are the two most common types of leases? (c) Distinguish between the two types of leases.

13. Orbison Company rents a warehouse on a month-to-month basis for the storage of its excess inventory. The company periodically must rent space when its production greatly exceeds actual sales. What is the nature of this type of lease agreement, and what accounting treatment should be used?

14. Costello Company entered into an agreement to lease 12 computers from Estes Electronics Inc. The present value of the lease payments is $186,300. Assuming that this is a capital lease, what entry would Costello Company make on the date of the lease agreement?

15. In general, what are the requirements for the financial statement presentation of long-term liabilities?

*16. Ginny Innis is discussing the advantages of the effective-interest method of bond amortization with her accounting staff. What do you think Ginny is saying?

*17. Redbone Corporation issues $500,000 of 9%, 5-year bonds on January 1, 2005, at 104. If Redbone uses the effective-interest method in amortizing the premium, will the annual interest expense increase or decrease over the life of the bonds? Explain.

*18. Vera Cruz and Swen Varberg are discussing how the market price of a bond is determined. Vera believes that the market price of a bond is solely a function of the amount of the principal payment at the end of the term of a bond. Is she right? Discuss.

*19. Explain the straight-line method of amortizing discount and premium on bonds payable.

*20. Fleming Corporation issues $300,000 of 8%, 5-year bonds on January 1, 2005, at 105. Assuming that the straight-line method is used to amortize the premium, what is the total amount of interest expense for 2005?

BRIEF EXERCISES

Compare bond versus stock financing.

(SO 1)

BE16-1 Shaffer Inc. is considering two alternatives to finance its construction of a new $2 million plant.

(a) Issuance of 200,000 shares of common stock at the market price of $10 per share.
(b) Issuance of $2 million, 8% bonds at par.

Complete the following table, and indicate which alternative is preferable.

	Issue Stock	Issue Bond
Income before interest and taxes	$900,000	$900,000
Interest expense from bonds	————	————
Income before income taxes	$	$
Income tax expense (30%)	————	————
Net income	$	$
Outstanding shares	————	500,000
Earnings per share	————	————

Prepare entries for bonds issued at face value.

(SO 2)

BE16-2 Quincy Corporation issued 4,000, 8%, 5-year, $1,000 bonds dated January 1, 2005, at 100.

(a) Prepare the journal entry to record the sale of these bonds on January 1, 2005.
(b) Prepare the journal entry to record the first interest payment on July 1, 2005 (interest payable semiannually), assuming no previous accrual of interest.
(c) Prepare the adjusting journal entry on December 31, 2005, to record interest expense.

Prepare entries for bonds sold at a discount and a premium.

(SO 2)

BE16-3 Sandstone Company issues $1 million, 10-year, 8% bonds at 97, with interest payable on July 1 and January 1.

(a) Prepare the journal entry to record the sale of these bonds on January 1, 2005.
(b) Assuming instead that the above bonds sold for 104, prepare the journal entry to record the sale of these bonds on January 1, 2005.

Prepare entries for bonds issued.

(SO 2)

BE16-4 Carrolla Company has issued three different bonds during 2005. Interest is payable semiannually on each of these bonds.

1. On January 1, 2005, 1,000, 8%, 5-year, $1,000 bonds dated January 1, 2005, were issued at face value.
2. On July 1, $500,000, 9%, 5-year bonds dated July 1, 2005, were issued at 102.
3. On September 1, $200,000, 7%, 5-year bonds dated September 1, 2005, were issued at 99.

Prepare the journal entry to record each bond transaction at the date of issuance.

Prepare entry for redemption of bonds.

(SO 3)

BE16-5 The balance sheet for Jones Company reports the following information on July 1, 2005.

Long-term liabilities		
Bonds payable	$1,000,000	
Less: Discount on bonds payable	60,000	$940,000

Jones decides to redeem these bonds at 103 after paying semiannual interest. Prepare the journal entry to record the redemption on July 1, 2005.

Prepare entries for long-term notes payable.

(SO 4)

BE16-6 McEntire Inc. issues a $400,000, 10%, 10-year mortgage note on December 31, 2005, to obtain financing for a new building. The terms provide for semiannual installment payments of $32,097. Prepare the entry to record the mortgage loan on December 31, 2005, and the first installment payment.

Contrast accounting for operating and capital lease.

(SO 5)

BE16-7 Prepare the journal entries that the lessee should make to record the following transactions.

1. The lessee makes a lease payment of $80,000 to the lessor in an operating lease transaction.
2. Zander Company leases a new building from Joel Construction, Inc. The present value of the lease payments is $900,000. The lease qualifies as a capital lease.

Prepare statement presentation of long-term liabilities.

(SO 6)

BE16-8 Presented below are long-term liability items for Saurez Company at December 31, 2005. Prepare the long-term liabilities section of the balance sheet for Saurez Company.

Bonds payable, due 2007	$500,000
Lease liability	50,000
Notes payable, due 2010	80,000
Discount on bonds payable	45,000

Determine present value.

(SO 7)

*BE16-9 **(a)** What is the present value of $10,000 due 8 periods from now, discounted at 10%?
(b) What is the present value of $10,000 to be received at the end of each of 6 periods, discounted at 8%?

Use effective-interest method of bond amortization.

(SO 8)

*BE16-10 Presented below is the partial bond discount amortization schedule for Cardosa Corp. Cardosa uses the effective-interest method of amortization.

Semiannual Interest Periods	Interest to Be Paid	Interest Expense to Be Recorded	Discount Amortization	Unamortized Discount	Bond Carrying Value
Issue date				$62,311	$937,689
1	$45,000	$46,884	$1,884	60,427	939,573
2	45,000	46,979	1,979	58,448	941,552

Instructions
(a) Prepare the journal entry to record the payment of interest and the discount amortization at the end of period 1.
(b) ▭▭▭▷ Explain why interest expense is greater than interest paid.
(c) Explain why interest expense will increase each period.

Prepare entries for bonds issued at a discount.

(SO 9)

*BE16-11 Bowie Company issues $3 million, 10-year, 9% bonds at 96, with interest payable on July 1 and January 1. The straight-line method is used to amortize bond discount.

(a) Prepare the journal entry to record the sale of these bonds on January 1, 2005.
(b) Prepare the journal entry to record interest expense and bond discount amortization on July 1, 2005, assuming no previous accrual of interest.

*BE16-12 Allman Inc. issues $2 million, 5-year, 10% bonds at 102, with interest payable on July 1 and January 1. The straight-line method is used to amortize bond premium.

(a) Prepare the journal entry to record the sale of these bonds on January 1, 2005.

(b) Prepare the journal entry to record interest expense and bond premium amortization on July 1, 2005, assuming no previous accrual of interest.

Prepare entries for bonds issued at a premium.

(SO 9)

EXERCISES

E16-1 Southeast Airlines is considering two alternatives for the financing of a purchase of a fleet of airplanes. These two alternatives are:

1. Issue 60,000 shares of common stock at $45 per share. (Cash dividends have not been paid nor is the payment of any contemplated).
2. Issue 10%, 10-year bonds at par for $2,700,000.

It is estimated that the company will earn $600,000 before interest and taxes as a result of this purchase. The company has an estimated tax rate of 30% and has 90,000 shares of common stock outstanding prior to the new financing.

Instructions
Determine the effect on net income and earnings per share for these two methods of financing.

Compare two alternatives of financing—issuance of common stock vs. issuance of bonds.

(SO 1)

E16-2 On January 1, Payne Company issued $200,000, 10%, 10-year bonds at par. Interest is payable semiannually on July 1 and January 1.

Instructions
Present journal entries to record the following.

(a) The issuance of the bonds.
(b) The payment of interest on July 1, assuming that interest was not accrued on June 30.
(c) The accrual of interest on December 31.

Prepare entries for issuance of bonds, and payment and accrual of bond interest.

(SO 2)

E16-3 On January 1, Hogan Company issued $200,000, 8%, 5-year bonds at face value. Interest is payable semiannually on July 1 and January 1.

Instructions
Prepare journal entries to record the following events.

(a) The issuance of the bonds.
(b) The payment of interest on July 1, assuming no previous accrual of interest.
(c) The accrual of interest on December 31.

Prepare entries for bonds issued at face value.

(SO 2)

E16-4 Pueblo Company issued $300,000 of 9%, 10-year bonds on January 1, 2004, at face value. Interest is payable semiannually on July 1 and January 1.

Instructions
Prepare the journal entries to record the following events.

(a) The issuance of the bonds.
(b) The payment of interest on July 1, assuming no previous accrual of interest.
(c) The accrual of interest on December 31.
(d) The redemption of bonds at maturity, assuming interest for the last interest period has been paid and recorded.

Prepare entries for bonds issued at face value.

(SO 2, 3)

E16-5 The following section is taken from Disch Corp.'s balance sheet at December 31, 2004.

Current liabilities	
Bond interest payable	$ 72,000
Long-term liabilities	
Bonds payable, 9%, due January 1, 2009	1,600,000

Interest is payable semiannually on January 1 and July 1. The bonds are callable on any interest date.

Instructions
(a) Journalize the payment of the bond interest on January 1, 2005.

Prepare entries for bond interest and redemption.

(SO 2, 3)

(b) Assume that on January 1, 2005, after paying interest, Disch calls bonds having a face value of $400,000. The call price is 104. Record the redemption of the bonds.

(c) Prepare the entry to record the payment of interest on July 1, 2005, assuming no previous accrual of interest on the remaining bonds.

Prepare entries for redemption of bonds and conversion of bonds into common stock.

(SO 3)

E16-6 Presented below are three independent situations.

1. Voris Corporation retired $130,000 face value, 12% bonds on June 30, 2005, at 102. The carrying value of the bonds at the redemption date was $107,500. The bonds pay semiannual interest, and the interest payment due on June 30, 2005, has been made and recorded.

2. Lamp Inc. retired $150,000 face value, 12.5% bonds on June 30, 2005, at 98. The carrying value of the bonds at the redemption date was $151,000. The bonds pay semiannual interest, and the interest payment due on June 30, 2005, has been made and recorded.

3. Keho Company has $80,000, 8%, 12-year convertible bonds outstanding. These bonds were sold at face value and pay semiannual interest on June 30 and December 31 of each year. The bonds are convertible into 30 shares of Keho $5 par value common stock for each $1,000 worth of bonds. On December 31, 2005, after the bond interest has been paid, $40,000 face value bonds were converted. The market value of Keho common stock was $44 per share on December 31, 2005.

Instructions

For each independent situation above, prepare the appropriate journal entry for the redemption or conversion of the bonds.

Prepare entries to record mortgage note and installment payments.

(SO 4)

E16-7 Tucki Co. receives $240,000 when it issues a $240,000, 10%, mortgage note payable to finance the construction of a building at December 31, 2005. The terms provide for semiannual installment payments of $16,000 on June 30 and December 31.

Instructions

Prepare the journal entries to record the mortgage loan and the first two installment payments.

E16-8 Presented below are two independent situations.

1. Speedy Car Rental leased a car to Rundgren Company for one year. Terms of the operating lease agreement call for monthly payments of $500.

Prepare entries for operating lease and capital lease.

(SO 5)

2. On January 1, 2005, Miles Inc. entered into an agreement to lease 20 computers from Halo Electronics. The terms of the lease agreement require three annual rental payments of $40,000 (including 10% interest) beginning December 31, 2005. The present value of the three rental payments is $99,474. Miles considers this a capital lease.

Instructions

(a) Prepare the appropriate journal entry to be made by Rundgren Company for the first lease payment.

(b) Prepare the journal entry to record the lease agreement on the books of Miles Inc. on January 1, 2005.

Prepare long-term liabilities section.

(SO 6)

E16-9 The adjusted trial balance for Matthews Corporation at the end of the current year contained the following accounts.

Bond Interest Payable	$ 9,000
Lease Liability	59,500
Bonds Payable, due 2013	180,000
Premium on Bonds Payable	32,000

Instructions

Prepare the long-term liabilities section of the balance sheet.

Prepare entries for issuance of bonds, payment of interest, and amortization of discount using effective-interest method

(SO 8)

*E16-10** Neagle Corporation issued $500,000, 9%, 10-year bonds on January 1, 2005, for $468,844. This price resulted in an effective-interest rate of 10% on the bonds. Interest is payable semiannually on July 1 and January 1. Neagle uses the effective-interest method to amortize bond premium or discount.

Instructions

Prepare the journal entries to record the following. (Round to the nearest dollar.)

(a) The issuance of the bonds.

(b) The payment of interest and the discount amortization on July 1, 2005, assuming that interest was not accrued on June 30.

(c) The accrual of interest and the discount amortization on December 31, 2005.

*E16-11 Hurley Company issued $400,000, 11%, 10-year bonds on January 1, 2005, for $424,925. This price resulted in an effective-interest rate of 10% on the bonds. Interest is payable semi-annually on July 1 and January 1. Hurley uses the effective-interest method to amortize bond premium or discount.

Prepare entries for issuance of bonds, payment of interest, and amortization of premium using effective-interest method.

(SO 8)

Instructions

Prepare the journal entries to record the following. (Round to the nearest dollar).

(a) The issuance of the bonds.
(b) The payment of interest and the premium amortization on July 1, 2005, assuming that interest was not accrued on June 30.
(c) The accrual of interest and the premium amortization on December 31, 2005.

*E16-12 Manilow Company issued $600,000, 9%, 20-year bonds on January 1, 2005, at 103. Interest is payable semiannually on July 1 and January 1. Manilow uses straight-line amortization for bond premium or discount.

Prepare entries to record issuance of bonds, payment of interest, amortization of premium, and redemption at maturity.

(SO 3, 9)

Instructions

Prepare the journal entries to record the following.

(a) The issuance of the bonds.
(b) The payment of interest and the premium amortization on July 1, 2005, assuming that interest was not accrued on June 30.
(c) The accrual of interest and the premium amortization on December 31, 2005.
(d) The redemption of the bonds at maturity, assuming interest for the last interest period has been paid and recorded.

*E16-13 Newton Company issued $600,000, 11%, 10-year bonds on December 31, 2004, for $550,000. Interest is payable semiannually on June 30 and December 31. Newton Company uses the straight-line method to amortize bond premium or discount.

Prepare entries to record issuance of bonds, payment of interest, amortization of discount, and redemption at maturity.

(SO 3, 9)

Instructions

Prepare the journal entries to record the following.

(a) The issuance of the bonds.
(b) The payment of interest and the discount amortization on June 30, 2005.
(c) The payment of interest and the discount amortization on December 31, 2005.
(d) The redemption of the bonds at maturity, assuming interest for the last interest period has been paid and recorded.

PROBLEMS: SET A

P16-1A On June 1, 2005, Hopkins Corp. issued $1,000,000, 8%, 5-year bonds at face value. The bonds were dated June 1, 2005, and pay interest semiannually on June 1 and December 1. Financial statements are prepared annually on December 31.

Prepare entries to record issuance of bonds, interest accrual, and bond redemption.

(SO 2, 3, 6)

Instructions

(a) Prepare the journal entry to record the issuance of the bonds.
(b) Prepare the adjusting entry to record the accrual of interest on December 31, 2005.
(c) Show the balance sheet presentation on December 31, 2005.
(d) Prepare the journal entry to record payment of interest on June 1, 2006, assuming no accrual of interest from January 1, 2006, to June 1, 2006.

(d) Int. exp. $33,333

(e) Prepare the journal entry to record payment of interest on December 1, 2006.
(f) Assume that on December 1, 2006, Hopkins calls the bonds at 101. Record the redemption of the bonds.

(f) Loss $10,000

P16-2A Formosa Co. sold $400,000, 9%, 10-year bonds on January 1, 2005. The bonds were dated January 1, and interest is paid on January 1 and July 1. The bonds were sold at 105.

Prepare entries to record issuance of bonds, interest accrual, and bond redemption.

(SO 2, 3, 6)

Instructions

(a) Prepare the journal entry to record the issuance of the bonds on January 1, 2005.
(b) At December 31, 2005, the balance in the Premium on Bonds Payable account is $18,000. Show the balance sheet presentation of accrued interest and the bond liability at December 31, 2005.

(c) On January 1, 2007, when the carrying value of the bonds was $416,000, the company redeemed the bonds at 105. Record the redemption of the bonds assuming that interest for the period has already been paid.

Prepare installment payments schedule and journal entries for a mortgage note payable.

(SO 4)

P16-3A Otto Electronics issues an $800,000, 8%, 10-year mortgage note on December 31, 2005, to help finance a plant expansion program. The terms provide for semiannual installment payments, not including real estate taxes and insurance, of $58,865. Payments are due June 30 and December 31.

Instructions

(b) June 30 Mortgage Notes Payable $26,865
(c) Current liability—2006: $59,276

(a) Prepare an installment payments schedule for the first 2 years.
(b) Prepare the entries for (1) the mortgage loan and (2) the first two installment payments.
(c) Show how the total mortgage liability should be reported on the balance sheet at December 31, 2006.

Analyze three different lease situations and prepare journal entries.

(SO 5)

P16-4A Presented below are three different lease transactions in which Ortiz Enterprises engaged in 2005. Assume that all lease transactions start on January 1, 2005. In no case does Ortiz receive title to the properties leased during or at the end of the lease term.

	Lessor		
	Schoen Co.	**Casey Co.**	**Lester Inc.**
Type of property	Bulldozer	Truck	Furniture
Bargain purchase option	None	None	None
Lease term	4 years	6 years	3 years
Estimated economic life	8 years	7 years	5 years
Yearly rental	$13,000	$15,000	$ 4,000
Fair market value of leased asset	$80,000	$72,000	$27,500
Present value of the lease rental payments	$48,000	$62,000	$12,000

Instructions

(a) Identify the leases above as operating or capital leases. Explain.
(b) How should the lease transaction for Casey Co. be recorded on January 1, 2005?
(c) How should the lease transaction for Lester Inc. be recorded in 2005?

Prepare entries to record issuance of bonds, payment of interest, and amortization of bond discount using effective-interest method.

(SO 2, 8)

*P16-5A On July 1, 2005, Kingston Satellites issued $3,600,000 face value, 9%, 10-year bonds at $3,375,680. This price resulted in an effective-interest rate of 10% on the bonds. Kingston uses the effective-interest method to amortize bond premium or discount. The bonds pay semiannual interest July 1 and January 1.

Instructions
(Round all computations to the nearest dollar.)

(b) Amortization $6,784

(c) Amortization $7,123

(d) Amortization $7,479

(a) Prepare the journal entry to record the issuance of the bonds on July 1, 2005.
(b) Prepare the journal entry to record the accrual of interest and the amortization of the discount on December 31, 2005.
(c) Prepare the journal entry to record the payment of interest and the amortization of the discount on July 1, 2006, assuming that interest was not accrued on June 30.
(d) Prepare the journal entry to record the accrual of interest and the amortization of the discount on December 31, 2006.
(e) Prepare an amortization table through December 31, 2006 (3 interest periods) for this bond issue.

Prepare entries to record issuance of bonds, payment of interest, and amortization of premium using effective-interest method. In addition, answer questions.

(SO 2, 8)

*P16-6A On July 1, 2005, S. Strigel Chemical Company issued $5,000,000 face value, 10%, 10-year bonds at $5,679,533. This price resulted in an 8% effective-interest rate on the bonds. Strigel uses the effective-interest method to amortize bond premium or discount. The bonds pay semiannual interest on each July 1 and January 1.

Instructions
(Round all computations to the nearest dollar.)

(a) Prepare the journal entries to record the following transactions.
  (1) The issuance of the bonds on July 1, 2005.
  (2) The accrual of interest and the amortization of the premium on December 31, 2005.

(a) (2) Amortization $22,819

(3) The payment of interest and the amortization of the premium on July 1, 2006, assuming no accrual of interest on June 30.

(a) (3) Amortization $23,731

(4) The accrual of interest and the amortization of the premium on December 31, 2006.

(a) (4) Amortization $24,681
(b) $5,608,302

(b) Show the proper balance sheet presentation for the liability for bonds payable on the December 31, 2006, balance sheet.

(c) ▭▬▬▷ Provide the answers to the following questions in letter form.

(1) What amount of interest expense is reported for 2006?

(2) Would the bond interest expense reported in 2006 be the same as, greater than, or less than the amount that would be reported if the straight-line method of amortization were used?

(3) Determine the total cost of borrowing over the life of the bond.

(4) Would the total bond interest expense be greater than, the same as, or less than the total interest expense if the straight-line method of amortization were used?

P16-7A Travis Company sold $2,000,000, 9%, 20-year bonds on January 1, 2005. The bonds were dated January 1, 2005, and pay interest on January 1 and July 1. Travis Company uses the straight-line method to amortize bond premium or discount. The bonds were sold at 96. Assume no interest is accrued on June 30.

Prepare entries to record issuance of bonds, interest accrual, and amortization for 2 years.

(SO 6, 9)

Instructions

(a) Prepare the journal entry to record the issuance of the bonds on January 1, 2005.

(b) Prepare a bond discount amortization schedule for the first 4 interest periods.

(c) Prepare the journal entries for interest and the amortization of the discount in 2005 and 2006.

(d) Show the balance sheet presentation of the bond liability at December 31, 2006.

(b) Amortization $2,000
(d) Discount on bonds payable $72,000

P16-8A Guehler Corporation sold $3,000,000, 8%, 10-year bonds on January 1, 2005. The bonds were dated January 1, 2005, and pay interest on July 1 and January 1. Guehler Corporation uses the straight-line method to amortize bond premium or discount. Assume no interest is accrued on June 30.

Prepare entries to record issuance of bonds, interest, and amortization of bond premium and discount.

(SO 6, 9)

Instructions

(a) Prepare all the necessary journal entries to record the issuance of the bonds and bond interest expense for 2005, assuming that the bonds sold at 103.

(b) Prepare journal entries as in part (a) assuming that the bonds sold at 96.

(c) Show balance sheet presentation for each bond issue at December 31, 2005.

(a) Amortization $4,500
(b) Amortization $6,000
(c) Premium on bonds payable $81,000
Discount on bonds payable $108,000

P16-9A The following is taken from the Jaggar Corp. balance sheet.

Prepare entries to record interest payments, discount amortization, and redemption of bonds.

(SO 2, 3 9)

JAGGAR CORPORATION
Balance Sheet (partial)
December 31, 2005

Current liabilities		
Bond interest payable (for 6 months		
from July 1 to December 31)		$ 96,000
Long-term liabilities		
Bonds payable, 8%, due		
January 1, 2016	$2,400,000	
Less: Discount on bonds payable	90,000	$2,310,000

Interest is payable semiannually on January 1 and July 1. The bonds are callable on any semi-annual interest date. Jaggar uses straight-line amortization for any bond premium or discount. From December 31, 2005, the bonds will be outstanding for an additional 10 years (120 months).

Instructions

(Round all computations to the nearest dollar).

(a) Journalize the payment of bond interest on January 1, 2006.

(b) Prepare the entry to amortize bond discount and to pay the interest due on July 1, 2006, assuming that interest was not accrued on June 30.

(b) Amortization $4,500

(c) Assume that on July 1, 2006, after paying interest, Jaggar Corp. calls bonds having a face value of $800,000. The call price is 102. Record the redemption of the bonds.

(c) Loss $44,500

(d) Prepare the adjusting entry at December 31, 2006, to amortize bond discount and to accrue interest on the remaining bonds.

(d) Amortization $3,000

PROBLEMS: SET B

Prepare entries to record issuance of bonds, interest accrual, and bond redemption.

(SO 2, 3, 6)

P16-1B On May 1, 2005, Sator Corp. issued $800,000, 9%, 5-year bonds at face value. The bonds were dated May 1, 2005, and pay interest semiannually on May 1 and November 1. Financial statements are prepared annually on December 31.

Instructions

(a) Prepare the journal entry to record the issuance of the bonds.

(b) Prepare the adjusting entry to record the accrual of interest on December 31, 2005.

(c) Show the balance sheet presentation on December 31, 2005.

(d) Int. exp. $24,000

(d) Prepare the journal entry to record payment of interest on May 1, 2006, assuming no accrual of interest from January 1, 2006, to May 1, 2006.

(e) Prepare the journal entry to record payment of interest on November 1, 2006.

(f) Loss $8,000

(f) Assume that on November 1, 2006, Sator calls the bonds at 101. Record the redemption of the bonds.

Prepare entries to record issuance of bonds, interest accrual, and bond redemption.

(SO 2, 3, 6)

P16-2B Hornung Electric sold $300,000, 10%, 10-year bonds on January 1, 2005. The bonds were dated January 1 and paid interest on January 1 and July 1. The bonds were sold at 104.

Instructions

(a) Prepare the journal entry to record the issuance of the bonds on January 1, 2005.

(b) At December 31, 2005, the balance in the Premium on Bonds Payable account is $10,800. Show the balance sheet presentation of accrued interest and the bond liability at December 31, 2005.

(c) Loss $5,400

(c) On January 1, 2007, when the carrying value of the bonds was $309,600, the company redeemed the bonds at 105. Record the redemption of the bonds assuming that interest for the period has already been paid.

Prepare installment payments schedule and journal entries for a mortgage note payable.

(SO 4)

P16-3B Hamilton Electronics issues a $600,000, 8%, 10-year mortgage note on December 31, 2004. The proceeds from the note are to be used in financing a new research laboratory. The terms of the note provide for semiannual installment payments, exclusive of real estate taxes and insurance, of $44,149. Payments are due June 30 and December 31.

Instructions

(a) Prepare an installment payments schedule for the first 2 years.

(b) June 30 Mortgage Notes Payable $20,149

(b) Prepare the entries for (1) the loan and (2) the first two installment payments.

(c) Current liability—2005: $44,458

(c) Show how the total mortgage liability should be reported on the balance sheet at December 31, 2005.

Analyze three different lease situations and prepare journal entries.

(SO 5)

P16-4B Presented below are three different lease transactions that occurred for Milo Inc. in 2005. Assume that all lease contracts start on January 1, 2005. In no case does Milo receive title to the properties leased during or at the end of the lease term.

	Lessor		
	Gibson Delivery	**Eller Co.**	**Louis Auto**
Type of property	Computer	Delivery equipment	Automobile
Yearly rental	$ 8,000	$ 4,200	$ 3,700
Lease term	6 years	4 years	2 years
Estimated economic life	7 years	7 years	5 years
Fair market value of lease asset	$44,000	$19,000	$11,000
Present value of the lease rental payments	$41,000	$13,000	$ 6,400
Bargain purchase option	None	None	None

Instructions

(a) Which of the leases above are operating leases and which are capital leases? Explain.

(b) How should the lease transaction for Eller Co. be recorded in 2005?

(c) How should the lease transaction for Gibson Delivery be recorded on January 1, 2005?

*P16-5B On July 1, 2005, Clintin Corporation issued $4,000,000 face value, 10%, 10-year bonds at $4,543,626. This price resulted in an effective-interest rate of 8% on the bonds. Clintin uses the effective-interest method to amortize bond premium or discount. The bonds pay semiannual interest July 1 and January 1.

Prepare entries to record issuance of bonds, payment of interest, and amortization of bond premium using effective-interest method.

(SO 2, 8)

Instructions

(Round all computations to the nearest dollar.)

(a) Prepare the journal entry to record the issuance of the bonds on July 1, 2005.

(b) Prepare the journal entry to record the accrual of interest and the amortization of the premium on December 31, 2005.

(b) Amortization $18,255

(c) Prepare the journal entry to record the payment of interest and the amortization of the premium on July 1, 2006, assuming no accrual of interest on June 30.

(c) Amortization $18,985

(d) Prepare the journal entry to record the accrual of interest and the amortization of the premium on December 31, 2006.

(d) Amortization $19,745

(e) Prepare an amortization table through December 31, 2006 (3 interest periods) for this bond issue.

*P16-6B On July 1, 2005, Wilkowski Company issued $2,000,000 face value, 8%, 10-year bonds at $1,750,757. This price resulted in an effective-interest rate of 10% on the bonds. Wilkowski uses the effective-interest method to amortize bond premium or discount. The bonds pay semiannual interest July 1 and January 1.

Prepare entries to record issuance of bonds, payment of interest, and amortization of discount using effective-interest method. In addition, answer questions.

(SO 2, 8)

Instructions

(Round all computations to the nearest dollar.)

(a) Prepare the journal entries to record the following transactions.

  (1) The issuance of the bonds on July 1, 2005.

  (2) The accrual of interest and the amortization of the discount on December 31, 2005.

  (3) The payment of interest and the amortization of the discount on July 1, 2006, assuming no accrual of interest on June 30.

(a) (3) Amortization $7,915

  (4) The accrual of interest and the amortization of the discount on December 31, 2006.

(a) (4) Amortization $8,311

(b) Show the proper balance sheet presentation for the liability for bonds payable on the December 31, 2006, balance sheet.

(b) $1,774,521

(c) ▭▭▭▷ Provide the answers to the following questions in letter form.

  (1) What amount of interest expense is reported for 2006?

  (2) Would the bond interest expense reported in 2006 be the same as, greater than, or less than the amount that would be reported if the straight-line method of amortization were used?

  (3) Determine the total cost of borrowing over the life of the bond.

  (4) Would the total bond interest expense be greater than, the same as, or less than the total interest expense that would be reported if the straight-line method of amortization were used?

*P16-7B Toshiba Electric sold $5,000,000, 10%, 10-year bonds on January 1, 2005. The bonds were dated January 1 and pay interest July 1 and January 1. Toshiba Electric uses the straight-line method to amortize bond premium or discount. The bonds were sold at 104. Assume no interest is accrued on June 30.

Prepare entries to record issuance of bonds, interest accrual, and amortization for 2 years.

(SO 6, 9)

Instructions

(a) Prepare the journal entry to record the issuance of the bonds on January 1, 2005.

(b) Prepare a bond premium amortization schedule for the first 4 interest periods.

(c) Prepare the journal entries for interest and the amortization of the premium in 2005 and 2006.

(b) Amortization $10,000
(d) Premium on bonds payable $160,000

(d) Show the balance sheet presentation of the bond liability at December 31, 2006.

*P16-8B McLain Company sold $2,000,000, 8%, 10-year bonds on July 1, 2005. The bonds were dated July 1, 2005, and pay interest July 1 and January 1. McLain Company uses the straight-line method to amortize bond premium or discount. Assume no interest is accrued on June 30.

Prepare entries to record issuance of bonds, interest, and amortization of bond premium and discount.

(SO 6, 9)
(a) Amortization $4,000
(b) Amortization $2,000
(c) Premium on bonds payable $76,000
Discount on bonds payable $38,000

Instructions

(a) Prepare all the necessary journal entries to record the issuance of the bonds and bond interest expense for 2005, assuming that the bonds sold at 104.

(b) Prepare journal entries as in part (a) assuming that the bonds sold at 98.

(c) Show balance sheet presentation for each bond issue at December 31, 2005.

Prepare entries to record interest payments, premium amortization, and redemption of bonds.

(SO 2, 3, 9)

*P16-9B The following is taken from the McGovern Company balance sheet.

MCGOVERN COMPANY
Balance Sheet (partial)
December 31, 2005

Current liabilities		
Bond interest payable (for 6 months		
from July 1 to December 31)		$ 120,000
Long-term liabilities		
Bonds payable, 8% due January 1, 2016	$3,000,000	
Add: Premium on bonds payable	200,000	$3,200,000

Interest is payable semiannually on January 1 and July 1. The bonds are callable on any semiannual interest date. McGovern uses straight-line amortization for any bond premium or discount. From December 31, 2005, the bonds will be outstanding for an additional 10 years (120 months).

Instructions

(a) Journalize the payment of bond interest on January 1, 2006

(b) Amortization $10,000

(b) Prepare the entry to amortize bond premium and to pay the interest due on July 1, 2006, assuming no accrual of interest on June 30.

(c) Gain $96,000

(c) Assume that on July 1, 2006, after paying interest, McGovern Company calls bonds having a face value of $1,800,000. The call price is 101. Record the redemption of the bonds.

(d) Amortization $4,000

(d) Prepare the adjusting entry at December 31, 2006, to amortize bond premium and to accrue interest on the remaining bonds.

COMPREHENSIVE PROBLEM: CHAPTERS 14–16

Plankton Corporation's trial balance at December 31, 2004, is presented below. All 2004 transactions have been recorded except for the items described on the next page.

	Debit	Credit
Cash	$ 18,000	
Accounts Receivable	51,000	
Merchandise Inventory	22,700	
Land	65,000	
Building	95,000	
Equipment	40,000	
Allowance for Doubtful Accounts		$ 450
Accumulated Depreciation—Building		30,000
Accumulated Depreciation—Equipment		14,400
Accounts Payable		19,300
Bond Interest Payable		–0–
Dividends Payable		–0–
Unearned Rent		8,000
Bonds Payable (10%)		50,000
Common Stock ($10 par)		30,000
Paid-in Capital in Excess of Par—Common Stock		6,000
Preferred Stock ($20 par)		–0–
Paid-in Capital in Excess of Par—Preferred Stock		–0–
Retained Earnings		75,050
Treasury Stock	–0–	
Cash Dividends Declared	–0–	
Sales		550,000
Rent Revenue		–0–
Bad Debts Expense	–0–	
Bond Interest Expense	2,500	
Cost of Goods Sold	385,000	
Depreciation Expense—Buildings	–0–	
Depreciation Expense—Equipment	–0–	
Other Operating Expenses	39,000	
Salaries Expense	65,000	
Total	$783,200	$783,200

Unrecorded transactions

1. On January 1, 2004, Plankton issued 1,000 shares of $20 par, 6% preferred stock for $22,000.
2. On January 1, 2004, Plankton also issued 500 shares of common stock for $23,000.
3. Plankton reacquired 300 shares of its common stock on July 1, 2004, for $49 per share.
4. On December 31, 2004, Plankton declared the annual preferred stock dividend and a $1.50 per share dividend on the outstanding common stock, all payable on January 15, 2005.
5. Plankton estimates that uncollectible accounts receivable at year-end is $5,100.
6. The building is being depreciated using the straight-line method over 30 years. The salvage value is $5,000.
7. The equipment is being depreciated using the straight-line method over 10 years. The salvage value is $4,000.
8. The unearned rent was collected on October 1, 2004. It was receipt of 4 months' rent in advance (October 1, 2004 through January 31, 2005).
9. The 10% bonds payable pay interest every January 1 and July 1. The interest for the 6 months ended December 31, 2004, has not been paid or recorded.

Instructions
(Ignore income taxes.)

(a) Prepare journal entries for the transactions listed above.
(b) Prepare an updated December 31, 2004, trial balance, reflecting the unrecorded transactions.
(c) Prepare an income statement for the year ending December 31, 2004.
(d) Prepare a statement of retained earnings for the year ending December 31, 2004.
(e) Prepare a classified balance sheet as of December 31, 2004.

BROADENING YOUR PERSPECTIVE

Financial Reporting and Analysis

■ FINANCIAL REPORTING PROBLEM: PepsiCo

BYP16-1 Refer to the financial statements of **PepsiCo** and the Notes to Consolidated Financial Statements in Appendix A.

Instructions
(a) What was PepsiCo's total long-term debt (excluding deferred income taxes) at December 28, 2002? What was the increase/decrease in total long-term debt (excluding deferred income taxes) from the prior year? What does Note 9 to the financial statements indicate about the composition of PepsiCo's long-term debt obligation?
(b) What type of leases, operating or capital, does PepsiCo report? (See Note 9.) Are these leases reported on PepsiCo's financial statements?
(c) What are the total long-term contractual commitments that PepsiCo reports as of December 28, 2002? (See Note 9.)

■ COMPARATIVE ANALYSIS PROBLEM: PepsiCo vs. Coca-Cola

BYP16-2 **PepsiCo**'s financial statements are presented in Appendix A. **Coca-Cola**'s financial statements are presented in Appendix B.

Instructions
(a) Based on the information contained in these financial statements, compute the following 2002 ratios for each company.
  (1) Debt (excluding "deferred income taxes") to total assets.
  (2) Times interest earned.
(b) What conclusions concerning the companies' long-run solvency can be drawn from these ratios?
(c) Which company has reported the greater amount of future long-term commitments for the 5 succeeding years?

■ **INTERPRETING FINANCIAL STATEMENTS: A Global Focus**

BYP16-3 Apache Corporation is an international, independent energy enterprise engaged in the exploration, development, production, gathering, processing, and marketing of natural gas and crude oil. Its corporate headquarters are located in Houston, Texas, and it has operations in North America, Australia, Egypt, Poland and the People's Republic of China.

The 1994 annual report of Apache Corporation disclosed the following information in its management discussion section.

APACHE CORPORATION
Management Discussion

In May 1994, Apache issued 9.25% bonds due 2002 in the principal amount of $100 million. The proceeds of $99 million from the offering were used to reduce bank debt, to pay off the 9.5% convertible debentures due 1996, and for general corporate purposes. In December 1994, the company privately placed 3.93% convertible notes due 1997 in the principal amount of $75 million. The notes are not redeemable before maturity and are convertible into Apache common stock at the option of the holders at any time prior to maturity, at a conversion price of $27 per share. Proceeds from the sale of the notes were used for the repayment of bank debt.

Instructions

(a) Identify the face amount, contractual interest rate, and selling price of the newly issued bonds due in 2002. Explain whether the bonds sold at a premium or a discount.

(b) For what purposes has Apache Corporation been incurring more debt?

■ **EXPLORING THE WEB**

BYP16-4 Bond or debt securities pay a stated rate of interest. This rate of interest is dependent on the risk associated with the investment. **Moody's Investment Service** provides rating for companies that issue debt securities.

Address: www.moodys.com, or go to www.wiley.com/college/weygandt

Steps: From Moody's homepage, choose **About Moody's** and **Moody's History**.

Instructions

(a) What year did Moody's introduce the first bond rating?

(b) List three basic principles Moody's uses in rating bonds.

(c) What is the definition of Moody's Aaa rating on long-term taxable debt?

Critical Thinking

■ **GROUP DECISION CASE**

*****BYP16-5** On January 1, 2003, Bailey Corporation issued $6,000,000 of 5-year, 8% bonds at 96; the bonds pay interest semiannually on July 1 and January 1. By January 1, 2005, the market rate of interest for bonds of risk similar to those of Bailey Corporation had risen. As a result the market value of these bonds was $5,000,000 on January 1, 2005—below their carrying value. Debbie Bailey, president of the company, suggests repurchasing all of these bonds in the open market at the $5,000,000 price. To do so the company will have to issue $5,000,000 (face value) of new 10-year, 11% bonds at par. The president asks you, as controller, "What is the feasibility of my proposed repurchase plan?"

Instructions

With the class divided into groups, answer the following.

(a) What is the carrying value of the outstanding Bailey Corporation 5-year bonds on January 1, 2005? (Assume straight-line amortization.)

(b) Prepare the journal entry to retire the 5-year bonds on January 1, 2005. Prepare the journal entry to issue the new 10-year bonds.

(c) Prepare a short memo to the president in response to her request for advice. List the economic factors that you believe should be considered for her repurchase proposal.

■ COMMUNICATION ACTIVITY

BYP16-6 Ken Robson, president of the Robson Corporation, is considering the issuance of bonds to finance an expansion of his business. He has asked you to (1) discuss the advantages of bonds over common stock financing, (2) indicate the type of bonds he might issue, and (3) explain the issuing procedures used in bond transactions.

Instructions
Write a memo to the president, answering his request.

■ ETHICS CASE

BYP16-7 Mel Horn is the president, founder, and majority owner of Wesley Medical Corporation, an emerging medical technology products company. Wesley is in dire need of additional capital to keep operating and to bring several promising products to final development, testing, and production. Mel, as owner of 51% of the outstanding stock, manages the company's operations. He places heavy emphasis on research and development and on long-term growth. The other principal stockholder is Mary Sommers who, as a nonemployee investor, owns 40% of the stock. Mary would like to deemphasize the R&D functions and emphasize the marketing function, to maximize short-run sales and profits from existing products. She believes this strategy would raise the market price of Wesley's stock.

All of Mel's personal capital and borrowing power is tied up in his 51% stock ownership. He knows that any offering of additional shares of stock will dilute his controlling interest because he won't be able to participate in such an issuance. But, Mary has money and would likely buy enough shares to gain control of Wesley. She then would dictate the company's future direction, even if it meant replacing Mel as president and CEO.

The company already has considerable debt. Raising additional debt will be costly, will adversely affect Wesley's credit rating, and will increase the company's reported losses due to the growth in interest expense. Mary and the other minority stockholders express opposition to the assumption of additional debt, fearing the company will be pushed to the brink of bankruptcy. Wanting to maintain his control and to preserve the direction of "his" company, Mel is doing everything to avoid a stock issuance. He is contemplating a large issuance of bonds, even if it means the bonds are issued with a high effective-interest rate.

Instructions
(a) Who are the stakeholders in this situation?
(b) What are the ethical issues in this case?
(c) What would you do if you were Mel?

Answers to Self-Study Questions
1. c   **2.** a   **3.** b   **4.** d   **5.** c   **6.** d   *7. b   *8. c   *9. d   *10. a

Answer to PepsiCo Review It Question 2, p. 639
An examination of **PepsiCo**'s statement of cash flows indicates the following reductions of debt: payments of long-term debt, $353 million, and payments of short-term borrowings of more than 3 months, $809 million.

☑ **REMEMBER** to go back to the Navigator box on the chapter-opening page and check off your completed work.

Investments

THE NAVIGATOR ✓

Understand **Concepts for Review**	❏
Read **Feature Story**	❏
Scan **Study Objectives**	❏
Read **Preview**	❏
Read text and answer **Before You Go On** p. 680 ❏ p. 686 ❏ p. 691 ❏	
Work **Demonstration Problem**	❏
Review **Summary of Study Objectives**	❏
Answer **Self-Study Questions**	❏
Complete **Assignments**	❏

CONCEPTS FOR REVIEW

Before studying this chapter, you should know or, if necessary, review:

How to record the issuance of bonds.
(Ch. 16, pp. 634–637)

How to compute and record interest.
(Ch. 3, pp. 101–102, Ch. 9, pp. 376–378, and Ch. 16, pp. 634–635, 640)

How to record amortization of bond discount and bond premium using the effective-interest method (Ch. 16, pp. 652–655) and the straight-line method.
(Ch. 16, pp. 656–659)

Where short-term and long-term investments are classified on a balance sheet.
(Ch. 4, pp. 152–153)

✓ THE NAVIGATOR

Is There Anything Else We Can Buy?

In a rapidly changing world you must change rapidly or suffer the consequences. In business, change requires investment.

A case in point is found in the entertainment industry. Technology is bringing about innovations so quickly that it is nearly impossible to guess which technologies will last and which will soon fade away. For example, will both satellite TV and cable TV survive, or will just one succeed, or will both be replaced by something else? Or consider the publishing industry. Will paper newspapers and magazines be replaced by online news via the World Wide Web? If you are a publisher, you have to make your best guess about what the future holds and invest accordingly.

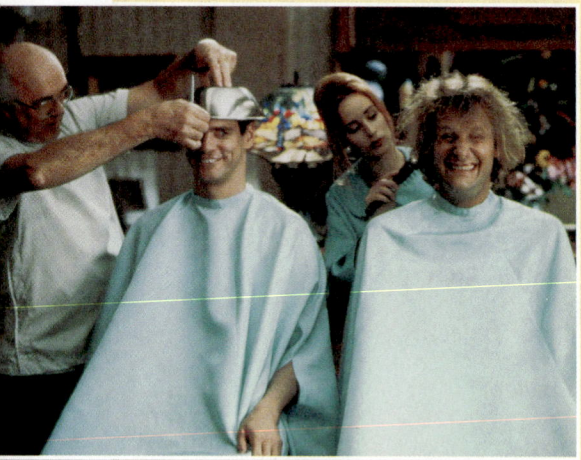

Time Warner, Inc. lives at the center of this arena. It is not an environment for the timid, and Time Warner's philosophy is anything but timid. It might be characterized as, "If we can't beat you, we will buy you." Its mantra is "invest, invest, invest." A list of Time Warner's holdings gives an idea of its reach. Magazines: *People, Time, Life, Sports Illustrated, Fortune.* Book publishers: Time-Life Books, Book-of-the-Month Club, Little, Brown & Co, Sunset Books. Music: Warner Bros. Records, Reprise, Atlantic, Rhino, Elektra, and Asylum, representing such artists as Hootie and the Blowfish, Tori Amos, Eric Clapton, and Madonna. Television and movies: Warner Bros. ("ER," "Friends," the WB Network), HBO, and movies like the *Dumb and Dumber* and *The Matrix* series. Broadcasting: TNT, CNN news, and Turner's library of thousands of classic movies. Internet: America Online, and AOL Anywhere. Time Warner owns more information and entertainment copyrights and brands than any other company in the world.

So what has Time Warner's aggressive acquisition spree meant for the bottom line? It has left the company with huge debt and massive interest costs. Also, some of the acquisitions have not come cheap, resulting in large amounts of reported goodwill and goodwill amortization. The merger of America Online (AOL) with Time Warner was billed as a merger of equals. But, it was AOL's phenomenal growth and astronomical stock price that made this merger possible. Unfortunately, investors involved in this merger have faired poorly. From a high of $95.80, Time Warner's stock price recently fell to $8.70 per share.

www.timewarner.com

After studying this chapter, you should be able to:

1. Discuss why corporations invest in debt and stock securities.
2. Explain the accounting for debt investments.
3. Explain the accounting for stock investments.
4. Describe the use of consolidated financial statements.
5. Indicate how debt and stock investments are valued and reported on the financial statements.
6. Distinguish between short-term and long-term investments.

Time Warner's management believed in aggressive growth through investing in the stock of existing companies. Besides purchasing stock, companies also purchase other securities such as bonds issued by corporations or by governments. Investments can be purchased for a short or long period of time, as a passive investment, or with the intent to control another company. As you will see in this chapter, the way in which a company accounts for its investments is determined by a number of factors.

The content and organization of Chapter 17 are as follows.

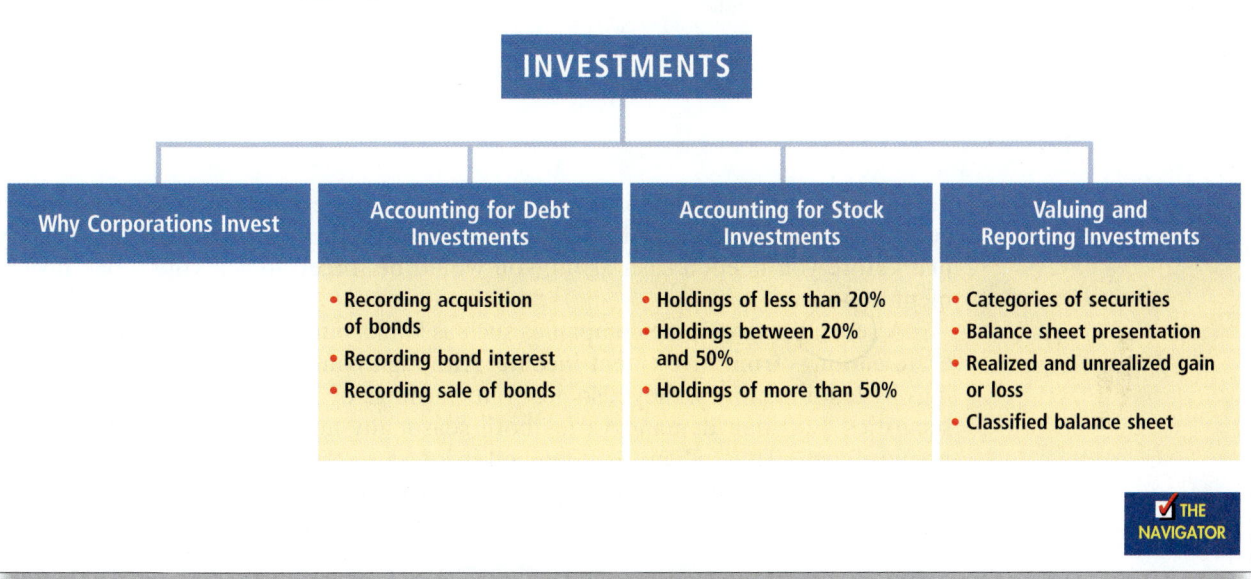

Why Corporations Invest

Corporations purchase investments in debt or stock securities generally for one of three reasons. First, a corporation may **have excess cash** that it does not need for the immediate purchase of operating assets. For example, many companies experience seasonal fluctuations in sales. A Cape Cod marina has more sales in the spring and summer than in the fall and winter. The reverse is true for an Aspen ski shop. At the end of an operating cycle, many companies have cash on hand that is temporarily idle until the start of another operating cycle. These companies may invest the excess funds to earn a greater return than they would get by just holding the funds in the bank. The role that such temporary investments play in the operating cycle is depicted in Illustration 17-1 (page 678).

Excess cash may also result from economic cycles. For example, when the economy is booming, **General Motors** generates considerable excess cash. It uses some of this cash to purchase new plant and equipment and pays out some of the cash in dividends. But it may also invest excess cash in liquid assets in anticipation of a future downturn in the economy. It can then liquidate these investments during a recession, when sales slow down and cash is scarce.

When investing excess cash for short periods of time, corporations invest in low-risk, highly liquid securities—most often short-term government securities. It is generally not wise to invest short-term excess cash in shares of common stock

Illustration 17-1
Temporary investments and
the operating cycle

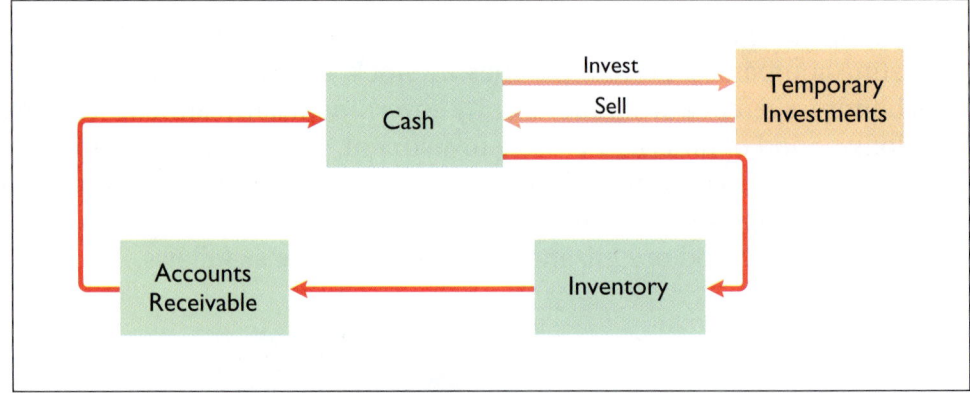

because stock investments can experience rapid price changes. If you did invest your short-term excess cash in stock and the price of the stock declined significantly just before you needed cash again, you would be forced to sell your stock investment at a loss.

A second reason some companies such as banks purchase investments is to generate **earnings from investment income**. Although banks make most of their earnings by lending money, they also generate earnings by investing in debt and equity securities. But loan demand varies both seasonally and with changes in the economic climate. Thus, when loan demand is low, a bank must find other uses for its cash. Bank regulators severely limit the ability of banks to invest in common stock because of the risk involved. Therefore, most investments held by banks are debt securities.

Pension funds and mutual funds are corporations that also regularly invest to generate earnings. However, they do so for **speculative reasons**. They are speculating that the investment will increase in value and thus result in positive returns. Therefore, they invest primarily in the common stock of other corporations. These investments are passive in nature. The pension fund or mutual fund does not usually take an active role in controlling the affairs of the companies in which they invest.

Companies also invest for **strategic reasons**. A company may purchase a noncontrolling interest in another company in a related industry in which it wishes to establish a presence. For example, **Time Warner** initially purchased an interest of less than 20 percent in **Turner Broadcasting** to have a stake in Turner's expanding business opportunities. At a later date **Time Warner** acquired the remaining 80 percent. Subsequently, Time Warner was merged into **AOL** and named **AOL Time Warner, Inc.** (Not even a huge corporation like Time Warner is at the top of the corporate "food-chain.") But, it is again just **Time Warner, Inc.**, having dropped the "AOL" from its name in late 2003. Or, a company can exercise some influence over a customer or supplier by purchasing a significant, but not controlling, interest in that company.

A corporation may also choose to purchase a controlling interest in another company. This might be done to enter a new industry without incurring the tremendous costs and risks associated with starting from scratch. Or a company might purchase another company in its same industry. The purchase of a company that is in your industry, but involved in a different activity, is called a **vertical acquisition**. For example, **Nike** might purchase a chain of athletic shoe stores, such as **The Athlete's Foot**. In a **horizontal acquisition** you purchase a company that does the same activity as your company. For example, Nike might purchase **Reebok**.

In summary, businesses invest in other companies for the reasons shown in Illustration 17-2.

Illustration 17-2
Why corporations invest

Reason	Typical Investment
To house excess cash until needed	Low-risk, high-liquidity, short-term securities such as government-issued securities
To generate earnings	Debt securities (banks and other financial institutions); and stock securities (mutual funds and pension funds)
To meet strategic goals	Stocks of companies in a related industry or in an unrelated industry that the company wishes to enter

Illustration 17-2
Why corporations invest

Accounting for Debt Investments

Debt investments are investments in government and corporation bonds. In accounting for debt investments, entries are required to record (1) the acquisition, (2) the interest revenue, and (3) the sale.

STUDY OBJECTIVE 2

Explain the accounting for debt investments.

Recording Acquisition of Bonds

At acquisition, the cost principle applies. Cost includes all expenditures necessary to acquire these investments, such as the price paid plus brokerage fees (commissions), if any. Assume, for example, that Kuhl Corporation acquires 50 Doan Inc. 8%, 10-year, $1,000 bonds on January 1, 2005, for $54,000, including brokerage fees of $1,000. The entry to record the investment is:

Jan. 1	Debt Investments	54,000	
	Cash		54,000
	(To record purchase of 50 Doan Inc. bonds)		

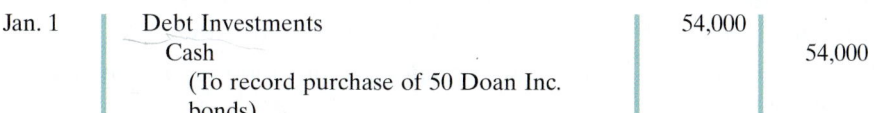

A = L + SE
+54,000
−54,000

Cash Flows
−54,000

Recording Bond Interest

The bonds pay interest of $2,000 semiannually on July 1 and January 1 ($50,000 × 8% × ½). The entry for the receipt of interest on July 1 is:

July 1	Cash	2,000	
	Interest Revenue		2,000
	(To record receipt of interest on Doan Inc. bonds)		

A = L + SE
+2,000   +2,000 Rev

Cash Flows
+2,000

If Kuhl Corporation's fiscal year ends on December 31, it is necessary to accrue the interest of $2,000 earned since July 1. The adjusting entry is:

Dec. 31	Interest Receivable	2,000	
	Interest Revenue		2,000
	(To accrue interest on Doan Inc. bonds)		

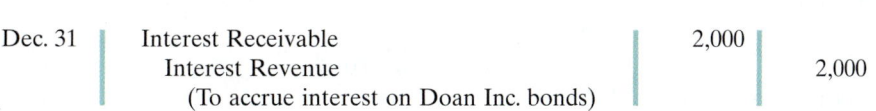

A = L + SE
+2,000   +2,000 Rev

Cash Flows
no effect

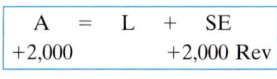

Interest Receivable is reported as a current asset in the balance sheet; Interest Revenue is reported under "Other revenues and gains" in the income statement.

When the interest is received on January 1, the entry is:

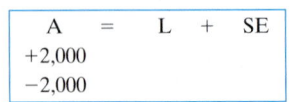

A	=	L	+	SE
+2,000				
−2,000				

Cash Flows
+2,000

Jan. 1	Cash	2,000	
	Interest Receivable		2,000
	(To record receipt of accrued interest)		

A credit to Interest Revenue at this time would be incorrect. Why? Because the interest revenue was earned and accrued in the preceding accounting period.

Recording Sale of Bonds

When the bonds are sold, it is necessary to credit the investment account for the cost of the bonds. Any difference between the net proceeds from the sale (sales price less brokerage fees) and the cost of the bonds is recorded as a gain or loss.

Assume, for example, that Kuhl Corporation receives net proceeds of $58,000 on the sale of the Doan Inc. bonds on January 1, 2006, after receiving the interest due. Since the securities cost $54,000, a gain of $4,000 has been realized. The entry to record the sale is:

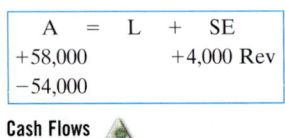

A	=	L	+	SE
+58,000				+4,000 Rev
−54,000				

Cash Flows
+54,000

Jan. 1	Cash	58,000	
	Debt Investments		54,000
	Gain on Sale of Debt Investments		4,000
	(To record sale of Doan Inc. bonds)		

The gain on sale of debt investments is reported under "Other revenues and gains" in the income statement.

BEFORE YOU GO ON...

Review It

1. Why might a company make investments in debt or stock securities?
2. What entries are required in accounting for debt investments?
3. How are gains and losses from the sale of bonds reported in the income statements?

Do It

Waldo Corporation had the following transactions pertaining to debt investments.

Jan. 1   Purchased 30 10%, $1,000 Hillary Co. bonds for $30,000, plus brokerage fees of $900. Interest is payable semiannually on July 1 and January 1.
July 1   Received semiannual interest on Hillary Co. bonds.
July 1   Sold 15 Hillary Co. bonds for $15,000, less $400 brokerage fees.

(a) Journalize the transactions, and (b) prepare the adjusting entry for the accrual of interest on December 31.

ACTION PLAN

■ Record bond investments at cost.
■ Record interest when received and/or accrued.
■ When bonds are sold, credit the investment account for the cost of the bonds.

■ Record any difference between the cost and the net proceeds as a gain or loss.

SOLUTION

(a)	Jan. 1	Debt Investments	30,900	
		Cash		30,900
		(To record purchase of 30 Hillary Co. bonds)		
	July 1	Cash	1,500	
		Interest Revenue ($30,000 × .10 × 6/12)		1,500
		(To record receipt of interest on Hillary Co. bonds)		
	July 1	Cash	14,600	
		Loss on Sale of Debt Investments	850	
		Debt Investments ($30,900 × 15/30)		15,450
		(To record sale of 15 Hillary Co. bonds)		
(b)	Dec. 31	Interest Receivable	750	
		Interest Revenue ($15,000 × .10 × 6/12)		750
		(To accrue interest on Hillary Co. bonds)		

Related exercise material: *BE17-1 and E17-1.*

✓ THE
NAVIGATOR

Accounting for Stock Investments

Stock investments are investments in the capital stock of corporations. When a company holds stock (and/or debt) of several different corporations, the group of securities is identified as an **investment portfolio**.

    The accounting for investments in common stock is based on the extent of the investor's influence over the operating and financial affairs of the issuing corporation (commonly called the **investee**). Illustration 17-3 shows the guidelines for three levels of influence.

STUDY OBJECTIVE 3

Explain the accounting for stock investments.

Investor's Ownership Interest in Investee's Common Stock	Presumed Influence on Investee	Accounting Guidelines
Less than 20%	Insignificant	Cost method
Between 20% and 50%	Significant	Equity method
More than 50%	Controlling	Consolidated financial statements

Illustration 17-3
Accounting guidelines for stock investments

The presumed influence may be negated by extenuating circumstances. For example, a company that acquires a 25% interest in another company in a "hostile" takeover may not have significant influence over the investee. Companies are required to use judgment instead of blindly following the guidelines.[1] On the following pages we will explain the application of each guideline.

Holdings of Less Than 20%

In accounting for stock investments of less than 20%, the cost method is used. Under the **cost method**, the investment is recorded at cost, and revenue is recognized only when cash dividends are received.

Recording Acquisition of Stock Investments

At acquisition, the cost principle applies. Cost includes all expenditures necessary to acquire these investments such as the price paid plus any brokerage fees (commissions). Assume, for example, that on July 1, 2005, Sanchez Corporation acquires 1,000 shares (10% ownership) of Beal Corporation common stock. Sanchez pays $40 per share plus brokerage fees of $500. The entry for the purchase is:

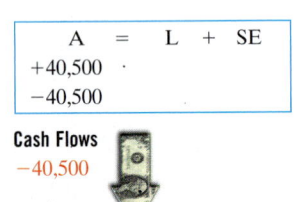

	A	=	L	+	SE
	+40,500				
	−40,500				

Cash Flows
−40,500

July 1	Stock Investments	40,500	
	Cash		40,500
	(To record purchase of 1,000 shares of Beal Corporation common stock)		

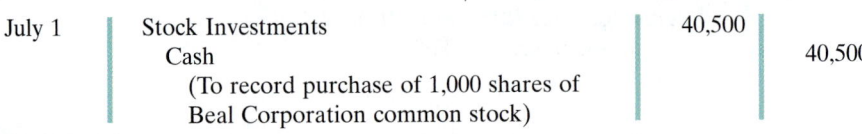

ACCOUNTING IN ACTION   **ⓔ Business Insight**

Amazon.com's Web site receives many "hits" each day. Because of this Amazon earns significant revenue by allowing other companies to advertise there. Many of them pay with stock in their company (since dot-coms often have very little cash). When Amazon receives the stock, it debits Investment in XYZ Company and credits Unearned Revenue for the market value of the shares on the day they are received. It then recognizes revenue over the life of the advertising agreement. In the future, Amazon hopes to do more cash deals and fewer stock deals.

Recording Dividends

During the time the stock is held, entries are required for any cash dividends received. If a $2.00 per share dividend is received by Sanchez Corporation on December 31, the entry is:

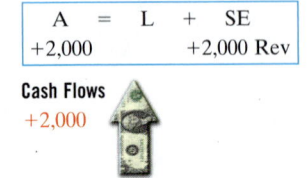

	A	=	L	+	SE
	+2,000				+2,000 Rev

Cash Flows
+2,000

Dec. 31	Cash (1,000 × $2)	2,000	
	Dividend Revenue		2,000
	(To record receipt of a cash dividend)		

---

[1]Among the questions that are considered in determining an investor's influence are these: (1) Does the investor have representation on the investee's board? (2) Does the investor participate in the investee's policy-making process? (3) Are there material transactions between the investor and investee? (4) Is the common stock held by other stockholders concentrated or dispersed?

Dividend Revenue is reported under "Other revenues and gains" in the income statement. Unlike interest on notes and bonds, dividends do not accrue. Therefore, adjusting entries are not made to accrue dividends.

Recording Sale of Stock

When stock is sold, the difference between the net proceeds from the sale (sales price less brokerage fees) and the cost of the stock is recognized as a gain or a loss. Assume that Sanchez Corporation receives net proceeds of $39,500 on the sale of its Beal stock on February 10, 2006. Because the stock cost $40,500, a loss of $1,000 has been incurred. The entry to record the sale is:

Feb. 10	Cash	39,500	
	Loss on Sale of Stock Investments	1,000	
	Stock Investments		40,500
	(To record sale of Beal common stock)		

A	=	L	+	SE
+39,500				−1,000 Exp
−40,500				

Cash Flows
+39,500

The loss account is reported under "Other expenses and losses" in the income statement. A gain on sale is shown under "Other revenues and gains."

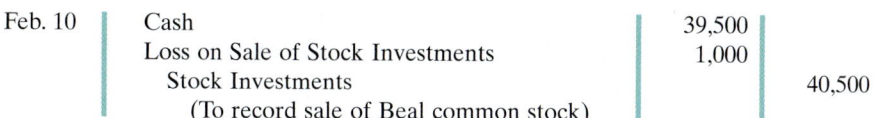

Holdings Between 20% and 50%

When an investor company owns only a small portion of the shares of stock of another company, the investor cannot exercise control over the investee. But, when an investor owns between 20% and 50% of the common stock of a corporation, it is presumed that the investor has significant influence over the financial and operating activities of the investee. The investor probably has a representative on the investee's board of directors. Through that representative, the investor begins to exercise some control over the investee. The investee company in some sense becomes part of the investor company. For example, even prior to purchasing all of Turner Broadcasting, **Time Warner** owned 20% of Turner and could exercise significant control over major decisions made by Turner.

Companies with stock holdings between 20% and 50% in an investee use an approach called the equity method. Under the **equity method**, **the investor records its share of the net income of the investee in the year when it is earned**. An alternative might be to delay recognizing the investor's share of net income until a cash dividend is declared. But that approach would ignore the fact that the investor and investee are, in some sense, one company, making the investor better off by the investee's earned income.

Under the equity method, the investment in common stock is initially recorded at cost. After that, the investment account is **adjusted annually** to show the investor's equity in the investee. Each year, the investor does the following: (1) It increases (debits) the investment account and increases (credits) revenue for its share of the investee's net income.[2] (2) The investor also decreases (credits) the investment account for the amount of dividends received. The investment account is reduced for dividends received because the net assets of the investee are decreased when a dividend is paid.

HELPFUL HINT

The entries for investments in common stock also apply to investments in preferred stock.

HELPFUL HINT

Under the equity method revenue is recognized on the accrual basis—i.e., when it is earned by the investee.

Recording Acquisition of Stock Investments

Assume that Milar Corporation acquires 30% of the common stock of Beck Company for $120,000 on January 1, 2005. The entry to record this transaction is:

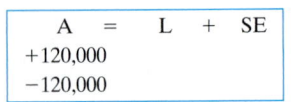

A	=	L	+	SE
+120,000				
−120,000				

Cash Flows

−120,000

Jan. 1	Stock Investments		120,000	
	Cash			120,000
	(To record purchase of Beck common stock)			

Recording Revenue and Dividends

For 2005, Beck reports net income of $100,000. It declares and pays a $40,000 cash dividend. Milar is required to record (1) its share of Beck's income, $30,000 (30% × $100,000) and (2) the reduction in the investment account for the dividends received, $12,000 ($40,000 × 30%). The entries are:

(1)

A	=	L	+	SE
+30,000				+30,000 Rev

Cash Flows
no effect

Dec. 31	Stock Investments		30,000	
	Revenue from Investment in Beck Company			30,000
	(To record 30% equity in Beck's 2005 net income)			

(2)

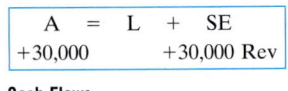

A	=	L	+	SE
+12,000				
−12,000				

Cash Flows

+12,000

Dec. 31	Cash		12,000	
	Stock Investments			12,000
	(To record dividends received)			

After posting the transactions for the year, the investment and revenue accounts will show the following.

Illustration 17-4
Investment and revenue accounts after posting

Stock Investments				Revenue from Investment in Beck Company		
Jan. 1	120,000	Dec. 31	**12,000**		Dec. 31	**30,000**
Dec. 31	**30,000**					
Dec. 31 Bal.	138,000					

During the year, the investment account has increased by $18,000. This $18,000 is Milar's 30% equity in the $60,000 increase in Beck's retained earnings ($100,000 − $40,000). In addition, Milar will report $30,000 of revenue from its investment, which is 30% of Beck's net income of $100,000. Note that the difference between reported revenue under the cost method and reported revenue under the equity method can be significant. For example, Milar would report only $12,000 of dividend revenue (30% × $40,000) if the cost method were used.

Holdings of More than 50%

STUDY OBJECTIVE 4

Describe the use of consolidated financial statements.

A company that owns more than 50% of the common stock of another entity is known as the **parent company**. The entity whose stock is owned by the parent company is called the **subsidiary (affiliated) company**. Because of its stock ownership, the parent company has a **controlling interest** in the subsidiary.

When a company owns more than 50% of the common stock of another company, **consolidated financial statements** are usually prepared. Consolidated financial statements present the total assets and liabilities controlled by the parent company.

They also present the total revenues and expenses of the subsidiary companies. Consolidated statements are prepared **in addition to** the financial statements for the parent and individual subsidiary companies. When Time Warner had a 20% investment in Turner, this investment was reported in a single line item—Other Investments—in Time Warner's balance sheet. After the merger, Time Warner instead consolidated Turner's results with its own. Under this approach, the individual assets and liabilities of Turner are included with those of Time Warner: its plant and equipment are added to Time Warner's plant and equipment, its receivables are added to Time Warner's receivables, and so on.

> **HELPFUL HINT**
>
> If parent (A) has three wholly owned subsidiaries (B, C, & D), there are four separate legal entities. But, from the viewpoint of the shareholders of the parent company, there is only one economic entity.

ACCOUNTING IN ACTION Business Insight

Time Warner, Inc. owns 100% of the common stock of **Home Box Office (HBO) Corporation**. The common stockholders of Time Warner elect the board of directors of the company, who, in turn, select the officers and managers of the company. Time Warner's board of directors controls the property owned by the corporation, which includes the common stock of HBO. Thus, they are in a position to elect the board of directors of HBO and, in effect, control its operations. These relationships are graphically illustrated here.

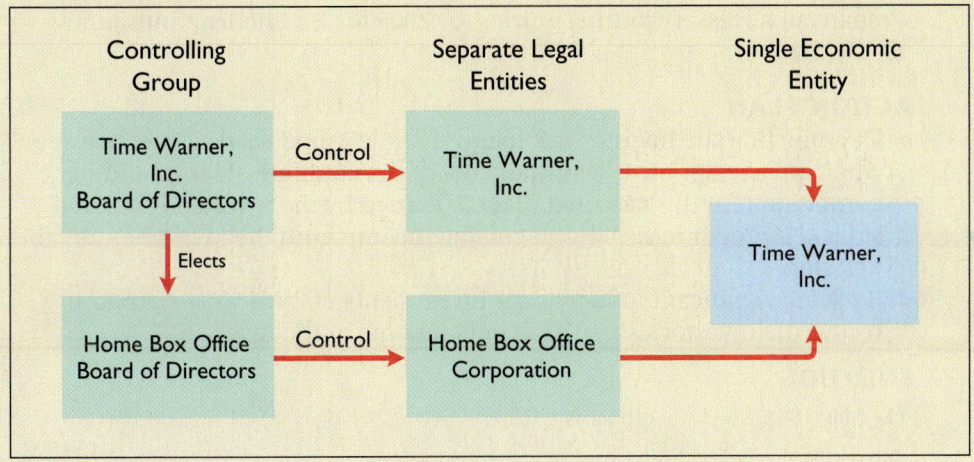

Consolidated statements are useful because they indicate the magnitude and scope of operations of the companies under common control. For example, regulators and the courts undoubtedly used the consolidated statements of **AT&T** to determine whether a breakup of AT&T was in the public interest. Listed below are three companies that prepare consolidated statements and some of the companies they have owned. Note that one, **Walt Disney**, is Time Warner's arch rival.

Toys "R" Us, Inc.	Cendant	The Walt Disney Company
Kids "R" Us	Howard Johnson	Capital Cities/ABC, Inc.
Babies "R" Us	Ramada Inn	Disneyland, Disney World
Imaginarium	Century 21	Mighty Ducks
Toysrus.com	Coldwell Banker	Anaheim Angels
	Avis	ESPN

BEFORE YOU GO ON...

Review It

1. What are the accounting entries for stock investments of less than 20%?
2. What entries are made under the equity method when (a) the investor receives a cash dividend from the investee and (b) the investee reports net income for the year?
3. What is the purpose of consolidated financial statements?
4. What does **PepsiCo** state regarding its accounting policy involving consolidated financial statements? The answer to this question is provided on page 708.

Do It

Presented below are two independent situations.

1. Rho Jean Inc. acquired 5% of the 400,000 shares of common stock of Stillwater Corp. at a total cost of $6 per share on May 18, 2005. On August 30, Stillwater declared and paid a $75,000 dividend. On December 31, Stillwater reported net income of $244,000 for the year.
2. Debbie, Inc. obtained significant influence over North Sails by buying 40% of North Sails' 60,000 outstanding shares of common stock at a cost of $12 per share on January 1, 2005. On April 15, North Sails declared and paid a cash dividend of $45,000. On December 31, North Sails reported net income of $120,000 for the year.

Prepare all necessary journal entries for 2005 for (1) Rho Jean Inc. and (2) Debbie, Inc.

ACTION PLAN

- Presume that the investor has relatively little influence over the investee when an investor owns less than 20% of the common stock of another corporation. In this case, net income earned by the investee is not considered a proper basis for recognizing income from the investment by the investor.
- Presume significant influence for investments of 20%–50%. Therefore, record the investor's share of the net income of the investee.

SOLUTION

(1) May 18	Stock Investments (20,000 × $6)		120,000	
	Cash			120,000
	(To record purchase of 20,000 shares of Stillwater Co. stock)			
Aug. 30	Cash		3,750	
	Dividend Revenue ($75,000 × 5%)			3,750
	(To record receipt of cash dividend)			
(2) Jan. 1	Stock Investments (60,000 × 40% × $12)		288,000	
	Cash			288,000
	(To record purchase of 24,000 shares of North Sails' stock)			
Apr. 15	Cash		18,000	
	Stock Investments ($45,000 × 40%)			18,000
	(To record receipt of cash dividend)			

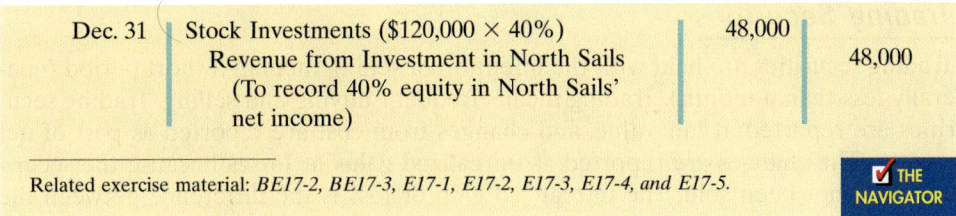

Dec. 31	Stock Investments ($120,000 × 40%)	48,000	
	Revenue from Investment in North Sails		48,000
	(To record 40% equity in North Sails' net income)		

Related exercise material: *BE17-2, BE17-3, E17-1, E17-2, E17-3, E17-4, and E17-5.*

☑ THE NAVIGATOR

Valuing and Reporting Investments

The value of debt and stock investments may fluctuate greatly during the time they are held. For example, in one 12-month period, the stock price of **Dell Computer Corp.** hit a high of $59.70 and a low of $16. In light of such price fluctuations, how should investments be valued at the balance sheet date? Valuation could be at cost, at fair value (market value), or at the lower of cost or market value. Many people argue that fair value offers the best approach because it represents the expected cash realizable value of securities. **Fair value** is the amount for which a security could be sold in a normal market. Others counter that, unless a security is going to be sold soon, the fair value is not relevant because the price of the security will likely change again.

STUDY OBJECTIVE 5

Indicate how debt and stock investments are valued and reported on the financial statements.

Categories of Securities

For purposes of valuation and reporting at a financial statement date, debt and stock investments are classified into three categories of securities:

1. **Trading securities** are securities bought and held primarily for sale in the near term to generate income on short-term price differences.
2. **Available-for-sale securities** are securities that are held with the intent of selling them sometime in the future.
3. **Held-to-maturity securities** are debt securities that the investor has the intent and ability to hold to maturity.[3]

The valuation guidelines for these securities are shown in Illustration 17-5. **These guidelines apply to all debt securities and all stock investments in which the holdings are less than 20%.**

Illustration 17-5
Valuation guidelines

---

[3]This category is provided for completeness. The accounting and valuation issues related to held-to-maturity securities are discussed in more advanced accounting courses.

Fair value = what you can sell it for

Trading Securities

Trading securities are held with the intention of selling them in a short period (generally less than a month). Trading means frequent buying and selling. Trading securities are reported at fair value, and changes from cost are reported as part of net income. The changes are reported as **unrealized gains or losses** because the securities have not been sold. The unrealized gain or loss is the difference between the **total cost** of trading securities and their **total fair value**.

Illustration 17-6 shows the cost and fair values for investments classified as trading securities for Pace Corporation on December 31, 2005. Pace has an unrealized gain of $7,000 because total fair value ($147,000) is $7,000 greater than total cost ($140,000).

Illustration 17-6
Valuation of trading securities

Trading Securities, December 31, 2005			
Investments	Cost	Fair Value	Unrealized Gain (Loss)
Yorkville Company bonds	$ 50,000	$ 48,000	$ (2,000)
Kodak Company stock	90,000	99,000	9,000
Total	$140,000	$147,000	$ 7,000

HELPFUL HINT

The fact that trading securities are short-term investments increases the likelihood that they will be sold at fair value (the company may not be able to time their sale) and the likelihood that there will be realized gains or losses.

A	=	L	+	SE
+7,000				+7,000 Rev

Cash Flows
no effect

Fair value and unrealized gain or loss are recorded through an adjusting entry at the time financial statements are prepared. In the entry, a valuation allowance account, Market Adjustment—Trading, is used to record the difference between the total cost and the total fair value of the securities. The adjusting entry for Pace Corporation is:

Dec. 31	Market Adjustment—Trading	7,000	
	Unrealized Gain—Income		7,000
	(To record unrealized gain on trading securities)		

The use of a Market Adjustment—Trading account enables the company to maintain a record of the investment cost. Actual cost is needed to determine the gain or loss realized when the securities are sold. The Market Adjustment—Trading balance is added to the cost of the investments to arrive at a fair value for the trading securities.

The fair value of the securities is the amount reported on the balance sheet. The unrealized gain is reported in the income statement in the "Other revenues and gains" section. The term "Income" is used in the account title to indicate that the gain affects net income.

When the total cost of the trading securities is greater than total fair value, an unrealized loss has occurred. In such a case, the adjusting entry is a debit to Unrealized Loss—Income and a credit to Market Adjustment—Trading. The unrealized loss is reported under "Other expenses and losses" in the income statement.

The market adjustment account is carried forward into future accounting periods. No entries are made to this account during the period. At the end of each reporting period, the balance in the account is adjusted to the difference between cost and fair value. For trading securities, the Unrealized Gain (Loss)—Income account is closed at the end of the reporting period.

Available-for-Sale Securities

As indicated earlier, available-for-sale securities are held with the intent of selling them sometime in the future. If the intent is to sell the securities within the next year or operating cycle, the securities are classified as current assets in the balance sheet. Otherwise, they are classified as long-term assets in the investments section of the balance sheet.

Available-for-sale securities are also reported at fair value. The procedure for determining fair value and the unrealized gain or loss for these securities is the same as for trading securities. To illustrate, assume that Ingrao Corporation has two securities that are classified as available-for-sale. Illustration 17-7 provides information on their valuation. There is an unrealized loss of $9,537 because total cost ($293,537) is $9,537 more than total fair value ($284,000).

Illustration 17-7
Valuation of available-for-sale securities

Available-for-Sale Securities, December 31, 2005			
Investments	Cost	Fair Value	Unrealized Gain (Loss)
Campbell Soup Corporation 8% bonds	$ 93,537	$103,600	$10,063
Hershey Corporation stock	200,000	180,400	(19,600)
Total	$293,537	$284,000	$(9,537)

Both the adjusting entry and the reporting of the unrealized gain or loss for available-for-sale securities differ from those illustrated for trading securities. The differences result because these securities are not expected to be sold in the near term. Thus, prior to actual sale it is more likely that changes in fair value may change either unrealized gains or losses. Therefore, an unrealized gain or loss is not reported in the income statement. Instead, it is reported as a **separate component of stockholders' equity**.

In the adjusting entry, the market adjustment account is identified with available-for-sale securities; the unrealized gain or loss account is identified with stockholders' equity. The adjusting entry to record the unrealized loss of $9,537 for Ingrao Corporation is as follows:

Dec. 31	Unrealized Gain or Loss—Equity	9,537	
	Market Adjustment—Available-for-Sale		9,537
	(To record unrealized loss on available-for-sale securities)		

A	=	L	+	SE
−9,537				−9,537 Exp

Cash Flows
no effect

If total fair value exceeds total cost, the adjusting entry would have a debit to the market adjustment account and a credit to an unrealized gain or loss account.

For available-for-sale securities, the unrealized gain or loss account is carried forward to future periods. At each future balance sheet date, it is adjusted with the market adjustment account to show the difference between cost and fair value at that time.

Balance Sheet Presentation

In the balance sheet, investments are classified as either short-term or long-term.

Short-Term Investments

Short-term investments are securities held by a company that are (1) **readily marketable** and (2) **intended to be converted into cash** within the next year or operating cycle, whichever is longer. Investments that do not meet **both criteria** are classified as **long-term investments**.

HELPFUL HINT

Trading securities are always classified as short-term. Available-for-sale securities can be either short-term or long-term.

READILY MARKETABLE.   An investment is readily marketable when it can be sold easily whenever the need for cash arises. Short-term paper[4] meets this criterion. It can be readily sold to other investors. Stocks and bonds traded on organized securities exchanges, such as the New York Stock Exchange, are readily marketable. They can be bought and sold daily. In contrast, there may be only a limited market for the securities issued by small corporations, and no market for the securities of a privately held company.

INTENT TO CONVERT.   Intent to convert means that management intends to sell the investment within the next year or operating cycle, whichever is longer. Generally, this criterion is satisfied when the investment is considered a resource that will be used whenever the need for cash arises. For example, a ski resort may invest idle cash during the summer months with the intent to sell the securities to buy supplies and equipment shortly before the next winter season. This investment is considered short-term even if lack of snow cancels the next ski season and eliminates the need to convert the securities into cash as intended.

Because of their high liquidity, short-term investments are listed immediately below cash in the current assets section of the balance sheet. They are reported at fair value. For example, Pace Corporation would report its trading securities as shown in Illustration 17-8.

Illustration 17-8
Presentation of short-term investments

PACE CORPORATION	
Balance Sheet (partial)	
Current assets	
Cash	$ 21,000
Short-term investments, at fair value	147,000

HELPFUL HINT

In a recent survey of 600 large U.S. companies, over 400 reported short-term investments.

Long-Term Investments

Long-term investments are generally reported in a separate section of the balance sheet immediately below current assets, as shown later in Illustration 17-11 (page 692). Long-term investments in available-for-sale securities are reported at fair value. Investments in common stock accounted for under the equity method are reported at their equity value.

Presentation of Realized and Unrealized Gain or Loss

Gains and losses on investments, whether realized or unrealized, must be presented in the financial statements. In the income statement, gains and losses are reported in the nonoperating activities section under the categories listed in Illustration 17-9. Interest and dividend revenue are also reported in that section.

Illustration 17-9
Nonoperating items related to investments

Other Revenue and Gains	**Other Expenses and Losses**
Interest Revenue	Loss on Sale of Investments
Dividend Revenue	Unrealized Loss—Income
Gain on Sale of Investments	
Unrealized Gain—Income	

---

[4]Short-term paper includes (1) certificates of deposit (CDs) issued by banks, (2) money market certificates issued by banks and savings and loan associations, (3) Treasury bills issued by the U.S. government, and (4) commercial paper (notes) issued by corporations with good credit ratings.

As indicated earlier, an unrealized gain or loss on available-for-sale securities is reported as a separate component of stockholders' equity. To illustrate, assume that Dawson Inc. has common stock of $3,000,000, retained earnings of $1,500,000, and an unrealized loss on available-for-sale securities of $100,000. The statement presentation of the unrealized loss is shown in Illustration 17-10.

Illustration 17-10
Unrealized loss in stockholders' equity section

DAWSON INC.
Balance Sheet (partial)

Stockholders' equity	
Common stock	$3,000,000
Retained earnings	1,500,000
Total paid-in capital and retained earnings	4,500,000
Less: **Unrealized loss on available-for-sale securities**	**(100,000)**
Total stockholders' equity	$4,400,000

Note that the loss decreases stockholders' equity. The cost of treasury stock is presented in the same way. An unrealized gain would be added to stockholders' equity. Reporting the unrealized gain or loss in the stockholders' equity section serves two important purposes: (1) It reduces the volatility of net income due to fluctuations in fair value. (2) It informs the financial statement user of the gain or loss that would occur if the securities were sold at fair value.

Accounting standards require that items such as this, which affect stockholders' equity but are not included in the calculation of net income, must be reported as part of a more inclusive measure called *comprehensive income*. Comprehensive income is discussed briefly in Chapter 19.

Classified Balance Sheet

Many sections of classified balance sheets have been presented in this and preceding chapters. The classified balance sheet in Illustration 17-11 on page 692 includes, in one place, key topics from previous chapters: the issuance of par value common stock, restrictions of retained earnings, and issuance of long-term bonds. From this chapter, the statement includes (highlighted in red) short-term and long-term investments. The investments in short-term securities are considered trading securities. The long-term investments in stock of less than 20% owned companies are considered available-for-sale securities. Illustration 17-11 also includes a long-term investment reported at equity and descriptive notations within the statement, such as the basis for valuing merchandise and one note to the statement.

BEFORE YOU GO ON...

Review It

1. What is the proper valuation and reporting of trading and available-for-sale securities on a balance sheet?

2. Explain how the unrealized gain or loss for both trading and available-for-sale securities is reported.

3. Explain where short-term and long-term investments are reported on a balance sheet.

Illustration 17-11
Classified balance sheet

PACE CORPORATION
Balance Sheet
December 31, 2005

Assets

Current assets

Cash			$ 21,000
Short-term investments, at fair value			**147,000**
Accounts receivable		$ 84,000	
Less: Allowance for doubtful accounts		4,000	80,000
Merchandise inventory, at FIFO cost			43,000
Prepaid insurance			23,000
Total current assets			314,000

Investments

Investments in stock of less than 20% owned companies, at fair value		**50,000**	
Investment in stock of 20–50% owned company, at equity		**150,000**	
Total investments			200,000

Property, plant, and equipment

Land			200,000
Buildings	$800,000		
Less: Accumulated depreciation	200,000	600,000	
Equipment	180,000		
Less: Accumulated depreciation	54,000	126,000	
Total property, plant, and equipment			926,000

Intangible assets

Goodwill			270,000
Total assets			$1,710,000

Liabilities and Stockholders' Equity

Current liabilities

Accounts payable		$185,000
Federal income taxes payable		60,000
Bond interest payable		10,000
Total current liabilities		255,000

Long-term liabilities

Bonds payable, 10%, due 2016	$ 300,000	
Less: Discount on bonds	10,000	
Total long-term liabilities		290,000
Total liabilities		545,000

Stockholders' equity

Paid-in capital

Common stock, $10 par value, 200,000 shares authorized, 80,000 shares issued and outstanding	800,000	
Paid-in capital in excess of par value	100,000	
Total paid-in capital	900,000	
Retained earnings (Note 1)	255,000	
Total paid-in capital and retained earnings	1,155,000	
Add: **Unrealized gain on available-for-sale securities**	**10,000**	
Total stockholders' equity		1,165,000
Total liabilities and stockholders' equity		$1,710,000

Note 1. Retained earnings of $100,000 is restricted for plant expansion.

DEMONSTRATION PROBLEM

In its first year of operations, DeMarco Company had the following selected transactions in stock investments that are considered trading securities.

June 1   Purchased for cash 600 shares of Sanburg common stock at $24 per share, plus $300 brokerage fees.
July 1   Purchased for cash 800 shares of Cey common stock at $33 per share, plus $600 brokerage fees.
Sept. 1   Received a $1 per share cash dividend from Cey Corporation.
Nov. 1   Sold 200 shares of Sanburg common stock for cash at $27 per share, less $150 brokerage fees.
Dec. 15   Received a $0.50 per share cash dividend on Sanburg common stock.

At December 31, the fair values per share were: Sanburg $25 and Cey $30.

Instructions

(a) Journalize the transactions.
(b) Prepare the adjusting entry at December 31 to report the securities at fair value.

SOLUTION TO DEMONSTRATION PROBLEM

(a) June 1	Stock Investments	14,700	
	Cash		14,700
	(To record purchase of 600 shares of Sanburg common stock)		
July 1	Stock Investments	27,000	
	Cash		27,000
	(To record purchase of 800 shares of Cey common stock)		
Sept. 1	Cash	800	
	Dividend Revenue		800
	(To record receipt of $1 per share cash dividend from Cey Corporation)		
Nov. 1	Cash	5,250	
	Stock Investments		4,900
	Gain on Sale of Stock Investments		350
	(To record sale of 200 shares of Sanburg common stock)		
Dec. 15	Cash	200	
	Dividend Revenue		200
	(To record receipt of $0.50 per share dividend from Sanburg Corporation)		
(b) Dec. 31	Unrealized Loss—Income	2,800	
	Market Adjustment—Trading		2,800
	(To record unrealized loss on trading securities)		

Investment	Cost	Fair Value	Unrealized Gain (Loss)
Sanburg common stock	$ 9,800	$10,000	$ 200
Cey common stock	27,000	24,000	(3,000)
Totals	$36,800	$34,000	$(2,800)

ACTION PLAN

- Include the price paid plus brokerage fees in the cost of the investment.
- Compute the gain or loss on sales as the difference between net selling price and the cost of the securities.
- Base the adjustment to fair value on the total difference between the cost and the fair value of the securities.

SUMMARY OF STUDY OBJECTIVES

1. **Discuss why corporations invest in debt and stock securities.** Corporations invest for three primary reasons: (a) They have excess cash. (b) They view investments as a significant revenue source. (c) They have strategic goals such as gaining control of a competitor or moving into a new line of business.

2. **Explain the accounting for debt investments.** Entries for investments in debt securities are required when the bonds are purchased, interest is received or accrued, and the bonds are sold. Gains or losses on the sale of bonds are reported in the "Other revenues and gains" or "Other expenses and losses" sections of the income statement.

3. **Explain the accounting for stock investments.** Entries for investments in common stock are required when the stock is purchased, dividends are received, and stock is sold. When ownership is less than 20%, the cost method is used. When ownership is between 20% and 50%, the equity method should be used. When ownership is more than 50%, consolidated financial statements should be prepared.

4. **Describe the use of consolidated financial statements.** When a company owns more than 50% of the common stock of another company, consolidated financial statements are usually prepared. These statements are useful because they indicate the magnitude and scope of operations of the companies under common control.

5. **Indicate how debt and stock investments are valued and reported on the financial statements.** Investments in debt and stock securities are classified as trading, available-for-sale, or held-to-maturity securities for valuation and reporting purposes. Trading securities are reported in current assets at fair value, with changes from cost reported in net income. Available-for-sale securities are also reported at fair value, with the changes from cost reported in stockholders' equity. Available-for-sale securities are classified as short-term or long-term depending on their expected realization.

6. **Distinguish between short-term and long-term investments.** Short-term investments are securities, held by a company, that are (a) readily marketable and (b) intended to be converted to cash within the next year or operating cycle, which-ever is longer. Investments that do not meet both criteria are classified as long-term investments.

GLOSSARY

Available-for-sale securities Securities that are held with the intent of selling them sometime in the future. (p. 687).

Consolidated financial statements Financial statements that present the assets and liabilities controlled by the parent company and the aggregate profitability of the affiliated companies. (p. 684).

Controlling interest Ownership of more than 50% of the common stock of another entity. (p. 684).

Cost method An accounting method in which the investment in common stock is recorded at cost, and revenue is recognized only when cash dividends are received. (p. 682).

Debt investments Investments in government and corporation bonds. (p. 679).

Equity method An accounting method in which the investment in common stock is initially recorded at cost, and the investment account is then adjusted annually to show the investor's equity in the investee. (p. 683).

Fair value Amount for which a security could be sold in a normal market. (p. 687).

Held-to-maturity securities Debt securities that the investor has the intent and ability to hold to their maturity date. (p. 687).

Investment portfolio A group of stocks in different corporations held for investment purposes. (p. 681).

Long-term investments Investments that are not readily marketable and that management does not intend to convert into cash within the next year or operating cycle, whichever is longer. (p. 689).

Parent company A company that owns more than 50% of the common stock of another entity. (p. 684).

Short-term investments Investments that are readily marketable and intended to be converted into cash within the next year or operating cycle, whichever is longer. (p. 689).

Stock investments Investments in the capital stock of corporations. (p. 681).

Subsidiary (affiliated) company A company in which more than 50% of its stock is owned by another company. (p. 684).

Trading securities Securities bought and held primarily for sale in the near term to generate income on short-term price differences. (p. 687).

SELF-STUDY QUESTIONS

Answers are at the end of the chapter.

(SO 2) **1.** Debt investments are initially recorded at:
- **a.** cost.
- **b.** cost plus accrued interest.
- **c.** fair value.
- **d.** None of the above.

(SO 2) **2.** Hanes Company sells debt investments costing $26,000 for $28,000, plus accrued interest that has been recorded. In journalizing the sale, credits are to:
- **a.** Debt Investments and Loss on Sale of Debt Investments.
- **b.** Debt Investments, Gain on Sale of Debt Investments, and Bond Interest Receivable.
- **c.** Stock Investments and Bond Interest Receivable.
- **d.** No correct answer given.

(SO 3) **3.** Pryor Company receives net proceeds of $42,000 on the sale of stock investments that cost $39,500. This transaction will result in reporting in the income statement a:
- **a.** loss of $2,500 under "Other expenses and losses."
- **b.** loss of $2,500 under "Operating expenses."
- **c.** gain of $2,500 under "Other revenues and gains."
- **d.** gain of $2,500 under "Operating revenues."

(SO 3) **4.** The equity method of accounting for long-term investments in stock should be used when the investor has significant influence over an investee and owns:
- **a.** between 20% and 50% of the investee's common stock.
- **b.** 20% or more of the investee's common stock.
- **c.** more than 50% of the investee's common stock.
- **d.** less than 20% of the investee's common stock.

(SO 4) **5.** Which of the following statements is *not true*? Consolidated financial statements are useful to:
- **a.** determine the profitability of specific subsidiaries.
- **b.** determine the total profitability of enterprises under common control.
- **c.** determine the breadth of a parent company's operations.
- **d.** determine the full extent of total obligations of enterprises under common control.

(SO 5) **6.** At the end of the first year of operations, the total cost of the trading securities portfolio is $120,000. Total fair value is $115,000. The financial statements should show:
- **a.** a reduction of an asset of $5,000 and a realized loss of $5,000.
- **b.** a reduction of an asset of $5,000 and an unrealized loss of $5,000 in the stockholders' equity section.
- **c.** a reduction of an asset of $5,000 in the current assets section and an unrealized loss of $5,000 in "Other expenses and losses."
- **d.** a reduction of an asset of $5,000 in the current assets section and a realized loss of $5,000 in "Other expenses and losses."

(SO 5) **7.** In the balance sheet, a debit balance in Unrealized Gain or Loss—Equity is reported as a:
- **a.** contra asset account.
- **b.** contra stockholders' equity account.
- **c.** loss in the income statement.
- **d.** loss in the retained earnings statement.

(SO 6) **8.** Short-term debt investments must be readily marketable and be expected to be sold within:
- **a.** 3 months from the date of purchase.
- **b.** the next year or operating cycle, whichever is shorter.
- **c.** the next year or operating cycle, whichever is longer.
- **d.** the operating cycle.

✓ THE NAVIGATOR

QUESTIONS

1. What are the reasons that corporations invest in securities?

2. (a) What is the cost of an investment in bonds? (b) When is interest on bonds recorded?

3. Jose Gonzalez is confused about losses and gains on the sale of debt investments. Explain to Jose (a) how the gain or loss is computed, and (b) the statement presentation of the gains and losses.

4. Sablow Company sells Gish's bonds costing $40,000 for $45,000, including $1,000 of accrued interest. In recording the sale, Sablow books a $5,000 gain. Is this correct? Explain.

5. What is the cost of an investment in stock?

6. To acquire Jackson Corporation stock, R. Toni pays $62,000 in cash, plus $1,500 broker's fees. What entry should be made for this investment, assuming the stock is readily marketable?

7. (a) When should a long-term investment in common stock be accounted for by the equity method? (b) When is revenue recognized under this method?

8. Diaz Corporation uses the equity method to account for its ownership of 25% of the common stock of Victor Packing. During 2005 Victor reported a net income of $80,000 and declares and pays cash dividends of $10,000. What recognition should Diaz Corporation give to these events?

9. What constitutes "significant influence" when an investor's financial interest is below the 50% level?

10. Distinguish between the cost and equity methods of accounting for investments in stocks.

11. What are consolidated financial statements?

12. What are the valuation guidelines for investments at a balance sheet date?

13. Jane Clemens is the controller of Nakoma Inc. At December 31, the company's investments in trading securities cost $74,000. They have a fair value of $72,000. Indicate how Jane would report these data in the financial statements prepared on December 31.

14. Using the data in question 13, how would Jane report the data if the investment were long-term and the securities were classified as available-for-sale?

15. Sajjad Company's investments in available-for-sale securities at December 31 show total cost of $195,000 and total fair value of $210,000. Prepare the adjusting entry.

16. Using the data in question 15, prepare the adjusting entry assuming the securities are classified as trading securities.

17. What is the proper statement presentation of the account Unrealized Loss—Equity (Available-for-Sale)?

18. What purposes are served by reporting Unrealized Gains (Losses)—Equity in the stockholders' equity section?

19. Jamaica Wholesale Supply owns stock in Ivy Corporation. Jamaica intends to hold the stock indefinitely because of some negative tax consequences if sold. Should the investment in Ivy be classified as a short-term investment? Why or why not?

BRIEF EXERCISES

Journalize entries for debt investments.

(SO 2)

BE17-1 Buslik Corporation purchased debt investments for $46,800 on January 1, 2005. On July 1, 2005, Buslik received cash interest of $2,340. Journalize the purchase and the receipt of interest. Assume that no interest has been accrued.

Journalize entries for stock investments.

(SO 3)

BE17-2 On August 1, Hyun Company buys 1,000 shares of Morgan common stock for $35,000 cash, plus brokerage fees of $600. On December 1, Hyun sells the stock investments for $40,000 in cash. Journalize the purchase and sale of the common stock.

Record transactions under the equity method of accounting.

(SO 3)

BE17-3 Iguana Company owns 30% of Hyde Company. For the current year Hyde reports net income of $180,000 and declares and pays a $50,000 cash dividend. Record Iguana's equity in Hyde's net income and the receipt of dividends from Hyde.

Prepare adjusting entry using fair value.

(SO 5)

BE17-4 The cost of the trading securities of Homura Company at December 31, 2005, is $64,000. At December 31, 2005, the fair value of the securities is $59,000. Prepare the adjusting entry to record the securities at fair value.

Indicate statement presentation using fair value.

(SO 5, 6)

BE17-5 For the data presented in BE17-4, show the financial statement presentation of the trading securities and related accounts.

Prepare adjusting entry using fair value.

(SO 5)

BE17-6 Karpman Corporation holds as a long-term investment available-for-sale stock securities costing $72,000. At December 31, 2005, the fair value of the securities is $68,000. Prepare the adjusting entry to record the securities at fair value.

Indicate statements presentation using fair value.

(SO 5, 6)

BE17-7 For the data presented in BE17-6, show the financial statement presentation of the available-for-sale securities and related accounts. Assume the available-for-sale securities are noncurrent.

Prepare investments section of balance sheet.

(SO 5, 6)

BE17-8 Dobbs Corporation has the following long-term investments: (1) Common stock of Kubek Co. (10% ownership) held as available-for-sale securities, cost $108,000, fair value $115,000. (2) Common stock of Ely Inc. (30% ownership), cost $210,000, equity $250,000. Prepare the investments section of the balance sheet.

EXERCISES

Journalize debt investment transactions and accrue interest.

(SO 2)

E17-1 Issel Corporation had the following transactions pertaining to debt investments.

Jan. 1   Purchased 60 8%, $1,000 Hollis Co. bonds for $60,000 cash plus brokerage fees of $900. Interest is payable semiannually on July 1 and January 1.

July 1   Received semiannual interest on Hollis Co. bonds.

July 1   Sold 30 Hollis Co. bonds for $34,000 less $500 brokerage fees.

Instructions

(a) Journalize the transactions.

(b) Prepare the adjusting entry for the accrual of interest at December 31.

E17-2 Satazar Company had the following transactions pertaining to stock investments.

Journalize stock investment transactions.

(SO 3)

Feb. 1 Purchased 800 shares of Hippo common stock (2%) for $8,000 cash, plus brokerage fees of $200.

July 1 Received cash dividends of $1 per share on Hippo common stock.

Sept. 1 Sold 300 shares of Hippo common stock for $4,400, less brokerage fees of $100.

Dec. 1 Received cash dividends of $1 per share on Hippo common stock.

Instructions

(a) Journalize the transactions.

(b) Explain how dividend revenue and the gain (loss) on sale should be reported in the income statement.

E17-3 Hermes Inc. had the following transactions pertaining to investments in common stock.

Journalize transactions for investments in stocks.

(SO 3)

Jan. 1 Purchased 2,000 shares of Lanier Corporation common stock (5%) for $140,000 cash plus $2,100 broker's commission.

July 1 Received a cash dividend of $3 per share.

Dec. 1 Sold 500 shares of Lanier Corporation common stock for $37,000 cash, less $800 broker's commission.

Dec. 31 Received a cash dividend of $3 per share.

Instructions

Journalize the transactions.

E17-4 On January 1 Jazz Corporation purchased a 30% equity in Snapper Corporation for $180,000. At December 31 Snapper declared and paid a $60,000 cash dividend and reported net income of $200,000.

Journalize and post transactions, and contrast cost and equity method results.

(SO 3)

Instructions

(a) Journalize the transactions.

(b) Determine the amount to be reported as an investment in Snapper stock at December 31.

E17-5 Presented below are two independent situations.

Journalize entries under cost and equity methods.

(SO 3)

1. Galex Cosmetics acquired 10% of the 200,000 shares of common stock of Yen Fashion at a total cost of $13 per share on March 18, 2002. On June 30, Yen declared and paid a $60,000 dividend. On December 31, Yen reported net income of $122,000 for the year. At December 31, the market price of Yen Fashion was $15 per share. The stock is classified as available-for-sale.

2. Smart, Inc., obtained significant influence over Gamma Corporation by buying 25% of Gamma's 30,000 outstanding shares of common stock at a total cost of $9 per share on January 1, 2005. On June 15, Gamma declared and paid a cash dividend of $30,000. On December 31, Gamma reported a net income of $80,000 for the year.

Instructions

Prepare all the necessary journal entries for 2005 for (a) Galex Cosmetics and (b) Smart, Inc.

E17-6 At December 31, 2005, the trading securities for Jeng, Inc. are as follows.

Prepare adjusting entry to record fair value, and indicate statement presentation.

(SO 5, 6)

Security	Cost	Fair Value
A	$17,500	$16,000
B	12,500	14,000
C	23,000	17,000
	$53,000	$47,000

Instructions

(a) Prepare the adjusting entry at December 31, 2005, to report the securities at fair value.

(b) Show the balance sheet and income statement presentation at December 31, 2005, after adjustment to fair value.

Prepare adjusting entry to record fair value, and indicate statement presentation.

(SO 5, 6)

E17-7   Data for investments in stock classified as trading securities are presented in E17-6. Assume instead that the investments are classified as available-for-sale securities. They have the same cost and fair value. The securities are considered to be a long-term investment.

Instructions

(a) Prepare the adjusting entry at December 31, 2005, to report the securities at fair value.
(b) Show the statement presentation at December 31, 2005, after adjustment to fair value.
(c)   M. Istanbel, a member of the board of directors, does not understand the reporting of the unrealized gains or losses. Write a letter to Mr. Istanbel explaining the reporting and the purposes that it serves.

Prepare adjusting entries for fair value, and indicate statement presentation for two classes of securities.

(SO 5, 6)

E17-8   Kanjo Company has the following data at December 31, 2005.

Securities	Cost	Fair Value
Trading	$120,000	$123,000
Available-for-sale	100,000	92,000

The available-for-sale securities are held as a long-term investment.

Instructions

(a) Prepare the adjusting entries to report each class of securities at fair value.
(b) Indicate the statement presentation of each class of securities and the related unrealized gain (loss) accounts.

PROBLEMS: SET A

Journalize debt investment transactions and show financial statement presentation.

(SO 2, 5, 6)

P17-1A   Strawder Farms is a grower of hybrid seed corn for DeKalb Genetics Corporation. It has had two exceptionally good years and has elected to invest its excess funds in bonds. The following selected transactions relate to bonds acquired as an investment by Strawder Farms, whose fiscal year ends on December 31.

2005

Jan.   1   Purchased at par $800,000 of Lesley Corporation 10-year, 9% bonds dated January 1, 2005, directly from the issuing corporation.
July   1   Received the semiannual interest on the Lesley bonds.
Dec. 31   Accrual of interest at year-end on the Lesley bonds.

(Assume that all intervening transactions and adjustments have been properly recorded and the number of bonds owned has not changed from December 31, 2005, to December 31, 2007.)

2008

Jan.   1   Received the semiannual interest on the Lesley bonds.
Jan.   1   Sold $400,000 Lesley bonds at 114. The broker deducted $7,000 for commissions and fees on the sale.
July   1   Received the semiannual interest on the Lesley bonds.
Dec. 31   Accrual of interest at year-end on the Lesley bonds.

Instructions

(a) Gain on sale of debt investments $49,000

(a) Journalize the listed transactions for the years 2005 and 2008.
(b) Assume that the fair value of the bonds at December 31, 2005, was $770,000. These bonds are classified as available-for-sale securities. Prepare the adjusting entry to record these bonds at fair value.
(c) Based on your analysis in part (b) show the balance sheet presentation of the bonds and interest receivable at December 31, 2005. Assume the investments are considered long-term. Indicate where any unrealized gain or loss is reported in the financial statements.

Journalize investment transactions, prepare adjusting entry, and show statement presentation.

(SO 2, 3, 5, 6)

P17-2A   In January 2005, the management of Ralley Company concludes that it has sufficient cash to purchase some short-term investments in debt and stock securities. During the year, the following transactions occurred.

Feb.   1   Purchased 600 shares of IBT common stock for $40,000, plus brokerage fees of $800.
Mar.   1   Purchased 500 shares of IMA common stock for $15,000, plus brokerage fees of $300.

Apr. 1 Purchased 60 $1,000, 12% CRE bonds for $60,000, plus $1,200 brokerage fees. Interest is payable semiannually on April 1 and October 1.
July 1 Received a cash dividend of $0.60 per share on the IBT common stock.
Aug. 1 Sold 300 shares of IBT common stock at $70 per share, less brokerage fees of $350.
Sept. 1 Received a $1 per share cash dividend on the IMA common stock.
Oct. 1 Received the semiannual interest on the CRE bonds.
Oct. 1 Sold the CRE bonds for $65,000, less $1,000 brokerage fees.

At December 31, the fair value of the IBT common stock was $66 per share. The fair value of the IMA common stock was $30 per share.

Instructions
(a) Journalize the transactions and post to the accounts Debt Investments and Stock Investments. (Use the T-account form.)
(b) Prepare the adjusting entry at December 31, 2005, to report the investments at fair value. All securities are considered to be trading securities.
(c) Show the balance sheet presentation of investment securities at December 31, 2005.
(d) Identify the income statement accounts and give the statement classification of each account.

(b) Unrealized loss $900

P17-3A On December 31, 2005, Carlin Associates owned the following securities, held as long-term investments.

Common Stock	Shares	Cost
Ace Co.	2,000	$50,000
Burns Co.	6,000	36,000
Cruz Co.	1,200	24,000

Journalize transactions and adjusting entry for stock investments.

(SO 3, 5, 6)

On this date, the total fair value of the securities was equal to its cost. The securities are not held for influence or control over the investees. In 2006, the following transactions occurred.

July 1 Received $1 per share semiannual cash dividend on Burns Co. common stock.
Aug. 1 Received $0.50 per share cash dividend on Ace Co. common stock.
Sept. 1 Sold 2,000 shares of Burns Co. common stock for cash at $7 per share, less brokerage fees of $300.
Oct. 1 Sold 600 shares of Ace Co. common stock for cash at $28 per share, less brokerage fees of $600.
Nov. 1 Received $1 per share cash dividend on Cruz Co. common stock.
Dec. 15 Received $0.50 per share cash dividend on Ace Co. common stock.
  31 Received $1 per share semiannual cash dividend on Burns Co. common stock.

At December 31, the fair values per share of the common stocks were: Ace Co. $24, Burns Co. $6, and Cruz Co. $19.

Instructions
(a) Journalize the 2006 transactions and post to the account Stock Investments. (Use the T-account form.)
(b) Prepare the adjusting entry at December 31, 2006, to show the securities at fair value. The stock should be classified as available-for-sale securities.
(c) Show the balance sheet presentation of the investments at December 31, 2006. At this date, Carlin Associates has common stock $2,000,000 and retained earnings $1,200,000.

(a) Gain on sale, $1,700 and $1,200

P17-4A Penny's Concrete acquired 25% of the outstanding common stock of Cardinal, Inc. on January 1, 2005, by paying $1,200,000 for 50,000 shares. Cardinal declared and paid a $0.50 per share cash dividend on June 30 and again on December 31, 2005. Cardinal reported net income of $600,000 for the year. At December 31, 2005, the market price of Cardinal's common stock was $30 per share.

Prepare entries under the cost and equity methods, and tabulate differences.

(SO 3)

Instructions
(a) Prepare the journal entries for Penny's Concrete for 2005 assuming Penny's cannot exercise significant influence over Cardinal. (Use the cost method and assume Cardinal common stock should be classified as available-for-sale.)
(b) Prepare the journal entries for Penny's Concrete for 2005, assuming Penny's can exercise significant influence over Cardinal. (Use the equity method.)
(c) In tabular form, indicate the investment and income account balances at December 31, 2005, under each method of accounting.

(a) Total dividend revenue $50,000

(b) Revenue from investments $150,000

Journalize stock investment transactions and show statement presentation.

(SO 3, 5, 6)

P17-5A The following are in Sanders Company's portfolio of long-term available-for-sale securities at December 31, 2005.

	Cost
500 shares of Bonds Corporation common stock	$26,000
700 shares of Ruth Corporation common stock	42,000
600 shares of Edmonds Corporation preferred stock	16,800

On December 31, the total cost of the portfolio equaled total fair value. Sanders Company had the following transactions related to the securities during 2006.

Jan.   7   Sold 500 shares of Bonds Corporation common stock at $58 per share, less brokerage fees of $700.

Jan. 10   Purchased 200 shares, $70 par value common stock of Schilling Corporation at $78 per share, plus brokerage fees of $240.

      26   Received a cash dividend of $1.15 per share on Ruth Corporation common stock.

Feb.   2   Received cash dividends of $0.40 per share on Edmonds Corporation preferred stock.

      10   Sold all 600 shares of Edmonds Corporation preferred stock at $25 per share less brokerage fees of $180.

July   1   Received a cash dividend of $1.00 per share on Ruth Corporation common stock.

Sept. 1   Purchased an additional 800 shares of the $70 par value common stock of Schilling Corporation at $75 per share, plus brokerage fees of $900.

Dec. 15   Received a cash dividend of $1.50 per share on Schilling Corporation common stock.

At December 31, 2006, the fair values of the securities were:

Ruth Corporation common stock	$63 per share
Schilling Corporation common stock	$72 per share

Sanders uses separate account titles for each investment, such as Investment in Ruth Corporation Common Stock.

(a) Loss on sale $1,980

(c) Unrealized loss $2,640

Instructions
(a) Prepare journal entries to record the transactions.
(b) Post to the investment accounts. (Use T accounts.)
(c) Prepare the adjusting entry at December 31, 2006, to report the portfolio at fair value.
(d) Show the balance sheet presentation at December 31, 2006.

Prepare a balance sheet.

(SO 5, 6)

P17-6A The following data, presented in alphabetical order, are taken from the records of Allison Corporation.

Accounts payable	$ 280,000
Accounts receivable	90,000
Accumulated depreciation—building	180,000
Accumulated depreciation—equipment	52,000
Allowance for doubtful accounts	6,000
Bonds payable (10%, due 2018)	400,000
Buildings	900,000
Cash	142,000
Common stock ($5 par value; 500,000 shares authorized, 300,000 shares issued)	1,500,000
Discount on bonds payable	20,000
Dividends payable	50,000
Equipment	275,000
Goodwill	200,000
Income taxes payable	120,000
Investment in Saratoga Inc. stock (30% ownership), at equity	600,000
Land	570,000
Merchandise inventory	170,000
Notes payable (due 2006)	70,000
Paid-in capital in excess of par value	200,000
Prepaid insurance	16,000
Retained earnings	310,000
Short-term stock investment, at fair value (and cost)	185,000

Instructions
Prepare a balance sheet at December 31, 2005.

Total assets $2,910,000

PROBLEMS: SET B

P17-1B Chelsea Carecenters Inc. provides financing and capital to the health-care industry, with a particular focus on nursing homes for the elderly. The following selected transactions relate to bonds acquired as an investment by Chelsea, whose fiscal year ends on December 31.

Journalize debt investment transactions and show financial statement presentation.

(SO 2, 5, 6)

2005

Jan.   1   Purchased at par $3,000,000 of Caring Nursing Centers, Inc., 10-year, 8% bonds dated January 1, 2005, directly from Caring.
July   1   Received the semiannual interest on the Caring bonds.
Dec. 31   Accrual of interest at year-end on the Caring bonds.

(Assume that all intervening transactions and adjustments have been properly recorded and that the number of bonds owned has not changed from December 31, 2005, to December 31, 2007.)

2008

Jan.   1   Received the semiannual interest on the Caring bonds.
Jan.   1   Sold $1,500,000 Caring bonds at 106. The broker deducted $6,000 for commissions and fees on the sale.
July   1   Received the semiannual interest on the Caring bonds.
Dec. 31   Accrual of interest at year-end on the Caring bonds.

Instructions
(a) Journalize the listed transactions for the years 2005 and 2008.
(b) Assume that the fair value of the bonds at December 31, 2005, was $3,300,000. These bonds are classified as available-for-sale securities. Prepare the adjusting entry to record these bonds at fair value.
(c) Based on your analysis in part (b), show the balance sheet presentation of the bonds and interest receivable at December 31, 2005. Assume the investments are considered long-term. Indicate where any unrealized gain or loss is reported in the financial statements.

(a) Gain on sale of debt investment $84,000

P17-2B In January 2005, the management of Match Company concludes that it has sufficient cash to permit some short-term investments in debt and stock securities. During the year, the following transactions occurred.

Journalize investment transactions, prepare adjusting entry, and show statement presentation.

(SO 2, 3, 5, 6)

Peachtree

Feb. 1   Purchased 600 shares of Loder common stock for $31,800, plus brokerage fees of $600.
Mar. 1   Purchased 800 shares of Greer common stock for $20,000, plus brokerage fees of $400.
Apr. 1   Purchased 50 $1,000, 8% Roy bonds for $50,000, plus $1,000 brokerage fees. Interest is payable semiannually on April 1 and October 1.
July 1   Received a cash dividend of $0.60 per share on the Loder common stock.
Aug. 1   Sold 200 shares of Loder common stock at $57 per share less brokerage fees of $200.
Sept. 1   Received a $1 per share cash dividend on the Greer common stock.
Oct. 1   Received the semiannual interest on the Roy bonds.
Oct. 1   Sold the Roy bonds for $49,000 less $1,000 brokerage fees.

At December 31, the fair value of the Loder common stock was $55 per share. The fair value of the Greer common stock was $23 per share.

Instructions
(a) Journalize the transactions and post to the accounts Debt Investments and Stock Investments. (Use the T-account form.)
(b) Prepare the adjusting entry at December 31, 2005, to report the investment securities at fair value. All securities are considered to be trading securities.
(c) Show the balance sheet presentation of investment securities at December 31, 2005.
(d) Identify the income statement accounts and give the statement classification of each account.

(a) Gain on stock sale $400

Journalize transactions and adjusting entry for stock investments.

(SO 3, 5, 6)

P17-3B On December 31, 2005, Mauro Associates owned the following securities, held as a long-term investment. The securities are not held for influence or control of the investee.

Common Stock	Shares	Cost
Kline Co.	3,000	$90,000
Mann Co.	5,000	45,000
Scott Co.	1,500	30,000

On this date, the total fair value of the securities was equal to its cost. In 2006, the following transactions occurred.

July 1 Received $1 per share semiannual cash dividend on Mann Co. common stock.
Aug. 1 Received $0.50 per share cash dividend on Kline Co. common stock.
Sept. 1 Sold 1,500 shares of Mann Co. common stock for cash at $8 per share, less brokerage fees of $300.
Oct. 1 Sold 800 shares of Kline Co. common stock for cash at $31 per share, less brokerage fees of $500.
Nov. 1 Received $1 per share cash dividend on Scott Co. common stock.
Dec. 15 Received $0.50 per share cash dividend on Kline Co. common stock.
31 Received $1 per share semiannual cash dividend on Mann Co. common stock.

At December 31, the fair values per share of the common stocks were: Kline Co. $32, Mann Co. $8, and Scott Co. $18.

Instructions

(a) Journalize the 2006 transactions and post to the account Stock Investments. (Use the T-account form.)

(b) Unrealized loss $2,100

(b) Prepare the adjusting entry at December 31, 2006, to show the securities at fair value. The stock should be classified as available-for-sale securities.

(c) Show the balance sheet presentation of the investments at December 31, 2006. At this date, Mauro Associates has common stock $1,500,000 and retained earnings $1,000,000.

Prepare entries under the cost and equity methods, and tabulate differences.

(SO 3)

P17-4B Marley Services acquired 25% of the outstanding common stock of Stevens Company on January 1, 2005, by paying $800,000 for the 40,000 shares. Stevens declared and paid $0.30 per share cash dividends on March 15, June 15, September 15, and December 15, 2005. Stevens reported net income of $320,000 for the year. At December 31, 2005, the market price of Stevens common stock was $24 per share.

Instructions

(a) Total dividend revenue $48,000

(a) Prepare the journal entries for Marley Services for 2005 assuming Marley cannot exercise significant influence over Stevens. (Use the cost method and assume that Stevens' common stock should be classified as a trading security.)

(b) Revenue from investments $80,000

(b) Prepare the journal entries for Marley Services for 2005, assuming Marley can exercise significant influence over Stevens. Use the equity method.

(c) In tabular form, indicate the investment and income statement account balances at December 31, 2005, under each method of accounting.

Journalize stock investment transactions and show statement presentation.

(SO 3, 5, 6)

P17-5B The following securities are in Morales Company's portfolio of long-term available-for-sale securities at December 31, 2005.

	Cost
1,000 shares of Abel Corporation common stock	$52,000
1,400 shares of HAL Corporation common stock	84,000
1,200 shares of Reese Corporation preferred stock	33,600

On December 31, 2005, the total cost of the portfolio equaled total fair value. Morales had the following transactions related to the securities during 2006.

Jan. 20 Sold 1,000 shares of Abel Corporation common stock at $54 per share less brokerage fees of $600.
28 Purchased 400 shares of $70 par value common stock of Nolan Corporation at $78 per share, plus brokerage fees of $480.
30 Received a cash dividend of $1.15 per share on HAL Corp. common stock.
Feb. 8 Received cash dividends of $0.40 per share on Reese Corp. preferred stock.
18 Sold all 1,200 shares of Reese Corp. preferred stock at $26 per share less brokerage fees of $360.

July 30 Received a cash dividend of $1.00 per share on HAL Corp. common stock.
Sept. 6 Purchased an additional 600 shares of $10 par value common stock of Nolan Corporation at $82 per share, plus brokerage fees of $800.
Dec. 1 Received a cash dividend of $1.50 per share on Nolan Corporation common stock.

At December 31, 2006, the fair values of the securities were:

HAL Corporation common stock	$64 per share
Nolan Corporation common stock	$72 per share

Morales Company uses separate account titles for each investment, such as "Investment in HAL Corporation Common Stock."

Instructions
(a) Prepare journal entries to record the transactions.
(b) Post to the investment accounts. (Use T accounts.)
(c) Prepare the adjusting entry at December 31, 2006 to report the portfolio at fair value.
(d) Show the balance sheet presentation at December 31, 2006.

(a) Loss on sale of preferred stock $2,760

(c) Unrealized loss $4,080

P17-6B The following data, presented in alphabetical order, are taken from the records of Lefever Corporation.

Prepare a balance sheet.

(SO, 5, 6)

Accounts payable	$ 210,000
Accounts receivable	140,000
Accumulated depreciation—building	180,000
Accumulated depreciation—equipment	52,000
Allowance for doubtful accounts	6,000
Bonds payable (10%, due 2016)	500,000
Buildings	950,000
Cash	42,000
Common stock ($10 par value; 500,000 shares authorized, 150,000 shares issued)	1,500,000
Dividends payable	80,000
Equipment	275,000
Goodwill	200,000
Income taxes payable	120,000
Investment in Dodge common stock (10% ownership), at cost	278,000
Investment in Portico common stock (30% ownership), at equity	380,000
Land	430,000
Market adjustment—available-for-sale securities (Dr)	8,000
Merchandise inventory	170,000
Notes payable (due 2006)	70,000
Paid-in capital in excess of par value	200,000
Premium on bonds payable	40,000
Prepaid insurance	16,000
Retained earnings	103,000
Short-term stock investment, at fair value (and cost)	180,000
Unrealized gain—available-for-sale securities	8,000

The investment in Dodge common stock is considered to be a long-term available-for-sale security.

Instructions
Prepare a balance sheet at December 31, 2005.

Total assets $2,831,000

PART I

Megan Bergeron and her two colleagues Jesse Ortiz and Tara Sheley are personal trainers at an upscale health spa/resort in Tampa, Florida. They want to start a health club that specializes in health plans for people in the 50+ age range. The growing population in this age range and strong consumer interest in the health benefits of physical activity have convinced them they can profitably operate their own club. In addition to many other decisions, they need to determine what type of business organization they want. Jesse believes there are more advantages to the corporate form than a partnership, but he hasn't yet convinced Megan and Tara. They have come to you, a small business consulting specialist, seeking information and advice regarding the choice of starting a partnership versus a corporation.

Instructions

(a) ▭▤▤▤▷ Prepare a memo (dated May 26, 2004) that describes the advantages and disadvantages of both partnerships and corporations. Advise Megan, Jesse, and Tara regarding which organizational form you believe would better serve their purposes. Make sure to include reasons supporting your advice.

PART II

After deciding to incorporate, each of the three investors receives 20,000 shares of $2 par common stock on June 12, 2004, in exchange for their co-owned building ($200,000 market value) and $100,000 total cash they contributed to the business. The next decision that Megan, Jesse, and Tara need to make is how to obtain financing for renovation and equipment. They understand the difference between equity securities and debt securities, but do not understand the tax, net income, and earnings per share consequences of equity versus debt financing on the future of their business.

Instructions

(b) Prepare notes for a discussion with the three entrepreneurs in which you will compare the consequences of using equity versus debt financing. As part of your notes, show the differences in interest and tax expense assuming $1,400,000 is financed with common stock, and then alternatively with debt. Assume that when common stock is used, 140,000 shares will be issued. When debt is used, assume the interest rate on debt is 9%, the tax rate is 32%, and income before interest and taxes is $200,000. (You may want to use an electronic spreadsheet.)

PART III

During the discussion about financing, Tara mentions that one of her clients, Antonio Cepeda, has approached her about buying a significant interest in the new club. Having an interested investor sways the three to issue equity securities to provide the financing they need. On July 21, 2004, Mr. Cepeda buys 140,000 shares at a price of $10 per share.

The club, LifePath Fitness, opens on January 12, 2005, and after a slow start, begins to produce the revenue desired by the owners. The owners decide to pay themselves a stock dividend, since cash has been less than abundant since they opened their doors. The 5% stock dividend is declared by the owners on July 27, 2005. The market value of the stock is $3 on the declaration date. The date of record is July 31, 2005 (there have been no changes in stock ownership since the initial issuance), and the issue date is August 15, 2005. By the middle of the fourth quarter of 2005, the cash flow of LifePath Fitness has improved to the point that the owners feel ready to pay themselves a cash dividend. They declare a $0.05 cash dividend on December 4, 2004. The record date is December 14, 2005, and the payment date is December 24, 2005.

Instructions

(c) (1) Record all of the transactions related to the common stock of LifePath Fitness during the years 2004 and 2005. **(2)** Indicate how many shares are issued and outstanding after the stock dividend is issued.

PART IV

Since the club opened, a major concern has been the pool facilities. Although the existing pool is adequate, Megan, Jesse, and Tara all desire to make LifePath a cutting-edge facility. Until the end of 2005, financing concerns prevented this improvement. However, because there has been steady growth in clientele, revenue, and income since the fourth quarter of 2005, the owners have explored possible financing options. They are hesitant to issue stock and change the ownership mix because they have been able to work together as a team with great effectiveness. They have formulated a plan to issue secured term bonds to raise the needed $500,000 for the pool facilities. By the end of April 2006 everything was in place for the bond issue to go ahead. On June 1, 2006, the bonds were issued for $456,000. The bonds pay semiannual interest of 3% (6% annual) on December 1 and June 1 of each year. The bonds mature in 10 years, and amortization is computed using the straight-line method.

Instructions

(d) Record **(1)** the issuance of the secured bonds, **(2)** the interest payment made on December 1, 2006, **(3)** the adjusting entry required at December 31, 2006, and **(4)** the interest payment made on June 1, 2007.

PART V

Mr. Cepeda's purchase of LifePath Fitness was done through his business. The investment has always been accounted for using the cost method on his firm's books. However, early in 2007 he decided to take his company public. He is preparing an IPO (initial public offering), and he needs to have the firm's financial statements audited. One of the issues to be resolved is to restate the investment in LifePath Fitness using the equity method, since Mr. Cepeda's ownership percentage is greater than 20%.

Instructions

(e) **(1)** Give the entries that would have been made on Cepeda's books if the equity method of accounting for investments had been used since the initial investment. Assume the following data for LifePath.

	2004	**2005**	**2006**
Net income	$30,000	$70,000	$105,000
Total cash dividends	$ 2,100	$20,000	$ 50,000

(2) Compute the balance in the LifePath Investment account at the end of 2006.

BROADENING YOUR PERSPECTIVE

Financial Reporting and Analysis

■ FINANCIAL REPORTING PROBLEM: PepsiCo

BYP17-1 The annual report of **PepsiCo. Inc.** is presented in Appendix A.

Instructions

(a) See Note 1 to the financial statements and indicate what the consolidated financial statements include.
(b) Using **PepsiCo**'s consolidated statement of cash flows, determine how much was spent for capital acquisitions during the current year.

■ COMPARATIVE ANALYSIS PROBLEM: PepsiCo vs. Coca-Cola

BYP17-2 **PepsiCo**'s financial statements are presented in Appendix A. **Coca-Cola**'s financial statements are presented in Appendix B.

Instructions

(a) Based on the information contained in these financial statements, determine each of the following for each company.
   (1) Net cash used for investing (investment) activities for the current year (from the statement of cash flows).
   (2) Cash used for capital expenditures during the current year.
(b) Each of PepsiCo's financial statements is labeled "consolidated." What has been consolidated? That is, from the contents of PepsiCo's annual report, identify by name the corporations that have been consolidated (parent and subsidiaries).

■ **INTERPRETING FINANCIAL STATEMENTS: A Global Focus**

BYP17-3 **Xerox Corporation** has a 50% investment interest in a joint venture with the Japanese corporation Fuji, called **Fuji Xerox**. Xerox accounts for this investment using the equity method. The following additional information regarding this investment was taken from a recent Xerox annual report (in millions).

Investment in Fuji Xerox per balance sheet	$ 1,354
Fuji Xerox net income	108
Xerox total assets	30,024
Xerox total liabilities	25,167
Fuji Xerox total assets	6,279
Fuji Xerox total liabilities	3,757

Instructions

(a) What alternative approaches are available for accounting for long-term investments in stock? Discuss whether Xerox is correct in using the equity method to account for this investment.

(b) Under the equity method, how does Xerox reports its investment in Fuji Xerox? If Xerox owned a majority of Fuji Xerox, it then would have to consolidate Fuji Xerox instead of using the equity method. Discuss how this would change Xerox's financial statements. That is, in what way and by how much would assets and liabilities change?

(c) The use of 50% joint ventures is becoming a fairly common practice. Why might companies like Xerox prefer to participate in a joint venture rather than own a majority share?

■ **EXPLORING THE WEB**

BYP17-4 The **Securities and Exchange Commission (SEC)** is the primary regulatory agency of U.S. financial markets. Its job is to ensure that the markets remain fair for all investors. The following SEC site provides useful information for investors.

Address: www.sec.gov/answers.shtml, or go to www.wiley.com/college/weygandt

Steps

Go to the site shown above.

Instructions

Find the definition of the following terms.

(a) Ask price.
(b) Margin account.
(c) Prospectus.
(d) Yield.

BYP17-5 Most publicly traded companies are analyzed by numerous analysts. These analysts often don't agree about a company's future prospects. In this exercise you will find analysts' ratings about companies and make comparisons over time and across companies in the same industry. You will also see to what extent the analysts experienced "earnings surprises." Earnings surprises can cause changes in stock prices.

Address: biz.yahoo.com/i, or go to www.wiley.com/college/weygandt

Steps

1. Choose a company.
2. Use the index to find the company's name.
3. Choose **Research**.

Instructions

(a) How many brokers rated the company?
(b) What percentage rated it a strong buy?
(c) What was the average rating for the week?
(d) Did the average rating improve or decline relative to the previous week?
(e) How do the brokers rank this company among all the companies in its industry?
(f) What was the amount of the earnings surprise during the last quarter?

Critical Thinking

■ GROUP DECISION CASE

BYP17-6 At the beginning of the question and answer portion of the annual stockholders' meeting of Reiley Corporation, stockholder Matt Finley asks, "Why did management sell the holdings in SRI Company at a loss when this company has been very profitable during the period its stock was held by Reiley?"

Since president Tony Garcia has just concluded his speech on the recent success and bright future of Reiley, he is taken aback by this question and responds, "I remember we paid $1,100,000 for that stock some years ago, and I am sure we sold that stock at a much higher price. You must be mistaken."

Finley retorts, "Well, right here in footnote number 7 to the annual report it shows that 240,000 shares, a 25% interest in SRI, were sold on the last day of the year. Also, it states that SRI earned $520,000 this year and paid out $160,000 in cash dividends. Further, a summary statement indicates that in past years, while Reiley held SRI stock, SRI earned $1,240,000 and paid out $440,000 in dividends. Finally, the income statement for this year shows a loss on the sale of SRI stock of $180,000. So, I doubt that I am mistaken."

Red-faced, president Garcia turns to you.

Instructions
With the class divided into groups, answer the following.

(a) What dollar amount did Reiley receive upon the sale of the SRI stock?
(b) Explain why both stockholder Finley and president Garcia are correct.

■ COMMUNICATION ACTIVITY

BYP17-7 Fargo Corporation has purchased two securities for its portfolio. The first is a stock investment in Tierney Corporation, one of its suppliers. Fargo purchased 10% of Tierney with the intention of holding it for a number of years, but has no intention of purchasing more shares. The second investment was a purchase of debt securities. Fargo purchased the debt securities because its analysts believe that changes in market interest rates will cause these securities to increase in value in a short period of time. Fargo intends to sell the securities as soon as they have increased in value.

Instructions
Write a memo to Dipak Ghosh, the chief financial officer, explaining how to account for each of these investments. Explain what the implications for reported income are from this accounting treatment.

■ ETHICS CASE

BYP17-8 Kreider Financial Services Company holds a large portfolio of debt and stock securities as an investment. The total fair value of the portfolio at December 31, 2005, is greater than total cost. Some securities have increased in value and others have decreased. Ann Lemke, the financial vice president, and Sue Greene, the controller, are in the process of classifying for the first time the securities in the portfolio.

Lemke suggests classifying the securities that have increased in value as trading securities in order to increase net income for the year. She wants to classify the securities that have decreased in value as long-term available-for-sale securities, so that the decreases in value will not affect 2005 net income.

Greene disagrees. She recommends classifying the securities that have decreased in value as trading securities and those that have increased in value as long-term available-for-sale securities. Greene argues that the company is having a good earnings year and that recognizing the losses now will help to smooth income for this year. Moreover, for future years, when the company may not be as profitable, the company will have built-in gains.

Instructions
(a) Will classifying the securities as Lemke and Greene suggest actually affect earnings as each says it will?
(b) Is there anything unethical in what Lemke and Greene propose? Who are the stakeholders affected by their proposals?

(c) Assume that Lemke and Greene properly classify the portfolio. Assume, at year-end, that Lemke proposes to sell the securities that will increase 2005 net income, and that Greene proposes to sell the securities that will decrease 2005 net income. Is this unethical?

Answers to Self-Study Questions
1. a   **2.** b   **3.** c   **4.** a   **5.** a   **6.** c   **7.** b   **8.** c

Answer to PepsiCo Review It Question 4, page 686
In Note 1, the following statement is made regarding **PepsiCo**'s consolidation policy:

> "Our financial statements include the consolidated accounts of PepsiCo, Inc. and the affiliates that we control. In addition, we include our share of the results of certain other affiliates based on our ownership interest. We do not control these other affiliates as our ownership in these other affiliates is generally less than fifty percent. Our share of the net income of noncontrolled bottling affiliates is reported in our income statement as bottling equity income. See Note 8 for additional information on our noncontrolled bottling affiliates. Our share of other noncontrolled affiliates is included in division operating profit. As a result of changes in the operations of our European snack joint venture, Snack Ventures Europe (SVE), we determined that effective in 2002, consolidation was required. Therefore, SVE's results of operations are consolidated with PepsiCo in 2002. Intercompany balances and transactions are eliminated."

The Statement of Cash Flows

CONCEPTS FOR REVIEW

Before studying this chapter, you should know or, if necessary, review:

The difference between the accrual basis and the cash basis of accounting.
(Ch. 3, pp. 90–91)

The major items included in a corporation's balance sheet.
(Ch. 17, pp. 691–692)

The major items included in a corporation's income statement.
(Ch. 15, pp. 610–611)

THE
NAVIGATOR

"Cash Is Cash, and Everything Else Is Accounting"

For Gerald Biby, vice president and chief financial officer of Kilian Community College in Sioux Falls, South Dakota, the statement of cash flows was the difference between being able to refinance a mortgage and being turned down by six local banks. "We recently wanted to refinance a $125,000 mortgage on a piece of property that we own," he says. "It was the statement of cash flows that finally showed our lender that we had the cash flow to service the debt."

As he explains, the traditional statement of cash flows for a not-for-profit, educational institution shows revenues and all expenditures, even the capital expenditures. According to this format, which the banks focused on initially, Kilian Community College was just breaking even. "In the business world, if we had spent $250,000 on a computer system, then we would have put that on a depreciation schedule. But in the non-profit arena, it's typical that the entire $250,000 is written off as an expense against the general fund." The statement of cash flows showed the bankers that one of the uses of funds was really the purchase of computer equipment that had several years of life.

The college's statement of cash flows has over 30 classifications including tuition, fees, bookstore revenues, and so on. The school has 250 students, charges $70 a credit hour (12 hours is a full-time schedule), and has five terms each year.

The bankers granted the refinancing when they saw that the college's sources of funds exceeded the loan repayments, including principal and interest, by a ratio of 3-to-1. Not only did the school get the loan, but it did so at a favorable rate. "We were able to cut the mortgage rate to prime plus 1 percent from prime plus 3 percent."

THE NAVIGATOR

After studying this chapter, you should be able to:

1. Indicate the usefulness of the statement of cash flows.
2. Distinguish among operating, investing, and financing activities.
3. Prepare a statement of cash flows using the indirect method.
4. Prepare a statement of cash flows using the direct method.
5. Analyze the statement of cash flows.

THE NAVIGATOR

As the story about Kilian Community College indicates, the balance sheet, income statement, and retained earnings statement do not always show the whole picture of the financial condition of a company or institution. In fact, looking at the financial statements of some well-known companies, a thoughtful investor might ask questions like these: How did Eastman Kodak finance cash dividends of $649 million in a year in which it earned only $17 million? How could United Airlines purchase new planes that cost $1.9 billion in a year in which it reported a net loss of over $2 billion? How did the companies that spent a combined fantastic $3.4 trillion on mergers and acquisitions in a recent year finance those deals? Answers to these and similar questions can be found in this chapter, which presents the statement of cash flows.

The content and organization of this chapter are as follows.

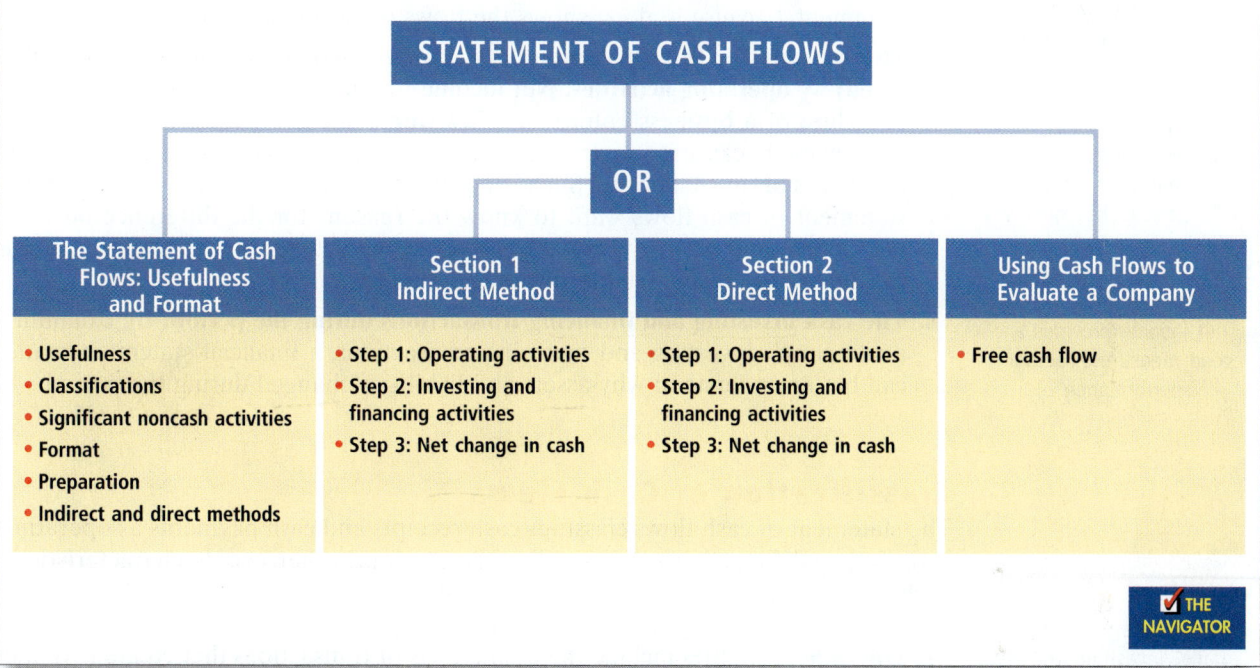

The Statement of Cash Flows: Usefulness and Format

The basic financial statements we have presented so far provide only limited information about a company's cash flows (cash receipts and cash payments). For example, comparative balance sheets show the increase in property, plant, and equipment during the year. But they do not show how the additions were financed or paid for. The income statement shows net income. But it does not indicate the amount of cash generated by operating activities. The retained earnings statement shows cash dividends declared but not the cash dividends paid during the year. None of these statements presents a detailed summary of where cash came from and how it was used.

> **HELPFUL HINT**
>
> Recall that the retained earnings statement is often presented in the statement of stockholders' equity.

Usefulness of the Statement of Cash Flows

The **statement of cash flows** reports the cash receipts, cash payments, and net change in cash resulting from operating, investing, and financing activities during a period. The information in a statement of cash flows should help investors, creditors, and others assess:

1. **The entity's ability to generate future cash flows.** By examining relationships between items in the statement of cash flows, investors and others can make predictions of the amounts, timing, and uncertainty of future cash flows better than they can from accrual basis data.

2. **The entity's ability to pay dividends and meet obligations.** If a company does not have adequate cash, it cannot pay employees, settle debts, or pay dividends. Employees, creditors, and stockholders should be particularly interested in this statement, because it alone shows the flows of cash in a business.

3. **The reasons for the difference between net income and net cash provided (used) by operating activities.** Net income provides information on the success or failure of a business enterprise. However, some are critical of accrual basis net income because it requires many estimates. As a result, the reliability of the number is often challenged. Such is not the case with cash. Many readers of the statement of cash flows want to know the reasons for the difference between net income and net cash provided by operating activities. Then they can assess for themselves the reliability of the income number.

4. **The cash investing and financing transactions during the period.** By examining a company's investing and financing transactions, a financial statement reader can better understand why assets and liabilities changed during the period.

Classification of Cash Flows

The statement of cash flows classifies cash receipts and cash payments as operating, investing, and financing activities. Transactions and other events characteristic of each kind of activity are described in the list below.

1. **Operating activities** include the cash effects of transactions that create revenues and expenses. They thus enter into the determination of net income.

2. **Investing activities** include (a) acquiring and disposing of investments and property, plant, and equipment, and (b) lending money and collecting the loans.

3. **Financing activities** include (a) obtaining cash from issuing debt and repaying the amounts borrowed, and (b) obtaining cash from stockholders and providing them with a return on their investment.

The category of operating activities is the most important. As noted above, it shows the cash provided by company operations. This source of cash is generally considered to be the best measure of a company's ability to generate sufficient cash to continue as a going concern.

Illustration 18-1 lists typical cash receipts and cash payments within each of the three classifications. **Study the list carefully.** It will prove very useful in solving homework exercises and problems.

Are we not factoring in the cash affect by current assets & curr. Lib ?

The Statement of Cash Flows: Usefulness and Format

Types of Cash Inflows and Outflows

Operating activities—Income statement items
Cash inflows:
   From sale of goods or services.
   From returns on loans (interest received) and on equity securities (dividends received).
Cash outflows:
   To suppliers for inventory.   *supplies ?*
   To employees for services.
   To government for taxes.
   To lenders for interest.
   To others for expenses.

Investing activities—Changes in investments and long-term assets
Cash inflows:
   From sale of property, plant, and equipment.
   From sale of debt or equity securities of other entities.   *lending + collecting*
   From collection of principal on loans to other entities.
Cash outflows:
   To purchase property, plant, and equipment.
   To purchase debt or equity securities of other entities.
   To make loans to other entities.

Financing activities—Changes in long-term liabilities and stockholders' equity
Cash inflows:
   From sale of common stock.
   From issuance of debt (bonds and notes).
Cash outflows:
   To stockholders as dividends.
   To redeem long-term debt or reacquire capital stock.

Operating activities

Investing activities

Financing activities

Note the following general guidelines: (1) Operating activities involve income statement items. (2) Investing activities involve cash flows resulting from changes in investments and long-term asset items. (3) Financing activities involve cash flows resulting from changes in long-term liability and stockholders' equity items.

Some cash flows related to investing or financing activities are classified as operating activities. For example, receipts of investment revenue (interest and dividends) are classified as operating activities. So are payments of interest to lenders. Why are these considered operating activities? **Because these items are reported in the income statement, where results of operations are shown.**

Significant Noncash Activities

Not all of a company's significant activities involve cash. Examples of significant noncash activities are:

1. Issuance of common stock to purchase assets.
2. Conversion of bonds into common stock.
3. Issuance of debt to purchase assets.
4. Exchanges of plant assets.

Significant financing and investing activities that do not affect cash are not reported in the body of the statement of cash flows. However, these activities are reported in either a **separate schedule** at the bottom of the statement of cash flows or in a **separate note or supplementary schedule** to the financial statements.

The reporting of these noncash activities in a separate schedule satisfies the **full disclosure principle**. In solving homework assignments you should present significant noncash investing and financing activities in a separate schedule at the bottom of the statement of cash flows. (See lower section of Illustration 18-2, below, for an example.)

ACCOUNTING IN ACTION   **Business Insight**

Net income is not the same as net cash provided by operations. The differences are illustrated by the following results from recent annual reports for 2002 ($ in millions). Note the wide disparity among these companies that all engaged in similar types of retail merchandising.

Company	Net Income	Net Cash Provided by Operations
Kmart Corporation	$(3,219)	$ 252
Wal-Mart Stores, Inc.	6,671	10,260
JCPenney Company, Inc.	378	1,329
Sears, Roebuck & Co.	1,578	2,467
Target Corporation	1,645	2,863

Format of the Statement of Cash Flows

The general format of the statement of cash flows presents the results of the three activities discussed previously—operating, investing, and financing—plus the significant noncash investing and financing activities. A widely used form of the statement of cash flows is shown in Illustration 18-2.

Illustration 18-2
Format of statement of cash flows

COMPANY NAME
Statement of Cash Flows
Period Covered

Cash flows from operating activities		
(List of individual items)	XX	
Net cash provided (used) by operating activities		XXX
Cash flows from investing activities		
(List of individual inflows and outflows)	XX	
Net cash provided (used) by investing activities		XXX
Cash flows from financing activities		
(List of individual inflows and outflows)	XX	
Net cash provided (used) by financing activities		XXX
Net increase (decrease) in cash		XXX
Cash at beginning of period		XXX
Cash at end of period		XXX
Noncash investing and financing activities		
(List of individual noncash transactions)		XXX

The cash flows from operating activities section always appears first. It is followed by the investing activities and the financing activities sections.

BEFORE YOU GO ON...

Review It

1. What is the primary purpose of a statement of cash flows?
2. Why is the statement of cash flows useful?
3. What are the major classifications of cash flows on the statement of cash flows?
4. In its 2002 statement of cash flows, what amounts are reported by **PepsiCo** for: (1) net cash provided by operating activities, (2) net cash used for investing activities, and (3) net cash used for financing activities? The answer to this question is provided on page 764.
5. What are some examples of significant noncash activities?
6. What is the general format of the statement of cash flows? In what sequence are the three types of business activities presented?

Do It

During its first week, Duffy & Stevenson Company had these transactions.

1. Issued 100,000 shares of $5 par value common stock for $800,000 cash.
2. Borrowed $200,000 from Castle Bank, signing a 5-year note bearing 8% interest.
3. Purchased two semi-trailer trucks for $170,000 cash.
4. Paid employees $12,000 for salaries and wages.
5. Collected $20,000 cash for services rendered.

Classify each of these transactions by type of cash flow activity.

ACTION PLAN

- Identify the three types of activities used to report all cash inflows and outflows.
- Report as operating activities the cash effects of transactions that create revenues and expenses and enter into the determination of net income.
- Report as investing activities transactions that (a) acquire and dispose of investments and productive long-lived assets and (b) lend money and collect loans.
- Report as financing activities transactions that (a) obtain cash from issuing debt and repay the amounts borrowed and (b) obtain cash from stockholders and pay them dividends.

SOLUTION

1. Financing activity
2. Financing activity
3. Investing activity
4. Operating activity
5. Operating activity

Related exercise material: *BE18-3, BE18-5, E18-1, and E18-6.*

Preparing the Statement of Cash Flows

The statement of cash flows is prepared differently from the three other basic financial statements. First, it is not prepared from an adjusted trial balance. The statement requires detailed information concerning the changes in account balances that occurred between two points in time. An adjusted trial balance will not provide the necessary data. Second, the statement of cash flows deals with cash receipts and payments. As a result, the effects of the use of accrual accounting **must be adjusted to determine cash flows**.

The information to prepare this statement usually comes from three sources:

- **Comparative balance sheets.** Information in the comparative balance sheets indicates the amount of the changes in assets, liabilities, and stockholders' equities from the beginning to the end of the period.
- **Current income statement.** Information in this statement helps determine the amount of cash provided or used by operations during the period.
- **Additional information.** Such information includes transaction data that are needed to determine how cash was provided or used during the period.

Preparing the statement of cash flows from these data sources involves three major steps, explained in Illustration 18-3.

Illustration 18-3
Three major steps in preparing the statement of cash flows

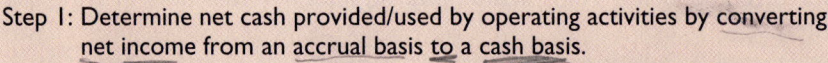

Step 1: Determine net cash provided/used by operating activities by converting net income from an accrual basis to a cash basis.

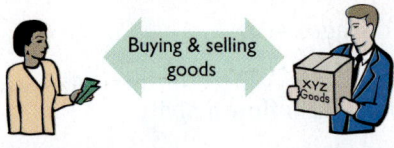

Buying & selling goods

This step involves analyzing not only the current year's income statement but also comparative balance sheets and selected additional data.

Step 2: Analyze changes in noncurrent asset and liability accounts and record as investing and financing activities, or as significant noncash transactions.

Investing   Financing

This step involves analyzing comparative balance sheet data and selected additional information for their effects on cash.

Step 3: Compare the net change in cash on the statement of cash flows with the change in the cash account reported on the balance sheet to make sure the amounts agree.

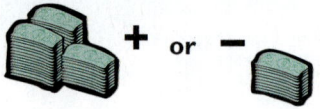

+ or −

The difference between the beginning and ending cash balances can be easily computed from comparative balance sheets.

Indirect and Direct Methods

In order to perform step 1, **net income must be converted from an accrual basis to a cash basis**. This conversion may be done by either of two methods: (1) the indirect method or (2) the direct method. **Both methods arrive at the same total amount** for "Net cash provided by operating activities." They differ in **how** they arrive at the amount.

The indirect method is used extensively in practice, as shown in the nearby chart.[1] Companies (98.7%) favor the indirect method for two reasons: (1) It is easier and less costly to prepare, and (2) it focuses on the differences between net income and net cash flow from operating activities.

The direct method shows operating cash receipts and payments, making it more consistent with the objective of a statement of cash flows. The FASB has expressed a preference for the direct method, but allows the use of either method.

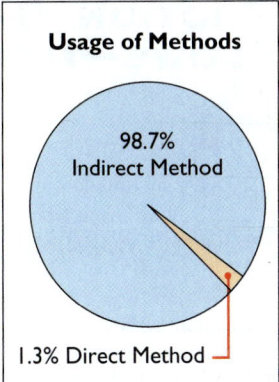

Usage of Methods

98.7%
Indirect Method

1.3% Direct Method

BEFORE YOU GO ON...

Review It

1. What is the primary difference between the indirect and direct approaches to the statement of cash flows? Which method is more commonly used in practice?

2. What are the three major steps in the preparation of a statement of cash flows?

THE NAVIGATOR

ACCOUNTING IN ACTION Ethics Insight

During the 1990s, analysts increasingly used cash-flow-based measures of income, such as cash flow provided by operations, instead of or in addition to net income. The reason for the change was that they were losing faith in accrual-accounting-based net income numbers. Sadly, these days even cash flow from operations isn't always what it seems to be. For example, in 2002 **WorldCom, Inc.** disclosed that it had improperly capitalized expenses: It moved $3.8 billion of cash outflows from the "Cash from operating activities" section of the cash flow statement to the "Investing activities" section, thereby greatly enhancing cash provided by operating activities. Similarly, in 2002 **Dynegy, Inc.** restated its cash flow statement for 2001 so that $300 million tied to its complex natural gas trading operation was removed from cash flow from operations and instead put into the financing section—a drop of 37% in cash flow from operations.

Source: Henny Sender, "Sadly, These Days Even Cash Flow Isn't Always What It Seems To Be," *Wall Street Journal Online* (May 8, 2002).

On the following pages, in two separate sections, we describe the use of the two methods. Section 1 illustrates the indirect method. Section 2 illustrates the direct method. These sections are independent of each other. *Only one or the other* need be covered in order to understand and prepare the statement of cash flows. When you have finished the section assigned by your instructor, turn to "Using Cash Flows to Evaluate a Company" on page 736.

---

[1]*Accounting Trends and Techniques—2002* (New York: American Institute of Certified Public Accountants, 2002).

SECTION ONE STATEMENT OF CASH FLOWS—INDIRECT METHOD

STUDY OBJECTIVE 3

Prepare a statement of cash flows using the indirect method.

To explain how to prepare a statement of cash flows using the indirect method, we use financial information from Computer Services Company. Illustration 18-4 presents Computer Services' current and previous-year balance sheets, its current-year income statement, and related financial information.

Illustration 18-4
Comparative balance sheets, income statement, and additional information for Computer Services Company

COMPUTER SERVICES COMPANY
Comparative Balance Sheets
December 31

Assets	2005	2004	Change in Account Balance Increase/Decrease
Current assets			
Cash	$ 55,000	$ 33,000	$ 22,000 Increase
Accounts receivable	20,000	30,000	10,000 Decrease
Merchandise inventory	15,000	10,000	5,000 Increase
Prepaid expenses	5,000	1,000	4,000 Increase
Property, plant, and equipment			
Land	130,000	20,000	110,000 Increase
Building	160,000	40,000	120,000 Increase
Accumulated depreciation—building	(11,000)	(5,000)	6,000 Increase
Equipment	27,000	10,000	17,000 Increase
Accumulated depreciation—equipment	(3,000)	(1,000)	2,000 Increase
Total	$398,000	$138,000	
Liabilities and Stockholders' Equity			
Current liabilities			
Accounts payable	$ 28,000	$ 12,000	$ 16,000 Increase
Income tax payable	6,000	8,000	2,000 Decrease
Long-term liabilities			
Bonds payable	130,000	20,000	110,000 Increase
Stockholders' equity			
Common stock	70,000	50,000	20,000 Increase
Retained earnings	164,000	48,000	116,000 Increase
Total liabilities and stockholders' equity	$398,000	$138,000	

COMPUTER SERVICES COMPANY
Income Statement
For the Year Ended December 31, 2005

Revenues		$507,000
Cost of goods sold	$150,000	
Operating expenses (excluding depreciation)	111,000	
Depreciation	9,000	
Interest expense	42,000	
Loss on sale of equipment	3,000	315,000
Income before income taxes		192,000
Income tax expense		47,000
Net income		$145,000

Additional information for 2005:

1. The company declared and paid a $29,000 cash dividend.
2. Issued $110,000 of long-term bonds in exchange for land.
3. A building costing $120,000 was purchased for cash. Equipment costing $25,000 was also purchased for cash.
4. The company sold equipment with a book value of $7,000 (cost $8,000, less accumulated depreciation $1,000) for $4,000 cash.
5. Issued common stock for $20,000 cash.
6. Depreciation expense was comprised of $6,000 for building and $3,000 for equipment.

We will now apply the three steps to the information provided for Computer Services Company.

Step 1: Operating Activities

DETERMINE NET CASH PROVIDED/USED BY OPERATING ACTIVITIES BY CONVERTING NET INCOME FROM AN ACCRUAL BASIS TO A CASH BASIS

To determine net cash provided by operating activities under the indirect method, **net income is adjusted in numerous ways.** A useful starting point is to understand **why** net income must be converted to net cash provided by operating activities. Under generally accepted accounting principles, most companies use the accrual basis of accounting. As you have learned, this basis requires that revenue be recorded when earned and that expenses be recorded when incurred. Earned revenues may include credit sales that have not yet been collected in cash. Expenses incurred may include some items that have not been paid in cash. Thus, under the accrual basis of accounting, net income is not the same as net cash provided by operating activities. Therefore, under the indirect method, net income must be adjusted to convert certain items to the cash basis. The **indirect method** (or reconciliation method) starts with net income and converts it to net cash provided by operating activities. Illustration 18-5 lists the three types of adjustments to net income.

Net Income	+/−	Adjustments	=	Net Cash Provided/Used by Operating Activities
		• Add back noncash expenses, such as depreciation expense, amortization, or depletion. • Deduct gains and add losses that resulted from investing and financing activities. • Analyze changes to noncash current asset and current liability accounts.		

Illustration 18-5
Three types of adjustments to convert net income to net cash provided by operating activities

The three types of adjustments are explained in the next three sections.

Depreciation Expense

Computer Services' income statement reports depreciation expense of $9,000. Although depreciation expense reduces net income, it does not reduce cash. In other words, depreciation expense is a noncash charge. It is added back to net income to

HELPFUL HINT

Depreciation is similar to any other expense in that it reduces net income. It differs in that it does not involve a current cash outflow; that is why it must be *added back* to net income to arrive at cash provided by operations.

arrive at net cash provided by operating activities. Depreciation expense is reported as follows in the statement of cash flows.

Illustration 18-6
Adjustment for depreciation

Cash flows from operating activities	
Net income	$145,000
Adjustments to reconcile net income to net cash provided by operating activities:	
Depreciation expense	**9,000**
Net cash provided by operating activities	$154,000

Depreciation and similar noncash charges such as amortization of intangible assets, and depletion expense are frequently listed in the statement of cash flows as the first adjustment to net income.

Loss on Sale of Equipment

Computer Services' income statement reports a $3,000 loss on the sale of equipment (book value $7,000, less cash received from sale of equipment $4,000). Illustration 18-1 states that cash received from the sale of plant assets should be reported in the investing activities section. Because of this, **all gains and losses must be eliminated from net income to arrive at cash from operating activities**. In our example, Computer Services Company's loss of $3,000 should not be included in the operating activities section of the statement of cash flows. Illustration 18-7 shows that the $3,000 loss is eliminated by adding $3,000 back to net income to arrive at net cash provided by operating activities.

Illustration 18-7
Adjustment for loss on sale of equipment

Cash flows from operating activities		
Net income		$145,000
Adjustments to reconcile net income to net cash provided by operating activities:		
Depreciation expense	$9,000	
Loss on sale of equipment	**3,000**	12,000
Net cash provided by operating activities		$157,000

If a gain on sale occurs, the gain is deducted from net income in order to determine net cash provided by operating activities. **In the case of either a gain or a loss, the actual amount of cash received from the sale is reported as a source of cash in the investing activities section of the statement of cash flows.**

Changes to Noncash Current Asset and Current Liability Accounts

A final adjustment in reconciling net income to net cash provided by operating activities involves examining all changes in current asset and current liability accounts. The accrual accounting process records revenues in the period earned and expenses in the period incurred. For example, Accounts Receivable is used to record amounts owed to the company for sales that have been made and cash collections have not yet been received. The Prepaid Insurance account is used to reflect insurance that has been paid for, but which has not yet expired, and therefore has not been expensed. Similarly, the Salaries Payable account reflects salaries expense that has been incurred by the company but has not been paid. As a result, we need to adjust net income for these accruals and prepayments to determine net cash provided by operating activities. Thus we must analyze the change in each current asset and current liability account to determine its impact on net income and cash.

Changes in Noncash Current Assets

The adjustments required for changes in noncash current asset accounts are as follows: **Increases in current asset accounts are deducted from net income, and decreases in current asset accounts are added to net income, to arrive at net cash provided by operating activities.** We can observe these relationships by analyzing the accounts of Computer Services Company.

DECREASE IN ACCOUNTS RECEIVABLE. Computer Services Company's accounts receivable decreases by $10,000 (from $30,000 to $20,000) during the period. For Computer Services Company this means that cash receipts were $10,000 higher than revenues. Illustration 18-8 shows that Computer Services Company had $507,000 in revenues (as reported on the income statement), but it collected $517,000 in cash. As shown in Illustration 18-9 (on page 722), to adjust net income to net cash provided by operating activities, the decrease of $10,000 in accounts receivable is added to net income.

	Accounts Receivable			
1/1/05	Balance	30,000	**Receipts from customers**	**517,000**
	Revenues	**507,000**		
12/31/05	Balance	20,000		

Illustration 18-8
Analysis of accounts receivable

When the Accounts Receivable balance increases, cash receipts are lower than revenue earned under the accrual basis. Therefore, the amount of the increase in accounts receivable is deducted from net income to arrive at net cash provided by operating activities.

INCREASE IN MERCHANDISE INVENTORY. Computer Services Company's Merchandise Inventory balance increases $5,000 (from $10,000 to $15,000) during the period. The Merchandise Inventory account reflects the difference between the amount of inventory that has been purchased and the amount which has been sold. For Computer Services this means that the cost of merchandise purchased exceeded the cost of goods sold by $5,000. As a result, cost of goods sold does not reflect $5,000 of cash payments made for merchandise. This inventory increase of $5,000 during the period is deducted from net income to arrive at net cash provided by operating activities (see Illustration 18-9, next page). If inventory decreases, the amount of the change is added to net income to arrive at net cash provided by operating activities.

INCREASE IN PREPAID EXPENSES. Prepaid expenses increased during the period by $4,000. This means that cash paid for expenses is higher than expenses reported on an accrual basis. Cash payments have been made in the current period, but expenses (as charges to the income statement) have been deferred to future periods. To adjust net income to net cash provided by operating activities, the $4,000 increase in prepaid expenses is deducted from net income (see Illustration 18-9).

If prepaid expenses decrease, reported expenses are higher than the expenses paid. Therefore, the decrease in prepaid expense is added to net income to arrive at net cash provided by operating activities.

Illustration 18-9
Adjustments for changes in
current asset accounts

Cash flows from operating activities		
Net income		$145,000
Adjustments to reconcile net income to net cash provided by operating activities:		
Depreciation expense	$ 9,000	
Loss on sale of equipment	3,000	
Decrease in accounts receivable	**10,000**	
Increase in merchandise inventory	**(5,000)**	
Increase in prepaid expenses	**(4,000)**	13,000
Net cash provided by operating activities		$158,000

Changes in Current Liabilities

The adjustments required for changes in current liability accounts are as follows: **Increases in current liability accounts are added to net income, and decreases in current liability accounts are deducted from net income, to arrive at net cash provided by operating activities.**

INCREASE IN ACCOUNTS PAYABLE. For Computer Services Company, Accounts Payable increased by $16,000 during the period. That means the company received $16,000 more in goods than it actually paid for. As shown in Illustration 18-10, to adjust net income to determine net cash provided by operating activities, the $16,000 increase in Accounts Payable is added to net income.

DECREASE IN INCOME TAXES PAYABLE. When a company incurs income tax expense but has not yet paid its taxes, it records income tax payable. A change in the Income Tax Payable account reflects the difference between income tax expense incurred and income tax actually paid. Computer Services' Income Tax Payable account decreased by $2,000. That means the $47,000 of income tax expense reported on the income statement was $2,000 less than the amount of taxes paid during the period of $49,000. As shown in Illustration 18-10, to adjust net income to a cash basis, net income must be reduced by $2,000.

Illustration 18-10
Adjustments for changes in
current liability accounts

Cash flows from operating activities		
Net income		$145,000
Adjustments to reconcile net income to net cash provided by operating activities:		
Depreciation expense	$ 9,000	
Loss on sale of equipment	3,000	
Decrease in accounts receivable	10,000	
Increase in merchandise inventory	(5,000)	
Increase in prepaid expenses	(4,000)	
Increase in accounts payable	**16,000**	
Decrease in income tax payable	**(2,000)**	27,000
Net cash provided by operating activities		$172,000

Illustration 18-10 shows that, after starting with net income of $145,000, the sum of all of the adjustments to net income was $27,000. This resulted in net cash provided by operating activities of $172,000.

Summary of Conversion to Net Cash Provided by Operating Activities—Indirect Method

As shown in the previous illustrations, the statement of cash flows prepared by the indirect method starts with net income. It then adds or deducts items to arrive at net cash provided by operating activities. The required adjustments are of three types: (1) noncash charges such as depreciation, amortization, and depletion; (2) gains and losses on the sale of plant assets; and (3) changes in noncash current asset and current liability accounts. A summary of these changes is provided in Illustration 18-11.

			Adjustment Required to Convert Net Income to Net Cash Provided by Operating Activities
Noncash Charges	{	Depreciation expense	Add
		Patent amortization expense	Add
		Depletion expense	Add
Gains and Losses	{	Loss on sale of plant asset	Add
		Gain on sale of plant asset	Deduct
Changes in Current Assets and Current Liabilities	{	Increase in current asset account	Deduct
		Decrease in current asset account	Add
		Increase in current liability account	Add
		Decrease in current liability account	Deduct

Illustration 18-11
Adjustments required to convert net income to net cash provided by operating activities

Step 2: Investing and Financing Activities

ANALYZE CHANGES IN NONCURRENT ASSET AND LIABILITY ACCOUNTS AND RECORD AS INVESTING AND FINANCING ACTIVITIES, OR AS NONCASH INVESTING AND FINANCING ACTIVITIES

INCREASE IN LAND. As indicated from the change in the Land account and the additional information, land of $110,000 was purchased through the issuance of long-term bonds. The issuance of bonds payable for land has no effect on cash. But it is a significant noncash investing and financing activity that merits disclosure in a separate schedule.

INCREASE IN BUILDING. As the additional data indicate, an office building was acquired for $120,000 cash. This is a cash outflow reported in the investing section.

INCREASE IN EQUIPMENT. The Equipment account increased $17,000. The additional information explains that this was a net increase that resulted from two transactions: (1) a purchase of equipment of $25,000 and (2) the sale for $4,000 of equipment costing $8,000. These transactions are classified as investing activities. Each transaction should be reported separately. Thus the purchase of equipment should be reported as an outflow of cash for $25,000. The sale should be reported as an inflow of cash for $4,000. The T account below shows the reasons for the change in this account during the year.

> **HELPFUL HINT**
>
> The investing and financing activities are measured and reported the same under both the direct and indirect methods.

Equipment				
1/1/05	Balance	10,000	Cost of equipment sold	8,000
	Purchase of equipment	**25,000**		
12/31/05	Balance	27,000		

Illustration 18-12
Analysis of equipment

The following entry shows the details of the equipment sale transaction.

Cash	4,000	
Accumulated Depreciation	1,000	
Loss on Sale of Equipment	3,000	
Equipment		8,000

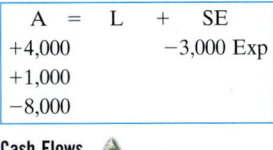

A	=	L	+	SE
+4,000				−3,000 Exp
+1,000				
−8,000				

Cash Flows
+4,000

INCREASE IN BONDS PAYABLE. The Bonds Payable account increased $110,000. As indicated in the additional information, land was acquired from the issuance of these bonds. This noncash transaction is reported in a separate schedule at the bottom of the statement.

INCREASE IN COMMON STOCK. The balance sheet reports an increase in Common Stock of $20,000. The additional information section notes that this increase resulted from the issuance of new shares of stock. This is a cash inflow reported in the financing section.

INCREASE IN RETAINED EARNINGS. Retained earnings increased $116,000 during the year. This increase can be explained by two factors: (1) Net income of $145,000 increased retained earnings. (2) Dividends of $29,000 decreased retained earnings. Net income is adjusted to net cash provided by operating activities in the operating activities section. Payment of the dividends is a **cash outflow that is reported as a financing activity**.

Statement of Cash Flows—2005

Using the previous information, we can now prepare a statement of cash flows for 2005 for Computer Services Company as shown in Illustration 18-13.

Illustration 18-13
Statement of cash flows, 2005—indirect method

COMPUTER SERVICES COMPANY Statement of Cash Flows—Indirect Method For the Year Ended December 31, 2005		
Cash flows from operating activities		
Net income		$145,000
Adjustments to reconcile net income to net cash provided by operating activities:		
Depreciation expense	$ 9,000	
Loss on sale of equipment	3,000	
Decrease in accounts receivable	10,000	
Increase in merchandise inventory	(5,000)	
Increase in prepaid expenses	(4,000)	
Increase in accounts payable	16,000	
Decrease in income tax payable	(2,000)	27,000
Net cash provided by operating activities		172,000
Cash flows from investing activities		
Purchase of building	(120,000)	
Purchase of equipment	(25,000)	
Sale of equipment	4,000	
Net cash used by investing activities		(141,000)
Cash flows from financing activities		
Issuance of common stock	20,000	
Payment of cash dividends	(29,000)	
Net cash used by financing activities		(9,000)
Net increase in cash		22,000
Cash at beginning of period		33,000
Cash at end of period		$ 55,000
Noncash investing and financing activities		
Issuance of bonds payable to purchase land		$110,000

Step 3: Net Change in Cash

COMPARE THE NET CHANGE IN CASH ON THE STATEMENT OF CASH FLOWS WITH THE CHANGE IN THE CASH ACCOUNT REPORTED ON THE BALANCE SHEET TO MAKE SURE THE AMOUNTS AGREE

Illustration 18-13 indicates that the net change in cash during the period was an increase of $22,000. This agrees with the change in Cash account reported on the balance sheet in Illustration 18-4 (page 718).

BEFORE YOU GO ON...

Review It

1. What is the format of the operating activities section of the statement of cash flows using the indirect method?

2. Where is depreciation expense shown on a statement of cash flows using the indirect method?

3. Where are significant noncash investing and financing activities shown in a statement of cash flows? Give some examples.

Do It

Presented below is information related to Reynolds Company. Use it to prepare a statement of cash flows using the indirect method.

REYNOLDS COMPANY
Comparative Balance Sheets
December 31

Assets	2005	2004	Change Increase/Decrease
Cash	$ 54,000	$ 37,000	$ 17,000 Increase
Accounts receivable	68,000	26,000	42,000 Increase
Inventories	54,000	–0–	54,000 Increase
Prepaid expenses	4,000	6,000	2,000 Decrease
Land	45,000	70,000	25,000 Decrease
Buildings	200,000	200,000	–0–
Accumulated depreciation—buildings	(21,000)	(11,000)	10,000 Increase
Equipment	193,000	68,000	125,000 Increase
Accumulated depreciation—equipment	(28,000)	(10,000)	18,000 Increase
Totals	$569,000	$386,000	
Liabilities and Stockholders' Equity			
Accounts payable	$ 23,000	$ 40,000	$ 17,000 Decrease
Accrued expenses payable	10,000	–0–	10,000 Increase
Bonds payable	110,000	150,000	40,000 Decrease
Common stock ($1 par)	220,000	60,000	160,000 Increase
Retained earnings	206,000	136,000	70,000 Increase
Totals	$569,000	$386,000	

REYNOLDS COMPANY
Income Statement
For the Year Ended December 31, 2005

Revenues		$890,000
Cost of goods sold	$465,000	
Operating expenses	221,000	
Interest expense	12,000	
Loss on sale of equipment	2,000	700,000
Income before income taxes		190,000
Income tax expense		65,000
Net income		$125,000

(*continued from p. 725*)

Additional information

1. Operating expenses include depreciation expense of $33,000 and charges from prepaid expenses of $2,000.
2. Land was sold at its book value for cash.
3. Cash dividends of $55,000 were declared and paid in 2005.
4. Interest expense of $12,000 was paid in cash.
5. Equipment with a cost of $166,000 was purchased for cash. Equipment with a cost of $41,000 and a book value of $36,000 was sold for $34,000 cash.
6. Bonds of $10,000 were redeemed at their book value for cash. Bonds of $30,000 were converted into common stock.
7. Common stock ($1 par) of $130,000 was issued for cash.
8. Accounts payable pertain to merchandise suppliers.

ACTION PLAN

- Determine net cash provided/used by operating activities by adjusting net income for items that did not affect cash.
- Determine net cash provided/used by investing activities and financing activities.
- Determine the net increase/decrease in cash.

SOLUTION

REYNOLDS COMPANY
Statement of Cash Flows—Indirect Method
For the Year Ended December 31, 2005

HELPFUL HINT

1. Determine net cash provided/used by operating activities, recognizing that operating activities generally relate to changes in current assets and current liabilities.

2. Determine net cash provided/used by investing activities, recognizing that investing activities generally relate to changes in noncurrent assets.

3. Determine net cash provided/used by financing activities, recognizing that financing activities generally relate to changes in long-term liabilities and stockholders' equity accounts.

Cash flows from operating activities		
Net income		$125,000
Adjustments to reconcile net income to net cash provided by operating activities:		
Depreciation expense	$ 33,000	
Loss on sale of equipment	2,000	
Increase in accounts receivable	(42,000)	
Increase in inventories	(54,000)	
Decrease in prepaid expenses	2,000	
Decrease in accounts payable	(17,000)	
Increase in accrued expenses payable	10,000	(66,000)
Net cash provided by operating activities		59,000
Cash flows from investing activities		
Sale of land	25,000	
Sale of equipment	34,000	
Purchase of equipment	(166,000)	
Net cash used by investing activities		(107,000)
Cash flows from financing activities		
Redemption of bonds	(10,000)	
Sale of common stock	130,000	
Payment of dividends	(55,000)	
Net cash provided by financing activities		65,000
Net increase in cash		17,000
Cash at beginning of period		37,000
Cash at end of period		$ 54,000
Noncash investing and financing activities		
Conversion of bonds into common stock		$ 30,000

Related exercise material: *BE18-1, BE18-2, BE18-4, E18-2, E18-3, E18-4, and E18-5.*

☑ THE NAVIGATOR

Note: This concludes Section 1 on preparation of the statement of cash flows using the indirect method. Unless your instructor assigns Section 2, turn to the concluding section of the chapter, "Using Cash Flows to Evaluate A Company," on p. 736.

SECTION TWO STATEMENT OF CASH FLOWS—DIRECT METHOD

To explain and illustrate the direct method, we will use the transactions of Juarez Company for 2005, to prepare an annual statement of cash flows. Illustration 18-14 presents information related to 2005 for Juarez Company.

STUDY OBJECTIVE 4

Prepare a statement of cash flows using the direct method.

Illustration 18-14
Comparative balance sheets, income statement, and additional information for Juarez Company

JUAREZ COMPANY
Comparative Balance Sheets
December 31

Assets	2005	2004	Change Increase/Decrease
Cash	$191,000	$159,000	$ 32,000 Increase
Accounts receivable	12,000	15,000	3,000 Decrease
Inventory	170,000	160,000	10,000 Increase
Prepaid expenses	6,000	8,000	2,000 Decrease
Land	140,000	80,000	60,000 Increase
Equipment	160,000	–0–	160,000 Increase
Accumulated depreciation—equipment	(16,000)	–0–	16,000 Increase
Total	$663,000	$422,000	
Liabilities and Stockholders' Equity			
Accounts payable	$ 52,000	$ 60,000	$ 8,000 Decrease
Accrued expenses payable	15,000	20,000	5,000 Decrease
Income taxes payable	12,000	–0–	12,000 Increase
Bonds payable	130,000	–0–	130,000 Increase
Common stock	360,000	300,000	60,000 Increase
Retained earnings	94,000	42,000	52,000 Increase
Total	$663,000	$422,000	

JUAREZ COMPANY
Income Statement
For the Year Ended December 31, 2005

Revenues		$975,000
Cost of goods sold	$660,000	
Operating expenses (excluding depreciation)	176,000	
Depreciation expense	18,000	
Loss on sale of store equipment	1,000	855,000
Income before income taxes		120,000
Income tax expense		36,000
Net income		$ 84,000

Additional information

1. In 2005, the company declared and paid a $32,000 cash dividend.
2. Bonds were issued at face value for $130,000 in cash.
3. Equipment costing $180,000 was purchased for cash.
4. Equipment costing $20,000 was sold for $17,000 cash when the book value of the equipment was $18,000.
5. Common stock of $60,000 was issued to acquire land.

To prepare a statement of cash flows under the direct approach, we will apply the three steps outlined in Illustration 18-3 (page 716).

Step 1: Operating Activities

DETERMINE NET CASH PROVIDED/USED BY OPERATING ACTIVITIES BY CONVERTING NET INCOME FROM AN ACCRUAL BASIS TO A CASH BASIS

Under the **direct method**, net cash provided by operating activities is computed by **adjusting each item in the income statement** from the accrual basis to the cash basis. To simplify and condense the operating activities section, **only major classes of operating cash receipts and cash payments are reported**. For these major classes, the difference between cash receipts and cash payments is the net cash provided by operating activities. These relationships are as shown in Illustration 18-15.

Illustration 18-15
Major classes of cash receipts and payments

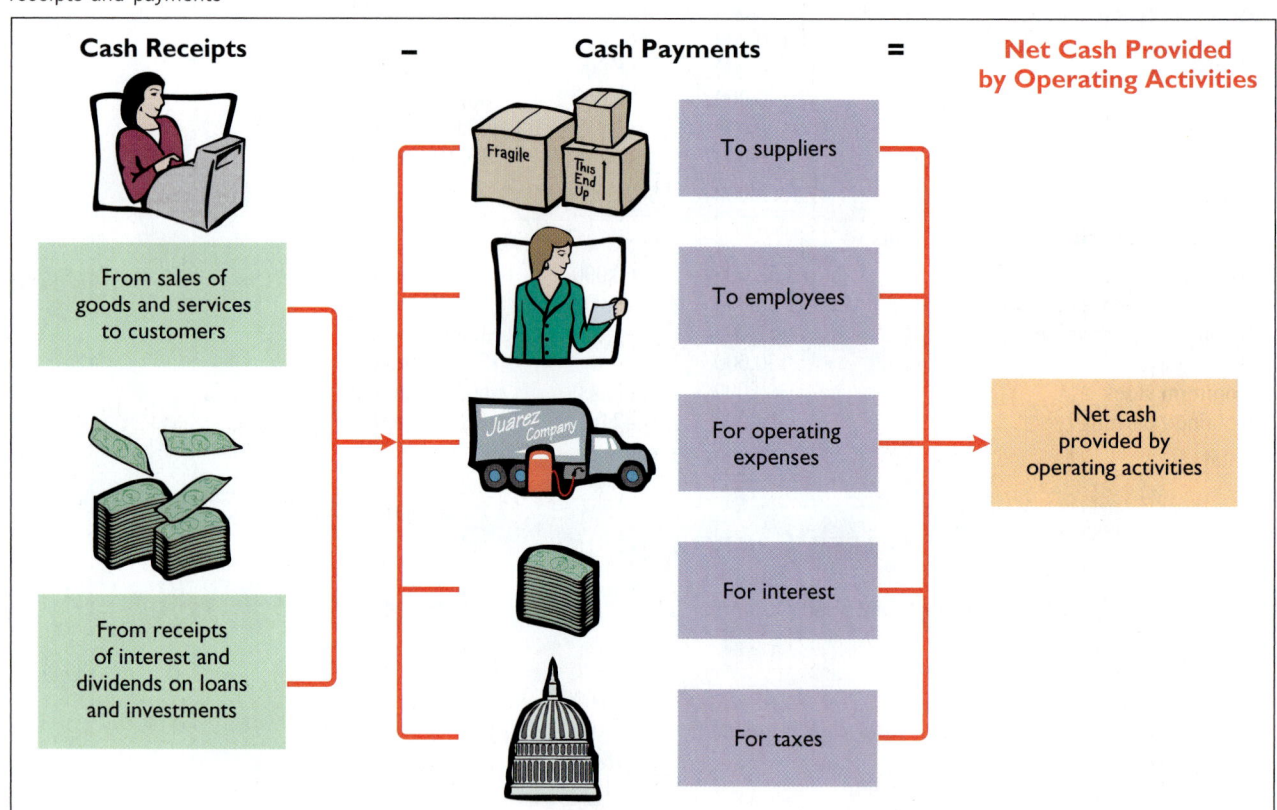

An efficient way to apply the direct method is to analyze the items reported in the income statement in the order in which they are listed. Cash receipts and cash payments related to these revenues and expenses are then determined. The direct method adjustments for Juarez Company in 2005 to determine net cash provided by operating activities are presented on the following pages.

CASH RECEIPTS FROM CUSTOMERS.   The income statement for Juarez Company reported revenues from customers of $975,000. How much of that was cash receipts? To answer that, it is necessary to consider the change in accounts receivable during the year. When accounts receivable increase during the year, revenues on an accrual basis are higher than cash receipts from customers. Operations led to revenues, but not all of these revenues resulted in cash receipts. To determine the amount of cash receipts, the increase in accounts receivable is deducted from sales revenues. On the other hand, there may be a decrease in accounts receivable. That would occur if cash receipts from customers exceeded sales revenues. In that case, the decrease in accounts receivable is added to sales revenues.

For Juarez Company, accounts receivable decreased $3,000. Thus, cash receipts from customers were $978,000, computed as follows.

Revenues from sales	$975,000
Add: Decrease in accounts receivable	3,000
Cash receipts from customers	**$978,000**

Illustration 18-16
Computation of cash receipts from customers

Cash receipts from customers may also be determined from an analysis of the Accounts Receivable account, as shown in Illustration 18-17.

Accounts Receivable			
1/1/05 Balance	15,000	**Receipts from customers**	**978,000**
Revenues from sales	975,000		
12/31/05 Balance	12,000		

Illustration 18-17
Analysis of accounts receivable

> **HELPFUL HINT**
>
> The T account shows that revenue plus decrease in receivables equals cash receipts.

The relationships among cash receipts from customers, revenues from sales, and changes in accounts receivable are shown in Illustration 18-18.

Cash Receipts from Customers	=	Revenues from Sales	+ Decrease in Accounts Receivable or − Increase in Accounts Receivable

Illustration 18-18
Formula to compute cash receipts from customers—direct method

CASH PAYMENTS TO SUPPLIERS. Juarez Company reported cost of goods sold of $660,000 on its income statement. How much of that was cash payments to suppliers? To answer that, it is first necessary to find purchases for the year. To find purchases, cost of goods sold is adjusted for the change in inventory. When inventory increases during the year, purchases for the year have exceeded cost of goods sold. As a result, to determine the amount of purchases, the increase in inventory is added to cost of goods sold.

In 2005, Juarez Company's inventory increased $10,000. Purchases are computed as follows.

Cost of goods sold	$660,000
Add: Increase in inventory	10,000
Purchases	**$670,000**

Illustration 18-19
Computation of purchases

After purchases are computed, cash payments to suppliers can be determined. This is done by adjusting purchases for the change in accounts payable. When accounts payable increase during the year, purchases on an accrual basis are higher than they are on a cash basis. As a result, to determine cash payments to suppliers, an increase in accounts payable is deducted from purchases. On the other hand, there may be a decrease in accounts payable. That would occur if cash payments to suppliers exceed purchases. In that case, the decrease in accounts payable is added to purchases.

For Juarez Company, cash payments to suppliers were $468,000, computed as follows.

Illustration 18-20
Computation of cash payments to suppliers

Purchases	$670,000
Add: Decrease in accounts payable	8,000
Cash payments to suppliers	**$678,000**

Cash payments to suppliers may also be determined from an analysis of the Accounts Payable account as shown in Illustration 18-21.

Illustration 18-21
Analysis of accounts payable

Accounts Payable					
Payments to suppliers	**678,000**	1/1/05	Balance		60,000
			Purchases		670,000
		12/31/05	Balance		52,000

HELPFUL HINT

The T account shows that purchases plus decrease in accounts payable equals payments to suppliers.

The relationships among cash payments to suppliers, cost of goods sold, changes in inventory, and changes in accounts payable are shown in the following formula.

Illustration 18-22
Formula to compute cash payments to suppliers—direct method

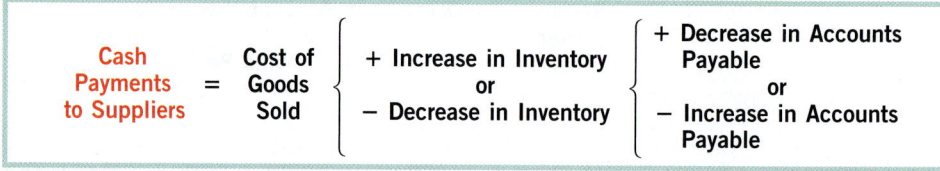

| Cash Payments to Suppliers | = | Cost of Goods Sold | { | + Increase in Inventory or − Decrease in Inventory | { | + Decrease in Accounts Payable or − Increase in Accounts Payable |

CASH PAYMENTS FOR OPERATING EXPENSES.   Operating expenses of $176,000 were reported on Juarez's income statement. How much of that amount was cash paid for operating expenses? To answer that, we need to adjust this amount for any changes in prepaid expenses and accrued expenses payable. For example, if prepaid expenses increased during the year, cash paid for operating expenses is higher than operating expenses reported on the income statement. To convert operating expenses to cash payments for operating expenses, the increase must be added to operating expenses. On the other hand, if prepaid expenses decrease during the year, the decrease must be deducted from operating expenses.

Operating expenses must also be adjusted for changes in accrued expenses payable. When accrued expenses payable increase during the year, operating expenses on an accrual basis are higher than they are on a cash basis. As a result, to determine cash payments for operating expenses, an increase in accrued expenses payable is deducted from operating expenses. On the other hand, a decrease in accrued expenses payable is added to operating expenses because cash payments exceed operating expenses.

Juarez Company's cash payments for operating expenses were $179,000, computed as follows.

Operating expenses	$176,000
Deduct: Decrease in prepaid expenses	(2,000)
Add: Decrease in accrued expenses payable	5,000
Cash payments for operating expenses	**$179,000**

Illustration 18-23
Computation of cash payments for operating expenses

The relationships among cash payments for operating expenses, changes in prepaid expenses, and changes in accrued expenses payable are shown in the following formula.

$$
\begin{array}{c}
\text{Cash} \\
\text{Payments for} \\
\text{Operating} \\
\text{Expenses}
\end{array}
=
\begin{array}{c}
\text{Operating} \\
\text{Expenses}
\end{array}
\left\{
\begin{array}{c}
\text{+ Increase in Prepaid} \\
\text{Expenses} \\
\text{or} \\
\text{- Decrease in Prepaid} \\
\text{Expenses}
\end{array}
\right.
\left\{
\begin{array}{c}
\text{+ Decrease in Accrued} \\
\text{Expenses Payable} \\
\text{or} \\
\text{- Increase in Accrued} \\
\text{Expenses Payable}
\end{array}
\right.
$$

Illustration 18-24
Formula to compute cash payments for operating expenses—direct method

DEPRECIATION EXPENSE AND LOSS ON SALE OF EQUIPMENT.
Operating expenses are shown exclusive of depreciation. Depreciation expense in 2005 was $18,000. Depreciation expense is not shown on a statement of cash flows because it is a noncash charge. If the amount for operating expenses includes depreciation expense, operating expenses must be reduced by the amount of depreciation to determine cash payments for operating expenses.

The loss on sale of equipment of $1,000 is also a noncash charge. The loss on sale of equipment reduces net income, but it does not reduce cash. Thus, the loss on sale of equipment is not reported on a statement of cash flows.

Other charges to expense that do not require the use of cash, such as the amortization of intangible assets, depletion expense, and bad debt expense, are treated in the same manner as depreciation.

CASH PAYMENTS FOR INCOME TAXES.   Income tax expense reported on the income statement was $36,000. Income taxes payable, however, increased $12,000. This increase means that $12,000 of the income taxes have not been paid. As a result, income taxes paid were less than income taxes reported in the income statement. Cash payments for income taxes were, therefore, $24,000 as shown below.

Income tax expense	$36,000
Deduct: Increase in income taxes payable	12,000
Cash payments for income taxes	**$24,000**

Illustration 18-25
Computation of cash payments for income taxes

The relationships among cash payments for income taxes, income tax expense, and changes in income taxes payable are shown in the following formula.

$$
\begin{array}{c}
\text{Cash} \\
\text{Payments for} \\
\text{Income Taxes}
\end{array}
=
\begin{array}{c}
\text{Income Tax} \\
\text{Expense}
\end{array}
\left\{
\begin{array}{c}
\text{+ Decrease in Income Taxes Payable} \\
\text{or} \\
\text{- Increase in Income Taxes Payable}
\end{array}
\right.
$$

Illustration 18-26
Formula to compute cash payments for income taxes—direct method

The results of the previous analysis are presented in the operating activities section of the statement of cash flows of Juarez Company in Illustration 18-27.

Illustration 18-27
Operating activities section of the statement of cash flows

Cash flows from operating activities		
Cash receipts from customers		$978,000
Cash payments:		
To suppliers	$678,000	
For operating expenses	179,000	
For income taxes	24,000	881,000
Net cash provided by operating activities		$ 97,000

When the direct method is used, the net cash flows from operating activities as computed under the indirect method must also be provided in a separate schedule.

Step 2: Investing and Financing Activities

ANALYZE CHANGES IN NONCURRENT ASSET AND LIABILITY ACCOUNTS AND RECORD AS INVESTING AND FINANCING ACTIVITIES, OR AS SIGNIFICANT NONCASH TRANSACTIONS

INCREASE IN LAND. Land increased $60,000. The additional information section indicates that common stock was issued to purchase the land. The issuance of common stock for land has no effect on cash. But it is a **significant noncash investing and financing transaction**. This transaction requires disclosure in a separate schedule at the bottom of the statement of cash flows.

INCREASE IN EQUIPMENT. The comparative balance sheets show that equipment increased $160,000 in 2005. The additional information in Illustration 18-14 (page 727) indicates that the increase resulted from two investing transactions: (1) Equipment costing $180,000 was purchased for cash. And (2) equipment costing $20,000 was sold for $17,000 cash when its book value was $18,000. The relevant data for the statement of cash flows is the cash paid for the purchase and the cash proceeds from the sale. For Juarez Company, the investing activities section will show the following: The $180,000 purchase of equipment as an outflow of cash, and the $17,000 sale of equipment also as an inflow of cash. The two amounts **should not be netted. Both individual outflows and inflows of cash should be shown**.

The analysis of the changes in equipment should include the related Accumulated Depreciation account. These two accounts for Juarez Company are shown in Illustration 18-28.

Illustration 18-28
Analysis of equipment and related accumulated depreciation

Equipment				
1/1/05	Balance	–0–	Cost of equipment sold	20,000
	Cash purchase	**180,000**		
12/31/05	Balance	160,000		

Accumulated Depreciation—Equipment					
Sale of equipment	2,000	1/1/05	Balance		–0–
			Depreciation expense		18,000
		12/31/05	Balance		16,000

INCREASE IN BONDS PAYABLE.   Bonds Payable increased $130,000. The additional information in Illustration 18-14 indicated that bonds with a face value of $130,000 were issued for $130,000 cash. The issuance of bonds is a financing activity. For Juarez Company, there is an inflow of cash of $130,000 from the issuance of bonds.

INCREASE IN COMMON STOCK.   The Common Stock account increased $60,000. The additional information indicated that land was acquired from the issuance of common stock. This transaction is a **significant noncash investing and financing transaction** that should be reported separately at the bottom of the statement.

INCREASE IN RETAINED EARNINGS.   The $52,000 net increase in Retained Earnings resulted from net income of $84,000 and the declaration and payment of a cash dividend of $32,000. **Net income is not reported in the statement of cash flows under the direct method.** Cash dividends paid of $32,000 are reported in the financing activities section as an outflow of cash.

Statement of Cash Flows—2005

The statement of cash flows for Juarez Company is shown in Illustration 18-29.

Illustration 18-29
Statement of cash flows, 2005—direct method

JUAREZ COMPANY Statement of Cash Flows—Direct Method For the Year Ended December 31, 2005		
Cash flows from operating activities		
Cash receipts from customers		$ 978,000
Cash payments:		
To suppliers	$ 678,000	
For operating expenses	179,000	
For income taxes	24,000	881,000
Net cash provided by operating activities		97,000
Cash flows from investing activities		
Purchase of equipment	(180,000)	
Sale of equipment	17,000	
Net cash used by investing activities		(163,000)
Cash flows from financing activities		
Issuance of bonds payable	130,000	
Payment of cash dividends	(32,000)	
Net cash provided by financing activities		98,000
Net increase in cash		32,000
Cash at beginning of period		159,000
Cash at end of period		$ 191,000
Noncash investing and financing activities		
Issuance of common stock to purchase land		$ 60,000

Step 3: Net Change in Cash

COMPARE THE NET CHANGE IN CASH ON THE STATEMENT OF CASH FLOWS WITH THE CHANGE IN THE CASH ACCOUNT REPORTED ON THE BALANCE SHEET TO MAKE SURE THE AMOUNTS AGREE

Illustration 18-29 indicates that the net change in cash during the period was an increase of $32,000. This agrees with the change in balances in the cash account reported on the balance sheets in Illustration 18-14.

BEFORE YOU GO ON...

Review It

1. What is the format of the operating activities section of the statement of cash flows using the direct method?
2. Where is depreciation expense shown on a statement of cash flows using the direct method?
3. Where are significant noncash investing and financing activities shown on a statement of cash flows? Give some examples.

Do It

Presented below is information related to Reynolds Company. Use it to prepare a statement of cash flows using the direct method.

REYNOLDS COMPANY
Comparative Balance Sheets
December 31

Assets	2005	2004	Change Increase/Decrease
Cash	$ 54,000	$ 37,000	$ 17,000 Increase
Accounts receivable	68,000	26,000	42,000 Increase
Inventories	54,000	–0–	54,000 Increase
Prepaid expenses	4,000	6,000	2,000 Decrease
Land	45,000	70,000	25,000 Decrease
Buildings	200,000	200,000	–0–
Accumulated depreciation—buildings	(21,000)	(11,000)	10,000 Increase
Equipment	193,000	68,000	125,000 Increase
Accumulated depreciation—equipment	(28,000)	(10,000)	18,000 Increase
Totals	$569,000	$386,000	
Liabilities and Stockholders' Equity			
Accounts payable	$ 23,000	$ 40,000	$ 17,000 Decrease
Accrued expenses payable	10,000	–0–	10,000 Increase
Bonds payable	110,000	150,000	40,000 Decrease
Common stock ($1 par)	220,000	60,000	160,000 Increase
Retained earnings	206,000	136,000	70,000 Increase
Totals	$569,000	$386,000	

REYNOLDS COMPANY
Income Statement
For the Year Ended December 31, 2005

Revenues		$890,000
Cost of goods sold	$465,000	
Operating expenses	221,000	
Interest expense	12,000	
Loss on sale of equipment	2,000	700,000
Income before income taxes		190,000
Income tax expense		65,000
Net income		$125,000

Additional information:

1. Operating expenses include depreciation expense of $33,000 and charges from prepaid expenses of $2,000.

2. Land was sold at its book value for cash.
3. Cash dividends of $55,000 were declared and paid in 2005.
4. Interest expense of $12,000 was paid in cash.
5. Equipment with a cost of $166,000 was purchased for cash. Equipment with a cost of $41,000 and a book value of $36,000 was sold for $34,000 cash.
6. Bonds of $10,000 were redeemed at their book value for cash. Bonds of $30,000 were converted into common stock.
7. Common stock ($1 par) of $130,000 was issued for cash.
8. Accounts payable pertain to merchandise suppliers.

ACTION PLAN

■ Determine net cash provided/used by operating activities by adjusting each item in the income statement from the accrual basis to the cash basis.
■ Determine net cash provided/used by investing activities.
■ Determine net cash provided/used by financing activities.
■ Determine the net increase/decrease in cash.

SOLUTION

REYNOLDS COMPANY
Statement of Cash Flows—Direct Method
For the Year Ended December 31, 2005

Cash flows from operating activities		
Cash receipts from customers		$848,000[a]
Cash payments:		
To suppliers	$536,000[b]	
For operating expenses	176,000[c]	
For interest expense	12,000	
For income taxes	65,000	789,000
Net cash provided by operating activities		59,000
Cash flows from investing activities		
Sale of land	25,000	
Sale of equipment	34,000	
Purchase of equipment	(166,000)	
Net cash used by investing activities		(107,000)
Cash flows from financing activities		
Redemption of bonds	(10,000)	
Sale of common stock	130,000	
Payment of dividends	(55,000)	
Net cash provided by financing activities		65,000
Net increase in cash		17,000
Cash at beginning of period		37,000
Cash at end of period		$ 54,000
Noncash investing and financing activities		
Conversion of bonds into common stock		$ 30,000

Computations:
[a]$848,000 = $890,000 − $42,000
[b]$536,000 = $465,000 + $54,000 + $17,000
[c]$176,000 = $221,000 − $33,000 − $2,000 − $10,000

Technically, an additional schedule reconciling net income to net cash provided by operating activities should be presented as part of the statement of cash flows when using the direct method.

Related exercise material: BE18-6, BE18-7, BE18-8, E18-7, E18-8, E18-9, and E18-10.

THE NAVIGATOR

HELPFUL HINT

1. Determine net cash provided/used by operating activities, recognizing that each item in the income statement must be adjusted to the cash basis.
2. Determine net cash provided/used by investing activities, recognizing that investing activities generally relate to changes in noncurrent assets.
3. Determine net cash provided/used by financing activities, recognizing that financing activities generally relate to changes in long-term liabilities and stockholders' equity accounts.

Note: This concludes Section 2 on preparation of the statement of cash flows using the direct method. You should now proceed to the concluding section of the chapter, "Using Cash Flows to Evaluate a Company."

Using Cash Flows to Evaluate a Company

STUDY OBJECTIVE 5

Analyze the statement of cash flows.

Traditionally, the ratios most commonly used by investors and creditors have been based on accrual accounting. In this section we introduce a cash-flow measure of analysis—free cash flow.

Free Cash Flow

In the statement of cash flows, cash provided by operating activities is intended to indicate the cash-generating capability of the company. Analysts have noted, however, that **cash provided by operating activities fails to take into account that a company must invest in new fixed assets** just to maintain its current level of operations. Companies also must at least **maintain dividends at current levels** to satisfy investors. A measurement to provide additional insight regarding a company's cash generating ability is free cash flow. **Free cash flow** describes the cash remaining from operations after adjustment for capital expenditures and dividends.

Consider the following example: Suppose that MPC produced and sold 10,000 personal computers this year. It reported $100,000 cash provided by operating activities. In order to maintain production at 10,000 computers, MPC invested $15,000 in equipment. It chose to pay $5,000 in dividends. Its free cash flow was $80,000 ($100,000 − $15,000 − $5,000). The company could use this $80,000 either to purchase new assets to expand the business or to pay an $80,000 dividend and continue to produce 10,000 computers. In practice, free cash flow is often calculated with the formula in Illustration 18-30. Alternative definitions also exist.

Illustration 18-30
Free cash flow

Free Cash Flow	=	Cash Provided by Operations	−	Capital Expenditures	−	Cash Dividends

Illustration 18-31 provides basic information excerpted from the 2002 statement of cash flows of **Microsoft Corporation**.

Illustration 18-31
Microsoft cash flow information ($ in millions)

MICROSOFT CORPORATION
Statement of Cash Flows (partial)
2002 (in millions)

Cash provided by operations		$11,426
Cash flows from investing activities		
Additions to property, plant, and equipment	$ (879)	
Purchases of investments	(42,290)	
Sales of investments	33,777	
Cash used by investing activities		(9,392)
Cash paid for dividends on preferred stock		(13)

Microsoft's free cash flow is calculated as shown in Illustration 18-32.

Illustration 18-32
Calculation of Microsoft's free cash flow ($ in millions)

Cash provided by operating activities	$11,426
Less: Expenditures on property, plant, and equipment	879
Dividends paid	13
Free cash flow	$10,534

This free cash flow of $10.534 billion is a tremendous amount of cash generated in a single year. It is available for the acquisition of new assets, the retirement of stock or debt, or the payment of dividends. It should also be noted that this amount far exceeds Microsoft's 2002 net income of $9,421 million. This lends additional credibility to Microsoft's income number as an indicator of potential future performance. If anything, Microsoft's net income might understate its actual performance.

Oracle Corporation is the world's largest seller of database software and information management services. Like Microsoft, its success depends on continuing to improve its existing products while developing new products to keep pace with rapid changes in technology. Oracle's free cash flow for 2002 was $2.965 billion. This is impressive, but significantly less than Microsoft's amazing ability to generate cash.

BEFORE YOU GO ON...

Review It

1. What is the difference between cash from operations and free cash flow?
2. What does it mean if a company has negative free cash flow?  THE NAVIGATOR

DEMONSTRATION PROBLEM

The income statement for the year ended December 31, 2005, for John Kosinski Manufacturing Company contains the following condensed information.

JOHN KOSINSKI MANUFACTURING COMPANY
Income Statement

Revenues		$6,583,000
Operating expenses (excluding depreciation)	$4,920,000	
Depreciation expense	880,000	5,800,000
Income before income taxes		783,000
Income tax expense		353,000
Net income		$ 430,000

Included in operating expenses is a $24,000 loss resulting from the sale of machinery for $270,000 cash. Machinery was purchased at a cost of $750,000.

The following balances are reported on Kosinski's comparative balance sheets at December 31.

JOHN KOSINSKI MANUFACTURING COMPANY
Comparative, Balance Sheets (partial)

	2005	2004
Cash	$672,000	$130,000
Accounts receivable	775,000	610,000
Inventories	834,000	867,000
Accounts payable	521,000	501,000

Income tax expense of $353,000 represents the amount paid in 2005. Dividends declared and paid in 2005 totaled $200,000.

Instructions

(a) Prepare the statement of cash flows using the indirect method.

OR

(b) Prepare the statement of cash flows using the direct method.

■ Apply the same data to
the preparation of a statement of cash flows under
both the indirect and di-
rect methods.

■ Note the similarities of
the two methods: Both
methods report the same
information in the investing and financing sections.

■ Note the differences between the two methods:
The cash flows from oper-
ating activities sections report different information
(but the amount of net
cash provided by operat-
ing activities is the same
for both methods).

SOLUTION TO DEMONSTRATION PROBLEM

(a)

JOHN KOSINSKI MANUFACTURING COMPANY
Statement of Cash Flows—**Indirect Method**
For the Year Ended December 31, 2005

Cash flows from operating activities		
Net income		$ 430,000
Adjustments to reconcile net income to net cash		
provided by operating activities:		
Depreciation expense	$ 880,000	
Loss on sale of machinery	24,000	
Increase in accounts receivable	(165,000)	
Decrease in inventories	33,000	
Increase in accounts payable	20,000	792,000
Net cash provided by operating activities		1,222,000
Cash flows from investing activities		
Sale of machinery	270,000	
Purchase of machinery	(750,000)	
Net cash used by investing activities		(480,000)
Cash flows from financing activities		
Payment of cash dividends		(200,000)
Net increase in cash		542,000
Cash at beginning of period		130,000
Cash at end of period		$ 672,000

(b)

JOHN KOSINSKI MANUFACTURING COMPANY
Statement of Cash Flows—**Direct Method**
For the Year Ended December 31, 2005

Cash flows from operating activities		
Cash receipts from customers		$6,418,000*
Cash payments:		
For operating expenses	$4,843,000**	
For income taxes	353,000	5,196,000
Net cash provided by operating activities		1,222,000
Cash flows from investing activities		
Sale of machinery	270,000	
Purchase of machinery	(750,000)	
Net cash used by investing activities		(480,000)
Cash flows from financing activities		
Payment of cash dividends		(200,000)
Net increase in cash		542,000
Cash at beginning of period		130,000
Cash at end of period		$ 672,000

Direct Method Computations:

* Computation of cash receipts from customers:	
Revenues per the income statement	$6,583,000
Less increase in accounts receivable	165,000
Cash receipts from customers	$6,418,000
** Computation of cash payments for operating expenses:	
Operating expenses per the income statement	$4,920,000
Deduct loss from sale of machinery	(24,000)
Deduct decrease in inventories	(33,000)
Deduct increase in accounts payable	(20,000)
Cash payments for operating expenses	$4,843,000

SUMMARY OF STUDY OBJECTIVES

1. **Indicate the usefulness of the statement of cash flows.** The statement of cash flows provides information about the cash receipts and cash payments during a period. A secondary objective is to provide information about the operating, investing, and financing activities during the period.

2. **Distinguish among operating, investing, and financing activities.** Operating activities include the cash effects of transactions that enter into the determination of net income. Investing activities involve cash flows resulting from changes in investments and long-term asset items. Financing activities involve cash flows resulting from changes in long-term liability and stockholders' equity items.

3. **Prepare a statement of cash flows using the indirect method.** The preparation of a statement of cash flows involves three major steps: (1) Determine net cash provided/used by operating activities, by converting net income from an accrual basis to a cash basis. (2) Analyze changes in noncurrent asset and liability accounts and record as investing and financing activities or as significant

noncash transactions. (3) Compare the net change in cash on the statement of cash flows with the change in the cash account reported on the balance sheet, to make sure the amounts agree.

4. **Prepare a statement of cash flows using the direct method.** The preparation of the statement of cash flows involves three major steps: (1) Determine net cash provided/used by operating activities, by converting net income from an accrual basis to a cash basis. (2) Analyze changes in noncurrent asset and liability accounts and record as investing and financing activities or as significant noncash transactions. (3) Compare the net change in cash on the statement of cash flows with the change in the cash account reported on the balance sheet, to make sure the amounts agree.

5. **Analyze the statement of cash flows.** The statement of cash flows can be used for cash-based ratio analysis. Free cash flow provides information about a company's cash-generating capabilities. It is calculated as cash from operations less capital expenditures and cash dividends.

GLOSSARY

Direct method A method of determining the net cash provided by operating activities by adjusting each item in the income statement from the accrual basis to the cash basis. (p. 728).

Financing activities Cash flow activities that include (a) obtaining cash from issuing debt and repaying the amounts borrowed and (b) obtaining cash from stockholders and providing them with a return on their investment. (p. 712).

Free cash flow Cash provided by operating activities adjusted for capital expenditures and dividends paid. (p. 736).

Indirect method A method of preparing a statement of cash flows in which net income is adjusted for items that did not affect cash, to determine net cash provided by operating activities. (p. 719).

Investing activities Cash flow activities that include (a) acquiring and disposing of investments and productive long-lived assets and (b) lending money and collecting on those loans. (p. 712).

Operating activities Cash flow activities that include the cash effects of transactions that create revenues and expenses and thus enter into the determination of net income. (p. 712).

Statement of cash flows A financial statement that provides information about the cash receipts and cash payments of an entity during a period, classified as operating, investing, and financing activities, in a format that reconciles the beginning and ending cash balances. (p. 712).

APPENDIX USING A WORK SHEET TO PREPARE THE STATEMENT OF CASH FLOWS—INDIRECT METHOD

When preparing a statement of cash flows, numerous adjustments of net income may be necessary. In such cases, **a work sheet is often used to assemble and classify the data that will appear on the statement**. The work sheet is merely an aid in the preparation of the statement. Its use is optional. The skeleton format of the work sheet for preparation of the statement of cash flows is shown in Illustration 18A-1.

STUDY OBJECTIVE 6

Explain the guidelines and procedural steps in using a work sheet to prepare the statement of cash flows using the indirect method.

Illustration 18A-1
Format of work sheet

	XYZ COMPANY			
	Work Sheet			
	Statement of Cash Flows			
	For the Year Ended . . .			

Balance Sheet Accounts	End of Last Year Balances	Reconciling Items Debits	Reconciling Items Credits	End of Current Year Balances
Debit balance accounts	XX	XX	XX	XX
	XX	XX	XX	XX
Totals	XXX			XXX
Credit balance accounts	XX	XX	XX	XX
	XX	XX	XX	XX
Totals	XXX			XXX
Statement of Cash Flows Effects				
Operating activities				
Net income		XX		
Adjustments to net income		XX	XX	
Investing activities				
Receipts and payments		XX	XX	
Financing activities				
Receipts and payments		XX	XX	
Totals		XXX	XXX	
Increase (decrease) in cash		(XX)	XX	
Totals		XXX	XXX	

The following guidelines are important in using a work sheet.

1. In the balance sheet accounts section, **accounts with debit balances are listed separately from those with credit balances.** This means, for example, that Accumulated Depreciation is listed under credit balances and not as a contra account under debit balances. The beginning and ending balances of each account are entered in the appropriate columns. The transactions that caused the change in the account balance during the year are entered as reconciling items in the two middle columns.

    After all reconciling items have been entered, each line pertaining to a balance sheet account should "foot across." That is, the beginning balance plus or minus the reconciling item(s) must equal the ending balance. When this agreement exists for all balance sheet accounts, all changes in account balances have been reconciled.

2. The bottom portion of the work sheet consists of the operating, investing, and financing activities sections. It provides the information necessary to prepare the formal statement of cash flows. **Inflows of cash are entered as debits in the reconciling columns. Outflows of cash are entered as credits in the reconciling columns.** Thus, in this section, the sale of equipment for cash at book value is entered as a debit under investing activities. Similarly, the purchase of land for cash is entered as a credit under investing activities.

3. **The reconciling items shown in the work sheet are not entered in any journal or posted to any account.** They do not represent either adjustments or corrections of the balance sheet accounts. They are used only to facilitate the preparation of the statement of cash flows.

Preparing the Work Sheet

As in the case of work sheets illustrated in earlier chapters, the preparation of a work sheet involves a series of prescribed steps. The steps in this case are:

1. Enter in the balance sheet accounts section the balance sheet accounts and their beginning and ending balances.

2. Enter in the reconciling columns of the work sheet the data that explain the changes in the balance sheet accounts other than cash and their effects on the statement of cash flows.

3. Enter on the cash line and at the bottom of the work sheet the increase or decrease in cash. This entry should enable the totals of the reconciling columns to be in agreement.

To illustrate the preparation of a work sheet, we will use the 2005 data for Computer Services Company. Your familiarity with these data should help you understand the use of a work sheet. For ease of reference, the comparative balance sheets, income statement, and selected data for 2005 are presented in Illustration 18A-2, below and on the next page.

COMPUTER SERVICES COMPANY
Comparative Balance Sheets
December 31

Assets	2005	2004	Change in Account Balance Increase/Decrease
Current assets			
Cash	$ 55,000	$ 33,000	$ 22,000 Increase
Accounts receivable	20,000	30,000	10,000 Decrease
Merchandise inventory	15,000	10,000	5,000 Increase
Prepaid expenses	5,000	1,000	4,000 Increase
Property, plant, and equipment			
Land	130,000	20,000	110,000 Increase
Building	160,000	40,000	120,000 Increase
Accumulated depreciation—building	(11,000)	(5,000)	6,000 Increase
Equipment	27,000	10,000	17,000 Increase
Accumulated depreciation—equipment	(3,000)	(1,000)	2,000 Increase
Total	$398,000	$138,000	
Liabilities and Stockholders' Equity			
Current liabilities			
Accounts payable	$ 28,000	$ 12,000	$ 16,000 Increase
Income tax payable	6,000	8,000	2,000 Decrease
Long-term liabilities			
Bonds payable	130,000	20,000	110,000 Increase
Stockholders' equity			
Common stock	70,000	50,000	20,000 Increase
Retained earnings	164,000	48,000	116,000 Increase
Total liabilities and stockholders' equity	$398,000	$138,000	

Illustration 18A-2
Comparative balance sheets, income statement, and additional information for Computer Services Company

COMPUTER SERVICES COMPANY
Income Statement
For the Year Ended December 31, 2005

Revenues		$507,000
Cost of goods sold	$150,000	
Operating expenses (excluding depreciation)	111,000	
Depreciation expense	9,000	
Interest expense	42,000	
Loss on sale of equipment	3,000	315,000
Income before income taxes		192,000
Income tax expense		47,000
Net income		$145,000

Additional information for 2005:

1. The company declared and paid a $29,000 cash dividend.
2. The company obtained land through the issuance of $110,000 of long-term bonds to the seller of the land.
3. A building costing $120,000 was purchased for cash. Equipment costing $25,000 was also purchased for cash.
4. The company sold equipment with a book value of $7,000 (cost $8,000, less accumulated depreciation $1,000) for $4,000 cash.
5. Issued common stock for $20,000 cash.
6. Depreciation expense was comprised of $6,000 for building and $3,000 for equipment.

Determining the Reconciling Items

Several approaches may be used to determine the reconciling items. For example, the changes affecting net cash provided by operating activities can be completed first, and then the effects of financing and investing transactions can be determined. Or, the balance sheet accounts can be analyzed in the order in which they are listed on the work sheet. We will follow this latter approach for Computer Services, except for cash. As indicated above, **cash is handled last**.

Accounts Receivable

The decrease of $10,000 in accounts receivable means that cash collections from revenues are higher than the revenues reported in the income statement. To convert net income to net cash provided by operating activities, the decrease of $10,000 is added to net income. The entry in the reconciling columns of the work sheet is:

(a)	Operating—Decrease in Accounts Receivable	10,000	
	Accounts Receivable		10,000

Merchandise Inventory

Computer Services Company's Merchandise Inventory balance increases $5,000 during the period. The Merchandise Inventory account reflects the difference between the amount of inventory that has been purchased and the amount which has been sold. For Computer Services this means that the cost of merchandise purchased exceeds the cost of goods sold by $5,000. As a result, cost of goods sold does not reflect $5,000 of cash payments made for merchandise. This inventory increase of $5,000 during the period is deducted from net income to arrive at net cash provided by operating activities. The work sheet entry is:

(b)	Merchandise Inventory	5,000	
	Operating—Increase in Merchandise Inventory		5,000

Prepaid Expenses

An increase of $4,000 in prepaid expenses means that expenses deducted in determining net income are less than expenses that were paid in cash. The increase of $4,000 must be deducted from net income in determining net cash provided by operating activities. The work sheet entry is:

| (c) | Prepaid Expenses | 4,000 | |
| | Operating—Increase in Prepaid Expenses | | 4,000 |

Land

The increase in land of $110,000 resulted from a purchase through the issuance of long-term bonds. This transaction should be reported as a significant noncash investing and financing activity. The work sheet entry is:

| (d) | Land | 110,000 | |
| | Bonds Payable | | 110,000 |

HELPFUL HINT

These amounts are asterisked in the work sheet to indicate that they result from a significant noncash transaction.

Building

The cash purchase of a building for $120,000 is an investing activity cash outflow. The entry in the reconciling columns of the work sheet is:

| (e) | Building | 120,000 | |
| | Investing—Purchase of Building | | 120,000 |

Equipment

The increase in equipment of $17,000 resulted from a cash purchase of $25,000 and the sale of equipment costing $8,000. The book value of the equipment was $7,000, the cash proceeds were $4,000, and a loss of $3,000 was recorded. The work sheet entries are:

| (f) | Equipment | 25,000 | |
| | Investing—Purchase of Equipment | | 25,000 |

(g)	Investing—Sale of Equipment	4,000	
	Operating—Loss on Sale of Equipment	3,000	
	Accumulated Depreciation—Equipment	1,000	
	Equipment		8,000

Accounts Payable

The increase of $16,000 in accounts payable must be added to net income to determine net cash provided by operating activities. The following work sheet entry is made.

| (h) | Operating—Increase in Accounts Payable | 16,000 | |
| | Accounts Payable | | 16,000 |

Income Taxes Payable

When a company incurs income tax expense but has not yet paid its taxes, it records income tax payable. A change in the Income Tax Payable account reflects the difference between income tax expense incurred and income tax actually paid. Computer Services' Income Tax Payable account decreases by $2,000. That means the $47,000 of income tax expense reported on the income statement was $2,000 less than the amount of taxes paid during the period of $49,000. To adjust net income to a cash basis, net income must be reduced by $2,000. The work sheet entry is:

| (i) | Income Taxes Payable | 2,000 | |
| | Operating—Decrease in Income Taxes Payable | | 2,000 |

Bonds Payable

The increase of $110,000 in this account resulted from the issuance of bonds for land. This is a significant noncash investing and financing activity. Work sheet entry (d) above is the only entry necessary.

Common Stock

The balance sheet reports an increase in Common Stock of $20,000. The additional information section notes that this increase resulted from the issuance of new shares of stock. This is a cash inflow reported in the financing section. The work sheet entry is:

| (j) | Financing—Issuance of Common Stock | 20,000 | |
| | Common Stock | | 20,000 |

Accumulated Depreciation—Building, and Accumulated Depreciation—Equipment

Increases in these accounts of $6,000 and $3,000, respectively, resulted from depreciation expense. Depreciation expense is a **noncash charge that must be added to net income** to determine net cash provided by operating activities. The work sheet entries are:

| (k) | Operating—Depreciation Expense—Building | 6,000 | |
| | Accumulated Depreciation—Building | | 6,000 |

| (l) | Operating—Depreciation Expense—Equipment | 3,000 | |
| | Accumulated Depreciation—Equipment | | 3,000 |

Retained Earnings

The $116,000 increase in retained earnings resulted from net income of $145,000 and the declaration and payment of a $29,000 cash dividend. Net income is included in net cash provided by operating activities, and the dividends are a financing activity cash outflow. The entries in the reconciling columns of the work sheet are:

| (m) | Operating—Net Income | 145,000 | |
| | Retained Earnings | | 145,000 |

| (n) | Retained Earnings | 29,000 | |
| | Financing—Payment of Dividends | | 29,000 |

Disposition of Change in Cash

The firm's cash increased $22,000 in 2005. The final entry on the work sheet, therefore, is:

| (o) | Cash | 22,000 | |
| | Increase in Cash | | 22,000 |

As shown in the work sheet, the increase in cash is entered in the reconciling credit column as a **balancing** amount. This entry should complete the reconciliation of the changes in the balance sheet accounts. Also, it should permit the totals of the reconciling columns to be in agreement. When all changes have been explained and the reconciling columns are in agreement, the reconciling columns are ruled to complete the work sheet. The completed work sheet for Computer Services Company is shown in Illustration 18A-3.

Illustration 18A-3
Completed work sheet—indirect method

COMPUTER SERVICES COMPANY
Work Sheet
Statement of Cash Flows
For the Year Ended December 31, 2006

Balance Sheet Accounts	Balance 12/31/04	Reconciling Items Debit		Reconciling Items Credit		Balance 12/31/05
Debits						
Cash	33,000	(o)	22,000			55,000
Accounts Receivable	30,000			(a)	10,000	20,000
Merchandise Inventory	10,000	(b)	5,000			15,000
Prepaid Expenses	1,000	(c)	4,000			5,000
Land	20,000	(d)	110,000*			130,000
Building	40,000	(e)	120,000			160,000
Equipment	10,000	(f)	25,000	(g)	8,000	27,000
Total	144,000					412,000
Credits						
Accounts Payable	12,000			(h)	16,000	28,000
Income Taxes Payable	8,000	(i)	2,000			6,000
Bonds Payable	20,000			(d)	110,000*	130,000
Accumulated Depreciation— Building	5,000			(k)	6,000	11,000
Accumulated Depreciation— Equipment	1,000	(g)	1,000	(l)	3,000	3,000
Common Stock	50,000			(j)	20,000	70,000
Retained Earnings	48,000	(n)	29,000	(m)	145,000	164,000
Total	144,000					412,000
Statement of Cash Flows Effects						
Operating activities						
Net income		(m)	145,000			
Decrease in accounts receivable		(a)	10,000			
Increase in merchandise inventory				(b)	5,000	
Increase in prepaid expenses				(c)	4,000	
Increase in accounts payable		(h)	16,000			
Decrease in income taxes payable				(i)	2,000	
Depreciation expense—building		(k)	6,000			
Depreciation expense—equipment		(l)	3,000			
Loss on sale of equipment		(g)	3,000			
Investing activities						
Purchase of building				(e)	120,000	
Purchase of equipment				(f)	25,000	
Sale of equipment		(g)	4,000			
Financing activities						
Issuance of common stock		(j)	20,000			
Payment of dividends				(n)	29,000	
Totals			525,000		503,000	
Increase in cash				(o)	22,000	
Totals			525,000		525,000	

*Significant noncash investing and financing activity.

Preparing the Statement

The statement of cash flows is prepared primarily from the data that appear in the work sheet under "Statement of Cash Flows Effects." The reconciling columns should also be scanned for any asterisked items that designate significant noncash activities. The formal statement was shown in Illustration 18-13 (page 724).

SUMMARY OF STUDY OBJECTIVE FOR APPENDIX

6. Explain the guidelines and procedural steps in using a work sheet to prepare the statement of cash flows using the indirect method. When there are numerous adjustments, a work sheet can be a helpful tool in preparing the statement of cash flows. Key guidelines for using a work sheet are: (1) List accounts with debit balances separately from those with credit balances. (2) In the reconciling columns in the bottom portion of the work sheet, show

cash inflows as debits and cash outflows as credits. (3) Do not enter reconciling items in any journal or account, but use them only to help prepare the statement of cash flows.

The steps in preparing the work sheet are: (1) Enter beginning and ending balances of balance sheet accounts. (2) Enter debits and credits in reconciling columns. (3) Enter the increase or decrease in cash in two places as a balancing amount.

*Note: All **asterisked** Questions, Exercises, and Problems relate to material in the appendix to the chapter.

SELF-STUDY QUESTIONS

Self-Study/Self-Test

Answers are at the end of the chapter.

(SO 1) **1.** Which of the following is *incorrect* about the statement of cash flows?
   a. It is a fourth basic financial statement.
   b. It provides information about cash receipts and cash payments of an entity during a period.
   c. It reconciles the ending cash account balance to the balance per the bank statement.
   d. It provides information about the operating, investing, and financing activities of the business.

(SO 2) **2.** The statement of cash flows classifies cash receipts and cash payments by the following activities:
   a. operating and nonoperating.
   b. investing, financing, and operating.
   c. financing, operating, and nonoperating.
   d. investing, financing, and nonoperating.

(SO 2) **3.** An example of a cash flow from an operating activity is:
   a. payment of cash to lenders for interest.
   b. receipt of cash from the sale of capital stock.
   c. payment of cash dividends to the company's stockholders.
   d. None of the above.

(SO 2) **4.** An example of a cash flow from an investing activity is:
   a. receipt of cash from the issuance of bonds payable.
   b. payment of cash to repurchase outstanding capital stock.
   c. receipt of cash from the sale of equipment.
   d. payment of cash to suppliers for inventory.

(SO 2) **5.** Cash dividends paid to stockholders are classified on the statement of cash flows as:
   a. operating activities.
   b. investing activities.

   c. a combination of the above.
   d. financing activities.

(SO **6.** An example of a cash flow from a financing activity is:
   a. receipt of cash from sale of land.
   b. issuance of debt for cash.
   c. purchase of equipment for cash.
   d. None of the above.

(SO **7.** Which of the following about the statement of cash flows is *incorrect?*
   a. The direct method may be used to report cash provided by operations.
   b. The statement shows the cash provided (used) for three categories of activity.
   c. The operating section is the last section of the statement.
   d. The indirect method may be used to report cash provided by operations.

Questions 8 and 9 apply only to the indirect method.

(SO **8.** Net income is $132,000. During the year, accounts payable increased $10,000, inventory decreased $6,000, and accounts receivable increased $12,000. Under the indirect method, net cash provided by operations is:
   a. $102,000.
   b. $112,000.
   c. $124,000.
   d. $136,000.

(SO **9.** Noncash charges that are added back to net income in determining cash provided by operations under the indirect method do *not* include:
   a. depreciation expense.
   b. an increase in inventory.
   c. amortization expense.
   d. loss on sale of equipment.

Questions 10 and 11 apply only to the direct method.

(SO 4) **10.** The beginning balance in accounts receivable is $44,000. The ending balance is $42,000. Sales during the period are $129,000. Cash receipts from customers are:
   a. $127,000.
   b. $129,000.
   c. $131,000.
   d. $141,000.

(SO 4) **11.** Which of the following items is reported on a cash flow statement prepared by the direct method?
   a. Loss on sale of building.
   b. Increase in accounts receivable.
   c. Depreciation expense.
   d. Cash payments to suppliers.

12. The statement of cash flows should *not* be used to eval- (SO 1) uate an entity's ability to:
   a. earn net income.
   b. generate future cash flows.
   c. pay dividends.
   d. meet obligations.

***13.** In a work sheet for the statement of cash flows, a de- (SO 6) crease in accounts receivable is entered in the reconciling columns as a credit to Accounts Receivable and a debit in the:
   a. investing activities section.
   b. operating activities section.
   c. financing activities section.
   d. None of the above.

QUESTIONS

1. What is the statement of cash flows?

2. Omar Morena maintains that the statement of cash flows is an optional financial statement. Do you agree? Explain.

3. Why is the statement of cash flows useful?

4. Distinguish among the three types of activities reported in the statement of cash flows.

5. What are the major sources (inflows) of cash in a statement of cash flows? What are the major uses (outflows) of cash?

6. Why is it important to disclose certain noncash transactions? How should they be disclosed?

7. George Burns and Gracie Allen were discussing the presentation format of the statement of cash flows of Classic Comedy Co. At the bottom of Classic Comedy's statement of cash flows was a separate section entitled "Noncash investing and financing activities." Give three examples of significant noncash transactions that would be reported in this section.

8. Why is it necessary to use comparative balance sheets, a current income statement, and certain transaction data in preparing a statement of cash flows?

9. Contrast the advantages and disadvantages of the direct and indirect methods. Are both methods acceptable? Which method is preferred by the FASB? Which method is more popular?

10. When the total cash inflows exceed the total cash outflows in the statement of cash flows, how and where is this excess identified?

11. Describe the indirect method for determining net cash provided by operating activities.

12. Why is it necessary to convert accrual-based net income to cash-basis income when preparing a statement of cash flows?

13. The president of Argot Company is puzzled. During the year, the company experienced a net loss of $800,000, yet its cash increased $300,000 during the same period. Explain to the president how this situation could occur.

14. Identify five items that are adjustments to reconcile net income to net cash provided by operating activities under the indirect method.

15. Why and how is depreciation expense reported in a statement prepared using the indirect method?

16. Identify two noncash charges other than depreciation expense that are treated like depreciation expense in a statement of cash flows.

17. During 2005, Brett Favre Company converted $1,600,000 of its total $2,000,000 of bonds payable into common stock. Indicate how the transaction would be reported on a statement of cash flows, if at all.

18. Describe the direct method for determining net cash provided by operating activities.

19. Give the formulas under the direct method for computing (a) cash receipts from customers and (b) cash payments to suppliers.

20. George Bell Inc. reported sales of $2 million for 2005. Accounts receivable decreased $400,000 and accounts payable increased $325,000. Compute cash receipts from customers, assuming that the receivable and payable transactions related to operations.

21. Why is depreciation expense not reported in the direct-method cash flow from operating activities section?

22. What does free cash flow indicate, and how is it calculated?

***23.** Why is it advantageous to use a work sheet when preparing a statement of cash flows? Is a work sheet required to prepare a statement of cash flows?

BRIEF EXERCISES

Compute cash provided by operating activities—indirect method.

(SO 3)

BE18-1 Blair Co. reported net income of $2.5 million in 2005. Depreciation for the year was $180,000, accounts receivable decreased $350,000, and accounts payable decreased $310,000. Compute net cash provided by operating activities using the indirect approach.

Compute cash provided by operating activities—indirect method.

(SO 3)

BE18-2 The net income for Karen Sepaniak Co. for 2005 was $280,000. For 2005, depreciation on plant assets was $60,000, and the company incurred a loss on sale of plant assets of $10,000. Compute net cash provided by operating activities under the indirect method.

Indicate statement presentation of selected transactions.

(SO 2)

BE18-3 Each of the following items must be considered in preparing a statement of cash flows for Catherine Janeway Co. for the year ended December 31, 2005. For each item, state how it should be shown in the statement of cash flows for 2005.

(a) Issued bonds for $300,000 cash.
(b) Purchased equipment for $140,000 cash.
(c) Sold land costing $20,000 for $20,000 cash.
(d) Declared and paid a $50,000 cash dividend.

Compute net cash provided by operating activities using indirect method.

(SO 3)

BE18-4 The comparative balance sheets for Mogilny Company show the following changes in noncash current asset accounts: accounts receivable decrease $75,000, prepaid expenses increase $16,000, and inventories increase $30,000. Compute net cash provided by operating activities using the indirect method, assuming that net income is $250,000.

Classify items by activities.

(SO 2)

BE18-5 Classify the following items as an operating, investing, or financing activity. Assume all items involve cash unless there is information to the contrary.

(a) Purchase of equipment.
(b) Sale of building.
(c) Redemption of bonds.
(d) Depreciation.
(e) Payment of dividends.
(f) Issuance of capital stock.

Compute receipts from customers using direct method.

(SO 4)

BE18-6 Beverly Crusher Co. has accounts receivable of $14,000 at January 1, 2005, and $21,000 at December 31, 2005. Sales revenues for 2005 were $470,000. What is the amount of cash receipts from customers in 2005?

Compute cash payments for income taxes using direct method.

(SO 4)

BE18-7 Pelican Company reported income taxes of $87,000 in its 2005 income statement and income taxes payable of $14,000 at December 31, 2004 and $9,000 at December 31, 2005. What amount of cash payments was made for income taxes during 2005?

Compute cash payments for operating expenses using direct method.

(SO 4)

BE18-8 Willis Company reports operating expenses of $100,000 excluding depreciation expense of $15,000 for 2005. During the year prepaid expenses decreased $6,600, and accrued expenses payable increased $2,900. Compute the cash payments for operating expenses in 2005.

Determine cash received in sale of equipment.

(SO 3, 4)

BE18-9 The T accounts for Equipment and the related Accumulated Depreciation for Wanda Landowski Company at the end of 2005 are as follows.

Equipment				Accumulated Depreciation			
Beg. bal.	80,000	Disposals	22,000	Disposals	5,500	Beg. bal.	44,500
Acquisitions	41,600					Depr.	12,000
End. bal.	99,600					End. bal.	51,000

Wanda Landowski Company's income statement reported a loss on the sale of equipment of $4,100. What amount was reported on the statement of cash flows as "Cash flow from sale of equipment"?

BE18-10 The following T account is a summary of the cash account of Martinez Company.

Cash (Summary Form)

Balance, 1/1/05	8,000		
Receipts from customers	364,000	Payments for goods	200,000
Dividends on stock investments	6,000	Payments for operating expenses	140,000
Proceeds from sale of equipment	36,000	Interest paid	10,000
Proceeds from issuance of bonds		Taxes paid	8,000
payable	200,000	Dividends paid	41,000
Balance, 12/31/05	215,000		

For Martinez Company what amount of net cash provided (used) by financing activities should be reported in the statement of cash flows?

BE18-11 Matt Damon Company reported cash from operations of $450,000, cash spent for capital assets of $110,000, and $40,000 of dividends paid. Calculate the free cash flow.

*BE18-12** Using the data in BE18-8, indicate how the changes in prepaid expenses and accrued expenses payable should be entered in the reconciling columns of a work sheet. Assume that beginning balances were: prepaid expenses $18,600 and accrued expenses payable $8,700.

EXERCISES

E18-1 Antoine Walteau Corporation had the following transactions during 2005.

1. Issued $50,000 par value common stock for cash.
2. Collected $11,000 of accounts receivable.
3. Declared and paid a cash dividend of $25,000.
4. Sold a long-term investment with a cost of $15,000 for $15,000 cash.
5. Issued $200,000 par value common stock upon conversion of bonds having a face value of $200,000.
6. Paid $14,000 on accounts payable.
7. Purchased a machine for $30,000, giving a long-term note in exchange.

Instructions

Analyze the transactions above and indicate whether each transaction resulted in a cash flow from **(a)** operating activities, **(b)** investing activities, **(c)** financing activities, or **(d)** noncash investing and financing activities.

E18-2 Duggan Company reported net income of $195,000 for 2005. Duggan also reported depreciation expense of $25,000, and a loss of $5,000 on the sale of equipment. The comparative balance sheets show an increase in accounts receivable of $15,000 for the year, an $8,000 increase in accounts payable, and a decrease in prepaid expenses $7,000.

Instructions

Prepare the operating activities section of the statement of cash flows for 2005 using the indirect method.

Prepare the operating activities section—indirect method.

(SO 3)

E18-3 The current sections of Blues Traveler Co. balance sheets at December 31, 2004 and 2005, are presented below.

BLUES TRAVELER CO.
Comparative Balance Sheets (partial)
December 31

	2005	2004
Current assets		
Cash	$105,000	$ 99,000
Accounts receivable	110,000	85,000
Inventory	171,000	186,000
Prepaid expenses	27,000	32,000
Total current assets	$413,000	$402,000
Current liabilities		
Accrued expenses payable	$ 15,000	$ 5,000
Accounts payable	$ 88,000	$ 92,000
Total current liabilities	$103,000	$ 97,000

Blues Traveler's net income for 2005 was $163,000. Depreciation expense was $30,000.

Instructions

Prepare the net cash provided by operating activities section of Blues Traveler's statement of cash flows for the year ended December 31, 2005, using the indirect method.

Prepare a partial statement of cash flows—indirect method.

(SO 3)

E18-4 Presented below are three accounts that appear in the general ledger of Karen Weller Co. during 2005.

Equipment

Date		Debit	Credit	Balance
Jan. 1	Balance			160,000
July 31	Purchase of equipment	70,000		230,000
Sept. 2	Cost of equipment constructed	53,000		283,000
Nov. 10	Cost of equipment sold		45,000	238,000

Accumulated Depreciation—Equipment

Date		Debit	Credit	Balance
Jan. 1	Balance			71,000
Nov. 10	Accumulated depreciation on equipment sold	35,000		36,000
Dec. 31	Depreciation for year		24,000	60,000

Retained Earnings

Date		Debit	Credit	Balance
Jan. 1	Balance			105,000
Aug. 23	Dividends (cash)	14,000		91,000
Dec. 31	Net income		61,000	152,000

Instructions

From the postings in the accounts above, indicate how the information is reported on a statement of cash flows by preparing a partial statement of cash flows using the indirect method. The loss on sale of equipment was $6,000.

E18-5 Comparative balance sheets for Will Smith Company are presented below.

Prepare a statement of cash flows—indirect method.

(SO 3, 5)

WILL SMITH COMPANY
Comparative Balance Sheets
December 31

Assets	2005	2004
Cash	$ 58,000	$ 22,000
Accounts receivable	85,000	76,000
Inventories	180,000	189,000
Land	80,000	100,000
Equipment	260,000	200,000
Accumulated depreciation	(66,000)	(42,000)
Total	$597,000	$545,000

Liabilities and Stockholders' Equity	2005	2004
Accounts payable	$ 34,000	$ 47,000
Bonds payable	150,000	200,000
Common stock ($1 par)	194,000	164,000
Retained earnings	219,000	134,000
Total	$597,000	$545,000

Additional information:

1. Net income for 2005 was $125,000.
2. Cash dividends of $40,000 were declared and paid.
3. Bonds payable amounting to $50,000 were redeemed for cash $50,000.
4. Common stock was issued for $30,000 cash.
5. Depreciation expense was $24,000.
6. Sales for the year were $978,000.

Instructions
(a) Prepare a statement of cash flows for 2005 using the indirect method.
(b) Compute free cash flow.

E18-6 An analysis of comparative balance sheets, the current year's income statement, and the general ledger accounts of Homer Winslow Corp. uncovered the following items. Assume all items involve cash unless there is information to the contrary.

Classify transactions by type of activity.

(SO 2)

1. Issuance of capital stock.
2. Amortization of patent.
3. Issuance of bonds for land.
4. Payment of interest on notes payable.
5. Conversion of bonds into common stock.
6. Sale of land at a loss.
7. Receipt of dividends on investment in stock.
8. Purchase of land.
9. Payment of dividends.
10. Sale of building at book value.
11. Exchange of land for patent.
12. Depreciation.
13. Redemption of bonds.
14. Receipt of interest on notes receivable.

Instructions
Indicate how the above items should be classified in the statement of cash flows using the following four major classifications: operating activity (indirect method), investing activity, financing activity, and significant noncash investing and financing activity.

E18-7 R. L. Stein Company has just completed its first year of operations on December 31, 2005. Its initial income statement showed that R. L. Stein had revenues of $137,000 and operating expenses of $81,000. Accounts receivable at year-end were $42,000. Accounts payable at year-end were $37,000. Assume that accounts payable related to operating expenses. Ignore income taxes.

Compute cash provided by operating activities—direct method.

(SO 4)

Instructions
Compute net cash provided by operating activities using the direct method.

Compute cash payments—direct method.

(SO 4)

E18-8 The income statement for Alatorre Company shows cost of goods sold $317,000 and operating expenses (exclusive of depreciation) $250,000. The comparative balance sheets for the year show that inventory increased $6,000, prepaid expenses decreased $6,000, accounts payable (merchandise suppliers) decreased $8,000, and accrued expenses payable increased $8,000.

Instructions

Using the direct method, compute (a) cash payments to suppliers and (b) cash payments for operating expenses.

Compute cash flow from operating activities—direct method.

(SO 2, 4)

E18-9 The 2005 accounting records of Eduardo Co. reveal the following transactions and events.

Payment of interest	$ 4,000	Collection of accounts receivable	$170,000
Cash sales	38,000	Payment of salaries and wages	65,000
Receipt of dividend revenue	14,000	Depreciation expense	24,000
Payment of income taxes	15,000	Proceeds from sale of aircraft	812,000
Net income	38,000	Purchase of equipment for cash	22,000
Payment of accounts payable		Loss on sale of aircraft	3,000
for merchandise	90,000	Payment of dividends	14,000
Payment for land	74,000	Payment of operating expenses	20,000

Instructions

Prepare the cash flows from operating activities section using the direct method. (Not all of the above items will be used.)

Calculate cash flows—direct method.

(SO 4)

E18-10 The following information is taken from the 2005 general ledger of Ed Bradley Company.

Rent	Rent expense	$ 33,000
	Prepaid rent, January 1	7,900
	Prepaid rent, December 31	3,000
Salaries	Salaries expense	$ 54,000
	Salaries payable, January 1	3,000
	Salaries payable, December 31	9,000
Sales	Revenue from sales	$180,000
	Accounts receivable, January 1	12,000
	Accounts receivable, December 31	7,000

Instructions

In each of the above cases, compute the amount that should be reported in the operating activities section of the statement of cash flows using the direct method.

Compare two companies by using cash-based ratios.

(SO 5)

E18-11 Presented here is information for two companies in the same industry: Pamela Corporation and Dean Corporation.

	Pamela Corporation	Dean Corporation
Cash provided by operations	$300,000	$300,000
Capital expenditures	50,000	150,000
Cash dividends	80,000	100,000
Net income	200,000	200,000
Sales	400,000	800,000

Instructions

Calculate the free cash flow for each company. Comment on each company's ability to generate cash.

Prepare a work sheet.

(SO 6)

*E18-12** Information for Will Smith Company is presented in E18-5.

Instructions

Use the data in E18-5 to prepare a work sheet for a statement of cash flows for 2005. Enter the reconciling items directly on the work sheet, presenting the entries alphabetically.

PROBLEMS: SET A

P18-1A The income statement of Noah's Ark is shown below.

Prepare the operating activities section—indirect method.

(SO 3)

NOAH'S ARK
Income Statement
For the Year Ended November 30, 2005

Sales		$6,800,000
Cost of goods sold		
Beginning inventory	$2,000,000	
Purchases	4,300,000	
Goods available for sale	6,300,000	
Ending inventory	1,400,000	
Cost of goods sold		4,900,000
Gross profit		1,900,000
Operating expenses		
Selling expenses	450,000	
Administrative expenses	600,000	1,050,000
Net income		$ 850,000

Additional information:

1. Accounts receivable decreased $230,000 during the year.
2. Prepaid expenses increased $150,000 during the year.
3. Accounts payable to suppliers of merchandise decreased $200,000 during the year.
4. Accrued expenses payable decreased $100,000 during the year.
5. Administrative expenses include depreciation expense of $90,000.

Instructions
Prepare the operating activities section of the statement of cash flows for the year ended November 30, 2005, for Noah's Ark using the indirect method.

Net cash provided
$1,320,000

P18-2A Data for Noah's Ark Company are presented in P18-1A.

Prepare the operating activities section—direct method.

(SO 4)

Instructions
Prepare the operating activities section of the statement of cash flows using the direct method.

Net cash provided
$1,320,000

P18-3A Ana Alicia Company's income statement for the year ended December 31, 2005, contained the following condensed information.

Prepare the operating activities section—direct method.

(SO 4)

Revenue from fees		$900,000
Operating expenses (excluding depreciation)	$624,000	
Depreciation expense	56,000	
Loss on sale of equipment	20,000	700,000
Income before income taxes		200,000
Income tax expense		60,000
Net income		$140,000

Alicia's balance sheet contained the following comparative data at December 31.

	2005	2004
Accounts receivable	$47,000	$57,000
Accounts payable	41,000	36,000
Income taxes payable	4,000	7,000

(Accounts payable pertains to operating expenses.)

Net cash provided $228,000

Instructions
Prepare the operating activities section of the statement of cash flows using the direct method.

Prepare the operating activities section—indirect method.
(SO 3)
Net cash provided $228,000

P18-4A Data for Ana Alicia Company are presented in P18-3A.

Instructions
Prepare the operating activities section of the statement of cash flows for Ana Alicia Company using the indirect method.

Prepare a statement of cash flows—indirect method, and perform analysis.
(SO 3, 5)

P18-5A The financial statements of Louis Zimmer Company appear below:

LOUIS ZIMMER COMPANY
Comparative Balance Sheets
December 31

Assets	2005	2004
Cash	$ 31,000	$ 13,000
Accounts receivable	28,000	14,000
Merchandise inventory	25,000	35,000
Property, plant, and equipment	60,000	78,000
Accumulated depreciation	(22,000)	(24,000)
Total	$122,000	$116,000
Liabilities and Stockholders' Equity		
Accounts payable	$ 27,000	$ 23,000
Income taxes payable	5,000	8,000
Bonds payable	27,000	35,000
Common stock	18,000	14,000
Retained earnings	45,000	36,000
Total	$122,000	$116,000

LOUIS ZIMMER COMPANY
Income Statement
For the Year Ended December 31, 2005

Sales		$220,000
Cost of goods sold		180,000
Gross profit		40,000
Selling expenses	$14,000	
Administrative expenses	8,000	22,000
Income from operations		18,000
Interest expense		1,000
Income before income taxes		17,000
Income tax expense		4,000
Net income		$ 13,000

Additional information:
1. Dividends declared and paid were $4,000.
2. During the year equipment was sold for $8,500 cash. This equipment cost $18,000 originally and had a book value of $8,500 at the time of sale.
3. All depreciation expense is in the selling expense category.
4. All sales and purchases are on account.

Instructions

(a) Net cash provided by operating activities $17,500

(a) Prepare a statement of cash flows using the indirect method.
(b) Compute free cash flow.

P18-6A Data for Louis Zimmer Company are presented in P18-5A. Further analysis reveals the following.

1. Accounts payable pertain to merchandise suppliers.
2. All operating expenses except for depreciation were paid in cash.

Instructions
(a) Prepare a statement of cash flows for Louis Zimmer Company using the direct method.
(b) Compute free cash flow.

P18-7A The financial statements of Ernest Banks Company appear below.

Prepare a statement of cash flows—direct method, and perform analysis.

(SO 4, 5)

(a) Cash receipts from customers $206,000

Prepare a statement of cash flows—indirect method.

(SO 3)

ERNEST BANKS COMPANY
Comparative Balance Sheets
December 31

Assets	2005	2004
Cash	$ 23,000	$ 13,000
Accounts receivable	24,000	33,000
Merchandise inventory	20,000	27,000
Prepaid expenses	20,000	13,000
Land	40,000	40,000
Property, plant, and equipment	200,000	225,000
Less: Accumulated depreciation	(50,000)	(67,500)
Total	$277,000	$283,500

Liabilities and Stockholders' Equity		
Accounts payable	$ 9,000	$ 18,500
Accrued expenses payable	9,500	7,500
Interest payable	1,000	1,500
Income taxes payable	3,000	2,000
Bonds payable	50,000	80,000
Common stock	123,000	105,000
Retained earnings	81,500	69,000
Total	$277,000	$283,500

ERNEST BANKS COMPANY
Income Statement
For the Year Ended December 31, 2005

Revenues		
Sales	$600,000	
Gain on sale of plant assets	2,500	$602,500
Less: Expenses		
Cost of goods sold	500,000	
Operating expenses (excluding depreciation)	60,000	
Depreciation expense	7,500	
Interest expense	5,000	
Income tax expense	9,000	581,500
Net income		$ 21,000

Additional information:

1. Plant assets were sold at a sales price of $62,500.
2. Additional equipment was purchased at a cost of $60,000.
3. Dividends of $8,500 were paid.
4. All sales and purchases were on account.
5. Bonds were redeemed at face value.
6. Additional shares of stock were issued for cash.

Instructions

Prepare a statement of cash flows for Ernest Banks Company for the year ended December 31, 2005, using the indirect method.

P18-8A Data for Ernest Banks Company is presented in P18-7A. Further analysis reveals the following.

1. Accounts payable relates to merchandise creditors.
2. All operating expenses, except depreciation expense, were paid in cash.

Instructions

Prepare a statement of cash flows for Ernest Banks Company for the year ended December 31, 2005, using the direct method.

P18-9A Presented below are the comparative balance sheets for Creative Works Company as of December 31.

CREATIVE WORKS COMPANY
Comparative Balance Sheets
December 31

Assets	2005	2004
Cash	$ 38,000	$ 45,000
Accounts receivable	49,500	52,000
Inventory	153,450	142,000
Prepaid expenses	15,780	21,000
Land	100,000	130,000
Equipment	228,000	155,000
Accumulated depreciation—equipment	(45,000)	(35,000)
Building	200,000	200,000
Accumulated depreciation—building	(60,000)	(40,000)
	$679,730	$670,000
Liabilities and Stockholders' Equity		
Accounts payable	$ 35,730	$ 40,000
Bonds payable	250,000	300,000
Common stock, $1 par	200,000	150,000
Retained earnings	194,000	180,000
	$679,730	$670,000

Additional information:

1. Operating expenses include depreciation expense of $42,000.
2. Land was sold for cash at book value.
3. Cash dividends of $24,000 were paid.
4. Net income for 2005 was $38,000.
5. Equipment was purchased for $95,000 cash. In addition, equipment costing $22,000 with a book value of $10,000 was sold for $8,100 cash.
6. Bonds were converted at face value by issuing 50,000 shares of $1 par value common stock.
7. Net sales for 2005 totaled $420,000.

Instructions

(a) Prepare a statement of cash flows for the year ended December 31, 2005, using the indirect method.

(b) Compute free cash flow for 2005.

*P18-10A** Data for Ernest Banks Company are presented in P18-7A.

Instructions

Prepare a work sheet for a statement of cash flows for 2005. Enter the reconciling entries directly on the work sheet, presenting the entries alphabetically.

P18-1B The income statement of Wayne Rogers Company is shown below.

Prepare the operating activities section—indirect method.

(SO 3)

WAYNE ROGERS COMPANY
Income Statement
For the Year Ended December 31, 2005

Sales		$7,200,000
Cost of goods sold		
Beginning inventory	$1,700,000	
Purchases	5,430,000	
Goods available for sale	7,130,000	
Ending inventory	1,920,000	
Cost of goods sold		5,210,000
Gross profit		1,990,000
Operating expenses		
Selling expenses	380,000	
Administrative expense	525,000	
Depreciation expense	95,000	
Amortization expense	30,000	1,030,000
Net income		$ 960,000

Additional information:

1. Accounts receivable increased $690,000 during the year.
2. Prepaid expenses increased $170,000 during the year.
3. Accounts payable to merchandise suppliers increased $35,000 during the year.
4. Accrued expenses payable decreased $190,000 during the year.

Instructions
Prepare the operating activities section of the statement of cash flows for the year ended December 31, 2005, for Wayne Rogers Company using the indirect method.

Net cash used $150,000

P18-2B Data for Wayne Rogers Company are presented in P18-1B.

Prepare the operating activities section—direct method.

(SO 4)

Instructions
Prepare the operating activities section of the statement of cash flows using the direct method.

Net cash used $150,000

P18-3B The income statement of Jurassic Park Co. for the year ended December 31, 2005, reported the following condensed information.

Prepare the operating activities section—direct method.

(SO 4)

Revenue from fees	$510,000
Operating expenses	280,000
Income from operations	230,000
Income tax expense	57,000
Net income	$173,000

Jurassic Park's balance sheet contained the following comparative data at December 31.

	2005	2004
Accounts receivable	$55,000	$60,000
Accounts payable	32,000	41,000
Income taxes payable	2,000	4,000

Jurassic Park has no depreciable assets. (Accounts payable pertains to operating expenses.)

Net cash provided $167,000

Instructions
Prepare the operating activities section of the statement of cash flows using the direct method.

Prepare the operating activities section—indirect method.

(SO 3)

Net cash provided $167,000

P18-4B Data for Jurassic Park Co. are presented in P18-3B.

Instructions
Prepare the operating activities section of the statement of cash flows using the indirect method.

Prepare a statement of cash flows—indirect method, and perform analysis.

(SO 3, 5)

P18-5B The financial statements of James Lyman Company appear below.

JAMES LYMAN COMPANY
Comparative Balance Sheets
December 31

Assets		2005		2004
Cash		$ 24,000		$ 16,000
Accounts receivable		20,000		11,000
Merchandise inventory		38,000		35,000
Property, plant, and equipment	$70,000		$78,000	
Less: Accumulated depreciation	(30,000)	40,000	(24,000)	54,000
Total		$122,000		$116,000

Liabilities and Stockholders' Equity		2005		2004
Accounts payable		$ 23,000		$ 33,000
Income taxes payable		15,000		20,000
Bonds payable		20,000		10,000
Common stock		25,000		25,000
Retained earnings		39,000		28,000
Total		$122,000		$116,000

JAMES LYMAN COMPANY
Income Statement
For the Year Ended December 31, 2005

Sales		$240,000
Cost of goods sold		180,000
Gross profit		60,000
Selling expenses	$23,000	
Administrative expenses	10,000	33,000
Income from operations		27,000
Interest expense		2,000
Income before income taxes		25,000
Income tax expense		7,000
Net income		$ 18,000

Additional information:

1. Dividends of $7,000 were declared and paid.
2. During the year equipment was sold for $11,000 cash. This equipment cost $15,000 originally and had a book value of $11,000 at the time of sale.
3. All depreciation expense, $10,000, is in the selling expense category.
4. All sales and purchases are on account.
5. Additional equipment was purchased for $7,000 cash.

Instructions

(a) Net cash provided by operating activities $1,000

(a) Prepare a statement of cash flows using the indirect method.
(b) Compute free cash flow.

P18-6B Data for James Lyman Company are presented in P18-5B. Further analysis reveals the following.

1. Accounts payable pertains to merchandise creditors.
2. All operating expenses except for depreciation are paid in cash.

Instructions
(a) Prepare a statement of cash flows using the direct method.
(b) Compute free cash flow.

Prepare a statement of cash flows—direct method, and perform analysis.

(SO 4, 5)

(a) Net cash provided by operating activities $1,000

P18-7B Condensed financial data of Daniel Barenboim Company appear below.

Prepare a statement of cash flows—indirect method.

(SO 3)

DANIEL BARENBOIM COMPANY
Comparative Balance Sheets
December 31

Assets	2005	2004
Cash	$ 98,700	$ 47,250
Accounts receivable	87,800	56,000
Inventories	121,900	103,650
Investments	81,500	87,000
Plant assets	250,000	205,000
Accumulated depreciation	(49,500)	(40,000)
	$590,400	$458,900

Liabilities and Stockholders' Equity	2005	2004
Accounts payable	$ 57,700	$ 48,280
Accrued expenses payable	12,100	18,830
Bonds payable	100,000	80,000
Common stock	250,000	200,000
Retained earnings	170,600	111,790
	$590,400	$458,900

DANIEL BARENBOIM COMPANY
Income Statement Data
For the Year Ended December 31, 2005

Sales		$312,500
Gain on sale of plant assets		8,750
		321,250
Less:		
Cost of goods sold	$99,460	
Operating expenses (excluding depreciation expense)	14,670	
Depreciation expense	49,700	
Income taxes	7,270	
Interest expense	2,940	174,040
Net income		$147,210

Additional information:

1. New plant assets costing $92,000 were purchased for cash during the year.
2. Investments were sold at cost.
3. Plant assets costing $47,000 were sold for $15,550, resulting in a gain of $8,750.
4. A cash dividend of $88,400 was declared and paid during the year.

Instructions
Prepare a statement of cash flows using the indirect method.

Net cash provided by operating activities $140,800
Investing activities used $70,950

Prepare a statement of cash flows—direct method.

(SO 4)

Cash receipts from customers $280,700
Investing activities used $70,950

Prepare a statement of cash flows—indirect method, and perform analysis.

(SO 3, 5)

P18-8B Data for Daniel Barenboim Company are presented in P18-7B. Further analysis reveals that accounts payable pertains to merchandise creditors.

Instructions

Prepare a statement of cash flows for Daniel Barenboim Company using the direct method.

P18-9B Presented below are the comparative balance sheets for Isao Aoki Company at December 31.

ISAO AOKI COMPANY
Comparative Balance Sheets
December 31

Assets	2005	2004
Cash	$ 45,000	$ 57,000
Accounts receivable	72,000	64,000
Inventory	132,000	147,000
Prepaid expenses	12,140	16,540
Land	125,000	150,000
Equipment	200,000	175,000
Accumulated depreciation—equipment	(60,000)	(49,000)
Building	250,000	250,000
Accumulated depreciation—building	(75,000)	(50,000)
	$701,140	$760,540

Liabilities and Stockholders' Equity		
Accounts payable	$ 44,000	$ 45,000
Bonds payable	235,000	265,000
Common stock, $1 par	280,000	250,000
Retained earnings	142,140	200,540
	$701,140	$760,540

Additional information:

1. Operating expenses include depreciation expense of $60,000 and charges from prepaid expenses of $4,400.
2. Land was sold for cash at cost.
3. Cash dividends of $105,290 were paid.
4. Net income for 2005 was $46,890.
5. Equipment was purchased for $65,000 cash. In addition, equipment costing $40,000 with a book value of $16,000 was sold for $14,000 cash.
6. Bonds were converted at face value by issuing 30,000 shares of $1 par value common stock.
7. Net sales in 2005 were $367,000.

Instructions

(a) Net cash provided by operating activities $119,290

(a) Prepare a statement of cash flows for 2005 using the indirect method.
(b) Compute free cash flow for 2005.

Prepare a work sheet

(SO 6)

Total reconciling columns $626,210

*P18-10B Data for Daniel Barenboim Company are presented in P18-7B.

Instructions

Prepare a work sheet for a statement of cash flows. Enter the reconciling items directly in the work sheet columns, identifying the debit and credit amounts alphabetically.

BROADENING YOUR PERSPECTIVE

Financial Reporting and Analysis

■ **FINANCIAL REPORTING PROBLEM: PepsiCo**

BYP18-1 Refer to the financial statements of **PepsiCo Inc.** presented in Appendix A, and answer the following questions.

(a) What was the amount of net cash provided by operating activities for the year ended December 28, 2002? For the year ended December 29, 2001?

(b) What was the amount of increase or decrease in cash and cash equivalents for the year ended December 28, 2002? For the year ended December 29, 2001?

(c) Which method of computing net cash provided by operating activities does PepsiCo use?

(d) From your analysis of the 2002 statement of cash flows, did the change in accounts and notes receivable require or provide cash? Did the change in inventories require or provide cash? Did the change in accounts payable and other current liabilities require or provide cash?

(e) What was the net outflow or inflow of cash from investing activities for the year ended December 28, 2002?

(f) What was the amount of interest paid in the year ended December 28, 2002? What was the amount of income taxes paid in the year ended December 28, 2002? (See Note 14.)

■ **COMPARATIVE ANALYSIS PROBLEM: PepsiCo vs. Coca-Cola**

BYP18-2 **PepsiCo**'s financial statements are presented in Appendix A. **Coca-Cola**'s financial statements are presented in Appendix B.

Instructions

(a) Based on the information contained in these financial statements, compute free cash flow for each company.

(b) What conclusions concerning the management of cash can be drawn from these data?

■ **INTERPRETING FINANCIAL STATEMENTS: A Global Focus**

BYP18-3 The statement of cash flows has become a commonly provided financial statement by companies throughout the world. It is interesting to note, however, that its format does vary across countries. The statement of cash flows on page 762 is from the 2001 financial statements of Irish pharmaceutical company **Elan Corporation**.

Instructions

(a) What similarities to U.S. cash flow statements do you notice in terms of general format, as well as terminology?

(b) What differences do you notice in terms of general format, as well as terminology?

ELAN CORPORATION
Consolidated Statement of Cash Flows

	Notes	Year Ended 31 December 2001 $m	2000 $m
Cash Flow from Operating Activities	28(a)	524.6	272.2
Returns on Investments and Servicing of Finance			
Interest received		80.3	111.8
Interest paid		(124.1)	(76.4)
Cash (outflow)/inflow from returns on investments and servicing of finance		(43.8)	35.4
Taxation		(6.5)	(3.6)
Capital Expenditure and Financial Investment			
Additions to property, plant and equipment		(120.8)	(64.4)
Receipts from disposal of property, plant and equipment		2.0	9.8
Payments to acquire intangible assets		(286.7)	(79.5)
Receipts from disposal of intangible assets		11.2	—
Payments to acquire financial current assets		(148.2)	(54.6)
Sale and maturity of financial current assets		143.3	100.1
Payments to acquire financial fixed assets		(624.3)	(411.9)
Receipts from disposal of financial fixed assets		76.2	6.7
Cash outflow from capital expenditure and financial investment		(947.3)	(493.8)
Acquisitions and Disposals			
Cash paid on acquisitions	28(d)	(9.5)	(8.0)
Receipts from part disposal of subsidiary		41.9	—
Cash inflow/(outflow) from acquisitions and disposals		32.4	(8.0)
Cash outflow before use of liquid resources and financing		(440.6)	(197.8)
Management of Liquid Resources	28(b)	106.8	399.1
Financing			
Proceeds from issue of share capital		304.8	76.9
Purchase of treasury shares		—	—
Issue of loan notes		1,185.7	444.1
Repayment of loans		(555.7)	(496.0)
Bank borrowing		342.8	200.0
Cash inflow from financing		1,277.6	225.0
Net increase in cash		943.8	426.3
Reconciliation of Net Cash Flow to Movement in Net Debt			
Increase in cash for the period		943.8	426.3
Cash inflow from movement in liquid resources		(106.8)	(399.1)
		837.0	27.2
Other borrowing		(347.4)	(200.0)
Repayment of loans		557.6	512.4
Issue of loan notes		(1,185.7)	(444.1)
Change in net debt resulting from cash flows		(138.5)	(104.5)
Liquid resources acquired with subsidiary undertaking		—	214.2
Loans acquired with subsidiary undertaking		(0.3)	(363.7)
Non-cash movement—translation differences		(1.4)	(1.1)
Non-cash movement—notes		255.3	(54.4)
Non-cash movement—other		1.1	(1.3)
Decrease/(increase) in net debt	28(c)	116.2	(310.8)

■ EXPLORING THE WEB

BYP18-4 Purpose: Learn about the SEC.

Address: www.sec.gov/index.html, or go to www.wiley.com/college/weygandt

From the SEC homepage, choose **About the SEC**.

Instructions
Answer the following questions.

(a) How many enforcement actions does the SEC take each year against securities law violators? What are typical infractions?

(b) After the Depression, Congress passed the Securities Acts of 1933 and 1934 to improve investor confidence in the markets. What two "common sense" notions are these laws based on?

(c) Who was the President of the United States at the time of the creation of the SEC? Who was the first SEC Chairperson?

BYP18-5 Purpose: Use the Internet to view SEC filings.

Address: biz.yahoo.com/i, or go to www.wiley.com/college/weygandt

Steps

1. Type in a company name.
2. Choose **Profile.**
3. Choose **SEC.** (This will take you to Yahoo-Edgar Online.)

Instructions
Answer the following questions.

(a) What company did you select?
(b) Which filing is the most recent? What is the date?
(c) What other recent SEC filings are available for your viewing?

Critical Thinking

■ GROUP DECISION CASE

BYP18-6 Kirby Garok and Jana Kingston are examining the following statement of cash flows for Poquito Trading Company for the year ended January 31, 2004.

POQUITO TRADING COMPANY
Statement of Cash Flows
For the Year Ended January 31, 2004

Sources of cash	
From sales of merchandise	$390,000
From sale of capital stock	420,000
From sale of investment (purchased below)	80,000
From depreciation	55,000
From issuance of note for truck	25,000
From interest on investments	6,000
Total sources of cash	976,000
Uses of cash	
For purchase of fixtures and equipment	320,000
For merchandise purchased for resale (all sold)	258,000
For operating expenses (including depreciation)	160,000
For purchase of investment	75,000
For purchase of truck by issuance of note	25,000
For purchase of treasury stock	10,000
For interest on note payable	3,000
Total uses of cash	851,000
Net increase in cash	$125,000

Kirby claims that Poquito's statement of cash flows is an excellent example of a superb first year, with cash increasing $125,000. Jana replies that it was not a superb first year—but rather, that the year was an operating failure. She says that the statement was incorrectly presented and that $125,000 is not the actual increase in cash. The cash balance at the beginning of the year was $140,000.

Instructions

With the class divided into groups, answer the following.

(a) With whom do you agree, Kirby or Jana? Explain your position.
(b) Using the data provided, prepare a statement of cash flows in proper form using the indirect method. The only noncash items in the income statement are depreciation and the gain from the sale of the investment.

■ COMMUNICATION ACTIVITY

BYP18-7 Gary Geek, the owner of Pocket Protector Company, is unfamiliar with the statement of cash flows which you, as his accountant, prepared. He asks for further explanation.

Instructions

Write him a brief memo explaining the form and content of the statement of cash flows as shown in Illustration 18-13 on page 724.

■ ETHICS CASE

BYP18-8 Tappit Corporation is a medium-sized wholesaler of automotive parts. It has ten stockholders, who have been paid a total of $1 million in cash dividends for eight consecutive years. The policy of the Board of Directors requires that in order for this dividend to be declared, net cash provided by operating activities as reported in Tappit's current year's statement of cash flows must be in excess of $1 million. President and CEO Ray Thomas's job is secure so long as he produces annual operating cash flows to support the usual dividend.

At the end of the current year, controller Jon Lawler presents president Thomas with some disappointing news: The net cash provided by operating activities is calculated, by the indirect method, to be only $970,000. The president says to Jon, "We must get that amount above $1 million. Isn't there some way to increase operating cash flow by another $30,000?" Jon answers, "These figures were prepared by my assistant. I'll go back to my office and see what I can do." The president replies, "I know you won't let me down, Jon."

Upon close scrutiny of the statement of cash flows, Jon concludes that he can get the operating cash flows above $1 million by reclassifying a $60,000, 2-year note payable listed in the financing activities section as "Proceeds from bank loan—$60,000." He will report the note instead as "Increase in payables—$60,000" and treat it as an adjustment of net income in the operating activities section. He returns to the president saying, "You can tell the Board to declare their usual dividend. Our net cash flow provided by operating activities is $1,030,000." "Good man, Jon! I knew I could count on you," exults the president.

Instructions

(a) Who are the stakeholders in this situation?
(b) Was there anything unethical about the president's actions? Was there anything unethical about the controller's actions?
(c) Are the Board members or anyone else likely to discover the misclassification?

Answers to Self-Study Questions
1. c   **2.** b   **3.** a   **4.** c   **5.** d   **6.** b   **7.** c   **8.** d   **9.** b   **10.** c
11. d   **12.** a   **13.** b

Answer to PepsiCo Review It Question 4, p. 715
In its 2002 statement of cash flows, **PepsiCo** reported:
(1) net cash provided by operating activities of $4.627 billion;
(2) net cash used for investing activities of $527 million; and
(3) net cash used for financing activities of $3.179 billion.

 ☑ **REMEMBER** to go back to the Navigator box on the chapter-opening page and check off your completed work.

Financial Statement Analysis

THE NAVIGATOR ✓

Understand **Concepts for Review**	❏
Read **Feature Story**	❏
Scan **Study Objectives**	❏
Read **Preview**	❏
Read text and answer **Before You Go On**	
p. 774 ❏ p. 785 ❏ p. 790 ❏ p. 792 ❏	
Work **Demonstration Problems**	❏
Review **Summary of Study Objectives**	❏
Answer **Self-Study Questions**	❏
Complete **Assignments**	❏

CONCEPTS FOR REVIEW

Before studying this chapter, you should know or, if necessary, review:

- The contents and classification of a balance sheet.
  (Ch. 4, pp. 152–157)

- The contents and classification of an income statement.
  (Ch. 5, pp. 195–199)

- Who are the various users of financial statement information.
  (Ch. 1, pp. 5–6)

- How to compute earnings per share (EPS).
  (Ch. 15, p. 611)

- How the liquidity of a company is determined.
  (Ch. 4, p. 155)

"Follow That Stock!"
If you thought cab drivers with cell phones were scary, how about a cab driver with a trading desk in the front seat?

When a stoplight turns red or traffic backs up, New York City cabby Carlos Rubino morphs into a day trader, scanning real-time quotes of his favorite stocks as they spew across a PalmPilot mounted next to the steering wheel. "It's kind of stressful," he says. "But I like it."

Itching to know how a particular stock is doing? Mr. Rubino is happy to look up quotes for passengers. Yahoo!, Amazon.com, and America Online are the most requested ones. He even lets customers use his Hitachi Traveler laptop to send urgent e-mails from the back seat. Aware of a new local law prohibiting cabbies from using cell phones while they're driving, Mr.

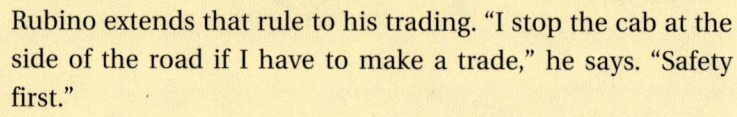

Rubino extends that rule to his trading. "I stop the cab at the side of the road if I have to make a trade," he says. "Safety first."

Originally from São Paulo, Brazil, Mr. Rubino has been driving his cab since 1987, and started trading stocks a few years ago. His curiosity grew as he began to educate himself by reading business publications. The Wall Street brokers he picks up are usually impressed with his knowledge, he says. But the feeling generally isn't mutual. Some of them "don't know much," he says. "They buy what people tell them to buy—they're like a toll collector."

Mr. Rubino is an enigma to his fellow cab drivers. A lot of his colleagues say they want to trade too. "But cab drivers are a little cheap," he says. "The [real-time] quotes cost $100 a month. The wireless Internet access is $54 a month."

Will he give up his brokerage firm on wheels for a stationary job? Not likely. Though he claims a 70 percent return on his investments in some months, he says he makes $1,300 and up a week driving his cab—more than he does trading. Besides, he adds, "Why go somewhere and have a boss?"

Source: Excerpted from Barbara Boydston, "With this Cab, People Jump in and Shout, 'Follow that Stock!'," *Wall Street Journal*, August 18, 1999, p. C1. Reprinted by permission of the Wall Street Journal © 1999 Dow Jones & Company, Inc. All Rights Reserved Worldwide.

After studying this chapter, you should be able to:

1. Discuss the need for comparative analysis.
2. Identify the tools of financial statement analysis.
3. Explain and apply horizontal analysis.
4. Describe and apply vertical analysis.
5. Identify and compute ratios, and describe their purpose and use in analyzing a firm's liquidity, profitability, and solvency.
6. Understand the concept of earning power, and indicate how material items not typical of regular operations are presented.
7. Recognize the limitations of financial statement analysis.

An important lesson can be learned from the Feature Story: Experience is the best teacher. By now you have learned a significant amount about financial reporting by U.S. corporations. Using some of the basic decision tools presented in this book, you can perform a rudimentary analysis on any U.S. company and draw basic conclusions about its financial health. Although it would not be wise for you to bet your life savings on a company's stock relying solely on your current level of knowledge, we strongly encourage you to practice your new skills wherever possible. Only with practice will you improve your ability to interpret financial numbers.

Before unleashing you on the world of high finance, we will present a few more important concepts and techniques, as well as provide you with one more comprehensive review of corporate financial statements. We use all of the decision tools presented in this text to analyze a single company—**Sears, Roebuck and Co.**, one of the country's oldest and largest retail store chains.

The content and organization of Chapter 19 are as follows.

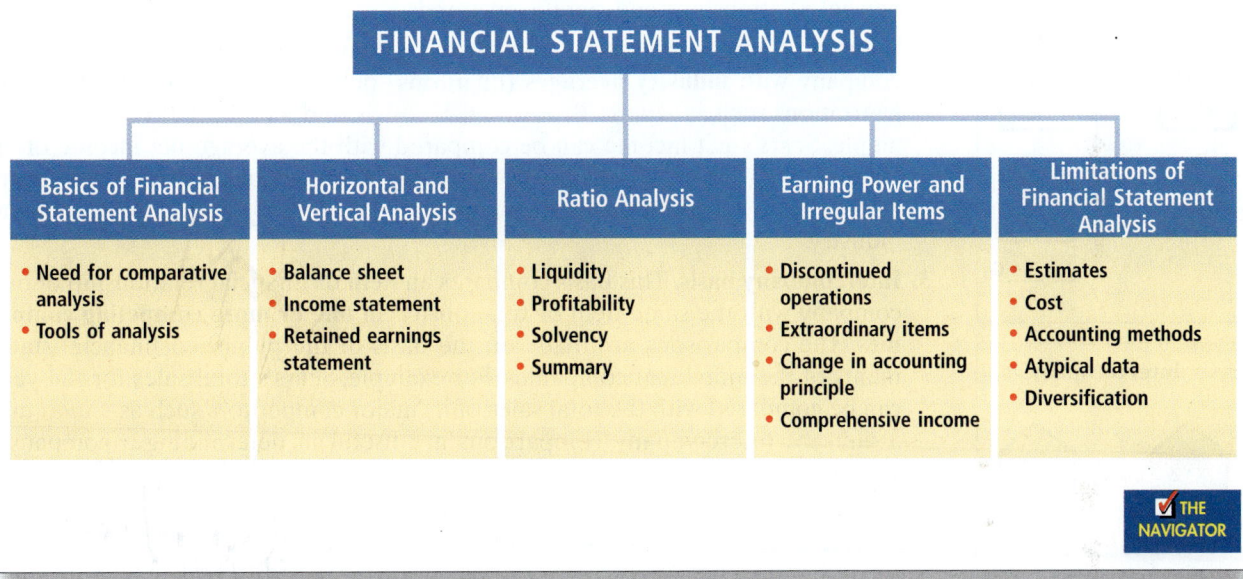

FINANCIAL STATEMENT ANALYSIS				
Basics of Financial Statement Analysis	**Horizontal and Vertical Analysis**	**Ratio Analysis**	**Earning Power and Irregular Items**	**Limitations of Financial Statement Analysis**
• Need for comparative analysis • Tools of analysis	• Balance sheet • Income statement • Retained earnings statement	• Liquidity • Profitability • Solvency • Summary	• Discontinued operations • Extraordinary items • Change in accounting principle • Comprehensive income	• Estimates • Cost • Accounting methods • Atypical data • Diversification

THE NAVIGATOR

Basics of Financial Statement Analysis

Analyzing financial statements involves evaluating three characteristics of a company: its liquidity, its profitability, and its solvency. A **short-term creditor**, such as a bank, is primarily interested in the ability of the borrower to pay obligations when they come due. The liquidity of the borrower is extremely important in evaluating the safety of a loan. A **long-term creditor**, such as a bondholder, however, looks to profitability and solvency measures that indicate the company's ability to survive over a long period of time. Long-term creditors consider such measures as the amount of debt in the company's capital structure and its ability to meet interest payments. Similarly, **stockholders** are interested in the profitability and solvency of the company. They want to assess the likelihood of dividends and the growth potential of the stock.

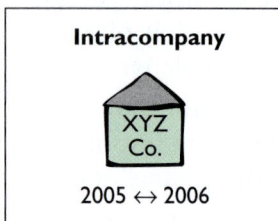

Intracompany

XYZ Co.

2005 ↔ 2006

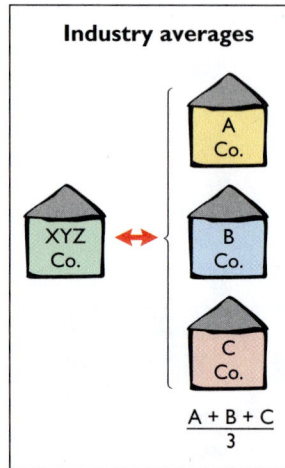

Industry averages

XYZ Co. ↔ A Co. / B Co. / C Co.

$$\frac{A + B + C}{3}$$

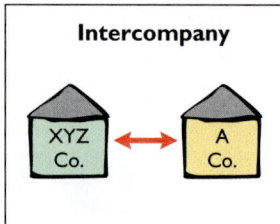

Intercompany

XYZ Co. ↔ A Co.

Need for Comparative Analysis

Every item reported in a financial statement has significance. When **Sears, Roebuck and Co.** reports cash of $729 million on its balance sheet, we know the company had that amount of cash on the balance sheet date. But, we do not know whether the amount represents an increase over prior years, or whether it is adequate in relation to the company's need for cash. To obtain such information, it is necessary to compare the amount of cash with other financial statement data.

Comparisons can be made on a number of different bases. Three are illustrated in this chapter.

1. **Intracompany basis.** This basis compares an item or financial relationship **within a company** in the current year with the same item or relationship in one or more prior years. For example, Sears, Roebuck and Co. can compare its cash balance at the end of the current year with last year's balance to find the amount of the increase or decrease. Likewise, Sears can compare the percentage of cash to current assets at the end of the current year with the percentage in one or more prior years. Intracompany comparisons are useful in detecting changes in financial relationships and significant trends.

2. **Industry averages.** This basis compares an item or financial relationship of a company with **industry averages** (or **norms**) published by financial ratings organizations such as **Dun & Bradstreet**, **Moody's**, and **Standard & Poor's**. For example, Sears's net income can be compared with the average net income of all companies in the retail chain-store industry. Comparisons with industry averages provide information as to a company's relative performance within the industry.

3. **Intercompany basis.** This basis compares an item or financial relationship of one company with the same item or relationship in **one or more competing companies.** The comparisons are made on the basis of the published financial statements of the individual companies. For example, Sears's total sales for the year can be compared with the total sales of its major competitors such as **Kmart** and **Wal-Mart**. Intercompany comparisons are useful in determining a company's competitive position.

Tools of Financial Statement Analysis

Various tools are used to evaluate the significance of financial statement data. Three commonly used tools are these:

- **Horizontal analysis** evaluates a series of financial statement data over a period of time.

- **Vertical analysis** evaluates financial statement data by expressing each item in a financial statement as a percent of a base amount.

- **Ratio analysis** expresses the relationship among selected items of financial statement data.

Horizontal analysis is used primarily in intracompany comparisons. Two features in published financial statements facilitate this type of comparison: First, each of the basic financial statements is presented on a comparative basis for a minimum of two years. Second, a summary of selected financial data is presented for a series of five to ten years or more. Vertical analysis is used in both intra- and intercompany comparisons. Ratio analysis is used in all three types of comparisons. In the following sections, we will explain and illustrate each of the three types of analysis.

Horizontal Analysis

Horizontal analysis, also called **trend analysis**, is a technique for evaluating a series of financial statement data over a period of time. Its purpose is to determine the increase or decrease that has taken place. This change may be expressed as either an amount or a percentage. For example, the recent net sales figures of **Sears, Roebuck and Co.** are as follows.

STUDY OBJECTIVE 3

Explain and apply horizontal analysis.

SEARS

SEARS, ROEBUCK AND CO.		
Net Sales (in millions)		
2002	**2001**	**2000**
$41,366	$40,990	$40,848

Illustration 19-1
Sears, Roebuck and Co.'s
net sales

If we assume that 2000 is the base year, we can measure all percentage increases or decreases from this base period amount as follows.

$$\text{Change Since Base Period} = \frac{\text{Current Year Amount} - \text{Base Year Amount}}{\text{Base Year Amount}}$$

Illustration 19-2
Formula for horizontal analysis of changes since base period

For example, we can determine that net sales for Sears increased from 2000 to 2001 approximately 0.3% [($40,990 − $40,848) ÷ $40,848]. Similarly, we can determine that net sales increased from 2000 to 2002 approximately 1.3% [($41,366 − $40,848) ÷ $40,848].

Alternatively, we can express current year sales as a percentage of the base period. This is done by dividing the current year amount by the base year amount, as shown below.

$$\text{Current Results in Relation to Base Period} = \frac{\text{Current Year Amount}}{\text{Base Year Amount}}$$

Illustration 19-3
Formula for horizontal analysis of current year in relation to base year

Illustration 19-4 presents this analysis for Sears for a three-year period using 2000 as the base period.

SEARS

SEARS, ROEBUCK AND CO.		
Net Sales (in millions)		
in relation to base period 2000		
2002	**2001**	**2000**
$41,366	$40,990	$40,848
101.3%	100.3%	100.0%

Illustration 19-4
Horizontal analysis of Sears, Roebuck and Co.'s net sales in relation to base period

Balance Sheet

To further illustrate horizontal analysis, we will use the financial statements of Quality Department Store Inc. It is a downtown, full-line department store in a southeastern city of 55,000 people. A horizontal analysis of its two-year condensed balance sheets, showing dollar and percentage changes, is presented in Illustration 19-5.

Illustration 19-5
Horizontal analysis of balance sheets

QUALITY DEPARTMENT STORE INC.
Condensed Balance Sheets
December 31

	2002	2001	Increase or (Decrease) during 2002 Amount	Percent
Assets				
Current assets	$1,020,000	$ 945,000	$ 75,000	7.9%
Plant assets (net)	800,000	632,500	167,500	26.5%
Intangible assets	15,000	17,500	(2,500)	(14.3%)
Total assets	$1,835,000	$1,595,000	$240,000	15.0%
Liabilities				
Current liabilities	$ 344,500	$ 303,000	$ 41,500	13.7%
Long-term liabilities	487,500	497,000	(9,500)	(1.9%)
Total liabilities	832,000	800,000	32,000	4.0%
Stockholders' Equity				
Common stock, $1 par	275,400	270,000	5,400	2.0%
Retained earnings	727,600	525,000	202,600	38.6%
Total stockholders' equity	1,003,000	795,000	208,000	26.2%
Total liabilities and stockholders' equity	$1,835,000	$1,595,000	$240,000	15.0%

The comparative balance sheets in Illustration 19-5 show that a number of significant changes have occurred in Quality Department Store's financial structure from 2001 to 2002. In the assets section, plant assets (net) increased $167,500, or 26.5%. In the liabilities section, current liabilities increased $41,500, or 13.7%. In the stockholders' equity section, retained earnings increased $202,600, or 38.6%. This suggests that the company expanded its asset base during 2002 and **financed this expansion primarily by retaining income** rather than assuming additional long-term debt.

Income Statement

Presented in Illustration 19-6 is a horizontal analysis of the two-year condensed income statements of Quality Department Store Inc. for the years 2002 and 2001.

Horizontal analysis of the income statements shows the following changes:

1. Net sales increased $260,000, or 14.2% ($260,000 ÷ $1,837,000).
2. Cost of goods sold increased $141,000, or 12.4% ($141,000 ÷ $1,140,000).
3. Total operating expenses increased $37,000, or 11.6% ($37,000 ÷ $320,000).

Overall, gross profit and net income were up substantially. Gross profit increased 17.1%, and net income, 26.5%. Quality's profit trend appears favorable.

Illustration 19-6
Horizontal analysis of income statements

QUALITY DEPARTMENT STORE INC.
Condensed Income Statements
For the Years Ended December 31

	2002	2001	Increase or (Decrease) during 2002 Amount	Percent
Sales	$2,195,000	$1,960,000	$235,000	12.0%
Sales returns and allowances	98,000	123,000	(25,000)	(20.3%)
Net sales	2,097,000	1,837,000	260,000	14.2%
Cost of goods sold	1,281,000	1,140,000	141,000	12.4%
Gross profit	816,000	697,000	119,000	17.1%
Selling expenses	253,000	211,500	41,500	19.6%
Administrative expenses	104,000	108,500	(4,500)	(4.1%)
Total operating expenses	357,000	320,000	37,000	11.6%
Income from operations	459,000	377,000	82,000	21.8%
Other revenues and gains				
Interest and dividends	9,000	11,000	(2,000)	(18.2%)
Other expenses and losses				
Interest expense	36,000	40,500	(4,500)	(11.1%)
Income before income taxes	432,000	347,500	84,500	24.3%
Income tax expense	168,200	139,000	29,200	21.0%
Net income	$ 263,800	$ 208,500	$ 55,300	26.5%

> **HELPFUL HINT**
>
> Note that though the amount column is additive (the total is $55,300), the percentage column is not additive (26.5% is not the total). A separate percentage has been calculated for each item.

Retained Earnings Statement

A horizontal analysis of Quality Department Store's comparative retained earnings statements is presented in Illustration 19-7. Analyzed horizontally, net income increased $55,300, or 26.5%, whereas dividends on the common stock increased only $1,200, or 2%. We saw in the horizontal analysis of the balance sheet that ending retained earnings increased 38.6%. As indicated earlier, the company retained a significant portion of net income to finance additional plant facilities.

Illustration 19-7
Horizontal analysis of retained earnings statements

QUALITY DEPARTMENT STORE INC.
Retained Earnings Statements
For the Years Ended December 31

	2002	2001	Increase or (Decrease) during 2002 Amount	Percent
Retained earnings, Jan. 1	$525,000	$376,500	$148,500	39.4%
Add: Net income	263,800	208,500	55,300	26.5%
	788,800	585,000	203,800	
Deduct: Dividends	61,200	60,000	1,200	2.0%
Retained earnings, Dec. 31	$727,600	$525,000	$202,600	38.6%

Horizontal analysis of changes from period to period is relatively straightforward and is quite useful. But complications can occur in making the computations. If an item has no value in a base year or preceding year and a value in the next year, no percentage change can be computed. Similarly, if a negative amount appears in the base or preceding period and a positive amount exists the following year (or vice versa), no percentage change can be computed.

Vertical Analysis

Vertical analysis, also called **common size analysis,** is a technique for evaluating financial statement data that expresses each item within a financial statement as a percent of a base amount. On a balance sheet we might say that current assets are 22% of total assets (total assets being the base amount). Or on an income statement, we might say that selling expenses are 16% of net sales (net sales being the base amount).

Balance Sheet

Presented in Illustration 19-8 is the vertical analysis of Quality Department Store Inc.'s comparative balance sheets. The base for the asset items is **total assets**. The base for the liability and stockholders' equity items is **total liabilities and stockholders' equity**.

Illustration 19-8
Vertical analysis of balance sheets

QUALITY DEPARTMENT STORE INC.
Condensed Balance Sheets
December 31

| | 2002 | | 2001 | |
	Amount	Percent	Amount	Percent
Assets				
Current assets	$1,020,000	55.6%	$ 945,000	59.2%
Plant assets (net)	800,000	43.6%	632,500	39.7%
Intangible assets	15,000	0.8%	17,500	1.1%
Total assets	$1,835,000	100.0%	$1,595,000	100.0%
Liabilities				
Current liabilities	$ 344,500	18.8%	$ 303,000	19.0%
Long-term liabilities	487,500	26.5%	497,000	31.2%
Total liabilities	832,000	45.3%	800,000	50.2%
Stockholders' Equity				
Common stock, $1 par	275,400	15.0%	270,000	16.9%
Retained earnings	727,600	39.7%	525,000	32.9%
Total stockholders' equity	1,003,000	54.7%	795,000	49.8%
Total liabilities and stockholders' equity	$1,835,000	100.0%	$1,595,000	100.0%

Vertical analysis shows the relative size of each category in the balance sheet. It also can show the **percentage change** in the individual asset, liability, and stockholders' equity items. For example, we can see that current assets decreased from 59.2% of total assets in 2001 to 55.6% in 2002 (even though the absolute dollar amount increased $75,000 in that time). Plant assets (net) have increased from 39.7% to 43.6% of total assets. Retained earnings have increased from 32.9% to 39.7% of total liabilities and stockholders' equity. These results reinforce the earlier observations that **Quality is choosing to finance its growth through retention of earnings rather than through issuing additional debt**.

Income Statement

Vertical analysis of Quality's income statements is shown in Illustration 19-9. We see that cost of goods sold as a percentage of net sales declined 1% (62.1% vs. 61.1%) and total operating expenses declined 0.4% (17.4% vs. 17.0%). As a result, it is not surprising to see net income as a percent of net sales increase from 11.4% to 12.6%. Quality appears to be a profitable enterprise that is becoming even more successful.

QUALITY DEPARTMENT STORE INC.
Condensed Income Statements
For the Years Ended December 31

	2002 Amount	2002 Percent	2001 Amount	2001 Percent
Sales	$2,195,000	104.7%	$1,960,000	106.7%
Sales returns and allowances	98,000	4.7%	123,000	6.7%
Net sales	2,097,000	100.0%	1,837,000	100.0%
Cost of goods sold	1,281,000	61.1%	1,140,000	62.1%
Gross profit	816,000	38.9%	697,000	37.9%
Selling expenses	253,000	12.0%	211,500	11.5%
Administrative expenses	104,000	5.0%	108,500	5.9%
Total operating expenses	357,000	17.0%	320,000	17.4%
Income from operations	459,000	21.9%	377,000	20.5%
Other revenues and gains				
Interest and dividends	9,000	0.4%	11,000	0.6%
Other expenses and losses				
Interest expense	36,000	1.7%	40,500	2.2%
Income before income taxes	432,000	20.6%	347,500	18.9%
Income tax expense	168,200	8.0%	139,000	7.5%
Net income	$ 263,800	12.6%	$ 208,500	11.4%

Illustration 19-9
Vertical analysis of income statements

HELPFUL HINT

The formula for calculating these income statement percentages is:

$$\frac{\text{Each item on I/S}}{\text{Net sales}} = \%$$

An associated benefit of vertical analysis is that it enables you to compare companies of different sizes. For example, Quality's main competitor is a Sears store in a nearby town. Using vertical analysis, the condensed income statements of the small local retail enterprise, Quality Department Store Inc., can be more meaningfully compared with the 2002 income statement of the giant international retailer, **Sears, Roebuck and Co.**, as shown in Illustration 19-10.

CONDENSED INCOME STATEMENTS
(in thousands)

	Quality Department Store Inc. Dollars	Quality Department Store Inc. Percent	Sears, Roebuck and Co.[1] Dollars	Sears, Roebuck and Co.[1] Percent
Net sales	$2,097	100.0%	$41,366,000	100.0%
Cost of goods sold	1,281	61.1%	25,646,000	62.0%
Gross profit	816	38.9%	15,720,000	38.0%
Selling and administrative expenses	357	17.0%	13,639,000	33.0%
Income from operations	459	21.9%	2,081,000	5.0%
Other expenses and revenues				
(including income taxes)	195	9.3%	705,000	1.7%
Net income	$ 264	12.6%	$ 1,376,000	3.3%

Illustration 19-10
Intercompany income statement comparison

[1] Sears, Roebuck and Co., *2002 Annual Report* (Hoffman Estates, Illinois).

Sears's net sales are 19,725 times greater than the net sales of relatively tiny Quality Department Store. But vertical analysis eliminates this difference in size. The percentages show that Quality's and Sears's gross profit rates were comparable at 38.9% and 38%. However, the percentages related to income from operations were significantly different at 21.9% and 5.0%. This disparity can be attributed to Quality's selling and administrative expense percentage (17%) which is much lower than Sears's (33.0%). Although Sears earned net income more than 5,211 times larger than Quality's, Sears's net income as a **percent of each sales dollar** (3.3%) is only 26% of Quality's (12.6%).

BEFORE YOU GO ON...

Review It

1. What are the different tools that might be used to compare financial information?

2. What is horizontal analysis?

3. What is vertical analysis?

4. Identify the specific sections in **PepsiCo**'s 2002 Annual Report where horizontal and vertical analysis of financial data is presented. The answer to this question is provided on page 814.

Do It

Summary financial information for Rosepatch Company is as follows.

	December 31, 2005	December 31, 2004
Current assets	$234,000	$180,000
Plant assets (net)	756,000	420,000
Total assets	$990,000	$600,000

Compute the amount and percentage changes in 2005 using horizontal analysis, assuming 2004 is the base year.

ACTION PLAN

■ Find the percentage change by dividing the amount of the increase by the 2004 amount (base year).

SOLUTION

	Increase in 2005	
	Amount	Percent
Current assets	$ 54,000	30% [($234,000 − $180,000) ÷ $180,000]
Plant assets (net)	336,000	80% [($756,000 − $420,000) ÷ $420,000]
Total assets	$390,000	65% [($990,000 − $600,000) ÷ $600,000]

Related exercise material: *BE19-1, BE19-3, BE19-4, BE19-6, E19-1, E19-3, and E19-4.*

Ratio Analysis

Ratio analysis expresses the relationship among selected items of financial statement data. A **ratio** expresses the mathematical relationship between one quantity and another. The relationship is expressed in terms of either a percentage, a rate, or a simple proportion. To illustrate, in 2002 **Nike, Inc.**, had current assets of $4,157.7

million and current liabilities of $1,836.2 million. The relationship is determined by dividing current assets by current liabilities. The alternative means of expression are:

Percentage: Current assets are 226% of current liabilities.
Rate: Current assets are 2.26 times current liabilities.
Proportion: The relationship of current assets to liabilities is 2.26:1.

For analysis of the primary financial statements, ratios can be used to evaluate liquidity, profitability, and solvency. These classifications are described and pictured in Illustration 19-11.

STUDY OBJECTIVE 5

Identify and compute ratios, and describe their purpose and use in analyzing a firm's liquidity, profitability, and solvency.

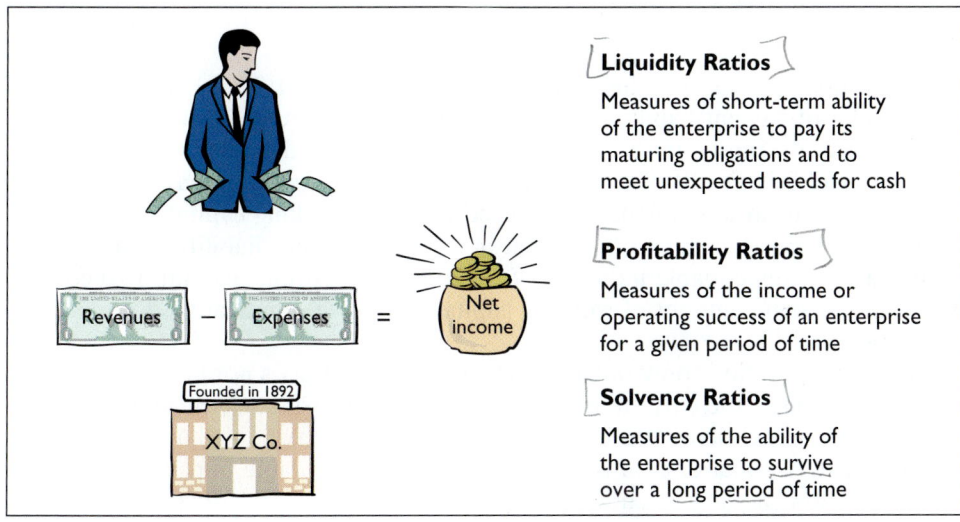

Illustration 19-11
Financial ratio classifications

Ratios can provide clues to underlying conditions that may not be apparent from individual financial statement components. However, a single ratio by itself is not very meaningful. Accordingly, in the discussion of ratios we will use the following types of comparisons.

1. **Intracompany comparisons** for two years for Quality Department Store.
2. **Industry average comparisons** based on median ratios for department stores.
3. **Intercompany comparisons** based on **Sears, Roebuck and Co.** as Quality Department Store's principal competitor.

Liquidity Ratios

Liquidity ratios measure the short-term ability of the enterprise to pay its maturing obligations and to meet unexpected needs for cash. Short-term creditors such as bankers and suppliers are particularly interested in assessing liquidity. The ratios that can be used to determine the enterprise's short-term debt-paying ability are the current ratio, the acid-test ratio, receivables turnover, and inventory turnover.

1. Current Ratio

The **current ratio** is a widely used measure for evaluating a company's liquidity and short-term debt-paying ability. The ratio is computed by dividing current assets by current liabilities.

The 2002 and 2001 current ratios for Quality Department Store and comparative data are shown in Illustration 19-12.

Illustration 19-12
Current ratio

$$\text{Current Ratio} = \frac{\text{Current Assets}}{\text{Current Liabilities}}$$

Quality Department Store

2002	2001
$\dfrac{\$1,020,000}{\$344,500} = 2.96:1$	$\dfrac{\$945,000}{\$303,000} = 3.1:1$
Industry average 1.28:1	Sears, Roebuck and Co. 2.19:1

What does the ratio actually mean? The 2002 ratio of 2.96:1 means that for every dollar of current liabilities, Quality has $2.96 of current assets. Quality's current ratio has decreased in the current year. But, compared to the industry average of 1.28:1, and Sears's 2.19:1 current ratio, Quality appears to be reasonably liquid.

The current ratio is sometimes referred to as the **working capital ratio** because **working capital** is the excess of current assets over current liabilities. The current ratio is a more dependable indicator of liquidity than working capital. Two companies with the same amount of working capital may have significantly different current ratios.

The current ratio is only one measure of liquidity. It does not take into account the composition of the current assets. For example, a satisfactory current ratio does not disclose the fact that a portion of the current assets may be tied up in slow-moving inventory. A dollar of cash would be more readily available to pay the bills than a dollar of slow-moving inventory.

ACCOUNTING IN ACTION   Business Insight

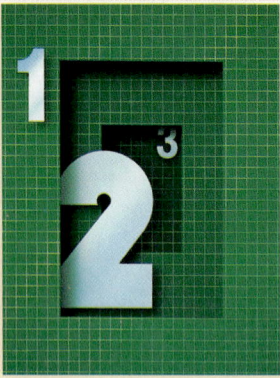

The apparent simplicity of the current ratio can have real-world limitations. An addition of equal amounts to both the numerator and the denominator causes the ratio to decrease. Assume, for example, that a company has $2,000,000 of current assets and $1,000,000 of current liabilities. Its current ratio is 2:1. If it purchases $1,000,000 of inventory on account, it will have $3,000,000 of current assets and $2,000,000 of current liabilities. Its current ratio will decrease to 1.5:1. If, instead, the company pays off $500,000 of its current liabilities, it will have $1,500,000 of current assets and $500,000 of current liabilities, and its current ratio will increase to 3:1. Any trend analysis should be done with care, since the ratio is susceptible to quick changes and is easily influenced by management.

2. Acid-Test Ratio

The **acid-test (quick) ratio** is a measure of a company's immediate short-term liquidity. It is computed by dividing the sum of cash, short-term investments, and net receivables by current liabilities. Thus, it is an important complement to the current ratio. For example, assume that the current assets of Quality Department Store for 2002 and 2001 consist of the following items.

Illustration 19-13
Current assets of Quality
Department Store

QUALITY DEPARTMENT STORE INC.
Balance Sheet (partial)

	2002	2001
Current assets		
Cash	$ 100,000	$155,000
Short-term investments	20,000	70,000
Receivables (net*)	230,000	180,000
Inventory	620,000	500,000
Prepaid expenses	50,000	40,000
Total current assets	$1,020,000	$945,000

*Allowance for doubtful accounts is $10,000 at the end of each year.

Cash, short-term investments, and receivables (net) are highly liquid compared to inventory and prepaid expenses. The inventory may not be readily saleable, and the prepaid expenses may not be transferable to others. Thus, the acid-test ratio measures **immediate** liquidity. The 2002 and 2001 acid-test ratios for Quality Department Store and comparative data are as follows.

Illustration 19-14
Acid-test ratio

$$\text{Acid-Test Ratio} = \frac{\text{Cash + Short-Term Investments + Receivables (Net)}}{\text{Current Liabilities}}$$

Quality Department Store

2002	2001
$\dfrac{\$100,000 + \$20,000 + \$230,000}{\$344,500} = 1.0:1$	$\dfrac{\$155,000 + \$70,000 + \$180,000}{\$303,000} = 1.3:1$
Industry average	Sears, Roebuck and Co.
0.33:1	1.81:1

The ratio has declined in 2002. Is an acid-test ratio of 1.0:1 adequate? When compared with the industry average of 0.33:1 and Sears's of 1.81:1, Quality's acid-test ratio seems adequate.

3. Receivables Turnover

Liquidity may be measured by how quickly certain assets can be converted to cash. How liquid, for example, are the receivables? The ratio used to assess the liquidity of the receivables is **receivables turnover**. It measures the number of times, on average, receivables are collected during the period. Receivables turnover is computed by dividing net credit sales (net sales less cash sales) by the average net receivables. Unless seasonal factors are significant, average net receivables can be computed from the beginning and ending balances of the net receivables.[2]

Assume that all sales are credit sales. The balance of net receivables at the beginning of 2001 is $200,000; at the end of 2001 it is $180,000, and at the end of 2002 it is $230,000. The receivables turnover for Quality Department Store and comparative data are shown in Illustration 19-15 (page 778). Quality's receivables turnover improved in 2002. The turnover of 9.8 times compares quite favorably with Sears's 1.4 times and is similar to the department store industry's average of 10.8 times.

---

[2]If seasonal factors are significant, the average receivables balance might be determined by using monthly amounts.

Illustration 19-15
Receivables turnover

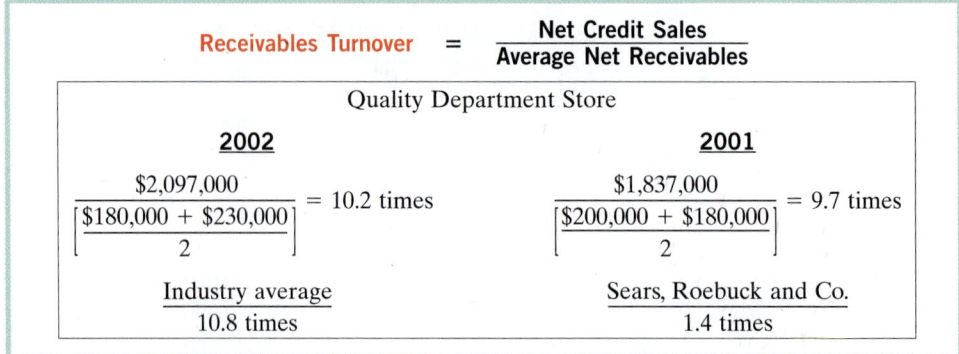

$$\text{Receivables Turnover} = \frac{\text{Net Credit Sales}}{\text{Average Net Receivables}}$$

Quality Department Store

2002

$$\frac{\$2,097,000}{\left[\dfrac{\$180,000 + \$230,000}{2}\right]} = 10.2 \text{ times}$$

Industry average
10.8 times

2001

$$\frac{\$1,837,000}{\left[\dfrac{\$200,000 + \$180,000}{2}\right]} = 9.7 \text{ times}$$

Sears, Roebuck and Co.
1.4 times

ACCOUNTING IN ACTION Business Insight

In some cases, receivables turnover may be misleading. Some companies, especially large retail chains, encourage credit and revolving charge sales. They may even slow collections in order to earn a healthy return on the outstanding receivables at interest rates of 18% to 22%. This may explain why **Sears**'s turnover is only 1.4 times. In general, however, the faster the turnover, the greater the reliance that can be placed on the current and acid-test ratios for assessing liquidity.

A popular variant of the receivables turnover ratio is to convert it to an **average collection period** in terms of days. This is done by dividing the receivables turnover ratio into 365 days. For example, the receivables turnover of 10.2 times is divided into 365 days to obtain approximately 36 days. This means that receivables are collected on average every 36 days, or about every 5 weeks. The average collection period is frequently used to assess the effectiveness of a company's credit and collection policies. The general rule is that the collection period should not greatly exceed the credit term period (the time allowed for payment).

4. Inventory Turnover

Inventory turnover measures the number of times on average the inventory is sold during the period. Its purpose is to measure the liquidity of the inventory. The inventory turnover is computed by dividing cost of goods sold by the average inventory. Unless seasonal factors are significant, average inventory can be computed from the beginning and ending inventory balances.

Assuming that the inventory balance for Quality Department Store at the beginning of 2001 was $450,000, its inventory turnover and comparative data are as shown in Illustration 19-16. Quality's inventory turnover declined slightly in 2002. The turnover of 2.3 times is relatively low compared with the industry average of 6.7 and Sears's 4.6. Generally, the faster the inventory turnover, the less cash that is tied up in inventory and the less the chance of inventory obsolescence. Inventory turnover ratios vary considerably among industries. For example, grocery store chains have a turnover of 10 times and an average selling period of 37 days. In contrast, jewelry stores have an average turnover of 1.3 times and an average selling period of 281 days.

Illustration 19-16
Inventory turnover

$$\text{Inventory Turnover} = \frac{\text{Cost of Goods Sold}}{\text{Average Inventory}}$$

Quality Department Store	
2002	**2001**
$\dfrac{\$1,281,000}{\left[\dfrac{\$500,000 + \$620,000}{2}\right]} = 2.3$ times	$\dfrac{\$1,140,000}{\left[\dfrac{\$450,000 + \$500,000}{2}\right]} = 2.4$ times
Industry average	Sears, Roebuck and Co.
6.7 times	4.6 times

A variant of inventory turnover is the **average days to sell the inventory**. It is calculated by dividing the inventory turnover into 365. For example, Quality's 2002 inventory turnover of 2.3 times divided into 365 is approximately 159 days. An average selling time of 159 days is also relatively high compared with the industry average of 54.5 days (365 ÷ 6.7) and Sears's 79.3 days (365 ÷ 4.6).

Profitability Ratios

Profitability ratios measure the income or operating success of an enterprise for a given period of time. Income, or the lack of it, affects the company's ability to obtain debt and equity financing. It also affects the company's liquidity position and the company's ability to grow. As a consequence, both creditors and investors are interested in evaluating earning power—profitability. Profitability is frequently used as the ultimate test of management's operating effectiveness.

5. Profit Margin

Profit margin is a measure of the percentage of each dollar of sales that results in net income. It is computed by dividing net income by net sales. Quality Department Store's profit margin and comparative data are shown in Illustration 19-17.

Illustration 19-17
Profit margin

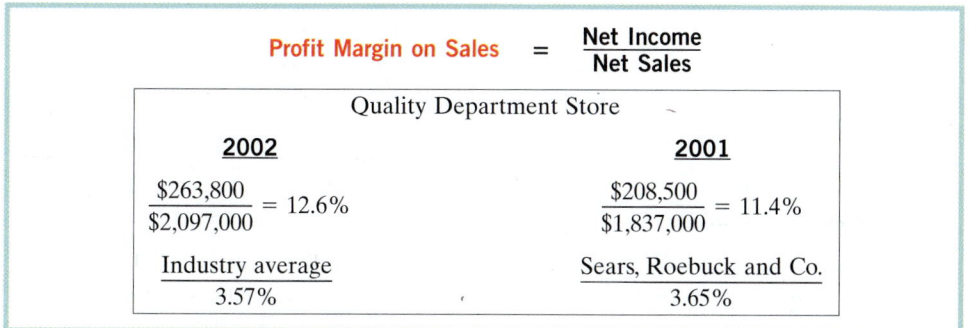

$$\text{Profit Margin on Sales} = \frac{\text{Net Income}}{\text{Net Sales}}$$

Quality Department Store	
2002	**2001**
$\dfrac{\$263,800}{\$2,097,000} = 12.6\%$	$\dfrac{\$208,500}{\$1,837,000} = 11.4\%$
Industry average	Sears, Roebuck and Co.
3.57%	3.65%

Quality experienced an increase in its profit margin from 2001 to 2002. Its profit margin is unusually high in comparison with the industry average of 3.57% and Sears's 3.65%.

High-volume (high inventory turnover) enterprises such as grocery stores (**Safeway** or **Kroger**) and discount stores (**Kmart** or **Wal-Mart**) generally experience low profit margins. In contrast, low-volume enterprises such as jewelry stores (**Tiffany & Co.**) or airplane manufacturers (**Boeing Co.**) have high profit margins.

6. Asset Turnover

Asset turnover measures how efficiently a company uses its assets to generate sales. It is determined by dividing net sales by average assets. The resulting number shows the dollars of sales produced by each dollar invested in assets. Unless seasonal factors are significant, average total assets can be computed from the beginning and ending balance of total assets. Assuming that total assets at the beginning of 2001 were $1,446,000, the 2002 and 2001 asset turnover for Quality Department Store and comparative data are as follows.

Illustration 19-18
Asset turnover

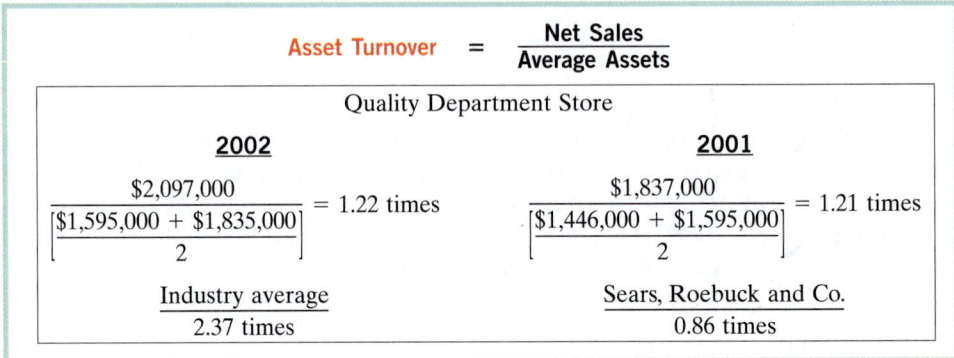

Asset turnover shows that in 2002 Quality generated sales of $1.22 for each dollar it had invested in assets. The ratio changed little from 2001 to 2002. Quality's asset turnover is below the industry average of 2.37 times but above Sears's ratio of 0.86 times.

Asset turnover ratios vary considerably among industries. For example, a large utility company like **Consolidated Edison** (New York) has a ratio of 0.49 times, and the large grocery chain **Kroger Stores** has a ratio of 4.34 times.

7. Return on Assets

An overall measure of profitability is **return on assets**. This ratio is computed by dividing net income by average assets. The 2002 and 2001 return on assets for Quality Department Store and comparative data are shown below.

Illustration 19-19
Return on assets

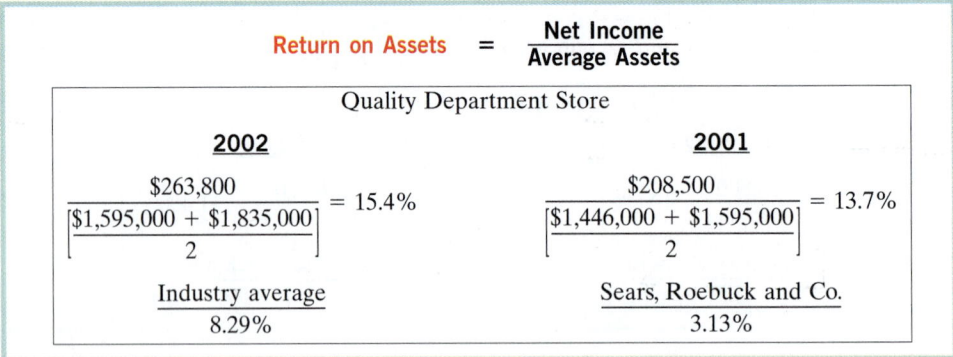

Quality's return on assets improved from 2001 to 2002. Its return of 15.4% is very high, compared with the department store industry average of 8.29% and Sears's 3.13%.

8. Return on Common Stockholders' Equity

Another widely used profitability ratio is **return on common stockholders' equity**. It measures profitability from the common stockholders' viewpoint. This ratio shows how many dollars of net income were earned for each dollar invested by the owners. It is computed by dividing net income by average common stockholders' equity. Assuming that common stockholders' equity at the beginning of 2001 was $667,000, the 2002 and 2001 ratios for Quality Department Store and comparative data are shown in Illustration 19-20.

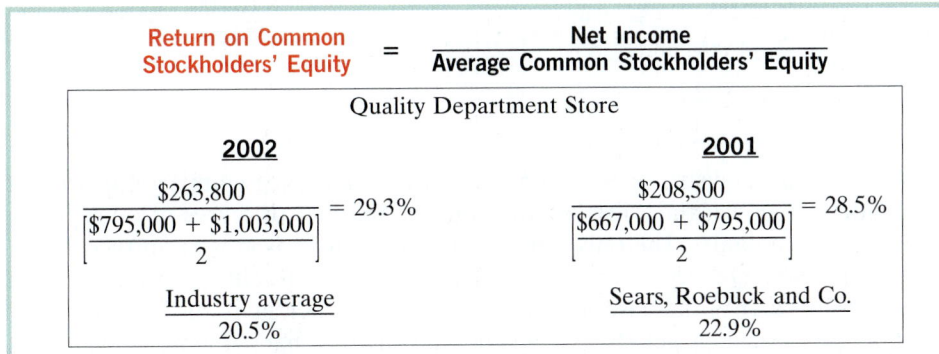

Illustration 19-20
Return on common stockholders' equity

Quality's rate of return on common stockholders' equity is high at 29.3%, considering an industry average of 20.5% and a rate of 22.9% for Sears.

When preferred stock is present, **preferred dividend** requirements are deducted from net income to compute income available to common stockholders. Similarly, the par value of preferred stock (or call price, if applicable) must be deducted from total stockholders' equity to determine the amount of common stock equity used in this ratio. The ratio then appears as follows.

$$\text{Return on Common Stockholders' Equity} = \frac{\text{Net Income} - \text{Preferred Dividends}}{\text{Average Common Stockholders' Equity}}$$

Illustration 19-21
Return on common stockholders' equity with preferred stock

ALTERNATIVE TERMINOLOGY

Trading on the equity is also called *leveraging*.

Note that Quality's rate of return on stockholders' equity (29.3%) is substantially higher than its rate of return on assets (15.4%). The reason is that Quality has made effective use of **leverage** or **trading on the equity** at a gain. Trading on the equity at a gain means that the company has borrowed money at a lower rate of interest than it is able to earn by using the borrowed money. Leverage enables Quality Department Store to use money supplied by nonowners to increase the return to the owners. A comparison of the rate of return on total assets with the rate of interest paid for borrowed money indicates the profitability of trading on the equity. Quality Department Store earns more on its borrowed funds than it has to pay in the form of interest. Thus the return to stockholders exceeds the return on the assets, benefiting from the positive leveraging.

9. Earnings per Share (EPS)

Earnings per share (EPS) is a measure of the net income earned on each share of common stock. It is computed by dividing net income by the number of weighted average common shares outstanding during the year. A measure of net income earned on a per share basis provides a useful perspective for determining profitability. Assuming that there is no change in the number of outstanding shares during 2001 and that the 2002 increase occurred midyear, the net income per share for Quality Department Store for 2002 and 2001 is computed as shown in Illustration 19-22 (page 782).

Illustration 19-22
Earnings per share

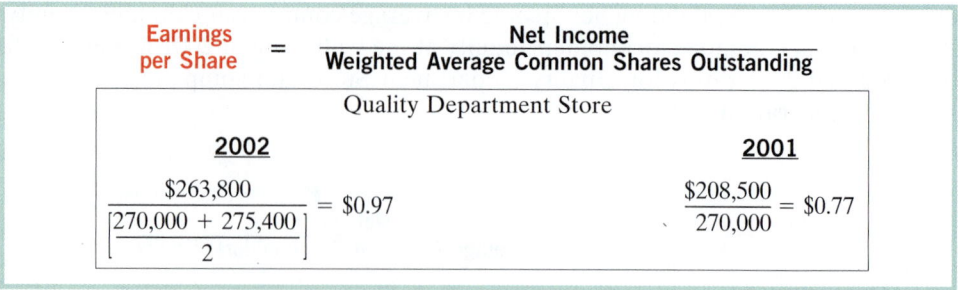

Note that no industry or Sears data are presented. Such comparisons are not meaningful because of the wide variations in the number of shares of outstanding stock among companies. The only meaningful EPS comparison is an intracompany trend comparison: Quality's earnings per share increased 20 cents per share in 2002. This represents a 26% increase over the 2001 earnings per share of 77 cents.

The terms "earnings per share" and "net income per share" refer to the amount of net income applicable to each share of **common stock**. Therefore, in computing EPS, if there are preferred dividends declared for the period, they must be deducted from net income to determine income available to the common stockholders.

10. Price-Earnings Ratio

The **price-earnings (P-E) ratio** is an oft-quoted measure of the ratio of the market price of each share of common stock to the earnings per share. The price-earnings (P-E) ratio reflects investors' assessments of a company's future earnings. It is computed by dividing the market price per share of the stock by earnings per share. Assuming that the market price of Quality Department Store Inc. stock is $8 in 2001 and $12 in 2002, the price-earnings ratio is computed as follows.

Illustration 19-23
Price-earnings ratio

In 2002 each share of Quality's stock sold for 12.4 times the amount that was earned on each share. Quality's price-earnings ratio is lower than the industry average of 26 times, but it is higher than the ratio of 7 times for Sears. The average price-earnings ratio for the stocks that constitute the Standard and Poor's 500 Index (500 largest U.S. firms) in June 2003 was an unusually high 24 times.

11. Payout Ratio

The **payout ratio** measures the percentage of earnings distributed in the form of cash dividends. It is computed by dividing cash dividends by net income. Companies that have high growth rates generally have low payout ratios because they reinvest most of their net income into the business. The 2002 and 2001 payout ratios for Quality Department Store are computed as follows.

Illustration 19-24
Payout ratio

$$\text{Payout Ratio} = \frac{\text{Cash Dividends}}{\text{Net Income}}$$

Quality Department Store

2002	2001
$\dfrac{\$61{,}200}{\$263{,}800} = 23.2\%$	$\dfrac{\$60{,}000}{\$208{,}500} = 28.8\%$
Industry average	Sears, Roebuck and Co.
16.0%	20.0%

Quality's payout ratio is comparable to Sears's payout ratio of 20.0%. As indicated earlier (page 770), Quality apparently has decided to fund its purchase of plant assets through retention of earnings.

ACCOUNTING IN ACTION   Business Insight

Many companies with stable earnings have high payout ratios. For example, Baltimore Gas and Electric had an 84% payout ratio over a recent five-year period. Omega Healthcare's dividends exceeded net income over the same period. Conversely, companies that are expanding rapidly, such as Toys "R" Us and Tellabs Inc. have never paid a cash dividend.

Solvency Ratios

Solvency ratios measure the ability of the company to survive over a long period of time. Long-term creditors and stockholders are particularly interested in a company's ability to pay interest as it comes due and to repay the face value of debt at maturity. Debt to total assets and times interest earned are two ratios that provide information about debt-paying ability.

12. Debt to Total Assets Ratio

The **debt to total assets ratio** measures the percentage of the total assets provided by creditors. It is computed by dividing total debt (both current and long-term liabilities) by total assets. This ratio indicates the company's degree of leverage. It also provides some indication of the company's ability to withstand losses without impairing the interests of creditors. The higher the percentage of debt to total assets, the greater the <u>risk</u> that the company may be unable to meet its maturing obligations. The 2002 and 2001 ratios for Quality Department Store and comparative data are as follows.

Illustration 19-25
Debt to total assets ratio

$$\text{Debt to Total Assets} = \frac{\text{Total Debt}}{\text{Total Assets}}$$

Quality Department Store

2002	2001
$\dfrac{\$832{,}000}{\$1{,}835{,}000} = 45.3\%$	$\dfrac{\$800{,}000}{\$1{,}595{,}000} = 50.2\%$
Industry average	Sears, Roebuck and Co.
40.1%	76.1%

A ratio of 45.3% means that creditors have provided 45.3% of Quality Department Store's total assets. Quality's 45.3% is above the industry average of 40.1%. But it is considerably below the high 76.1% ratio of Sears. The lower the ratio, the more equity "buffer" there is available to the creditors. Thus, from the creditors' point of view, a low ratio of debt to total assets is usually desirable.

The adequacy of this ratio is often judged in the light of the company's earnings. Generally, companies with relatively stable earnings (such as public utilities) have higher debt to total assets ratios than cyclical companies with widely fluctuating earnings (such as many high-tech companies).

13. Times Interest Earned

Times interest earned provides an indication of the company's ability to meet interest payments as they come due. It is computed by dividing income before interest expense and income taxes by interest expense. The 2002 and 2001 ratios for Quality Department Store and comparative data are shown in Illustration 19-26. Note that times interest earned uses income before income taxes and interest expense. This represents the amount available to cover interest. For Quality Department Store the 2002 amount of $468,000 is computed by taking the income before income taxes of $432,000 and adding back the $36,000 of interest expense.

Illustration 19-26
Times interest earned

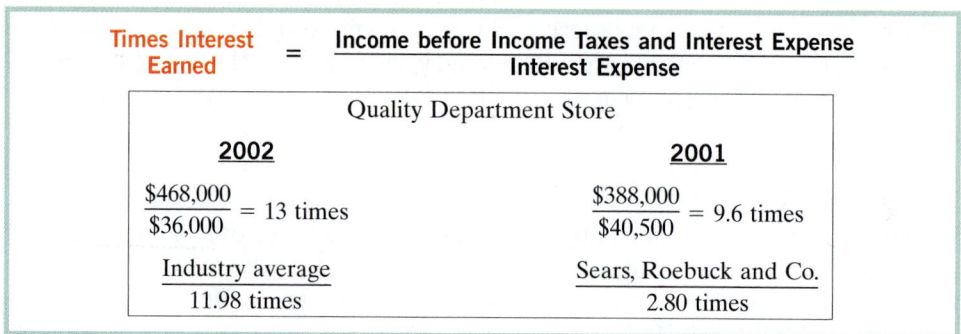

$$\text{Times Interest Earned} = \frac{\text{Income before Income Taxes and Interest Expense}}{\text{Interest Expense}}$$

Quality Department Store

2002	2001
$\dfrac{\$468,000}{\$36,000} = 13$ times	$\dfrac{\$388,000}{\$40,500} = 9.6$ times
Industry average	Sears, Roebuck and Co.
11.98 times	2.80 times

Quality's interest expense is well covered at 13 times, compared with the industry average of 11.98 times and Sears's 2.80 times.

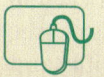 

ACCOUNTING IN ACTION e Business Insight

Today, investors have access to information provided by corporate managers that used to be available only to professional analysts. Corporate managers have always made themselves available to security analysts for questions at the end of every quarter. Now, because of a combination of new corporate disclosure requirements by the Securities and Exchange Commission and technologies that make communication to large numbers of people possible at a very low price, the average investor can listen in on these discussions. For example, one individual investor, Matthew Johnson, a **Nortel Networks** local area network engineer in Belfast, Northern Ireland, "stayed up past midnight to listen to **Apple Computer**'s recent Internet conference call. Hearing the company's news 'from the dog's mouth,' he says 'gave me better information' than hunting through chat-rooms."

Source: Jeff D. Opdyke, "Individuals Pick Up on Conference Calls," *Wall Street Journal*, November 20, 2000.

Summary of Ratios

A summary of the ratios discussed in the chapter is presented in Illustration 19-27. The summary includes the formula and purpose or use of each ratio.

Illustration 19-27
Summary of liquidity, profitability, and solvency ratios

Ratio	Formula	Purpose or Use
Liquidity Ratios		
1. Current ratio	$\dfrac{\text{Current assets}}{\text{Current liabilities}}$	Measures short-term debt-paying ability.
2. Acid-test (quick) ratio	$\dfrac{\text{Cash + Short-term investments + Receivables (net)}}{\text{Current liabilities}}$	Measures immediate short-term liquidity.
3. Receivables turnover	$\dfrac{\text{Net credit sales}}{\text{Average net receivables}}$	Measures liquidity of receivables.
4. Inventory turnover	$\dfrac{\text{Cost of goods sold}}{\text{Average inventory}}$	Measures liquidity of inventory.
Profitability Ratios		
5. Profit margin	$\dfrac{\text{Net income}}{\text{Net sales}}$	Measures net income generated by each dollar of sales.
6. Asset turnover	$\dfrac{\text{Net sales}}{\text{Average assets}}$	Measures how efficiently assets are used to generate sales.
7. Return on assets	$\dfrac{\text{Net income}}{\text{Average assets}}$	Measures overall profitability of assets.
8. Return on common stockholders' equity	$\dfrac{\text{Net income}}{\text{Average common stockholders' equity}}$	Measures profitability of owners' investment.
9. Earnings per share (EPS)	$\dfrac{\text{Net income}}{\text{Weighted average common shares outstanding}}$	Measures net income earned on each share of common stock.
10. Price-earnings (P-E) ratio	$\dfrac{\text{Market price per share of stock}}{\text{Earnings per share}}$	Measures the ratio of the market price per share to earnings per share.
11. Payout ratio	$\dfrac{\text{Cash dividends}}{\text{Net income}}$	Measures percentage of earnings distributed in the form of cash dividends.
Solvency Ratios		
12. Debt to total assets ratio	$\dfrac{\text{Total debt}}{\text{Total assets}}$	Measures the percentage of total assets provided by creditors.
13. Times interest earned	$\dfrac{\text{Income before income taxes and interest expense}}{\text{Interest expense}}$	Measures ability to meet interest payments as they come due.

BEFORE YOU GO ON...

Review It

1. What are liquidity ratios? Explain the current ratio, acid-test ratio, receivables turnover, and inventory turnover.

2. What are profitability ratios? Explain the profit margin, asset turnover ratio, return on assets, return on common stockholders' equity, earnings per share, price-earnings ratio, and payout ratio.

3. What are solvency ratios? Explain the debt to total assets ratio and times interest earned.

Do It

Selected financial data for Drummond Company at December 31, 2005, are as follows: cash $60,000; receivables (net) $80,000; inventory $70,000; current liabilities $140,000. Compute the current and acid-test ratios.

ACTION PLAN

■ Use the formula for the current ratio: Current assets ÷ Current liabilities.
■ Use the formula for the acid-test ratio: Cash + Short-term investments + Receivables (net) ÷ Current liabilities.

SOLUTION The current ratio is 1.5:1 ($210,000 ÷ $140,000). The acid-test ratio is 1:1 ($140,000 ÷ $140,000).

Related exercise material: *BE19-7, BE19-8, BE19-9, BE19-10, BE19-11, E19-5, E19-6, and E19-7, E19-8, E19-9, and E19-10.*

THE NAVIGATOR

Earning Power and Irregular Items

STUDY OBJECTIVE 6

Understand the concept of earning power, and indicate how material items not typical of regular operations are presented.

Users of financial statements are interested in the concept of "earning power." Earning power means the normal level of income to be obtained in the future. Earning power differs from actual net income by the amount of irregular revenues, expenses, gains, and losses. Users are interested in earning power because it helps them derive an estimate of future earnings without the "noise" of irregular items.

For users of financial statements to determine "earning power" or regular income, the "irregular" items are separately identified on the income statement. Three types of "irregular" items are reported:

1. Discontinued operations.
2. Extraordinary items.
3. Changes in accounting principle.

All these "irregular" items are reported net of income taxes. That is, income tax is first calculated for the income before "irregular" items. Then it is calculated for each of the listed "irregular" items. The general concept is "let the tax follow income or loss."

Discontinued Operations

Discontinued operations refers to the disposal of a **significant segment** of a business. Examples are the cessation of an entire activity and the elimination of a major class of customers. **Kmart**'s decision to terminate its interest in four business activities, including **PACE Membership Warehouse** and **PayLess Drug Stores Northwest**, was reported as discontinued operations. On the other hand, the phasing out of a model such as the **GM** Chevette or part of a line of business is not considered to be a disposal of a segment.

Following the disposal of a significant segment, the income statement should report both income from continuing operations and income (or loss) from discontinued operations. **The income (loss) from discontinued operations consists of two parts: the income (loss) from operations and the gain (loss) on disposal of the segment.**

To illustrate, assume that during 2005 Acro Energy Inc. has income before income taxes of $800,000. During 2005 Acro discontinued and sold its unprofitable chemical division. The loss in 2005 from chemical operations (net of $60,000 taxes) was $140,000. The loss on disposal of the chemical division (net of $30,000 taxes) was $70,000. Assuming a 30% tax rate on income, the income statement presentation is shown below.

Illustration 19-28
Statement presentation of discontinued operations

ACRO ENERGY INC. Income Statement (partial) For the Year Ended December 31, 2005		
Income before income taxes		$800,000
Income tax expense		240,000
Income from continuing operations		560,000
Discontinued operations		
Loss from operations of chemical division, net of $60,000 income tax saving	**$140,000**	
Loss from disposal of chemical division, net of $30,000 income tax saving	**70,000**	**210,000**
Net income		$350,000

HELPFUL HINT

Observe the dual disclosures: (1) The results of operations of the discontinued division must be eliminated from the results of continuing operations. (2) The disposal of the operation must also be reported.

Note that the caption "Income from continuing operations" is used and that a new section "Discontinued operations" is added. **Within the new section, both the operating loss and the loss on disposal are reported net of applicable income taxes.** This presentation clearly indicates the separate effects of continuing operations and discontinued operations on net income.

Extraordinary Items

Extraordinary items are events and transactions that meet two conditions: They are (1) **unusual in nature and** (2) **infrequent in occurrence**. To be "unusual," the item should be abnormal and only incidentally related to the company's customary activities. To be "infrequent," the item should not be reasonably expected to recur in the foreseeable future. Both criteria must be evaluated in terms of the company's operating environment. Thus, **Weyerhaeuser Co.** reported the $36 million in damages to its timberland caused by the volcanic eruption of Mount St. Helens as an extraordinary item. The eruption was both unusual and infrequent. In contrast, Florida Citrus Company does not report frost damage to its citrus crop as an extraordinary item. Frost damage is not viewed as infrequent. Illustration 19-29 (page 788) shows the classification of extraordinary and ordinary items.

ACCOUNTING IN ACTION **Business Insight**

In the recession of the early 1990s, many companies closed plants and reduced their work forces. The costs incurred in these activities are called plant restructuring costs. Such costs are reported as other expenses and losses in the income statement. They are not considered an extraordinary item because plant closings are neither unusual nor infrequent in many industries.

Plant restructuring costs often have a significant effect on net income. For example, **Union Pacific Corp.** had a $585 million after-tax charge, of which $492 million applied to the disposal of 7,100 miles of the Union Pacific Railroad.

Illustration 19-29
Examples of extraordinary and ordinary items

Extraordinary items	Ordinary items

1. Effects of major casualties (acts of God), if rare in the area.

1. Effects of major casualties (acts of God), not uncommon in the area.

2. Expropriation (takeover) of property by a foreign government.

2. Write-down of inventories or write-off of receivables.

3. Effects of a newly enacted law or regulation, such as a condemnation action.

3. Losses attributable to labor strikes.

4. Gains or losses from sales of property, plant, or equipment.

Extraordinary items are reported net of taxes in a separate section of the income statement immediately below discontinued operations. To illustrate, assume that in 2005 a foreign government expropriated property held as an investment by Acro Energy Inc. If the loss is $70,000 before applicable income taxes of $21,000, the income statement will report a deduction of $49,000 as shown in Illustration 19-30. When there is an extraordinary item to report, the caption "Income before extraordinary item" is added immediately before the section for the extraordinary item. This presentation clearly indicates the effect of the extraordinary item on net income.

Illustration 19-30
Statement presentation of extraordinary items

ACRO ENERGY INC.
Income Statement (partial)
For the Year Ended December 31, 2005

Income before income taxes		$800,000
Income tax expense		240,000
Income from continuing operations		560,000
Discontinued operations		
Loss from operations of chemical division, net of $60,000 income tax saving	$140,000	
Loss from disposal of chemical division, net of $30,000 income tax saving	70,000	210,000
Income before extraordinary item		350,000
Extraordinary item		
Expropriation of investment, net of $21,000 income tax saving		**49,000**
Net income		$301,000

HELPFUL HINT

If there are no discontinued operations, the third line of the income statement would be labeled "Income before extraordinary item."

What if a transaction or event meets one (but not both) of the criteria for an extraordinary item? In that case it is reported under either "Other revenues and gains" or "Other expenses and losses" at its gross amount (not net of tax). This is true, for example, of gains (losses) resulting from the sale of property, plant, and equipment, as explained in Chapter 10. It has become quite common for companies to use the label "Nonrecurring charges" for losses that do not meet the extraordinary item criteria.

Change in Accounting Principle

For ease of comparison, financial statements are expected to be prepared on a basis **consistent** with the preceding period. Where a choice of accounting principles is available, the principle initially chosen should be consistently applied from period to period. A **change in accounting principle** occurs when the principle used in the current year is different from the one used in the preceding year. Examples include a change in depreciation methods (declining-balance to straight-line) and a change in inventory costing methods (FIFO to average cost). When is a change in accounting principle permitted? When two conditions are met: (1) management can show that the new principle is preferable to the old principle, and (2) the effects of the change are clearly disclosed in the income statement.

When a change in accounting principle has occurred:

1. The new principle should be used in reporting the results of operations of the current year.
2. The cumulative effect of the change on all prior year income statements should be disclosed net of applicable taxes in a special section immediately preceding net income.

To illustrate, assume that at the beginning of 2005, Acro Energy Inc. changes from the straight-line method of depreciation to the declining-balance method for equipment purchased on January 1, 2002. The cumulative effect on prior year income statements (statements for 2002–2004) is to increase depreciation expense and decrease income before income taxes by $24,000. Assuming a 30 percent tax rate, the net-of-tax effect of the change is $16,800 ($24,000 × 70%). The income statement presentation for the change in accounting principle is shown in Illustration 19-31.

Illustration 19-31
Statement presentation of cumulative effect of change in accounting principle

ACRO ENERGY INC. Income Statement (partial) For the Year Ended December 31, 2005		
Income before income taxes		$800,000
Income tax expense		240,000
Income from continuing operations		560,000
Discontinued operations		
Loss from operations of chemical division, net of $60,000 income tax saving	$140,000	
Loss from disposal of chemical division, net of $30,000 income tax saving	70,000	210,000
Income before extraordinary item and cumulative effect of change in accounting principle		350,000
Extraordinary item		
Expropriation of investment, net of $21,000 income tax saving		49,000

Cumulative effect of change in accounting principle
  Effect on prior years of change in depreciation
    method, net of $7,200 income tax saving
		16,800

Net income		$284,200

HELPFUL HINT

If a company does not have either discontinued operations or extraordinary items, the label "Income before cumulative effect of change in accounting principle" is used in place of "Income from continuing operations."

The income statement for Acro Energy will also show depreciation expense for the current year. The amount is based on the new depreciation method. The caption "Income before extraordinary item and cumulative effect of change in accounting principle" is inserted immediately following the effects of discontinued operations. This presentation clearly indicates the cumulative effect of the change on prior years' income.

A complete income statement showing all material items not typical of regular operations is illustrated in the Demonstration Problem (page 794).

Comprehensive Income

Most revenues, expenses, gains, and losses recognized during the period are included in income. However, over time, specific exceptions to this general practice have developed. Certain items now bypass income and are reported directly in stockholders' equity. For example, in Chapter 17 you learned that unrealized gains and losses on available-for-sale securities are not included in income but instead are reported in the balance sheet as adjustments to stockholders' equity.

Why are these gains and losses on available-for-sale securities excluded from net income? Because disclosing them separately (1) reduces the volatility of net income due to fluctuations in fair value, yet (2) informs the financial statement user of the gain or loss that would be incurred if the securities were sold at fair value.

Many analysts have expressed concern over the significant increase in the number of items that bypass the income statement. They feel that this has reduced the usefulness of the income statement. To address this concern, the FASB now requires that, in addition to reporting net income, a company must also report comprehensive income. **Comprehensive income** includes all changes in stockholders' equity during a period except those resulting from investments by stockholders and distributions to stockholders. A number of alternative formats for reporting comprehensive income are allowed. These formats are discussed in advanced accounting courses.

BEFORE YOU GO ON...

Review It

1. What are the similarities and differences in reporting material items not typical of regular operations?
2. What is included in comprehensive income?

Do It

In its proposed 2005 income statement, AIR Corporation reports income before income taxes $400,000, extraordinary loss $100,000, income taxes (30%) $120,000, and net income $210,000. Prepare a correct income statement, beginning with income before income taxes.

ACTION PLAN
- Recall that the loss is extraordinary because it meets the criteria of being both unusual and infrequent.
- Disclose the income tax effect of each component of income, beginning with income before any irregular items.
- Report irregular items net of any income tax effect.

SOLUTION

AIR CORPORATION
Income Statement (partial)

Income before income taxes	$400,000
Income tax expense (30%)	120,000
Income before extraordinary item	280,000
Extraordinary loss net of $30,000 income tax saving	70,000
Net income	$210,000

Related exercise material: *BE19-12, BE19-13, BE19-14, E19-11, and E19-12.*

☑ THE NAVIGATOR

Limitations of Financial Statement Analysis

Significant business decisions are frequently made using one or more of the analytical tools illustrated in this chapter. But, you should be aware of the limitations of these tools and of the financial statements on which they are based.

STUDY OBJECTIVE 7

Recognize the limitations of financial statement analysis.

Estimates
Financial statements contain numerous estimates. Estimates are used in determining the allowance for uncollectible receivables, periodic depreciation, the costs of warranties, and contingent losses. To the extent that these estimates are inaccurate, the financial ratios and percentages are inaccurate.

Cost
Traditional financial statements are based on cost. They are not adjusted for price-level changes. Comparisons of unadjusted financial data from different periods may be rendered invalid by significant inflation or deflation. For example, a five-year comparison of Sears's revenues might show a growth of 36%. But this growth trend would be misleading if the general price level had increased significantly during the same period.

Alternative Accounting Methods
Companies vary in the generally accepted accounting principles they use. Such variations may hamper comparability. For example, one company may use the FIFO method of inventory costing; another company in the same industry may use LIFO. If inventory is a significant asset to both companies, it is unlikely that their current ratios are comparable. For example, if **General Motors Corporation** had used FIFO instead of LIFO in valuing its inventories, its inventories would have been 26% higher. This difference would significantly affect the current ratio (and other ratios as well). In addition to differences in inventory costing methods, differences also exist in reporting such items as depreciation, depletion, and amortization. These differences in accounting methods might be detectable from reading the notes to the financial statements. But, adjusting the financial data to compensate for the different methods is difficult, if not impossible in some cases.

Atypical Data

Fiscal year-end data may not be typical of the financial condition during the year. Firms frequently establish a fiscal year-end that coincides with the low point in operating activity or in inventory levels. Therefore, certain account balances (cash, receivables, payables, and inventories) may not be representative of the balances in the accounts during the year.

Diversification of Firms

Diversification within a global environment also limits the usefulness of financial analysis. Many firms today are so diversified that they cannot be classified by a single industry—they are true [conglomerates. Others appear to be comparable but are not.

BEFORE YOU GO ON...

Review It

1. What are some limitations of financial statement analysis?
2. Give examples of alternative accounting methods that hamper comparability.
3. In what way does diversification limit the usefulness of financial statement analysis?

 THE NAVIGATOR

DEMONSTRATION PROBLEM 1

The condensed financial statements ot The Estée Lauder Companies, Inc., for the years ended June 30, 2002 and 2001, are presented below.

THE ESTÉE LAUDER COMPANIES, INC.
Balance Sheets
June 30

Assets	(in millions) 2002	2001
Current assets		
Cash and cash equivalents	$ 546.9	$ 346.7
Accounts receivable (net)	624.8	580.6
Inventories	544.5	630.3
Prepaid expenses and other current assets	211.4	181.3
Total current assets	1,927.6	1,738.9
Property, plant, and equipment (net)	580.7	528.7
Investments	30.3	41.0
Intangibles and other assets	877.9	910.2
Total assets	$3,416.5	$3,218.8
Liabilities and Stockholders' Equity		
Current liabilities	$ 959.6	$ 856.7
Long-term liabilities	635.0	650.0
Stockholders' equity—common	1,821.9	1,712.1
Total liabilities and stockholders' equity	$3,416.5	$3,218.8

THE ESTÉE LAUDER COMPANIES, INC.
Income Statements
For the Year Ended June 30

	(in millions)	
	2002	**2001**
Revenues	$4,751.5	$4,682.1
Costs and expenses		
Cost of goods sold	1,273.4	1,226.4
Selling and administrative expenses	3,133.6	2,947.6
Interest expense	17.6	26.7
Total costs and expenses	4,424.6	4,200.7
Income before income taxes	326.9	481.4
Income tax expense	114.4	174.0
Net income	$ 212.5	$ 307.4

Instructions

Compute the following ratios for 2002 and 2001.

(a) Current ratio.
(b) Inventory turnover. (Inventory on 6/30/00 was $546.3.)
(c) Profit margin ratio.
(d) Return on assets. (Assets on 6/30/00 were $3,043.3.)
(e) Return on common stockholders' equity. (Equity on 6/30/00 was $1,520.3.)
(f) Debt to total assets ratio.
(g) Times interest earned.

SOLUTION TO DEMONSTRATION PROBLEM 1

	2002	2001
(a) Current ratio:		
$1,927.6 ÷ $959.6 =	2.0:1	
$1,738.9 ÷ $856.7 =		2.0:1
(b) Inventory turnover:		
$1,273.4 ÷ [($544.5 + $630.3) ÷ 2] =	2.2 times	
$1,226.4 ÷ [($630.3 + $546.3) ÷ 2] =		2.1 times
(c) Profit margin:		
$212.5 ÷ $4,751.5	4.5%	
$307.4 ÷ $4,682.1		6.6%
(d) Return on assets:		
$212.5 ÷ [($3,416.5 + $3,218.8) ÷ 2] =	6.4%	
$307.4 ÷ [($3,218.8 + $3,043.3) ÷ 2] =		9.8%
(e) Return on common stockholders' equity:		
$212.5 ÷ [($1,821.9 + $1,712.1) ÷ 2] =	12%	
$307.4 ÷ [($1,712.1 + $1,520.3) ÷ 2] =		19%
(f) Debt to total assets ratio:		
($959.6 + $635.0) ÷ $3,416.5 =	47%	
($856.7 + $650.0) ÷ $3,218.8 =		47%
(g) Times interest earned:		
($212.5 + $114.4 + $17.6) ÷ $17.6 =	19.6 times	
($307.4 + $174.0 + $26.7) ÷ $26.7 =		19.0 times

THE NAVIGATOR

ACTION PLAN

- Remember that the current ratio includes all current assets. The acid-test ratio uses only cash, temporary investments, and net receivables.

- Use average balances for turnover ratios like inventory, receivables, and assets.

- Remember that return on assets is less than or equal to return on common stockholders' equity depending on cost of debt.

DEMONSTRATION PROBLEM 2

The events and transactions of Dever Corporation for the year ending December 31, 2005, resulted in the following data.

Cost of goods sold	$2,600,000
Net sales	4,400,000
Other expenses and losses	9,600
Other revenues and gains	5,600
Selling and administrative expenses	1,100,000
Income from operations of plastics division	70,000
Gain from disposal of plastics division	500,000
Loss from tornado disaster (extraordinary loss)	600,000
Cumulative effect of changing from straight-line depreciation to double-declining-balance (increase in depreciation expense)	300,000

Analysis reveals that:

1. All items are before the applicable income tax rate of 30%.
2. The plastics division was sold on July 1.
3. All operating data for the plastics division have been segregated.

Instructions

Prepare an income statement for the year.

SOLUTION TO DEMONSTRATION PROBLEM 2

ACTION PLAN

- Report material items not typical of operations in separate sections, net of taxes.
- Associate income taxes with the item that affects the taxes.
- Apply the corporate tax rate to income before income taxes to determine tax expense.
- Recall that all data presented in determining income before income taxes are the same as for unincorporated companies.

DEVER CORPORATION
Income Statement
For the Year Ended December 31, 2005

Net sales			$4,400,000
Cost of goods sold			2,600,000
Gross profit			1,800,000
Selling and administrative expenses			1,100,000
Income from operations			700,000
Other revenues and gains		$ 5,600	
Other expenses and losses		9,600	4,000
Income before income taxes			696,000
Income tax expense ($696,000 × 30%)			208,800
Income from continuing operations			487,200
Discontinued operations			
Income from operations of plastics division, net of $21,000 income taxes ($70,000 × 30%)		49,000	
Gain from disposal of plastics division, net of $150,000 income taxes ($500,000 × 30%)		350,000	399,000
Income before extraordinary item and cumulative effect of change in accounting principle			886,200
Extraordinary item			
Tornado loss, net of $180,000 income tax saving ($600,000 × 30%)			420,000
Cumulative effect of change in accounting principle			
Effect on prior years of change in depreciation method, net of $90,000 income tax saving ($300,000 × 30%)			210,000
Net income			$ 256,200

☑ THE NAVIGATOR

SUMMARY OF STUDY OBJECTIVES

1. **Discuss the need for comparative analysis.** There are three bases of comparison: (1) Intracompany, which compares an item or financial relationship with other data within a company. (2) Industry, which compares company data with industry averages. (3) Intercompany, which compares an item or financial relationship of a company with data of one or more competing companies.

2. **Identify the tools of financial statement analysis.** Financial statements can be analyzed horizontally, vertically, and with ratios.

3. **Explain and apply horizontal (trend) analysis.** Horizontal analysis is a technique for evaluating a series of data over a period of time to determine the increase or decrease that has taken place, expressed as either an amount or a percentage.

4. **Describe and apply vertical analysis.** Vertical analysis is a technique that expresses each item within a financial statement in terms of a percentage of a relevant total or a base amount.

5. **Identify and compute ratios, and describe their purpose and use in analyzing a firm's liquidity, profitability, and solvency.** The formula and purpose of each ratio was presented in Illustration 19-27.

6. **Understand the concept of earning power, and indicate how material items not typical of regular operations are presented.** Earning power refers to a company's ability to sustain its profits from operations. "Irregular items"—discontinued operations, extraordinary items, and changes in accounting principles—are presented net of tax below income from continuing operations to highlight their unusual nature.

7. **Recognize the limitations of financial statement analysis.** The usefulness of analytical tools is limited by the use of estimates, the cost basis, the application of alternative accounting methods, atypical data at year-end, and the diversification of firms.

GLOSSARY

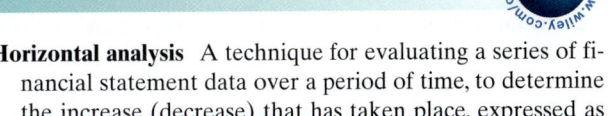

Acid-test (quick) ratio A measure of a company's immediate short-term liquidity; computed by dividing the sum of cash, short-term investments, and net receivables by current liabilities. (p. 776).

Asset turnover A measure of how efficiently a company uses its assets to generate sales; computed by dividing net sales by average assets. (p. 780).

Change in accounting principle The use of a principle in the current year that is different from the one used in the preceding year. (p. 789).

Comprehensive income Includes all changes in stockholders' equity during a period except those resulting from investments by stockholders and distributions to stockholders. (p. 790).

Current ratio A measure used to evaluate a company's liquidity and short-term debt-paying ability; computed by dividing current assets by current liabilities. (p. 775).

Debt to total assets ratio Measures the percentage of total assets provided by creditors; computed by dividing total debt by total assets. (p. 783).

Discontinued operations The disposal of a significant segment of a business. (p. 786).

Earnings per share (EPS) The net income earned on each share of common stock; computed by dividing net income by the number of weighted average common shares outstanding. (p. 781).

Extraordinary items Events and transactions that are unusual in nature and infrequent in occurrence. (p. 787).

Horizontal analysis A technique for evaluating a series of financial statement data over a period of time, to determine the increase (decrease) that has taken place, expressed as either an amount or a percentage. (p. 769).

Inventory turnover A measure of the liquidity of inventory; computed by dividing cost of goods sold by average inventory. (p. 778).

Leverage See Trading on the equity.

Liquidity ratios Measures of the short-term ability of the enterprise to pay its maturing obligations and to meet unexpected needs for cash. (p. 775).

Payout ratio Measures the percentage of earnings distributed in the form of cash dividends; computed by dividing cash dividends by net income. (p. 782).

Price-earnings (P-E) ratio Measures the ratio of the market price of each share of common stock to the earnings per share; computed by dividing the market price of the stock by earnings per share. (p. 782).

Profit margin Measures the percentage of each dollar of sales that results in net income; computed by dividing net income by net sales. (p. 779).

Profitability ratios Measures of the income or operating success of an enterprise for a given period of time. (p. 779).

Ratio An expression of the mathematical relationship between one quantity and another. The relationship may be expressed either as a percentage, a rate, or a simple proportion. (p. 774).

Ratio analysis A technique for evaluating financial statements that expresses the relationship between selected financial statement data. (p. 774).

Receivables turnover A measure of the liquidity of receivables; computed by dividing net credit sales by average net receivables. (p. 777).

Return on assets An overall measure of profitability; computed by dividing net income by average assets. (p. 780).

Return on common stockholders' equity Measures the dollars of net income earned for each dollar invested by the owners; computed by dividing net income by average common stockholders' equity. (p. 780).

Solvency ratios Measures of the ability of the enterprise to survive over a long period of time. (p. 783).

Times interest earned Measures a company's ability to meet interest payments as they come due; computed by dividing income before interest expense and income taxes by interest expense. (p. 784).

Trading on the equity (leverage) Borrowing money at a lower rate of interest than can be earned by using the borrowed money. (p. 781).

Vertical analysis A technique for evaluating financial statement data that expresses each item within a financial statement as a percent of a base amount. (p. 772).

SELF-STUDY QUESTIONS

Self-Study/Self-Test

Answers are at the end of the chapter.

(SO 1) **1.** Comparisons of data within a company are an example of the following comparative basis:
   a. Industry averages.
   b. Intracompany.
   c. Intercompany.
   d. Both (b) and (c).

(SO 3) **2.** In horizontal analysis, each item is expressed as a percentage of the:
   a. net income amount.
   b. stockholders' equity amount.
   c. total assets amount.
   d. base year amount.

(SO 4) **3.** In vertical analysis, the base amount for depreciation expense is generally:
   a. net sales.
   b. depreciation expense in a previous year.
   c. gross profit.
   d. fixed assets.

(SO 4) **4.** The following schedule is a display of what type of analysis?

	Amount	Percent
Current assets	$200,000	25%
Property, plant, and equipment	600,000	75%
Total assets	$800,000	

   a. Horizontal analysis.
   b. Differential analysis.
   c. Vertical analysis.
   d. Ratio analysis.

(SO 3) **5.** Sammy Corporation reported net sales of $300,000, $330,000, and $360,000 in the years, 2003, 2004, and 2005, respectively. If 2003 is the base year, what is the trend percentage for 2005?
   a. 77%.
   b. 108%.

   c. 120%.
   d. 130%.

(SO **6.** Which of the following measures is an evaluation of a firm's ability to pay current liabilities?
   a. Acid-test ratio.
   b. Current ratio.
   c. Both (a) and (b).
   d. None of the above.

(SO **7.** A measure useful in evaluating the efficiency in managing inventories is:
   a. inventory turnover.
   b. average days to sell inventory.
   c. Both (a) and (b).
   d. None of the above.

(SO **8.** In reporting discontinued operations, the income statement should show in a special section:
   a. gains and losses on the disposal of the discontinued segment.
   b. gains and losses from operations of the discontinued segment.
   c. Both (a) and (b).
   d. Neither (a) nor (b).

(SO **9.** Scout Corporation has income before taxes of $400,000 and an extraordinary loss of $100,000. If the income tax rate is 25% on all items, the income statement should show income before extraordinary items and extraordinary items, respectively, of:
   a. $325,000 and $100,000.
   b. $325,000 and $75,000.
   c. $300,000 and $100,000
   d. $300,000 and $75,000.

(SO **10.** Which of the following is generally *not* considered to be a limitation of financial analysis?
   a. Use of estimates.
   b. Use of ratio analysis.
   c. Use of cost.
   d. Use of alternative accounting methods.

QUESTIONS

1. (a) Alan Rodriquez believes that the analysis of financial statements is directed at two characteristics of a company: liquidity and profitability. Is Alan correct? Explain.

   (b) Are short-term creditors, long-term creditors, and stockholders interested primarily in the same characteristics of a company? Explain.

2. (a) Distinguish among the following bases of comparison: (1) intracompany, (2) industry averages, and (3) intercompany.

   (b) Give the principal value of using each of the three bases of comparison.

3. Two popular methods of financial statement analysis are horizontal analysis and vertical analysis. Explain the difference between these two methods.

4. (a) If Roberts Company had net income of $480,000 in 2005 and it experienced a 24.5% increase in net income for 2006, what is its net income for 2006?

   (b) If six cents of every dollar of Roberts revenue is net income in 2005, what is the dollar amount of 2005 revenue?

5. What is a ratio? What are the different ways of expressing the relationship of two amounts? What information does a ratio provide?

6. Name the major ratios useful in assessing (a) liquidity and (b) solvency.

7. Angeles Ochoa is puzzled. His company had a profit margin of 10% in 2005. He feels that this is an indication that the company is doing well. Celia Cruz, his accountant, says that more information is needed to determine the firm's financial well-being. Who is correct? Why?

8. What do the following classes of ratios measure? (a) Liquidity ratios. (b) Profitability ratios. (c) Solvency ratios.

9. What is the difference between the current ratio and the acid-test ratio?

10. Bloom Company, a retail store, has a receivables turnover of 4.5 times. The industry average is 12.5 times. Does Bloom have a collection problem with its receivables?

11. Which ratios should be used to help answer the following questions?

   (a) How efficient is a company in using its assets to produce sales?

   (b) How near to sale is the inventory on hand?

   (c) How many dollars of net income were earned for each dollar invested by the owners?

   (d) How able is a company to meet interest charges as they fall due?

12. The price-earnings ratio of **General Motors** (automobile builder) was 8, and the price-earnings ratio of **Microsoft** (computer software) was 38. Which company did the stock market favor? Explain.

13. What is the formula for computing the payout ratio? Would you expect this ratio to be high or low for a growth company?

14. Holding all other factors constant, indicate whether each of the following changes generally signals good or bad news about a company.

   (a) Increase in profit margin.

   (b) Decrease in inventory turnover.

   (c) Increase in the current ratio.

   (d) Decrease in earnings per share.

   (e) Increase in price-earnings ratio.

   (f) Increase in debt to total assets ratio.

   (g) Decrease in times interest earned.

15. The return on total assets for Wyeth Corporation is 7.6%. During the same year Wyeth's return on common stockholders' equity is 12.8%. What is the explanation for the difference in the two rates?

16. Which two ratios do you think should be of greatest interest to:

   (a) A pension fund considering the purchase of 20-year bonds?

   (b) A bank contemplating a short-term loan?

   (c) A common stockholder?

17. Why must preferred stock dividends be subtracted from net income in computing earnings per share?

18. (a) What is meant by trading on the equity?

   (b) How would you determine the profitability of trading on the equity?

19. Jackson Inc. has net income of $210,000, weighted average shares of common stock outstanding of 50,000, and preferred dividends for the period of $40,000. What is Jackson's earnings per share of common stock? Kate Jackson, the president of Jackson Inc., believes the computed EPS of the company is high. Comment.

20. Why is it important to report discontinued operations separately from income from continuing operations?

21. You are considering investing in Cederno Transportation. The company reports 2005 earnings per share of $6.50 on income before extraordinary items and $4.75 on net income. Which EPS figure would you consider more relevant to your investment decision? Why?

22. MCE Inc. reported 2004 earnings per share of $3.20 and had no extraordinary items. In 2005, EPS on income before extraordinary items was $2.99, and EPS on net income was $3.49. Is this a favorable trend?

23. Indicate which of the following items would be reported as an extraordinary item in Weiland Corporation's income statement.

   (a) Loss from damages caused by volcano eruption.

   (b) Loss from sale of temporary investments.

   (c) Loss attributable to a labor strike.

   (d) Loss caused when manufacture of a product was prohibited by the Food and Drug Administration.

   (e) Loss from flood damage. (The nearby Black River floods every 2 to 3 years.)

   (f) Write-down of obsolete inventory.

   (g) Expropriation of a factory by a foreign government.

24. When studying for an accounting test, a fellow student says, "Changes in accounting principle are reported in the retained earnings statement." Is your friend correct, or should he study harder?

25. Identify and briefly explain five limitations of financial analysis.

26. Explain how the choice of one of the following accounting methods over the other raises or lowers a company's net income during a period of continuing inflation.

(a) Use of FIFO instead of LIFO for inventory costing.
(b) Use of a 6-year life for machinery instead of a 9-year life.
(c) Use of straight-line depreciation instead of accelerated declining-balance depreciation.

BRIEF EXERCISES*

Prepare horizontal analysis.
(SO 3)

BE19-1 Using the following data from the comparative balance sheet of Jane Hull Company, illustrate horizontal analysis.

	December 31, 2006	December 31, 2005
Accounts receivable	$ 540,000	$ 400,000
Inventory	$ 840,000	$ 600,000
Total assets	$ 3,640,000	$2,800,000

Prepare vertical analysis.
(SO 4)

BE19-2 Using the same data presented above in BE19-1 for Jane Hull Company, illustrate vertical analysis.

Calculate percentage of change.
(SO 3)

BE19-3 Net income was $500,000 in 2004, $400,000 in 2005, and $508,000 in 2006. What is the percentage of change from (a) 2004 to 2005 and (b) 2005 to 2006? Is the change an increase or a decrease?

Calculate net income.
(SO 3)

BE19-4 If Alana Company had net income of $650,000 in 2006 and it experienced a 30% increase in net income over 2005, what was its 2005 net income?

Calculate change in net income.
(SO 4)

BE19-5 Vertical analysis (common size) percentages for Osborne Company's sales, cost of goods sold, and expenses are shown below.

Vertical Analysis	2006	2005	2004
Sales	100.0	100.0	100.0
Cost of goods sold	59.2	62.4	64.5
Expenses	25.0	26.6	27.5

Did Osborne's net income as a percent of sales increase, decrease, or remain unchanged over the 3-year period? Provide numerical support for your answer.

Calculate change in net income.
(SO 3)

BE19-6 Horizontal analysis (trend analysis) percentages for Klamoth Company's sales, cost of goods sold, and expenses are shown below.

Horizontal Analysis	2006	2005	2004
Sales	96.2	106.8	100.0
Cost of goods sold	102.0	97.0	100.0
Expenses	109.6	98.4	100.0

Did Klamoth's net income increase, decrease, or remain unchanged over the 3-year period?

---

*Follow the rounding procedures used in the chapter.

BE19-7 Selected condensed data taken from a recent balance sheet of Kutenai Inc. are as follows.

Calculate liquidity ratios.

(SO 5)

KUTENAI INC.

Balance Sheet (partial)

Cash	$ 8,041,000
Short-term investments	1,947,000
Accounts receivable	12,545,000
Inventories	14,814,000
Other current assets	5,571,000
Total current assets	$42,918,000
Total current liabilities	$40,644,000

What are the **(a)** working capital, **(b)** current ratio, and **(c)** acid-test ratio?

BE19-8 Augusta Corporation has net income of $11.44 million and net revenue of $88 million in 2005. Its assets are $14 million at the beginning of the year and $18 million at the end of the year. What are **(a)** Augusta's asset turnover and **(b)** profit margin?

Calculate profitability ratios.

(SO 5)

BE19-9 The following data are taken from the financial statements of Abbado Company.

Evaluate collection of accounts receivable.

(SO 5)

	2006	**2005**
Accounts receivable (net), end of year	$ 550,000	$ 520,000
Net sales on account	3,850,000	3,100,000
Terms for all sales are 1/10, n/60.		

(a) Compute for each year (1) the receivables turnover and (2) the average collection period. At the end of 2004, accounts receivable (net) was $490,000.
(b) What conclusions about the management of accounts receivable can be drawn from these data?

BE19-10 The following data are from the income statements of Kristi Thomas Company.

Evaluate management of inventory.

(SO 5)

	2006	**2005**
Sales	$6,420,000	$6,240,000
Beginning inventory	960,000	860,000
Purchases	4,540,000	4,661,000
Ending inventory	1,020,000	960,000

(a) Compute for each year (1) the inventory turnover and (2) the average days to sell the inventory. **(b)** What conclusions concerning the management of the inventory can be drawn from these data?

BE19-11 Watson Company has owners' equity of $400,000 and net income of $54,000. It has a payout ratio of 20% and a rate of return on assets of 15%. How much did Watson pay in cash dividends, and what were its average assets?

Calculate profitability ratios.

(SO 5)

BE19-12 An inexperienced accountant for Omar Corporation showed the following in the income statement: income before income taxes and extraordinary item $400,000, and extraordinary loss from flood (before taxes) $70,000. The extraordinary loss and taxable income are both subject to a 25% tax rate. Prepare a correct income statement.

Prepare income statement including extraordinary items.

(SO 6)

BE19-13 On June 30, Tanner Corporation discontinued its operations in Mexico. During the year, the operating loss was $300,000 before taxes. On September 1, Tanner disposed of the Mexico facility at a pretax loss of $160,000. The applicable tax rate is 30%. Show the discontinued operations section of the income statement.

Prepare discontinued operations section of income statement.

(SO 6)

BE19-14 On January 1, 2005, Ramirez Inc. changed from the straight-line method of depreciation to the declining-balance method. The cumulative effect of the change was to increase prior years' depreciation by $60,000 and 2005 depreciation by $8,000. Show the change in accounting principle section of the 2005 income statement, assuming the tax rate is 30%.

Prepare change in accounting principle section of income statement.

(SO 6)

EXERCISES*

Prepare horizontal analysis.

(SO 3)

E19-1 Financial information for Marysara Inc. is presented below.

	December 31, 2006	December 31, 2005
Current assets	$125,000	$100,000
Plant assets (net)	380,000	330,000
Current liabilities	91,000	70,000
Long-term liabilities	140,000	95,000
Common stock, $1 par	135,000	115,000
Retained earnings	139,000	150,000

Instructions

Prepare a schedule showing a horizontal analysis for 2006 using 2005 as the base year.

Prepare vertical analysis.

(SO 4)

E19-2 Operating data for Jessi Corporation are presented below.

	2006	2005
Sales	$800,000	$600,000
Cost of goods sold	472,000	390,000
Selling expenses	120,000	72,000
Administrative expenses	76,000	54,000
Income tax expense	33,000	21,000
Net income	99,000	63,000

Instructions

Prepare a schedule showing a vertical analysis for 2006 and 2005.

Prepare horizontal and vertical analyses.

(SO 3, 4)

E19-3 The comparative balance sheets of Ramsey Corporation are presented below.

RAMSEY CORPORATION
Comparative Balance Sheets
December 31

	2006	2005
Assets		
Current assets	$ 76,000	$ 80,000
Property, plant, and equipment (net)	99,000	90,000
Intangibles	25,000	40,000
Total assets	$200,000	$210,000
Liabilities and stockholders' equity		
Current liabilities	$ 40,800	$ 48,000
Long-term liabilities	143,000	150,000
Stockholders' equity	16,200	12,000
Total liabilities and stockholders' equity	$200,000	$210,000

Instructions

(a) Prepare a horizontal analysis of the balance sheet data for Ramsey Corporation using 2005 as a base.

(b) Prepare a vertical analysis of the balance sheet data for Ramsey Corporation in columnar form for 2006.

---

*Follow the rounding procedures used in the chapter.

E19-4 The comparative income statements of Accra Corporation are shown below.

Prepare horizontal and vertical analyses.

(SO 3, 4)

ACCRA CORPORATION
Comparative Income Statements
For the Years Ended December 31

	2006	2005
Net sales	$600,000	$500,000
Cost of goods sold	480,000	420,000
Gross profit	120,000	80,000
Operating expenses	57,200	44,000
Net income	$ 62,800	$ 36,000

Instructions
(a) Prepare a horizontal analysis of the income statement data for Accra Corporation using 2005 as a base. (Show the amounts of increase or decrease.)
(b) Prepare a vertical analysis of the income statement data for Accra Corporation in columnar form for both years.

E19-5 **Nordstrom, Inc.** operates department stores in numerous states. Selected financial statement data for the year ending January 31, 2002, are as follows.

Compute liquidity ratios and compare results.

(SO 5)

NORDSTROM

NORDSTROM, INC.
Balance Sheet (partial)

(in millions)	End-of-Year	Beginning-of-Year
Cash and cash equivalents	$ 331	$ 25
Receivables (less allowance of 23 and 17)	699	722
Merchandise inventory	888	946
Prepaid expenses	37	29
Other current assets	102	91
Total current assets	$2,057	$1,813
Total current liabilities	$ 950	$ 951

For the year, net sales were $5,634, and cost of goods sold was $3,766.

Instructions
(a) Compute the four liquidity ratios at the end of the current year.
(b) Using the data in the chapter, compare Nordstrom's liquidity with (1) that of **Sears, Roebuck and Co.**, and (2) the industry averages for department stores.

E19-6 Seliz Incorporated had the following transactions occur involving current assets and current liabilities during February 2005.

Perform current and acid-test ratio analysis.

(SO 5)

Feb. 3	Accounts receivable of $15,000 are collected.
7	Equipment is purchased for $28,000 cash.
11	Paid $3,000 for a 3-year insurance policy.
14	Accounts payable of $12,000 are paid.
18	Cash dividends of $5,000 are declared.

Additional information:

1. As of February 1, 2005, current assets were $140,000, and current liabilities were $50,000.
2. As of February 1, 2005, current assets included $15,000 of inventory and $2,000 of prepaid expenses.

Instructions
(a) Compute the current ratio as of the beginning of the month and after each transaction.
(b) Compute the acid-test ratio as of the beginning of the month and after each transaction.

Compute selected ratios.

(SO 5)

E19-7 Marcus Company has the following comparative balance sheet data.

MARCUS COMPANY
Balance Sheets
December 31

	2005	2004
Cash	$ 15,000	$ 30,000
Receivables (net)	70,000	60,000
Inventories	60,000	50,000
Plant assets (net)	200,000	180,000
	$345,000	$320,000
Accounts payable	$ 40,000	$ 60,000
Mortgage payable (15%)	100,000	100,000
Common stock, $10 par	140,000	120,000
Retained earnings	65,000	40,000
	$345,000	$320,000

Additional information for 2005:

1. Net income was $25,000.
2. Sales on account were $420,000. Sales returns and allowances were $20,000.
3. Cost of goods sold was $198,000.
4. The allowance for doubtful accounts was $2,500 on December 31, 2005, and $2,000 on December 31, 2004.

Instructions
Compute the following ratios at December 31, 2005.

(a) Current.
(b) Acid-test.
(c) Receivables turnover.
(d) Inventory turnover.

Compute selected ratios.

(SO 5)

E19-8 Selected comparative statement data for Crimson Tide Products Company are presented below. All balance sheet data are as of December 31.

	2006	2005
Net sales	$800,000	$720,000
Cost of goods sold	480,000	440,000
Interest expense	7,000	5,000
Net income	60,000	42,000
Accounts receivable	120,000	100,000
Inventory	85,000	75,000
Total assets	580,000	500,000
Total common stockholders' equity	430,000	325,000

Instructions
Compute the following ratios for 2006.

(a) Profit margin.
(b) Asset turnover.
(c) Return on assets.
(d) Return on common stockholders' equity.

E19-9 The income statement for Nancy Kwan, Inc., appears below.

Compute selected ratios.
(SO 5)

NANCY KWAN, INC.
Income Statement
For the Year Ended December 31, 2005

Sales	$400,000
Cost of goods sold	230,000
Gross profit	170,000
Expenses (including $16,000 interest and $24,000 income taxes)	100,000
Net income	$ 70,000

Additional information:

1. The weighted average common shares outstanding in 2005 were 30,000 shares.
2. The market price of Nancy Kwan, Inc. stock was $13 in 2005.
3. Cash dividends of $23,000 were paid, $5,000 of which were to preferred stockholders.

Instructions
Compute the following ratios for 2005.

(a) Earnings per share.
(b) Price-earnings.
(c) Payout.
(d) Times interest earned.

E19-10 Sosa Corporation experienced a fire on December 31, 2006, in which its financial records were partially destroyed. It has been able to salvage some of the records and has ascertained the following balances.

Compute amounts from ratios.
(SO 5)

	December 31, 2006	December 31, 2005
Cash	$ 30,000	$ 10,000
Receivables (net)	72,500	126,000
Inventory	200,000	180,000
Accounts payable	50,000	90,000
Notes payable	30,000	60,000
Common stock, $100 par	400,000	400,000
Retained earnings	113,500	101,000

Additional information:

1. The inventory turnover is 3.2 times.
2. The return on common stockholders' equity is 22%. The company had no additional paid-in capital.
3. The receivables turnover is 8.4 times.
4. The return on assets is 20%.
5. Total assets at December 31, 2005, were $605,000.

Instructions
Compute the following for Sosa Corporation.

(a) Cost of goods sold for 2006.
(b) Net sales (credit) for 2006.
(c) Net income for 2006.
(d) Total assets at December 31, 2006.

Prepare a correct income statement.

(SO 6)

E19-11 For its fiscal year ending October 31, 2005, Moreno Corporation reports the following partial data.

Income before income taxes	$540,000
Income tax expense (30% × $440,000)	132,000
Income before extraordinary items	408,000
Extraordinary loss from flood	100,000
Net income	$308,000

The flood loss is considered an extraordinary item. The income tax rate is 30% on all items.

Instructions

(a) Prepare a correct income statement, beginning with income before income taxes.

(b) 🖉 Explain in memo form why the income statement data are misleading.

Prepare income statement.

(SO 6)

E19-12 Servia Corporation has income from continuing operations of $240,000 for the year ended December 31, 2005. It also has the following items (before considering income taxes).

1. An extraordinary loss of $80,000.
2. A gain of $30,000 on the discontinuance of a division.
3. A cumulative change in an accounting principle that resulted in an increase in prior years' depreciation of $40,000.
4. A correction of an error in last year's financial statements that resulted in a $10,000 understatement of 2004 net income.

Assume all items are subject to income taxes at a 30% tax rate.

Instructions

(a) Prepare an income statement, beginning with income from continuing operations.

(b) Indicate the statement presentation of any item not included in (a) above.

PROBLEMS *

Prepare vertical analysis and comment on profitability.

(SO 4, 5)

P19-1 Comparative statement data for Rocking Company and Rolling Company, two competitors, appear below. All balance sheet data are as of December 31, 2006, and December 31, 2005.

	Rocking Company		Rolling Company	
	2006	**2005**	**2006**	**2005**
Net sales	$1,549,035		$339,038	
Cost of goods sold	1,080,490		241,000	
Operating expenses	292,275		79,000	
Interest expense	8,980		2,252	
Income tax expense	44,500		6,650	
Current assets	325,975	$312,410	83,336	$ 79,467
Plant assets (net)	521,310	500,000	139,728	125,812
Current liabilities	70,325	75,815	35,348	30,281
Long-term liabilities	108,500	90,000	29,620	25,000
Common stock, $10 par	500,000	500,000	120,000	120,000
Retained earnings	168,460	146,595	38,096	29,998

Instructions

(a) Prepare a vertical analysis of the 2006 income statement data for Rocking Company and Rolling Company in columnar form.

(b) 🖉 Comment on the relative profitability of the companies by computing the return on assets and the return on common stockholders' equity ratios for both companies.

---

*Follow the rounding procedures used in the chapter.

P19-2 The comparative statements of Taylor Tool Company are presented below.

Compute ratios from balance sheet and income statement.

(SO 5)

TAYLOR TOOL COMPANY
Income Statement
For the Year Ended December 31

	2005	2004
Net sales	$1,818,500	$1,750,500
Cost of goods sold	1,011,500	996,000
Gross profit	807,000	754,500
Selling and administrative expense	506,000	479,000
Income from operations	301,000	275,500
Other expenses and losses		
Interest expense	18,000	14,000
Income before income taxes	283,000	261,500
Income tax expense	84,000	77,000
Net income	$199,000	$184,500

TAYLOR TOOL COMPANY
Balance Sheets
December 31

Assets	2005	2004
Current assets		
Cash	$ 60,100	$ 64,200
Short-term investments	69,000	50,000
Accounts receivable (net)	107,800	102,800
Inventory	133,000	115,500
Total current assets	369,900	332,500
Plant assets (net)	600,300	520,300
Total assets	$970,200	$852,800
Liabilities and Stockholders' Equity		
Current liabilities		
Accounts payable	$160,000	$145,400
Income taxes payable	43,500	42,000
Total current liabilities	203,500	187,400
Bonds payable	200,000	200,000
Total liabilities	403,500	387,400
Stockholders' equity		
Common stock ($5 par)	280,000	300,000
Retained earnings	286,700	165,400
Total stockholders' equity	566,700	465,400
Total liabilities and stockholders' equity	$970,200	$852,800

All sales were on account. The allowance for doubtful accounts was $3,200 on December 31, 2005, and $3,000 on December 31, 2004.

Instructions
Compute the following ratios for 2005. (Weighted average common shares in 2005 were 57,000.)

(a) Earnings per share.
(b) Return on common stockholders' equity.
(c) Return on assets.
(d) Current.
(e) Acid-test.

(f) Receivables turnover.
(g) Inventory turnover.
(h) Times interest earned.
(i) Asset turnover.
(j) Debt to total assets.

Perform ratio analysis, and
evaluate financial position and
operating results.

(SO 5)

P19-3 Condensed balance sheet and income statement data for Jeff Malone Corporation appear below.

JEFF MALONE CORPORATION
Balance Sheets
December 31

	2006	2005	2004
Cash	$ 25,000	$ 20,000	$ 18,000
Receivables (net)	50,000	45,000	48,000
Other current assets	90,000	95,000	64,000
Investments	75,000	70,000	45,000
Plant and equipment (net)	400,000	370,000	358,000
	$640,000	$600,000	$533,000
Current liabilities	$ 75,000	$ 80,000	$ 70,000
Long-term debt	80,000	85,000	50,000
Common stock, $10 par	340,000	310,000	300,000
Retained earnings	145,000	125,000	113,000
	$640,000	$600,000	$533,000

JEFF MALONE CORPORATION
Income Statement
For the Year Ended December 31

	2006	2005
Sales	$740,000	$700,000
Less: Sales returns and allowances	40,000	50,000
Net sales	700,000	650,000
Cost of goods sold	420,000	400,000
Gross profit	280,000	250,000
Operating expenses (including income taxes)	232,000	218,000
Net income	$ 48,000	$ 32,000

Additional information:

1. The market price of Malone's common stock was $4.00, $5.00, and $8.00 for 2004, 2005, and 2006, respectively.
2. All dividends were paid in cash.

Instructions

(a) Compute the following ratios for 2005 and 2006.

(1) Profit margin.
(2) Asset turnover.
(3) Earnings per share. (Weighted average common shares in 2006 were 32,000 and in 2005 were 31,000.)
(4) Price-earnings.
(5) Payout.
(6) Debt to total assets.

(b) ▭▭▭▷ Based on the ratios calculated, discuss briefly the improvement or lack thereof in financial position and operating results from 2005 to 2006 of Jeff Malone Corporation.

P19-4 Financial information for Fat Cat Company is presented below.

Compute ratios, and comment on overall liquidity and profitability.

(SO 5)

FAT CAT COMPANY
Balance Sheets
December 31

Assets	2006	2005
Cash	$ 70,000	$ 65,000
Short-term investments	52,000	40,000
Receivables (net)	94,000	90,000
Inventories	129,000	125,000
Prepaid expenses	29,000	23,000
Land	130,000	130,000
Building and equipment (net)	180,000	175,000
	$684,000	$648,000

Liabilities and Stockholders' Equity		
Notes payable	$100,000	$100,000
Accounts payable	48,000	42,000
Accrued liabilities	50,000	40,000
Bonds payable, due 2009	150,000	150,000
Common stock, $10 par	200,000	200,000
Retained earnings	136,000	116,000
	$684,000	$648,000

FAT CAT COMPANY
Income Statement
For the Years Ended December 31

	2006	2005
Sales	$850,000	$790,000
Cost of goods sold	620,000	575,000
Gross profit	230,000	215,000
Operating expenses	194,000	180,000
Net income	$ 36,000	$ 35,000

Additional information:

1. Inventory at the beginning of 2005 was $118,000.
2. Receivables (net) at the beginning of 2005 were $88,000. The allowance for doubtful accounts was $4,000 at the end of 2006, $3,800 at the end of 2005, and $3,700 at the beginning of 2005.
3. Total assets at the beginning of 2005 were $630,000.
4. No common stock transactions occurred during 2005 or 2006.
5. All sales were on account.

Instructions

(a) Indicate, by using ratios, the change in liquidity and profitability of Fat Cat Company from 2005 to 2006. (*Note:* Not all profitability ratios can be computed.)
(b) Given below are three independent situations and a ratio that may be affected. For each situation, compute the affected ratio (1) as of December 31, 2006, and (2) as of December 31, 2007, after giving effect to the situation. Net income for 2007 was $45,000. Total assets on December 31, 2007, were $700,000.

Situation	Ratio
(1) 18,000 shares of common stock were sold at par on July 1, 2007.	Return on common stockholders' equity
(2) All of the notes payable were paid in 2007. The only change in liabilities was that the notes payable were paid.	Debt to total assets
(3) Market price of common stock was $9 on December 31, 2006, and $12.80 on December 31, 2007.	Price-earnings ratio

Compute selected ratios, and compare liquidity, profitability, and solvency for two companies.

(SO 5)

P19-5 Selected financial data of **Target** and **Wal-Mart** for 2001 are presented here (in millions).

	Target Corporation	Wal-Mart Stores, Inc.
	Income Statement Data for Year	
Net sales	$39,176	$217,799
Cost of goods sold	27,246	171,562
Selling and administrative expenses	9,962	36,173
Interest expense	464	1,326
Other income (expense)	712	2,013
Income tax expense	842	3,897
Net income	$ 1,374	$ 6,854
	Balance Sheet Data (End of Year)	
Current assets	$ 9,648	$ 28,246
Noncurrent assets	14,506	55,205
Total assets	$24,154	$ 83,451
Current liabilities	$ 7,054	$ 27,282
Long-term debt	9,240	21,067
Total stockholders' equity	7,860	35,102
Total liabilities and stockholders' equity	$24,154	$ 83,451
	Beginning-of-Year Balances	
Total assets	$19,490	$ 78,130
Total stockholders' equity	6,519	31,343
Current liabilities	6,301	28,949
Total liabilities	12,971	46,787
	Other Data	
Average net receivables	$ 1,916	$ 1,884
Average inventory	4,349	22,028
Net cash provided by operating activities	1,992	10,260

Instructions

(a) For each company, compute the following ratios.

(1) Current.	**(7)** Asset turnover.
(2) Receivables turnover.	**(8)** Return on assets.
(3) Average collection period.	**(9)** Return on common stockholders' equity.
(4) Inventory turnover.	**(10)** Debt to total assets.
(5) Days in inventory.	**(11)** Times interest earned.
(6) Profit margin.	

(b) Compare the liquidity, solvency, and profitability of the two companies.

Compute numerous ratios.

(SO 5)

P19-6 The comparative statements of Enis Company are presented below.

ENIS COMPANY
Income Statement
For Year Ended December 31

	2006	2005
Net sales (all on account)	$600,000	$520,000
Expenses		
Cost of goods sold	415,000	354,000
Selling and administrative	123,800	114,800
Interest expense	7,800	6,000
Income tax expense	18,000	14,000
Total expenses	564,600	488,800
Net income	$ 35,400	$ 31,200

ENIS COMPANY
Balance Sheets
December 31

Assets	2006	2005
Current assets		
Cash	$ 21,000	$ 18,000
Short-term investments	18,000	15,000
Accounts receivable (net)	92,000	74,000
Inventory	84,000	70,000
Total current assets	215,000	177,000
Plant assets (net)	423,000	383,000
Total assets	$638,000	$560,000

Liabilities and Stockholders' Equity		
Current liabilities		
Accounts payable	$122,000	$110,000
Income taxes payable	23,000	20,000
Total current liabilities	145,000	130,000
Long-term liabilities		
Bonds payable	120,000	80,000
Total liabilities	265,000	210,000
Stockholders' equity		
Common stock ($5 par)	150,000	150,000
Retained earnings	223,000	200,000
Total stockholders' equity	373,000	350,000
Total liabilities and stockholders' equity	$638,000	$560,000

Additional data:

The common stock recently sold at $19.50 per share.

The year-end balance in the allowance for doubtful accounts was $3,000 for 2006 and $2,400 for 2005.

Instructions

Compute the following ratios for 2006.

(a) Current.

(b) Acid-test.

(c) Receivables turnover.

(d) Inventory turnover.

(e) Profit margin.

(f) Asset turnover.

(g) Return on assets.

(h) Return on common stockholders' equity.

(i) Earnings per share.

(j) Price-earnings.

(k) Payout.

(l) Debt to total assets.

(m) Times interest earned.

Compute missing information given a set of ratios.

(SO 5)

P19-7 Presented below is an incomplete income statement and an incomplete comparative balance sheet of Sulu Corporation.

SULU CORPORATION
Income Statement
For the Year Ended December 31, 2006

Sales	$11,000,000
Cost of goods sold	?
Gross profit	?
Operating expenses	1,204,600
Income from operations	?
Other expenses and losses	
Interest expense	?
Income before income taxes	?
Income tax expense	560,000
Net income	$?

SULU CORPORATION
Balance Sheets
December 31

Assets	2006	2005
Current assets		
Cash	$ 450,000	$ 249,000
Accounts receivable (net)	?	1,076,000
Inventory	?	1,720,000
Total current assets	?	3,045,000
Plant assets (net)	4,912,500	3,955,000
Total assets	$?	$7,000,000
Liabilities and Stockholders' Equity		
Current liabilities	$?	$ 825,000
Long-term notes payable	?	2,800,000
Total liabilities	?	3,625,000
Common stock, $1 par	3,000,000	3,000,000
Retained earnings	400,000	375,000
Total stockholders' equity	3,400,000	3,375,000
Total liabilities and stockholders' equity	$?	$7,000,000

Additional information:

1. The receivables turnover for 2006 is 10 times.
2. All sales are on account.
3. The profit margin for 2006 is 11.5%.
4. Return on assets is 16% for 2006.
5. The current ratio on December 31, 2006, is 3.0.
6. The inventory turnover for 2006 is 3.8 times.

Instructions

Compute the missing information given the ratios above. Show computations. (*Note*: Start with one ratio and derive as much information as possible from it before trying another ratio. List all missing amounts under the ratio used to find the information.)

P19-8 Clinton Corporation owns a number of cruise ships and a chain of hotels. The hotels, which have not been profitable, were discontinued on September 1, 2005. The 2005 operating results for the company were as follows.

Prepare income statement with discontinued operations and extraordinary loss.

(SO 6)

Operating revenues	$12,850,000
Operating expenses	8,700,000
Operating income	$ 4,150,000

Analysis discloses that these data include the operating results of the hotel chain, which were: operating revenues $2,500,000 and operating expenses $3,000,000. The hotels were sold at a gain of $200,000 before taxes. This gain is not included in the operating results. During the year, Clinton suffered an extraordinary loss of $600,000 before taxes, which is not included in the operating results. In 2005, the company had other revenues and gains of $100,000, which are not included in the operating results. The corporation is in the 30% income tax bracket.

Instructions
Prepare a condensed income statement.

P19-9 The ledger of Iceland Corporation at December 31, 2005, contains the following summary data.

Prepare income statement with nontypical items.

(SO 6)

Net sales	$1,700,000	Cost of goods sold	$1,100,000
Selling expenses	120,000	Administrative expenses	130,000
Other revenues and gains	20,000	Other expenses and losses	28,000

Your analysis reveals the following additional information that is not included in the above data.

1. The entire puzzles division was discontinued on August 31. The income from operations for this division before income taxes was $20,000. The puzzles division was sold at a loss of $70,000 before income taxes.
2. On May 15, company property was expropriated for an interstate highway. The settlement resulted in an extraordinary gain of $90,000 before income taxes.
3. During the year, Iceland changed its depreciation method from double-declining balance to straight-line. The cumulative effect of the change on prior years' net income was an increase of $80,000 before taxes. (Assume that depreciation under the new method is correctly included in the ledger data.)
4. The income tax rate on all items is 30%.

Instructions
Prepare an income statement for the year ended December 31, 2005. Use the format illustrated in the Demonstration Problem 2 (p. 794).

BROADENING YOUR PERSPECTIVE

Financial Reporting and Analysis

■ FINANCIAL REPORTING PROBLEM: PepsiCo

BYP19-1 Your parents are considering investing in **PepsiCo Inc.**, common stock. They ask you, as an accounting expert, to make an analysis of the company for them. Fortunately, excerpts from a current annual report of PepsiCo are presented in Appendix A of this textbook. Note that all dollar amounts are in millions.

Instructions
(Follow the approach in the chapter for rounding numbers.)

(a) Make a 5-year trend analysis, using 1998 as the base year, of (1) net sales and (2) net income. Comment on the significance of the trend results.
(b) Compute for 2002 and 2001 the (1) profit margin, (2) asset turnover, (3) return on assets, and (4) return on common stockholders' equity. How would you evaluate PepsiCo's profitability? Total assets at December 31, 2000, were $20,757, and total stockholders' equity at December 31, 2000, was $7,604.

(c) Compute for 2002 and 2001 the (1) debt to total assets and (2) times interest earned ratio. How would you evaluate PepsiCo's long-term solvency?

(d) What information outside the annual report may also be useful to your parents in making a decision about PepsiCo, Inc.?

■ **COMPARATIVE ANALYSIS PROBLEM: PepsiCo vs. Coca-Cola**

BYP19-2 PepsiCo's financial statements are presented in Appendix A. **Coca-Cola Company**'s financial statements are presented in Appendix B.

Instructions

(a) Based on the information contained in these financial statements, determine each of the following for each company.

  (1) The percentage increase (decrease) in (i) net sales and (ii) net income from 2001 to 2002.

  (2) The percentage increase in (i) total assets and (ii) total common stockholders' (shareholders') equity from 2001 to 2002.

  (3) The basic earnings per share and price-earnings ratio for 2000. (For Coca-Cola, use the basic earnings per share before the accounting change.) Coca-Cola's common stock had a market price of $43.84 at the end of fiscal-year 2002.

(b) What conclusions concerning the two companies can be drawn from these data?

■ **INTERPRETING FINANCIAL STATEMENTS: A Global Focus**

BYP19-3 In England, the railroads were run by the government until recently. Eight years ago, **Railtrack Group PLC** became a publicly traded company. The largest railroad company in the United States is **Burlington Northern Railroad Company**. The following data were taken from the 1998 financial statements of each company.

Financial Highlights	Railtrack Group (pounds in millions)		Burlington Northern (dollars in millions)	
	1998	**1997**	**1998**	**1997**
Cash and short-term investments	£ 380	£ 26	$ 95	$ –0–
Accounts receivable	434	402	676	632
Total current assets	909	521	1,357	1,197
Total assets	7,095	5,760	22,725	21,199
Current liabilities	1,128	1,209	2,175	2,089
Total liabilities	3,882	2,888	14,497	14,176
Total stockholders' equity	3,213	2,872	8,228	7,023
Sales	2,573		8,936	
Operating costs	2,102		6,781	
Interest expense	93		293	
Income tax expense	3		733	
Net income	425		1,206	
Cash provided by operations	988		2,107	

Instructions

(a) Calculate the following 1998 liquidity ratios and discuss the relative liquidity of the two companies.

  (1) Current ratio.

  (2) Acid-test.

  (3) Receivables turnover.

(b) Calculate the following 1998 solvency ratios and discuss the relative solvency of the two companies.

  (1) Debt to total assets.

  (2) Times interest earned.

(c) Calculate the following 1998 profitability ratios and discuss the relative profitability of the two companies.

  (1) Asset turnover.

  (2) Profit margin.

  (3) Return on assets.

  (4) Return on common stockholders' equity.

(d) What other issues must you consider when comparing these two companies?

■ EXPLORING THE WEB

BYP19-4 The Management Discussion and Analysis section of an annual report addresses corporate performance for the year, and sometimes uses financial ratios to support its claims.

Address: www.ibm.com/financialguide, or go to www.wiley.com/college/weygandt

Steps

1. From IBM's Financial Guide, choose **Getting Started.**
2. Choose **What's an Annual Report.**
3. Choose **Anatomy of an Annual Report.**

Instructions
Using the information from the above site, answer the following questions.

(a) What are the optional elements that are often included in an annual report?
(b) What are the elements of an annual report that are required by the SEC?
(c) Describe the contents of the Management Discussion.
(d) Describe the contents of the Auditors' Report.
(e) Describe the contents of the Selected Financial Data.

Critical Thinking

■ GROUP DECISION CASE

BYP19-5 As the CPA for Roenick Manufacturing Inc., you have been asked to develop some key ratios from the comparative financial statements. This information is to be used to convince creditors that the company is solvent and will continue as a going concern. The data requested and the computations developed from the financial statements follow.

	2003	2002
Current ratio	3.1 times	2.1 times
Acid-test ratio	.8 times	1.4 times
Asset turnover	2.8 times	2.2 times
Net income	Up 32%	Down 8%
Earnings per share	$3.30	$2.50
Book value per share	Up 8%	Up 11%

Instructions
With the class divided into groups, answer the following.

(a) Roenick Manufacturing Inc. asks you to prepare a list of brief comments stating how each of these items supports the solvency and going-concern potential of the business. The company wishes to use these comments to support its presentation of data to its creditors. You are to prepare the comments as requested, giving the implications and the limitations of each item separately. Then prepare a collective inference that may be drawn from the individual items about Roenick's solvency and going-concern potential.
(b) What warnings should you offer these creditors about the limitations of ratio analysis for the purpose stated here?

BYP19-6 General Dynamics develops, produces, and supports innovative, reliable, and highly sophisticated military and commercial products. In July of a recent year, the corporation announced that its Quincy Shipbuilding Division (Quincy) will be closed following the completion of the Maritime Prepositioning Ship construction program.

Prior to discontinuance, the operating results of Quincy were net sales $246.8 million, income from operations before income taxes $28.3 million, and income taxes $12.5 million. The corporation's loss on disposition of Quincy was $5.0 million, net of $4.3 million income tax benefits.

From its other operating activities, General Dynamics' financial results were net sales $8,163.8 million, cost of goods sold $6,958.8 million, and selling and administrative expenses $537.0 million. In addition, the corporation had interest expense of $17.2 million and interest revenue of $3.6 million. Income taxes were $282.9 million.

General Dynamics had an average of 42.3 million shares of common stock outstanding during the year.

Instructions

With the class divided into groups, answer the following.

(a) Prepare the income statement for the year, assuming that the year ended on December 31, 2005. Show earnings per share data on the income statement. All dollars should be stated in millions, except for per share amounts. (For example, $8 million would be shown as $8.0)

(b) In the preceding year, Quincy's earnings were $51.6 million before income taxes of $22.8 million. For comparative purposes, General Dynamics reported earnings per share of $0.61 from discontinued operations for Quincy in the preceding year.

    (1) What was the average number of common shares outstanding during the preceding year?

    (2) If earnings per share from continuing operations was $7.47, what was income from continuing operations during the preceding year? (Round to two decimals.)

■ COMMUNICATION ACTIVITY

BYP19-7 Dawn Flutie is the CEO of Tomorrow's Electronics. Flutie is an expert engineer but a novice in accounting. She asks you to explain (1) the bases for comparison in analyzing Tomorrow's financial statements, and (2) the limitations, if any, in financial statement analysis.

Instructions

Write a letter to Dawn Flutie that explains the bases for comparison and the limitations of financial statement analysis.

■ ETHICS CASE

BYP19-8 Mike Singletary, president of Singletary Industries, wishes to issue a press release to bolster his company's image and maybe even its stock price, which has been gradually falling. As controller, you have been asked to provide a list of twenty financial ratios along with some other operating statistics relative to Singletary Industries' first quarter financials and operations.

    Two days after you provide the ratios and data requested, Curtis Conway, the public relations director of Singletary, asks you to prove the accuracy of the financial and operating data contained in the press release written by the president and edited by Curtis. In the news release, the president highlights the sales increase of 25% over last year's first quarter and the positive change in the current ratio from 1.5:1 last year to 3:1 this year. He also emphasizes that production was up 50% over the prior year's first quarter.

    You note that the press release contains only positive or improved ratios and none of the negative or deteriorated ratios. For instance, no mention is made that the debt to total assets ratio has increased from 35% to 55%, that inventories are up 89%, and that while the current ratio improved, the acid-test ratio fell from 1:1 to .5:1. Nor is there any mention that the reported profit for the quarter would have been a loss had not the estimated lives of Singletary's plant and machinery been increased by 30%. Curtis emphasized, "The prez wants this release by early this afternoon."

Instructions

(a) Who are the stakeholders in this situation?

(b) Is there anything unethical in president Singletary's actions?

(c) Should you as controller remain silent? Does Curtis have any responsibility?

Answers to Self-Study Questions

1. b   **2.** d   **3.** a   **4.** c   **5.** c   **6.** c   **7.** c   **8.** c   **9.** d   **10.** b

Answer to PepsiCo Review It Question 4, p. 774

PepsiCo presents horizontal analyses in its "Financial Highlights" section and its Management's Discussion and Analysis section. Vertical analysis is used in discussions presented in the Management's Discussion and Analysis section.

Managerial Accounting

THE NAVIGATOR ✓

Understand **Concepts for Review** ☐

Read **Feature Story** ☐

Scan **Study Objectives** ☐

Read **Preview** ☐

Read text and answer **Before You Go On**
p. 820 ☐   p. 822 ☐   p. 831 ☐

Work **Demonstration Problems** ☐

Review **Summary of Study Objectives** ☐

Answer **Self-Study Questions** ☐

Complete **Assignments** ☐

CONCEPTS FOR REVIEW

Before studying this chapter, you should know or, if necessary, review:

- The cost principle.
  (Ch. 1, p. 10)

- Ethics in accounting.
  (Ch. 1, p. 9)

- The computation of cost of goods sold.
  (Ch. 6, pp. 235–240)

- The adjusting and closing process used in a merchandising firm.
  (Ch. 5, pp. 193–194)

- The use of a work sheet in the preparation of financial statements.
  (Ch. 4, pp. 135–141, and Ch. 5, pp. 207–209)

THE
NAVIGATOR

What a Difference a Day Makes

In January 1998 Compaq Computer had just become the largest seller of personal computers, and it was *Forbes* magazine's "company of the year." Its chief executive, Eckhard Pfeiffer, was riding high. But during the next two years Compaq lost $2 billion. The company was in chaos, and Mr. Pfeiffer was out of a job. And, in May 2002, Compaq Computer was sold to Hewlett-Packard. What happened?

First, Dell happened. Dell Computer pioneered a new way of making and selling personal computers. Its customers "custom design" their computer over the Internet or phone. Dell reengineered its "supply chain": It coordinated its efforts with its suppliers and stream-

lined its order-taking and production process, and it can ship a computer within two days of taking an order. Personal computers lose 1 percent of their value every week they sit on a shelf. Thus, having virtually no inventory is a great advantage to Dell. Compaq tried to adopt Dell's approach, but with limited success.

The second shock to Compaq came when it acquired a company even larger than itself—Digital Equipment. Digital was famous as much for its technical service as it was for its products. Mr. Pfeiffer believed that the purchase of Digital, with its huge and respected technical sales force, opened new opportunities for Compaq as a global service company. Now it could sell to and service high-end corporate customers. But combining the two companies proved to be hugely expensive and extremely complicated.

The saga of Compaq Computer indicates that managers in today's rapidly changing global environment often must make decisions that determine their company's fate, and their own. The remaining chapters of this text discuss techniques used to assist managers in making these decisions.

www.compaq.com
www.dell.com
www.hp.com

After studying this chapter, you should be able to:

1. Explain the distinguishing features of managerial accounting.
2. Identify the three broad functions of management.
3. Define the three classes of manufacturing costs.
4. Distinguish between product and period costs.
5. Explain the difference between a merchandising and a manufacturing income statement.
6. Indicate how cost of goods manufactured is determined.
7. Explain the difference between a merchandising and a manufacturing balance sheet.

Beginning with this chapter, we turn our attention to issues illustrated in the Feature Story about **Compaq Computer**. To this point in the text, we have described the form and content of **financial statements** for **external users** such as stockholders and creditors. These statements represent the principal end-product of financial accounting. The remaining chapters of this textbook focus primarily on the preparation of **reports** for **internal users**, such as the managers and officers of a company. These reports are an integral part of managerial accounting. Managerial accounting provides tools for assisting management in making decisions and for evaluating the effectiveness of those decisions.

The content and organization of Chapter 20 are as follows.

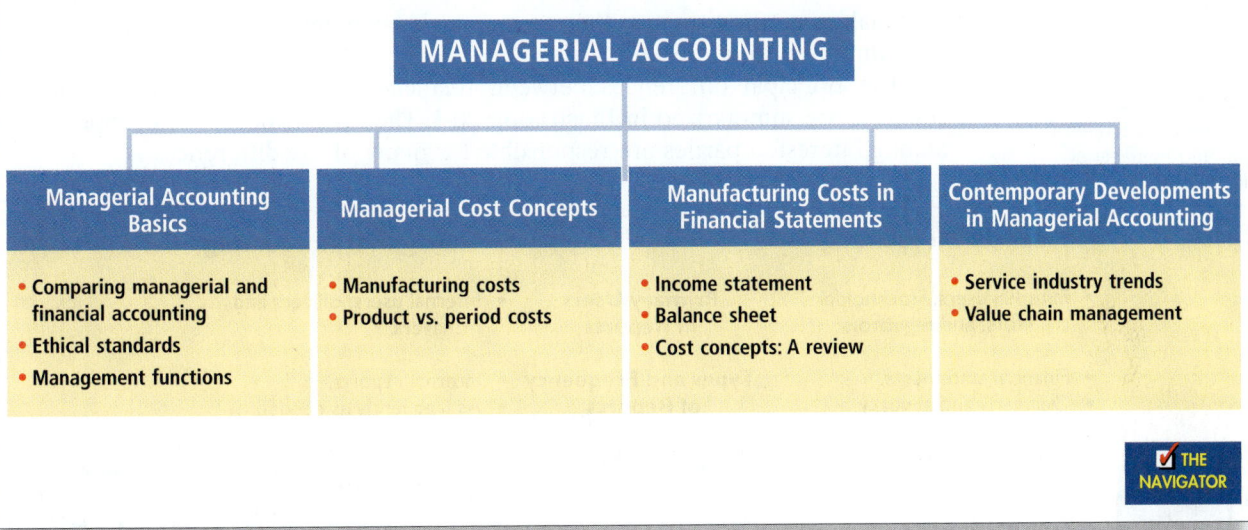

Managerial Accounting Basics

Managerial accounting, also called **management accounting**, is a field of accounting that provides economic and financial information for managers and other internal users. The activities that are part of managerial accounting (and the chapters in which they are discussed) are as follows:

1. Explaining manufacturing and nonmanufacturing costs and how they are reported in the financial statements (Chapter 20).
2. Computing the cost of providing a service or manufacturing a product (Chapters 21 and 22).
3. Determining the behavior of costs and expenses as activity levels change and analyzing cost–volume–profit relationships within a company (Chapter 23).
4. Assisting management in profit planning and formalizing these plans in the form of budgets (Chapter 24).
5. Providing a basis for controlling costs and expenses by comparing actual results with planned objectives and standard costs (Chapters 25 and 26).
6. Accumulating and presenting relevant data for management decision making (Chapter 27).

Managerial accounting applies to all types of businesses—service, merchandising, and manufacturing. It also applies to all forms of business organizations—proprietorships, partnerships, and corporations. Managerial accounting is needed in not-for-profit entities as well as in profit-oriented enterprises.

Not long ago, the managerial accountant was primarily engaged in cost accounting—collecting and reporting manufacturing costs to management. Today, the managerial accountant's responsibilities extend to **strategic cost management**—providing managers with data on the efficient use of company resources in both manufacturing and service industries.

Comparing Managerial and Financial Accounting

There are both similarities and differences between managerial and financial accounting. First, each field of accounting deals with the economic events of a business. Thus, their interests overlap. For example, determining the unit cost of manufacturing a product is part of managerial accounting. Reporting the total cost of goods manufactured and sold is part of financial accounting. In addition, both managerial and financial accounting require that a company's economic events be quantified and communicated to interested parties.

Illustration 20-1
Differences between financial and managerial accounting

The principal differences between financial accounting and managerial accounting are summarized in Illustration 20-1. The diverse needs for economic data among interested parties are responsible for many of the differences.

Financial Accounting		Managerial Accounting
• External users: stockholders, creditors, and regulators.	**Primary Users of Reports**	• Internal users: officers and managers.
• Financial statements. • Quarterly and annually.	**Types and Frequency of Reports**	• Internal reports. • As frequently as needed.
• General-purpose.	**Purpose of Reports**	• Special-purpose for specific decisions.
• Pertains to business as a whole. • Highly aggregated (condensed). • Limited to double-entry accounting and cost data. • Generally accepted accounting principles.	**Content of Reports**	• Pertains to subunits of the business. • Very detailed. • Extends beyond double-entry accounting to any relevant data. • Standard is relevance to decisions.
• Audit by CPA.	**Verification Process**	• No independent audits.

Ethical Standards for Managerial Accountants

We have emphasized throughout the textbook the importance of ethics in business and in accounting. Managerial accountants recognize that they have an ethical obligation to their companies and the public. To provide guidance for managerial accountants, the Institute of Management Accountants (IMA) has developed a code of ethical standards, entitled *Standards of Ethical Conduct for Management Accountants.* This code divides the managerial accountants' responsibilities into four areas: (1) competence, (2) confidentiality, (3) integrity, and (4) objectivity. The code states that management accountants should not commit acts in violation of these standards. Nor should they condone such acts by others within their organizations.

Management Functions

Management's activities and responsibilities can be classified into three broad functions:

1. Planning.
2. Directing and motivating.
3. Controlling.

In performing these functions, managers make decisions that have a significant impact on the organization.

Planning requires management to look ahead and to establish objectives. These objectives are often diverse: maximizing short-term profits and market share, maintaining a commitment to environmental protection, contributing to social programs. A key objective of management is to add **value** to the business under its control. Value is usually measured by the trading price of the company's stock and by the potential selling price of the company.

Directing and **motivating** involves coordinating a company's diverse activities and human resources to produce a smooth-running operation. This function relates to implementing planned objectives and providing necessary incentives. For example, in manufacturers such as **Campbell Soup Company**, **General Motors**, and **Dell Computer**, purchasing, manufacturing, warehousing, and selling must be coordinated. Service corporations such as **American Airlines**, **Federal Express**, and **AT&T** must coordinate scheduling, sales, and equipment and supply acquisitions. Directing also involves selecting executives, appointing managers and supervisors, and hiring and training employees. Most companies prepare **organization charts** to show the interrelationship of activities and the delegation of authority and responsibility within the company.

The third management function, **controlling**, is the process of keeping the firm's activities on track. In controlling operations, managers determine whether planned goals are being met. When there are deviations from targeted objectives, they must decide what changes are needed to get back on track.

How do managers achieve control? A smart manager in a small operation should make personal observations, ask good questions, and know how to evaluate the answers. But such a system in a large organization would be chaotic. Imagine the president of **IBM** attempting to determine whether planned objectives are being met without some record of what has happened and what is expected to occur. Thus, a formal system of evaluation is typically used in large businesses. It would include such items as budgets, responsibility centers, and performance evaluation reports.

Decision making is not a separate management function. Rather, it is the outcome of the exercise of good judgment in planning, directing, motivating, and controlling.

You are now ready to study specific applications of managerial accounting. As you study the managerial chapters, you will encounter many new terms, concepts, and reports. At the same time, you will find some new uses and interpretations of a number of familiar financial accounting terms.

ACCOUNTING IN ACTION   e Business Insight

The trend toward more automated and computerized factories has changed the way managers and employees interact. For one thing, managers have fewer direct labor employees to supervise because fewer are needed on the line. Instead of standing in one spot all day, employees and managers have become more mobile, monitoring the computers that handle the production, and involving themselves in a variety of jobs.

Recently, two technology giants, **General Electric** and **Cisco Systems**, joined forces to build computerized infrastructures for manufacturers. Their goal is to improve productivity by making better use of data generated by factory-automation equipment. Ultimately their systems should provide a closer link between the factory and corporate offices.

BEFORE YOU GO ON...

Review It

1. Compare financial accounting and managerial accounting, identifying the principal differences.
2. Identify and discuss the three broad functions of management.

 THE NAVIGATOR

Managerial Cost Concepts

To perform the three management functions effectively, management needs information. One very important type of information is related to costs. For example, questions such as the following should be asked.

1. What costs are involved in making a product or providing a service?
2. If production volume is decreased, will costs decrease?
3. What impact will automation have on total costs?
4. How can costs best be controlled?

To answer these questions, management needs reliable and relevant cost information. We now explain and illustrate the costs that management uses.

STUDY OBJECTIVE 3

Define the three classes of manufacturing costs.

Manufacturing Costs

Manufacturing consists of activities and processes that convert raw materials into finished goods. Contrast this type of operation with merchandising, which sells merchandise in the form in which it is purchased. Manufacturing costs are typically classified as shown in Illustration 20-2.

Illustration 20-2
Classifications of manufacturing costs

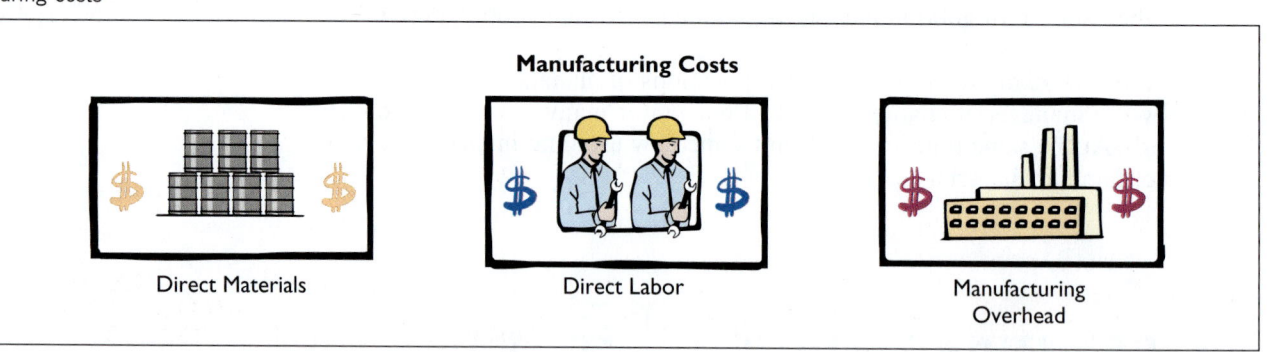

Direct Materials   Direct Labor   Manufacturing Overhead

Direct Materials

To obtain the materials that will be converted into the finished product, the manufacturer purchases raw materials. **Raw materials** are the basic materials and parts used in the manufacturing process. For example, auto manufacturers such as **General Motors**, **Ford**, and **DaimlerChrysler** use steel, plastics, and tires as raw materials in making cars.

Raw materials that can be physically and directly associated with the finished product during the manufacturing process are called **direct materials**. Examples include flour in the baking of bread, syrup in the bottling of soft drinks, and steel in the making of automobiles. In the Feature Story, direct materials for **Dell Computer** and **Hewlett-Packard** include plastic, glass, hard drives, and processing chips.

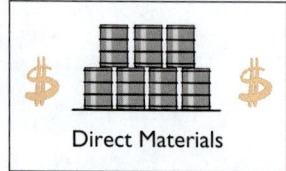
Direct Materials

But some raw materials cannot be easily associated with the finished product. These are considered indirect materials. **Indirect materials** (1) do not physically become part of the finished product, such as lubricants and polishing compounds, or (2) cannot be traced because their physical association with the finished product is too small in terms of cost, such as cotter pins and lock washers. Indirect materials are accounted for as part of **manufacturing overhead**.

Direct Labor

The work of factory employees that can be physically and directly associated with converting raw materials into finished goods is considered **direct labor**. Bottlers at **Coca-Cola**, bakers at **Sara Lee**, and typesetters at **TechBooks** are employees whose activities are usually classified as direct labor. In contrast, the wages of maintenance people, time-keepers, and supervisors are usually identified as **indirect labor**. Their efforts have no physical association with the finished product, or it is impractical to trace the costs to the goods produced. Like indirect materials, indirect labor is classified as **manufacturing overhead**.

Direct Labor

Manufacturing Overhead

Manufacturing overhead consists of costs that are indirectly associated with the manufacture of the finished product. These costs may also be manufacturing costs that cannot be classified as direct materials or direct labor. Manufacturing overhead includes indirect materials, indirect labor, depreciation on factory buildings and machines, and insurance, taxes, and maintenance on factory facilities.

One study found the following magnitudes of the three different product costs in terms of the total product cost: direct materials 54.4 percent, direct labor 12.9 percent, and manufacturing overhead 32.6 percent. Note that the direct labor component is the smallest. This component of product cost is dropping substantially because of automation. In some companies, direct labor has become as little as 5 percent of the total cost.

Allocating materials and labor costs to specific products is fairly straightforward. But dealing with overhead presents problems. How much of the purchasing agent's salary is attributable to the hundreds of products made in the same plant? What about the grease that keeps the machines humming, or the computers that make sure paychecks come out on time? Boiled down to its simplest form, the question becomes: Which products cause which costs? In subsequent chapters we show various methods of allocating overhead to products.

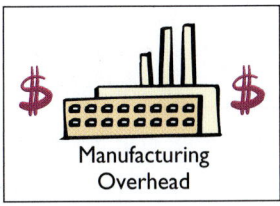
Manufacturing Overhead

ALTERNATIVE TERMINOLOGY

Terms such as *factory overhead*, *indirect manufacturing costs*, and *burden* are sometimes used instead of manufacturing overhead.

Product cost ——— D: Labor
D-material
overhead

Product Versus Period Costs

Each of the manufacturing cost components (direct materials, direct labor, and manufacturing overhead) are product costs. As the term suggests, **product costs** are costs that are a necessary and integral part of producing the finished product. Product costs are recorded as inventory when incurred. Under the matching principle, these costs do not become expenses until the finished goods inventory is sold. The expense is cost of goods sold.

Period costs are costs that are matched with the revenue of a specific time period rather than included as part of the cost of a salable product. These are non-manufacturing costs. Period costs include selling and administrative expenses. They are deducted from revenues in the period in which they are incurred.

The foregoing relationships and cost terms are summarized in Illustration 20-3. Our main concern in this chapter is with product costs.

Illustration 20-3
Product versus period costs

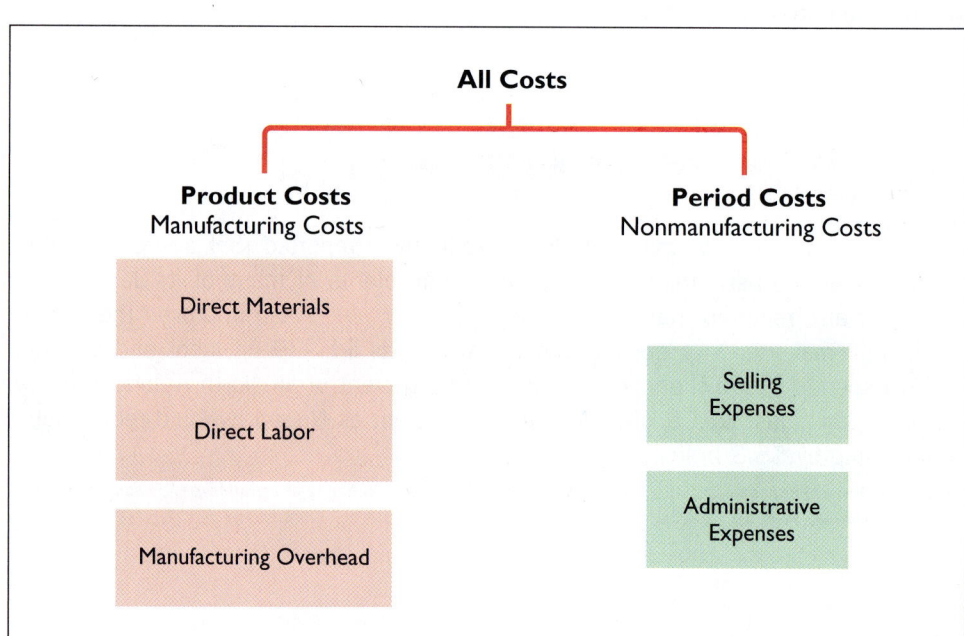

BEFORE YOU GO ON...

Review It

1. What are the major cost classifications involved in manufacturing a product?
2. What are product and period costs, and what is their relationship to the manufacturing process?

Do It

In making bicycles, a company has the following costs: tires, salaries of employees who put tires on the wheels, factory building depreciation, wheel nuts, spokes, salary of factory foreman, handle bars, and salaries of factory maintenance employees. Classify each cost as direct materials, direct labor, or manufacturing overhead.

Manufacturing Costs in Financial Statements

The financial statements of a manufacturing company are very similar to those of a merchandising company. The principal differences pertain to the cost of goods sold section in the income statement and the current assets section in the balance sheet.

Income Statement

Under a periodic inventory system, the income statements of a merchandiser and a manufacturer differ in the cost of goods sold section. For a merchandiser, cost of goods sold is computed by adding the beginning merchandise inventory and the **cost of goods purchased** and subtracting the ending merchandise inventory. For a manufacturer, cost of goods sold is computed by adding the beginning finished goods inventory and **cost of goods manufactured** and subtracting the ending finished goods inventory. The different components are shown in Illustration 20-4.

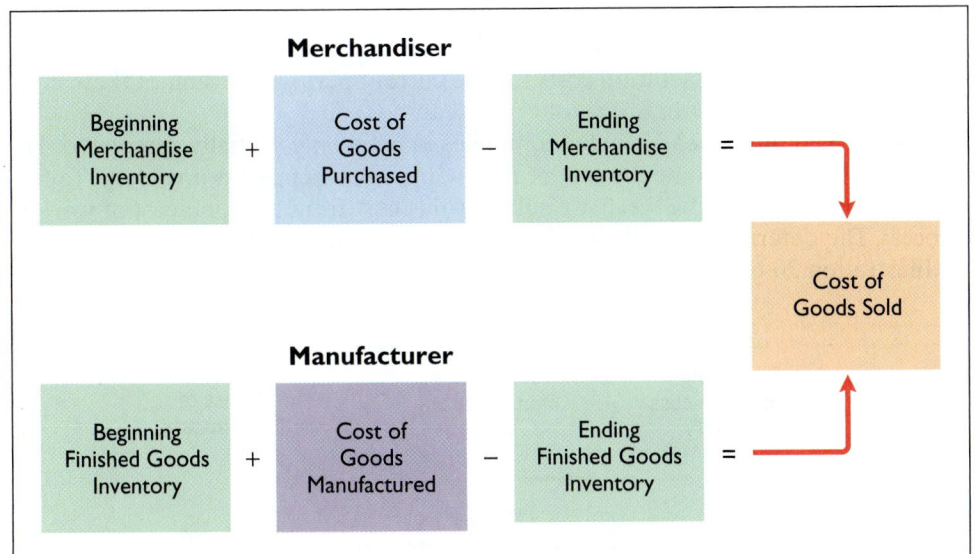

Illustration 20-4
Cost of goods sold components

Illustration 20-5
Cost of goods sold sections
of merchandising and manufacturing income statements

The cost of goods sold sections for merchandising and manufacturing companies in Illustration 20-5 show the different presentations.

| MERCHANDISE COMPANY | | MANUFACTURING COMPANY | |
| Income Statement (partial) | | Income Statement (partial) | |
For the Year Ended December 31, 2005		For the Year Ended December 31, 2005	
Cost of goods sold		Cost of goods sold	
Merchandise inventory, January 1	$ 70,000	Finished goods inventory, January 1	$ 90,000
Cost of goods purchased	650,000	Cost of goods manufactured	
		(see Illustration 20-7)	370,000
Cost of goods available for sale	720,000	Cost of goods available for sale	460,000
Merchandise inventory, December 31	400,000	Finished goods inventory, December 31	80,000
Cost of goods sold	$320,000	Cost of goods sold	$380,000

The other sections of an income statement are similar for merchandisers and manufacturers.

A number of accounts are involved in determining the cost of goods manufactured. To eliminate excessive detail, it is customary to show in the income statement
only the total cost of goods manufactured. The details are presented in a Cost of
Goods Manufactured Schedule. The form and content of this schedule are shown in
Illustration 20-7 (page 825).

Determining the Cost of Goods Manufactured

An example may help show how the cost of goods manufactured is determined. Assume that **Ford Motor Company** has a number of automobiles in various stages of
production on January 1. In total, these partially completed units are called **beginning
work in process inventory**. The costs assigned to beginning work in process inventory are based on the **manufacturing costs incurred in the prior period**.

The manufacturing costs incurred in the current year are used first to complete
the work in process on January 1. They then are used to start the production of other
automobiles. The sum of the direct materials costs, direct labor costs, and manufacturing overhead incurred in the current year is the **total manufacturing costs** for the
current period.

We now have two cost amounts: (1) the cost of the beginning work in process
and (2) the total manufacturing costs for the current period. The sum of these costs
is the **total cost of work in process** for the year.

At the end of the year, some automobiles may be only partially completed. The
costs of these units become the cost of the **ending work in process inventory**. To find
the **cost of goods manufactured**, we subtract this cost from the total cost of work in
process. The determination of the cost of goods manufactured is shown graphically
in Illustration 20-6.

Illustration 20-6
Cost of goods manufactured
formula

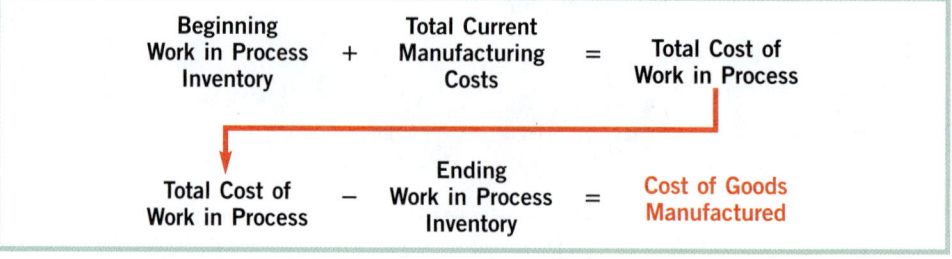

Cost of Goods Manufactured Schedule

An internal report shows each of the cost elements shown in Illustration 20-6. This report is called the **cost of goods manufactured schedule**. The schedule for Olsen Manufacturing Company (using assumed data) is shown in Illustration 20-7. Note that the schedule presents detailed data for direct materials and for manufacturing overhead.

Illustration 20-7
Cost of goods manufactured schedule

OLSEN MANUFACTURING COMPANY		
Cost of Goods Manufactured Schedule		
For the Year Ended December 31, 2005		
Work in process, January 1		$ 18,400
Direct materials		
Raw materials inventory, January 1	$ 16,700	
Raw materials purchases	152,500	
Total raw materials available for use	169,200	
Less: Raw materials inventory, December 31	22,800	
Direct materials used		$146,400
Direct labor		175,600
Manufacturing overhead		
Indirect labor	14,300	
Factory repairs	12,600	
Factory utilities	10,100	
Factory depreciation	9,440	
Factory insurance	8,360	
Total manufacturing overhead		54,800
Total current manufacturing costs		376,800
Total cost of work in process		395,200
Less: Work in process, December 31		25,200
Cost of goods manufactured		$370,000

Review Illustration 20-6 and then examine the cost of goods manufactured schedule in Illustration 20-7. You should be able to distinguish between "Total current manufacturing costs" and "Cost of goods manufactured." The difference is the effect of the change in work in process during the period.

Balance Sheet

The balance sheet for a merchandising company shows just one category of inventory. In contrast, the balance sheet for a manufacturer may have three inventory accounts. They are:

STUDY OBJECTIVE 7

Explain the difference between a merchandising and a manufacturing balance sheet.

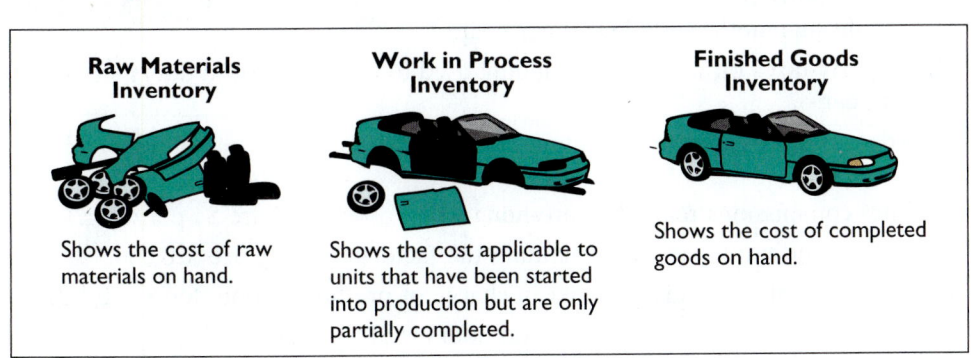

Raw Materials Inventory
Shows the cost of raw materials on hand.

Work in Process Inventory
Shows the cost applicable to units that have been started into production but are only partially completed.

Finished Goods Inventory
Shows the cost of completed goods on hand.

Illustration 20-8
Inventory accounts for a manufacturer

Finished Goods Inventory is to a manufacturer what Merchandise Inventory is to a merchandiser. It represents the goods that are available for sale.

The current assets sections presented in Illustration 20-9 contrast the presentations of inventories for merchandising and manufacturing companies. Manufacturing inventories are generally listed in the order of their liquidity—the order in which they are expected to be realized in cash. Thus, finished goods inventory is listed first. The remainder of the balance sheet is similar for the two types of companies.

Illustration 20-9
Current assets sections of merchandising and manufacturing balance sheets

MERCHANDISING COMPANY		MANUFACTURING COMPANY		
Balance Sheet		Balance Sheet		
December 31, 2005		December 31, 2005		
Current assets		Current assets		
Cash	$100,000	Cash		$180,000
Receivables (net)	210,000	Receivables (net)		210,000
Merchandise inventory	400,000	Inventories		
Prepaid expenses	22,000	Finished goods	$80,000	
		Work in process	25,200	
Total current assets	$732,000	Raw materials	22,800	128,000
		Prepaid expenses		18,000
		Total current assets		$536,000

For expanded coverage, see Chapter 20—Accounting Cycle (Work Sheet) for a Manufacturing Company

Each step in the accounting cycle for a merchandiser applies to a manufacturer. For example, prior to preparing financial statements, adjusting entries are required. The adjusting entries are essentially the same as those of a merchandiser. The closing entries are also similar for manufacturers and merchandisers.

Cost Concepts—A Review

You have learned a number of cost concepts in this chapter. Because many of these concepts are new, we believe an extended example will help illustrate how they are used. Assume that Northridge Company manufactures and sells pre-hung metal doors. Recently, it has decided to start selling pre-hung wood doors also. An old warehouse that the company owns will be used to manufacture the new product. Northridge identifies the following costs associated with manufacturing and selling the pre-hung wood doors.

1. The material cost (wood) for each door is $10.
2. Labor costs involved in constructing a wood door are $8 per door.
3. Depreciation on the new equipment used to make the wood doors using the straight-line method is $25,000 per year.
4. Property taxes on the factory building used to make the wood doors are $6,000 per year.
5. Advertising costs for the pre-hung wood doors total $2,500 per month or $30,000 per year.
6. Sales commissions related to pre-hung wood doors sold are $4 per door.
7. Salaries for employees who maintain the factory building are $28,000.
8. The salary of the plant manager in charge of pre-hung wood doors is $70,000.
9. The cost of shipping pre-hung wood doors is $12 per door sold.

These manufacturing and selling costs can be assigned to the various categories shown in Illustration 20-10.

Illustration 20-10
Assignment of costs to cost categories

| Cost Item | Product Costs | | | Period Costs |
	Direct Materials	Direct Labor	Manufacturing Overhead	
1. Material cost ($10) per door	X			
2. Labor costs ($8) per door		X		
3. Depreciation on new equipment ($25,000 per year)			X	
4. Property taxes (factory) ($6,000 per year)			X	
5. Advertising costs ($30,000 per year)				X
6. Sales commissions ($4 per door)				X
7. Maintenance salaries (factory) ($28,000 per year)			X	
8. Salary of plant manager ($70,000)			X	
9. Cost of shipping pre-hung doors ($12 per door)				X

Remember that total manufacturing costs are the sum of the product costs—direct materials, direct labor, and manufacturing overhead. If Northridge Company produces 10,000 pre-hung wood doors the first year, the total manufacturing costs would be:

Illustration 20-11
Computation of total manufacturing costs

Cost Number and Item	Manufacturing Cost
1. Material cost ($10 × 10,000)	$100,000
2. Labor cost ($8 × 10,000)	80,000
3. Depreciation on factory equipment	25,000
4. Property taxes (factory)	6,000
7. Maintenance salaries (factory)	28,000
8. Salary of plant manager	70,000
Total manufacturing costs	**$309,000**

Knowing the total manufacturing costs, Northridge can compute the manufacturing cost per unit, assuming 10,000 units: The cost to produce one pre-hung wood door is $30.90 ($309,000 ÷ 10,000 units).

The cost concepts above will be used extensively in subsequent chapters. Study Illustration 20-10 carefully. If you do not understand any of these classifications, go back and reread the appropriate section in this chapter.

Contemporary Developments in Managerial Accounting

The competitive environment for U.S. businesses has changed significantly in recent years. Within the United States, for example, the airline, financial services, and telecommunications industries have been deregulated. Global competition has intensified, particularly in the automotive and electronics industries. Today, business managers demand from managerial accountants different and better information than they needed just a few years ago. Factors such as those discussed below will contribute to the expanding role of managerial accounting in the twenty-first century.

Service Industry Trends

The Feature Story notes that at the peak of its success as a personal computer manufacturer, **Compaq** purchased **Digital Equipment**. In doing so, management indicated its belief that the future of computing lies in providing computer services, rather than in manufacturing hardware. In fact, during the most recent decade, the U.S. economy in general shifted toward an emphasis on providing services, rather than goods. Today over 50 percent of U.S. workers are employed by service companies, and that percentage is projected to increase in coming years. Much of this chapter focused on manufacturers. But most of the techniques that you will learn in this course are equally applicable to service entities.

In some respects, the challenges for managerial accounting are greater in service companies than in manufacturing companies. Further complicating matters, as indicated earlier, many service industries have been deregulated (for example: trucking, airlines, telecommunications, and banking). In a deregulated environment the information provided by managerial accounting is even more important. Illustration 20-12 presents examples of questions faced by service-company managers.

Illustration 20-12
Service industries and companies and the managerial accounting questions they face

	Industry/Company	Questions Faced by Service-Company Managers
	Transportation (**American Airlines**, **Amtrak**)	Whether to buy new or used planes? Whether to service a new route?
	Package delivery services (**FedEx**, **UPS**)	What fee structure to use? What mode of transportation to use?
	Telecommunications (**AT&T**, **Time Warner**)	What fee structure to use? Whether to service a new community? How many households will it take to break even? Whether to invest in a new satellite or lay new cable?
	Professional services (attorneys, accountants, physicians)	How much to charge for particular services? How much office overhead to allocate to particular jobs? How efficient and productive are individual staff members?
	Financial institutions (**Wells Fargo**, **Merrill Lynch**)	Which services to charge for, and which to provide for free? Whether to build a new branch office or to install a new ATM? Should fees vary depending on the size of the customers' accounts?
	Health care (**Blue Cross-Blue Shield**, HMOs)	Whether to invest in new equipment? How much to charge for various services? How to measure the quality of services provided?

Managers of service companies look to managerial accounting to answer these questions. In some instances the managerial accountant may need to develop new systems for measuring the cost of serving individual customers. In others, he or she may need new operating controls to improve the quality and efficiency of specific services. Many of the examples we present in subsequent chapters will be based on service companies.

ACCOUNTING IN ACTION Business Insight

At **South Central Bell (Telephone)**, management accountants have shed their score-keeping image. A corporate reorganization plan challenged the accountants to "show their stuff." They took on the roles of interpreter, advisor, and partner. To do so, they had to understand what the accounting numbers mean, relate the numbers to business activity, and recommend alternative courses of action. In addition, they evaluate alternatives and make decisions to maximize business efficiency.

Value Chain Management

The **value chain** is the term that describes all activities associated with providing a product or service. The value chain includes activities such as research and development, ordering raw materials, manufacturing, marketing, delivery, and customer relations. Each of these activities should be designed and operated so that they add value to the product or service. A critical component of the value chain is the supply chain. The **supply chain** is all of the activities from receipt of an order to delivery of a product or service. A number of factors affect efforts to manage the value chain and supply chain.

Technological Change

Many companies now employ **enterprise resource planning (ERP)** software systems to manage their value chain. ERP systems provide a comprehensive, centralized, integrated source of information used to manage all major business processes, from purchasing to manufacturing to human resource records. In large companies, an ERP system might replace as many as 200 individual software packages. For example, an ERP system can eliminate the need for individual software packages for personnel, inventory management, receivables, and payroll. Because the value chain extends beyond the walls of the company, ERP systems often collect and provide information from and to the company's major suppliers, customers, and business partners.

Technology is also affecting the value chain through business-to-business e-commerce on the Internet. The Internet has dramatically changed the way corporations do business with one another. It enables customers and suppliers to share information nearly instantaneously. In addition, it has changed the marketplace, often having the effect of cutting out the "middle man." Industries such as the automobile, airline, hotel, and electronics industries have made commitments to purchase some or all of their supplies and raw materials in the huge business-to-business electronic marketplaces. For example, **Hilton Hotels** committed to purchase as much as $1.5 billion of bed sheets, pest control services, and other items from an Internet supplier, **PurchasePro.com**.

Just-in-Time Inventory Methods

Many companies have significantly lowered inventory levels and costs using **just-in-time (JIT) inventory** methods. Under a just-in-time method, goods are manufactured or purchased just in time for use. As noted in the Feature Story, **Dell Computer** is famous for having developed a system for making computers in response to individual customer requests. Even though each computer is custom-made to meet each customer's particular specifications, it takes Dell less than 48 hours to assemble the computer and put it on a truck. By integrating its information systems with those of its suppliers, Dell reduced its inventories to nearly zero. This is a huge advantage in an industry where products become obsolete nearly overnight.

Produced only when needed

Quality

JIT inventory systems require an increased emphasis on product quality. If products are produced only as they are needed, it is very costly for the company to have to stop production because of defects or machine breakdowns. Many companies have installed **total quality management (TQM)** systems to reduce defects in finished products. The goal is to achieve zero defects. These systems require timely data on defective products, rework costs, and the cost of honoring warranty contracts. Often this information is used to help redesign the product in a way that makes it less prone to defect. Or it may be used to reengineer the production process to reduce setup time and decrease the potential for error. TQM systems also provide information on nonfinancial measures such as customer satisfaction, number of service calls, and time to generate reports. Attention to these measures, which employees can control, leads to increased profitability.

ACCOUNTING IN ACTION Business Insight

When it comes to total quality management, few companies can compare with **Chiquita Brands International**. Grocery store customers are very picky about bananas—bad bananas are consistently the number one grocery store complaint. Because bananas often account for up to 3 percent of a grocery store's sales, Chiquita goes to great lengths to protect the popular fruit. While bananas are in transit from Central America, "black box" recording devices attached to shipping crates ensure that they are kept in an environment of 90 percent humidity and an unvarying 55-degree temperature. Upon arrival in the U.S. bananas are ripened in airtight warehouses that use carefully monitored levels of ethylene gas. Regular checks are made of each warehouse using ultrasonic detectors that can detect leaks the size of a pinhole. Says one grocery store executive, "No other item in the store has this type of attention and resources devoted to it."

Source: Devon Spurgeon, "When Grocers in U.S. Go Bananas Over Bad Fruit, They Call Laubenthal," *Wall Street Journal*, August 14, 2000, p. A1.

Focus on Activities

As discussed earlier, overhead costs have become an increasingly large component of product and service costs. By definition, overhead costs cannot be directly traced to individual products. But to determine each product's cost, overhead must be allocated to the various products. In order to obtain more accurate product costs, many companies now allocate overhead using **activity-based costing (ABC)**. Under ABC, overhead is allocated based on each product's use of activities in making the product. For example, the company can keep track of the cost of setting up machines for each batch of a production process. Then a particular product can be allocated part of the total set-up cost based on the number of set-ups that product required. Activity-based costing is beneficial because it results in more accurate product costing and in more careful scrutiny of all activities in the value chain. For example, if a product's cost is high because it requires a high number of set-ups, management will be motivated to determine how to produce the product using the optimal number of machine set-ups.

BEFORE YOU GO ON...

Review It

1. How does the content of an income statement for a merchandiser differ from that for a manufacturer?
2. How are the work in process inventories reported in the cost of goods manufactured schedule?
3. What amounts are reported for PepsiCo in its 2002 annual report for (1) raw materials inventory (2) work in process inventory and (3) finished goods inventory? The answer to this question is provided on page 849.
4. How does the content of the balance sheet for a merchandiser differ from that for a manufacturer?

DEMONSTRATION PROBLEM 1

Superior Manufacturing Company has the following cost and expense data for the year ending December 31, 2005.

Raw materials, 1/1/05	$ 30,000	Insurance, factory	$ 14,000
Raw materials, 12/31/05	20,000	Property taxes, factory building	6,000
Raw materials purchased	205,000	Sales (net)	1,500,000
Indirect materials	15,000	Delivery expenses	100,000
Work in process, 1/1/05	80,000	Sales commissions	150,000
Work in process, 12/31/05	50,000	Indirect labor	90,000
Finished goods, 1/1/05	110,000	Factory machinery rent	40,000
Finished goods, 12/31/05	120,000	Factory utilities	65,000
Direct labor	350,000	Depreciation, factory building	24,000
Factory manager's salary	35,000	Administrative expenses	300,000

Instructions

(a) Prepare a cost of goods manufactured schedule for Superior Company for 2005.

(b) Prepare an income statement for Superior Company for 2005.

(c) Assume that Superior Company's ledgers show the balances of the following current asset accounts: Cash $17,000, Accounts Receivable (net) $120,000, Prepaid Expenses $13,000, and Short-term Investments $26,000. Prepare the current assets section of the balance sheet for Superior Company as of December 31, 2005.

(*continued from p. 831*)

ACTION PLAN

- Start with beginning work in process as the first item in the cost of goods manufactured schedule.
- Sum direct materials used, direct labor, and total manufacturing overhead to determine total current manufacturing costs.
- Sum beginning work in process and total current manufacturing costs to determine total cost of work in process.
- Cost of goods manufactured is the total cost of work in process less ending work in process.
- In the cost of goods sold section of the income statement, show beginning and ending finished goods inventory and cost of goods manufactured.
- In the balance sheet, list manufacturing inventories in the order of their expected realization in cash, with finished goods first.

SOLUTION TO DEMONSTRATION PROBLEM 1

(a)

SUPERIOR MANUFACTURING COMPANY
Cost of Goods Manufactured Schedule
For the Year Ended December 31, 2005

Work in process, 1/1			$ 80,000
Direct materials			
Raw materials inventory, 1/1	$ 30,000		
Raw materials purchased	205,000		
Total raw materials available for use	235,000		
Less: Raw materials inventory, 12/31	20,000		
Direct materials used		$215,000	
Direct labor		350,000	
Manufacturing overhead			
Indirect labor	90,000		
Factory utilities	65,000		
Factory machinery rent	40,000		
Factory manager's salary	35,000		
Depreciation on building	24,000		
Indirect materials	15,000		
Factory insurance	14,000		
Property taxes	6,000		
Total manufacturing overhead		289,000	
Total current manufacturing costs			854,000
Total cost of work in process			934,000
Less: Work in process, 12/31			50,000
Cost of goods manufactured			$884,000

(b)

SUPERIOR MANUFACTURING COMPANY
Income Statement
For the Year Ended December 31, 2005

Sales (net)		$1,500,000
Cost of goods sold		
Finished goods inventory, January 1	$110,000	
Cost of goods manufactured	884,000	
Cost of goods available for sale	994,000	
Less: Finished goods inventory, December 31	120,000	
Cost of goods sold		874,000
Gross profit		626,000
Operating expenses		
Administrative expenses	300,000	
Sales commissions	150,000	
Delivery expenses	100,000	
Total operating expenses		550,000
Net income		$ 76,000

(c)   **SUPERIOR MANUFACTURING COMPANY**
                            Balance Sheet (partial)
                             December 31, 2005

Current assets		
Cash		$ 17,000
Short-term investments		26,000
Accounts receivable (net)		120,000
Inventories		
Finished goods	$120,000	
Work in process	50,000	
Raw materials	20,000	190,000
Prepaid expenses		13,000
Total current assets		$366,000

☑ THE
NAVIGATOR

DEMONSTRATION PROBLEM 2

Giant Company specializes in manufacturing different models of racing bicycles. A new model, the Jaguar, has been well accepted. As a result, the company has established a separate manufacturing facility to produce these bicycles. The company produces 1,000 bicycles per month. Giant's monthly manufacturing cost and other expenses data related to these bicycles are as follows.

1. Rent on manufacturing equipment (lease cost) $2,000/month
2. Insurance on manufacturing building $750/month
3. Raw materials (frames, tires, etc.) $80/bicycle
4. Utility costs for manufacturing facility $1,000/month
5. Supplies for general office $800/month
6. Wages for assembly line workers in manufacturing facility $30/bicycle
7. Depreciation on office equipment $650/month
8. Miscellaneous materials (lubricants, solders, etc.) $1.20/bicycle
9. Property taxes on manufacturing building $2,400/year
10. Manufacturing supervisor's salary $3,000/month
11. Advertising for bicycles $30,000/year
12. Sales commissions $10/bicycle
13. Depreciation on manufacturing building $1,500/month

Instructions

(a) Prepare an answer sheet with the following column headings.

	Product Costs			
Cost Item	**Direct Materials**	**Direct Labor**	**Manufacturing Overhead**	**Period Costs**

Enter each cost item on your answer sheet, placing an "X" mark under the appropriate headings.

(b) Compute total manufacturing costs for the month.

(continued from p. 833)

ACTION PLAN

- Make sure you are doing the computations for the appropriate period: month, year, unit, etc.
- Recall that period costs are not manufacturing costs and, therefore, are not inventoriable.
- Recall that product costs are manufacturing costs and are inventoriable.

SOLUTION TO DEMONSTRATION PROBLEM 2

(a)

Cost Item	Product Costs			Period Costs
	Direct Materials	**Direct Labor**	**Manufacturing Overhead**	
1. Rent on equipment ($2,000/month)			X	
2. Insurance on manufacturing building ($750/month)			X	
3. Raw materials ($80/bicycle)	X			
4. Manufacturing utilities ($1,000/month)			X	
5. Office supplies ($800/month)				X
6. Wages for workers ($30/bicycle)		X		
7. Depreciation on office equipment ($650/month)				X
8. Miscellaneous materials ($1.20/bicycle)			X	
9. Property taxes on building ($2,400/year)			X	
10. Manufacturing supervisor's salary ($3,000/month)			X	
11. Advertising cost ($30,000/year)				X
12. Sales commissions ($10/bicycle)				X
13. Depreciation on manufacturing building ($1,500/month)			X	

(b)

Cost Item	Manufacturing Cost
Rent on equipment	$ 2,000
Insurance	750
Raw materials ($80 × 1,000)	80,000
Manufacturing utilities	1,000
Labor ($30 × 1,000)	30,000
Miscellaneous materials ($1.20 × 1,000)	1,200
Property taxes ($2,400 ÷ 12)	200
Manufacturing supervisor's salary	3,000
Depreciation on building	1,500
Total manufacturing costs	$119,650

☑ THE NAVIGATOR

SUMMARY OF STUDY OBJECTIVES

1. **Explain the distinguishing features of managerial accounting.** The distinguishing features of managerial accounting are:

   Primary users of reports—internal users, who are officers and managers.

   Type and frequency of reports—internal reports that are issued as frequently as the need arises.

   Purpose of reports—to provide special-purpose information for specific decisions.

   Content of reports—pertains to subunits of the business and may be very detailed; may extend beyond double-entry accounting system; the reporting standard is relevance to the decision being made.

   Verification of reports—no independent audits.

2. **Identify the three broad functions of management.** The three functions are planning, directing and motivating, and controlling. Planning requires management to look ahead and to establish objectives. Directing and motivating involves coordinating the diverse activities and human resources of a company to produce a smooth-running operation. Controlling is the process of keeping the activities on track.

3. **Define the three classes of manufacturing costs.** Manufacturing costs are typically classified as either (1) direct materials, (2) direct labor, or (3) manufacturing overhead. Raw materials that can be physically and directly associated with the finished product during the manufacturing process are called direct materials. The work of factory employees that can be physically and directly associated with converting raw materials into finished goods is considered direct labor. Manufacturing overhead consists of costs that are indirectly associated with the manufacture of the finished product.

4. **Distinguish between product and period costs.** Product costs are costs that are a necessary and integral part of producing the finished product. Product costs are also called inventoriable costs. Under the matching principle, these costs do not become expenses until the inventory to which they attach is sold. Period costs are costs that are matched with the revenue of a specific time period rather than included as part of the cost of a salable product. These costs relate to nonmanufacturing costs and therefore are not inventoriable costs.

5. **Explain the difference between a merchandising and a manufacturing income statement.** The difference between a merchandising and a manufacturing income statement is in the cost of goods sold section. A manufacturing cost of goods sold section shows beginning and ending finished goods inventories and the cost of goods manufactured.

6. **Indicate how cost of goods manufactured is determined.** The cost of the beginning work in process is added to the total manufacturing costs for the current year to arrive at the total cost of work in process for the year. The ending work in process is then subtracted from the total cost of work in process to arrive at the cost of goods manufactured.

7. **Explain the difference between a merchandising and a manufacturing balance sheet.** The difference between a manufacturing and a merchandising balance sheet is in the current assets section. In the current assets section of a manufacturing company's balance sheet, three inventory accounts are presented: finished goods inventory, work in process inventory, and raw materials inventory.

GLOSSARY

Activity-based costing (ABC) A method of allocating overhead based on each product's use of activities in making the product. (p. 831).

Cost of goods manufactured Total cost of work in process less the cost of the ending work in process inventory. (p. 824).

Direct labor The work of factory employees that can be physically and directly associated with converting raw materials into finished goods. (p. 821).

Direct materials Raw materials that can be physically and directly associated with manufacturing the finished product. (p. 820).

Enterprise resource planning (ERP) system Software that provides a comprehensive, centralized, integrated source of information used to manage all major business processes. (p. 829).

Indirect labor Work of factory employees that has no physical association with the finished product, or for which it is impractical to trace the costs to the goods produced. (p. 821).

Indirect materials Raw materials that do not physically become part of the finished product or cannot be traced because their physical association with the finished product is too small. (p. 821).

Just-in-time (JIT) inventory Inventory system in which goods are manufactured or purchased just in time for use. (p. 830).

Managerial accounting A field of accounting that provides economic and financial information for managers and other internal users. (p. 817).

Manufacturing overhead Manufacturing costs that are indirectly associated with the manufacture of the finished product. (p. 821).

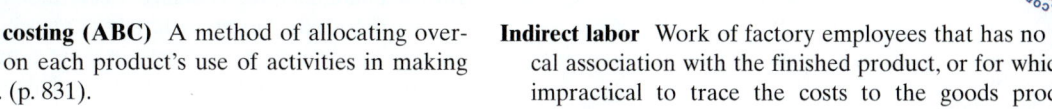

Period costs Costs that are matched with the revenue of a specific time period and charged to expense as incurred. (p. 822).

Product costs Costs that are a necessary and integral part of producing the finished product. (p. 822).

Supply chain All activities from receipt of an order to delivery of a product or service. (p. 829).

Total cost of work in process Cost of the beginning work in process plus total manufacturing costs for the current period. (p. 824).

Total manufacturing costs The sum of direct materials, direct labor, and manufacturing overhead incurred in the current period. (p. 824).

Total quality management (TQM) Systems implemented to reduce defects in finished products with the goal of achieving zero defects. (p. 830).

Value chain All activities associated with providing a product or service. (p. 829).

SELF-STUDY QUESTIONS

Self-Study/Self-Test

Answers are at the end of the chapter.

(SO 1) **1.** Managerial accounting:
- **a.** is governed by generally accepted accounting principles.
- **b.** places emphasis on special-purpose information.
- **c.** pertains to the entity as a whole and is highly aggregated.
- **d.** is limited to cost data.

(SO 1) **2.** Which of the following is *not* one of the categories in *Standards of Ethical Conduct for Management Accountants?*
- **a.** Confidentiality.
- **b.** Competence.
- **c.** Integrity.
- **d.** Independence.

(SO 2) **3.** The management of an organization performs several broad functions. They are:
- **a.** planning, directing and motivating, and selling.
- **b.** planning, directing and motivating, and controlling.
- **c.** planning, manufacturing, and controlling.
- **d.** directing and motivating, manufacturing, and controlling.

(SO 3) **4.** Direct materials are a:

	Product Cost	Manufacturing Overhead Cost
a.	Yes	Yes
b.	Yes	No
c.	Yes	Yes
d.	No	No

(SO 4) **5.** Indirect labor is a:
- **a.** nonmanufacturing cost.
- **b.** raw material cost.
- **c.** product cost.
- **d.** period cost.

(SO) **6.** Which of the following costs would be included in manufacturing overhead of a computer manufacturer?
- **a.** The cost of the CD drives.
- **b.** The wages earned by computer assemblers.
- **c.** The cost of the memory chips.
- **d.** Depreciation on testing equipment.

(SO) **7.** Which of the following is *not* an element of manufacturing overhead?
- **a.** Sales manager's salary.
- **b.** Plant manager's salary.
- **c.** Factory repairman's wages.
- **d.** Product inspector's salary.

(SO) **8.** For the year, Redder Company has cost of goods manufactured of $600,000, beginning finished goods inventory of $200,000, and ending finished goods inventory of $250,000. The cost of goods sold is:
- **a.** $450,000.
- **b.** $500,000.
- **c.** $550,000.
- **d.** $600,000.

(SO) **9.** A cost of goods manufactured schedule shows beginning and ending inventories for:
- **a.** raw materials and work in process only.
- **b.** work in process only.
- **c.** raw materials only.
- **d.** raw materials, work in process, and finished goods.

(SO) **10.** In a manufacturer's balance sheet, three inventories may be reported: (1) raw materials, (2) work in process, and (3) finished goods. Indicate in what sequence these inventories generally appear on a balance sheet.
- **a.** (1), (2), (3)
- **b.** (2), (3), (1)
- **c.** (3), (1), (2)
- **d.** (3), (2), (1)

QUESTIONS

1. (a) "Managerial accounting is a field of accounting that provides economic information for all interested parties." Do you agree? Explain.
(b) Juan Ortiz believes that managerial accounting serves only manufacturing firms. Is Juan correct? Explain.

2. Distinguish between managerial and financial accounting as to (a) primary users of reports, (b) types and frequency of reports, and (c) purpose of reports.

3. How does the content of reports and the verification of reports differ between managerial and financial accounting?

4. (a) Identify the four categories of ethical standards for management accountants.

   (b) Is the responsibility of the management accountant limited to only his or her own acts? Explain.

5. Marie Carne is studying for the accounting mid-term examination. Summarize for Marie what she should know about management functions.

6. "Decision making is management's most important function." Do you agree? Why or why not?

7. Ann Hurley is studying for her next accounting examination. Explain to Ann what she should know about the differences between the income statements for a manufacturing and for a merchandising company.

8. Jim Parin is unclear as to the difference between the balance sheets of a merchandising company and a manufacturing company. Explain the difference to Jim.

9. How are manufacturing costs classified?

10. Dean Saber claims that the distinction between direct and indirect materials is based entirely on physical association with the product. Is Dean correct? Why?

11. Sally Scope is confused about the differences between a product cost and a period cost. Explain the differences to Sally.

12. Identify the differences in the cost of goods sold section of an income statement between a merchandising company and a manufacturing company.

13. The determination of the cost of goods manufactured involves the following factors: (A) beginning work in process inventory, (B) total manufacturing costs, and (C) ending work in process inventory. Identify the meaning of x in the following formulas:

   (a) $A + B = x$
   (b) $A + B - C = x$

14. Jorge Manufacturing has beginning raw materials inventory $12,000, ending raw materials inventory $18,000, and raw materials purchases $150,000. What is the cost of direct materials used?

15. Ely Manufacturing Inc. has beginning work in process $27,200, direct materials used $260,000, direct labor $200,000, total manufacturing overhead $150,000, and ending work in process $32,000. What are total manufacturing costs?

16. Using the data in Q15, what are (a) the total cost of work in process and (b) the cost of goods manufactured?

17. In what order should manufacturing inventories be listed in a balance sheet?

BRIEF EXERCISES

BE20-1 Complete the following comparison table between managerial and financial accounting.

Distinguish between managerial and financial accounting.
(SO 1)

	Financial Accounting	Managerial Accounting
Primary users		
Type of reports		
Frequency of reports		
Purpose of reports		
Content of reports		
Verification		

BE20-2 The Institute of Management Accountants has promulgated ethical standards for managerial accountants. Identify the four specific standards.

Identify ethical standards.
(SO 1)

BE20-3 Listed below are three functions of the management of an organization:

1. Planning   **2.** Directing and motivating   **3.** Controlling

Identify each of the following statements that best describes each of the above functions.

(a) ____ require(s) management to look ahead and to establish objectives. A key objective of management appears to be to add value to the business.

(b) ____ involve(s) coordinating the diverse activities and human resources of a company to produce a smooth-running operation. This function relates to the implementation of planned objectives.

(c) ____ is the process of keeping the activities on track. Management must determine whether goals are being met and what changes are necessary when there are deviations.

Identify the three management functions.
(SO 2)

BE20-4 Determine whether each of the following costs should be classified as direct materials (DM), direct labor (DL), or manufacturing overhead (MO).

(a) ____ Frames and tires used in manufacturing bicycles.
(b) ____ Wages paid to production workers.
(c) ____ Insurance on factory equipment and machinery.
(d) ____ Depreciation on factory equipment.

Classify manufacturing costs.
(SO 3)

Classify manufacturing costs.

(SO 3)

BE20-5 Indicate whether each of the following costs of an automobile manufacturer would be classified as direct materials, direct labor, or manufacturing overhead:

(a) ____ Windshield.

(b) ____ Engine.

(c) ____ Wages of assembly line worker.

(d) ____ Depreciation of factory machinery.

(e) ____ Factory machinery lubricants.

(f) ____ Tires.

(g) ____ Steering wheel.

(h) ____ Salary of painting supervisor.

Identify product and period costs.

(SO 4)

BE20-6 Identify whether each of the following costs should be classified as product costs or period costs.

(a) ____ Manufacturing overhead.

(b) ____ Selling expenses.

(c) ____ Administrative expenses.

(d) ____ Advertising expenses.

(e) ____ Direct labor.

(f) ____ Direct material.

Classify manufacturing costs.

(SO 3, 4)

BE20-7 Presented below are Torre Company's monthly manufacturing cost data related to its personal computer products.

(a) Utilities for manufacturing equipment	$116,000
(b) Raw materials (CPU, chips, etc.)	$ 85,000
(c) Depreciation on manufacturing building	$880,000
(d) Wages for production workers	$191,000

Enter each cost item in the following table, placing an "X" under the appropriate headings.

	Product Costs		
	Direct Materials	**Direct Labor**	**Factory Overhead**
(a)			
(b)			
(c)			
(d)			

Compute total manufacturing costs and total cost of work in process.

(SO 6)

BE20-8 Garcia Manufacturing Company has the following data: direct labor $260,000, direct materials used $180,000, total manufacturing overhead $208,000, and beginning work in process $25,000. Compute (a) total manufacturing costs and (b) total cost of work in process.

Prepare current assets section.

(SO 7)

BE20-9 In alphabetical order below are current asset items for Scheer Company's balance sheet at December 31, 2005. Prepare the current assets section (including a complete heading).

Accounts receivable	$200,000
Cash	62,000
Finished goods	95,000
Prepaid expenses	38,000
Raw materials	68,000
Work in process	87,000

Determine missing amounts in computing total manufacturing costs.

(SO 6)

BE20-10 Presented below are incomplete 2005 manufacturing cost data for Ling Corporation. Determine the missing amounts.

	Direct Materials Used	**Direct Labor Used**	**Factory Overhead**	**Total Manufacturing Costs**
(a)	$35,000	$40,000	$ 50,000	?
(b)	?	$75,000	$120,000	$296,000
(c)	$55,000	?	$111,000	$300,000

Determine missing amounts in computing cost of goods manufactured.

(SO 6)

BE20-11 Use the same data from BE20-10 above and the data below. Determine the missing amounts.

	Total Manufacturing Costs	**Work in Process (1/1)**	**Work in Process (12/31)**	**Cost of Goods Manufactured**
(a)	?	$120,000	$86,000	?
(b)	$296,000	?	$98,000	$321,000
(c)	$300,000	$463,000	?	$515,000

EXERCISES

E20-1 Presented below is a list of costs and expenses usually incurred by Omega Corporation, a manufacturer of furniture, in its factory.

Classify costs into three classes of manufacturing costs.

(SO 3)

1. Salaries for assembly line inspectors.
2. Insurance on factory machines.
3. Property taxes on the factory building.
4. Factory repairs.
5. Upholstery used in manufacturing furniture.
6. Wages paid to assembly line workers.
7. Factory machinery depreciation.
8. Glue, nails, paint, and other small parts used in production.
9. Factory supervisors' salaries.
10. Wood used in manufacturing furniture.

Instructions

Classify the above items into the following categories: **(a)** direct materials, **(b)** direct labor, and **(c)** manufacturing overhead.

E20-2 Sandoval Company reports the following costs and expenses in May.

Determine the total amount of various types of costs.

(SO 3, 4)

Factory utilities	$ 8,500	Direct labor	$69,100
Depreciation on factory		Sales salaries	49,400
equipment	12,650	Property taxes on factory	
Depreciation on delivery trucks	3,500	building	2,500
Indirect factory labor	48,900	Repairs to office equipment	1,300
Indirect materials	89,800	Factory repairs	2,000
Direct materials used	157,600	Advertising	18,000
Factory manager's salary	6,000	Office supplies used	2,640

Instructions

From the information, determine the total amount of:

(a) Manufacturing overhead.
(b) Product costs.
(c) Period costs.

E20-3 Tierney Company is a manufacturer of personal computers. Various costs and expenses associated with its operations are as follows.

Classify various costs into different cost categories.

(SO 3, 4)

1. Property taxes on the factory building.
2. Production superintendents' salaries.
3. Memory boards and chips used in assembling computers.
4. Depreciation on the factory equipment.
5. Salaries for assembly line quality control inspectors.
6. Sales commissions paid to sell personal computers.
7. Electrical wiring in assembling computers.
8. Wages of workers assembling personal computers.
9. Soldering materials used on factory assembly lines.
10. Salaries for the night security guards for the factory building.

The company intends to classify these costs and expenses into the following categories: **(a)** direct materials, **(b)** direct labor, **(c)** manufacturing overhead, and **(d)** period costs.

Instructions

List the items 1–10. For each item, indicate the cost category to which the item belongs.

Determine missing amounts in cost of goods manufactured schedule.

(SO 6)

E20-4 The cost of goods manufactured schedule shows each of the cost elements. Complete the following schedule for Orlando Manufacturing Company.

ORLANDO MANUFACTURING COMPANY
Cost of Goods Manufactured Schedule
For the Year Ended December 31, 2005

Work in process (1/1)		$200,000
Direct materials		
Raw materials inventory (1/1)	$?	
Add: Raw materials purchases	178,000	
Less: Raw materials inventory (12/31)	7,500	
Direct materials used		$190,000
Direct labor		?
Manufacturing overhead		
Indirect labor	$ 18,000	
Factory depreciation	36,000	
Factory utilities	68,000	
Total overhead		122,000
Total manufacturing costs		?
Total cost of work in process		$?
Less: Work in process (12/31)		151,000
Cost of goods manufactured		$560,000

Determine the missing amount of different cost items.

(SO 6)

E20-5 Manufacturing cost data for Pirie Company are presented below.

	Case A	Case B	Case C
Direct materials used	(a)	$68,400	$130,000
Direct labor	$ 57,000	86,000	(g)
Manufacturing overhead	42,500	51,600	102,000
Total manufacturing costs	160,650	(d)	317,000
Work in process 1/1/05	(b)	16,500	(h)
Total cost of work in process	221,500	(e)	327,000
Work in process 12/31/05	(c)	9,000	70,000
Cost of goods manufactured	185,275	(f)	(i)

Instructions
Indicate the missing amount for each letter.

Determine the missing amount of different cost items, and prepare a condensed cost of goods manufactured schedule.

(SO 5, 6)

E20-6 Incomplete manufacturing cost data for Ramon Company for 2005 are presented as follows.

	Direct Materials Used	Direct Labor Used	Manufacturing Overhead	Total Manufacturing Costs	Work in Process 1/1	Work in Process 12/31	Cost of Goods Manufactured
(1)	$137,000	$140,000	$ 77,000	(a)	$30,000	(b)	$360,000
(2)	(c)	200,000	132,000	$410,000	(d)	$40,000	470,000
(3)	80,000	100,000	(e)	240,000	60,000	80,000	(f)
(4)	70,000	(g)	75,000	324,000	45,000	(h)	270,000

Instructions
(a) Indicate the missing amount for each letter.
(b) Prepare a condensed cost of goods manufactured schedule for situation (1) for the year ended December 31, 2005.

E20-7 Duggan Corporation has the following cost records for June 2005.

Prepare a cost of goods manufactured schedule and a partial income statement.

(SO 5, 6)

Indirect factory labor	$ 4,500	Factory utilities	$ 400
Direct materials used	15,000	Depreciation, factory equipment	1,400
Work in process, 6/1/05	3,000	Direct labor	25,000
Work in process, 6/30/05	5,500	Maintenance, factory equipment	1,300
Finished goods, 6/1/05	5,000	Indirect materials	2,200
Finished goods, 6/30/05	9,500	Factory manager's salary	3,000

Instructions
(a) Prepare a cost of goods manufactured schedule for June 2005.
(b) Prepare an income statement through gross profit for June 2005 assuming net sales are $98,100.

E20-8 Abbott Manufacturing Company produces blankets. From its accounting records it prepares the following schedule and financial statements on a yearly basis.

Indicate in which schedule or financial statement(s) different cost items will appear.

(SO 5, 6, 7)

(a) Cost of goods manufactured schedule
(b) Income statement
(c) Balance sheet

The following items are found in its ledger and accompanying data.

1. Direct labor
2. Raw materials inventory, 1/1
3. Work in process inventory, 12/31
4. Finished goods inventory, 1/1
5. Indirect labor
6. Depreciation on factory machinery
7. Work in process, 1/1
8. Finished goods inventory, 12/31
9. Factory maintenance salaries
10. Cost of goods manufactured
11. Depreciation on delivery equipment
12. Cost of goods available for sale
13. Direct materials used
14. Heat and electricity for factory
15. Repairs to roof of factory building
16. Cost of raw materials purchases

Instructions
List the items 1–16. For each item, indicate by using the appropriate letter or letters, the schedule and/or financial statement(s) in which the item will appear.

E20-9 An analysis of the accounts of Aaron Manufacturing reveals the following manufacturing cost data for the month ended June 30, 2005.

Prepare a cost of goods manufactured schedule, and present the ending inventories of the balance sheet.

(SO 5, 6, 7)

Inventories	Beginning	Ending
Raw materials	$7,000	$11,100
Work in process	5,000	9,000
Finished goods	8,000	6,000

Costs incurred:
Raw materials purchases $64,000, direct labor $50,000, manufacturing overhead $30,000. The specific overhead costs were: indirect labor $15,600, factory insurance $4,000, machinery depreciation $4,000, machinery repairs $1,800, factory utilities $3,100, miscellaneous factory costs $1,500.

Instructions
(a) Prepare the cost of goods manufactured schedule for the month ended June 30, 2005.
(b) Show the presentation of the ending inventories on the June 30, 2005, balance sheet.

E20-10 Kelso Motor Company manufactures automobiles. During September 2005 the company purchased 5,000 head lamps at a cost of $8 per lamp. Kelso withdrew 4,650 lamps from the warehouse during the month. Fifty of these lamps were used to replace the head lamps in autos used by traveling sales staff. The remaining 4,600 lamps were put in autos manufactured during the month.

Of the autos put into production during September 2005, 90% were completed and transferred to the company's storage lot. Of the cars completed during the month, 70% were sold by September 30.

Determine the amount of cost to appear in various accounts, and indicate in which financial statements these accounts would appear.

(SO 5, 6, 7)

Instructions

(a) Determine the cost of head lamps that would appear in each of the following accounts at September 30, 2005: Raw Materials, Work in Process, Finished Goods, Cost of Goods Sold, and Selling Expenses.

(b) ▭▭▭▷ Write a short memo to the chief accountant, indicating whether and where each of the accounts in (a) would appear on the income statement or on the balance sheet at September 30, 2005.

PROBLEMS: SET A

Classify manufacturing costs into different categories and compute the unit cost.

(SO 3, 4)

P20-1A Mantle Company specializes in manufacturing motorcycles. The company has enough orders to keep the factory production at 1,000 motorcycles per month. Mantle's monthly manufacturing cost and other expense data are as follows.

Maintenance costs on factory building	$ 300
Factory manager's salary	6,000
Advertising for motorcycles	10,000
Sales commissions	5,000
Depreciation on factory building	700
Rent on factory equipment	5,000
Insurance on factory building	3,000
Raw materials (frames, tires, etc.)	20,000
Utility costs for factory	800
Supplies for general office	200
Wages for assembly line workers	35,000
Depreciation on office equipment	500
Miscellaneous materials (lubricants, solders, etc.)	1,000

Instructions

(a) Prepare an answer sheet with the following column headings.

		Product Costs		
Cost Item	Direct Materials	Direct Labor	Manufacturing Overhead	Period Costs

(a) DM $20,000
DL $35,000
MO $16,800
PC $15,700

Enter each cost item on your answer sheet, placing the dollar amount under the appropriate headings. Total the dollar amounts in each of the columns.

(b) Compute the cost to produce one motorcycle.

Classify manufacturing costs into different categories and compute the unit cost.

(SO 3, 4)

P20-2A Willow Company, a manufacturer of tennis rackets, started production in November 2005. For the preceding 5 years Willow had been a retailer of sports equipment. After a thorough survey of tennis racket markets, Willow decided to turn its retail store into a tennis racket factory.

Raw materials cost for a tennis racket will total $20 per racket. Workers on the production lines are paid on average $14 per hour. A racket usually takes 2 hours to complete. In addition, the rent on the equipment used to produce rackets amounts to $1,000 per month. Indirect materials cost $3 per racket. A supervisor was hired to oversee production; her monthly salary is $3,500.

Janitorial costs are $1,200 monthly. Advertising costs for the rackets will be $6,000 per month. The factory building depreciation expense is $8,400 per year. Property taxes on the factory building will be $4,320 per year.

Instructions

(a) Prepare an answer sheet with the following column headings.

(a) DM $50,000
DL $70,000
MO $14,260
PC $6,000

		Product Costs		
Cost Item	Direct Materials	Direct Labor	Manufacturing Overhead	Period Costs

Assuming that Willow manufactures, on average, 2,500 tennis rackets per month, enter each cost item on your answer sheet, placing the dollar amount per month under the appropriate headings. Total the dollar amounts in each of the columns.

(b) Compute the cost to produce one racket.

P20-3A Incomplete manufacturing costs, expenses, and selling data for two different cases are as follows.

Indicate the missing amount of different cost items, and prepare a condensed cost of goods manufactured schedule, an income statement, and a partial balance sheet.

(SO 5, 6, 7)

	Case	
	1	**2**
Direct Materials Used	$ 8,000	$ (g)
Direct Labor	3,000	4,000
Manufacturing Overhead	4,000	5,000
Total Manufacturing Costs	(a)	20,000
Beginning Work in Process Inventory	1,000	(h)
Ending Work in Process Inventory	(b)	2,000
Sales	21,500	(i)
Sales Discounts	1,500	1,200
Cost of Goods Manufactured	12,800	21,000
Beginning Finished Goods Inventory	(c)	4,000
Goods Available for Sale	15,300	(j)
Cost of Goods Sold	(d)	(k)
Ending Finished Goods Inventory	1,200	2,500
Gross Profit	(e)	7,000
Operating Expenses	2,700	(l)
Net Income	(f)	2,800

Instructions

(a) Indicate the missing amount for each letter.

(b) Prepare a condensed cost of goods manufactured schedule for Case 1.

(c) Prepare an income statement and the current assets section of the balance sheet for Case 1. Assume that in Case 1 the other items in the current assets section are as follows: Cash $3,000, Receivables (net) $10,000, Raw Materials $700, and Prepaid Expenses $200.

(b) CGM $12,800
(c) Total current assets $18,300

P20-4A The following data were taken from the records of Portico Manufacturing Company for the year ended December 31, 2005.

Prepare a cost of goods manufactured schedule, a partial income statement, and a partial balance sheet.

(SO 5, 6, 7)

Raw Materials		Factory Insurance	$ 5,400
Inventory 1/1/05	$ 40,000	Factory Machinery	
Raw Materials		Depreciation	7,700
Inventory 12/31/05	44,200	Freight-in on Raw Materials	
Finished Goods		Purchased	3,900
Inventory 1/1/05	85,000	Factory Utilities	15,900
Finished Goods		Office Utilities Expense	8,600
Inventory 12/31/05	72,800	Sales	495,000
Work in Process		Sales Discounts	3,500
Inventory 1/1/05	9,500	Plant Manager's Salary	40,000
Work in Process		Factory Property Taxes	6,100
Inventory 12/31/05	8,000	Factory Repairs	800
Direct Labor	145,100	Raw Materials Purchases	64,600
Indirect Labor	19,100	Cash	28,000
Accounts Receivable	27,000		

Instructions

(a) Prepare a cost of goods manufactured schedule.

(b) Prepare an income statement through gross profit.

(c) Prepare the current assets section of the balance sheet at December 31.

Totals
(a) $305,900
(b) $173,400
(c) $180,000

Prepare a cost of goods manu-factured schedule and a correct income statement.

(SO 5, 6)

P20-5A Harmon Company is a manufacturer of toys. Its controller, Gina Harmon, resigned in August 2005. An inexperienced assistant accountant has prepared the following income statement for the month of August 2005.

HARMON COMPANY
Income Statement
For the Month Ended August 31, 2005

Sales (net)		$690,000
Less: Operating expenses		
Raw materials purchased	$230,000	
Direct labor cost	150,000	
Advertising expense	75,000	
Selling and administrative salaries	70,000	
Rent on factory facilities	60,000	
Depreciation on sales equipment	55,000	
Depreciation on factory equipment	35,000	
Indirect labor cost	20,000	
Utilities expense	10,000	
Insurance expense	5,000	710,000
Net loss		$(20,000)

Prior to August 2005 the company had been profitable every month. The company's president is concerned about the accuracy of the income statement. As her friend, you have been asked to review the income statement and make necessary corrections. After examining other manufacturing cost data, you have acquired additional information as follows.

1. Inventory balances at the beginning and end of August were:

	August 1	**August 31**
Raw materials	$19,500	$33,000
Work in process	25,000	26,000
Finished goods	40,000	62,000

2. Only 60% of the utilities expense and 70% of the insurance expense apply to factory operations; the remaining amounts should be charged to selling and administrative activities.

Instructions

(a) CGM $490,000
(b) NI $16,500

(a) Prepare a cost of goods manufactured schedule for August 2005.
(b) Prepare a correct income statement for August 2005.

PROBLEMS: SET B

Classify manufacturing costs into different categories and compute the unit cost.

(SO 3, 4)

P20-1B McClain Company specializes in manufacturing a unique model of bicycle helmet. The model is well accepted by consumers, and the company has enough orders to keep the factory production at 10,000 helmets per month (80% of its full capacity). McClain's monthly manufacturing cost and other expense data are as follows.

Rent on factory equipment	$ 8,000
Insurance on factory building	1,500
Raw materials (plastics, polystyrene, etc.)	70,000
Utility costs for factory	900
Supplies for general office	300
Wages for assembly line workers	41,000
Depreciation on office equipment	800
Miscellaneous materials (lubricants, solders, etc.)	1,100
Factory manager's salary	5,700
Property taxes on factory building	400
Advertising for helmets	13,000
Sales commissions	7,000
Depreciation on factory building	1,500

Instructions

(a) Prepare an answer sheet with the following column headings:

	Product Costs			
Cost Item	Direct Materials	Direct Labor	Manufacturing Overhead	Period Costs

(a) DM $70,000
DL $41,000
MO $19,100
PC $21,100

Enter each cost item on your answer sheet, placing the dollar amount under the appropriate headings. Total the dollar amounts in each of the columns.

(b) Compute the cost to produce one helmet.

P20-2B Phelps Company, a manufacturer of stereo systems, started its production in October 2005. For the preceding 3 years Phelps had been a retailer of stereo systems. After a thorough survey of stereo system markets, Phelps decided to turn its retail store into a stereo equipment factory.

Classify manufacturing costs into different categories and compute the unit cost.

(SO 3, 4)

Raw materials cost for a stereo system will total $70 per unit. Workers on the production lines are on average paid $12 per hour. A stereo system usually takes 5 hours to complete. In addition, the rent on the equipment used to assemble stereo systems amounts to $4,500 per month. Indirect materials cost $5 per system. A supervisor was hired to oversee production; her monthly salary is $2,700.

Janitorial costs were $1,300 monthly. Advertising costs for the stereo system will be $8,500 per month. The factory building depreciation expense is $7,200 per year. Property taxes on the factory building will be $6,000 per year.

Instructions

(a) Prepare an answer sheet with the following column headings:

	Product Costs			
Cost Item	Direct Materials	Direct Labor	Manufacturing Overhead	Period Costs

(a) DM $105,000
DL $90,000
MO $17,100
PC $8,500

Assuming that Phelps manufactures, on average, 1,500 stereo systems per month, enter each cost item on your answer sheet, placing the dollar amount per month under the appropriate headings. Total the dollar amounts in each of the columns.

(b) Compute the cost to produce one stereo system.

P20-3B Incomplete manufacturing costs, expenses, and selling data for two different cases are as follows.

Indicate the missing amount of different cost items, and prepare a condensed cost of goods manufactured schedule, an income statement, and a partial balance sheet.

(SO 5, 6, 7)

	Case	
	1	**2**
Direct Materials Used	$ 7,000	$ (g)
Direct Labor	6,000	8,000
Manufacturing Overhead	5,000	4,000
Total Manufacturing Costs	(a)	21,000
Beginning Work in Process Inventory	1,000	(h)
Ending Work in Process Inventory	(b)	3,000
Sales	24,500	(i)
Sales Discounts	2,500	1,400
Cost of Goods Manufactured	16,000	22,000
Beginning Finished Goods Inventory	(c)	4,300
Goods Available for Sale	20,000	(j)
Cost of Goods Sold	(d)	(k)
Ending Finished Goods Inventory	2,400	2,500
Gross Profit	(e)	7,000
Operating Expenses	2,500	(l)
Net Income	(f)	2,000

Instructions

(a) Indicate the missing amount for each letter.

(b) CGM $16,000
(c) Total current assets
    $25,400

(b) Prepare a condensed cost of goods manufactured schedule for Case 1.

(c) Prepare an income statement and the current assets section of the balance sheet for Case 1. Assume that in Case 1 the other items in the current assets section are as follows: Cash $4,000, Receivables (net) $15,000, Raw Materials $600, and Prepaid Expenses $400.

Prepare a cost of goods manu-factured schedule, a partial income statement, and a partial balance sheet.

(SO 5, 6, 7)

P20-4B The following data were taken from the records of Lionel Manufacturing Company for the fiscal year ended June 30, 2005.

Raw Materials		Factory Insurance	$ 4,600
Inventory 7/1/04	$ 43,000	Factory Machinery	
Raw Materials		Depreciation	15,000
Inventory 6/30/05	39,600	Freight-in on Raw Materials	
Finished Goods		Purchased	8,600
Inventory 7/1/04	96,000	Factory Utilities	24,600
Finished Goods		Office Utilities Expense	8,650
Inventory 6/30/05	85,900	Sales	577,000
Work in Process		Sales Discounts	4,200
Inventory 7/1/04	19,800	Plant Manager's Salary	42,000
Work in Process		Factory Property Taxes	9,600
Inventory 6/30/05	17,600	Factory Repairs	1,400
Direct Labor	147,250	Raw Materials Purchases	89,800
Indirect Labor	24,460	Cash	32,000
Accounts Receivable	27,000		

Totals
(a) $372,910
(b) $189,790
(c) $202,100

Instructions

(a) Prepare a cost of goods manufactured schedule.

(b) Prepare an income statement through gross profit.

(c) Prepare the current assets section of the balance sheet at June 30, 2005.

Prepare a cost of goods manu-factured schedule and a correct income statement.

(SO 5, 6)

P20-5B Lieberman Company is a manufacturer of computers. Its controller resigned in October 2005. An inexperienced assistant accountant has prepared the following income statement for the month of October 2005.

LIEBERMAN COMPANY
Income Statement
For the Month Ended October 31, 2005

Sales (net)		$800,000
Less: Operating expenses		
Raw materials purchased	$270,000	
Direct labor cost	190,000	
Advertising expense	92,000	
Selling and administrative salaries	75,000	
Rent on factory facilities	60,000	
Depreciation on sales equipment	45,000	
Depreciation on factory equipment	35,000	
Indirect labor cost	25,000	
Utilities expense	12,000	
Insurance expense	8,000	812,000
Net loss		$(12,000)

Prior to October 2005 the company had been profitable every month. The company's president is concerned about the accuracy of the income statement. As his friend, you have been asked to review the income statement and make necessary corrections. After examining other manufacturing cost data, you have acquired additional information as follows.

1. Inventory balances at the beginning and end of October were:

	October 1	October 31
Raw materials	$18,000	$31,000
Work in process	16,000	19,000
Finished goods	30,000	48,000

2. Only 70% of the utilities expense and 60% of the insurance expense apply to factory operations. The remaining amounts should be charged to selling and administrative activities.

Instructions
(a) Prepare a schedule of cost of goods manufactured for October 2005.
(b) Prepare a correct income statement for October 2005.

(a) CGM $577,200
(b) NI $22,000

BROADENING YOUR PERSPECTIVE

Group Decision Case

BYP20-1 Wendall Manufacturing Company specializes in producing fashion outfits. On July 31, 2005, a tornado touched down at its factory and general office. The inventories in the warehouse and the factory were totally damaged due to heavy rain and moisture. The general office nearby was completely destroyed. Next morning, through a careful search of the disaster site, however, Jim Wolfe, the company's controller, and Betty Francis, the cost accountant, were able to recover a small part of manufacturing cost data for the current month.

"What a horrible experience," sighed Jim. "And the worst part is that we may not have enough records to use in filing an insurance claim."

"It was terrible," replied Betty. "However, I managed to recover some of the manufacturing cost data that I was working on yesterday afternoon. The data indicate that our direct labor cost in July totaled $225,000 and that we had purchased $355,000 of raw materials. Also, I recall that the raw materials used for July was $350,000. But I'm not sure this information will help. The rest of our records are blown away."

"Well, not exactly," said Jim. "I was working on the year-to-date income statement when the tornado warning was announced. My recollection is that our sales in July were $1,200,000 and our gross profit ratio has been 40% of sales. Also, I can remember that our cost of goods available for sale was $740,000 for July."

"Maybe we can work something out from this information!" exclaimed Betty. "My experience tells me that our manufacturing overhead is usually 60% of direct labor."

"Hey, look what I just found," cried Betty. "It's a copy of this June's balance sheet, and it shows that our inventories as of June 30 are Finished goods $36,000, Work in process $22,000, and Raw materials $19,000."

"Super," yelled Jim. "Let's go work something out."

In order to file an insurance claim Wendall Company must determine the amount of its inventories as of July 31, 2005, the date of the tornado touchdown.

Instructions
With the class divided into groups, determine the amount of cost in the Raw Materials, Work in Process, and Finished Goods inventory accounts as of the date of the tornado touchdown.

Managerial Analysis

BYP20-2 Tennis, Anyone? is a fairly large manufacturing company located in the southern United States. The company manufactures tennis rackets, tennis balls, tennis clothing, and tennis shoes, all bearing the company's distinctive logo, a large green question mark on a white flocked tennis ball. The company's sales have been increasing over the past 10 years.

The tennis racket division has recently implemented several advanced manufacturing techniques. Robot arms hold the tennis rackets in place while glue dries, and machine vision systems check for defects. The engineering and design team uses computerized drafting and testing of new products. The following managers work in the tennis racket division.

Peter Davis, Sales Manager (supervises all sales representatives)
Tom Stevens, technical specialist (supervises computer programmers)
Kevin Chaney, cost accounting manager (supervises cost accountants)
Jack Marler, production supervisor (supervises all manufacturing employees)
Sharon Ruth, engineer (supervises all new product design teams)

Instructions
(a) What are the primary information needs of each manager?
(b) Which, if any, financial accounting report(s) is each likely to use?
(c) Name one special-purpose management accounting report that could be designed for each manager. Include the name of the report, the information it would contain, and how frequently it should be issued.

Real-World Focus

BYP20-3 **Anchor Glass Container Corporation**, the third largest manufacturer of glass containers in the U.S., supplies beverage and food producers and consumer products manufacturers nationwide. Parent company **Consumers Packaging Inc.** (*Toronto Stock Exchange*: CGC) is a leading international designer and manufacturer of glass containers.

The following management discussion appeared in a recent annual report of Anchor Glass.

ANCHOR GLASS CONTAINER CORPORATION
Management Discussion

Cost of Products Sold Cost of products sold as a percentage of net sales was 89.3% in the current year compared to 87.6% in the prior year. The increase in cost of products sold as a percentage of net sales principally reflected the impact of operational problems during the second quarter of the current year at a major furnace at one of the Company's plants, higher downtime, and costs and expenses associated with an increased number of scheduled capital improvement projects, increases in labor, and certain other manufacturing costs (with no corresponding selling price increases in the current year). Reduced fixed costs from the closing of the Streator, Illinois, plant in June of the current year and productivity and efficiency gains partially offset these cost increases.

Instructions
What factors affect the costs of products sold at Anchor Glass Container Corporation?

Exploring the Web

BYP20-4 **The Institute of Management Accountants (IMA)** is the largest organization of its kind in the world, dedicated to excellence in the practice of management accounting and financial management.

Address: www.imanet.org., or go to www.wiley.com/college/weygandt

Instructions
At the IMA's home page, locate the answers to the following questions.

(a) How many members does the IMA have, and what are their job titles?
(b) What are some of the benefits of joining the IMA as a student?
(c) Use the chapter locator function to locate the IMA chapter nearest you, and find the name of the chapter president.

Communication Activity

BYP20-5 Refer to Problem 20-5A and add the following requirement.

Prepare a letter to the president of the company, Becky Mintor, describing the changes you made. Explain clearly why net income is different after the changes. Keep the following points in mind as you compose your letter.

1. This is a letter to the president of a company, who is your friend. The style should be generally formal, but you may relax some requirements. For example, you may call the president by her first name.
2. Executives are very busy. Your letter should tell the president your main results first (for example, the amount of net income).
3. You should include brief explanations so that the president can understand the changes you made in the calculations.

Ethics Case

BYP20-6 Juan Ramirez, controller for Warren Industries, was reviewing production cost reports for the year. One amount in these reports continued to bother him—advertising. During the year, the company had instituted an expensive advertising campaign to sell some of its slower-moving products. It was still too early to tell whether the advertising campaign was successful.

There had been much internal debate as how to report advertising costs. The vice president of finance argued that advertising costs should be reported as a cost of production, just like direct materials and direct labor. He therefore recommended that this cost be identified as manufacturing overhead and reported as part of inventory costs until sold. Others disagreed. Ramirez believed that this cost should be reported as an expense of the current period, based on the conservatism principle. Others argued that it should be reported as Prepaid Advertising and reported as a current asset.

The president finally had to decide the issue. He argued that these costs should be reported as inventory. His arguments were practical ones. He noted that the company was experiencing financial difficulty and expensing this amount in the current period might jeopardize a planned bond offering. Also, by reporting the advertising costs as inventory rather than as prepaid advertising, less attention would be directed to it by the financial community.

Instructions
(a) Who are the stakeholders in this situation?
(b) What are the ethical issues involved in this situation?
(c) What would you do if you were Juan Ramirez?

Answers to Self-Study Questions
1. b   **2.** d   **3.** b   **4.** b   **5.** c   **6.** d   **7.** a   **8.** c   **9.** a   **10.** d

Answer to PepsiCo Review It Question 3, page 831
In Note 14, **PepsiCo** reports raw materials inventory of $525 million, work-in-process inventory of $214 million, and finished goods inventory of $603 million.

 ☑ **REMEMBER** to go back to the Navigator box on the chapter-opening page and check off your completed work.

Job Order Cost Accounting

THE NAVIGATOR ✓

Understand **Concepts for Review** ❏

Read **Feature Story** ❏

Scan **Study Objectives** ❏

Read **Preview** ❏

Read text and answer **Before You Go On**
p. 855 ❏   p. 865 ❏   p. 870 ❏

Work **Demonstration Problem** ❏

Review **Summary of Study Objectives** ❏

Answer **Self-Study Questions** ❏

Complete **Assignments** ❏

CONCEPTS FOR REVIEW

Before studying this chapter, you should know or, if necessary, review:

- How a perpetual inventory system works.
  (Ch. 5, pp. 186–192)

- The three classifications of manufacturing costs.
  (Ch. 20, pp. 820–821)

- The difference between product and period costs.
  (Ch. 20, p. 822)

- The form and content of a cost of goods manufactured schedule.
  (Ch. 20, p. 825)

THE
NAVIGATOR

"... And We'd Like It in Red"

Western States Fire Apparatus, Inc., of Cornelius, Oregon, is one of the few U.S. companies that makes fire trucks. The company builds about 25 trucks per year. Founded in 1941, the company is run by the children and grandchildren of the original founder.

"We buy the chassis, which is the cab and the frame," says Susan Scott, the company's bookkeeper. "In our computer, we set up an account into which all of the direct material that

is purchased for that particular job is charged." Other direct materials include the water pump—which can cost $10,000—the lights, the siren, ladders, and hoses.

As for direct labor, the production workers fill out job sheets that tell what jobs they worked on. Usually, the company is building four trucks at any one time. On payday, the controller allocates the payroll to the appropriate job record.

Indirect materials, such as nuts and bolts, wiring, lubricants, and abrasives, are allocated to each job in proportion to direct material dollars. Other costs, such as insurance and supervisors' salaries, are allocated based on direct labor hours. "We need to allocate overhead in order to know what kind of price we have to charge when we submit our bids," she says.

Western gets orders through a "blind-bidding" process. That is, Western submits its bid without knowing the bid prices made by its competitors. "If we bid too low, we won't make a profit. If we bid too high, we don't get the job."

Regardless of the final price for the truck, the quality had better be first-rate. "The fire departments let you know if they don't like what you did, and you usually end up fixing it."

After studying this chapter, you should be able to:

1. Explain the characteristics and purposes of cost accounting.
2. Describe the flow of costs in a job order cost accounting system.
3. Explain the nature and importance of a job cost sheet.
4. Indicate how the predetermined overhead rate is determined and used.
5. Prepare entries for jobs completed and sold.
6. Distinguish between under- and overapplied manufacturing overhead.

The Feature Story about **Western States Fire Apparatus** described the manufacturing costs used in making a fire truck. It demonstrated that accurate costing is critical to the company's success. For example, in order to submit accurate bids on new jobs and to know whether it profited from past jobs, the company needs a good costing system. This chapter illustrates how these manufacturing costs would be assigned to specific jobs, such as the manufacture of individual fire trucks. We begin the discussion in this chapter with an overview of the flow of costs in a job order cost accounting system. We then use a case study to explain and illustrate the documents, entries, and accounts in this type of cost accounting system.

The content and organization of Chapter 21 are as follows.

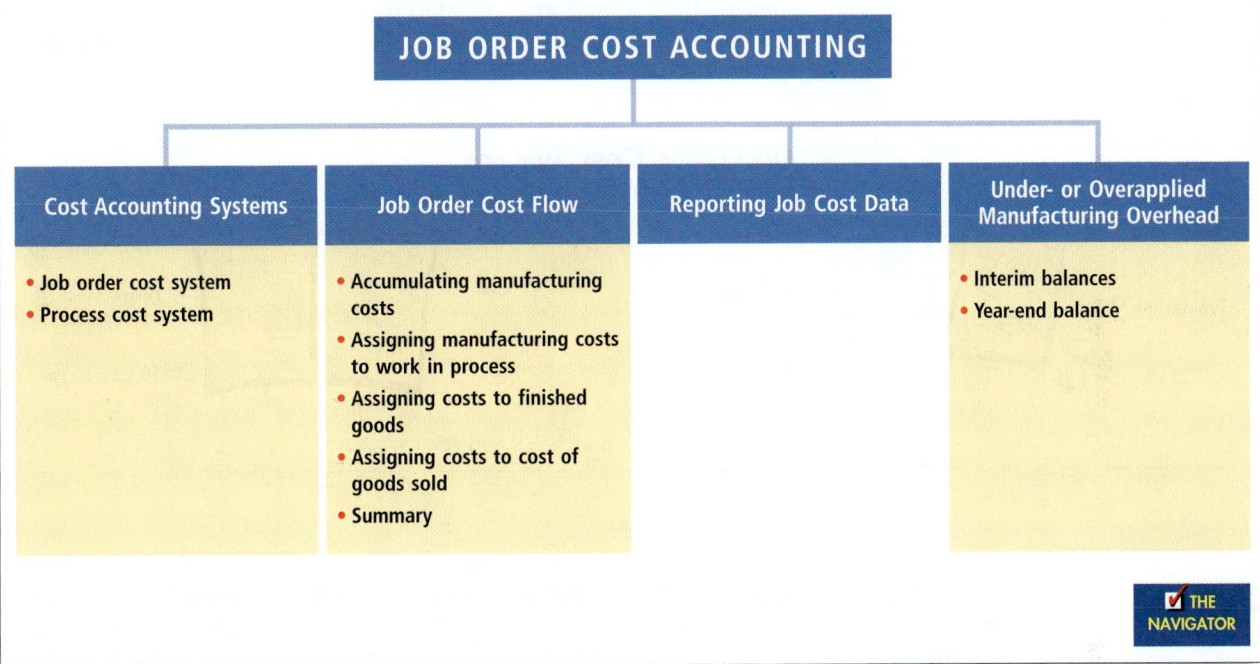

JOB ORDER COST ACCOUNTING

Cost Accounting Systems	Job Order Cost Flow	Reporting Job Cost Data	Under- or Overapplied Manufacturing Overhead
• Job order cost system • Process cost system	• Accumulating manufacturing costs • Assigning manufacturing costs to work in process • Assigning costs to finished goods • Assigning costs to cost of goods sold • Summary		• Interim balances • Year-end balance

☑ THE NAVIGATOR

Cost Accounting Systems

Cost accounting involves the measuring, recording, and reporting of product costs. From the data accumulated, both the total cost and the unit cost of each product is determined. The accuracy of the product cost information produced by the cost accounting system is critical to the success of the company. As you will see in later chapters, this information is used to determine which products to produce, what price to charge, and the amounts to produce. Accurate product cost information is also vital for effective evaluation of employee performance.

A **cost accounting system** consists of accounts for the various manufacturing costs. These accounts are fully integrated into the general ledger of a company. **An important feature of a cost accounting system is the use of a perpetual inventory system.** Such a system **provides immediate, up-to-date information on the cost of a product**. There are two basic types of cost accounting systems: (1) a job order cost system and (2) a process cost system. Although cost accounting systems differ widely from company to company, most are based on one of these two traditional product costing systems.

STUDY OBJECTIVE 1

Explain the characteristics and purposes of cost accounting.

(handwritten margin note) batch = a multitude of the same thing w/ntdspecificunit qty accounted as one unit.

Job Order Cost System

Under a **job order cost system**, costs are assigned to each **job** or to each **batch** of goods. An example of a job would be the manufacture of a mainframe computer by **IBM**, the production of a movie by **Disney**, or the making of a fire truck by **Western States**. An example of a batch would be the printing of 225 wedding invitations by a local print shop, or the printing of a weekly issue of *Fortune* magazine by a hi-tech printer such as **Quad Graphics**. Jobs or batches may be completed to fill a specific customer order or to replenish inventory.

An important feature of job order costing is that each job (or batch) has its own distinguishing characteristics. For example, each house is custom built, each consulting engagement by a CPA firm is unique, and each printing job is different. **The objective is to compute the cost per job.** At each point in the manufacturing of a product or the providing of a service, the job and its associated costs can be identified. A job order cost system measures costs for each completed job, rather than for set time periods. The recording of costs in a job order cost system is shown in Illustration 21-1.

Illustration 21-1
Job order cost system

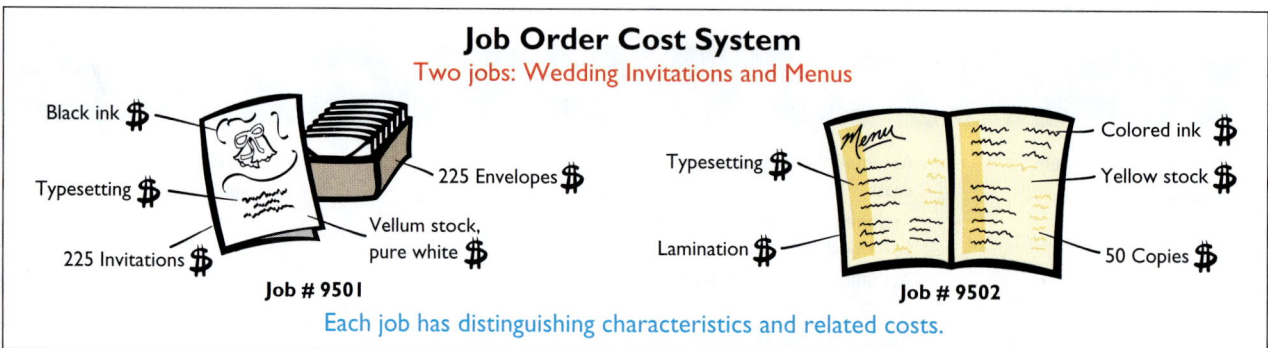

Job Order Cost System
Two jobs: Wedding Invitations and Menus

Black ink $ Colored ink $
Typesetting $ Typesetting $ Yellow stock $
225 Invitations $ 225 Envelopes $ Lamination $ 50 Copies $
Vellum stock, pure white $

Job # 9501   **Job # 9502**

Each job has distinguishing characteristics and related costs.

Process Cost System

A **process cost system** is used when a series of connected manufacturing processes or departments produce a large volume of similar products. Production is continuous to ensure that adequate inventories of the finished product(s) are on hand. A process cost system is used in the manufacture of cereal by **Kellogg**, the refining of petroleum by **ExxonMobil**, and the production of automobiles by **General Motors**. Process costing accumulates product-related costs **for a period of time** (such as a week or a month) instead of assigning costs to specific products or job orders. In process costing, the costs are assigned to departments or processes for a set period of time. The recording of costs in a process cost system is shown in Illustration 21-2. The process cost system will be discussed further in Chapter 22.

Illustration 21-2
Process cost system

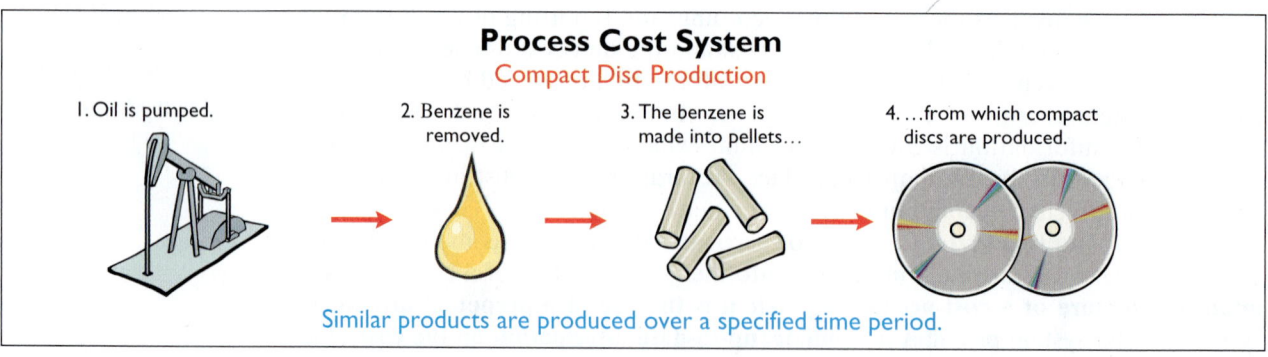

Process Cost System
Compact Disc Production

1. Oil is pumped.   2. Benzene is removed.   3. The benzene is made into pellets...   4. ...from which compact discs are produced.

Similar products are produced over a specified time period.

A company may use both types of cost systems. For example, **General Motors** uses process cost accounting for its standard model cars, such as Saturns and Corvettes, and job order cost accounting for a custom-made limousine for the President of the United States. The objective of both systems is to provide unit cost information for product pricing, cost control, inventory valuation, and financial statement presentation. End-of-period inventory values are computed by using unit cost data.

ACCOUNTING IN ACTION   Business Insight

Many companies suffer from poor cost accounting. As a result, they sometimes make products they ought not to be selling at all and buy others that they could more profitably make themselves. Also, inaccurate cost data lead companies to misallocate capital and frustrate efforts by plant managers to improve efficiency.

For example, consider the case of a diversified company in the business of rebuilding diesel locomotives. The managers thought they were making money, but a consulting firm found that costs had been seriously underestimated. The company bailed out of the business, and not a moment too soon. Says the consultant who advised the company: "The more contracts it won, the more money it lost."

BEFORE YOU GO ON...

Review It

1. What is cost accounting?
2. What does a cost accounting system consist of?
3. How does a job order cost system differ from a process cost system?

☑ THE NAVIGATOR

Job Order Cost Flow

The flow of costs (direct materials, direct labor, and manufacturing overhead) in job order cost accounting parallels the physical flow of the materials as they are converted into finished goods. As shown in Illustration 21-3, manufacturing costs are assigned to the Work in Process Inventory account. When a job is completed, the cost of the job is transferred to Finished Goods Inventory. Later when the goods are sold, their cost is transferred to Cost of Goods Sold.

STUDY OBJECTIVE 2

Describe the flow of costs in a job order cost accounting system.

Illustration 21-3
Flow of costs in job order cost accounting

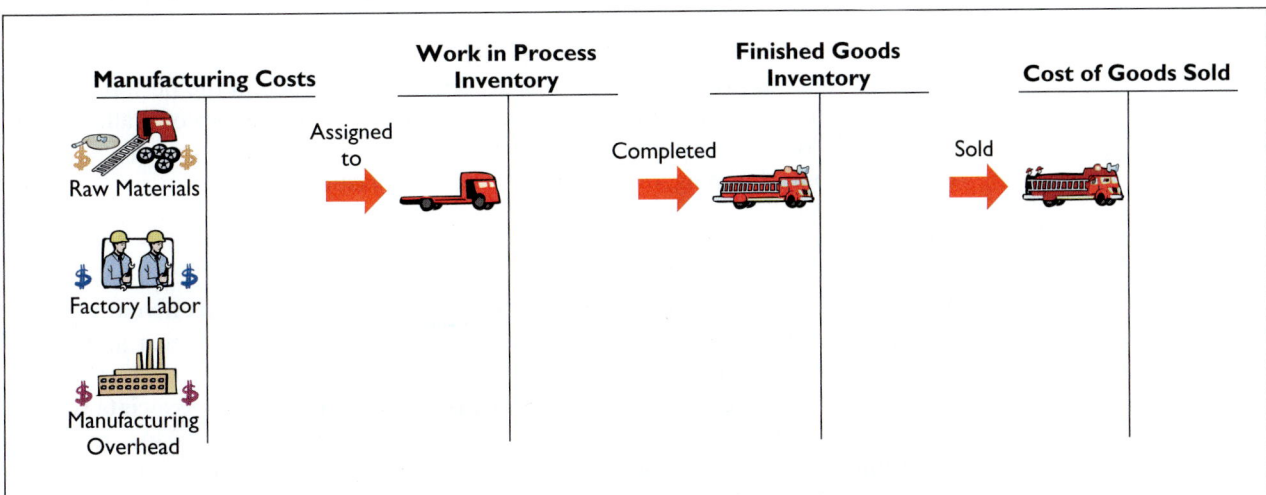

Illustration 21-3 provided a basic overview of the flow of costs in a manufacturing setting. A more detailed presentation of the flow of costs is shown in Illustration 21-4. It indicates that there are two major steps in the flow of costs: (1) *accumulating* the manufacturing costs incurred and (2) *assigning* the accumulated costs to the work done. As shown, manufacturing costs incurred are accumulated in entries 1–3 by debits to Raw Materials Inventory, Factory Labor, and Manufacturing Overhead. When these costs are incurred no attempt is made to associate the costs with specific jobs. The remaining entries (entries 4–8) assign manufacturing costs incurred. On the following pages we will use a case study to explain how a job order system operates.

Illustration 21-4
Job order cost accounting system

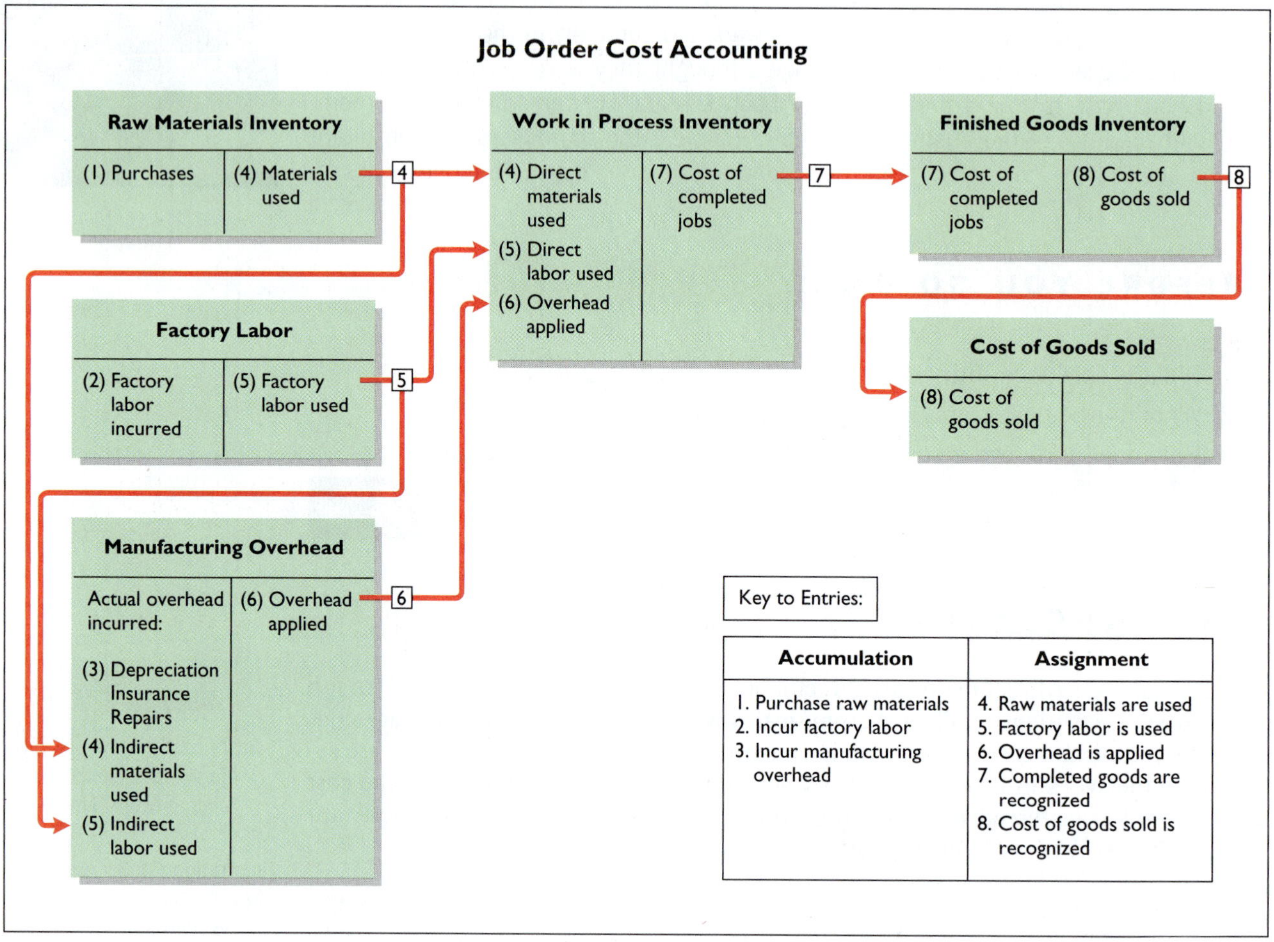

Job Order Cost Accounting

Raw Materials Inventory	
(1) Purchases	(4) Materials used

4

Work in Process Inventory	
(4) Direct materials used	(7) Cost of completed jobs
(5) Direct labor used	
(6) Overhead applied	

7

Finished Goods Inventory	
(7) Cost of completed jobs	(8) Cost of goods sold

8

Factory Labor	
(2) Factory labor incurred	(5) Factory labor used

5

Cost of Goods Sold	
(8) Cost of goods sold	

Manufacturing Overhead	
Actual overhead incurred:	(6) Overhead applied
(3) Depreciation Insurance Repairs	
(4) Indirect materials used	
(5) Indirect labor used	

6

Key to Entries:

Accumulation	Assignment
1. Purchase raw materials	4. Raw materials are used
2. Incur factory labor	5. Factory labor is used
3. Incur manufacturing overhead	6. Overhead is applied
	7. Completed goods are recognized
	8. Cost of goods sold is recognized

Accumulating Manufacturing Costs

In a job order cost system, manufacturing costs are recorded in the period in which they are incurred. To illustrate, we will use the January transactions of Wallace Manufacturing Company, which makes machine tools and dies. (Dies are devices used for cutting out, stamping, or forming metals and plastics.)

Raw Materials Costs

The costs of raw materials purchased are debited to Raw Materials Inventory when the materials are received. This account is debited for the invoice cost and freight costs chargeable to the purchaser. It is credited for purchase discounts taken and purchase returns and allowances. **No effort is made at this point to associate the cost of materials with specific jobs or orders.** The procedures for ordering, receiving, recording, and paying for raw materials are similar to the purchasing procedures of a merchandising company.

To illustrate, assume that Wallace Manufacturing purchases 2,000 handles (Stock No. AA2746) at $5 per unit ($10,000) and 800 modules (Stock No. AA2850) at $40 per unit ($32,000) for a total cost of $42,000 ($10,000 + $32,000). The entry to record this purchase on January 4 is:

(1)

Jan. 4	Raw Materials Inventory	42,000	
	Accounts Payable		42,000
	(Purchase of raw materials on account)		

Raw Materials Inventory is a control account. The subsidiary ledger consists of individual records for each item of raw materials. The records may take the form of accounts (or cards) that are manually or mechanically prepared. Or the records may be kept as data files maintained electronically on disks or magnetic tape. The records are referred to as **materials inventory records** (or **stores ledger cards**). The card for Stock No. AA2746 following the purchase is shown in Illustration 21-5.

Also serves as subsidiary

Illustration 21-5
Materials inventory card

Item: Handles								Part No: AA2746		
	Receipts			Issues			Balance			
Date	Units	Cost	Total	Units	Cost	Total	Units	Cost	Total	
1/4	2,000	$5	$10,000				2,000	$5	$10,000	

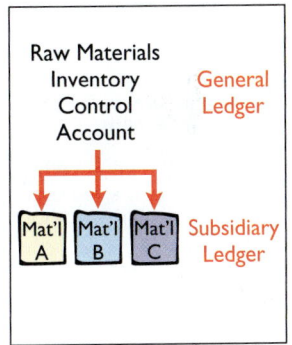

Raw Materials Inventory Control Account — General Ledger

Mat'l A   Mat'l B   Mat'l C — Subsidiary Ledger

Postings are made daily to the subsidiary ledger. After all postings have been completed, the sum of the balances in the raw materials subsidiary ledger should equal the balance in the Raw Materials Inventory control account.

Factory Labor Costs

The procedures for accumulating factory labor costs are similar to those for computing the payroll for a merchandising company. Time clocks and time cards are used to determine total hours worked; gross and net earnings for each employee are listed in a payroll register; and individual employee earnings records are maintained. To help ensure the accuracy of data, a company should follow the principles of internal control for payrolls described in Chapter 11.

In a manufacturing company, the cost of factory labor consists of (1) gross earnings of factory workers, (2) employer payroll taxes on such earnings, and (3) fringe benefits (such as sick pay, pensions, and vacation pay) incurred by the employer. **Labor costs are debited to Factory Labor when they are incurred.**

To illustrate, assume that Wallace Manufacturing incurs $32,000 of factory labor costs. Of that amount, $27,000 relates to wages payable and $5,000 relates to payroll taxes payable in January. The entry is:

(2)

Jan. 31	Factory Labor	32,000	
	Factory Wages Payable		27,000
	Employer Payroll Taxes Payable		5,000
	(To record factory labor costs)		

Factory labor is subsequently assigned to work in process and manufacturing overhead, as explained later in the chapter.

Manufacturing Overhead Costs

A company may have many types of overhead costs. These costs may be recognized **daily**, as in the case of machinery repairs and the use of indirect materials and indirect labor. Or overhead costs may be recorded **periodically** through adjusting entries. Property taxes, depreciation, and insurance are recorded periodically, for example. Using assumed data, a **summary entry** for manufacturing overhead in Wallace Manufacturing Company is:

HELPFUL HINT

This is referred to as a **summary entry** because it summarizes the totals from multiple transactions.

(3)

Jan. 31	Manufacturing Overhead	13,800	
	Utilities Payable		4,800
	Prepaid Insurance		2,000
	Accounts Payable (for repairs)		2,600
	Accumulated Depreciation		3,000
	Property Taxes Payable		1,400
	(To record overhead costs)		

Manufacturing Overhead is a control account. The subsidiary ledger consists of individual accounts for each type of cost, such as Factory Utilities, Factory Insurance, and Factory Repairs.

Assigning Manufacturing Costs to Work in Process

STUDY OBJECTIVE 3

Explain the nature and importance of a job cost sheet.

As shown in Illustration 21-4, assigning manufacturing costs to work in process results in the following entries: (1) **Debits** are made to Work in Process Inventory. (2) **Credits** are made to Raw Materials Inventory, Factory Labor, and Manufacturing Overhead. Journal entries to assign costs to work in process are usually made and posted **monthly**.

An essential accounting record in assigning costs to jobs is a **job cost sheet** shown in Illustration 21-6. A **job cost sheet** is a form used to record the costs chargeable to a specific job and to determine the total and unit costs of the completed job.

Illustration 21-6
Job cost sheet

ETHICS NOTE

The misallocation of costs in a job order system can be a serious legal and ethical problem. For example, the Department of Defense sued **General Dynamics Corporation** at one time for over-allocating production costs that were not related to the underlying contract for U.S. Navy nuclear submarines.

Job Cost Sheet

Job No. _____   Quantity _____
Item _____   Date Requested _____
For _____   Date Completed _____

Date	Direct Materials	Direct Labor	Manufacturing Overhead

Cost of completed job
  Direct materials $ _____
  Direct labor   _____
  Manufacturing overhead   _____
Total cost $ _____
Unit cost (total dollars ÷ quantity) $ _____

Postings to job cost sheets are made daily, directly from supporting documents.

A separate job cost sheet is kept for each job. The job cost sheets constitute the subsidiary ledger for the Work in Process Inventory account. **Each entry to Work in Process Inventory must be accompanied by a corresponding posting to one or more job cost sheets.**

Raw Materials Costs

Raw materials costs are assigned when the materials are issued by the storeroom. To achieve effective internal control over the issuance of materials, the storeroom worker should receive a written authorization before materials are released to production. Such authorization for issuing raw materials is made on a prenumbered **materials requisition slip**. This form is signed by an authorized employee such as a department supervisor. The materials issued may be used directly on a job, or they may be considered indirect materials. As shown in Illustration 21-7, the requisition should indicate the quantity and type of materials withdrawn and the account to be charged. Direct materials will be charged to Work in Process Inventory, and indirect materials to Manufacturing Overhead.

Illustration 21-7
Materials requisition slip

Wallace Manufacturing Company
Materials Requisition Slip

| Deliver to: | Assembly Department | | Req. No. | R247 |
| Charge to: | Work in Process–Job No. 101 | | Date: | 1/6/05 |

Quantity	Description	Stock No.	Cost per Unit	Total
200	Handles	AA2746	$5.00	$1,000

Requested by _Bruce Howart_   Received by _Herb Crowley_

Approved by _Kap Shin_   Costed by _Heather Remmers_

The requisition is prepared in duplicate. A copy is retained in the storeroom as evidence of the materials released. The original is sent to accounting, where the cost per unit and total cost of the materials used are determined. Any of the inventory costing methods (FIFO, LIFO, or average cost) may be used in costing the requisitions. After the requisition slips have been costed, they are posted daily to the materials inventory records. Also, **requisitions for direct materials are posted daily to the individual job cost sheets**.

Periodically, the requisitions are sorted, totaled, and journalized. For example, if $24,000 of direct materials and $6,000 of indirect materials are used in Wallace Manufacturing in January, the entry is:

	(4)		
Jan. 31	Work in Process Inventory	24,000	
	Manufacturing Overhead	6,000	
	Raw Materials Inventory		30,000
	(To assign materials to jobs and overhead)		

The requisition slips show total direct materials costs of $12,000 for Job No. 101, $7,000 for Job No. 102, and $5,000 for Job No. 103. The posting of requisition slip R247 and other assumed postings to the job cost sheets for materials are shown in Illustration 21-8. After all postings have been completed, the sum of the direct materials columns of the job cost sheets should equal the direct materials debited to Work in Process Inventory.

Illustration 21-8
Job cost sheets—direct materials

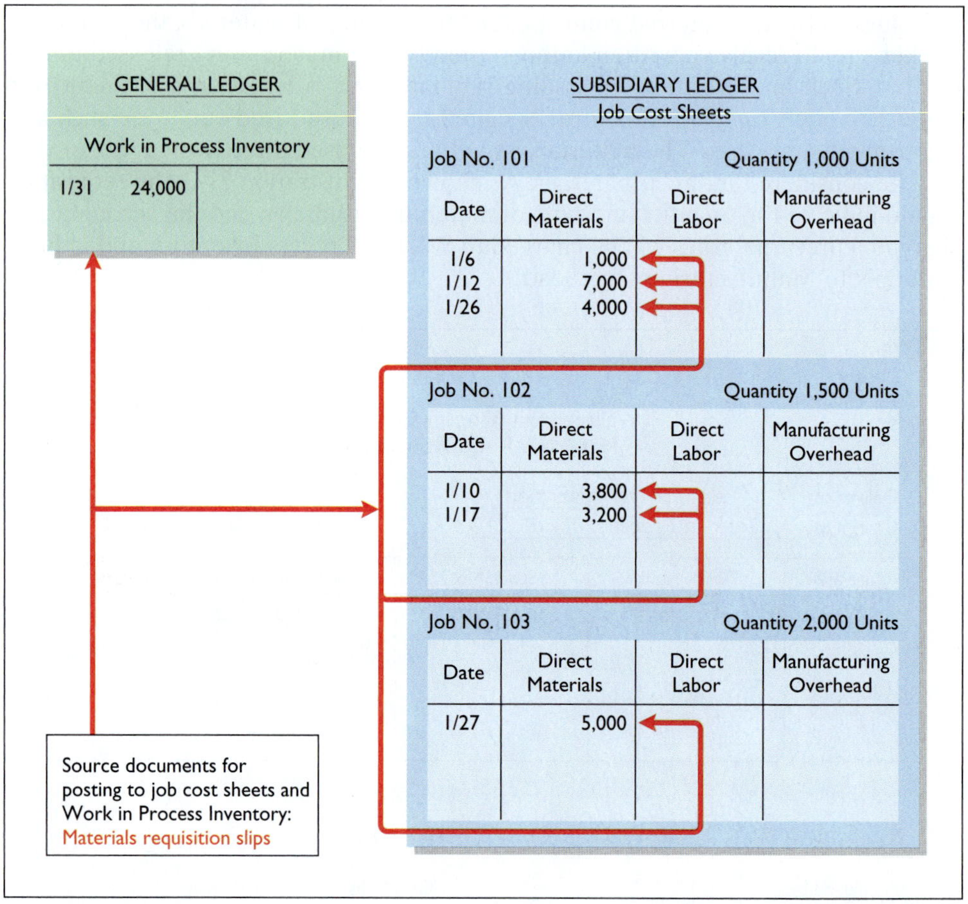

HELPFUL HINT
Postings to control accounts are made monthly, and postings to job cost sheets are made daily.

The materials inventory record for Part No. AA2746 is shown in Illustration 21-9. It shows the posting of requisition slip R247 and an assumed requisition slip for 760 handles costing $3,800 on January 10 for Job 102.

Illustration 21-9
Materials inventory card following issuances

Item: Handles — Part No: AA2746

	Receipts			Issues			Balance		
Date	Units	Cost	Total	Units	Cost	Total	Units	Cost	Total
1/4	2,000	$5	$10,000				2,000	$5	$10,000
1/6				200	$5	$1,000	1,800	$5	9,000
1/10				760	$5	3,800	1,040	$5	5,200

Factory Labor Costs

Factory labor costs are assigned to jobs on the basis of time tickets prepared when the work is performed. The time ticket should indicate the employee, the hours worked, the account and job to be charged, and the total labor cost. In many companies these data are accumulated through the use of bar coding and scanning devices. When they start and end work, employees scan bar codes on their identification badges and bar codes associated with each job they work on. The account Work in Process Inventory is debited for direct labor, and Manufacturing Overhead is debited for indirect labor. When direct labor is involved, the job number must be indicated, as shown in Illustration 21-10. All time tickets should be approved by the employee's supervisor.

Illustration 21-10
Time ticket

Wallace Manufacturing Company
Time Ticket

			Date:	1/6/05
Employee	John Nash		Employee No.	124
Charge to:	Work in Process		Job No.	101

Time			Hourly Rate	Total Cost
Start	Stop	Total Hours		
0800	1200	4	10.00	40.00

Approved by *Bob Kadler*   Costed by *M Cher*

The time tickets are later sent to the payroll department. There, the total time reported for an employee for a pay period is reconciled with total hours worked, as shown on the employee's time card. Then the employee's hourly wage rate is applied, and the total labor cost is computed. Finally, the time tickets are sorted, totaled, and journalized. For example, if the $32,000 total factory labor cost consists of $28,000 of direct labor and $4,000 of indirect labor, the entry is:

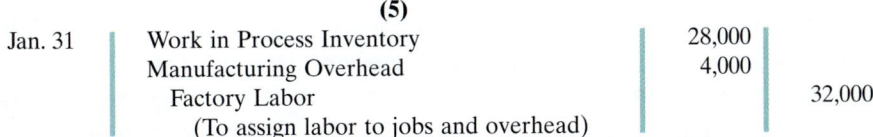

	(5)		
Jan. 31	Work in Process Inventory	28,000	
	Manufacturing Overhead	4,000	
	Factory Labor		32,000
	(To assign labor to jobs and overhead)		

As a result of this entry, Factory Labor is left with a zero balance, and gross earnings are assigned to the appropriate manufacturing accounts.

Let's assume that the labor costs chargeable to Wallace's three jobs are $15,000, $9,000, and $4,000. The Work in Process Inventory and job cost sheets after posting are shown in Illustration 21-11 (page 862). As in the case of direct materials, the postings to the direct labor columns of the job cost sheets should equal the posting of direct labor to Work in Process Inventory.

Illustration 21-11
Job cost sheets—direct labor

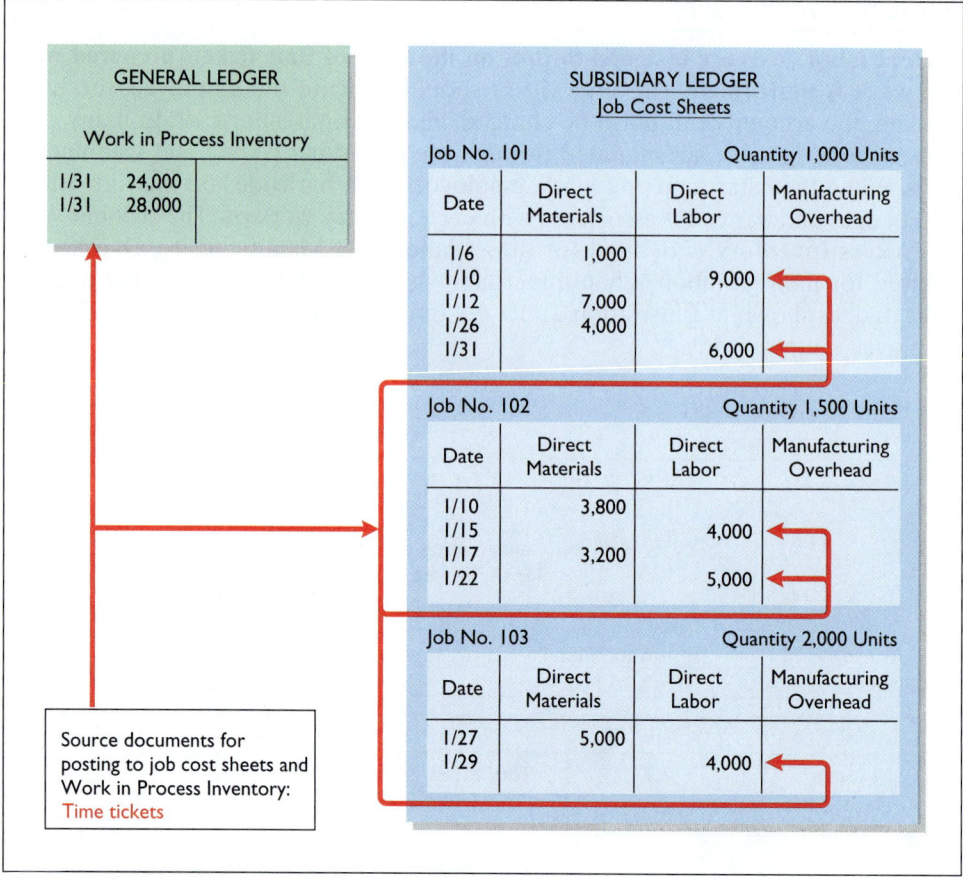

Manufacturing Overhead Costs

STUDY OBJECTIVE 4

Indicate how the predetermined overhead rate is
determined and used.

We've seen that direct materials and direct labor can be applied to specific jobs. In
contrast, manufacturing overhead relates to production operations **as a whole**. As a
result, overhead costs cannot be assigned to specific jobs on the basis of actual costs
incurred. Instead, manufacturing overhead is assigned to work in process and to specific jobs **on an estimated basis through the use of a predetermined overhead rate**.

ACCOUNTING IN ACTION   **Business Insight**

A job cost computer program provides summaries of material and labor costs by
job. The program accumulates costs by jobs, provides data to accounts receivable
for billings, assigns overhead costs, and provides up-to-date management reports.
The reports generated by such systems are basically the same as those shown for
Wallace Manufacturing. The major difference between manual and computerized
systems is the time involved in converting data into information and in getting
feedback (reports) to management.

The **predetermined overhead rate** is based on the relationship between estimated annual overhead costs and expected annual operating activity. This relationship is expressed in terms of a common **activity base**. The activity may be stated in

terms of direct labor costs, direct labor hours, machine hours, or any other measure that will provide an equitable basis for applying overhead costs to jobs. The predetermined overhead rate is established at the beginning of the year. Small companies often will have a single, company-wide predetermined overhead rate. Large companies, however, often have rates that vary from department to department. The formula for a predetermined overhead rate is:

Estimated Annual Overhead Costs	÷	Expected Annual Operating Activity	=	Predetermined Overhead Rate

Illustration 21-12
Formula for predetermined overhead rate

We indicated earlier that overhead relates to production operations as a whole. In order to know what "the whole" is, the logical thing would be to wait until the end of the year's operations, when all costs for the period would be available. But as a practical matter, that wouldn't work: managers could not wait that long before having information about product costs of specific jobs completed during the year. Instead, using a predetermined overhead rate enables a cost to be determined for the job immediately. Illustration 21-13 indicates how manufacturing overhead is assigned to work in process.

HELPFUL HINT

In contrast to overhead, actual costs for direct materials and direct labor are used to assign costs to Work in Process.

Illustration 21-13
Using predetermined overhead rates

Wallace Manufacturing uses direct labor cost as the activity base. Assuming that annual overhead costs are expected to be $280,000 and that $350,000 of direct labor costs are anticipated for the year, the overhead rate is 80%, computed as follows:

$$\$280,000 \div \$350,000 = 80\%$$

This means that for every dollar of direct labor, 80 cents of manufacturing overhead will be assigned to a job. The use of a predetermined overhead rate enables the company to determine the approximate total cost of each job **when the job is completed**.

Historically, direct labor costs or direct labor hours have often been used as the activity base. The reason was the relatively high correlation between direct labor and manufacturing overhead. In recent years, **there has been a trend toward use of machine hours as the activity base, due to increased reliance on automation in manufacturing operations**. Or, as mentioned in Chapter 20, activity-based costing has resulted in more accurate allocation of overhead costs based on the activities that give rise to the costs.

A company may use more than one activity base. For example, if a job order is manufactured in more than one factory department, each department may have its own overhead rate. In the Feature Story about fire trucks, two bases were used in assigning overhead to jobs: direct materials dollars for indirect materials, and direct labor hours for such costs as insurance and supervisors' salaries.

For Wallace Manufacturing, the total amount of manufacturing overhead is assigned to work in process. It then is **charged to jobs when direct labor costs are assigned**. Overhead applied for January is $22,400 ($28,000 × 80%). This application is recorded through the following entry.

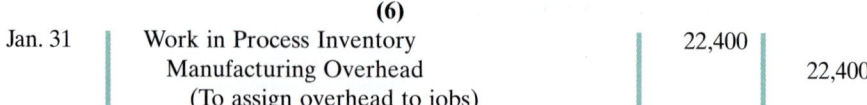

	(6)		
Jan. 31	Work in Process Inventory	22,400	
	Manufacturing Overhead		22,400
	(To assign overhead to jobs)		

The overhead assigned to each job will be 80 percent of the direct labor cost of the job for the month. After posting, the Work in Process Inventory account and the job cost sheets will appear as shown in Illustration 21-14. Note that the debit of $22,400 to Work in Process Inventory equals the sum of the overhead assigned to jobs: Job 101 $12,000 + Job 102 $7,200 + Job 103 $3,200.

Illustration 21-14
Job cost sheets—manufacturing overhead applied

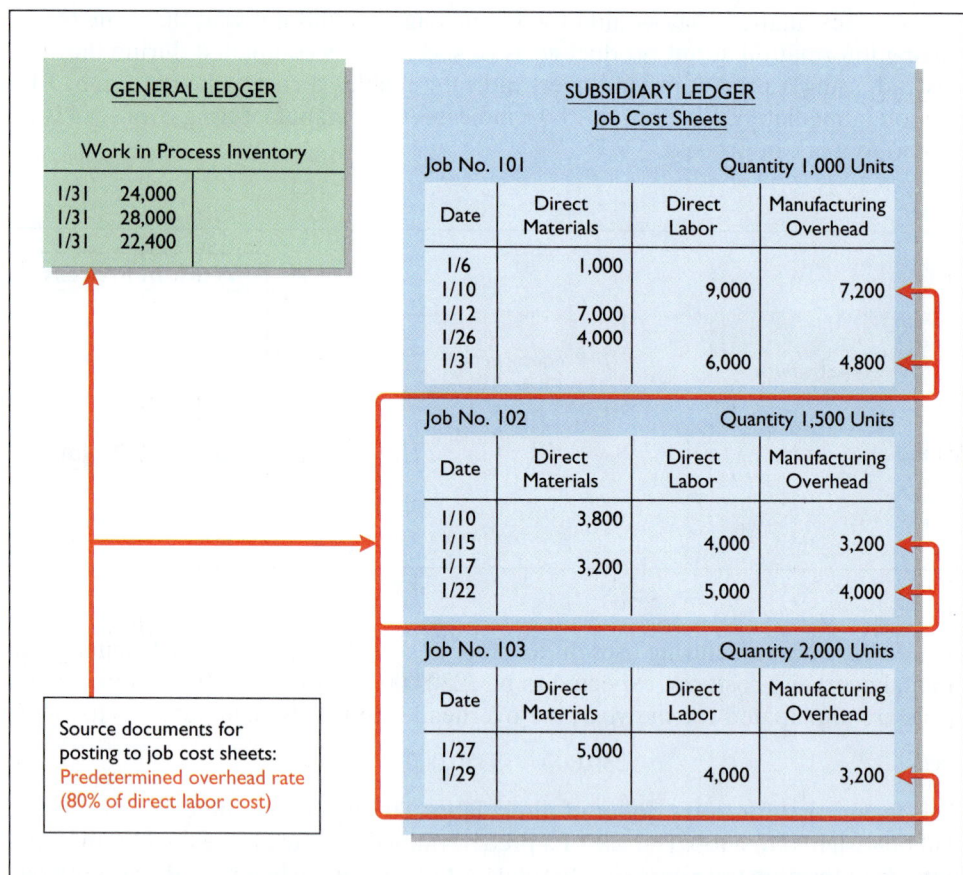

At the end of each month, **the balance in Work in Process Inventory should equal the sum of the costs shown on the job cost sheets of unfinished jobs**. Assuming that all jobs are unfinished, proof of the agreement of the control and subsidiary accounts in Wallace Manufacturing is shown below.

Illustration 21-15
Proof of job cost sheets to work in process inventory

Work in Process Inventory		**Job Cost Sheets**	
Jan. 31	24,000	No. 101	$39,000
31	28,000	102	23,200
31	22,400	103	12,200
	74,400		**$74,400**

BEFORE YOU GO ON...

Review It

1. What source documents are used in assigning manufacturing costs to Work in Process Inventory?

2. What is a job cost sheet, and what is its primary purpose?

3. What is the formula for computing a predetermined overhead rate?

Do It

Danielle Company is working on two job orders. The job cost sheets show the following:

  Direct materials—Job 120 $6,000, Job 121 $3,600
  Direct labor—Job 120 $4,000, Job 121 $2,000
  Manufacturing overhead—Job 120 $5,000, Job 121 $2,500

Prepare the three summary entries to record the assignment of costs to Work in Process from the data on the job cost sheets.

ACTION PLAN

- Recognize that Work in Process Inventory is the control account for all unfinished job cost sheets.
- Debit Work in Process Inventory for the materials, labor, and overhead charged to the job cost sheets.
- Credit the accounts that were debited when the manufacturing costs were accumulated.

SOLUTION   The three summary entries are:

Work in Process Inventory ($6,000 + $3,600)	9,600	
Raw Materials Inventory		9,600
(To assign materials to jobs)		
Work in Process Inventory ($4,000 + $2,000)	6,000	
Factory Labor		6,000
(To assign labor to jobs)		
Work in Process Inventory ($5,000 + $2,500)	7,500	
Manufacturing Overhead		7,500
(To assign overhead to jobs)		

Related exercise material: *BE21-3, BE21-4, BE21-7, E21-2, E21-3 E21-7, and E21-8.*

THE NAVIGATOR

Assigning Costs to Finished Goods

When a job is completed, the costs are summarized and the lower portion of the applicable job cost sheet is completed. For example, if we assume that Job No. 101 is completed on January 31, the job cost sheet in Illustration 21-16 (page 866) shows the details of Job No. 101.

STUDY OBJECTIVE 5

Prepare entries for jobs completed and sold.

Illustration 21-16
Completed job cost sheet

Job Cost Sheet

Job No. _____101_____ Quantity _____1,000_____
Item ___Magnetic Sensors___ Date Requested ___February 5___
For ___Tanner Company___ Date Completed ___January 31___

Date	Direct Materials	Direct Labor	Manufacturing Overhead
1/6	$ 1,000		
1/10		$ 9,000	$ 7,200
1/12	7,000		
1/26	4,000		
1/31		6,000	4,800
	$12,000	$15,000	$12,000

Cost of completed job		
Direct materials	$	12,000
Direct labor		15,000
Manufacturing overhead		12,000
Total cost	$	39,000
Unit cost ($39,000 ÷ 1,000)	$	39.00

When a job is finished, an entry is made to transfer its total cost to finished goods inventory. The entry for Wallace Manufacturing is:

(7)

Jan. 31	Finished Goods Inventory	39,000	
	Work in Process Inventory		39,000
	(To record completion of Job No. 101)		

Finished Goods Inventory is a control account. It controls individual finished goods records in a finished goods subsidiary ledger. Postings to the receipts columns are made directly from completed job cost sheets. The finished goods inventory record for Job No. 101 is shown in Illustration 21-17.

Illustration 21-17
Finished goods record

Item: Magnetic Sensors   Job No: 101

	Receipts			Issues			Balance		
Date	Units	Cost	Total	Units	Cost	Total	Units	Cost	Total
1/31	1,000	$39	$39,000				1,000	$39	$39,000
2/2				1000	$39	$39,000			–0–

Assigning Costs to Cost of Goods Sold

Cost of goods sold is recognized when each sale occurs. To illustrate the entries when a completed job is sold, assume that on January 31 Wallace Manufacturing sells on account Job 101, costing $39,000, for $50,000.

The entries to record the sale and recognize cost of goods sold are:

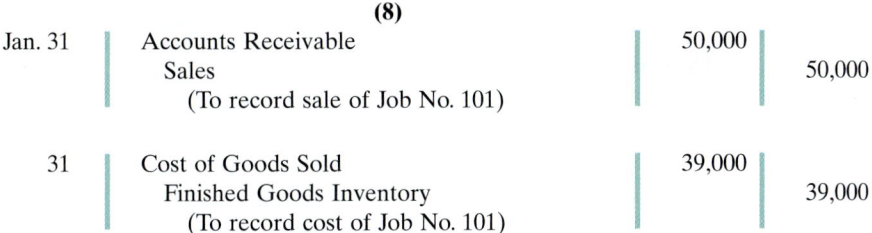

		(8)		
Jan. 31	Accounts Receivable		50,000	
	Sales			50,000
	(To record sale of Job No. 101)			
31	Cost of Goods Sold		39,000	
	Finished Goods Inventory			39,000
	(To record cost of Job No. 101)			

The units sold, the cost per unit, and the total cost of goods sold for each job sold are recorded in the issues section of the finished goods record, as shown in Illustration 21-17.

Summary of Job Order Cost Flows

A completed flow chart for a job order cost accounting system is shown in Illustration 21-18. All postings are keyed to entries 1–8 in Wallace Manufacturing's accounts presented in the cost flow graphic in Illustration 21-4.

Illustration 21-18
Flow of costs in a job order cost system

Flow of Costs

Raw Materials Inventory

(1)	42,000	(4)	30,000 → 4
Bal.	12,000		

Factory Labor

(2)	32,000	(5)	32,000 → 5

Manufacturing Overhead

(3)	13,800	(6)	22,400 → 6
(4)	6,000		
(5)	4,000		
Bal.	1,400		

Work in Process Inventory

(4)	24,000	(7)	39,000 → 7
(5)	28,000		
(6)	22,400		
Bal.	35,400		

Finished Goods Inventory

(7)	39,000	(8)	39,000 → 8

Cost of Goods Sold

(8)	39,000

Key to Entries:

Accumulation	Assignment
1. Purchase raw materials	4. Raw materials are used
2. Incur factory labor	5. Factory labor is used
3. Incur manufacturing overhead	6. Overhead is applied
	7. Completed goods are recognized
	8. Cost of goods sold is recognized

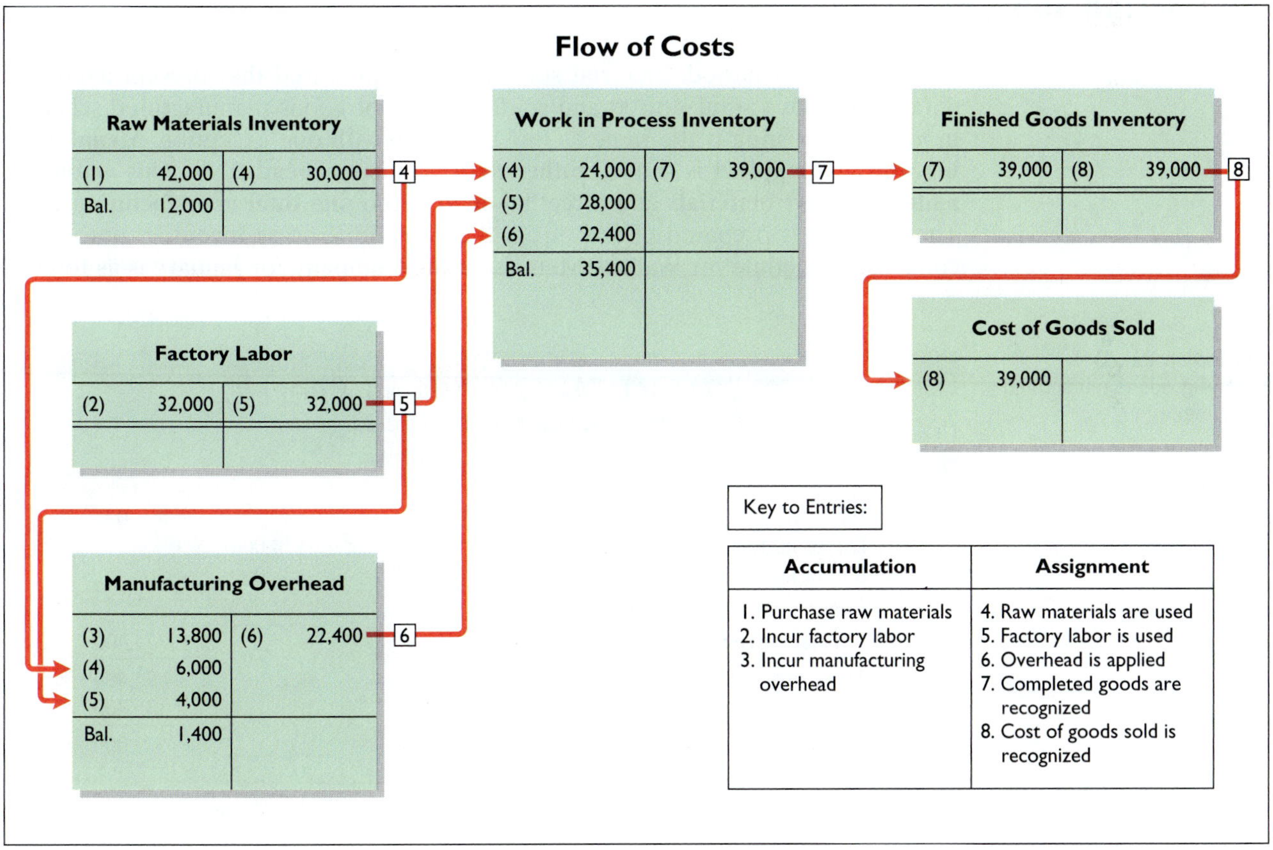

Illustration 21-19 (page 868) provides a summary of the flow of documents in a job order cost system.

Illustration 21-19
Flow of documents in a job
order cost system

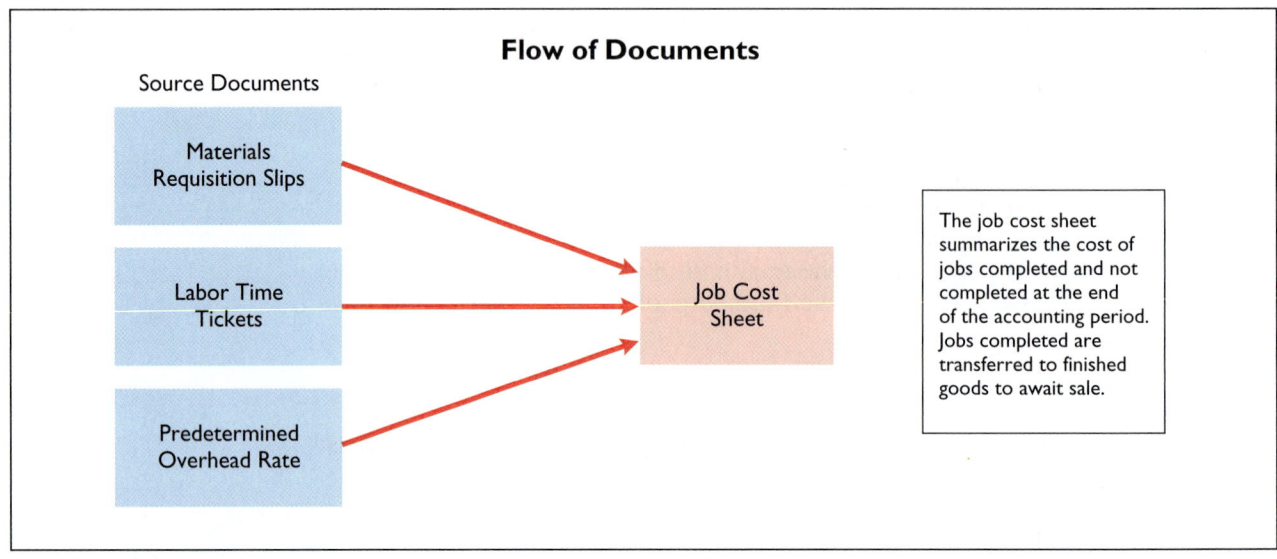

Reporting Job Cost Data

At the end of a period, financial statements are prepared that present aggregate data on all jobs manufactured and sold. The cost of goods manufactured schedule in job order costing is the same as in Chapter 20 with one exception: **Manufacturing overhead applied is shown, rather than actual overhead costs. This amount is added to direct materials and direct labor to determine total manufacturing costs.** The schedule is prepared directly from the Work in Process Inventory account. A condensed schedule for Wallace Manufacturing Company for January is as follows.

Illustration 21-20
Cost of goods manufactured
schedule

WALLACE MANUFACTURING COMPANY		
Cost of Goods Manufactured Schedule		
For the Month Ended January 31, 2005		
Work in process, January 1		$ –0–
Direct materials used	$24,000	
Direct labor	28,000	
Manufacturing overhead applied	**22,400**	
Total current manufacturing costs		74,400
Total cost of work in process		74,400
Less: Work in process, January 31		35,400
Cost of goods manufactured		$39,000

Note that the cost of goods manufactured ($39,000) agrees with the amount transferred from Work in Process Inventory to Finished Goods Inventory in journal entry no. 7 in Illustration 21-18.

The income statement and balance sheet are the same as those illustrated in Chapter 20. For example, the partial income statement for Wallace Manufacturing for the month of January is as follows.

Illustration 21-21
Partial income statement

WALLACE MANUFACTURING Income Statement (partial) For the Month Ending January 31, 2005		
Sales		$50,000
Cost of goods sold		
Finished goods inventory, January 1	$ –0–	
Cost of goods manufactured (See Illustration 21-20)	39,000	
Cost of goods available for sale	39,000	
Less: Finished goods inventory, January 31	–0–	
Cost of goods sold		39,000
Gross profit		$11,000

Under- or Overapplied Manufacturing Overhead

When Manufacturing Overhead has a **debit balance**, overhead is said to be under-applied. Underapplied overhead means that the overhead assigned to work in process is less than the overhead incurred. Conversely, when manufacturing overhead has a **credit balance**, overhead is overapplied. Overapplied overhead means that the overhead assigned to work in process is greater than the overhead incurred. These concepts are shown in Illustration 21-22.

STUDY OBJECTIVE 6

Distinguish between under- and overapplied manufacturing overhead.

Illustration 21-22
Under- and overapplied overhead

	Manufacturing Overhead	
	Actual (Costs incurred)	Applied (Costs assigned)

Manufacturing Overhead

If actual is *greater* than applied, manufacturing overhead is underapplied.

If actual is *less* than applied, manufacturing overhead is overapplied.

Interim Balances

The existence of under- or overapplied overhead at the end of a month is expected. It usually does not require corrective action by management. Monthly differences between actual and applied overhead will usually be offsetting over the course of the year.

When monthly financial statements are prepared, under- or overapplied overhead is reported on the balance sheet. **Underapplied overhead is shown as a prepaid expense in the current assets section. Overapplied overhead is reported as unearned revenue in the current liabilities section.**

Year-End Balance

At the end of the year, all manufacturing overhead transactions are complete. There is no further opportunity for offsetting events to occur. Accordingly, any balance in Manufacturing Overhead is eliminated by an adjusting entry. Usually, under- or overapplied overhead is considered to be an **adjustment to cost of goods sold**. Thus, **underapplied overhead is debited to Cost of Goods Sold. Overapplied overhead is credited to Cost of Goods Sold.** To illustrate, assume that Wallace Manufacturing has a $2,500 credit balance in Manufacturing Overhead at December 31. The adjusting entry for the overapplied overhead is:

Dec. 31	Manufacturing Overhead	2,500	
	Cost of Goods Sold		2,500
	(To transfer overapplied overhead to cost		
	of goods sold)		

After this entry is posted, Manufacturing Overhead will have a zero balance. In preparing an income statement for the year, the amount reported for cost of goods sold will be the account balance **after the adjustment** for either under- or over-applied overhead.

ACCOUNTING IN ACTION Business Insight

Overhead also applies in nonmanufacturing companies. The State of Michigan found that auto dealers were charging documentary and service fees ranging from $18 to $445 per automobile and inspection fees from $88 to $360. These fees often were charged auto buyers after a base sales price for the car had been negotiated. The Attorney General of the State of Michigan ruled that auto dealers cannot charge customers additional fees for routine overhead costs. The attorney general said: "Overhead is part of the sales price of a motor vehicle. Processing paper work, dealer incurred costs, and inspection fees to qualify cars for extended warranty plans are ordinary overhead expenses."

Conceptually, it can be argued that under- or overapplied overhead at the end of the year should be allocated among ending work in process, finished goods, and cost of goods sold. However, most management accountants do not believe allocation is worth the cost and effort. The bulk of the under- or overapplied amount will be allocated to cost of goods sold anyway, because most of the jobs will be sold during the year.

BEFORE YOU GO ON...

Review It

1. When are entries made to record the completion and sale of a job?
2. What costs are included in total manufacturing costs in the cost of goods manufactured schedule?
3. How is under- or overapplied manufacturing overhead reported in monthly financial statements?

DEMONSTRATION PROBLEM

During February, Cardella Manufacturing works on two jobs: A16 and B17. Summary data concerning these jobs are as follows.

Manufacturing Costs Incurred:

Purchased $54,000 of raw materials on account.
Factory labor $76,000, plus $4,000 employer payroll taxes.
Manufacturing overhead exclusive of indirect materials and indirect labor $59,800.

Assignment of Costs:

Direct materials: Job A16 $27,000, Job B17 $21,000
Indirect materials: $3,000
Direct labor: Job A16 $52,000, Job B17 $26,000
Indirect labor: $2,000
Manufacturing overhead rate: 80% of direct labor costs.

Job A16 was completed and sold on account for $150,000. Job B17 was only partially completed.

Instructions

(a) Journalize the February transactions in the sequence followed in the chapter.
(b) What was the amount of under- or overapplied manufacturing overhead?

SOLUTION TO DEMONSTRATION PROBLEM

(a)

1.

Feb. 28	Raw Materials Inventory	54,000	
	Accounts Payable		54,000
	(Purchase of raw materials on account)		

2.

28	Factory Labor	80,000	
	Factory Wages Payable		76,000
	Employer Payroll Taxes Payable		4,000
	(To record factory labor costs)		

3.

28	Manufacturing Overhead	59,800	
	Accounts Payable, Accumulated		
	Depreciation, and Prepaid Insurance		59,800
	(To record overhead costs)		

4.

28	Work in Process Inventory	48,000	
	Manufacturing Overhead	3,000	
	Raw Materials Inventory		51,000
	(To assign raw materials to production)		

5.

28	Work in Process Inventory	78,000	
	Manufacturing Overhead	2,000	
	Factory Labor		80,000
	(To assign factory labor to production)		

6.

28	Work in Process Inventory	62,400	
	Manufacturing Overhead		62,400
	(To assign overhead to jobs —80% × $78,000)		

7.

Feb. 28	Finished Goods Inventory		120,600	
	Work in Process Inventory			120,600
	(To record completion of Job A16: direct			
	materials $27,000, direct labor $52,000, and			
	manufacturing overhead $41,600)			

8.

28	Accounts Receivable		150,000	
	Cost of Goods Sold		120,600	
	Sales			150,000
	Finished Goods Inventory			120,600
	(To record sale of Job A16)			

(b) Manufacturing Overhead has a debit balance of $2,400 as shown below.

Manufacturing Overhead

(3)	59,800	(6)	62,400
(4)	3,000		
(5)	2,000		
Bal.	2,400		

Thus, manufacturing overhead is underapplied for the month.

SUMMARY OF STUDY OBJECTIVES

1. **Explain the characteristics and purposes of cost accounting.** Cost accounting involves the procedures for measuring, recording, and reporting product costs. From the data accumulated, the total cost and the unit cost of each product is determined. The two basic types of cost accounting systems are job order cost and process cost.

2. **Describe the flow of costs in a job order cost accounting system.** In job order cost accounting, manufacturing costs are first accumulated in three accounts: Raw Materials Inventory, Factory Labor, and Manufacturing Overhead. The accumulated costs are then assigned to Work in Process Inventory and eventually to Finished Goods Inventory and Cost of Goods Sold.

3. **Explain the nature and importance of a job cost sheet.** A job cost sheet is a form used to record the costs chargeable to a specific job and to determine the total and unit cost of the completed job. Job cost sheets constitute the subsidiary ledger for the Work in Process Inventory control account.

4. **Indicate how the predetermined overhead rate is determined and used.** The predetermined overhead rate is based on the relationship between estimated annual overhead costs and expected annual operating activity. This is expressed in terms of a common activity base, such as direct labor cost. The rate is used in assigning overhead costs to work in process and to specific jobs.

5. **Prepare entries for jobs completed and sold.** When jobs are completed, the cost is debited to Finished Goods Inventory and credited to Work in Process Inventory. When a job is sold the entries are: (a) Debit Cash or Accounts Receivable and credit Sales for the selling price, and (b) debit Cost of Goods Sold and credit Finished Goods Inventory for the cost of the goods.

6. **Distinguish between under- and overapplied manufacturing overhead.** Underapplied manufacturing overhead means that the overhead assigned to work in process is less than the overhead incurred. Overapplied overhead means that the overhead assigned to work in process is greater than the overhead incurred.

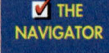

GLOSSARY

Cost accounting An area of accounting that involves the measuring, recording, and reporting of product costs. (p. 853).

Cost accounting system Manufacturing cost accounts that are fully integrated into the general ledger of a company. (p. 853).

Job cost sheet A form used to record the costs chargeable to a job and to determine the total and unit costs of the completed job. (p. 858)

Job order cost system A cost accounting system in which costs are assigned to each job or batch. (p. 854).

Materials requisition slip A document authorizing the issuance of raw materials from the storeroom to production. (p. 859).

Overapplied overhead A situation in which overhead assigned to work in process is greater than the overhead incurred. (p. 869).

Predetermined overhead rate A rate based on the relationship between estimated annual overhead costs and expected annual operating activity, expressed in terms of a common activity base. (p. 862).

Process cost system A system of accounting used by companies that manufacture relatively homogeneous products through a series of continuous processes or operations. (p. 854).

Summary entry A journal entry that summarizes the totals from multiple transactions. (p. 858)

Time ticket A document that indicates the employee, the hours worked, the account and job to be charged, and the total labor cost. (p. 861).

Underapplied overhead A situation in which overhead assigned to work in process is less than the overhead incurred. (p. 869).

SELF-STUDY QUESTIONS

Self-Study/Self-Test

Answers are at the end of the chapter.

(SO 1) **1.** Cost accounting involves the measuring, recording, and reporting of:
   a. product costs.
   b. future costs.
   c. manufacturing processes.
   d. managerial accounting decisions.

(SO 2) **2.** In accumulating raw materials costs, the cost of raw materials purchased in a perpetual system is debited to:
   a. Raw Materials Purchases.
   b. Raw Materials Inventory.
   c. Purchases.
   d. Work in Process.

(SO 2) **3.** When incurred, factory labor costs are debited to:
   a. Work in Process.
   b. Factory Wages Expense.
   c. Factory Labor.
   d. Factory Wages Payable.

(SO 3) **4.** The source documents for assigning costs to job cost sheets are:
   a. invoices, time tickets, and the predetermined overhead rate.
   b. materials requisition slips, time tickets, and the actual overhead costs.
   c. materials requisition slips, payroll register, and the predetermined overhead rate.
   d. materials requisition slips, time tickets, and the predetermined overhead rate.

(SO 3) **5.** In recording the issuance of raw materials in a job order cost system, it would be *incorrect* to:
   a. debit Work in Process Inventory.
   b. debit Finished Goods Inventory.
   c. debit Manufacturing Overhead.
   d. credit Raw Materials Inventory.

(SO 3) **6.** The entry when direct factory labor is assigned to jobs is a debit to:
   a. Work in Process Inventory and a credit to Factory Labor.
   b. Manufacturing Overhead and a credit to Factory Labor.
   c. Factory Labor and a credit to Manufacturing Overhead.
   d. Factory Labor and a credit to Work in Process Inventory.

(SO 4) **7.** The formula for computing the predetermined manufacturing overhead rate is estimated annual overhead costs divided by an expected annual operating activity, expressed as:
   a. direct labor cost.
   b. direct labor hours.
   c. machine hours.
   d. any of the above.

(SO 4) **8.** In Cleo Company, the predetermined overhead rate is 80% of direct labor cost. During the month, $210,000 of factory labor costs are incurred, of which $180,000 is direct labor and $30,000 is indirect labor. Actual overhead incurred was $200,000. The amount of overhead debited to Work in Process Inventory should be:
   a. $120,000.
   b. $144,000.
   c. $168,000.
   d. $160,000.

(SO 5) **9.** In BAC Company, Job No. 26 is completed at a cost of $4,500 and later sold for $7,000 cash. A correct entry is:
   a. Debit Finished Goods Inventory $7,000 and credit Work in Process Inventory $7,000.
   b. Debit Cost of Goods Sold $7,000 and credit Finished Goods Inventory $7,000.
   c. Debit Finished Goods Inventory $4,500 and credit Work in Process Inventory $4,500.
   d. Debit Accounts Receivable $7,000 and credit Sales $7,000.

(SO 6) **10.** In preparing monthly financial statements, overapplied overhead is reported in the balance sheet as a(an):
   a. prepaid expense.
   b. unearned revenue.
   c. noncurrent asset.
   d. noncurrent liability.

✔ THE NAVIGATOR

QUESTIONS

1. Tim Turner is studying for an accounting midterm examination. What should Tim know about how management may use job cost data?

2. (a) Kent Krause is not sure about the differences between cost accounting and a cost accounting system. Explain the difference to Kent. (b) What is an important feature of a cost accounting system?

3. (a) Distinguish between the two types of cost accounting systems. (b) May a company use both types of cost accounting systems?

4. What type of industry is likely to use a job order cost system? Give some examples.

5. What type of industry is likely to use a process cost system? Give some examples.

6. Your roommate asks your help in understanding the major steps in the flow of costs in a job order cost system. Identify the steps for your roommate.

7. There are three inventory control accounts in a job order system. Identify the control accounts and their subsidiary ledgers.

8. What source documents are used in accumulating direct labor costs?

9. "Entries to manufacturing overhead normally are only made daily." Do you agree? Explain.

10. Alan Bruski is confused about the source documents used in assigning materials and labor costs. Identify the documents and give the entry for each document.

11. What is the purpose of a job cost sheet?

12. Indicate the source documents that are used in charging costs to specific jobs.

13. Differentiate between a "materials inventory record" and a "materials requisition slip" as used in a job order cost system.

14. Joe Gruber believes actual manufacturing overhead should be charged to jobs. Do you agree? Why or why not?

15. What relationships are involved in computing a predetermined overhead rate?

16. How can the agreement of Work in Process Inventory and job cost sheets be verified?

17. Jane Jelk believes that the cost of goods manufactured schedule in job order cost accounting is the same as in manufacturing accounting. Is Jane correct? Explain.

18. Alex Cesska is confused about under- and overapplied manufacturing overhead. Define the terms for Alex, and indicate the balance in the manufacturing overhead account applicable to each term.

19. "Under- or overapplied overhead is reported in the income statement when monthly financial statements are prepared." Do you agree? If not, indicate the proper presentation.

20. "At the end of the year, under- or overapplied overhead is closed to Income Summary." Is this correct? If not, indicate the customary treatment of this account.

BRIEF EXERCISES

Prepare a flowchart of a job order cost accounting system, and identify transactions.

(SO 2)

BE21-1 Sandy Tool & Die begins operations on January 1. Because all work is done to customer specifications, the company decides to use a job cost accounting system. Prepare a flow chart of a typical job order system with arrows showing the flow of costs. Identify the eight transactions.

Prepare entries in accumulating manufacturing costs.

(SO 2)

BE21-2 During the first month of operations, Sandy Tool & Die accumulated the following manufacturing costs: raw materials $3,000 on account, factory labor $5,000 of which $4,500 relates to factory wages payable and $500 relates to payroll taxes payable, and utilities payable $2,000. Prepare separate journal entries for each type of manufacturing cost.

Prepare entry for the assignment of raw materials costs.

(SO 2)

BE21-3 In January, Sandy Tool & Die requisitions raw materials for production as follows: Job 1 $900, Job 2 $1,200, Job 3 $500, and general factory use $600. Prepare a summary journal entry to record raw materials used.

Prepare entry for the assignment of factory labor costs.

(SO 2)

BE21-4 Factory labor data for Sandy Tool & Die is given in BE21-2. During January, time tickets show that the factory labor of $5,000 was used as follows: Job 1 $1,200, Job 2 $1,600 Job 3 $1,700, and general factory use $500. Prepare a summary journal entry to record factory labor used.

Prepare job cost sheets.

(SO 3)

BE21-5 Data pertaining to job cost sheets for Sandy Tool & Die are given in BE21-3 and BE21-4. Prepare the job cost sheets for each of the three jobs. (*Note*: You may omit the column for Manufacturing Overhead.)

BE21-6 Burrand Company estimates that annual manufacturing overhead costs will be $600,000. Estimated annual operating activity bases are: direct labor cost $500,000, direct labor hours 50,000, and machine hours 100,000. Compute the predetermined overhead rate for each activity base.

Compute predetermined overhead rates.
(SO 4)

BE21-7 During the first quarter, Sota Company incurs the following direct labor costs: January $40,000, February $30,000, and March $50,000. For each month, prepare the entry to assign overhead to production using a predetermined rate of 120% of direct labor cost.

Assign manufacturing overhead to production.
(SO 4)

BE21-8 In March, Caroline Company completes Jobs 10 and 11. Job 10 cost $25,000 and Job 11 $32,000. On March 31, Job 10 is sold to the customer for $35,000 in cash. Journalize the entries for the completion of the two jobs and the sale of Job 10.

Prepare entries for completion and sale of completed jobs.
(SO 5)

BE21-9 On September 30, balances in Manufacturing Overhead are: Madlock Company—debit $2,000, Blanco Company—credit $3,000. Indicate how each company should report its balance at September 30, assuming each company prepares annual financial statements on December 31.

Indicate statement classification of under- or overapplied overhead.
(SO 6)

BE21-10 At December 31, balances in Manufacturing Overhead are: Apex Company—debit $1,200, Lopez Company—credit $900. Prepare the adjusting entry for each company at December 31, assuming the adjustment is made to cost of goods sold.

Prepare adjusting entries for under- and overapplied overhead.
(SO 6)

EXERCISES

E21-1 The gross earnings of the factory workers for Darlinda Company during the month of January are $80,000. The employer's payroll taxes for the factory payroll are $8,000. The fringe benefits to be paid by the employer on this payroll are $4,000. Of the total accumulated cost of factory labor, 85% is related to direct labor and 15% is attributable to indirect labor.

Prepare entries for factory labor.
(SO 2)

Instructions
(a) Prepare the entry to record the factory labor costs for the month of January.
(b) Prepare the entry to assign factory labor to production.

E21-2 Dooley Manufacturing uses a job order cost accounting system. On May 1, the company has a balance in Work in Process Inventory of $3,200 and two jobs in process: Job No. 429 $2,000, and Job No. 430 $1,200. During May, a summary of source documents reveals the following.

Prepare journal entries for manufacturing costs.
(SO 2, 3, 4, 5)

Job Number	Materials Requisition Slips	Labor Time Tickets
429	$ 2,500	$ 2,400
430	3,500	3,000
431	4,400	7,600
General use	800	1,200
	$11,200	$14,200

Dooley Manufacturing applies manufacturing overhead to jobs at an overhead rate of 90% of direct labor cost. Job No. 429 is completed during the month.

Instructions
(a) Prepare summary journal entries to record the requisition slips, time tickets, the assignment of manufacturing overhead to jobs, and the completion of Job No. 429.
(b) Post the entries to Work in Process Inventory, and prove the agreement of the control account with the job cost sheets.

Analyze a job cost sheet and prepare entries for manufacturing costs.

(SO 2, 3, 4, 5)

E21-3 A job order cost sheet for Bjerg Company is shown below.

Job No. 92			For 2,000 Units
Date	Direct Materials	Direct Labor	Manufacturing Overhead
Beg. bal. Jan. 1	5,000	6,000	4,200
8	6,000		
12		8,000	6,400
25	2,000		
27		4,000	3,200
	13,000	18,000	13,800

Cost of completed job:	
Direct materials	$13,000
Direct labor	18,000
Manufacturing overhead	13,800
Total cost	$44,800
Unit cost ($44,800 ÷ 2,000)	$22.40

Instructions

(a) On the basis of the foregoing data answer the following questions.
  (1) What was the balance in Work in Process Inventory on January 1 if this was the only unfinished job?
  (2) If manufacturing overhead is applied on the basis of direct labor cost, what overhead rate was used in each year?
(b) Prepare summary entries at January 31 to record the current year's transactions pertaining to Job No. 92.

Analyze costs of manufacturing and determine missing amounts.

(SO 2, 5)

E21-4 Manufacturing cost data for Copa Company, which uses a job order cost system, are presented below.

	Case A	Case B	Case C
Direct materials	$ (a)	$ 83,000	$ 63,150
Direct labor used	50,000	100,000	(h)
Manufacturing overhead applied	42,500	(d)	(i)
Total manufacturing costs	165,650	(e)	250,000
Work in process 1/1/05	(b)	15,500	18,000
Total cost of work in process	201,500	(f)	(j)
Work in process 12/31/05	(c)	11,800	(k)
Cost of goods manufactured	192,300	(g)	262,000

Instructions

Indicate the missing amount for each letter. Assume that in all cases manufacturing overhead is applied on the basis of direct labor cost and the rate is the same.

Compute the manufacturing overhead rate and under- or overapplied overhead.

(SO 4, 6)

E21-5 Rodriquez Company applies manufacturing overhead to jobs on the basis of machine hours used. Overhead costs are expected to total $300,000 for the year, and machine usage is estimated at 125,000 hours.

In January, $28,000 of overhead costs are incurred and 12,000 machine hours are used. For the remainder of the year, $294,000 of overhead costs are incurred and 118,000 machine hours are worked.

Instructions

(a) Compute the manufacturing overhead rate for the year.
(b) What is the amount of under- or overapplied overhead at January 31? How should this amount be reported in the financial statements prepared on January 31?
(c) What is the amount of under- or overapplied overhead at December 31?
(d) Assuming the under- or overapplied overhead for the year is not allocated to inventory accounts, prepare the adjusting entry to assign the amount to cost of goods sold.

E21-6 A job cost sheet of Battle Company is given below.

Job Cost Sheet

JOB NO.   469   Quantity   2,000

ITEM   White Lion Cages   Date Requested   7/2

FOR   Tesla Company   Date Completed   7/31

Date	Direct Materials	Direct Labor	Manufacturing Overhead
7/10	825		
12	900		
15		440	528
22		380	456
24	1,600		
27	1,500		
31		540	648

Cost of completed job:

Direct materials   _____

Direct labor   _____

Manufacturing overhead   _____

Total cost   _____

Unit cost   _____

Instructions

(a) Answer the following questions.

    (1) What are the source documents for direct materials, direct labor, and manufacturing overhead costs assigned to this job?

    (2) What is the predetermined manufacturing overhead rate?

    (3) What are the total cost and the unit cost of the completed job?

(b) Prepare the entry to record the completion of the job.

E21-7 Laird Corporation incurred the following transactions.

1. Purchased raw materials on account $46,300.

2. Raw Materials of $36,000 were requisitioned to the factory. An analysis of the materials requisition slips indicated that $8,800 was classified as indirect materials.

3. Factory labor costs incurred were $53,900, of which $49,000 pertained to factory wages payable and $4,900 pertained to employer payroll taxes payable.

4. Time tickets indicated that $50,000 was direct labor and $3,900 was indirect labor.

5. Overhead costs incurred on account were $80,500.

6. Manufacturing overhead was applied at the rate of 150% of direct labor cost.

7. Goods costing $88,000 were completed and transferred to finished goods.

8. Finished goods costing $75,000 to manufacture were sold on account for $103,000.

Instructions

Journalize the transactions. (Omit explanations.)

E21-8 Tombert Printing Corp. uses a job order cost system. The following data summarize the operations related to the first quarter's production.

1. Materials purchased on account $192,000, and factory wages incurred $87,300.

2. Materials requisitioned and factory labor used by job:

Job Number	Materials	Factory Labor
A20	$ 32,240	$18,000
A21	42,920	22,000
A22	36,100	15,000
A23	39,270	25,000
General factory use	4,470	7,300
	$155,000	$87,300

3. Manufacturing overhead costs incurred on account $39,500.
4. Depreciation on machinery and equipment $14,550.
5. Manufacturing overhead rate is 70% of direct labor cost.
6. Jobs completed during the quarter: A20, A21, and A23.

Instructions
Prepare entries to record the operations summarized above. (Prepare a schedule showing the individual cost elements and total cost for each job in item 6.)

Prepare a cost of goods manufactured schedule and partial financial statements.

(SO 2, 5)

E21-9 At May 31, 2005, the accounts of Yellow Knife Manufacturing Company show the following.

1. May 1 inventories—finished goods $12,600, work in process $14,700, and raw materials $8,200.
2. May 31 inventories—finished goods $11,500, work in process $17,900, and raw materials $7,100.
3. Debit postings to work in process were: direct materials $62,400, direct labor $32,000, and manufacturing overhead applied $48,000.
4. Sales totaled $200,000.

Instructions
(a) Prepare a condensed cost of goods manufactured schedule.
(b) Prepare an income statement for May through gross profit.
(c) Indicate the balance sheet presentation of the manufacturing inventories at May 31, 2005.

Compute work in process and finished goods from job cost sheets.

(SO 3, 5)

E21-10 Tomlin Company begins operations on April 1. Information from job cost sheets shows the following.

	Manufacturing Costs Assigned		
Job Number	**April**	**May**	**June**
10	$5,200	$4,400	
11	6,100	3,900	$3,000
12	1,200		
13		4,700	4,500
14		3,900	3,600

Job 12 was completed in April. Job 10 was completed in May. Jobs 11 and 13 were completed in June. Each job was sold for 50% above its cost in the month following completion.

Instructions
(a) What is the balance in Work in Process Inventory at the end of each month?
(b) What is the balance in Finished Goods Inventory at the end of each month?
(c) What is the gross profit for May, June, and July?

PROBLEMS: SET A

Prepare entries in a job cost system and job costs sheets.

(SO 2, 3, 4, 5, 6)

P21-1A Elite Manufacturing uses a job order cost system and applies overhead to production on the basis of direct labor hours. On January 1, 2005, Job No. 25 was the only job in process. The costs incurred prior to January 1 on this job were as follows: direct materials $10,000; direct labor $6,000; and manufacturing overhead $9,000. Job No. 23 had been completed at a cost of $45,000 and was part of finished goods inventory. There was a $5,000 balance in the Raw Materials inventory account.

During the month of January, the company began production on Jobs 26 and 27, and completed Jobs 25 and 26. Jobs 23 and 25 were sold on account during the month for $67,000 and $74,000, respectively. The following additional events occurred during the month.

1. Purchased additional raw materials of $45,000 on account.
2. Incurred factory labor costs of $35,500. Of this amount $6,500 related to employer payroll taxes.

3. Incurred manufacturing overhead costs as follows: indirect materials $10,000; indirect labor $7,500; depreciation expense $12,000; and various other manufacturing overhead costs on account $6,000.
4. Assigned direct materials and direct labor to jobs as follows.

Job No.	Direct Materials	Direct Labor
25	$ 5,000	$ 3,000
26	20,000	12,000
27	15,000	9,000

5. The company uses direct labor hours as the activity base to assign overhead. Direct labor hours incurred on each job were as follows: Job No. 25, 200; Job No. 26, 800; and Job No. 27, 600.

Instructions
(a) Calculate the predetermined overhead rate for the year 2005, assuming Elite Manufacturing estimates total manufacturing overhead costs of $400,000, direct labor costs of $300,000, and direct labor hours of 20,000 for the year.
(b) Open job cost sheets for Jobs 25, 26, and 27. Enter the January 1 balances on the job cost sheet for Job No. 25.
(c) Prepare the journal entries to record the purchase of raw materials, the factory labor costs incurred, and the manufacturing overhead costs incurred during the month of January.
(d) Prepare the journal entries to record the assignment of direct materials, direct labor, and manufacturing overhead costs to production. In assigning manufacturing overhead costs, use the overhead rate calculated in (a). Post all costs to the job cost sheets as necessary.
(e) Total the job cost sheets for any job(s) completed during the month. Prepare the journal entry (or entries) to record the completion of any job(s) during the month.   *(e) Job 25, $37,000*
                                                                                                            Job 26, $48,000
(f) Prepare the journal entry (or entries) to record the sale of any job(s) during the month.
(g) What is the balance in the Work in Process Inventory account at the end of the month? What does this balance consist of?
(h) What is the amount of over- or underapplied overhead for the month? How would this be reported on the financial statements for the month of January?

P21-2A For the year ended December 31, 2005, the job cost sheets of Sprague Company contained the following data.   *Prepare entries in a job cost system and partial income statement.*

(SO 2, 3, 4, 5, 6)

Job Number	Explanation	Direct Materials	Direct Labor	Manufacturing Overhead	Total Costs
7650	Balance 1/1	$18,000	$20,000	$25,000	$ 63,000
	Current year's costs	27,000	30,000	37,500	94,500
7651	Balance 1/1	12,000	18,000	22,500	52,500
	Current year's costs	28,000	40,000	50,000	118,000
7652	Current year's costs	40,000	64,000	80,000	184,000

Other data:
1. Raw materials inventory totaled $20,000 on January 1. During the year, $100,000 of raw materials were purchased on account.
2. Finished goods on January 1 consisted of Job No. 7648 for $98,000 and Job No. 7649 for $62,000.
3. Job No. 7650 and Job No. 7651 were completed during the year.
4. Job Nos. 7648, 7649, and 7650 were sold on account for $490,000.
5. Manufacturing overhead incurred on account totaled $120,000.
6. Other manufacturing overhead consisted of indirect materials $12,000, indirect labor $18,000 and depreciation on factory machinery $19,500.

Instructions
(a) Prove the agreement of Work in Process Inventory with job cost sheets pertaining to unfinished work. *Hint:* Use a single T account for Work in Process Inventory. Calculate each of the following, then post each to the T account: (1) beginning balance, (2) direct materials, (3) direct labor, (4) manufacturing overhead, and (5) completed jobs.

(a) (1) $115,500
(4) $167,500
Unfinished job 7652, $184,000

(b) Amount = $2,000

(c) $170,500

Prepare entries in a job cost system and cost of goods manufactured schedule.

(SO 2, 3, 4, 5)

(b) Prepare the adjusting entry for manufacturing overhead, assuming the balance is allocated entirely to cost of goods sold.
(c) Determine the gross profit to be reported for 2005.

P21-3A Steve Taylor is a contractor specializing in custom-built jacuzzis. On May 1, 2005, his ledger contains the following data.

Raw Materials Inventory	$30,000
Work in Process Inventory	12,600
Manufacturing Overhead	2,500 (dr.)

The Manufacturing Overhead account has debit totals of $12,500 and credit totals of $10,000. Subsidiary data for Work in Process Inventory on May 1 include:

Job Cost Sheets

Job by Customer	Direct Materials	Direct Labor	Manufacturing Overhead
Farley	$2,500	$2,000	$1,600
Hendricks	2,000	1,200	960
Minor	900	800	640
	$5,400	$4,000	$3,200

A summary of materials requisition slips and time tickets for the month of May reveals the following.

Job by Customer	Materials Requisition Slips	Time Tickets
Farley	$ 500	$ 400
Hendricks	600	1,000
Minor	2,300	1,300
Bennett	2,400	3,300
	5,800	6,000
General use	1,500	2,000
	$7,300	$8,000

During May, the following costs were incurred: (a) raw materials purchased on account $5,000, (b) labor paid $8,000, (c) manufacturing overhead paid $1,400. Overhead was charged to jobs on the basis of direct labor cost at the same rate as in the previous month.

The jacuzzis for customers Farley, Hendricks, and Minor were completed during May. Each jacuzzi was sold for $12,500 cash.

Instructions
(a) Prepare journal entries for the May transactions.
(b) Post the entries to Work in Process Inventory.
(c) Reconcile the balance in Work in Process Inventory with the costs of unfinished jobs.
(d) Prepare a cost of goods manufactured schedule for May.

(d) Cost of goods manufactured $20,860

Compute predetermined overhead rates, apply overhead, and indicate statement presentation of under- or overapplied overhead.

(SO 4, 6)

P21-4A Acquatic Manufacturing uses a job order cost system in each of its three manufacturing departments. Manufacturing overhead is applied to jobs on the basis of direct labor cost in Department A, direct labor hours in Department B, and machine hours in Department C.

In establishing the predetermined overhead rates for 2005 the following estimates were made for the year.

	Department		
	A	**B**	**C**
Manufacturing overhead	$930,000	$800,000	$750,000
Direct labor cost	$600,000	$100,000	$600,000
Direct labor hours	50,000	40,000	40,000
Machine hours	100,000	120,000	150,000

During January, the job cost sheets showed the following costs and production data.

	Department		
	A	**B**	**C**
Direct materials used	$92,000	$86,000	$64,000
Direct labor cost	$48,000	$35,000	$50,400
Manufacturing overhead incurred	$76,000	$74,000	$61,500
Direct labor hours	4,000	3,500	4,200
Machine hours	8,000	10,500	12,600

Instructions
(a) Compute the predetermined overhead rate for each department.
(b) Compute the total manufacturing costs assigned to jobs in January in each department.
(c) Compute the under- or overapplied overhead for each department at January 31.
(d) Indicate the statement presentation of the under- or overapplied overhead at January 31.
(e) If the amount in (d) was the same at December 31, how would it be reported in the year-end financial statements?

(a) 155%, $20, $5
(b) $214,400, $191,000
   $177,400
(c) $1,600, $4,000,
   $(1,500)

P21-5A Freedo Company's fiscal year ends on June 30. The following accounts are found in its job order cost accounting system for the first month of the new fiscal year.

Analyze manufacturing accounts and determine missing amounts.
(SO 2, 3, 4, 5, 6)

Raw Materials Inventory

July 1	Beginning balance	19,000	July 31	Requisitions	(a)
31	Purchases	90,400			
July 31	Ending balance	(b)			

Work in Process Inventory

July 1	Beginning balance	(c)	July 31	Jobs completed	(f)
31	Direct materials	80,000			
31	Direct labor	(d)			
31	Overhead	(e)			
July 31	Ending balance	(g)			

Finished Goods Inventory

July 1	Beginning balance	(h)	July 31	Cost of goods sold	(j)
31	Completed jobs	(i)			
July 31	Ending balance	(k)			

Factory Labor

July 31	Factory wages	(l)	July 31	Wages assigned	(m)

Manufacturing Overhead

July 31	Indirect materials	8,900	July 31	Overhead applied	117,000
31	Indirect labor	16,000			
31	Other overhead	(n)			

Other data:

1. On July 1, two jobs were in process: Job No. 4085 and Job No. 4086, with costs of $19,000 and $8,200, respectively.
2. During July, Job Nos. 4087, 4088, and 4089 were started. On July 31, only Job No. 4089 was unfinished. This job had charges for direct materials $2,000 and direct labor $1,000, plus manufacturing overhead.
3. On July 1, Job No. 4084, costing $135,000, was in the finished goods warehouse. On July 31, Job No. 4088, costing $143,000, was in finished goods.
4. Manufacturing overhead was applied at the rate of 130% of direct labor cost. Overhead was $3,000 underapplied in July.

Instructions
List the letters (a) through (n) and indicate the amount pertaining to each letter. Show computations.

Prepare entries in a job cost system and job cost sheets.

(SO 2, 3, 4, 5, 6)

P21-1B Medina Manufacturing uses a job order cost system and applies overhead to production on the basis of direct labor costs. On January 1, 2005, Job No. 50 was the only job in process. The costs incurred prior to January 1 on this job were as follows: direct materials $20,000, direct labor $12,000, and manufacturing overhead $16,000. As of January 1, Job No. 49 had been completed at a cost of $90,000 and was part of finished goods inventory. There was a $15,000 balance in the Raw Materials inventory account.

During the month of January, Medina Manufacturing began production on Jobs 51 and 52, and completed Jobs 50 and 51. Jobs 49 and 50 were also sold on account during the month for $122,000 and $158,000, respectively. The following additional events occurred during the month.

1. Purchased additional raw materials of $90,000 on account.
2. Incurred factory labor costs of $65,000. Of this amount $13,000 related to employer payroll taxes.
3. Incurred manufacturing overhead costs as follows: indirect materials $14,000; indirect labor $15,000; depreciation expense $19,000, and various other manufacturing overhead costs on account $20,000.
4. Assigned direct materials and direct labor to jobs as follows.

Instructions

Job No.	Direct Materials	Direct Labor
50	$10,000	$ 5,000
51	39,000	25,000
52	30,000	20,000

(a) Calculate the predetermined overhead rate for 2005, assuming Medina Manufacturing estimates total manufacturing overhead costs of $980,000, direct labor costs of $700,000, and direct labor hours of 20,000 for the year.

(b) Open job cost sheets for Jobs 50, 51, and 52. Enter the January 1 balances on the job cost sheet for Job No. 50.

(c) Prepare the journal entries to record the purchase of raw materials, the factory labor costs incurred, and the manufacturing overhead costs incurred during the month of January.

(d) Prepare the journal entries to record the assignment of direct materials, direct labor, and manufacturing overhead costs to production. In assigning manufacturing overhead costs, use the overhead rate calculated in (a). Post all costs to the job cost sheets as necessary.

(e) Job 50, $70,000
Job 51, $99,000

(e) Total the job cost sheets for any job(s) completed during the month. Prepare the journal entry (or entries) to record the completion of any job(s) during the month.

(f) Prepare the journal entry (or entries) to record the sale of any job(s) during the month.

(g) What is the balance in the Finished Goods Inventory account at the end of the month? What does this balance consist of?

(h) What is the amount of over- or underapplied overhead for the month? How would this be reported on the financial statements for the month of January?

Prepare entries in a job cost system and partial income statement.

(SO 2, 3, 4, 5, 6)

P21-2B For the year ended December 31, 2005, the job cost sheets of Amend Company contained the following data.

Job Number	Explanation	Direct Materials	Direct Labor	Manufacturing Overhead	Total Costs
7640	Balance 1/1	$25,000	$24,000	$28,800	$ 77,800
	Current year's costs	30,000	36,000	43,200	109,200
7641	Balance 1/1	11,000	18,000	21,600	50,600
	Current year's costs	40,000	48,000	57,600	145,600
7642	Current year's costs	48,000	50,000	60,000	158,000

Other data:

1. Raw materials inventory totaled $15,000 on January 1. During the year, $140,000 of raw materials were purchased on account.

2. Finished goods on January 1 consisted of Job No. 7638 for $87,000 and Job No. 7639 for $92,000.
3. Job No. 7640 and Job No. 7641 were completed during the year.
4. Job Nos. 7638, 7639, and 7641 were sold on account for $530,000.
5. Manufacturing overhead incurred on account totaled $115,000.
6. Other manufacturing overhead consisted of indirect materials $14,000, indirect labor $20,000, and depreciation on factory machinery $8,000.

Instructions
(a) Prove the agreement of Work in Process Inventory with job cost sheets pertaining to unfinished work. *Hint:* Use a single T account for Work in Process Inventory. Calculate each of the following, then post each to the T account: (1) beginning balance, (2) direct materials, (3) direct labor, (4) manufacturing overhead, and (5) completed jobs.
(b) Prepare the adjusting entry for manufacturing overhead, assuming the balance is allocated entirely to Cost of Goods Sold.
(c) Determine the gross profit to be reported for 2005.

(a) $158,000; Job 7642: $158,000

(b) Amount = $3,800

(c) $158,600

P21-3B Zion Inc. is a construction company specializing in custom patios. The patios are constructed of concrete, brick, fiberglass, and lumber, depending upon customer preference. On June 1, 2005, the general ledger for Zion Inc. contains the following data.

Prepare entries in a job cost system and cost of goods manufactured schedule.
(SO 2, 3, 4, 5)

Raw Materials Inventory	$4,200	Manufacturing Overhead Applied	$32,640
Work in Process Inventory	$5,540	Manufacturing Overhead Incurred	$31,650

Subsidiary data for Work in Process Inventory on June 1 are as follows.

Job Cost Sheets

	Customer Job		
Cost Element	**Powell**	**Aurora**	**Hayden**
Direct materials	$ 600	$ 800	$ 900
Direct labor	320	540	580
Manufacturing overhead	400	675	725
	$1,320	$2,015	$2,205

A summary of materials requisition slips and time tickets for June shows the following.

Customer Job	Materials Requisition Slips	Time Tickets
Powell	$ 800	$ 450
Elgin	2,000	800
Aurora	500	360
Hayden	1,300	800
Powell	300	390
	4,900	2,800
General use	1,500	1,200
	$6,400	$4,000

During June, raw materials purchased on account were $3,900, and all wages were paid. Additional overhead costs consisted of depreciation on equipment $700 and miscellaneous costs of $400 incurred on account. Overhead was charged to jobs at the same rate that was used in May. The patios for customers Powell, Aurora, and Hayden were completed during June and sold for a total of $18,900. Each customer paid in full.

Instructions
(a) Journalize the June transactions.
(b) Post the entries to Work in Process Inventory.
(c) Reconcile the balance in Work in Process Inventory with the costs of unfinished jobs.
(d) Prepare a cost of goods manufactured schedule for June.

(d) Cost of goods manufactured $12,940

P21-4B Stein Manufacturing Company uses a job order cost system in each of its three manufacturing departments. Manufacturing overhead is applied to jobs on the basis of direct labor cost in Department D, direct labor hours in Department E, and machine hours in Department K.

In establishing the predetermined overhead rates for 2006 the following estimates were made for the year.

	Department		
	D	**E**	**K**
Manufacturing overhead	$1,200,000	$1,500,000	$900,000
Direct labor costs	$1,500,000	$1,250,000	$450,000
Direct labor hours	100,000	125,000	40,000
Machine hours	400,000	500,000	120,000

During January, the job cost sheets showed the following costs and production data.

	Department		
	D	**E**	**K**
Direct materials used	$140,000	$126,000	$78,000
Direct labor costs	$120,000	$110,000	$37,500
Manufacturing overhead incurred	$ 98,000	$129,000	$74,000
Direct labor hours	8,000	11,000	3,500
Machine hours	34,000	45,000	10,400

Instructions

(a) Compute the predetermined overhead rate for each department.
(b) Compute the total manufacturing costs assigned to jobs in January in each department.
(c) Compute the under- or overapplied overhead for each department at January 31.
(d) Indicate the statement presentation of the under- or overapplied overhead at January 31.
(e) If the amount in (d) was the same at December 31, how would it be reported in the year-end financial statements?

P21-5B Vargas Corporation's fiscal year ends on November 30. The following accounts are found in its job order cost accounting system for the first month of the new fiscal year.

Raw Materials Inventory

Dec. 1	Beginning balance	(a)	Dec. 31	Requisitions	16,850
31	Purchases	19,225			
Dec. 31	Ending balance	7,975			

Work in Process Inventory

Dec. 1	Beginning balance	(b)	Dec. 31	Jobs completed	(f)
31	Direct materials	(c)			
31	Direct labor	8,800			
31	Overhead	(d)			
Dec. 31	Ending balance	(e)			

Finished Goods Inventory

Dec. 1	Beginning balance	(g)	Dec. 31	Cost of goods sold	(i)
31	Completed jobs	(h)			
Dec. 31	Ending balance	(j)			

Factory Labor

Dec. 31	Factory wages	12,025	Dec. 31	Wages assigned	(k)

Manufacturing Overhead

Dec. 31	Indirect materials	1,900	Dec. 31	Overhead applied	(m)
31	Indirect labor	(l)			
31	Other overhead	1,245			

Other data:

1. On December 1, two jobs were in process: Job No. 154 and Job No. 155. These jobs had combined direct materials costs of $9,750 and direct labor costs of $15,000. Overhead was applied at a rate that was 75% of direct labor cost.
2. During December, Job Nos. 156, 157, and 158 were started. On December 31, Job No. 158 was unfinished. This job had charges for direct materials $3,800 and direct labor $4,800, plus manufacturing overhead. All jobs, except for Job No. 158, were completed in December.
3. On December 1, Job No. 153 was in the finished goods warehouse. It had a total cost of $5,000. On December 31, Job No. 157 was the only job finished that was not sold. It had a cost of $4,000.
4. Manufacturing overhead was $230 overapplied in December.

Instructions
List the letters (a) through (m) and indicate the amount pertaining to each letter.

BROADENING YOUR PERSPECTIVE

Group Decision Case

BYP21-1 Wang Products Company uses a job order cost system. For a number of months there has been an ongoing rift between the sales department and the production department concerning a special-order product, TC-1. TC-1 is a seasonal product that is manufactured in batches of 1,000 units. TC-1 is sold at cost plus a markup of 40% of cost.

The sales department is unhappy because fluctuating unit production costs significantly affect selling prices. Sales personnel complain that this has caused excessive customer complaints and the loss of considerable orders for TC-1.

The production department maintains that each job order must be fully costed on the basis of the costs incurred during the period in which the goods are produced. Production personnel maintain that the only real solution to the problem is for the sales department to increase sales in the slack periods.

Sandra Devona, president of the company, asks you as the company accountant to collect quarterly data for the past year on TC-1. From the cost accounting system, you accumulate the following production quantity and cost data.

| | | Quarter | | |
Costs	1	2	3	4
Direct materials	$100,000	$220,000	$ 80,000	$200,000
Direct labor	60,000	132,000	48,000	120,000
Manufacturing overhead	105,000	153,000	97,000	125,000
Total	$265,000	$505,000	$225,000	$445,000
Production in batches	5	11	4	10
Unit cost (per batch)	$ 53,000	$ 45,909	$ 56,250	$ 44,500

Instructions
With the class divided into groups, answer the following questions.

(a) What manufacturing cost element is responsible for the fluctuating unit costs? Why?
(b) What is your recommended solution to the problem of fluctuating unit cost?
(c) Restate the quarterly data on the basis of your recommended solution.

Managerial Analysis

BYP21-2 In the course of routine checking of all journal entries prior to preparing month-end reports, Sally Yount discovered several strange entries. She recalled that the president's son Ken had come in to help out during an especially busy time and that he had recorded some journal entries. She was relieved that there were only a few of his entries, and even more relieved that he had included rather lengthy explanations. The entries Ken made were:

1.

| Work in Process Inventory | 25,000 | |
| Cash | | 25,000 |

(This is for materials put into process. I don't find the record that we paid for these, so I'm crediting Cash, because I know we'll have to pay for them sooner or later.)

2.

| Manufacturing Overhead | 12,000 | |
| Cash | | 12,000 |

(This is for bonuses paid to salespeople. I know they're part of overhead, and I can't find an account called "Non-factory Overhead" or "Other Overhead" so I'm putting it in Manufacturing Overhead. I have the check stubs, so I know we paid these.)

3.

| Wages Expense | 120,000 | |
| Cash | | 120,000 |

(This is for the factory workers' wages. I have a note that payroll taxes are $12,000. I still think that's part of wages expense, and that we'll have to pay it all in cash sooner or later, so I credited Cash for the wages and the taxes.)

4.

| Work in Process Inventory | 3,000 | |
| Raw Materials Inventory | | 3,000 |

(This is for the glue used in the factory. I know we used this to make the products, even though we didn't use very much on any one of the products. I got it out of inventory, so I credited an inventory account.)

Instructions

(a) How should Ken have recorded each of the four events?

(b) If the entry was not corrected, which financial statements (income statement or balance sheet) would be affected? What balances would be overstated or understated?

Real-World Focus

BYP21-3   Founded in 1970, **Parlex Corporation** is a world leader in the design and manufacture of flexible interconnect products. Utilizing proprietary and patented technologies, Parlex produces custom flexible interconnects including flexible circuits, polymer thick film, laminated cables, and value-added assemblies for sophisticated electronics used in automotive, telecommunications, computer, diversified electronics, and aerospace applications. In addition to manufacturing sites in Methuen, Massachusetts; Salem, New Hampshire; Cranston, Rhode Island; San Jose, California; Shanghai, China; Isle of Wight, UK; and Empalme, Mexico, Parlex has logistic support centers and strategic alliances throughout North America, Asia, and Europe.

The following information was provided in the company's annual report.

PARLEX COMPANY
Notes to the Financial Statements

The Company's products are manufactured on a job order basis to customers' specifications. Customers submit requests for quotations on each job, and the Company prepares bids based on its own cost estimates. The Company attempts to reflect the impact of changing costs when establishing prices. However, during the past several years, the market conditions for flexible circuits and the resulting price sensitivity haven't always allowed this to transpire. Although still not satisfactory, the Company was able to reduce the cost of products sold as a percentage of sales to 85% this year versus 87% that was experienced in the two immediately preceding years. Management continues to focus on improving operational efficiency and further reducing costs.

Instructions

(a) Parlex management discusses the job order cost system employed by their company. What are several advantages of using the job order approach to costing?

(b) Contrast the products produced in a job order environment, like Parlex, to those produced when process cost systems are used.

Exploring the Web

BYP21-4 The Institute of Management Accountants sponsors a certification for management accountants, allowing them to obtain the title of Certified Management Accountant.

Address: www.imanet.org, or go to www.wiley.com/college/weygandt

Steps

1. Go to the site shown above.

2. Choose **Certification**.

Instructions

(a) What are the objectives of the certification program?

(b) What is the "experience requirement"?

(c) How many hours of continuing education are required, and what types of courses qualify?

Communication Activity

BYP21-5 You are the management accountant for Clemente Manufacturing. Your company does custom carpentry work and uses a job order cost accounting system. Clemente sends detailed job cost sheets to its customers, along with an invoice. The job cost sheets show the date materials were used, the dollar cost of materials, and the hours and cost of labor. A predetermined overhead application rate is used, and the total overhead applied is also listed.

Cindy Stein is a customer who recently had custom cabinets installed. Along with her check in payment for the work done, she included a letter. She thanked the company for including the detailed cost information but questioned why overhead was estimated. She stated that she would be interested in knowing exactly what costs were included in overhead, and she thought that other customers would, too.

Instructions

Prepare a letter to Ms. Stein (address: 123 Cedar Lane, Altoona, Kansas 66651) and tell her why you did not send her information on exact costs of overhead included in her job. Respond to her suggestion that you provide this information.

Ethics Case

BYP21-6 ESU Printing provides printing services to many different corporate clients. Although ESU bids most jobs, some jobs, particularly new ones, are often negotiated on a "cost-plus" basis. Cost-plus means that the buyer is willing to pay the actual cost plus a return (profit) on these costs to ESU.

Clara Biggio, controller for ESU, has recently returned from a meeting where ESU's president stated that he wanted her to find a way to charge most costs to any project that was on a cost-plus basis. The president noted that the company needed more profits to meet its stated goals this period. By charging more costs to the cost-plus projects and therefore less cost to the jobs that were bid, the company should be able to increase its profits for the current year.

Clara knew why the president wanted to take this action. Rumors were that he was looking for a new position and if the company reported strong profits, the president's opportunities would be enhanced. Clara also recognized that she could probably increase the cost of certain jobs by changing the basis used to allocate manufacturing overhead.

Instructions

(a) Who are the stakeholders in this situation?

(b) What are the ethical issues in this situation?

(c) What would you do if you were Clara Biggio?

Answers to Self-Study Questions

1. a   **2.** b   **3.** c   **4.** d   **5.** b   **6.** a   **7.** d   **8.** b   **9.** c   **10.** b

 ✓ **REMEMBER** to go back to the Navigator box on the chapter-opening page and check off your completed work.

Process Cost Accounting

THE NAVIGATOR ✓

Understand **Concepts for Review** ❏

Read **Feature Story** ❏

Scan **Study Objectives** ❏

Read **Preview** ❏

Read text and answer **Before You Go On**
p. 896 ❏   p. 905 ❏   p. 908 ❏

Work **Demonstration Problem** ❏

Review **Summary of Study Objectives** ❏

Answer **Self-Study Questions** ❏

Complete **Assignments** ❏

CONCEPTS FOR REVIEW

Before studying this chapter, you should know or, if necessary, review:

- The three manufacturing cost elements.
  (Ch. 20, pp. 820–821)

- How manufacturing costs are accumulated in the accounts.
  (Ch. 21, pp. 856–858)

- How manufacturing costs are assigned to work in process, finished goods, and cost of goods sold.
  (Ch. 21, pp. 858–867)

- The flow of costs and supporting documents in a job order cost accounting system.
  (Ch. 21, pp. 855–856)

THE NAVIGATOR

Ben & Jerry's Tracks Its Mix-Ups

At one time, one of the fastest growing companies in the nation was **Ben & Jerry's Homemade, Inc.**, based in Waterbury, Vermont. The ice cream company that started out of a garage in 1978 is now one of the largest players in the ice cream market.

Making ice cream is a process—a movement of product from a mixing department to a prepping department to a pint department. The mixing department is where the ice cream is created. The prep area is where extras such as cherries and walnuts are added to make plain ice cream into "Cherry Garcia." And the pint department is where the ice cream is actually put into containers. As the product is processed from one department to the next, the appropriate materials, labor, and overhead are added to it.

"The incoming ingredients from the shipping and receiving departments are stored in certain locations, either in a freezer or dry warehouse," says Beecher Eurich, staff accountant. "As ingredients get added, so do the costs associated with them." How much ice cream is actually produced? Running the plant around the clock, 24,000 pints are produced per 8-hour shift, or 72,000 pints per day.

Using a process costing system, Eurich can tell you how much a certain batch of ice cream costs to make—its materials, labor, and overhead in each of the production departments. She generates reports for the production department heads, but makes sure not to overdo it. "You can get bogged down in numbers," says Eurich. "If you're generating a report that no one can use, then that's a waste of time." More likely, though, Ben & Jerry's production people want to know how efficient they are.

www.benjerry.com

After studying this chapter, you should be able to:

1. Understand who uses process cost systems.
2. Explain the similarities and differences between job order cost and process cost systems.
3. Explain the flow of costs in a process cost system.
4. Make the journal entries to assign manufacturing costs in a process cost system.
5. Compute equivalent units.
6. Explain the four steps necessary to prepare a production cost report.
7. Prepare a production cost report.
8. Explain just-in-time (JIT) processing.
9. Explain activity-based costing (ABC).

THE NAVIGATOR

The cost accounting system used by companies such as Ben & Jerry's is called a **process cost accounting** system. In contrast to job order cost accounting, which focuses on the individual job, process cost accounting focuses on the processes involved in mass-producing products that are identical or very similar in nature. The primary objective of the chapter is to explain and illustrate process cost accounting.

The content and organization of Chapter 22 are as follows.

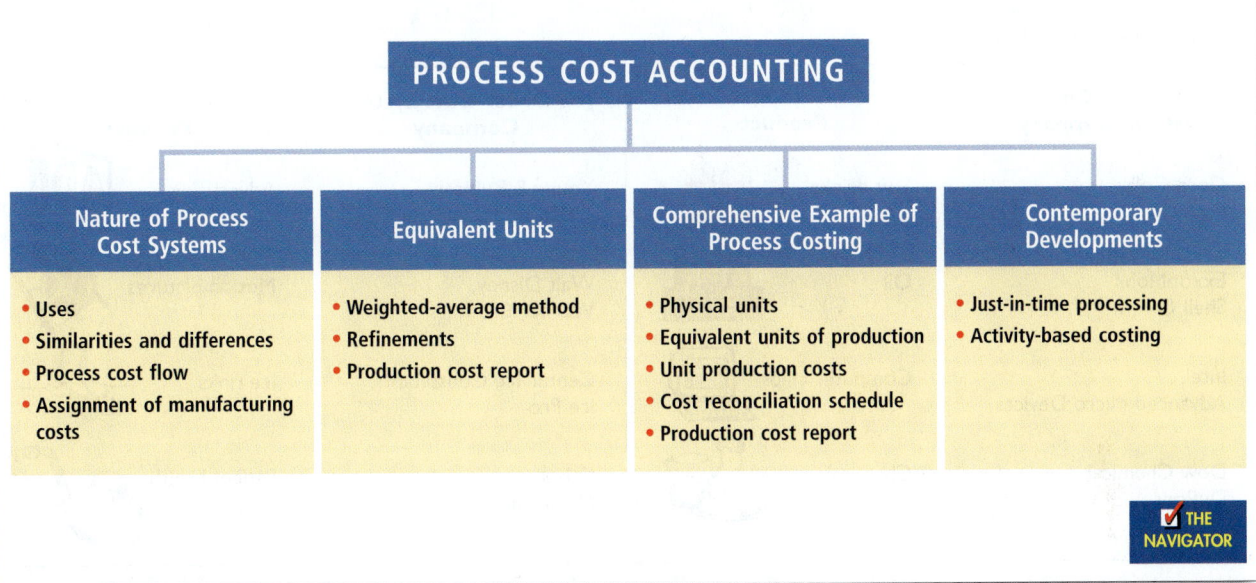

PROCESS COST ACCOUNTING

Nature of Process Cost Systems	Equivalent Units	Comprehensive Example of Process Costing	Contemporary Developments
• Uses • Similarities and differences • Process cost flow • Assignment of manufacturing costs	• Weighted-average method • Refinements • Production cost report	• Physical units • Equivalent units of production • Unit production costs • Cost reconciliation schedule • Production cost report	• Just-in-time processing • Activity-based costing

☑ THE NAVIGATOR

The Nature of Process Cost Systems

Uses of Process Cost Systems

Process cost systems are used to apply costs to similar products that are mass-produced in a continuous fashion. Ben & Jerry's uses a process cost system: Production of the ice cream, once it begins, continues until the ice cream emerges, and the processing is the same for the entire run—with precisely the same amount of materials, labor, and overhead. Each finished pint of ice cream is indistinguishable from another.

A company such as **USX** uses process costing in the manufacturing of steel. **Kellogg** and **General Mills** use process costing for cereal production. **ExxonMobil** uses process costing for its oil refining. And **Sherwin Williams** uses process costing for its paint products. At a bottling company like **Coca-Cola**, the manufacturing process begins with the blending of the beverages. Next the beverage is dispensed into bottles that are moved into position by automated machinery. The bottles are then capped, packaged, and forwarded to the finished goods warehouse. This process is shown in Illustration 22-1.

STUDY OBJECTIVE 1

Understand who uses process cost systems.

Illustration 22-1
Manufacturing processes

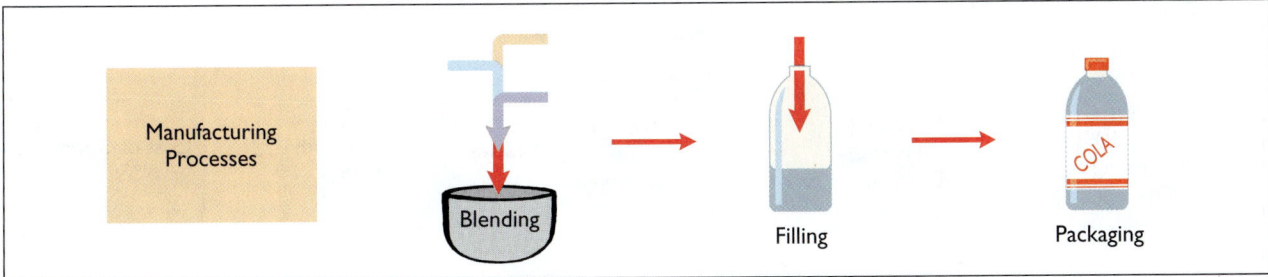

Manufacturing Processes → Blending → Filling → Packaging

For Coca-Cola, as well as the other companies just mentioned, once the production begins, it continues until the finished product emerges, and each unit of finished product is like every other unit.

In comparison, costs in a job order cost system are assigned to a specific job. Examples are the construction of a customized home, the making of a motion picture, or the manufacturing of a specialized machine. Illustration 22-2 provides examples of companies that primarily use either a process cost system or a job order cost system.

Illustration 22-2
Process cost and job order cost companies and products

Process Cost System Company	Product	Job Order Cost System Company	Product
Coca-Cola, PepsiCo	Soft drinks	Young & Rubicam, J. Walter Thompson	Advertising
ExxonMobil Shell Oil	Oil	Walt Disney, Warner Brothers	Motion pictures
Intel, Advanced Micro Devices	Computer chips	Center Ice Consultants, Ice Pro	Ice rinks
Dow Chemical, DuPont	Chemicals	Kaiser, Mayo Clinic	Patient health care

STUDY OBJECTIVE 2

Explain the similarities and differences between job order cost and process cost systems.

Similarities and Differences Between Job Order Cost and Process Cost Systems

In a job order cost system, costs are assigned to each job. In a process cost system, costs are tracked through a series of connected manufacturing processes or departments, rather than by individual jobs. Thus, process cost systems are used when a large volume of uniform or relatively homogeneous products are produced. The basic flow of costs in these two systems is shown in Illustration 22-3.

Illustration 22-3
Job order cost and process cost flow

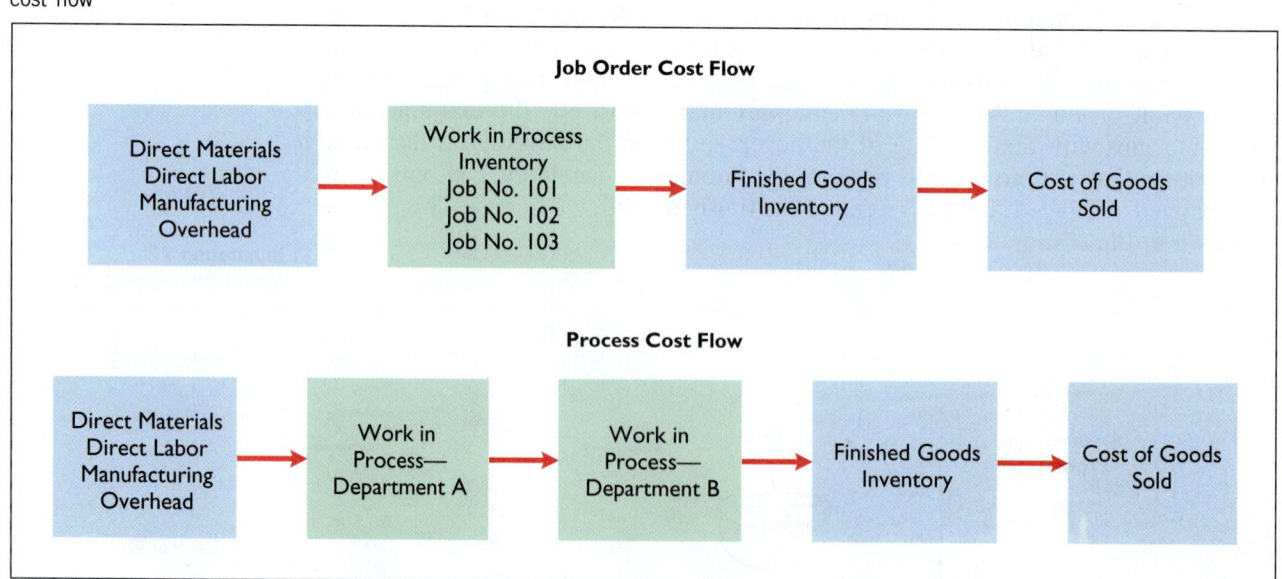

The basic similarities and differences between these two systems are highlighted in the following analysis.

Similarities

Job order cost and process cost systems are similar in three ways:

1. **The manufacturing cost elements.** Both a job order cost and a process cost system track the same three manufacturing cost elements—direct materials, direct labor, and manufacturing overhead.

2. **The accumulation of the costs of materials, labor, and overhead.** In both costing systems, all raw materials are debited to Raw Materials Inventory; all factory labor is debited to Factory Labor; and all manufacturing overhead costs are debited to Manufacturing Overhead.

3. **The flow of costs.** As noted above, all manufacturing costs are accumulated by debits to Raw Materials Inventory, Factory Labor, and Manufacturing Overhead. These costs are then assigned to the same accounts in both costing systems—Work in Process, Finished Goods Inventory, and Cost of Goods Sold. **The methods of assigning costs, however, differ significantly.** These differences are explained and illustrated later in the chapter.

Differences

The differences between a job order cost and a process cost system are as follows.

1. **The number of work in process accounts used.** In a job order cost system, only one work in process account is used. In a process cost system, multiple work in process accounts are used; separate accounts are maintained for each production department or manufacturing process.

2. **Documents used to track costs.** In a job order cost system, costs are charged to individual jobs and summarized in a job cost sheet. In a process cost system, costs are summarized in a production cost report for each department.

3. **The point at which costs are totaled.** In a job order cost system, total costs are determined when the job is completed. In a process cost system, total costs are determined at the end of a period of time, such as a month or year.

4. **Unit cost computations.** In a job order cost system, the unit cost is the total cost per job divided by the units produced. In a process cost system, the unit cost is total manufacturing costs for the period divided by the units produced during the period.

The major differences between a job order cost and a process cost system are summarized in Illustration 22-4.

Features	Job Order Cost System	Process Cost System
Work in process accounts	• One for each job	• One for each process
Documents used	• Job cost sheets	• Production cost reports
Determination of total manufacturing costs	• Each job	• Each period
Unit-cost computations	• Cost of each job ÷ Units produced for the job	• Total manufacturing costs ÷ Units produced during the period

Illustration 22-4
Job order versus process cost systems

Process Cost Flow

Illustration 22-5 shows the flow of costs in the process cost system for Tyler Company. Tyler Company manufactures automatic can openers that are sold to retail outlets. Manufacturing consists of two processes: machining and assembly. In the Machining Department, the raw materials are shaped, honed, and drilled. In the Assembly Department, the parts are assembled and packaged.

Illustration 22-5
Flow of costs in process cost system

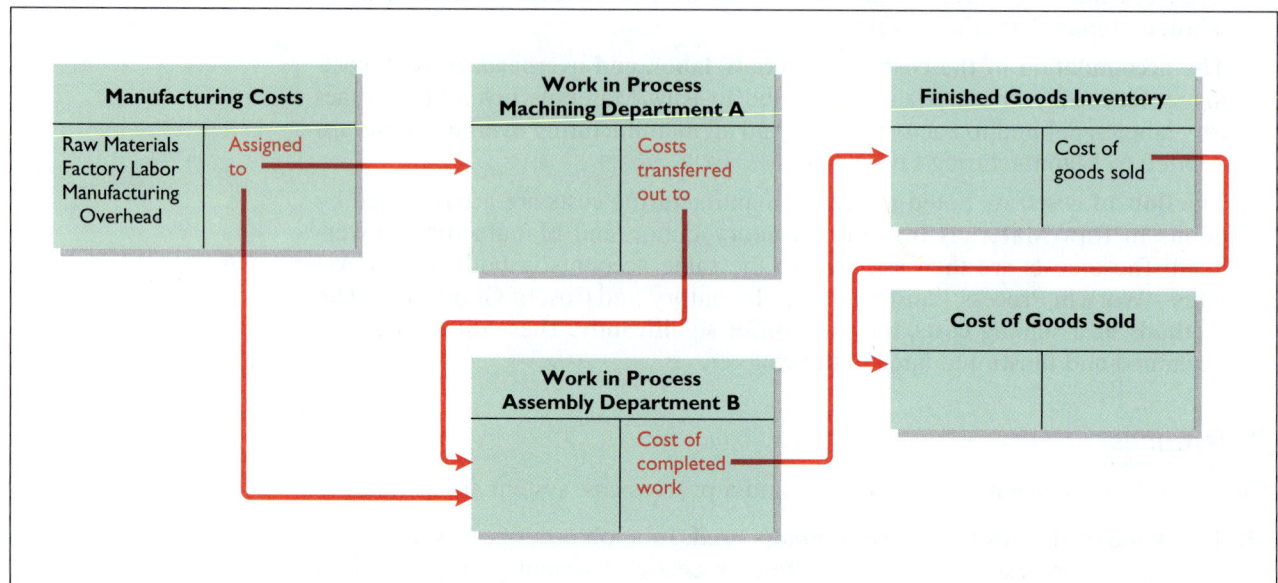

As the flow of costs indicates, materials, labor, and manufacturing overhead can be added in both the Machining and Assembly Departments. When the Machining Department finishes its work, the partially completed units are transferred to the Assembly Department. In the Assembly Department, the goods are finished and are then transferred to the finished goods inventory. Upon sale, the goods are removed from the finished goods inventory. Within each department, a similar set of activities is performed on each unit processed.

Assignment of Manufacturing Costs—Journal Entries

As indicated earlier, the accumulation of the costs of materials, labor, and manufacturing overhead is the same in a process cost system as in a job order cost system. All raw materials are debited to Raw Materials Inventory when the materials are purchased. All factory labor is debited to Factory Labor when the labor costs are incurred. And overhead costs are debited to Manufacturing Overhead as they are incurred. However, the assignment of the three manufacturing cost elements to Work in Process in a process cost system is different from a job order cost system. Here we'll look at how these manufacturing cost elements are assigned in a process cost system.

Materials Costs

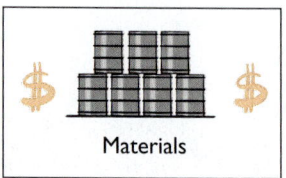

Materials

All raw materials issued for production are a materials cost to the producing department. Materials requisition slips may be used in a process cost system, but **fewer requisitions are generally required than in a job order cost system**, **because the materials are used for processes rather than for specific jobs**. Requisitions are issued less frequently in a process cost system because the requisitions are for larger quantities.

Materials are usually added to production at the beginning of the first process. However, in subsequent processes, other materials may be added at various points.

For example, in the manufacture of **Hershey** candy bars, the chocolate and other ingredients are added at the beginning of the first process, and the wrappers and cartons are added at the end of the packaging process. At Tyler Company, materials are entered at the beginning of each process. The entry to record the materials used is:

Work in Process—Machining	XXXX	
Work in Process—Assembly	XXXX	
Raw Materials Inventory		XXXX
(To record materials used)		

In the Feature Story at the beginning of the chapter, materials are added to the ice cream in three departments: milk and flavoring in the mixing department; extras such as cherries and walnuts in the prepping department; and cardboard containers in the pinting (packaging) department.

Factory Labor Costs

In a process cost system, as in a job order cost system, time tickets may be used to determine the cost of labor assignable to production departments. Since labor costs are assigned to a process rather than a job, the labor cost chargeable to a process can be obtained from the payroll register or departmental payroll summaries.

All labor costs incurred within a producing department are a cost of processing the raw materials. Thus, labor costs for the Machining Department will include the wages of employees who shape, hone, and drill the raw materials. The entry to assign these costs for Tyler Company is:

Factory Labor

Work in Process—Machining	XXXX	
Work in Process—Assembly	XXXX	
Factory Labor		XXXX
(To assign factory labor to production)		

Manufacturing Overhead Costs

The objective in assigning overhead in a process cost system is to allocate the overhead costs to the production departments on an objective and equitable basis. That basis is the activity that "drives" or causes the costs. A primary driver of overhead costs in continuous manufacturing operations is **machine time used**, not direct labor. Thus, **machine hours are widely used** in allocating manufacturing overhead costs. The entry to allocate overhead to the two processes is:

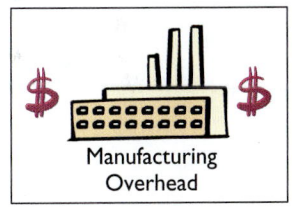
Manufacturing Overhead

Work in Process—Machining	XXXX	
Work in Process—Assembly	XXXX	
Manufacturing Overhead		XXXX
(To assign overhead to production)		

 ACCOUNTING IN ACTION   Business Insight

In one of **Caterpillar**'s automated cost centers, work is fed into the cost center, processed by robotic machines, and transferred to the next cost center without human intervention. One person tends all of the machines and spends more time maintaining machines than operating them. In such cases, overhead rates based on direct labor hours may be misleading. Surprisingly, some companies continue to assign manufacturing overhead on the basis of direct labor despite the fact that there is no cause-and-effect relationship between labor and overhead.

Transfer to Next Department

At the end of the month, an entry is needed to record the cost of the goods transferred out of the department. In this case, the transfer is to the Assembly Department, and the following entry is made:

Work in Process—Assembly	XXXXX	
Work in Process—Machining		XXXXX
(To record transfer of units to the Assembly		
Department)		

Transfer to Finished Goods

The units completed in the Assembly Department are transferred to the finished goods warehouse. The entry for this transfer is as follows.

Finished Goods Inventory	XXXXX	
Work in Process—Assembly		XXXXX
(To record transfer of units to finished goods)		

Transfer to Cost of Goods Sold

When finished goods are sold, the entry to record the cost of goods sold is as follows.

Cost of Goods Sold	XXXXX	
Finished Goods Inventory		XXXXX
(To record cost of units sold)		

BEFORE YOU GO ON...

Review It

1. What type of manufacturing companies might use a process cost accounting system?
2. What are the principal similarities and differences between a job order cost system and a process cost system?

Do It

Ruth Company manufactures ZEBO through two processes: Blending and Bottling. In June, raw materials used were Blending $18,000 and Bottling $4,000. Factory labor costs were Blending $12,000 and Bottling $5,000. Manufacturing overhead costs were Blending $6,000 and Bottling $2,500. Units completed at a cost of $19,000 in the Blending Department are transferred to the Bottling Department. Units completed at a cost of $11,000 in the Bottling Department are transferred to Finished Goods. Journalize the assignment of these costs to the two processes and the transfer of units as appropriate.

ACTION PLAN

- In process cost accounting, keep separate work in process accounts for each process.
- When the costs are assigned to production, debit the separate work in process accounts.
- Transfer cost of completed units to the next process or to Finished Goods.

SOLUTION The entries are:

Work in Process—Blending	18,000	
Work in Process—Bottling	4,000	
Raw Materials Inventory		22,000
(To record materials used)		
Work in Process—Blending	12,000	
Work in Process—Bottling	5,000	
Factory Labor		17,000
(To assign factory labor to production)		
Work in Process—Blending	6,000	
Work in Process—Bottling	2,500	
Manufacturing Overhead		8,500
(To assign overhead to production)		
Work in Process—Bottling	19,000	
Work in Process—Blending		19,000
(To record transfer of units to the Bottling Department)		
Finished Goods Inventory	11,000	
Work in Process—Bottling		11,000
(To record transfer of units to finished goods)		

Related exercise material: *BE22-1, BE22-2, BE22-3, E22-7, and E22-10.*

☑ THE NAVIGATOR

Equivalent Units

Suppose you were asked to compute the cost of instruction at your college per full-time equivalent student. You are provided the following information.

STUDY OBJECTIVE 5

Compute equivalent units.

Illustration 22-6
Information for full-time student example

Costs:	
Total cost of instruction	$900,000
Student population:	
Full-time students	900
Part-time students	1,000

Part-time students take 60 percent of the classes of a full-time student during the year. To compute the number of full-time equivalent students per year, you would make the following computation.

Illustration 22-7
Full-time equivalent unit computation

Full-time Students	+	Equivalent Units of Part-time Students	=	Full-time Equivalent Students
900	+	(60% × 1,000)	=	**1,500**

The cost of instruction per full-time equivalent student is therefore the total cost of instruction ($900,000) divided by the number of full-time equivalent students (1,500), which is $600 ($900,000 ÷ 1,500).

In a process cost system, the same idea, called equivalent units of production, is used. **Equivalent units of production** measure the work done during the period, expressed in fully completed units. This concept is used to determine the cost per unit of completed product.

Weighted-Average Method

The formula to compute equivalent units of production is as follows.

Illustration 22-8
Equivalent units of production formula

Units Completed and Transferred Out	+	Equivalent Units of Ending Work in Process	=	Equivalent Units of Production

To better understand this concept of equivalent units, consider the following two examples.

Example 1: The Blending Department's entire output during the period consists of ending work in process of 4,000 units which are 60 percent complete as to materials, labor, and overhead. The equivalent units of production for the Blending Department are therefore 2,400 units (4,000 × 60%).

Example 2: The Packaging Department's output during the period consists of 10,000 units completed and transferred out, and 5,000 units in ending work in process which are 70 percent completed. The equivalent units of production are therefore 13,500 [10,000 + (5,000 × 70%)].

This method of computing equivalent units is referred to as the **weighted-average method**. It considers the degree of completion (weighting) of the units completed and transferred out and the ending work in process. It is the method most widely used in practice. Another method, called the FIFO method, is discussed in advanced cost accounting courses.

Refinements on the Weighted-Average Method

Kellogg Company has produced Eggo® Waffles since 1970. Three departments are used to produce these waffles: Mixing, Baking, and Freezing and Packaging. In the Mixing Department dry ingredients, including flour, salt, and baking powder, are mixed with liquid ingredients, including eggs and vegetable oil, to make waffle batter. Information related to the Mixing Department at the end of June is provided in Illustration 22-9.

Illustration 22-9
Information for Mixing Department

Mixing Department			
		Percentage Complete	
	Physical Units	**Materials**	**Conversion Costs**
Work in process, June 1	100,000	100%	70%
Started into production	800,000		
Total units	900,000		
Units transferred out	700,000		
Work in process, June 30	200,000	100%	60%
Total units	900,000		

Illustration 22-9 indicates that the beginning work in process is 100 percent complete as to materials cost and 70 percent complete as to conversion costs (labor and overhead). In other words, both the dry and liquid ingredients (materials) are added at the beginning of the process to make Eggo® Waffles. The conversion costs related to the mixing of these ingredients were incurred uniformly and are 70 percent complete. The ending work in process is 100 percent complete as to materials cost and 60 percent complete as to conversion costs.

We then use the Mixing Department information to determine equivalent units. **In computing equivalent units, the beginning work in process is not part of the equivalent units of production formula.** The units transferred out to the Baking Department are fully complete as to both materials and conversion costs. The ending work in process is fully complete as to materials, but only 60 percent complete as to conversion cost. **Two equivalent unit computations are therefore necessary:** one for materials and the other for conversion costs. Illustration 22-10 shows these computations.

	Equivalent Units	
	Materials	**Conversion Costs**
Units transferred out	700,000	700,000
Work in process, June 30		
200,000 × 100%	200,000	
200,000 × 60%		120,000
Total equivalent units	900,000	820,000

Illustration 22-10
Computation of equivalent units—Mixing Department

The earlier formula used to compute equivalent units of production can be refined to show the computations for materials and for conversion costs, as follows.

Units Completed and Transferred Out— Materials	+	Equivalent Units of Ending Work in Process—Materials	=	Equivalent Units of Production— Materials
Units Completed and Transferred Out— Conversion Costs	+	Equivalent Units of Ending Work in Process—Conversion Costs	=	Equivalent Units of Production— Conversion Costs

Illustration 22-11
Refined equivalent unit of production formula

Production Cost Report

As mentioned earlier, a production cost report is prepared for each department in a process cost system. A **production cost report** is the key document used by management to understand the activities in a department. It shows the production quantity and cost data related to that department. For example, in producing Eggo® Waffles, **Kellogg Company** would have three production cost reports: Mixing, Baking, and Freezing and Packaging. Illustration 22-12 shows the flow of costs to make an Eggo® Waffle and the related production cost reports for each department.

Illustration 22-12
Flow of costs in making Eggo® Waffles

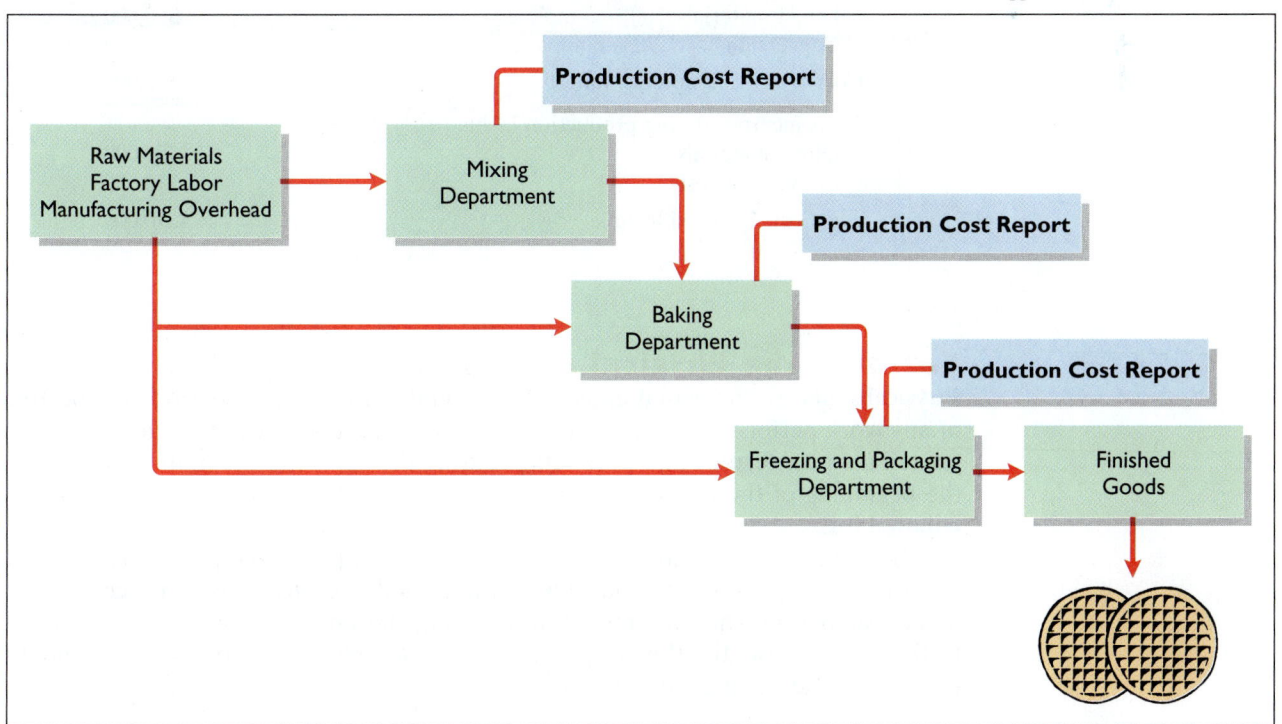

In order to be ready to complete a production cost report, the company must perform four steps:

1. Compute the physical unit flow.

2. Compute the equivalent units of production.

3. Compute unit production costs.

4. Prepare a cost reconciliation schedule.

As a whole, these four steps make up the process costing system. The next section explores these steps in an extended example.

Comprehensive Example of Process Costing

Assumed data for the Mixing Department at **Kellogg Company** for the month of June are shown in Illustration 22-13. We will use this information to complete a production cost report for the Mixing Department.

Illustration 22-13
Unit and cost data—Mixing Department

Mixing Department	
Units:	
Work in process, June 1	100,000
Direct materials: 100% complete	
Conversion costs: 70% complete	
Units started into production during June	800,000
Units completed and transferred out to Baking Department	700,000
Work in process, June 30	200,000
Direct materials: 100% complete	
Conversion costs: 60% complete	
Costs:	
Work in process, June 1	
Direct materials: 100% complete	$50,000
Conversion costs: 70% complete	35,000
Cost of work in process, June 1	$85,000
Costs incurred during production in June	
Direct materials	$400,000
Conversion costs	170,000
Costs incurred in June	$570,000

Compute the Physical Unit Flow (Step 1)

Physical units are the actual units to be accounted for during a period, irrespective of any work performed. To keep track of these units, it is necessary to add the units started (or transferred) into production during the period to the units in process at the beginning of the period. This amount is referred to as the **total units to be accounted for**.

The total units then are accounted for by the output of the period. The output consists of units transferred out during the period and any units in process at the end of the period. This amount is referred to as the **total units accounted for**. Illustration 22-14 shows the flow of physical units for Kellogg Company for the month of June for the Mixing Department.

Mixing Department	
	Physical Units
Units to be accounted for	
Work in process, June 1	100,000
Started (transferred) into production	800,000
Total units	**900,000**
Units accounted for	
Completed and transferred out	700,000
Work in process, June 30	200,000
Total units	**900,000**

Illustration 22-14
Physical unit flow—Mixing Department

The records indicate that 900,000 units must be accounted for in the Mixing Department. Of this sum, 700,000 units were transferred to the Baking Department and 200,000 units were still in process.

Compute Equivalent Units of Production (Step 2)

Once the physical flow of the units is established, it is necessary to measure the Mixing Department's productivity in terms of equivalent units of production. In the Mixing Department, materials are added at the beginning of the process, and conversion costs are incurred uniformly during the process. Thus, two computations of equivalent units are required: one for materials and one for conversion costs. The equivalent unit computation is as follows.

	Equivalent Units	
	Materials	**Conversion Costs**
Units transferred out	700,000	700,000
Work in process, June 30		
200,000 × 100%	200,000	
200,000 × 60%		120,000
Total equivalent units	**900,000**	**820,000**

Illustration 22-15
Computation of equivalent units—Mixing Department

Remember that the beginning work in process is ignored in this computation.

Compute Unit Production Costs (Step 3)

Armed with the knowledge of the equivalent units of production, we can now compute the unit production costs. **Unit production costs** are costs expressed in terms of equivalent units of production. When equivalent units of production are different for materials and conversion costs, three unit costs are computed: (1) materials, (2) conversion, and (3) total manufacturing.

The computation of total materials cost related to Eggo® Waffles is as follows.

Work in process, June 1	
Direct materials cost	$ 50,000
Costs added to production during June	
Direct materials cost	400,000
Total materials cost	**$450,000**

Illustration 22-16
Materials cost computation

The computation of unit materials cost is as follows.

Illustration 22-17
Unit materials cost computation

Total Materials Cost	÷	Equivalent Units of Materials	=	Unit Materials Cost
$450,000	÷	900,000	=	**$0.50**

The computation of total conversion costs is as follows.

Illustration 22-18
Conversion costs computation

Work in process, June 1	
Conversion costs	$ 35,000
Costs added to production during June	
Conversion costs	170,000
Total conversion costs	**$205,000**

The computation of unit conversion cost is as follows.

Illustration 22-19
Unit conversion cost computation

Total Conversion Costs	÷	Equivalent Units of Conversion Costs	=	Unit Conversion Cost
$205,000	÷	820,000	=	**$0.25**

Total manufacturing cost per unit is therefore computed as follows.

Illustration 22-20
Total manufacturing cost per unit

Unit Materials Cost	+	Unit Conversion Cost	=	Total Manufacturing Cost per Unit
$0.50	+	$0.25	=	**$0.75**

Prepare a Cost Reconciliation Schedule (Step 4)

We are now ready to determine the cost of goods transferred out of the Mixing Department to the Baking Department and the costs in ending work in process. The total costs that were charged to the Mixing Department in June are as follows.

Illustration 22-21
Costs charged to Mixing Department

Costs to be accounted for	
Work in process, June 1	$ 85,000
Started into production	570,000
Total costs	**$655,000**

The total costs charged to the Mixing Department in June are therefore $655,000. A cost reconciliation schedule is then prepared to assign these costs to (1) units transferred out to the Baking Department and (2) ending work in process.

Illustration 22-22
Cost reconciliation schedule—Mixing Department

Mixing Department Cost Reconciliation Schedule		
Costs accounted for		
Transferred out (700,000 × $0.75)		$525,000
Work in process, June 30		
Materials (200,000 × $0.50)	$100,000	
Conversion costs (120,000 × $0.25)	30,000	130,000
Total costs		**$655,000**

The total manufacturing cost per unit, $0.75, is used in costing the units completed and transferred to the Baking Department. In contrast, the unit cost of materials and the unit cost of conversion are needed in costing units in process. The **cost reconciliation schedule** shows that the **total costs accounted for** (Illustration 22-22) equal the **total costs to be accounted for** (see Illustration 22-21).

Preparing the Production Cost Report

At this point, we are ready to prepare the production cost report for the Mixing Department. As indicated earlier, this report is an internal document for management that shows production quantity and cost data for a production department.

There are four steps in preparing a production cost report. They are: (1) Prepare a physical unit schedule. (2) Compute equivalent units. (3) Compute unit costs. (4) Prepare a cost reconciliation schedule. The production cost report for the Mixing Department is shown in Illustration 22-23. The four steps are identified in the report.

STUDY OBJECTIVE 7

Prepare a production cost report.

Illustration 22-23
Production cost report

Mixing Department
Production Cost Report
For the Month Ended June 30, 2005

	Physical Units	Equivalent Units	
		Materials	Conversion Costs
QUANTITIES	Step 1	Step 2	
Units to be accounted for			
Work in process, June 1	100,000		
Started into production	800,000		
Total units	900,000		
Units accounted for			
Transferred out	700,000	700,000	700,000
Work in process, June 30	200,000	200,000	120,000 (200,000 × 60%)
Total units	900,000	900,000	820,000

COSTS		Materials	Conversion Costs	Total
Unit costs Step 3				
Costs in June	(a)	$450,000	$205,000	$655,000
Equivalent units	(b)	900,000	820,000	
Unit costs [(a) ÷ (b)]		$0.50	$0.25	$0.75

Costs to be accounted for			
Work in process, June 1			$ 85,000
Started into production			570,000
Total costs			$655,000
Cost Reconciliation Schedule Step 4			
Costs accounted for			
Transferred out (700,000 × $0.75)			$525,000
Work in process, June 30			
Materials (200,000 × $0.50)		$100,000	
Conversion costs (120,000 × $0.25)		30,000	130,000
Total costs			$655,000

HELPFUL HINT

The two self-checks in the report are: (1) Total physical units accounted for must equal the total units to be accounted for. (2) Total costs accounted for must equal the total costs to be accounted for.

ETHICS NOTE

Because production cost reports are used as the basis for evaluating department productivity and efficiency, the units, costs, and computations reported therein should be independently accumulated and analyzed to prevent misstatements by department managers.

Production cost reports provide a basis for evaluating the productivity of a department. In addition, the cost data can be used to assess whether unit costs and total costs are reasonable. By comparing the quantity and cost data with predetermined goals, top management can also judge whether current performance is meeting planned objectives.

ACCOUNTING IN ACTION Business Insight

Frequently when we think of service companies we think of specific, nonroutine tasks, such as rebuilding an automobile engine, providing consulting services on a business acquisition, or working on a major lawsuit. Clearly, such nonroutine situations would call for job order costing. However, many service companies specialize in performing repetitive, routine aspects of a particular business. For example, auto-care vendors such as **Jiffy Lube** focus on the routine aspects of car care. **H&R Block** focuses on the routine aspects of basic tax practice, and many large law firms focus on routine legal services, such as uncomplicated divorces. For service companies that perform routine, repetitive services, process costing provides a simple solution to their accounting needs. In fact, since in many instances there is little or no work in process at the end of the period, applying process costing in this setting can be even easier than for a manufacturer.

Final Comments

Companies often use a combination of a process cost and a job order cost system, called **operations costing**. Operations costing is similar to process costing in that standardized methods are used to manufacture the product. At the same time, the product may have some customized, individual features that require the use of a job order cost system. Consider, for example, the automobile manufacturer **Ford Motor Company**. Each automobile at a given plant goes through the same assembly line, but different materials (such as seat coverings, paint, and tinted glass) may be used for different automobiles. Similarly, **Kellogg's** Pop-Tarts Toaster Pastries® go through numerous processes—mixing, filling, baking, frosting, and packaging. The pastry dough, however, comes in three flavors—plain, chocolate, and graham—and fillings include Smucker's® real fruit, chocolate fudge, vanilla creme, brown sugar cinnamon, and S'mores.

A cost–benefit tradeoff occurs as a company decides which costing system to use. A job order system, for example, provides detailed information related to the cost of the product. Because each job has its own distinguishing characteristics, an accurate cost per job can be provided. This information is useful in controlling costs and pricing products. However, the cost of implementing a job order cost system is often expensive because of the accounting costs involved.

On the other hand, for a company like **Intel**, which makes computer chips, is there a benefit in knowing whether the cost of the one hundredth chip produced is different from the one thousandth chip produced? Probably not. An average cost of the product will suffice for control and pricing purposes. In summary, when deciding to use one of these systems, or a combination system, a company must weigh the cost of implementing the system against the benefits from the additional information provided.

BEFORE YOU GO ON...

Review It

1. How do physical units differ from equivalent units of production?
2. What are the formulas for computing unit costs of production?
3. How are costs assigned to units transferred out and in process?
4. What are the four sections of a production cost report?
5. What is operations costing, and in what circumstances would a manufacturer use operations costing instead of process costing?
6. Describe the cost-benefit tradeoff involved in deciding what costing system to use.

Do It

In March, Rodayo Manufacturing had the following unit production costs: materials $6 and conversion costs $9. On March 1, it had zero work in process. During March, 12,000 units were transferred out, and 800 units that were 25 percent complete as to conversion costs and 100 percent complete as to materials were in ending work in process at March 31. Assign the costs to the units transferred out and in process.

ACTION PLAN

- Assign the total manufacturing cost of $15 per unit to the 12,000 units transferred.
- Assign the materials cost and conversion cost based on equivalent units of production to units in process.

SOLUTION   The assignment of costs is as follows:

Costs accounted for		
Transferred out (12,000 × $15)		$180,000
Work in process, March 31		
Materials (800 × $6)	$4,800	
Conversion costs (200[a] × $9)	1,800	6,600
Total costs		$186,600
[a]800 × 25%		

Related exercise material: *BE22-4, BE22-5, BE22-6, BE22-7, BE22-8, BE22-9, BE22-10, E22-1, E22-2, E22-3, E22-4, E22-5, E22-6, E22-8, E22-9, and E22-10.*

 ✓ THE NAVIGATOR

Contemporary Developments

As indicated in Chapter 20, two contemporary developments in managerial accounting are just-in-time processing and activity-based costing. We explain these innovations in the following sections.

Just-In-Time Processing

Traditionally, continuous process manufacturing has been based on a **just-in-case** philosophy: Inventories of raw materials are maintained **just in case** some items are of poor quality or a key supplier is shut down by a strike. Subassembly parts are manufactured and stored **just in case** they are needed later in the manufacturing process. Finished goods are completed and stored **just in case** unexpected and rush customer orders are received. This philosophy often results in a **"push approach"**:

STUDY OBJECTIVE 8

Explain just-in-time (JIT) processing.

Raw materials and subassembly parts are pushed through each process. Traditional processing often results in the buildup of extensive manufacturing inventories.

Primarily in response to foreign competition, many U.S. firms have switched to **just-in-time (JIT) processing**. JIT manufacturing is dedicated to producing the right products (or parts) at the right time as they are needed. Under JIT processing, raw materials are received **just in time** for use in production, subassembly parts are completed **just in time** for use in finished goods, and finished goods are completed **just in time** to be sold. Illustration 22-24 shows the sequence of activities in just-in-time processing.

Illustration 22-24
Just-in-time processing

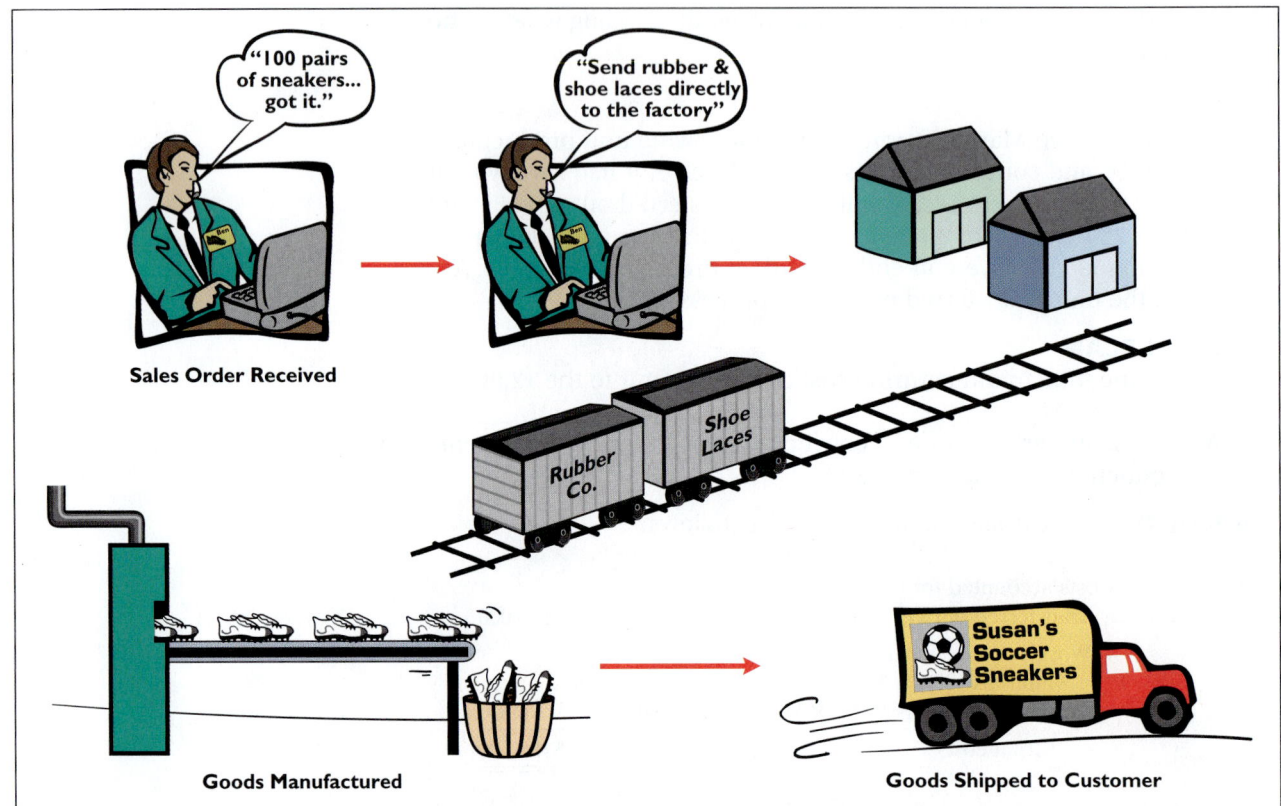

Objective of JIT Processing

A primary objective of JIT is to eliminate all manufacturing inventories. Inventories are considered to have an adverse effect on net income because they tie up funds and storage space that could be made available for more productive purposes. JIT strives to eliminate inventories by using a **"pull approach"** in manufacturing: At the final process (work station) a signal is sent via a computer to the next preceding work station. This signal indicates the exact materials (parts and subassemblies) needed to complete the production of a specified product for a specified time period (such as an eight-hour shift). The preceding process, in turn, sends its signal to other processes back up the line. The goal is a smooth continuous flow in the manufacturing process and no buildup of inventories at any point.

Elements of JIT Processing

There are three important elements in JIT processing:

1. A company must have **dependable suppliers**. Suppliers must be willing to deliver on short notice exact quantities of raw materials according to precise

quality specifications (even including multiple deliveries within the same day). Suppliers must also be willing to deliver the raw materials at specified work stations rather than at a central receiving department. This type of purchasing requires constant and direct communication. Such communication is facilitated by an online computer linkage between the company and its suppliers.

2. A **multiskilled workforce** must be developed. Under JIT, machines are often strategically grouped around work cells or work stations. Much of the work is automated. As a result, one worker may have the responsibility to operate and maintain several different types of machines.

3. A **total quality control system** must be established throughout the manufacturing operations. Total quality control means **no defects**. Since only required quantities are signaled by the **pull approach**, any defects at any work station will shut down operations at subsequent work stations. Total quality control requires continuous monitoring by both employees and supervisors at each work station.

Benefits of JIT Processing

The major benefits of JIT processing are:

1. Manufacturing inventories are significantly reduced or eliminated.
2. Product quality is enhanced.
3. Rework costs and inventory storage costs are reduced or eliminated.
4. Production cost savings are realized from the improved flow of goods through the processes.

One of the major accounting benefits of JIT is the elimination of raw materials and work in process inventory accounts. In place of these accounts is **one account**, Raw and In-Process Inventory. All materials and conversion costs are charged to this account. Because of the reduction (or elimination) of in-process inventories, the computation of equivalent units of production is simplified.

ACCOUNTING IN ACTION Business Insight

JIT first hit the United States in the early 1980s when it was adopted by automobile companies to meet foreign competition. It is now being successfully used in many companies, including **General Electric**, **Caterpillar**, and **Harley-Davidson**. The effects in most cases have been dramatic. For example, after using JIT for two years, a major division of **Hewlett-Packard** found that work-in-process inventories (in dollars) were down 82 percent, scrap/rework costs were down 30 percent, space utilization was down 40 percent, and labor efficiency improved 50 percent. As indicated, JIT not only reduces inventory but also enables a manufacturer to produce a better product faster and with less waste.

Activity-Based Costing

Activity-based costing (ABC) is a development in product costing that has received much attention in recent years. **Activity-based costing** focuses on the activities performed in producing a product. An ABC system is similar to conventional costing systems in accounting for direct materials and direct labor, but it differs in regard to manufacturing overhead.

In a conventional cost system, a **single unit-level** basis is used to allocate overhead costs to products. The basis may be direct labor or machine hours used to

STUDY OBJECTIVE 9

Explain activity-based costing (ABC).

manufacture the product. The assumption in this approach is that as volume of units produced increases, so does the cost of overhead. However, in recent years the amount of direct labor used in many industries has greatly decreased, and total overhead costs resulting from depreciation on expensive equipment and machinery, utilities, repairs, and maintenance have significantly increased.

In ABC, the cost of a product is equal to the sum of the costs of all activities performed to manufacture it. ABC recognizes that to have accurate and meaningful cost data, **more than one basis** of allocating activity costs to products is needed.

In selecting the allocation basis, ABC seeks to identify the **cost drivers** that measure the activities performed on the product. A cost driver may be any factor or activity that has a direct cause–effect relationship with the resources consumed. Examples of activities and possible cost drivers are as follows.

Illustration 22-25
Activities and cost drivers
in ABC

Activity	Cost Driver
Ordering raw materials	Ordering hours; number of orders
Receiving raw materials	Receiving hours; number of shipments
Materials handling	Number of requisitions; weight of materials; handling hours
Production scheduling	Number of orders
Machine setups	Setup hours; number of setups
Machining (fabricating, assembling, etc.)	Machine hours
Quality control inspections	Number of inspections
Factory supervision	Number of employees

Two important assumptions must be met in order to obtain accurate product costs under ABC:

1. All overhead costs related to the activity must be driven by the cost driver used to assign costs to products.

2. All overhead costs related to the activity should respond proportionally to changes in the activity level of the cost driver.

For example, if there is little or no correlation between changes in the cost driver and consumption of the overhead cost, inaccurate product costs are inevitable. A case example in the use of ABC is explained and illustrated in the appendix at the end of this chapter.

Activity-based costing may be used with either a job order or a process cost accounting system. The primary benefit of ABC is more accurate and meaningful product costing. Also, improved cost data about an activity can lead to reduced costs for the activity. In sum, ABC makes managers realize that it is activities and not products that determine the profitability of a company—a realization that should lead to better management decisions.

BEFORE YOU GO ON...

Review It

1. What are the principal accounting effects of just-in-time (JIT) processing?

2. What are the primary differences between activity-based costing (ABC) and traditional costing?

DEMONSTRATION PROBLEM

Essence Company manufactures a high-end after-shave lotion, called Eternity, in 10-ounce plastic bottles. Because the market for after-shave lotion is highly competitive, the company is very concerned about keeping its costs under control. Eternity is manufactured through three processes: mixing, filling, and corking. Materials are added at the beginning of the process, and labor and overhead are incurred uniformly throughout each process. The company uses a weighted-average method to cost its product. A partially completed production cost report for the month of May for the Mixing Department is shown below.

ESSENCE COMPANY
Mixing Department
Production Cost Report
For the Month Ended May 31, 2005

| | | Equivalent Units | |
QUANTITIES	Physical Units	Materials	Conversion Costs
Units to be accounted for	Step 1		Step 2
Work in process, May 1	1,000		
Started into production	2,000		
Total units	3,000		
Units accounted for			
Transferred out	2,200	?	?
Work in process, May 31	800	?	?
Total units	3,000	?	?

COSTS		Materials	Conversion Costs	Total
Unit costs Step 3				
Costs in May	(a)	?	?	?
Equivalent units	(b)	?	?	
Unit costs [(a) ÷ (b)]		?	?	?
Costs to be accounted for				
Work in process, May 1				$ 56,300
Started into production				119,320
Total costs				$175,620

Cost Reconciliation Schedule Step 4

Costs accounted for			
Transferred out			?
Work in process, May 31			
Materials		?	
Conversion costs		?	?
Total costs			?

Additional information:
Work in process, May 1, 1000 units		
Materials cost, 1,000 units (100% complete)	$49,100	
Conversion costs, 1,000 units (70% complete)	7,200	$ 56,300
Materials cost for May, 2,000 units		$100,000

Work in process, May 31, 800 units, 100% complete as to materials and 50% complete as to conversion costs.

(continued from p. 909)

Instructions

(a) Prepare a production cost report for the Mixing Department for the month of May.

(b) Prepare the journal entry to record the transfer of goods from the Mixing Department to the Filling Department.

(c) Explain why Essence Company is using a process cost system to account for its costs.

ACTION PLAN

- Compute the physical unit flow—that is, the total units to be accounted for.
- Compute the equivalent units of production.
- Compute the unit production costs, expressed in terms of equivalent units of production.
- Prepare a cost reconciliation schedule, which shows that the total costs accounted for equal the total costs to be accounted for.

SOLUTION

(a) A completed production cost report for the Mixing Department is shown below. Computations to support the amounts reported follow the report.

ESSENCE COMPANY
Mixing Department
Production Cost Report
For the Month Ended May 31, 2005

QUANTITIES	Physical Units	Equivalent Units Materials	Conversion Costs
Units to be accounted for	Step 1	Step 2	
Work in process, May 1	1,000		
Started into production	2,000		
Total units	3,000		
Units accounted for			
Transferred out	2,200	2,200	2,200
Work in process, May 31	800	800	400 (800 × 50%)
Total units	3,000	3,000	2,600

COSTS		Materials	Conversion Costs	Total
Unit costs Step 3				
Costs in May	(a)	$149,100	$26,520	$175,620
Equivalent units	(b)	3,000	2,600	
Unit costs [(a) ÷ (b)]		$49.70	$10.20	$59.90
Costs to be accounted for				
Work in process, May 1				$ 56,300
Started into production				119,320
Total costs				$175,620

Cost Reconciliation Schedule Step 4			
Costs accounted for			
Transferred out (2,200 × $59.90)			$131,780
Work in process, May 31			
Materials (800 × $49.70)		$39,760	
Conversion costs (400 × $10.20)		4,080	43,840
Total costs			$175,620

Additional computations to support production cost report data:
Materials cost—$49,100 + $100,000
Conversion costs—$7,200 + $19,320 ($119,320 − $100,000)

(b) Work in Process—Filling   131,780

       Work in Process—Mixing   131,780

(c) Process cost systems are used to apply costs to similar products that are mass-produced in a continuous fashion. Essence Company uses a process cost system: production of the after-shave lotion, once it begins, continues until the after-shave lotion emerges. The processing is the same for the entire run—with precisely the same amount of materials, labor, and overhead. Each bottle of Eternity after-shave lotion is indistinguishable from another.

☑ THE NAVIGATOR

SUMMARY OF STUDY OBJECTIVES

1. **Understand who uses process cost systems.** Process cost systems are used by companies that mass-produce similar products in a continuous fashion. Once production begins, it continues until the finished product emerges. Each unit of finished product is indistinguishable from every other unit.

2. **Explain the similarities and differences between job order cost and process cost systems.** Job order cost systems are similar to process cost systems in three ways: (1) Both systems track the same cost elements—direct materials, direct labor, and manufacturing overhead. (2) Costs are accumulated in the same accounts—Raw Materials Inventory, Factory Labor, and Manufacturing Overhead. (3) Accumulated costs are assigned to the same accounts—Work in Process, Finished Goods Inventory, and Cost of Goods Sold. However, the method of assigning costs differs significantly.

 There are four main differences between the two cost systems: (1) A process cost system uses separate accounts for each production department or manufacturing process, rather than only one work in process account used in a job order cost system. (2) In a process cost system, costs are summarized in a production cost report for each department. In a job cost system, costs are charged to individual jobs and summarized in a job cost sheet. (3) Costs are totaled at the end of a time period in a process cost system and at the completion of a job in a job cost system. (4) In a process cost system, unit cost is calculated as: Total manufacturing costs for the period ÷ Units produced during the period. Unit cost in a job cost system is: Total cost per job ÷ Units produced.

3. **Explain the flow of costs in a process cost system.** Manufacturing costs for raw materials, labor, and overhead are assigned to work in process accounts for various departments or manufacturing processes. The costs of units completed in a department are transferred from one department to another as those units move through the manufacturing process. The costs of completed work are transferred to Finished Goods Inventory. When inventory is sold, costs are transferred to Cost of Goods Sold.

4. **Make the journal entries to assign manufacturing costs in a process cost system.** Entries to assign the costs of raw materials, labor, and overhead consist of a credit to Raw Materials Inventory, Factory Labor, and Manufacturing Overhead, and a debit to Work in Process for each of the departments doing the processing. Entries to record the cost of goods transferred to another department are a credit to Work in Process for the department whose work is finished and a debit to the department to which the goods are transferred. The entry to record units completed and transferred to the warehouse is a credit for the department whose work is finished and a debit to Finished Goods Inventory. Finally, the entry to record the sale of goods is a credit to Finished Goods Inventory and a debit to Cost of Goods Sold.

5. **Compute equivalent units.** Equivalent units of production measure work done during a period, expressed in fully completed units. This concept is used to determine the cost per unit of completed product. Equivalent units are the sum of units completed and transferred out plus equivalent units of ending work in process.

6. **Explain the four steps necessary to prepare a production cost report.** The four steps to complete a production cost report are: (1) Compute the physical unit flow—that is, the total units to be accounted for. (2) Compute the equivalent units of production. (3) Compute the unit production costs, expressed in terms of equivalent units of production. (4) Prepare a cost reconciliation schedule, which shows that the total costs accounted for equal the total costs to be accounted for.

7. **Prepare a production cost report.** The production cost report contains both quantity and cost data for a production department. There are four sections in the report: (1) number of physical units, (2) equivalent units determination, (3) unit costs, and (4) cost reconciliation schedule.

8. **Explain just-in-time (JIT) processing.** JIT is a manufacturing technique dedicated to producing the right products at the right time as needed. One of the principal accounting effects is that a Raw and In-Process Inventory account replaces both the raw materials and work in process inventory accounts.

9. **Explain activity-based costing (ABC).** ABC is a method of product costing that focuses on the activities performed to produce products. It assigns the cost of the activities to products by using cost drivers that measure the activities performed. The primary objective of ABC is accurate and meaningful product costs.

☑ THE NAVIGATOR

GLOSSARY

Activity-based costing A cost accounting system that focuses on the activities performed in manufacturing a specific product. (p. 907).

Cost reconciliation schedule A schedule that shows that the total costs accounted for equal the total costs to be accounted for. (p. 903).

Equivalent units of production A measure of the work done during the period, expressed in fully completed units. (p. 897).

Just-in-time processing A processing system dedicated to producing the right products (or parts) as they are needed. (p. 906).

Operations costing A combination of a process cost and a job order cost system, in which products are manufactured primarily by standardized methods, with some customization. (p. 904).

Physical units Actual units to be accounted for during a period, irrespective of any work performed. (p. 900).

Process cost systems An accounting system used to apply costs to similar products that are mass-produced in a continuous fashion. (p. 891).

Production cost report An internal report for management that shows both production quantity and cost data for a production department. (p. 899).

Total units (costs) accounted for The sum of the units (costs) transferred out during the period plus the units (costs) in process at the end of the period. (pp. 900, 903).

Total units (costs) to be accounted for The sum of the units (costs) started (or transferred) into production during the period plus the units (costs) in process at the beginning of the period. (pp. 900, 903).

Unit production costs Costs expressed in terms of equivalent units of production. (p. 901).

Weighted-average method Method used to compute equivalent units of production which considers the degree of completion (weighting) of the units completed and transferred out and the ending work in process. (p. 898).

APPENDIX CASE EXAMPLE OF TRADITIONAL COSTING VERSUS ACTIVITY-BASED COSTING

Production and Cost Data

STUDY OBJECTIVE 10

Apply activity-based costing to specific company data.

In this appendix we present a case example that compares activity-based costing to traditional costing. Assume that Atlas Company produces two products, The Boot and The Club. The Boot is a high-volume item totaling 25,000 units annually. The Club is a low-volume item totaling only 5,000 units per year. Each product requires one hour of direct labor for completion. Therefore, total annual direct labor hours are 30,000 (25,000 + 5,000). Expected annual manufacturing overhead costs are $900,000. The predetermined overhead rate is $30 ($900,000 ÷ 30,000) per direct labor hour.

The direct materials cost per unit is $40 for The Boot and $30 for The Club. The direct labor cost is $12 per unit for each product.

Unit Costs Under Traditional Costing

The unit cost for each product under traditional costing is shown below.

Illustration 22A-1
Units costs—traditional costing

Manufacturing Costs	Product	
	The Boot	**The Club**
Direct materials	$40	$30
Direct labor	12	12
Overhead	30*	30*
Total unit cost	**$82**	**$72**

*Predetermined overhead rate × direct labor hours ($30 × 1 hr = $30).

Determining Overhead Rates Under ABC

Analysis reveals that Atlas Company's expected annual overhead costs of $900,000 relate to three activities—machine setups, machining, and inspections. The cost driver and overhead rate for each activity are shown in Illustration 22A-2.

Activity	Cost Driver	Total Expected Overhead Cost	Total Expected Use of Driver	Activity Based Overhead Rate
Machine setups	Number of setups	$300,000	1,500	$200 per setup
Machining	Machine hours	500,000	50,000	$ 10 per machine hour
Inspections	Number of inspections	100,000	2,000	$ 50 per inspection

Illustration 22A-2
Computing overhead rates—ABC

Assigning Overhead Costs to Products Under ABC

In assigning costs, it is necessary to know the expected number of cost drivers for each product. Because of its low volume, The Club requires more setups and inspections than The Boot. The expected number of cost drivers for each product is as follows.

Cost Driver	Product		Total Usage
	The Boot	The Club	
Number of machine setups	500	1,000	1,500
Machine hours	30,000	20,000	50,000
Number of inspections	500	1,500	2,000

Illustration 22A-3
Expected number of cost drivers

Using these data, Atlas can assign the expected annual overhead cost to each product as follows.

Activity	The Boot		The Club		Total Cost
	Number	Cost	Number	Cost	
Machine setups ($200)	500	$100,000	1,000	$200,000	$300,000
Machining ($10)	30,000	300,000	20,000	200,000	500,000
Inspections ($50)	500	25,000	1,500	75,000	100,000
Total assigned costs (a)		$425,000		$475,000	$900,000
Units produced (b)		25,000		5,000	
Overhead cost per unit [(a) ÷ (b)]		$17		$95	

Illustration 22A-4
Assignment of overhead costs to products

These data show that under ABC, overhead costs are shifted from the high-volume product (The Boot) to the low-volume product (The Club). This shift results in more accurate costing for two reasons:

1. Low-volume products often require more special handling, such as more machine setups and inspections, than high-volume products. This is true for Atlas Company. Thus, the low-volume product frequently is responsible for more overhead costs per unit than a high-volume product.

2. The overhead costs incurred by the low-volume product often are disproportionate to a traditional allocation base. For example, direct labor hours is usually a poor cost driver for assigning overhead costs to low-volume products. When overhead is properly assigned in ABC, it will usually increase the unit cost of low-volume products.

Comparing Unit Costs

A comparison of unit manufacturing costs under traditional costing and ABC shows the following significant differences.

Illustration 22A-5
Comparison of unit product costs

	The Boot		The Club	
Manufacturing Costs	**Traditional Costing**	**ABC**	**Traditional Costing**	**ABC**
Direct materials	$40	$40	$30	$ 30
Direct labor	12	12	12	12
Overhead	30	17	30	95
Total cost per unit	**$82**	**$69**	**$72**	**$137**
		Overstated		Understated
		$13		$65

The comparison shows that unit costs under traditional costing have been significantly distorted. The cost of The Boot has been overstated $13 per unit ($82 − $69). The cost of The Club has been understated $65 per unit ($137 − $72). The differences are attributable to how manufacturing overhead is assigned. A likely consequence of the differences is that Atlas Company has been overpricing The Boot and possibly losing market share to competitors. It also has been sacrificing profitability by underpricing The Club.

As illustrated in the above case, ABC involves the following steps.

1. Identify the major activities that pertain to the manufacture of specific products.
2. Accumulate manufacturing overhead costs by activities.
3. Identify the cost driver(s) that accurately measure(s) each activity's contribution to the finished product.
4. Assign manufacturing overhead costs for each activity to products, using the cost driver(s).

Benefits and Limitations of Activity-based Costing

We have already seen that a primary benefit of ABC is more accurate product costing. In addition, ABC offers the following other benefits:

1. **Control over overhead costs** is enhanced. Many overhead costs are incurred directly by activities. Thus, managers become more aware of their responsibility to control the activities that generate the costs.
2. **Better management decisions** can be made. More accurate product costing should contribute to setting selling prices that will achieve desired profitability levels. The cost data also should be helpful in deciding whether to discontinue or expand a product line or whether to make or buy a component.

The principal disadvantages of ABC generally focus on two factors. First, **the expense of obtaining the cost data** required by the system is relatively high. ABC requires data that are not normally generated within a company. Examples of such data are the number of setups, inspections, orders placed, and orders received. In addition, many computations are involved in assigning overhead costs to individual products.

ACCOUNTING IN ACTION   Business Insight

ABC enabled **Digital Communications Associates**, a computer hardware and software manufacturer, to discover why profit margins slipped from 18.6 percent to 8 percent over a three-year period. Digital boiled down 600 production activities to 136. ABC helped Digital and its 1,300 employees to bring costs under control.

Second, **ABC does not eliminate arbitrary assignments** of overhead. For example, plant-wide overhead costs such as depreciation, insurance, and property taxes on the factory building should be allocated to the activity centers in determining the cost of a product. With ABC, these allocations may be more difficult to do accurately because of the increased number of activity centers. As a result, accuracy of product costs could be adversely affected.

SUMMARY OF STUDY OBJECTIVE FOR APPENDIX

10. **Apply activity-based costing to specific company data.** In applying ABC, it is necessary to compute the overhead rate for each activity by dividing total expected overhead by the total expected usage of the cost driver. The overhead cost for each activity is then assigned to products on the basis of each product's use of the cost driver.

*Note: All **asterisked** Questions, Exercises, and Problems relate to material contained in the appendix to the chapter.

SELF-STUDY QUESTIONS

Self-Study/Self-Test

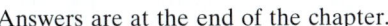

Answers are at the end of the chapter.

(SO 1) **1.** Which of the following items is *not* a characteristic of a process cost system?
  a. Once production begins, it continues until the finished product emerges.
  b. The products produced are heterogeneous in nature.
  c. The focus is on continually producing homogeneous products.
  d. When the finished product emerges, all units have precisely the same amount of materials, labor, and overhead.

(SO 2) **2.** Indicate which of the following statements is *not* correct.
  a. Both a job order and a process cost system track the same three manufacturing cost elements—direct materials, direct labor, and manufacturing overhead.
  b. In a job order cost system, only one work in process account is used, whereas in a process cost system, multiple work in process accounts are used.
  c. Manufacturing costs are accumulated the same way in a job order and in a process cost system.
  d. Manufacturing costs are assigned the same way in a job order and in a process cost system.

(SO 3) **3.** In a process cost system, costs are assigned only:
  a. to one work in process account.
  b. to work in process and finished goods inventory.

  c. to work in process, finished goods, and cost of goods sold.
  d. to work in process accounts.

4. In making the journal entry to assign raw materials costs: (SO 4)
  a. the debit is to Finished Goods Inventory.
  b. the debit is often to two or more work in process accounts.
  c. the credit is generally to two or more work in process accounts.
  d. the credit is to Finished Goods Inventory.

5. The Mixing Department's output during the period con-   (SO 5) sists of 20,000 units completed and transferred out, and 5,000 units in ending work in process 60% complete as to materials and conversion costs. Beginning inventory is 1,000 units, 40% complete as to materials and conversion costs. The equivalent units of production are:
  a. 22,600.   **c.** 24,000.
  b. 23,000.   **d.** 25,000.

6. In RYZ Company, there are zero units in beginning work   (SO 6) in process, 7,000 units started into production, and 500 units in ending work in process 20% completed. The physical units to be accounted for are:
  a. 7,000.   **c.** 7,600.
  b. 7,360.   **d.** 7,340.

(SO 6) **7.** Stock Company has 2,000 units in beginning work in process, 20% complete as to conversion costs, 23,000 units transferred out to finished goods, and 3,000 units in ending work in process 33⅓% complete as to conversion costs. The beginning and ending inventory is fully complete as to materials costs. Equivalent units for materials and conversion costs are, respectively:

   a. 22,000, 24,000.   **c.** 26,000, 24,000.
   b. 24,000, 26,000.   **d.** 26,000, 26,000.

(SO 6) **8.** Fortner Company has no beginning work in process; 9,000 units are transferred out and 3,000 units in ending work in process are one-third finished as to conversion costs and fully complete as to materials cost. If total materials cost is $60,000, the unit materials cost is:

   a. $5.00.
   b. $5.45 rounded.
   c. $6.00.
   d. No correct answer is given.

(SO 6) **9.** Largo Company has unit costs of $10 for materials and $30 for conversion costs. If there are 2,500 units in ending work in process, 40% complete as to conversion costs, and fully complete as to materials cost, the total cost assignable to the ending work in process inventory is:

   a. $45,000.   **c.** $75,000.
   b. $55,000.   **d.** $100,000.

10. A production cost report   (SO
   a. is an external report.
   b. shows costs charged to a department and costs accounted for.
   c. shows equivalent units of production but not physical units.
   d. contains six sections.

11. Just-in-time processing (JIT):   (SO
   a. strives to eliminate inventories.
   b. uses a pull approach in manufacturing.
   c. Neither of the above.
   d. Both (a) and (b).

12. Activity-based costing (ABC):   (SO
   a. can be used only in a process cost system.
   b. focuses on units of production.
   c. focuses on activities performed to produce a product.
   d. uses only a single basis of allocation.

***13.** The overhead rate for Machine Setups is $100 per setup. (SO Products A and B have 80 and 60 setups, respectively. The overhead assigned to each product is:
   a. Product A $8,000, Product B $8,000.
   b. Product A $8,000, Product B $6,000.
   c. Product A $6,000, Product B $6,000.
   d. Product A $6,000, Product B $8,000.

QUESTIONS

1. Identify which costing system—job order or process cost—the following companies would use: (a) **Quaker Oats**, (b) **Ford Motor Company**, (c) **Kinko's Print Shop**, and (d) **Warner Bros. Motion Pictures**.

2. Contrast the primary focus of job order cost accounting and of process cost accounting.

3. What are the similarities between a job order and a process cost system?

4. Your roommate is confused about the features of process cost accounting. Identify and explain the distinctive features for your roommate.

5. Hal Adelman believes there are no significant differences in the flow of costs between job order cost accounting and process cost accounting. Is Adelman correct? Explain.

6. (a) What source documents are used in assigning (1) materials and (2) labor to production?
   (b) What criterion and basis are commonly used in allocating overhead to processes?

7. At Yen Company, overhead is assigned to production departments at the rate of $10 per machine hour. In July, machine hours were 3,000 in the Machining Department and 2,400 in the Assembly Department. Prepare the entry to assign overhead to production.

8. Marc Tucci is uncertain about the steps used to prepare a production cost report. State the procedures that are required in the sequence in which they are performed.

9. Phil Remmers is confused about computing physical units. Explain to Phil how physical units to be accounted for and physical units accounted for are determined.

10. What is meant by the term "equivalent units of production"?

11. How are equivalent units of production computed?

12. Tomko Company had zero units of beginning work in process. During the period, 7,000 units were completed, and there were 600 units of ending work in process. What were the units started into production?

13. Carnes Co. has zero units of beginning work in process. During the period 12,000 units were completed, and there were 500 units of ending work in process one-fifth complete as to conversion cost and 100% complete as to materials cost. What were the equivalent units of production for (a) materials and (b) conversion costs?

14. Jorge Co. started 3,000 units for the period. Its beginning inventory is 800 units one-fourth complete as to conversion costs and 100% complete as to materials cost. Its ending inventory is 200 units one-fifth complete as to conversion cost and 100% complete as to materials costs. How many units were transferred out this period?

15. Simon Company transfers out 14,000 units and has 2,000 units of ending work in process that are 25% complete. Materials are entered at the beginning of the process and there is no beginning work in process. Assuming unit materials costs of $3 and unit conversion costs of $7, what are the costs to be assigned to units (a) transferred out and (b) in ending work in process?

16. (a) Pam Smith believes the production cost report is an external report for stockholders. Is Pam correct? Explain.
    (b) Identify the sections in a production cost report.

17. What purposes are served by a production cost report?

18. At Crowl Company, there are 800 units of ending work in process that are 100% complete as to materials and 40% complete as to conversion costs. If the unit cost of materials is $4 and the costs assigned to the 800 units is $7,000, what is the per-unit conversion cost?

19. What is the difference between operations costing and a process costing system?

20. How does a company decide whether to use a job order or a process cost system?

21. (a) Describe the philosophy and approach of just-in-time processing.
    (b) Identify the major elements of JIT processing.

22. (a) What are the principal differences between activity-based costing (ABC) and traditional product costing?
    (b) What assumptions must be met for ABC costing to be useful?

23. Ghosh Co. identifies the following activities that pertain to manufacturing overhead: Materials Handling, Machine Setups, Factory Machine Maintenance, Factory Supervision, and Quality Control. For each activity identify an appropriate cost driver.

*24. (a) Identify the steps that pertain to activity-based costing.
    (b) What are the advantages of ABC costing?

BRIEF EXERCISES

BE22-1 Sinason Manufacturing purchases $45,000 of raw materials on account, and it incurs $40,000 of factory labor costs. Journalize the two transactions on March 31 assuming the labor costs are not paid until April.

Journalize entries for accumulating costs.

(SO 4)

BE22-2 Data for Sinason Manufacturing are given in BE22-1. Supporting records show that (a) the Assembly Department used $24,000 of raw materials and $30,000 of the factory labor, and (b) the Finishing Department used the remainder. Journalize the assignment of the costs to the processing departments on March 31.

Journalize the assignment of materials and labor costs.

(SO 4)

BE22-3 Factory labor data for Sinason Manufacturing are given in BE22-2. Manufacturing overhead is assigned to departments on the basis of 200% of labor costs. Journalize the assignment of overhead to the Assembly and Finishing Departments.

Journalize the assignment of overhead costs.

(SO 4)

BE22-4 Carlos Manufacturing Company has the following production data for selected months.

Compute physical units of production.

(SO 6)

Month	Beginning Work in Process	Units Transferred Out	Ending Work in Process Units	Ending Work in Process % Complete as to Conversion Cost
January	–0–	30,000	10,000	40%
March	–0–	40,000	4,000	75
July	–0–	40,000	12,000	25

Compute the physical units for each month.

BE22-5 Using the data in BE22-4, compute equivalent units of production for materials and conversion costs, assuming materials are entered at the beginning of the process.

Compute equivalent units of production.

(SO 5)

BE22-6 In Santana Company, total material costs are $32,000, and total conversion costs are $48,000. Equivalent units of production are materials 10,000 and conversion costs 12,000. Compute the unit costs for materials, conversion costs, and total manufacturing costs.

Compute unit costs of production.

(SO 6)

BE22-7 Wendy Company has the following production data for April: units transferred out 40,000, and ending work in process 5,000 units that are 100% complete for materials and 40% complete for conversion costs. If unit materials cost is $6 and unit conversion cost is $9, determine the costs to be assigned to the units transferred out and the units in ending work in process.

Assign costs to units transferred out and in process.

(SO 6)

Compute unit costs.
(SO 6)

BE22-8 Production costs chargeable to the Finishing Department in June in Sanchez Company are materials $10,000, labor $29,500, overhead $18,000. Equivalent units of production are materials 20,000 and conversion costs 19,000. Compute the unit costs for materials and conversion costs.

Prepare cost reconciliation schedule.
(SO 6)

BE22-9 Data for Sanchez Company are given in BE22-8. Production records indicate that 18,000 units were transferred out, and 2,000 units in ending work in process were 50% complete as to conversion cost and 100% complete as to materials. Prepare a cost reconciliation schedule.

Compute equivalent units of production.
(SO 5)

BE22-10 The Smelting Department of Cerrato Manufacturing Company has the following production and cost data for November.

Production: Beginning work in process 2,000 units that are 100% complete as to materials and 20% complete as to conversion costs; units transferred out 8,000 units; and ending work in process 3,000 units that are 100% complete as to materials and 40% complete as to conversion costs.

Compute the equivalent units of production for **(a)** materials and **(b)** conversion costs for the month of November.

Compute overhead rates for activities.
(SO 10)

*BE22-11 Mahmoud Company identifies three activities in its manufacturing process: machine setups, machining, and inspections. Estimated annual overhead cost for each activity is $150,000, $300,000, and $70,000, respectively. The cost driver for each activity and the expected annual usage are: number of setups 1,000, machine hours 25,000, and number of inspections 2,000. Compute the overhead rate for each activity.

EXERCISES

Compute physical units and equivalent units of production.
(SO 5, 6)

E22-1 In Alvarez Company, materials are entered at the beginning of each process. Work in process inventories, with the percentage of work done on conversion costs, and production data for its Sterilizing Department in selected months during 2005 are as follows.

	Beginning Work in Process		**Units**	**Ending Work in Process**	
Month	**Units**	**Conversion Cost%**	**Transferred Out**	**Units**	**Conversion Cost%**
January	–0–	—	7,000	1,000	60
March	–0–	—	12,000	3,000	30
May	–0–	—	16,000	5,000	80
July	–0–	—	10,000	2,500	40

Instructions
(a) Compute the physical units for January and May.
(b) Compute the equivalent units of production for (1) materials and (2) conversion costs for each month.

Determine equivalent units, unit costs, and assignment of costs.
(SO 5, 6)

E22-2 The Cutting Department of Stanfree Manufacturing has the following production and cost data for July.

Production	**Costs**	
1. Transferred out 9,000 units.	Beginning work in process	$ –0–
2. Started 1,000 units that are 60% complete as to conversion costs and 100% complete as to materials at July 31.	Materials	45,000
	Labor	14,700
	Manufacturing overhead	18,900

Materials are entered at the beginning of the process. Conversion costs are incurred uniformly during the process.

Instructions
(a) Determine the equivalent units of production for (1) materials and (2) conversion costs.
(b) Compute unit costs and prepare a cost reconciliation schedule.

E22-3 The Sanding Department of Lopez Furniture Company has the following production and manufacturing cost data for March 2005.

> Production: 17,000 units finished and transferred out; 3,000 units started that are 100% complete as to materials and 20% complete as to conversion costs.
> Manufacturing costs: Materials $33,000; labor $30,000; overhead $36,000.

Prepare a production cost report.

(SO 5, 6, 7)

Instructions
Prepare a production cost report.

E22-4 The Blending Department of Serrano Company has the following cost and production data for the month of April.

Determine equivalent units, unit costs, and assignment of costs.

(SO 5, 6)

Costs:	
Work in process, April 1	
Direct materials: 100% complete	$100,000
Conversion costs: 20% complete	70,000
Cost of work in process, April 1	$170,000
Costs incurred during production in April	
Direct materials	$ 800,000
Conversion costs	353,000
Costs incurred in April	$1,153,000

Units transferred out totaled 9,000. Ending work in process was 1,000 units that are 100% complete as to materials and 40% complete as to conversion costs.

Instructions
(a) Compute the equivalent units of production for (1) materials and (2) conversion costs for the month of April.
(b) Compute the unit costs for the month.
(c) Determine the costs to be assigned to the units transferred out and in ending work in process.

E22-5 Jeff Berry has recently been promoted to production manager, and so he has just started to receive various managerial reports. One of the reports he has received is the production cost report that you prepared. It showed that his department had 2,000 equivalent units in ending inventory. His department has had a history of not keeping enough inventory on hand to meet demand. He has come to you, very angry, and wants to know why you credited him with only 2,000 units when he knows he had at least twice that many on hand.

Explain the production cost report.

(SO 7)

Instructions
▭▭▭▷ Explain to him why his production cost report showed only 2,000 equivalent units in ending inventory. Write an informal memo. Be kind and explain very clearly why he is mistaken.

E22-6 The ledger of Barajas Company has the following work in process account.

Answer questions on costs and production.

(SO 3, 5, 6)

Work in Process—Painting						
5/1	Balance	3,590	5/31	Transferred out		?
5/31	Materials	5,160				
5/31	Labor	2,200				
5/31	Overhead	1,650				
5/31	Balance	?				

Production records show that there were 700 units in the beginning inventory, 30% complete, 1,100 units started, and 1,200 units transferred out. The beginning work in process had materials cost of $2,040 and conversion costs of $1,550. The units in ending inventory were 40% complete. Materials are entered at the beginning of the painting process.

Instructions
(a) How many units are in process at May 31?
(b) What is the unit materials cost for May?
(c) What is the unit conversion cost for May?
(d) What is the total cost of units transferred out in May?
(e) What is the cost of the May 31 inventory?

Journalize transactions for two processes.

(SO 4)

E22-7 Tidrick Manufacturing Company has two production departments: Cutting and Assembly. July 1 inventories are Raw Materials $4,200, Work in Process—Cutting $2,900, Work in Process—Assembly $10,600, and Finished Goods $31,000. During July, the following transactions occurred.

1. Purchased $62,500 of raw materials on account.
2. Incurred $56,000 of factory labor. (Credit Wages Payable.)
3. Incurred $70,000 of manufacturing overhead; $40,000 was paid and the remainder is unpaid.
4. Requisitioned materials for Cutting $15,700 and Assembly $8,900.
5. Used factory labor for Cutting $29,000 and Assembly $27,000.
6. Applied overhead at the rate of $20 per machine hour. Machine hours were Cutting 1,680 and Assembly 1,720.
7. Transferred goods costing $77,600 from the Cutting Department to the Assembly Department.
8. Transferred goods costing $134,900 from Assembly to Finished Goods.
9. Sold goods costing $150,000 for $200,000 on account.

Instructions
Journalize the transactions. (Omit explanations.)

Compute equivalent units, unit costs, and costs assigned.

(SO 5, 6)

E22-8 The Polishing Department of Ramirez Manufacturing Company has the following production and manufacturing cost data for September. Materials are entered at the beginning of the process.

Production: Beginning inventory 1,600 units that are 100% complete as to materials and 30% complete as to conversion costs; units started during the period are 15,400; ending inventory of 3,000 units 10% complete as to conversion costs.

Manufacturing costs: Beginning inventory costs, comprised of $20,000 of materials and $43,180 of conversion costs; materials costs added in Polishing during the month, $177,200; labor and overhead applied in Polishing during the month, $100,080 and $257,140, respectively.

Instructions
(a) Compute the equivalent units of production for materials and conversion costs for the month of September.
(b) Compute the unit costs for materials and conversion costs for the month.
(c) Determine the costs to be assigned to the units transferred out and in process.

Prepare a production cost report.

(SO 5, 6, 7)

E22-9 The Welding Department of Tejada Manufacturing Company has the following production and manufacturing cost data for February 2005. All materials are added at the beginning of the process.

Manufacturing Costs			**Production Data**	
Beginning work in process			Beginning work in process	15,000 units
Materials	$18,000			1/10 complete
Conversion costs	14,175	$32,175	Units transferred out	64,000
Materials		180,000	Units started	75,000
Labor		35,100	Ending work in process	26,000 units
Overhead		61,445		1/5 complete

Instructions
Prepare a production cost report for the Welding Department for the month of February.

E22-10 Corrales Company manufactures pizza sauce through two production departments: Cooking and Canning. In each process, materials and conversion costs are incurred evenly throughout the process. For the month of April, the work in process accounts show the following debits.

Journalize transactions.
(SO 3, 4)

	Cooking	Canning
Beginning work in process	$ –0–	$ 4,000
Materials	18,000	6,000
Labor	8,500	7,000
Overhead	29,500	25,800
Costs transferred in		50,000

Instructions
Journalize the April transactions.

*E22-11** Chicago Instrument Inc. manufactures two products: missile range instruments and space pressure gauges. During January, 50 range instruments and 300 pressure gauges were produced, and overhead costs of $73,000 were incurred. An analysis of overhead costs reveals the following activities.

Compute overhead rates and assign overhead using ABC.
(SO 10)

Activity	Cost Driver	Total Cost
1. Materials handling	Number of requisitions	$25,000
2. Machine setups	Number of setups	27,000
3. Quality inspections	Number of inspections	21,000

The cost driver volume for each product was as follows.

Cost Driver	Instruments	Gauges	Total
Number of requisitions	400	600	1,000
Number of setups	150	300	450
Number of inspections	200	400	600

Instructions
(a) Determine the overhead rate for each activity.
(b) Assign the manufacturing overhead costs for January to the two products using activity-based costing.
(c) ▭▭▭▭▷ Write a memo to the president of Chicago Instrument, explaining the benefits of activity-based costing.

PROBLEMS: SET A

P22-1A Hopkins Corporation manufactures water skis through two processes: Molding and Packaging. In the Molding Department fiberglass is heated and shaped into the form of a ski. In the Packaging Department, the skis are placed in cartons and sent to the finished goods warehouse. Materials are entered at the beginning of both processes. Labor and manufacturing overhead are incurred uniformly throughout each process. Production and cost data for the Molding Department for January 2005 are presented below.

Complete four steps necessary to prepare a production cost report.
(SO 5, 6, 7)

Production Data	January
Beginning work in process units	–0–
Units started into production	42,500
Ending work in process units	2,500
Percent complete—ending inventory	40%

Cost Data	
Materials	$595,000
Labor	96,000
Overhead	232,000
Total	$923,000

Instructions

(a) Compute the physical units of production.

(b) Determine the equivalent units of production for materials and conversion costs.

(c) Compute the unit costs of production.

(d) Determine the costs to be assigned to the units transferred out and in process.

(e) Prepare a production cost report for the Molding Department for the month of January.

Complete four steps necessary to prepare a production cost report.

(SO 5, 6, 7)

P22-2A Jaytag Corporation manufactures in separate processes refrigerators and freezers for homes. In each process, materials are entered at the beginning and conversion costs are incurred uniformly. Production and cost data for the first process in making two products in two different manufacturing plants are as follows.

| | **Stamping Department** | |
| | **Plant A** | **Plant B** |
Production Data—June	**R12 Refrigerators**	**F24 Freezers**
Work in process units, June 1	–0–	–0–
Units started into production	21,000	18,000
Work in process units, June 30	2,000	2,500
Work in process percent complete	75	60

Cost Data—June		
Work in process, June 1	$ –0–	$ –0–
Materials	840,000	684,000
Labor	236,000	251,000
Overhead	420,000	191,000
Total	$1,496,000	$1,126,000

Instructions

(a) For each plant:

(1) Compute the physical units of production.

(2) Compute equivalent units of production for materials and for conversion costs.

(3) Determine the unit costs of production.

(4) Show the assignment of costs to units transferred out and in process.

(b) Prepare the production cost report for Plant A for June 2005.

Journalize transactions.

(SO 3, 4)

P22-3A Du Page Company manufactures a nutrient, Everlife, through two manufacturing processes: Blending and Packaging. All materials are entered at the beginning of each process. On August 1, 2005, inventories consisted of Raw Materials $5,000, Work in Process—Blending $0, Work in Process—Packaging $3,945, and Finished Goods $7,500. The beginning inventory for Packaging consisted of 500 units, two-fifths complete as to conversion costs and fully complete as to materials. During August, 9,000 units were started into production in Blending, and the following transactions were completed.

1. Purchased $25,000 of raw materials on account.

2. Issued raw materials for production: Blending $18,930 and Packaging $7,140.

3. Incurred labor costs of $20,770.

4. Used factory labor: Blending $13,320 and Packaging $7,450.

5. Incurred $41,500 of manufacturing overhead on account.

6. Applied manufacturing overhead at the rate of $30 per machine hour. Machine hours were Blending 900 and Packaging 300.

7. Transferred 8,200 units from Blending to Packaging at a cost of $54,940.

8. Transferred 8,600 units from Packaging to Finished Goods at a cost of $72,490.

9. Sold goods costing $62,000 for $90,000 on account.

Instructions

Journalize the August transactions.

P22-4A Modine Company has several processing departments. Costs charged to the Assembly Department for October 2005 totaled $1,357,600 as follows.

Assign costs and prepare production cost report.

(SO 5, 6, 7)

Work in process, October 1		
Materials	$29,000	
Conversion costs	26,200	$ 55,200
Materials added		1,071,000
Labor		90,000
Overhead		141,400

Production records show that 25,000 units were in beginning work in process 40% complete as to conversion cost, 375,000 units were started into production, and 40,000 units were in ending work in process 20% complete as to conversion costs. Materials are entered at the beginning of each process.

Instructions

(a) Determine the equivalent units of production and the unit costs for the Assembly Department.

(b) Determine the assignment of costs to goods transferred out and in process.

(c) Prepare a production cost report for the Assembly Department.

P22-5A Rossi Company manufactures bicycles and tricycles. For both products, materials are added at the beginning of the production process, and conversion costs are incurred uniformly. Production and cost data for the month of May are as follows.

Determine equivalent units and unit costs and assign costs.

(SO 5, 6, 7)

Production Data—Bicycles	Units	Percent Complete
Work in process units, May 1	500	80%
Units started in production	1,100	
Work in process units, May 31	600	10%

Cost Data—Bicycles		
Work in process, May 1		
Materials	$10,000	
Conversion costs	9,280	$ 19,280
Direct materials		50,000
Direct labor		19,020
Manufacturing overhead		30,000

Instructions

(a) Calculate the following.

(1) The equivalent units of production for materials and conversion.

(2) The unit costs of production for materials and conversion costs.

(3) The assignment of costs to units transferred out and in process at the end of the accounting period.

(b) Prepare a production cost report for the month of May for the bicycles.

Compute equivalent units and complete production cost report.

(SO 5, 7)

P22-6A Traynor Cleaner Company uses a weighted-average process costing system and manufactures a single product—an all-purpose liquid cleaner. The manufacturing activity for the month of March has just been completed. A partially completed production cost report for the month of March for the mixing and blending department is shown below.

TRAYNOR CLEANER COMPANY
Mixing and Blending Department
Production Cost Report
For the Month Ended March 31

		Equivalent Units	
QUANTITIES	Physical Units	Materials	Conversion Costs
Units to be accounted for			
Work in process, March 1 (40% materials, 20% conversion costs)	10,000		
Started into production	100,000		
Total units	110,000		
Units accounted for			
Transferred out	80,000	?	?
Work in process, March 31 (2/3 materials, 1/3 conversion costs)	30,000	?	?
Total units accounted for	110,000	?	?

COSTS			
Unit costs	Materials	Conversion Costs	Total
Costs in March	$170,000	$90,000	$260,000
Equivalent units	?	?	
Unit costs	$? +	$? =	$?
Costs to be accounted for			
Work in process, March 1			$ 15,700
Started into production			244,300
Total costs			$260,000

Cost Reconciliation Schedule

Costs accounted for			
Transferred out			$?
Work in process, March 31			
Materials		?	
Conversion costs		?	?
Total costs			?

Instructions
(a) Prepare a schedule that shows how the equivalent units were computed so that you can complete the "Quantities: Units accounted for" equivalent units section shown in the production cost report above, and compute March unit costs.
(b) Complete the "Cost Reconciliation Schedule" part of the production cost report above.

Assign overhead to products using ABC.

(SO 10)

***P22-7A** Baker Electronics manufactures two large-screen television models: the Royale which sells for $1,500, and a new model, the Majestic, which sells for $1,200. The production cost per unit for each model in 2005 was as follows.

	Royale	Majestic
Direct materials	$ 700	$420
Direct labor ($20 per hour)	100	80
Manufacturing overhead ($40 per DLH)	200	160
Total per unit cost	$1,000	$660

In 2005, Baker manufactured 30,000 units of the Royale and 10,000 units of the Majestic. The overhead rate of $40 per direct labor hour was determined by dividing total expected manufacturing overhead of $7,600,000 by the total direct labor hours (190,000) for the two models.

The gross profit on the model was: Royale $500 ($1,500 − $1,000) and Majestic $540 ($1,200 − $660). Because of this difference, management is considering phasing out the Royale model and increasing the production of the Majestic model.

Before finalizing its decision, management asks the controller, Patty Sherrick, to prepare an analysis using activity-based costing. Patty accumulates the following information about overhead for the year ended December 31, 2005.

Activity	Cost Driver	Total Cost	Cost Driver Volume	Overhead Rate
Purchase orders	Number of orders	$1,500,000	30,000	$50
Machine setups	Number of setups	600,000	15,000	40
Machining	Machine hours	4,800,000	160,000	30
Quality control	Number of inspections	700,000	35,000	20

The cost driver volume for each product was:

Cost Driver	Royale	Majestic	Total
Purchase orders	16,000	14,000	30,000
Machine setups	5,000	10,000	15,000
Machine hours	100,000	60,000	160,000
Inspections	10,000	25,000	35,000

Instructions
(a) Assign the total 2005 manufacturing overhead costs to the two products using activity-based costing (ABC).
(b) What was the cost per unit and gross profit of each model using ABC costing?
(c) Are management's future plans for the two models sound?

PROBLEMS: SET B

P22-1B Peoria Company manufactures bowling balls through two processes: Molding and Packaging. In the Molding Department, the urethane, rubber, plastics, and other materials are molded into bowling balls. In the Packaging Department, the balls are placed in cartons and sent to the finished goods warehouse. All materials are entered at the beginning of each process. Labor and manufacturing overhead are incurred uniformly throughout each process. Production and cost data for the Molding Department during June 2005 are presented below.

Complete four steps necessary to prepare a production cost report.

(SO 5, 6, 7)

Production Data	June
Beginning work in process units	–0–
Units started into production	22,000
Ending work in process units	2,000
Percent complete—ending inventory	45%

Cost Data	
Materials	$198,000
Labor	50,400
Overhead	116,800
Total	$365,200

Instructions

(a) Prepare a schedule showing physical units of production.

(b) Determine the equivalent units of production for materials and conversion costs.

(c) Compute the unit costs of production.

(d) Determine the costs to be assigned to the units transferred and in process for June.

(e) Prepare a production cost report for the Molding Department for the month of June.

Complete four steps necessary to prepare a production cost report.

(SO 5, 6, 7)

P22-2B Moline Industries Inc. manufactures in separate processes furniture for homes. In each process, materials are entered at the beginning, and conversion costs are incurred uniformly. Production and cost data for the first process in making two products in two different manufacturing plants are as follows.

| | Cutting Department | |
Production Data—July	Plant 1 T12-Tables	Plant 2 C10-Chairs
Work in process units, July 1	–0–	–0–
Units started into production	19,000	16,000
Work in process units, July 31	1,000	500
Work in process percent complete	60	80

Cost Data—July		
Work in process, July 1	$ –0–	$ –0–
Materials	380,000	288,000
Labor	175,000	125,900
Overhead	104,000	96,700
Total	$659,000	$510,600

Instructions

(a) For each plant:

    (1) Compute the physical units of production.

    (2) Compute equivalent units of production for materials and for conversion costs.

    (3) Determine the unit costs of production.

    (4) Show the assignment of costs of units transferred out and in process.

(b) Prepare the production cost report for Plant 1 for July 2005.

Journalize transactions.

(SO 3, 4)

P22-3B Urbana Company manufactures its product, Vitadrink, through two manufacturing processes: Mixing and Packaging. All materials are entered at the beginning of each process. On October 1, 2005, inventories consisted of Raw Materials $26,000, Work in Process—Mixing $0, Work in Process—Packaging $250,000, and Finished Goods $289,000. The beginning inventory for Packaging consisted of 10,000 units that were 50% complete as to conversion costs and fully complete as to materials. During October, 50,000 units were started into production in the Mixing Department and the following transactions were completed.

1. Purchased $300,000 of raw materials on account.
2. Issued raw materials for production: Mixing $210,000 and Packaging $45,000.
3. Incurred labor costs of $248,900.
4. Used factory labor: Mixing $182,500 and Packaging $66,400.
5. Incurred $790,000 of manufacturing overhead on account.
6. Applied indirect manufacturing overhead on the basis of $25 per machine hour. Machine hours were 28,000 in Mixing and 6,000 in Packaging.
7. Transferred 45,000 units from Mixing to Packaging at a cost of $999,000.
8. Transferred 53,000 units from Packaging to Finished Goods at a cost of $1,355,000.
9. Sold goods costing $1,640,000 for $2,500,000 on account.

Instructions

Journalize the October transactions.

P22-4B Rockford Company has several processing departments. Costs charged to the Assembly Department for November 2005 totaled $2,123,800 as follows.

Assign costs and prepare production cost report.
(SO 5, 6, 7)

Work in process, November 1		
Materials	$69,000	
Conversion costs	48,150	$ 117,150
Materials added		1,405,000
Labor		225,920
Overhead		375,730

Production records show that 37,000 units were in beginning work in process 30% complete as to conversion costs, 700,000 units were started into production, and 25,000 units were in ending work in process 40% complete as to conversion costs. Materials are entered at the beginning of each process.

Instructions
(a) Determine the equivalent units of production and the unit costs for the Assembly Department.
(b) Determine the assignment of costs to goods transferred out and in process.
(c) Prepare a production cost report for the Assembly Department.

P22-5B Ying Company manufactures basketballs. Materials are added at the beginning of the production process and conversion costs are incurred uniformly. Production and cost data for the month of July 2005 are as follows.

Determine equivalent units and unit costs and assign costs.
(SO 5, 6, 7)

Production Data—Basketballs	Units	Percent Complete
Work in process units, July 1	500	60%
Units started into production	1,300	
Work in process units, July 31	600	40%

Cost Data—Basketballs		
Work in process, July 1		
Materials	$750	
Conversion costs	600	$1,350
Direct materials		2,400
Direct labor		1,580
Manufacturing overhead		1,060

Instructions
(a) Calculate the following.
  (1) The equivalent units of production for materials and conversion.
  (2) The unit costs of production for materials and conversion costs.
  (3) The assignment of costs to units transferred out and in process at the end of the accounting period.
(b) Prepare a production cost report for the month of July for the basketballs.

P22-6B Han Wu Processing Company uses a weighted-average process costing system and manufactures a single product—a premium rug shampoo and cleaner. The manufacturing activity for the month of October has just been completed. A partially completed production cost report for the month of October for the mixing and cooking department is shown on page 928.

Compute equivalent units and complete production cost report.
(SO 5, 7)

Instructions
(a) Prepare a schedule that shows how the equivalent units were computed so that you can complete the "Quantities: Units accounted for" equivalent units section shown in the production cost report above, and compute October unit costs.
(b) Complete the "Cost Reconciliation Schedule" part of the production cost report on page 928.

HAN WU PROCESSING COMPANY
Mixing and Cooking Department
Production Cost Report
For the Month Ended October 31

QUANTITIES	Physical Units	Equivalent Units	
		Materials	**Conversion Costs**
Units to be accounted for			
Work in process, October 1 (all materials, 70% conversion costs)	20,000		
Started into production	160,000		
Total units	180,000		
Units accounted for			
Transferred out	130,000	?	?
Work in process, October 31 (40% materials, 20% conversion costs)	50,000	?	?
Total units accounted for	180,000	?	?

COSTS	Materials	Conversion Costs	Total
Unit costs			
Costs in October	$240,000	$105,000	$345,000
Equivalent units	?	?	
Unit costs	$? +	$? =	$?
Costs to be accounted for			
Work in process, October 1			$ 30,000
Started into production			315,000
Total costs			$345,000

Cost Reconciliation Schedule

Costs accounted for		
Transferred out		$?
Work in process, October 31		
Materials	?	
Conversion costs	?	?
Total costs		?

BROADENING YOUR PERSPECTIVE

Group Decision Case

BYP22-1 Atlantic Beach Company manufactures suntan lotion, called Surtan, in 11-ounce plastic bottles. Surtan is sold in a competitive market. As a result, management is very cost-conscious. Surtan is manufactured through two processes: mixing and filling. Materials are entered at the beginning of each process and labor and manufacturing overhead occur uniformly throughout each process. Unit costs are based on the cost per gallon of Surtan using the weighted-average costing approach.

On June 30, 2005, Sara Simmons, the chief accountant for the past 20 years, opted to take early retirement. Her replacement, Ira Jacobs, had extensive accounting experience with motels in the area but only limited contact with manufacturing accounting. During July, Ira correctly accumulated the following production quantity and cost data for the Mixing Department.

Production quantities: Work in process, July 1, 8,000 gallons 75% complete; started into production 100,000 gallons; work in process, July 31, 5,000 gallons 20% complete. Materials are added at the beginning of the process.

Production costs: Beginning work in process $88,000, comprised of $21,000 of materials costs and $67,000 of conversion costs; incurred in July: materials $573,000, conversion costs $765,000.

Ira then prepared a production cost report on the basis of physical units started into production. His report showed a production cost of $14.26 per gallon of Surtan. The management of Atlantic Beach was surprised at the high unit cost. The president comes to you, as Sara's top assistant, to review Ira's report and prepare a correct report if necessary.

Instructions

With the class divided into groups, answer the following questions.

(a) Show how Ira arrived at the unit cost of $14.26 per gallon of Surtan.
(b) What error(s) did Ira make in preparing his production cost report?
(c) Prepare a correct production cost report for July.

Managerial Analysis

BYP22-2   Sauer Furniture Company manufactures living room furniture through two departments: Framing and Upholstering. Materials are entered at the beginning of each process. For May, the following cost data are obtained from the two work in process accounts.

	Framing	Upholstering
Work in process, May 1	$ –0–	$?
Materials	420,000	?
Conversion costs	280,000	330,000
Costs transferred in	–0–	550,000
Costs transferred out	550,000	?
Work in process, May 31	150,000	?

Instructions

Answer the following questions.

(a) If 3,500 sofas were started into production on May 1 and 2,500 sofas were transferred to Upholstering, what was the unit cost of materials for May in the Framing Department?
(b) Using the data in (a) above, what was the per unit conversion cost of the sofas transferred to Upholstering?
(c) Continuing the assumptions in (a) above, what is the percentage of completion of the units in process at May 31 in the Framing Department?

Real-World Focus

BYP22-3   General Microwave Corp. is engaged primarily in the design, development, manufacture, and marketing of microwave, electronic, and fiber optic test equipment, components, and subsystems. A substantial portion of the company's microwave product is sold to manufacturers and users of microwave systems and equipment for applications in the defense electronics industry. General Microwave Corp. reports the following information in one of the notes to its financial statements.

GENERAL MICROWAVE CORPORATION
Notes to the Financial Statement

Work in process inventory reflects all accumulated production costs, which are comprised of direct production costs and overhead, reduced by amounts attributable to units delivered. Work in process inventory is reduced to its estimated net realizable value by a charge to cost of sales in the period [in which] excess costs are identified. Raw materials and finished goods inventories are reflected at the lower of cost or market.

Instructions

(a) What types of manufacturing costs are accumulated in work in process inventory?

(b) What types of information must General Microwave have to be able to compute equivalent units of production?

(c) How does General Microwave assign costs to the units transferred out of work in process that are completed?

Exploring the Web

BYP22-4 Search the Internet and find the Web sites of two manufacturers that you think are likely to use process costing. Are there any specifics included in their Web sites that confirm the use of process costing for each of these companies?

Communication Activity

BYP22-5 Nancy Beeman was a good friend of yours in high school and is from your home town. While you chose to major in accounting when you both went away to college, she majored in marketing and management. You have recently been promoted to accounting manager for the Snack Foods Division of Sauder Enterprises, and your friend was promoted to regional sales manager for the same division of Sauder. Nancy recently telephoned you. She explained that she was familiar with job cost sheets, which had been used by the Special Projects division where she had formerly worked. She was, however, very uncomfortable with the production cost reports prepared by your division. She faxed you a list of her particular questions:

1. Since Sauder occasionally prepares snack foods for special orders in the Snack Foods Division, why don't we track costs of the orders separately?

2. What is an equivalent unit?

3. Why am I getting four production cost reports? Isn't there one Work in Process account?

Instructions

Prepare a memo to Nancy. Answer her questions, and include any additional information you think would be helpful. You may write informally, but do use proper grammar and punctuation.

Ethics Case

BYP22-6 R. B. Shannon Company manufactures a high-tech component that passes through two production processing departments, Molding and Assembly. Department managers are partially compensated on the basis of units of products completed and transferred out relative to units of product put into production. This was intended as encouragement to be efficient and to minimize waste.

Ann Meyers is the department head in the Molding Department, and Tony Terrago is her quality control inspector. During the month of June, Ann had three new employees who were not yet technically skilled. As a result, many of the units produced in June had minor molding defects. In order to maintain the department's normal high rate of completion, Ann told Tony to pass through inspection and on to the Assembly Department all units that had defects nondetectable to the human eye. "Company and industry tolerances on this product are too high anyway," says Ann. "Less than 2% of the units we produce are subjected in the market to the stress tolerance we've designed into them. The odds of those 2% being any of this month's units are even less. Anyway, we're saving the company money."

Instructions

(a) Who are the potential stakeholders involved in this situation?

(b) What alternatives does Tony have in this situation? What might the company do to prevent this situation from occurring?

Answers to Self-Study Questions

1. b   **2.** d   **3.** c   **4.** b   **5.** b   **6.** a   **7.** c   **8.** a   **9.** b   **10.** b   **11.** d
12. c   **13.** b

 REMEMBER to go back to the Navigator box on the chapter-opening page and check off your completed work.

Cost-Volume-Profit Relationships

THE NAVIGATOR ✓

Understand **Concepts for Review**	❏
Read **Feature Story**	❏
Scan **Study Objectives**	❏
Read **Preview**	❏
Read text and answer **Before You Go On** p. 939 ❏ p. 946 ❏ p. 951 ❏	
Work **Demonstration Problems**	❏
Review **Summary of Study Objectives**	❏
Answer **Self-Study Questions**	❏
Complete **Assignments**	❏

CONCEPTS FOR REVIEW

Before studying this chapter, you should know or, if necessary, review:

The three manufacturing cost elements.
(Ch. 20, pp. 820–821)

The difference between product and period costs.
(Ch. 20, p. 822)

The income statement for a manufacturing company.
(Ch. 20, pp. 823–825)

THE NAVIGATOR

Growing by Leaps and Leotards

When the last of her three children went off to school, Amy began looking for a job. At this same time, her daughter asked to take dance classes. The nearest dance studio was over 20 miles away, and Amy didn't know how she would balance a new job and drive her daughter to dance class. Suddenly it hit her—why not start her own dance studio?

Amy sketched out a business plan: A local church would rent its basement for $6 per hour. The size of the basement limited the number of students she could teach, but the rent was low. Insurance for a small studio was $50 per month. Initially she would teach classes only for young kids since that was all she felt qualified to do. She thought she could charge $2.50 for a one-hour class. There was room for 8 students per class. She wouldn't get rich—but at least it would be fun, and she didn't have much at risk.

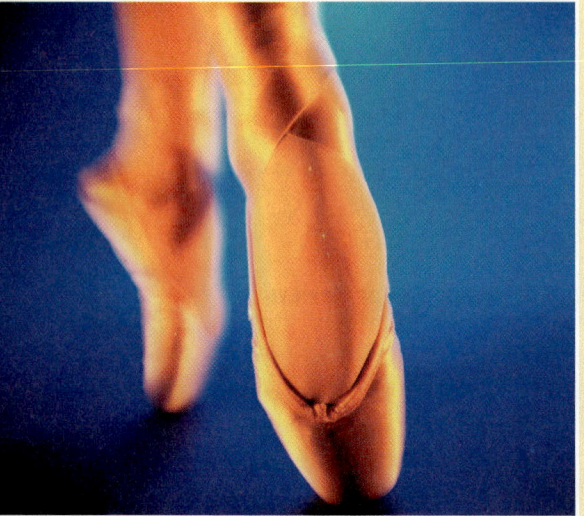

Amy soon realized that the demand for dance classes far exceeded her capacity. She considered renting a bigger space that could serve 15 students per class. But her rent would also increase significantly. Also, rather than paying rent by the hour, she would have to pay $600 per month, even during the summer months when demand for dance classes was low. She also would have to pay utilities—roughly $70 per month.

However, with a bigger space Amy could offer classes for teens and adults. Teens and adults would pay a higher fee— $5 per hour—though the number of students per class would have to be smaller, probably only 8 per class. She could hire a part-time instructor at about $18 per hour to teach advanced classes. Insurance costs could increase to $100 per month. In addition, she would need a part-time administrator at $100 per month to keep records. Amy also realized she could increase her income by selling dance supplies such as shoes, towels, and leotards.

Amy laid out a new business plan based on these estimates. If she failed, she stood to lose real money. Convinced she could make a go of it, she made the big plunge.

Her planning paid off: Within 10 years of starting her business in a church basement Amy had over 800 students, seven instructors, two administrators, and a facility with three separate studios.

THE NAVIGATOR

After studying this chapter, you should be able to:

1. Distinguish between variable and fixed costs.
2. Explain the significance of the relevant range.
3. Explain the concept of mixed costs.
4. List the five components of cost-volume-profit analysis.
5. Indicate what contribution margin is and how it can be expressed.
6. Identify the three ways to determine the break-even point.
7. Define margin of safety and give the formulas for computing it.
8. Give the formulas for determining sales required to earn target net income.
9. Describe the essential features of a cost-volume-profit income statement.

THE NAVIGATOR

As the Feature Story indicates, to manage any size business you must understand how costs respond to changes in sales volume and the effect of costs and revenues on profits. A prerequisite to understanding cost-volume-profit (CVP) relationships is knowledge of how costs behave. In this chapter, we first explain the considerations involved in cost behavior analysis. Then we discuss and illustrate CVP analysis.

The content and organization of Chapter 23 are as follows.

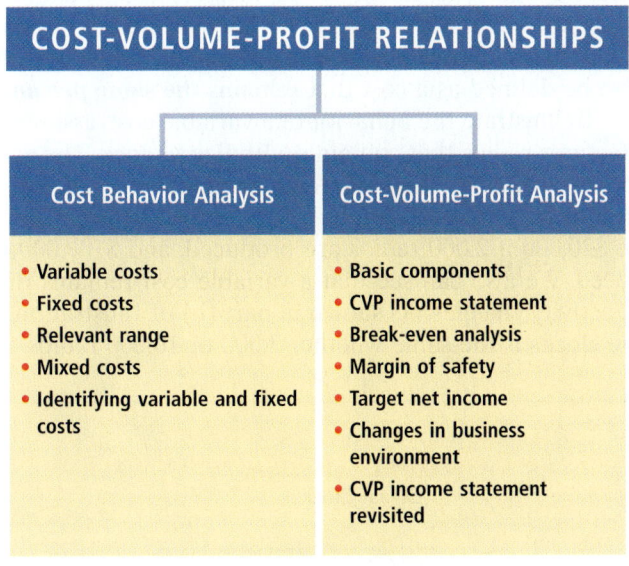

Cost Behavior Analysis

Cost behavior analysis is the study of how specific costs respond to changes in the level of business activity. As you might expect, some costs change, and others remain the same. For example, for an airline company such as **Southwest** or **United**, the longer the flight the higher the fuel costs. On the other hand, **Massachusetts General Hospital**'s employee costs to run the emergency room on any given night are relatively constant regardless of the number of patients serviced. A knowledge of cost behavior helps management plan operations and decide between alternative courses of action. Cost behavior analysis applies to all types of entities, as the Feature Story about Amy's dance studio indicates.

The starting point in cost behavior analysis is measuring the key business activities. Activity levels may be expressed in terms of sales dollars (in a retail company), miles driven (in a trucking company), room occupancy (in a hotel), or dance classes taught (by a dance studio). Many companies use more than one measurement base. A manufacturer, for example, may use direct labor hours or units of output for manufacturing costs and sales revenue or units sold for selling expenses.

For an activity level to be useful in cost behavior analysis, changes in the level or volume of activity should be correlated with changes in costs. The activity level selected is referred to as the activity (or volume) index. The **activity index** identifies the activity that causes changes in the behavior of costs. With an appropriate activity index, it is possible to classify the behavior of costs in response to changes in activity levels into three categories: variable, fixed, or mixed.

Variable Costs

Variable costs are costs that vary **in total** directly and proportionately with changes in the activity level. If the level increases 10 percent, total variable costs will increase 10 percent. If the level of activity decreases by 25 percent, variable costs will decrease 25 percent. Examples of variable costs include direct materials and direct labor for a manufacturer; cost of goods sold, sales commissions, and freight-out for a merchandiser; and gasoline in airline and trucking companies. A variable cost may also be defined as a cost that **remains the same *per unit* at every level of activity**.

To illustrate the behavior of a variable cost, assume that Damon Company manufactures radios that contain a $10 digital clock. The activity index is the number of radios produced. As each radio is manufactured, the total cost of the clocks increases by $10. As shown in part (a) of Illustration 23-1, total cost of the clocks will be $20,000 if 2,000 radios are produced, and $100,000 when 10,000 radios are produced. We also can see that a variable cost remains the same per unit as the level of activity changes. As shown in part (b) of Illustration 23-1, the unit cost of $10 for the clocks is the same whether 2,000 or 10,000 radios are produced.

Illustration 23-1
Behavior of total and unit variable costs

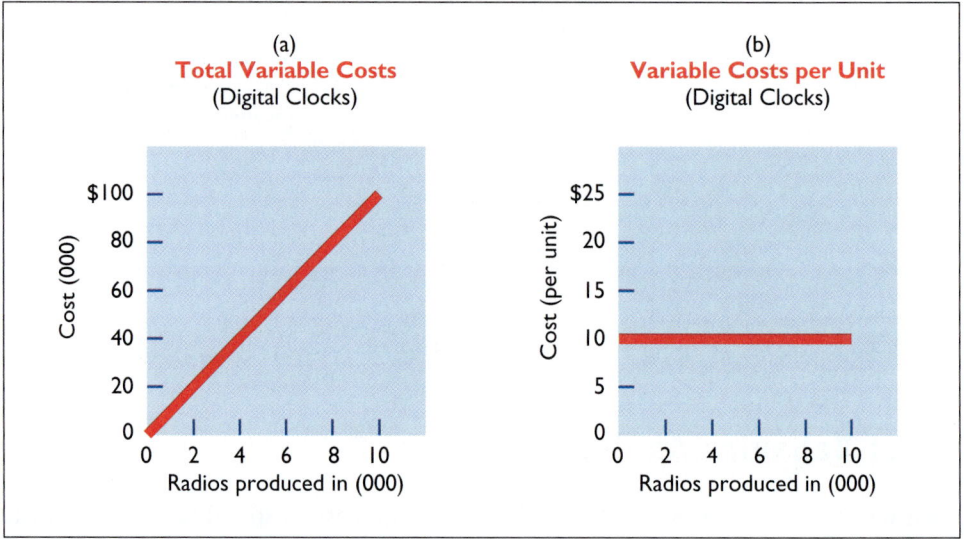

Companies that rely heavily on labor to manufacture a product, such as **Nike** or **Reebok**, or to provide a service, such as **Hilton** or **Marriott**, are likely to have many variable costs. In contrast, companies that use a high proportion of machinery and equipment in producing revenue, such as **ATT** or **Duke Energy Co.**, may have few variable costs.

Fixed Costs

Fixed costs are costs that **remain the same in total** regardless of changes in the activity level. Examples include property taxes, insurance, rent, supervisory salaries, and depreciation on buildings and equipment. Because total fixed costs remain constant as activity changes, it follows that **fixed costs *per unit* vary inversely with activity: As volume increases, unit cost declines, and vice versa**.

To illustrate the behavior of fixed costs, assume that Damon Company leases its productive facilities at a cost of $10,000 per month. Total fixed costs of the facilities will remain constant at every level of activity, as shown in part (a) of Illustration 23-2. But, on a per unit basis, the cost of rent will decline as activity increases, as shown in part (b) of Illustration 23-2. At 2,000 units, the unit cost is $5 ($10,000 ÷ 2,000). When 10,000 radios are produced, the unit cost is only $1 ($10,000 ÷ 10,000).

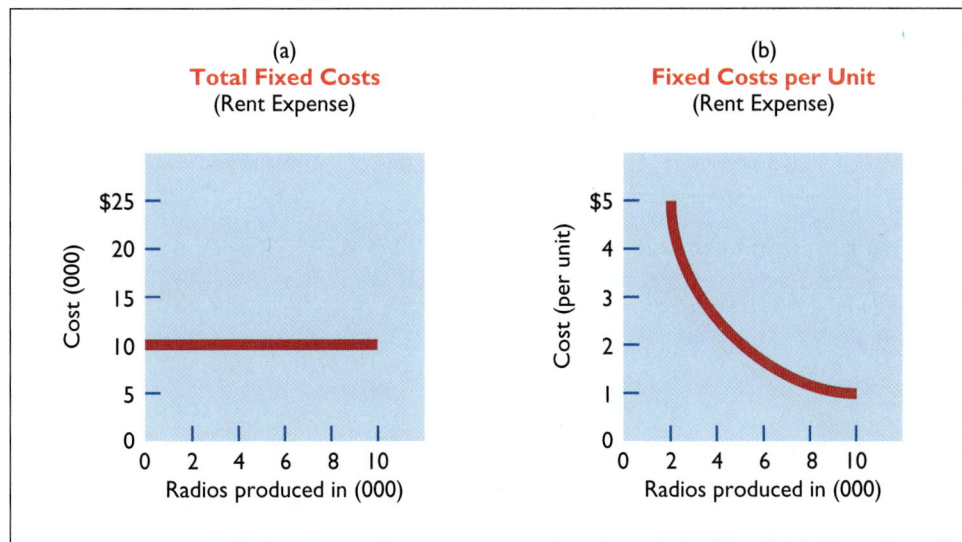

Illustration 23-2
Behavior of total and unit fixed costs

The trend for many manufacturers is to have more fixed costs and fewer variable costs. This trend is the result of increased use of automation and less use of employee labor. As a result, depreciation and lease charges (fixed costs) increase, whereas direct labor costs (variable costs) decrease.

ACCOUNTING IN ACTION Business Insight

When Thomas Moser quit teaching communications at Bates College 25 years ago, he turned to what he loved doing—furniture woodworking. Today he has over 120 employees. In a business where profit margins are seldom thicker than wood shavings, cost control is everything. Moser keeps no inventory; a 50 percent deposit buys the wood. Because computer-driven machines cut most of the standardized parts and joints, "we're free to be inefficient in assembly and finishing work, where the craft is most obviously expressed," says Moser. Direct labor costs are a manageable 30 percent of revenues. By keeping a tight lid on costs and running an efficient operation, Moser is free to spend most of his time doing what he enjoys most—designing furniture.

Source: Excerpts from "Out of the Woods," *Forbes*, April 5, 1999, p. 74.

Relevant Range

In Illustrations 23-1 and 23-2, straight lines were drawn throughout the entire activity index for total variable costs and total fixed costs. In essence, the assumption was made that the costs were **linear**. It is now necessary to ask: Is the straight-line relationship realistic? Does the linear assumption produce useful data for CVP analysis?

In most business situations, a straight-line relationship **does not exist** for variable costs throughout the entire range of possible activity. At abnormally low levels of activity, it may be impossible to be cost efficient. Small-scale operations may not allow the company to obtain quantity discounts for raw materials or to use specialized labor. In contrast, at abnormally high levels of activity, labor costs may increase sharply because of overtime pay. Also at high activity levels, materials costs may jump signifi-

STUDY OBJECTIVE 2

Explain the significance of the relevant range.

cantly because of excess spoilage caused by worker fatigue. As a result, in the real world, the relationship between the behavior of a variable cost and changes in the activity level is often **curvilinear**, as shown in part (a) of Illustration 23-3.

Illustration 23-3
Nonlinear behavior of variable and fixed costs

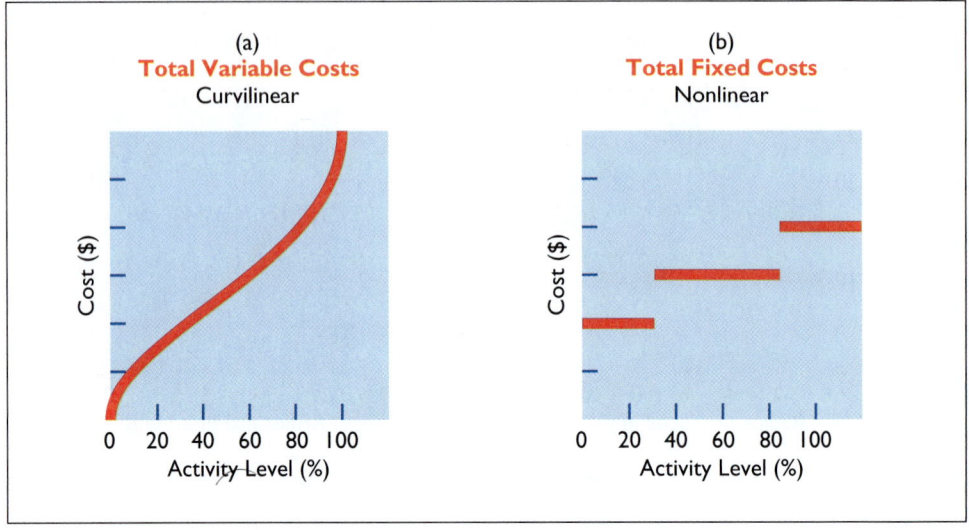

Total fixed costs also do not have a straight-line relationship over the entire range of activity. Some fixed costs will not change. But it is possible for management to change other fixed costs. For example, in the Feature Story the dance studio's rent was originally variable and then became fixed at a certain amount. It then increased to a new fixed amount when the size of the studio increased beyond a certain point. An example of the behavior of total fixed costs through all potential levels of activity is shown in part (b) of Illustration 23-3.

For most companies, operating at almost zero or at 100 percent capacity is the exception rather than the rule. Instead, companies often operate over a somewhat narrower range, such as 40–80 percent of capacity. The range over which a company expects to operate during a year is called the **relevant range** of the activity index. Within the relevant range, as shown in both diagrams in Illustration 23-4, a straight-line relationship generally exists for both variable and fixed costs.

Illustration 23-4
Linear behavior within relevant range

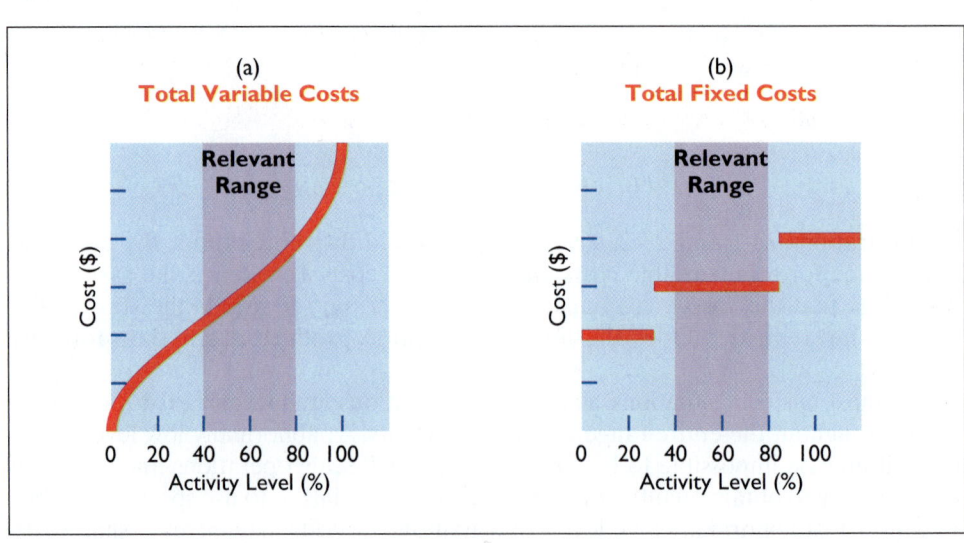

As you can see, although the straight-line relationship may not be completely realistic, **the linear assumption produces useful data for CVP analysis as long as the level of activity remains within the relevant range**.

Mixed Costs

Mixed costs are costs that contain both a variable element and a fixed element. Sometimes called **semivariable costs, mixed costs change in total but not proportionately with changes in the activity level**. The rental of a U-Haul truck is a good example of a mixed cost. Assume that local rental terms for a 17-foot truck, including insurance, are $50 per day plus 50 cents per mile. The per diem charge is a fixed cost with respect to miles driven, whereas the mileage charge is a variable cost. The graphic presentation of the rental cost for a one-day rental is as follows.

STUDY OBJECTIVE 3

Explain the concept of mixed costs.

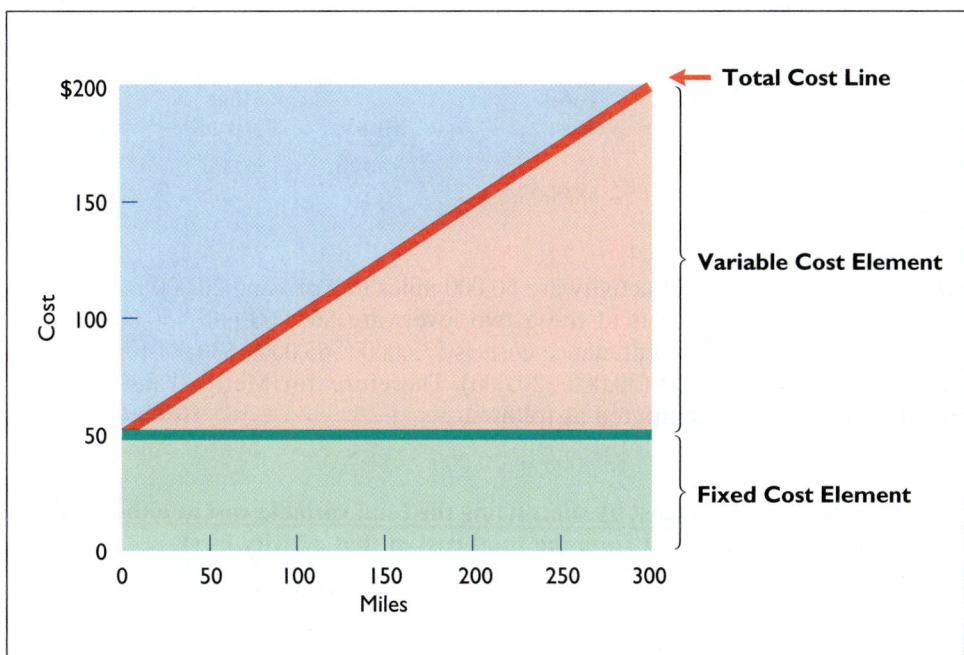

Illustration 23-5
Behavior of a mixed cost

In this case, the fixed cost element is the cost of having the service available. The variable cost element is the cost of actually using the service. Another example of a mixed cost is utility costs (electric, telephone, and so on), where there is a flat service fee plus a usage charge.

For purposes of CVP analysis, **mixed costs must be classified into their fixed and variable elements**. How does management make the classification? One possibility is to determine the variable and fixed components each time a mixed cost is incurred. But because of time and cost constraints, this approach is rarely followed. Instead, the customary approach is to determine variable and fixed costs on an **aggregate basis at the end of a period of time**. The company does this by using its past experience with the behavior of the mixed cost at various levels of activity. Management may use any of several methods in making the determination. We will explain the **high-low method** here. Other methods are more appropriately explained in cost accounting courses.[1]

---

[1]Other methods include the scatter diagram method and least squares regression analysis.

High-Low Method

The **high-low method** uses the total costs incurred at the high and low levels of activity. The difference in costs between the high and low levels represents variable costs, since only the variable cost element can change as activity levels change. The steps in computing fixed and variable costs under this method are as follows.

1. **Determine variable cost per unit from the following formula.**

Illustration 23-6
Formula for variable cost per unit using high-low method

Change in Total Costs	÷	High minus Low Activity Level	=	Variable Cost per Unit

To illustrate, assume that Metro Transit Company has the following maintenance costs and mileage data for its fleet of buses over a 4-month period.

Illustration 23-7
Assumed maintenance costs and mileage data

Month	Miles Driven	Total Cost	Month	Miles Driven	Total Cost
January	20,000	$30,000	March	35,000	$49,000
February	40,000	48,000	April	50,000	63,000

The high and low levels of activity are 50,000 miles in April and 20,000 miles in January. The maintenance costs at these two levels are $63,000 and $30,000, respectively. The difference in maintenance costs is $33,000 ($63,000−$30,000) and the difference in miles is 30,000 (50,000−20,000). Therefore, for Metro Transit, variable cost per unit is $1.10, computed as follows.

$$\$33,000 \div 30,000 = \$1.10$$

2. **Determine the fixed cost by subtracting the total variable cost at either the high or the low activity level from the total cost at that activity level.**

For Metro Transit, the computations are shown in Illustration 23-8.

Illustration 23-8
High-low method computation of fixed costs

	Activity Level	
	High	**Low**
Total cost	$63,000	$30,000
Less: Variable costs		
50,000 × $1.10	55,000	
20,000 × $1.10		22,000
Total fixed costs	$ 8,000	$ 8,000

Maintenance costs are therefore $8,000 per month plus $1.10 per mile. For example, at 45,000 miles, estimated maintenance costs would be $8,000 fixed and $49,500 variable (45,000 × $1.10).

The high-low method generally produces a reasonable estimate for analysis. However, it does not produce a precise measurement of the fixed and variable elements in a mixed cost because other activity levels are ignored in the computation.

Importance of Identifying Variable and Fixed Costs

Why is it important to segregate costs into variable and fixed elements? The answer may become apparent if we look at the following four business decisions.

1. If **American Airlines** is to make a profit when it reduces all domestic fares by 30 percent, what reduction in costs or increase in passengers will be required? **Answer**: To make a profit when it cuts domestic fares by 30 percent, American Airlines will have to increase the number of passengers or cut its variable costs for those flights. Its fixed costs will not change.

2. If **Ford Motor Company** meets the United Auto Workers' demands for higher wages, what increase in sales revenue will be needed to maintain current profit levels? **Answer**: Higher wages to UAW members at Ford Motor Company will increase the variable costs of manufacturing automobiles. To maintain present profit levels, Ford will have to cut other variable costs or increase the price of its automobiles.

3. If **U.S. Steel**'s program to modernize plant facilities reduces the work force by 50 percent, what will be the effect on the cost of producing one ton of steel? **Answer**: The modernizing of plant facilities at U.S. Steel changes the proportion of fixed and variable costs of producing one ton of steel. Fixed costs increase because of higher depreciation charges, whereas variable costs decrease due to the reduction in the number of steelworkers.

4. What happens if **Kellogg Company** increases its advertising expenses but cannot increase prices because of competitive pressure? **Answer**: Sales volume must be increased to cover three items: (1) the increase in advertising, (2) the variable cost of the increased sales volume, and (3) the desired additional net income.

BEFORE YOU GO ON...

Review It

1. What are the effects on (a) a variable cost and (b) a fixed cost due to a change in activity?
2. What is the relevant range, and how do costs behave within this range?
3. What are the steps in applying the high-low method to mixed costs?

Do It

Helena Company reports the following total costs at two levels of production.

	10,000 units	20,000 units
Direct materials	$20,000	$40,000
Maintenance	8,000	10,000
Depreciation	4,000	4,000

Classify each cost as either variable, fixed, or mixed.

ACTION PLAN

- Recall that a variable cost varies in total directly and proportionately with each change in activity.
- Recall that a fixed cost remains the same in total with each change in activity.
- Recall that a mixed cost changes in total but not proportionately with each change in activity.

SOLUTION   Direct materials is a variable cost. Maintenance is a mixed cost. Depreciation is a fixed cost.

Related exercise material: *BE23-1, E23-1, and E23-2.*

 THE NAVIGATOR

Cost-Volume-Profit Analysis

STUDY OBJECTIVE 4

List the five components of cost-volume-profit analysis.

Cost-volume-profit (CVP) analysis is the study of the effects of changes in costs and volume on a company's profits. CVP analysis is important in profit planning. It also is a critical factor in such management decisions as setting selling prices, determining product mix, and maximizing use of production facilities.

Basic Components

CVP analysis considers the interrelationships among the components shown in Illustration 23-9.

Illustration 23-9
Components of CVP analysis

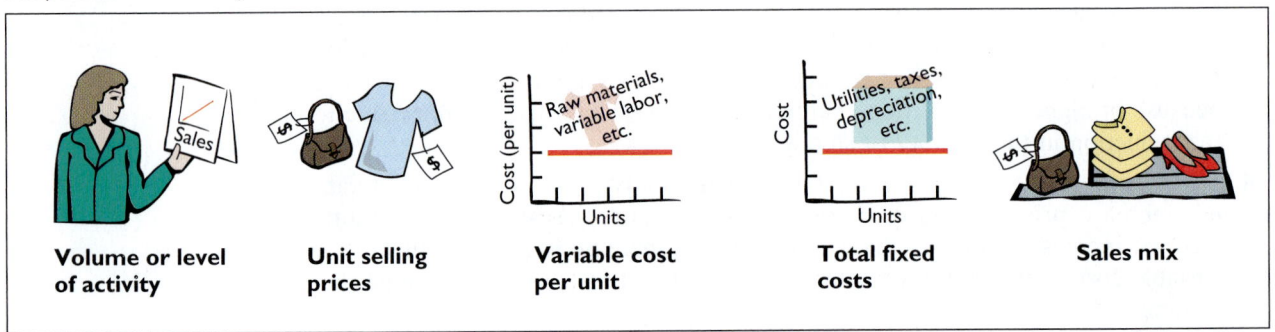

Volume or level of activity	Unit selling prices	Variable cost per unit	Total fixed costs	Sales mix

The following assumptions underlie each CVP analysis.

1. The behavior of both costs and revenues is linear throughout the relevant range of the activity index.
2. All costs can be classified with reasonable accuracy as either variable or fixed.
3. Changes in activity are the only factors that affect costs.
4. All units produced are sold.
5. When more than one type of product is sold, the sales mix will remain constant. That is, the percentage that each product represents of total sales will stay the same. Sales mix complicates CVP analysis because different products will have different cost relationships. In this chapter we assume a single product. Sales mix issues are addressed in advanced accounting courses.

When these five assumptions are not valid, the results of CVP analysis may be inaccurate.

CVP Income Statement

STUDY OBJECTIVE 5

Indicate what contribution margin is and how it can be expressed.

Because CVP is so important for decision making, management often wants this information reported in a **CVP income statement format** for internal use. The CVP income statement classifies costs as variable and fixed and computes a contribution margin. **Contribution margin** is the amount of revenue remaining after deducting variable costs. It is often stated both as a total amount and on a per unit basis. We will use Vargo Video Company to illustrate a CVP income statement. Relevant data for the CD/DVD players made by this company are as follows.

Illustration 23-10
Assumed selling and cost data for Vargo Video

Unit selling price of CD/DVD player	$500
Unit variable costs	$300
Total monthly fixed costs	$200,000
Units sold	1,600

The CVP income statement for Vargo Video therefore would be reported as follows.

VARGO VIDEO COMPANY
CVP Income Statement
For the Month Ended June 30, 2005

	Total	Per Unit
Sales (1,600 CD/DVD players)	$800,000	$500
Variable costs	480,000	300
Contribution margin	**320,000**	**$200**
Fixed costs	200,000	
Net income	**$120,000**	

Illustration 23-11
CVP income statement, with net income

A traditional income statement and a CVP income statement both report the same bottom-line net income of $120,000. However a traditional income statement does not classify costs as variable and fixed, and therefore a contribution margin would not be reported. In addition, both a total and a per unit amount are often shown on a CVP income statement to facilitate CVP analysis. In the applications of CVP analysis that follow, we will assume that the term "cost" includes all costs and expenses pertaining to production and sale of the product. That is, cost includes manufacturing costs plus selling and administrative expenses.

Contribution Margin Per Unit

From Vargo Video's CVP income statement, we can see that the contribution margin is $320,000, and the contribution margin per unit is $200 ($500 − $300). The formula for **contribution margin per unit** and the computation for Vargo Video are:

Unit Selling Price	−	Unit Variable Costs	=	Contribution Margin per Unit
$500	−	$300	=	$200

Illustration 23-12
Formula for contribution margin per unit

Contribution margin per unit indicates that for every CD/DVD player sold, Vargo will have $200 to cover fixed costs and contribute to net income. Because Vargo Video has fixed costs of $200,000, it must sell 1,000 CD/DVD players ($200,000 ÷ $200) before it earns any net income. Vargo's CVP income statement, assuming sales of 1,000 units, reports net income of zero.

Illustration 23-13
CVP income statement, with zero net income

VARGO VIDEO COMPANY
CVP Income Statement
For the Month Ended June 30, 2005

	Total	Per Unit
Sales (1,000 CD/DVD players)	$500,000	$500
Variable costs	300,000	300
Contribution margin	**200,000**	**$200**
Fixed costs	200,000	
Net income	**$ −0−**	

It follows that for every CD/DVD player sold above 1,000 units, net income is increased $200. For example, assume that Vargo sold one more CD/DVD player, for a total of 1,001 CD/DVDs players sold. In this case it would report net income of $200 as shown in Illustration 23-14.

Illustration 23-14
CVP income statement, with net income

VARGO VIDEO COMPANY
CVP Income Statement
For the Month Ended June 30, 2005

	Total	Per Unit
Sales (1,001 CD/DVD players)	$500,500	$500
Variable costs	300,300	300
Contribution margin	200,200	$200
Fixed costs	200,000	
Net income	$ 200	

Contribution Margin Ratio

Some managers prefer to use a contribution margin ratio in CVP analysis. The **contribution margin ratio** is the contribution margin per unit divided by the unit selling price. For Vargo Video, the ratio is as follows.

Illustration 23-15
Formula for contribution margin ratio

Contribution Margin per Unit	÷	Unit Selling Price	=	Contribution Margin Ratio
$200	÷	$500	=	40%

The contribution margin ratio of 40 percent means that $0.40 of each sales dollar ($1 × 40%) is available to apply to fixed costs and to contribute to net income.

This expression of contribution margin is very helpful in determining the effect of changes in sales on net income. For example, net income will increase $40,000 (40% × $100,000) if sales increase $100,000. Thus, by using the contribution margin ratio, managers can quickly determine increases in net income from any change in sales. We can also see this effect through a CVP income statement. Assume that Vargo Video's current sales are $500,000 and it wants to know the effect of a $100,000 increase in sales. It could prepare a comparative CVP income statement analysis as follows.

Illustration 23-16
Comparative CVP income statements

VARGO VIDEO COMPANY
CVP Income Statements
For the Month Ended June 30, 2005

	No Change		With Change	
	Total	Per Unit	Total	Per Unit
Sales	$500,000	$500	$600,000	$500
Variable costs	300,000	300	360,000	300
Contribution margin	200,000	$200	240,000	$200
Fixed costs	200,000		200,000	
Net income	$ –0–		$ 40,000	

Study these CVP income statements carefully. The concepts used in these statements will be used extensively in this and later chapters.

Break-Even Analysis

A key relationship in CVP analysis is the level of activity at which total revenues equal total costs (both fixed and variable). This level of activity is called the **break-even point**. At this volume of sales, the company will realize no income and will suffer no loss. The process of finding the break-even point is called **break-even analysis**. Knowledge of the break-even point is useful to management when it decides whether to introduce new product lines, change sales prices on established products, or enter new market areas.

The break-even point can be:

1. Computed from a mathematical equation.
2. Computed by using contribution margin.
3. Derived from a cost-volume-profit (CVP) graph.

The break-even point can be expressed **either in sales units or sales dollars**.

Mathematical Equation

A common equation used for cost-volume-profit (CVP) analysis is shown in Illustration 23-17.

Sales	=	**Variable Costs**	+	**Fixed Costs**	+	**Net Income**

Illustration 23-17
Basic CVP equation

Identifying the break-even point is a special case of CVP analysis. Because at the break-even point net income is zero, **break-even occurs where total sales equal variable costs plus fixed costs**.

The break-even point **in units** can be computed directly from the equation in Illustration 23-17 by **using unit selling prices** and **unit variable costs**. The computation of the break-even point in units for Vargo Video is:

$$\$500Q = \$300Q + \$200{,}000 + \$0$$
$$\$200Q = \$200{,}000$$
$$Q = \textbf{1{,}000 units}$$

where
$$Q = \text{sales volume}$$
$$\$500 = \text{selling price}$$
$$\$300 = \text{variable cost per unit}$$
$$\$200{,}000 = \text{total fixed costs}$$

Illustration 23-18
Computation of break-even point in units

Thus, Vargo Video must sell 1,000 units to break even.

To find **sales dollars** required to break even, we multiply the units sold at the break-even point times the selling price per unit, as shown below.

$$1{,}000 \times \$500 = \$500{,}000 \text{ (break-even sales dollars)}$$

Contribution Margin Technique

We know that contribution margin equals total revenues less variable costs. It follows that at the break-even point, **contribution margin must equal total fixed costs**. On the basis of this relationship, we can compute the break-even point using either the contribution margin per unit or the contribution margin ratio.

When the contribution margin per unit is used, the formula to compute break-even point in units is as follows.

Illustration 23-19
Formula for break-even point in units using contribution margin

Fixed Costs	÷	Contribution Margin per Unit	=	Break-even Point in Units

For Vargo Video, the contribution margin per unit is $200, as explained earlier. Thus, the break-even point in units is:

$$\$200,000 \div \$200 = 1,000 \text{ units}$$

When the contribution margin ratio is used, the formula to compute break-even point in dollars is:

Illustration 23-20
Formula for break-even point in dollars using contribution margin ratio

Fixed Costs	÷	Contribution Margin Ratio	=	Break-even Point in Dollars

We know that the contribution margin ratio for Vargo Video is 40 percent. Thus, the break-even point in dollars is:

$$\$200,000 \div 40\% = \$500,000$$

Graphic Presentation

An effective way to find the break-even point is to prepare a break-even graph. Because this graph also shows costs, volume, and profits, it is referred to as a **cost-volume-profit (CVP) graph**.

As shown in the CVP graph in Illustration 23-21, sales volume is recorded along the horizontal axis. This axis should extend to the maximum level of expected sales.

Both total revenues (sales) and total costs (fixed plus variable) are recorded on the vertical axis.

The construction of the graph, using the data for Vargo Video, is as follows.

1. Plot the total-revenue line, starting at the zero activity level. For every CD/DVD player sold, total revenue increases by $500. For example, at 200 units, sales are $100,000. At the upper level of activity (1,800 units), sales are $900,000. Note that the revenue line is assumed to be linear throughout the full range of activity.

2. Plot the total fixed cost using a horizontal line. For the CD/DVD players, this line is plotted at $200,000. The fixed cost is the same at every level of activity.

3. Plot the total cost line. This starts at the fixed-cost line at zero activity. It increases by the variable cost at each level of activity. For each CD/DVD player, variable costs are $300. Thus, at 200 units, total variable cost is $60,000, and total cost is $260,000. At 1,800 units, total variable cost is $540,000, and total cost is $740,000. On the graph, the amount of variable cost can be derived from the difference between the total cost and fixed cost lines at each level of activity.

4. Determine the break-even point from the intersection of the total cost line and the total revenue line. The break-even point in dollars is found by drawing a horizontal line from the break-even point to the vertical axis. The break-even point in units is found by drawing a vertical line from the break-even point to the horizontal axis. For the CD/DVD players, the break-even point is $500,000 of sales, or 1,000 units. At this sales level, Vargo Video will cover costs but make no profit.

The CVP graph also shows both the net income and net loss areas. Thus, the amount of income or loss at each level of sales can be derived from the total sales and total cost lines.

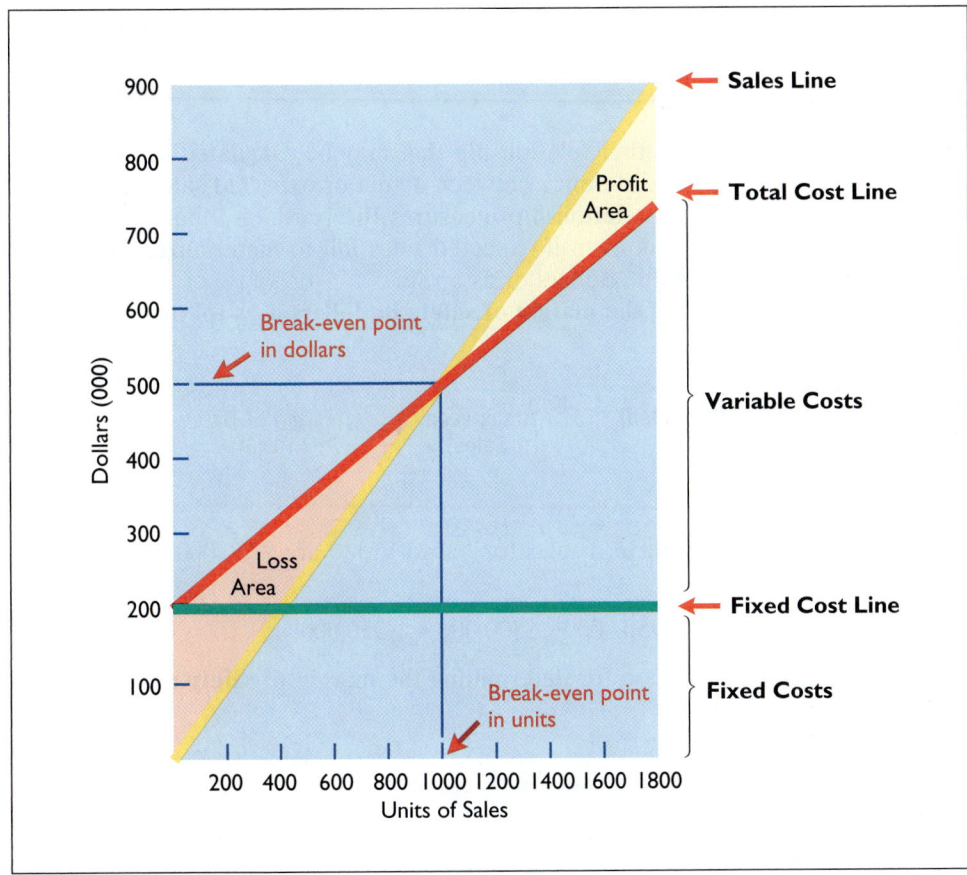

Illustration 23-21
CVP graph

A CVP graph is useful because the effects of a change in any element in the CVP analysis can be quickly seen. For example, a 10 percent increase in selling price will change the location of the total revenue line. Likewise, the effects on total costs of wage increases can be quickly observed.

BEFORE YOU GO ON...

Review It

1. What are the assumptions that underlie each CVP application?
2. What is contribution margin, and how can it be expressed?
3. How can the break-even point be determined?

Do It

Lombardi Company has a unit selling price of $400, variable costs per unit of $240, and fixed costs of $160,000. Compute the break-even point in units using (a) a mathematical equation and (b) contribution margin per unit.

ACTION PLAN

■ Apply the formula: Sales = Variable costs + Fixed costs + Net income.
■ Apply the formula: Fixed costs ÷ Contribution margin per unit = Break-even point in units.

SOLUTION (a) The formula is $400Q = $240Q + $160,000. The break-even point in units is 1,000 ($160,000 ÷ $160Q). (b) Contribution margin per unit is $160 ($400 − $240). The formula is $160,000 ÷ $160, and the break-even point in units is 1,000.

Related exercise material: *BE23-5, BE23-6, E23-3, E23-4, E23-5, E23-6, and E23-7.*

Margin of Safety

STUDY OBJECTIVE 7

Define margin of safety, and give the formulas for computing it.

The margin of safety is another relationship that may be calculated in CVP analysis. **Margin of safety** is the difference between actual or expected sales and sales at the break-even point. This relationship measures the "cushion" that management has, allowing it to still break even if expected sales fail to materialize. The margin of safety may be expressed in dollars or as a ratio.

The formula for stating the **margin of safety in dollars** is as follows.

Illustration 23-22
Formula for margin of safety in dollars

Actual (Expected) Sales	−	Break-even Sales	=	Margin of Safety in Dollars

Assuming that actual (expected) sales for Vargo Video are $750,000, the computation is:

$$\$750,000 - \$500,000 = \$250,000$$

The formula and computation for determining the **margin of safety ratio** are:

Illustration 23-23
Formula for margin of safety ratio

Margin of Safety in Dollars	÷	Actual (Expected) Sales	=	Margin of Safety Ratio
$250,000	÷	$750,000	=	33%

The higher the dollars or the percentage, the greater the margin of safety. The adequacy of the margin of safety should be evaluated by management in terms of such factors as the vulnerability of the product to competitive pressures and to downturns in the economy.

ACCOUNTING IN ACTION   Business Insight

Computation of break-even and margin of safety is important for service companies as well. Consider how the promoter for the Rolling Stones' tour used the break-even point and margin of safety. For example, one outdoor show should bring 70,000 individuals for a gross of $2.45 million. The promoter guarantees $1.2 million to the Rolling Stones. In addition, 20 percent of gross, or approximately $500,000, goes to the stadium in which the performance is staged. Add another $400,000 for other expenses such as ticket takers, parking attendants, advertising, and so on. This leaves $350,000 to the promoter per show, if it sells out. At 75 percent, the promoter breaks about even. At 50 percent, the promoter loses hundreds of thousands of dollars. However, the promoter also shares in sales of T-shirts and memorabilia for which the promoter will net over $7 million during the tour. From a successful Rolling Stones' tour, the promoter could make $35 million!

Target Net Income

Management usually sets an income objective for individual product lines. This objective is called **target net income**. It indicates the sales necessary to achieve a specified level of income. The sales necessary to achieve target net income can be determined from each of the approaches used to determine break-even sales.

STUDY OBJECTIVE 8

Give the formulas for determining sales required to earn target net income.

Mathematical Equation

We know that at the break-even point no profit or loss results for the company. By instead adding an amount for target net income to the same basic equation, we obtain the following formula for determining required sales.

Required Sales	=	Variable Costs	+	Fixed Costs	+	Target Net Income

Illustration 23-24
Formula for required sales to meet target net income

Required sales may be expressed in **either sales units or sales dollars**. Assuming that target net income is $120,000 for Vargo Video, the computation of required sales in units is as follows.

$$\$500Q = 300Q + \$200,000 + \$120,000$$
$$\$200Q = \$320,000$$
$$Q = \textbf{1,600 units}$$

where:
$$Q = \text{sales volume}$$
$$\$500 = \text{selling price}$$
$$\$300 = \text{variable costs per unit}$$
$$\$200,000 = \text{total fixed costs}$$
$$\$120,000 = \text{target net income}$$

Illustration 23-25
Computation of required sales

The sales dollars required to achieve the target net income is found by multiplying the units sold by the unit selling price [(1,600 × $500) = $800,000].

Contribution Margin Technique

As in the case of break-even sales, the sales required to meet a target net income can be computed in either units or dollars. The formula using the contribution margin per unit is as follows.

Illustration 23-26
Formula for required sales in units using contribution margin per unit

Fixed Costs + Target Net Income	÷	Contribution Margin Per Unit	=	Required Sales in Units

The computation for Vargo Video is as follows.

$$($200,000 + $120,000) \div $200 = 1,600 \text{ units}$$

The formula using the contribution margin ratio is as follows.

Illustration 23-27
Formula for required sales in dollars using contribution margin ratio

Fixed Costs + Target Net Income	÷	Contribution Margin Ratio	=	Required Sales in Dollars

The computation for Vargo Video is as follows.

$$$320,000 \div 40\% = $800,000$$

Graphic Presentation

The CVP graph in Illustration 23-21 (on page 945) can also be used to find the sales required to meet target net income. In the profit area of the graph, the distance between the sales line and the total cost line at any point equals net income. Required sales are found by analyzing the differences between the two lines until the desired net income is found.

CVP and Changes in the Business Environment

When the **IBM** personal computer (PC) was introduced, it sold for $2,500. Today the same type of computer sells for much less. Recently, when oil prices rose, the break-even point for airline companies such as **American**, **Southwest**, and **United** rose dramatically. Because of lower prices for imported steel, the demand for domestic steel dropped significantly. The point should be clear: Business conditions change rapidly, and management must respond intelligently to these changes. CVP analysis can help.

To illustrate how CVP analysis can be used in responding to change, we will look at three independent situations that might occur at Vargo Video. Each case is based on the original CD/DVD-player sales and cost data, which were:

Illustration 23-28
Original CD/DVD-player sales and cost data

Unit selling price	$500
Unit variable cost	$300
Total fixed costs	$200,000
Break-even sales	$500,000 or 1,000 units

CASE I.   A competitor is offering a 10% discount on the selling price of its CD/DVD players. Management must decide whether to offer a similar discount. **Question**: What effect will a 10 percent discount on selling price have on the break-even point for the product? **Answer**: A 10 percent discount on selling price reduces the selling price per unit to $450 [$500 − ($500 × 10%)]. Variable costs per unit remain unchanged at $300. Thus, the contribution margin per unit is $150. Assuming no change in fixed costs, break-even sales are 1,333 units, computed as follows.

Fixed Costs	÷	Contribution Margin per Unit	=	Break-even Sales
$200,000	÷	$150	=	1,333 units (rounded)

Illustration 23-29
Computation of break-even sales in units

For Vargo Video, this change would require monthly sales to increase by 333 units, or 33⅓ percent, in order to break even. In reaching a conclusion about offering a 10 percent discount to customers, management must determine how likely it is to achieve the increased sales. Also, management should estimate the possible loss of sales if the competitor's discount price is not matched.

CASE II.   To meet the threat of foreign competition, management invests in new robotic equipment that will lower the amount of direct labor required to make CD/DVD players. It is estimated that total fixed costs will increase 30 percent and that variable cost per unit will decrease 30 percent. **Question**: What effect will the new equipment have on the sales volume required to break even? **Answer**: Total fixed costs become $260,000 [$200,000 + (30% × $200,000)]. The variable cost per unit becomes $210 [$300 − (30% × $300)]. The new break-even point is approximately 900 units, computed as follows.

Fixed Costs	÷	Contribution Margin per Unit	=	Break-even Sales
$260,000	÷	($500 − $210)	=	900 units (rounded)

Illustration 23-30
Computation of break-even sales in units

These changes appear to be advantageous for Vargo Video. The break-even point is reduced by 100 units, or 10 percent.

CASE III.   Vargo's principal supplier of raw materials has just announced a price increase. The higher cost is expected to increase the variable cost of CD/DVD players by $25 per unit. Management would like to hold the line on the selling price of the product. It plans a cost-cutting program that will save $17,500 in fixed costs per month. Vargo is currently realizing monthly net income of $80,000 on sales of 1,400 CD/DVD players. **Question**: What increase in units sold will be needed to maintain the same level of net income? **Answer**: The variable cost per unit increases to $325 ($300 + $25). Fixed costs are reduced to $182,500 ($200,000 − $17,500). Because of the change in variable cost, the contribution margin per unit becomes $175 ($500 − $325). The required number of units sold to achieve the target net income is computed as follows.

Fixed Costs + Target Net Income	÷	Contribution Margin per Unit	=	Required Sales in Units
($182,500 + $80,000)	÷	$175	=	1,500

Illustration 23-31
Computation of required sales in units

To achieve the required sales, 1,500 CD/DVD players will have to be sold, an increase of 100 units. If this does not seem to be a reasonable expectation, management will either have to make further cost reductions or accept less net income if the selling price remains unchanged.

When analyzing an Internet business, the so-called "conversion rate" is closely watched. It is calculated by dividing the number of people who actually take action at an Internet site (e.g., buy something) by the total number of people who visit the site. Average conversion rates are from 3 to 5 percent. A rate below 2 percent is poor, while a rate above 10 percent is great.

Conversion rates have an obvious effect on break-even point. Suppose you spend $10,000 on your site, and you attract 5,000 visitors. If you get a 2 percent conversion rate (100 purchases), your site costs $100 per purchase ($10,000 ÷ 100). A 4 percent conversion rate gets you down to a cost of $50 per transaction, and an 8 percent conversion rate gets you down to $25. Studies have shown that conversion rates increase if the site has an easy-to-use interface, fast-performing screens, a convenient ordering process, and advertising that is both clever and clear.

Source: J. William Gurley, "The One Internet Metric That Really Counts," *Fortune*, March 6, 2000, p. 392.

CVP Income Statement Revisited

STUDY OBJECTIVE 9

Describe the essential features of a cost-volume-profit income statement.

At the beginning of the chapter we presented a simple CVP income statement. When companies prepare a CVP income statement, they provide more detail about specific variable and fixed-cost items.

To illustrate a more detailed CVP income statement, we will assume that Vargo Video reaches its target net income of $120,000 (see Illustration 23-25 on page 947). The following information is obtained on the $680,000 of costs that were incurred in June.

Illustration 23-32
Assumed cost and expense data

	Variable	Fixed	Total
Cost of goods sold	$400,000	$120,000	$520,000
Selling expenses	60,000	40,000	100,000
Administrative expenses	20,000	40,000	60,000
	$480,000	$200,000	$680,000

The detailed CVP income statement for Vargo is shown below.

Illustration 23-33
Detailed CVP income statement

VARGO VIDEO COMPANY
CVP Income Statement
For the Month Ended June 30, 2005

		Total	Per Unit
Sales		$800,000	$500
Variable expenses			
Cost of goods sold	$400,000		
Selling expenses	60,000		
Administrative expenses	20,000		
Total variable expenses		480,000	300
Contribution margin		**320,000**	**$200**
Fixed expenses			
Cost of goods sold	120,000		
Selling expenses	40,000		
Administrative expenses	40,000		
Total fixed expenses		200,000	
Net income		**$120,000**	

BEFORE YOU GO ON...

Review It

1. What is the formula for computing the margin of safety (a) in dollars and (b) as a ratio?
2. What is the equation to compute target net income?

☑ THE NAVIGATOR

DEMONSTRATION PROBLEM 1

Mabo Company makes calculators that sell for $20 each. For the coming year, management expects fixed costs to total $220,000 and variable costs to be $9 per unit.

Instructions

(a) Compute break-even point in units using the mathematical equation.
(b) Compute break-even point in dollars using the contribution margin (CM) ratio.
(c) Compute the margin of safety percentage assuming actual sales are $500,000.
(d) Compute the sales required in dollars to earn net income of $165,000.

SOLUTION TO DEMONSTRATION PROBLEM 1

(a) Sales = Variable costs + Fixed costs + Net income
$$\$20Q = \$9Q + \$220,000 + \$0$$
$$\$11Q = \$220,000$$
$$Q = 20,000 \text{ units}$$

(b) Contribution margin per unit = Unit selling price − Unit variable costs
$$\$11 = \$20 - \$9$$
Contribution margin ratio = Contribution margin per unit ÷ Unit selling price
$$55\% = \$11 \div \$20$$
Break-even point in dollars = Fixed cost ÷ Contribution margin ratio
$$= \$220,000 \div 55\%$$
$$= \$400,000$$

(c) Margin of safety = $\dfrac{\text{Actual sales} - \text{Break-even sales}}{\text{Actual sales}}$

$$= \frac{\$500,000 - \$400,000}{\$500,000}$$

$$= 20\%$$

(d) Required sales = Variable costs + Fixed costs + Net income
$$\$20Q = \$9Q + \$220,000 + \$165,000$$
$$\$11Q = \$385,000$$
$$Q = 35,000 \text{ units}$$
35,000 units × $20 = $700,000 required sales

☑ THE NAVIGATOR

ACTION PLAN

- Know the formulas.
- Recognize that variable costs change with sales volume; fixed costs do not.
- Avoid computational errors.

DEMONSTRATION PROBLEM 2

B.T. Hernandez Company, maker of high-quality flashlights, has experienced steady growth over the last 6 years. However, increased competition has led Mr. Hernandez, the president, to believe that an aggressive campaign is needed next year to maintain the company's present growth. The company's accountant has presented Mr. Hernandez with the following data for the current year, 2005, for use in preparing next year's advertising campaign.

ACTION PLAN

- Know the formulas.
- Recognize that variable costs change with sales volume; fixed costs do not.
- Avoid computational errors.

Cost Schedules

Variable costs	
Direct labor per flashlight	$ 8.00
Direct materials	4.00
Variable overhead	3.00
Variable cost per flashlight	$15.00
Fixed costs	
Manufacturing	$ 25,000
Selling	40,000
Administrative	70,000
Total fixed costs	$135,000
Selling price per flashlight	$25.00
Expected sales, 2005 (20,000 flashlights)	$500,000

Mr. Hernandez has set the sales target for the year 2006 at a level of $550,000 (22,000 flashlights).

Instructions

(Ignore any income tax considerations.)

(a) What is the projected operating income for 2005?

(b) What is the contribution margin per unit for 2005?

(c) What is the break-even point in units for 2005?

(d) Mr. Hernandez believes that to attain the sales target in the year 2006, the company must incur an additional selling expense of $10,000 for advertising in 2006, with all other costs remaining constant. What will be the break-even point in dollar sales for 2006 if the company spends the additional $10,000?

(e) If the company spends the additional $10,000 for advertising in 2006, what is the sales level in dollars required to equal 2005 operating income?

SOLUTION TO DEMONSTRATION PROBLEM 2

(a)

Expected sales		$500,000
Less:		
Variable cost (20,000 flashlights × $15)	300,000	
Fixed costs	135,000	
Projected operating income		$ 65,000

(b)

Selling price per flashlight	$25
Variable cost per flashlight	15
Contribution margin per unit	$10

(c) Fixed costs ÷ Contribution margin per unit = Break-even point in units
$135,000 ÷ $10 = 13,500 units

(d) Fixed costs ÷ Contribution margin ratio = Break-even point in dollars

$145,000 ÷ 40% = $362,500

Fixed costs (from 2005)	$135,000
Additional advertising expense	10,000
Fixed costs (2006)	$145,000

Contribution margin per unit (b) $10
Contribution margin ratio = Contribution margin per unit ÷ Unit selling price
40% = $10 ÷ 25

(e) Required sales = (Fixed costs + Target net income) ÷ Contribution margin ratio

$525,000 = ($145,000 + $65,000) ÷ 40%

☑ THE NAVIGATOR

SUMMARY OF STUDY OBJECTIVES

1. **Distinguish between variable and fixed costs.** Variable costs are costs that vary in total directly and proportionately with changes in the activity index. Fixed costs are costs that remain the same in total regardless of changes in the activity index.

2. **Explain the significance of the relevant range.** The relevant range is the range of activity in which a company expects to operate during a year. It is important in CVP analysis because the behavior of costs is linear throughout the relevant range.

3. **Explain the concept of mixed costs.** Mixed costs increase in total but not proportionately with changes in the activity level. For purposes of CVP analysis, mixed costs must be classified into their fixed and variable elements. One method that management may use is the high-low method.

4. **List the five components of cost-volume-profit analysis.** The five components of CVP analysis are (a) volume or level of activity, (b) unit selling prices, (c) variable cost per unit, (d) total fixed costs, and (e) sales mix.

5. **Indicate what contribution margin is and how it can be expressed.** Contribution margin is the amount of revenue remaining after deducting variable costs. It can be expressed as a per unit amount or as a ratio.

6. **Identify the three ways to determine the break-even point.** The break-even point can be (a) computed from a mathematical equation, (b) computed by using a contribution margin technique, and (c) derived from a CVP graph.

7. **Define margin of safety, and give the formulas for computing it.** Margin of safety is the difference between actual or expected sales and sales at the break-even point. The formulas for margin of safety are: Actual (expected) sales − Break-even sales = Margin of safety in dollars; Margin of safety in dollars ÷ Actual (expected) sales = Margin of safety ratio.

8. **Give the formulas for determining sales required to earn target net income.** One formula is: Required sales = Variable costs + Fixed costs + Target net income. Another formula is: Fixed costs + Target net income ÷ Contribution margin ratio = Required sales.

9. **Describe the essential features of a cost-volume-profit income statement.** The CVP income statement classifies costs and expenses as variable or fixed and reports contribution margin in the body of the statement.

☑ THE NAVIGATOR

GLOSSARY

Activity index The activity that causes changes in the behavior of costs. (p. 933)

Break-even point The level of activity at which total revenues equal total costs. (p. 943)

Contribution margin (CM) The amount of revenue remaining after deducting variable costs. (p. 940)

Contribution margin per unit The amount of revenue remaining per unit after deducting variable costs; calculated as unit selling price minus unit variable cost. (p. 941)

Contribution margin ratio The percentage of each dollar of sales that is available to contribute to net income; calculated as contribution margin per unit divided by unit selling price. (p. 942)

Cost behavior analysis The study of how specific costs respond to changes in the level of business activity. (p. 933)

Cost-volume-profit (CVP) analysis The study of the effects of changes in costs and volume on a company's profits. (p. 940)

Cost-volume-profit (CVP) graph A graph showing the relationship between costs, volume, and profits. (p. 944)

Cost-volume-profit (CVP) income statement A statement for internal use that classifies costs and expenses as fixed or variable and reports contribution margin in the body of the statement. (p. 940)

Fixed costs Costs that remain the same in total regardless of changes in the activity level. (p. 934)

High-low method A mathematical method that uses the total costs incurred at the high and low levels of activity. (p. 938)

Margin of safety The difference between actual or expected sales and sales at the break-even point. (p. 946)

Mixed costs Costs that contain both a variable and a fixed cost element and change in total but not proportionately with changes in the activity level. (p. 937)

Relevant range The range of the activity index over which the company expects to operate during the year. (p. 936)

Target net income The income objective for individual product lines. (p. 947)

Variable costs Costs that vary in total directly and proportionately with changes in the activity level. (p. 934)

APPENDIX VARIABLE COSTING

<table>
<tr><td>

STUDY OBJECTIVE 10

Explain the difference between absorption costing and variable costing.

</td></tr>
</table>

In the earlier chapters, both variable and fixed manufacturing costs have been classified as product costs. In job order costing, for example, a job is assigned the costs of direct materials, direct labor, and both variable and fixed manufacturing overhead. This costing approach is referred to as **full** or **absorption costing**. It is so named because all manufacturing costs are charged to, or absorbed by, the product.

An alternative approach is to use variable costing. Under **variable costing** only direct materials, direct labor, and variable manufacturing overhead costs are considered product costs. Fixed manufacturing overhead costs are recognized as period costs (expenses) when incurred. The difference between absorption costing and variable costing is shown in Illustration 23A-1 as follows.

Illustration 23A-1
Difference between absorption costing and variable costing

Selling and administrative expenses are period costs under both absorption and variable costing.

To illustrate the computation of unit production cost under absorption and variable costing, assume that Premium Products Corporation manufactures a polyurethane sealant called Fix-it for car windshields. Relevant data for Fix-it in January 2005, the first month of production, are as follows.

Illustration 23A-2
Sealant sales and cost data for Premium Products Corporation

Selling price	$20 per unit.
Units	Produced 30,000; sold 20,000; beginning inventory zero.
Variable unit costs	Manufacturing $9 (direct materials $5, direct labor $3, and variable overhead $1). Selling and administrative expenses $2.
Fixed costs	Manufacturing overhead $120,000. Selling and administrative expenses $15,000.

The per unit production cost under each costing approach is:

Type of Cost	Absorption Costing	Variable Costing
Direct materials	$ 5	$5
Direct labor	3	3
Variable manufacturing overhead	1	1
Fixed manufacturing overhead		
($120,000 ÷ 30,000 units produced)	4	0
Total unit cost	**$13**	**$9**

Illustration 23A-3
Computation of per unit production cost

The total unit cost is $4 ($13−$9) higher for absorption costing. This occurs because fixed manufacturing costs are a product cost under absorption costing. They are a period cost under variable costing and so are expensed, instead. Based on these data, each unit sold and each unit remaining in inventory is costed at $13 under absorption costing and at $9 under variable costing.

Effects of Variable Costing on Income

The income statements under the two costing approaches are shown in Illustrations 23A-4 and 23A-5 (page 956). The traditional income statement format is used with absorption costing. The cost-volume-profit format is used with variable costing. Computations are inserted parenthetically in the statements to facilitate your understanding of the amounts.

Income from operations under absorption costing shown in Illustration 23A-4 is $40,000 higher than under variable costing ($85,000 − $45,000) shown in Illustration 23A-5 (page 956).

As highlighted in the two income statements, there is a $40,000 difference in the ending inventories ($130,000 under absorption costing versus $90,000 under variable costing). Under absorption costing, $40,000 of the fixed overhead costs (10,000 units × $4) has been deferred to a future period as a product cost. In contrast, under variable costing the entire fixed manufacturing costs are expensed when incurred.

Illustration 23A-4
Absorption costing income statement

PREMIUM PRODUCTS CORPORATION		
Income Statement		
For the Month Ended January 31, 2005		
(Absorption Costing)		
Sales (20,000 units × $20)		$400,000
Cost of goods sold		
Inventory, January 1	$ –0–	
Cost of goods manufactured (30,000 units × $13)	390,000	
Cost of goods available for sale	390,000	
Inventory, January 31 (10,000 units × $13)	**130,000**	
Cost of goods sold (20,000 units × $13)		260,000
Gross profit		140,000
Selling and administrative expenses		
(Variable 20,000 units × $2 + fixed $15,000)		55,000
Income from operations		**$ 85,000**

HELPFUL HINT

This is the traditional statement that would result from job order and processing costing explained in Chapters 21 and 22.

Illustration 23A-5
Variable costing income statement

PREMIUM PRODUCTS CORPORATION		
Income Statement		
For the Month Ended January 31, 2005		
(Variable Costing)		
Sales (20,000 units × $20)		$400,000
Variable expenses		
Variable cost of goods sold		
Inventory, January 1	$ –0–	
Variable manufacturing costs (30,000 units × $9)	270,000	
Cost of goods available for sale	270,000	
Inventory, January 31 (10,000 units × $9)	**90,000**	
Variable cost of goods sold	180,000	
Variable selling and administrative expenses		
(20,000 units × $2)	40,000	
Total variable expenses		220,000
Contribution margin		180,000
Fixed expenses		
Manufacturing overhead	120,000	
Selling and administrative expenses	15,000	
Total fixed expenses		135,000
Income from operations		**$ 45,000**

HELPFUL HINT

Note the difference in the computation of the ending inventory: $9 per unit here, $13 per unit in Illustration 23A-4.

As shown, when units produced exceed units sold, income under absorption costing is higher. When units produced are less than units sold, income under absorption costing is lower.

When units produced and sold are the same, income from operations will be equal under the two costing approaches. In this case, there is no increase in ending inventory. So fixed overhead costs of the current period are not deferred to future periods through the ending inventory.

The foregoing effects of the two costing approaches on income from operations may be summarized as follows.

Illustration 23A-6
Summary of income effects

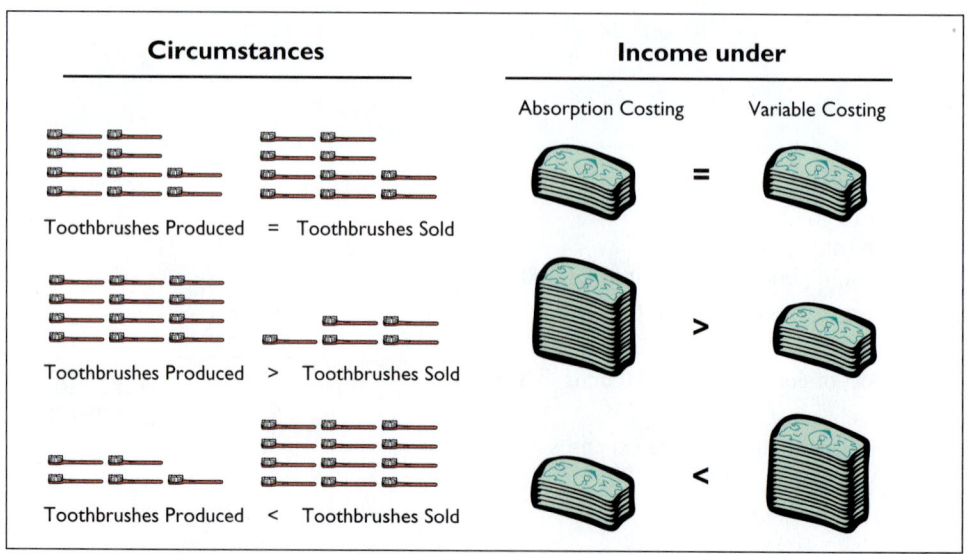

Rationale for Variable Costing

The rationale for variable costing centers on the purpose of fixed manufacturing costs. That purpose is **to have productive facilities available for use**. These costs are incurred whether a company operates at zero or at 100 percent of capacity. Thus, proponents of variable costing argue that these costs should be expensed in the period in which they are incurred.

Supporters of absorption costing defend the assignment of fixed manufacturing overhead costs to inventory. They say that these costs are as much a cost of getting a product ready for sale as direct materials or direct labor. Accordingly, these costs should not be matched with revenues until the product is sold.

The use of variable costing is acceptable **only for internal use by management**. It cannot be used in determining product costs in financial statements prepared in accordance with generally accepted accounting principles because it understates inventory costs. To comply with the matching principle, a company must use absorption costing for its work in process and finished goods inventories. Similarly, absorption costing must be used for income tax purposes.

SUMMARY OF STUDY OBJECTIVE FOR APPENDIX

10. **Explain the difference between absorption costing and variable costing.** Under absorption costing, fixed manufacturing costs are product costs. Under variable costing, fixed manufacturing costs are period costs.

GLOSSARY FOR APPENDIX

Absorption costing A costing approach in which all manufacturing costs are charged to the product. (p. 954)

Variable costing A costing approach in which only variable manufacturing costs are product costs, and fixed manufacturing costs are period costs (expenses). (p. 954)

*__Note__: All **asterisked** Questions, Exercises, and Problems relate to material in the appendix to the chapter.

SELF-STUDY QUESTIONS

Self-Study/Self-Test

Answers are at the end of the chapter.

(SO 1) **1.** Variable costs are costs that:
   a. vary in total directly and proportionately with changes in the activity level.
   b. remain the same per unit at every activity level.
   c. Neither of the above.
   d. Both (a) and (b) above.

(SO 2) **2.** The relevant range is:
   a. the range of activity in which variable costs will be curvilinear.
   b. the range of activity in which fixed costs will be curvilinear.
   c. the range over which the company expects to operate during a year.
   d. usually from zero to 100% of operating capacity.

3. Mixed costs consist of a: (SO 3)
   a. variable cost element and a fixed cost element.
   b. fixed cost element and a controllable cost element.
   c. relevant cost element and a controllable cost element.
   d. variable cost element and a relevant cost element.

4. One of the following is *not* involved in CVP analysis.   (SO 4)
   That factor is:
   a. sales mix.
   b. unit selling prices.
   c. fixed costs per unit.
   d. volume or level of activity.

5. Contribution margin: (SO 5)
   a. is revenue remaining after deducting variable costs.
   b. may be expressed as contribution margin per unit.
   c. is selling price less cost of goods sold.
   d. Both (a) and (b) above.

(SO 6)   **6.** Gossen Company is planning to sell 200,000 pliers for $4 per unit. The contribution margin ratio is 25%. If Gossen will break even at this level of sales, what are the fixed costs?
   a. $100,000.
   b. $160,000.
   c. $200,000.
   d. $300,000.

(SO 7)   **7.** Marshall Company had actual sales of $600,000 when break-even sales were $420,000. What is the margin of safety ratio?
   a. 25%.   **c.** 33⅓%.
   b. 30%.   **d.** 45%.

(SO 8)   **8.** The mathematical equation for computing required sales to obtain target net income is: Required sales =
   a. Variable costs + Target net income.
   b. Variable costs + Fixed costs + Target net income.
   c. Fixed costs + Target net income.
   d. No correct answer is given.

9. Cournot Company sells 100,000 wrenches for $12 a unit.   (SO
Fixed costs are $300,000, and net income is $200,000. What should be reported as variable expenses in the CVP income statement?
   a. $700,000.   **c.** $500,000.
   b. $900,000.   **d.** $1,000,000.

*10. Under variable costing, fixed manufacturing costs are   (SO
classified as:
   a. period costs.
   b. product costs.
   c. both (a) and (b).
   d. neither (a) nor (b).

QUESTIONS

1. (a) What is cost behavior analysis?
   (b) Why is cost behavior analysis important to management?

2. (a) Marti Abair asks your help in understanding the term "activity index." Explain the meaning and importance of this term for Marti.
   (b) State the two ways that variable costs may be defined.

3. Contrast the effects of changes in the activity level on total fixed costs and on unit fixed costs.

4. F. X. Rodriguez claims that the relevant range concept is important only for variable costs.
   (a) Explain the relevant range concept.
   (b) Do you agree with F.X.'s claim? Explain.

5. "The relevant range is indispensable in cost behavior analysis." Is this true? Why or why not?

6. Eric Sautbine is confused. He does not understand why rent on his apartment is a fixed cost and rent on a Hertz rental truck is a mixed cost. Explain the difference to Eric.

7. How should mixed costs be classified in CVP analysis? What approach is used to effect the appropriate classification?

8. At the high and low levels of activity during the month, direct labor hours are 90,000 and 40,000, respectively. The related costs are $180,000 and $100,000. What are the fixed and variable costs at any level of activity?

9. "Cost-volume-profit (CVP) analysis is based entirely on unit costs." Do you agree? Explain.

10. Sara Maas defines contribution margin as the amount of profit available to cover operating expenses. Is there any truth in this definition? Discuss.

11. Lomas Company's Speedo pocket calculator sells for $40. Variable costs per unit are estimated to be $22. What are the contribution margin per unit and the contribution margin ratio?

12. "Break-even analysis is of limited use to management because a company cannot survive by just breaking even." Do you agree? Explain.

13. Total fixed costs are $22,000 for Ewig Inc. It has a contribution margin per unit of $15, and a contribution margin ratio of 25%. Compute the break-even sales in dollars.

14. Julie Zuniga asks your help in constructing a CVP graph. Explain to Julie (a) how the break-even point is plotted, and (b) how the level of activity and dollar sales at the break-even point are determined.

15. Define the term "margin of safety." If Rypel Company expects to sell 1,600 units of its product at $12 per unit, and break-even sales for the product are $12,000, what is the margin of safety ratio?

16. Kujawa Company's break-even sales are $600,000. Assuming fixed costs are $240,000, what sales volume is needed to achieve a target net income of $60,000?

17. The traditional income statement for Prosen Company shows sales $900,000, cost of goods sold $600,000, and operating expenses $200,000. Assuming all costs and expenses are 70% variable and 30% fixed, prepare a CVP income statement through contribution margin.

*18. Distinguish between absorption costing and variable costing.

*19. (a) What is the major rationale for the use of variable costing? (b) Discuss why variable costing may not be used for financial reporting purposes.

BRIEF EXERCISES

BE23-1 Monthly production costs in Ribarchek Company for two levels of production are as follows.

Cost	3,000 units	6,000 units
Indirect labor	$10,000	$20,000
Supervisory salaries	5,000	5,000
Maintenance	4,000	6,000

Classify costs as variable, fixed, or mixed.
(SO 1, 3)

Indicate which costs are variable, fixed, and mixed, and give the reason for each answer.

BE23-2 For Kutil Company, the relevant range of production is 40–80% of capacity. At 40% of capacity, a variable cost is $2,000 and a fixed cost is $6,000. Diagram the behavior of each cost within the relevant range assuming the behavior is linear.

Diagram the behavior of costs within the relevant range.
(SO 2)

BE23-3 For Biro Company, a mixed cost is $40,000 plus $16 per direct labor hour. Diagram the behavior of the cost using increments of 500 hours up to 2,500 hours on the horizontal axis and increments of $20,000 up to $80,000 on the vertical axis.

Diagram the behavior of a mixed cost.
(SO 3)

BE23-4 Favero Company accumulates the following data concerning a mixed cost, using miles as the activity level.

	Miles Driven	Total Cost		Miles Driven	Total Cost
January	8,000	$14,150	March	8,500	$15,000
February	7,500	13,300	April	8,200	14,490

Determine variable and fixed cost elements using the high-low method.
(SO 3)

Compute the variable and fixed cost elements using the high-low method.

BE23-5 Determine the missing amounts.

	Unit Selling Price	Unit Variable Costs	Contribution Margin per Unit	Contribution Margin Ratio
1.	$250	$160	(a)	(b)
2.	$500	(c)	$200	(d)
3.	(e)	(f)	$360	30%

Determine missing amounts for contribution margin.
(SO 5)

BE23-6 Minot Company has a unit selling price of $400, variable costs per unit of $260, and fixed costs of $168,000. Compute the break-even point in units using (a) the mathematical equation and (b) contribution margin per unit.

Compute the break-even point.
(SO 6)

BE23-7 For Ehlers Company actual sales are $1,400,000 and break-even sales are $900,000. Compute (a) the margin of safety in dollars and (b) the margin of safety ratio.

Compute the margin of safety and the margin of safety ratio.
(SO 7)

BE23-8 For Niezgoda Company, variable costs are 70% of sales, and fixed costs are $180,000. Management's net income goal is $60,000. Compute the required sales needed to achieve management's target net income of $60,000. (Use the mathematical equation approach.)

Compute sales for target net income.
(SO 8)

BE23-9 Ojeda Manufacturing Inc. has sales of $1,900,000 for the first quarter of 2005. In making the sales, the company incurred the following costs and expenses.

	Variable	Fixed
Cost of goods sold	$760,000	$540,000
Selling expenses	95,000	60,000
Administrative expenses	79,000	66,000

Prepare CVP income statement.
(SO 9)

Prepare a CVP income statement for the quarter ended March 31, 2005.

Compute net income under absorption and variable costing.

(SO 10)

*BE23-10 Houk Company's fixed overhead costs are $4 per unit, and its variable overhead costs are $8 per unit. In the first month of operations, 50,000 units are produced, and 47,000 units are sold. Write a short memo to the chief financial officer explaining which costing approach will produce the higher income and what the difference will be.

EXERCISES

Define and classify variable, fixed, and mixed costs.

(SO 1, 3)

E23-1 Enk Company manufactures a single product. Annual production costs incurred in the manufacturing process are shown below for two levels of production.

	Costs Incurred			
Production in Units	**5,000**		**10,000**	
Production Costs	**Total Cost**	**Cost/ Unit**	**Total Cost**	**Cost/ Unit**
Direct materials	$8,250	$1.65	$16,500	$1.65
Direct labor	9,500	1.90	19,000	1.90
Utilities	1,500	0.30	2,500	0.25
Rent	4,000	0.80	4,000	0.40
Maintenance	800	0.16	1,100	0.11
Supervisory salaries	1,000	0.20	1,000	0.10

Instructions
(a) Define the terms variable costs, fixed costs, and mixed costs.
(b) Classify each cost above as either variable, fixed, or mixed.

Determine fixed and variable costs using the high-low method and prepare graph.

(SO 1, 3)

E23-2 The controller of Bluhm Industries has collected the following monthly expense data for use in analyzing the cost behavior of maintenance costs.

Month	Total Maintenance Costs	Total Machine Hours
January	$2,900	300
February	3,000	400
March	3,600	600
April	4,500	790
May	3,200	500
June	4,900	800

Instructions
(a) Determine the fixed and variable cost components using the high-low method.
(b) Prepare a graph showing the behavior of maintenance costs, and identify the fixed and variable cost elements. Use 200 unit increments and $1,000 cost increments.

Compute contribution margin, break-even point, and margin of safety.

(SO 5, 6, 7)

E23-3 In the month of June, Mandeep's Beauty Salon gave 2,700 haircuts, shampoos, and permanents at an average price of $30. During the month, fixed costs were $18,000 and variable costs were 75% of sales.

Instructions
(a) Determine the contribution margin in dollars, per unit, and as a ratio.
(b) Using the contribution margin technique, compute the break-even point in dollars and in units.
(c) Compute the margin of safety in dollars and as a ratio.

Prepare a CVP graph and compute break-even point and margin of safety.

(SO 6, 7)

E23-4 Eisling Company estimates that variable costs will be 50% of sales, and fixed costs will total $800,000. The selling price of the product is $4.

Instructions
(a) Prepare a CVP graph, assuming maximum sales of $3,200,000. (*Note*: Use $400,000 increments for sales and costs and 100,000 increments for units.)

(b) Compute the break-even point in (1) units and (2) dollars.
(c) Compute the margin of safety in (1) dollars and (2) as a ratio, assuming actual sales are $2.4 million.

E23-5 In 2005, Filipak Company had a break-even point of $350,000 based on a selling price of $7 per unit and fixed costs of $140,000. In 2006, the selling price and the variable cost per unit did not change, but the break-even point increased to $420,000.

Compute variable cost per unit, contribution margin ratio, and increase in fixed costs.

(SO 5)

Instructions
(a) Compute the variable cost per unit and the contribution margin ratio for 2005.
(b) Compute the increase in fixed costs for 2006.

E23-6 Jung Company had $150,000 of net income in 2005 when the selling price per unit was $150, the variable costs per unit were $90, and the fixed costs were $750,000. Management expects per unit data and total fixed costs to remain the same in 2006. The president of Jung Company is under pressure from stockholders to increase net income by $90,000 in 2006.

Compute various components to derive target net income under different assumptions.

(SO 6, 8)

Instructions
(a) Compute the number of units sold in 2005.
(b) Compute the number of units that would have to be sold in 2006 to reach the stockholders' desired profit level.
(c) Assume that Jung Company sells the same number of units in 2006 as it did in 2005. What would the selling price have to be in order to reach the stockholders' desired profit level?

E23-7 Gonyo Company reports the following operating results for the month of August: Sales $320,000 (units 5,000); variable costs $210,000; and fixed costs $90,000. Management is considering the following independent courses of action to increase net income.

Compute net income under different alternatives.

(SO 8)

1. Increase selling price by 10% with no change in total variable costs.
2. Reduce variable costs to 65% of sales.
3. Reduce fixed costs by $10,000.

Instructions
Compute the net income to be earned under each alternative. Which course of action will produce the highest net income?

E23-8 Hrubec Company had sales in 2005 of $1,500,000 on 60,000 units. Variable costs totaled $720,000, and fixed costs totaled $500,000.

Prepare a CVP income statement before and after changes in business environment.

(SO 9)

A new raw material is available that will decrease the variable costs per unit by 20% (or $2.40). However, to process the new raw material, fixed operating costs will increase by $60,000. Management feels that one-half of the decline in the variable costs per unit should be passed on to customers in the form of a sales price reduction. The marketing department expects that this sales price reduction will result in a 7% increase in the number of units sold.

Instructions
Prepare a CVP income statement for 2005, assuming the changes are made as described.

*E23-9 Waala Equipment Company manufactures and distributes industrial air compressors. The following costs are available for the year ended December 31, 2005. The company has no beginning inventory. In 2005, 1,500 units were produced, but only 1,300 units were sold. The unit selling price was $4,500. Costs and expenses were:

Compute total product cost and prepare an income statement using variable costing.

(SO 10)

Variable costs per unit	
Direct materials	$ 800
Direct labor	1,500
Variable manufacturing overhead	300
Variable selling and administrative expenses	70
Annual fixed costs and expenses	
Manufacturing overhead	$1,300,000
Selling and administrative expenses	100,000

Instructions
(a) Compute the manufacturing cost of one unit of product using variable costing.
(b) Prepare a 2005 income statement for Waala Company using variable costing.

PROBLEMS: SET A

Determine variable and fixed costs, compute break-even point, prepare a CVP graph, and determine net income.

(SO 1, 3, 5, 6)

P23-1A The Campus Barber Shop employs four barbers. One barber, who also serves as the manager, is paid a salary of $2,200 per month. The other barbers are paid $1,400 per month. In addition, each barber is paid a commission of $4 per haircut. Other monthly costs are: store rent $700 plus 60 cents per haircut, depreciation on equipment $500, barber supplies 40 cents per haircut, utilities $300, and advertising $100. The price of a haircut is $10.

Instructions
(a) Determine the variable cost per haircut and the total monthly fixed costs.
(b) Compute the break-even point in units and dollars.
(c) Prepare a CVP graph, assuming a maximum of 1,800 haircuts in a month. Use increments of 300 haircuts on the horizontal axis and $3,000 increments on the vertical axis.
(d) Determine the net income, assuming 1,700 haircuts are given in a month.

Prepare a CVP income statement, compute break-even point, contribution margin ratio, margin of safety ratio, and sales for target net income.

(SO 5, 6, 7, 8, 9)

P23-2A Rosen Company bottles and distributes No-FIZZ, a fruit drink. The beverage is sold for 50 cents per 16-ounce bottle to retailers, who charge customers 70 cents per bottle. For the year 2005, management estimates the following revenues and costs.

Net sales	$2,000,000	Selling expenses—variable	$ 100,000
Direct materials	360,000	Selling expenses—fixed	150,000
Direct labor	670,000	Administrative expenses—	
Manufacturing overhead—		variable	40,000
variable	270,000	Administrative expenses—	
Manufacturing overhead—		fixed	50,000
fixed	220,000		

Instructions
(a) Prepare a CVP income statement for 2005 based on management's estimates.
(b) Compute the break-even point in (1) units and (2) dollars.
(c) Compute the contribution margin ratio and the margin of safety ratio.
(d) Determine the sales dollars required to earn net income of $196,000.

Compute break-even point under alternative courses of action.

(SO 5, 6)

P23-3A Galati Manufacturing had a bad year in 2005. For the first time in its history it operated at a loss. The company's income statement showed the following results from selling 60,000 units of product: Net sales $1,500,000; total costs and expenses $1,740,000; and net loss $240,000. Costs and expenses consisted of the following.

	Total	Variable	Fixed
Cost of goods sold	$1,200,000	$780,000	$420,000
Selling expenses	420,000	65,000	355,000
Administrative expenses	120,000	55,000	65,000
	$1,740,000	$900,000	$840,000

Management is considering the following independent alternatives for 2006.

1. Increase unit selling price 20% with no change in costs, expenses, and sales volume.
2. Change the compensation of salespersons from fixed annual salaries totaling $200,000 to total salaries of $30,000 plus a 6% commission on net sales.
3. Purchase new high-tech factory machinery that will change the proportion between variable and fixed cost of goods sold to 50:50.

Instructions
(a) Compute the break-even point in dollars for 2005.
(b) Compute the break-even point in dollars under each of the alternative courses of action. Which course of action do you recommend?

Compute break-even point and margin of safety ratio, and prepare a CVP income statement before and after changes in business environment.

(SO 6, 7, 9)

P23-4A Mimi Tomchek is the advertising manager for Thrifty Shoe Store. She is currently working on a major promotional campaign. Her ideas include the installation of a new lighting system and increased display space that will add $32,000 in fixed costs to the $238,000 currently spent. In addition, Mimi is proposing that a 6⅔% price decrease (from $30 to $28) will produce an increase in sales volume from 17,000 to 21,000 units. Variable costs will remain at $13 per pair of shoes. Management is impressed with Mimi's ideas but concerned about the effects that these changes will have on the break-even point and the margin of safety.

Instructions
(a) Compute the current break-even point in units, and compare it to the break-even point in units if Mimi's ideas are used.
(b) Compute the margin of safety ratio for current operations and after Mimi's changes are introduced. (Round to nearest full percent.)
(c) Prepare a CVP income statement for current operations and after Mimi's changes are introduced. Would you make the changes suggested?

*P23-5A Zilles Metal Company produces the steel wire that goes into the production of paper clips. In 2005, the first year of operations, Zilles produced 50,000 miles of wire and sold 40,000 miles. In 2006, the production and sales results were exactly reversed. In each year, selling price per mile was $80, variable manufacturing costs were 25% of the sales price, variable selling expenses were $7.00 per mile sold, fixed manufacturing costs were $1,200,000, and fixed administrative expenses were $230,000.

Prepare income statements under absorption and variable costing.

(SO 10)

Instructions
(a) Prepare comparative income statements for each year using variable costing.
(b) Prepare comparative income statements for each year using absorption costing.
(c) Reconcile the differences each year in income from operations under the two costing approaches.
(d) Comment on the effects of production and sales on net income under the two costing approaches.

PROBLEMS: SET B

P23-1B Doug Stahl owns the Somonauk Barber Shop. He employs five barbers and pays each a base rate of $1,200 per month. One of the barbers serves as the manager and receives an extra $500 per month. In addition to the base rate, each barber also receives a commission of $3.50 per haircut.

   Other costs are as follows.

Determine variable and fixed costs, compute break-even point, prepare a CVP graph, and determine net income.

(SO 1, 3, 5, 6)

Advertising	$200 per month
Rent	$900 per month
Barber supplies	$0.30 per haircut
Utilities	$175 per month plus $0.20 per haircut
Magazines	$25 per month

Doug currently charges $10 per haircut.

Instructions
(a) Determine the variable cost per haircut and the total monthly fixed costs.
(b) Compute the break-even point in units and dollars.
(c) Prepare a CVP graph, assuming a maximum of 1,800 haircuts in a month. Use increments of 300 haircuts on the horizontal axis and $3,000 on the vertical axis.
(d) Determine net income, assuming 1,600 haircuts are given in a month.

P23-2B Tritz Company bottles and distributes Livit, a diet soft drink. The beverage is sold for 50 cents per 16-ounce bottle to retailers, who charge customers 75 cents per bottle. For the year 2005, management estimates the following revenues and costs.

Prepare a CVP income statement, compute break-even point, contribution margin ratio, margin of safety ratio, and sales for target net income.

(SO 5, 6, 7, 8, 9)

Net sales	$1,800,000	Selling expenses—variable	$70,000
Direct materials	430,000	Selling expenses—fixed	65,000
Direct labor	280,000	Administrative expenses—	
Manufacturing overhead—		variable	20,000
variable	316,000	Administrative expenses—	
Manufacturing overhead—		fixed	51,000
fixed	283,000		

Instructions

(a) Prepare a CVP income statement for 2005 based on management's estimates.

(b) Compute the break-even point in (1) units and (2) dollars.

(c) Compute the contribution margin ratio and the margin of safety ratio. (Round to full percents.)

(d) Determine the sales dollars required to earn net income of $190,000.

Compute break-even point under alternative courses of action.

(SO 5, 6)

P23-3B Cusick manufacturing's sales slumped badly in 2005. For the first time in its history, it operated at a loss. The company's income statement showed the following results from selling 600,000 units of product: Net sales $2,400,000; total costs and expenses $2,600,000; and net loss $200,000. Costs and expenses consisted of the following.

	Total	Variable	Fixed
Cost of goods sold	$2,100,000	$1,440,000	$ 660,000
Selling expenses	300,000	72,000	228,000
Administrative expenses	200,000	48,000	152,000
	$2,600,000	$1,560,000	$1,040,000

Management is considering the following independent alternatives for 2006.

1. Increase unit selling price 20% with no change in costs, expenses, and sales volume.

2. Change the compensation of salespersons from fixed annual salaries totaling $210,000 to total salaries of $60,000 plus a 5% commission on net sales.

3. Purchase new automated equipment that will change the proportion between variable and fixed cost of goods sold to 54% variable and 46% fixed.

Instructions

(a) Compute the break-even point in dollars for 2005.

(b) Compute the break-even point in dollars under each of the alternative courses of action. (Round to nearest full percent.) Which course of action do you recommend?

Compute break-even point and margin of safety ratio, and prepare a CVP income statement before and after changes in business environment.

(SO 6, 7, 9)

P23-4B Laura Benavente is the advertising manager for Value Shoe Store. She is currently working on a major promotional campaign. Her ideas include the installation of a new lighting system and increased display space that will add $32,000 in fixed costs to the $288,000 currently spent. In addition, Laura is proposing that a 5% price decrease ($40 to $38) will produce a 20% increase in sales volume (20,000 to 24,000). Variable costs will remain at $22 per pair of shoes. Management is impressed with Laura's ideas but concerned about the effects that these changes will have on the break-even point and the margin of safety.

Instructions

(a) Compute the current break-even point in units, and compare it to the break-even point in units if Laura's ideas are used.

(b) Compute the margin of safety ratio for current operations and after Laura's changes are introduced. (Round to nearest full percent.)

(c) Prepare a CVP income statement for current operations and after Laura's changes are introduced. Would you make the changes suggested?

Prepare income statements under absorption and variable costing.

(SO 10)

*P23-5B** KDS produces plastic that is used for injection molding applications such as gears for small motors. In 2005, the first year of operations, KDS produced 6,000 tons of plastic and sold 5,000 tons. In 2006, the production and sales results were exactly reversed. In each year, selling price per ton was $2,000, variable manufacturing costs were 15% of the sales price of units produced, variable selling expenses were 10% of the selling price of units sold, fixed manufacturing costs were $2,400,000, and fixed administrative expenses were $500,000.

Instructions

(a) Prepare comparative income statements for each year using variable costing.

(b) Prepare comparative income statements for each year using absorption costing.

(c) Reconcile the differences each year in income from operations under the two costing approaches.

(d) Comment on the effects of production and sales on net income under the two costing approaches.

BROADENING YOUR PERSPECTIVE

Group Decision Case

BYP23-1 Costello Company has decided to introduce a new product. The new product can be manufactured by either a capital-intensive method or a labor-intensive method. The manufacturing method will not affect the quality of the product. The estimated manufacturing costs by the two methods are as follows.

	Capital-Intensive	Labor-Intensive
Direct materials	$5 per unit	$5.50 per unit
Direct labor	$6 per unit	$7.20 per unit
Variable overhead	$3 per unit	$4.50 per unit
Fixed manufacturing costs	$2,508,000	$1,538,000

Costello's market research department has recommended an introductory unit sales price of $30. The incremental selling expenses are estimated to be $460,000 annually plus $2 for each unit sold, regardless of manufacturing method.

Instructions

With the class divided into groups, answer the following.

(a) Calculate the estimated break-even point in annual unit sales of the new product if Costello Company uses the:
  (1) capital-intensive manufacturing method.
  (2) labor-intensive manufacturing method.
(b) Determine the annual unit sales volume at which Costello Company would be indifferent between the two manufacturing methods.
(c) Explain the circumstance under which Costello should employ each of the two manufacturing methods.

(CMA adapted)

Managerial Analysis

BYP23-2 The condensed income statement for the Randi and Sandy partnership for 2005 is as follows.

RANDI AND SANDY COMPANY
Income Statement
For the Year Ended December 31, 2005

Sales (200,000 units)		$1,200,000
Cost of goods sold		800,000
Gross profit		400,000
Operating expenses		
Selling	$320,000	
Administrative	160,000	480,000
Net loss		($80,000)

A cost behavior analysis indicates that 75% of the cost of goods sold are variable, 50% of the selling expenses are variable, and 25% of the administrative expenses are variable.

Instructions

(Round to nearest unit, dollar, and percentage, where necessary. Use the CVP income statement format in computing profits.)

(a) Compute the break-even point in total sales dollars and in units for 2005.
(b) Randi has proposed a plan to get the partnership "out of the red" and improve its profitability. She feels that the quality of the product could be substantially improved by

spending $0.55 more per unit on better raw materials. The selling price per unit could be increased to only $6.50 because of competitive pressures. Randi estimates that sales volume will increase by 30%. What effect would Randi's plan have on the profits and the break-even point in dollars of the partnership?

(c) Sandy was a marketing major in college. He believes that sales volume can be increased only by intensive advertising and promotional campaigns. He therefore proposed the following plan as an alternative to Randi's. (1) Increase variable selling expenses to $0.90 per unit, (2) lower the selling price per unit by $0.25, and (3) increase fixed selling expenses by $25,000. Sandy quoted an old marketing research report that said that sales volume would increase by 60% if these changes were made. What effect would Sandy's plan have on the profits and the break-even point in dollars of the partnership?

(d) Which plan should be accepted? Explain your answer.

Real-World Focus

BYP23-3 The Coca-Cola Company hardly needs an introduction. A line taken from the cover of a recent annual report says it all: If you measured time in servings of Coca-Cola, "a billion Coca-Cola's ago was yesterday morning." On average, every U.S. citizen drinks 363 8-ounce servings of Coca-Cola products each year. Coca-Cola's primary line of business is the making and selling of syrup to bottlers. These bottlers then sell the finished bottles and cans of Coca-Cola to the consumer.

In the annual report of Coca-Cola, the following information was provided.

THE COCA-COLA COMPANY
Management Discussion

Our gross margin declined to 61 percent this year from 62 percent in the prior year, primarily due to costs for materials such as sweeteners and packaging.

The increases [in selling expenses] in the last two years were primarily due to higher marketing expenditures in support of our Company's volume growth.

We measure our sales volume in two ways: (1) gallon shipments of concentrates and syrups and (2) unit cases of finished product (bottles and cans of Coke sold by bottlers).

Instructions

Answer the following questions.

(a) Are sweeteners and packaging a variable cost or a fixed cost? What is the impact on the contribution margin of an increase in the per unit cost of sweeteners or packaging? What are the implications for profitability?

(b) In your opinion, are marketing expenditures a fixed cost, variable cost, or mixed cost to The Coca-Cola Company? Give justification for your answer.

(c) Which of the two measures cited for measuring volume represents the activity index as defined in this chapter? Why might Coca-Cola use two different measures?

Exploring the Web

BYP23-4 Ganong Bros. Ltd., located in St. Stephen, New Brunswick, is Canada's oldest independent candy company. Its products are distributed worldwide. In 1885, Ganong invented the popular "chicken bone," a cinnamon flavored, pink, hard candy jacket over a chocolate center. The home page of Ganong, listed below, includes information about the company and its products.

Address: www.ganong.com/index.cfm?section=3&page=10, or go to www.wiley.com/college/weygandt

Instructions

Read the description of "chicken bones," and answer the following.

(a) Describe the steps in making "chicken bones."

(b) Identify at least two variable and two fixed costs that are likely to affect the production of "chicken bones."

Communication Activity

BYP23-5 Your roommate asks your help on the following questions about CVP analysis formulas.

(a) How can the mathematical equation for break-even sales show both sales units and sales dollars?

(b) How do the formulas differ for contribution margin per unit and contribution margin ratio?

(c) How can contribution margin be used to determine break-even sales in units and in dollars?

Instructions

Write a memo to your roommate stating the relevant formulas and answering each question.

Ethics Case

BYP23-6 Robby Doggett is an accountant for Millott Company. Early this year Robby made a highly favorable projection of sales and profits over the next 3 years for Millott hot-selling computer PLEX. As a result of the projections Robby presented to senior management, they decided to expand production in this area. This decision led to dislocations of some plant personnel who were reassigned to one of the company's newer plants in another state. However, no one was fired, and in fact the company expanded its work force slightly.

Unfortunately Robby rechecked his computations on the projections a few months later and found that he had made an error that would have reduced his projections substantially. Luckily, sales of PLEX have exceeded projections so far, and management is satisfied with its decision. Robby, however, is not sure what to do. Should he confess his honest mistake and jeopardize his possible promotion? He suspects that no one will catch the error because sales of PLEX have exceeded his projections, and it appears that profits will materialize close to his projections.

Instructions

(a) Who are the stakeholders in this situation?

(b) Identify the ethical issues involved in this situation.

(c) What are the possible alternative actions for Robby? What would you do in Robby's position?

Answers to Self-Study Questions

1. d   **2.** c   **3.** a   **4.** c   **5.** d   **6.** c   **7.** b   **8.** b   **9.** a   **10.** a

 ✓ **REMEMBER** to go back to the Navigator box on the chapter-opening page and check off your completed work.

Budgetary Planning

CONCEPTS FOR REVIEW

Before studying this chapter, you should know or, if necessary, review:

The meaning of the management function of planning.
(Ch. 20, p. 819)

The difference between variable costs and fixed costs.
(Ch. 23, pp. 934–938)

The Next Amazon.Com? Not Quite

The bursting of the dot-com bubble resulted in countless stories of dot-com failures. Many of these ventures were half-baked, get-rich-quick schemes, rarely based on sound business practices. Initially they saw money flowing in faster than they knew what to do with—which was precisely the problem. Without proper planning and budgeting, much of the money went to waste. In some cases, failure was actually brought on by rapid, uncontrolled growth.

One such example was the Web site www.PositivelyYou.com, an online discount bookseller. One of the co-founders, Lyle Bowline, had never run a business. However, his experience as an assistant director of an entrepreneurial center had provided him with knowledge

about the do's and don'ts of small business. To minimize costs, he started the company off small and simple. He invested $5,000 in computer equipment and ran the business out of his basement. In the early months, even though sales were only about $2,000 a month, the company actually made a profit because it kept its costs low (a feat few other dot-coms could boast of).

Things changed dramatically when the company received national publicity in the financial press. Suddenly the company's sales increased to $50,000 a month—fully 25 times the previous level. The "simple" little business suddenly needed a business plan, a strategic plan, and a budget. It needed to rent office space and to hire employees. Initially, members of a local book club donated time to help meet the sudden demand. But quickly the number of paid employees ballooned. The sudden growth necessitated detailed planning and budgeting. The need for a proper budget was accentuated by the fact that the company's gross profit was only 16 cents on each dollar of goods sold. This meant that after paying for its inventory, the company had only 16 cents of every dollar to cover its remaining operating costs.

Unfortunately, the company never got things under control. Within a few months, sales had plummeted to $12,000 per month. At this level of sales the company could not meet the mountain of monthly expenses that it had accumulated in trying to grow. Ironically, the company's sudden success, and the turmoil it created, appears to have been what eventually caused the company to fail.

THE NAVIGATOR

After studying this chapter, you should be able to:

1. Indicate the benefits of budgeting.
2. State the essentials of effective budgeting.
3. Identify the budgets that comprise the master budget.
4. Describe the sources for preparing the budgeted income statement.
5. Explain the principal sections of a cash budget.
6. Indicate the applicability of budgeting in nonmanufacturing companies.

THE NAVIGATOR

Budgeting is an integral part of our society. As a student, you budget your study time and your money. Families budget income and expenses. Governmental agencies budget revenues and expenditures. As the Feature Story about PositivelyYou.com indicates, business enterprises use budgets in planning and controlling their operations.

Our primary focus in this chapter is budgeting—specifically, how budgeting is used as a *planning tool* by management. Through budgeting, it should be possible for management to maintain enough cash to pay creditors, to have sufficient raw materials to meet production requirements, and to have adequate finished goods to meet expected sales.

The content and organization of Chapter 24 are as follows.

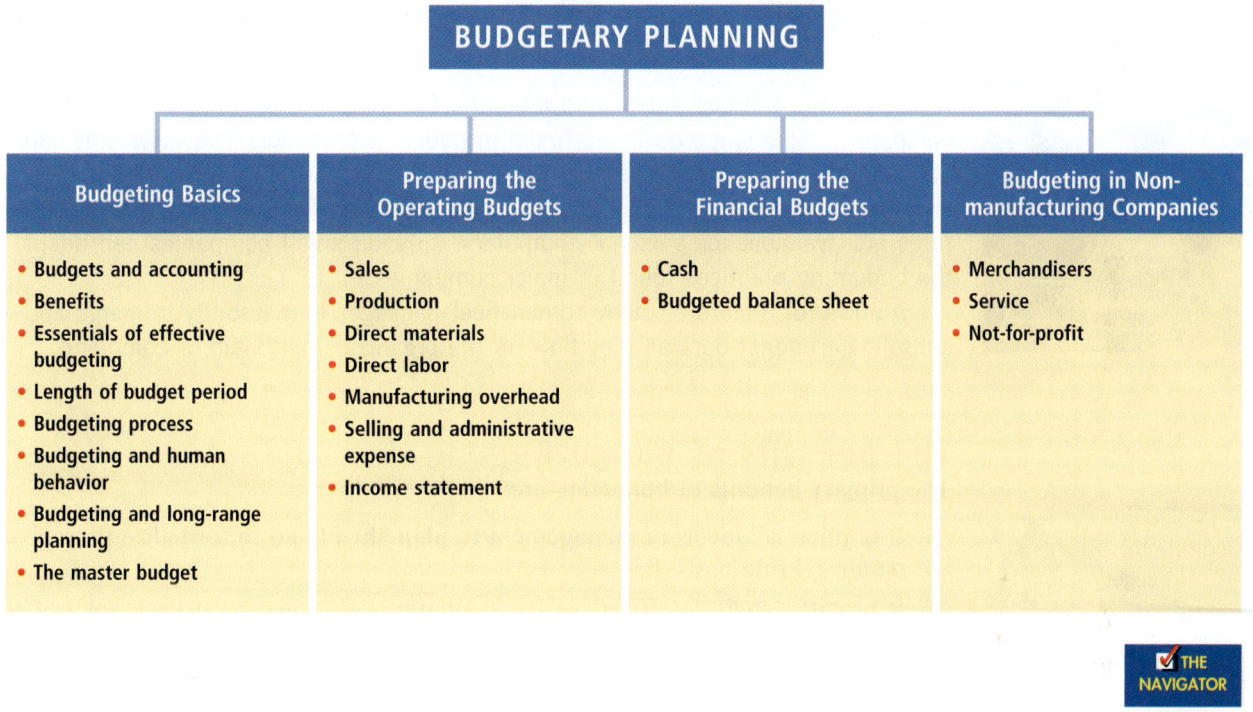

BUDGETARY PLANNING			
Budgeting Basics	**Preparing the Operating Budgets**	**Preparing the Financial Budgets**	**Budgeting in Non-manufacturing Companies**
• Budgets and accounting • Benefits • Essentials of effective budgeting • Length of budget period • Budgeting process • Budgeting and human behavior • Budgeting and long-range planning • The master budget	• Sales • Production • Direct materials • Direct labor • Manufacturing overhead • Selling and administrative expense • Income statement	• Cash • Budgeted balance sheet	• Merchandisers • Service • Not-for-profit

☑ THE NAVIGATOR

Budgeting Basics

One of management's major responsibilities is planning. As explained in Chapter 20, **planning** is the process of establishing enterprise-wide objectives. A successful organization makes both long-term and short-term plans. These plans set forth the objectives of the company and the proposed way of accomplishing them.

A budget is a formal written statement of management's plans for a specified future time period, expressed in financial terms. It normally represents the primary method of communicating agreed-upon objectives throughout the organization. Once adopted, a budget becomes an important basis for evaluating performance. It promotes efficiency and serves as a deterrent to waste and inefficiency. We consider the role of budgeting as a **control device** in Chapter 25.

Budgets and Accounting

Accounting information makes major contributions to the budgeting process. From the accounting records, historical data on revenues, costs, and expenses can be obtained. These data may be helpful in formulating future budget goals.

Normally, accountants have the responsibility for expressing management's budgeting goals in financial terms. In this role, they translate management's plans and communicate the budget to all areas of responsibility. Accountants also prepare periodic budget reports that provide the basis for measuring performance and comparing actual results with planned objectives. The budget itself, and the administration of the budget, however, are entirely management responsibilities.

ACCOUNTING IN ACTION  **ⓔ Business Insight**

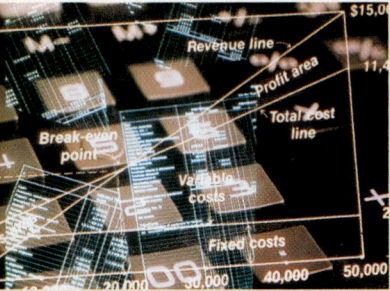

In large firms, the computer is an essential tool in the budgeting process. Many computer programs are designed to aid in budget preparation. These systems can also be integrated into the general ledger. They can provide a complete reporting package for monitoring budgeted versus actual results. Packages with similar features are available for personal computers, so even small companies can adopt the budgeting practices found in major companies.

A powerful feature of many spreadsheet packages is the ability to merge and consolidate budget data as they flow up the organizational chain of command.

The Benefits of Budgeting

STUDY OBJECTIVE 1

Indicate the benefits of budgeting.

The primary benefits of budgeting are:

1. It requires all levels of management to **plan ahead** and to formalize their goals on a recurring basis.
2. It provides **definite objectives** for evaluating performance at each level of responsibility.
3. It creates an **early warning system** for potential problems. With early warning, management has time to make changes before things get out of hand.
4. It facilitates the **coordination of activities** within the business. It does this by correlating the goals of each segment with overall company objectives. Thus, production and sales promotion can be integrated with expected sales.
5. It results in greater **management awareness** of the entity's overall operations and the impact on operations of external factors, such as economic trends.
6. It **motivates personnel** throughout the organization to meet planned objectives.

A budget is an aid to management; it is not a substitute for management. A budget cannot operate or enforce itself. The benefits of budgeting will be realized only when budgets are carefully prepared and properly administered by management.

Essentials of Effective Budgeting

STUDY OBJECTIVE 2

State the essentials of effective budgeting.

Effective budgeting depends on a **sound organizational structure**. In such a structure, authority and responsibility for all phases of operations are clearly defined. Budgets based on **research and analysis** should result in realistic goals that will contribute to the growth and profitability of a company. And, the effectiveness of a budget program is directly related to its **acceptance by all levels of management**.

Once the budget has been adopted, it should be an important tool for evaluating performance. Variations between actual and expected results should be systematically and periodically reviewed to determine their cause(s). However, individuals should not be held responsible for variations that are beyond their control.

Length of the Budget Period

The budget period is not necessarily one year in length. **A budget may be prepared for any period of time.** Various factors influence the length of the budget period. These factors include the type of budget, the nature of the organization, the need for periodic appraisal, and prevailing business conditions. For example, cash may be budgeted monthly, and a plant expansion budget may cover a ten-year period.

The budget period should be long enough to provide an attainable goal under normal business conditions. Ideally, the time period should minimize the impact of seasonal or cyclical fluctuations. On the other hand, the budget period should not be so long that reliable estimates are impossible.

The **most common budget period is one year**. The annual budget, in turn, is often supplemented by monthly and quarterly budgets. Many companies use **continuous twelve-month budgets**. These budgets drop the month just ended and add a future month. One advantage of continuous budgeting is that it keeps management planning a full year ahead.

The Budgeting Process

The development of the budget for the coming year generally starts several months before the end of the current year. The budgeting process usually begins with the collection of data from each organizational unit of the company. Past performance is often the starting point from which future budget goals are formulated.

The budget is developed within the framework of a **sales forecast**. This forecast shows potential sales for the industry and the company's expected share of such sales. Sales forecasting involves a consideration of various factors: (1) general economic conditions, (2) industry trends, (3) market research studies, (4) anticipated advertising and promotion, (5) previous market share, (6) changes in prices, and (7) technological developments. The input of sales personnel and top management are essential to the sales forecast.

In many companies, responsibility for coordinating the preparation of the budget is assigned to a **budget committee**. The committee ordinarily includes the president, treasurer, chief accountant (controller), and management personnel from each of the major areas of the company, such as sales, production, and research. The budget committee serves as a review board where managers can defend their budget goals and requests. Differences are reviewed, modified if necessary, and reconciled. The budget is then put in its final form by the budget committee, approved, and distributed.

Budgeting and Human Behavior

A budget can have a significant impact on human behavior. It may inspire a manager to higher levels of performance. Or, it may discourage additional effort and pull down the morale of a manager. Why do these diverse effects occur? The answer is found in how the budget is developed and administered.

In **developing the budget**, each level of management should be invited to participate. The overall goal is to reach agreement on a budget that the manager considers fair and achievable. When this objective is met, the budget will have a positive effect on the manager. In contrast, if the manager views the budget as being unfair and unrealistic, he or she may feel discouraged and uncommitted to the budget goals. The risk of having unrealistic budgets is generally greater when the budget is developed from top management down to lower management than vice versa. Illustration 24-1 (page 974) graphically displays the appropriate flow of budget data from bottom to top in an organization.

Illustration 24-1
Flow of budget data from lower levels of management to top

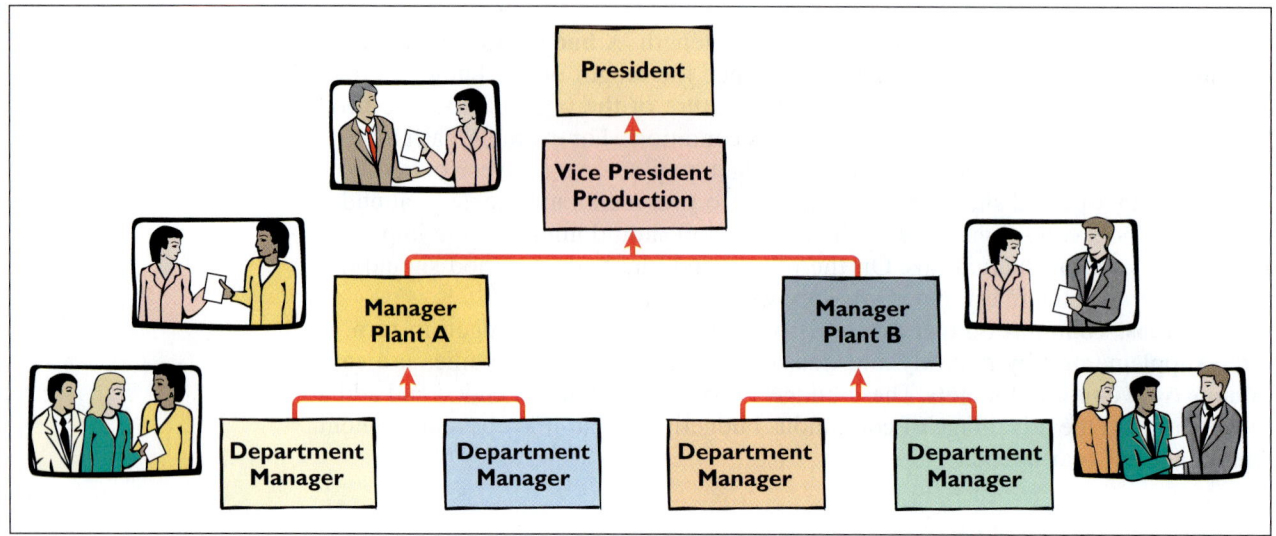

Administering the budget relates to how the budget is used by top management. As explained earlier, the budget should have the complete support of top management. The budget also should be an important basis for evaluating performance. The effect of an evaluation will be positive when top management tempers criticism with advice and assistance. In contrast, a manager is likely to respond negatively if the budget is used exclusively to assess blame.

A budget may be used improperly as a pressure device to force improved performance. Or, it can be used as a positive aid in achieving projected goals. In sum, a budget can become a manager's friend or a foe.

Budgeting and Long-Range Planning

In business, you may hear talk about the need for long-range planning. Budgeting and long-range planning are not the same. One important difference is the **time period involved**. The maximum length of a budget is usually one year, and budgets are often prepared for shorter periods of time, such as a month or a quarter. In contrast, long-range planning usually encompasses a period of at least five years.

A second significant difference is in **emphasis**. Budgeting focuses on achieving specific short-term goals, such as meeting annual profit objectives. **Long-range planning**, on the other hand, identifies long-term goals, selects strategies to achieve those goals, and develops policies and plans to implement the strategies. In long-range planning, management also considers anticipated trends in the economic and political environment and how the company should cope with them.

The final difference between budgeting and long-range planning pertains to the **amount of detail presented**. Budgets, as you will see in this chapter, can be very detailed. Long-range plans contain considerably less detail. The data in long-range plans are intended more for a review of progress toward long-term goals than as a basis of control for achieving specific results. The primary objective of long-range planning is to develop the best strategy to maximize the company's performance over an extended future period.

The Master Budget

The term "budget" is actually a shorthand term to describe a variety of budget documents. All of these documents are combined from all sources into a master budget.

The **master budget** is a set of interrelated budgets that constitutes a plan of action for a specified time period. The individual budgets included in a master budget are pictured in Illustration 24-2.

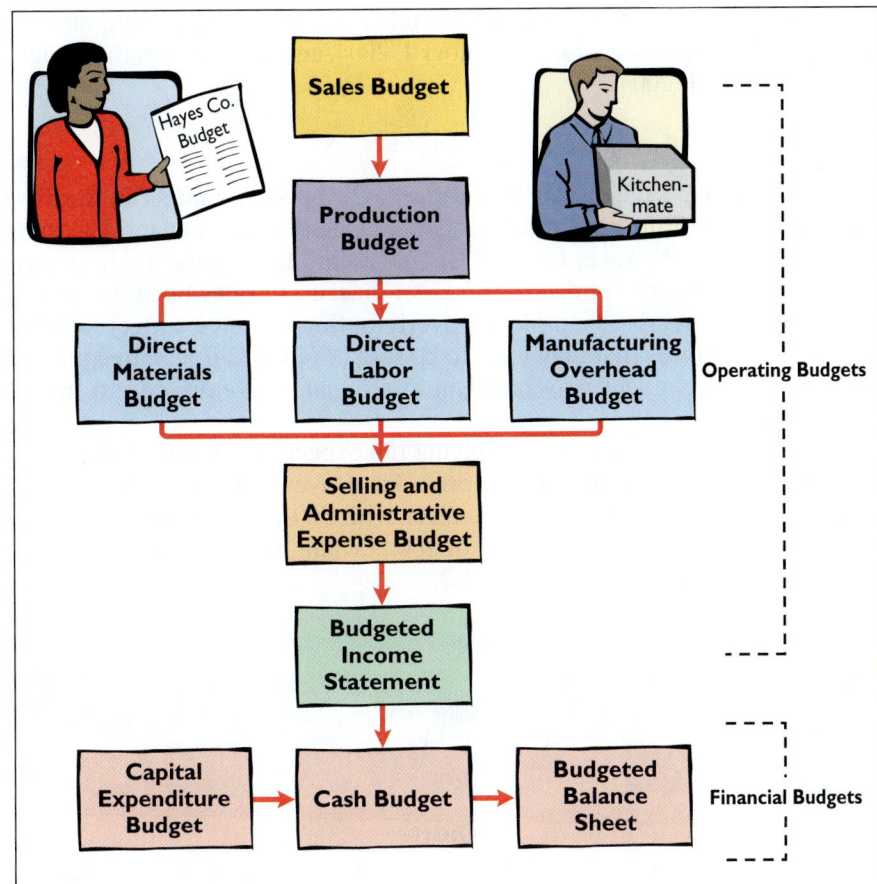

Illustration 24-2
Components of the master budget

As the illustration shows, the master budget contains two classes of budgets. **Operating budgets** are the individual budgets that result in the preparation of the budgeted income statement. These budgets establish goals for the company's sales and production personnel. In contrast, **financial budgets** are the cash budget and the budgeted balance sheet. These budgets focus primarily on the cash resources needed to fund expected operations and planned capital expenditures.

The master budget is prepared in the sequence shown in Illustration 24-2. The operating budgets are developed first, beginning with the sales budget. Then the financial budgets are prepared. We will explain and illustrate each budget shown in Illustration 24-2 except the capital expenditure budget. This budget is discussed under the topic Capital Budgeting in Chapter 27.

BEFORE YOU GO ON...

Review It

1. What are the benefits of budgeting?
2. What are the factors essential to effective budgeting?
3. How does the budget process work?
4. How does budgeting differ from long-range planning?
5. What is a master budget?

THE NAVIGATOR

Preparing the Operating Budgets

A case study of Hayes Company will be used in preparing the operating budgets. Hayes manufactures and sells a single product, Kitchen-mate. The budgets will be prepared by quarters for the year ending December 31, 2005. Hayes Company begins its annual budgeting process on September 1, 2004, and it completes the budget for 2005 by December 1, 2004.

Sales Budget

As shown in the master budget in Illustration 24-2, **the sales budget is the first budget prepared**. Each of the other budgets depends on the sales budget. The **sales budget** is derived from the sales forecast. It represents management's best estimate of sales revenue for the budget period. An inaccurate sales budget may adversely affect net income. For example, an overly optimistic sales budget may result in excessive inventories that may have to be sold at reduced prices. In contrast, an unduly conservative budget may result in loss of sales revenue due to inventory shortages.

The sales budget is prepared by multiplying the expected unit sales volume for each product by its anticipated unit selling price. For Hayes Company, sales volume is expected to be 3,000 units in the first quarter with 500-unit increments in each succeeding quarter. Based on a sales price of $60 per unit, the sales budget for the year, by quarters, is shown in Illustration 24-3.

Illustration 24-3
Sales budget

HAYES COMPANY					
Sales Budget					
For the Year Ending December 31, 2005					
	Quarter				
	1	**2**	**3**	**4**	**Year**
Expected unit sales	3,000	3,500	4,000	4,500	15,000
Unit selling price	× $60	× $60	× $60	× $60	× $60
Total sales	$180,000	$210,000	$240,000	$270,000	$900,000

Some companies classify the anticipated sales revenue as cash or credit sales and by geographical regions, territories, or salespersons.

Production Budget

The **production budget** shows the units that must be produced to meet anticipated sales. Production requirements are determined from the following formula.[1]

Illustration 24-4
Production requirements formula

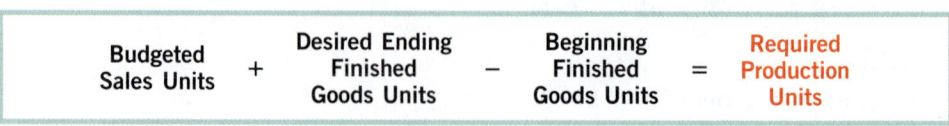

Budgeted Sales Units	+	Desired Ending Finished Goods Units	−	Beginning Finished Goods Units	=	Required Production Units

---

[1]This formula ignores any work in process inventories, which are assumed to be nonexistent in Hayes Company.

A realistic estimate of ending inventory is essential in scheduling production requirements. Excessive inventories in one quarter may lead to cutbacks in production and employee layoffs in a subsequent quarter. On the other hand, inadequate inventories may result either in added costs for overtime work or in lost sales. Hayes Company believes it can meet future sales requirements by maintaining an ending inventory equal to 20 percent of the next quarter's budgeted sales volume. For example, the ending finished goods inventory for the first quarter is 700 units (20% × anticipated second-quarter sales of 3,500 units). The production budget is shown in Illustration 24-5.

Illustration 24-5
Production budget

HAYES COMPANY					
Production Budget					
For the Year Ending December 31, 2005					
	Quarter				
	1	**2**	**3**	**4**	**Year**
Expected unit sales (Illustration 24-3)	3,000	3,500	4,000	4,500	
Add: Desired ending finished goods units[a]	700	800	900	1,000[b]	
Total required units	3,700	4,300	4,900	5,500	
Less: Beginning finished goods units	600[c]	700	800	900	
Required production units	**3,100**	**3,600**	**4,100**	**4,600**	**15,400**

[a]20% of next quarter's sales
[b]Expected 2006 first-quarter sales, 5,000 units × 20%
[c]20% of estimated first-quarter 2005 sales units

The production budget, in turn, provides the basis for determining the budgeted costs for each manufacturing cost element, as explained in the following pages.

Direct Materials Budget

The **direct materials budget** shows both the quantity and cost of direct materials to be purchased. The quantities of direct materials are derived from the following formula.

Illustration 24-6
Formula for direct materials
quantities

The budgeted cost of direct materials to be purchased is then computed by multiplying the required units of direct materials by the anticipated cost per unit.

The desired ending inventory is again a key component in the budgeting process. For example, inadequate inventories could result in temporary shutdowns of production. Because of its close proximity to suppliers, Hayes Company has found that an ending inventory of raw materials equal to 10 percent of the next quarter's production is sufficient. The manufacture of each Kitchen-mate requires 2 pounds of raw materials, and the expected cost per pound is $4. The direct materials budget is shown in Illustration 24-7 (page 978).

Illustration 24-7
Direct materials budget

HAYES COMPANY
Direct Materials Budget
For the Year Ending December 31, 2005

	Quarter				
	1	**2**	**3**	**4**	**Year**
Units to be produced (Illustration 24-5)	3,100	3,600	4,100	4,600	
Direct materials per unit	× 2	× 2	× 2	× 2	
Total pounds needed for production	6,200	7,200	8,200	9,200	
Add: Desired ending direct materials (pounds)[a]	720	820	920	1,020[b]	
Total materials required	6,920	8,020	9,120	10,220	
Less: Beginning direct materials (pounds)	620[c]	720	820	920	
Direct materials purchases	6,300	7,300	8,300	9,300	
Cost per pound	× $4	× $4	× $4	× $4	
Total cost of direct materials purchases	**$25,200**	**$29,200**	**$33,200**	**$37,200**	**$124,800**

[a]10% of next quarter's production
[b]Estimated 2006 first-quarter pounds needed for production, 10,200 × 10%
[c]10% of estimated first-quarter pounds needed for production

Direct Labor Budget

Like the direct materials budget, the **direct labor budget** contains the quantity (hours) and cost of direct labor necessary to meet production requirements. Direct labor hours are determined from the production budget. At Hayes Company, two hours of direct labor are required to produce each unit of finished goods. The anticipated hourly wage rate is $10. These data are shown in Illustration 24-8.

Illustration 24-8
Direct labor budget

> **HELPFUL HINT**
>
> An important assumption here is that the company can add to and subtract from its work force as needed so that the $10 per hour labor cost applies to a wide range of possible production activity.

HAYES COMPANY
Direct Labor Budget
For the Year Ending December 31, 2005

	Quarter				
	1	**2**	**3**	**4**	**Year**
Units to be produced (Illustration 24-5)	3,100	3,600	4,100	4,600	
Direct labor time (hours) per unit	× 2	× 2	× 2	× 2	
Total required direct labor hours	6,200	7,200	8,200	9,200	
Direct labor cost per hour	× $10	× $10	× $10	× $10	
Total direct labor cost	**$62,000**	**$72,000**	**$82,000**	**$92,000**	**$308,000**

The direct labor budget is critical in maintaining a labor force that can meet the expected levels of production.

Manufacturing Overhead Budget

The **manufacturing overhead budget** shows the expected manufacturing overhead costs for the budget period. As shown in Illustration 24-9, **this budget distinguishes between variable and fixed overhead costs**. Hayes Company expects variable costs to fluctuate with production volume on the basis of the following rates per direct labor hour: indirect materials $1.00, indirect labor $1.40, utilities $0.40, and maintenance $0.20. Thus, for 6,200 direct labor hours, budgeted indirect materials are $6,200 (6,200 × $1), and budgeted indirect labor is $8,680 (6,200 × $1.40). Hayes also recognizes that some maintenance is fixed. The amounts reported for fixed costs are assumed.

At Hayes Company, overhead is applied to production on the basis of direct labor hours. Thus, as shown in Illustration 24-9, the annual rate is $8 per hour ($246,400 ÷ 30,800).

Illustration 24-9
Manufacturing overhead budget

HAYES COMPANY
Manufacturing Overhead Budget
For the Year Ending December 31, 2005

	Quarter				
	1	**2**	**3**	**4**	**Year**
Variable costs					
Indirect materials	$ 6,200	$ 7,200	$ 8,200	$ 9,200	$ 30,800
Indirect labor	8,680	10,080	11,480	12,880	43,120
Utilities	2,480	2,880	3,280	3,680	12,320
Maintenance	1,240	1,440	1,640	1,840	6,160
Total variable	18,600	21,600	24,600	27,600	92,400
Fixed costs					
Supervisory salaries	20,000	20,000	20,000	20,000	80,000
Depreciation	3,800	3,800	3,800	3,800	15,200
Property taxes and insurance	9,000	9,000	9,000	9,000	36,000
Maintenance	5,700	5,700	5,700	5,700	22,800
Total fixed	38,500	38,500	38,500	38,500	154,000
Total manufacturing overhead	**$57,100**	**$60,100**	**$63,100**	**$66,100**	**$246,400**
Direct labor hours	**6,200**	**7,200**	**8,200**	**9,200**	**30,800**
Manufacturing overhead rate per direct labor hour ($246,400 ÷ 30,800)					**$8.00**

Selling and Administrative Expense Budget

Hayes Company combines its operating expenses into one budget, the **selling and administrative expense budget**. This budget projects anticipated selling and administrative expenses for the budget period. In this budget, as in the preceding one, expenses are classified as either variable or fixed. In this case, the variable expense rates per unit of sales are sales commissions $3.00 and freight-out $1.00. Variable expenses per quarter are based on the unit sales from the sales budget (Illustration 24-3). For example, sales in the first quarter are expected to be 3,000 units. Thus, Sales Commissions Expense is $9,000 (3,000 × $3), and Freight-out is $3,000 (3,000 × $1). Fixed expenses are based on assumed data. The selling and administrative expense budget is shown in Illustration 24-10 (page 980).

Illustration 24-10
Selling and administrative
expense budget

HAYES COMPANY
Selling and Administrative Expense Budget
For the Year Ending December 31, 2005

	Quarter				
	1	**2**	**3**	**4**	**Year**
Variable expenses					
Sales commissions	$ 9,000	$10,500	$12,000	$13,500	$ 45,000
Freight-out	3,000	3,500	4,000	4,500	15,000
Total variable	12,000	14,000	16,000	18,000	60,000
Fixed expenses					
Advertising	5,000	5,000	5,000	5,000	20,000
Sales salaries	15,000	15,000	15,000	15,000	60,000
Office salaries	7,500	7,500	7,500	7,500	30,000
Depreciation	1,000	1,000	1,000	1,000	4,000
Property taxes and insurance	1,500	1,500	1,500	1,500	6,000
Total fixed	30,000	30,000	30,000	30,000	120,000
Total selling and administrative expenses	**$42,000**	**$44,000**	**$46,000**	**$48,000**	**$180,000**

ACCOUNTING IN ACTION   e Business Insight

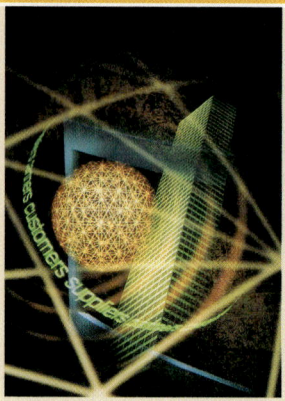

Good budgeting depends on good information. And good information is what e-business is all about. As manufacturers, suppliers, and customers become electronically linked, each benefits by being better informed. **Dell Computer** not only is directly linked to **Solectron**, one of its main suppliers, but also to **Texas Instruments**, one of the main suppliers of parts to Solectron. This linking takes a lot of guesswork out of planning and budgeting for all three companies.

To further improve planning and budgeting, Dell hopes that some day everyone in its industry will anonymously provide their up-to-the-minute production and sales information at a central, electronic exchange. A centralized database such as this would provide valuable information about the supply and demand of computer goods in the marketplace. This information might dramatically improve sales projections, leading to significant improvements in the budgeting process.

Source: "E-Management," *The Economist*, November 11, 2000.

Budgeted Income Statement

STUDY OBJECTIVE 4

Describe the sources for
preparing the budgeted
income statement.

The **budgeted income statement** is the important end-product of the operating budgets. This budget indicates the expected profitability of operations for the budget period. The budgeted income statement provides the basis for evaluating company performance.

As you would expect, this budget is prepared from the various operating budgets. For example, to find the cost of goods sold, it is first necessary to determine the total unit cost of producing one Kitchen-mate, as follows.

Illustration 24-11
Computation of total unit cost

	Cost of One Kitchen-mate			
Cost Element	**Illustration**	**Quantity**	**Unit Cost**	**Total**
Direct materials	24-7	2 pounds	$ 4.00	$ 8.00
Direct labor	24-8	2 hours	$10.00	20.00
Manufacturing overhead	24-9	2 hours	$ 8.00	16.00
Total unit cost				**$44.00**

Cost of goods sold can then be determined by multiplying the units sold by the unit cost. For Hayes Company, budgeted cost of goods sold is $660,000 (15,000 × $44). All data for the statement are obtained from the individual operating budgets except the following: (1) interest expense is expected to be $100 and (2) income taxes are estimated to be $12,000. The budgeted income statement is shown in Illustration 24-12.

Illustration 24-12
Budgeted income statement

HAYES COMPANY
Budgeted Income Statement
For the Year Ending December 31, 2005

Sales (Illustration 24-3)	$900,000
Cost of goods sold (15,000 × $44)	660,000
Gross profit	240,000
Selling and administrative expenses (Illustration 24-10)	180,000
Income from operations	60,000
Interest expense	100
Income before income taxes	59,900
Income tax expense	12,000
Net income	$ 47,900

Preparing the Financial Budgets

As shown in Illustration 24-2 (page 975), the financial budgets consist of the capital expenditure budget, the cash budget, and the budgeted balance sheet. The capital expenditure budget is discussed in Chapter 27; the other budgets are explained in the following sections.

Cash Budget

The **cash budget** shows anticipated cash flows. Because cash is so vital, this budget is considered to be the most important output in preparing financial budgets. The cash budget contains three sections (cash receipts, cash disbursements, and financing) and the beginning and ending cash balances, as shown in Illustration 24-13 (page 982).

The **cash receipts section** includes expected receipts from the company's principal source(s) of revenue. These are usually cash sales and collections from customers on credit sales. This section also shows anticipated receipts of interest and dividends, and proceeds from planned sales of investments, plant assets, and the company's capital stock.

STUDY OBJECTIVE 5

Explain the principal sections of a cash budget.

Illustration 24-13
Basic form of a cash budget

ANY COMPANY Cash Budget	
Beginning cash balance	$X,XXX
Add: Cash receipts (Itemized)	X,XXX
Total available cash	X,XXX
Less: Cash disbursements (Itemized)	X,XXX
Excess (deficiency) of available cash over cash disbursements	X,XXX
Financing	X,XXX
Ending cash balance	$X,XXX

The **cash disbursements section** shows expected cash payments. Such payments include direct materials, direct labor, manufacturing overhead, and selling and administrative expenses. This section also includes projected payments for income taxes, dividends, investments, and plant assets.

The **financing section** shows expected borrowings and the repayment of the borrowed funds plus interest. This section is needed when there is a cash deficiency or when the cash balance is below management's minimum required balance.

Data in the cash budget must be prepared in sequence. The ending cash balance of one period becomes the beginning cash balance for the next period. Data for preparing the cash budget are obtained from other budgets and from information provided by management. In practice, cash budgets are often prepared for the year on a monthly basis.

To minimize detail, we will assume that Hayes Company prepares an annual cash budget by quarters. The cash budget for Hayes Company is based on the following assumptions.

1. The January 1, 2005, cash balance is expected to be $38,000.

2. Sales (Illustration 24-3): 60 percent are collected in the quarter sold and 40 percent are collected in the following quarter. Accounts receivable of $60,000 at December 31, 2004, are expected to be collected in full in the first quarter of 2005.

3. Short-term investments are expected to be sold for $2,000 cash in the first quarter.

4. Direct materials (Illustration 24-7): 50 percent are paid in the quarter purchased and 50 percent are paid in the following quarter. Accounts payable of $10,600 at December 31, 2004, are expected to be paid in full in the first quarter of 2005.

5. Direct labor (Illustration 24-8): 100 percent is paid in the quarter incurred.

6. Manufacturing overhead (Illustration 24-9) and selling and administrative expenses (Illustration 24-10): All items except depreciation are paid in the quarter incurred.

7. Management plans to purchase a truck in the second quarter for $10,000 cash.

8. Hayes makes equal quarterly payments of its estimated annual income taxes.

9. Loans are repaid in the earliest quarter in which there is sufficient cash (i.e., when the cash on hand exceeds the $15,000 minimum required balance).

In preparing the cash budget, it is useful to prepare schedules for collections from customers (assumption No. 2, above) and cash payments for direct materials (assumption No. 4, above). The schedules are shown in Illustrations 24-14 and 24-15.

The cash budget for Hayes Company is shown in Illustration 24-16. The budget indicates that $3,000 of financing will be needed in the second quarter to maintain a minimum cash balance of $15,000. Since there is an excess of available cash over disbursements of $22,500 at the end of the third quarter, the borrowing is repaid in this quarter plus $100 interest.

Illustration 24-14
Collections from customers

Schedule of Expected Collections from Customers

	Quarter			
	1	**2**	**3**	**4**
Accounts receivable, 12/31/04	$ 60,000			
First quarter ($180,000)	108,000	$ 72,000		
Second quarter ($210,000)		126,000	$ 84,000	
Third quarter ($240,000)			144,000	$ 96,000
Fourth quarter ($270,000)				162,000
Total collections	$168,000	$198,000	$228,000	$258,000

Illustration 24-15
Payments for direct materials

Schedule of Expected Payments for Direct Materials

	Quarter			
	1	**2**	**3**	**4**
Accounts payable, 12/31/04	$10,600			
First quarter ($25,200)	12,600	$12,600		
Second quarter ($29,200)		14,600	$14,600	
Third quarter ($33,200)			16,600	$16,600
Fourth quarter ($37,200)				18,600
Total payments	$23,200	$27,200	$31,200	$35,200

Illustration 24-16
Cash budget

HAYES COMPANY
Cash Budget
For the Year Ending December 31, 2005

		Quarter			
	Assumption	**1**	**2**	**3**	**4**
Beginning cash balance	1	$ 38,000	$ 25,500	$ 15,000	$ 19,400
Add: Receipts					
Collections from customers	2	168,000	198,000	228,000	258,000
Sale of securities	3	2,000	0	0	0
Total receipts		170,000	198,000	228,000	258,000
Total available cash		208,000	223,500	243,000	277,400
Less: Disbursements					
Direct materials	4	23,200	27,200	31,200	35,200
Direct labor	5	62,000	72,000	82,000	92,000
Manufacturing overhead	6	53,300[1]	56,300	59,300	62,300
Selling and administrative expenses	6	41,000[2]	43,000	45,000	47,000
Purchase of truck	7	0	10,000	0	0
Income tax expense	8	3,000	3,000	3,000	3,000
Total disbursements		182,500	211,500	220,500	239,500
Excess (deficiency) of available cash over disbursements		25,500	12,000	22,500	37,900
Financing					
Borrowings		0	3,000	0	0
Repayments—plus $100 interest	9	0	0	3,100	0
Ending cash balance		$ 25,500	$ 15,000	$ 19,400	$ 37,900

[1]$57,100 − $3,800 depreciation
[2]$42,000 − $1,000 depreciation

A cash budget contributes to more effective cash management. It can show when additional financing will be necessary well before the actual need arises. And, it can indicate when excess cash will be available for investments or other purposes.

Budgeted Balance Sheet

The **budgeted balance sheet** is a projection of financial position at the end of the budget period. This budget is developed from the budgeted balance sheet for the preceding year and the budgets for the current year. Pertinent data from the budgeted balance sheet at December 31, 2004, are as follows.

Building and equipment	$182,000	Common stock	$225,000
Accumulated depreciation	$ 28,800	Retained earnings	$ 46,480

The budgeted balance sheet at December 31, 2005, is shown below.

Illustration 24-17
Budgeted balance sheet

HAYES COMPANY
Budgeted Balance Sheet
December 31, 2005

Assets

Cash		$ 37,900
Accounts receivable		108,000
Finished goods inventory		44,000
Raw materials inventory		4,080
Buildings and equipment	$192,000	
Less: Accumulated depreciation	48,000	144,000
Total assets		$337,980

Liabilities and Stockholders' Equity

Accounts payable	$ 18,600
Common stock	225,000
Retained earnings	94,380
Total liabilities and stockholders' equity	$337,980

The computations and sources of the amounts are explained below.

Cash: Ending cash balance $37,900, shown in the cash budget (Illustration 24-16).

Accounts receivable: 40 percent of fourth-quarter sales $270,000, shown in the schedule of expected collections from customers (Illustration 24-14).

Finished goods inventory: Desired ending inventory 1,000 units, shown in the production budget (Illustration 24-5) times the total unit cost $44 (shown in Illustration 24-11).

Raw materials inventory: Desired ending inventory 1,020 pounds, times the cost per pound $4, shown in the direct materials budget (Illustration 24-7).

Buildings and equipment: December 31, 2004, balance $182,000, plus purchase of truck for $10,000.

Accumulated depreciation: December 31, 2004, balance $28,800, plus $15,200 depreciation shown in manufacturing overhead budget (Illustration 24-9) and $4,000 depreciation shown in selling and administrative expense budget (Illustration 24-10).

Accounts payable: 50 percent of fourth-quarter purchases $37,200, shown in schedule of expected payments for direct materials (Illustration 24-15).

Common stock: Unchanged from the beginning of the year.

Retained earnings: December 31, 2004, balance $46,480, plus net income $47,900, shown in budgeted income statement (Illustration 24-12).

ACCOUNTING IN ACTION 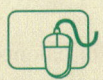 e Business Insight

After the budgeting data are entered into the computer, the various budgets (sales, cash, etc.) can be prepared, as well as the budgeted financial statements. Management can also manipulate the budgets in "what if" (sensitivity) analyses based on different hypothetical assumptions. For example, suppose that sales were budgeted to be 10 percent higher in the coming quarter. What impact would the change have on the rest of the budgeting process and the financing needs of the business? The computer can quickly "play out" the impact of the various assumptions on the budgets. Armed with these analyses, management can make more informed decisions about the impact of various projects. They also can anticipate future problems and business opportunities. Budgeting is one of the top uses of electronic spreadsheets. Template versions of every one of the Hayes Company budgets shown in this chapter can easily be prepared.

BEFORE YOU GO ON...

Review It

1. What are the two classifications of the individual budgets in the master budget?
2. What is the sequence for preparing the budgets that comprise the operating budgets?
3. Identify some of the source documents that would be used in preparing each of the operating budgets.
4. What are the three principal sections of the cash budget?
5. Obviously, **PepsiCo** does not present its detailed budgets in its 2002 Annual Report. But, in its "Management's Discussion and Analysis" section and its "Notes to Consolidated Financial Statements," what expectations and plans does PepsiCo have for the future (2003 and beyond)? The answer to this question is provided on page 1003.

Do It

In Martian Company, management wants to maintain a minimum monthly cash balance of $15,000. At the beginning of March, the cash balance is $16,500, expected cash receipts for March are $210,000, and cash disbursements are expected to be $220,000. How much cash, if any, must be borrowed to maintain the desired minimum monthly balance?

ACTION PLAN

 Write down the basic form of the cash budget, starting with the beginning cash balance, adding cash receipts for the period, deducting cash disbursements, and identifying the needed financing to achieve the desired minimum ending cash balance.

(continued from p. 985)

■ Insert the data given into the outlined form of the cash budget.

SOLUTION

MARTIAN COMPANY
Cash Budget
For the Month Ending March 31, 2005

Beginning cash balance	$ 16,500
Add: Cash receipts for March	210,000
Total available cash	226,500
Less: Cash disbursements for March	220,000
Excess of available cash over cash disbursements	6,500
Financing	8,500
Ending cash balance	$ 15,000

To maintain the desired minimum cash balance of $15,000, Martian Company must borrow $8,500 of cash.

Related exercise material: *BE24-9 and E24-9.*

Budgeting in Nonmanufacturing Companies

STUDY OBJECTIVE 6

Indicate the applicability of budgeting in nonmanufacturing companies.

Budgeting is not limited to manufacturers. Budgets may also be used by merchandisers, service enterprises, and not-for-profit organizations.

Merchandisers

As in manufacturing operations, the sales budget for a merchandiser is both the starting point and the key factor in the development of the master budget. The major differences between the master budgets of a merchandiser and a manufacturer are these: (1) A merchandiser **uses a merchandise purchases budget instead of a production budget**. (2) A merchandiser **does not use the manufacturing budgets (direct materials, direct labor, and manufacturing overhead)**. The **merchandise purchases budget** shows the estimated cost of goods to be purchased to meet expected sales. The formula for determining budgeted merchandise purchases is:

Illustration 24-18
Merchandise purchases formula

Budgeted Cost of Goods Sold	+	Desired Ending Merchandise Inventory	−	Beginning Merchandise Inventory	=	Required Merchandise Purchases

To illustrate, assume that the budget committee of Lima Company is preparing the merchandise purchases budget for July. It estimates that budgeted sales will be $300,000 in July and $320,000 in August. Cost of goods sold is expected to be 70 percent of sales. The company's desired ending inventory is 30 percent of the following month's cost of goods sold. Required merchandise purchases for July are $214,200, as shown in Illustration 24-19.

Budgeted cost of goods sold (budgeted sales for July, $300,000 × 70%)	$210,000
Desired ending merchandise inventory (budgeted sales for August, $320,000 × 70% × 30%)	67,200
Total	277,200
Less: Beginning merchandise inventory (budgeted sales for July, $300,000 × 70% × 30%)	63,000
Required merchandise purchases for July	**$214,200**

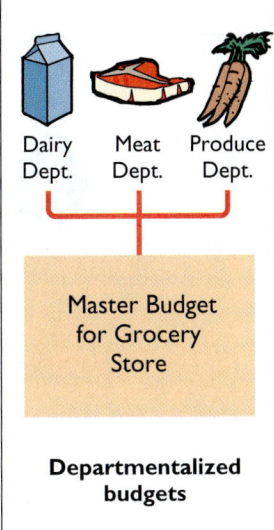

Illustration 24-19
Computation of required merchandise purchases

When a merchandiser is departmentalized, separate budgets are prepared for each department. For example, a grocery store may start by preparing sales budgets and purchases budgets for each of its major departments, such as dairy, meat, and produce. These budgets are then combined into a master budget for the store. When a retailer has branch stores, separate master budgets are prepared for each store. Then these budgets are incorporated into the master budget for the company as a whole.

Service Enterprises

In service enterprises, such as a public accounting firm, a law office, or a medical practice, the critical factor in budgeting is **coordinating professional staff needs with anticipated services**. If a firm is overstaffed, several problems may result: (1) Labor costs will be disproportionately high. (2) Profits will be lower because of the additional salaries. (3) Staff turnover may increase because of lack of challenging work. In contrast, if an enterprise is understaffed, revenue may be lost because existing and prospective client needs for service cannot be met. Also, professional staff may seek other jobs because of excessive work loads.

Budget data for service revenue may be obtained from **expected output** or **expected input**. When output is used, it is necessary to determine the expected billings of clients for services rendered. In a public accounting firm, for example, output would be the sum of its billings in auditing, tax, and consulting services. When input data are used, each professional staff member is required to project his or her billable time. Billing rates are then applied to billable time to produce expected service revenue.

Not-for-Profit Organizations

Budgeting is just as important for not-for-profit organizations as for profit-oriented enterprises. The budget process, however, is significantly different. In most cases not-for-profit entities budget **on the basis of cash flows (expenditures and receipts), rather than on a revenue and expense basis**. Further, the starting point in the process is usually expenditures, not receipts. For the not-for-profit entity, management's task generally is to find the receipts needed to support the planned expenditures. The activity index is also likely to be significantly different. For example, in a not-for-profit entity, such as a university, budgeted faculty positions may be based on full-time equivalent students or credit hours expected to be taught in a department.

For some governmental units, the budget must be approved by voters. In other cases, such as state governments and the federal government, legislative approval is required. After the budget is adopted, it must be strictly followed. Overspending is often illegal. In governmental budgets, authorizations tend to be on a line-by-line basis. That is, the budget for a municipality may have a specified authorization for police and fire protection, garbage collection, street paving, and so on. The line-item authorization of governmental budgets significantly limits the amount of discretion management can exercise. The city manager often cannot use savings from one line item, such as street paving, to cover increased spending in another line item, such as snow removal.

BEFORE YOU GO ON...

Review It

1. What is the formula for computing required merchandise purchases?
2. How does budgeting in service and not-for-profit organizations differ from budgeting for manufacturers and merchandisers?

THE NAVIGATOR

DEMONSTRATION PROBLEM

The Soroco Company is preparing its master budget for 2005. Relevant data pertaining to its sales and production budgets are as follows:

Sales: Sales for the year are expected to total 1,200,000 units. Quarterly sales are 20%, 25%, 30%, and 25% respectively. The sales price is expected to be $50 per unit for the first three quarters and $55 per unit beginning in the fourth quarter. Sales in the first quarter of 2006 are expected to be 10% higher than the budgeted sales volume for the first quarter of 2005.

Production: Management desires to maintain ending finished goods inventories at 25% of the next quarter's budgeted sales volume.

Instructions

Prepare the sales budget and production budget by quarters for 2005.

ACTION PLAN

- Know the form and content of the sales budget.
- Prepare the sales budget first as the basis for the other budgets.
- Determine the units that must be produced to meet anticipated sales.
- Know how to compute the beginning and ending finished goods units.

SOLUTION TO DEMONSTRATION PROBLEM

SOROCO COMPANY
Sales Budget
For the Year Ending December 31, 2005

	Quarter				
	1	**2**	**3**	**4**	**Year**
Expected unit sales	240,000	300,000	360,000	300,000	1,200,000
Unit selling price	× $50	× $50	× $50	× $55	—
	$12,000,000	$15,000,000	$18,000,000	$16,500,000	$61,500,000

SOROCO COMPANY
Production Budget
For the Year Ending December 31, 2005

	Quarter				
	1	**2**	**3**	**4**	**Year**
Expected unit sales	240,000	300,000	360,000	300,0000	
Add: Desired ending finished goods units	75,000	90,000	75,000	66,000[1]	
Total required units	315,000	390,000	435,000	366,000	
Less: Beginning finished goods units	60,000[2]	75,000	90,000	75,000	
Units to be produced	255,000	315,000	345,000	291,000	1,206,000

[1]Estimated first-quarter 2006 sales volume 240,000 + (240,000 × 10%) = 264,000; 264,000 × 25%.
[2]25% of estimated first-quarter 2005 sales units.

THE NAVIGATOR

SUMMARY OF STUDY OBJECTIVES

1. **Indicate the benefits of budgeting.** The primary advantages of budgeting are that it (a) requires management to plan ahead, (b) provides definite objectives for evaluating performance, (c) creates an early warning system for potential problems, (d) facilitates coordination of activities, (e) results in greater management awareness, and (f) motivates personnel to meet planned objectives.

2. **State the essentials of effective budgeting.** The essentials of effective budgeting are (a) sound organizational structure, (b) research and analysis, and (c) acceptance by all levels of management.

3. **Identify the budgets that comprise the master budget.** The master budget consists of the following budgets: (a) sales, (b) production, (c) direct materials, (d) direct labor, (e) manufacturing overhead, (f) selling and administrative expense, (g) budgeted income statement, (h) capital expenditure budget, (i) cash budget, and (j) budgeted balance sheet.

4. **Describe the sources for preparing the budgeted income statement.** The budgeted income statement is prepared from (a) the sales budget, (b) the budgets for direct materials, direct labor, and manufacturing overhead, and (c) the selling and administrative expense budget.

5. **Explain the principal sections of a cash budget.** The cash budget has three sections (receipts, disbursements, and financing) and the beginning and ending cash balances.

6. **Indicate the applicability of budgeting in nonmanufacturing companies.** Budgeting may be used by merchandisers for development of a master budget. In service enterprises budgeting is a critical factor in coordinating staff needs with anticipated services. In not-for-profit organizations, the starting point in budgeting is usually expenditures, not receipts.

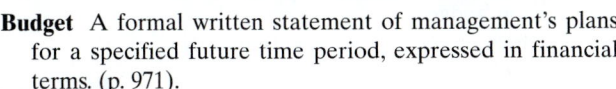

GLOSSARY

Budget A formal written statement of management's plans for a specified future time period, expressed in financial terms. (p. 971).

Budget committee A group responsible for coordinating the preparation of the budget. (p. 973).

Budgeted balance sheet A projection of financial position at the end of the budget period. (p. 984).

Budgeted income statement An estimate of the expected profitability of operations for the budget period. (p. 980).

Cash budget A projection of anticipated cash flows. (p. 981).

Direct labor budget A projection of the quantity and cost of direct labor to be incurred to meet production requirements. (p. 978).

Direct materials budget An estimate of the quantity and cost of direct materials to be purchased. (p. 977).

Financial budgets Individual budgets that indicate the cash resources needed for expected operations and planned capital expenditures. (p. 975).

Long-range planning A formalized process of selecting strategies to achieve long-term goals and developing policies and plans to implement the strategies. (p. 974).

Manufacturing overhead budget An estimate of expected manufacturing overhead costs for the budget period. (p. 979).

Master budget A set of interrelated budgets that constitutes a plan of action for a specific time period. (p. 975).

Merchandise purchases budget The estimated cost of goods to be purchased by a merchandiser to meet expected sales. (p. 986).

Operating budgets Individual budgets that result in a budgeted income statement. (p. 975).

Production budget A projection of the units that must be produced to meet anticipated sales. (p. 976).

Sales budget An estimate of expected sales for the budget period. (p. 976).

Sales forecast The projection of potential sales for the industry and the company's expected share of such sales. (p. 973).

Selling and administrative expense budget A projection of anticipated selling and administrative expenses for the budget period. (p. 979).

SELF-STUDY QUESTIONS

Answers are at the end of the chapter.

(O 1) **1.** The benefits of budgeting include *all but one* of the following:
   a. Management can plan ahead.

b. An early warning system is provided for potential problems.

c. It enables disciplinary action to be taken at every level of responsibility.

d. The coordination of activities is facilitated.

(SO 2)   **2.** The essentials of effective budgeting do *not* include:
   a. top-down budgeting.
   b. management acceptance.
   c. research and analysis.
   d. sound organizational structure.

(SO 2)   **3.** Compared to budgeting, long-range planning generally has the:
   a. same amount of detail.
   b. longer time period.
   c. same emphasis.
   d. same time period.

(SO 3)   **4.** A sales budget is:
   a. derived from the production budget.
   b. management's best estimate of sales revenue for the year.
   c. not the starting point for the master budget.
   d. prepared only for credit sales.

(SO 3)   **5.** The formula for the production budget is budgeted sales in units plus:
   a. desired ending merchandise inventory less beginning merchandise inventory.
   b. beginning finished goods units less desired ending finished goods units.
   c. desired ending direct materials units less beginning direct materials units.
   d. desired ending finished goods units less beginning finished goods units.

(SO 3)   **6.** Direct materials inventories are kept in pounds in Byrd Company, and the total pounds of direct materials needed for production is 9,500. If the beginning inventory is 1,000 pounds and the desired ending inventory is 2,200 pounds, the total pounds to be purchased is:

   a. 9,400.   **c.** 9,700.
   b. 9,500.   **d.** 10,700.

7. The formula for computing the direct labor cost budget (SO is to multiply the direct labor cost per hour by the:
   a. total required direct labor hours.
   b. physical units to be produced.
   c. equivalent units to be produced.
   d. No correct answer is given.

8. Each of the following budgets is used in preparing the (SO budgeted income statement *except* the:
   a. sales budget.
   b. selling and administrative budget.
   c. capital expenditure budget.
   d. direct labor budget.

9. Expected direct materials purchases in Read Company (SO are $70,000 in the first quarter and $90,000 in the second quarter. Forty percent of the purchases are paid in cash as incurred, and the balance is paid in the following quarter. The budgeted cash payments for purchases in the second quarter are:
   a. $96,000.   **c.** $78,000.
   b. $90,000.   **d.** $72,000.

10. The budget for a merchandiser differs from a budget for (SO a manufacturer because:
   a. a merchandise purchases budget replaces the production budget.
   b. the manufacturing budgets are not applicable.
   c. None of the above.
   d. Both (a) and (b) above.

QUESTIONS

1. (a) What is a budget?
   (b) How does a budget contribute to good management?

2. Donna Cox and Tony Carpino are discussing the benefits of budgeting. They ask you to identify the primary advantages of budgeting. Comply with their request.

3. Kate Coulter asks your help in understanding the essentials of effective budgeting. Identify the essentials for Kate.

4. (a) "Accounting plays a relatively unimportant role in budgeting." Do you agree? Explain.
   (b) What responsibilities does management have in budgeting?

5. What criteria are helpful in determining the length of the budget period? What is the most common budget period?

6. Ann Wilkins maintains that the only difference between budgeting and long-range planning is time. Do you agree? Why or why not?

7. Distinguish between a master budget and a sales forecast.

8. What budget is the starting point in preparing the master budget? What may result if this budget is inaccurate?

9. "The production budget shows both unit production data and unit cost data." Is this true? Explain.

10. Alov Company has 10,000 beginning finished goods units. Budgeted sales units are 160,000. If management desires 20,000 ending finished goods units, what are the required units of production?

11. In preparing the direct materials budget for Quan Company, management concludes that required purchases are 54,000 units. If 52,000 direct materials units are required in production and there are 7,000 units of beginning direct materials, what is the desired units of ending direct materials?

12. The production budget of Layden Company calls for 90,000 units to be produced. If it takes 30 minutes to make one unit and the direct labor rate is $16 per hour, what is the total budgeted direct labor cost?

13. Marrero Company's manufacturing overhead budget shows total variable costs of $168,000 and total fixed costs of $162,000. Total production in units is expected to be 160,000. It takes 15 minutes to make one unit, and the direct labor rate is $15 per hour. Express the manufacturing overhead rate as (a) a percentage of direct labor cost, and (b) an amount per direct labor hour.

14. Ankiel Company's variable selling and administrative expenses are 10% of net sales. Fixed expenses are $60,000 per quarter. The sales budget shows expected sales of $200,000 and $250,000 in the first and second quarters, respectively. What are the total budgeted selling and administrative expenses for each quarter?

15. For Tomko Company, the budgeted cost for one unit of product is direct materials $10, direct labor $20, and manufacturing overhead 80% of direct labor cost. If 25,000 units are expected to be sold at $69 each, what is the budgeted gross profit?

16. Indicate the supporting schedules used in preparing a budgeted income statement through gross profit for a manufacturer.

17. Identify the three sections of a cash budget. What balances are also shown in this budget?

18. Springer Company has credit sales of $400,000 in January. Past experience suggests that 45% is collected in the month of sale, 50% in the month following the sale, and 4% in the second month following the sale. Compute the cash collections from January sales in January, February, and March.

19. What is the formula for determining required merchandise purchases for a merchandiser?

20. How may expected revenues in a service enterprise be computed?

BRIEF EXERCISES

BE24-1 Russo Manufacturing Company uses the following budgets: Balance Sheet, Capital Expenditure, Cash, Direct Labor, Direct Materials, Income Statement, Manufacturing Overhead, Production, Sales, and Selling and Administrative. Prepare a diagram of the interrelationships of the budgets in the master budget. Indicate whether each budget is an operating or a financial budget.

Prepare a diagram of a master budget.
(SO 3)

BE24-2 Maltz Company estimates that unit sales will be 10,000 in quarter 1; 12,000 in quarter 2; 14,000 in quarter 3; and 18,000 in quarter 4. Using a sales price of $70 per unit, prepare the sales budget by quarters for the year ending December 31, 2005.

Prepare a sales budget.
(SO 3)

BE24-3 Sales budget data for Maltz Company are given in BE24-2. Management desires to have an ending finished goods inventory equal to 25% of the next quarter's expected unit sales. Prepare a production budget by quarters for the first 6 months of 2005.

Prepare a production budget for 2 quarters.
(SO 3)

BE24-4 Gomez Company has 1,600 pounds of raw materials in its December 31, 2005, ending inventory. Required production for January and February are 4,000 and 5,000 units, respectively. Two pounds of raw materials are needed for each unit, and the estimated cost per pound is $6. Management desires an ending inventory equal to 20% of next month's materials requirements. Prepare the direct materials budget for January.

Prepare a direct materials budget for 1 month.
(SO 3)

BE24-5 For Tracey Company, units to be produced are 5,000 in quarter 1 and 6,000 in quarter 2. It takes 1.8 hours to make a finished unit, and the expected hourly wage rate is $14 per hour. Prepare a direct labor budget by quarters for the 6 months ending June 30, 2005.

Prepare a direct labor budget for 2 quarters.
(SO 3)

BE24-6 For Savage Inc. variable manufacturing overhead costs are expected to be $20,000 in the first quarter of 2005 with $2,000 increments in each of the remaining three quarters. Fixed overhead costs are estimated to be $35,000 in each quarter. Prepare the manufacturing overhead budget by quarters for the year.

Prepare a manufacturing overhead budget.
(SO 3)

BE24-7 Rado Company classifies its selling and administrative expense budget into variable and fixed components. Variable expenses are expected to be $25,000 in the first quarter, and $3,000 increments are expected in the remaining quarters of 2005. Fixed expenses are expected to be $40,000 in each quarter. Prepare the selling and administrative expense budget by quarters for 2005.

Prepare a selling and administrative expense budget.
(SO 3)

BE24-8 Stoker Company has completed all of its operating budgets. The sales budget for the year shows 50,000 units and total sales of $2,000,000. The total unit cost of making one unit of sales is $24. Selling and administrative expenses are expected to be $300,000. Income taxes are estimated to be $150,000. Prepare a budgeted income statement for the year ending December 31, 2005.

Prepare a budgeted income statement for the year.
(SO 4)

Prepare data for a cash budget.

(SO 5)

BE24-9 Chow Industries expects credit sales for January, February, and March to be $200,000, $260,000, and $310,000, respectively. It is expected that 70% of the sales will be collected in the month of sale, and 30% will be collected in the following month. Compute cash collections from customers for each month.

Determine required merchandise purchases for 1 month.

(SO 6)

BE24-10 Reebles Wholesalers is preparing its merchandise purchases budget. Budgeted sales are $400,000 for April and $450,000 for May. Cost of goods sold is expected to be 60% of sales. The company's desired ending inventory is 20% of the following month's cost of goods sold. Compute the required purchases for April.

EXERCISES

Prepare a sales budget for 2 quarters.

(SO 3)

E24-1 Vosser Electronics Inc. produces and sells two models of pocket calculators, XQ-103 and XQ-104. The calculators sell for $12 and $25, respectively. Because of the intense competition Vosser faces, management budgets sales semiannually. Its projections for the first 2 quarters of 2005 are as follows.

	Unit Sales	
Product	**Quarter 1**	**Quarter 2**
XQ-103	30,000	25,000
XQ-104	12,000	13,000

No changes in selling prices are anticipated.

Instructions
Prepare a sales budget for the 2 quarters ending June 30, 2005. List the products and show for each quarter and for the 6 months, units, selling price, and total sales by product and in total.

Prepare quarterly production budgets.

(SO 3)

E24-2 Wayans Company produces and sells two types of automobile batteries, the heavy-duty HD-240 and the long-life LL-250. The 2005 sales budget for the two products is as follows.

Quarter	**HD-240**	**LL-250**
1	5,000	10,000
2	7,000	18,000
3	8,000	20,000
4	10,000	35,000

The January 1, 2005, inventory of HD-240 and LL-250 units is 2,000 and 4,000, respectively. Management desires an ending inventory each quarter equal to 40% of the next quarter's sales. Sales in the first quarter of 2006 are expected to be 30% higher than sales in the same quarter in 2005.

Instructions
Prepare separate quarterly production budgets for each product by quarters for 2005.

Prepare a direct materials purchases budget.

(SO 3)

E24-3 Samano Industries has adopted the following production budget for the first 4 months of 2006.

Month	**Units**	**Month**	**Units**
January	10,000	March	5,000
February	8,000	April	4,000

Each unit requires 5 pounds of raw materials costing $2.00 per pound. On December 31, 2005, the ending raw materials inventory was 15,000 pounds. Management wants to have a raw materials inventory at the end of the month equal to 30% of next month's production requirements.

Instructions
Prepare a direct materials purchases budget by months for the first quarter.

E24-4 The Sanchez Company budget committee has reached agreement on the following data for the 6 months ending June 30, 2006.

Prepare production and direct materials budgets by quarters for 6 months.

(SO 3)

Sales units:	First quarter 5,000; second quarter 8,000
Ending raw materials inventory:	50% of the next quarter's production requirements
Ending finished goods inventory:	30% of the next quarter's expected sales units

The ending raw materials and finished goods inventories at December 31, 2005, follow the same percentage relationships to production and sales that occur in 2006. Three pounds of raw materials are required to make each unit of finished goods. Raw materials purchased are expected to cost $4 per pound. Sales of 7,000 units and required production of 7,250 units are expected in the third quarter of 2006.

Instructions
(a) Prepare a production budget by quarters for the 6 months.
(b) Prepare a direct materials budget by quarters for the 6 months.

E24-5 Pacer, Inc., is preparing its direct labor budget for 2005 from the following production budget based on a calendar year.

Prepare a direct labor budget.
(SO 3)

Quarter	Units	Quarter	Units
1	20,000	3	35,000
2	25,000	4	30,000

Each unit requires 1.2 hours of direct labor.

Instructions
Prepare a direct labor cost budget for 2005. Wage rates are expected to be $15 for the first 2 quarters and $16 for quarters 3 and 4.

E24-6 Keyser Company is preparing its manufacturing overhead budget for 2005. Relevant data consist of the following.

Prepare a manufacturing overhead budget for the year.
(SO 3)

Units to be produced (by quarters): 10,000, 12,000, 14,000, 16,000.

Direct labor: Time is 1.5 hours per unit.

Variable overhead costs per direct labor hour: Indirect materials $0.70; indirect labor $1.20; and maintenance $0.30.

Fixed overhead costs per quarter: Supervisory salaries $35,000; depreciation $16,000; and maintenance $12,000.

Instructions
Prepare the manufacturing overhead budget for the year, showing quarterly data.

E24-7 Lockwood Company combines its operating expenses for budget purposes in a selling and administrative expense budget. For the first 6 months of 2005, the following data are available.

Prepare a selling and administrative expense budget for 2 quarters.

(SO 3)

1. Sales: 20,000 units quarter 1; 24,000 units quarter 2.
2. Variable costs per dollar of sales: Sales commissions 5%, delivery expense 2%, and advertising 3%.
3. Fixed costs per quarter: Sales salaries $10,000, office salaries $6,000, depreciation $4,200, insurance $1,500, utilities $800, and repairs expense $600.
4. Unit selling price: $20.

Instructions
Prepare a selling and administrative expense budget by quarters for the first 6 months of 2005.

E24-8 Haven Company has accumulated the following budget data for the year 2005.

Prepare a budgeted income statement for the year.

(SO 3, 4)

1. Sales: 40,000 units, unit selling price $80.
2. Cost of one unit of finished goods: Direct materials 2 pounds at $5 per pound, direct labor 3 hours at $12 per hour, and manufacturing overhead $6 per direct labor hour.
3. Inventories (raw materials only): Beginning, 10,000 pounds; ending, 15,000 pounds.
4. Raw materials cost: $5 per pound.
5. Selling and administrative expenses: $200,000.
6. Income taxes: 30% of income before income taxes.

Instructions

Prepare a budgeted income statement for 2005. Show the computation of cost of goods sold.

Prepare a cash budget for 2 months.

(SO 5)

E24-9 Nunez Company expects to have a cash balance of $46,000 on January 1, 2005. Relevant monthly budget data for the first 2 months of 2005 are as follows.

Collections from customers: January $75,000, February $150,000.

Payments to suppliers: January $45,000, February $70,000.

Direct labor: January $30,000, February $45,000. Wages are paid in the month they are incurred.

Manufacturing overhead: January $21,000, February $30,000. These costs include depreciation of $1,000 per month. All other overhead costs are paid as incurred.

Selling and administrative expenses: January $15,000, February $20,000. These costs are exclusive of depreciation. They are paid as incurred.

Sales of marketable securities in January are expected to realize $10,000 in cash. Nunez Company has a line of credit at a local bank that enables it to borrow up to $25,000. The company wants to maintain a minimum monthly cash balance of $20,000.

Instructions

Prepare a cash budget for January and February.

Prepare a purchases budget and budgeted income statement for a merchandiser.

(SO 6)

E24-10 In May 2005, the budget committee of Loebs Stores assembles the following data in preparation of budgeted merchandise purchases for the month of June.

1. Expected sales: June $550,000, July $600,000.
2. Cost of goods sold is expected to be 70% of sales.
3. Desired ending merchandise inventory is 40% of the following (next) month's cost of goods sold.
4. The beginning inventory at June 1 will be the desired amount.

Instructions

(a) Compute the budgeted merchandise purchases for June.
(b) Prepare the budgeted income statement for June through gross profit on sales.

PROBLEMS: SET A

Prepare a budgeted income statement and supporting budgets.

(SO 3, 4)

P24-1A Tilger Farm Supply Company manufactures and sells a fertilizer called Basic II. The following data are available for preparing budgets for Basic II for the first 2 quarters of 2005.

1. Sales: Quarter 1, 40,000 bags; quarter 2, 55,000 bags. Selling price is $60 per bag.
2. Direct materials: Each bag of Basic II requires 6 pounds of Crup at a cost of $3 per pound and 10 pounds of Dert at $1.50 per pound.
3. Desired inventory levels:

Type of Inventory	January 1	April 1	July 1
Basic II (bags)	10,000	15,000	20,000
Crup (pounds)	9,000	12,000	15,000
Dert (pounds)	15,000	20,000	25,000

4. Direct labor: Direct labor time is 15 minutes per bag at an hourly rate of $12 per hour.
5. Selling and administrative expenses are expected to be 10% of sales plus $150,000 per quarter.
6. Income taxes are expected to be 30% of income from operations.

Your assistant has prepared two budgets: (1) The manufacturing overhead budget shows expected costs to be 100% of direct labor cost. (2) The direct materials budget for Dert which shows the cost of Dert to be $682,500 in quarter 1 and $907,500 in quarter 2.

Instructions

Net income $787,500
Cost per bag $39.00

Prepare the budgeted income statement for the first 6 months of 2005 and all required supporting budgets by quarters. (*Note*: Use variable and fixed in the selling and administrative expense budget.)

P24-2A Greish Inc. is preparing its annual budgets for the year ending December 31, 2005. Accounting assistants furnish the following data.

Prepare sales, production, direct materials, direct labor, and income statement budgets.

(SO 3, 4)

	Product LN 35	Product LN 40
Sales budget:		
Anticipated volume in units	350,000	180,000
Unit selling price	$20.00	$30.00
Production budget:		
Desired ending finished goods units	30,000	25,000
Beginning finished goods units	20,000	15,000
Direct materials budget:		
Direct materials per unit (pounds)	2	3
Desired ending direct materials pounds	50,000	20,000
Beginning direct materials pounds	40,000	10,000
Cost per pound	$2.00	$3.00
Direct labor budget:		
Direct labor time per unit	0.5	0.75
Direct labor rate per hour	$10.00	$10.00
Budgeted income statement:		
Total unit cost	$10.00	$20.00

An accounting assistant has prepared the detailed manufacturing overhead budget and the selling and administrative expense budget. The latter shows selling expenses of $560,000 for product LN 35 and $440,000 for product LN 40, and administrative expenses of $420,000 for product LN 35 and $380,000 for product LN 40. Income taxes are expected to be 30%.

Instructions

Prepare the following budgets for the year. Show data for each product. Quarterly budgets should not be prepared.

(a) Sales
(b) Production
(c) Direct materials
(d) Direct labor
(e) Income statement (*Note*: Income taxes are
     not allocated to the products.)

(a) Total sales $12,400,000
(b) Required production units:
    LN 35, 360,000
    LN 40, 190,000
(c) Total cost of direct materials purchases $3,200,000
(d) Total direct labor cost
    $3,225,000
(e) Net income $2,450,000

P24-3A Hirsch Industries has sales in 2005 of $5,250,000 (750,000 units) and gross profit of $1,587,500. Management is considering two alternative budget plans to increase its gross profit in 2006.

Prepare sales and production budgets and compute cost per unit under two plans.

(SO 3, 4)

Plan A would increase the selling price per unit from $7.00 to $7.60. Sales volume would decrease by 10% from its 2005 level. Plan B would decrease the selling price per unit by 5%. The marketing department expects that the sales volume would increase by 100,000 units.

At the end of 2005, Hirsch has 75,000 units on hand. If Plan A is accepted, the 2006 ending inventory should be equal to 90,000 units. If Plan B is accepted, the ending inventory should be equal to 100,000 units. Each unit produced will cost $2.00 in direct materials, $1.50 in direct labor, and $0.50 in variable overhead. The fixed overhead for 2006 should be $965,000.

Instructions

(a) Prepare a sales budget for 2006 under (1) Plan A and (2) Plan B.
(b) Prepare a production budget for 2006 under (1) Plan A and (2) Plan B.
(c) Compute the cost per unit under (1) Plan A and (2) Plan B. Explain why the cost per unit is different for each of the two plans. (Round to two decimals.)
(d) Which plan should be accepted? (*Hint*: Compute the gross profit under each plan.)

(c) Unit cost: Plan A $5.40,
    Plan B $5.10
(d) Gross profit:
    Plan A $1,485,000
    Plan B $1,317,500

P24-4A Lorch Company prepares monthly cash budgets. Relevant data from operating budgets for 2006 are:

Prepare cash budget for 2 months.

(SO 5)

	January	February
Sales	$360,000	$400,000
Direct materials purchases	100,000	110,000
Direct labor	100,000	115,000
Manufacturing overhead	60,000	75,000
Selling and administrative expenses	75,000	80,000

All sales are on account. Collections are expected to be 60% in the month of sale, 30% in the first month following the sale, and 10% in the second month following the sale. Thirty percent (30%) of direct materials purchases are paid in cash in the month of purchase, and the balance due is paid in the month following the purchase. All other items above are paid in the month incurred. Depreciation has been excluded from manufacturing overhead and selling and administrative expenses.

Other data:

1. Credit sales: November 2005, $200,000; December 2005, $280,000.
2. Purchases of direct materials: December 2005, $90,000.
3. Other receipts: January—Collection of December 31, 2005, interest receivable $3,000; February—Proceeds from sale of securities $5,000.
4. Other disbursements: February—payment of $20,000 for land.

The company's cash balance on January 1, 2006, is expected to be $60,000. The company wants to maintain a minimum cash balance of $50,000.

(a) January:
  collections $320,000
  payments $93,000
(b) Ending cash balance:
  January $55,000
  February $50,000

Instructions

(a) Prepare schedules for (1) expected collections from customers and (2) expected payments for direct materials purchases.
(b) Prepare a cash budget for January and February in columnar form.

Prepare purchases and income statement budgets for a merchandiser.

(SO 6)

P24-5A The budget committee of Ridder Company collects the following data for its Westwood Store in preparing budgeted income statements for July and August 2005.

1. Expected sales: July $400,000, August $450,000, September $500,000.
2. Cost of goods sold is expected to be 60% of sales.
3. Company policy is to maintain ending merchandise inventory at 25% of the following month's cost of goods sold.
4. Operating expenses are estimated to be:

Sales salaries	$30,000 per month
Advertising	4% of monthly sales
Delivery expense	2% of monthly sales
Sales commissions	3% of monthly sales
Rent expense	$3,000 per month
Depreciation	$700 per month
Utilities	$500 per month
Insurance	$300 per month

5. Income taxes are estimated to be 30% of income from operations.

(a) Purchases: July $247,500
  August $277,500
(b) Net income: July $62,650
  August $73,500

Instructions

(a) Prepare the merchandise purchases budget for each month in columnar form.
(b) Prepare budgeted income statements for each month in columnar form. Show the details of cost of goods sold in the statements.

Prepare budgeted income statement and balance sheet.

(SO 3, 4)

P24-6A Kurian Industries' balance sheet at December 31, 2005, is presented below.

KURIAN INDUSTRIES
Balance Sheet
December 31, 2005

Assets

Current assets		
Cash		$ 7,500
Accounts receivable		82,500
Finished goods inventory (2,000 units)		30,000
Total current assets		120,000
Property, plant, and equipment		
Equipment	$40,000	
Less: Accumulated depreciation	10,000	30,000
Total assets		$150,000

Liabilities and Stockholders' Equity

Liabilities		
Notes payable		$ 25,000
Accounts payable		45,000
Total liabilities		70,000
Stockholders' equity		
Common stock	$50,000	
Retained earnings	30,000	
Total stockholders' equity		80,000
Total liabilities and stockholders' equity		$150,000

Additional information accumulated for the budgeting process is as follows.
  Budgeted data for the year 2006 include the following.

	4th Qtr. of 2006	Year 2006 Total
Sales budget (8,000 units at $30)	$70,000	$240,000
Direct materials used	17,000	69,400
Direct labor	8,500	38,600
Manufacturing overhead applied	10,000	54,000
Selling and administrative expenses	18,000	76,000

   To meet sales requirements and to have 3,000 units of finished goods on hand at December 31, 2006, the production budget shows 9,000 required units of output. The total unit cost of production is expected to be $18. Kurian Industries uses the first-in, first-out (FIFO) inventory costing method. Selling and administrative expenses include $4,000 for depreciation on equipment. Interest expense is expected to be $3,500 for the year. Income taxes are expected to be 30% of income before income taxes.

   All sales and purchases are on account. It is expected that 60% of quarterly sales are collected in cash within the quarter and the remainder is collected in the following quarter. Direct materials purchased from suppliers are paid 50% in the quarter incurred and the remainder in the following quarter. Purchases in the fourth quarter were the same as the materials used. In 2006, the company expects to purchase additional equipment costing $14,000. It expects to pay $8,000 on notes payable plus all interest due and payable to December 31 (included in interest expense $3,500, above). Accounts payable at December 31, 2006, includes amounts due suppliers (see above) plus other accounts payable of $10,700. In 2006, the company expects to declare and pay a $5,000 cash dividend. Unpaid income taxes at December 31 will be $5,000. The company's cash budget shows an expected cash balance of $9,950 at December 31, 2006.

Instructions
Prepare a budgeted income statement for 2006 and a budgeted balance sheet at December 31, 2006. In preparing the income statement, you will need to compute cost of goods manufactured (materials + labor + overhead) and finished goods inventory (December 31, 2006).

Net income $15,750
Total assets $131,950

PROBLEMS: SET B

P24-1B Wahlen Farm Supply Company manufactures and sells a pesticide called Snare. The following data are available for preparing budgets for Snare for the first 2 quarters of 2006.

1. Sales: Quarter 1, 28,000 bags; quarter 2, 40,000 bags. Selling price is $60 per bag.
2. Direct materials: Each bag of Snare requires 4 pounds of Gumm at a cost of $3 per pound and 6 pounds of Tarr at $1.50 per pound.
3. Desired inventory levels:

Prepare budgeted income statement and supporting budgets.

(SO 3, 4)

Type of Inventory	January 1	April 1	July 1
Snare (bags)	8,000	12,000	18,000
Gumm (pounds)	9,000	10,000	13,000
Tarr (pounds)	14,000	20,000	25,000

4. Direct labor: Direct labor time is 15 minutes per bag at an hourly rate of $14 per hour.
5. Selling and administrative expenses are expected to be 15% of sales plus $175,000 per quarter.
6. Income taxes are expected to be 30% of income from operations.

Your assistant has prepared two budgets: (1) The manufacturing overhead budget shows expected costs to be 150% of direct labor cost. (2) The direct materials budget for Tarr shows the cost of Tarr to be $297,000 in quarter 1 and $421,500 in quarter 2.

Instructions

Net income $766,500
Cost per bag $29.75

Prepare the budgeted income statement for the first 6 months and all required supporting budgets by quarters. (*Note*: Use variable and fixed in the selling and administrative expense budget).

Prepare sales, production, direct materials, direct labor, and income statement budgets.

(SO 3, 4)

P24-2B Lasorda Inc. is preparing its annual budgets for the year ending December 31, 2006. Accounting assistants furnish the following data.

	Product JB 50	Product JB 60
Sales budget:		
Anticipated volume in units	450,000	200,000
Unit selling price	$20.00	$25.00
Production budget:		
Desired ending finished goods units	25,000	15,000
Beginning finished goods units	30,000	10,000
Direct materials budget:		
Direct materials per unit (pounds)	2	3
Desired ending direct materials pounds	30,000	15,000
Beginning direct materials pounds	40,000	10,000
Cost per pound	$3.00	$4.00
Direct labor budget:		
Direct labor time per unit	0.4	0.6
Direct labor rate per hour	$10.00	$10.00
Budgeted income statement:		
Total unit cost	$12.00	$20.00

An accounting assistant has prepared the detailed manufacturing overhead budget and the selling and administrative expense budget. The latter shows selling expenses of $660,000 for product JB 50 and $360,000 for product JB 60, and administrative expenses of $540,000 for product JB 50 and $340,000 for product JB 60. Income taxes are expected to be 30%.

(a) Total sales $14,000,000
(b) Required production units:
JB 50, 445,000
JB 60, 205,000
(c) Total cost of direct materials purchases $5,120,000
(d) Total direct labor cost $3,010,000
(e) Net income $1,890,000

Instructions

Prepare the following budgets for the year. Show data for each product. Quarterly budgets should not be prepared.

(a) Sales
(b) Production
(c) Direct materials

(d) Direct labor
(e) Income statement (*Note*: Income taxes are not allocated to the products.)

Prepare sales and production budgets and compute cost per unit under two plans.

(SO 3, 4)

P24-3B Tick Industries had sales in 2005 of $6,000,000 and gross profit of $1,500,000. Management is considering two alternative budget plans to increase its gross profit in 2006.

Plan A would increase the selling price per unit from $8.00 to $8.40. Sales volume would decrease by 5% from its 2005 level. Plan B would decrease the selling price per unit by $0.50. The marketing department expects that the sales volume would increase by 150,000 units.

At the end of 2005, Tick has 30,000 units of inventory on hand. If Plan A is accepted, the 2006 ending inventory should be equal to 4% of the 2006 sales. If Plan B is accepted, the ending inventory should be equal to 40,000 units. Each unit produced will cost $1.80 in direct labor, $2.00 in direct materials, and $1.20 in variable overhead. The fixed overhead for 2006 should be $1,800,000.

Instructions

(a) Prepare a sales budget for 2006 under each plan.
(b) Prepare a production budget for 2006 under each plan.

(c) Compute the production cost per unit under each plan. Why is the cost per unit different for each of the two plans? (Round to two decimals.)

(d) Which plan should be accepted? (*Hint*: Compute the gross profit under each plan.)

(c) Unit cost: Plan A $7.53
Plan B $6.98
(d) Gross profit:
Plan A $619,875
Plan B $468,000

P24-4B Nigh Company prepares monthly cash budgets. Relevant data from operating budgets for 2006 are:

Prepare cash budget for 2 months.

(SO 5)

	January	February
Sales	$350,000	$400,000
Direct materials purchases	120,000	130,000
Direct labor	80,000	100,000
Manufacturing overhead	70,000	75,000
Selling and administrative expenses	79,000	81,000

All sales are on account. Collections are expected to be 50% in the month of sale, 30% in the first month following the sale, and 20% in the second month following the sale. Sixty percent (60%) of direct materials purchases are paid in cash in the month of purchase, and the balance due is paid in the month following the purchase. All other items above are paid in the month incurred except for selling and administrative expenses that include $1,000 of depreciation per month.

Other data:

1. Credit sales: November 2005, $260,000; December 2005, $300,000.
2. Purchases of direct materials: December 2005, $100,000.
3. Other receipts: January—Collection of December 31, 2005, notes receivable $15,000; February—Proceeds from sale of securities $6,000.
4. Other disbursements: February—Withdrawal of $5,000 cash for personal use of owner, Dewey Yaeger.

The company's cash balance on January 1, 2006, is expected to be $60,000. The company wants to maintain a minimum cash balance of $50,000.

Instructions

(a) Prepare schedules for (1) expected collections from customers and (2) expected payments for direct materials purchases.

(b) Prepare a cash budget for January and February in columnar form.

(a) January:
collections $317,000
payments $112,000
(b) Ending cash balance:
January $52,000
February $50,000

P24-5B The budget committee of Lococo Company collects the following data for its San Miguel Store in preparing budgeted income statements for May and June 2006.

Prepare purchases and income statement budgets for a merchandiser.

(SO 6)

1. Sales for May are expected to be $600,000. Sales in June and July are expected to be 10% higher than the preceding month.
2. Cost of goods sold is expected to be 75% of sales.
3. Company policy is to maintain ending merchandise inventory at 20% of the following month's cost of goods sold.
4. Operating expenses are estimated to be:

Sales salaries	$30,000 per month
Advertising	5% of monthly sales
Delivery expense	3% of monthly sales
Sales commissions	4% of monthly sales
Rent expense	$5,000 per month
Depreciation	$800 per month
Utilities	$600 per month
Insurance	$500 per month

5. Income taxes are estimated to be 30% of income from operations.

Instructions

(a) Prepare the merchandise purchases budget for each month in columnar form.

(b) Prepare budgeted income statements for each month in columnar form. Show in the statements the details of cost of goods sold.

(a) Purchases:
May $459,000
June $504,900
(b) Net income:
May $28,770
June $34,230

BROADENING YOUR PERSPECTIVE

Group Decision Case

BYP24-1   Peters Corporation operates on a calendar-year basis. It begins the annual budgeting process in late August when the president establishes targets for the total dollar sales and net income before taxes for the next year.

The sales target is given first to the marketing department. The marketing manager formulates a sales budget by product line in both units and dollars. From this budget, sales quotas by product line in units and dollars are established for each of the corporation's sales districts. The marketing manager also estimates the cost of the marketing activities required to support the target sales volume and prepares a tentative marketing expense budget.

The executive vice president uses the sales and profit targets, the sales budget by product line, and the tentative marketing expense budget to determine the dollar amounts that can be devoted to manufacturing and corporate office expense. The executive vice president prepares the budget for corporate expenses. She then forwards to the production department the product-line sales budget in units and the total dollar amount that can be devoted to manufacturing.

The production manager meets with the factory managers to develop a manufacturing plan that will produce the required units when needed within the cost constraints set by the executive vice president. The budgeting process usually comes to a halt at this point because the production department does not consider the financial resources allocated to be adequate.

When this standstill occurs, the vice president of finance, the executive vice president, the marketing manager, and the production manager meet together to determine the final budgets for each of the areas. This normally results in a modest increase in the total amount available for manufacturing costs and cuts in the marketing expense and corporate office expense budgets. The total sales and net income figures proposed by the president are seldom changed. Although the participants are seldom pleased with the compromise, these budgets are final. Each executive then develops a new detailed budget for the operations in his or her area.

None of the areas has achieved its budget in recent years. Sales often run below the target. When budgeted sales are not achieved, each area is expected to cut costs so that the president's profit target can be met. However, the profit target is seldom met because costs are not cut enough. In fact, costs often run above the original budget in all functional areas (marketing, production, and corporate office).

The president is disturbed that Peters has not been able to meet the sales and profit targets. He hired a consultant with considerable experience with companies in Peters's industry. The consultant reviewed the budgets for the past 4 years. He concluded that the product-line sales budgets were reasonable and that the cost and expense budgets were adequate for the budgeted sales and production levels.

Instructions

With the class divided into groups, answer the following.

(a) Discuss how the budgeting process employed by Peters Corporation contributes to the failure to achieve the president's sales and profit targets.
(b) Suggest how Peters Corporation's budgeting process could be revised to correct the problems.
(c) Should the functional areas be expected to cut their costs when sales volume falls below budget? Explain your answer.   (CMA adapted.)

Managerial Analysis

BYP24-2   Prasad & Green Inc. manufactures ergonomic devices for computer users. Some of their more popular products include glare screens (for computer monitors), keyboard stands with wrist rests, and carousels that allow easy access to magnetic (floppy) disks. Over the past 5 years, they experienced rapid growth, with sales of all products increasing 20% to 50% each year.

Last year, some of the primary manufacturers of computers began introducing new products with some of the ergonomic designs, such as glare screens and wrist rests, already built in. As a result, sales of Prasad & Green's accessory devices have declined somewhat. The company believes that the disk carousels will probably continue to show growth, but that the other products will probably continue to decline. When the next year's budget was prepared, increases were built in to research and development so that replacement products could be developed or the company could expand into some other product line. Some product lines being considered are general-purpose ergonomic devices including back supports, foot rests, and sloped writing pads.

The most recent results have shown that sales decreased more than was expected for the glare screens. As a result, the company may have a shortage of funds. Top management has therefore asked that all expenses be reduced 10% to compensate for these reduced sales. Summary budget information is as follows.

Raw materials	$240,000
Direct labor	110,000
Insurance	50,000
Depreciation	90,000
Machine repairs	30,000
Sales salaries	50,000
Office salaries	80,000
Factory salaries (indirect labor)	50,000
Total	$700,000

Instructions

Using the information above, answer the following questions.

(a) What are the implications of reducing each of the costs? For example, if the company reduces raw materials costs, it may have to do so by purchasing lower-quality materials. This may affect sales in the long run.

(b) Based on your analysis in (a), what do you think is the best way to obtain the $70,000 in cost savings requested? Be specific. Are there any costs that cannot or should not be reduced? Why?

Real-World Focus

BYP24-3 **Network Computing Devices Inc.** was founded in 1988 in Mountain View, Calif. The company develops software products such as X-terminals, Z-mail, PC X-ware, and related hardware products. Presented below is a discussion by management in its annual report.

NETWORK COMPUTING DEVICES, INC.
Management Discussion

The Company's operating results have varied significantly, particularly on a quarterly basis, as a result of a number of factors, including general economic conditions affecting industry demand for computer products, the timing and market acceptance of new product introductions by the Company and its competitors, the timing of significant orders from large customers, periodic changes in product pricing and discounting due to competitive factors, and the availability of key components, such as video monitors and electronic subassemblies, some of which require substantial order lead times. The Company's operating results may fluctuate in the future as a result of these and other factors, including the Company's success in developing and introducing new products, its product and customer mix, and the level of competition which it experiences. The Company operates with a small backlog. Sales and operating results, therefore, generally depend on the volume and timing of orders received, which are difficult to forecast. The Company has experienced slowness in orders from some customers during the first quarter of each calendar year due to budgeting cycles common in the computer industry. In addition, sales in Europe typically are adversely affected in the third calendar quarter as many European customers reduce their business activities during the month of August.

Due to the Company's rapid growth rate and the effect of new product introductions on quarterly revenues, these seasonal trends have not materially impacted the Company's results of operations to date. However, as the Company's product lines mature and its rate of revenue growth declines, these seasonal factors may become more evident. Additionally, the Company's international sales are denominated in U.S. dollars, and an increase or decrease in the value of the U.S. dollar relative to foreign currencies could make the Company's products less or more competitive in those markets.

Instructions

(a) Identify the factors that affect the budgeting process at Network Computing Devices, Inc.

(b) Explain the additional budgeting concerns created by the international operations of the company.

Exploring the Web

BYP24-4 The opportunities for business consulting in the areas of corporate planning, budgeting, and strategy are almost limitless as new, more powerful software continues to be developed. This exercise takes you to the Web site of **CP Corporate Planning**, a European consulting firm.

Address: www.corporate-planning.com/home/fse_home.html, or go to www.wiley.com/college/weygandt

Steps: Go to the site above.

Instructions

Choose three case studies, and in each case identify the problem the company faced and how the situation was resolved.

Communication Activity

BYP24-5 In order to better serve their rural patients, Drs. Ken and Dick Ginavan (brothers) began giving safety seminars. Especially popular were their "emergency-preparedness" talks given to farmers. Many people asked whether the "kit" of materials the doctors recommended for common farm emergencies was commercially available.

After checking with several suppliers, the doctors realized that no other company offered the supplies they recommended in their seminars, packaged in the way they described. Their wives, Nancy and Sue, agreed to make a test package by ordering supplies from various medical supply companies and assembling them into a "kit" that could be sold at the seminars. When these kits proved a runaway success, the sisters-in-law decided to market them. At the advice of their accountant, they organized this venture as a separate company, called Life Protection Products (LPP), with Nancy Ginavan as CEO and Sue Ginavan as Secretary-Treasurer.

LPP soon started receiving requests for the kits from all over the country, as word spread about their availability. Even without advertising, LPP was able to sell its full inventory every month. However, the company was becoming financially strained. Nancy and Sue had about $100,000 in savings, and they invested about half that amount initially. They believed that this venture would allow them to make money. However, at the present time, only about $30,000 of the cash remains, and the company is constantly short of cash.

Nancy Ginavan has come to you for advice. She does not understand why the company is having cash flow problems. She and Sue have not even been withdrawing salaries. However, they have rented a local building and have hired two more full-time workers to help them cope with the increasing demand. They do not think they could handle the demand without this additional help.

Nancy is also worried that the cash problems mean that the company may not be able to support itself. She has prepared the cash budget shown on the next page. All seminar customers pay for their products in full at the time of purchase. In addition, several large companies have ordered the kits for use by employees who work in remote sites. They have requested credit terms and have been allowed to pay in the month following the sale. These large purchasers amount to about 25% of the sales at the present time. LPP purchases the materials for the kits about 2 months ahead of time. Nancy and Sue are considering slowing the growth of the company by simply purchasing less materials, which will mean selling fewer kits.

The workers are paid in cash weekly. Nancy and Sue need about $15,000 cash on hand at the beginning of the month to pay for purchases of raw materials. Right now they have been using cash from their savings, but as noted, only $30,000 is left.

The cash budget that Nancy Ginavan has given you is shown at the top of the next page.

Instructions

Write a response to Nancy Ginavan. Explain why LPP is short of cash. Will this company be able to support itself? Explain your answer. Make any recommendations you deem appropriate.

LIFE PROTECTION PRODUCTS
Cash Budget
For the Quarter Ending June 30, 2006

	April	May	June
Cash balance, beginning	$15,000	$15,000	$15,000
Cash received			
From prior month sales	5,000	7,500	12,500
From current sales	15,000	22,500	37,500
Total cash on hand	35,000	45,000	65,000
Cash payments			
To employees	3,000	3,000	3,000
For products	25,000	35,000	45,000
Miscellaneous expenses	5,000	6,000	7,000
Postage	1,000	1,000	1,000
Total cash payments	34,000	45,000	56,000
Cash balance	$ 1,000	$ 0	$ 9,000
Borrow from savings	$14,000	$15,000	$ 1,000
Borrow from bank?	$ 0	$ 0	$ 5,000

Ethics Case

BYP24-6 You are an accountant in the budgetary, projections, and special projects department of National Conductor, Inc., a large manufacturing company. The president, Richard Sheen, asks you on very short notice to prepare some sales and income projections covering the next 2 years of the company's much heralded new product lines. He wants these projections for a series of speeches he is making while on a 2-week trip to eight East Coast brokerage firms. The president hopes to bolster National's stock sales and price.

You work 23 hours in 2 days to compile the projections, hand deliver them to the president, and are swiftly but graciously thanked as he departs. A week later you find time to go over some of your computations and discover a miscalculation that makes the projections grossly overstated. You quickly inquire about the president's itinerary and learn that he has made half of his speeches and has half yet to make. You are in a quandary as to what to do.

Instructions
(a) What are the consequences of telling the president of your gross miscalculations?
(b) What are the consequences of *not* telling the president of your gross miscalculations?
(c) What are the ethical considerations to you and the president in this situation?

Answers to Self-Study Questions
1. c   **2.** a   **3.** b   **4.** b   **5.** d   **6.** d   **7.** a   **8.** c   **9.** c   **10.** d

Answer to PepsiCo Review It Question 5, page 985

In its MD & A section, under "Cautionary Statements," **PepsiCo** makes the following statement: "We discuss expectations regarding our future performance, such as our business outlook, in our annual and quarterly reports, press releases, and other written and oral statements. These 'forward-looking statements' are based on currently available competitive, financial and economic data and our operating plans. They are inherently uncertain, and investors must recognize that events could turn out to be significantly different from our expectations."

In addition, PepsiCo makes statements in its Management's Discussion and Analysis section about expectations in 2003 and beyond and futuristic statements in its Notes to Consolidated Financial Statements.

 ✓**REMEMBER** to go back to the Navigator box on the chapter-opening page and check off your completed work.

Budgetary Control and Responsibility Accounting

CONCEPTS FOR REVIEW

Before studying this chapter, you should know or, if necessary, review:

The meaning and scope of the management function of controlling.
(Ch. 20, p. 819)

The cost elements that produce a total cost per unit of finished goods.
(Ch. 20, pp. 820–822)

How variable costs differ from fixed costs.
(Ch. 23, pp. 934–938)

Trying to Avoid an Electric Shock

Budgets are critical to evaluating an organization's success. They are based on management's expectations of what is most likely to happen in the future. In order to be useful, they must be accurate. But what if management's expectations are wrong? Estimates are never exactly correct, and sometimes, especially in volatile industries, estimates can be "off by a mile."

In recent years the electric utility industry has become very volatile. Deregulation; volatile prices for natural gas, coal, and oil; changes in environmental regulations; and economic

swings have all contributed to large changes in the profitability of electric utility companies. This means that for planning and budgeting purposes, utilities must plan and budget based on multiple "what if" scenarios that take into account factors beyond management's control. For example, in recent years, **Duke Energy Corporation**, headquartered in Charlotte, North Carolina, built budgeting and planning models based on three different scenarios of what the future might hold. One scenario assumes that the U.S. economy will slow considerably. A second scenario assumes that the company will experience "pricing pressure" as the market for energy becomes more efficient as a result of more energy being traded in Internet auctions. A third scenario assumes a continuation of the current environment of rapid growth, changing regulation, and large swings in the prices for the fuels the company uses to create energy.

Compounding this budgeting challenge is the fact that changes in many indirect costs can also significantly affect the company. For example, even a tiny change in market interest rates has a huge effect on the company because it has massive amounts of outstanding debt. And finally, as a result of the California energy crisis, there is mounting pressure for government intervention and regulation. This pressure has resulted in setting "rate caps" that limit the amount that utilities and energy companies can charge, thus lowering profits. The bottom line is that for budgeting and planning purposes, utility companies must remain alert and flexible.

STUDY OBJECTIVES

After studying this chapter, you should be able to:

1. Describe the concept of budgetary control.
2. Evaluate the usefulness of static budget reports.
3. Explain the development of flexible budgets and the usefulness of flexible budget reports.
4. Describe the concept of responsibility accounting.
5. Indicate the features of responsibility reports for cost centers.
6. Identify the content of responsibility reports for profit centers.
7. Explain the basis and formula used in evaluating performance in investment centers.

In Chapter 24 you learned how budgets are used for planning. In this chapter we consider how budgets are used by management to control operations. In the Feature Story on Duke Energy, we saw that budgeting must take into account factors beyond management's control. This chapter focuses on two aspects of management control: (1) budgetary control and (2) responsibility accounting.

The content and organization of Chapter 25 are as follows.

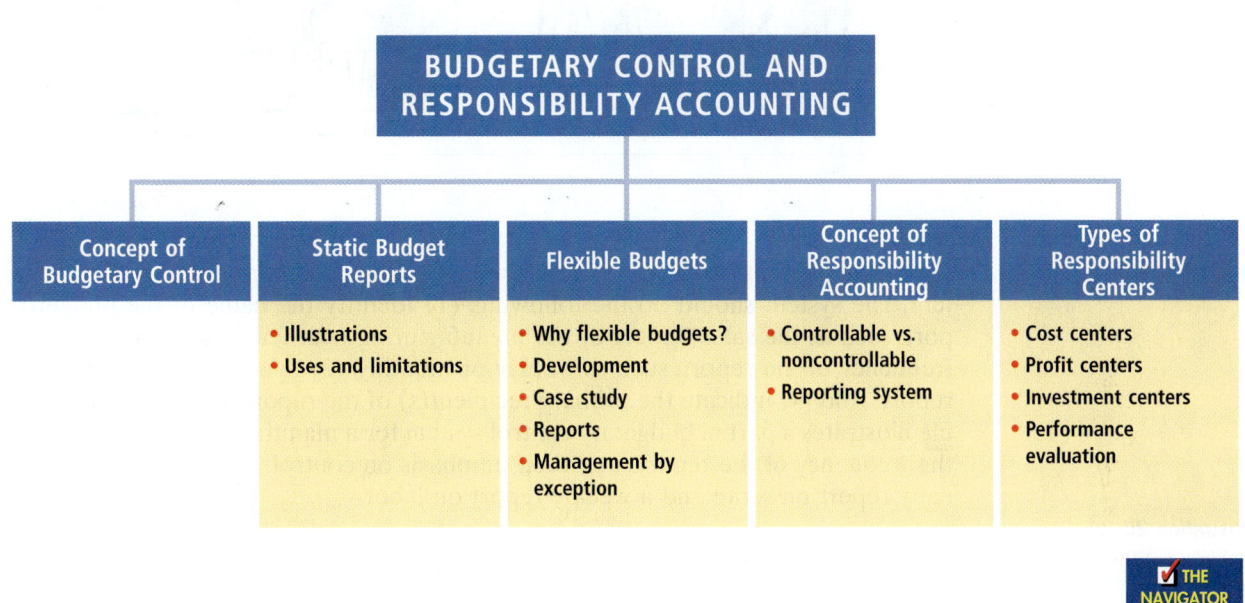

Concept of Budgetary Control

One of management's major functions is to control company operations. Control consists of the steps taken by management to see that planned objectives are met. We now ask: How do budgets contribute to control of operations?

The use of budgets in controlling operations is known as **budgetary control**. Such control takes place by means of **budget reports** that compare actual results with planned objectives. The use of budget reports is based on the belief that planned objectives lose much of their potential value without some monitoring of progress along the way. Just as your professors give midterm exams to evaluate your progress, so top management requires periodic reports on the progress of department managers toward their planned objectives.

Budget reports provide management with feedback on operations. The feedback for a crucial objective, such as having enough cash on hand to pay bills, may be made daily. For other objectives, such as meeting budgeted annual sales and operating expenses, monthly budget reports may suffice. Budget reports can be prepared as frequently as needed. From these reports, management analyzes any differences between actual and planned results and determines their causes. Management then may take corrective action, or it may decide to modify future plans.

Budgetary control involves the activities shown in Illustration 25-1 (page 1008).

STUDY OBJECTIVE 1

Describe the concept of budgetary control.

Illustration 25-1
Budgetary control

Budgetary control works best when a company has a formalized reporting system. The system should do the following: (1) Identify the name of the budget report, such as the sales budget or the manufacturing overhead budget. (2) State the frequency of the report, such as weekly or monthly. (3) Specify the purpose of the report. And (4) indicate the primary recipient(s) of the report. The following schedule illustrates a partial budgetary control system for a manufacturing company. Note the frequency of the reports and their emphasis on control. For example, there is a daily report on scrap and a weekly report on labor.

Illustration 25-2
Budgetary control reporting system

Name of Report	Frequency	Purpose	Primary Recipient(s)
Sales	Weekly	Determine whether sales goals are being met	Top management and sales manager
Labor	Weekly	Control direct and indirect labor costs	Vice president of production and production department managers
Scrap	Daily	Determine efficient use of materials	Production manager
Departmental overhead costs	Monthly	Control overhead costs	Department manager
Selling expenses	Monthly	Control selling expenses	Sales manager
Income statement	Monthly and quarterly	Determine whether income objectives are being met	Top management

Static Budget Reports

STUDY OBJECTIVE 2

Evaluate the usefulness of static budget reports.

You learned in Chapter 24 that the master budget formalizes management's planned objectives for the coming year. When used in budgetary control, each budget included in the master budget is considered to be static. A **static budget** is a projection of budget data at one level of activity. Data for different levels of activity are ignored. As a result, actual results are always compared with budget data at the activity level used in developing the master budget.

Illustrations

To illustrate the role of a static budget in budgetary control, we will use selected data prepared for Hayes Company in Chapter 24. Budget and actual sales data for the Kitchen-mate product in the first and second quarters of 2005 are as follows.

Illustration 25-3
Budget and actual sales data

Sales	First Quarter	Second Quarter	Total
Budgeted	$180,000	$210,000	$390,000
Actual	179,000	199,500	378,500
Difference	$ 1,000	$ 10,500	$ 11,500

The sales budget report for Hayes Company's first quarter is shown below. The rightmost column reports the difference between the budgeted and actual amounts.

Illustration 25-4
Sales budget report—first quarter

HAYES COMPANY
Sales Budget Report
For the Quarter Ended March 31, 2005

Product Line	Budget	Actual	Difference Favorable F Unfavorable U
Kitchen-mate[a]	$180,000	$179,000	$1,000 U

[a] In practice, each product line would be included in the report.

ALTERNATIVE TERMINOLOGY

The difference between budget and actual is sometimes called a *budget variance*.

The report shows that sales are $1,000 under budget—an unfavorable result. This difference is less than 1 percent of budgeted sales ($1,000 ÷ $180,000 = .0056). Top management's reaction to unfavorable differences is often influenced by the materiality (significance) of the difference. Since the difference of $1,000 is immaterial in this case, we will assume that Hayes Company management takes no specific corrective action.

The budget report for the second quarter is presented in Illustration 25-5. It contains one new feature: cumulative year-to-date information. This report indicates that sales for the second quarter were $10,500 below budget. This is 5 percent of budgeted sales ($10,500 ÷ $210,000). Top management may now conclude that the difference between budgeted and actual sales requires investigation.

Illustration 25-5
Sales budget report—second quarter

HAYES COMPANY
Sales Budget Report
For the Quarter Ended June 30, 2005

Product Line	Second Quarter			Year-to-Date		
	Budget	Actual	Difference Favorable F Unfavorable U	Budget	Actual	Difference Favorable F Unfavorable U
Kitchen-mate	$210,000	$199,500	$10,500 U	$390,000	$378,500	$11,500 U

Management's analysis should start by asking the sales manager the cause(s) of the shortfall. The need for corrective action should be considered. For example, management may decide to spur sales by offering sales incentives to customers or by increasing the advertising of Kitchen-mates. Or, if management concludes that a downturn in the economy is responsible for the lower sales, it may modify planned sales and profit goals for the remainder of the year.

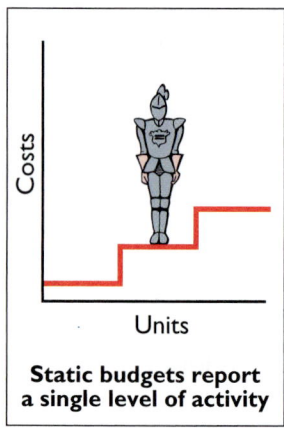

Static budgets report a single level of activity

Uses and Limitations

From these examples, you can see that a master sales budget is useful in evaluating the performance of a sales manager. It is now necessary to ask: Is the master budget appropriate for evaluating a manager's performance in controlling costs? Recall that in a static budget, data are not modified or adjusted, regardless of changes in activity. It follows, then, that a static budget is appropriate in evaluating a manager's effectiveness in controlling costs when:

1. The actual level of activity closely approximates the master budget activity level, and/or
2. The behavior of the costs in response to changes in activity is fixed.

A static budget report is, therefore, appropriate for **fixed manufacturing costs** and for **fixed selling and administrative expenses**. But, as you will see shortly, static budget reports may not be a proper basis for evaluating a manager's performance in controlling variable costs.

Flexible Budgets

STUDY OBJECTIVE 3

Explain the development of flexible budgets and the usefulness of flexible budget reports.

In contrast to a static budget, which is based on one level of activity, a flexible budget projects budget data for various levels of activity. In essence, **the flexible budget is a series of static budgets at different levels of activity.** The flexible budget recognizes that the budgetary process is more useful if it is adaptable to changed operating conditions.

Flexible budgets can be prepared for each of the types of budgets included in the master budget. For example, **Marriott Hotels** can budget revenues and net income on the basis of 60 percent, 80 percent, and 100 percent of room occupancy. Similarly, **American Van Lines** can budget its operating expenses on the basis of various levels of truck miles driven. Likewise, in the Feature Story, **Duke Energy** can budget revenue and net income on the basis of estimated billions of kwh (Kilowatt hours) of residential, commercial, and industrial electricity generated. In the following pages, we will illustrate a flexible budget for manufacturing overhead.

Why Flexible Budgets?

Assume that you are the manager in charge of manufacturing overhead in the Forging Department of Barton Steel. In preparing the manufacturing overhead budget for 2005, you prepare the following static budget based on a production volume of 10,000 units of steel ingots.

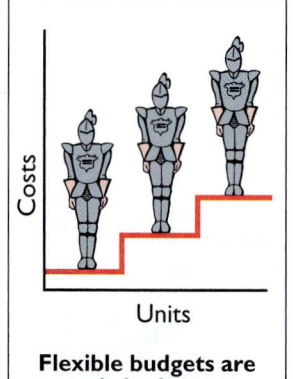

Flexible budgets are static budgets at different activity levels

Illustration 25-6
Static overhead budget

HELPFUL HINT

The static budget is the master budget of Chapter 24.

BARTON STEEL
Manufacturing Overhead Budget (Static)
Forging Department
For the Year Ended December 31, 2005

Budgeted production in units (steel ingots)	10,000
Budgeted costs	
Indirect materials	$ 250,000
Indirect labor	260,000
Utilities	190,000
Depreciation	280,000
Property taxes	70,000
Supervision	50,000
	$1,100,000

Fortunately for the company, the demand for steel ingots has increased, and 12,000 units are produced and sold during the year, rather than 10,000. You are elated: Increased sales means increased profitability, which should mean a bonus or a raise for you and the employees in your department. Unfortunately, a comparison of Forging Department actual and budgeted costs has put you on the spot. The budget report is shown below.

Illustration 25-7
Static overhead budget
report

BARTON STEEL
Manufacturing Overhead Budget Report (Static)
Forging Department
For the Year Ended December 31, 2005

	Budget	Actual	Difference Favorable F Unfavorable U
Production in units	10,000	12,000	
Costs			
Indirect materials	$ 250,000	$ 295,000	$ 45,000 U
Indirect labor	260,000	312,000	52,000 U
Utilities	190,000	225,000	35,000 U
Depreciation	280,000	280,000	–0–
Property taxes	70,000	70,000	–0–
Supervision	50,000	50,000	–0–
	$1,100,000	$1,232,000	$132,000 U

This comparison uses budget data based on the original activity level (10,000 steel ingots). It indicates that the Forging Department is significantly **over budget** for three of the six overhead costs. And, there is a total unfavorable difference of $132,000, which is 12 percent over budget ($132,000 ÷ $1,100,000). Your supervisor is very unhappy! Instead of sharing in the company's success, you may find yourself looking for another job. What went wrong?

When you calm down and carefully examine the manufacturing overhead budget, you identify the problem: The budget data are not relevant! At the time the budget was developed, the company anticipated that only 10,000 units of steel ingots would be produced, **not** 12,000 ingots. Comparing actual with budgeted variable costs is meaningless. As production increases, the budget allowances for variable costs should increase both directly and proportionately. The variable costs in this example are indirect materials, indirect labor, and utilities.

Analyzing the budget data for these costs at 10,000 units, you arrive at the following per unit results.

> **HELPFUL HINT**
>
> A static budget will not work if a company has substantial variable costs.

Illustration 25-8
Variable costs per unit

Item	Total Cost	Per Unit
Indirect materials	$250,000	$25
Indirect labor	260,000	26
Utilities	190,000	19
	$700,000	$70

You then can calculate the budgeted variable costs at 12,000 units as follows.

Illustration 25-9
Budgeted variable costs,
12,000 units

Item	Computation	Total
Indirect materials	$25 × 12,000	$300,000
Indirect labor	26 × 12,000	312,000
Utilities	19 × 12,000	228,000
		$840,000

Because fixed costs do not change in total as activity changes, the budgeted amounts for these costs remain the same. The budget report based on the flexible budget for **12,000 units** of production is shown in Illustration 25-10. (Compare this with Illustration 25-7.)

Illustration 25-10
Flexible overhead budget
report

BARTON STEEL
Manufacturing Overhead Budget Report (Flexible)
Forging Department
For the Year Ended December 31, 2005

	Budget	Actual	Difference Favorable F Unfavorable U
Production in units	12,000	12,000	
Variable costs			
Indirect materials	$ 300,000	$ 295,000	$5,000 F
Indirect labor	312,000	312,000	–0–
Utilities	228,000	225,000	3,000 F
Total variable	840,000	832,000	8,000 F
Fixed costs			
Depreciation	280,000	280,000	–0–
Property taxes	70,000	70,000	–0–
Supervision	50,000	50,000	–0–
Total fixed	400,000	400,000	–0–
Total costs	$1,240,000	$1,232,000	$8,000 F

This report indicates that the Forging Department is below budget—a favorable difference. Instead of worrying about being fired, you may be in line for a bonus or a raise after all! As this analysis shows, the only appropriate comparison is between actual costs at 12,000 units of production and budgeted costs at 12,000 units. Flexible budget reports provide this comparison.

Developing the Flexible Budget

The flexible budget uses the master budget as its basis. To develop the flexible budget, management should take the following steps.

1. Identify the activity index and the relevant range of activity.

2. Identify the variable costs, and determine the budgeted variable cost per unit of activity for each cost.

3. Identify the fixed costs, and determine the budgeted amount for each cost.

4. Prepare the budget for selected increments of activity within the relevant range.

The activity index chosen should be one that significantly influences the costs that are being budgeted. For manufacturing overhead costs, for example, the activity index is usually the same as the index used in developing the predetermined overhead rate—that is, direct labor hours or machine hours. For selling and administrative expenses, the activity index usually is sales or net sales.

The choice of the increment of activity is largely a matter of judgment. For example, if the relevant range is 8,000 to 12,000 direct labor hours, increments of 1,000 hours may be selected. The flexible budget is then prepared for each increment within the relevant range.

Flexible Budget—A Case Study

To illustrate the flexible budget, we will use Fox Manufacturing Company. Fox's management wants to use a **flexible budget for monthly comparisons** of actual and budgeted manufacturing overhead costs of the Finishing Department. The master budget for the year ending December 31, 2005, shows expected annual operating capacity of 120,000 direct labor hours and the following overhead costs.

Variable Costs		Fixed Costs	
Indirect materials	$180,000	Depreciation	$180,000
Indirect labor	240,000	Supervision	120,000
Utilities	60,000	Property taxes	60,000
Total	$480,000	Total	$360,000

Illustration 25-11
Master budget data

The four steps for developing the flexible budget are applied as follows.

Step 1. Identify the activity index and the relevant range of activity. The activity index is direct labor hours. Management concludes that the relevant range is 8,000–12,000 direct labor hours per month.

Step 2. Identify the variable costs, and determine the budgeted variable cost per unit of activity for each cost. There are three variable costs. The variable cost per unit is found by dividing each total budgeted cost by the direct labor hours used in preparing the master budget (120,000 hours). For Fox Manufacturing, the computations are:

Variable Cost	Computation	Variable Cost per Direct Labor Hour
Indirect materials	$180,000 ÷ 120,000	$1.50
Indirect labor	240,000 ÷ 120,000	2.00
Utilities	60,000 ÷ 120,000	0.50
Total		$4.00

Illustration 25-12
Computation of variable costs per direct labor hour

Step 3. Identify the fixed costs, and determine the budgeted amount for each cost. There are three fixed costs. Since Fox desires **monthly budget data**, the budgeted amount is found by dividing each annual budgeted cost by 12. For Fox Manufacturing, the monthly budgeted fixed costs are: depreciation $15,000, supervision $10,000, and property taxes $5,000.

Step 4. Prepare the budget for selected increments of activity within the relevant range. Management decides to prepare the budget in increments of 1,000 direct labor hours.

The flexible budget is shown in Illustration 25-13.

Illustration 25-13
Flexible monthly overhead budget

FOX MANUFACTURING COMPANY Flexible Monthly Manufacturing Overhead Budget Finishing Department For the Year 2005					
Activity level					
Direct labor hours	8,000	9,000	10,000	11,000	12,000
Variable costs					
Indirect materials	$12,000	$13,500	$15,000	$16,500	$18,000
Indirect labor	16,000	18,000	20,000	22,000	24,000
Utilities	4,000	4,500	5,000	5,500	6,000
Total variable	32,000	36,000	40,000	44,000	48,000
Fixed costs					
Depreciation	15,000	15,000	15,000	15,000	15,000
Supervision	10,000	10,000	10,000	10,000	10,000
Property taxes	5,000	5,000	5,000	5,000	5,000
Total fixed	30,000	30,000	30,000	30,000	30,000
Total costs	$62,000	$66,000	$70,000	$74,000	$78,000

From the budget, the following formula may be used to determine total budgeted costs at any level of activity.

Illustration 25-14
Formula for total budgeted costs

$$\text{Fixed Costs} + \text{Variable Costs*} = \text{Total Budgeted Costs}$$

*Total variable cost per unit times activity level.

For Fox Manufacturing, fixed costs are $30,000, and total variable cost per unit is $4.00. Thus, at 9,000 direct labor hours, total budgeted costs are $66,000 [$30,000 + ($4.00 × 9,000)]. Similarly, at 8,622 direct labor hours, total budgeted costs are $64,488 [$30,000 + ($4.00 × 8,622)].

Total budgeted costs can also be shown graphically, as in Illustration 25-15. In the graph, the activity index is shown on the horizontal axis, and costs are indicated on the vertical axis. The graph highlights two activity levels (10,000 and 12,000). As shown, total budgeted costs at these activity levels are $70,000 [$30,000 + ($4.00 × 10,000)] and $78,000 [$30,000 + ($4.00 × 12,000)], respectively.

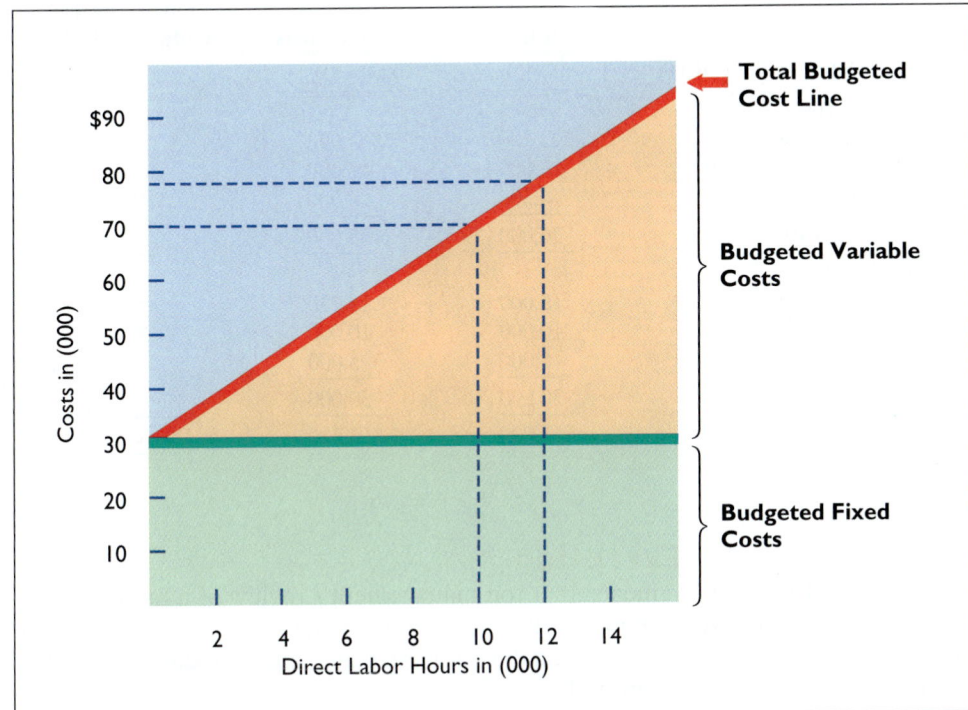

Illustration 25-15
Graphic flexible budget data highlighting 10,000 and 12,000 activity levels

Flexible Budget Reports

Flexible budget reports are another type of internal report produced by managerial accounting. The flexible budget report consists of two sections: (1) production data for a selected activity index, such as direct labor hours, and (2) cost data for variable and fixed costs. The report provides a basis for evaluating a manager's performance in two areas: production control and cost control. Flexible budget reports are widely used in production and service departments.

A budget report for the Finishing Department of Fox Company for the month of January is shown in Illustration 25-16 (page 1016). In this month, 9,000 hours were worked. The budget data are therefore based on the flexible budget for 9,000 hours in Illustration 25-13. The actual cost data are assumed.

How appropriate is this report in evaluating the Finishing Department manager's performance in controlling overhead costs? The report clearly provides a reliable basis. Both actual and budget costs are based on the activity level worked during January. Since variable costs generally are incurred directly by the department, the difference between the budget allowance for those hours and the actual costs are the responsibility of the department manager.

In subsequent months, other flexible budget reports will be prepared. For each month, the budget data are based on the actual activity level attained. In February that level may be 11,000 direct labor hours, in July 10,000, and so on.

> **HELPFUL HINT**
>
> An assembly department is a production department, and a maintenance department is a service department, as explained on page 1022.

Illustration 25-16
Flexible overhead budget report

FOX MANUFACTURING COMPANY
Flexible Manufacturing Overhead Budget Report
Finishing Department
For the Month Ended January 31, 2005

	Budget	Actual Costs	Difference Favorable F Unfavorable U
Direct labor hours (DLH)	9,000 DLH	9,000 DLH	
Variable costs			
Indirect materials	$13,500	$14,000	$ 500 U
Indirect labor	18,000	17,000	1,000 F
Utilities	4,500	4,600	100 U
Total variable	36,000	35,600	400 F
Fixed costs			
Depreciation	15,000	15,000	–0–
Supervision	10,000	10,000	–0–
Property taxes	5,000	5,000	–0–
Total fixed	30,000	30,000	–0–
Total costs	$66,000	$65,600	$ 400 F

HELPFUL HINT

Note that this flexible budget is based on a single cost driver. A more accurate budget often can be developed using the activity-based costing concepts explained in Chapter 22.

Management by Exception

Management by exception means that top management's review of a budget report is focused either entirely or primarily on differences between actual results and planned objectives. This approach enables top management to focus on problem areas. Management by exception does not mean that top management will investigate every difference. For this approach to be effective, there must be guidelines for identifying an exception. The usual criteria are materiality and controllability.

Materiality

Without quantitative guidelines, management would have to investigate every budget difference regardless of the amount. Materiality is usually expressed as a percentage difference from budget. For example, management may set the percentage difference at 5 percent for important items and 10 percent for other items. All differences either over or under budget by the specified percentage will be investigated. Costs over budget warrant investigation to determine why they were not controlled. Likewise, costs under budget merit investigation to determine whether costs critical to profitability are being curtailed. For example, if maintenance costs are budgeted at $80,000 but only $40,000 is spent, major unexpected breakdowns in productive facilities may occur in the future.

Alternatively, a company may specify a single percentage difference from budget for all items and supplement this guideline with a minimum dollar limit. For example, the exception criteria may be stated at 5 percent of budget or more than $10,000.

Controllability of the Item

Exception guidelines are more restrictive for controllable items than for items that are not controllable by the manager. In fact, there may be no guidelines for noncontrollable items. For example, a large unfavorable difference between actual and budgeted property tax expense may not be flagged for investigation because the only possible causes are an unexpected increase in the tax rate or in the assessed value of the property. An investigation into the difference will be useless: the manager cannot control either cause.

The Concept of Responsibility Accounting

Like budgeting, responsibility accounting is an important part of management accounting. **Responsibility accounting** involves accumulating and reporting costs (and revenues, where relevant) on the basis of the manager who has the authority to make the day-to-day decisions about the items. Under responsibility accounting, a manager's performance is evaluated on matters directly under that manager's control. Responsibility accounting can be used at every level of management in which the following conditions exist.

STUDY OBJECTIVE 4

Describe the concept of responsibility accounting.

1. Costs and revenues can be directly associated with the specific level of management responsibility.
2. The costs and revenues are controllable at the level of responsibility with which they are associated.
3. Budget data can be developed for evaluating the manager's effectiveness in controlling the costs and revenues.

Levels of responsibility for controlling costs are depicted in Illustration 25-17.

Under responsibility accounting, any individual who has control and is accountable for a specified set of activities can be recognized as a responsibility center. Thus, responsibility accounting may extend from the lowest level of control to the top strata of management. Once responsibility has been established, the effec-

Illustration 25-17
Responsibility for controllable costs at varying levels of management

Responsibility accounting gives managers responsibility for *controllable costs* at each level of authority

tiveness of the individual's performance is first measured and reported for the specified activity. It is then reported upward throughout the organization.

Responsibility accounting is especially valuable in a decentralized company. **Decentralization** means that the control of operations is delegated to many managers throughout the organization. The term **segment** is sometimes used to identify an area of responsibility in decentralized operations. Under responsibility accounting, segment reports are prepared periodically such as monthly, quarterly, and annually, to evaluate managers' performance.

Responsibility accounting is an essential part of any effective system of budgetary control. The reporting of costs and revenues under responsibility accounting differs from budgeting in two respects.

1. A distinction is made between controllable and noncontrollable items.
2. Performance reports either emphasize or include only items controllable by the individual manager.

Responsibility accounting applies to both profit and not-for-profit entities. The former seek to maximize net income. The latter wish to minimize the cost of providing services.

ACCOUNTING IN ACTION   **Business Insight**

Since devising its budgeting and control system, **JKL, Inc.**, a large New York advertising agency, has become aware of which specific customer accounts are unprofitable and the reasons why. As a result, the agency has dropped several unprofitable accounts that otherwise would have gone unnoticed. Account managers now feel responsible for the profitability of their accounts. They carefully monitor actual hours spent on each account to make sure the account is being managed and run as efficiently as possible. For example, an account manager noticed a large amount of supervisory creative time was being spent on one account. Further investigation showed that the supervisors, rather than the creative department, were doing the actual creative work. The account manager pointed this out, and a junior creative team was appointed to the account, saving JKL a great deal of money.

Controllable versus Noncontrollable Revenues and Costs

All costs and revenues are controllable at some level of responsibility within a company. This truth underscores the adage by the CEO of any organization that "the buck stops here." Under responsibility accounting, the critical issue is **whether the cost or revenue is controllable at the level of responsibility with which it is associated**.

A cost is considered to be controllable at a given level of managerial responsibility if the manager has the power to incur it within a given period of time. From this criterion, it follows that:

1. All costs are controllable by top management because of the broad range of its authority.
2. Fewer costs are controllable as one moves down to each lower level of managerial responsibility because of the manager's decreasing authority.

In general, **costs incurred directly by a level of responsibility are controllable at that level**. In contrast, costs incurred indirectly and allocated to a responsibility level are considered to be noncontrollable at that level.

HELPFUL HINT

There are more controllable costs as you move to higher levels of management.

Responsibility Reporting System

A responsibility reporting system involves the preparation of a report for each level of responsibility in the company's organization chart. To illustrate such a system, we will use the partial organization chart and production departments of Francis Chair Company in Illustration 25-18.

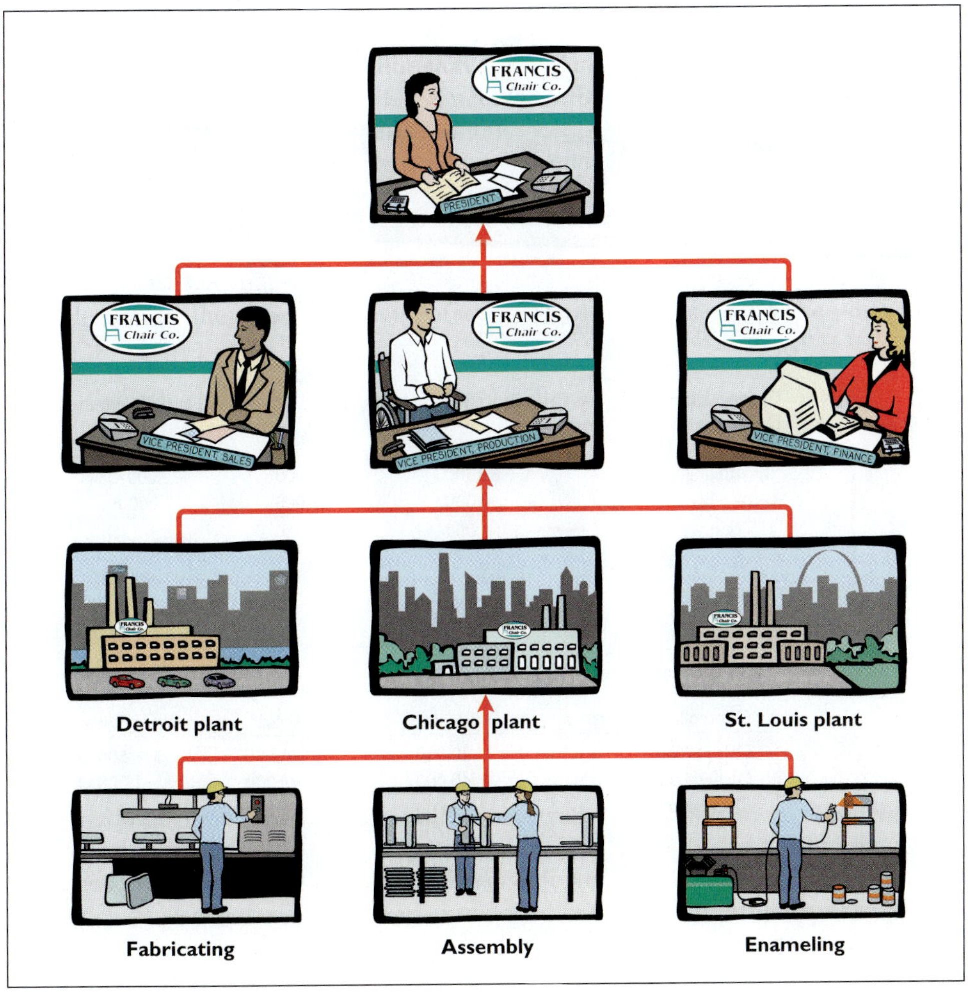

Illustration 25-18
Partial organization chart

Report A
President sees summary data of vice presidents.

Report B
Vice president sees summary of controllable costs in his/her functional area.

Report C
Plant manager sees summary of controllable costs for each department in the plant.

Report D
Department manager sees controllable costs of his/her department.

The responsibility reporting system begins with the lowest level of responsibility for controlling costs and moves upward to each higher level. The connections between levels are detailed below in Illustration 25-19. A brief description of the four reports for Francis Chair Company is as follows.

1. **Report D** is typical of reports that go to managers at the lowest level of responsibility shown in the organization chart—department managers. Similar

Illustration 25-19
Responsibility reporting system

Report A
President sees summary data of vice presidents.

Report B
Vice president sees summary of controllable costs in his/her functional area.

Report C
Plant manager sees summary of controllable costs for each department in the plant.

Report D
Department manager sees controllable costs of his/her department.

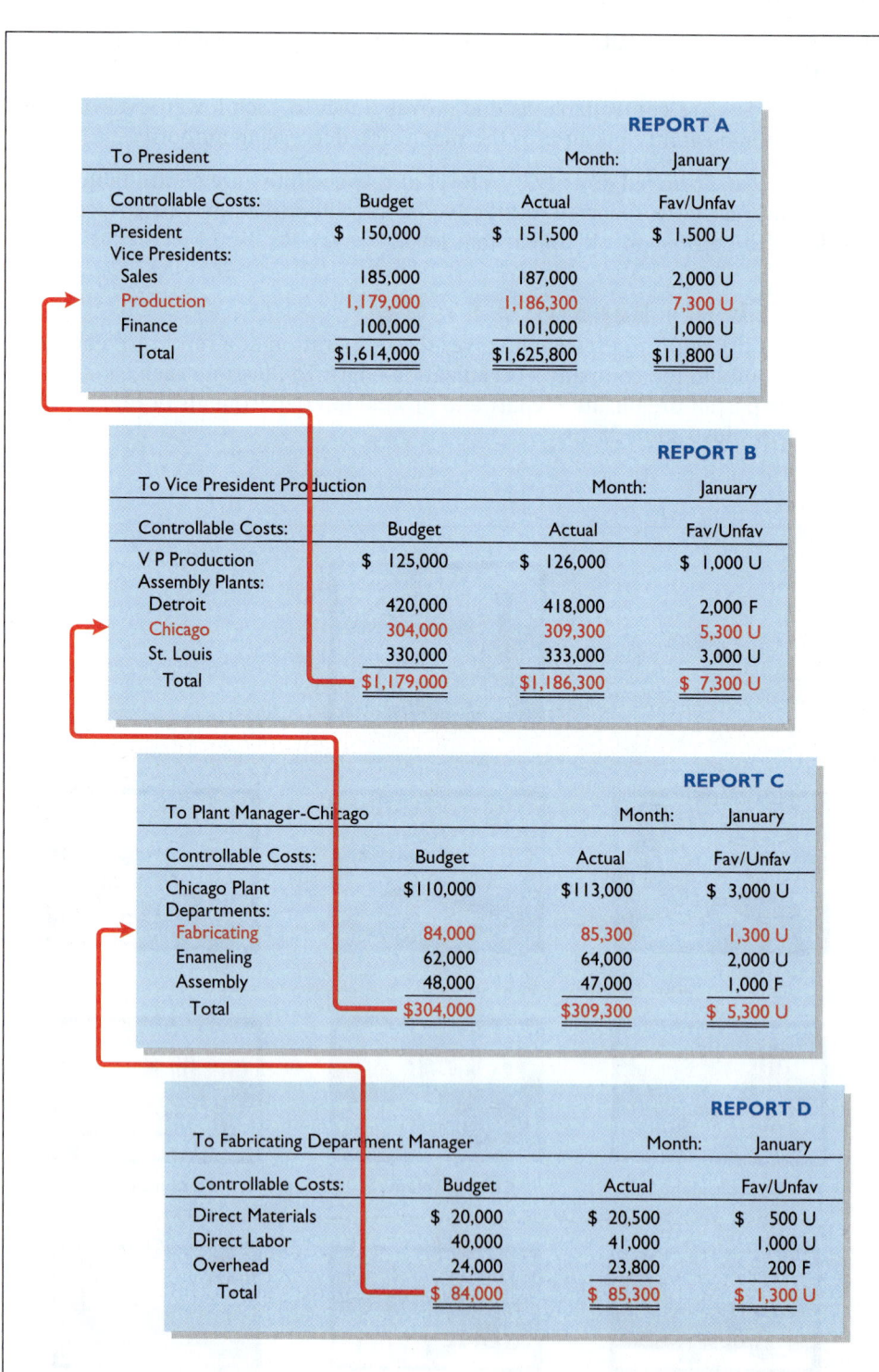

REPORT A

To President			Month:	January
Controllable Costs:	Budget	Actual		Fav/Unfav
President	$ 150,000	$ 151,500		$ 1,500 U
Vice Presidents:				
Sales	185,000	187,000		2,000 U
Production	1,179,000	1,186,300		7,300 U
Finance	100,000	101,000		1,000 U
Total	$1,614,000	$1,625,800		$11,800 U

REPORT B

To Vice President Production			Month:	January
Controllable Costs:	Budget	Actual		Fav/Unfav
V P Production	$ 125,000	$ 126,000		$ 1,000 U
Assembly Plants:				
Detroit	420,000	418,000		2,000 F
Chicago	304,000	309,300		5,300 U
St. Louis	330,000	333,000		3,000 U
Total	$1,179,000	$1,186,300		$ 7,300 U

REPORT C

To Plant Manager-Chicago			Month:	January
Controllable Costs:	Budget	Actual		Fav/Unfav
Chicago Plant	$110,000	$113,000		$ 3,000 U
Departments:				
Fabricating	84,000	85,300		1,300 U
Enameling	62,000	64,000		2,000 U
Assembly	48,000	47,000		1,000 F
Total	$304,000	$309,300		$ 5,300 U

REPORT D

To Fabricating Department Manager			Month:	January
Controllable Costs:	Budget	Actual		Fav/Unfav
Direct Materials	$ 20,000	$ 20,500		$ 500 U
Direct Labor	40,000	41,000		1,000 U
Overhead	24,000	23,800		200 F
Total	$ 84,000	$ 85,300		$ 1,300 U

reports are prepared for the managers of the Fabricating, Assembling, and Enameling Departments.

2. **Report C** is an example of reports that are sent to plant managers. It shows the costs of the Chicago plant that are controllable at the second level of responsibility. In addition, Report C shows summary data for each department that is controlled by the plant manager. Similar reports are prepared for the Detroit and St. Louis plant managers.

3. **Report B** illustrates the reports at the third level of responsibility. It shows the controllable costs of the vice president of production and summary data on the three assembly plants for which this officer is responsible.

4. **Report A** is typical of the reports that go to the top level of responsibility—the president. This report shows the controllable costs and expenses of this office and summary data on the vice presidents that are accountable to the president.

A responsibility reporting system permits management by exception at each level of responsibility. And, each higher level of responsibility can obtain the detailed report for each lower level of responsibility. For example, the vice president of production in the Francis Chair Company may request the Chicago plant manager's report because this plant is $5,300 over budget.

This type of reporting system also permits comparative evaluations. In Illustration 25-19, the Chicago plant manager can easily rank the department managers' effectiveness in controlling manufacturing costs. Comparative rankings provide further incentive for a manager to control costs. For example, the Detroit plant manager will want to continue to be No. 1 in the report to the vice president of production. The Chicago plant manager will not want to remain No. 3 in future reporting periods.

ACCOUNTING IN ACTION   Business Insight

In Chapter 20 we discussed enterprise resource planning (ERP) software packages that collect all information regarding the results of the supply chain. A recent innovation is to attach enterprise application systems (EAS) to ERP systems. EAS systems are budgeting and planning tools. By attaching an EAS system called Hyperion Pillar to its ERP system, **Fujitsu Computer Products of America** found that it could more easily compare its budgeted amounts to its actual results. It also reduced its typical time spent on planning and budgeting from 6 to 8 weeks down to 10 to 15 days. Finally, the new system has enabled the company to respond quickly to new developments. For example, the software forewarned the company of a potential oversupply problem, and provided recommendations for changes in staffing and capital needs.

Source: Russ Banham, "Better Budgets," *Journal of Accountancy*, February 2000, p. 37.

Types of Responsibility Centers

There are three basic types of responsibility centers: cost centers, profit centers, and investment centers. These centers indicate the degree of responsibility the manager has for the performance of the center.

A **cost center** incurs costs (and expenses) but does not directly generate revenues. Managers of cost centers have the authority to incur costs. They are evaluated on their ability to control costs. **Cost centers are usually either production departments or service departments.** The former participate directly in making the product. The latter provide only support services. In a **Ford Motor Company** automobile plant, the welding, painting, and assembling departments are production departments; the maintenance, cafeteria, and human resources departments are service departments. All of them are cost centers.

A **profit center** incurs costs (and expenses) and also generates revenues. Managers of profit centers are judged on the profitability of their centers. Examples of profit centers include the individual departments of a retail store, such as clothing, furniture, and automotive products, and branch offices of banks.

Like a profit center, an **investment center** incurs costs (and expenses) and generates revenues. In addition, an investment center has control over the investment funds available for use. Managers of investment centers are evaluated on both the profitability of the center and the rate of return earned on the funds invested. Investment centers are often associated with subsidiary companies. For example, **General Mills's** product lines include cereals, helper dinner mixes, fruit snacks, popcorn, and yogurt. And, our Feature Story utility company, **Duke Energy**, has operating divisions such as electric utility, energy, trading, and natural gas. The manager of the investment center (product line) is able to control or significantly influence investment decisions pertaining to such matters as plant expansion and entry into new market areas. These three types of responsibility centers are depicted in Illustration 25-20.

The evaluation of a manager's performance in each type of responsibility center is explained in the remainder of this chapter.

Illustration 25-20
Types of responsibility centers

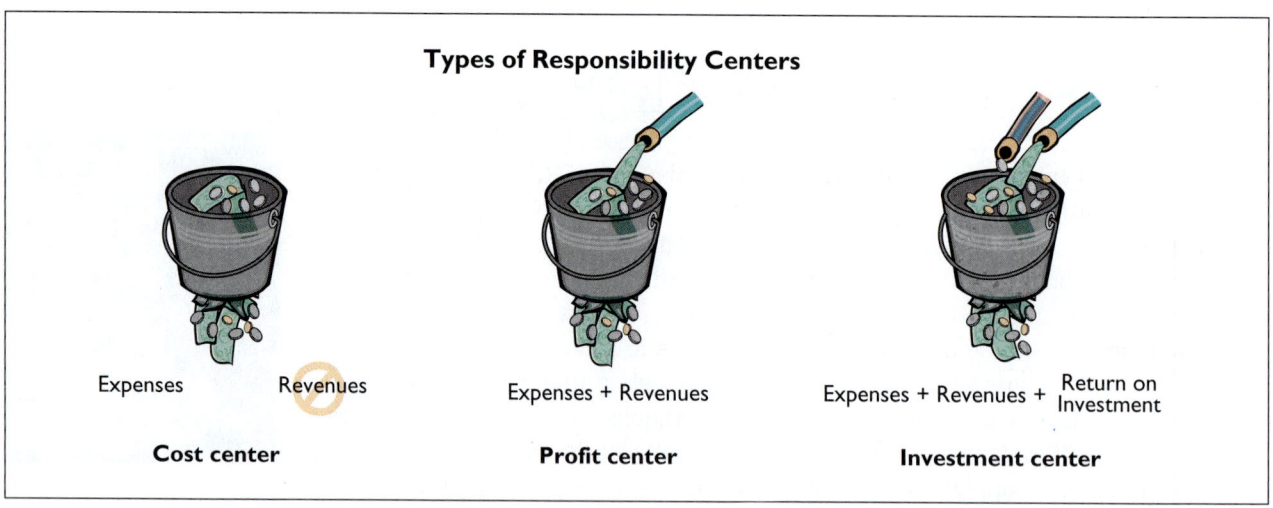

Types of Responsibility Centers

Expenses   Revenues

Cost center

Expenses + Revenues

Profit center

Expenses + Revenues + Return on Investment

Investment center

Responsibility Accounting for Cost Centers

The evaluation of a manager's performance for cost centers is based on his or her ability to meet budgeted goals for controllable costs. **Responsibility reports for cost centers compare actual controllable costs with flexible budget data.**

A responsibility report is illustrated in Illustration 25-21. The report is adapted from the budget report for Fox Manufacturing Company in Illustration 25-16 on page 1016. It assumes that the Finishing Department manager is able to control all manufacturing overhead costs except depreciation, property taxes, and his own monthly salary of $6,000. The remaining $4,000 of supervision costs are assumed to apply to other supervisory personnel within the Finishing Department, whose salaries are controllable by the manager.

Illustration 25-21
Responsibility report for a
cost center

FOX MANUFACTURING COMPANY
Finishing Department
Responsibility Report
For the Month Ended January 31, 2005

Controllable Cost	Budget	Actual	Difference Favorable F Unfavorable U
Indirect materials	$13,500	$14,000	$ 500 U
Indirect labor	18,000	17,000	1,000 F
Utilities	4,500	4,600	100 U
Supervision	4,000	4,000	–0–
	$40,000	$39,600	$ 400 F

Only controllable costs are included in the report, and no distinction is made between variable and fixed costs. The responsibility report continues the concept of management by exception. In this case, top management may request an explanation of the $1,000 favorable difference in indirect labor and/or the $500 unfavorable difference in indirect materials.

Responsibility Accounting for Profit Centers

To evaluate the performance of a manager of a profit center, detailed information is needed about both controllable revenues and controllable costs. The operating revenues earned by a profit center, such as sales, are controllable by the manager. All variable costs (and expenses) incurred by the center are also controllable by the manager because they vary with sales. However, to determine the controllability of fixed costs, it is necessary to distinguish between direct and indirect fixed costs.

STUDY OBJECTIVE 6

Identify the content of
responsibility reports for
profit centers.

Direct and Indirect Fixed Costs

A profit center may have both direct and indirect fixed costs. **Direct fixed costs** are costs that relate specifically to one center and are incurred for the sole benefit of that center. Examples of such costs include the salaries established by the profit center manager for supervisory personnel and the cost of a timekeeping department for the center's employees. Since these fixed costs can be traced directly to a center, they are also called **traceable costs. Most direct fixed costs are controllable by the profit center manager.**

In contrast, **indirect fixed costs** pertain to a company's overall operating activities and are incurred for the benefit of more than one profit center. Indirect fixed costs are allocated to profit centers on some type of equitable basis. For example, property taxes on a building occupied by more than one center may be allocated on the basis of square feet of floor space used by each center. Or, the costs of a company's human resources department may be allocated to profit centers on the basis of the number of employees in each center. Because these fixed costs apply to more than one center, they are also called **common costs. Most indirect fixed costs are not controllable by the profit center manager.**

Responsibility Report

The responsibility report for a profit center shows budgeted and actual **controllable revenues and costs.** The report is prepared using the cost-volume-profit income statement explained in Chapter 23. In the report:

1. Controllable fixed costs are deducted from contribution margin.
2. The excess of contribution margin over controllable fixed costs is identified as **controllable margin**.
3. Noncontrollable fixed costs are not reported.

The responsibility report for the manager of the Marine Division, a profit center of Mantle Manufacturing Company, is shown in Illustration 25-22. For the year, the Marine Division also had $60,000 of indirect fixed costs that were not controllable by the profit center manager.

Illustration 25-22
Responsibility report for profit center

MANTLE MANUFACTURING COMPANY
Marine Division
Responsibility Report
For the Year Ended December 31, 2005

	Budget	Actual	Difference Favorable F Unfavorable U
Sales	$1,200,000	$1,150,000	$50,000 U
Variable costs			
Cost of goods sold	500,000	490,000	10,000 F
Selling and administrative	160,000	156,000	4,000 F
Total	660,000	646,000	14,000 F
Contribution margin	540,000	504,000	36,000 U
Controllable fixed costs			
Cost of goods sold	100,000	100,000	–0–
Selling and administrative	80,000	80,000	–0–
Total	180,000	180,000	–0–
Controllable margin	**$ 360,000**	**$ 324,000**	**$36,000 U**

Controllable margin is considered to be the best measure of the manager's performance **in controlling revenues and costs.** This report shows that the manager's performance was below budgeted expectations by approximately 10 percent ($36,000 ÷ $360,000). Top management would likely investigate the causes of this unfavorable result. Note that the report does not show the Marine Division's noncontrollable fixed costs of $60,000. These costs would be included in a report on the profitability of the profit center.

Responsibility reports for profit centers may also be prepared monthly. In addition, they may include cumulative year-to-date results.

BEFORE YOU GO ON...

Review It

1. What conditions are essential for responsibility accounting?
2. What is involved in a responsibility reporting system?

3. What is the primary objective of a responsibility report for a cost center?

4. How does contribution margin differ from controllable margin in a responsibility report for a profit center?

Do It

Midwest Division operates as a profit center. It reports the following actual results for the year: Sales $1,700,000, variable costs $800,000, controllable fixed costs $400,000, noncontrollable fixed costs $200,000. Annual budgeted amounts were $1,500,000, $700,000, $400,000, and $200,000, respectively. Prepare a responsibility report for the Midwest Division for December 31, 2005.

ACTION PLAN

- Deduct variable costs from sales to show contribution margin.
- Deduct controllable fixed costs from the contribution margin to show controllable margin.
- Do not report noncontrollable fixed costs.

SOLUTION

MIDWEST DIVISION
Responsibility Report
For the Year Ended December 31, 2005

	Budget	Actual	Difference Favorable F Unfavorable U
Sales	$1,500,000	$1,700,000	$200,000 F
Variable costs	700,000	800,000	100,000 U
Contribution margin	800,000	900,000	100,000 F
Controllable fixed costs	400,000	400,000	–0–
Controllable margin	$ 400,000	$ 500,000	$100,000 F

Related exercise material: *BE25-7 and E25-9.*

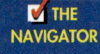 THE NAVIGATOR

Responsibility Accounting for Investment Centers

As explained earlier, an investment center manager can control or significantly influence the investment funds available for use. Thus, the primary basis for evaluating the performance of a manager of an investment center is **return on investment (ROI)**. The return on investment is considered to be a useful performance measure because it shows the **effectiveness of the manager in utilizing the assets at his or her disposal**.

STUDY OBJECTIVE 7

Explain the basis and formula used in evaluating performance in investment centers.

Return on Investment (ROI)

The formula for computing ROI for an investment center, together with assumed illustrative data, is shown in Illustration 25-23 (page 1026). Both factors in the formula are controllable by the investment center manager. Operating assets consist of current assets and plant assets used in operations by the center and controlled by the manager. Nonoperating assets such as idle plant assets and land held for future use are excluded. Average operating assets are usually based on the cost or book value of the assets at the beginning and end of the year.

Illustration 25-23
ROI formula

Controllable Margin	÷	Average Operating Assets	=	Return on Investment (ROI)
$1,000,000	÷	$5,000,000	=	20%

Responsibility Report

The scope of the investment center manager's responsibility significantly affects the content of the performance report. Since an investment center is an independent entity for operating purposes, **all fixed costs are controllable by its manager**. For example, the manager is responsible for depreciation on investment center assets. Therefore, more fixed costs are identified as controllable in the performance report for an investment center manager than in a performance report for a profit center manager. The report also shows budgeted and actual ROI below controllable margin.

To illustrate this responsibility report, we will now assume that the Marine Division of Mantle Manufacturing Company is an investment center. It has budgeted and actual average operating assets of $2,000,000. We now will assume that the manager can control the $60,000 of fixed costs that were not controllable when the division was a profit center. The responsibility report is shown in Illustration 25-24.

Illustration 25-24
Responsibility report for investment center

MANTLE MANUFACTURING COMPANY
Marine Division
Responsibility Report
For the Year Ended December 31, 2005

	Budget	Actual	Difference Favorable F Unfavorable U
Sales	$1,200,000	$1,150,000	$50,000 U
Variable costs			
Cost of goods sold	500,000	490,000	10,000 F
Selling and administrative	160,000	156,000	4,000 F
Total	660,000	646,000	14,000 F
Contribution margin	540,000	504,000	36,000 U
Controllable fixed costs			
Cost of goods sold	100,000	100,000	–0–
Selling and administrative	80,000	80,000	–0–
Other fixed costs	**60,000**	**60,000**	**–0–**
Total	240,000	240,000	–0–
Controllable margin	**$300,000**	**$ 264,000**	**$36,000 U**
Return on investment	15%	13.2%	1.8% U
	(a)	(b)	(c)

(a) $\dfrac{\$300,000}{\$2,000,000}$ (b) $\dfrac{\$264,000}{\$2,000,000}$ (c) $\dfrac{\$36,000}{\$2,000,000}$

The report shows that the manager's performance based on ROI was 12 percent below budget expectations (1.8% ÷ 15%). Top management would likely want an explanation of the reasons for this unfavorable result.

Judgmental Factors in ROI

The return on investment approach includes two judgmental factors:

1. **Valuation of operating assets.** Operating assets may be valued at acquisition cost, book value, appraised value, or market value. The first two bases are readily available from the accounting records.

2. **Margin (income) measure.** This measure may be controllable margin, income from operations, or net income.

Each of the alternative values for operating assets can provide a reliable basis for evaluating a manager's performance as long as it is consistently applied between reporting periods. However, the use of income measures other than controllable margin will not result in a valid basis for evaluating the performance of an investment center manager.

Improving ROI

The manager of an investment center can improve ROI in two ways: (1) increase controllable margin, and/or (2) reduce average operating assets. To illustrate, we will use the following assumed data for the Marine Division of Mantle Manufacturing.

Sales	$2,000,000
Variable cost	1,100,000
Contribution margin (45%)	900,000
Controllable fixed costs	300,000
Controllable margin (a)	$ 600,000
Average operating assets (b)	$5,000,000
Return on investment (a) ÷ (b)	12%

Illustration 25-25
Assumed data for Marine Division

INCREASING CONTROLLABLE MARGIN. Controllable margin can be increased by increasing sales or by reducing variable and controllable fixed costs as follows.

1. **Increase sales 10 percent.** Sales will increase $200,000 ($2,000,000 × .10). Assuming no change in the contribution margin percentage of 45 percent, contribution margin will increase $90,000 ($200,000 × .45). Controllable margin will increase by the same amount because controllable fixed costs will not change. Thus, controllable margin becomes $690,000 ($600,000 + $90,000). The new ROI is 13.8 percent, computed as follows.

$$\text{ROI} = \frac{\text{Controllable margin}}{\text{Average operating assets}} = \frac{\$690,000}{\$5,000,000} = \textbf{13.8\%}$$

Illustration 25-26
ROI computation—increase in sales

An increase in sales benefits both the investment center and the company if it results in new business. It would not benefit the company if the increase was achieved at the expense of other investment centers.

2. **Decrease variable and fixed costs 10 percent.** Total costs will decrease $140,000 [($1,100,000 + $300,000) × .10]. This reduction will result in a corresponding increase in controllable margin. Thus, controllable margin becomes $740,000 ($600,000 + $140,000). The new ROI is 14.8 percent, computed as follows.

Illustration 25-27
ROI computation—decrease in costs

$$\text{ROI} = \frac{\text{Controllable margin}}{\text{Average operating assets}} = \frac{\$740,000}{\$5,000,000} = \textbf{14.8\%}$$

This course of action is clearly beneficial when waste and inefficiencies are eliminated. But, a reduction in vital costs such as required maintenance and inspections is not likely to be acceptable to top management.

REDUCING AVERAGE OPERATING ASSETS. Assume that average operating assets are reduced 10 percent or $500,000 ($5,000,000 × .10). Average operating assets become $4,500,000 ($5,000,000 − $500,000). Since controllable margin remains unchanged at $600,000, the new ROI is 13.3 percent, computed as follows.

Illustration 25-28
ROI computation—decrease in operating assets

$$\text{ROI} = \frac{\text{Controllable margin}}{\text{Average operating assets}} = \frac{\$600,000}{\$4,500,000} = \textbf{13.3\%}$$

Reductions in operating assets may or may not be prudent. It is beneficial to eliminate overinvestment in inventories and to dispose of excessive plant assets. However, it is unwise to reduce inventories below expected needs or to dispose of essential plant assets.

Principles of Performance Evaluation

Performance evaluation is at the center of responsibility accounting. **Performance evaluation** is a management function that compares actual results with budget goals. It is based on internal reports prepared by the managerial accountant. Performance evaluation involves both behavioral and reporting principles.

Behavioral Principles

The human factor is critical in evaluating performance. Behavioral principles include the following.

1. **Managers of responsibility centers should have direct input into the process of establishing budget goals of their area of responsibility.** Without such input, managers may view the goals as unrealistic or arbitrarily set by top management. Such views adversely affect the managers' motivation to meet the targeted objectives.

2. **The evaluation of performance should be based entirely on matters that are controllable by the manager being evaluated.** Criticism of a manager on matters outside his or her control reduces the effectiveness of the evaluation process. It leads to negative reactions by a manager and to doubts about the fairness of the company's evaluation policies.

3. **Top management should support the evaluation process.** As explained earlier, the evaluation process begins at the lowest level of responsibility and extends upward to the highest level of management. Managers quickly lose faith in the process when top management ignores, overrules, or bypasses established procedures for evaluating a manager's performance.

4. **The evaluation process must allow managers to respond to their evaluations.** Evaluation is not a one-way street. Managers should have the opportunity to

defend their performance. Evaluation without feedback is both impersonal and ineffective.

5. **The evaluation should identify both good and poor performance.** Praise for good performance is a powerful motivating factor for a manager. This is especially true when a manager's compensation includes rewards for meeting budget goals.

Reporting Principles of Performance Evaluation

Performance evaluation under responsibility accounting should be based on certain reporting principles. These principles pertain primarily to the internal reports that provide the basis for evaluating performance. Performance reports should:

1. Contain only data that are controllable by the manager of the responsibility center.
2. Provide accurate and reliable budget data to measure performance.
3. Highlight significant differences between actual results and budget goals.
4. Be tailor-made for the intended evaluation.
5. Be prepared at reasonable intervals.

BEFORE YOU GO ON...

Review It

1. What is the formula for computing return on investment (ROI)?
2. Identify three actions a manager may take to improve ROI.
3. What responsibility centers (investment type) might **PepsiCo** be utilizing in determining ROI? (*Hint:* Review "Management's Discussion and Analysis.") The answer to this question is provided on page 1046.

☑ THE NAVIGATOR

DEMONSTRATION PROBLEM

Glenda Company uses a flexible budget for manufacturing overhead based on direct labor hours. For 2005 the master overhead budget for the Packaging Department at normal capacity of 300,000 direct labor hours was as follows.

Variable Costs		Fixed Costs	
Indirect labor	$360,000	Supervision	$ 60,000
Supplies and lubricants	150,000	Depreciation	24,000
Maintenance	210,000	Property taxes	18,000
Utilities	120,000	Insurance	12,000
	$840,000		$114,000

During July, 24,000 direct labor hours were worked. The company incurred the following variable costs in July: indirect labor $30,200, supplies and lubricants $11,600, maintenance $17,500, and utilities $9,200. Actual fixed overhead costs were the same as monthly budgeted fixed costs.

Instructions

Prepare a flexible budget report for the Packaging Department for July.

(continued from p. 1029)

ACTION PLAN

- Use budget data for actual direct labor hours worked.
- Classify each cost as variable or fixed.
- Determine the difference between budgeted and actual costs.
- Identify the difference as favorable or unfavorable.
- Determine the difference in total variable costs, total fixed costs, and total costs.

SOLUTION TO DEMONSTRATION PROBLEM

GLENDA COMPANY
Manufacturing Overhead Budget Report (Flexible)
Packaging Department
For the Month Ended July 31, 2005

	Budget	Actual Costs	Difference Favorable F Unfavorable U
Direct labor hours (DLH)	24,000 DLH	24,000 DLH	
Variable costs			
Indirect labor	$28,800	$30,200	$1,400 U
Supplies and lubricants	12,000	11,600	400 F
Maintenance	16,800	17,500	700 U
Utilities	9,600	9,200	400 F
Total variable	67,200	68,500	1,300 U
Fixed costs			
Supervision	5,000	5,000	–0–
Depreciation	2,000	2,000	–0–
Property taxes	1,500	1,500	–0–
Insurance	1,000	1,000	–0–
Total fixed	9,500	9,500	–0–
Total costs	$76,700	$78,000	$1,300 U

☑ THE NAVIGATOR

SUMMARY OF STUDY OBJECTIVES

1. **Describe the concept of budgetary control.** Budgetary control consists of (a) preparing periodic budget reports that compare actual results with planned objectives, (b) analyzing the differences to determine their causes, (c) taking appropriate corrective action, and (d) modifying future plans, if necessary.

2. **Evaluate the usefulness of static budget reports.** Static budget reports are useful in evaluating the progress toward planned sales and profit goals. They are also appropriate in assessing a manager's effectiveness in controlling costs when (a) actual activity closely approximates the master budget activity level and/or (b) the behavior of the costs in response to changes in activity is fixed.

3. **Explain the development of flexible budgets and the usefulness of flexible budget reports.** To develop the flexible budget it is necessary to:
   (a) Identify the activity index and the relevant range of activity.
   (b) Identify the variable costs, and determine the budgeted variable cost per unit of activity for each cost.
   (c) Identify the fixed costs, and determine the budgeted amount for each cost.
   (d) Prepare the budget for selected increments of activity within the relevant range.

   Flexible budget reports permit an evaluation of a manager's performance in controlling production and costs.

4. **Describe the concept of responsibility accounting.** Responsibility accounting involves accumulating and reporting revenues and costs on the basis of the individual manager who has the authority to make the day-to-day decisions about the items. The evaluation of a manager's performance is based on the matters directly under the manager's control. In responsibility accounting, it is necessary to distinguish between controllable and noncontrollable fixed costs and to identify three types of responsibility centers: cost, profit, and investment.

5. **Indicate the features of responsibility reports for cost centers.** Responsibility reports for cost centers compare actual costs with flexible budget data. The reports show only controllable costs, and no distinction is made between variable and fixed costs.

6. **Identify the content of responsibility reports for profit centers.** Responsibility reports show contribution margin, controllable fixed costs, and controllable margin for each profit center.

7. **Explain the basis and formula used in evaluating performance in investment centers.** The primary basis for evaluating performance in investment centers is return on investment (ROI). The formula for computing ROI for investment centers is: Controllable margin (in dollars) ÷ Average operating assets.

☑ THE NAVIGATOR

GLOSSARY

Budgetary control The use of budgets to control operations. (p. 1007).

Controllable costs Costs that a manager has the authority to incur within a given period of time. (p. 1019).

Controllable margin Contribution margin less controllable fixed costs. (p. 1024).

Cost center A responsibility center that incurs costs but does not directly generate revenues. (p. 1021).

Decentralization Control of operations is delegated to many managers throughout the organization. (p. 1018).

Direct fixed costs Costs that relate specifically to a responsibility center and are incurred for the sole benefit of the center. (p. 1023).

Flexible budget A projection of budget data for various levels of activity. (p. 1010).

Indirect fixed costs Costs that are incurred for the benefit of more than one profit center. (p. 1023).

Investment center A responsibility center that incurs costs, generates revenues, and has control over the investment funds available for use. (p. 1022).

Management by exception The review of budget reports by top management focused entirely or primarily on differences between actual results and planned objectives. (p. 1016).

Noncontrollable costs Costs incurred indirectly and allocated to a responsibility center that are not controllable at that level. (p. 1019).

Profit center A responsibility center that incurs costs and also generates revenues. (p. 1022).

Responsibility accounting A part of management accounting that involves accumulating and reporting revenues and costs on the basis of the manager who has the authority to make the day-to-day decisions about the items. (p. 1017).

Responsibility reporting system The preparation of reports for each level of responsibility in the company's organization chart. (p. 1019).

Return on investment (ROI) A measure of management's effectiveness in utilizing assets at its disposal in an investment center. (p. 1025).

Segment An area of responsibility in decentralized operations. (p. 1018).

Static budget A projection of budget data at one level of activity. (p. 1008).

SELF-STUDY QUESTIONS

Self-Study/Self-Test

Answers are at the end of the chapter.

(SO 1) 1. Budgetary control involves *all but one* of the following:
   a. modifying future plans.
   b. analyzing differences.
   c. using static budgets.
   d. determining differences between actual and planned results.

(SO 2) 2. A static budget is useful in controlling costs when cost behavior is:
   a. mixed.   c. variable.
   b. fixed.   d. linear.

(SO 3) 3. At zero direct labor hours in a flexible budget graph, the total budgeted cost line intersects the vertical axis at $30,000. At 10,000 direct labor hours, a horizontal line drawn from the total budgeted cost line intersects the vertical axis at $90,000. Fixed and variable costs may be expressed as:
   a. $30,000 fixed plus $6 per direct labor hour variable.
   b. $30,000 fixed plus $9 per direct labor hour variable.
   c. $60,000 fixed plus $3 per direct labor hour variable.
   d. $60,000 fixed plus $6 per direct labor hour variable.

(SO 3) 4. At 9,000 direct labor hours, the flexible budget for indirect materials is $27,000. If $28,000 of indirect materials costs are incurred at 9,200 direct labor hours, the flexible budget report should show the following difference for indirect materials:
   a. $1,000 unfavorable.
   b. $1,000 favorable.
   c. $400 favorable.
   d. $400 unfavorable.

(SO 4) 5. Under responsibility accounting, the evaluation of a manager's performance is based on matters that the manager:
   a. directly controls.
   b. directly and indirectly controls.
   c. indirectly controls.
   d. has for shared responsibility with another manager.

(SO 4) 6. Responsibility centers include:
   a. cost centers.
   b. profit centers.
   c. investment centers.
   d. all of the above.

(SO 5) 7. Responsibility reports for cost centers:
   a. distinguish between fixed and variable costs.
   b. use static budget data.
   c. include both controllable and noncontrollable costs.
   d. include only controllable costs.

(SO 6) **8.** In a responsibility report for a profit center, controllable fixed costs are deducted from contribution margin to show:
  a. profit center margin.
  b. controllable margin.
  c. net income.
  d. income from operations.

(SO 7) **9.** In the formula for return on investment (ROI), the factors for controllable margin and operating assets are, respectively:
  a. controllable margin percentage and total operating assets.

  b. controllable margin dollars and average operating assets.
  c. controllable margin dollars and total assets.
  d. controllable margin percentage and average operating assets.

10. A manager of an investment center can improve ROI by: (SO
  a. increasing average operating assets.
  b. reducing sales.
  c. increasing variable costs.
  d. reducing variable and/or controllable fixed costs.

QUESTIONS

1. (a) What is budgetary control?
  (b) Ken Leask is describing budgetary control. What steps should be included in Ken's description?

2. The following purposes are part of a budgetary reporting system: (a) Determine efficient use of materials. (b) Control overhead costs. (c) Determine whether income objectives are being met. For each purpose, indicate the name of the report, the frequency of the report, and the primary recipient(s) of the report.

3. How may a budget report for the second quarter differ from a budget report for the first quarter?

4. Mary Flynn questions the usefulness of a master sales budget in evaluating sales performance. Is there justification for Mary's concern? Explain.

5. Under what circumstances may a static budget be an appropriate basis for evaluating a manager's effectiveness in controlling costs?

6. "A flexible budget is really a series of static budgets." Is this true? Why?

7. The static manufacturing overhead budget based on 40,000 direct labor hours shows budgeted indirect labor costs of $56,000. During March, the department incurs $65,000 of indirect labor while working 45,000 direct labor hours. Is this a favorable or unfavorable performance? Why?

8. A static overhead budget based on 40,000 direct labor hours shows Factory Insurance $6,400 as a fixed cost. At the 50,000 direct labor hours worked in March, factory insurance costs were $6,200. Is this a favorable or unfavorable performance? Why?

9. Lori Scott is confused about how a flexible budget is prepared. Identify the steps for Lori.

10. Milner Company has prepared a graph of flexible budget data. At zero direct labor hours, the total budgeted cost line intersects the vertical axis at $35,000. At 10,000 direct labor hours, the line drawn from the total budgeted

cost line intersects the vertical axis at $85,000. How may the fixed and variable costs be expressed?

11. The flexible budget formula is fixed costs $40,000 plus variable costs of $3 per direct labor hour. What is the total budgeted cost at (a) 9,000 hours and (b) 12,345 hours?

12. What is management by exception? What criteria may be used in identifying exceptions?

13. What is responsibility accounting? Explain the purpose of responsibility accounting.

14. Val Wheaton is studying for an accounting examination. Describe for Val what conditions are necessary for responsibility accounting to be used effectively.

15. Distinguish between controllable and noncontrollable costs.

16. How do responsibility reports differ from budget reports?

17. What is the relationship, if any, between a responsibility reporting system and a company's organization chart?

18. Distinguish among the three types of responsibility centers.

19. (a) What costs are included in a performance report for a cost center? (b) In the report, are variable and fixed costs identified?

20. How do direct fixed costs differ from indirect fixed costs? Are both types of fixed costs controllable?

21. Sharon Manion is confused about controllable margin reported in an income statement for a profit center. How is this margin computed, and what is its primary purpose?

22. What is the primary basis for evaluating the performance of the manager of an investment center? Indicate the formula for this basis.

23. Explain the ways that ROI can be improved.

24. Indicate two behavioral (performance evaluation) principles that pertain to (a) the manager being evaluated and (b) top management.

BRIEF EXERCISES

BE25-1 For the quarter ended March 31, 2005, Westphal Company accumulates the following sales data for its product, Garden-Tools: $315,000 budget; $304,000 actual. Prepare a static budget report for the quarter.

Prepare static budget report.
(SO 2)

BE25-2 Data for Westphal Company are given in BE25-1. In the second quarter, budgeted sales were $380,000, and actual sales were $386,000. Prepare a static budget report for the second quarter and for the year to date.

Prepare static budget report for 2 quarters.
(SO 2)

BE25-3 In Hinsdale Company, direct labor is $20 per hour. The company expects to operate at 10,000 direct labor hours each month. In January 2005, direct labor totaling $205,000 is incurred in working 10,400 hours. Prepare (a) a static budget report and (b) a flexible budget report. Evaluate the usefulness of each report.

Show usefulness of flexible budgets in evaluating performance.
(SO 3)

BE25-4 Dukane Company expects to produce 1,200,000 units of Product XX in 2005. Monthly production is expected to range from 80,000 to 120,000 units. Budgeted variable manufacturing costs per unit are: direct materials $4, direct labor $6, and overhead $9. Prepare a flexible manufacturing budget for the relevant range value using 20,000 unit increments.

Prepare a flexible budget for variable costs.
(SO 3)

BE25-5 Data for Dukane Company are given in BE25-4. In March 2005, the company incurs the following costs in producing 100,000 units: direct materials $425,000, direct labor $590,000, and variable overhead $915,000. Prepare a flexible budget report for March. Were costs controlled?

Prepare flexible budget report.
(SO 3)

BE25-6 In the Assembly Department of Emil Company, budgeted and actual manufacturing overhead costs for the month of April 2005 were as follows.

Prepare a responsibility report for a cost center.
(SO 5)

	Budget	**Actual**
Indirect materials	$15,000	$14,300
Indirect labor	20,000	20,800
Utilities	10,000	10,750
Supervision	5,000	5,000

All costs are controllable by the department manager. Prepare a responsibility report for April for the cost center.

BE25-7 Advent Manufacturing Company accumulates the following summary data for the year ending December 31, 2005, for its Water Division which it operates as a profit center: sales—$2,000,000 budget, $2,080,000 actual; variable costs—$1,000,000 budget, $1,030,000 actual; and controllable fixed costs—$300,000 budget, $310,000 actual. Prepare a responsibility report for the Water Division.

Prepare a responsibility report for a profit center.
(SO 6)

BE25-8 For the year ending December 31, 2005, Nathan Company accumulates the following data for the Plastics Division which it operates as an investment center: contribution margin—$700,000 budget, $715,000 actual; controllable fixed costs—$300,000 budget, $305,000 actual. Average operating assets for the year were $2,000,000. Prepare a responsibility report for the Plastics Division beginning with contribution margin.

Prepare a responsibility report for an investment center.
(SO 7)

BE25-9 For its three investment centers, Stahl Company accumulates the following data:

Compute return on investment using the ROI formula.
(SO 7)

	I	**II**	**III**
Sales	$2,000,000	$3,000,000	$ 4,000,000
Controllable margin	1,200,000	2,000,000	3,000,000
Average operating assets	6,000,000	8,000,000	10,000,000

Compute the return on investment (ROI) for each center.

BE25-10 Data for the investment centers for Stahl Company are given in BE25-9. The centers expect the following changes in the next year: (I) increase sales 15%; (II) decrease costs $200,000; (III) decrease average operating assets $400,000. Compute the expected return on investment (ROI) for each center. Assume center I has a contribution margin percentage of 80%.

Compute return on investment under changed conditions.
(SO 7)

EXERCISES

Prepare flexible manufacturing overhead budget.

(SO 3)

E25-1 Twyla Company uses a flexible budget for manufacturing overhead based on direct labor hours. Variable manufacturing overhead costs per direct labor hour are as follows.

Indirect labor	$1.00
Indirect materials	0.60
Utilities	0.40

Fixed overhead costs per month are: Supervision $4,000, Depreciation $1,500, and Property Taxes $800. The company believes it will normally operate in a range of 7,000–10,000 direct labor hours per month.

Instructions
Prepare a monthly flexible manufacturing overhead budget for 2005 for the expected range of activity, using increments of 1,000 direct labor hours.

Prepare flexible budget reports for manufacturing overhead costs, and comment on findings.

(SO 3)

E25-2 Using the information in E25-1, assume that in July 2005, Twyla Company incurs the following manufacturing overhead costs.

Variable Costs		**Fixed Costs**	
Indirect labor	$8,700	Supervision	$4,000
Indirect materials	5,300	Depreciation	1,500
Utilities	3,200	Property taxes	800

Instructions
(a) Prepare a flexible budget performance report, assuming that the company worked 9,000 direct labor hours during the month.
(b) Prepare a flexible budget performance report, assuming that the company worked 8,500 direct labor hours during the month.
(c) Comment on your findings.

Prepare flexible selling expense budget.

(SO 3)

E25-3 Vincent Company uses flexible budgets to control its selling expenses. Monthly sales are expected to range from $170,000 to $200,000. Variable costs and their percentage relationship to sales are: Sales Commissions 6%, Advertising 4%, Traveling 3%, and Delivery 2%. Fixed selling expenses will consist of Sales Salaries $32,000, Depreciation on Delivery Equipment $7,000, and Insurance on Delivery Equipment $1,000.

Instructions
Prepare a monthly flexible budget for each $10,000 increment of sales within the relevant range for the year ending December 31, 2005.

Prepare flexible budget reports for selling expenses.

(SO 3)

E25-4 The actual selling expenses incurred in March 2005 by Vincent Company are as follows.

Variable Expenses		**Fixed Expenses**	
Sales commissions	$11,000	Sales salaries	$32,000
Advertising	7,000	Depreciation	7,000
Travel	5,100	Insurance	1,000
Delivery	3,500		

Instructions
(a) Prepare a flexible budget performance report for March using the budget data in E25-3, assuming that March sales were $170,000. Expected and actual sales are the same.
(b) Prepare a flexible budget performance report, assuming that March sales were $180,000. Expected sales and actual sales are the same.
(c) Comment on the importance of using flexible budgets in evaluating the performance of the sales manager.

E25-5 Sublette Company's manufacturing overhead budget for the first quarter of 2005 contained the following data.

Prepare flexible budget and responsibility report for manufacturing overhead.
(SO 3, 5)

Variable Costs		Fixed Costs	
Indirect materials	$12,000	Supervisory salaries	$36,000
Indirect labor	10,000	Depreciation	7,000
Utilities	8,000	Property taxes and insurance	8,000
Maintenance	5,000	Maintenance	5,000

Actual variable costs were: indirect materials $13,800, indirect labor $9,600, utilities $8,700, and maintenance $4,200. Actual fixed costs equaled budgeted costs except for property taxes and insurance, which were $8,400.

All costs are considered controllable by the production department manager except for depreciation, and property taxes and insurance.

Instructions

(a) Prepare a flexible overhead budget report for the first quarter.

(b) Prepare a responsibility report for the first quarter.

E25-6 As sales manager, Shawn Keyser was given the following static budget report for selling expenses in the Clothing Department of Dunham Company for the month of October.

Prepare flexible budget report, and answer question.
(SO 2, 3)

DUNHAM COMPANY
Clothing Department
Budget Report
For the Month Ended October 31, 2005

	Budget	Actual	Difference Favorable F Unfavorable U
Sales in units	8,000	10,000	2,000 F
Variable costs			
Sales commissions	$ 2,000	$ 2,600	$ 600 U
Advertising expense	800	850	50 U
Travel expense	4,400	4,900	500 U
Free samples given out	1,600	1,300	300 F
Total variable	8,800	9,650	850 U
Fixed costs			
Rent	1,500	1,500	–0–
Sales salaries	1,200	1,200	–0–
Office salaries	800	800	–0–
Depreciation—autos (sales staff)	500	500	–0–
Total fixed	4,000	4,000	–0–
Total costs	$12,800	$13,650	$ 850 U

As a result of this budget report, Shawn was called into the president's office and congratulated on his fine sales performance. He was reprimanded, however, for allowing his costs to get out of control. Shawn knew something was wrong with the performance report that he had been given. However, he was not sure what to do, and comes to you for advice.

Instructions

(a) Prepare a budget report based on flexible budget data to help Shawn.

(b) Should Shawn have been reprimanded? Explain.

E25-7 Sherrer Company has two production departments, Fabricating and Assembling. At a department managers' meeting, the controller uses flexible budget graphs to explain total budgeted costs. Separate graphs based on direct labor hours are used for each department. The graphs show the following.

State total budgeted cost formulas, and prepare flexible budget graph.
(SO 3)

1. At zero direct labor hours, the total budgeted cost line and the fixed cost line intersect the vertical axis at $40,000 in the Fabricating Department and $35,000 in the Assembling Department.

2. At normal capacity of 50,000 direct labor hours, the line drawn from the total budgeted cost line intersects the vertical axis at $160,000 in the Fabricating Department, and $110,000 in the Assembling Department.

Instructions

(a) State the total budgeted cost formula for each department.

(b) Compute the total budgeted cost for each department, assuming actual direct labor hours worked were 53,000 and 47,000, in the Fabricating and Assembling Departments, respectively.

(c) Prepare the flexible budget graph for the Fabricating Department, assuming the maximum direct labor hours in the relevant range is 100,000. Use increments of 10,000 direct labor hours on the horizontal axis and increments of $50,000 on the vertical axis.

Prepare reports in a responsibility reporting system.

(SO 4)

E25-8 Marcum Company's organization chart includes the president; the vice president of production; three assembly plants—Dallas, Atlanta, and Tucson; and two departments within each plant—Machining and Finishing. Budget and actual manufacturing cost data for July 2005 are as follows:

Finishing Department—Dallas: Direct materials $41,000 actual, $45,000 budget; direct labor $83,000 actual, $82,000 budget; manufacturing overhead $51,000 actual, $49,200 budget.

Machining Department—Dallas: Total manufacturing costs $220,000 actual, $214,000 budget.

Atlanta Plant: Total manufacturing costs $424,000 actual, $421,000 budget.

Tucson Plant: Total manufacturing costs $494,000 actual, $499,000 budget.

The Dallas plant manager's office costs were $95,000 actual and $92,000 budget. The vice president of production's office costs were $132,000 actual and $130,000 budget. Office costs are not allocated to departments and plants.

Instructions

Using the format on page 1020, prepare the reports in a responsibility system for:

(a) The Finishing Department—Dallas.

(b) The plant manager—Dallas.

(c) The vice president of production.

Compute missing amounts in responsibility reports for three profit centers, and prepare a report.

(SO 6)

E25-9 Longhead Manufacturing Inc. has three divisions which are operated as profit centers. Actual operating data for the divisions listed alphabetically are as follows.

Operating Data	Women's Shoes	Men's Shoes	Children's Shoes
Contribution margin	$250,000	(3)	$170,000
Controllable fixed costs	100,000	(4)	(5)
Controllable margin	(1)	$ 90,000	96,000
Sales	600,000	450,000	(6)
Variable costs	(2)	320,000	250,000

Instructions

(a) Compute the missing amounts. Show computations.

(b) Prepare a responsibility report for the Women's Shoe Division assuming (1) the data are for the month ended June 30, 2005, and (2) all data equal budget except variable costs which are $10,000 over budget.

Compute ROI for current year and for possible future changes.

(SO 7)

E25-10 The Green Division of Campana Company reported the following data for the current year.

Sales	$3,000,000
Variable costs	1,800,000
Controllable fixed costs	600,000
Average operating assets	5,000,000

Top management is unhappy with the investment center's return on investment (ROI). It asks the manager of the Green Division to submit plans to improve ROI in the next year. The manager believes it is feasible to consider the following independent courses of action.

1. Increase sales by $320,000 with no change in the contribution margin percentage.

2. Reduce variable costs by $100,000.

3. Reduce average operating assets by 4%.

Instructions

(a) Compute the return on investment (ROI) for the current year.

(b) Using the ROI formula, compute the ROI under each of the proposed courses of action. (Round to one decimal.)

PROBLEMS: SET A

P25-1A Alcore Company estimates that 240,000 direct labor hours will be worked during 2005 in the Assembly Department. On this basis, the following budgeted manufacturing overhead data are computed.

Prepare flexible budget and budget report for manufacturing overhead.

(SO 3)

Variable Overhead Costs		Fixed Overhead Costs	
Indirect labor	$ 72,000	Supervision	$ 72,000
Indirect materials	48,000	Depreciation	36,000
Repairs	24,000	Insurance	9,600
Utilities	38,400	Rent	9,000
Lubricants	9,600	Property taxes	6,000
	$192,000		$132,600

It is estimated that direct labor hours worked each month will range from 18,000 to 24,000 hours.

During January, 20,000 direct labor hours were worked and the following overhead costs were incurred.

Variable Overhead Costs		Fixed Overhead Costs	
Indirect labor	$ 6,200	Supervision	$ 6,000
Indirect materials	3,600	Depreciation	3,000
Repairs	1,600	Insurance	800
Utilities	2,500	Rent	800
Lubricants	830	Property taxes	500
	$14,730		$11,100

Instructions

(a) Prepare a monthly flexible manufacturing overhead budget for each increment of 2,000 direct labor hours over the relevant range for the year ending December 31, 2005.

(b) Prepare a manufacturing overhead budget report for January.

(c) ▭▭▭▷ Comment on management's efficiency in controlling manufacturing overhead costs in January.

(a) Total costs: 18,000 DLH, $25,450; 24,000 DLH, $30,250

(b) Budget, $27,050 Actual, $25,830

P25-2A Borealis Manufacturing Company produces one product, Kebo. Because of wide fluctuations in demand for Kebo, the Assembly Department experiences significant variations in monthly production levels.

The annual master manufacturing overhead budget is based on 300,000 direct labor hours. In July 27,500 labor hours were worked. The master manufacturing overhead budget for the year and the actual overhead costs incurred in July are as follows.

Prepare flexible budget, budget report, and graph for manufacturing overhead.

(SO 3)

Overhead Costs	Master Budget (annual)	Actual in July
Variable		
Indirect labor	$ 300,000	$26,000
Indirect materials	210,000	17,000
Utilities	90,000	8,100
Maintenance	60,000	5,400
Fixed		
Supervision	180,000	15,000
Depreciation	120,000	10,000
Insurance and taxes	60,000	5,000
Total	$1,020,000	$86,500

Instructions

(a) Total costs: 22,500 DLH,
$79,500; 30,000 DLH,
$96,000
(b) Budget $90,500
Actual $86,500

(a) Prepare a monthly flexible overhead budget for the year ending December 31, 2005, assuming monthly production levels range from 22,500 to 30,000 direct labor hours. Use increments of 2,500 direct labor hours.

(b) Prepare a budget performance report for the month of July 2005 comparing actual results with budget data based on the flexible budget.

(c) ✏️➤ Were costs effectively controlled? Explain.

(d) State the formula for computing the total monthly budgeted costs in Borealis Company.

(e) Prepare the flexible budget graph showing total budgeted costs at 25,000 and 27,500 direct labor hours. Use increments of 5,000 on the horizontal axis and increments of $10,000 on the vertical axis.

State total budgeted cost formula, and prepare flexible budget reports for 2 time periods.

(SO 2, 3)

P25-3A Chambers Company uses budgets in controlling costs. The May 2005 budget report for the company's Packaging Department is as follows.

CHAMBERS COMPANY
Budget Report
Packaging Department
For the Month Ended May 31, 2005

Manufacturing Costs	Budget	Actual	Difference Favorable F Unfavorable U
Variable costs			
Direct materials	$ 35,000	$ 37,500	$2,500 U
Direct labor	50,000	53,000	3,000 U
Indirect materials	15,000	15,200	200 U
Indirect labor	12,500	13,000	500 U
Utilities	7,500	7,100	400 F
Maintenance	5,000	5,200	200 U
Total variable	125,000	131,000	6,000 U
Fixed costs			
Rent	8,000	8,000	–0–
Supervision	9,000	9,000	–0–
Depreciation	5,000	5,000	–0–
Total fixed	22,000	22,000	–0–
Total costs	$147,000	$153,000	$6,000 U

The budget amounts in the report were based on the master budget for the year, which assumed that 600,000 units would be produced (50,000 per month). (*Hint:* The budget amounts above are one-twelfth of the master budget for the year.)

The company president was displeased with the department manager's performance. The department manager, who thought he had done a good job, could not understand the unfavorable results. In May, 55,000 units were produced.

Instructions

(a) State the total budgeted cost formula.

(b) Budget $159,500

(b) Prepare a budget report for May using flexible budget data. Why does this report provide a better basis for evaluating performance than the report based on static budget data?

(c) Budget $122,000
Actual $126,800

(c) In June, 40,000 units were produced. Prepare the budget report using flexible budget data, assuming (1) each variable cost was 20% less in June than its actual cost in May, and (2) fixed costs were the same in the month of June as in May.

Prepare responsibility report for a profit center.

(SO 6)

P25-4A Korene Manufacturing Inc. operates the Home Appliance Division as a profit center. Operating data for this division for the year ended December 31, 2005, are as shown on the next page.

	Budget	Difference from Budget
Sales	$2,400,000	$80,000 U
Cost of goods sold		
Variable	1,200,000	47,000 U
Controllable fixed	200,000	10,000 F
Selling and administrative		
Variable	240,000	8,000 F
Controllable fixed	60,000	6,000 U
Noncontrollable fixed costs	50,000	2,000 U

In addition, Korene Manufacturing incurs $150,000 of indirect fixed costs that were budgeted at $155,000. Twenty percent (20%) of these costs are allocated to the Home Appliance Division. None of these costs are controllable by the division manager.

Instructions
(a) Prepare a responsibility report for the Home Appliance Division (a profit center) for the year.
(b) ▭▭▭▭▶ Comment on the manager's performance in controlling revenues and costs.
(c) Identify any costs excluded from the responsibility report and explain why they were excluded.

(a) Contribution margin
$119,000 U
Controllable margin
$115,000 U

P25-5A Chudzik Manufacturing Company manufactures a variety of garden and lawn equipment. The company operates through three divisions. Each division is an investment center. Operating data for the Lawnmower Division for the year ended December 31, 2005, and relevant budget data are as follows.

Prepare responsibility report for an investment center, and compute ROI.
(SO 7)

	Actual	Comparison with Budget
Sales	$3,000,000	$150,000 unfavorable
Variable cost of goods sold	1,400,000	100,000 unfavorable
Variable selling and administrative expenses	300,000	50,000 favorable
Controllable fixed cost of goods sold	270,000	On target
Controllable fixed selling and administrative expenses	130,000	On target

Average operating assets for the year for the Lawnmower Division were $5,000,000 which was also the budgeted amount.

Instructions
(a) Prepare a responsibility report (in thousands of dollars) for the Lawnmower Division.
(b) Evaluate the manager's performance. Which items will likely be investigated by top management?
(c) Compute the expected ROI in 2006 for the Lawnmower Division, assuming the following independent changes.
  (1) Variable cost of goods sold is decreased by 15%.
  (2) Average operating assets are decreased by 20%.
  (3) Sales are increased by $500,000 and this increase is expected to increase contribution margin by $200,000.

(a) Controllable margin:
Budget $1,100
Actual $900

P25-6A Kojak Company uses a responsibility reporting system. It has divisions in Denver, Seattle, and San Diego. Each division has three production departments: Cutting, Shaping, and Finishing. The responsibility for each department rests with a manager who reports to the division production manager. Each division manager reports to the vice president of production. There are also vice presidents for marketing and finance. All vice presidents report to the president.

In January 2005, controllable actual and budget manufacturing overhead cost data for the departments and divisions were as shown on the next page.

Prepare reports for cost centers under responsibility accounting, and comment on performance of managers.
(SO 4)

Manufacturing Overhead	Actual	Budget
Individual costs—Cutting Department—Seattle		
Indirect labor	$ 73,000	$ 70,000
Indirect materials	46,700	46,000
Maintenance	20,500	18,000
Utilities	20,100	17,000
Supervision	22,000	20,000
	$ 182,300	$ 171,000
Total costs		
Shaping Department—Seattle	$ 158,000	$ 148,000
Finishing Department—Seattle	210,000	208,000
Denver division	676,000	673,000
San Diego division	722,000	715,000

Additional overhead costs were incurred as follows: Seattle division production manager—actual costs $52,500, budget $51,000; vice president of production—actual costs $65,000, budget $64,000; president—actual costs $76,400, budget $74,200. These expenses are not allocated.

The vice presidents who report to the president, other than the vice president of production, had the following expenses.

Vice president	Actual	Budget
Marketing	$133,600	$130,000
Finance	108,000	105,000

Instructions

(a) (1) $11,300 U
(2) $24,800 U
(3) $35,800 U
(4) $44,600 U

(a) Using the format on page 1020, prepare the following responsibility reports.
  (1) Manufacturing overhead—Cutting Department manager—Seattle division.
  (2) Manufacturing overhead—Seattle division manager.
  (3) Manufacturing overhead—vice president of production.
  (4) Manufacturing overhead and expenses—president.
(b) Comment on the comparative performances of:
  (1) Department managers in the Seattle division.
  (2) Division managers.
  (3) Vice presidents.

PROBLEMS: SET B

Prepare flexible budget and budget report for manufacturing overhead.

(SO 3)

P25-1B Oakley Company estimates that 360,000 direct labor hours will be worked during the coming year, 2005, in the Packaging Department. On this basis, the following budgeted manufacturing overhead cost data are computed for the year.

Fixed Overhead Costs		Variable Overhead Costs	
Supervision	$ 90,000	Indirect labor	$144,000
Depreciation	60,000	Indirect materials	90,000
Insurance	30,000	Repairs	54,000
Rent	36,000	Utilities	72,000
Property taxes	18,000	Lubricants	18,000
	$234,000		$378,000

It is estimated that direct labor hours worked each month will range from 27,000 to 36,000 hours.

During October, 27,000 direct labor hours were worked and the following overhead costs were incurred.

Fixed overhead costs: Supervision $7,500, Depreciation $5,000, Insurance $2,470, Rent $3,000, and Property taxes $1,500.

Variable overhead costs: Indirect labor $11,760, Indirect materials, $6,400, Repairs $4,000, Utilities $5,700, and Lubricants $1,640.

(a) Prepare a monthly flexible manufacturing overhead budget for each increment of 3,000 direct labor hours over the relevant range for the year ending December 31, 2005.

(b) Prepare a flexible budget report for October.

(c) ▢▤▱▷ Comment on management's efficiency in controlling manufacturing overhead costs in October.

(a) Total costs: DLH 27,000, $47,850; DLH 36,000, $57,300
(b) Total $1,120 U

P25-2B Hindu Company manufactures tablecloths. Sales have grown rapidly over the past 2 years. As a result, the president has installed a budgetary control system for 2005. The follow-ing data were used in developing the master manufacturing overhead budget for the Ironing Department, which is based on an activity index of direct labor hours.

Prepare flexible budget, budget report, and graph for manu-facturing overhead.

(SO 3)

Variable Costs	Rate per Direct Labor Hour	Annual Fixed Costs	
Indirect labor	$0.40	Supervision	$30,000
Indirect materials	0.60	Depreciation	18,000
Factory utilities	0.30	Insurance	12,000
Factory repairs	0.20	Rent	24,000

The master overhead budget was prepared on the expectation that 480,000 direct labor hours will be worked during the year. In June, 42,000 direct labor hours were worked. At that level of activity, actual costs were as follows.

Variable—per direct labor hour: Indirect labor $0.43, Indirect materials $0.58, Factory util-ities $0.32, and Factory repairs $0.24.
Fixed: same as budgeted.

Instructions

(a) Prepare a monthly flexible manufacturing overhead budget for the year ending December 31, 2005, assuming production levels range from 35,000 to 50,000 direct labor hours. Use in-crements of 5,000 direct labor hours.

(b) Prepare a budget performance report for June comparing actual results with budget data based on the flexible budget.

(c) Were costs effectively controlled? Explain.

(d) State the formula for computing the total budgeted costs for Hindu Company.

(e) Prepare the flexible budget graph, showing total budgeted costs at 35,000 and 45,000 direct labor hours. Use increments of 5,000 direct labor hours on the horizontal axis and incre-ments of $10,000 on the vertical axis.

(a) Total costs: 35,000 DLH, $59,500; 50,000 DLH, $82,000
(b) Budget $70,000
Actual $72,940

P25-3B Yaeger Company uses budgets in controlling costs. The August 2005 budget report for the company's Assembling Department is as follows.

State total budgeted cost for-mula, and prepare flexible budget reports for 2 time periods.

(SO 2, 3)

YAEGER COMPANY
Budget Report
Assembling Department
For the Month Ended August 31, 2005

Manufacturing Costs	Budget	Actual	Difference Favorable F Unfavorable U
Variable costs			
Direct materials	$ 48,000	$ 47,000	$1,000 F
Direct labor	66,000	62,700	3,300 F
Indirect materials	24,000	24,200	200 U
Indirect labor	18,000	17,500	500 F
Utilities	15,000	14,900	100 F
Maintenance	9,000	9,200	200 U
Total variable	180,000	175,500	4,500 F
Fixed costs			
Rent	12,000	12,000	–0–
Supervision	17,000	17,000	–0–
Depreciation	7,000	7,000	–0–
Total fixed	36,000	36,000	–0–
Total costs	$216,000	$211,500	$4,500 F

The budget data in the report are based on the master budget for the year, which assumed that 720,000 units would be produced (60,000 per month). The Assembling Department manager is pleased with the report and expects a raise, or at least praise for a job well done. The company president, however, is unhappy with the results for August, because only 58,000 units were produced. (*Hint:* The budget amounts above are one-twelfth of the master budget.)

Instructions

(b) Budget $210,000

(c) Budget $228,000
Actual $229,050

(a) State the total monthly budgeted cost formula.
(b) Prepare a budget report for August using flexible budget data. Why does this report provide a better basis for evaluating performance than the report based on static budget data?
(c) In September, 64,000 units were produced. Prepare the budget report using flexible budget data, assuming (1) each variable cost was 10% higher than its actual cost in August, and (2) fixed costs were the same in September as in August.

Prepare responsibility report for a profit center.

(SO 6)

P25-4B Henning Manufacturing Inc. operates the Patio Furniture Division as a profit center. Operating data for this division for the year ended December 31, 2005, are as follows.

	Budget	**Difference from Budget**
Sales	$2,500,000	$70,000 F
Cost of goods sold		
Variable	1,300,000	33,000 F
Controllable fixed	200,000	5,000 U
Selling and administrative		
Variable	220,000	7,000 U
Controllable fixed	50,000	2,000 U
Noncontrollable fixed costs	70,000	4,000 U

In addition, Henning Manufacturing incurs $180,000 of indirect fixed costs that were budgeted at $175,000. Twenty percent (20%) of these costs are allocated to the Patio Furniture Division.

Instructions

(a) Contribution margin
$96,000 F
Controllable margin
$89,000 F

(a) Prepare a responsibility report for the Patio Furniture Division for the year.
(b) ▭▭▭▷ Comment on the manager's performance in controlling revenues and costs.
(c) Identify any costs excluded from the responsibility report and explain why they were excluded.

Prepare responsibility report for an investment center, and compute ROI.

(SO 7)

P25-5B Alosio Manufacturing Company manufactures a variety of tools and industrial equipment. The company operates through three divisions. Each division is an investment center. Operating data for the Home Division for the year ended December 31, 2005, and relevant budget data are as follows.

	Actual	**Comparison with Budget**
Sales	$1,550,000	$100,000 favorable
Variable cost of goods sold	700,000	70,000 unfavorable
Variable selling and administrative expenses	125,000	25,000 unfavorable
Controllable fixed cost of goods sold	170,000	On target
Controllable fixed selling and administrative		
expenses	100,000	On target

Average operating assets for the year for the Home Division were $2,500,000 which was also the budgeted amount.

Instructions

(a) Controllable margin:
Budget $450;
Actual $455

(a) Prepare a responsibility report (in thousands of dollars) for the Home Division.
(b) Evaluate the manager's performance. Which items will likely be investigated by top management?
(c) Compute the expected ROI in 2006 for the Home Division, assuming the following independent changes to actual data.
   (1) Variable cost of goods sold is decreased by 6%.
   (2) Average operating assets are decreased by 10%.
   (3) Sales are increased by $200,000, and this increase is expected to increase contribution margin by $90,000.

BROADENING YOUR PERSPECTIVE

Group Decision Case

BYP25-1 Z-Bar Pastures is a 400-acre farm on the outskirts of the Kentucky Bluegrass, specializing in the boarding of broodmares and their foals. A recent economic downturn in the thoroughbred industry has led to a decline in breeding activities, and it has made the boarding business extremely competitive. To meet the competition, Z-Bar Pastures planned in 2005 to entertain clients, advertise more extensively, and absorb expenses formerly paid by clients such as veterinary and blacksmith fees.

The budget report for 2005 is presented below. As shown, the static income statement budget for the year is based on an expected 21,900 boarding days at $25 per mare. The variable expenses per mare per day were budgeted: Feed $5, Veterinary fees $3, Blacksmith fees $0.30, and Supplies $0.70. All other budgeted expenses were either semifixed or fixed.

During the year, management decided not to replace a worker who quit in March, but it did issue a new advertising brochure and did more entertaining of clients.[1]

Z-BAR PASTURES
Static Budget Income Statement
Year Ended December 31, 2005

	Actual	Master Budget	Difference
Number of mares	52	60	8*
Number of boarding days	18,980	21,900	2,920*
Sales	$379,600	$547,500	$167,900*
Less variable expenses:			
Feed	104,390	109,500	5,110
Veterinary fees	58,838	65,700	6,862
Blacksmith fees	6,074	6,570	496
Supplies	12,954	15,330	2,376
Total variable expenses	182,256	197,100	14,844
Contribution margin	197,344	350,400	153,056*
Less fixed expenses:			
Depreciation	40,000	40,000	–0–
Insurance	11,000	11,000	–0–
Utilities	12,000	14,000	2,000
Repairs and maintenance	10,000	11,000	1,000
Labor	88,000	96,000	8,000
Advertisement	12,000	8,000	4,000*
Entertainment	7,000	5,000	2,000*
Total fixed expense	180,000	185,000	5,000
Net income	$ 17,344	$165,400	$148,056*

*Unfavorable.

Instructions
With the class divided into groups, answer the following.

(a) Based on the static budget report:
  (1) What was the primary cause(s) of the loss in net income?
  (2) Did management do a good, average, or poor job of controlling expenses?
  (3) Were management's decisions to stay competitive sound?
(b) Prepare a flexible budget report for the year.

---

[1]Data for this case are based on Hans Sprohge and John Talbott, "New Applications for Variance Analysis," *Journal of Accountancy* (AICPA, New York), April 1989, pp. 137–141.

(c) Based on the flexible budget report, answer the three questions in part (a) above.

(d) What course of action do you recommend for the management of Z-Bar Pastures?

Managerial Analysis

BYP25-2 Castle Company manufactures expensive watch cases sold as souvenirs. Three of its sales departments are: Retail Sales, Wholesale Sales, and Outlet Sales. The Retail Sales Department is a profit center. The Wholesale Sales Department is a cost center. Its managers merely take orders from customers who purchase through the company's wholesale catalog. The Outlet Sales Department is an investment center, because each manager is given full responsibility for an outlet store location. The manager can hire and discharge employees, purchase, maintain, and sell equipment, and in general is fairly independent of company control.

Sara Sutton is a manager in the Retail Sales Department. Gilbert Lewis manages the Wholesale Sales Department. Jose Lopez manages the Golden Gate Club outlet store in San Francisco. The following are the budget responsibility reports for each of the three departments.

Budget

	Retail Sales	Wholesale Sales	Outlet Sales
Sales	$ 750,000	$ 400,000	$200,000
Variable costs			
Cost of goods sold	150,000	100,000	25,000
Advertising	100,000	30,000	5,000
Sales salaries	75,000	15,000	3,000
Printing	10,000	20,000	5,000
Travel	20,000	30,000	2,000
Fixed costs			
Rent	50,000	30,000	10,000
Insurance	5,000	2,000	1,000
Depreciation	75,000	100,000	40,000
Investment in assets	$1,000,000	$1,200,000	$800,000

Actual Results

	Retail Sales	Wholesale Sales	Outlet Sales
Sales	$ 750,000	$ 400,000	$200,000
Variable costs			
Cost of goods sold	195,000	120,000	26,250
Advertising	100,000	30,000	5,000
Sales salaries	75,000	15,000	3,000
Printing	10,000	20,000	5,000
Travel	15,000	20,000	1,500
Fixed costs			
Rent	40,000	50,000	12,000
Insurance	5,000	2,000	1,000
Depreciation	80,000	90,000	60,000
Investment in assets	$1,000,000	$1,200,000	$800,000

Instructions

(a) Determine which of the items should be included in the responsibility report for each of the three managers.

(b) Compare the budgeted measures with the actual results. Decide which results should be called to the attention of each manager.

Real-World Focus

BYP25-3 **Computer Associates International, Inc.**, the world's leading business software company, delivers the end-to-end infrastructure to enable e-business through innovative technology, services, and education. CA has 19,000 employees worldwide and had revenue of over $6 billion for the fiscal year ended March 31, 2000.

Presented below is information from the company's annual report.

COMPUTER ASSOCIATES INTERNATIONAL
Management Discussion

The Company has experienced a pattern of business whereby revenue for its third and fourth fiscal quarters reflects an increase over first- and second-quarter revenue. The Company attributes this increase to clients' increased spending at the end of their calendar year budgetary periods and the culmination of its annual sales plan. Since the Company's costs do not increase proportionately with the third- and fourth-quarters' increase in revenue, the higher revenue in these quarters results in greater profit margins and income. Fourth-quarter profitability is traditionally affected by significant new hirings, training, and education expenditures for the succeeding year.

Instructions
(a) Why don't the company's costs increase proportionately as the revenues increase in the third and fourth quarters?
(b) What type of budgeting seems appropriate for the Computer Associates situation?

Exploring the Web

BYP25-4 Genelle and Doug have recorded the story of their wedding planning. They are on a strict budget and need help in preparing what they call "a somewhat flexible budget."

Address: www.wednet.com/inspire/wedstory/story1.htm, or go to
www.wiley.com/college/weygandt

Steps
1. Go to Genelle and Doug's Web site, and read about their trials and tribulations in planning a wedding.
2. Review the **Planning and Budgeting** section in "Part 1" of their story. They mention that this is a "somewhat flexible budget" for 250 guests, totalling $7,150. They would like to reduce their total costs to $7,000, if at all possible.

Instructions
Recast Genelle and Doug's budget into a truly flexible budget so that they can see the effects on their total costs of reducing the number of invited guests to 225 or 200.

Communication Activity

BYP25-5 The manufacturing overhead budget for Dillons Company contains the following items.

Variable expenses	
Indirect materials	$28,000
Indirect labor	12,000
Maintenance expenses	10,000
Manufacturing supplies	6,000
Total variable	$56,000
Fixed expenses	
Supervision	$18,000
Inspection costs	1,000
Insurance expenses	2,000
Depreciation	15,000
Total fixed	$36,000

The budget was based on an estimated 2,000 units being produced. During the past month, 1,500 units were produced, and the following costs incurred.

Variable expenses	
Indirect materials	$28,200
Indirect labor	13,500
Maintenance expenses	8,200
Manufacturing supplies	5,100
Total variable	$55,000
Fixed expenses	
Supervision	$19,300
Inspection costs	1,200
Insurance expenses	2,200
Depreciation	14,700
Total fixed	$37,400

Instructions

(a) Determine which items would be controllable by Jeff Howell, the production manager.
(b) How much should have been spent during the month for the manufacture of the 1,500 units?
(c) Prepare a flexible manufacturing overhead budget report for Mr. Howell.
(d) Prepare a responsibility report. Include only the costs that would have been controllable by Mr. Howell. In an attached memo, describe clearly for Mr. Howell the areas in which his performance needs to be improved.

Ethics Case

BYP25-6 American Products Corporation participates in a highly competitive industry. In order to meet this competition and achieve profit goals, the company has chosen the decentralized form of organization. Each manager of a decentralized investment center is measured on the basis of profit contribution, market penetration, and return on investment. Failure to meet the objectives established by corporate management for these measures has not been acceptable and usually has resulted in demotion or dismissal of an investment center manager.

An anonymous survey of managers in the company revealed that the managers feel the pressure to compromise their personal ethical standards to achieve the corporate objectives. For example, at certain plant locations there was pressure to reduce quality control to a level which could not assure that all unsafe products would be rejected. Also, sales personnel were encouraged to use questionable sales tactics to obtain orders, including gifts and other incentives to purchasing agents.

The chief executive officer is disturbed by the survey findings. In his opinion such behavior cannot be condoned by the company. He concludes that the company should do something about this problem.

Instructions

(a) Who are the stakeholders (the affected parties) in this situation?
(b) Identify the ethical implications, conflicts, or dilemmas in the above described situation.
(c) What might the company do to reduce the pressures on managers and decrease the ethical conflicts?

(CMA adapted)

Answers to Self-Study Questions
1. c **2.** b **3.** a **4.** d **5.** a **6.** d **7.** d **8.** b **9.** b **10.** d

Answer to PepsiCo Review It Question 3, p. 1029
In its Management's Discussion and Analysis section, under the heading "Results of Operations—Division Review," **PepsiCo** reports six divisions. These are: Frito-Lay North America, Frito-Lay International, Pepsi-Cola North America, Gatorade/Tropicana North America, PepsiCo Beverages International, and Quaker Foods North America.

 REMEMBER to go back to the Navigator box on the chapter-opening page and check off your completed work.

Performance Evaluation through Standard Costs

CONCEPTS FOR REVIEW

Before studying this chapter, you should know or, if necessary, review:

- The flow of costs in a job order and process cost accounting system.
  (Ch. 21, pp. 855–856, and Ch. 22, p. 892)

- How manufacturing overhead is applied to work in process.
  (Ch. 21, pp. 862–864)

- The management by exception principle.
  (Ch. 25, p. 1016)

- How to prepare a flexible manufacturing overhead budget.
  (Ch. 25, pp. 1012–1016)

THE NAVIGATOR

Highlighting Performance Efficiency

There's a very good chance that the highlighter you're holding in your hand was made by Sanford, a maker of permanent markers and other writing instruments. Sanford, headquartered in Illinois, annually sells hundreds of millions of dollars' worth of ACCENT highlighters, fine-point pens, Sharpie permanent markers, Expo dry-erase markers for overhead projectors, and other writing instruments.

Since Sanford makes literally billions of writing utensils per year, the company must keep tight control over manufacturing costs. A very important part of Sanford's manufacturing process is determining how much direct materials, labor, and overhead should cost. These costs are then compared to actual costs to assess performance efficiency. Raw materials for Sanford's markers include a barrel, plug, cap, ink reservoir, and a nib (tip). These parts are assembled by machine to produce thousands of units per hour. A major component of manufacturing overhead is machine maintenance—some fixed, some variable.

"Labor costs are associated with material handling and equipment maintenance functions. Although the assembly process is highly automated, labor is still required to move raw materials to the machine and to package the finished product. In addition, highly skilled technicians are required to service and maintain each piece of equipment," says Mike Orr, vice president, operations.

Labor rates are predictable because the hourly workers are covered by a union contract. The story is the same with the fringe benefits and some supervisory salaries. Even volume levels are fairly predictable—demand for the product is high—so fixed overhead is efficiently absorbed. Raw material standard costs are based on the previous year's actual prices plus any anticipated inflation. Lately, though, inflation has been so low that the company is considering any price increase in raw material to be unfavorable because its standards will remain unchanged.

www.sandfordcorp.com

THE NAVIGATOR

After studying this chapter, you should be able to:

1. Distinguish between a standard and a budget.
2. Identify the advantages of standard costs.
3. Describe how standards are set.
4. State the formulas for determining direct materials and direct labor variances.
5. State the formulas for determining manufacturing overhead variances.
6. Discuss the reporting of variances.
7. Enumerate the features of a standard cost accounting system.

THE NAVIGATOR

In this chapter we continue the study of controlling costs. Here we consider additional measures that permit the evaluation of performance.

The content and organization of Chapter 26 are as follows.

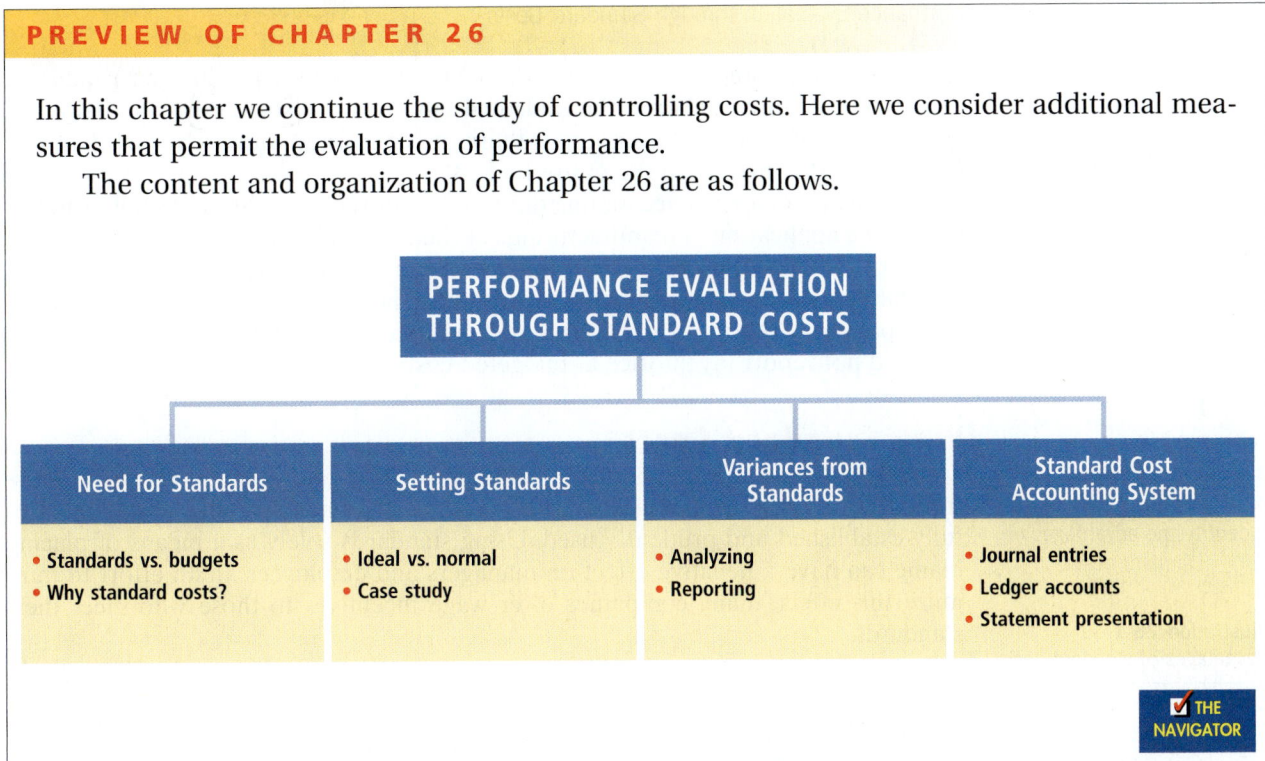

In this chapter we continue the study of controlling costs.

The diagram shows:

PERFORMANCE EVALUATION THROUGH STANDARD COSTS

Need for Standards	Setting Standards	Variances from Standards	Standard Cost Accounting System
• Standards vs. budgets • Why standard costs?	• Ideal vs. normal • Case study	• Analyzing • Reporting	• Journal entries • Ledger accounts • Statement presentation

☑ THE NAVIGATOR

The Need for Standards

Standards are a fact of life. You met the admission standards for the school you are attending. The vehicle that you drive had to meet certain governmental emissions standards. The hamburgers and salads you eat in a restaurant have to meet certain health and nutritional standards before they can be sold. The reason for standards in these cases is very simple: They help to ensure that overall product quality is high. Without standards, quality control is lost.

Standards are also common in business. Those imposed by government agencies are often called **regulations**. They include the Fair Labor Standards Act, the Equal Employment Opportunity Act, and a multitude of environmental standards. Standards established internally by a company may extend to personnel matters, such as employee absenteeism and ethical codes of conduct, quality control standards for products, and standard costs for goods and services. In managerial accounting, **standard costs** are predetermined unit costs, which are used as measures of performance.

We will focus on manufacturing operations in the remainder of this chapter. But you should also recognize that standard costs also apply to many types of service businesses as well. For example, a fast-food restaurant such as **McDonald's** knows the price it should pay for pickles, beef, buns, and other ingredients. It also knows how much time it should take an employee to flip hamburgers. If too much is paid for pickles or too much time is taken to prepare Big Macs, the deviations are noticed and corrective action is taken. Standard costs also may be used in not-for-profit enterprises such as universities, charitable organizations, and governmental agencies.

Distinguishing between Standards and Budgets

In concept, **standards** and **budgets** are essentially the same. Both are predetermined costs, and both contribute to management planning and control. There is a difference, however, in the way the terms are expressed. A standard is a **unit** amount. A budget is a **total** amount. Thus, it is customary to state that the standard cost of

STUDY OBJECTIVE 1

Distinguish between a standard and a budget.

direct labor for a unit of product is $10. If 5,000 units of the product are produced, the $50,000 of direct labor is the **budgeted** labor cost. A standard is the budgeted cost per unit of product. A standard is therefore concerned with each individual cost component that makes up the entire budget.

There are important accounting differences between budgets and standards. Except in the application of manufacturing overhead to jobs and processes, budget data are not journalized in cost accounting systems. In contrast, as will be illustrated in the chapter, standard costs may be incorporated into cost accounting systems. Also, a company may report its inventories at standard cost in its financial statements, but it would not report inventories at budgeted costs.

Why Standard Costs?

STUDY OBJECTIVE 2

Identify the advantages of standard costs.

Standard costs offer a number of advantages to an organization, as shown in Illustration 26-1. These advantages will be realized only when standard costs are carefully established and prudently used. Using standards solely as a means of placing blame can have a negative effect on managers and employees. In an effort to minimize this effect, many companies offer wage incentives to those who meet their standards.

Illustration 26-1
Advantages of standard costs

Advantages of standard costs

Facilitate management planning

Promote greater economy by making employees more "cost-conscious"

Useful in setting selling prices

Contribute to management control by providing basis for evaluation of cost control

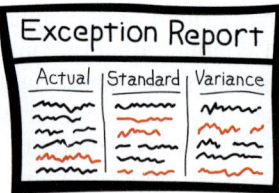

Useful in highlighting variances in management by exception

Simplify costing of inventories and reduce clerical costs

Setting Standard Costs—A Difficult Task

STUDY OBJECTIVE 3

Describe how standards are set.

The setting of standard costs to produce a unit of product is a difficult task. It requires input from all persons who have responsibility for costs and quantities. To determine the standard cost of direct materials, management may have to consult purchasing agents, product managers, quality control engineers, and production supervisors. In setting the cost standard for direct labor, pay rate data are obtained from the payroll department, and the labor time requirements may be determined by industrial engineers. The managerial accountant provides important input into the standards-setting process by accumulating historical cost data and by knowing how costs respond to changes in activity levels.

To be effective in controlling costs, standard costs need to be current at all times. Thus, standards should be under continuous review. They should be changed whenever it is determined that the existing standard is not a good measure of performance. Circumstances that may warrant revision of a standard include changed wage rates resulting from a new union contract, a change in product specifications, or the implementation of a new manufacturing method.

Ideal versus Normal Standards

Standards may be set at one of two levels: ideal or normal. **Ideal standards** represent optimum levels of performance under perfect operating conditions. **Normal standards** represent efficient levels of performance that are attainable under expected operating conditions.

Some managers believe ideal standards will stimulate workers to ever-increasing improvement. However, most managers believe that ideal standards lower the morale of the entire workforce because they are so difficult, if not impossible, to meet. Very few companies use ideal standards.

Most companies that use standards set them at a normal level. Properly set, normal standards should be **rigorous but attainable**. Normal standards allow for rest periods, machine breakdowns, and other "normal" contingencies in the production process. It will be assumed in the remainder of this chapter that standard costs are set at a normal level.

> **ETHICS NOTE**
>
> When standards are set too high, employees sometimes feel pressure to consider unethical practices to meet these standards.

A Case Study

To establish the standard cost of producing a product, it is necessary to establish standards for each manufacturing cost element—direct materials, direct labor, and manufacturing overhead. The standard for each element is derived from the standard price to be paid and the standard quantity to be used. To illustrate, we will look at a case study of how standard costs are set. In this extended example, we will assume that Xonic, Inc. wishes to use standard costs to measure performance in filling an order for 1,000 gallons of Weed-O, a liquid weed killer.

Direct Materials

The **direct materials price standard** is the cost per unit of direct materials that should be incurred. This standard should be based on the purchasing department's best estimate of the **cost of raw materials**. This is frequently based on current purchase prices. The price standard should also include an amount for related costs such as receiving, storing, and handling. The materials price standard per pound of material for Xonic's weed killer is:

Item	Price
Purchase price, net of discounts	$2.70
Freight	0.20
Receiving and handling	0.10
Standard direct materials price per pound	**$3.00**

Illustration 26-2
Setting direct materials price standard

The **direct materials quantity standard** is the quantity of direct materials that should be used per unit of finished goods. This standard is expressed as a physical measure, such as pounds, barrels, or board feet. In setting the standard, management should consider both the quality and quantity of materials required to manufacture the product. The standard should include allowances for unavoidable waste and normal spoilage. The standard quantity per unit for Xonic, Inc. is as follows.

Illustration 26-3
Setting direct materials quantity standard

Item	Quantity (Pounds)
Required materials	3.5
Allowance for waste	0.4
Allowance for spoilage	0.1
Standard direct materials quantity per unit	**4.0**

The standard direct materials cost per unit is the standard direct materials price times the standard direct materials quantity. For Xonic, Inc., the standard direct materials cost per gallon of Weed-O is $12.00 ($3.00 × 4.0 pounds).

Direct Labor

ALTERNATIVE TERMINOLOGY

The direct labor price standard is also called the *direct labor rate standard*.

The **direct labor price standard** is the rate per hour that should be incurred for direct labor. This standard is based on current wage rates, adjusted for anticipated changes such as cost of living adjustments (COLAs). The price standard also generally includes employer payroll taxes and fringe benefits, such as paid holidays and vacations. For Xonic, Inc., the direct labor price standard is as follows.

Illustration 26-4
Setting direct labor price standard

Item	Price
Hourly wage rate	$ 7.50
COLA	0.25
Payroll taxes	0.75
Fringe benefits	1.50
Standard direct labor rate per hour	**$10.00**

ALTERNATIVE TERMINOLOGY

The direct labor quantity standard is also called the *direct labor efficiency standard*.

The **direct labor quantity standard** is the time that should be required to make one unit of the product. This standard is especially critical in labor-intensive companies. Allowances should be made in this standard for rest periods, cleanup, machine setup, and machine downtime. For Xonic, Inc., the direct labor quantity standard is as follows.

Illustration 26-5
Setting direct labor quantity standard

Item	Quantity (Hours)
Actual production time	1.5
Rest periods and cleanup	0.2
Setup and downtime	0.3
Standard direct labor hours per unit	**2.0**

The standard direct labor cost per unit is the standard direct labor rate times the standard direct labor hours. For Xonic, Inc., the standard direct labor cost per gallon of Weed-O is $20 ($10.00 × 2.0 hours).

Manufacturing Overhead

For manufacturing overhead, a **standard predetermined overhead rate** is used in setting the standard. This overhead rate is determined by dividing budgeted overhead costs by an expected standard activity index. For example, the index may be standard direct labor hours or standard machine hours.

As discussed in Chapter 22, many companies employ **activity-based costing** (ABC) to allocate overhead costs. Because ABC uses multiple activity indices to allocate overhead costs, it results in a better correlation between activities and costs incurred. As a result, the use of ABC can significantly improve the usefulness of a standard costing system for management decision making.

Xonic, Inc. uses standard direct labor hours as the activity index. The company expects to produce 13,200 gallons of Weed-O during the year at normal capacity. Since it takes 2 direct labor hours for each gallon, total standard direct labor hours are 26,400 (13,200 × 2). At this level of activity, overhead costs are budgeted to be $132,000. Of that amount, $79,200 are variable and $52,800 are fixed. The standard predetermined overhead rates are computed as shown in Illustration 26-6.

Calculating the overhead rate

Overhead ÷ Standard activity index

Budgeted Overhead Costs	Amount	÷	Standard Direct Labor Hours	=	Overhead Rate per Direct Labor Hour
Variable	$ 79,200		26,400		**$3.00**
Fixed	52,800		26,400		**2.00**
Total	$132,000		26,400		**$5.00**

Illustration 26-6
Computing predetermined overhead rates

The standard manufacturing overhead rate per unit is the predetermined overhead rate times the activity index quantity standard. For Xonic, Inc., which uses direct labor hours as its activity index, the standard manufacturing overhead rate per gallon of Weed-O is $10 ($5 × 2 hours).

Total Standard Cost per Unit

Now that the standard quantity and price have been established per unit of product, the total standard cost can be determined. The total standard cost per unit is the sum of the standard costs of direct materials, direct labor, and manufacturing overhead. For Xonic, Inc., the total standard cost per gallon of Weed-O is $42, as shown on the following standard cost card.

Illustration 26-7
Standard cost per gallon of Weed-O

Product: Weed-O			Unit Measure: Gallon	
Manufacturing Cost Elements	Standard Quantity	×	Standard Price	= Standard Cost
Direct materials	4 pounds		$ 3.00	$12.00
Direct labor	2 hours		$10.00	20.00
Manufacturing overhead	2 hours		$ 5.00	10.00
				$42.00

A standard cost card is prepared for each product. This card provides the basis for determining variances from standards.

ACCOUNTING IN ACTION Business Insight

Setting standards can be difficult. Consider **Susan's Chili Factory**, which manufactures and sells chili. The cost of manufacturing Susan's chili consists of the costs of raw materials, labor to convert the basic ingredients to chili, and overhead. We will use material cost as an example. Three standards need to be developed: (1) What should be the formula (mix) of ingredients for one gallon of chili? (2) What should be the normal wastage (or shrinkage) for the individual ingredients? (3) What should be the standard cost for the individual ingredients that go into the chili?

Susan's Chili Factory also illustrates how standard costs can be used by management in controlling costs. Suppose that summer droughts have reduced crop yields. As a result, prices have doubled for beans, onions, and peppers. In this case, actual costs will be significantly higher than standard costs, which will cause management to evaluate the situation. Management might decide to increase the price charged for a gallon of chili. It might reexamine the product mix to see if other types of ingredients can be used. Or it might curtail production until ingredients can be purchased at or near standard costs. Similarly, assume that poor maintenance caused the onion-dicing blades to become dull. As a result, usage of onions to make a gallon of chili tripled. Because this deviation is quickly highlighted through standard costs, corrective action can be promptly taken.

Source: Adapted from David R. Beran, "Cost Reduction Through Control Reporting," *Management Accounting*, April 1982, pp. 29–33.

BEFORE YOU GO ON...

Review It

1. How do standards differ from budgets?

2. What are the advantages of standard costs to an organization?

3. Distinguish between normal standards and ideal standards. Which standard is more widely used? Why?

Do It

The management of Arapahoe Company has decided to use standard costs. Management asks you to explain the components used in setting the standard cost per unit for direct materials, direct labor, and manufacturing overhead.

ACTION PLAN

■ Differentiate between the two components of each standard: price and quantity.

SOLUTION   The standard direct materials cost per unit is the standard direct materials price times the standard direct materials quantity. The standard direct labor cost per unit is the standard direct labor rate times the standard direct labor hours. The standard manufacturing overhead rate per unit is the standard predetermined overhead rate times the activity index quantity standard.

Related exercise material: *BE26-2, BE26-3, and E26-1.*

☑ THE NAVIGATOR

Variances from Standards

One of the major management uses of standard costs is to identify variances from standards. **Variances** are the differences between total actual costs and total standard costs. To illustrate, we will assume that in producing 1,000 gallons of Weed-O in the month of June, Xonic, Inc. incurred the following costs.

ALTERNATIVE TERMINOLOGY

In business, the term *variance* is also used to indicate differences between total budgeted and total actual costs.

Direct materials	$13,020
Direct labor	20,580
Variable overhead	6,500
Fixed overhead	4,400
Total actual costs	$44,500

Illustration 26-8
Actual production costs

Total standard costs are determined by multiplying the units produced by the standard cost per unit. The total standard cost of Weed-O is $42,000 (1,000 gallons × $42). Thus, the total variance is $2,500, as shown below.

Actual costs	$44,500
Standard costs	42,000
Total variance	**$ 2,500**

Illustration 26-9
Computation of total variance

Note that the variance is expressed in total dollars and not on a per unit basis.

When actual costs exceed standard costs, the variance is **unfavorable**. The $2,500 variance in June for Weed-O is unfavorable. An unfavorable variance has a negative connotation. It suggests that too much was paid for one or more of the manufacturing cost elements or that the elements were used inefficiently.

If actual costs are less than standard costs, the variance is **favorable**. A favorable variance has a positive connotation. It suggests efficiencies in incurring manufacturing costs and in using direct materials, direct labor, and manufacturing overhead. However, be careful: A favorable variance could be obtained by using inferior materials. In printing wedding invitations, for example, a favorable variance could result from using an inferior grade of paper. Or, a favorable variance might be achieved in installing tires on an automobile assembly line by tightening only half of the lug bolts. The point should be obvious: A variance is not favorable if quality control standards have been sacrificed.

Analyzing Variances

To interpret properly the significance of a variance, you must analyze it to determine the underlying factors. Analyzing variances begins by determining the cost elements that comprise the variance. **For each manufacturing cost element, a total dollar variance is computed. Then this variance is analyzed into a price variance and a quantity variance.** The relationships are shown graphically in Illustration 26-10.

Illustration 26-10
Variance relationships

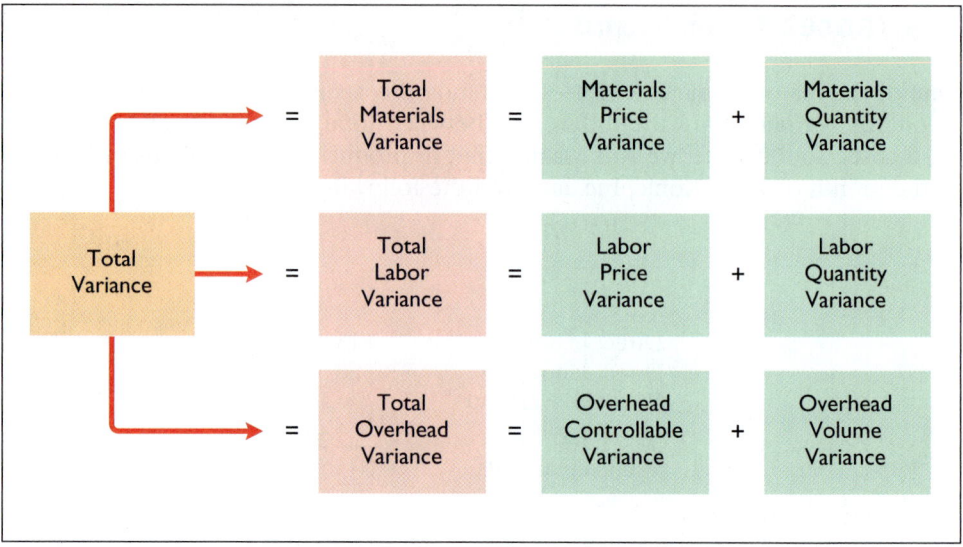

Each of the variances is explained below.

STUDY OBJECTIVE 4

State the formulas for determining direct materials and direct labor variances.

Direct Materials Variances

In completing the order for 1,000 gallons of Weed-O, Xonic used 4,200 pounds of direct materials. These were purchased at a cost of $3.10 per unit. The **total materials variance** is computed from the following formula.

Illustration 26-11
Formula for total materials variance

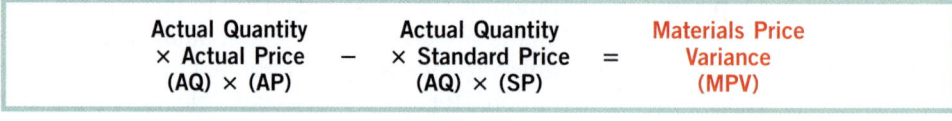

Actual Quantity × Actual Price (AQ) × (AP)	−	Standard Quantity × Standard Price (SQ) × (SP)	=	Total Materials Variance (TMV)

For Xonic, Inc., the total materials variance is $1,020 ($13,020 − $12,000) unfavorable as shown below.

$$(4,200 \times \$3.10) - (4,000 \times \$3.00) = \$1,020 \text{ U}$$

Next, the total variance is analyzed to determine the amount attributable to price (costs) and to quantity (use). The **materials price variance** is computed from the following formula.[1]

Illustration 26-12
Formula for materials price variance

Actual Quantity × Actual Price (AQ) × (AP)	−	Actual Quantity × Standard Price (AQ) × (SP)	=	Materials Price Variance (MPV)

For Xonic, Inc., the materials price variance is $420 ($13,020 − $12,600) unfavorable as shown below.

$$(4,200 \times \$3.10) - (4,200 \times \$3.00) = \$420 \text{ U}$$

The price variance can also be computed by multiplying the actual quantity purchased by the difference between the actual and standard price per unit. The computation in this case is $4,200 \times (\$3.10 - \$3.00) = \$420$ U.

HELPFUL HINT

The alternative formula is:

$$\boxed{AQ} \times \boxed{AP-SP} = \boxed{MPV}$$

---

[1]We will assume that all materials purchased during the period are used in production and that no units remain in inventory at the end of the period.

The **materials quantity variance** is determined from the following formula.

Actual Quantity × Standard Price (AQ) × (SP)	−	Standard Quantity × Standard Price (SQ) × (SP)	=	Materials Quantity Variance (MQV)

Illustration 26-13
Formula for materials quantity variance

For Xonic, Inc., the materials quantity variance is $600 ($12,600 − $12,000) unfavorable, as shown below.

$$(4,200 \times \$3.00) - (4,000 \times \$3.00) = \$600 \text{ U}$$

This variance can also be computed by applying the standard price to the difference between actual and standard quantities used. The computation in this example is $3.00 × (4,200 − 4,000) = $600 U.

The total materials variance of $1,020 U, therefore, consists of the following.

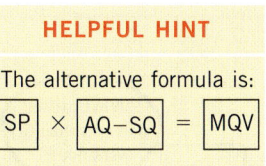

HELPFUL HINT

The alternative formula is:

$$\boxed{SP} \times \boxed{AQ-SQ} = \boxed{MQV}$$

Materials price variance	$ 420 U
Materials quantity variance	600 U
Total materials variance	**$1,020 U**

Illustration 26-14
Summary of materials variance

A matrix is sometimes used to analyze a variance. **When the matrix is used, the formulas for each cost element are computed first and then the variances.** The completed matrix for the direct materials variance for Xonic, Inc. is shown in Illustration 26-15. The matrix provides a convenient structure for determining each variance.

Illustration 26-15
Matrix for direct materials variance

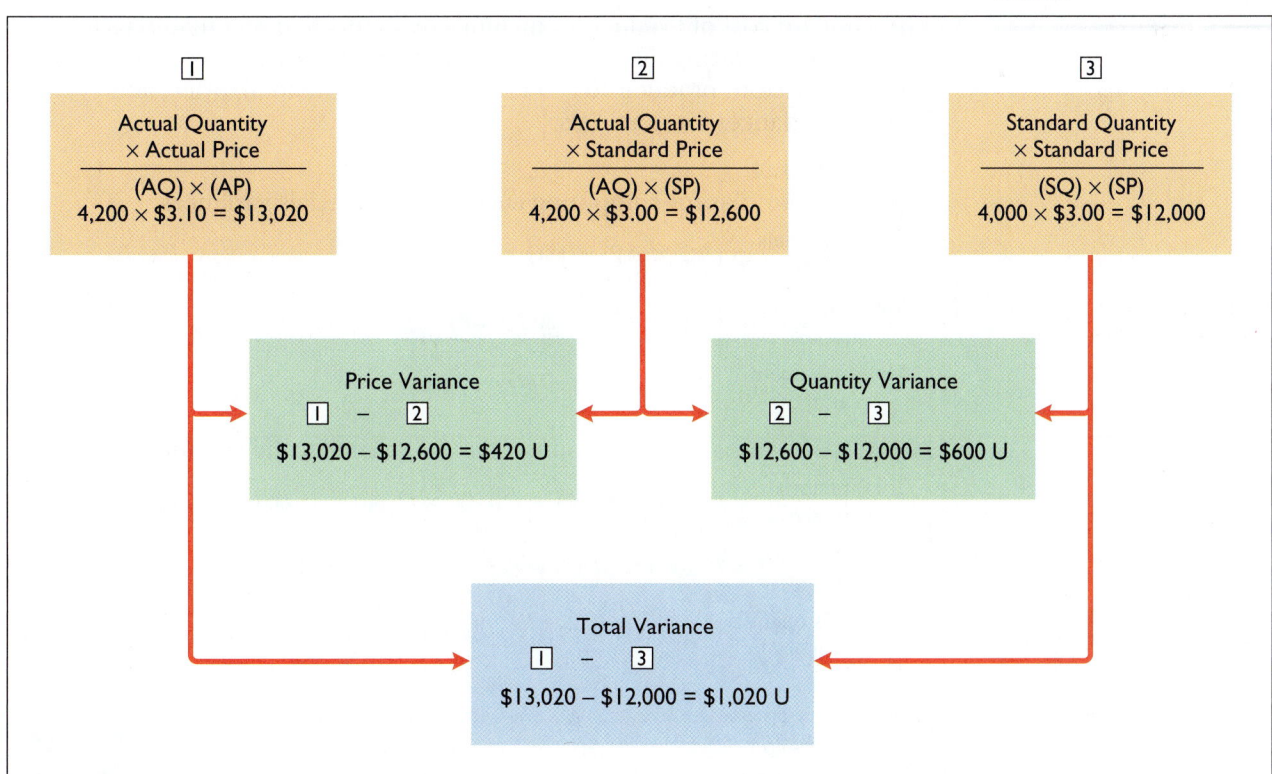

"What caused materials price variances?"

Purchasing Dept.

"What caused materials quantity variances?"

Production Dept.

CAUSES OF MATERIALS VARIANCES. What are the causes of a variance? The causes may relate to both internal and external factors. **The investigation of a materials price variance usually begins in the purchasing department.** Many factors affect the price paid for raw materials. These include the delivery method used, availability of quantity and cash discounts, and the quality of the materials requested. To the extent that these factors have been considered in setting the price standard, the purchasing department should be responsible for any variances.

However, a variance may be beyond the control of the purchasing department. Sometimes, for example, prices may rise faster than expected. Moreover, actions by groups over which the company has no control, such as the OPEC nations' oil price increases, may cause an unfavorable variance. There are also times when a production department may be responsible for the price variance. This may occur when a rush order forces the company to pay a higher price for the materials.

The starting point for determining the cause(s) of an unfavorable **materials quantity variance** is in the **production department**. If the variances are due to inexperienced workers, faulty machinery, or carelessness, the production department would be responsible. However, if the materials obtained by the purchasing department were of inferior quality, then the purchasing department should be responsible.

BEFORE YOU GO ON...

Review It

1. The total variance from standard cost is comprised of what three elements?
2. What are the formulas for computing the total, price, and quantity variances for direct materials?

Do It

The standard cost of Product XX includes two units of direct materials at $8.00 per unit. During July, 22,000 units of direct materials are purchased at $7.50 and used to produce 10,000 units. Compute the total, price, and quantity variances for materials.

ACTION PLAN

■ Use the formulas for computing each of the materials variances:

$$\text{Total materials variance} = (AQ \times AP) - (SQ \times SP)$$

$$\text{Materials price variance} = (AQ \times AP) - (AQ \times SP)$$

$$\text{Materials quantity variance} = (AQ \times SP) - (SQ \times SP)$$

SOLUTION   Substituting amounts into the formulas, the variances are:

$$\text{Total materials variance} = (22{,}000 \times \$7.50) - (20{,}000 \times \$8.00) = \$5{,}000 \text{ unfavorable.}$$

$$\text{Materials price variance} = (22{,}000 \times \$7.50) - (22{,}000 \times \$8.00) = \$11{,}000 \text{ favorable.}$$

$$\text{Materials quantity variance} = (22{,}000 \times \$8.00) - (20{,}000 \times \$8.00) = \$16{,}000 \text{ unfavorable.}$$

Related exercise material: *BE26-4, BE26-5, BE26-6, BE26-7, BE26-8, E26-2, E26-3, E26-4, E26-6, E26-7, E26-8, E26-9, and E26-12.*

☑ THE NAVIGATOR

Direct Labor Variances

The process of determining direct labor variances is the same as for determining the direct materials variances. In completing the Weed-O order, Xonic, Inc. incurred 2,100 direct labor hours at an average hourly rate of $9.80. The standard hours allowed for the units produced were 2,000 hours (1,000 units × 2 hours). The standard labor rate was $10 per hour. The **total labor variance** is obtained from the following formula.

Actual Hours × Actual Rate (AH) × (AR)	−	Standard Hours × Standard Rate (SH) × (SR)	=	Total Labor Variance (TLV)

Illustration 26-16
Formula for total labor variance

The total labor variance is $580 ($20,580 − $20,000) unfavorable, as shown below.

$$(2,100 \times \$9.80) - (2,000 \times \$10.00) = \$580 \text{ U}$$

The formula for the **labor price variance** is:

Actual Hours × Actual Rate (AH) × (AR)	−	Actual Hours × Standard Rate (AH) × (SR)	=	Labor Price Variance (LPV)

Illustration 26-17
Formula for labor price variance

For Xonic, Inc., the labor price variance is $420 ($20,580 − $21,000) favorable as shown below.

$$(2,100 \times \$9.80) - (2,100 \times \$10.00) = \$420 \text{ F}$$

This variance can also be computed by multiplying actual hours worked by the difference between the actual pay rate and the standard pay rate. The computation in this example is 2,100 × ($10.00 − $9.80) = $420 F.

The **labor quantity variance** is derived from the following formula.

HELPFUL HINT

The alternative formula is:

$$AH \times \boxed{AR - SR} = \boxed{LPV}$$

Actual Hours × Standard Rate (AH) × (SR)	−	Standard Hours × Standard Rate (SH) × (SR)	=	Labor Quantity Variance (LQV)

Illustration 26-18
Formula for labor quantity variance

For Xonic, Inc., the labor quantity variance is $1,000 ($21,000 − $20,000) unfavorable:

$$(2,100 \times \$10.00) - (2,000 \times \$10.00) = \$1,000 \text{ U}$$

The same result can be obtained by multiplying the standard rate by the difference between actual hours worked and standard hours allowed. In this case the computation is $10.00 × (2,100 − 2,000) = $1,000 U.

The total direct labor variance of $580 U, therefore, consists of:

HELPFUL HINT

The alternative formula is:

$$SR \times \boxed{AH - SH} = \boxed{LQV}$$

Labor price variance	$ 420 F
Labor quantity variance	1,000 U
Total direct labor variance	**$ 580 U**

Illustration 26-19
Summary of labor variances

These results can also be obtained from the matrix in Illustration 26-20.

Illustration 26-20
Matrix for direct labor variances

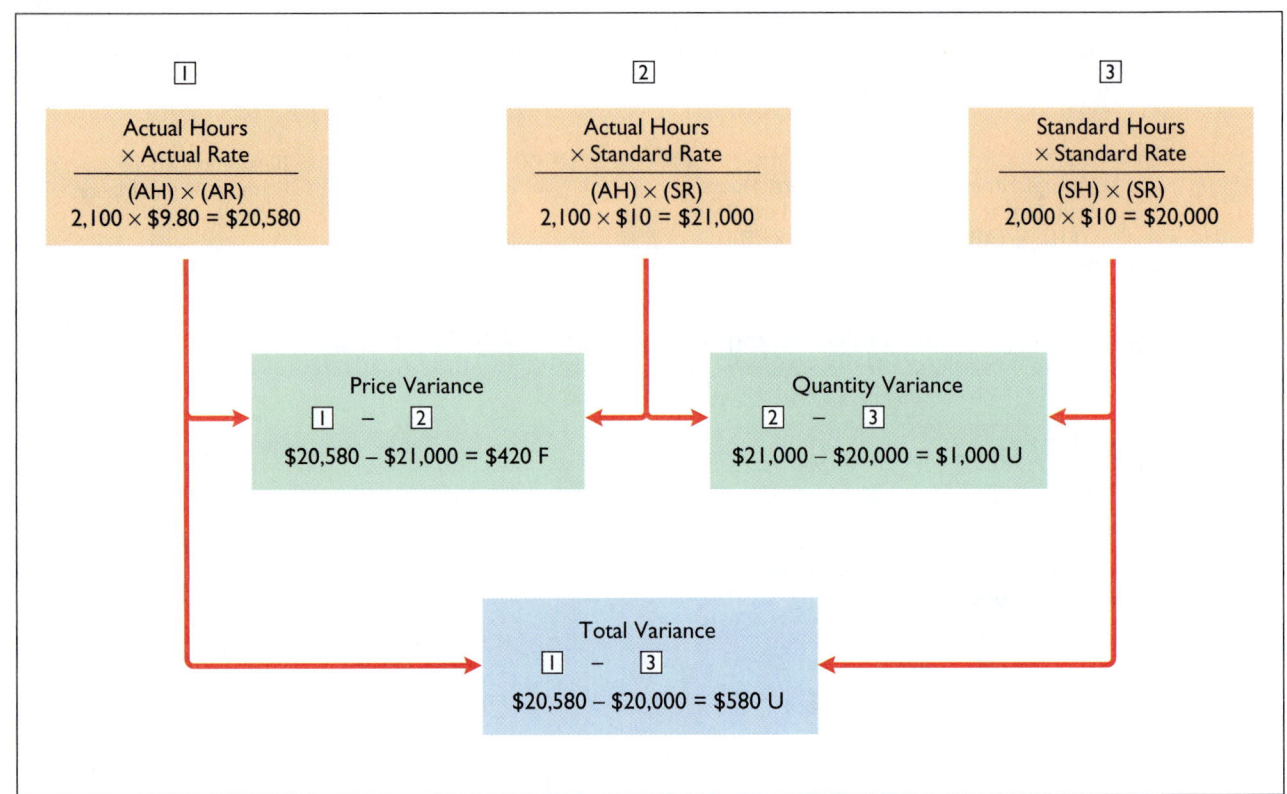

CAUSES OF LABOR VARIANCES.   **Labor price variances** usually result from two factors: (1) paying workers **higher wages than expected**, and **(2) misallocation of workers.** In companies where pay rates are determined by union contracts, labor price variances should be infrequent. When workers are not unionized, there is a much higher likelihood of such variances. The responsibility for these variances rests with the manager who authorized the wage increase.

Misallocation of the workforce refers to using skilled workers in place of unskilled workers and vice versa. The use of an inexperienced worker instead of an experienced one will result in a favorable price variance because of the lower pay rate of the unskilled worker. An unfavorable price variance would result if a skilled worker were substituted for an inexperienced one. The production department generally is responsible for labor price variances resulting from misallocation of the workforce.

Labor quantity variances relate to the **efficiency of workers.** The cause of a quantity variance generally can be traced to the production department. The causes of an unfavorable variance may be poor training, worker fatigue, faulty machinery, or carelessness. These causes are the responsibility of the **production department.** However, if the excess time is due to inferior materials, the responsibility falls outside the production department.

ACCOUNTING IN ACTION Business Insight

At **United Parcel Service (UPS)** performance standards are set by industrial engineers for many tasks performed by UPS employees. For example, a UPS driver is expected to walk at a pace of three feet per second when going to a customer's door and knock rather than take the time to look for a doorbell. UPS executives attribute the company's success to its ability to manage and hold labor accountable.

Manufacturing Overhead Variances

The computation of the manufacturing overhead variances is conceptually the same as the computation of the materials and labor variances. However, one difference is that for manufacturing overhead, both variable and fixed overhead costs must be considered.

STUDY OBJECTIVE 5

State the formulas for determining manufacturing overhead variances.

TOTAL OVERHEAD VARIANCE. The **total overhead variance** is the difference between actual overhead costs and overhead costs applied to work done. As indicated earlier, manufacturing overhead costs incurred by Xonic were $10,900, as follows.

Variable overhead	$ 6,500
Fixed overhead	4,400
Total actual overhead	**$10,900**

Illustration 26-21
Actual overhead costs

Under a standard costing system, manufacturing overhead costs are applied to work in process on the basis of the **standard hours allowed** for the work done. **Standard hours allowed** are the hours that should have been worked for the units produced. For the Weed-O order, the standard hours allowed for the 1,000 units produced are 2,000 (1,000 units × 2 hours). The predetermined overhead rate is $5 per direct labor hour ($132,000 ÷ 26,400, per Illustration 26-6 on page 1053.) Thus, overhead applied is $10,000 (2,000 × $5). Note that actual hours of direct labor (2,100) are not used in applying manufacturing overhead.

The formula for the total overhead variance is:

Actual Overhead	−	**Overhead Applied***	=	**Total Overhead Variance**

*Based on standard hours allowed.

Illustration 26-22
Formula for total overhead variance

Thus, for Xonic, Inc., the total overhead variance is $900 unfavorable as shown below:

$$\$10,900 - \$10,000 = \$900 \text{ U}$$

The overhead variance is analyzed through a price variance and a quantity variance. The name usually given to the price variance is the **overhead controllable variance**, whereas the quantity variance is referred to as the **overhead volume variance**.

ALTERNATIVE TERMINOLOGY

The overhead controllable variance is also called the *budget* or *spending variance*.

OVERHEAD CONTROLLABLE VARIANCE. The overhead controllable variance shows whether overhead costs were effectively controlled. To compute this variance, actual overhead costs incurred are compared with budgeted costs for the **standard hours allowed**. The budgeted costs are determined from the flexible manufacturing overhead budget.

The budget for Xonic, Inc. is shown in Illustration 26-23.

Illustration 26-23
Flexible budget using standard direct labor hours

XONIC, INC. Flexible Manufacturing Overhead Budget				
Activity Index				
Standard direct labor hours	1,800	**2,000**	2,200	2,400
Costs				
Variable costs				
Indirect materials	$1,800	**$ 2,000**	$ 2,200	$ 2,400
Indirect labor	2,700	**3,000**	3,300	3,600
Utilities	900	**1,000**	1,100	1,200
Total variable	5,400	**6,000**	6,600	7,200
Fixed costs				
Supervision	3,000	**3,000**	3,000	3,000
Depreciation	1,400	**1,400**	1,400	1,400
Total fixed	4,400	**4,400**	4,400	4,400
Total costs	$9,800	**$10,400**	$11,000	$11,600

As shown, the budgeted costs for 2,000 standard hours are $10,400 ($6,000 variable and $4,400 fixed).

The formula for the overhead controllable variance is:

Illustration 26-24
Formula for overhead controllable variance

Actual Overhead	−	**Overhead Budgeted***	=	**Overhead Controllable Variance**

*Based on standard hours allowed.

The overhead controllable variance for Xonic, Inc. is $500 unfavorable as shown below.

$$\$10,900 - \$10,400 = \$500 \text{ U}$$

Most controllable variances are associated with variable costs, which are controllable costs. Fixed costs are usually known at the time the budget is prepared. At Xonic, Inc., the variance is accounted for by comparing the actual variable overhead costs ($6,500, as shown in Illustration 26-21) with the budgeted variable costs ($6,000).

Management can compare actual and budgeted overhead for each manufacturing overhead cost that contributes to the controllable variance. In addition, cost and quantity variances can be developed for each overhead cost, such as indirect materials and indirect labor.

OVERHEAD VOLUME VARIANCE. The overhead volume variance is the difference between normal capacity hours and standard hours allowed times the fixed overhead rate. The overhead volume variance relates to whether fixed costs were under- or over-applied during the year. For example, the overhead volume variance answers the question of whether Xonic effectively used its fixed costs. If Xonic produces less Weed-O than normal capacity would allow, an unfavorable variance results. Conversely, if Xonic produces more Weed-O than what is considered normal capacity, a favorable variance results.

The formula for computing the overhead volume variance is as follows.

Fixed Overhead Rate	×	Normal Capacity (in hours) − Standard Hours Allowed	=	Overhead Volume Variance

Illustration 26-25
Formula for overhead volume variance

To illustrate the fixed overhead rate computation, recall that Xonic Inc. budgeted fixed overhead cost for the year of $52,800 (Illustration 26-6 on p. 1053). At normal capacity, 26,400 standard direct labor hours are required. The fixed overhead rate is therefore $2 ($52,800 ÷ 26,400).

Xonic Co produced 1,000 units of Weed-O in June. As indicated earlier, the standard hours allowed for the 1,000 units produced in June is 2,000 (1,000 units × 2 hours). For Xonic, standard direct labor hours for June at normal capacity is 2,200 (26,400 annual hours ÷ 12 months). The computation of the overhead volume variance in this case is as follows.

$$\$2 \times (2,200 - 2,000) = \$400 \text{ U}$$

In Xonic's case, a $400 unfavorable volume variance results. The volume variance is unfavorable because Xonic did not produce up to the normal capacity level in the month of June. As a result, it underapplied fixed overhead for that period.

In computing the overhead variances, it is important to remember the following.

1. Standard hours allowed are used in each of the variances.
2. Budgeted costs for the controllable variance are derived from the flexible budget.
3. The controllable variance generally pertains to variable costs.
4. The volume variance pertains solely to fixed costs.

CAUSES OF MANUFACTURING OVERHEAD VARIANCES. Since the **controllable variance** relates to variable manufacturing costs, the responsibility for the variance rests with the **production department**. The cause of an unfavorable variance may be: (1) **higher than expected use** of indirect materials, indirect labor, and factory supplies, or (2) **increases in indirect manufacturing costs**, such as fuel and maintenance costs.

The **overhead volume variance** is the responsibility of the **production department** if the cause is inefficient use of direct labor or machine breakdowns. When the cause is a **lack of sales orders**, the responsibility rests **outside** the production department.

"What caused manufacturing overhead variances?"

Controllable Variance	Overhead Volume Variance
Production Dept.	**Production or Sales Dept.**

Reporting Variances

All variances should be reported to appropriate levels of management as soon as possible. The sooner management is informed, the sooner problems can be evaluated and corrective actions taken if necessary.

The form, content, and frequency of variance reports vary considerably among companies. One approach is to prepare a weekly report for each department that has primary responsibility for cost control. Under this approach, materials price variances are reported to the purchasing department, and all other variances are reported to the production department that did the work. The following report for Xonic, Inc., with the materials for the Weed-O order listed first, illustrates this approach.

Illustration 26-26
Materials price variance report

XONIC, INC.
Variance Report—Purchasing Department
For Week Ended June 8, 2005

Type of Materials	Quantity Purchased	Actual Price	Standard Price	Price Variance	Explanation
X100	4,200 lbs.	$3.10	$3.00	$420 U	Rush order
X142	1,200 units	2.75	2.80	60 F	Quantity discount
A 85	600 doz.	5.20	5.10	60 U	Regular supplier on strike
Total price variance				**$420 U**	

The explanation column is completed after consultation with the purchasing department manager.

Variance reports facilitate the principle of "management by exception" explained in Chapter 25. For example, the vice president of purchasing can use the report shown above to evaluate the effectiveness of the purchasing department manager. Or, the vice president of production can use production department variance reports to determine how well each production manager is controlling costs. In using variance reports, top management normally looks for **significant variances**. These may be judged on the basis of some quantitative measure, such as more than 10 percent of the standard or more than $1,000.

ACCOUNTING IN ACTION   e Business Insight

Computerized standard cost systems represent one of the most complex accounting systems to develop and maintain. The standard cost system must be fully integrated into the general ledger. It must allow for the creation and timely maintenance of the database of standard usage and costs for every product. It must perform variance computations. And it must also produce variance reports by product, department, or employee. With the increased use of automation and robotics, the computerized standard cost system may even be tied directly into the manufacturing process to gather variance information.

BEFORE YOU GO ON...

Review It
1. What are the formulas for computing the total, price, and quantity variances for direct labor?
2. What are the formulas for computing the total, controllable, and volume variances for manufacturing overhead?

 THE NAVIGATOR

Standard Cost Accounting System

A **standard cost accounting system** is a double-entry system of accounting. In this system, standard costs are used in making entries, and variances are formally recognized in the accounts. A standard cost system may be used with either job order or process costing. At this point, we will explain and illustrate a **standard cost, job order cost accounting system**. The system is based on two important assumptions: (1) Variances from standards are recognized at the earliest opportunity. (2) The Work in Process account is maintained exclusively on the basis of standard costs. In practice, there are many variations among standard cost systems. The system described here should prepare you for systems you see in the "real world."

STUDY OBJECTIVE 7

Enumerate the features of a standard cost accounting system.

Journal Entries
We will use the transactions of Xonic, Inc. to illustrate the journal entries. Note that the major difference between the entries here and those for the job order cost accounting system in Chapter 21 is the **variance accounts**.

1. Purchase raw materials on account for $13,020 when the standard cost is $12,600.

Raw Materials Inventory	12,600	
Materials Price Variance	420	
Accounts Payable		13,020
(To record purchase of materials)		

The inventory account is debited for actual quantities at standard cost. This enables the perpetual materials records to show actual quantities. The price variance, which is unfavorable, is debited to Materials Price Variance.

2. Incur direct labor costs of $20,580 when the standard labor cost is $21,000.

Factory Labor	21,000	
Labor Price Variance		420
Wages Payable		20,580
(To record direct labor costs)		

Like the raw materials inventory account, Factory Labor is debited for actual hours worked at the standard hourly rate of pay. In this case, the labor variance is favorable. Thus, Labor Price Variance is credited.

3. Incur actual manufacturing overhead costs of $10,900.

Manufacturing Overhead	10,900	
Accounts Payable/Cash/Acc. Depreciation		10,900
(To record overhead incurred)		

The controllable overhead variance is not recorded at this time. It depends on standard hours applied to work in process. This amount is not known at the time overhead is incurred.

4. Issue raw materials for production at a cost of $12,600 when the standard cost is $12,000.

Work in Process Inventory	12,000	
Materials Quantity Variance	600	
Raw Materials Inventory		12,600
(To record issuance of raw materials)		

Work in Process Inventory is debited for standard materials quantities used at standard prices. The variance account is debited because the variance is unfavorable. Raw Materials Inventory is credited for actual quantities at standard prices.

5. Assign factory labor to production at a cost of $21,000 when standard cost is $20,000.

Work in Process Inventory	20,000	
Labor Quantity Variance	1,000	
Factory Labor		21,000
(To assign factory labor to jobs)		

Work in Process Inventory is debited for standard labor hours at standard rates. The unfavorable variance is debited to Labor Quantity Variance. The credit to Factory Labor produces a zero balance in this account.

6. Applying manufacturing overhead to production $10,000.

Work in Process Inventory	10,000	
Manufacturing Overhead		10,000
(To assign overhead to jobs)		

Work in Process Inventory is debited for standard hours allowed multiplied by the standard overhead rate.

7. Transfer completed work to finished goods $42,000.

Finished Goods Inventory	42,000	
Work in Process Inventory		42,000
(To record transfer of completed work		
to finished goods)		

In this example, both inventory accounts are at standard cost.

8. The 1,000 gallons of Weed-O are sold for $60,000.

Accounts Receivable	60,000	
Cost of Goods Sold	42,000	
Sales		60,000
Finished Goods Inventory		42,000
(To record sale of finished goods and the		
cost of goods sold)		

Cost of Goods Sold is debited at standard cost. Gross profit, in turn, is the difference between sales and the standard cost of goods sold.

9. Recognize unfavorable overhead variances: controllable, $500; volume, $400.

Overhead Controllable Variance	500	
Overhead Volume Variance	400	
Manufacturing Overhead		900
(To recognize overhead variances)		

Prior to this entry, a debit balance of $900 existed in Manufacturing Overhead. This entry therefore produces a zero balance in the Manufacturing Overhead account. The information needed for this entry is often not available until the end of the accounting period.

Ledger Accounts

The cost accounts for Xonic, Inc., after posting the entries, are shown in Illustration 26-27 below. Note that six variance accounts are included in the ledger. The remaining accounts are the same as those illustrated for a job order cost system in Chapter 21, in which only actual costs were used.

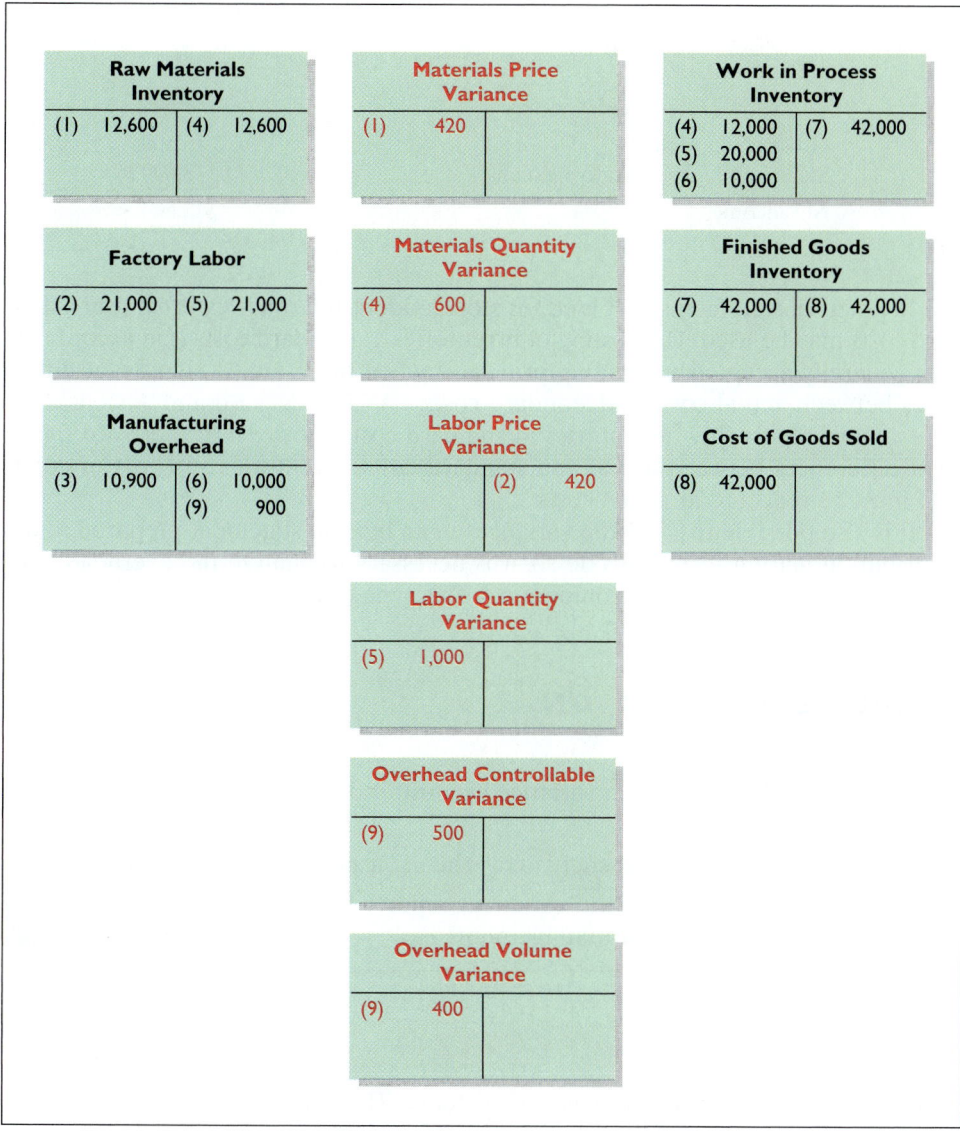

Illustration 26-27
Cost accounts with variances

HELPFUL HINT

All debit balances in variance accounts indicate unfavorable variances; all credit balances indicate favorable variances.

Statement Presentation of Variances

In income statements **prepared for management** under a standard cost accounting system, **cost of goods sold is stated at standard cost and the variances are separately disclosed**, as shown in Illustration 26-28 on the next page. The statement shown is based entirely on the production and sale of Weed-O. It assumes selling and administrative costs of $3,000. Observe that each variance is shown, as well as the total net variance. In this example, variations from standard costs reduced net income by $2,500.

Illustration 26-28
Variances in income statement for management

XONIC, INC.
Income Statement
For the Month Ended June 30, 2005

Sales		$60,000
Cost of goods sold (at standard)		42,000
Gross profit (at standard)		18,000
Variances		
Materials price	$ 420	
Materials quantity	600	
Labor price	(420)	
Labor quantity	1,000	
Overhead controllable	500	
Overhead volume	400	
Total variance unfavorable		2,500
Gross profit (actual)		15,500
Selling and administrative expenses		3,000
Net income		$12,500

In financial statements prepared for stockholders and other external users, standard costs may be used. The costing of inventories at standard costs is in accordance with generally accepted accounting principles when there are no significant differences between actual costs and standard costs. **Hewlett-Packard** and **Jostens, Inc.,** for example, report their inventories at standard costs. However, if there are significant differences between actual and standard costs, inventories and cost of goods sold must be reported at actual costs.

It is also possible to show the variances in an income statement prepared in the contribution margin format. To do so, it is necessary to analyze the overhead variances into variable and fixed components. This type of analysis is explained in cost accounting textbooks.

BEFORE YOU GO ON...

Review It
1. Does a debit balance in a variance account indicate favorable or unfavorable performance?
2. What entry is made to recognize overhead variances in the accounts?
3. How are standard costs and variances reported in income statements prepared for management?

DEMONSTRATION PROBLEM

Manlow Company makes a cologne called Allure. The standard cost for one bottle of Allure is as follows.

	Standard			
Manufacturing Cost Elements	**Quantity**	**×**	**Price**	**= Cost**
Direct materials	6 oz.	×	$ 0.90	= $ 5.40
Direct labor	0.5 hrs.	×	$12.00	= 6.00
Manufacturing overhead	0.5 hrs.	×	$ 4.80	= 2.40
				$13.80

During the month, the following transactions occurred in manufacturing 10,000 bottles of Allure.

1. 58,000 ounces of materials were purchased at $1.00 per ounce.
2. All the materials purchased were used to produce the 10,000 bottles of Allure.
3. 4,900 direct labor hours were worked at a total labor cost of $56,350.
4. Variable manufacturing overhead incurred was $15,000 and fixed overhead incurred was $10,400.

Normal capacity is 5,200 direct labor hours. The total overhead budget at this capacity is $10,400 fixed and $14,560 variable. The predetermined manufacturing overhead rate is $4.80 ($2.00 fixed and $2.80 variable).

Instructions

Compute the total variance and the variances for each of the manufacturing cost elements.

SOLUTION TO DEMONSTRATION PROBLEM

Total Variance

Actual costs incurred:	
Direct materials	$ 58,000
Direct labor	56,350
Manufacturing overhead	25,400
	139,750
Standard cost (10,000 × $13.80)	138,000
Total variance	$ 1,750 U

Direct Materials Variances

Total	=	$58,000 (58,000 × $1.00)	−	$54,000 (60,000 × $0.90)	=	$4,000 U
Price	=	$58,000 (58,000 × $1.00)	−	$52,200 (58,000 × $0.90)	=	$5,800 U
Quantity	=	$52,200 (58,000 × $0.90)	−	$54,000 (60,000 × $0.90)	=	$1,800 F

Direct Labor Variances

Total	=	$56,350 (4,900 × $11.50)	−	$60,000 (5,000 × $12.00)	=	$3,650 F
Price	=	$56,350 (4,900 × $11.50)	−	$58,800 (4,900 × $12.00)	=	$2,450 F
Quantity	=	$58,800 (4,900 × $12.00)	−	$60,000 (5,000 × $12.00)	=	$1,200 F

Overhead Variances

Total	=	$25,400 ($15,000 + $10,400)	−	$24,000 (5,000 × $4.80)	=	$1,400 U
Controllable	=	$25,400 ($15,000 + $10,400)	−	$24,400 ($14,000 + $10,400)	=	$1,000 U
Volume	=	$2	×	(5,200 − 5,000)*	=	$ 400 U

*(10,000 × .5)

ACTION PLAN

- Check to make sure the total variance and the sum of the individual variances are equal.
- Find the price variance first, then the quantity variance.
- Base budgeted overhead costs on flexible budget data.
- Base overhead applied on standard hours allowed.
- Ignore actual hours worked in computing overhead variances.
- Relate the overhead volume variance solely to fixed costs.

✓ THE NAVIGATOR

SUMMARY OF STUDY OBJECTIVES

1. Distinguish between a standard and a budget. Both standards and budgets are predetermined costs. The primary difference is that a standard is a unit amount, whereas a budget is a total amount. A standard may be regarded as the budgeted cost per unit of product.

2. Identify the advantages of standard costs. Standard costs offer a number of advantages. They (a) facilitate management planning, (b) promote greater economy and efficiency, (c) are useful in setting selling prices, (d) contribute to management control, (e) permit "management by exception," and (f) simplify the costing of inventories and reduce clerical costs.

3. Describe how standards are set. The direct materials price standard should be based on the delivered cost of raw materials plus an allowance for receiving and handling. The direct materials quantity standard should establish the required quantity plus an allowance for waste and spoilage.

The direct labor price standard should be based on current wage rates and anticipated adjustments such as COLAs. It also generally includes payroll taxes and fringe benefits. Direct labor quantity standards should be based on required production time plus an allowance for rest periods, cleanup, machine setup, and machine downtime.

For manufacturing overhead, a standard predetermined overhead rate is used. It is based on an expected standard activity index such as standard direct labor hours or standard direct labor cost.

4. State the formulas for determining direct materials and direct labor variances. The formulas for the direct materials variances are:

$$\left(\begin{array}{c}\text{Actual quantity} \\ \times \text{ Actual price}\end{array}\right) - \left(\begin{array}{c}\text{Standard quantity} \\ \times \text{ Standard price}\end{array}\right) = \begin{array}{c}\text{Total} \\ \text{materials} \\ \text{variance}\end{array}$$

$$\left(\begin{array}{c}\text{Actual quantity} \\ \times \text{ Actual price}\end{array}\right) - \left(\begin{array}{c}\text{Actual quantity} \\ \times \text{ Standard price}\end{array}\right) = \begin{array}{c}\text{Materials} \\ \text{price} \\ \text{variance}\end{array}$$

$$\left(\begin{array}{c}\text{Actual quantity} \\ \times \text{ Standard price}\end{array}\right) - \left(\begin{array}{c}\text{Standard quantity} \\ \times \text{ Standard price}\end{array}\right) = \begin{array}{c}\text{Materials} \\ \text{quantity} \\ \text{variance}\end{array}$$

The formulas for the direct labor variances are:

$$\left(\begin{array}{c}\text{Actual hours} \\ \times \text{ Actual rate}\end{array}\right) - \left(\begin{array}{c}\text{Standard hours} \\ \times \text{ Standard rate}\end{array}\right) = \begin{array}{c}\text{Total} \\ \text{labor} \\ \text{variance}\end{array}$$

$$\left(\begin{array}{c}\text{Actual hours} \\ \times \text{ Actual rate}\end{array}\right) - \left(\begin{array}{c}\text{Actual hours} \\ \times \text{ Standard rate}\end{array}\right) = \begin{array}{c}\text{Labor} \\ \text{price} \\ \text{variance}\end{array}$$

$$\left(\begin{array}{c}\text{Actual hours} \\ \times \text{ Standard rate}\end{array}\right) - \left(\begin{array}{c}\text{Standard hours} \\ \times \text{ Standard rate}\end{array}\right) = \begin{array}{c}\text{Labor} \\ \text{quantity} \\ \text{variance}\end{array}$$

5. State the formulas for determining manufacturing overhead variances. The formulas for the manufacturing overhead variances are:

$$\begin{array}{c}\text{Actual} \\ \text{overhead}\end{array} - \begin{array}{c}\text{Overhead} \\ \text{applied}\end{array} = \begin{array}{c}\text{Total overhead} \\ \text{variance}\end{array}$$

$$\begin{array}{c}\text{Actual} \\ \text{overhead}\end{array} - \begin{array}{c}\text{Overhead} \\ \text{budgeted}\end{array} = \begin{array}{c}\text{Overhead control-} \\ \text{lable variance}\end{array}$$

$$\begin{array}{c}\text{Fixed} \\ \text{overhead}\end{array} \times \left(\begin{array}{c}\text{Normal capacity} \\ - \text{ Standard} \\ \text{hours allowed}\end{array}\right) = \begin{array}{c}\text{Overhead} \\ \text{volume} \\ \text{variance}\end{array}$$

6. Discuss the reporting of variances. Variances are reported to management in variance reports. The reports facilitate management by exception by highlighting significant differences.

7. Enumerate the features of a standard cost accounting system. In a standard cost accounting system, standard costs are journalized and posted, and separate variance accounts are maintained in the ledger. When differences between actual costs and standard costs do not differ significantly, inventories may be reported at standard costs.

GLOSSARY

Direct labor price standard The rate per hour that should be incurred for direct labor. (p. 1052).

Direct labor quantity standard The time that should be required to make one unit of product. (p. 1052).

Direct materials price standard The cost per unit of direct materials that should be incurred. (p. 1051).

Direct materials quantity standard The quantity of direct materials that should be used per unit of finished goods. (p. 1051).

Ideal standards Standards based on the optimum level of performance under perfect operating conditions. (p. 1051).

Labor price variance The difference between the actual hours times the actual rate and the actual hours times the standard rate for labor. (p. 1059).

Labor quantity variance The difference between actual hours times the standard rate and standard hours times the standard rate for labor. (p. 1059).

Materials price variance The difference between the actual quantity times the actual price and the actual quantity times the standard price for materials. (p. 1056).

Materials quantity variance The difference between the actual quantity times the standard price and the standard quantity times the standard price for materials. (p. 1057).

Normal standards Standards based on an efficient level of performance that are attainable under expected operating conditions. (p. 1051).

Overhead controllable variance The difference between actual overhead incurred and overhead budgeted for the standard hours allowed. (p. 1062).

Overhead volume variance The difference between normal capacity hours and standard hours allowed times the fixed overhead rate. (p. 1063).

Standard cost accounting system A double-entry system of accounting in which standard costs are used in making entries and variances are recognized in the accounts. (p. 1065).

Standard costs Predetermined unit costs which are used as measures of performance. (p. 1049).

Standard hours allowed The hours that should have been worked for the units produced. (p. 1061).

Standard predetermined overhead rate An overhead rate determined by dividing budgeted overhead costs by an expected standard activity index. (p. 1053).

Total labor variance The difference between actual hours times the actual rate and standard hours times the standard rate for labor. (p. 1059).

Total materials variance The difference between the actual quantity times the actual price and the standard quantity times the standard price of materials. (p. 1056).

Total overhead variance The difference between actual overhead costs and overhead costs applied to work done. (p. 1061).

Variances The difference between total actual costs and total standard costs. (p. 1055).

SELF-STUDY QUESTIONS   Self-Study/Self-Test

Answers are at the end of the chapter.

(SO 1)   1. Standards differ from budgets in that:
   a. budgets but not standards may be used in valuing inventories.
   b. budgets but not standards may be journalized and posted.
   c. budgets are a total amount and standards are a unit amount.
   d. only budgets contribute to management planning and control.

(SO 2)   2. The advantages of standard costs include all of the following *except*:
   a. management by exception may be used.
   b. management planning is facilitated.
   c. they may simplify the costing of inventories.
   d. management must use a static budget.

(SO 3)   3. The setting of standards is:
   a. a managerial accounting decision.
   b. a management decision.
   c. a worker decision.
   d. preferably set at the ideal level of performance.

(SO 4)   4. Each of the following formulas is correct *except*:
   a. Labor price variance = (Actual hours × Actual rate) − (Actual hours × Standard rate).
   b. Overhead controllable variance = Actual overhead − Overhead budgeted.
   c. Materials price variance = (Actual quantity × Actual cost) − (Standard quantity × Standard cost).
   d. Overhead volume variance = Overhead budgeted − Overhead applied.

(SO 4)   5. In producing product AA, 6,300 pounds of direct materials were used at a cost of $1.10 per pound. The standard was 6,000 pounds at $1 per pound. The direct materials quantity variance is:
   a. $330 unfavorable.
   b. $300 unfavorable.
   c. $600 unfavorable.
   d. $630 unfavorable.

6. In producing product ZZ, 14,800 direct labor hours were **(SO 4)** used at a rate of $8.20 per hour. The standard was 15,000 hours at $8.00 per hour. Based on these data, the direct labor:
   a. quantity variance is $1,600 favorable.
   b. quantity variance is $1,600 unfavorable.
   c. price variance is $2,960 favorable.
   d. price variance is $3,000 unfavorable.

7. Which of the following is *correct* about overhead variances? **(SO 5)**
   a. The controllable variance generally pertains to fixed overhead costs.
   b. The volume variance pertains solely to variable overhead costs.
   c. Standard hours actually worked are used in each variance.
   d. Budgeted overhead costs are based on the flexible overhead budget.

8. The formula for computing the total overhead variance **(SO 5)** is:
   a. actual overhead less overhead applied.
   b. overhead budgeted less overhead applied.
   c. actual overhead less overhead budgeted.
   d. no correct answer given.

9. Which of the following is *incorrect* about variance **(SO 6)** reports?
   a. They facilitate "management by exception."
   b. They should only be sent to the top level of management.
   c. They should be prepared as soon as possible.
   d. They may vary in form, content, and frequency among companies.

10. Which of the following is *incorrect* about a standard cost **(SO 7)** accounting system?
   a. It is applicable to job order costing.
   b. It is applicable to process costing.
   c. It is a single-entry system.
   d. It keeps separate accounts for each variance.

QUESTIONS

1. (a) "Standard costs are the expected total cost of completing a job." Is this correct? Explain.
(b) "A standard imposed by a governmental agency is known as a regulation." Do you agree? Explain.

2. (a) Explain the similarities and differences between standards and budgets.
(b) Contrast the accounting for standards and budgets.

3. Standard costs facilitate management planning. What are the other advantages of standard costs?

4. Contrast the roles of the management accountant and management in setting standard costs.

5. Distinguish between an ideal standard and a normal standard.

6. What factors should be considered in setting (a) the direct materials price standard and (b) the direct materials quantity standard?

7. "The objective in setting the direct labor quantity standard is to determine the aggregate time required to make one unit of product." Do you agree? What allowances should be made in setting this standard?

8. How is the predetermined overhead rate determined when standard costs are used?

9. What is the difference between a favorable cost variance and an unfavorable cost variance?

10. In each of the following formulas, supply the words that should be inserted for each number in parentheses.
(a) (Actual quantity × (1)) − (Standard quantity × (2)) = Total materials variance
(b) ((3) × Actual price) − (Actual quantity × (4)) = Materials price variance
(c) (Actual quantity × (5)) − ((6) × Standard price) = Materials quantity variance

11. In the direct labor variance matrix, there are three factors: (1) Actual hours × Actual rate, (2) Actual hours × Standard rate, and (3) Standard hours × Standard rate. Using the numbers, indicate the formulas for each of the direct labor variances.

12. Keene Company's standard predetermined overhead rate is $8.00 per direct labor hour. For the month of June, 26,000 actual hours were worked, and 27,500 standard hours were allowed. Normal capacity hours were 28,000. How much overhead was applied?

13. If the $8.00 per hour overhead rate in question 12 includes $5.00 variable, and actual overhead costs were $218,000, what is the overhead controllable variance for June? Is the variance favorable or unfavorable?

14. Using the data in questions 12 and 13, what is the overhead volume variance for June? Is the variance favorable or unfavorable?

15. What is the purpose of computing the overhead volume variance? What is the basic formula for this variance?

16. Nancy Morgan does not understand why the overhead volume variance indicates that fixed overhead costs are under- or overapplied. Clarify this matter for Nancy.

17. Mike Darby is attempting to outline the important points about overhead variances on a class examination. List four points that Mike should include in his outline.

18. How often should variances be reported to management? What principle may be used with variance reports?

19. What circumstances may cause the purchasing department to be responsible for both an unfavorable materials price variance and an unfavorable materials quantity variance?

20. (a) Explain the basic features of a standard cost accounting system. (b) What type of balance will exist in the variance account when (1) the materials price variance is unfavorable and (2) the labor quantity variance is favorable?

21. (a) How are variances reported in income statements prepared for management? (b) May standard costs be used in preparing financial statements for stockholders? Explain.

BRIEF EXERCISES

Distinguish between a standard and a budget.
(SO 1)

BE26-1 Valdez Company uses both standards and budgets. For the year, estimated production of Product X is 500,000 units. Total estimated cost for materials and labor are $1,000,000 and $1,600,000. Compute the estimates for (a) a standard cost and (b) a budgeted cost.

Set direct materials standard.
(SO 3)

BE26-2 Hideo Company accumulates the following data concerning raw materials in making one gallon of finished product: (1) Price—net purchase price $3.20, freight-in $0.20 and receiving and handling $0.10. (2) Quantity—required materials 2.6 pounds, allowance for waste and spoilage 0.4 pounds. Compute the following.

(a) Standard direct materials price per gallon.
(b) Standard direct materials quantity per gallon.
(c) Total standard material cost per gallon.

BE26-3 Labor data for making one gallon of finished product in Hideo Company are as follows: (1) Price—hourly wage rate $10.00, payroll taxes $0.80, and fringe benefits $1.20. (2) Quantity—actual production time 1.2 hours, rest periods and clean up 0.25 hours, and setup and downtime 0.15 hours. Compute the following.

Set direct labor standard.
(SO 3)

(a) Standard direct labor rate per hour.
(b) Standard direct labor hours per gallon.
(c) Standard labor cost per gallon.

BE26-4 Sprague Company's standard materials cost per unit of output is $10 (2 pounds × $5.00). During July, the company purchases and uses 3,300 pounds of materials costing $16,731 in making 1,500 units of finished product. Compute the total, price, and quantity materials variances.

Compute direct materials variances.
(SO 4)

BE26-5 Talbot Company's standard labor cost per unit of output is $20 (2 hours × $10.00 per hour). During August, the company incurs 1,900 hours of direct labor at an hourly cost of $9.60 per hour in making 1,000 units of finished product. Compute the total, price, and quantity labor variances.

Compute direct labor variances.
(SO 4)

BE26-6 In October, Russo Company reports 21,000 actual direct labor hours, and it incurs $96,000 of manufacturing overhead costs. Standard hours allowed for the work done is 20,000 hours. The predetermined overhead rate is $5.00 per direct labor hour. Compute the total manufacturing overhead variance.

Compute total manufacturing overhead variance.
(SO 5)

BE26-7 Some overhead data for Russo Company are given in BE26-6. In addition, the flexible manufacturing overhead budget shows that budgeted costs are $4.00 variable per direct labor hour and $25,000 fixed. Compute the manufacturing overhead controllable variance.

Compute the manufacturing overhead controllable variance.
(SO 5)

BE26-8 Using the data in BE26-6 and BE26-7, compute the manufacturing overhead volume variance. Normal capacity was 25,000 direct labor hours.

Compute overhead volume variance.
(SO 5)

BE26-9 Journalize the following transactions for McBee Manufacturing.

Journalize materials variances.
(SO 7)

(a) Purchased 6,000 units of raw materials on account for $11,500. The standard cost was $12,000.
(b) Issued 5,600 units of raw materials for production. The standard units were 5,800.

BE26-10 Journalize the following transactions for Worrel Manufacturing.

Journalize labor variances.
(SO 7)

(a) Incurred direct labor costs of $24,000 for 3,000 hours. The standard labor cost was $24,600.
(b) Assigned 3,000 direct labor hours costing $24,000 to production. Standard hours were 3,100.

EXERCISES

E26-1 Raul Mondesi manufactures and sells homemade wine, and he wants to develop a standard cost per gallon. The following are required for production of a 50-gallon batch.

Compute standard materials costs.
(SO 3)

3,000 ounces of grape concentrate at $0.04 per ounce
54 pounds of granulated sugar at $0.30 per pound
60 lemons at $0.60 each
50 yeast tablets at $0.25 each
50 nutrient tablets at $0.20 each
2,500 ounces of water at $0.003 per ounce

Raul estimates that 4% of the grape concentrate is wasted, 10% of the sugar is lost, and 20% of the lemons cannot be used.

Instructions
Compute the standard cost of the ingredients for one gallon of wine. (Carry computations to three decimal places.)

E26-2 The standard cost of Product B manufactured by Gomez Company includes three units of direct materials at $5.00 per unit. During June, 27,600 units of direct materials are purchased at a cost of $4.70 per unit, and 27,600 units of direct materials are used to produce 9,000 units of Product B.

Compute materials price and quantity variances.
(SO 4)

Instructions
(a) Compute the materials price and quantity variances.
(b) Repeat (a), assuming the purchase price is $5.20 and the quantity purchased and used is 26,400 units.

Compute labor price and quantity variances.

(SO 4)

E26-3 Pagley Company's standard labor cost of producing one unit of Product DD is 4 hours at the rate of $12.00 per hour. During August, 40,500 hours of labor are incurred at a cost of $12.10 per hour to produce 10,000 units of Product DD.

Instructions
(a) Compute the total labor variance.
(b) Compute the labor price and quantity variances.
(c) Repeat (b), assuming the standard is 4.2 hours of direct labor at $12.20 per hour.

Compute materials and labor variances.

(SO 4)

E26-4 Kopecky Inc., which produces a single product, has prepared the following standard cost sheet for one unit of the product.

Direct materials (8 pounds at $2.50 per pound)	$20.00
Direct labor (3 hours at $12.00 per hour)	$36.00

During the month of April, the company manufactures 240 units and incurs the following actual costs.

Direct materials (1,900 pounds)	$4,940
Direct labor (700 hours)	$8,120

Instructions
Compute the total, price, and quantity variances for materials and labor.

Journalize entries for materials and labor variances.

(SO 7)

E26-5 Data for Kopecky Inc. are given in E26-4.

Instructions
Journalize the entries to record the materials and labor variances.

Compute the materials and labor variances and list reasons for unfavorable variances.

(SO 4, 6)

E26-6 The following direct materials and direct labor data pertain to the operations of Batista Manufacturing Company for the month of August.

Costs		Quantities	
Actual labor rate	$13.00 per hour	Actual hours incurred and used	4,250 hours
Actual materials price	$128.00 per ton	Actual quantity of materials purchased and used	1,250 tons
Standard labor rate	$12.00 per hour	Standard hours used	4,300 hours
Standard materials price	$130.00 per ton	Standard quantity of materials used	1,200 tons

Instructions
(a) Compute the total, price, and quantity variances for materials and labor.
(b) ▭▭▭▭▷ Provide two possible explanations for each of the unfavorable variances calculated above, and suggest where responsibility for the unfavorable result might be placed.

Compute manufacturing overhead variances and interpret findings.

(SO 5)

E26-7 The following information was taken from the annual manufacturing overhead cost budget of Fernetti Company.

Variable manufacturing overhead costs	$33,000
Fixed manufacturing overhead costs	$21,450
Normal production level in labor hours	16,500
Normal production level in units	4,125
Standard labor hours per unit	4

During the year, 4,000 units were produced, 16,100 hours were worked, and the actual manufacturing overhead was $54,000. Actual fixed manufacturing overhead costs equaled budgeted fixed manufacturing overhead costs. Overhead is applied on the basis of direct labor hours.

Instructions

(a) Compute the total, fixed, and variable predetermined manufacturing overhead rates.

(b) Compute the total, controllable, and volume overhead variances.

(c) ▰▰▰▰▶ Briefly interpret the overhead controllable and volume variances computed in (b).

E26-8 Manufacturing overhead data for the production of Product H by Rondell Company are as follows.

Compute overhead variances and journalize transactions and adjusting entry.

(SO 5, 7)

Overhead incurred for 52,000 actual direct labor hours worked		$213,000
Overhead rate (variable $3.00; fixed $1.00) at normal capacity of 54,000		
direct labor hours		$ 4.00
Standard hours allowed for work done		52,000

Instructions

(a) Compute the total, controllable, and volume overhead variances.

(b) Journalize the incurrence of the overhead costs and the application of overhead to the job, assuming a standard cost accounting system is used.

(c) Prepare the adjusting entry for the overhead variances.

E26-9 During March 2005, Garner Tool & Die Company worked on four jobs. A review of direct labor costs reveals the following summary data.

Prepare a variance report for direct labor.

(SO 4, 6)

Job	Actual		Standard		Total
Number	Hours	Costs	Hours	Costs	Variance
A257	220	$ 4,400	225	$4,500	$ 100 F
A258	450	10,350	430	8,600	1,750 U
A259	300	6,150	300	6,000	150 U
A260	115	2,070	110	2,200	130 F
Total variance					$1,670 U

Analysis reveals that Job A257 was a repeat job. Job A258 was a rush order that required overtime work at premium rates of pay. Job A259 required a more experienced replacement worker on one shift. Work on Job A260 was done for one day by a new trainee when a regular worker was absent.

Instructions

Prepare a report for the plant supervisor on direct labor cost variances for March. The report should have columns for (1) Job No., (2) Actual Hours, (3) Standard Hours, (4) Labor Quantity Variance, (5) Actual Rate, (6) Standard Rate, (7) Labor Price Variance, and (8) Explanations.

E26-10 Carlos Company uses a standard cost accounting system. During January, the company reported the following manufacturing variances.

Prepare income statement for management.

(SO 7)

Materials price variance	$1,250 debit	Labor quantity variance	$ 725 debit
Materials quantity variance	700 credit	Overhead controllable	200 credit
Labor price variance	525 debit	Overhead volume	1,000 debit

In addition, 6,000 units of product were sold at $8.00 per unit. Each unit sold had a standard cost of $6.00. Selling and administrative expenses were $6,000 for the month.

Instructions

Prepare an income statement for management for the month ending January 31, 2005.

E26-11 Marley Company installed a standard cost system on January 1. Selected transactions for the month of January are as follows.

Journalize entries in a standard cost accounting system.

(SO 7)

1. Purchased 18,000 units of raw materials on account at a cost of $4.50 per unit. Standard cost was $4.25 per unit.

2. Issued 18,000 units of raw materials for jobs that required 17,600 standard units of raw materials.

3. Incurred 15,200 actual hours of direct labor at an actual rate of $4.80 per hour. The standard rate is $5.25 per hour. (Credit Wages Payable)
4. Performed 15,200 hours of direct labor on jobs when standard hours were 15,400.
5. Applied overhead to jobs at the rate of 100% of direct labor cost for standard hours allowed.

Instructions
Journalize the January transactions.

Answer questions concerning missing entries and balances.
(SO 4, 5, 7)

E26-12 Tovar Company uses a standard cost accounting system. Some of the ledger accounts have been destroyed in a fire. The controller asks your help in reconstructing some missing entries and balances.

Instructions
Answer the following questions.

(a) Materials Price Variance shows a $3,000 favorable balance. Accounts Payable shows $128,000 of raw materials purchases. What was the amount debited to Raw Materials Inventory for raw materials purchased?

(b) Materials Quantity Variance shows a $3,000 unfavorable balance. Raw Materials Inventory shows a zero balance. What was the amount debited to Work in Process Inventory for direct materials used?

(c) Labor Price Variance shows a $1,500 unfavorable balance. Factory Labor shows a debit of $150,000 for wages incurred. What was the amount credited to Wages Payable?

(d) Factory Labor shows a credit of $150,000 for direct labor used. Labor Quantity Variance shows a $900 unfavorable balance. What was the amount debited to Work in Process for direct labor used?

(e) Overhead applied to Work in Process totaled $165,000. If the total overhead variance was $1,000 unfavorable, what was the amount of overhead costs debited to Manufacturing Overhead?

(f) Overhead Controllable Variance shows a debit balance of $1,500. What was the amount and type of balance (debit or credit) in Overhead Volume Variance?

PROBLEMS: SET A

Compute variances, and prepare income statement.
(SO 4, 5, 7)

P26-1A Soriano Manufacturing Company uses a standard cost accounting system. In July 2005, it accumulates the following data relative to jobs started and finished.

Cost and Production Data	Actual	Standard
Raw materials		
Units purchased	17,400	
Units used	17,400	18,000
Unit cost	$3.40	$3.00
Direct labor		
Hours worked	2,900	3,000
Hourly rate	$11.80	$12.20
Manufacturing overhead		
Incurred	$87,500	
Applied		$93,750

Manufacturing overhead was applied on the basis of direct labor hours. Normal capacity for the month was 2,800 direct labor hours. At normal capacity, budgeted overhead costs were: variable $56,000 and fixed $31,500.

Jobs finished during the month were sold for $240,000. Selling and administrative expenses were $25,000.

Instructions
(a) Compute all of the variances for (1) direct materials, (2) direct labor, and (3) manufacturing overhead.
(b) Prepare an income statement for management. Ignore income taxes.

P26-2A Inman Corporation manufactures a single product. The standard cost per unit of product is as follows.

Compute variances.
(SO 4, 5)

Direct materials—2 pounds of plastic at $5.00 per pound	$10.00
Direct labor—2 hours at $12.00 per hour	24.00
Variable manufacturing overhead	12.00
Fixed manufacturing overhead	6.00
Total standard cost per unit	$52.00

The master manufacturing overhead budget for the year based on normal productive capacity of 180,000 direct labor hours (90,000 units) shows total variable costs of $1,080,000 and total fixed costs of $540,000. Overhead is applied on the basis of direct labor hours. Actual costs for November in producing 7,600 units were as follows.

Direct materials (15,000 pounds)	$ 73,500
Direct labor (14,900 hours)	181,780
Variable overhead	88,990
Fixed overhead	44,000
Total manufacturing costs	$388,270

The purchasing department normally buys the quantities of raw materials that are expected to be used in production each month. Raw materials inventories, therefore, can be ignored.

Instructions
Compute all of the materials, labor, and overhead variances.

P26-3A Kohler Clothiers manufactures women's business suits. The company uses a standard cost accounting system. In March 2005, 11,800 suits were made. The following standard and actual cost data applied to the month of March when normal capacity was 15,000 direct labor hours. All materials purchased were used in production.

Compute variances, journalize entries, and identify significant variances.
(SO 4, 5, 6, 7)

Cost Element	Standard (per unit)	Actual
Direct materials	5 yards at $7.00 per yard	$410,400 for 57,000 yards ($7.20 per yard)
Direct labor	1.0 hours at $12.00 per hour	$125,440 for 11,200 hours ($11.20 per hour)
Overhead	1.0 hours at $9.30 per hour (fixed $6.30; variable $3.00)	$90,000 fixed overhead $42,000 variable overhead

Overhead is applied on the basis of direct labor hours. At normal capacity, budgeted fixed overhead costs were $94,500, and budgeted variable overhead costs were $45,000.

Instructions
(a) Compute the total, price, and quantity variances for (1) materials and (2) labor, and compute the total, controllable, and volume variances for manufacturing overhead.
(b) Journalize the entries to record the variances assuming (1) all purchases of materials were on account, and (2) Wages Payable was credited for factory labor incurred.
(c) ▱▱▱▱▷ Which of the materials and labor variances should be investigated if management considers a variance of more than 6% from standard to be significant?

P26-4A Fayman Manufacturing Company uses standard costs with its job order cost accounting system. In January, an order (Job 84) was received for 3,900 units of Product D. The standard cost of 1 unit of Product D is as follows.

Journalize and post standard cost entries, and prepare income statement.
(SO 4, 5, 7)

Direct materials—1.4 pounds at $4.00 per pound	$ 5.60
Direct labor—1 hour at $9.00 per hour	9.00
Overhead—1 hour (variable $7.40; fixed $10.00)	17.40
Standard cost per unit	$32.00

Overhead is applied on the basis of direct labor hours. Normal capacity for the month of January was 4,500 direct labor hours. During January, the following transactions applicable to Job No. 84 occurred.

1. Purchased 6,200 pounds of raw materials on account at $3.60 per pound.
2. Requisitioned 6,200 pounds of raw materials for production.
3. Incurred 3,700 hours of direct labor at $9.25 per hour.
4. Worked 3,700 hours of direct labor on Job No. 84.
5. Incurred $73,650 of manufacturing overhead on account.
6. Applied overhead to Job No. 84 on the basis of direct labor hours.
7. Transferred Job No. 84 to finished goods.
8. Billed customer for Job No. 84 at a selling price of $250,000.
9. Incurred selling and administrative expenses on account $61,000.

Instructions
(a) Journalize the transactions.
(b) Post to the job order cost accounts.
(c) Prepare the entry to recognize the overhead variances.
(d) Prepare the income statement for management for January 2005.

Answer questions about variances.

(SO 4, 5, 7)

P26-5A Crede Manufacturing Company uses a standard cost accounting system. In 2005, 33,000 units were produced. Each unit took several pounds of direct materials and 1⅓ standard hours of direct labor at a standard hourly rate of $12.00. Normal capacity was 42,000 direct labor hours. During the year, 132,000 pounds of raw materials were purchased at $0.90 per pound. All pounds purchased were used during the year.

Instructions
(a) If the materials price variance was $3,960 unfavorable, what was the standard materials price per pound?
(b) If the materials quantity variance was $2,871 favorable, what was the standard materials quantity per unit?
(c) What were the standard hours allowed for the units produced?
(d) If the labor quantity variance was $8,400 unfavorable, what were the actual direct labor hours worked?
(e) If the labor price variance was $4,470 favorable, what was the actual rate per hour?
(f) If total budgeted manufacturing overhead was $327,600 at normal capacity, what was the predetermined overhead rate?
(g) What was the standard cost per unit of product?
(h) How much overhead was applied to production during the year?
(i) If the fixed overhead rate was $2.50, what was the overhead volume variance?
(j) If the overhead controllable variance was $3,000 favorable, what were the total variable overhead costs incurred?
(k) Using selected answers above, what were the total costs assigned to work in process?

PROBLEMS: SET B

Compute variances, and prepare income statement.

(SO 4, 5, 7)

P26-1B Finley Manufacturing Corporation accumulates the following data relative to jobs started and finished during the month of June 2005.

Costs and Production Data	Actual	Standard
Raw materials purchases, 10,400 units	$ 23,400	$20,800
Raw materials units used	10,400	10,000
Direct labor payroll	$124,100	$120,000
Direct labor hours worked	14,600	15,000
Manufacturing overhead incurred	$182,500	
Manufacturing overhead applied		$189,000
Machine hours expected to be used at normal capacity		42,500
Budgeted fixed overhead for June		$51,000
Variable overhead rate per hour		$3.00

Overhead is applied on the basis of standard machine hours. Three hours of machine time are required for each direct labor hour. The jobs were sold for $400,000. Selling and administrative expenses were $40,000.

Instructions
(a) Compute all of the variances for (1) direct materials, (2) direct labor, and (3) manufacturing overhead.
(b) Prepare an income statement for management. Ignore income taxes.

P26-2B Ranier Corporation manufactures a single product. The standard cost per unit of product is shown below.

Compute variances.

(SO 4, 5)

Direct materials—1 pound plastic at $7.00 per pound	$ 7.00
Direct labor—1.5 hours at $12.00 per hour	18.00
Variable manufacturing overhead	11.25
Fixed manufacturing overhead	3.75
Total standard cost per unit	$40.00

The predetermined manufacturing overhead rate is $10 per direct labor hour ($15.00 ÷ 1.5). This rate was computed from a master manufacturing overhead budget based on normal production of 90,000 direct labor hours (60,000 units) for the year. The master budget showed total variable costs of $675,000 and total fixed costs of $225,000. Actual costs for October in producing 4,800 units were as follows.

Direct materials (5,100 pounds)	$ 37,230
Direct labor (7,000 hours)	87,500
Variable overhead	56,170
Fixed overhead	19,680
Total manufacturing costs	$200,580

The purchasing department normally buys the quantities of raw materials that are expected to be used in production each month. Raw materials inventories, therefore, can be ignored.

Instructions
Compute all of the materials, labor, and overhead variances.

P26-3B Merando Clothiers is a small company that manufactures tall-men's suits. The company has used a standard cost accounting system. In May 2005, 11,200 suits were produced. The following standard and actual cost data applied to the month of May when normal capacity was 14,000 direct labor hours. All materials purchased were used.

Compute variances, journalize entries, and identify significant variances.

(SO 4, 5, 6, 7)

Cost Element	Standard (per unit)	Actual
Direct materials	8 yards at $4.50 per yard	$371,050 for 90,500 yards ($4.10 per yard)
Direct labor	1.2 hours at $13.00 per hour	$201,630 for 14,300 hours ($14.10 per hour)
Overhead	1.2 hours at $6.00 per hour (fixed $3.50; variable $2.50)	$49,000 fixed overhead $36,000 variable overhead

Overhead is applied on the basis of direct labor hours. At normal capacity, budgeted fixed overhead costs were $49,000, and budgeted variable overhead was $35,000.

Instructions
(a) Compute the total, price, and quantity variances for (1) materials and (2) labor, and the total, controllable, and volume variances for manufacturing overhead.
(b) Journalize the entries to record the variances assuming (1) all purchases of materials were on account, and (2) Wages Payable was credited for factory labor incurred.
(c) ▭▭▭▭▷ Which of the materials and labor variances should be investigated if management considers a variance of more than 7% from standard to be significant?

*Journalize and post standard
cost entries, and prepare
income statement.*

(SO 4, 5, 7)

P26-4B Berman Corporation uses standard costs with its job order cost accounting system. In January, an order (Job No. 12) for 1,950 units of Product B was received. The standard cost of one unit of Product B is as follows.

Direct materials	3 pounds at $1.00 per pound	$ 3.00
Direct labor	1 hour at $8.00 per hour	8.00
Overhead	2 hours (variable $4.00 per machine hour;	
	fixed $2.25 per machine hour)	12.50
Standard cost per unit		$23.50

Normal capacity for the month was 4,200 machine hours. During January, the following transactions applicable to Job No. 12 occurred.

1. Purchased 6,250 pounds of raw materials on account at $1.04 per pound.
2. Requisitioned 6,250 pounds of raw materials for Job No. 12.
3. Incurred 2,200 hours of direct labor at a rate of $7.75 per hour.
4. Worked 2,200 hours of direct labor on Job No. 12.
5. Incurred manufacturing overhead on account $25,800.
6. Applied overhead to Job No. 12 on basis of standard machine hours used.
7. Completed Job No. 12.
8. Billed customer for Job No. 12 at a selling price of $70,000.
9. Incurred selling and administrative expenses on account $2,000.

Instructions
(a) Journalize the transactions.
(b) Post to the job order cost accounts.
(c) Prepare the entry to recognize the overhead variances.
(d) Prepare the January 2005 income statement for management.

*Answer questions about
variances.*

(SO 4, 5, 7)

P26-5B Harbaugh Manufacturing Company uses a standard cost accounting system. In 2005, 30,000 units were produced. Each unit took several pounds of direct materials and 1½ standard hours of direct labor at a standard hourly rate of $12.00. Normal capacity was 50,000 direct labor hours. During the year, 133,000 pounds of raw materials were purchased at $0.92 per pound. All pounds purchased were used during the year.

Instructions
(a) If the materials price variance was $5,320 favorable, what was the standard materials price per pound?
(b) If the materials quantity variance was $3,840 unfavorable, what was the standard materials quantity per unit?
(c) What were the standard hours allowed for the units produced?
(d) If the labor quantity variance was $7,200 unfavorable, what were the actual direct labor hours worked?
(e) If the labor price variance was $9,120 favorable, what was the actual rate per hour?
(f) If total budgeted manufacturing overhead was $340,000 at normal capacity, what was the predetermined overhead rate?
(g) What was the standard cost per unit of product?
(h) How much overhead was applied to production during the year?
(i) If the fixed overhead rate was $2.00, what was the overhead volume variance?
(j) If the overhead controllable variance is $3,000 unfavorable, what were the total variable overhead costs incurred?
(k) Using one or more answers above, what were the total costs assigned to work in process?

BROADENING YOUR PERSPECTIVE

Group Decision Case

BYP26-1 Agmar Professionals, a management consulting firm, specializes in strategic planning for financial institutions. Tim Agler and Jill Marlin, partners in the firm, are assembling a new strategic planning model for use by clients. The model is designed for use on most personal computers and replaces a rather lengthy manual model currently marketed by the firm. To market the new model Tim and Jill will need to provide clients with an estimate of the number of labor hours and computer time needed to operate the model. The model is currently being test marketed at five small financial institutions. These financial institutions are listed below, along with the number of combined computer/labor hours used by each institution to run the model one time.

Financial Institutions	Computer/Labor Hours Required
Midland National	25
First State	45
Financial Federal	40
Pacific America	30
Lakeview National	30
Total	170
Average	34

Any company that purchases the new model will need to purchase user manuals to access and operate the system. Also required are specialized computer forms that are sold only by Agmar Professionals. User manuals will be sold to clients in cases of 20, at a cost of $300 per case. One manual must be used each time the model is run because each manual includes a nonreusable computer accessed password for operating the system. The specialized computer forms are sold in packages of 250, at a cost of $50 per package. One application of the model requires the use of 50 forms. This amount includes two forms that are generally wasted in each application due to printer alignment errors. The overall cost of the strategic planning model to user clients is $12,000. Most clients will use the model four times annually.

Agmar Professionals must provide its clients with estimates of ongoing costs incurred in operating the new strategic planning model. They would like to provide this information in the form of standard costs.

Instructions

With the class divided into groups, answer the following.

(a) What factors should be considered in setting a standard for computer/labor hours?
(b) What alternatives for setting a standard for computer/labor hours might be used?
(c) What standard for computer/labor hours would you select? Justify your answer.
(d) Determine the standard materials cost associated with the user manuals and computer forms for each application of the strategic planning model.

Managerial Analysis

BYP26-2 Mo Vaughn and Associates is a medium-sized company located near a large metropolitan area in the Midwest. The company manufactures cabinets of mahogany, oak, and other fine woods for use in expensive homes, restaurants, and hotels. Although some of the work is custom, many of the cabinets are a standard size.

One such non-custom model is called Luxury Base Frame. Normal production is 1,000 units. Each unit has a direct labor hour standard of 5 hours. Overhead is applied to production based on standard direct labor hours. During the most recent month, only 900 units were produced; 4,500 direct labor hours were allowed for standard production, but only 4,000 hours were used. Standard and actual overhead costs were as follows.

	Standard (1,000 units)	Actual (900 units)
Indirect materials	$ 12,000	$ 12,300
Indirect labor	48,000	51,000
(Fixed) Manufacturing supervisors salaries	22,000	22,000
(Fixed) Manufacturing office employees salaries	13,000	11,500
(Fixed) Engineering costs	26,000	25,000
Computer costs	10,000	10,000
Electricity	2,500	2,500
(Fixed) Manufacturing building depreciation	8,000	8,000
(Fixed) Machinery depreciation	3,000	3,000
(Fixed) Trucks and forklift depreciation	1,500	1,500
Small tools	700	1,400
(Fixed) Insurance	500	500
(Fixed) Property taxes	300	300
Total	$147,500	$149,000

Instructions
(a) Determine the overhead application rate.
(b) Determine how much overhead was applied to production.
(c) Calculate the controllable overhead variance and the overhead volume variance.
(d) Decide which overhead variances should be investigated.
(e) Discuss causes of the overhead variances. What can management do to improve its performance next month?

Real-World Focus

BYP26-3 Glassmaster Co. was incorporated in 1946 as Koolvent Metal Awning Company. Its current name was adopted in 1982 to reflect the more general nature of its products. The company is organized as two divisions and one subsidiary. One division focuses on the manufacture of filaments such as fishing line and sewing thread; the other division manufactures antennas and specialty fiberglass products. Its subsidiary manufactures flexible steel wire controls and molded control panels.

The annual report of Glassmaster provides the following information.

GLASSMASTER COMPANY
Management Discussion

Gross profit margins for the year improved to 20.9% of sales compared to last year's 18.5%. All operations reported improved margins due in large part to improved operating efficiencies as a result of cost reduction measures implemented during the second and third quarters of the fiscal year and increased manufacturing throughout due to higher unit volume sales. Contributing to the improved margins was a favorable materials price variance due to competitive pricing by suppliers as a result of soft demand for petrochemical-based products. This favorable variance is temporary and will begin to reverse itself as stronger worldwide demand for commodity products improves in tandem with the economy. Partially offsetting these positive effects on profit margins were competitive pressures on sales prices of certain product lines. The company responded with pricing strategies designed to maintain and/or increase market share.

Instructions
(a) Is it apparent from the information whether Glassmaster utilizes standard costs?
(b) Do you think the price variance experienced should lead to changes in standard costs for the next fiscal year?

Exploring the Web

BYP26-4 The Caelus Management System (CMS), is a real-time fully, integrated decision support, operational control, and financial management system.

Address: www.caelus.com, or go to www.wiley.com/college/weygandt

Steps

1. Choose **CMS Product Info** and answer part (a), below.
2. Choose **Standard Cost** and answer parts (b) and (c).

Instructions

(a) List some of the modules that are familiar to you from either financial accounting topics or managerial accounting topics.
(b) What types of decisions does this module of the software support?
(c) Does this product distinguish between fixed and variable costs?
(d) The flexibility of this software allows managers to evaluate costs in a variety of different ways. Why is this important?

Communication Activity

BYP26-5 The setting of standards is critical to the effective use of standards in evaluating performance.

Instructions

Explain the following in a memo to your instructor.

(a) The comparative advantages and disadvantages of ideal versus normal standards.
(b) The factors that should be included in setting the price and quantity standards for direct materials, direct labor, and manufacturing overhead.

Ethics Case

BYP26-6 At Camden Manufacturing Company, production workers in the Painting Department are paid on the basis of productivity. The labor time standard for a unit of production is established through periodic time studies conducted by the Foster Management Department. In a time study, the actual time required to complete a specific task by a worker is observed. Allowances are then made for preparation time, rest periods, and clean-up time. Dan Renfro is one of several veterans in the Painting Department.

Dan is informed by Foster Management that he will be used in the time study for the painting of a new product. The findings will be the basis for establishing the labor time standard for the next 6 months. During the test, Dan deliberately slows his normal work pace in an effort to obtain a labor time standard that will be easy to meet. Because it is a new product, the Foster Management representative who conducted the test is unaware that Dan did not give the test his best effort.

Instructions

(a) Who was benefited and who was harmed by Dan's actions?
(b) Was Dan ethical in the way he performed the time study test?
(c) What measure(s) might the company take to obtain valid data for setting the labor time standard?

Answers to Self-Study Questions

1. c **2.** d **3.** b **4.** c **5.** b **6.** a **7.** d **8.** a **9.** b **10.** c

---

 ✓ REMEMBER to go back to the Navigator box on the chapter-opening page and check off your completed work.

Incremental Analysis and Capital Budgeting

CONCEPTS FOR REVIEW

Before studying this chapter, you should know or, if necessary, review:

- The difference between variable and fixed costs.
  (Ch. 23, pp. 934–938)

- The meaning of the term contribution margin.
  (Ch. 23, pp. 940–942)

- How to use present value tables.
  (Appendix C)

Soup Is Good Food

When you hear the word *Campbell's*, what is the first thing that comes to mind? Soup. Campbell's *is* soup. It sells 38 percent of all the soup—including homemade—consumed in the United States. But can a company survive on soup alone? In an effort to expand its operations and to lessen its reliance on soup, Campbell Soup Company began searching for an additional line of business in 1990. Campbell's management believed it saw an opportunity in convenient meals that were low in fat, nutritionally rich, and had therapeutic value for heart patients and diabetics. This venture would require a huge investment—but the rewards were potentially tremendous.

The initial investment required building food labs, hiring nutritional scientists, researching prototype products, constructing new production facilities, and marketing the new products. Management predicted that with an initial investment of roughly $55 million, the company might generate sales of $200 million per year.

By 1994 the company had created 24 meals, and an extensive field-study revealed considerable health benefits from the products. Unfortunately, initial sales of the new product line, called Intelligent Quisine, were less than stellar. In 1997 a consulting firm was hired to evaluate whether the project should be continued. Product development of the new line was costing $20 million per year—a sum that some managers felt could be better spent developing new products in other divisions, or expanding overseas operations. In 1998 the project was discontinued.

Campbell's was not giving up on growth, but simply had decided to refocus its efforts on soup. The company's annual report stated management's philosophy: "Soup will be our growth engine." Campbell's is now selling off many of its non-soup businesses and in a recent year introduced twenty new soup products.

Source: Vanessa O'Connell, "Food for Thought: How Campbell Saw a Breakthrough Menu Turn into Leftovers," *Wall Street Journal*, October 6, 1998.

www.campbellsoup.com

☑ THE NAVIGATOR

STUDY OBJECTIVES

After studying this chapter, you should be able to:

1. Identify the steps in management's decision-making process.
2. Describe the concept of incremental analysis.
3. Identify the relevant costs in accepting an order at a special price.
4. Identify the relevant costs in a make-or-buy decision.
5. Give the decision rule for whether to sell or process materials further.
6. Identify the factors to be considered in retaining or replacing equipment.
7. Explain the relevant factors in deciding whether to eliminate an unprofitable segment.
8. Determine which products to make and sell when resources are limited.
9. Contrast the annual rate of return and cash payback techniques in capital budgeting.
10. Distinguish between the net present value and internal rate of return methods.

☑ THE NAVIGATOR

An important purpose of management accounting is to provide relevant information for decision making. Examples of these decisions include the following: (1) **Campbell Soup**'s decision to produce "therapeutic meals" rather than some other food product. (2) **Boeing**'s strategic decisions to spend $5 billion to build a plane for the 21st century—the B-777—and to cancel development of a larger version of the B-747. (3) **The Coca-Cola Company**'s decision to spend $750 million to build twelve plants in Russia.

This chapter begins with an explanation of management's decision-making process. It then considers the topics of incremental analysis and capital budgeting.

The content and organization of Chapter 27 are as follows.

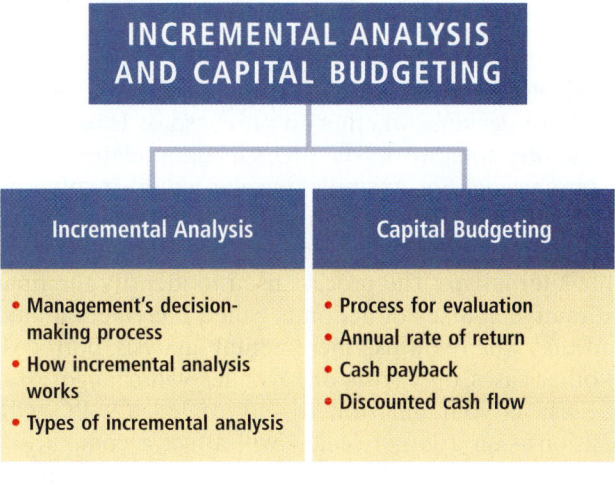

SECTION 1 INCREMENTAL ANALYSIS

Management's Decision-Making Process

Making decisions is an important management function. Management's decision-making process does not always follow a set pattern, because decisions vary significantly in their scope, urgency, and importance. It is possible, though, to identify some steps that are frequently involved in the process. These steps are shown in Illustration 27-1 (page 1088).

Accounting's contribution to the decision-making process occurs primarily in Steps 2 and 4—evaluating possible courses of action, and reviewing the results. In Step 2, for each possible course of action, relevant revenue and cost data are provided. These show the expected overall effect on net income. In Step 4, internal reports are prepared that review the actual impact of the decision.

In making business decisions, management ordinarily considers both financial and nonfinancial information. **Financial** information is related to revenues and costs and their effect on the company's overall profitability. **Nonfinancial** information relates to such factors as the effect of the decision on employee turnover, the environment, or the overall image of the company in the community. Although the nonfinancial information can be as important as the financial information, we will focus primarily on financial information that is relevant to the decision.

STUDY OBJECTIVE 1

Identify the steps in management's decision-making process.

Illustration 27-1
Management's decision-
making process

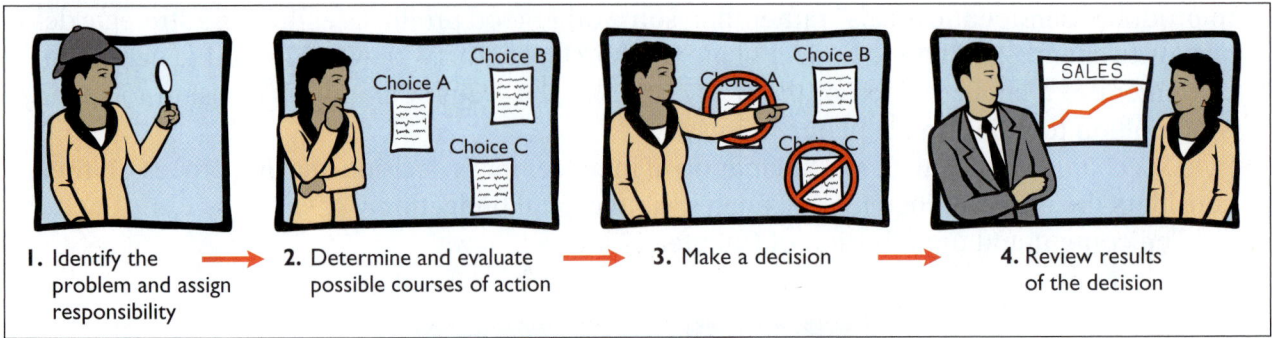

I. Identify the problem and assign responsibility   →   2. Determine and evaluate possible courses of action   →   3. Make a decision   →   4. Review results of the decision

Decisions involve a choice among alternative courses of action. Suppose that you were deciding whether to purchase or lease a computer for use in doing your accounting homework. The financial data relate to the cost of leasing versus the cost of purchasing. For example, leasing would involve periodic lease payments; purchasing would require "up-front" payment of the purchase price. In other words, the financial data relevant to the decision are the data that would vary among the possible alternatives. The process used to identify the financial data that change under alternative courses of action is called **incremental analysis**. In some cases, you will find that when you use incremental analysis, both costs **and** revenues will change. In other cases, only costs **or** revenues will change.

Just as your decision to buy or lease a PC will affect your future, similar decisions—on a larger scale—will affect a company's future. Incremental analysis identifies the probable effects of those decisions on future earnings. Such analysis inevitably involves estimates and uncertainty. Gathering data for incremental analyses may involve market analysts, engineers, and accountants. In quantifying the data, the accountant is expected to produce the most reliable information available at the time the decision must be made.

How Incremental Analysis Works

The basic approach in incremental analysis is illustrated in the following example.

Illustration 27-2
Basic approach in incremental analysis

	Alternative A	Alternative B	Net Income Increase (Decrease)
Revenues	$125,000	$110,000	$(15,000)
Costs	100,000	80,000	20,000
Net income	$ 25,000	$ 30,000	$ 5,000

In this example, alternative B is being compared with alternative A. The net income column shows the differences between the alternatives. In this case, incremental revenue will be $15,000 less under alternative B than under alternative A. But a $20,000 incremental cost saving will be realized.[1] Thus, alternative B will produce $5,000 more net income than alternative A.

---

[1]Although income taxes are sometimes important in incremental analysis, they are ignored in the chapter for simplicity's sake.

Incremental analysis sometimes involves changes that at first glance might seem contrary to your intuition. For example, sometimes variable costs **do not** change under the alternative courses of action. Also, sometimes fixed costs **do** change. For example, direct labor, normally a variable cost, is not an incremental cost in deciding between two new factory machines if each asset requires the same amount of direct labor. In contrast, rent expense, normally a fixed cost, is an incremental cost in a decision to continue occupancy of a building or to purchase or lease a new building.

Types of Incremental Analysis

A number of different types of decisions involve incremental analysis. The more common types of decisions are whether to:

1. Accept an order at a special price.
2. Make or buy.
3. Sell or process further.
4. Retain or replace equipment.
5. Eliminate an unprofitable business segment.
6. Allocate limited resources.

We will consider each of these types of analysis in the following pages.

Accept an Order at a Special Price

Sometimes, a company may have an opportunity to obtain additional business if it is willing to make a major price concession to a specific customer. To illustrate, assume that Sunbelt Company produces 100,000 automatic blenders per month, which is 80 percent of plant capacity. Variable manufacturing costs are $8 per unit. Fixed manufacturing costs are $400,000, or $4 per unit. The blenders are normally sold directly to retailers at $20 each. Sunbelt has an offer from Mexico Co. (a foreign wholesaler) to purchase an additional 2,000 blenders at $11 per unit. Acceptance of the offer would not affect normal sales of the product, and the additional units can be manufactured without increasing plant capacity. What should management do?

If management makes its decision on the basis of the total cost per unit of $12 ($8 + $4), the order would be rejected, because costs ($12) would exceed revenues ($11) by $1 per unit. However, since the units can be produced within existing plant capacity, the special order **will not increase fixed costs**. The relevant data for the decision, therefore, are the variable manufacturing costs per unit of $8 and the expected revenue of $11 per unit. Thus, as shown in Illustration 27-3, Sunbelt will increase its net income by $6,000 by accepting this special order.

> **STUDY OBJECTIVE 3**
>
> Identify the relevant costs in accepting an order at a special price.

> **HELPFUL HINT**
>
> This is a good example of different costs for different purposes. In the long-run all costs are relevant, but for this decision only costs that change are relevant.

	Reject Order	Accept Order	Net Income Increase (Decrease)
Revenues	$–0–	$22,000	**$22,000**
Costs	–0–	16,000	**(16,000)**
Net income	$–0–	$ 6,000	**$ 6,000**

Illustration 27-3
Incremental analysis—accepting an order at a special price

Two points should be emphasized: First, it is assumed that sales of the product in other markets would not be affected by this special order. If other sales were affected, then Sunbelt would have to consider the lost sales in making the decision.

Second, if Sunbelt is operating at full capacity, it is likely that the special order would be rejected. Under such circumstances, the company would have to expand plant capacity. In that case, the special order would have to absorb these additional fixed manufacturing costs, as well as the variable manufacturing costs.

Make or Buy

STUDY OBJECTIVE 4

Identify the relevant costs in a make-or-buy decision.

When a manufacturer assembles component parts in producing a finished product, management must decide whether to make or buy the components. For example, **General Motors Corporation** may either make or buy the batteries, tires, and radios used in its cars. Similarly, **Zenith Corporation** may make or buy the electronic circuitry, cabinets, and speakers for its television sets. The decision to make or buy components should be made on the basis of incremental analysis.

To illustrate the analysis, assume that Baron Company incurs the following annual costs in producing 25,000 ignition switches for motor scooters.

Illustration 27-4
Annual product cost data

Direct materials	$ 50,000
Direct labor	75,000
Variable manufacturing overhead	40,000
Fixed manufacturing overhead	60,000
Total manufacturing costs	$225,000
Total cost per unit ($225,000 ÷ 25,000)	**$9.00**

Or, instead of making its own switches, Baron Company might purchase the ignition switches from Ignition, Inc. at a price of $8 per unit. The question again is, "What should management do?"

At first glance, it appears that management should purchase the ignition switches for $8, rather than make them at a cost of $9. However, a review of operations indicates that if the ignition switches are purchased from Ignition, Inc., *all* of Baron's variable costs but only $10,000 of its fixed manufacturing costs will be eliminated. Thus, $50,000 of the fixed manufacturing costs will remain if the ignition switches are purchased. The relevant costs for incremental analysis are as follows.

Illustration 27-5
Incremental analysis—
make or buy

	Make	Buy	Net Income Increase (Decrease)
Direct materials	$ 50,000	$ –0–	$ 50,000
Direct labor	75,000	–0–	75,000
Variable manufacturing costs	40,000	–0–	40,000
Fixed manufacturing costs	60,000	50,000	10,000
Purchase price (25,000 × $8)	–0–	200,000	(200,000)
Total annual cost	$225,000	$250,000	$ (25,000)

ETHICS NOTE

In the make-or-buy decision it is important for management to take into account the social impact of their choice. For instance, buying may be the most economically feasible solution, but such action could result in the closure of a manufacturing plant that employs many good workers.

This analysis indicates that Baron Company will incur $25,000 of additional cost by buying the ignition switches. Therefore, Baron should continue to make the ignition switches, even though the total manufacturing cost is $1 higher than the purchase price. The reason is that if the company purchases the ignition switches, it will still have fixed costs of $50,000 to absorb.

The foregoing analysis is complete only if the productive capacity used to make the ignition switches cannot be converted to another purpose. If there is an opportunity to use this productive capacity in some other manner, then this opportunity cost must be considered. **Opportunity cost** is the potential benefit that may be obtained by following an alternative course of action.

To illustrate, assume that through buying the switches, Baron Company can use the released productive capacity to generate additional income of $28,000. This lost income is an additional cost of continuing to make the switches in the make-or-buy decision. This opportunity cost therefore is added to the "Make" column, for comparison. As shown, it is now advantageous to buy the ignition switches.

	Make	Buy	Net Income Increase (Decrease)
Total annual cost	$225,000	$250,000	$(25,000)
Opportunity cost	**28,000**	–0–	**28,000**
Total cost	$253,000	$250,000	$ 3,000

Illustration 27-6
Incremental analysis—make or buy, with opportunity cost

The qualitative factors in this decision include the possible loss of jobs for employees who produce the ignition switches. In addition, management must assess how long the supplier will be able to satisfy the company's quality control standards at the quoted price per unit.

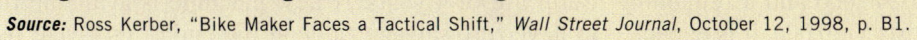

ACCOUNTING IN ACTION Business Insight

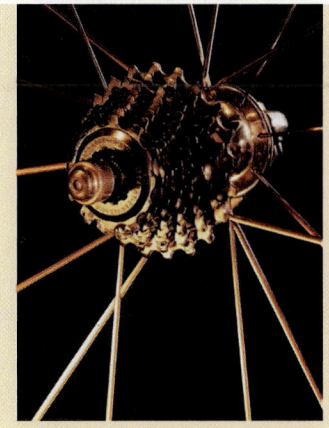

In the bicycle industry, nearly all bikes of quality are made with **Shimano** parts. This dominance by a single supplier has made bikes a sort of commodity. That is, if all bikes are made from the same parts, then what does it matter what brand of bike you buy? As a consequence, the majority of profits go to Shimano, with bike manufacturers that use Shimano parts having to accept an increasingly small profit margin.

To break this trend, and increase its profit margins, **Cannondale Corporation** has decided to take "the approach that we manufacture the whole bicycle, not just taking a frame and putting somebody's parts on it." Similar steps are being taken by **Trek Bicycle Corporation** and **Specialized Bicycle Components Inc**. These companies recognize that they are taking a risk. In order to compete with Shimano, they will have to dramatically step up their research and development efforts and significantly increase their efficiency in the manufacture of parts. This will be difficult given Shimano's huge volume advantage.

Source: Ross Kerber, "Bike Maker Faces a Tactical Shift," *Wall Street Journal*, October 12, 1998, p. B1.

Sell or Process Further

Many manufacturers have the option of selling products at a given point in the production cycle or continuing to process with the expectation of selling them at a higher price. For example, a bicycle manufacturer such as **Schwinn** could sell its 10-speed bicycles to retailers either unassembled or assembled, and a furniture manufacturer such as **Ethan Allen** could sell its dining room sets to furniture stores either unfinished or finished. The sell-or-process further decision should be made on the basis of incremental analysis. The basic decision rule is: **Process further as long as the incremental revenue from such processing exceeds the incremental processing costs.**

STUDY OBJECTIVE 5

Give the decision rule for whether to sell or process materials further.

Assume, for example, that Woodmasters Inc. makes tables. The cost to manufacture an unfinished table is $35, computed as follows.

Illustration 27-7
Per unit cost of unfinished table

Direct material	$15
Direct labor	10
Variable manufacturing overhead	6
Fixed manufacturing overhead	4
Manufacturing cost per unit	**$35**

The selling price per unfinished unit is $50. Woodmasters currently has unused productive capacity that is expected to continue indefinitely. Management concludes that some of this capacity can be used to finish the tables and sell them at $60 per unit. For a finished table, direct materials will increase $2 and direct labor costs will increase $4. Variable manufacturing overhead costs will increase by $2.40 (60% of direct labor). No increase is anticipated in fixed manufacturing overhead. The incremental analysis on a per unit basis is as follows.

Illustration 27-8
Incremental analysis—sell or process further

HELPFUL HINT

Current net income is known. Net income from processing further is an estimate. In making its decision, management could add a "risk" factor for the estimate.

	Sell	Process Further	Net Income Increase (Decrease)
Sales per unit	$50.00	$60.00	**$10.00**
Cost per unit			
Direct materials	15.00	17.00	**(2.00)**
Direct labor	10.00	14.00	**(4.00)**
Variable manufacturing overhead	6.00	8.40	**(2.40)**
Fixed manufacturing overhead	4.00	4.00	**–0–**
Total	$35.00	$43.40	**$(8.40)**
Net income per unit	$15.00	$16.60	**$ 1.60**

It would be advantageous for Woodmaster to process the tables further. The incremental revenue of $10.00 from the additional processing is $1.60 higher than the incremental processing costs of $8.40.

Retain or Replace Equipment

STUDY OBJECTIVE 6

Identify the factors to be considered in retaining or replacing equipment.

Management often has to decide whether to continue using an asset or replace it. To illustrate, assume that Jeffcoat Company has a factory machine with a book value of $40,000 and a remaining useful life of 4 years. A new machine is available that costs $120,000. It is expected to have zero salvage value at the end of its 4-year useful life. If the new machine is acquired, variable manufacturing costs are expected to decrease from $160,000 to $125,000 annually, and the old unit will be scrapped. The incremental analysis for the 4-year period is as follows.

Illustration 27-9
Incremental analysis—retain or replace equipment

	Retain Equipment	Replace Equipment	Net Income Increase (Decrease)
Variable manufacturing costs	$640,000[a]	$500,000[b]	**$140,000**
New machine cost		120,000	**(120,000)**
Total	$640,000	$620,000	**$ 20,000**

[a](4 years × $160,000)
[b](4 years × $125,000)

In this case, it would be to the company's advantage to replace the equipment. The lower variable manufacturing costs due to replacement more than offset the cost of the new equipment.

One other point should be mentioned regarding Jeffcoat's decision: **The book value of the old machine does not affect the decision.** Book value is a sunk cost, which is a cost that cannot be changed by any present or future decision. Sunk costs **are not relevant in incremental analysis**. In this example, if the asset is retained, book value will be depreciated over its remaining useful life. Or, if the new unit is acquired, book value will be recognized as a loss of the current period. Thus, the effect of book value on current and future earnings is the same regardless of the replacement decision. **Any trade-in allowance or cash disposal value of the existing asset, however, is relevant** to the decision, because this value will not be realized if the asset is continued in use.

Eliminate an Unprofitable Segment

Management sometimes must decide whether to eliminate an unprofitable business segment. Again, the key is to focus on the relevant amounts—the data that change under the alternative courses of action. To illustrate, assume that Martina Company manufactures tennis racquets in three models: Pro, Master, and Champ. Pro and Master are profitable lines. Champ (highlighted in color in the table below) operates at a loss. Condensed income statement data are:

STUDY OBJECTIVE 7

Explain the relevant factors in deciding whether to eliminate an unprofitable segment.

	Pro	Master	Champ	Total
Sales	$800,000	$300,000	**$100,000**	$1,200,000
Variable expenses	520,000	210,000	**90,000**	820,000
Contribution margin	280,000	90,000	**10,000**	380,000
Fixed expenses	80,000	50,000	**30,000**	160,000
Net income	$200,000	$ 40,000	**$(20,000)**	$ 220,000

Illustration 27-10
Segment income data

It might be expected that total net income will increase by $20,000 to $240,000 if the unprofitable line of racquets is eliminated. However, **net income may decrease if the Champ line is discontinued**. The reason is that the fixed expenses allocated to the Champ racquets will have to be absorbed by the other products. To illustrate, assume that the $30,000 of fixed costs applicable to the unprofitable segment are allocated ⅔ and ⅓ to the Pro and Master product lines, respectively. Fixed expenses will increase to $100,000 ($80,000 + $20,000) in the Pro line and to $60,000 ($50,000 + $10,000) in the Master line. The revised income statement is:

HELPFUL HINT

A decision to discontinue a segment based solely on the bottom line—net loss—is inappropriate.

	Pro	Master	Total
Sales	$800,000	$300,000	$1,100,000
Variable expenses	520,000	210,000	730,000
Contribution margin	280,000	90,000	370,000
Fixed expenses	**100,000**	**60,000**	160,000
Net income	$180,000	$ 30,000	**$ 210,000**

Illustration 27-11
Income data after eliminating unprofitable product line

Total net income has decreased $10,000 ($220,000 − $210,000). This result is also obtained in the following incremental analysis of the Champ racquets.

Illustration 27-12
Incremental analysis—eliminating an unprofitable segment

	Continue	Eliminate	Net Income Increase (Decrease)
Sales	$100,000	$ –0–	$(100,000)
Variable expenses	90,000	–0–	90,000
Contribution margin	10,000	–0–	(10,000)
Fixed expenses	30,000	30,000	–0–
Net income	$(20,000)	$(30,000)	$ (10,000)

The loss in net income is attributable to the contribution margin ($10,000) that will not be realized if the segment is discontinued.

In deciding on the future status of an unprofitable segment, management should consider the effect of elimination on related product lines. It may be possible for continuing product lines to obtain some or all of the sales lost by the discontinued product line. In some businesses, services or products may be linked—for example, free checking accounts at a bank, or coffee at a donut shop. In addition, management should consider the effect of eliminating the product line on employees who may have to be discharged or retrained.

ACCOUNTING IN ACTION Business Insight

In 1994 Quaker Oats paid $1.7 billion for one of America's hottest new beverage companies. While some observers thought that Quaker Oats had overpaid, Quaker's management believed it was an exciting purchase because it would make a great strategic partner for Quaker Oats' famous sport drink—Gatorade. For a variety of reasons, the acquisition didn't work out. One of those reasons was that at about the same time, several other major beverage manufacturers decided to begin producing and selling competing fruit and tea drinks. Worse yet, the processing methods used by these other manufacturers appeared to allow them to produce their drinks much more inexpensively. Only a few years after purchasing the beverage company, Quaker Oats sold it and took a $1.4 billion loss. Management stated that by selling this division, the company could reduce its debt burden and focus on its cereal brands and Gatorade.

Allocate Limited Resources

STUDY OBJECTIVE 8

Determine which products to make and sell when resources are limited.

Everyone's resources are limited. For a company, the limited resource may be floor space in a retail department store, or raw materials, direct labor hours, or machine capacity in a manufacturing company. When a company has limited resources, management must decide which products to make and sell in order to maximize net income.

To illustrate, assume that Collins Company manufactures deluxe and standard pen and pencil sets. The limiting resource is machine capacity, which is 3,600 hours per month. Relevant data consist of the following.

Illustration 27-13
Contribution margin and machine hours

	Deluxe Sets	Standard Sets
Contribution margin per unit	$8	$6
Machine hours required	0.4	0.2

The deluxe sets may appear to be more profitable: they have a higher contribution margin ($8) than the standard sets ($6). However, note that the standard sets take fewer machine hours to produce than the deluxe sets. Therefore, it is necessary to find the **contribution margin per unit of limited resource**, in this case, contribution margin per machine hour. This is obtained by dividing the contribution margin per unit of each product by the number of units of the limited resource required for each product.

HELPFUL HINT

CM alone is not enough in this decision. The key factor is CM per limited resource.

	Deluxe Sets	Standard Sets
Contribution margin per unit (a)	$8	$6
Machine hours required (b)	0.4	0.2
Contribution margin per unit of limited resource [(a) ÷ (b)]	**$20**	**$30**

Illustration 27-14
Contribution margin per unit of limited resource

The computation shows that the standard sets have a higher contribution margin per unit of limited resource. If Collins Company is able to increase machine capacity from 3,600 hours to 4,200 hours, the additional 600 hours could be used to produce either the standard or deluxe pen and pencil sets. The total contribution margin under each alternative is found by multiplying the machine hours by the contribution margin per unit of limited resource as shown below.

	Produce Deluxe Sets	Produce Standard Sets
Machine hours (a)	600	600
Contribution margin per unit of limited resource (b)	$20	$30
Contribution margin [(a) × (b)]	**$12,000**	**$18,000**

Illustration 27-15
Incremental analysis—computation of total contribution margin

From this analysis, we can see that to maximize net income, all of the increased capacity should be used to make and sell the standard sets.

BEFORE YOU GO ON...

Review It

1. Give three examples of how incremental analysis might be used.
2. What is the decision rule in deciding to sell or process products further?
3. How may the elimination of an unprofitable segment decrease the overall net income of a company?
4. What is the critical factor in allocating limited resources?

Do It

Cobb Company incurs a cost of $28 per unit, of which $18 is variable, to make a product that normally sells for $42. A foreign wholesaler offers to buy 5,000 units at $25 each. Cobb will incur shipping costs of $1 per unit. Compute the net income (loss) Cobb will realize by accepting the special order, assuming Cobb has excess operating capacity. Should Cobb Company accept the special order?

(continued from p. 1095.)

ACTION PLAN

■ Identify all revenues that will change as a result of accepting the order.
■ Identify all costs that will change as a result of accepting the order, and net this amount against the change in revenues.

SOLUTION

	Reject	Accept	Net Income Increase (Decrease)
Revenues	$–0–	$125,000	$125,000
Costs	–0–	95,000*	(95,000)
Net income	$–0–	$ 30,000	$ 30,000

*(5,000 × $18) + (5,000 × $1)

Given the result of the above analysis, Cobb Company should accept the special order.

Related exercise material: *BE27-2, BE27-3, and E27-1.*

☑ THE NAVIGATOR

www.wiley.com/college/weygandt

DEMONSTRATION PROBLEM 1

Juanita Company must decide whether to make or buy some of its components. The costs of producing 50,000 electrical cords for its floor lamps are as follows.

Direct materials	$60,000	Variable overhead	$12,000
Direct labor	30,000	Fixed overhead	8,000

Instead of making the electrical cords at an average cost per unit of $2.20 ($110,000 ÷ 50,000), the company has an opportunity to buy the cords at $2.15 per unit. If the cords are purchased, all variable costs and one-half of the fixed costs will be eliminated.

Instructions

(a) Prepare an incremental analysis showing whether the company should make or buy the electrical cords.
(b) Will your answer be different if the released productive capacity will generate additional income of $25,000?

ACTION PLAN

■ Look for the costs that change.
■ Ignore the costs that do not change.
■ Use the format in the chapter for your answer.
■ Recognize that opportunity cost can make a difference.

SOLUTION TO DEMONSTRATION PROBLEM 1

(a)	Make	Buy	Net Income Increase (Decrease)
Direct materials	$ 60,000	$ –0–	$ 60,000
Direct labor	30,000	–0–	30,000
Variable manufacturing costs	12,000	–0–	12,000
Fixed manufacturing costs	8,000	4,000	4,000
Purchase price	–0–	107,500	(107,500)
Total cost	$110,000	$111,500	$ (1,500)

This analysis indicates that Juanita Company will incur $1,500 of additional costs if it buys the electrical cords.

(b)

	Make	Buy	Net Income Increase (Decrease)
Total cost	$110,000	$111,500	$ (1,500)
Opportunity cost	25,000		25,000
Total cost	$135,000	$111,500	$ 23,500

Yes, the answer is different because the analysis shows that net income will be increased by $23,500 if the electrical cords are purchased.

☑ THE NAVIGATOR

SECTION 2 CAPITAL BUDGETING

Individuals make capital expenditures when they buy a new home, car, or television set. Similarly, businesses make capital expenditures when they modernize plant facilities or expand operations. Companies like **Campbell Soup** must constantly determine how to invest their resources. Other examples: Hollywood studios recently built 25 new sound stage projects to allow for additional filming in future years. And **Union Pacific Resources Group Inc.** announced that it would cut its capital budget by 19 percent in a recent year in order to use the funds to reduce its outstanding debt.

In business, as for individuals, the amount of possible capital expenditures usually exceeds the funds available for such expenditures. Thus, the resources available must be allocated (budgeted) among the competing alternatives. The process of making capital expenditure decisions in business is known as **capital budgeting**. Capital budgeting involves choosing among various capital projects to find the one(s) that will maximize a company's return on investment.

Process for Evaluation

Many companies follow a standard process in capital budgeting. At least once a year, proposals for projects are requested from each department. The proposals are screened by a capital budgeting committee, which submits its findings to the officers of the company. The officers, in turn, select the projects they believe to be most worthy of funding. They submit this list to the board of directors. Ultimately, the directors approve the capital expenditure budget for the year.

The involvement of top management and the board of directors in the process demonstrates the importance of capital budgeting decisions. These decisions often have a significant impact on a company's future profitability. In fact, poor capital budgeting decisions have led to the bankruptcy of some companies. Accounting data are indispensable in assessing the probable effects of capital expenditures.

To provide management with relevant data for capital budgeting decisions, you should be familiar with the quantitative techniques that may be used. The three most common techniques are: (1) annual rate of return, (2) cash payback, and (3) discounted cash flow. To illustrate the three quantitative techniques, assume that Tappan Company is considering an investment of $130,000 in new equipment. The new equipment is expected to last 10 years. It will have zero salvage value at the end of its useful life. The straight-line method of depreciation is used for accounting purposes. The expected annual revenues and costs of the new product that will be produced from the investment are:

Illustration 27-16
Estimated annual net income from capital expenditure

Sales		$200,000
Less: Costs and expenses		
Manufacturing costs (exclusive of depreciation)	$145,000	
Depreciation expenses ($130,000 ÷ 10)	13,000	
Selling and administrative expenses	22,000	180,000
Income before income taxes		20,000
Income tax expense		7,000
Net income		$ 13,000

Annual Rate of Return

STUDY OBJECTIVE 9

Contrast the annual rate of return and cash payback techniques in capital budgeting.

The **annual rate of return technique** is based directly on accounting data. It indicates **the profitability of a capital expenditure** by dividing expected annual net income by the average investment. The formula for computing annual rate of return is shown in Illustration 27-17.

Illustration 27-17
Annual rate of return formula

$$\text{Expected Annual Net Income} \div \text{Average Investment} = \text{Annual Rate of Return}$$

Expected annual net income is obtained from the projected income statement. Tappan Company's expected annual net income is $13,000. Average investment is derived from the following formula.

Illustration 27-18
Formula for computing average investment

$$\text{Average investment} = \frac{\text{Original Investment} + \text{Value at End of Useful Life}}{2}$$

The value at the end of useful life is equal to the asset's salvage value, if any. For Tappan Company, average investment is $65,000 [($130,000 + $0) ÷ 2]. The expected annual rate of return for Tappan Company's investment in new equipment is therefore 20 percent, computed as follows:

$$\$13,000 \div \$65,000 = 20\%$$

Management then compares this annual rate of return with its required minimum rate of return for investments of similar risk. The minimum rate of return (also called the **hurdle rate** or **cutoff rate**) is generally based on the company's **cost of capital**. The cost of capital is the rate of return that management expects to pay on all borrowed and equity funds. It does not relate to the cost of funding a specific project. The decision rule is: **A project is acceptable if its rate of return is greater than management's minimum rate of return. It is unacceptable when the reverse is true.** When the rate of return technique is used in deciding among several acceptable projects, **the higher the rate of return for a given risk, the more attractive the investment**.

The principal advantages of this technique are simplicity of calculation and management's familiarity with the accounting terms used in the computation. A

HELPFUL HINT

A capital budgeting decision based on only one technique may be misleading. It is often wise to analyze the investment from a number of different perspectives.

major limitation of the annual rate of return approach is that it does not consider the time value of money. For example, no consideration is given as to whether cash inflows will occur early or late in the life of the investment. As explained in Appendix C, recognition of the time value of money can make a significant difference between the future value and the present value of an investment.

Cash Payback

The **cash payback technique** identifies the time period required to recover the cost of the capital investment from the annual cash inflow produced by the investment. The formula for computing the cash payback period is:

Cost of Capital Investment	÷	Annual Cash Inflow	=	Cash Payback Period

Illustration 27-19
Cash payback formula

Annual (or **net**) **cash inflow** is approximated by taking net income and adding back depreciation expense. Depreciation expense is added back because depreciation on the capital expenditure does not involve an annual outflow of cash. Accordingly, the depreciation deducted in determining net income must be added back to determine annual cash inflows. In the Tappan Company example, annual cash inflow is $26,000, as shown below.

HELPFUL HINT

Annual cash inflow can also be approximated by net cash provided by operating activities from the statement of cash flows.

Net income	$13,000
Add: Depreciation expense	13,000
Annual cash inflow	**$26,000**

Illustration 27-20
Computation of annual cash inflow

The cash payback period in this example is therefore 5 years, computed as follows.

$$\$130,000 \div \$26,000 = 5 \text{ years}$$

The evaluation of the payback period is often related to the expected useful life of the asset. For example, assume that at Tappan Company a project is unacceptable if the payback period is longer than 60 percent of the asset's expected useful life. The 5-year payback period in this case is 50 percent of the project's expected useful life. Thus, the project is acceptable. It follows that when the payback technique is used to decide among acceptable alternative projects, **the shorter the payback period, the more attractive the investment**. This is true for two reasons: (1) The earlier the investment is recovered, the sooner the cash funds can be used for other purposes. And (2) the risk of loss from obsolescence and changed economic conditions is less in a shorter payback period.

The computation of the cash payback period above assumes equal cash flows in each year of the investment's life. In many cases, this assumption is not valid. In the case of **uneven** cash flows, the cash payback period is determined when the cumulative cash flows from the investment equal the cost of the investment. To illustrate, assume that Chan Company proposes an investment in a new Web site which is estimated to cost $300,000. The proposed investment cost, annual cash inflows, cumulative cash inflows, and the cash payback period are shown in Illustration 27-21 (page 1100).

As indicated from Illustration 27-21, at the end of year 3, cumulative cash inflow of $240,000 is less than the investment cost of $300,000, but at the end of year 4 the cumulative cash inflow of $360,000 exceeds the investment cost. The cash

Year	Investment	Annual Cash Inflow	Cumulative Cash Inflow
0	$300,000		
1		$ 60,000	$ 60,000
2		90,000	150,000
3		90,000	240,000
4		120,000	360,000
5		100,000	460,000

Cash payback period = **3.5 years**

inflow needed in year 4 to equal the investment cost is $60,000 ($300,000 − $240,000). Assuming the cash inflow occurred evenly during year 4, this amount is then divided by the annual cash inflow in year 4 ($120,000) to determine the point during the year when the cash payback occurs. Thus, .50 ($60,000/$120,000), or half of the year, is computed, and the cash payback period is 3.5 years.

The cash payback technique may be useful as an initial screening tool. It also may be the most critical factor in the capital budgeting decision for a company that desires a fast turnaround of its investment because of a weak cash position. Like the annual rate of return, cash payback is relatively easy to compute and understand.

However, cash payback should not ordinarily be the only basis for the capital budgeting decision because it ignores the expected profitability of the project. To illustrate, assume that Projects A and B have the same payback period, but Project A's useful life is double the useful life of Project B's. Project A's earning power, therefore, is twice as long as Project B's. A further disadvantage of this technique is that it ignores the time value of money.

Discounted Cash Flow

The **discounted cash flow technique** is generally recognized as the best conceptual approach to making capital budgeting decisions. This technique considers both the estimated total cash inflows from the investment and the time value of money. The expected total cash inflow consists of the sum of the annual cash inflows plus the estimated liquidation proceeds when the asset is sold for salvage at the end of its useful life. But because liquidation proceeds are generally immaterial, they are ignored in subsequent discussions.

Two methods are used with the discounted cash flow technique: (1) net present value and (2) internal rate of return. **Before we discuss the methods, we recommend that you examine Appendix C if you need a review of present value concepts.**

Net Present Value Method

Under the **net present value method**, cash inflows are discounted to their present value and then compared with the capital outlay required by the investment. The difference between these two amounts is referred to as **net present value**. The interest rate to be used in discounting the future cash inflows is the required minimum rate of return. The decision rule is this: **A proposal is acceptable when net present value is zero or positive.** This means that the rate of return on the investment equals or exceeds the required rate of return. When net present value is negative, the project is unacceptable. Illustration 27-22 shows the net present value decision criteria.

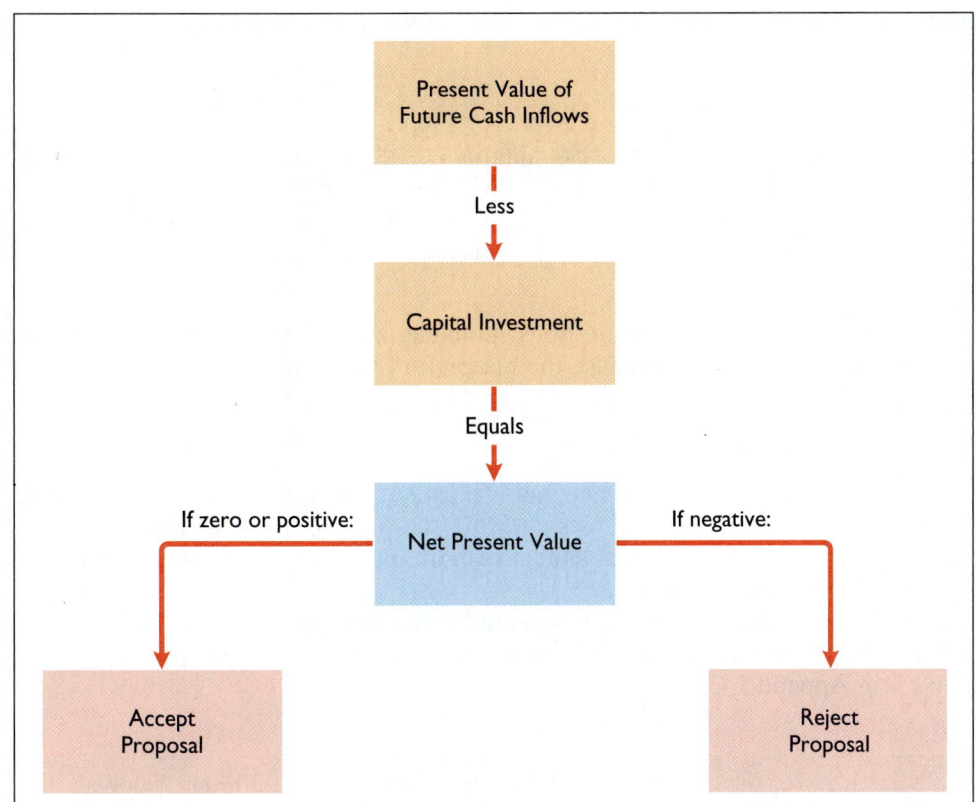

Illustration 27-22
Net present value decision criteria

When making a selection among acceptable proposals, **the higher the positive net present value, the more attractive the investment**. The application of this method to two cases is described in the next two sections. In each case, we will assume that the investment has no salvage value.

Equal Annual Cash Inflows

Tappan Company's annual cash inflows are $26,000. If we assume this amount **is uniform over the asset's useful life**, the present value of the annual cash inflows can be computed by using the present value of an annuity of 1 for 10 periods (in Table 2, Appendix C). The computations at rates of return of 12 percent and 15 percent, respectively, are:

ETHICS NOTE

Discounted future cash flows may not take into account all of the important considerations needed to make an informed capital budgeting decision. Other issues, for example, could include worker safety, product quality, and environmental impact.

	Present Values at Different Discount Rates	
	12%	**15%**
Discount factor for 10 periods	5.65022	5.01877
Present value of cash inflows:		
$26,000 × 5.65022	**$146,906**	
$26,000 × 5.01877		**$130,488**

Illustration 27-23
Present value of annual cash inflows

The analysis of the proposal by the net present value method is as follows:

Illustration 27-24
Computations of net present value

	12%	15%
Present value of future cash inflows	$146,906	$130,488
Capital investment	130,000	130,000
Positive (negative) net present value	**$ 16,906**	**$ 488**

The proposed capital expenditure is acceptable at a required rate of return of both 12 percent and 15 percent because the net present values are positive.

Unequal Annual Cash Inflows

When annual cash inflows are unequal, we cannot use annuity tables to calculate their present value. Instead, tables showing the **present value of a single future amount must be applied to each annual cash inflow**. To illustrate, assume that Tappan Company management expects the same aggregate annual cash inflow ($260,000) but a declining market demand for the new product over the life of the equipment. The present value of the annual cash flows is calculated as follows using Table 1 in Appendix C.

Illustration 27-25
Computing present value of unequal annual cash inflows

Year	Assumed Annual Cash Inflows	Discount Factor 12%	Discount Factor 15%	Present Value 12%	Present Value 15%
	(1)	(2)	(3)	(1) × (2)	(1) × (3)
1	$ 36,000	.89286	.86957	$ 32,143	$ 31,305
2	32,000	.79719	.75614	25,510	24,196
3	29,000	.71178	.65752	20,642	19,068
4	27,000	.63552	.57175	17,159	15,437
5	26,000	.56743	.49718	14,753	12,927
6	24,000	.50663	.43233	12,159	10,376
7	23,000	.45235	.37594	10,404	8,647
8	22,000	.40388	.32690	8,885	7,192
9	21,000	.36061	.28426	7,573	5,969
10	20,000	.32197	.24719	6,439	4,944
	$260,000			**$155,667**	**$140,061**

Therefore, the analysis of the proposal by the net present value method is as follows.

Illustration 27-26
Analysis of proposal using net present value method

	12%	15%
Present value of future cash inflows	$155,667	$140,061
Capital investment	130,000	130,000
Positive (negative) net present value	**$ 25,667**	**$ 10,061**

In this example, the present values of the cash inflows are greater than the $130,000 capital investment. Thus, the project is acceptable at both a 12 percent and 15 percent required rate of return. The difference between the present values using the 12 percent rate under equal cash inflows ($146,906) and unequal cash inflows ($155,667) is due to the pattern of the inflows.

ACCOUNTING IN ACTION   Business Insight

Inaccurate trend forecasting and market positioning are often more detrimental to a capital budget decision than using the wrong discount rate. **Ampex** patented the VCR, but failed to see its market potential. **Westinghouse** made the same mistake with flat-screen video display. More often, companies adopt projects or businesses but later discontinue them in response to market changes. **Texas Instruments** announced it would stop manufacturing computer chips, after investing to become one of the world's leading suppliers. The company has dropped out of some twelve business lines in recent years.

Source: World Research Advisory Inc. (London), August 1998, page 4.

Internal Rate of Return Method

The **internal rate of return method** finds the **interest yield of the potential investment**. The **internal rate of return** is the rate that will cause the present value of the proposed capital expenditure to equal the present value of the expected annual cash inflows. The determination of the internal rate of return involves two steps.

Step 1. Compute the internal rate of return factor. The formula for this factor is:

Capital Investment	÷	Annual Cash Inflows	=	Internal Rate of Return Factor

Illustration 27-27
Formula for internal rate of return factor

The computation for the Tappan Company, assuming equal annual cash inflows,[2] is:

$$\$130,000 \div \$26,000 = 5.0$$

Step 2. Use the factor and the present value of an annuity of 1 table to find the internal rate of return. Table 2 of Appendix C is used in this step. The internal rate of return is found by locating the discount factor that is closest to the internal rate of return factor for the time period covered by the annual cash flows.

In Tappan Company, the annual cash inflows are expected to continue for 10 years. Thus, it is necessary to read across the period-10 row in Table 2 to find the discount factor. Row 10 is reproduced below for your convenience.

(*n*) Periods	5%	6%	8%	9%	10%	11%	12%	15%
10	7.72173	7.36009	6.71008	6.41766	6.14457	5.88923	5.65022	**5.01877**

TABLE 2
PRESENT VALUE OF AN ANNUITY OF 1

In this case, the closest discount factor to 5.0 is 5.01877, which represents an interest rate of approximately 15 percent. The rate of return can be further determined by interpolation, but since we are using estimated annual cash flows such precision is seldom required.

---

[2]When annual cash inflows are equal, the internal rate of return factor is the same as the cash payback period.

The internal rate of return that has been determined is then compared to management's required minimum rate of return. The decision rule is: **Accept the project when the internal rate of return is equal to or greater than the required rate of return. Reject the project when the internal rate of return is less than the required rate.** These relationships are shown graphically in Illustration 27-28. Assuming the minimum required rate of return is 10 percent for Tappan Company, the project is acceptable because the 15 percent internal rate of return is greater than the required rate.

The internal rate of return method is widely used in practice. Most managers find the internal rate of return easy to interpret.

Illustration 27-28
Internal rate of return decision criteria

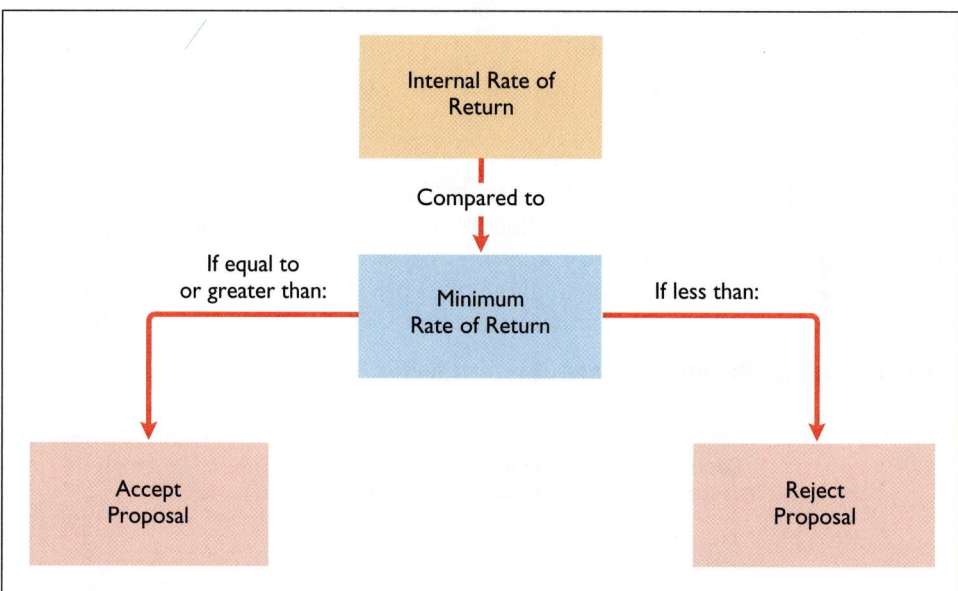

Comparison of Discounted Cash Flow Methods

A comparison of the two discounted cash flow methods—net present value and internal rate of return—is presented in Illustration 27-29. When properly used, either method will provide management with relevant quantitative data for making capital budgeting decisions.

Illustration 27-29
Comparison of discounted cash flow methods

Item	Net Present Value	Internal Rate of Return
1. Objective	Compute net present value (a dollar amount).	Compute internal rate of return (a percentage).
2. Decision rate	If net present value is zero or positive, accept the proposal. If net present value is negative, reject the proposal.	If internal rate of return is equal to or greater than the minimum required rate of return, accept the proposal. If internal rate of return is less than the minimum rate, reject the proposal.

BEFORE YOU GO ON...

Review It

1. What is the formula for and the decision rule in using the annual rate of return method?
2. What is the formula for the cash payback method?

3. When is a proposal acceptable under (a) the net present value method and (b) the internal rate of return method?

4. What does **PepsiCo** report as its capital spending for 2001 and 2002? (See **PepsiCo**'s financial highlights section.) The answer to this question is provided on page 1120.

☑ THE NAVIGATOR

DEMONSTRATION PROBLEM 2

Sierra Company is considering a long-term capital investment project called ZIP. The project will require an investment of $120,000, and it will have a useful life of 4 years. Annual net income for ZIP is expected to be: Year 1, $12,000; Year 2, $10,000; Year 3, $8,000; and Year 4, $6,000. Depreciation is computed by the straight-line method with no salvage value. The company's cost of capital is 12%.

Instructions

(Round all computations to two decimal places.)

(a) Compute the annual rate of return for the project.
(b) Compute the cash payback period for the project. (Round to two decimals.)
(c) Compute the net present value for the project. (Round to nearest dollar.)
(d) Should the project be accepted? Why?

ACTION PLAN

■ To compute annual rate of return, divide expected annual net income by average investment.

■ To compute cash payback, divide cost of the investment by annual cash inflows.

■ Recall that annual cash inflow equals annual net income plus annual depreciation expense.

■ Be careful to use the correct discount factor in using the net present value method.

SOLUTION TO DEMONSTRATION PROBLEM 2

(a) $9,000 ($36,000 ÷ 4) ÷ $60,000 ($120,000 ÷ 2) = 15%
(b) Depreciation expense is $120,000 ÷ 4 years = $30,000.
　　Annual cash inflows are:
　　Year 1　　$12,000 + $30,000 = $42,000
　　Year 2　　$10,000 + $30,000 = $40,000
　　Year 3　　$8,000　+ $30,000 = $38,000
　　Year 4　　$6,000　+ $30,000 = $36,000

　Cumulative cash inflows would be $82,000 ($42,000 + $40,000) at the end of year 2 and $120,000 ($42,000 + $40,000 + $38,000) at the end of year 3. Since the cumulative cash flows at the end of year 3 exactly equal the initial cash investment of $120,000, the cash payback period is 3 years.

(c)

Year	Discount Factor	Cash Inflow	Present Value
1	.89286	$42,000	$ 37,500
2	.79719	40,000	31,888
3	.71178	38,000	27,048
4	.63552	36,000	22,879
			119,315
		Capital investment	120,000
		Negative net present value	$ (685)

(d) The annual rate of return of 15% is good. However, the cash payback period is 75% of the project's useful life, and net present value is negative. The recommendation is to reject the project.

☑ THE NAVIGATOR

SUMMARY OF STUDY OBJECTIVES

1. **Identify the steps in management's decision-making process.** Management's decision-making process consists of (a) identifying the problem or opportunity, (b) assigning responsibility for the decision, (c) determining possible courses of action, (d) developing data relevant to each course of action, (e) making the decision, and (f) reviewing the results of the decision.

2. **Describe the concept of incremental analysis.** Incremental analysis is the process that is used to identify financial data that change under alternative courses of action. These data are relevant to the decision because they will vary in the future among the possible alternatives.

3. **Identify the relevant costs in accepting an order at a special price.** The relevant information in accepting an order at a special price is the difference between the variable manufacturing costs to produce the special order and expected revenues.

4. **Identify the relevant costs in a make-or-buy decision.** In a make-or-buy decision, the relevant costs are (a) the variable manufacturing costs that will be saved, (b) the purchase price, and (c) opportunity costs.

5. **Give the decision rule for whether to sell or process materials further.** The decision rule for whether to sell or process materials further is: Process further as long as the incremental revenue from processing exceeds the incremental processing costs.

6. **Identify the factors to be considered in retaining or replacing equipment.** The factors to be considered in determining whether equipment should be retained or replaced are the effects on variable costs and the cost of the new equipment. Also, any disposal value of the existing asset must be considered.

7. **Explain the relevant factors in deciding whether to eliminate an unprofitable segment.** In deciding whether to eliminate an unprofitable segment, it is necessary to determine the contribution margin, if any, produced by the segment and the disposition of the segment's fixed expenses.

8. **Determine which products to make and sell when resources are limited.** When a company has limited resources, it is necessary to find the contribution margin per unit of limited resource. Then multiply this amount by the units of limited resource to determine which product maximizes net income.

9. **Contrast the annual rate of return and cash payback techniques in capital budgeting.** The annual rate of return is obtained by dividing expected annual net income by the average investment. The higher the rate of return, the more attractive the investment. The cash payback technique identifies the time period to recover the cost of the investment. The formula is: Cost of capital expenditure divided by estimated annual cash inflow equals cash payback period. The shorter the payback period, the more attractive the investment.

10. **Distinguish between the net present value and internal rate of return methods.** Under the net present value method, the present value of future cash inflows is compared with the capital investment to determine net present value. The decision rule is: Accept the project if net present value is zero or positive. Reject the investment if net present value is negative.

    Under the internal rate of return method, the objective is to find the interest yield of the potential investment. The decision rule is: Accept the project when the internal rate of return is equal to or greater than the required rate of return. Reject the project when the internal rate of return is less than the required rate.

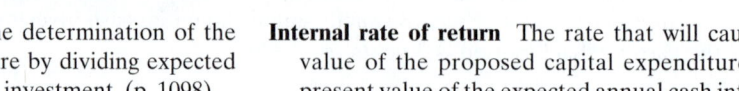

GLOSSARY

Annual rate of return technique The determination of the profitability of a capital expenditure by dividing expected annual net income by the average investment. (p. 1098).

Capital budgeting The process of making capital expenditure decisions in business. (p. 1097).

Cash payback technique A capital budgeting technique that identifies the time period required to recover the cost of a capital investment from the annual cash inflow produced by the investment. (p. 1099).

Cost of capital The rate of return that management expects to pay on all borrowed and equity funds. (p. 1098).

Discounted cash flow technique A capital budgeting technique that considers both the estimated total cash inflows from the investment and the time value of money. (p. 1100).

Incremental analysis The process of identifying the financial data that change under alternative courses of action. (p. 1088).

Internal rate of return The rate that will cause the present value of the proposed capital expenditure to equal the present value of the expected annual cash inflows. (p. 1103).

Internal rate of return method A method used in capital budgeting that results in finding the interest yield of the potential investment. (p. 1103).

Net present value The difference that results when the original capital outlay is subtracted from the discounted cash inflows. (p. 1100).

Net present value method A method used in capital budgeting in which cash inflows are discounted to their present value and then compared to the capital outlay required by the investment. (p. 1100).

Opportunity cost The potential benefit that may be obtained from following an alternative course of action. (p. 1091).

Sunk cost A cost that cannot be changed by any present or future decision. (p. 1093).

SELF-STUDY QUESTIONS

Answers are at the end of the chapter.

(SO 1) **1.** Three of the steps in management's decision process are: (1) Review results of decision. (2) Develop data relevant to each course of action. (3) Make the decision. The steps are performed in the following order.
   a. (1), (2), (3).
   b. (3), (2), (1).
   c. (2), (1), (3).
   d. (2), (3), (1).

(SO 2) **2.** Incremental analysis is the process of identifying the financial data that:
   a. do not change under alternative courses of action.
   b. change under alternative courses of action.
   c. are mixed under alternative courses of action.
   d. No correct answer is given.

(SO 3) **3.** It costs a company $14 of variable costs and $6 of fixed costs to produce product A that sells for $30. A foreign buyer offers to purchase 3,000 units at $18 each. If the special offer is accepted and produced with unused capacity, net income will:
   a. decrease $6,000.
   b. increase $6,000.
   c. increase $12,000.
   d. increase $9,000.

(SO 4) **4.** In a make-or-buy decision, relevant costs are:
   a. manufacturing costs that will be saved.
   b. the purchase price of the units.
   c. opportunity costs.
   d. all of the above.

(SO 5) **5.** The decision rule in a sell-or-process-further decision is: Process further as long as the incremental revenue from processing exceeds:
   a. incremental processing costs.
   b. variable processing costs.
   c. fixed processing costs.
   d. No correct answer is given.

6. In a decision to retain or replace equipment, the book (SO 6) value of the old equipment is a(n):
   a. opportunity cost.
   b. sunk cost.
   c. incremental cost.
   d. marginal cost.

7. If an unprofitable segment is eliminated: (SO 7)
   a. net income will always increase.
   b. variable expenses of the eliminated segment will have to be absorbed by other segments.
   c. fixed expenses allocated to the eliminated segment will have to be absorbed by other segments.
   d. net income will always decrease.

8. If the contribution margin per unit is $15 and it takes 3.0 (SO 8) machine hours to produce the unit, the contribution margin per unit of limited resource is:
   a. $25.
   b. $5.
   c. $45.
   d. No correct answer is given.

9. Which of the following is *incorrect* about the annual rate (SO 9) of return technique?
   a. The calculation is simple.
   b. The accounting terms used are familiar to management.
   c. The timing of the cash inflows is not considered.
   d. The time value of money is considered.

10. A positive net present value means that the: (SO 10)
   a. project's rate of return is less than the cutoff rate.
   b. project's rate of return exceeds the required rate of return.
   c. project's rate of return equals the required rate of return.
   d. project is unacceptable.

QUESTIONS

1. What steps are frequently involved in management's decision-making process?

2. Your roommate, Larry Hook, contends that accounting contributes to most of the steps in management's decision-making process. Is your roommate correct? Explain.

3. "Incremental analysis involves the accumulation of information concerning a single course of action. "Do you agree? Why?

4. Trent Webb asks your help concerning the relevance of variable and fixed costs in incremental analysis. Help Trent with his problem.

5. What data are relevant in deciding whether to accept an order at a special price?

6. Weston Company has an opportunity to buy parts at $7 each that currently cost $10 to make. What manufacturing costs are relevant to this make-or-buy decision?

7. Define the term "opportunity cost." How may this cost be relevant in a make-or-buy decision?

8. What is the decision rule in deciding whether to sell a product or process it further?

9. Your roommate, Shelly Harris, is confused about sunk costs. Explain to your roommate the meaning of sunk costs and their relevance to a decision to retain or replace equipment.

10. Privat Inc. has one product line that is unprofitable. What circumstances may cause overall company net income to be lower if the unprofitable product line is eliminated?

11. How is the contribution margin per unit of limited resources computed?

12. Describe the process a company may use in screening and approving the capital expenditure budget.

13. Your classmate, Grace Carson, is confused about the factors that are included in the annual rate of return technique. What is the formula for this technique?

14. Manny Gomez is trying to understand the term "cost of capital." Define the term, and indicate its relevance to the decision rule under the annual rate of return technique.

15. Will Truman claims the formula for the cash payback technique is the same as the formula for the annual rate of return technique. Is Will correct? What is the formula for the cash payback technique?

16. What are the advantages and disadvantages of the cash payback technique?

17. Two types of present value tables may be used with the discounted cash flow technique. Identify the tables and the circumstance(s) when each table should be used.

18. What is the decision rule under the net present value method?

19. Identify the steps required in using the internal rate of return method.

20. Cartwright Company uses the internal rate of return method. What is the decision rule for this method?

BRIEF EXERCISES

Identify the steps in management's decision-making process.

(SO 1)

BE27-1 The steps in management's decision-making process are listed in random order below. Indicate the order in which the steps should be executed.

___ Make a decision.
___ Identify the problem and assign responsibility.
___ Review results of the decision.
___ Determine and evaluate possible courses of action.

Determine incremental changes.

(SO, 2)

BE27-2 Chen Company is considering two alternatives. Alternative A will have sales of $150,000 and costs of $100,000. Alternative B will have sales of $180,000 and costs of $125,000. Compare Alternative A to Alternative B showing incremental revenues, costs, and net income.

Determine whether to accept a special order.

(SO 3)

BE27-3 In Appolo Company it costs $30 per unit ($20 variable and $10 fixed) to make a product that normally sells for $45. A foreign wholesaler offers to buy 4,000 units at $22 each. Appolo will incur special shipping costs of $1 per unit. Assuming that Appolo has excess operating capacity, indicate the net income (loss) Appolo would realize by accepting the special order.

Determine whether to make or buy a part.

(SO 4)

BE27-4 Dearing Manufacturing incurs unit costs of $8 ($5 variable and $3 fixed) in making a sub-assembly part for its finished product. A supplier offers to make 10,000 of the part at $5.50 per unit. If the offer is accepted, Dearing will save all variable costs but no fixed costs. Prepare an analysis showing the total cost saving, if any, Dearing will realize by buying the part.

Determine whether to sell or process further.

(SO 5)

BE27-5 Hawkins Inc. makes unfinished bookcases that it sells for $60. Production costs are $30 variable and $10 fixed. Because it has unused capacity, Hawkins is considering finishing the bookcases and selling them for $72. Variable finishing costs are expected to be $6 per unit with no increase in fixed costs. Prepare an analysis on a per unit basis showing whether Hawkins should sell unfinished or finished bookcases.

Determine whether to retain or replace equipment.

(SO 6)

BE27-6 Roscoe Company has a factory machine with a book value of $90,000 and a remaining useful life of 4 years. A new machine is available at a cost of $200,000. This machine will have a 4-year useful life with no salvage value. The new machine will lower annual variable manufacturing costs from $600,000 to $480,000. Prepare an analysis showing whether the old machine should be retained or replaced.

Determine whether to eliminate an unprofitable segment.

(SO 7)

BE27-7 Handy, Inc. manufactures golf clubs in three models. For the year, the Eagle line has a net loss of $20,000 from sales $200,000, variable expenses $180,000, and fixed expenses $40,000. If the Eagle line is eliminated, $30,000 of fixed costs will remain. Prepare an analysis showing whether the Eagle line should be eliminated.

Show allocation of limited resources.

(SO 8)

BE27-8 In Parker Company, data concerning two products are: Contribution margin per unit—Product A $10, Product B $12; machine hours required for one unit—Product A 2, Product B 2.5. Compute the contribution margin per unit of limited resource for each product.

Compute the cash payback period for a capital investment.

(SO 9)

BE27-9 Burns Company is considering purchasing new equipment for $400,000. It is expected that the equipment will produce annual net income of $10,000 over its 10-year useful life. Annual depreciation will be $40,000. Compute the payback period.

BE27-10 Purdy Company accumulates the following data concerning a proposed capital investment: cash cost $225,000, annual cash inflow $36,000, present value factor of cash inflows for 10 years 6.71 (rounded). Determine the net present value, and indicate whether the investment should be made.

Compute net present value of an investment.

(SO 10)

EXERCISES

E27-1 Yanu Company manufactures toasters. For the first 8 months of 2006, the company reported the following operating results while operating at 75% of plant capacity.

Make incremental analysis for special order.

(SO 3)

Sales (400,000 units)	$4,000,000
Cost of goods sold	2,400,000
Gross profit	1,600,000
Operating expenses	900,000
Net income	$ 700,000

Cost of goods sold was 70% variable and 30% fixed. Operating expenses were 60% variable and 40% fixed.

In September, Yanu Company receives a special order for 20,000 toasters at $6.00 each from Alazar Company of Mexico City. Acceptance of the order would result in $5,000 of shipping costs but no increase in fixed operating expenses.

Instructions
(a) Prepare an incremental analysis for the special order.
(b) ▭▭▭▷ Should Yanu Company accept the special order? Why or why not?

E27-2 Maxwell Inc. has been manufacturing its own shades for its table lamps. The company is currently operating at 100% of capacity. Variable manufacturing overhead is charged to production at the rate of 50% of direct labor cost. The direct materials and direct labor cost per unit to make the lamp shades are $4.00 and $6.00, respectively. Normal production is 50,000 table lamps per year.

Make incremental analysis for make-or-buy decision.

(SO 4)

A supplier offers to make the lamp shades at a price of $13.60 per unit. If Maxwell Inc. accepts the supplier's offer, all variable manufacturing costs will be eliminated, but the $40,000 of fixed manufacturing overhead currently being charged to the lamp shades will have to be absorbed by other products.

Instructions
(a) Prepare the incremental analysis for the decision to make or buy the lamp shades.
(b) ▭▭▭▷ Should Maxwell Inc. buy the lamp shades?
(c) ▭▭▭▷ Would your answer be different in (b) if the productive capacity released by not making the lamp shades could be used to produce income of $35,000?

E27-3 Mandy McGuire recently opened her own basketweaving studio. She sells finished baskets in addition to the raw materials needed by customers to weave baskets of their own. Mandy has put together a variety of raw material kits, each including materials at various stages of completion. Unfortunately, owing to space limitations, Mandy is unable to carry all varieties of kits originally assembled and must choose between two basic packages.

Make incremental analysis for further processing of materials.

(SO 5)

The basic introductory kit includes undyed, uncut reeds (with dye included) for weaving one basket. This basic package costs Mandy $12 and sells for $27. The second kit, called Stage 2, includes cut reeds that have already been dyed. With this kit the customer need only soak the reeds and weave the basket. Mandy is able to produce the second kit by using the basic materials included in the first kit and adding one hour of her own time (to produce two kits), which she values at $20 per hour. Because she is more efficient at cutting and dying reeds than her average customer, Mandy is able to make two kits of the dyed reeds, in one hour, from one kit of undyed reeds. The kit of dyed and cut reeds sells for $36.

Instructions
Determine whether Mandy's basketweaving shop should carry the basic introductory kit with undyed and uncut reeds, or the Stage 2 kit with reeds already dyed and cut. Prepare an incremental analysis to support your answer.

Make incremental analysis for retaining or replacing equipment.

(SO 6)

E27-4 Newby Enterprises uses a word processing computer to handle its sales invoices. Lately, business has been so good that it takes an extra 3 hours per night, plus every third Saturday, to keep up with the volume of sales invoices. Management is considering updating its computer with a faster model that would eliminate all of the overtime processing.

	Current Machine	**New Machine**
Original purchase cost	$15,000	$21,000
Accumulated depreciation	6,000	—
Estimated operating costs	24,000	19,000
Useful life	5 years	5 years

If sold now, the current machine would have a salvage value of $3,000. If operated for the remainder of its useful life, the current machine would have zero salvage value. The new machine is expected to have zero salvage value after 5 years.

Instructions

Should the current machine be replaced? (Ignore the time value of money.)

Make incremental analysis concerning elimination of division.

(SO 7)

E27-5 Barb Newell, a recent graduate of Rolling's accounting program, evaluated the operating performance of Renfro Company's six divisions. Barb made the following presentation to Renfro Board of Directors and suggested the Ketchum Division be eliminated. "If the Ketchum Division is eliminated," she said, "our total profits would increase by $16,870."

	The Other Five Divisions	**Ketchum Division**	**Total**
Sales	$1,664,200	$ 98,200	$1,762,400
Cost of goods sold	978,520	76,470	1,054,990
Gross profit	685,680	21,730	707,410
Operating expenses	527,940	38,600	566,540
Net income	$ 157,740	$(16,870)	$ 140,870

In the Ketchum Division, cost of goods sold is $58,000 variable and $18,470 fixed, and operating expenses are $14,000 variable and $24,600 fixed. None of the Ketchum Division's fixed costs will be eliminated if the division is discontinued.

Instructions

Is Barb right about eliminating the Ketchum Division? Prepare a schedule to support your answer.

Compute contribution margin and determine the product to be manufactured.

(SO 8)

E27-6 Carsen Company manufactures and sells three products. Relevant per unit data concerning each product are given below.

	Product		
	A	**B**	**C**
Selling price	$10	$12	$14
Variable costs and expenses	$ 4	$ 8	$ 9
Machine hours to produce	2	1	2

Instructions

(a) Compute the contribution margin per unit of the limited resource (machine hour) for each product.

(b) Assuming 3,000 additional machine hours are available, which product should be manufactured?

(c) Prepare an analysis showing the total contribution margin if the additional hours are (1) divided equally among the products, and (2) allocated entirely to the product identified in (b) above.

E27-7 Billings Service Center just purchased an automobile hoist for $13,000. The hoist has a 5-year life and an estimated salvage value of $960. Installation costs were $2,900, and freight charges were $740. Billings uses straight-line depreciation.

The new hoist will be used to replace mufflers and tires on automobiles. Billings estimates that the new hoist will enable his mechanics to replace four extra mufflers per week. Each muffler sells for $65 installed. The cost of a muffler is $35, and the labor cost to install a muffler is $10.

Compute cash payback period and annual rate of return.

(SO 9)

Instructions
(a) Compute the payback period for the new hoist.
(b) Compute the annual rate of return for the new hoist. (Round to one decimal.)

E27-8 Nakoma Manufacturing Company is considering three new projects, each requiring an equipment investment of $21,000. Each project will last for 3 years and produce the following cash inflows.

Compute cash payback period and net present value.

(SO 9, 10)

Year	AA	BB	CC
1	$ 7,000	$ 9,500	$13,000
2	9,000	9,500	10,000
3	15,000	9,500	11,000
Total	$31,000	$28,500	$34,000

The equipment's salvage value is zero. Nakoma uses straight-line depreciation. Nakoma will not accept any project with a payback period over 2 years. Nakoma's minimum required rate of return is 12%.

Instructions
(a) Compute each project's payback period, indicating the most desirable project and the least desirable project using this method. (Round to two decimals.)
(b) Compute the net present value of each project. Does your evaluation change? (Round to nearest dollar.)

E27-9 Costello Company is considering a capital investment of $150,000 in additional productive facilities. The new machinery is expected to have a useful life of 5 years with no salvage value. Depreciation is by the straight-line method. During the life of the investment, annual net income and cash inflows are expected to be $15,000 and $45,000, respectively. Costello has a 12% cost of capital rate, which is the minimum acceptable rate of return on the investment.

Compute annual rate of return, cash payback period, and net present value.

(SO 9, 10)

Instructions
(Round to two decimals.)
(a) Compute (1) the annual rate of return and (2) the cash payback period on the proposed capital expenditure.
(b) Using the discounted cash flow technique, compute the net present value.

E27-10 Alpha Company is considering three capital expenditure projects. Relevant data for the projects are as follows.

Determine internal rate of return.

(SO 10)

Project	Investment	Annual Income	Life of Project
22A	$240,000	$13,300	6 years
23A	270,000	19,000	9 years
24A	288,000	18,400	8 years

Annual income is constant over the life of the project. Each project is expected to have zero salvage value at the end of the project. Alpha Company uses the straight-line method of depreciation.

Instructions
(a) Determine the internal rate of return for each project. Round the internal rate of return factor to three decimals.
(b) If Alpha Company's minimum required rate of return is 10%, which projects are acceptable?

PROBLEMS: SET A

Make incremental analysis for special order, and identify non-financial factors in decision.

(SO 3)

P27-1A Hi-Tech Inc. manufactures basketballs for the National Basketball Association (NBA). For the first 6 months of 2006, the company reported the following operating results while operating at 90% of plant capacity.

	Amount	Per Unit
Sales	$4,500,000	$50.00
Cost of goods sold	3,600,000	40.00
Selling and administrative expenses	360,000	4.00
Net income	$ 540,000	$ 6.00

Fixed costs for the period were: Cost of goods sold $900,000, and selling and administrative expenses $135,000.

In July, normally a slack manufacturing month, Hi-Tech receives a special order for 8,000 basketballs at $35 each from the Italian Basketball Association (IBA). Acceptance of the order would increase variable selling and administrative expenses $0.50 per unit because of shipping costs but would not increase fixed costs and expenses.

Instructions
(a) Prepare an incremental analysis for the special order.
(b) Should Hi-Tech Inc. accept the special order?
(c) What is the minimum selling price on the special order to produce net income of $3.00 per ball?
(d) ▭▭▭▭▷ What nonfinancial factors should management consider in making its decision?

Make incremental analysis related to make or buy; consider opportunity cost, and identify nonfinancial factors.

(SO 4)

P27-2A The management of Sycamore Manufacturing Company is trying to decide whether to continue manufacturing a part or to buy it from an outside supplier. The part, called WISCO, is a component of the company's finished product.

The following information was collected from the accounting records and production data for the year ending December 31, 2006.

1. 9,000 units of WISCO were produced in the Machining Department.
2. Variable manufacturing costs applicable to the production of each WISCO unit were: direct materials $4.75, direct labor $4.80, indirect labor $0.45, utilities $0.35.
3. Fixed manufacturing costs applicable to the production of WISCO were:

Cost Item	Direct	Allocated
Depreciation	$1,600	$ 900
Property taxes	400	200
Insurance	900	600
	$2,900	$1,700

All variable manufacturing and direct fixed costs will be eliminated if WISCO is purchased. Allocated costs will have to be absorbed by other production departments.
4. The lowest quotation for 9,000 WISCO units from a supplier is $99,000.
5. If WISCO units are purchased, freight and inspection costs would be $0.30 per unit, and receiving costs totaling $750 per year would be incurred by the Machining Department.

Instructions
(a) Prepare an incremental analysis for WISCO. Your analysis should have columns for (1) Make WISCO, (2) Buy WISCO, and (3) Net Income Increase/Decrease.
(b) Based on your analysis, what decision should management make?
(c) Would the decision be different if Sycamore Company has the opportunity to produce $8,000 of net income with the facilities currently being used to manufacture WISCO? Show computations.
(d) ▭▭▭▭▷ What nonfinancial factors should management consider in making its decision?

P27-3A Scott Manufacturing Company has four operating divisions. During the first quarter of 2006, the company reported aggregate income from operations of $155,000 and the following divisional results.

Compute contribution margin, and prepare incremental analysis concerning elimination of divisions.

(SO 7)

	Division			
	I	**II**	**III**	**IV**
Sales	$490,000	$410,000	$ 295,000	$195,000
Cost of goods sold	300,000	250,000	270,000	180,000
Selling and administrative expenses	60,000	80,000	35,000	60,000
Income (loss) from operations	$130,000	$ 80,000	$ (10,000)	$(45,000)

Analysis reveals the following percentages of variable costs in each division.

	I	**II**	**III**	**IV**
Cost of goods sold	70%	80%	75%	90%
Selling and administrative expenses	40	50	60	70

Discontinuance of any division would save 50% of the fixed costs and expenses for that division.
    Top management is very concerned about the unprofitable divisions (III and IV). Consensus is that one or both of the divisions should be discontinued.

Instructions
(a) Compute the contribution margin for Divisions III and IV.
(b) Prepare an incremental analysis concerning the possible discontinuance of (1) Division III and (2) Division IV. What course of action do you recommend for each division?
(c) Prepare a columnar condensed income statement for Scott Manufacturing, assuming Division IV is eliminated. Use the CVP format. Division IV's unavoidable fixed costs are allocated equally to the continuing divisions.
(d) Reconcile the total income from operations ($155,000) with the total income from operations without Division IV.

P27-4A Nimitz Corporation is considering three long-term capital investment proposals. Each investment has a useful life of 5 years. Relevant data on each project are as follows.

Compute annual rate of return, cash payback, and net present value.

(SO 9, 10)

	Project Tic	**Project Tac**	**Project Toe**
Capital investment	$150,000	$160,000	$200,000
Annual net income:			
Year 1	13,000	18,000	27,000
2	13,000	17,000	22,000
3	13,000	16,000	21,000
4	13,000	12,000	13,000
5	13,000	9,000	12,000
Total	$ 65,000	$ 72,000	$ 95,000

Depreciation is computed by the straight-line method with no salvage value. The company's cost of capital is 15%.

Instructions
(a) Compute the annual rate of return for each project. (Round to two decimals.)
(b) Compute the cash payback period for each project. (Round to two decimals.)
(c) Compute the net present value for each project. (Round to nearest dollar.)
(d) Rank the projects on each of the foregoing bases. Which project do you recommend?

P27-5A Angie Sheeley is an accounting major at a midwestern state university located approximately 60 miles from a major city. Many of the students attending the university are from the metropolitan area and visit their homes regularly on the weekends. Angie, an entrepreneur at heart, realizes that few good commuting alternatives are available for students doing weekend travel. She believes that a weekend commuting service could be organized

Compute annual rate of return, cash payback, and net present value.

(SO, 9, 10)

and run profitably from several suburban and downtown shopping mall locations. Angie has gathered the following investment information.

1. Six used vans would cost a total of $90,000 to purchase and would have a 3-year useful life with negligible salvage value. Angie plans to use straight-line depreciation.
2. Ten drivers would have to be employed at a total payroll expense of $65,000.
3. Other annual out of pocket expenses associated with running the commuter service would include Gasoline $12,000, Maintenance $2,800, Repairs $3,500, Insurance $3,200, Advertising $1,500. (Exclude interest expense.)
4. Angie has visited several financial institutions to discuss funding for her new venture. The best interest rate she has been able to negotiate is 10%. Use this rate for cost of capital.
5. Angie expects each van to make nine round trips weekly and carry an average of five students each trip. The service is expected to operate 30 weeks each years. Each student will be charged $15.00 for a round-trip ticket.

Instructions
(a) Determine the annual (1) net income, and (2) cash inflow for the commuter service.
(b) Compute (1) the annual rate of return, and (2) the cash payback period. (Round to two decimals.)
(c) Compute the net present value of the commuter service. (Round to the nearest dollar.)
(d) ▭▭▭▷ What should Angie conclude from these computations?

PROBLEMS: SET B

Make incremental analysis for special order, and identify non-financial factors in decisions.

(SO 3)

P27-1B Lotto Company is currently producing 20,000 units per month, which is 80% of its production capacity. Variable manufacturing costs are currently $8.00 per unit. Fixed manufacturing costs are $50,000 per month. Lotto pays a 9% sales commission to its sales people, has $30,000 in fixed administrative expenses per month, and is averaging $320,000 in sales per month.

A special order received from a foreign company would enable Lotto Company to operate at 100% capacity. The foreign company offered to pay 75% of Lotto's current selling price per unit. If the order is accepted, Lotto will have to spend an extra $2.00 per unit to package the product for overseas shipping. Also, Lotto Company would need to lease a new stamping machine to imprint the foreign company's logo on the product, at a monthly cost of $2,500. The special order would require a sales commission of $3,000.

Instructions
(a) Compute the number of units involved in the special order and the foreign company's offered price per unit.
(b) What is the manufacturing cost of producing one unit of Lotto's product for regular customers?
(c) Prepare an incremental analysis of the special order. Should management accept the order?
(d) What is the lowest price that Lotto could accept for the special order to earn net income of $1.20 per unit?
(e) ▭▭▭▷ What nonfinancial factors should management consider in making its decision?

Make incremental analysis related to make or buy; consider opportunity cost, and identify nonfinancial factors.

(SO 4)

P27-2B The management of Gonzalez Manufacturing Company has asked for your assistance in deciding whether to continue manufacturing a part or to buy it from an outside supplier. The part, called Tropica, is a component of Gonzalez's finished product.

An analysis of the accounting records and the production data revealed the following information for the year ending December 31, 2005.

1. The Machinery Department produced 48,000 units of Tropica.
2. Each Tropica unit requires 10 minutes to produce. Four people in the Machinery Department work full time (2,000 hours per year) producing Tropica. Each person is paid $11.00 per hour.
3. The cost of materials per Tropica unit is $2.00.
4. Manufacturing costs directly applicable to the production of Tropica are: indirect labor, $5,500; utilities, $1,300; depreciation, $1,600; property taxes and insurance, $1,000. All of the costs will be eliminated if Tropica is purchased.

5. The lowest price for a Tropica from an outside supplier is $3.80 per unit. Freight charges will be $0.30 per unit, and a part-time receiving clerk at $8,500 per year will be required.

6. If Tropica is purchased, the excess space will be used to store Gonzalez's finished product. Currently, Gonzalez rents storage space at approximately $0.60 per unit stored per year. Approximately 6,000 units per year are stored in the rented space.

Instructions

(a) Prepare an incremental analysis for the make-or-buy decision. Should Gonzalez make or buy the part? Why?

(b) Prepare an incremental analysis, assuming the released facilities can be used to produce $10,000 of net income in addition to the savings on the rental of storage space. What decision should now be made?

(c) ▣▤▭▷ What nonfinancial factors should be considered in the decision?

P27-3B Konerko Manufacturing Company has four operating divisions. During the first quarter of 2005 the company reported total income from operations of $61,000 and the following results for the divisions.

Compute contribution margin, and prepare incremental analysis concerning elimination of divisions.

(SO 7)

	Division			
	Denver	**Miami**	**San Diego**	**Tacoma**
Sales	$445,000	$730,000	$920,000	$525,000
Cost of goods sold	380,000	480,000	576,000	430,000
Selling and administrative expenses	120,000	207,000	246,000	120,000
Income (loss) from operations	$ (55,000)	$ 43,000	$ 98,000	$ (25,000)

Analysis reveals the following percentages of variable costs in each division.

	Denver	**Miami**	**San Diego**	**Tacoma**
Cost of goods sold	95%	80%	90%	90%
Selling and administrative expenses	80	60	70	60

Discontinuance of any division would save 60% of the fixed costs and expenses for that division.

Top management is deeply concerned about the unprofitable divisions (Denver and Tacoma). The consensus is that one or both of the divisions should be eliminated.

Instructions

(a) Compute the contribution margin for the two unprofitable divisions.

(b) Prepare an incremental analysis concerning the possible elimination of (1) the Denver Division and (2) the Tacoma Division. What course of action do you recommend for each division?

(c) Prepare a columnar condensed income statement using the CVP format for Konerko Manufacturing Company, assuming (1) the Denver Division is eliminated, and (2) the unavoidable fixed costs and expenses of the Denver Division are allocated 30% to Miami, 50% to San Diego, and 20% to Tacoma.

(d) Compare the total income from operations with the Denver Division ($61,000) to total income from operations without this division.

P27-4B Quarles Corporation is considering three long-term capital investment proposals. Relevant data on each project are as follows.

Compute annual rate of return, cash payback, and net present value.

(SO 9, 10)

	Project		
	Brown	**Red**	**Yellow**
Capital investment	$200,000	$225,000	$250,000
Annual net income:			
Year 1	25,000	20,000	26,000
2	16,000	20,000	24,000
3	13,000	20,000	23,000
4	10,000	20,000	22,000
5	8,000	20,000	20,000
Total	$ 72,000	$100,000	$115,000

Salvage value is expected to be zero at the end of each project. Depreciation is computed by the straight-line method. The company's minimum rate of return is the company's cost of capital which is 12%.

Instructions
(a) Compute the average annual rate of return for each project. (Round to two decimals.)
(b) Compute the cash payback period for each project. (Round to two decimals.)
(c) Compute the net present value for each project. (Round to nearest dollar.)
(d) Rank the projects on each of the foregoing bases. Which project do you recommend?

Compute annual rate of return, cash payback, and net present value.

(SO 9, 10)

P27-5B Vicky Bunker managing director of the Emporia Day Care Center. Emporia is currently set up as a full-time child care facility for children between the ages of 12 months and 6 years. Vicky is trying to determine whether the center should expand its facilities to incorporate a newborn care room for infants between the ages of 6 weeks and 12 months. The necessary space already exists. An investment of $25,000 would be needed, however, to purchase cribs, high chairs, etc. The equipment purchased for the room would have a 5-year useful life with zero salvage value.

The newborn nursery would be staffed to handle 12 infants on a full-time basis. The parents of each infant would be charged $175 weekly, and the facility would operate 52 weeks of the year. Staffing the nursery would require two full-time specialists and five part-time assistants at an annual cost of $88,500. Food, diapers, and other miscellaneous supplies are expected to total $14,000 annually.

Instructions
(a) Determine (1) annual net income and (2) cash inflow for the new nursery.
(b) Compute (1) the annual rate of return and (2) the cash payback period for the new nursery. (Round to two decimals.)
(c) Assuming that Emporia can borrow the money needed for expansion at 10%, compute the net present value of the new room. (Round to the nearest dollar.)
(d) ▭▬▭▬▷ What should Vicky conclude from these computations?

COMPREHENSIVE PROBLEM: CHAPTERS 20 TO 27

You would like to start a business manufacturing a unique model of bicycle helmet. In preparation for an interview with the bank to discuss your financing needs, you develop answers to the following questions. A number of assumptions are required; clearly note all assumptions that you make.

Instructions
(a) Identify the types of costs that would likely be involved in making this product.
(b) Set up five columns as indicated.

	Product Costs			
Item	**Direct Materials**	**Direct Labor**	**Manufacturing Overhead**	**Period Costs**

Classify the costs you identified in (a) into the manufacturing cost classifications of product costs (direct materials, direct labor, and manufacturing overhead) and period costs.
(c) Assign hypothetical monthly dollar figures to the costs you identified in (a) and (b).
(d) Assume you have no raw materials or work in process beginning or ending inventories. Prepare a projected cost of goods manufactured schedule for the first month of operations.
(e) Project the number of helmets you expect to produce the first month of operations. Compute the cost to produce one bicycle helmet. Review the result to ensure it is reasonable; if not, return to part (c) and adjust the monthly dollar figures you assigned accordingly.
(f) What type of cost accounting system will you likely use—job order or process costing?
(g) Explain how you would assign costs in either the job order or process costing system you plan to use.
(h) Classify your costs as either variable or fixed costs. For simplicity, assign all costs to either variable or fixed, assuming there are no mixed costs, using the format shown.

Item	**Variable Costs**	**Fixed Costs**	**Total Costs**

(i) Compute the unit variable cost, using the production number you determined in (e).

(j) Project the number of helmets you anticipate selling the first month of operations. Set a unit selling price, and compute both the contribution margin per unit and the contribution margin ratio.

(k) Determine your break-even point in dollars and in units.

(l) Prepare projected operating budgets (sales, production, direct materials, direct labor, manufacturing overhead, selling and administrative expense, and income statement).

Assumptions will be required for each of the following:

Direct materials budget:	Quantity of direct materials required to produce one helmet; cost per unit of quantity; desired ending direct materials (assume none).
Direct labor budget:	Direct labor time required per helmet; direct labor cost per hour.
Budgeted income statement:	Income tax expense is 45% of income from operations.

(m) Prepare a cash budget for the month.

Assume the percentage of sales that will be collected from customers is 75%, and the percentage of direct materials that will be paid in the current month is 75%.

(n) Determine a relevant range of activity, using the number of helmets produced as your activity index. Recast your manufacturing overhead budget into a flexible monthly budget for two additional activity levels.

(o) Identify one potential cause of materials, direct labor, and manufacturing overhead variances for your product.

(p) Assume that you wish to purchase production equipment that costs $720,000. Determine the cash payback period, utilizing the monthly cash flow that you computed in part (m) multiplied by 12 months (for simplicity).

(q) Identify any non-quantitative factors that should be considered before commencing your business venture.

BROADENING YOUR PERSPECTIVE

Group Decision Case

BYP27-1 Constantive Company is considering the purchase of a new machine. The invoice price of the machine is $150,000, freight charges are estimated to be $4,000, and installation costs are expected to be $6,000. Salvage value of the new equipment is expected to be zero after a useful life of 4 years. Existing equipment could be retained and used for an additional 4 years if the new machine is not purchased. At that time, the salvage value of the equipment would be zero. If the new machine is purchased now, the existing machine would be scrapped. Constantive's accountant, Diane Gallup, has accumulated the following data regarding annual sales and expenses with and without the new machine.

1. Without the new machine, Constantive can sell 10,000 units of product annually at a per unit selling price of $100. If the new unit is purchased, the number of units produced and sold would increase by 20%. The selling price would remain the same.

2. The new machine is faster than the old machine, and it is more efficient in its usage of materials. With the old machine the gross profit rate will be 25% of sales. With the new machine the rate will be 28% of sales.

3. Annual selling expenses are $140,000 with the current equipment. Because the new equipment would produce a greater number of units to be sold, annual selling expenses are expected to increase by 10% if it is purchased.

4. Annual administrative expenses are expected to be $100,000 with the old machine and $113,000 with the new machine.

5. The current book value of the existing machine is $36,000. Constantive uses straight-line depreciation.

6. Constantive's management wants a minimum rate of return of 15% on its investment and a payback period of no more than 3 years.

Instructions

With the class divided into groups, answer the following. (Ignore income tax effects.)

(a) Prepare an incremental analysis for the 4 years showing whether Constantive should keep the existing machine or buy the new machine.

(b) Calculate the annual rate of return for the new machine. (Round to two decimals.)

(c) Compute the payback period for the new machine. (Round to two decimals.)

(d) Compute the net present value of the new machine. (Round to the nearest dollar.)

(e) On the basis of the foregoing data, would you recommend that Constantive buy the machine? Why?

Managerial Analysis

BYP27-2 Marino Company manufactures private-label small electronic products, such as alarm clocks, calculators, kitchen timers, stopwatches, and automatic pencil sharpeners. Some of the products are sold as sets, and others are sold individually. Products are studied as to their sales potential, and then cost estimates are made. The Engineering Department develops production plans, and then production begins. The company has generally had very successful product introduction. Only two products introduced by the company have been discontinued.

One of the products currently sold is a multi-alarm alarm clock. The clock has four alarms that can be programmed to sound at various times and for varying lengths of time. The company has experienced a great deal of difficulty in making the circuit boards for the clocks. The production process has never operated smoothly. The product is unprofitable at the present time, primarily because of warranty repairs and product recalls. Two models of the clocks were recalled, for example, because they sometimes caused an electric shock when the alarms were being shut off. The Engineering Department is attempting to revise the manufacturing process, but the revision will take another 6 months at least.

The clocks were very popular when they were introduced, and since they are private-label, the company has not suffered much from the recalls. Presently, the company has a very large order for several items from Kmart Stores. The order includes 5,000 of the multi-alarm clocks. When the company suggested that Kmart purchase the clocks from another manufacturer, Kmart threatened to rescind the entire order unless the clocks were included.

The company has therefore investigated the possibility of having another company make the clocks for them. The clocks were bid for the Kmart order, based on an estimated $5.50 cost to manufacture, as follows.

Circuit board, 1 each @ $1.00	$1.00
Plastic case, 1 each @ $0.50	0.50
Alarms, 4 @ $0.15 each	0.60
Labor, 15 minutes @ $12/hour	3.00
Overhead, $1.60 per labor hour	0.40

Marino could purchase clocks to fill the Kmart order for $10 from Silver Star, a Korean manufacturer with a very good quality record. Silver Star has offered to reduce the price to $7.50 after Marino has been a customer for 6 months, placing an order of at least 1,000 units per month. If Marino becomes a "preferred customer" by purchasing 15,000 units per year, the price would be reduced still further to $4.50.

Alpha Products, a local manufacturer, has also offered to make clocks for Marino. They have offered to sell 5,000 clocks for $3 each. However, Alpha Products has been in business for only 6 months. They have experienced significant turnover in their labor force, and the local media have reported that the owners may soon face tax evasion charges. The owner of Alpha Products is an electronic engineer, however, and the quality of the clocks is likely to be good.

If Marino decides to purchase the clocks from either Silver Star or Alpha, all the costs to manufacturer could be avoided, except a total of $5,000 in overhead costs for machine depreciation. The machinery is fairly new, and has no alternate use.

Instructions

(a) What is the difference in profit under each of the alternatives if the clocks are to be sold for $13.00 each to Kmart?

(b) What are the most important nonfinancial factors that Marino should consider when making this decision?

(c) What should Marino do in regard to the Kmart order? What should it do in regard to continuing to manufacture the multi-alarm alarm clocks? Be prepared to defend your answer.

Real-World Focus

BYP27-3 Founded in 1983, the **Beverly Hills Fan Company** is located in Woodland Hills, California. With 23 employees and sales of less than $10 million, the company is relatively small. Management feels that there is potential for growth in the upscale market for ceiling fans and lighting. They are particularly optimistic about growth in Mexican and Canadian markets.

Presented below is information from the president's letter in the company's annual report.

BEVERLY HILLS FAN COMPANY
President's Letter

An aggressive product development program was initiated during the past year resulting in new ceiling fan models planned for introduction in 1993. Award winning industrial designer Ron Rezek created several new fan models for the Beverly Hills Fan and L.A. Fan lines, including a new Showroom Collection, designed specifically for the architectural and designer markets. Each of these models has received critical acclaim, and order commitments for 1993 have been outstanding. Additionally, our Custom Color and special order fans continued to enjoy increasing popularity and sales gains as more and more customers desire fans that match their specific interior decors. Currently, Beverly Hills Fan Company offers a product line of over 100 models of contemporary, traditional, and transitional ceiling fans.

Instructions

(a) What points did the company management need to consider before deciding to offer the special-order fans to customers?

(b) How would incremental analysis be employed to assist in this decision?

Exploring the Web

BYP27-4 **Campbell Soup Company** is an international provider of soup products. Management is very interested in continuing to grow the company in its core business, while "spinning off" those businesses that are not part of its core operation.

Address: www.campbellsoups.com, or go to www.wiley.com/college/weygandt

Steps

1. Go to the home page of Campbell Soup Company at the address shown above.

2. Choose **Investor Center**.

3. Choose **Financial Reports**.

4. Choose the 2002 annual report, or the current annual report if 2002 is no longer available.

Instructions

Review the financial statements and management's discussion and analysis, and answer the following questions.

(a) What was the total amount reported as "Purchases of Plant Assets" in the 2002 statement of cash flows? How does this amount compare with the previous year?

(b) What range of interest rates does the company report on its long-term liabilities in the notes to its financial statements?

(c) Assume that this year's capital expenditures are expected to increase cash flows by $35 million. What is the expected internal rate of return (IRR) for these capital expenditures? (Assume a 10-year period for the cash flows.)

Communication Activity

BYP27-5 Refer back to Exercise 27-7 to address the following.

Instructions

Prepare a memo to Diane Pepco, your supervisor. Show your calculations from E27-7, parts **(a)** and **(b)**. In one or two paragraphs, discuss important nonfinancial considerations. Make any assumptions you believe to be necessary. Make a recommendation, based on your analysis.

Ethics Case

BYP27-6 Romano Company operates in a state where corporate taxes and workmen's compensation insurance rates have recently doubled. Romano's president has assigned you the task of preparing an economic analysis and making a recommendation about whether to move the company's entire operation to Missouri. The president is slightly in favor of such a move because Missouri is his boyhood home, and he also owns a fishing lodge there.

You have just completed building your dream house, moved in, and sodded the lawn. Your children are all doing well in school and sports and, along with your spouse, want no part of a move to Missouri. If the company does move, so will you because your town is a one-industry community, and you and your spouse will have to move to have employment. Moving when everyone else does will cause you to take a big loss on the sale of your house. The same hardships will be suffered by your coworkers, and the town will be devastated.

In compiling the costs of moving versus not moving, you have latitude in the assumptions you make, the estimates you compute, and the discount rates and time periods you project. You are in a position to influence the decision singlehandedly.

Instructions
(a) Who are the stakeholders in this situation?
(b) What are the ethical issues in this situation?
(c) What would you do in this situation?

Answers to Self-Study Questions
1. d **2.** b **3.** c **4.** d **5.** a **6.** b **7.** c **8.** b **9.** d **10.** b

Answer to PepsiCo Review It Question 4, p. 1105
PepsiCo's capital spending for 2001 is $1,324,000,000 and for 2002 is $1,437,000,000.

Specimen Financial Statements:
PepsiCo, Inc.

THE ANNUAL REPORT

Once each year a corporation communicates to its stockholders and other interested parties by issuing a complete set of audited financial statements. The **annual report**, as this communication is called, summarizes the financial results of its operations for the year and its plans for the future. Many annual reports have become attractive, multicolored, glossy public relations pieces containing pictures of corporate officers and directors as well as photos and descriptions of new products and new buildings. Yet the basic function of every annual report is to report **financial information**, almost all of which is a product of the corporation's accounting system.

The content and organization of corporate annual reports have become fairly standardized. Excluding the public relations part of the report (pictures and products), the following items are the traditional financial portions of the annual report:

Financial Highlights
Letter to the Stockholders
Auditor's Report
Management's Responsibility for Financial Statements
Management Discussion and Analysis
Financial Statements and Accompanying Notes
Five- or Ten-Year Summary

In this appendix we illustrate current financial reporting with a comprehensive set of corporate financial statements. They have been prepared in accordance with generally accepted accounting principles and audited by an international independent certified public accounting firm. We are grateful for permission to use the actual financial statements and other accompanying financial information from the annual report of a large, publicly held company, **PepsiCo, Inc.**

The financial information herein is reprinted with permission from the PepsiCo, Inc. 2002 Annual Report. The complete financial statements are available through a link at the book's companion Web site and with new copies of the textbook.

Financial Highlights

The financial highlights section is usually presented inside the front cover or on the first two pages of the annual report. This section generally reports the total or per share amounts for five to ten financial items for the current year and one or more previous years. Financial items from the income statement and the balance sheet that typically are presented are sales, income from continuing operations, net income, net income per share, dividends per common share, and the amount of capital expenditures. The financial highlights section from PepsiCo's Annual Report is shown below.

Financial Highlights
PepsiCo 2002 and 2001
($ in millions except per share amounts; all per share amounts assume dilution)

	2002	2001	%Chg(a)
Summary of Operations			
Division net sales (b)	**$25,005**	$24,074	4
Division operating profit (b)	**$5,316**	$4,784	11
Net income			
Reported	**$3,313**	$2,662	24
Comparable (c)	**$3,503**	$3,105	13
Net income per common share			
Reported	**$1.85**	$1.47	26
Comparable (c)	**$1.96**	$1.72	14
Other Data			
Net cash provided by operating activities	**$4,627**	$3,820	21
Common share repurchases	**$2,192**	$1,716	28
Dividends paid	**$1,041**	$994	5
Long-term debt	**$2,187**	$2,651	(18)
Capital spending	**$1,437**	$1,324	9

(a) Percentage changes are based on unrounded amounts.

(b) For additional information on net sales and operating profit, see Note 1 to our consolidated financial statements.

(c) Comparable amounts exclude the costs associated with our merger with The Quaker Oats Company and other impairment and restructuring charges. In addition, 2001 amounts reflect the adoption of Statement of Financial Accounting Standards No.142 and the impact of the consolidation of our European snack joint venture as if they had occurred at the beginning of 2001. For additional information on these items, see "Items Affecting Comparability" in Management's Discussion and Analysis. The comparable information does not comply with and should not be considered an alternative to United States Generally Accepted Accounting Principles.

As shown above, PepsiCo chose also to present the percent change from last year to the current year for each of the reported items.

Letter to the Stockholders

Nearly every annual report contains a letter to the stockholders from the Chairman of the Board or the President (or both). This letter typically discusses the company's accomplishments during the past year. It also highlights significant events such as mergers and acquisitions, new products, operating achievements, business philosophy, changes in officers or directors, financing commitments, expansion plans, and future prospects. The first page of the letter to the stockholders signed by Steve Reinemund, President and Chief Executive Officer of PepsiCo, is shown on page A3.

Dear Fellow Shareholders:

I am pleased to report that PepsiCo made solid progress in 2002 and posted strong financial results:

- Reported earnings per share grew 26% and comparable earnings per share grew 14%, as we marked our 13th consecutive quarter of 13%-or-better growth.

- Division operating profit grew 11%.

- Volume and division net sales grew 4%.

- Return on invested capital rose more than 2 points to 28% on a comparable basis.

- Operating cash flow grew 27% to $3.3 billion, after capital spending and contributions to our pension plans.

- We repurchased 53.4 million shares of PepsiCo stock.

- Annual cost savings from the Quaker merger reached approximately $250 million, exceeding our target.

- We gained market share in all our key categories.

We took important steps to strengthen our organization:

- We focused our most senior leaders squarely on our greatest opportunities.

- We moved beyond the boundaries of our traditional product portfolios and ramped up activity at our convenient foods unit to develop products that leverage the brand and distribution strengths of Frito-Lay and Quaker.

- We forged strategic partnerships with respected medical and fitness experts to address growing consumer interest in nutrition and wellness — and named a senior executive to facilitate and advance our efforts.

- We expanded our diversity efforts to include training for every U.S. salaried employee in an effort to make PepsiCo a better workplace and more competitive in the marketplace.

OUR GAME PLAN FOR GROWTH

Steve Reinemund
Chairman and Chief Executive Officer

Auditor's Report

All publicly held corporations, as well as many other enterprises and organizations (both profit and not-for-profit, large and small) engage the services of independent certified public accountants who will provide an objective, expert report on their financial statements. Based on a comprehensive examination of the company's accounting system and records, and of the financial statements, the outside CPA issues the auditor's report.

The standard auditor's report consists of three pieces of information, expressed in separate sentences or paragraphs: (1) a responsibilities statement, (2) a scope statement, and (3) the opinion. In the **responsibilities statement**, the auditor identifies who and what was audited and indicates the responsibilities of management and the auditor relative to the financial statements. In the **scope statement**, the auditor states that the audit was conducted in accordance with generally accepted auditing standards and discusses the nature and limitations of the audit. In the **opinion statement**, the auditor expresses an informed opinion as to (1) the fairness of the financial statements and (2) their conformity with generally accepted accounting principles. The **Report of KPMG, Independent Public Accountants**, appearing in PepsiCo's Annual Report is shown below.

Board of Directors and Shareholders
PepsiCo, Inc.:

We have audited the accompanying Consolidated Balance Sheet of PepsiCo, Inc. and Subsidiaries as of December 28, 2002 and December 29, 2001 and the related Consolidated Statements of Income, Cash Flows and Common Shareholders' Equity for each of the years in the three-year period ended December 28, 2002. These consolidated financial statements are the responsibility of PepsiCo, Inc.'s management. Our responsibility is to express an opinion on these consolidated financial statements based on our audits.

We conducted our audits in accordance with auditing standards generally accepted in the United States of America. Those standards require that we plan and perform the audit to obtain reasonable assurance about whether the financial statements are free of material misstatement. An audit includes examining, on a test basis, evidence supporting the amounts and disclosures in the financial statements. An audit also includes assessing the accounting principles used and significant estimates made by management, as well as evaluating the overall financial statement presentation. We believe that our audits provide a reasonable basis for our opinion.

In our opinion, the consolidated financial statements referred to above present fairly, in all material respects, the financial position of PepsiCo, Inc. and Subsidiaries as of December 28, 2002 and December 29, 2001, and the results of their operations and their cash flows for each of the years in the three-year period ended December 28, 2002, in conformity with accounting principles generally accepted in the United States of America.

As discussed in Note 4 to the consolidated financial statements, PepsiCo, Inc. in 2002 adopted the provisions of the Financial Accounting Standards Board's Statement of Financial Accounting Standard No. 142, "Goodwill and Other Intangible Assets."

KPMG LLP

KPMG LLP
New York, New York
February 6, 2003

The auditor's report issued on PepsiCo's financial statements is **unqualified** or "clean." That is, it contains no qualifications or exceptions. The auditor conformed completely with generally accepted auditing standards in performing the audit, and the financial statements conformed in all material respects with generally accepted accounting principles.

When the financial statements do not conform with generally accepted accounting principles, the auditor must issue a **qualified** opinion and describe the exception. If the lack of conformity with GAAP is sufficiently material, the auditor is compelled to issue an **adverse** or negative opinion. An adverse opinion means that the financial statements do not present fairly the company's financial condition and/or the results of the company's operations at the dates and for the periods reported.

In circumstances where the auditor is unable to perform all the auditing procedures necessary to reach a conclusion as to the fairness of the financial statements, a **disclaimer** must be issued. In these rare instances, the auditor must report the reason for failure to reach a conclusion on the fairness of the financial statements.

Companies strive to obtain an unqualified auditor's report. Hence, only infrequently are you likely to encounter anything other than this type of opinion on the financial statements.

Management's Responsibility for Financial Statements

A relatively recent addition to corporate annual reports is the statement made by management about its role in and responsibility for the accuracy and integrity of the financial statements. PepsiCo's management letter is entitled **Management's Responsibility for Financial Statements**. In it, the Chairman of the Board along with the President and Chief Financial Officer, and Senior Vice President and Controller on behalf of management, do the following: They (1) assume primary responsibility for the financial statements and the related notes, (2) declare the financial statements in conformity with generally accepted accounting principles, (3) comment on the audit by the certified public accountant, (4) outline and assess the company's internal control system, and (5) disclose the composition and role of the Audit Committee of the Board of Directors. PepsiCo's management report is presented below.

MANAGEMENT'S RESPONSIBILITY FOR FINANCIAL STATEMENTS

To Our Shareholders:

Management is responsible for the reliability of the consolidated financial statements and related notes. The financial statements were prepared in conformity with generally accepted accounting principles and include amounts based upon our estimates and assumptions, as required. The financial statements have been audited by our independent auditors, KPMG LLP, who were given free access to all financial records and related data, including minutes of the meetings of the Board of Directors and Committees of the Board. We believe that our representations to the independent auditors are valid and appropriate.

Management maintains a system of internal controls designed to provide reasonable assurance as to the reliability of the financial statements, as well as to safeguard assets from unauthorized use or disposition. The system is supported by formal policies and procedures, including an active Code of Conduct program intended to ensure employees adhere to the highest standards of personal and professional integrity. Our internal audit function monitors and reports on the adequacy of and compliance with the internal control system, and appropriate actions are taken to address significant control deficiencies and other opportunities for improving the system as they are identified. The Audit Committee of the Board of Directors consists solely of directors who are not salaried employees and who are, in the opinion of the Board of Directors, free from any relationship that would interfere with the exercise of independent judgment as a committee member. The Committee meets during the year with representatives of management, including internal auditors and the independent auditors to review our financial reporting process and our controls to safeguard assets. Both our independent auditors and internal auditors have free access to the Audit Committee.

Although no cost-effective internal control system will preclude all errors and irregularities, we believe our controls as of December 28, 2002 provide reasonable assurance that the financial statements are reliable and that our assets are reasonably safeguarded.

Peter Bridgman

Peter A. Bridgman
Senior Vice President and Controller

Indra Nooyi

Indra K. Nooyi
President and Chief Financial Officer

Steven S Reinemund

Steven S Reinemund
Chairman of the Board and Chief Executive Officer

Management's Discussion and Analysis

The **management's discussion and analysis (MD&A)** section covers three financial aspects of a company: its results of operations, its ability to pay near-term obligations, and its ability to fund operations and expansion. Management must highlight favorable or unfavorable trends and identify significant events and uncertainties that affect these three factors. This discussion obviously involves a number of subjective estimates and opinions. The MD&A section of PepsiCo's annual report is presented on the following pages.

MANAGEMENT'S DISCUSSION AND ANALYSIS AND CONSOLIDATED FINANCIAL STATEMENTS

[We have extracted from Management's Discussion and Analysis two items: (1) "OUR BUSINESS," consisting of "Our Operations," "Our Customers," "Our Distribution Network," "Our Competition," and "Our Market Risks"; and (2) "RESULTS OF OPERATIONS—DIVISION REVIEW," consisting of analyses of results of operations by divisions and product lines. To read this extracted material, go to PepsiCo's hard-copy 2002 Annual Report or the textbook's Web site.]

CAUTIONARY STATEMENTS

We discuss expectations regarding our future performance, such as our business outlook, in our annual and quarterly reports, press releases, and other written and oral statements. These "forward-looking statements" are based on currently available competitive, financial and economic data and our operating plans. They are inherently uncertain, and investors must recognize that events could turn out to be significantly different from our expectations.

You should consider the following key factors when evaluating our trends and future results:
- continued demand for our products, which is dependent on successful product introductions and other innovations, effectiveness of our sales incentives, advertising campaigns and marketing programs,

seasonal weather conditions, relationships with key customers (including our bottlers), and our response to consumer health concerns and changes in product category consumption;
- competitive product and pricing pressures;
- continued success from our productivity initiatives, which is dependent upon our ability to implement and leverage these programs;
- continued success of acquisition integrations, including our ability to achieve cost savings and revenue enhancement opportunities from the Quaker merger;
- unforeseen economic changes and political unrest, which may result in business interruption, foreign currency devaluation, inflation,

deflation and decreased demand, particularly in areas outside North America, such as in Latin America and the Middle East;
- maintenance of our profit margin in the face of a consolidating retail environment;
- changes in laws and regulations, including changes in food and drug laws, accounting standards, taxation requirements (including tax rate changes, new tax laws and revised tax law interpretations) and environmental laws; and
- fluctuations in manufacturing costs and the availability of raw materials.

The discussion of these risks and uncertainties is by no means all inclusive but is designed to highlight what we believe are important factors to consider.

OUR CRITICAL ACCOUNTING POLICIES

An understanding of our accounting policies is necessary to completely analyze our financial results. Our critical accounting policies require management to make difficult and subjective judgments regarding uncertainties. As a result, estimates are included in and may significantly impact our financial results. The precision of these estimates and the likelihood of future changes depend on a number of underlying variables and a range of possible outcomes. We applied our estimation methods consistently in all periods presented.

Our critical accounting policies arise in conjunction with the following:
- revenue recognition,
- brands and goodwill,
- income taxes, and
- pension and retiree medical plans.

REVENUE RECOGNITION

Our products are sold for cash or on credit terms. Our credit terms, which are established in accordance with local and industry practices, typically require payment within 30 days of delivery and may allow discounts for early payment. We recognize revenue upon delivery to our customers in accordance with written sales terms that do not allow for a right of return. However, our policy for direct-store-delivery and chilled products is to remove and replace out-of-date products from store shelves to ensure that consumers receive the product quality and freshness that they expect. Based on our historical experience with this practice, we have reserved for anticipated out-of-date product. Our bottlers have a similar replacement policy and are responsible for our products that they distribute.

We offer sales incentives through various programs to customers, consumers and, for PCNA, directly to certain retailers. Sales incentives are accounted for as a reduction of sales and totaled $5.5 billion in 2002, $4.7 billion in 2001 and $4.3 billion in 2000. A number of these programs, such as bottler funding and customer volume rebates, are based on annual targets, and accruals are established during the year for the expected payout. The accruals are based on our previous experience with similar programs. The terms of most of our incentive arrangements do not exceed a year. However, we have arrangements, such as fountain pouring rights, which extend up to 12 years. Costs incurred to obtain these rights are recognized over the life of the contract as a reduction of sales, and the outstanding balance is included in other assets in our Consolidated Balance Sheet.

We estimate and reserve for our bad debt exposure from credit sales based on our experience. Our method of determining the reserves has not changed during the years presented in the consolidated financial statements. Bad debt expense is classified within selling, general and administrative expenses in our Consolidated Income Statement.

We recognize revenue upon delivery to our customers.

BRANDS AND GOODWILL

We sell products under a number of brand names around the world, many of which were developed by us. The brand development costs are expensed as incurred. We also purchase brands and goodwill in acquisitions. Upon acquisition, the purchase price is first allocated to identifiable assets and liabilities, including brands, based on estimated fair value, with any remaining purchase price recorded as goodwill. Goodwill and perpetual brands are not amortized.

We believe that a brand has an indefinite life if it has significant market share in a stable macroeconomic environment, and a history of strong revenue and cash flow performance that we expect to continue for the foreseeable future. If these perpetual brand criteria are not met, brands are amortized over their expected useful lives, which generally range from five to twenty years. Determining the expected life of a brand requires considerable management judgment and is based on an evaluation of a number of factors, including the competitive environment, market share, brand history and the macroeconomic environment of the country in which the brand is sold.

Perpetual brands and goodwill are assessed for impairment at least annually to ensure that future cash flows continue to exceed the related book value. A perpetual brand is impaired if its book value exceeds its fair value. Goodwill is evaluated for impairment if the book value of its reporting unit exceeds its fair value. A reporting unit can be a division or business. If the fair value of an evaluated asset is less than its book value, the asset is written down based on its discounted future cash flows to fair value.

Amortizable brands are only evaluated for impairment upon a significant change in the operating or macroeco-

The determination of the expected life of our brands is primarily based on:
- **competitive environment,**
- **market share,**
- **brand history, and**
- **macroeconomic environment.**

nomic environment. If an evaluation of the undiscounted cash flows indicates impairment, the asset is written down to its estimated fair value, which is generally based on discounted future cash flows.

Considerable management judgment is necessary to evaluate the impact of operating and macroeconomic changes and to estimate future cash flows. Assumptions used in our impairment evaluations, such as forecasted growth rates and our cost of capital, are consistent with our internal projections and operating plans.

We did not recognize any impairment charges for perpetual brands or goodwill during 2002. As of December 28, 2002, we had over $4 billion of perpetual brands and goodwill, of which 75% related to Tropicana and Walkers. In our most recent impairment evaluations for Tropicana and Walkers, no impairment charges would have resulted even if operating profit growth were assumed to be 5% lower.

> **Over 75% of our perpetual brands and goodwill relate to Tropicana and Walkers.**

INCOME TAXES

Our reported effective tax rate was 31.9% for 2002. Excluding the impact of nondeductible merger-related costs, our effective tax rate was 31.2%. For 2003, our effective tax rate, excluding the impact of nondeductible merger-related costs, is expected to be 30.5%. The decrease from 2002 primarily reflects the impact of our new concentrate plant.

Our effective tax rate is based on expected income, statutory tax rates and tax planning opportunities available to us in the various jurisdictions in which we operate. Significant judgment is required in determining our effective tax rate and in evaluating our tax positions. We establish reserves when, despite our belief that our tax return positions are

> **Our effective tax rate was 31.9% in 2002. Excluding nondeductible merger costs, our effective tax rate was 31.2%.**

> **Our effective tax rate is based on:**
> • **expected income,**
> • **statutory rates, and**
> • **tax planning opportunities.**

fully supportable, we believe that certain positions are likely to be challenged and that we may not succeed. We adjust these reserves in light of changing facts and circumstances, such as the progress of a tax audit. Our effective tax rate includes the impact of reserve provisions and changes to reserves that we consider appropriate, as well as related interest. This rate is then applied to our quarterly operating results. In the event that there is a significant unusual or one-time item recognized in our operating results, the tax attributable to that item would be separately calculated and recorded at the same time as the unusual or one-time item. We consider the Quaker merger-related costs to be a significant one-time item.

Tax regulations require items to be included in the tax return at different times than the items are reflected in the financial statements. As a result, our effective tax rate reflected in our financial statements is different than that reported in our tax return. Some of these differences are permanent, such as expenses which are not deductible on our tax return, and some are timing differences, such as depreciation expense. Timing differences create deferred tax assets and liabilities. Deferred tax assets generally represent items that can be used as a tax deduction or credit in our tax return in future years for which we have already recorded the tax benefit in our income statement. We establish valuation allowances for our deferred tax assets when the amount of expected future taxable income is not likely to support the use of the deduction or credit. Deferred tax liabilities generally represent tax expense recognized in our financial statements for which payment has been deferred or expense for which we have already taken a deduction on our tax return, but have not yet recognized as expense in our financial statements. We have not recognized any United States tax expense on undistributed international earnings since we intend to reinvest the earnings outside the United States for the foreseeable future. These undistributed earnings are approximately $7.5 billion at December 28, 2002.

A number of years may elapse before a particular matter, for which we have established a reserve, is audited and finally resolved. The number of years with open tax audits varies depending on the tax jurisdiction. In the United States, the audits for 1991 through 1993 remain open for certain items and the Internal Revenue Service is currently examining our tax returns for 1994 through 1997. While it is often difficult to predict the final outcome or the timing of resolution of any particular tax matter, we believe that our reserves reflect the probable outcome of known tax contingencies. Unfavorable settlement of any particular issue would require use of our cash. Favorable resolution would be recognized as a reduction to our effective tax rate in the year of resolution. Our tax reserves are presented in the balance sheet within other liabilities, except for amounts relating to items we expect to settle in the coming year which are classified as current.

PENSION AND RETIREE MEDICAL PLANS

Our pension plans cover full-time U.S. employees and certain international employees. Benefits are determined based on either years of service or a combination of years of service and earnings. U.S. employees are also eligible for medical and life insurance benefits (retiree medical) if they meet age and service requirements and qualify for retirement benefits. Generally, our retiree medical costs are capped at a specified dollar amount, with retirees contributing the remainder.

The expected benefit to be paid is expensed over the employees' expected service. Management must make many assumptions to determine the expected benefit and expected service, including:

- the interest rate used to determine the present value of liabilities (discount rate),
- the expected return on plan assets for plans funded by us,
- the rate of salary increases for plans where benefits are based on earnings,
- health care cost trend rates for retiree medical plans, and
- certain employee-related factors, such as turnover, retirement age and mortality.

We make contributions to trusts maintained to provide plan benefits for certain pension plans. These contributions are made in accordance with applicable tax regulations that provide for current tax deductions for our contributions and taxation to the employee only upon receipt of plan benefits. We do not generally fund pension plans and retiree medical plans when our contributions would not be tax deductible or when the employee would be taxed prior to receipt of benefit. Pension plan investment guidelines are established based upon an evaluation of market conditions, risk tolerance and plan investment horizon.

Weighted-average assumptions for pension and retiree medical expense:	2003	2002	2001	2000
Pension				
Expense discount rate	6.7%	7.4%	7.7%	7.7%
Expected rate of return on plan assets	8.2%	9.1%	9.8%	9.9%
Rate of salary increases	4.4%	4.4%	4.6%	4.5%
Retiree medical				
Expense discount rate	6.7%	7.5%	7.8%	7.8%

The assets, liabilities and assumptions used to measure pension and retiree medical expense are determined as of September 30 of the preceding year (measurement date). Since the liabilities are measured on a discounted basis, the discount rate is a significant assumption. It is based on interest rates for high-quality, long-term corporate debt at each measurement date. The expected return on pension plan assets is based on our historical experience and our expectations for long-term rates of return. To measure pension expense, we use a calculated value for plan assets which recognizes changes in fair value over five years rather than the current fair value at each measurement date. The other assumptions also reflect our historical experience and management's best judgment regarding future expectations.

Gains and losses resulting from actual experience differing from our assumptions are determined at each measurement date. If the net total gain or loss exceeds 10% of the greater of plan assets or liabilities, a portion of the net gain or loss is included in expense for the next year. The cost or benefit of plan changes, such as increasing or decreasing benefits for prior employee service, is included in expense over the expected service of the employees.

We review our assumptions at least at the annual measurement date. During 2002, we completed a review of our pension investment and funding strategy for our U.S. pension plans. As a result, we revised our U.S. investment allocation to a maximum of 65% equities with the balance in fixed income securities. As a result of the mid-year 2002 investment funding and strategy changes, we remeasured pension expense for our U.S. plans to incorporate a reduction in the rate of return on plan assets to 8.2%, as well as changes to employee-related assumptions based on current data. This mid-year valuation resulted in a weighted average expected return on plan assets for 2002 of 9.1% and increased the balance of year pension expense by $29 million. This increase is reported in Corporate selling, general and administrative expenses.

Health care cost trend rates have an impact on the retiree medical plan expense. A 1 percentage point increase in the assumed health care trend rate would increase the service and interest costs by $4 million for 2003 and a 1 percentage point decrease would reduce these costs by $4 million.

Pension expense for 2003 is estimated to be approximately $160 million and retiree medical expense is estimated to be approximately $120 million compared to 2002 pension expense of $111 million and retiree medical expense of $88 million. These estimates incorporate the 2003 assumptions as well as the impact of the increased pension plan assets resulting from our contributions to funded plans.

- **Pension plans cover full-time U.S. and certain international employees.**
- **The expected benefit to be paid is expensed over the employees' service period.**
- **The assumed rate of return on assets was reduced to 8.2%.**
- **Mid-year 2002 changes resulted in increased pension expense of $29 million.**

ITEMS AFFECTING COMPARABILITY

The year-over-year comparisons of our financial results are affected by the following one-time items and accounting changes:

	2002	2001	2000
Net Sales			
SVE consolidation	–	$706	$648
53rd week in 2000	–	–	$(294)
Operating Profit			
Merger-related costs	$224	$356	–
SFAS 142 adoption	–	$23	$88
SVE consolidation	–	$13	$16
Other impairment and restructuring charges	–	$31	$184
53rd week in 2000	–	–	$(62)
Other	–	$(2)	$17
Bottling Equity Income			
SFAS 142 adoption	–	$65	$70
53rd week in 2000	–	–	$(5)
Net Income			
Merger-related costs	$190	$322	–
SFAS 142 adoption	–	$102	$151
Other impairment and restructuring charges	–	$19	$111
53rd week in 2000	–	–	$(44)
Net Income per Common Share – Diluted			
Merger-related costs	$0.11	$0.18	–
SFAS 142 adoption	–	$0.06	$0.08
Other impairment and restructuring charges	–	$0.01	$0.06
53rd week in 2000	–	–	$(0.02)

Merger-Related Costs
We incurred costs associated with our merger with Quaker. We expect to incur additional costs of approximately $50 million in 2003 to complete the integration of the two companies. For additional information, see Note 3 to our consolidated financial statements.

SFAS 142 Adoption
In 2002, we adopted SFAS 142, *Goodwill and Other Intangible Assets*, which eliminated amortization of goodwill and perpetual brands (our nonamortizable

intangibles), and resulted in the acceleration of the amortization of certain of our other intangibles. The prior year adjustments in the above table reflect the impact that would have resulted if adoption had occurred at the beginning of 2000. For additional information, see "Our Critical Accounting Policies" and Note 4 to our consolidated financial statements.

SVE Consolidation
As a result of changes in the operations of Snack Ventures Europe (SVE), we

determined that consolidation was required, and we consolidated SVE in 2002. The prior year adjustments in the table reflect the impact that would have resulted if consolidation had occurred at the beginning of 2000. For further information on our consolidation of SVE, see Note 1 to our consolidated financial statements.

Other Impairment and Restructuring Charges
We incurred costs for Quaker's supply chain reconfiguration and manufacturing and distribution optimization project.

53rd Week in 2000
Our fiscal year ends on the last Saturday in December, and as a result, a 53rd week is added every five or six years. Comparisons of 2002 and 2001 to 2000 are affected by an additional week of results in 2000.

Other
This adjustment primarily reflects the reclassification of our prepaid forward contracts. Beginning in 2001, in connection with the adoption of the accounting standard on derivative instruments, gains or losses on prepaid forward contracts, which are used to hedge a portion of our deferred compensation liability, were reclassified to Corporate selling, general and administrative expenses. These amounts were previously reported in interest income. For more information on these prepaid forward contracts, see "Our Market Risks."

Pending Accounting Changes
Current pending accounting standards are not expected to have a material impact on our financial statements. For a description of these new accounting standards see Note 2 to our consolidated financial statements.

RESULTS OF OPERATIONS – CONSOLIDATED REVIEW

In the discussions of net sales and operating profit below, *effective net pricing* reflects the year-over-year impact of discrete pricing actions, sales incentive activities and mix resulting from selling varying products in different package sizes and in different countries.

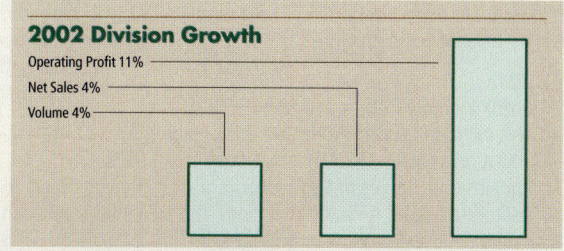

2002 Division Growth
Operating Profit 11%
Net Sales 4%
Volume 4%

SERVINGS

> **Servings increased 4% in 2002 and 2001.**

Since our divisions each use different measures of physical unit volume (e.g., kilos, pounds, case sales, gallons, etc.), a common servings metric is necessary to reflect our consolidated physical unit volume. Our divisions' physical volume measures are converted into servings based on U.S. Food and Drug Administration guidelines for single-serving sizes of our products.

Total servings increased 4% in 2002 compared to 2001 due to volume gains across all divisions led by beverages. Total servings increased 4% in 2001 compared to 2000 primarily due to contributions from our international divisions and Pepsi-Cola North America.

NET SALES AND TOTAL OPERATING PROFIT

2002
Net sales increased 7% and operating profit increased 18% driven by volume gains across all divisions, the consolidation of SVE, higher concentrate pricing and favorable mix. These gains were partially offset by increased promotional spending at Gatorade/Tropicana North America and Frito-Lay North America and net unfavorable foreign currency movement. The consolidation of SVE increased net sales growth by 3 percentage points and operating profit by 1 percentage point. In addition, operating profit growth improved 5 percentage points from the impact of lower merger-related costs, the absence of other impairment and restructuring costs and the adoption of SFAS 142.

The impact of net unfavorable foreign currency movements reduced net sales growth by 1 percentage point. Operating profit growth was not materially affected by foreign currency movements.

Our operating profit margin increased 1.7 percentage points primarily due to lower costs reflecting merger synergies of approximately $250 million, lower merger costs and productivity. We expect our operating margins to continue to improve as a result of Quaker merger-related synergies that are expected to reach $400 million a year by 2004 and by our ongoing productivity initiatives.

2001
Net sales and operating profit increased 5% primarily reflecting increased volume and higher effective net pricing of snacks and beverages, as well as the acquisition of South Beach Beverage Company, LLC (SoBe), which contributed nearly 1 percentage point to net sales growth. These gains were partially offset by the inclusion of the 53rd week in 2000, which reduced net sales growth by more than 1 percentage point and operating profit growth by 1.5 percentage points, and a net unfavorable foreign currency impact. In addition, operating profit was reduced by merger-related costs and higher general and administrative expenses, partially offset by lower costs for the Quaker supply chain project. Merger-related costs and lower supply chain costs reduced operating profit growth by approximately 5 percentage points.

The unfavorable foreign currency impact, primarily in Brazil and Europe, reduced net sales growth by more than 1 percentage point. Operating profit growth was reduced nearly 1 percentage point as a result of unfavorable foreign currency movements.

	2002	2001	2000	Change 2002	2001
Net sales	$25,112	$23,512	$22,337	7%	5%
Operating profit	$4,730	$4,021	$3,818	18%	5%
Operating profit margin	18.8%	17.1%	17.1%	1.7	–

BOTTLING EQUITY INCOME

Bottling equity income includes our share of the net income or loss of our noncontrolled bottling affiliates as described in "Our Customers." Our interest in these bottling investments may change from

	2002	2001	2000	% Change 2002	2001
Bottling equity income	$280	$160	$130	75	23

time to time. Any gains or losses from these changes, as well as other transactions related to our bottling investments, are also included on a pre-tax basis.

2002

Bottling equity income increased 75%. This increase primarily reflects the adoption of SFAS 142. The impact of impairment charges of $35 million related to a Latin American bottling investment was more than offset by the settlement of issues upon the sale of our investment in Pepsi-Gemex, our Mexican bottling affiliate, and the absence of

one-time items discussed in 2001 below. Excluding these items, bottling equity income increased approximately 13% reflecting improved performance of our international bottling investments, and the contribution of our North American anchor bottlers.

2001

Bottling equity income increased 23%, primarily reflecting the strong performance of PBG. Results for 2001 also include a gain of $59 million from the sale of approximately 2 million shares of PBG stock, and a net credit of $23 million

related to the resolution of issues for which a prior year accrual was established in connection with the creation of our anchor bottler system. Bottling equity income in 2001 also benefited from $5 million of losses from the 53rd week in 2000. These increases were offset by impairment charges of $62 million related to certain international bottling investments, primarily our equity investment in Turkey and a charge of $27 million for our share of a charge recorded by PepsiAmericas for environmental liabilities related to discontinued operations.

INTEREST EXPENSE, NET

2002

Net interest expense declined 6% primarily due to lower average debt levels, partially offset by increased losses of $10 million on investments used to hedge a portion of our deferred compensation liability. Decreases in borrowing rates were offset by decreases in investment rates.

2001

Net interest expense declined 19%.

| | | | | % Change | |
	2002	2001	2000	2002	2001
Interest expense, net	$(142)	$(152)	$(187)	6	19

Interest expense declined primarily as a result of significantly lower average debt levels. Interest income declined as 2000 includes $19 million in gains from prepaid forward contracts. Excluding the prepaid forward contracts, interest

income increased slightly as the impact of higher average investment balances was largely offset by lower average interest rates and losses on the investments hedging a portion of our deferred compensation liability.

EFFECTIVE TAX RATE

2002

The effective tax rate decreased 2 percentage points compared to prior year. The adoption of SFAS 142 reduced the rate by 0.8 percentage points. The impact of nondeductible merger-related costs on the rate decreased from 1.9 percentage points in 2001 to 0.7 percentage points in 2002. Excluding the impact of nondeductible merger-

	2002	2001	2000
Effective tax rate	31.9%	33.9%	32.4%

related costs in 2002, our effective tax rate would have been 31.2%.

2001

The effective tax rate increased 1.5 per-

centage points primarily due to limited tax benefits associated with merger-related costs, partially offset by lower taxes on foreign results.

NET INCOME AND NET INCOME PER COMMON SHARE

2002

Net income increased 24% and the related net income per common share increased 26%. These increases primarily reflect the solid operating profit growth, lower merger-related costs and the adoption of SFAS 142. Net income per common share also reflects the benefit of a reduction in average shares outstanding primarily as a result of increased share buyback activity. Merger-related costs reduced net income per common share by $0.11 in 2002.

| | | | | % Change | |
	2002	2001	2000	2002	2001
Net income	$3,313	$2,662	$2,543	24	5
Net income per common share – diluted	$1.85	$1.47	$1.42	26	4

2001

Net income increased 5% and the related net income per common share increased 4%. These increases primarily reflect increased operating profit,

reduced other impairment and restructuring costs, lower net interest expense, and a lower effective tax rate, partially offset by merger-related costs.

OUR LIQUIDITY AND CAPITAL RESOURCES

Our strong cash-generating capability and financial condition give us ready access to capital markets throughout the world.

Our principal source of liquidity is operating cash flows, which are derived from net income. This cash-generating capability is one of our fundamental strengths and provides us with substantial financial flexibility in meeting operating, investing and financing needs. We focus on management operating cash flow as a key element in achieving maximum shareholder value.

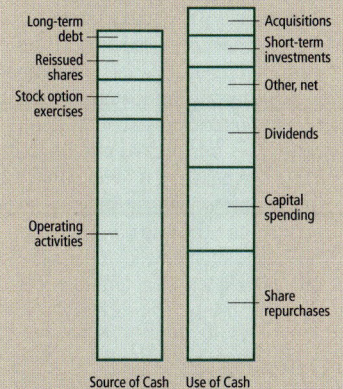

2002 Cash Utilization

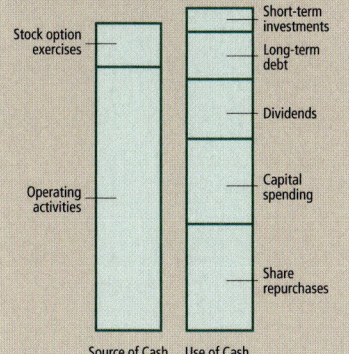

2001 Cash Utilization

2000 Cash Utilization

Operating Activities

In 2002, net cash provided by operating activities of $4.6 billion primarily reflects our solid business results and our emphasis on working capital efficiencies. Net cash provided by operating activities includes pension plan contributions of $820 million and a net tax refund of approximately $250 million in 2002. We expect pension plan contributions to be at a significantly lower level in 2003.

In 2001, net cash provided by operating activities of $3.8 billion primarily reflects our solid business results less cash paid for merger-related costs and other restructuring charges.

Investing Activities

In 2002, net cash used in investing activities of $0.5 billion primarily reflects capital spending and acquisitions, primarily the Wotsits brand in the United Kingdom, partially offset by maturities of short-term investments of $0.8 billion and proceeds from the Pepsi-Gemex transaction.

In 2001, net cash used in investing activities of $2.3 billion primarily reflects capital spending, the acquisition of SoBe and purchases of short-term investments of $0.5 billion.

Capital spending was $1.4 billion in 2002, $1.3 billion in 2001 and $1.4 billion in 2000. We expect capital spending to continue at a rate of approximately 5.5% to 6% of net sales.

Financing Activities

In 2002, cash used for financing activities of $3.2 billion primarily reflects share repurchases of $2.2 billion and dividend payments of $1 billion. Our policy is to pay dividends equal to approximately one-third of our previous year's net income.

In 2001, cash used for financing activities of $1.9 billion primarily reflects share repurchases of $1.7 billion and dividend payments of $1.0 billion. These payments were partially offset by the net proceeds of $524 million from the issuance of 13.2 million shares of our repurchased common stock to qualify for pooling-of-interests accounting treatment in connection with the merger with Quaker.

In 2002, our Board of Directors authorized a share repurchase program of up to $5 billion over a three-year period. In 2003, we expect share repurchases to continue at a level consistent with the years presented. In 2001, subsequent to our merger with Quaker, we repurchased shares of our common stock, as permitted by the emergency and exemptive orders from the Securities and Exchange Commission aimed at facilitating the reopening of the United States equities market on September 17, 2001, following the events of September 11th. Our Board of Directors authorized the repurchase of up to $2 billion worth of our common stock during the terms of these orders. Repurchases under these orders did not compromise our accounting for the Quaker merger. All prior authorizations for share repurchases had been rescinded as a result of the PepsiCo and Quaker merger.

Management Operating Cash Flow

> **Management operating cash flow is the primary measure management uses to monitor cash flow performance. It is not a measure calculated under United States generally accepted accounting principles.**

We believe capital spending is a recurring and essential use of cash necessary to maintain our operating capabilities. The table below reconciles net cash provided by operating activities as reflected in our Consolidated Statement of Cash Flows to our management operating cash flow.

Management operating cash flow was used primarily to fund share repurchases and dividend payments. In 2000, management operating cash flow was also used to reduce long-term debt. We expect management operating cash flow for fiscal year 2003 to remain strong and at levels consistent with the years presented. However, see "Cautionary Statements" for certain factors that may impact our operating cash flows.

Credit Ratings

Our debt ratings of A1 from Moody's and A from Standard & Poor's contribute to our ability to access global capital markets. Each rating is considered a strong investment grade bond rating with strong debt protection measures. These ratings reflect the third highest rankings out of nine-tier ranking systems. They reflect our strong operating cash flows and include the

> **Our debt ratings of A1 from Moody's and A from Standard & Poor's represent a strong investment grade bond rating with strong debt protection measures.**

impact of the cash flows and debt of our anchor bottlers. We have maintained these healthy ratings since 1989, demonstrating the stability of our operating cash flows.

Credit Facilities and Long-Term Contractual Commitments

See Note 9 to our consolidated financial statements for a description of our credit facilities and long-term contractual commitments.

Off-Balance Sheet Arrangements

It is not our business practice to enter into off-balance sheet arrangements nor is it our policy to issue guarantees to our bottlers, noncontrolled affiliates or third parties. However, certain guarantees were necessary to facilitate the separation of our bottling and restaurant operations from us. As of year-end 2002, we believe it is remote that these guarantees would require any cash payment. See Note 9 to our consolidated financial statements for a description of our off-balance sheet arrangements.

	2002	2001	2000
Net cash provided by operating activities	$ 4,627	$ 3,820	$ 4,178
Capital spending	(1,437)	(1,324)	(1,352)
Sales of property, plant and equipment	89	–	57
After-tax interest and forex	10	87	116
Management operating cash flow	$ 3,289	$ 2,583	$ 2,999

Financial Statements and Accompanying Notes

The standard set of financial statements consists of: (1) a comparative statement of income (statement of operations) for three years, (2) a comparative balance sheet for two years, (3) a comparative statement of cash flows for three years, (4) a statement of stockholders' (or shareholders') equity for three years, and (5) a set of accompanying notes that are considered an integral part of the financial statements. The auditor's report, unless stated otherwise, covers the financial statements and the accompanying notes. The financial statements and accompanying notes plus some supplementary data for PepsiCo, Inc. appear on the following pages.

CONSOLIDATED STATEMENT OF INCOME

PEPSICO

PepsiCo, Inc. and Subsidiaries
Fiscal years ended December 28, 2002, December 29, 2001 and December 30, 2000

(in millions except per share amounts)	2002	2001	2000
Net Sales	**$25,112**	$23,512	$22,337
Cost of sales	11,497	10,750	10,226
Selling, general and administrative expenses	8,523	8,189	7,962
Amortization of intangible assets	138	165	147
Merger-related costs	224	356	–
Other impairment and restructuring charges	–	31	184
Operating Profit	**4,730**	4,021	3,818
Bottling equity income	280	160	130
Interest expense	(178)	(219)	(272)
Interest income	36	67	85
Income before Income Taxes	**4,868**	4,029	3,761
Provision for Income Taxes	**1,555**	1,367	1,218
Net Income	**$ 3,313**	$ 2,662	$ 2,543
Net Income per Common Share			
Basic	**$1.89**	$1.51	$1.45
Diluted	**$1.85**	$1.47	$1.42

See accompanying notes to consolidated financial statements.

PEPSICO

CONSOLIDATED BALANCE SHEET

PepsiCo, Inc. and Subsidiaries
December 28, 2002 and December 29, 2001

(in millions except per share amounts)	2002	2001
ASSETS		
Current Assets		
Cash and cash equivalents	$ 1,638	$ 683
Short-term investments, at cost	207	966
	1,845	1,649
Accounts and notes receivable, net	2,531	2,142
Inventories	1,342	1,310
Prepaid expenses and other current assets	695	752
Total Current Assets	6,413	5,853
Property, Plant and Equipment, net	7,390	6,876
Amortizable Intangible Assets, net	801	875
Nonamortizable Intangible Assets	4,418	3,966
Investments in Noncontrolled Affiliates	2,611	2,871
Other Assets	1,841	1,254
Total Assets	$23,474	$21,695
LIABILITIES AND SHAREHOLDERS' EQUITY		
Current Liabilities		
Short-term obligations	$ 562	$ 354
Accounts payable and other current liabilities	4,998	4,461
Income taxes payable	492	183
Total Current Liabilities	6,052	4,998
Long-Term Debt Obligations	2,187	2,651
Other Liabilities	4,226	3,876
Deferred Income Taxes	1,718	1,496
Preferred Stock, no par value	41	41
Repurchased Preferred Stock	(48)	(15)
Common Shareholders' Equity		
Common stock, par value 1 $^2/_3$¢ per share (issued 1,782 shares)	30	30
Capital in excess of par value	–	13
Retained earnings	13,464	11,519
Accumulated other comprehensive loss	(1,672)	(1,646)
	11,822	9,916
Less: repurchased common stock, at cost (60 and 26 shares, respectively)	(2,524)	(1,268)
Total Common Shareholders' Equity	9,298	8,648
Total Liabilities and Shareholders' Equity	$23,474	$21,695

See accompanying notes to consolidated financial statements.

CONSOLIDATED STATEMENT OF CASH FLOWS

PepsiCo, Inc. and Subsidiaries
Fiscal years ended December 28, 2002, December 29, 2001 and December 30, 2000

(in millions)	2002	2001	2000
Operating Activities			
Net income	$ 3,313	$ 2,662	$ 2,543
Adjustments to reconcile net income to net cash provided by operating activities			
Depreciation and amortization	1,112	1,082	1,093
Merger-related costs	224	356	–
Other impairment and restructuring charges	–	31	184
Cash payments for merger-related costs and other restructuring charges	(123)	(273)	(38)
Pension plan contributions	(820)	(446)	(103)
Bottling equity income, net of dividends	(222)	(103)	(74)
Deferred income taxes	288	162	33
Deferred compensation – ESOP	–	48	36
Other noncash charges and credits, net	263	209	303
Changes in operating working capital, excluding effects			
of acquisitions and dispositions			
Accounts and notes receivable	(260)	7	(52)
Inventories	(53)	(75)	(51)
Prepaid expenses and other current assets	(78)	(6)	(35)
Accounts payable and other current liabilities	426	(236)	219
Income taxes payable	278	394	335
Net change in operating working capital	313	84	416
Other	279	8	(215)
Net Cash Provided by Operating Activities	4,627	3,820	4,178
Investing Activities			
Capital spending	(1,437)	(1,324)	(1,352)
Sales of property, plant and equipment	89	–	57
Acquisitions and investments in noncontrolled affiliates	(351)	(432)	(98)
Divestitures	376	–	33
Short-term investments, by original maturity			
More than three months – purchases	(62)	(2,537)	(4,950)
More than three months – maturities	833	2,078	4,585
Three months or less, net	(14)	(41)	(9)
Snack Ventures Europe consolidation	39	–	–
Net Cash Used for Investing Activities	(527)	(2,256)	(1,734)
Financing Activities			
Proceeds from issuances of long-term debt	11	324	130
Payments of long-term debt	(353)	(573)	(879)
Short-term borrowings, by original maturity			
More than three months – proceeds	707	788	198
More than three months – payments	(809)	(483)	(155)
Three months or less, net	40	(397)	1
Cash dividends paid	(1,041)	(994)	(949)
Share repurchases – common	(2,158)	(1,716)	(1,430)
Share repurchases – preferred	(32)	(10)	–
Quaker share repurchases	–	(5)	(254)
Proceeds from reissuance of shares	–	524	–
Proceeds from exercises of stock options	456	623	690
Net Cash Used for Financing Activities	(3,179)	(1,919)	(2,648)
Effect of exchange rate changes on cash and cash equivalents	34	–	(4)
Net Increase/(Decrease) in Cash and Cash Equivalents	955	(355)	(208)
Cash and Cash Equivalents, Beginning of Year	683	1,038	1,246
Cash and Cash Equivalents, End of Year	$ 1,638	$ 683	$ 1,038

See accompanying notes to consolidated financial statements.

CONSOLIDATED STATEMENT OF COMMON SHAREHOLDERS' EQUITY   **PEPSICO**

PepsiCo, Inc. and Subsidiaries
Fiscal years ended December 28, 2002, December 29, 2001 and December 30, 2000

(in millions)	2002 Shares	2002 Amount	2001 Shares	2001 Amount	2000 Shares	2000 Amount
Common Stock						
Balance, beginning of year	1,782	$ 30	2,029	$ 34	2,030	$ 34
Quaker share repurchases	–	–	–	–	(9)	–
Stock option exercises	–	–	6	–	–	–
Quaker stock option exercises	–	–	3	–	8	–
Shares issued to effect merger	–	–	(256)	(4)	–	–
Balance, end of year	1,782	30	1,782	30	2,029	34
Capital in Excess of Par Value						
Balance, beginning of year		13		375		559
Quaker share repurchases		–		–		(236)
Stock option exercises[a]		(9)		82		52
Reissued shares		–		150		–
Shares issued to effect merger		–		(595)		–
Other		(4)		1		–
Balance, end of year		–		13		375
Deferred Compensation						
Balance, beginning of year		–		(21)		(45)
Net activity		–		21		24
Balance, end of year		–		–		(21)
Retained Earnings						
Balance, beginning of year		11,519		16,510		14,921
Net income[b]		3,313		2,662		2,543
Shares issued to effect merger		–		(6,644)		–
Cash dividends declared – common		(1,042)		(1,005)		(950)
Cash dividends declared – preferred		(4)		(4)		(4)
Stock option exercises[a]		(322)		–		–
Balance, end of year		13,464		11,519		16,510
Accumulated Other Comprehensive Loss						
Balance, beginning of year		(1,646)		(1,374)		(1,085)
Currency translation adjustment[b]		56		(218)		(289)
Cash flow hedges, net of tax[b]		18		(18)		–
Minimum pension liability adjustment, net of tax[b]		(99)		(38)		(2)
Other[b]		(1)		2		2
Balance, end of year		(1,672)		(1,646)		(1,374)
Repurchased Common Stock						
Balance, beginning of year	(26)	(1,268)	(280)	(7,920)	(271)	(7,306)
Share repurchases	(53)	(2,192)	(35)	(1,716)	(38)	(1,430)
Stock option exercises	19	931	20	751	29	816
Reissued shares	–	–	13	374	–	–
Shares issued to effect merger	–	–	256	7,243	–	–
Other	–	5	–	–	–	–
Balance, end of year	(60)	(2,524)	(26)	(1,268)	(280)	(7,920)
Total Common Shareholders' Equity		$ 9,298		$ 8,648		$ 7,604

(a) Includes total tax benefit of $143 million in 2002, $212 million in 2001 and $177 million in 2000.

(b) Combined these amounts represent total comprehensive income of $3,287 million in 2002, $2,390 million in 2001 and $2,254 million in 2000.

See accompanying notes to consolidated financial statements.

NOTES TO CONSOLIDATED FINANCIAL STATEMENTS

NOTE 1 – BASIS OF PRESENTATION AND OUR DIVISIONS

Basis of Presentation
Our financial statements include the consolidated accounts of PepsiCo, Inc. and the affiliates that we control. In addition, we include our share of the results of certain other affiliates based on our ownership interest. We do not control these other affiliates as our ownership in these other affiliates is generally less than fifty percent. Our share of the net income of noncontrolled bottling affiliates is reported in our income statement as bottling equity income. See Note 8 for additional information on our noncontrolled bottling affiliates. Our share of other noncontrolled affiliates is included in division operating profit. As a result of changes in the operations of our European snack joint venture, Snack Ventures Europe (SVE), we determined that effective in 2002, consolidation was required. Therefore, SVE's results of operations are consolidated with PepsiCo in 2002. Intercompany balances and transactions are eliminated.

The preparation of our consolidated financial statements in conformity with generally accepted accounting principles requires us to make estimates and assumptions that affect reported amounts of assets, liabilities, revenues, expenses and disclosure of contingent assets and liabilities. Actual results could differ from these estimates.

Our fiscal year ends on the last Saturday in December and, as a result, a 53rd week is added every fifth or sixth year. The fiscal year ended December 30, 2000 consisted of fifty-three weeks.

The impact of the 53rd week and certain other items, such as merger-related costs (described in Note 3), the adoption of SFAS 142 (described in Note 4) and the SVE consolidation affect the comparability of our consolidated results. For additional unaudited information on these items, see "Our Divisions" below and "Items Affecting Comparability" in Management's Discussion and Analysis.

Tabular dollars are in millions, except per share amounts. All per share amounts reflect common per share amounts, assume dilution unless noted, and are based on unrounded amounts. Certain reclassifications were made to prior year amounts to conform to the 2002 presentation.

We manufacture, market and sell a variety of salty, sweet and grain-based snacks, carbonated and noncarbonated beverages, and foods through our North American and international business divisions. Our North American divisions include the United States and Canada. The accounting policies for the divisions are the same as those described in Note 2.

Division results are based on how our Chief Executive Officer manages our divisions. Beginning in 2003, we will combine our North American beverage businesses as PepsiCo Beverages North America and our international food and beverage businesses as PepsiCo International to reflect operating and management changes. Merger-related costs and significant other impairment and restructuring charges are not included in division results. In addition, prior year division results are adjusted to reflect the adoption of SFAS 142 and consolidation of SVE, and exclude divested businesses. For additional unaudited information on our divisions, see "Our Operations" in Management's Discussion and Analysis.

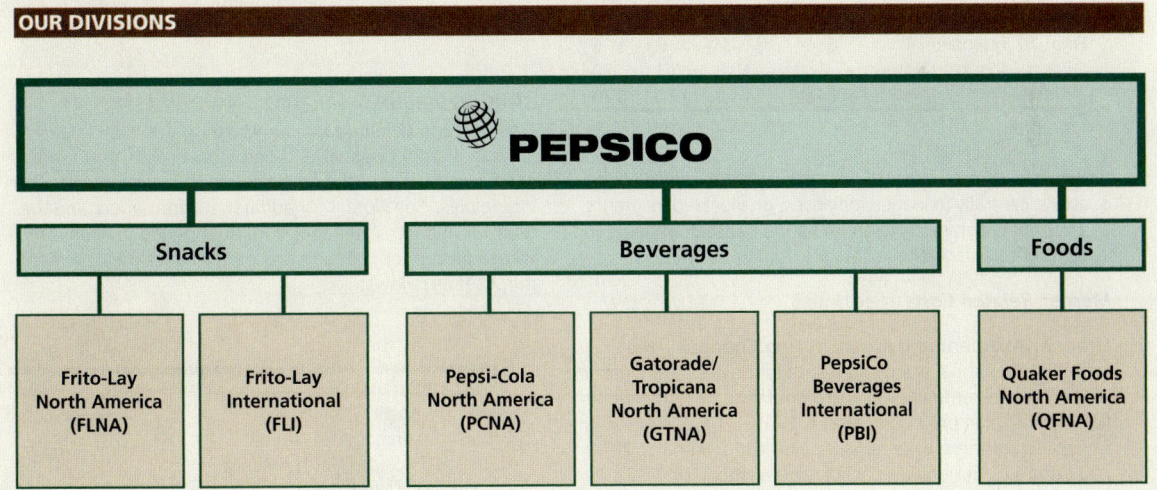

OUR DIVISIONS

	2002	2001	2000	2002	2001	2000
		Net Sales			**Operating Profit**	
Snacks						
– FLNA	$ 8,565	$ 8,216	$ 7,769	**$2,216**	$2,056	$1,875
– FLI	**5,713**	5,492	5,172	**781**	651	577
Beverages						
– PCNA	**3,365**	3,189	2,657	**987**	881	820
– GTNA	**3,835**	3,699	3,514	**590**	585	554
– PBI	**2,036**	2,012	1,981	**261**	212	161
QFNA	**1,491**	1,466	1,453	**481**	399	369
Total division	**25,005**	24,074	22,546	**5,316**	4,784	4,356
Divested businesses	**107**	144	145	**15**	29	36
Corporate				**(377)**	(371)	(331)
	25,112	24,218	22,691	**4,954**	4,442	4,061
Merger-related costs	**–**	–	–	**(224)**	(356)	–
Other impairment and restructuring charges	**–**	–	–	**–**	(31)	(184)
Other	**–**	–	–	**–**	2	(17)
SVE consolidation	**–**	(706)	(648)	**–**	(13)	(16)
SFAS 142 adoption	**–**	–	–	**–**	(23)	(88)
53rd week in 2000	**–**	–	294	**–**	–	62
Total	**$25,112**	$23,512	$22,337	**$4,730**	$4,021	$3,818

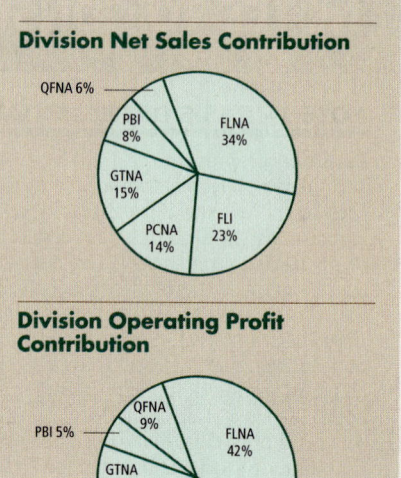

Division Net Sales Contribution

Division Operating Profit Contribution

Divested Businesses – During 2002, we sold our Quaker Foods North America bagged cereal business and our Frito-Lay International food businesses in Colombia and Venezuela. A net loss of $5 million was recorded on the sale of these businesses. The net loss and results prior to the divestitures are presented as divested businesses. Prior year division operating results have been reclassified as follows:

	2001	2000	2001	2000
				Operating
	Net Sales			Profit
Frito-Lay International	$ 44	$ 41	$ 6	$ 6
Quaker Foods North America	100	104	23	30
	$144	$145	$29	$36

Corporate – Corporate includes costs of our corporate head-quarters, centrally managed initiatives, unallocated insurance and benefit programs, foreign exchange transaction gains and losses and certain one-time charges.

Merger-Related Costs – See Note 3.

Other Impairment and Restructuring Changes – We incurred other impairment and restructuring costs for Quaker's supply chain reconfiguration and manufacturing and distribution optimization project initiated in 1999. Approximately $14 million of these costs remain payable at December 28, 2002 and $23 million was payable at December 29, 2001.

Other – This adjustment primarily reflects the reclassification of our prepaid forward contracts. For more unaudited information on these prepaid forward contracts, see "Items Affecting Comparability" in Management's Discussion and Analysis.

The following items are necessary to reconcile division results to consolidated results since, as noted above, division results are presented as managed.

SVE Consolidation – We have consolidated SVE in 2002. As a result, prior period amounts were adjusted to include SVE for planning and performance measurement purposes as follows:

	2001	2000
Frito-Lay International net sales	$706	$648
Frito-Lay International operating profit	$14	$17
Corporate	$(1)	$(1)

SFAS 142 Adoption – In 2002, we adopted SFAS 142, *Goodwill and Other Intangible Assets*, which eliminated amortization of goodwill and perpetual brands, and resulted in an acceleration of the amortization of certain of our other intangibles. See Note 4 for additional information, and the after-tax impact. After adoption, prior period division results were adjusted for planning and performance measurement purposes as follows:

	2001	2000
Frito-Lay International	$ 18	$ 32
Pepsi-Cola North America	(50)	–
PepsiCo Beverages International	(21)	(20)
Gatorade/Tropicana North America	69	69
Quaker Foods North America	7	7
	$ 23	$ 88

53rd Week in 2000 – Since we manage our results on a fifty-two week basis, the impact of the 53rd week in 2000 is excluded as shown.

	Net Sales	Operating Profit
Frito-Lay North America	$164	$40
Frito-Lay International	61	10
Pepsi-Cola North America	36	13
Gatorade/Tropicana North America	33	5
	$294	68
Corporate		(6)
		$62

OTHER DIVISION INFORMATION

	2002	2001	2000	2002	2001	2000
	Total Assets			**Capital Spending**		
Snacks						
– FLNA	$ 5,099	$ 4,623	$ 4,282	$ 523	$ 514	$ 524
– FLI[a]	5,131	4,321	4,278	337	290	276
Beverages						
– PCNA	1,380	1,325	836	135	70	59
– GTNA	4,311	4,078	3,893	232	289	261
– PBI	2,144	2,038	2,202	136	95	98
QFNA	1,001	878	917	50	55	95
Total division	19,066	17,263	16,408	1,413	1,313	1,313
Divested businesses	–	58	80	1	3	3
Corporate[b]	2,072	1,927	1,737	23	8	36
Investments in bottling affiliates	2,336	2,447	2,532	–	–	–
	$23,474	$21,695	$20,757	$1,437	$1,324	$1,352

	Amortization of Intangible Assets			**Depreciation and Other Amortization**		
Snacks						
– FLNA	$ 3	$ 7	$ 7	$399	$377	$374
– FLI	27	31	13	219	211	206
Beverages						
– PCNA	70	69	2	69	64	94
– GTNA	–	–	–	137	129	118
– PBI	37	37	36	81	99	111
QFNA	1	1	1	37	41	49
Total division	138	145	59	942	921	952
Divested businesses	–	–	–	3	4	3
Corporate	–	–	–	29	18	16
SVE consolidation	–	(3)	–	–	(26)	(25)
SFAS 142 adoption	–	23	88	–	–	–
	$138	$165	$147	$974	$917	$946

	Net Sales			**Long-Lived Assets[c]**		
United States	$16,588	$15,976	$15,076	$ 9,767	$ 9,439	$ 9,035
Mexico	2,686	2,609	2,404	764	1,065	934
United Kingdom	1,106	954	946	1,529	1,104	1,156
Canada	967	896	866	410	375	367
All other countries	3,765	3,077	3,045	2,750	2,605	2,759
	$25,112	$23,512	$22,337	$15,220	$14,588	$14,251

Total Assets
FLNA 22% · FLI 22% · GTNA 18% · PBI 9% · QFNA 4% · Other 19% · PCNA 6%

Capital Spending
FLNA 36% · FLI 23% · PCNA 9% · GTNA 16% · PBI 10% · QFNA 4% · Other 2%

Net Sales
United States 66% · Mexico 11% · United Kingdom 4% · Canada 4% · Other 15%

Long-Lived Assets
United States 64% · Mexico 5% · United Kingdom 10% · Canada 3% · Other 18%

(a) Frito-Lay International assets include investments in noncontrolled affiliates, principally Productos SAS, of $145 million in 2002 and $155 million in 2001.

(b) Corporate assets consist principally of cash and cash equivalents, short-term investments primarily held outside the United States and property, plant and equipment.

(c) Long-lived assets represent net property, plant and equipment, nonamortizable and net amortizable intangible assets and investments in noncontrolled affiliates.

NOTE 2 – OUR SIGNIFICANT ACCOUNTING POLICIES

Revenue Recognition

We recognize revenue upon delivery to our customers in accordance with written sales terms that do not allow for a right of return. However, our policy for direct-store-delivery and chilled products is to remove and replace out-of-date products from store shelves to ensure that our consumers receive the product quality and freshness that they expect. Based on our historical experience with this practice, we have reserved for anticipated out-of-date product. For additional unaudited information on our revenue recognition and related policies, see "Our Critical Accounting Policies" in Management's Discussion and Analysis.

Sales Incentives and Other Marketplace Spending

We offer sales incentives through various programs to our customers, consumers and, for PCNA, directly to certain retailers. Sales incentives are accounted for as a reduction to sales and totaled $5.5 billion in 2002, $4.7 billion in 2001 and $4.3 billion in 2000. These sales incentives include the impact of adopting EITF 01-9, *Accounting for Consideration Given by a Vendor to a Customer or a Reseller of the Vendor's Products*, which reduced our net sales by $3.4 billion in 2001 and $3.1 billion in 2000, with selling, general and administrative expenses reduced by the same amounts. Most of these incentive arrangements have terms of no more than one year. However, we have arrangements, such as fountain pouring rights, which extend up to twelve years. Costs incurred to obtain these rights are expensed over the contract period and the remaining balance of $349 million at December 28, 2002 and $374 million at December 29, 2001 is primarily reported in other assets in the Consolidated Balance Sheet. For additional unaudited information on our sales incentives, see "Our Critical Accounting Policies" in Management's Discussion and Analysis.

Other marketplace spending includes the costs of advertising and other marketing activities and is reported as selling, general and administrative expenses. Advertising expenses were $1.5 billion in 2002 and $1.7 billion in 2001 and 2000. Deferred advertising costs are not expensed until the year first used and consist of:

- media and personal service prepayments,
- promotional materials in inventory, and
- production costs of future media advertising.

Deferred advertising costs of $147 million at year-end 2002 and $111 million at year-end 2001 are classified as prepaid expenses in the Consolidated Balance Sheet.

Distribution Costs

Distribution costs, including the costs of shipping and handling activities, are reported as selling, general and administrative expenses for direct-store-delivery distribution systems. For our other distribution systems, these costs are reported in cost of sales. Shipping and handling expenses classified as selling, general and administrative expenses were $2.8 billion in 2002, $2.6 billion in 2001 and $2.5 billion in 2000.

Cash Equivalents

Cash equivalents are investments with original maturities of three months or less.

Commitments and Contingencies

We are subject to various claims and contingencies related to lawsuits, taxes and environmental matters, as well as commitments under contractual and other commercial obligations. We recognize liabilities for contingencies and commitments when a loss is probable and estimable. For additional information on our commitments and other contractual and commercial obligations, see Note 9.

Other Significant Accounting Policies

Our other significant accounting policies are disclosed as follows:

- *Income Taxes* – Note 5 and, for additional unaudited information, see "Our Critical Accounting Policies" in Management's Discussion and Analysis.
- *Pension and Retiree Medical Plans* – Note 6 and, for additional unaudited information, see "Our Critical Accounting Policies" in Management's Discussion and Analysis.
- *Employee Stock Options* – Note 7.
- *Risk Management* – Note 10 and, for additional unaudited information, see "Our Market Risks" in Management's Discussion and Analysis.
- *Property, Plant and Equipment and Intangible Assets* – Note 4 and, for additional unaudited information on brands and goodwill, see "Our Critical Accounting Policies" in Management's Discussion and Analysis.

Pending Accounting Changes

In June 2001, the FASB issued SFAS 143, *Accounting for Asset Retirement Obligations*. SFAS 143 addresses the financial accounting and reporting for obligations associated with the retirement of tangible long-lived assets. It requires that we recognize the fair value of a liability for an asset retirement obligation in the period in which it is incurred if a reasonable estimate of fair value can be made. We currently have no significant asset retirement obligations, and therefore, adoption will have no impact on our consolidated financial statements.

In June 2002, the FASB issued SFAS 146, *Accounting for Costs Associated with Exit or Disposal Activities*. SFAS 146 addresses the accounting and reporting for costs associated with restructuring activities. This new standard changes the timing of the recognition of restructuring charges. Liabilities for restructuring costs will be required to be recognized when the liability is incurred rather than when we commit to the plan. SFAS 146 is effective for restructuring activity initiated after December 31, 2002.

NOTE 3 – OUR MERGER WITH QUAKER

On August 2, 2001, we completed our merger with Quaker. Under the terms of the merger agreement, we issued approximately 306 million shares of our common stock in exchange for all the outstanding common stock of Quaker.

The merger was accounted for as a tax-free transaction and as a pooling-of-interests. As a result, all prior period consolidated financial statements presented have been restated to include the results of operations, financial position and cash flows of both companies as if they had always been combined. Certain reclassifications were made to conform the presentation of the financial statements, and the fiscal calendar and certain interim reporting policies were also conformed. There were no material transactions between pre-merger PepsiCo and Quaker.

We have recognized the following costs associated with our merger with Quaker:

	2002	2001
Transaction costs	$ –	$ 117
Integration and restructuring costs	224	239
Total merger-related costs	$ 224	$ 356
After-tax	$ 190	$ 322
Per share	$0.11	$0.18

Transaction costs were incurred to complete the merger and consist primarily of fees and expenses for investment bankers, attorneys and accountants, SEC filing fees, stock exchange listing fees and financial printing and other related charges.

Integration and restructuring costs represent incremental one-time merger-related costs. Such costs include consulting fees and expenses, employee-related costs, information system integration costs, asset impairments and other costs related to the integration of Quaker. Employee-related costs include retirement benefit and severance costs and expenses related to change-in-control provisions of pre-merger employment contracts. As of December 28, 2002, an accrual has been recorded for costs associated with the termination of approximately 1,100 corporate, sales, distribution, manufacturing, research, information technology and marketing employees, a majority of which have occurred. We expect to incur additional costs in 2003 to integrate the two companies.

Merger-related integration and restructuring reserves are included within accounts payable and other current liabilities in the Consolidated Balance Sheet.

Merger-related integration and restructuring reserves:

	Integration	Employee Related	Asset Impairment	Facility and Other Exit	Total
2001 costs	$124	$106	$ 1	$ 8	$ 239
Cash payments	(80)	(33)	–	(2)	(115)
Reclassification to retiree medical/postemployment liabilities	–	(22)	–	–	(22)
Other noncash utilization	(22)	–	(1)	(2)	(25)
Reserves, December 29, 2001	22	51	–	4	77
2002 costs	90	53	56	25	224
Cash payments	(62)	(43)	–	(13)	(118)
Reclassification to retiree medical/postemployment liabilities	(7)	(9)	–	–	(16)
Other noncash utilization	–	(4)	(56)	(10)	(70)
Reserves, December 28, 2002	$ 43	$ 48	$ –	$ 6	$ 97

NOTE 4 – PROPERTY, PLANT AND EQUIPMENT AND INTANGIBLE ASSETS

	Useful Life	2002	2001	2000
Property, plant and equipment, net				
Land and improvements		$ 504	$ 464	
Buildings and improvements	20 - 40 yrs.	3,119	2,846	
Machinery and equipment, including fleet	5 - 15	9,005	8,135	
Construction in progress		767	735	
		13,395	12,180	
Accumulated depreciation		(6,005)	(5,304)	
		$ 7,390	$ 6,876	
Depreciation expense		$929	$843	$840
Amortizable intangible assets, net				
Brands	5 - 40	$ 938	$ 869	
Other identifiable intangibles	3 - 15	203	207	
		1,141	1,076	
Accumulated amortization		(340)	(201)	
		$ 801	$ 875	
Amortization expense		$138	$165	$147

Depreciation and amortization are recognized on a straight-line basis over an asset's estimated useful life. Land is not depreciated and construction in progress is not depreciated until ready for service. Amortization for each of the next five years, based on existing intangible assets and 2002 foreign exchange rates, is expected to be $138 million in 2003, $129 million in 2004 and 2005 and $19 million thereafter.

No impairment charges resulted from the adoption of SFAS 144, *Accounting for the Impairment or Disposal of Long-Lived Assets.* Depreciable and amortizable assets are only evaluated for impairment upon a significant change in the operating or macroeconomic environment. In these circumstances, if an evaluation of the undiscounted cash flows indicates impairment, the asset is written down to its estimated fair value, which is generally based on discounted future cash flows. Useful lives are periodically evaluated to determine whether events or circumstances have occurred which indicate the need to revise the useful lives. For additional unaudited information on our amortizable brand policies, see "Our Critical Accounting Policies" in Management's Discussion and Analysis.

Nonamortizable Intangible Assets

Perpetual brands and goodwill are assessed for impairment at least annually to ensure that future cash flows continue to exceed the related book value. A perpetual brand is impaired if its book value exceeds its fair value. Goodwill is evaluated for impairment if the book value of its reporting unit exceeds its fair value. A reporting unit can be a division or business. If the fair value of an evaluated asset is less than its book value, the asset is written down based on its discounted future cash flows to fair value. No impairment charges resulted from the required impairment evaluations in 2002. The change in the book value of nonamortizable intangible assets during 2002 is as shown.

	Balance, Beginning of Year	Acquisitions	Translation and Other	Balance, End of Year
Frito-Lay North America				
Goodwill	$ 107	$ –	$ 2	$ 109
Frito-Lay International(a)				
Goodwill	788	39	109	936
Brands	427	248	45	720
	1,215	287	154	1,656
Gatorade/Tropicana North America				
Goodwill	2,148	–	1	2,149
Brands	59	–	–	59
	2,207	–	1	2,208
PepsiCo Beverages International				
Goodwill	250	–	–	250
Quaker Foods North America				
Goodwill	187	–	–	187
Corporate				
Pension intangible	–	–	8	8
Total goodwill	3,480	39	112	3,631
Total brands	486	248	45	779
Total pension intangible	–	–	8	8
	$ 3,966	$ 287	$ 165	$ 4,418

(a) Beginning of year balance includes the impact of consolidating Snack Ventures Europe in 2002 for Frito-Lay International.

We adopted SFAS 142, *Goodwill and Other Intangible Assets*, in 2002. Prior to the adoption of SFAS 142, our nonamortizable intangible assets had useful lives ranging from 20 to 40 years. The table to the right provides pro forma disclosure of the elimination of goodwill and perpetual brands amortization and the acceleration of certain other amortization as if SFAS 142 had been adopted in 2000.

For additional unaudited information on our goodwill and nonamortizable brand policies, see "Our Critical Accounting Policies" in Management's Discussion and Analysis.

	2001	2000
Reported net income	$2,662	$2,543
Cease goodwill amortization	112	112
Adjust brands amortization	(67)	(22)
Cease equity investee goodwill amortization	57	61
Adjusted net income	$2,764	$2,694
Reported earnings per common share – basic	$ 1.51	$ 1.45
Cease goodwill amortization	0.06	0.06
Adjust brands amortization	(0.03)	(0.01)
Cease equity investee goodwill amortization	0.03	0.03
Adjusted earnings per common share – basic	$ 1.57	$ 1.53
Reported earnings per common share – diluted	$ 1.47	$ 1.42
Cease goodwill amortization	0.06	0.06
Adjust brands amortization	(0.03)	(0.01)
Cease equity investee goodwill amortization	0.03	0.03
Adjusted earnings per common share – diluted	$ 1.53	$ 1.50

NOTE 5 – INCOME TAXES

	2002	2001	2000
Income before income taxes			
U.S.	$3,516	$2,922	$2,574
Foreign	1,352	1,107	1,187
	$4,868	$4,029	$3,761
Provision for income taxes			
Current: U.S. Federal	$ 956	$ 926	$ 958
Foreign	256	226	165
State	55	53	62
	1,267	1,205	1,185
Deferred: U.S. Federal	255	159	31
Foreign	11	(8)	(7)
State	22	11	9
	288	162	33
	$1,555	$1,367	$1,218
Tax rate reconciliation			
U.S. Federal statutory tax rate	35.0%	35.0%	35.0%
State income tax, net of U.S. Federal tax benefit	1.0	1.0	1.2
Lower taxes on foreign results	(3.9)	(4.3)	(2.9)
Merger-related costs and other impairment and restructuring charges	0.9	2.3	(0.2)
Other, net	(1.1)	(0.1)	(0.7)
Effective tax rate	31.9%	33.9%	32.4%
Deferred tax liabilities			
Investments in noncontrolled affiliates	$ 753	$ 702	
Property, plant and equipment	746	804	
Safe harbor leases	57	82	
Zero coupon notes	61	68	
Intangible assets other than nondeductible goodwill	127	121	
Other	669	480	
Gross deferred tax liabilities	2,413	2,257	
Deferred tax assets			
Net carryforwards	504	538	
Retiree medical benefits	315	320	
Various current and noncurrent liabilities	642	805	
Gross deferred tax assets	1,461	1,663	
Valuation allowances	(487)	(511)	
Deferred tax assets, net	974	1,152	
Net deferred tax liabilities	$1,439	$1,105	
Included within:			
Prepaid expenses and other current assets	$279	$391	
Deferred income taxes	$1,718	$1,496	

Operating loss carryforwards totaling $3.3 billion at year-end 2002 are being carried forward in a number of foreign and state jurisdictions where we are permitted to use tax operating losses from prior periods to reduce future taxable income. These operating losses will expire as follows: $0.1 billion in 2003, $2.9 billion between 2004 and 2018 and $0.3 billion may be carried forward indefinitely. In addition, certain tax credits generated in prior periods of approximately $72 million are available to reduce certain foreign tax liabilities through 2011. We establish valuation allowances for our deferred tax assets when the amount of expected future taxable income is not likely to support the use of the deduction or credit.

We have not recognized any United States tax expense on undistributed international earnings since we have the intention to reinvest the earnings outside the United States for the foreseeable future. These undistributed earnings are approximately $7.5 billion at December 28, 2002.

Analysis of valuation allowances:	2002	2001	2000
Balance, beginning of year	$511	$ 813	$804
(Benefit)/provision	(22)	(300)	7
Other (deductions)/additions	(2)	(2)	2
Balance, end of year	$487	$ 511	$813

For additional unaudited information on our income tax policies, see "Our Critical Accounting Policies" in Management's Discussion and Analysis.

NOTE 6 – PENSION AND RETIREE MEDICAL PLANS

Our pension plans cover full-time U.S. employees and certain international employees. Benefits are determined based on either years of service or a combination of years of service and earnings. U.S. employees are also eligible for medical and life insurance benefits (retiree medical) if they meet age and service requirements and qualify for retirement benefits. We use a September 30 measurement date. Prior service costs are amortized on a straight-line basis over the average remaining service period of employees expected to receive benefits.

For additional unaudited information on our pension and retiree medical plans and related accounting policies and assumptions, see "Our Critical Accounting Policies" in Management's Discussion and Analysis.

	2002	2001	2000
Weighted average pension assumptions			
Liability discount rate	6.7%	7.4%	7.7%
Expected return on plan assets	9.1%	9.8%	9.9%
Rate of salary increases	4.4%	4.6%	4.5%
Components of pension expense			
Service cost	$ 156	$ 127	$ 120
Interest cost	265	233	221
Expected return on plan assets	(329)	(301)	(277)
Amortization of transition asset	(1)	(2)	(3)
Amortization of prior service costs	6	8	13
Amortization of experience loss/(gain)	5	(9)	(18)
Pension expense	102	56	56
Curtailment/settlement loss	–	1	6
Special termination benefits	9	26	–
Total	$ 111	$ 83	$ 62

	2002	2001	2000
Liability discount rate	**6.7%**	7.5%	7.8%
Components of retiree medical expense			
Service cost	**$25**	$20	$22
Interest cost	**66**	63	58
Amortization of prior service costs	**(7)**	(12)	(12)
Amortization of experience loss/(gain)	**3**	–	(1)
Retiree medical expense	**87**	71	67
Curtailment loss	**–**	–	2
Special termination benefits	**1**	1	–
Total	**$88**	$72	$69

	2002	2001	2002	2001
	Pension		Retiree Medical	
Change in benefit liability				
Liability at beginning of year	**$3,556**	$3,170	**$ 911**	$834
Service cost	**156**	127	**25**	20
Interest cost	**265**	233	**66**	63
Plan amendments	**12**	10	**(25)**	1
Participant contributions	**6**	5	**–**	–
Experience loss	**514**	170	**205**	50
Benefit payments	**(234)**	(170)	**(63)**	(58)
Curtailment loss	**–**	2	**–**	–
Special termination benefits	**9**	26	**1**	1
Foreign currency adjustment	**40**	(17)	**–**	–
Liability at end of year	**$4,324**	$3,556	**$1,120**	$911
Change in fair value of plan assets				
Fair value at beginning of year	**$3,129**	$3,251	**$ –**	$ –
Actual loss on plan assets	**(221)**	(382)	**–**	–
Employer contributions	**820**	446	**63**	58
Participant contributions	**6**	5	**–**	–
Benefit payments	**(234)**	(170)	**(63)**	(58)
Foreign currency adjustment	**37**	(21)	**–**	–
Fair value at end of year	**$3,537**	$3,129	**$ –**	$ –
Funded status as recognized in the Consolidated Balance Sheet				
Funded status at end of year	**$ (787)**	$(427)	**$(1,120)**	$ (911)
Unrecognized prior service cost	**44**	38	**(23)**	(5)
Unrecognized experience loss	**1,631**	548	**294**	91
Unrecognized transition asset	**(1)**	(2)	**–**	–
Net amounts recognized	**$ 887**	$ 157	**$ (849)**	$ (825)

	2002	2001	2002	2001
	Pension		Retiree Medical	
Net amounts as recognized in the Consolidated Balance Sheet				
Other assets	**$1,097**	$ 396	**$ –**	$ –
Intangible assets	**8**	–	**–**	–
Accrued benefit liability	**(283)**	(261)	**(849)**	(825)
Accumulated other comprehensive income	**65**	22	**–**	–
Net amounts recognized	**$ 887**	$ 157	**$(849)**	$(825)
Selected information for plans with liability to date in excess of plan assets				
Liability for service to date	**$(419)**	$(252)	**$(1,120)**	$(911)
Projected benefit liability	**$(656)**	$(419)	**$(1,120)**	$(911)
Fair value of plan assets	**$182**	$51	**–**	–

Of the total projected pension benefit liability at year-end 2002, $416 million relates to plans that we do not fund because of unfavorable tax treatment.

Pension Assets
Pension assets include approximately 5.5 million shares of PepsiCo common stock with a market value of $202 million in 2002, and 4.7 million shares with a market value of $227 million in 2001. Our investment policy limits the investment in PepsiCo stock to 10% of the fair value of plan assets.

Retiree Medical Cost Trend Rates
An average increase of 10% in the cost of covered retiree medical benefits is assumed for 2003. This average increase is then projected to decline gradually to 4.5% in 2007 and thereafter. Generally, our costs are capped at a specified dollar amount, with retirees contributing the remainder. These assumed health care cost trend rates have a significant impact on the retiree medical plan expense and liability. A 1 percentage point change in the assumed health care trend rate would have the following effects:

	1% Increase	1% Decrease
2002 service and interest cost components	$7	$(6)
2002 benefit liability	$37	$(34)

NOTE 7 – EMPLOYEE STOCK OPTIONS

Our stock option program is a broad-based program designed to attract and retain talent while creating alignment with the interests of our shareholders. Employees at all levels participate in our stock option program. In addition, members of our Board of Directors receive stock options for their service on our Board. Stock options are granted to employees under the following active plans.

SharePower Stock Option Plan (SharePower)
SharePower options are awarded to all eligible employees based on annual earnings and tenure, become exercisable after three years and have a 10-year term. SharePower options represent approximately 20% of our annual employee option grants. At year-end 2002, 35.1 million shares were available for future awards under SharePower.

Long-Term Incentive Plan (LTIP)
All senior management and certain middle management are awarded LTIP grants, generally based on a multiple of base salary. LTIP options generally become exercisable at the end of three years and have a 10-year term. Beginning in 2001, the entire award was made in stock options. Prior to 2001, two-thirds of the award consisted of stock options with the balance in stock options or paid in cash based on the employee's selection. Amounts expensed for expected cash payments were $18 million in 2002 and $37 million in 2001 and 2000. At year-end 2002, 36.6 million shares were available for future awards under the LTIP.

Stock Option Incentive Plan (SOIP)
SOIP options are available to middle management employees based on a multiple of base salary. SOIP options generally become exercisable at the end of three years and have a 10-year term. At year-end 2002, 29.3 million shares were available for future awards under the SOIP.

Accounting Policy
We account for employee stock options using the intrinsic value method rather than the fair value method. Under the intrinsic value method, compensation expense is measured as the excess, if any, of the market value of PepsiCo common stock at the award date over the amount the employee must pay for the stock (exercise price). Our policy is to award stock options with an exercise price equal to the market value at the date of award, and accordingly, no compensation expense is recognized. If the fair value method of accounting had been used, compensation expense would have been recognized over the vesting period of the awards resulting in lower net income and net income per common share as shown. We have no current plans to change our intrinsic value accounting. We believe there are a number of valuation issues

with the fair value method that still need to be resolved as well as potential changes necessary to reconcile international and United States standards. Upon resolution of these matters, we will be better able to consider implementation of the fair value method.

	2002	2001	2000
Pro forma impact of fair value method			
Reported net income	**$3,313**	$2,662	$2,543
Less: fair value impact of employee stock compensation	**(360)**	(306)	(200)
Pro forma net income	**$2,953**	$2,356	$2,343
Earnings per common share			
Basic – as reported	**$1.89**	$1.51	$1.45
Diluted – as reported	**$1.85**	$1.47	$1.42
Basic – pro forma	**$1.68**	$1.33	$1.34
Diluted – pro forma	**$1.65**	$1.30	$1.31
Weighted average Black-Scholes fair value assumptions			
Risk free interest rate	**4.4%**	4.8%	6.7%
Expected life	**6 yrs.**	5 yrs.	5 yrs.
Expected volatility	**27%**	29%	29%
Expected dividend yield	**1.14%**	0.98%	1.08%

Stock option activity[a]:

	2002 Options	2002 Average Price[b]	2001 Options	2001 Average Price[b]	2000 Options	2000 Average Price[b]
Outstanding at beginning of year	**176,922**	**$32.35**	170,640	$28.08	188,661	$25.82
Granted	**37,376**	**48.75**	40,432	43.53	28,660	31.92
Exercised	**(19,558)**	**23.32**	(29,064)	21.59	(37,039)	18.40
Forfeited/expired	**(4,308)**	**39.01**	(5,086)	34.83	(9,642)	33.93
Outstanding at end of year	**190,432**	**36.45**	176,922	32.35	170,640	28.08
Exercisable at end of year	**82,620**	**$30.14**	83,521	$26.32	75,129	$21.27
Weighted average fair value of options granted		**$15.20**		$13.53		$12.04

Stock options outstanding and exercisable at December 28, 2002[a]:

Range of Exercise Price	Options Outstanding Options	Average Life[c]	Average Price[b]	Options Exercisable Options	Average Price[b]
$ 5.95 to $18.37	8,867	1.39 yrs.	$14.78	8,867	$14.78
$18.58 to $35.53	77,856	5.30	29.32	38,278	25.55
$36.50 to $51.50	103,709	7.84	43.69	35,475	39.04
	190,432	6.46	36.45	82,620	30.14

(a) Options in thousands and include options granted under Quaker plans.
(b) Weighted average exercise price.
(c) Weighted average contractual life remaining in years.

NOTE 8 – NONCONTROLLED BOTTLING AFFILIATES

Our most significant noncontrolled bottling affiliates are The Pepsi Bottling Group (PBG) and PepsiAmericas (PAS). These affiliates account for over 40% of our worldwide bottler case sales.

The Pepsi Bottling Group

In addition to approximately 38% of PBG's outstanding common stock that we own at year-end 2002, we own 100% of PBG's class B common stock and approximately 7% of the equity of Bottling Group, LLC, PBG's principal operating subsidiary. This gives us economic ownership of approximately 42% of PBG's combined operations. PBG's summarized financial information is as follows:

	2002	2001
Current assets	$ 1,737	$1,548
Noncurrent assets	8,290	6,309
Total assets	$10,027	$7,857
Current liabilities	$1,248	$1,081
Noncurrent liabilities	6,607	4,856
Minority interest	348	319
Total liabilities	$8,203	$6,256
Our investment	$1,107	$962

	2002	2001	2000
Net sales	$9,216	$8,443	$7,982
Gross profit	$4,215	$3,863	$3,577
Operating profit	$898	$676	$590
Net income	$428	$305	$229

In December 2002, PBG acquired Pepsi-Gemex, a franchise bottler in Mexico, in which we previously held a 34% ownership interest. Under the terms of the agreement, we received the cash tender price for our Pepsi-Gemex shares, net of a payment of $17 million to PBG. Including the gain from our net investment hedge, the transaction resulted in an after-tax loss of approximately $8 million. The table above includes the results of Pepsi-Gemex from the transaction date forward.

Our investment in PBG was $118 million higher than our ownership interest in their net assets at year-end 2002. Based upon the quoted closing price of PBG shares at year-end 2002, the calculated market value of our shares in PBG, excluding our investment in Bottling Group, LLC, exceeded our investment balance by approximately $1.9 billion.

PepsiAmericas

PepsiAmericas was formed in December 2000 when two of our bottling affiliates, Whitman and PepsiAmericas, merged. At year-end 2002, we owned approximately 39% of the combined company. PepsiAmericas' summarized financial information is as follows:

	2002	2001
Current assets	$ 550	$ 481
Noncurrent assets	3,013	2,938
Total assets	$3,563	$3,419
Current liabilities	$ 698	$ 643
Noncurrent liabilities	1,416	1,346
Total liabilities	$2,114	$1,989
Our investment	$782	$746

	2002	2001	2000
Net sales	$3,240	$3,144	$2,511
Gross profit	$1,272	$1,232	$1,017
Operating profit	$301	$268	$223
Income from continuing operations	$136	$90	$72
Net income	$130	$19	$80

The above financial information for 2000 includes the results of the former PepsiAmericas after the date of the merger with Whitman.

Our investment in PAS was $215 million higher than our ownership interest in their net assets at year-end 2002. Based upon the quoted closing price of PAS shares at year-end 2002, the calculated market value of our shares in PepsiAmericas was less than our investment balance by approximately $27 million.

Related Party Transactions

Our significant related party transactions involve our noncontrolled bottling affiliates. We sell concentrate to these affiliates that is used in the production of carbonated soft drinks and noncarbonated beverages. The sale of concentrate is reported net of bottler funding. We also sell certain finished goods to these affiliates and we receive royalties for the use of our trademark for certain products. For further unaudited information on these bottlers, see "Our Customers" in Management's Discussion and Analysis. These transactions with our bottling affiliates are reflected in the Consolidated Statement of Income as shown.

	2002	2001	2000
Net sales	$3,455	$2,262	$1,978
Selling, general and administrative expenses	$83	$57	$5

As of December 28, 2002, the receivables from these bottling affiliates were $126 million and payables to these affiliates were $122 million. As of December 29, 2001, the receivables from these bottling affiliates were $119 million and payables to these affiliates were $108 million. Such amounts are settled on terms consistent with other trade receivables and payables. See Note 9 regarding our guarantee of certain PBG debt.

In addition, we coordinate, on an aggregate basis, the negotiation and purchase of sweeteners and other raw materials requirements for certain of our bottlers with suppliers. Once we have negotiated the contracts, the bottlers order and take delivery directly from the supplier and pay the suppliers directly. Consequently, these transactions are not reflected in our consolidated financial statements. As the contracting party, we could be liable to these suppliers in the event of any nonpayment by our anchor bottlers, but we consider this exposure to be remote.

NOTE 9 – DEBT OBLIGATIONS AND COMMITMENTS

	2002	2001
Short-term debt obligations		
Current maturities of long-term debt	$ 485	$ 319
Other borrowings (5.7% and 6.4%)	452	410
Amounts reclassified to long-term debt	(375)	(375)
	$ 562	$ 354
Long-term debt obligations		
Short-term borrowings, reclassified	$ 375	$ 375
Notes due 2003-2026 (4.0% and 4.1%)	1,716	1,986
Zero coupon notes, $625 million		
due 2003-2012 (12.6%)	338	356
Other, due 2003-2015 (7.6% and 6.9%)	243	253
	2,672	2,970
Less: current maturities of		
long-term debt obligations	(485)	(319)
	$2,187	$2,651

Short-term borrowings are reclassified to long-term when we have the intent and ability, through the existence of the unused lines of credit, to refinance these borrowings on a long-term basis. The weighted average interest rates in the table shown include the impact of outstanding interest rate swaps at year-end. See Note 10 for additional information on our interest rate swaps.

At year-end 2002, we maintained $750 million in corporate lines of credit subject to normal banking terms and conditions. These credit facilities support short-term debt issuances and remained unused at year-end 2002. Of the $750 million, $375 million expires in June 2003 with the remaining $375 million expiring in June 2007. Upon consent of PepsiCo and the lenders, these facilities can be extended an additional year. In addition, $270 million of our debt was outstanding on various lines of credit maintained for our international divisions. These lines of credit are subject to normal banking terms and conditions and are committed to the extent of our borrowings.

Long-Term Contractual Commitments and Off-Balance Sheet Arrangements

		Payments Due by Year			
	Total	Less than 1 Year	1-3 Years	3-5 Years	More than 5 Years
Long-term contractual commitments[a]					
Long-term debt obligations[b]	$2,187	$ –	$ 603	$ 699	$ 885
Non-cancelable operating leases	526	129	169	91	137
Purchasing commitments	3,307	773	1,006	569	959
Capital equipment commitments	34	34	–	–	–
Marketing commitments	251	75	115	52	9
Other commitments	31	23	8	–	–
	$6,336	$1,034	$1,901	$1,411	$1,990

(a) Reflects non-cancelable commitments as of December 28, 2002 based on year-end foreign exchange rates.

(b) Excludes current maturities of long-term debt of $485 million which are classified within current liabilities.

Long-term contractual commitments, except for our long-term debt obligations, are not recorded in our Consolidated Balance Sheet. Non-cancelable purchasing, capital equipment and marketing commitments are in the normal course of our business for our projected needs. Our non-cancelable capital equipment commitments primarily relate to our new concentrate plant in Ireland. As bottler funding is negotiated on an annual basis, these commitments are not reflected in our long-term contractual commitments. See Note 8 regarding our commitments to noncontrolled bottling affiliates.

Off-Balance Sheet Arrangements

It is not our business practice to enter into off-balance sheet arrangements nor is it our policy to issue guarantees to our bottlers, noncontrolled affiliates or third parties. However, certain guarantees were necessary to facilitate the separation of our bottling and restaurant operations from us. In connection with these transactions, we have guaranteed $2.3 billion of Bottling Group, LLC's long-term debt through 2012 and $68 million of YUM! Brands, Inc. (YUM) outstanding obligations, primarily property leases. The terms of our Bottling Group, LLC debt guarantee are intended to preserve the structure of PBG's separation from us and our payment obligation would be triggered if Bottling Group, LLC failed to perform under these debt obligations or the structure significantly changed. Our guarantees of certain obligations ensured YUM's continued use of these properties. These guarantees would require our cash payment if YUM failed to perform under these lease obligations.

NOTE 10 – RISK MANAGEMENT

We are exposed to the risk of loss arising from adverse changes in:
- commodity prices, affecting the cost of our raw materials and fuel;
- foreign exchange risks;
- interest rates on our debt and short-term investment portfolios; and
- stock prices.

In the normal course of business, we manage these risks through a variety of strategies, including the use of derivative instruments designated as cash flow and fair value hedges. See "Our Market Risks" in Management's Discussion and Analysis for further unaudited information on our hedges.

For cash flow hedges, changes in fair value are generally deferred in accumulated other comprehensive loss within shareholders' equity until the underlying hedged item is recognized in net income. For fair value hedges, changes in fair value are recognized immediately in earnings, consistent with the underlying hedged item. Hedging transactions are limited to an underlying exposure. As a result, any change in the value of our derivative instruments would be substantially offset by an opposite change in the value of the underlying hedged items. Hedging ineffectiveness and a net earnings impact occur when the change in the value of the hedge does not offset the change in the value of the underlying hedged item. We do not use derivative instruments for trading or speculative purposes and, to manage credit risk, we limit our exposure to individual counterparties.

Commodity Prices

We are subject to commodity price risk because our ability to recover increased costs through higher pricing may be limited in the competitive environment in which we operate. This risk is managed through the use of fixed-price purchase orders, pricing agreements, geographic diversity and cash flow hedges. We use cash flow hedges, with terms of no more than two years, to hedge price fluctuations in a portion of our anticipated commodity purchases, primarily for corn, natural gas, oats, packaging materials and wheat. Any ineffectiveness is recorded immediately. However, our commodity hedges have not had any material ineffectiveness. We classify both the earnings and cash flow impact from these hedges consistent with the underlying hedged item.

During the next 12 months, we expect to reclassify gains of approximately $4 million from accumulated other comprehensive loss into net income.

Foreign Exchange

Our operations outside of the United States generated 34% of our net sales of which Mexico, the United Kingdom and Canada contributed 19%. As a result, we are exposed to foreign currency risks from unforeseen economic changes and political unrest. On occasion, we enter into fair value hedges, primarily forward contracts, to reduce the effect of foreign exchange rates. Ineffectiveness resulting from our fair value hedges was not material to our results of operations.

In 2002, we hedged 2.1 billion Mexican pesos related to our net investment in Pepsi-Gemex which resulted in a $5 million gain upon our disposal of Pepsi-Gemex described in Note 8.

Interest Rates

We centrally manage our debt and investment portfolios considering investment opportunities and risks, tax consequences and overall financing strategies. We have used interest rate swaps to effectively change the interest rate of specific debt issuances, with the objective of reducing our overall borrowing costs.

Late in 2002, we terminated the majority of our interest rate swaps resulting in a gain of approximately $23 million which will be amortized over the remaining term of the related debt. As a result, 12% of our debt at year-end 2002 is exposed to variable interest rates compared to approximately 45% at year-end 2001.

Stock Prices

The portion of our deferred compensation liability that is based on our stock price is subject to market risk. We hold prepaid forward contracts to manage this risk. Changes in the fair value of these contracts are recognized immediately in earnings and are offset by changes in the related compensation liability.

Fair Value

All derivative instruments are recognized in our Consolidated Balance Sheet at fair value. The fair value of our derivative instruments is generally based on quoted market prices. Book and fair values of our derivative and financial instruments are as follows:

	2002		2001	
	Book Value	**Fair Value**	Book Value	Fair Value
Assets				
Cash and cash equivalents	**$1,638**	**$1,638**	$683	$683
Short-term investments[a]	**$207**	**$207**	$966	$966
Forward exchange contracts[b]	**$2**	**$2**	$6	$6
Commodity contracts[b]	**$6**	**$6**	$1	$1
Prepaid forward contracts[b]	**$96**	**$96**	$65	$65
Interest rate swaps[b]	**$1**	**$1**	$32	$32
Liabilities				
Forward exchange contracts[c]	**$3**	**$3**	$2	$2
Commodity contracts[c]	**$2**	**$2**	$17	$17
Debt obligations	**$2,749**	**$3,134**	$3,005	$3,270

Included in the Consolidated Balance Sheet under the captions noted above or as indicated below.

(a) Includes $82 million at December 28, 2002 and $89 million at December 29, 2001 of mutual fund investments used to manage a portion of market risk arising from our deferred compensation liability.

(b) Included within prepaid expenses and other current assets.

(c) Included within accounts payable and other current liabilities.

This table excludes guarantees, including our guarantee of $2.3 billion of Bottling Group, LLC's long-term debt. The guarantee had a fair value of $35 million at December 28, 2002 and $59 million at December 29, 2001 based on an external estimate of the cost to us of transferring the liability to an independent financial institution. See Note 9 for additional information on our guarantees.

NOTE 11 – NET INCOME PER COMMON SHARE

Basic net income per common share is net income available to common shareholders divided by the weighted average of common shares outstanding during the period. Diluted net income per common share is calculated using the weighted average of common shares outstanding adjusted to include the effect that would occur if in-the-money employee stock options were exercised and preferred shares were converted into common shares. Options to purchase 69.4 million shares in 2002, 0.4 million shares in 2001 and 0.1 million shares in 2000 were not included in the calculation of diluted earnings per common share because these options were out-of-the-money.

The computations of basic and diluted net income per common share are as shown.

	2002		2001		2000	
	Income	Shares[a]	Income	Shares[a]	Income	Shares[a]
Net income	$3,313		$2,662		$2,543	
Preferred shares:						
Dividends	(4)		(4)		(4)	
Redemption	–		(1)		–	
Net income available for common shareholders	$3,309	1,753	$2,657	1,763	$2,539	1,748
Basic net income per common share	$1.89		$1.51		$1.45	
Net income available for common shareholders	$3,309	1,753	$2,657	1,763	$2,539	1,748
Dilutive securities:						
Stock options	–	32	–	39	–	38
ESOP convertible preferred stock	3	3	3	4	2	4
Unvested stock awards	–	1	–	1	–	1
Diluted	$3,312	1,789	$2,660	1,807	$2,541	1,791
Diluted net income per common share	$1.85		$1.47		$1.42	

(a) Weighted average common shares outstanding.

NOTE 12 – PREFERRED AND COMMON STOCK

As of December 28, 2002, there were 3.6 billion shares of common stock and 3 million shares of convertible preferred stock authorized. The preferred stock was issued only for an employee stock ownership plan (ESOP) established by Quaker and these shares are redeemable by the ESOP participants. The preferred stock accrues dividends at an annual rate of $5.46 per share. At year-end 2002, there are 803,953 preferred shares issued and 602,353 shares outstanding. Each share is convertible at the option of the holder into 4.9625 shares of common stock. The preferred shares may be called by us upon written notice at $78 per share plus accrued and unpaid dividends.

As of December 28, 2002, 0.6 million outstanding shares of preferred stock with a fair value of $127 million and 20 million shares of common stock were held in the accounts of ESOP participants. Quaker made the final award to its ESOP plan in June 2001.

Preferred stock activity:

	2002		2001		2000	
	Shares	Amount	Shares	Amount	Shares	Amount
Preferred stock						
Balance, beginning of year	0.8	$41	1.3	$100	1.3	$100
Adjustment to effect merger	–	–	(0.5)	(59)	–	–
Balance, end of year	0.8	$41	0.8	$ 41	1.3	$100
Repurchased preferred stock						
Balance, beginning of year	0.1	$15	0.5	$ 51	0.4	$ 39
Redemptions	0.1	33	0.1	23	0.1	12
Adjustment to effect merger	–	–	(0.5)	(59)	–	–
Balance, end of year	0.2	$48	0.1	$ 15	0.5	$ 51

NOTE 13 – ACCUMULATED OTHER COMPREHENSIVE LOSS

Comprehensive income is a measure of income which includes both net income and other comprehensive loss. Other comprehensive loss results from items deferred on the balance sheet in shareholders' equity. Other comprehensive loss was $26 million in 2002, $272 million in 2001 and $289 million in 2000. The accumulated balances for each component of other comprehensive loss were as shown.

	2002	2001	2000
Currency translation adjustment	$(1,531)	$(1,587)	$(1,369)
Cash flow hedges, net of tax[a]	–	(18)	–
Minimum pension liability adjustment[b]	(142)	(43)	(5)
Other	1	2	–
Accumulated other comprehensive loss	$(1,672)	$(1,646)	$(1,374)

(a) Includes $4 million in 2002 and $7 million in 2001 for our share of our equity investees' accumulated derivative losses. In addition, 2001 includes $3 million related to the cumulative effect of adopting SFAS 133.

(b) Net of taxes of $72 million in 2002, $22 million in 2001 and $3 million in 2000. Also, includes $99 million in 2002 and $29 million in 2001 for our share of our equity investees' minimum pension liability adjustments.

NOTE 14 – SUPPLEMENTAL FINANCIAL INFORMATION

	2002	2001	2000
Accounts receivable			
Trade receivables	$1,924	$1,663	
Other receivables	723	600	
	2,647	2,263	
Allowance, beginning of year	121	126	$109
Charged to expense	38	41	42
Other additions[a]	3	2	8
Deductions[b]	(46)	(48)	(33)
Allowance, end of year	116	121	$126
Net receivables	$2,531	$2,142	
Inventory[c]			
Raw materials	$ 525	$ 535	
Work-in-process	214	205	
Finished goods	603	570	
	$1,342	$1,310	
Accounts payable and other liabilities			
Accounts payable	$1,543	$1,238	
Accrued selling, advertising and marketing	716	861	
Accrued compensation and benefits	806	789	
Dividends payable	259	255	
Insurance accruals	168	158	
Other current liabilities	1,506	1,160	
	$4,998	$4,461	
Other liabilities[d]	$4,226	$3,876	
Other supplemental information			
Rent expense	$194	$165	$171
Interest paid	$119	$159	$226
Income taxes paid	$1,056	$857	$876
Acquisitions[e]			
Fair value of assets acquired	$ 626	$ 604	$ 80
Cash paid and debt issued	(351)	(432)	(98)
Liabilities assumed	$ 275	$ 172	$(18)

(a) Includes acquisitions and currency translation effects.

(b) Includes accounts written off and currency translation effects.

(c) Inventories are valued at the lower of cost or market. Cost is determined using the average, first-in, first-out (FIFO) or last-in, first-out (LIFO) methods. Approximately 19% in 2002 and 20% in 2001 of the inventory cost was computed using the LIFO method. The differences between LIFO and FIFO methods of valuing these inventories are not material.

(d) Includes reserves for tax positions when, despite our belief that our position is fully supportable, we believe that our position is likely to be challenged and that we may not succeed.

(e) Includes our acquisition of the Wotsits brand in the United Kingdom for $228 million and the SoBe brand in the United States for $337 million in 2001.

Five- or Ten-Year Summary

Usually presented in close proximity to the audited financial statements is a five- or ten-year summary of selected financial data. From such a summary, one can determine trends and growth patterns over a fairly long period of time. PepsiCo presents five years of selected financial data that includes operating data, financial position data, and selected statistics and ratios.

PEPSICO

5-YEAR SUMMARY
(in millions except per share amounts, unaudited)

	2002	2001	2000	1999	1998
Net sales	$25,112	23,512	22,337	22,183	24,605
Net income	$ 3,313	2,662	2,543	2,505	2,278
Income per common share – basic	$ 1.89	1.51	1.45	1.41	1.27
Income per common share – diluted	$ 1.85	1.47	1.42	1.38	1.23
Cash dividends declared per common share	$ 0.595	0.575	0.555	0.535	0.515
Total assets	$23,474	21,695	20,757	19,948	25,170
Long-term debt	$ 2,187	2,651	3,009	3,527	4,823

As a result of the adoption of SFAS 142 and the consolidation of SVE in 2002, the bottling deconsolidation in 1999, the Tropicana acquisition late in 1998 and items identified below, the data provided above is not comparable.

- Net sales have been restated to reflect the adoption of EITF 01-9 in 2002 which reduced net sales and selling, general and administrative expenses by $3.4 billion in 2001, $3.1 billion in 2000, $2.9 billion in 1999 and $2.6 billion in 1998.

- Includes merger-related costs of:

	2002	2001
Pre-tax	$224	$356
After-tax	$190	$322
Per share	$0.11	$0.18

- Includes other impairment and restructuring charges of:

	2001	2000	1999	1998
Pre-tax	$31	$184	$73	$482
After-tax	$19	$111	$45	$379
Per share	$0.01	$0.06	$0.02	$0.21

- The 2000 fiscal year consisted of fifty-three weeks compared to fifty-two weeks in our normal fiscal year. The 53rd week increased 2000 net sales by an estimated $294 million and net income by an estimated $44 million (or $0.02 per share).

- In 1999, includes a net gain on bottling transactions of $1.0 billion ($270 million after-tax or $0.15 per share) and a tax provision related to the PepCom transaction of $25 million ($0.01 per share), and a Quaker favorable tax adjustment of $59 million (or $0.03 per share).

- In 1998, includes a tax benefit of $494 million (or $0.27 per share) related to final agreement with the IRS to settle a case related to concentrate operations in Puerto Rico.

- Cash dividends per common share are those of pre-merger PepsiCo prior to the effective date of the merger.

Specimen Financial Statements: The Coca-Cola Company

CONSOLIDATED STATEMENTS OF INCOME
The Coca-Cola Company and Subsidiaries

YEAR ENDED DECEMBER 31, *(In millions except per share data)*	2002	2001	2000
NET OPERATING REVENUES	$ 19,564	$ 17,545	$ 17,354
Cost of goods sold	7,105	6,044	6,204
GROSS PROFIT	12,459	11,501	11,150
Selling, general and administrative expenses	7,001	6,149	6,016
Other operating charges	—	—	1,443
OPERATING INCOME	5,458	5,352	3,691
Interest income	209	325	345
Interest expense	199	289	447
Equity income (loss)	384	152	(289)
Other income (loss)—net	(353)	39	99
Gains on issuances of stock by equity investee	—	91	—
INCOME BEFORE INCOME TAXES AND CUMULATIVE EFFECT OF ACCOUNTING CHANGE	5,499	5,670	3,399
Income taxes	1,523	1,691	1,222
NET INCOME BEFORE CUMULATIVE EFFECT OF ACCOUNTING CHANGE	3,976	3,979	2,177
Cumulative effect of accounting change for SFAS No. 142, net of income taxes:			
Company operations	(367)	—	—
Equity investees	(559)	—	—
Cumulative effect of accounting change for SFAS No. 133, net of income taxes	—	(10)	—
NET INCOME	$ 3,050	$ 3,969	$ 2,177
BASIC NET INCOME PER SHARE			
Before accounting change	$ 1.60	$ 1.60	$ .88
Cumulative effect of accounting change	(.37)	—	—
	$ 1.23	$ 1.60	$ .88
DILUTED NET INCOME PER SHARE			
Before accounting change	$ 1.60	$ 1.60	$ .88
Cumulative effect of accounting change	(.37)	—	—
	$ 1.23	$ 1.60	$ .88
AVERAGE SHARES OUTSTANDING	2,478	2,487	2,477
Effect of dilutive securities	5	—	10
AVERAGE SHARES OUTSTANDING ASSUMING DILUTION	2,483	2,487	2,487

See Notes to Consolidated Financial Statements.

The financial information herein is reprinted with permission from The Coca-Cola Company 2002 Annual Report. The accompanying Notes are an integral part of the consolidated financial statements. The complete financial statements are available through a link at the book's companion Web site.

CONSOLIDATED BALANCE SHEETS
The Coca-Cola Company and Subsidiaries

DECEMBER 31,	2002	2001
(In millions except share data)		
ASSETS		
CURRENT		
Cash and cash equivalents	$ 2,126	$ 1,866
Marketable securities	219	68
	2,345	1,934
Trade accounts receivable, less allowances of $55 in 2002 and $59 in 2001	2,097	1,882
Inventories	1,294	1,055
Prepaid expenses and other assets	1,616	2,300
TOTAL CURRENT ASSETS	7,352	7,171
INVESTMENTS AND OTHER ASSETS		
Equity method investments:		
Coca-Cola Enterprises Inc.	972	788
Coca-Cola Hellenic Bottling Company S.A.	872	791
Coca-Cola Amatil Limited	492	432
Other, principally bottling companies	2,401	3,117
Cost method investments, principally bottling companies	254	294
Other assets	2,694	2,792
	7,685	8,214
PROPERTY, PLANT AND EQUIPMENT		
Land	385	217
Buildings and improvements	2,332	1,812
Machinery and equipment	5,888	4,881
Containers	396	195
	9,001	7,105
Less allowances for depreciation	3,090	2,652
	5,911	4,453
TRADEMARKS WITH INDEFINITE LIVES	1,724	1,697
GOODWILL AND OTHER INTANGIBLE ASSETS	1,829	882
TOTAL ASSETS	$ 24,501	$ 22,417
LIABILITIES AND SHARE-OWNERS' EQUITY		
CURRENT		
Accounts payable and accrued expenses	$ 3,692	$ 3,679
Loans and notes payable	2,475	3,743
Current maturities of long-term debt	180	156
Accrued income taxes	994	851
TOTAL CURRENT LIABILITIES	7,341	8,429
LONG-TERM DEBT	2,701	1,219
OTHER LIABILITIES	2,260	961
DEFERRED INCOME TAXES	399	442
SHARE-OWNERS' EQUITY		
Common stock, $.25 par value		
Authorized: 5,600,000,000 shares; issued: 3,490,818,627 shares in 2002 and 3,491,465,016 shares in 2001	873	873
Capital surplus	3,857	3,520
Reinvested earnings	24,506	23,443
Accumulated other comprehensive income (loss) and unearned compensation on restricted stock	(3,047)	(2,788)
	26,189	25,048
Less treasury stock, at cost (1,019,839,490 shares in 2002; 1,005,237,693 shares in 2001)	14,389	13,682
	11,800	11,366
TOTAL LIABILITIES AND SHARE-OWNERS' EQUITY	$ 24,501	$ 22,417

See Notes to Consolidated Financial Statements.

CONSOLIDATED STATEMENTS OF CASH FLOWS

The Coca-Cola Company and Subsidiaries

YEAR ENDED DECEMBER 31, *(In millions)*	2002	2001	2000
OPERATING ACTIVITIES			
Net income	$ 3,050	$ 3,969	$ 2,177
Depreciation and amortization	806	803	773
Stock-based compensation expense	365	41	43
Deferred income taxes	40	56	3
Equity income or loss, net of dividends	(256)	(54)	380
Foreign currency adjustments	(76)	(60)	196
Gain on issuances of stock by equity investee	—	(91)	—
(Gains) losses on sales of assets, including bottling interests	3	(85)	(127)
Cumulative effect of accounting changes	926	10	—
Other operating charges	—	—	916
Other items	291	(17)	76
Net change in operating assets and liabilities	(407)	(462)	(852)
Net cash provided by operating activities	4,742	4,110	3,585
INVESTING ACTIVITIES			
Acquisitions and investments, principally trademarks and bottling companies	(544)	(651)	(397)
Purchases of investments and other assets	(156)	(456)	(508)
Proceeds from disposals of investments and other assets	243	455	290
Purchases of property, plant and equipment	(851)	(769)	(733)
Proceeds from disposals of property, plant and equipment	69	91	45
Other investing activities	52	142	138
Net cash used in investing activities	(1,187)	(1,188)	(1,165)
FINANCING ACTIVITIES			
Issuances of debt	1,622	3,011	3,671
Payments of debt	(2,378)	(3,937)	(4,256)
Issuances of stock	107	164	331
Purchases of stock for treasury	(691)	(277)	(133)
Dividends	(1,987)	(1,791)	(1,685)
Net cash used in financing activities	(3,327)	(2,830)	(2,072)
EFFECT OF EXCHANGE RATE CHANGES ON CASH AND CASH EQUIVALENTS	32	(45)	(140)
CASH AND CASH EQUIVALENTS			
Net increase during the year	260	47	208
Balance at beginning of year	1,866	1,819	1,611
Balance at end of year	$ 2,126	$ 1,866	$ 1,819

See Notes to Consolidated Financial Statements.

CONSOLIDATED STATEMENTS OF SHARE–OWNERS' EQUITY

The Coca-Cola Company and Subsidiaries

YEAR ENDED DECEMBER 31,	2002	2001	2000
(In millions except per share data)			
NUMBER OF COMMON SHARES OUTSTANDING			
Balance at beginning of year	2,486	2,485	2,472
Stock issued to employees exercising stock options	3	7	12
Purchases of stock for treasury [1]	(14)	(6)	(2)
Restricted stock and other stock plans, less cancellations	—	—	3
Adoption of SFAS No. 123	(4)	—	—
Balance at end of year	2,471	2,486	2,485
COMMON STOCK			
Balance at beginning of year	$ 873	$ 870	$ 867
Stock issued to employees exercising stock options	1	2	2
Restricted stock and other stock plans, less cancellations	—	1	1
Adoption of SFAS No. 123	(1)	—	—
Balance at end of year	873	873	870
CAPITAL SURPLUS			
Balance at beginning of year	3,520	3,196	2,584
Stock issued to employees exercising stock options	111	162	329
Tax benefit from employees' stock option and restricted stock plans	11	58	116
Stock-based compensation	365	—	—
Restricted stock and other stock plans, less amortization and cancellations	—	132	167
Unearned restricted stock adjustment	—	(28)	—
Adoption of SFAS No. 123	(150)	—	—
Balance at end of year	3,857	3,520	3,196
REINVESTED EARNINGS			
Balance at beginning of year	23,443	21,265	20,773
Net income	3,050	3,969	2,177
Dividends (per share—$.80, $.72 and $.68 in 2002, 2001 and 2000, respectively)	(1,987)	(1,791)	(1,685)
Balance at end of year	24,506	23,443	21,265
OUTSTANDING RESTRICTED STOCK			
Balance at beginning of year	(150)	(195)	(59)
Adoption of SFAS No. 123	150	—	—
Restricted stock and other stock plans, less cancellations	—	(24)	(160)
Amortization of restricted stock	—	41	24
Unearned restricted stock adjustment	—	28	—
Balance at end of year	—	(150)	(195)
ACCUMULATED OTHER COMPREHENSIVE INCOME (LOSS)			
Balance at beginning of year	(2,638)	(2,527)	(1,492)
Translation adjustments	(95)	(207)	(965)
Cumulative effect of adoption of SFAS No. 133	—	50	—
Net gain (loss) on derivatives	(186)	92	—
Net change in unrealized gain (loss) on available-for-sale securities	67	(29)	(60)
Net change in minimum pension liability	(195)	(17)	(10)
Net other comprehensive income adjustments	(409)	(111)	(1,035)
Balance at end of year	(3,047)	(2,638)	(2,527)
TREASURY STOCK			
Balance at beginning of year	(13,682)	(13,293)	(13,160)
Purchases of treasury stock	(707)	(277)	(133)
Restricted stock and other stock plans, less cancellations	—	(112)	—
Balance at end of year	(14,389)	(13,682)	(13,293)
TOTAL SHARE–OWNERS' EQUITY	$ 11,800	$ 11,366	$ 9,316
COMPREHENSIVE INCOME			
Net income	$ 3,050	$ 3,969	$ 2,177
Net other comprehensive income adjustments	(409)	(111)	(1,035)
TOTAL COMPREHENSIVE INCOME	$ 2,641	$ 3,858	$ 1,142

[1] Common stock purchased from employees exercising stock options numbered .2 million, .3 million and 2.2 million shares for the years ended December 31, 2002, 2001 and 2000, respectively.

See Notes to Consolidated Financial Statements.

Present Value Concepts

Business enterprises borrow and invest large sums of money. Both of these types of transactions involve the use of **present value computations**. A present value computation is based on the concept of the **time value of money**. For example, would you rather be given $1,000 today or be given $1,000 a year from today? If you get the $1,000 today and invest it to earn 10% per year, the $1,000 will accumulate to $1,100 ($1,000 plus the $100 interest) one year from today. The $1,000 received today is the present value amount that is equivalent to $1,100 one year from now. The present value, therefore, is based on three variables: (1) the dollar amount to be received (the future amount), (2) the length of time until the amount is received (the number of periods), and (3) the interest rate (the discount rate). The process of determining the present value is referred to as **discounting the future amount**. The relationship of these fundamental variables is depicted in the following time diagram.

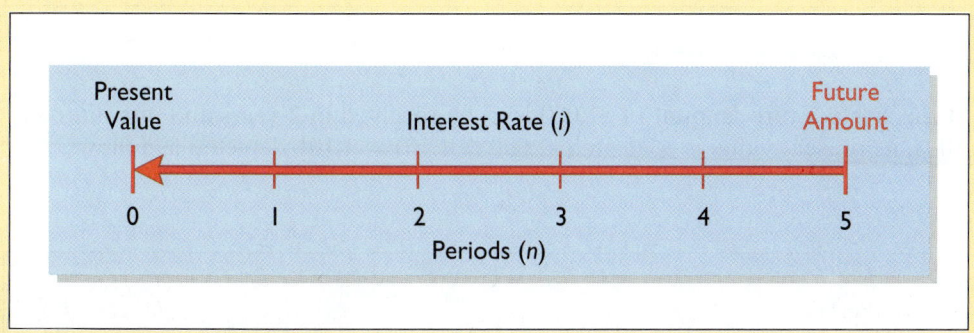

Illustration C-1
Time diagram

To better understand the variables involved in present value analysis, we encourage you to use time diagrams such as the one in Illustration C-1.

In this textbook, present value computations are used in measuring several items. For example, in Chapter 16, to determine the market price of a bond, the present value of the principal and interest payments is computed. In addition, finding the amount to be reported for notes payable and lease liability involves present value computations. And, in Chapter 27, the discounted cash flow technique and the net present value method for capital budget decisions use present value computations.

PRESENT VALUE OF A SINGLE FUTURE AMOUNT

To illustrate present value concepts, assume that you are willing to invest a sum of money that will yield $1,000 at the end of one year. In other words, what amount would you need to invest today to have $1,000 one year from now? If you want a

10% rate of return, the investment or present value is \$909.09 (\$1,000 ÷ 1.10). The computation of this amount is shown in Illustration C-2.

Illustration C-2
Present value computation—\$1,000 discounted at 10% for 1 year

Present value × (1 + Interest rate)	= Future amount
Present value × (1 + 10%)	= \$1,000
Present value	= \$1,000 ÷ 1.10
Present value	**= \$909.09**

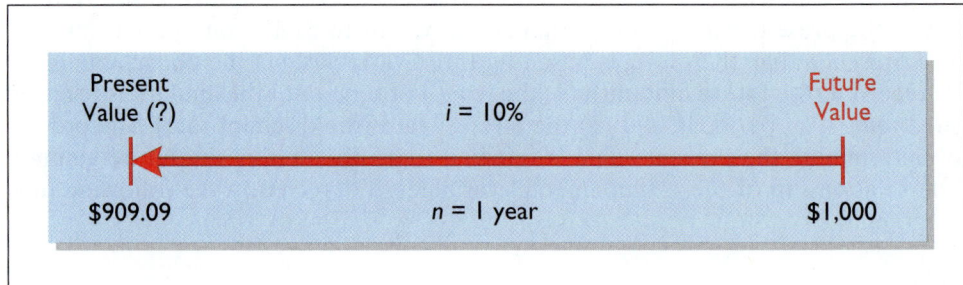

The future amount (\$1,000), the discount rate (10%), and the number of periods (1) are known. The variables in this situation can be depicted in the time diagram in Illustration C-3.

Illustration C-3
Finding present value if discounted for one period

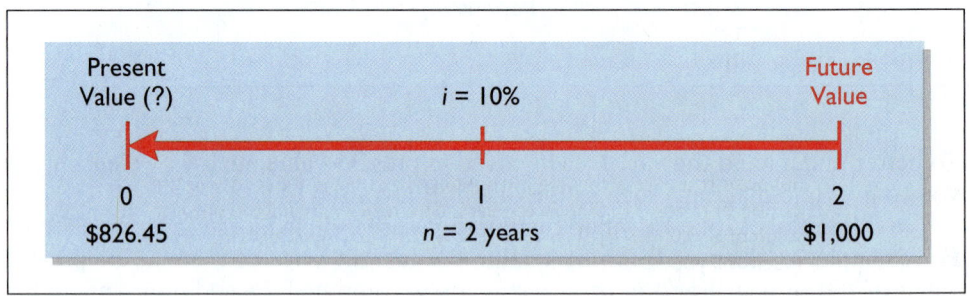

If the single future amount of \$1,000 is to be received **in 2 years** and discounted at 10%, its present value is \$826.45 [(\$1,000 ÷ 1.10) ÷ 1.10], depicted as follows.

Illustration C-4
Finding present value if discounted for two periods

The present value of 1 may also be determined through tables that show the present value of 1 for *n* periods. In Table C-1 (on the next page), *n* is the number of discounting periods involved. The percentages are the periodic interest rates or discount rates, and the 5-digit decimal numbers in the respective columns are the factors for the present value of 1.

When Table C-1 is used, the future amount is multiplied by the present value factor specified at the intersection of the number of periods and the discount rate. For example, the present value factor for 1 period at a discount rate of 10% is .90909, which equals the \$909.09 (\$1,000 × .90909) computed in Illustration C-2.

TABLE C-1
Present Value of 1

(*n*) Periods	4%	5%	6%	8%	9%	10%	11%	12%	15%
1	.96154	.95238	.94340	.92593	.91743	.90909	.90090	.89286	.86957
2	.92456	.90703	.89000	.85734	.84168	.82645	.81162	.79719	.75614
3	.88900	.86384	.83962	.79383	.77218	.75132	.73119	.71178	.65752
4	.85480	.82270	.79209	.73503	.70843	.68301	.65873	.63552	.57175
5	.82193	.78353	.74726	.68058	.64993	.62092	.59345	.56743	.49718
6	.79031	.74622	.70496	.63017	.59627	.56447	.53464	.50663	.43233
7	.75992	.71068	.66506	.58349	.54703	.51316	.48166	.45235	.37594
8	.73069	.67684	.62741	.54027	.50187	.46651	.43393	.40388	.32690
9	.70259	.64461	.59190	.50025	.46043	.42410	.39092	.36061	.28426
10	.67556	.61391	.55839	.46319	.42241	.38554	.35218	.32197	.24719
11	.64958	.58468	.52679	.42888	.38753	.35049	.31728	.28748	.21494
12	.62460	.55684	.49697	.39711	.35554	.31863	.28584	.25668	.18691
13	.60057	.53032	.46884	.36770	.32618	.28966	.25751	.22917	.16253
14	.57748	.50507	.44230	.34046	.29925	.26333	.23199	.20462	.14133
15	.55526	.48102	.41727	.31524	.27454	.23939	.20900	.18270	.12289
16	.53391	.45811	.39365	.29189	.25187	.21763	.18829	.16312	.10687
17	.51337	.43630	.37136	.27027	.23107	.19785	.16963	.14564	.09293
18	.49363	.41552	.35034	.25025	.21199	.17986	.15282	.13004	.08081
19	.47464	.39573	.33051	.23171	.19449	.16351	.13768	.11611	.07027
20	.45639	.37689	.31180	.21455	.17843	.14864	.12403	.10367	.06110

For 2 periods at a discount rate of 10%, the present value factor is .82645, which equals the $826.45 ($1,000 × .82645) computed previously.

Note that **a higher discount rate produces a smaller present value**. For example, using a 15% discount rate, the present value of $1,000 due one year from now is $869.57. At 10%, it is $909.09. You also should recognize that **the further removed from the present the future amount is, the smaller the present value**. For example, using the same discount rate of 10%, the present value of $1,000 due **in 5 years** is $620.92. The present value of $1,000 due in **1** year is $909.09.

The following two demonstration problems (Illustrations C-5, below and C-6, on the next page) illustrate how to use Table C-1.

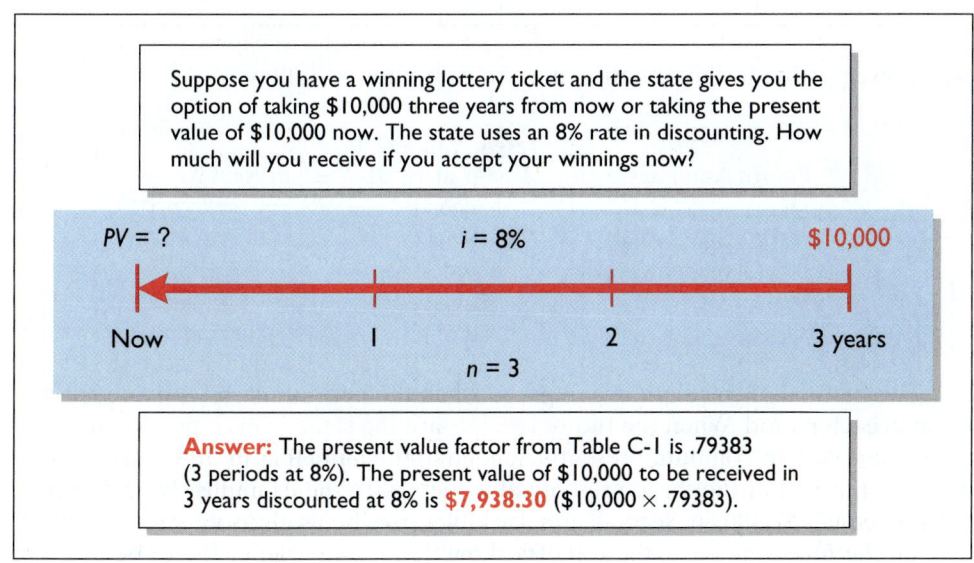

Illustration C-5
Demonstration Problem—
Using Table C-1 for PV of 1

Suppose you have a winning lottery ticket and the state gives you the option of taking $10,000 three years from now or taking the present value of $10,000 now. The state uses an 8% rate in discounting. How much will you receive if you accept your winnings now?

PV = ?   i = 8% $10,000

Now   1   2   3 years

n = 3

Answer: The present value factor from Table C-1 is .79383 (3 periods at 8%). The present value of $10,000 to be received in 3 years discounted at 8% is **$7,938.30** ($10,000 × .79383).

Illustration C-6
Demonstration Problem—
Using Table C-1 for PV of 1

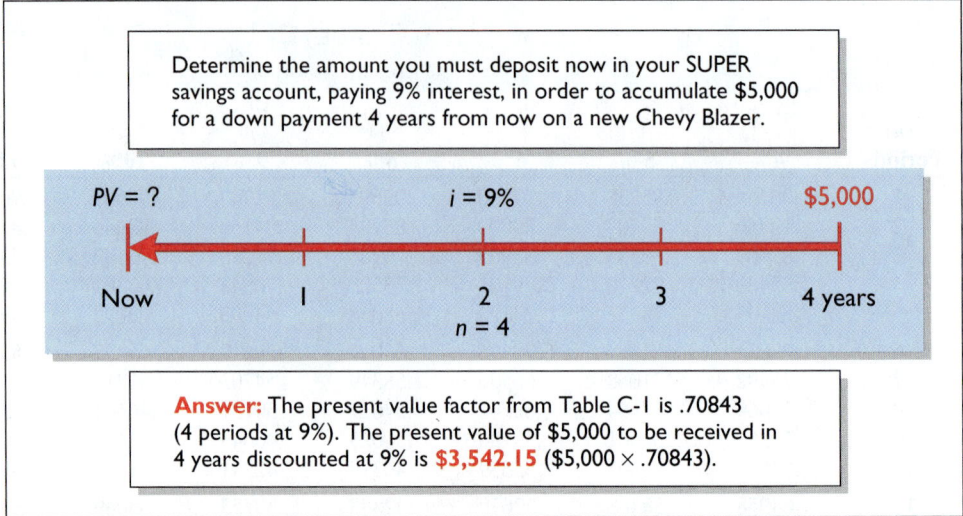

Determine the amount you must deposit now in your SUPER savings account, paying 9% interest, in order to accumulate $5,000 for a down payment 4 years from now on a new Chevy Blazer.

PV = ?   i = 9% $5,000

Now   1   2   3   4 years
         n = 4

Answer: The present value factor from Table C-I is .70843 (4 periods at 9%). The present value of $5,000 to be received in 4 years discounted at 9% is **$3,542.15** ($5,000 × .70843).

Present Value of a Series of Future Amounts (Annuities)

The preceding discussion involved the discounting of only a single future amount. Businesses and individuals frequently engage in transactions in which a series of equal dollar amounts are to be received or paid periodically. Examples of a series of periodic receipts or payments are loan agreements, installment sales, mortgage notes, lease (rental) contracts, and pension obligations. These series of periodic receipts or payments are called **annuities**. In computing the present value of an annuity, it is necessary to know (1) the discount rate, (2) the number of discount periods, and (3) the amount of the periodic receipts or payments. To illustrate the computation of the present value of an annuity, assume that you will receive $1,000 cash annually for 3 years and the discount rate is 10%. This situation is depicted in the following time diagram.

Illustration C-7
Time diagram for a 3-year annuity

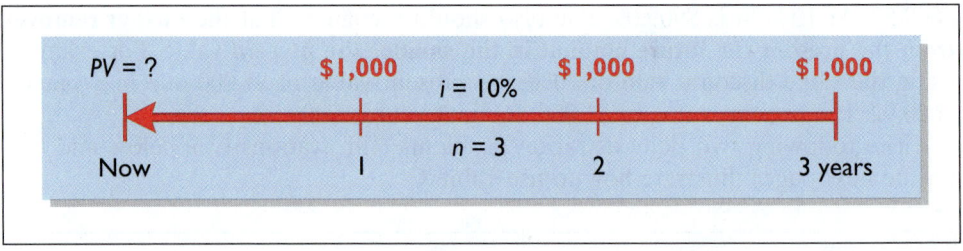

PV = ? $1,000 $1,000 $1,000
               i = 10%
Now   1   n = 3   2   3 years

The present value in this situation may be computed as follows.

Illustration C-8
Present value of a series of future amounts computation

Future Amount	×	Present Value of 1 Factor at 10%	=	Present Value
$1,000 (1 year away)		.90909		$ 909.09
1,000 (2 years away)		.82645		826.45
1,000 (3 years away)		.75132		751.32
		2.48686		**$2,486.86**

This method of calculation is required when the periodic cash flows are not uniform in each period. When the future receipts are the same in each period, there are two other ways to compute present value. First, the annual cash flow can be multiplied by the sum of the three present value factors. In the example above, $1,000 × 2.48686 equals $2,486.86. Second, annuity tables may be used. As illustrated in Table C-2 on the following page, these tables show the present value of 1 to be received periodically for a given number of periods.

TABLE C-2
Present Value of an Annuity of 1

(*n*) Periods	4%	5%	6%	8%	9%	10%	11%	12%	15%
1	.96154	.95238	.94340	.92593	.91743	.90909	.90090	.89286	.86957
2	1.88609	1.85941	1.83339	1.78326	1.75911	1.73554	1.71252	1.69005	1.62571
3	2.77509	2.72325	2.67301	2.57710	2.53130	2.48685	2.44371	2.40183	2.28323
4	3.62990	3.54595	3.46511	3.31213	3.23972	3.16986	3.10245	3.03735	2.85498
5	4.45182	4.32948	4.21236	3.99271	3.88965	3.79079	3.69590	3.60478	3.35216
6	5.24214	5.07569	4.91732	4.62288	4.48592	4.35526	4.23054	4.11141	3.78448
7	6.00205	5.78637	5.58238	5.20637	5.03295	4.86842	4.71220	4.56376	4.16042
8	6.73274	6.46321	6.20979	5.74664	5.53482	5.33493	5.14612	4.96764	4.48732
9	7.43533	7.10782	6.80169	6.24689	5.99525	5.75902	5.53705	5.32825	4.77158
10	8.11090	7.72173	7.36009	6.71008	6.41766	6.14457	5.88923	5.65022	5.01877
11	8.76048	8.30641	7.88687	7.13896	6.80519	6.49506	6.20652	5.93770	5.23371
12	9.38507	8.86325	8.38384	7.53608	7.16073	6.81369	6.49236	6.19437	5.42062
13	9.98565	9.39357	8.85268	7.90378	7.48690	7.10336	6.74987	6.42355	5.58315
14	10.56312	9.89864	9.29498	8.24424	7.78615	7.36669	6.98187	6.62817	5.72448
15	11.11839	10.37966	9.71225	8.55948	8.06069	7.60608	7.19087	6.81086	5.84737
16	11.65230	10.83777	10.10590	8.85137	8.31256	7.82371	7.37916	6.97399	5.95424
17	12.16567	11.27407	10.47726	9.12164	8.54363	8.02155	7.54879	7.11963	6.04716
18	12.65930	11.68959	10.82760	9.37189	8.75563	8.20141	7.70162	7.24967	6.12797
19	13.13394	12.08532	11.15812	9.60360	8.95012	8.36492	7.83929	7.36578	6.19823
20	13.59033	12.46221	11.46992	9.81815	9.12855	8.51356	7.96333	7.46944	6.25933

From Table C-2 you can see that the present value factor of an annuity of 1 for three periods at 10% is 2.48685.[1] This present value factor is the total of the three individual present value factors as shown in Illustration C-8. Applying this amount to the annual cash flow of $1,000 produces a present value of $2,486.85.

The following demonstration problem (Illustration C-9) illustrates how to use Table C-2.

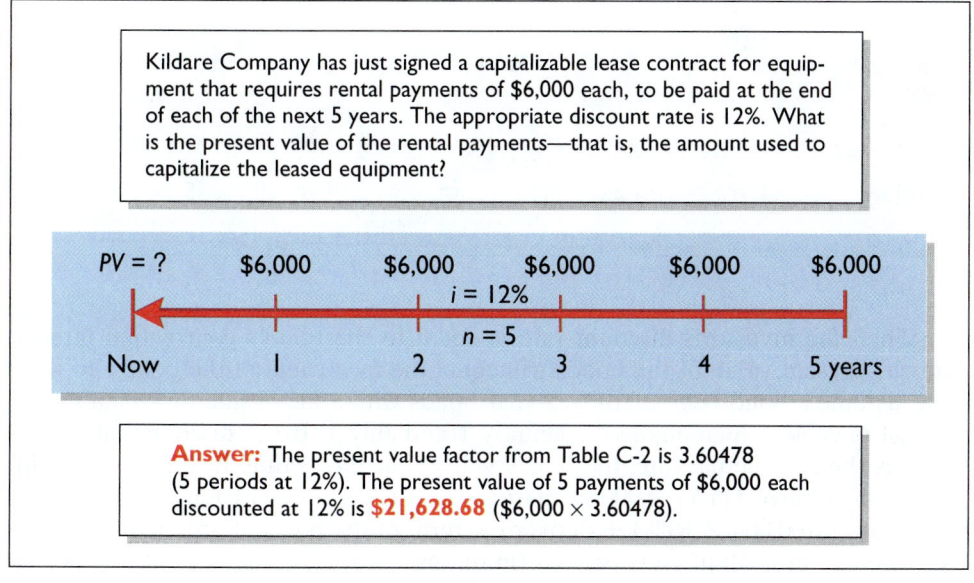

Kildare Company has just signed a capitalizable lease contract for equipment that requires rental payments of $6,000 each, to be paid at the end of each of the next 5 years. The appropriate discount rate is 12%. What is the present value of the rental payments—that is, the amount used to capitalize the leased equipment?

PV = ? $6,000 $6,000 $6,000 $6,000 $6,000

i = 12%
n = 5

Now   1   2   3   4   5 years

Answer: The present value factor from Table C-2 is 3.60478 (5 periods at 12%). The present value of 5 payments of $6,000 each discounted at 12% is **$21,628.68** ($6,000 × 3.60478).

Illustration C-9
Demonstration Problem—
Using Table C-2 for PV of an annuity of 1

---

[1] The difference of .00001 between 2.48686 and 2.48685 is due to rounding.

Time Periods and Discounting

In the preceding calculations, the discounting has been done on an annual basis using an annual interest rate. Discounting may also be done over shorter periods of time, such as monthly, quarterly, or semiannually. When the time frame is less than one year, it is necessary to convert the annual interest rate to the shorter time frame. Assume, for example, that the investor in Illustration C-8 received $500 **semiannually** for 3 years instead of $1,000 annually. In this case, the number of periods becomes 6 (3 × 2), the discount rate is 5% (10% ÷ 2), the present value factor from Table C-2 is 5.07569, and the present value of the future cash flows is $2,537.85 (5.07569 × $500). This amount is slightly higher than the $2,486.86 computed in Illustration C-8 because interest is computed twice during the same year. That is, interest is earned on the first half year's interest.

Computing the Present Value of a Bond

The present value (or market price) of a bond is a function of three variables: (1) the payment amounts, (2) the length of time until the amounts are paid, and (3) the discount rate.

The first variable (dollars to be paid) is made up of two elements: (1) a series of interest payments (an annuity) and (2) the principal amount (a single sum). To compute the present value of the bond, both the interest payments and the principal amount must be discounted. This is done in two different computations. The time diagrams for a bond due in 5 years are shown in Illustration C-10.

Illustration C-10
Time diagram for the present value of a bond

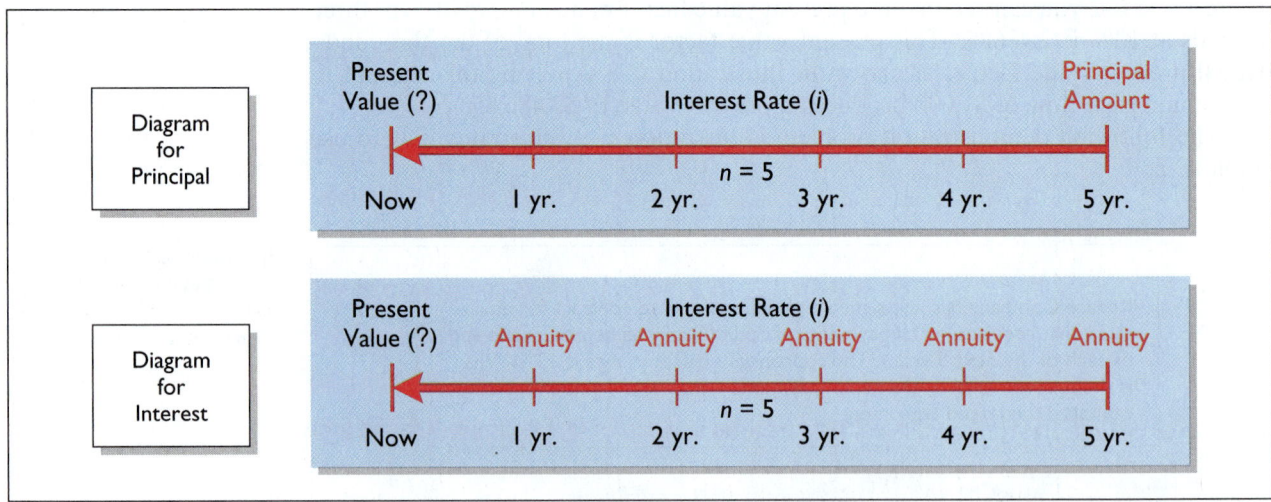

When the investor's discount rate is equal to the bond's contractual interest rate, the present value of the bonds will equal the face value of the bonds. To illustrate, assume a bond issue of 10%, 5-year bonds with a face value of $100,000 with interest payable **semiannually** on January 1 and July 1. If the discount rate is the same as the contractual rate, the bonds will sell **at face value**. In this case, the investor will receive (1) $100,000 at maturity and (2) a series of ten $5,000 interest payments [($100,000 × 10%) ÷ 2] over the term of the bonds. The length of time is expressed in terms of interest periods (in this case, 10) and the discount rate per interest period (5%). The following time diagram (Illustration C-11) depicts the variables involved in this discounting situation.

Illustration C-11
Time diagram for the present value of a 10%, 5-year bond paying interest semiannually

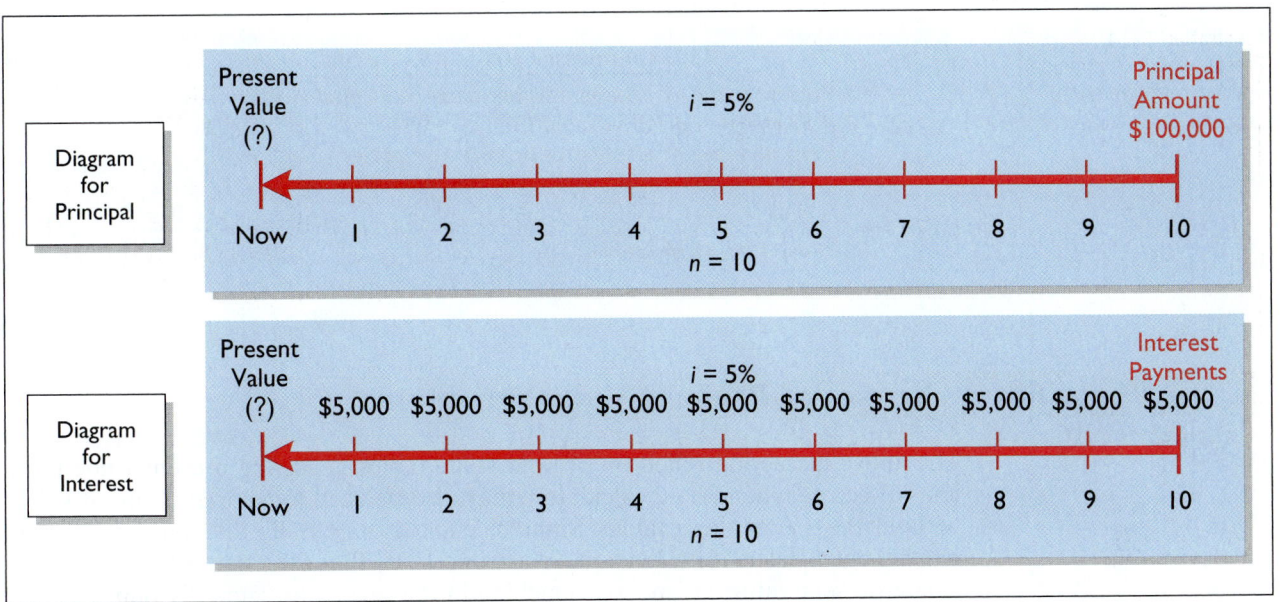

The computation of the present value of these bonds is shown below.

Illustration C-12
Present value of principal and interest (face value)

10% Contractual Rate—10% Discount Rate	
Present value of principal to be received at maturity	
$100,000 × PV of 1 due in 10 periods at 5%	
$100,000 × .61391 (Table C-1)	$ 61,391
Present value of interest to be received periodically over the term of the bonds	
$5,000 × PV of 1 due periodically for 10 periods at 5%	
$5,000 × 7.72173 (Table C-2)	38,609*
Present value of bonds	**$100,000**

*(Rounded).

Now assume that the investor's required rate of return is 12%, not 10%. The future amounts are again $100,000 and $5,000, respectively. But now a discount rate of 6% (12% ÷ 2) must be used. The present value of the bonds is $92,639, as computed below.

Illustration C-13
Present value of principal and interest (discount)

10% Contractual Rate—12% Discount Rate	
Present value of principal to be received at maturity	
$100,000 × .55839 (Table C-1)	$55,839
Present value of interest to be received periodically over the term of the bonds	
$5,000 × 7.36009 (Table C-2)	36,800
Present value of bonds	**$92,639**

If the discount rate is 8% and the contractual rate is 10%, the present value of the bonds is $108,111, computed as follows.

Illustration C-14
Present value of principal and interest (premium)

10% Contractual Rate—8% Discount Rate	
Present value of principal to be received at maturity	
$100,000 × .67556 (Table C-1)	$ 67,556
Present value of interest to be received periodically over the term of the bonds	
$5,000 × 8.11090 (Table C-2)	40,555
Present value of bonds	**$108,111**

Use of Calculators to Solve Present Value Problems

The above discussion relied on present value tables in solving present value problems. Electronic hand-held calculators may also be used to compute present values without the use of these tables. Some calculators, especially the "business" or "financial" type calculators, have present value (PV) functions that allow you to calculate present values by merely punching in the proper amount, discount rate, periods, and pressing the PV key. Whether you use a calculator or tables to solve present value problems, you should make sure that you fully understand the important concepts that underlie the calculations.

ACCOUNTING IN ACTION  **Business Perspective**

As discussed in this appendix, the selling price of bonds can be determined by present value formulas. Many computer spreadsheets and computer programs can perform the discounting functions given the basic information of the situation.

BRIEF EXERCISES (Use Tables to Solve Exercises)

Using present value tables.

BEC-1 For each of the following cases, indicate (a) to what interest rate columns and (b) to what number of periods you would refer in looking up the discount rate.

1. In Table C-1 (present value of 1):

	Annual Rate	**Number of Years Involved**	**Discounts Per Year**
(a)	12%	6	Annually
(b)	10%	15	Annually
(c)	8%	10	Semiannually

2. In Table C-2 (present value of an annuity of 1):

	Annual Rate	**Number of Years Involved**	**Number of Payments Involved**	**Frequency of Payments**
(a)	8%	20	20	Annually
(b)	10%	5	5	Annually
(c)	12%	4	8	Semiannually

BEC-2 **(a)** What is the present value of $20,000 due 8 periods from now, discounted at 8%? **(b)** What is the present value of $20,000 to be received at the end of each of 6 periods, discounted at 9%?

Determining present values.

BEC-3 Gonzalez Company is considering an investment that will return a lump sum of $500,000 5 years from now. What amount should Gonzalez Company pay for this investment in order to earn a 10% return?

Compute the present value of a single-sum investment.

BEC-4 Lasorda Company earns 9% on an investment that will return $875,000 8 years from now. What is the amount Lasorda should invest now in order to earn this rate of return?

Compute the present value of a single-sum investment.

BEC-5 McNeil Company sold a 5-year, zero-interest-bearing $27,000 note receivable to Valley Inc. Valley wishes to earn 10% over the remaining 4 years of the note. How much cash will McNeil receive upon sale of the note?

Compute the present value of a single-sum zero-interest-bearing note.

BEC-6 Clemente Company issues a 3-year, zero-interest-bearing $80,000 note. The interest rate used to discount the zero-interest-bearing note is 8%. What are the cash proceeds that Clemente Company should receive?

Compute the present value of a single-sum zero-interest-bearing note.

BEC-7 Bosco Company is considering investing in an annuity contract that will return $30,000 annually at the end of each year for 15 years. What amount should Bosco Company pay for this investment if it earns a 6% return?

Compute the present value of an annuity investment.

BEC-8 Modine Enterprises earns 11% on an investment that pays back $120,000 at the end of each of the next 4 years. What is the amount Modine Enterprises invested to earn the 11% rate of return?

Compute the present value of an annuity investment.

BEC-9 Midwest Railroad Co. is about to issue $100,000 of 10-year bonds paying a 10% interest rate, with interest payable semiannually. The discount rate for such securities is 8%. How much can Midwest expect to receive for the sale of these bonds?

Compute the present value of bonds.

BEC-10 Assume the same information as in BEC-9 except that the discount rate is 10% instead of 8%. In this case, how much can Midwest expect to receive from the sale of these bonds?

Compute the present value of bonds.

BEC-11 Lounsbury Company receives a $50,000, 6-year note bearing interest of 8% (paid annually) from a customer at a time when the discount rate is 9%. What is the present value of the note received by Lounsbury Company?

Compute the present value of a note.

BEC-12 Hartzler Enterprises issued 8%, 8-year, $2,000,000 par value bonds that pay interest semiannually on October 1 and April 1. The bonds are dated April 1, 2005, and are issued on that date. The discount rate of interest for such bonds on April 1, 2005, is 10%. What cash proceeds did Hartzler receive from issuance of the bonds?

Compute the present value of bonds.

BEC-13 Vinny Carpino owns a garage and is contemplating purchasing a tire retreading machine for $16,280. After estimating costs and revenues, Vinny projects a net cash flow from the retreading machine of $3,000 annually for 8 years. Vinny hopes to earn a return of 11% on such investments. What is the present value of the retreading operation? Should Vinny Carpino purchase the retreading machine?

Compute the value of a machine for purposes of making a purchase decision.

BEC-14 Rodriguez Company issues a 10%, 6-year mortgage note on January 1, 2005, to obtain financing for new equipment. Land is used as collateral for the note. The terms provide for semiannual installment payments of $56,413. What were the cash proceeds received from the issuance of the note?

Compute the present value of a note.

BEC-15 Goltra Company is considering purchasing equipment. The equipment will produce the following cash flows: Year 1, $30,000; Year 2, $40,000; Year 3, $50,000. Goltra requires a minimum rate of return of 12%. What is the maximum price Goltra should pay for this equipment?

Compute the maximum price to pay for a machine.

BEC-16 If Maria Sanchez invests $3,152 now, she will receive $10,000 at the end of 15 years. What annual rate of interest will Maria earn on her investment? (*Hint:* Use Table C-1.)

Compute the interest rate on a single sum.

BEC-17 Lori Burke has been offered the opportunity of investing $42,410 now. The investment will earn 10% per year and at the end of that time will return Lori $100,000. How many years must Lori wait to receive $100,000? (*Hint:* Use Table C-1.)

Compute the number of periods of a single sum.

Compute the interest rate on an annuity.

BEC-18 Nancy Burns purchased an investment for $12,462.21. From this investment, she will receive $1,000 annually for the next 20 years, starting one year from now. What rate of interest will Nancy's investment be earning for her? (*Hint:* Use Table C-2.)

Compute the number of periods of an annuity.

BEC-19 Betty Estes invests $7,536.08 now for a series of $1,000 annual returns, beginning one year from now. Betty will earn a return of 8% on the initial investment. How many annual payments of $1,000 will Betty receive? (*Hint:* Use Table C-2.)

Standards of Ethical Conduct for Management Accountants

Management accountants have an obligation to the organizations they serve, their profession, the public, and themselves to maintain the highest standards of ethical conduct. In recognition of this obligation, the **Institute of Management Accountants**, formerly the National Association of Accountants, has published and promoted the following standards of ethical conduct for management accountants. Adherence to these standards is integral to achieving the *Objectives of Management Accounting*.[1] Management accountants shall not commit acts contrary to these standards nor shall they condone the commission of such acts by others within their organizations.

COMPETENCE

Management accountants have a responsibility to:

- Maintain an appropriate level of professional competence by ongoing development of their knowledge and skills.
- Perform their professional duties in accordance with relevant laws, regulations, and technical standards.
- Prepare complete and clear reports and recommendations after appropriate analyses of relevant and reliable information.

CONFIDENTIALITY

Management accountants have a responsibility to:

- Refrain from disclosing confidential information acquired in the course of their work except when authorized, unless legally obligated to do so.
- Inform subordinates as appropriate regarding the confidentiality of information acquired in the course of their work and monitor their activities to assure the maintenance of that confidentiality.
- Refrain from using or appearing to use confidential information acquired in the course of their work for unethical or illegal advantage either personally or through third parties.

---

[1]Institute of Management Accountants, formerly National Association of Accountants, *Statements on Management Accounting: Objectives of Management Accounting,* Statement No. 1B, June 17, 1982.

Integrity

Management accountants have a responsibility to:

- Avoid actual or apparent conflicts of interest and advise all appropriate parties of any potential conflict.
- Refrain from engaging in any activity that would prejudice their ability to carry out their duties ethically.
- Refuse any gift, favor, or hospitality that would influence or would appear to influence their actions.
- Refrain from either actively or passively subverting the attainment of the organization's legitimate and ethical objectives.
- Recognize and communicate professional limitations or other constraints that would preclude responsible judgment or successful performance of an activity.
- Communicate unfavorable as well as favorable information and professional judgments or opinions.
- Refrain from engaging in or supporting any activity that would discredit the profession.

Objectivity

Management accountants have a responsibility to:

- Communicate information fairly and objectively.
- Disclose fully all relevant information that could reasonably be expected to influence an intended user's understanding of the reports, comments, and recommendations presented.

PHOTO CREDITS

Ed Honowitz/ Stone/Getty Images. Page 870: Royalty-Free/ Corbis Images. Page 886: Information was provided by Parlex Corporation.

Chapter 22   Opener: Foodfolio/Alamy Images. Page 895: John Wilkinson/Corbis Images. Page 904: PhotoDisc, Inc./Getty Images. Page 907: Jennie Oppenheimer/Stock Illustration Source/Images.com. Page 915: Margie & Howard Fullmer/ Stock Illustration Source/Images.com. Page 929: Courtesy General Microwave.

Chapter 23   Opener: Dave Crosier/Stone/Getty Images. Page 935: Martin Schreiber/Stone/Getty Images. Page 944: Royalty-Free/Corbis Images. Page 947: Yael/Retna. Page 950: Micheal Simpson/Taxi/Getty Images.

Chapter 24   Opener: ©2000 Artville/Getty Images. Page 972: Gary Conner/Index Stock. Page 980: Ralph Mercer/

Stone/Getty Images. Page 985: Paul Muns/Stock Illustration Source/Images.com. Page 1001: Courtesy Network Computing Devices Inc.

Chapter 25   Opener: ©EyeWire/Getty Images. Page 1018: ©2000 Artville/Getty Images. Page 1021: EyeWire/Getty Images.

Chapter 26   Opener: Dick Luria/Taxi/Getty Images. Page 1054: John Syoboda/FoodPix/Getty Images. Page 1061: Courtesy of United Parcel Service. Page 1064: Garry Gay/The Image Bank/Getty Images. Page 1082: Courtesy Glassmaster Company.

Chapter 27   Opener: Royalty-Free/Corbis Images. Page 1091: Ed Eckstein/Corbis Images. Page 1094: William Tautic/ Corbis Stock Market. Page 1103: Tim Jonke/The Image Bank/ Getty Images. Page 792-793: Jan Cobb/The Image Bank/Getty Images.

COMPANY INDEX